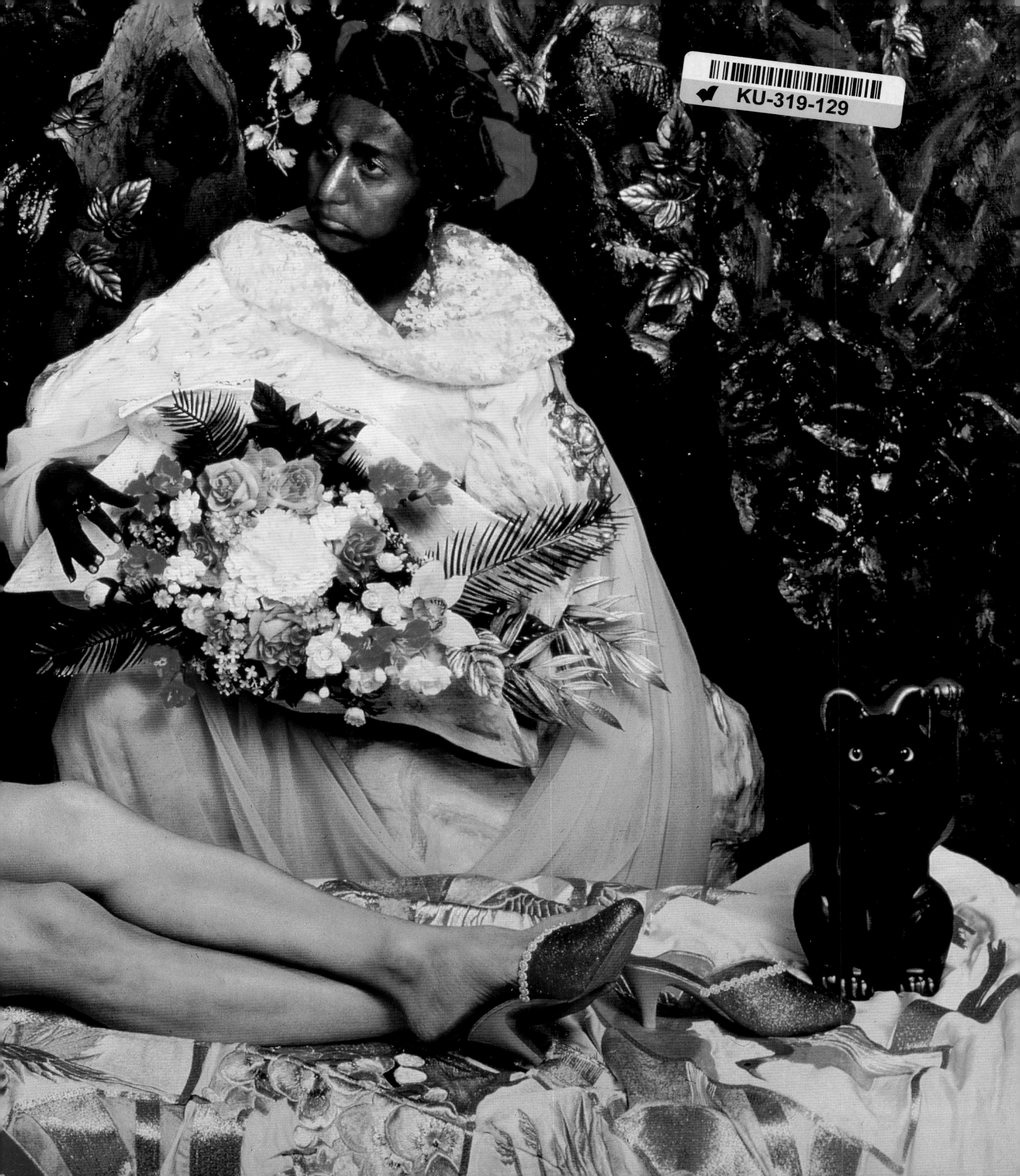

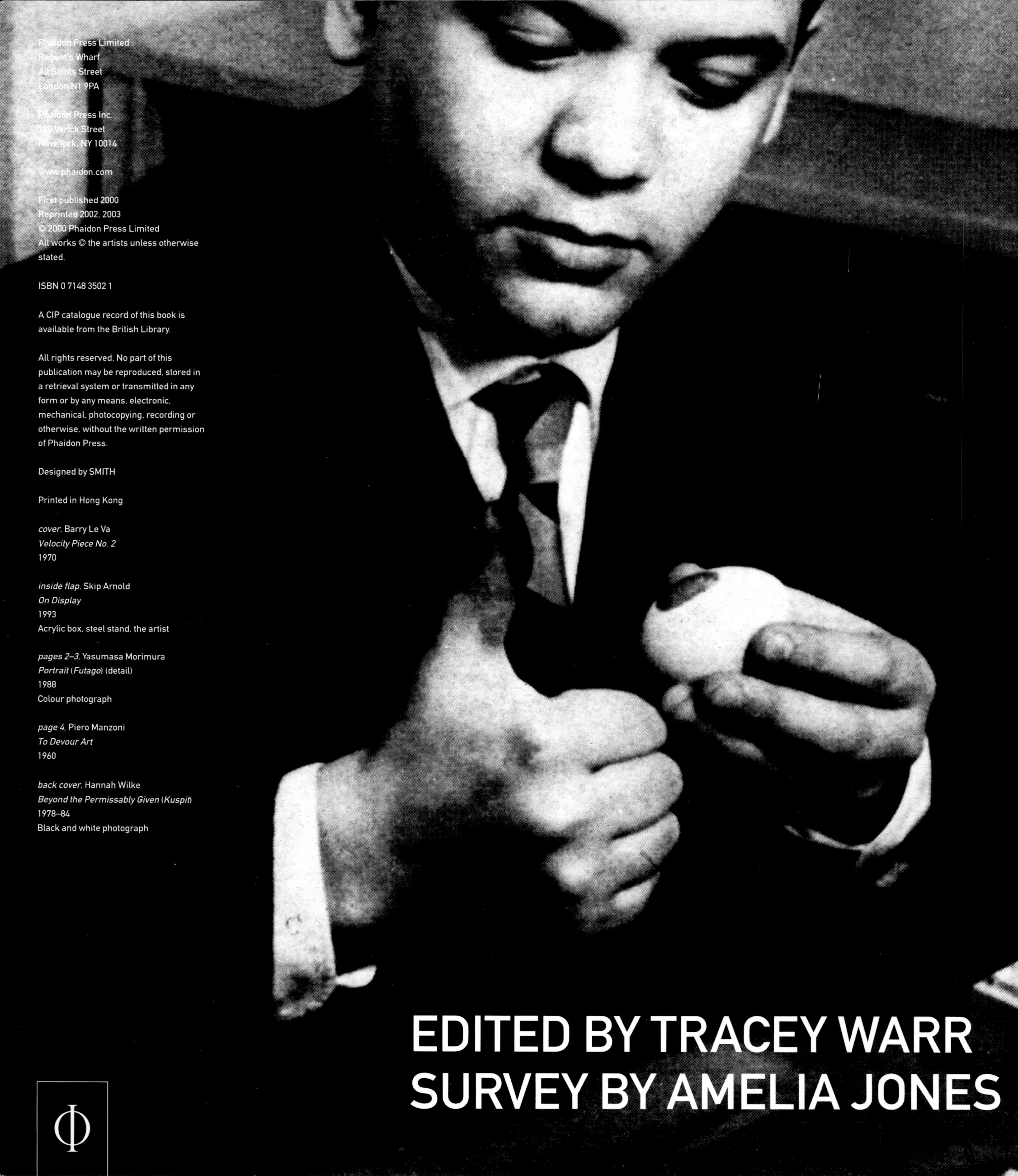

Phaidon Press Limited
Regent's Wharf
All Saints Street
London N1 9PA

Phaidon Press Inc.
180 Varick Street
New York, NY 10014

www.phaidon.com

First published 2000
Reprinted 2002, 2003

ISBN 0 7148 3502 1

A CIP catalogue record of this book is available from the British Library.

Designed by SMITH

Printed in Hong Kong

cover, Barry Le Va
Velocity Piece No. 2
1970

inside flap, Skip Arnold
On Display
1993
Acrylic box, steel stand, the artist

pages 2–3, Yasumasa Morimura
Portrait (*Futago*) (detail)
1988
Colour photograph

page 4, Piero Manzoni
To Devour Art
1960

back cover, Hannah Wilke
Beyond the Permissably Given (*Kuspit*)
1978–84
Black and white photograph

EDITED BY TRACEY WARR
SURVEY BY AMELIA JONES

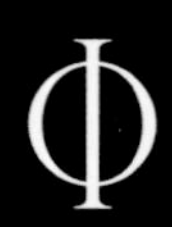

Twentieth-century art has increasingly seen the artist's body used as both the subject and the object of artists' work. Bound or beaten, naked or painted, still or spasmodic: the body is presented in all possible guises, as the artist quite literally lives his or her art either publicly, in performances, or privately, in video and photography. Expanding and renewing the age-old tradition of self-portraiture, body and performance artists are part of the tradition of artists moving art out of the gallery, into unexpected spaces and media. Breaking down the barriers between art and life, visual experience and sensual experience, these artists well represent the sense of angst and individual disorientation at the close of the twentieth century.

Beginning with such key artists as Marcel Duchamp and Jackson Pollock, this book examines a selection of the most significant players who have used their bodies to create their art – among them, in the 1960s, Carolee Schneemann, Rudolf Schwarzkogler, Yoko Ono; in the 1970s, Chris Burden, Ana Mendieta, Vito Acconci, Marina Abramović; up to the present, with works by Matthew Barney, Yasumasa Morimura and Mona Hatoum. Survey author Amelia Jones, among the world's leading experts in the field, discusses these performance and body artists against the background of the social history of the times. The Documents section, edited by Tracey Warr, is parallel to the illustrated works of art, and combines texts by critics who shaped the movement, from Lucy R. Lippard to Thomas McEvilley. Alongside these are writings by philosophers and thinkers such as Georges Bataille and Gilles Deleuze who have contributed on a theoretical level to the discussion around the body – a prevalent theme in late twentieth-century cultural theory.

THEMES AND MOVEMENTS

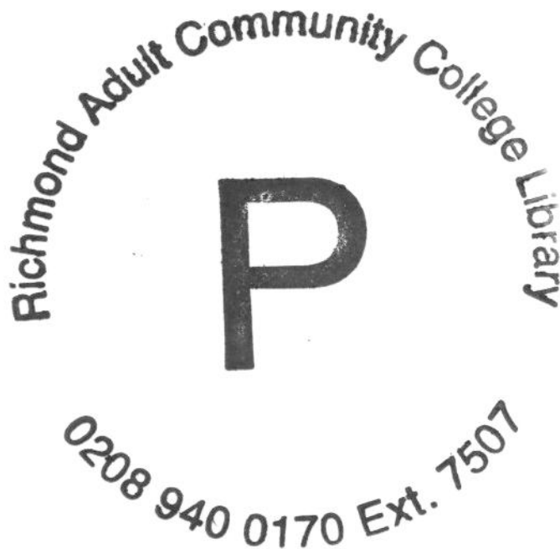

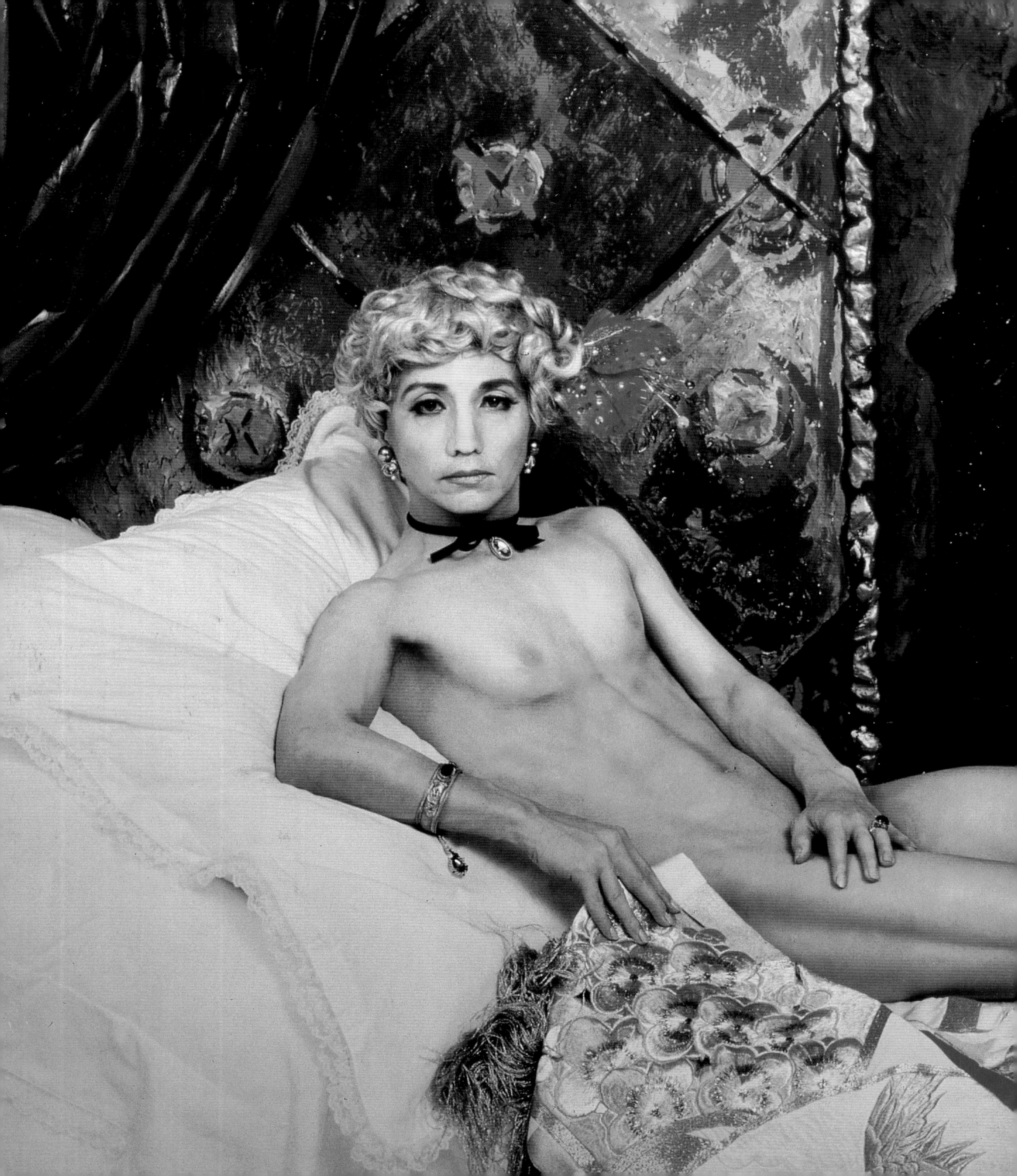

THE ARTIST'S BODY

PREFACE TRACEY WARR
page 10
SURVEY AMELIA JONES
page 16

WORKS page 48
PAINTING BODIES page 49
GESTURING BODIES page 70
RITUALISTIC AND TRANSGRESSIVE BODIES page 92
BODY BOUNDARIES page 114
PERFORMING IDENTITY page 134
ABSENT BODIES page 162
EXTENDED AND PROSTHETIC BODIES page 178

DOCUMENTS page 190
PAINTING BODIES page 193
GESTURING BODIES page 201
RITUALISTIC AND TRANSGRESSIVE BODIES page 216
BODY BOUNDARIES page 230
PERFORMING IDENTITY page 247
ABSENT BODIES page 275
EXTENDED AND PROSTHETIC BODIES page 284

ARTISTS' BIOGRAPHIES page 288
AUTHORS' BIOGRAPHIES page 296
BIBLIOGRAPHY page 298
INDEX page 301
ACKNOWLEDGEMENTS page 304

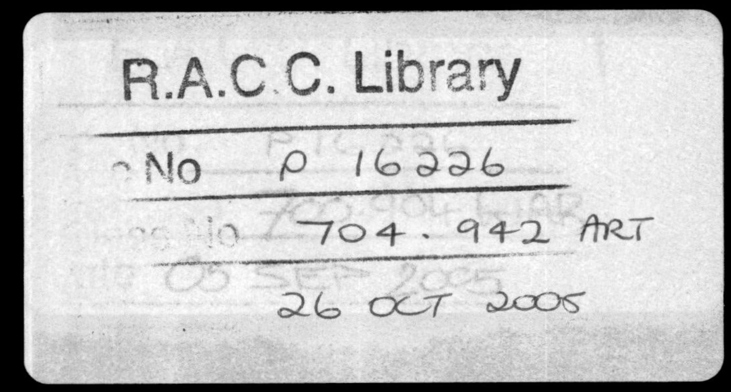

WORKS page 48

PAINTING BODIES page 49

Marcel DUCHAMP Paysage fautif (Wayward landscape) 1946 page 49

Georges MATHIEU Homage to General Hideyoshi, 1957 page 50

Jackson POLLOCK Painting in his studio, *c.* 1950 page 51

Saburo MURAKAMI Breaking Through Many Paper Screens, 1956 page 52

Kazuo SHIRAGA Challenging Mud, 1955 page 53

Shozo SHIMAMOTO Making a Painting by Throwing Bottles of Paint, 1956 page 53

Yves KLEIN Anthropometry of the Blue Epoch, 1960 page 54

Yves KLEIN Untitled Anthropometry, 1960 page 55

Yves KLEIN Untitled (Anthropometry with Male and Female Figures), 1960 page 56

Niki de SAINT-PHALLE First Shooting Impasse Ronsin, 1961 page 57

Claes OLDENBURG Snapshots from the City, 1960 page 58

Allan KAPROW 18 Happenings in 6 Parts, 1959 page 59

Jim DINE The Smiling Workman, 1960 page 59

Nam June PAIK Performing La Monte Young's *Composition 1960 No. 10* to Bob Morris (Zen for Head), 1962 page 60

Carolee SCHNEEMANN Meat Joy, 1964 page 60

Carolee SCHNEEMANN Eye Body: 36 Transformative Actions, 1963 page 61

Shigeko KUBOTA Vagina Painting, 1965 page 62

Paul McCARTHY Face Painting – Floor, White Line, 1972 page 63

Ana MENDIETA Body Tracks, 1974 page 63

Stuart BRISLEY Moments and Decision and Indecision, 1975 page 64

Andy WARHOL Oxidation Painting, 1978 page 65

Andres SERRANO Untitled XIII (Ejaculate in Trajectory), 1989 page 65

Janine ANTONI Loving Care, 1992 page 66

Rachel LACHOWICZ Red not Blue, 1992 page 67

Cheryl DONEGAN Kiss My Royal Irish Ass (K.M.R.I.A.), 1993 page 67

Keith BOADWEE Untitled (Purple Squirt), 1995 page 68

Jenny SAVILLE and Glen LUCHFORD Closed Contact No. 10, 1995-97 page 68

Tracey EMIN Exorcism of the Last Painting I Ever Made, 1996 page 69

GESTURING BODIES page 70

Yves KLEIN Leap into the Void, 1960 page 70

Robert MORRIS I-Box, 1962 page 71

Dick HIGGINS and Alison KNOWLES Danger Music No.2, 1962 page 72

Tetsumi KUDO Philosophy of Impotence, 1962 page 72

Ben VAUTIER Geste: Rentrer dans l'eau [Gesture: To enter the water], 1964/72 page 72, 73

Yoko ONO Cut Piece, 1964 page 74

Milan KNÍŽÁK Demonstration for all the Senses, 1964 page 75

HI-RED CENTER Maquette of the Hi Red Center Shelter (Hotel Event), 1964 page 76

Joseph BEUYS I Like America and America Likes Me, 1974 page 76

Joseph BEUYS How to Explain Pictures to a Dead Hare, 1965 page 77

Bruce NAUMAN Art Make-up Films No. 1: Green, 1967–68 page 78

Bruce NAUMAN Self-Portrait as a Fountain, 1966-67 page 78

Paul COTTON The People's Prick, 1969 page 79

Bruce NAUMAN Walking in an Exaggerated Manner Around the Perimeter of a Square, 1967–68 page 80–81

Yayoi KUSAMA Grand Orgy to Awaken the Dead at MoMA, 1969 page 82

GILBERT & GEORGE The Singing Sculpture, 1970 page 83

Dennis OPPENHEIM Parallel Stress, 1970 page 84

Joan JONAS Mirror Check, 1970 page 85

Bas Jan ADER I'm Too Sad to Tell You, 1970 page 85

Giuseppe PENONE Rovesciare i propri occhi [To reverse one's eyes], 1970 page 86

Bruce McLEAN Pose Work for Plinths, 1970 page 86

Eleanor ANTIN Carving: A Traditional Sculpture, 1973 page 87

Charles RAY Plank Piece I & II, 1973 page 88

Bonnie SHERK Public Lunch, 1971 page 89

Mierle Laderman UKELES Hartford Wash: Washing, Tracks, Maintenance: Outside, 1973 page 89

Carolee SCHNEEMANN Up To And Including Her Limits, 1976 page 90

Skip ARNOLD On Display, 1993 page 91

Oleg KULIK I Bite America and America Bites Me, 1997 page 91

RITUALISTIC AND TRANSGRESSIVE BODIES page 92

Hermann NITSCH 1st Action, 1962 page 92

Hermann NITSCH 80th Action: Orgies Mysteries Theatre, 1984 page 93

Otto MÜHL Material Action No.1: Degradation of a Venus, 1963 page 94

Otto MÜHL Gymnastics Class in Food, 1965 page 94

Otto MÜHL Pissaction, 1969 page 95

Günter BRUS Art and Revolution, 1968 page 95

Günter BRUS Self-painting, Self-mutilation, 1965 page 96

Wolf VOSTELL You-Happening, 1964 page 97

Rudolf SCHWARZKOGLER Action 1: Wedding, 1965 page 97

Michel JOURNIAC Messe pour un corps (Mass for a body), 1969 page 98

Rafael Montañez ORTIZ The Birth and Death of White Henny, 1967 page 98

Arnulf RAINER Face Farces, 1969 page 98

Lucas SAMARAS Photo-Transformation, 1974 page 99

Ana MENDIETA Rape Scene, 1973 page 100

Ana MENDIETA Death of a Chicken, 1972 page 101

Gina PANE Death Control, 1974 page 101

Chris BURDEN Icarus, 1973 page 102

Gideon GECHTMAN Naked, 1974 page 102

Chris BURDEN Trans-Fixed, 1974 page 103

Paul McCARTHY Hot Dog, 1974 page 104

Mike PARR Cathartic Action: Social Gestus No. 5, 1977 page 105

John DUNCAN Blind Date, 1980 page 105

Mike KELLEY Plato's Cave, Rothko's Chapel, Lincoln's Profile, 1986 page 105

Cindy SHERMAN Untitled No. 175, 1987 page 106

Andres SERRANO Piss Christ, 1987 page 107

Karen FINLEY We Keep Our Victims Ready, 1989 page 108

Bob FLANAGAN and Sheree ROSE Visiting Hours, 1992 page 109

Bob FLANAGAN Auto-Erotic S&M, 1989 page 109

Annie SPRINKLE Post-Porn Modernist Show, 1992 page 110

Ron ATHEY 4 Scenes in a Harsh Life, 1994 page 110

FRANKO B Mama, I Can't Sing, 1996 page 110

Elke KRYSTUFEK Satisfaction, 1996 page 111

Marina ABRAMOVIĆ Balkan Baroque, 1997 page 112–113

BODY BOUNDARIES page 114

Peter WEIBEL and Valie EXPORT Aus der Mappe der Hundigkeit [From the Portfolio of Doggishness], 1968 page 114

Yayoi KUSAMA Kusama's Peep Show or Endless Love Show, 1966 page 115

Dennis OPPENHEIM and Bob FÍORE Arm and Wire, 1969 page 116

Valie EXPORT Eros/ion, 1971 page 116

Barbara SMITH Feed Me, 1973 page 116

Vito ACCONCI Seedbed, 1972 page 117

Dennis OPPENHEIM Reading Position for a Second Degree Burn, 1970 page 118

Vito ACCONCI Trademarks, 1970 page 119

Vito ACCONCI and Kathy DILLON Pryings, 1971 page 119

Gina PANE Le Lait Chaud [Warm milk], 1972 page 120

Barry LE VA Velocity Piece No.2, 1970 page 121

Chris BURDEN Shoot, 1971 page 122

William WEGMAN Family Combinations, 1972 page 122

Gianni PISANI Each Morning Before Going Out, 1973 page 122

Klaus RINKE Deplazierung [Changing loctation according to points in time], 1972 page 123

Marina ABRAMOVIĆ Rhythm 2, 1974 page 124

ABRAMOVIĆ and ULAY Imponderabilia, 1977 page124

Marina ABRAMOVIĆ Rhythm 0, 1975 page 125

Susan HILLER Dream Mapping, 1974 page 126

PetrŠTEMBERA Grafting, 1975 page 126

Bill VIOLA Space between the Teeth, 1976 page 127

Raúl ZURITA No, no puedo mas [No, I can't stand it any longer], 1979 page 128

Diamela ELTIT Maipu, 1980 page 128

Zbigniew WARPECHOWSKI Nail Driven Through the Hand, 1980 page 128

Linda MONTANO and Tehching HSIEH A Year Spent Tied at the Waist, 1983–84 page 129

Jayne PARKER K, 1989 page 130

Teresa MURAK Seed, 1989 page 131

Pepe ESPALIÚ Carrying, 1992 page 131

Mona HATOUM Corps étranger, 1994 page 132, 133

PERFORMING IDENTITY page 134

Yayoi KUSAMA Untitled, *c.* 1966 page 134

Pierre MOLINIER The Spur of Love, 1966-68 page 135

Vito ACCONCI Conversions, 1971 page 136

Judy CHICAGO Boxing Ring, 1970 page 137

Faith WILDING Waiting, 1971 page 137

Urs LÜTHI Self-Portrait with Ecky, 1974 page 138

Adrian PIPER The Mythic Being, 1975 page 139

Adrian PIPER Catalysis, 1971–71 page 139

Jürgen KLAUKE Transformer, 1973 page 140

Katharina SIEVERDING Transformer 1 A/B, 1973 page 141

Lynda BENGLIS Untitled, 1974 page 142

Robert MORRIS Untitled, 1974 page 143

Mary Beth EDELSON Goddess Head, 1975 page 144

Carolee SCHNEEMANN Interior Scroll, 1975 page 145

Paul McCARTHY Sailor's Meat, 1975 page 146

Ulrike ROSENBACH Don't believe I am an Amazon, 1975 page 147

Carlos LEPPE Perchero [Coat Hanger], 1975 page 147

Hannah WILKE Exchange Values (Marx), 1978–84 page 148

Hannah WILKE Opportunity Makes Relations as it Makes Thieves (Goethe), 1978–84 page 148

Hannah WILKE His Farced Epistol (Joyce), 1978–84 page 148

Hannah WILKE (with Donald GODDARD) Intra Venus, 1993 page 149

Robert MAPPLETHORPE Self-Portrait with Bullwhip, 1978 page 150

Sherman FLEMING Something Akin to Living, 1979 page 150

Mona HATOUM The Negotiating Table, 1983 page 150

Cindy SHERMAN Untitled No. 15, 1978 page 151

Cindy SHERMAN Untitled No. 131, 1983 page 151

Andy WARHOL Self-Portrait in Drag, 1986 page 152

Pipilotti RIST I'm Not the Girl Who Misses Much, 1986 page 153

James LUNA The Artifact Piece, 1987 page 154

Lorna SIMPSON Guarded Conditions, 1989 page 154

Lyle Ashton HARRIS and Renée COX Queen, Alias & Id: The Child, 1994 page 155

Yasamasa MORIMURA Doublenage (Marcel), 1988 page 155

Jeff KOONS Untitled, 1989 page 156

Laura AGUILAR In Sandy's Room (Self-Portrait), 1991 page 157

John COPLANS Self-Portrait (Standing, Side View, Three Panels, No. 5), 1993 page 158

Oladélé Ajiboyé BAMGBOYÉ Celebrate, 1994 page 159

Coco FUSCO and Guillermo GÓMEZ-PEÑA Two Undiscovered Amerindians Visit Madrid, 1992 page 159

Mariko MORI Miko no Inori (Last Departure), 1996 page 160

Shirin NESHAT Faceless, 1994 page 161

ABSENT BODIES page 162

Marcel DUCHAMP With My Tongue in My Cheek, 1959 page 162

Piero MANZONI Artist's Breath, 1960 page 163

Piero MANZONI Artist's Shit, 1961 page 163

Bruce NAUMAN From Hand to Mouth, 1967 page 164

Terry FOX Levitation, 1970 page 165

Richard LONG A Line Made by Walking, 1967 page 166

Howard FRIED All My Dirty Blue Clothes, 1970 page 166

CÉSAR Masque XXIII (Mask XXIII), 1968 page 166

Giuseppe PENONE Piede (Foot), 1972 page 167

Alan SONFIST Last Will and Testament, 1973 page 168

Ana MENDIETA Untitled (from the 'Silueta' series), 1976 page 169

Francesca WOODMAN House No. 4, Providence, Rhode Island, 1975–76 page 170

Francesca WOODMAN Untitled (from the 'Angel' Series, Rome), 1977–78 page 171

Antony GORMLEY Bed, 1981 page 172

Helen CHADWICK Viral Landscape No. 3, 1988–89 page 173

Marc QUINN Self, 1991 page 174

Charles RAY Oh Charley, Charley, Charley . . . , 1992 page 174

Miroslaw BALKA 2 × /o2,5 × 167 × 15/, 1990 page 176

Janine ANTONI Eureka, 1993 page 177

Mona HATOUM Recollection, 1995 page 177

EXTENDED AND PROSTHETIC BODIES page 178

Atsuko TANAKA Electric Dress, 1956 page 178

Nam June PAIK and Charlotte MOORMAN Human Cello (Interpreting John Cage's '26'1.1499 for a String Player), 1965 page 179

Nam June PAIK and Charlotte MOORMAN TV Bra for a Living Sculpture, 1969 page 179

Lygia CLARK Dialogo de Maos [Dialogue of Hands], 1966 page 180

Lygia CLARK The I and the You : Clothing/Body/Clothing, 1967 page 181

Hélio OITICICA Wearing Parangolé P19 Capa 15, Gileasa: to Gilberto Gil, 1968 page 181

James Lee BYARS Five in a Dress, 1969 page 182

Louise BOURGEOIS Costume for 'A Banquet', 1975 page 182

Rebecca HORN Arm-Extensione (Arm Extensions), 1970 page 183

Rebecca HORN Fingerhandschule (Finger Gloves), 1972 page 183

STELARC Event for Stretched Skin, 1976 page 184

STELARC The Third Hand, 1976-80 page 184

ORLAN Omnipresence, 1993 page 185

Matthew BARNEY BLIND PERINEUM, 1991 page 186

Heli REKULA Hyperventilation, 1993 page 187

Leigh BOWERY Leigh Bowery in Performance at the Anthony D'Offay Gallery, 11–15 October 1988, 1988 page 187

Lucy ORTA The Unit, 1996 page 187

Stahl STENSLIE and Kirk WOLFORD CyberSM, 1994 page 188

Bruce GILCHRIST (with Jonathan BRADLEY) Divided by Resistance, 1996 page 188

Eglė RAKAUSKAITĖ In Honey, 1996 page 189

DOCUMENTS page 190

PAINTING BODIES page 193

Georges BATAILLE Primitive Art, 1929 page 193

Harold ROSENBERG The American Action Painters, 1952 page 193

Jiro YOSHIHARA Gutai Manifesto, 1956 page 194

Allan KAPROW The Legacy of Jackson Pollock, 1958 page 194

Yves KLEIN Truth Becomes Reality, 1960 page 195

Maurice MERLEAU-PONTY Eye and Mind, 1961 page 196

Susan SONTAG Happenings: An Art of Radical Juxtaposition, 1962 page 197

Carolee SCHNEEMANN Eye Body, 1963 page 197

Gilles DELEUZE The Body, the Meat and the Spirit: Becoming Animal, 1981 page 197

Helen MOLESWORTH Before *Bed*, 1993 page 198

GESTURING BODIES page 201

Neo-Concretist Manifesto, 1959 page 201

George MACIUNAS Fluxus Manifesto, 1963 page 201

Milan KNÍŽÁK Demonstration for All the Senses, 1964 page 202

Yayoi KUSAMA Artist's statement on WABC Radio, 1965 page 202

Joseph BEUYS Statement on How to Explain Pictures to a Dead Hare, 1965 page 202

Dick HIGGINS Statement on Intermedia, 1966 page 203

Michael FRIED Art and Objecthood, 1967 page 203

Lucy R. LIPPARD John CHANDLER, The Dematerialization of Art, 1968 page 203

ART & LANGUAGE Concerning the article 'The Dematerialization of Art', 1968 page 205

Robert MORRIS Anti-Form, 1968 page 206

Carolee SCHNEEMANN Naked Action Lecture, 1968 page 206

Mierle Laderman UKELES Maintenance Art, 1969 page 206

Marcia TUCKER Phenaumanology, 1970 page 207

GILBERT & GEORGE A Day in the Life of George & Gilbert, the Sculptors, 1971 page 209

Ben VAUTIER Art = Ben, 1973 page 209

Thomas MCEVILLEY Diogenes of Sinope: Selected Performance Pieces, 1983 page 210

Kristine STILES Between Water and Stone – Fluxus Performance: A Metaphysics of Acts, 1993 page 211

Jean-Jacques LEBEL Interview by Arnaud Labelle-Rojoux, 1994 page 214

Kathy O'DELL Displacing the Haptic: Performance Art, the Photographic Document and the 1970s, 1997 page 215

RITUALISTIC AND TRANSGRESSIVE BODIES page 216

Antonin ARTAUD The Theatre and Cruelty, 1933 page 216

Hermann NITSCH The Blood Organ, 1962 page 216

Otto MÜHL Materialaktion: Manifesto, 1964 page 217

Rudolf SCHWARZKOGLER Script for a Wedding, 1965 page 217

Günter BRUS Artist's statement, 1965 page 217

Wolf VOSTELL You: A Decollage Happening for Bob and Rhett Brown, 1964 page 218

François PLUCHART Body Art, 1974 page 218

Peter WEIBEL Artist's statement, 1978 page 219

François PLUCHART Risk as the Practice of Thought, 1978 page 219

Thomas McEVILLEY Art in the Dark, 1983 page 222

Kristine STILES Survival Ethos and Destruction Art, 1992 page 227

Meiling CHENG Bob Flanagan's Body Double, 1998 page 229

BODY BOUNDARIES page 230

Herbert MARCUSE An Essay on Liberation: Introduction, 1969 page 230

Willoughby SHARP Body Works – A Pre-critical, Non-definitive Survey of Very Recent Works Using the Human Body or Parts Thereof, 1970 page 231

Cindy NEMSER Subject – Object: Body Art, 1971 page 233

Jonathan BENTHALL The Body as a Medium of Expression: A Manifesto, 1972 page 235

Lea VERGINE Bodylanguage, 1974 page 236

Catherine FRANCBLIN Body-Object, Woman-Object, 1975 page 238

Moira ROTH Towards a History of California Performance: Part One, 1978 page 238

Moira ROTH Towards a History of California Performance: Part Two, 1978 page 240

Julia KRISTEVA Approaching Abjection, 1980 page 242

Elaine SCARRY The Structure of Belief and Its Modulation into Material Making, 1985 page 243

Nelly RICHARD The Rhetoric of the Body, 1986 page 244

Rob LA FRENAIS The Pit and the Pendulum: An Anatomy of Real Performance, 1993 page 245

RoseLee GOLDBERG Here and Now, 1995 page 246

PERFORMING IDENTITY page 247

Sigmund FREUD Parapraxes: Introduction, 1916 page 247

Jacques LACAN The Mirror Stage as Formative of the Function of the I as Revealed in Psychoanalytic Experience, 1949 page 248

Max KOZLOFF Pygmalion Revisited, 1975 page 248

Severo SARDUY The Transvestites, Kallima on a Body: Painting, Idol, 1975 page 250

Carolee SCHNEEMANN Interior Scroll, 1975 page 250

Ira LICHT Bodyworks, 1975 page 251

Lucy R. LIPPARD The Pains and Pleasures of Rebirth: Women's Body Art, 1976 page 252

Hannah WILKE Intercourse with ... , 1976 page 256

Gloria Feman ORENSTEIN The Re-emergence of the Archetype of the Great Goddess in Art by Contemporary Woman, 1978 page 257

Mary KELLY Woman - Desire - Image, 1984 page 257

Donald KUSPIT The New Subjectivism: Inside Cindy Sherman, 1987 page 258

Francesco BONAMI Yasamasa Morimura, 1992 page 259

Peggy PHELAN Developing the Negative, 1993 page 259

Leslie C. JONES Transgressive Femininity: Art and Gender in the1960s and 1970s, 1993 page 260

Judith BUTLER Bodies That Matter, 1993 page 263

Coco FUSCO The Other History of Intercultural Performance, 1994 page 265

Amelia JONES Dis/playing The Phallus: Male Artists Perform Their Masculinities,1994 page 265

Eve Kosofsky SEDGWICK Queer Performativity: Warhol's Whiteness/Warhol's Shyness, 1996 page 271

Rebecca SCHNEIDER Gender in Perspective: Have We Really Gone Beyond?, 1997 page 273

ABSENT BODIES page 275

Piero MANZONI Some Realizations, Some Experiments, Some Projects, 1962 page 275

Robert PINCUS-WITTEN Theatre of the Conceptual: Autobiography and Myth, 1973 page 276

Rosalind KRAUSS Video: The Aesthetics of Narcissism, 1976 page 277

Helen CHADWICK Soliloquy to Flesh, 1989 page 280

Miroslaw BALKA Conversation with Jaromir Jedlinski, 1991 page 281

Francésco BONAMI Charles Ray: A Telephone Conversation, 1992 page 281

Miwon KWON Bloody Valentines: Afterimages by Ana Mendieta, 1996 page 282

Margaret SUNDELL Vanishing Points: The Photography of Francesca Woodman, 1996 page 283

EXTENDED AND PROSTHETIC BODIES page 284

Lygia CLARK About the Act, 1965 page 284

Rebecca HORN Arm Extensions, 1968 page 285

STELARC Artist's statement, 1977 page 285

Howard JUNKER James Lee Byars: Performance as Protective Colouration, 1978 page 285

Donna HARAWAY A Cyborg Manifesto: Science, Technology and Socialist-Feminism in the Late Twentieth Century, 1985 page 286

Stuart MORGAN Matthew Barney: Of Goats and Men, 1995 page 287

Paul VIRILIO Urban Armour, 1996 page 287

PRE-FACE

BY TRACEY WARR

Throughout history artists have drawn, sculpted and painted the human form. Recent art history, however, reveals a significant shift in artists' perceptions of the body, which has been used not simply as the 'content' of the work, but also as canvas, brush, frame and platform. Over the course of the last hundred years artists and others have interrogated the way in which the body has been depicted and how it has been conceived. The idea of the physical and mental self as a stable and finite form has gradually eroded, echoing influential twentieth-century developments in the fields of psychoanalysis, philosophy, anthropology, medicine and science. Artists have investigated the temporality, contingency and instability of the body, and have explored the notion that identity is 'acted out' within and beyond cultural boundaries, rather than being an inherent quality. They have explored the notion of consciousness, reaching to express the self that is invisible, formless and liminal. They have addressed issues of risk, fear, death, danger and sexuality, at times when the body has been most threatened by these things.

The history of work by artists using their own body as the material of their work reveals a cross-fertilization of ideas and ideologies from different disciplines and cultures. At the turn of the century Sigmund Freud's theories of the unconscious began to influence the way in which the mind and body were understood. Although many of his theories have been challenged and reformulated since then, Freud's idea that the unconscious mind affects behaviour in ways that the subject is not necessarily aware of has changed the way in which the relationship between mind, body and behaviour are perceived. In the 1910s and 1920s Dada artists such as Tristian Tzara and Kurt Schwitters used irreverent, performative and multi-disciplinary tactics in order to incorporate physical bodily realities as a challenge to the 'pretence' of traditional representation in art. Escaping from the conventional museum with its wall- and plinth-based art, Dadaists made art in places they considered more 'real' and more relevant: cafés, cabaret halls, newspapers, the street. Surrealism, which developed out of Dada, introduced a psychological twist and helped to popularize the Freudian fascination with sex, dreams and the unconscious, epitomized by a work such as Max Ernst's *Pietà or Revolution by Night* (1923). The collage, photomontage, installation, performance, environments and assemblages of Dada and Surrealism broke out of the frame and the flat plane of painting and began to engage with everyday life.

The Surrealists' interest in dreams and the unconscious was evident in their paintings, sculptures, actions and manifestos[1] and was also fuelled by the anthropological research of their contemporaries[2] and by further developments in psychoanalysis. Modern art has been notoriously fascinated by distant peoples, exemplified by Picasso's admiration for 'primitive art' clearly apparent in such paintings as *Les Demoiselles d'Avignon* (1907). Exhibitions of peoples and artifacts from 'exotic' colonial countries provoked a popular hunger for information about these different cultures. The challenge posed by this representation of non-Western cultures had a profound impact on many artists who were attracted to these different traditions of 'self': traditions in which altered states of mind such as dreaming, insanity, hallucination and near-death experiences were directly related to the body as forms of somatic knowledge. Anthropology was a fertile source for an alternative semantics of the body, which had been suppressed by layers of Western rationalism. Non-Western cultures were not so focused on a notion of the individual as a central, cumulative point, but rather on an understanding of self as part of a continuum in time, a community, an environment, a cosmos. Ecstatic rites, alien social customs such as human sacrifice, ritual initiation, circumcision, body painting, scarification, tattooing and piercing, were observed to use the body as access to another plane.

The physical and philosophical impacts of the First World War in Europe were immense. In 1918 Viennese artist Oskar Schlemmer wrote from the battlefield, 'the new artistic medium is a much more direct one: the human body'.[3] The scale of death and destruction brought the reality of corporeal existence into sharp focus, dislodging previously held beliefs and values and altering the status quo in terms of race, class and gender. By the dawn of the Second World War, erupting into a world that had hardly had time to heal from the physical and emotional wounds of the First, attitudes to the body had altered irrevocably.

After the Second World War, during a period of relative prosperity in both Europe and America, artists such as John Cage, Marcel Duchamp, Allan Kaprow, Yves Klein, and in Japan, Kazuo Shiraga and the Gutai group, took advantage of developing non-gallery spaces and alternative ideologies to create process-based, multi-disciplinary work, often using performance – or 'action' – to express their ideas. For example, in America Jackson Pollock's radical horizontal positioning of the canvas in the studio changed the relation of the body to the painting; the movement of his body around the flat canvas became an integral part of the work. Other artists, for example Allan Kaprow and Jim Dine, organized 'Happenings' which recreated the canvas as a three-dimensional space. In Europe Yves Klein used his models as 'brushes', directing their movements as they 'painted' with their bodies. In Japan Kazuo Shiraga 'painted' his canvases with his feet, literally placing his body in the work.

The brutal treatment of the human body in battles, death camps and barbarous medical experiments during the two world wars informed the Viennese Actionists' symbolic language of slaughter, torture, operation and sacrifice. Work by artists using their own bodies, among them Günter Brus, Hermann Nitsch and Otto Mühl, has proved too difficult for many to assimilate, and has often been neutralized through marginalization, mythologization or its simple omission from art history. Audiences and critics have frequently found body art disturbing, and reacted by characterizing it as psychotic and exhibitionist, an aberration in art history. The sensationalist reception of the Actionists' work, for example, often continues to overlook the fact that their mutilations, torture and coprophilia were mostly theatricalized, fictionalized or staged for the camera. Actionism can be seen as a direct response to the post-war situation in Germany and Austria, although its use of ritualized and extreme self-mutilation has been influential in the work of other artists outside Austria. Less extreme, although equally significant, examples of analogous work that deals with breaking down taboos and boundaries can be found in the work of such US-based artists as Nam June Paik, Carolee Schneemann and Paul McCarthy.

By the 1960s writers such as Susan Sontag were disputing the position of formalist Greenbergian critics who separated style and content. New writers argued against interpretations that posited an artwork as a fixed synopsis of the artist's intentions – incontrovertible and fundamental in meaning. Philosopher Roland Barthes' assertion that in literature the true voice is not in the writing but in the reading, could as well be applied to art and its audience, i.e., the reception is as crucial as the creation of art.[4]

This distrust of individual authorship was reflected by Fluxus artists in the 1960s, among them Hi Red Center, George Maciunas and Yoko Ono. Their international membership and manifestation shared the Duchampian emphasis on idea, gesture and behaviour over visual production. Other artists such as Yves Klein and Piero Manzoni, echoing Duchamp's early Dada gestures (for example, a star-shaped haircut), made performative works often involving the public 'signing' of objects and bodies both as ironic authentifications and, more ambivalently, as projections of self. In a similar vein, artists in America such as Claes Oldenburg and Carolee Schneemann began to organize events or Happenings which overtly incorporated the audience into the artwork and addressed its co-operative, creative role in the process. In all of this, the active, participatory body of the artist remained central. Artists' work with the body was resistant to the mythology of the artist-as-individual-genius through the sheer ephemerality of the product. For example, Brazilian artist Lygia Clark's work was often a therapeutic ritualistic costume which could not be divorced from the wearer and his or her actions, i.e. from the event.

Artists making performative work have sought to demonstrate that the represented body has a language and that this language of the body, like other semantic systems, is unstable. Compared to verbal language or visual symbolism, the 'parts of speech' of corporeal language are relatively imprecise. The body as a language is at once inflexible and too flexible. Much can be expressed, whether deliberately or not, through the body's behaviour. Use of the body is often ritualized in an effort to contextualize and more precisely fix its meaning. Wildly contradictory reactions to the work of Chris Burden, Orlan, Gina Pane or Hannah Wilke are evidence of the difficulty of controlling and using the body as a language. This is particularly apparent in the reactions to the work of female artists whose work involves the use of their own naked bodies. Even sympathetic critics have often come to the conclusion that artists' use of their bodies as art objects is sometimes the equivalent of self-abuse or exhibitionism. Feminist commentators such as Catherine Francblin have criticized female artists who used their own nude bodies as colluding with the objectification of women. No amount of critical contextualizing or artists' insistence on intention can stabilize the language of the body.

Since the 1960s artists using their bodies have explored the constructed visual and linguistic identities of gender, sexuality and race, offering up these representations as hierarchies of power. For example, from Hannah Wilke to Mary Kelly, female artists have sought to show the constructed identity of femininity. This is taken to a further extreme by an artist such as Cindy Sherman, who employs costume as disguise to stage images of feminine stereotypes. The way in which we dress or the hairstyle we adopt can reflect the controlling social norms and expectations. Artists have used their bodies to dismantle the parameters of these norms and disrupt accepted signifiers of identity. Provocative revisions of gender and sexuality have sprung from inventive reformulations of identity, spurred on by both fantastic visions and political imperatives. Paul McCarthy describes his cross-gender personae as 'pretending to be female, but obviously male'.[5] The transvestism of Jürgen Klauke, Carlos Leppe or Urs Lüthi does not merely question the stereotyped category of male gender and the representation of femininity; it questions the notion of a stable identity and sense of self. The body is a fluid signifying system, which in the twentieth century is continuously undergoing challenging and liberating transformations. The boundaries of the individual shift constantly as the boundaries between public and private, and the notion of the individual, change. The idea of a hermeneutic, essentialist self – what Amelia Jones refers to as 'the Cartesian subject' – is no longer simply accepted.

Technology has already vastly extended our life expectancy, our physical environment, our perceptions and our memories. New, constantly created hybrid forms break down static categories and suggest new technologies of the body. The results are contemporary visions of cyborgs: ambitious, intelligent machine-people. These depictions of bodies, which employ highly crafted theatricality, also display a contemporary ambivalence about the body and its link with technology: a balance between technophilia and technophobia. Stelarc's work contends that the body is obsolete, no longer able to cope with its physical environment, overloaded by undigested information and intimidated by its own technology.[6] Recent revisionist theories applied to semantics, gender, sexuality, class and race have examined and exposed the fictitious state of many notions that we previously cherished as authoritative truths, among them the different roles of men and women or the site of private or sexual acts. Postmodernist critiques presented by theorists such as Judith Butler or Donna Haraway have instead delineated the means of self-empowerment based on new social codes. Explorations and extension of the body's physical, empirical reality, for example in the work of Bruce Gilchrist or Stahl Stenslie, further our understanding of the limits and possibilities of the body.

Witnessing a live performance rather than experiencing the work vicariously by looking at the resulting documentation leaves the viewer with a very different impression. Peggy Phelan and Rob La Frenais are among critics who have cogently argued for the authentic witnessing and cathartic physical experience of performance for both the performer(s) and the audience. La Frenais suggests that 'real performance' is defined by a 'zone of entropy', a non-closure, a refusal of crystallization.[7] Phelan emphasizes that performance is about disappearance, rather than preservation, about tracelessness and valuing what is lost. 'Performance indicates the possibility of revaluing ... emptiness.' It plunges momentarily into visibility 'in a maniacally charged present – and disappears into memory'.[8] Within this special environment, which is often laid open to accusations of exclusivity and essentialism, not only personal but also wider cultural fears and fantasies might be enacted. Michel Feher sums up our three current obsessions with the body as a search for values which will protect us against an epidemic fed by our carnal desires, a confusion between human and machine, and a dissociation of procreation and sexuality.[9] AIDS and scientific and medical technologies have fuelled a new, metaphorical heightening of death, carnal sin and aberration, as explored in the work of artists such as Ron Athey and Orlan.

The belief that the body can produce knowledge which is not purely rational or empirical is prevalent at the end of the twentieth century. Evidence of somatic or sensual knowledge can be seen to some degree in the rise in popularity of the notion of a healthy body leading to a healthy mind. Nevertheless, efforts to use subjective evidence, techniques and expression in the West are still rudimentary. Many non-Western cultures appear to use the body to gain access to ancient, constant knowledge through the use of shamanic ritual, trance and hallucination. In the West, alternatives to the long-dominant rationalist epistemology have been in evidence throughout the century and become visible at moments when the inherited orthodoxies become untenable. At these moments the voices of women, non-Western and indigenous peoples, and those deemed 'aberrant' for reasons of sexuality, disability or disease are joined by those who are concerned with the needs of our environment and the voices of the non-dominant culture.

The themes around which artists have chosen to use their own bodies as both the subject and the object of the artwork form the different chapters in this volume. Chapter one, 'Painting Bodies', concerns work that shows the trace, stain or imprint of the artist's body in response to the age-old paint-on-canvas tradition. Chapter two, 'Gesturing Bodies', examines artists who transform the body – its acts, its gesture – into art; gesture, behaviour and situations are used in place of art objects. Chapter three, 'Ritualistic and Transgressive Bodies', looks at work which uses the body to enact challenges to the social expecations of the body, often in rituals that perform a cathartic function. Mutilation and sacrifice are used to rupture personal and social homogeneity. Chapter four, 'Body Boundaries', examines boundaries between the individual body and the social environment and between the inside and outside of the body itself. Chapter five, 'Performing Identity', looks at issues of representation and identity. In chapter six, 'Absent Bodies', absence and the mortality of the body are explored through photography, casting, imprints or remnants of the body. In chapter seven, 'Extended and Prosthetic Bodies', the body is extended through prosthetics or technology, to explore cyberspace and alternative states of consciousness.

Much of the work presented here is performative and therefore temporary and ephemeral in nature, and we are greatly indebted to the photographers who have recorded these events. We are moreover grateful to the many critics and writers who have tackled this unprecedented, complex art practice in order to explain its political, social and formal significance in art history, and above all we thank all the artists, who have lived their art literally and courageously on their own skin.

1 French poet André Breton articulated the meaning of the term 'surreal' in the first 'Manifesto of Surrealism' (1924). The term was first coined by French poet Guillaume Apollinaire to refer to his play *Les Mamelles de Tirésias*.

2 For example, the reseach and writings of Emile Durkheim and Marcel Mauss.

3 Tut Schlemmer, ed., *The Letters and Diaries of Oskar Schlemmer*, trans. Krishna Winston (Middletown, Connecticut: Wesleyan University Press, 1972) 50.

4 Roland Barthes, 'The Death of the Author', *Image, Music, Text*, trans. Stephen Heath (London: Fontana/Collins, 1977) 142-148.

5 Paul McCarthy, quoted in Michael Duncan, 'Daddy's Little Helper', *frieze*, 10 (May 1993) 22.

6 Stelarc, 'Von Psycho - zu Cyberstrategien: Prothetik, Robotik und Tele-Existenz', *Kunstforum International*, 132 (November 1995 – January 1996) 72-81. Author's own translation.

7 Rob La Frenais, 'The Pit and the Pendulum', Gottfried Hattinger, ed., *Relikte und Sedimente* (Linz: Offenes Kulturhaus, 1993) 11-15. Author's own translation.

8 Peggy Phelan, *Unmarked: The Politics of Performance* (New York and London: Routledge, 1993) 148.

9 Michel Feher, Ramona Naddaff and Nadia Tazi, eds., *Fragments for a History of the Human Body*, Part 1 (New York: Zone, 1989) 12.

SUR-
BY AMELIA JONES
VEY

[Go] back to the
body,
which is where all the
splits
in Western Culture occur.

Carolee Schneemann, *Ask the Goddess*, 1991[1]

'There is no gap between the social and the biological.'
– Marcel Mauss

'Our embodiment is a necessary requirement of our social identification.'
– Bryan Turner

'We know, we conceive, we even imagine only the signifying body ... The body can belong to the community only by being itself meaningful.'
– Jean-Luc Nancy[2]

In her important book of 1974 on body art,[3] the Italian curator and writer Lea Vergine laid out terms for understanding the obsessive performative surfacing of the artist's body in the visual arts that had burst on to the Euro-American scene in the 1960s and early 1970s. Vergine's gloriously hyperbolic text proclaims that the body artist is 'obsessed by the obligation to exhibit himself in order to be able to *be* ... The choice of the body as a means of expression is an attempt to deal with something *repressed* that subsequently returns to the surface of experience with all the narcissism that surrounds it.' Such a dramatic display of the artist's body – which had, as Vergine suggests, remained largely repressed in the Modernist regime – marks a violent transformation in the very conception of what visual art *is*. Correlatively, it also signals the disruption of how the subjects of making and viewing function in relation to the social matrix in which visual artworks are produced and experienced. The artist's body is viscerally enacted such that the social dimension of human artistic production, which had been repressed since the demise of the historic avant-gardes in the 1910s, 1920s and 1930s, is brought to the surface again.[4] The body, as the work of Marxist urban theorist Henri Lefebvre suggests, is the means by which we produce ourselves as social beings, by which we produce 'social space'.[5]

There is a telling parallel between body art's dislocation of the coherent Cartesian subject of artistic Modernism (centred and made transcendent, as in Descartes' famous dictum 'I think therefore I am') and the contemporaneous post-Structuralist critique of this subject.[6] This points to two related questions, both connected to the primarily Euro-American context of the Western art world: why was the artist's body largely veiled or repressed within Modernism to the extent that it could not be fully 'seen' until the 1960s?; and, what happens to our conception of the artistic subject (the subject who creates) – and of the subject in general – when we begin to 'see' that body after 1960?

Modernist art history and criticism, derived from Kantian aesthetic discourse, are predicated upon the suppression of the particular, embodied, desiring subject; the artist and the critic must remain transcendent rather than immanent (embodied).[7] The radicalizing antics of the historic avant-garde (Dada in particular) aside, the body has served for over two centuries as the 'phobic object' of artistic Modernism, threatening to undermine or even feminize the transcendent Cartesian subject.[8] At the same time, Modernism can be said to have developed the aesthetic in a 'systematic retreat in philosophy from understanding the social and historical meanings of representational practices':[9] that is, Modernism suppresses social context in its fixation on individual genius or experimentation. The repression of the body marks a refusal of Modernism to acknowledge that all cultural practices and objects are embedded in society, since it is the body that inexorably links the subject to her or his social environment. The question of why the artist's body is largely veiled or repressed within Modernism is thus at least partly explained by the stakes of the aesthetic. Its philosophical structure privileged a certain 'disinterested' and thus resolutely disembodied subject – usually the white, Western male: the allegedly universal subject or transcendent, disembodied *cogito* of Descartes' philosophy of being. This subject is recognized at the expense of other, 'primitive' or 'feminine' subjects who, conversely, seem to be tied inexorably to the weighty flesh of their thoroughly 'interested' and socially embedded bodies.[10] The veiling of the body in Modernism is ideologically and practically linked to the structures of patriarchy, with all of the colonialist, classist and heterosexist pretensions it produces and sustains.

Why, in the Euro-American context, do we not 'see' the artist's body fully until the 1960s? The newly re-emerging artists' bodies from around 1960 to the present *enact* the dramatic social and cultural shifts we now define as indicative of a 'post' Modernist episteme. The body, which previously had to be veiled to confirm the Modernist regime of meaning and value, has more and more aggressively surfaced during this period *as a locus of the self and the site where the public domain meets the private, where the social is negotiated, produced and made sense of.*

A phenomenological model of meaning and experience acknowledges intersubjectivity and the full imbrication of the embodied subject in the social, allowing for an analysis of the social effects of various body art practices during this period. As philosopher Maurice Merleau-Ponty has argued, '[w]e must return to the social with which we are in contact by the mere fact of existing, and which we carry about with us before any objectification'. The history of a period does not exist as an 'object' to be identified; the history of body-oriented practices since 1960 'is what *comes about* on the fringes of all perspectives and on which they are all erected'. It is in this way that body-oriented practices reveal themselves in their full historicity and sociality: in their capacity to link subjects (and thus bodies) across and through the thickness of time.[11]

The emergence of the artist's body in the radicalizing 1960s is linked to the problems of subjectivity and sociality endemic to late or 'pan' capitalism, characterized by a single

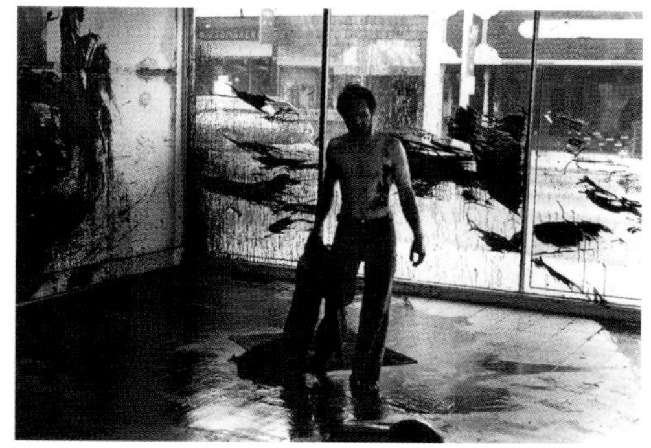

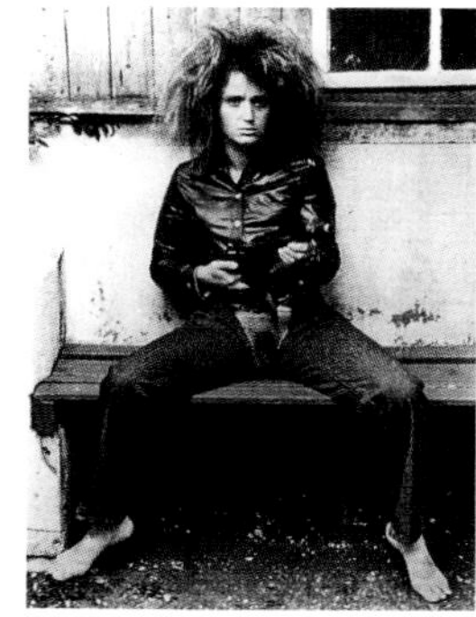

'globally dominant political economy' that demands that individuals submit their bodies so that they can function more efficiently under its 'obsessively rational imperatives ... (production, consumption and order)'.[12] In pancapitalism, subjects become objects of the commodity system with its never-ending processes of exchange. The display, performance and often fragmented referencing of the artist's body thus negotiate the pancapitalist social system, with its commodification of all aspects of everyday life, its attempted conversion of all lived experience into what Martin Heidegger called a 'world picture', where every subject becomes a viewable object in a framed scenario of visual pleasure.[13] The emergence of the artist's body addresses this voracious commodification and, in particular, the marketing of the artist (via the artist's body) as commodity fetish.[14]

The artist's body becomes a gesturing, expressive body, sometimes an aggressively *activist body* (in tune with the protest movements of the 1960s and early 1970s), or perhaps a parodic, self-commodified body. Developing out of the existentialist and individualist rhetoric of the 1950s (from Sartre to the Beats), with its action-painting heroes and Cold War anxieties about conformity, body art initially becomes a mode of projecting the suffering self into 'authenticity' – as in the tragically self-destructive figure of Jackson Pollock, photographed or filmed in the act of painting.[15] In the late 1950s and early 1960s body art is largely aimed towards an exhibition of the self in its full embodiment as a way of laying claim to 'being' itself. (It is in this sense that, as Vergine notes in the above quote, the individual is obsessed by 'the obligation to exhibit himself in order to be able to *be* ...') At the same time, this 'authentic', existentialist artistic self begins to self-implode through its own histrionic excessiveness. The exaggerated 'genius' personae of Yves Klein and Piero Manzoni (who goes so far as to sell cans of his own shit as 'art') and the elevation by Fluxus and Happenings artists of deadpan 'everyday' behaviours to art phenomena in the early 1960s,

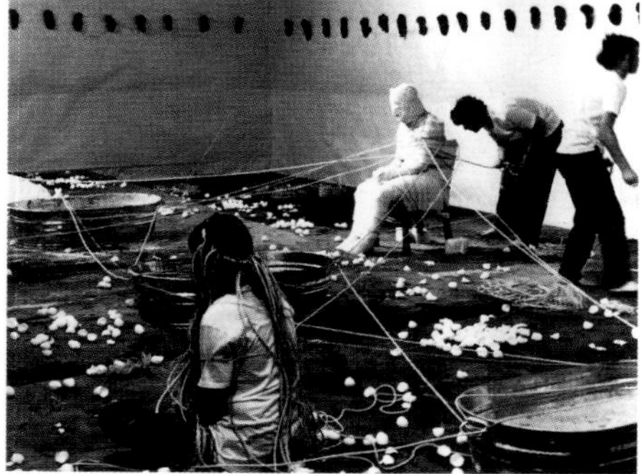

articulate a new artistic subject who holds a parodic, or at least ambivalent, relationship to the 'authentic' image of Pollock painting.

In the 1970s body art becomes increasingly frenzied, violent and excessive as the 'mechanics of alienation' take over the celebratory sexual frenzy of works such as Carolee Schneemann's 1964 Happening *Meat Joy* and the repetitiveness of other Fluxus and Happening events.[16] The tragic existentialist artist-hero becomes an exaggeratedly, even facetiously macho (as in the works of Paul McCarthy, Vito Acconci, Bruce Nauman and Chris Burden) or hyper-sexualized feminist – and often explicitly activist – subject of the work of art (for example in the work of Ana Mendieta, Mierle Laderman Ukeles and Hannah Wilke). The aggressive self-enactments by artists such as Schneemann, Shigeko Kubota, Yoko Ono, Lynda Benglis, Martha Rosler and Valie Export negotiate Modernism's repression of the artist's body by proposing fully embedded and socially relevant feminist bodies that are also specific 'selves'. Especially in US feminist performances, the histrionically virile action painting body is converted into an overtly wounded but politically activated feminist subject. This can

Paul MCCARTHY Whipping a Wall and a Window with Paint, 1974
Valie EXPORT Genital Panic, 1969
Judy CHICAGO, Suzanne LACY, Sandra ORGEL and Aviva RAHMANI Ablutions, 1972

be seen in the violent rape re-enactment of *Ablutions* (1972; produced collaboratively by Judy Chicago, Suzanne Lacy, Sandra Orgel and Aviva Rahmani) or the parodic enactment of gender difference in the 1970 *Cock and Cunt Play*, written by Judy Chicago and performed by Faith Wilding and Jan Lester.[17]

From the 1970s to the 1980s body art dissipates, splitting off into 'performance art' proper and photographic self-portraiture. The former has come to designate practices that are far more theatrical, narrative performances dependent on the traditional staged relationship with a relatively passive audience. In the latter, the self is insistently objectified and fetishized such that the process of commodification is exaggerated, rather than ignored or critiqued. By the Reagan-Thatcher era, characterized by a wide-scale embrace of consumerist culture at least in US and British contexts, the body/self is experienced in a more and more alienated, commodified form, calling for an increasingly dramatic mode of representation. In the 1980s exaggeration rather than critique thus becomes the dominant means of negotiating the alienation of everyday life in pancapitalism.

Art historian Kathy O'Dell writes of the 1970s as proposing 'more and more a floating subject', calling for a 'desire on the part of the artists to render [the body's] ... objecthood so concretely that their actions would illustrate the [alienation of the body/self experienced] ... in the arena of [the Vietnam] war ... and in society at large ... '.[18] While the subject is more and more alienated by the tendency to understand 'identity' as communicated through surface appurtenances (dress, body care, race- and gender-coded attributes), the 1970s are not in any simple way typified by a greater and greater desire to confirm the 'objecthood' of the body. Rather, the 1970s is a period marked by a dual development: the performance of the body in activist work, where it serves as a signifier of individual-turned-collective political engagement, and a move towards the simulacral self – the performance of the self-as-image – a move solidified in the 1980s. Thus, the anti-commercial, sober enactments of everyday experience in Fluxus in the early 1960s give way to the activist projects of, for example, Hi Red Center, the Guerrilla Art Action Group, Suzanne Lacy and Mierle Laderman Ukeles, and the simulacral self-masquerades of Yayoi Kusama, Urs Lüthi, Eleanor Antin, Hannah Wilke, Cindy Sherman, Robert Mapplethorpe, Laurie Anderson, Jeff Koons and Lyle Ashton Harris.

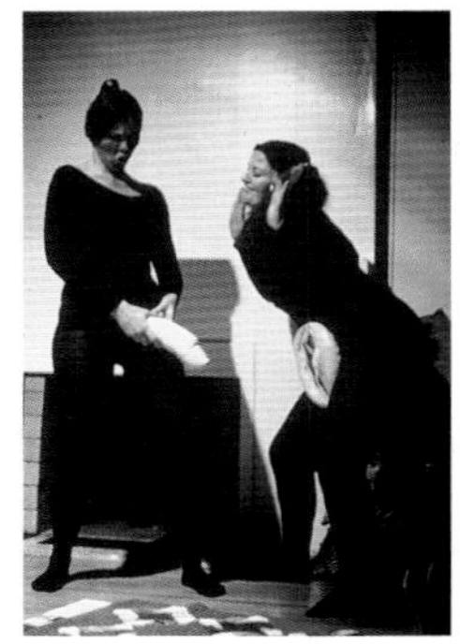

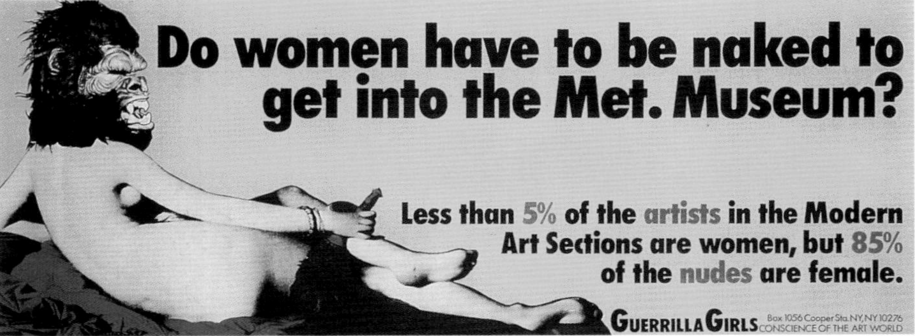

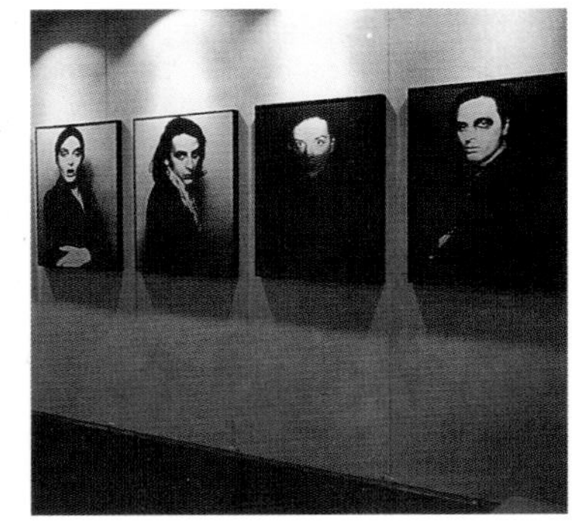

Judy CHICAGO Cock and Cunt Play, 1970, performed by Faith WILDING and Jan LESTER
Poster by the GUERRILLA GIRLS, 1989
Urs LÜTHI Tell Me Who Stole Your Smile, 1974

By the 1990s what Vergine calls the 'love of romance of the self'[19] in earlier body art makes way for a return to the art object or staged installation. But this return is one in which the body is obsessively referenced – as fragmented, splintered and/or staged via elaborate video transfers and/or disruptive installations. This new articulation of the artist's body as shattered, technologically mediated and otherwise resolutely incomplete is paralleled by American scholar Michel Feher's formulation about the meaning of the body in contemporary life:

'*the body is at once the ... actualizer of power relations – and that which resists power ... [I]t resists power not in the name of trans-historical needs but because of the new desires and constraints that each new regime develops. The situation therefore is one of permanent battle, with the body as the shifting field where mechanisms of power constantly meet new techniques of resistance and escape. So the body is not a site of resistance to a power which exists outside it; within the body there is a constant tension between mechanisms of power and techniques of resistance.*'[20]

Artists in the 1990s tend to perform this body as exploded from within as well as from without, prompted by the frenzied tensions of pancapitalism, in which the body is the site of both resistance and power.

The artist's body has functioned as a kind of 'resistance to a power' in relation to the body itself *through its performance as socially determined and determining*. The emergence or unveiling of the artist's body in the 1960s can be viewed as a means of enacting and asserting the self within the social. Because the body is the site through which public and private powers are articulated, it then becomes the site of protest where the revolutionary ideals of the rights movements that resist Modernism's repressive, exclusionary and colonizing logic can be articulated. Addressing the artist's body with a focus on developments within the last forty years is a way of excavating what Feher calls the 'constant tension between mechanisms of power and techniques of resistance', a tension that lingers within the embodied subject.

The Existentialist, Gesturing Artist's Body

It was the 'action painting' body of Jackson Pollock that provided one of the most powerful performative inspirations for artists who looked to activate the body in relation to the work of art. Pollock's body had been obscured in critical discourse throughout the heyday of Abstract Expressionism (from Clement Greenberg, in his typically Kantian, 'disinterested' claims for the immutable value of Pollock's canvases, to Harold Rosenberg, coiner and celebrator of an unnamed but clearly Pollock-inspired 'action' painter). However, Hans Namuth's internationally circulated photographs of Pollock in the act of flinging paint onto prone canvases disseminated the seeds of Pollock's paternal influence from the US to Europe and the Gutai artists in Japan. As Allan Kaprow's famous paean to the artist, the 1958 essay 'The Legacy of Jackson Pollock', makes clear, Pollock, as the photographic, and thus embodied, action-painting hero, becomes the major figure for subsequent generations of artists to negotiate.[21]

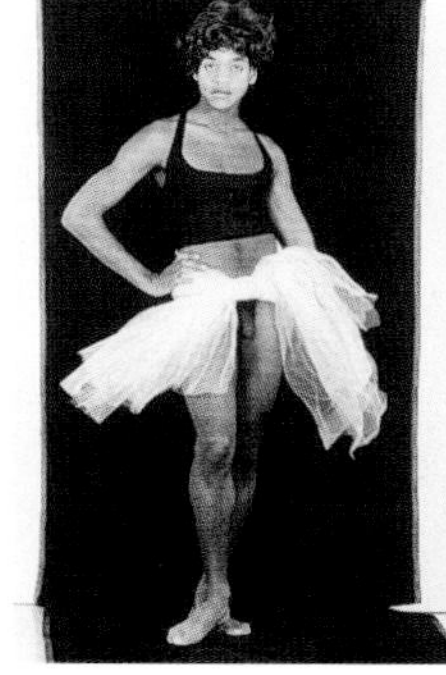

Lyle Ashton HARRIS Construct No. 10, 1989

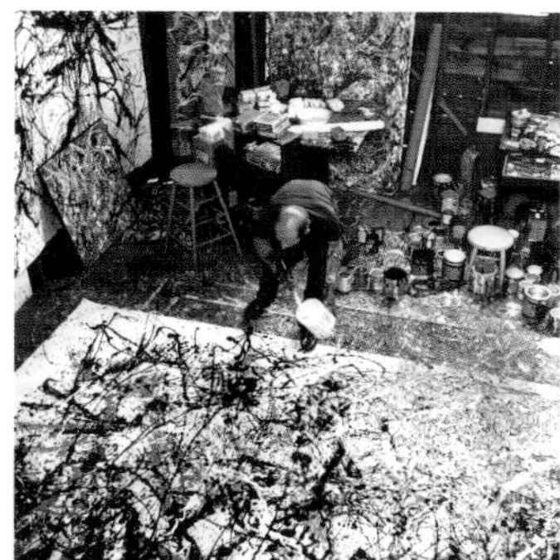

Jackson POLLOCK photographed by Hans Namuth in his studio, 1950

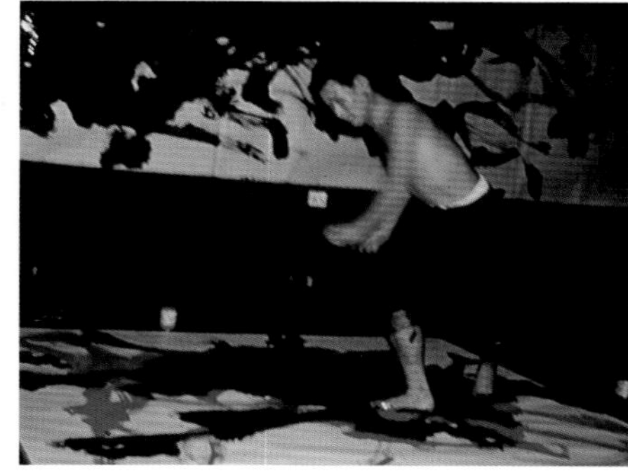

Kazuo SHIRAGA Painting with his Feet, 1956

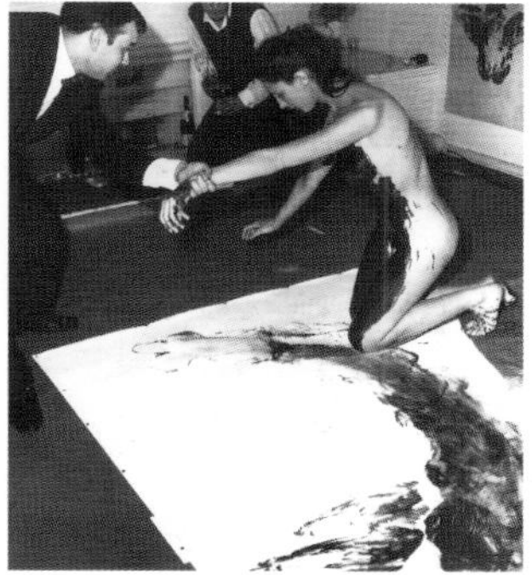

Yves KLEIN Anthropometry, c. 1960

The deification of Pollock during the 1950s (and perhaps especially after his death in 1956) was supported by the strangely intertwined discourses of existentialism and Cold War individualism in US culture in this period. Rosenberg described Pollock as the toiling existentialist action painter – the 'cosmic "I"' who 'will realize his total personality' through the transcendent and mystical act of painting – at the same time as the popular media promoted him as the quintessential Cold War hero, the anti-conformist who promises to transcend the homogenization of subjectivity under Soviet bloc-style totalitarianism.[22] Within the context of the 1950s, Pollock, then, came to be viewed as proof of the free will of the subject – or, in Jean-Paul Sartre's existentialist terms, the fact that every person makes himself what he is and is condemned to be free.[23] This formulation ensured the coherence of the (male) subject in the face of the increasingly terrifying social realm of the post-Second World War period, with the threat of nuclear war, the pressures of commodity capitalism and memories of the holocaust still fresh.

As critic Thomas McEvilley has noted, this configuration of action painting, its emphasis on Pollock in the act of painting, placed 'the direct expression of the artist's unique personality' in the foreground, preparing 'for the claim that the artist's person *was in fact the art*'. For later generations of artists, 'through the survival in the art realm of the Romantic idea of the specially inspired individual, it was possible to confer on an artist the status of a royal or sacred being who is on display to other humans'.[24] The parodistic dimension of such 'homages' to Pollock becomes more explicit as the 1960s roll into the 1970s. None the less, McEvilley clearly highlights the fixation – from Rosenberg onwards and in environments as diverse as New York and Tokyo – on the artist, specifically via his body as pictured in the act of painting. Pollock comes to exemplify not only the existentialist individual, but the newly won hegemony of US culture over defeated France, the former centre of Modernist art production and reception. Pollock, one could argue (as several, if indirectly, have), is marketed around the 'free' world as symbol of the 'freedom' of democratic cultures.[25]

This 'gesturing body' is thus foregrounded, exaggerated and often parodied into the 1960s and beyond. The usual genealogy would trace increasingly overt performances of the act of making a work of art from Pollock through the dynamic art enactments of the Japanese Gutai artists and Georges Mathieu's exaggeratedly Pollockian performances in France and Japan.[26] This lineage would extend through the ironic restaging of performative painting by European artists such as Yves Klein and Piero Manzoni, and would continue into the 1960s with the work of artists referencing the painting body in such a way that the still-lingering Modernist model of artistic genius is politicized. (One thinks here of Shigeko Kubota's Fluxus *Vagina Painting* [1965], for which the artist attached a paintbrush to her crotch and indecorously squatted over the canvas in a parody of Pollock's painterly gesture.)

The still-powerful force of Pollock's example in the 1960s is evident in the plethora of practices that negotiate, often in a kind of parodic homage, the photographic model of Pollock painting. These include Carolee Schneemann's 1963 performance-installation *Eye Body*, which is known through a series of photographs and textual documentation in her book *More Than Meat Joy* (1979),[27] and Brazilian artist Lygia Clark's *Relational Objects*, produced from the mid 1960s into the 1970s. Both transform the Pollockian impulse to register the 'presence' of the artist in the traces of gestural marks on the canvas, themselves 'proof' of the vigorous act of making. Schneemann's transformation turns Pollock's desire to be 'in the painting' into a feminist desire to 'have the painting be on her body', legitimating her body as the wilful subject.[28] *Eye Body* makes the act of painting an environmental, performative and technologized event, one in which the female body is also the body of the artist. As Schneemann describes the piece, '[c]overed in paint, grease, chalk, ropes, plastic, I establish my body as visual territory. Not only am I an image maker, but I explore the image values of flesh as [the] material I choose to work with'. Her painted flesh is surrounded by an environment 'built of large panels interlocked by rhythmic colour units, broken mirrors and glass, lights, moving umbrellas and motorized parts'.[29] *Eye Body* thus represents the interest in sustaining a certain Pollockian notion of painting as an activity, but also marks a striking shift away from the veiled body of Modernism's conception of Pollock.

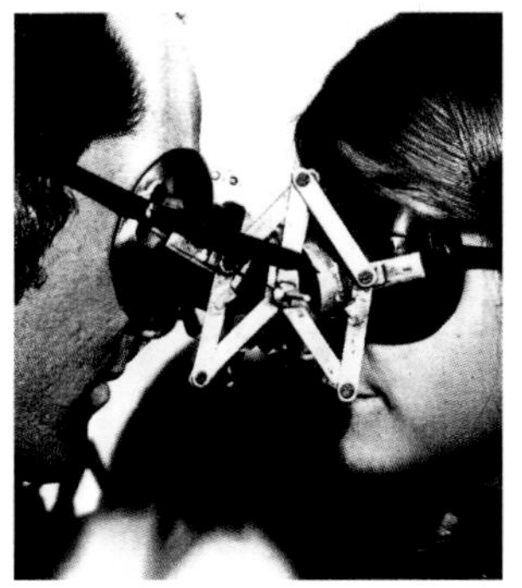

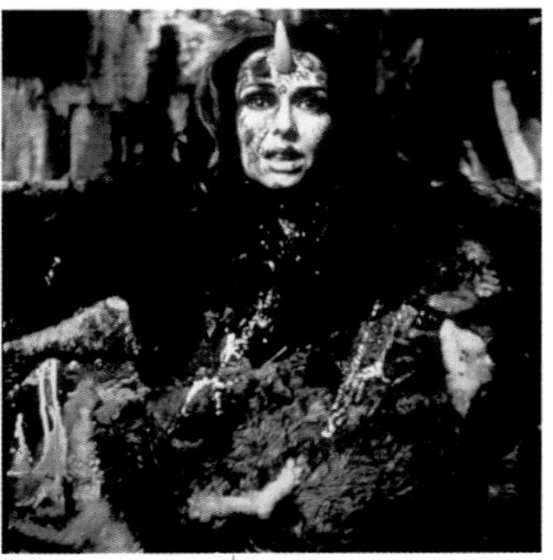

Lygia CLARK Dialogue, 1968
Carolee SCHNEEMANN Eye Body: 36 Transformative Actions, 1963
Joan MITCHELL Chez ma Soeur, 1981-82

While the embodied subject, 'Pollock', had clearly been key to Greenberg and Rosenberg, who regarded action painting or Abstract Expressionism as the epitome of high Modernism, the artist's body was consistently veiled: that is, the critic claimed to extract meaning from the resulting art work, not from the specific body that laboured to produce the work. Its overt appearance would have confused the 'disinterested' position of the critics in privileging the works as transcendent. Schneemann unveils the making body of the artist but simultaneously produces herself as female nude: '*Eye Body* suggested embodied vision, a bodily eye – sighted eyes – artist's eyes – not only in the seer, but in the body of the seen.'[30] In the feminist/existentialist terms of Simone de Beauvoir, Schneemann thrusts the 'immanent' female subject into the domain of the 'transcendent', active male.[31] In *Eye Body* the female nude *looks back*.

Schneemann extends the painterly gesture into a series of actions that confirm life:

'*Take basic stroke of hand nerve pulse to brush, eye to hand, paint to canvas as related, integral organic rhythm: Monet, Velázquez, Rembrandt, Pollock, Joan Mitchell. Event. Particle of universe action. Microcosmic movement building a world moment by moment, motion by motion!*'[32]

Thus, putting the artist's body – as female body – in movement radicalizes the painterly female nude, denying that it is necessarily only the object of a 'male gaze' (here, Willem de Kooning's *Woman* series might be a more accurate foil than Pollock's drip paintings).[33]

In Brazil, at around the same time, with her series of 'vestimentary sculptures' and 'relational objects', Lygia Clark expanded Schneemann's enlivening of the artist on the public stage, focusing on the engagement of an active spectator: 'What I wanted was for the spectator to take an active part in ... [the] space created by these objects.'[34] Clark works obliquely in relation to the history of Euro-American discourses about painting, producing objects that aim to address the psychic state of the subject in a gesture that could be viewed as an exaggeration of the existentialist dimension of Pollock rather than its antithesis. Clark later vehemently rejected altogether what she saw to be the theatrical terms of performance art and the notion of a singular spectator, operating on the premise that the object is 'a mere vehicle for bodily experience', which itself is only fully expressed through a collective body whose relation to the object is psychotherapeutic and evocative of social memories.[35] Expanding on psychoanalysis, each relational object – such as the 1966 *Ar e pedra* (*Air and Stone*), a sealed plastic bag filled with air on which a stone is placed, to hang, fall and 'rise again like a floater'[36] as the participant manipulates it with her hands – exists only in relation to the body that holds it. The individual body that experiences the object is thus marked in its 'relational' – social – dimension.

While Schneemann attempts to press her objectivity into her subjectivity (a gesture that had radical implications for a woman artist at the time), Clark turns the subject inside out,

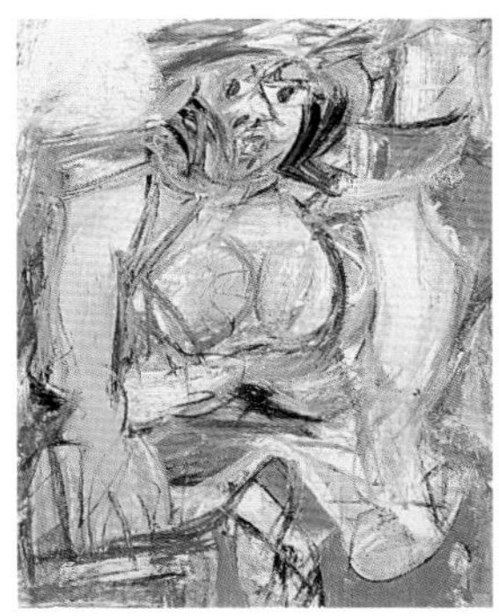

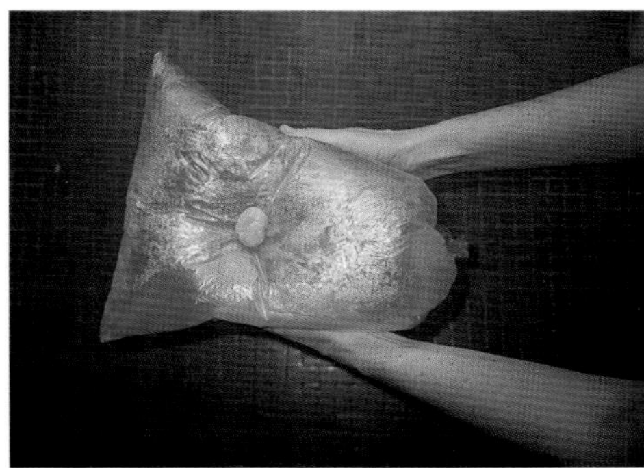

Willem de KOONING Woman IV, 1952-53
Lygia CLARK Ar e Pedra (Air and Stone), 1966

exposing the relationship between the interior subject and her environment. Her embodied artistic subject introjects 'the cosmos' and, at the same time, is 'my own ego crystallized as an object in space'. The subject, Clark insists, 'no longer has a static physiognomy that is self-defining'.[37] While Schneemann makes the body itself into an action painting, merging her flesh into the 'flesh' of her environment, Clark makes the inside of the subject reveal itself by bringing to the surface the collective flow of embodied thoughts, feelings and ideas that constitute the social being. For Clark, the 'exchange between people of their intimate psychology' through environmental situations is the work of art.[38] Viewed from a US perspective that highlights Pollock, Clark brings Pollock full circle, producing performative works that expose to view the 'insides' of the body/mind complex.

Clark's is an idealist (if also deeply conceptual) practice that, like Schneemann's *Eye Body*, returns us to the belief in 'pure' gesture that gave Pollock's works (and the images of him making them) their cultural power. This premium on expressivity is negatively linked (as a rebellious response) to the increasing overlap with mass-media technologies such as television and video in the 1960s, and the cultural and social production of the body/self. That is, an increasingly intimate relationship emerges between the mass cultural heroization of celebrity and the art world's production of the heroic artistic subject (viz Pollock's 1949 appearance in *Life* magazine).[39] In a sense, both Schneemann and Clark are reclaiming this heroic and popularly acknowledged authorial position for those subjects who had been for centuries excluded from its purview – women, non-Westerners and anyone else perceived as being outside Euro-American cultural traditions.

The newly activated, marginalized subjects of Schneemann and Clark – given meaning and significance through the pressure of their flesh upon the world – produce the body/self as 'authentic', capable of bringing about social and personal change. At the same time, these artists' process-based works exaggerate the performative dimension of the Modernist model (i.e., Pollock's performativity), reinforcing the tendency of commodity culture to threaten the notion of art making as a divinely inspired, incorporeal practice, even as it thrives on the ecomonic value of authorial 'genius'. Schneemann and Clark perform bodies that are overtly marked in their social contingency.

The 'Everyday' Artist's Body

The painting, imprinting, gesturing bodies of the 1950s to the 1960s seem to enact an antagonistic relationship to the hypocrisies and violence of Cold War value systems (perhaps especially the militaristic nationalism of this period, which burgeoned in the US and continued to exist, if underground, in Germany and Japan), and to the increasingly alienating effects of mass-communication technologies such as television. In relation to a similarly politicized cultural environment in Chile, critic Nelly Richard highlights precisely the embodied subject's social nature:

'*It is at the level of what we understand as everyday life, namely the intersubjective microcircuits existing within the couple or the family, work, domestic organization, urban movements, etc., that the division between* the public *(the sphere of social productivity) and* the private *(everything outside that sphere) can be traced. The body is the stage on which this division primarily leaves its mark.*'[40]

As the 'meeting-place' of the individual and the collective, the site where the private and public spheres of everyday life 'can be traced', the body is mobilized by artists to activate and, in some cases, to erase the division between self and other, body and space. Thus, Clark's performance *I and You/Clothing-Body-Clothing* (1967) poses a blindfolded couple in plastic suits that literally veil the particularity of their bodies. By manipulating the clothing and its orifices, each member of the couple comes to know the other – and thus her or himself – through sensorial experiences, 'discovering' the subject of art.[41] Similarly, in Senga Nengudi's *Studio Performance with R.S.V.P.* (1976), the art object and exhibition space become extensions of the performer's very flesh. Dressed all in black so that the boundary between her body and the rest of the piece is indistinct, Nengudi pulls ritualistically at the attenuated leg of a pair of pantyhose braced with weights and attached to the gallery wall. While the 'sculpture' is itself a kind of flesh, Nengudi merges with its objecthood, as if

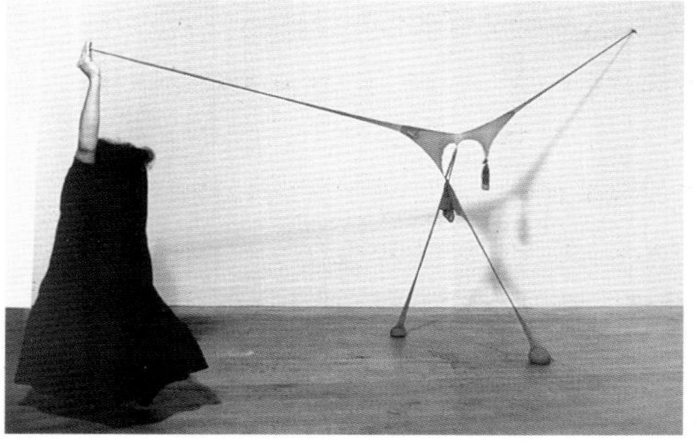

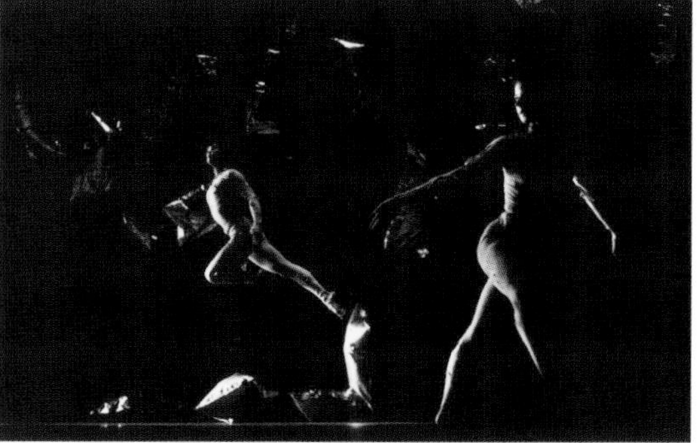

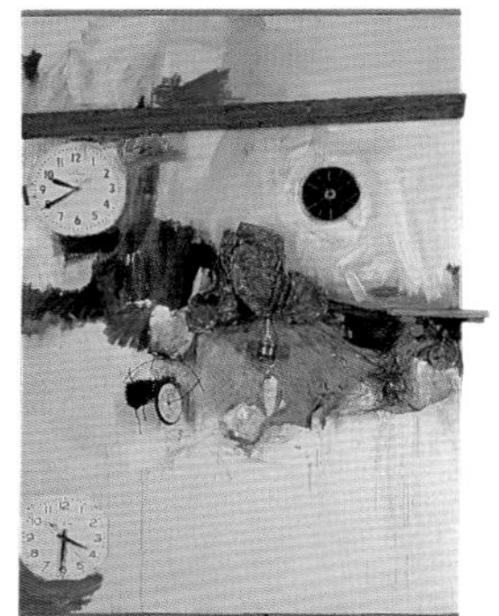

Senga NENGUDI Studio Performance with R.S.V.P., 1976
Merce CUNNINGHAM Rain Forest (with Andy Warhol), 1968
Robert RAUSCHENBERG Reservoir, 1961

enacting Merleau-Ponty's observations about the reciprocal relation of the body to the world:

'*The openness through flesh: the two leaves of my body and the leaves of the visible world ... It is between these intercalated leaves that there is visibility ... all this means: the world, the flesh not as fact or sum of facts, but as the locus of an inscription of truth ...*'[42]

The impulse to activate the everyday in performance work after 1960 also attaches itself to this 'excavation of the flesh of the world'. Works by artists associated with the Fluxus and Happening movements in the early 1960s thus focus on the 'everyday', mimicking and denaturalizing life through repetitive actions – with Dada's earlier merging of art and life a kind of historical echo and the strategic banality of contemporary dance (in particular the work of Merce Cunningham, the Judson Dance Theater and Contact Improvisation providing a crucial backdrop). The interconnections among dance, the visual arts, theatre (in particular the New York-based Living Theater[43]), Fluxus and Happenings events are well documented. Cunningham's everyday gestures – 'found movements' – were ritualized into repetitive dance structures. Not coincidentally – given the links between Cunningham and his partner, musician John Cage, Robert Rauschenberg and subsequently the Judson Dance Group[44] – these paralleled the impulse towards registering the everyday in art via collage or performance with artists such as Rauschenberg in the 1950s and in avant-garde dance in New York City in the 1960s.

Dancers in this period put into motion a radical rethinking about the body in movement. While ballet had veiled the strenuous effort required to complete its tortuous moves – just as Modernist art criticism had veiled the embodied subject responsible for 'pure' abstraction – experimental dance of the 1960s insistently *unveiled* the labouring body of the dancer.[45] As with Clark and Nengudi, contemporary dancers explored intersubjective and collective experience through the stored memory of the body. Thus, in early Contact Improvisation performances from around 1972 to 1976, dancers improvised, often in pairs, and involved viewers in the work by soliciting and sharing in their anticipation. As dance historian Karen Schaffman has argued, Contact Improvisation 'relies on the collective body as choreographer'; it recognizes that the body's actions stem from the conjunction of body language and learned patterns of social behaviour. Contact Improvisation opposes itself to the tradition of an authoritative choreographer who, like the centred, veiled Modernist artist, determines the form and meaning of an artistic practice.[46]

As these dancers recognized, the desire to register the body's everyday activities, while perhaps a sign of social anxiety sublimated into activism, can also be viewed as a productive gesture of debasement. In dance-historian Sally Banes' terms this kind of gesture 'degrades' the human form, 'bringing its subjects down to earth [and] ... re-embod[ying] ... what official culture had disembodied or etherealized';[47] it also mocks its pathos as flesh-bound, wounded or otherwise grotesque. The hyper-awareness of the body's vulnerability is clearly related to anxieties raised by the Cold War, and by the conflicts in Korea and, later, Vietnam. It is also linked to the sex-celebratory, drug-inflected Euro-American counterculture of the 1960s. (It has been suggested that the exhibitionism and riskiness of much body art in the late 1960s and early 1970s was facilitated by drug use.[48])

The democratizing impulse within art practice in this period can be understood in relation to the politically countercultural thrust of the era. No longer are private acts – the fine art of drawing the human figure or the expression of personal feelings – considered the *modi operandi* of art production. Rather, artists now began to produce scripts that could be enacted by anyone as 'art' to solicit rage, compassion and other emotions which would presumably break down the apathy and passivity promoted by corporate bureaucracy. Body art's impulse to democratize leads in two directions from this period: the production of mundane actions (primarily among artists associated with Fluxus and Happenings); and what art historian Helen Molesworth has referred to as the registering of the body – in our case the everyday (desiring, fleshy) body – within the work of art.[49]

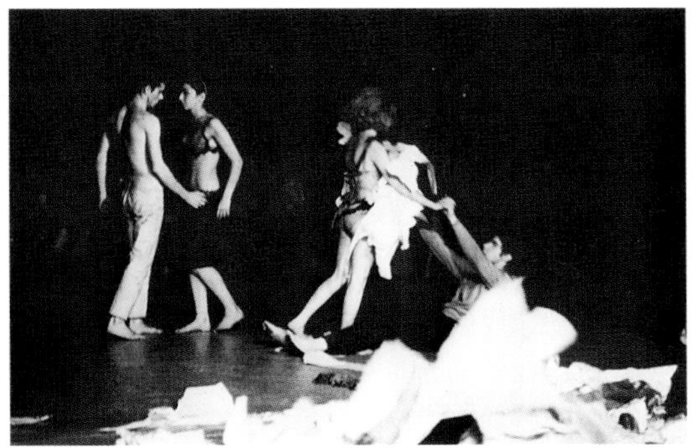
Carolee SCHNEEMANN Meat Joy, 1964

This stinking, breathing, needy, everyday body, which enacts the body/self of the 1960s free love movement, asserts both particular and collective relationships within a carnivalesque, orgiastic piece such as Schneemann's *Meat Joy*. This work definitively 'registers' the body and resolutely insists on the collective dimension of sexual being. A 'fluid, unpredictable performance', in Schneemann's own words, *Meat Joy* 'has the character of an erotic rite: excessive, indulgent, a celebration of flesh as material'. Almost naked male and female performers roll around, rubbing each other with paint and raw meat, in a 'propulsion towards the ecstatic – shifting and turning between tenderness, wildness, precision, abandon: qualities which could at any moment be sensual, comic, joyous, repellent'. Popular songs and tapes of Paris street sounds increase the sense of carnal abandon. It is not only the performing bodies in *Meat Joy* that are enacted as sexually free: as in Contact Improvisation, the audience is seated 'as close to the performance area as possible' to 'heighten ... the sense of communality'.[50]

Meat Joy proposes just the kind of collective liberation from restrictive 1950s ideals of national and individual propriety, of hard work and family values, which the enormously influential social theorist Herbert Marcuse was to argue for in his influential tract of 1969, *An Essay on Liberation*. This revolution would overthrow artistic Modernism to ensure a radical cancellation of capitalism's alienation of labour and commodification of pleasure. Marcuse excoriated the 'global dominion of corporate capitalism', its 'neo-colonial empire' and 'unshaken capacity to subject the majority of the underlying population to its overwhelming productivity and force'. He called for a 'Great Refusal' to break up 'the repressive continuum' of what we are terming here pancapitalism. Works such as *Meat Joy* are surely paradigmatic of Marcuse's conception of a radical counterculture, which celebrates erotic and emotional feeling and 'expresses the ascent of the life instincts over aggressiveness and guilt' to overthrow the puritanism of the 'Establishment'.[51]

In Marcuse's terms, then, the desiring bodies of *Meat Joy* are anarchic and antagonistic to the existing order. In theorizing what she terms the joyous, sexualized and similarly anarchic 'effervescent body' of 1960s performance, Banes goes on to cite cultural theorist Michel Bakhtin on the body of carnivalesque performance:

'*... the body constructed by the rules of polite conduct is turned inside out – by emphasizing food, digestion, excretion and procreation – and upside down – by stressing the lower stratum* (*sex and excretion*) *over the upper stratum* (*the head and all that it implies*). *And ... the effervescent, grotesque body challenges ... the closed, private, psychologized and singular body ... of the modern, post-Renaissance world of individual self-sufficiency. For it speaks of the body as a historical as well as a collective entity.*'[52]

The sexually charged, excreting body is necessarily a collective one, refuting both the modern ('closed, private, psychologized and singular') body and the Cartesian pure mind that leaves the body behind through a masculine transcendence. The everyday also meets the desiring, sexualized, carnivalesque body (a body extraordinary in its excess, and yet mundane in its daily insistence) in the sense that everyday experience, both singularly and collectively, has the potential to thwart the rationalism and spectacular thrust of pancapitalist society. As urban theorist Michel de Certeau has noted, the everyday escapes 'the imaginary totalizations' that are 'produced by the eye' and which encourage the capitalist desire to possess one's environment in commodity form.[53]

In a 1962 Happening performed in Paris, Wolf Vostell instructed the audience to board a city bus, ride around Paris and take note of their aural and visual experiences. Highlighting the transitional status of Happenings and Fluxus, still linked to many of the metaphysical presuppositions of action painting, in 1968 Vostell connected his Happenings to the appropriation of ordinary mass-produced objects as artworks by Dada artists. In existentialist terms, he declared art to be,

'*the* total *event ... a merging of elements, so that life* (*man*) *can be art ...* [*A*] *happening is* direct *art in a cathartic sense: realization of raw experiences and psychic recovery through conscious use of the inner freedom in man*.'[54]

Vostell argued that, by 'taking everyday occurrences out of their context', spectators (and perhaps also artists?) will be encouraged to be more open to understanding 'the absurdities and demands of life'. In a Brechtian move, Vostell hopes thereby to 'shock ... the audience and prompt ... them to reflect and react'. As with Contact Improvisation, it is the *chance* effects of everyday life that intervene and 'shift the environment into new contexts', creating new meanings by breaking up the old and allowing the spectator/participant to 'experience indeterminacy as a creative force'.[55] Vostell's Happenings activate spectators as participants in the flux of more or less spontaneous actions, which themselves mimic the indeterminacy of everyday life.

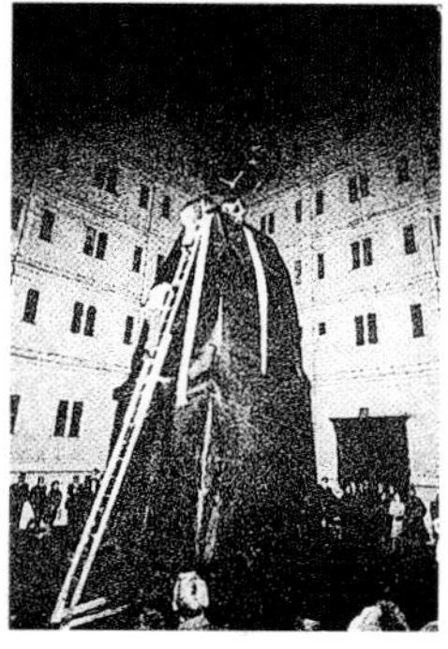

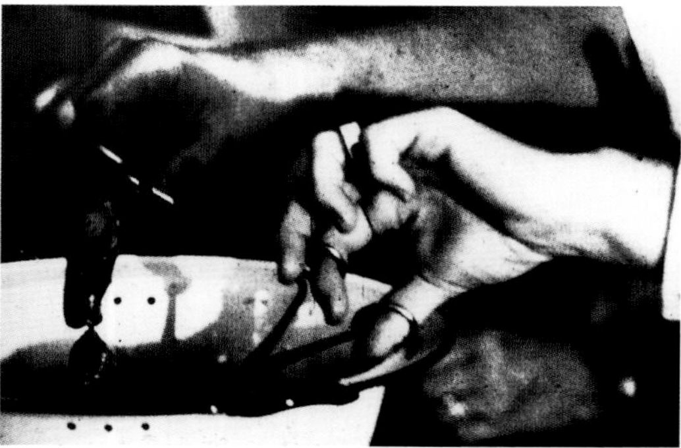

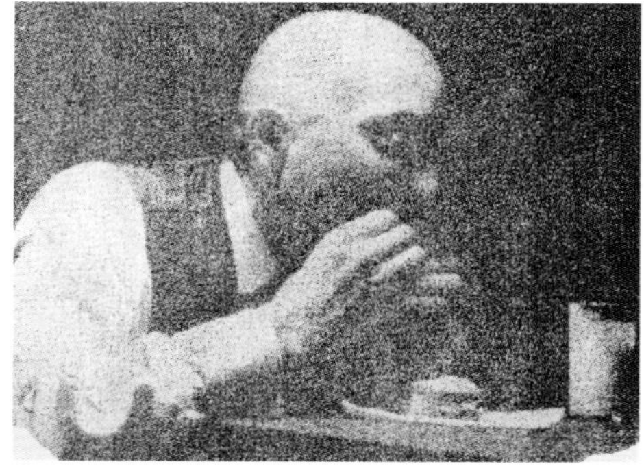

Allan KAPROW The Courtyard, 1962
Barbara SMITH Ritual Meal, 1968
Alison KNOWLES Identical Lunch (version with George Maciunas), 1973

Key to the Happening was the elicitation of the chance effects that mould and shape our experience; in Allan Kaprow's terms, 'a Happening cannot be reproduced'.[56] The loosely scripted actions of the Happening are generally unrehearsed and deliberately mismatched to produce dislocating effects. Thus, in Kaprow's *The Courtyard*, performed at the Greenwich Hotel in New York City in 1962, at one point two workmen enter a courtyard with brooms and begin to sweep; then, as the script demands, '[d]uring this action, MAN WITH BICYCLE enters and rides through crowd, ringing handlebar bell in a quiet way'.[57] The actions take place in everyday spaces ('old lofts, basements, vacant stores, natural surroundings and the street'[58]), which commingle 'audience' with 'artists' into a mass of performers. The Happening proposes to erase the division between viewer and maker, between the everyday and the artistically produced, making all of these performers newly aware of the power of the mundane to join bodies across social spaces.

As Kaprow insisted of Happenings, '[t]he line between art and life should be kept as fluid, and perhaps indistinct as possible' and actions or material could be used from any context '*except* from the arts'.[59] The Happening event still, however, takes its meaning from its point of enunciation – if not the artist as transcendent genius, then the embodied artist existing within the art world as a site of cultural empowerment. The same tension is at work in the extremely simplified actions choreographed under the rubric of Fluxus. Related to Los Angeles-based artist Barbara Smith's *Ritual Meal* (1968), where sixteen guests ate a six-course meal with surgical tools, Fluxus artist Alison Knowles' *Identical Lunch* (1969) was comprised of the daily routine of eating the 'same lunch at the same time at the same place', a monotony that was frequently disrupted by the chance interruptions of everyday events.[60] Maintaining the seriousness of Abstract Expressionism with an occasional edge of quirky humour, the Fluxus event was pared down to the bare bones of banality. Yet, just as the Happenings take their meaning from the art context, so Fluxus events such as *Identical Lunch* become meaningful as philosophically based acts in relation to the complex Fluxus framework. After all, eating the same lunch every day would be nothing *but* banal when performed through habit rather than as a work of art.

Fluxus and, to a certain extent, Happenings, produced an emphatically social artist's body by scripting it into repetitive everyday actions, encouraging our observation of the structure and meaning of daily life and in some senses re-authenticating actions that had been commodified by consumer culture, such as eating or performing household chores, both spectacularized in television advertisements and shows. As Fluxus leader George Maciunas has claimed, Fluxus had an explicitly pedagogical function and aimed to 'redirect the use of materials and human ability into socially constructive purposes'. Fluxus, he continues, is 'against art as a medium for the artist's ego ... and tends therefore towards the spirit of the collective, to anonymity and ANTI-INDIVIDUALISM'.[61] Through Fluxus and Happening events the artists self-consciously cast their bodies within a collective sphere of inquiry, thereby producing socially engaged spectators who would no longer buy into or promote the marketing of false individualism in post-war culture. At the same time the social meaning of their performances, mundane events produced within the art world context, relies on the authorial structures of this context, that is, on the authority of the artist. As far as the art world has incorporated Fluxus, it is via the author names of artists such as Maciunas, Vostell and Knowles.

The impulse to reconsider the everyday persists through almost all performative work using the artist's body from around 1960 onwards – from Tom Marioni's 1970s performances or Linda Montano's numerous 1970s pieces of 'art in everyday life' to Janine Antoni's *Slumber* (1994), in which the artist sleeps at night in the gallery and weaves during the day.[62] The performance of everyday acts as art at least partially denaturalizes the 'private' actions being regularly turned into artifice by television sit-coms, dramas and advertisements. By turning private activities into public manifestos of contemporary being, the artists who activate everyday bodies also activate both these bodies and the spaces they occupy and enliven, whether galleries and museums, or other public (non-art) spaces. As de Certeau argues,

'[*p*]*laces are fragmentary and inward-turning histories, pasts that others are not allowed to read, accumulated times that can be unfolded but like stories held in reserve, remaining in an enigmatic state, symbolizations encysted in the pain or pleasure of the body*'.[63]

Moving dramatically away from the collapsed dimensionality of action painting, with its gestural but veiled artistic bodies, these artists of the everyday mark the historical and social dimension of living with their performative bodies.

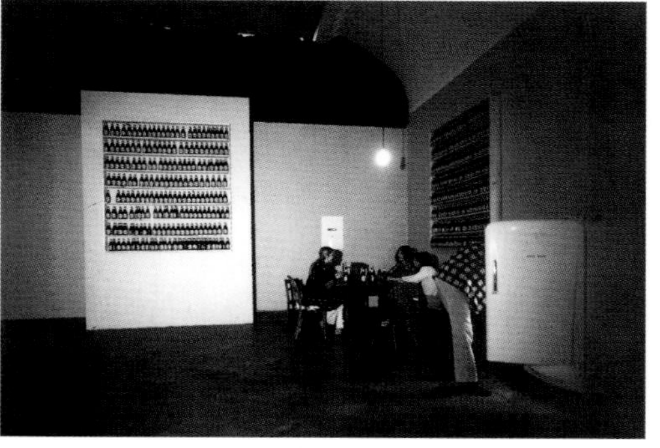

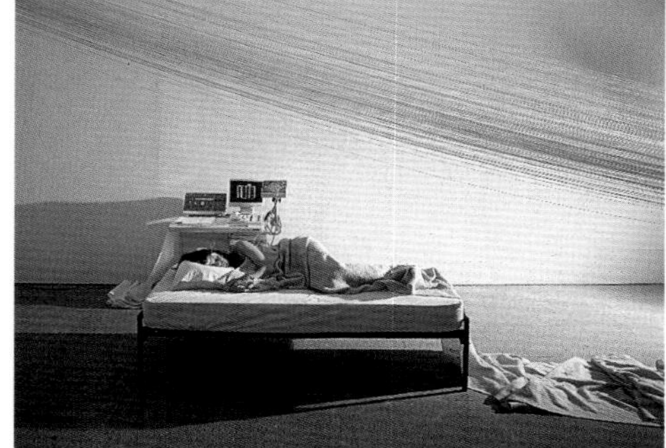

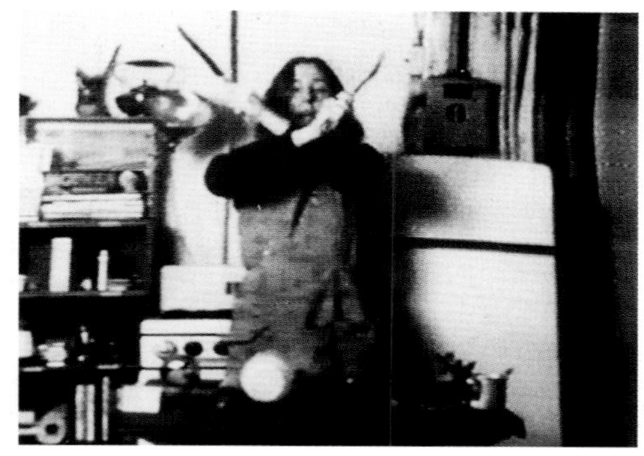

Tom MARIONI Free Beer on Friday, 1979
Janine ANTONI Slumber, 1994
Martha ROSLER Semiotics of the Kitchen, 1975

The 'Authentic' Activist Artist's Body

From the mid 1960s into the 1970s – parallelling the explosion of the rights movements as well as the self-searching and sometimes hedonistic earth-goddess, free-love and drug cultures – the artist's body is mobilized through a deadpan, ironicized or rapturous attachment to its capacity, as repository of an 'authentic' self, to 'defeat ... technological and scientific determinism'.[64] Thus, Barbara Smith claims of her performance *Pure Food* (1973) that it literally transcended its industrial surroundings: 'I sat all day in a favourite field in Costa Mesa on a bluff overlooking the sea (and the nearby oil wells) receiving the pure cosmic rays of sun and cosmos which are totally satisfying.'[65] In a 1971 article entitled 'The Body as a Medium of Expression' and suggestively illustrated by a captioned picture of 'Racial protest at the Olympic Games, Mexico, 16 October 1968', Jonathan Benthall exposes the preoccupation of that heatedly activist time, writing in Marcusian terms:

'*Demonstrations, street art and sit-ins are literally and palpably embodying arguments to challenge verbal mystification and lies ... / all repressed groups will tend to find their most effective and confident expression through the body's wider resources rather than within* [*only*] *the enclosure of verbal language, in so far as they opt for self-assertion rather than for integrating with the norms of the majority.*'[66]

Benthall's comments highlight the sense in which the overtly performative bodies in visual arts practices must be seen as coextensive with the activist bodies of the rights movements (most obviously, perhaps, in the case of feminism). These bodies laboured to produce and secure the enunciatory 'presence' of non-normative subjects, from African Americans and women to the youth who resisted the reified traditions of mainstream culture.

As Marcuse argues in *An Essay on Liberation,* all resistance movements were ultimately about challenging the 'global dominion of corporate capitalism'.[67] Thus, US videographer and critical documentary photographer Martha Rosler comments that 'it was very important to de-aestheticize your relation to the work so that it didn't become formalized into an aesthetic commodity [in the late 1960s and early 1970s] ... '. And the French artist Yves Klein proclaimed his desire to 'leave my mark on the world', to subvert the technological force of 'rockets, Sputniks and missiles' through the 'affective atmosphere of the flesh itself'.[68] While the important performance-art historian Kristine Stiles takes Klein's statements and works at their apparent face value – as proof of the artist's heartfelt activist impulse during the 1960s in particular – one could also read them as more ambiguous, as ironic, uncertain or parodic. The 'authentic' body was often proclaimed within or in relation to body-oriented works from this period. However, there was a frequent tension between this apparently straightforward, openly proclaimed yearning for authenticity (as in relation to, say, the goddess impersonations of Mary Beth Edelson in the early 1970s[69]) and the ambivalent bodies that emerged within this work. The claims of the artists are not transparently 'truthful', nor was the activist body positioned in such simple terms as singularly resistant to state power and technologies gone awry.

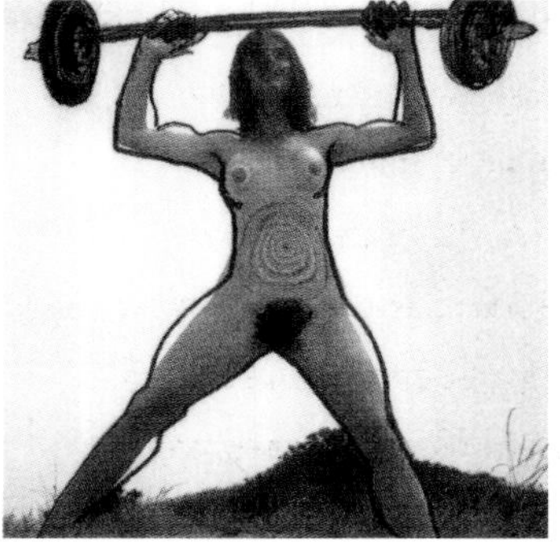

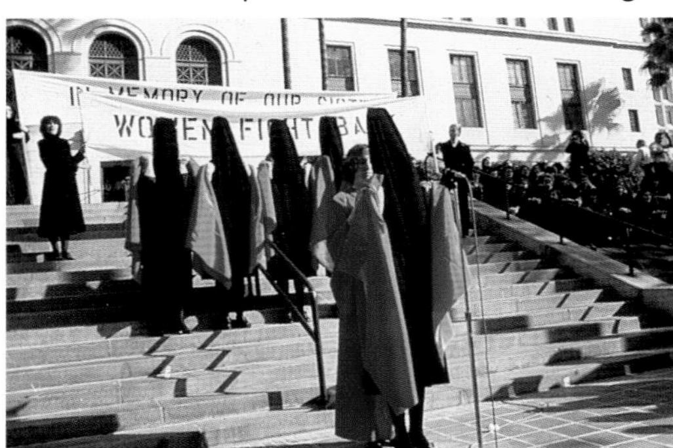

Mary Beth EDELSON Strong Medicine, 1973
Suzanne LACY and Leslie LABOWITZ In Mourning and in Rage, 1977

The activist performance of the 'authentic' body, linked to artists' participation in activist groups such as the Art Worker's Coalition, Women Artists in Revolution, the Women, Students and Artists for Black Art Liberation, the Artists' Protest Committee and the Los Angeles Council of Women Artists, can be understood as a dramatic re-embodiment of the hollowed-out contemporary subject in the service of social ideals.[70] A trajectory within feminist body-art practice, from Edelson's goddess impersonations, to Suzanne Lacy's overtly activist, large-scale performance projects, to Ana Mendieta's impressions of her body into the earth as symbolic enactments of Santería goddesses,[71] shows the power but also the apparent limits of attempting to counter the simulacral thrust of contemporary life through claims of authenticity. In Marcuse's terms such claims retain the language of commodity capitalism and thus fail to revolutionize as true 'anti-art' would do.[72]

Suzanne Lacy is one of the best-known activist performance artists, producing large-scale events that integrate not only *her* body but call upon the collective social bodies relevant to each piece to produce 'sophisticated forms for meaningful social action through art'.[73] Lacy's 1977 *Three Weeks in May* included approximately thirty events held across Los Angeles, including speak-outs, performances, demonstrations and media-orchestrated coverage. Lacy publicly staged performances such as *In Mourning and in Rage* (created with Leslie Labowitz), an anti-rape protest on the steps of City Hall by a group of women veiled in black, and documented the sites of rapes and counselling organizations for its victims on two enormous maps of the city hung in the Los Angeles City Hall shopping mall.[74]

In the early 1970s Lacy was a founding member of the Feminist Art Program in Southern California, a radical pedagogical programme to train women artists and designers. Linked to this important position within the burgeoning feminist art movement, her work is paradigmatic of the intersecting of feminist art and performance art during this period. The idealism of 1970s Californian feminism excavated not only an 'authentic body' for feminist art production (taking 'woman' away from her position solely as object of art) but a universal feminine symbology (or a 'female imagery'[75]). These could both be mobilized by newly empowered women artists. This idealist thrust in feminism parallels the frequent tendency to claim authenticity and full, unmediated presence in performance or body art. Thus, in a 1972–73 essay, critic Rosemary Mayer writes that body art is 'not mediated through canvas ... or the materials of sculpture' but presents itself transparently to the audience.[76]

The yearning towards an authentic body and/or self in the

late 1960s and early 1970s is on one level negatively linked to the threat of commodity culture, or the 'precession of simulacra' – the understanding of the world as pure simulation with no grounded, pre-existing 'real' – which we now understand to be endemic to the postmodern condition.[77] We might read this yearning as an attempt to articulate a gestural self-expression that returns a kind of legitimating weight and mass to the embodied subject, that is, the artist as constituted in, but also productive of, social space. Such an understanding produces the body as socially engaged but also open to transformation or, in Marcuse's terms, resistance. The articulation of the artist's body as activist is linked to collective promises to wrest the subject from the grip of commodity culture, which in contrast seeks to produce a flattened experience of the body as a commodifiable possession (as itself a simulacrum).[78]

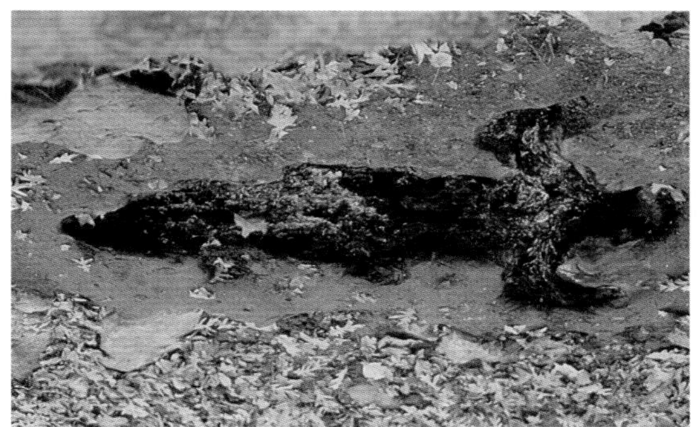

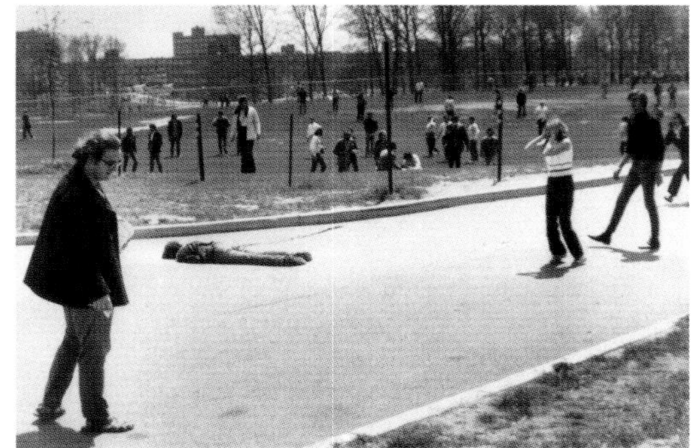

Ana MENDIETA Silueta de Cenizas (Silhouette of Ashes), 1975
Demonstrations at Kent State University, Ohio, 1968

As Catherine Francblin has pointed out, the female body is still the quintessential commodified 'object' within the pancapitalist regime – an alignment that explains the efficacy of the feminist artistic negotiation of narcissism, played out in the production of the body/self as two-dimensional image, as in Hannah Wilke's seemingly endless series of exaggeratedly posed self-portraits. The ritual actions of Lacy's works challenging violence against women thus, in Francblin's terms, 'disappropriate' the woman's body as sexual object, refusing its objectification as image. This kind of refusal puts into play the 'resistance to processes of substitution, displacement, sublimation' – those processes that set the postmodern precession of simulacra in motion.[79]

It is in the same way that Mendieta's *Silueta* Series from the 1970s resists the fetishization and commodification of the body of the artist, the woman, the racially other. She initially performs her body in nature to claim a connection with the earth and the Santería goddess Yemayá (the protector of women) and eventually, in the later works from the series, removes her body entirely, marking its absent form with gashes of dirt or flames. While Lacy counts on the activist 'presence' of the body within the social sphere to make her political point, Mendieta's later *Siluetas* offer another way of negotiating commodity culture. She chooses, in contrast, to absent the self (the artist) as 'origin' of the work, as starting and ending point of artistic meaning. Mendieta's absence forces us to reconsider our attachment to the unveiled and seemingly 'authentic' (but here disappeared) bodies of Postmodernism.[80] The violence of this disappearing (the violence of the fetishization of women's bodies and of coloured bodies under white patriarchy) is signalled by Mendieta's use of fire and wound imagery.

The activist feminist work also negotiates the loss at the centre of social subjectivity – specifically through activism and/or the enactment of the body within social relations. A series of other refusals is thus put into play: of fetishization and commodification; of our projection of ourselves into technologized objects (hence the emphasis on 'authenticity'); and of the injuries inflicted on the subject (particularly the female, non-white, or otherwise queer subject) by war technologies, rape and other forms of contemporary violence. As the locus where social trauma is registered, the body becomes the site of protest, the site 'for transgressing the constraints of meaning or ... normality'.[81]

The tension of the period from the mid 1960s to the mid 1970s between state power (which in the US context was exposed in its fascist dimensions by the killings at Kent State University, the 1968 Democratic convention and the Vietnam war) and the ideological and activist domain of what Herb Blau calls the 'theatricalizing consciousness' of desublimating cultural discourse (as at Woodstock in 1969) proved to be both productive and destructive.[82] This tension was unfortunately resolved in the late 1970s and into the 1980s by a vast incorporation of 'transgressive' behaviours into the commodity system. Thus by the early 1980s the efforts of the Reagan and Thatcher regimes to homogenize culture and promote pancapitalism on a global scale merge almost seamlessly into the simulacral re-enactments of hippy and disco fashion by internationally disseminated celebrities such as Madonna, Michael Jackson and their followers.

Even the 'authentic' activist body becomes commodified.

Performance art splits off in the 1980s from its modest base in dance and the visual arts to form a separate domain of large-scale theatrical productions performed at large-capacity venues such as the Brooklyn Academy of Music. What Laurie Anderson's performances of the 1980s and 1990s, more like rock concerts than 1970s body-art presentations, make clear is that the 'authentic' body was not only never fully present, it was always incorporated into the machinations of pancapitalism. In the 1990s Edelson's sincere self-performances as an ancient goddess dangle at the edges of art history (rescued only by their potentially fetishistic documentation in self-published catalogues and obscure journal articles) while the antics of the Spice Girls have become perhaps equally empowering, if hyper-commodified, models for young girls.

The Body in Pain / The Personal is Political

The performance of bodily pain and decrepitude has become a crucial strategy to imprint the psychic sufferings of individual and collective subjects on to the social screen. As Kathy O'Dell has argued, artists such as Vito Acconci, Chris Burden, Gina Pane and the Ulay/Abramović team deployed masochistic bodily mutilation to 'reveal symbolically the structure of agreements that we make as we try to come to terms with an unsettling, indeterminate consciousness of our own bodies'. For O'Dell, the use of masochism in 1970s body art is a means of countering the broken social contract evidenced by the tragedies of the Vietnam war.[83]

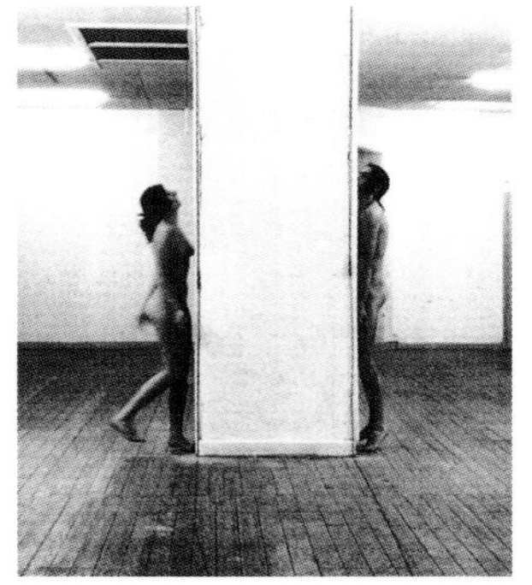

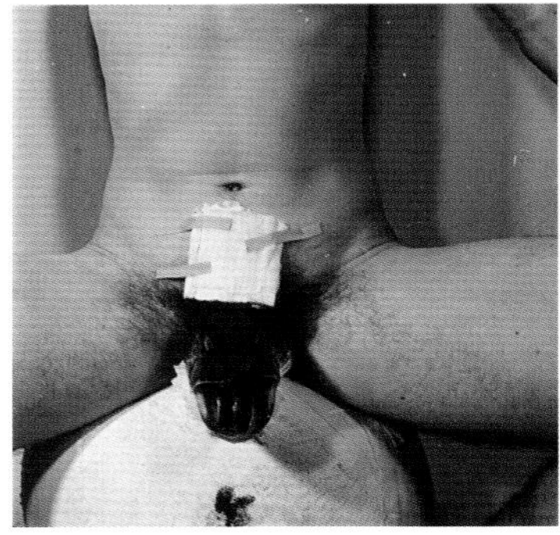

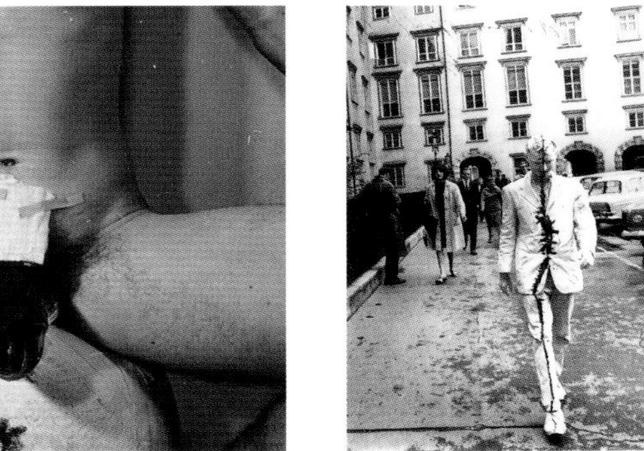

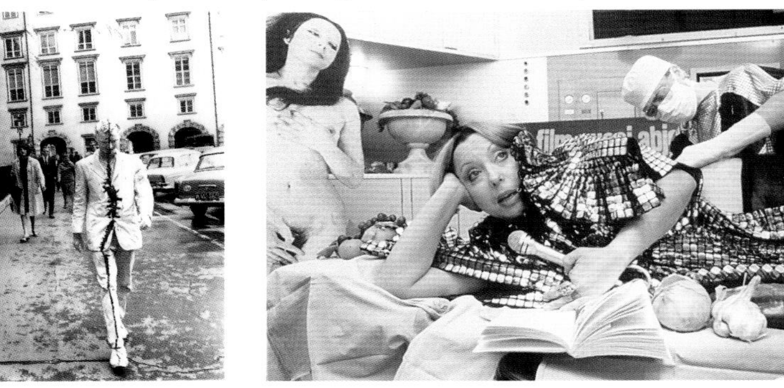

ULAY/ABRAMOVIĆ Interruption in Space, 1977
Rudolf SCHWARZKOGLER Aktion 3, 1965
Günter BRUS Vienna Walk, 1965
ORLAN Omnipresence, 1993

The rather understated, symbolic violence of Mendieta's earth-bound fiery gashes is exaggerated, its sincerity undermined, in the pseudo-violent works of artists such as Paul McCarthy and the Viennese Actionist group during this period. Most notably, the violence of Rudolf Schwarzkogler's famous 1969 histrionic castration performance, documented by the seemingly incontrovertible evidence of the black and white photograph, was nonetheless faked, like most of the bloodshed in the Actionists' works. In performances and videos from the 1970s to the present Paul McCarthy produces a more ironic, perhaps even anti-macho male body, in his performance of himself as a ketchup-covered 'bloody' body-in-pain.[84]

It seems no accident that such performative displays of simulated bodily suffering are executed almost entirely by melodramatic, castration-anxious heterosexual male body artists. Even Chris Burden, who notoriously had himself 'really' wounded in public – in pieces such as *Shoot* of 1971, in which he was shot in the arm by a friend – carefully choreographed and thus to a certain extent controlled, these violent actions. Conversely, Ron Athey, an HIV-positive gay artist, and the queer (if heterosexually identified) sadomasochistic team of Bob Flanagan and Sheree Rose have in the past ten years performed lacerating bodily mutilations before live audiences. Both Athey and Flanagan/Rose use performative violence – which they accept cheerfully or even ecstatically – as if to exorcize the internal violence being done on their bodies by illness (Flanagan suffered from cystic fibrosis, from which he died in 1996).[85]

That the body in pain is a body on the edge of sociality – even a body poised between life and the extinguishing unknown of death – seems to be the point of Gina Pane's self-lacerating body-art works of the 1970s. Pane, one of the only woman artists to carve and wound her own body (making literal what Ana Mendieta and Hannah Wilke had metaphorized through symbolic wounding) until the recent public plastic surgeries of French artist Orlan, tests the integrity of the embodied self by literally slicing through its boundaries. While Chris Burden's body woundings act as tests to ensure and reinforce the ultimate impermeability of his masculine subjectivity (his masochism is linked to the exhibitionistic suffering associated with Christian martyrdom[86]), Pane's seem to collapse the flesh of the self into the flesh of the world. Thus, in the 1971 piece *Escalade non-anesthésiée* (*Non-anesthesized climb*), Pane climbs up and down a metal grid whose footholds are lined with razor-sharp protrusions (her actions possibly signifying the bodily agonies sublimated in Modernist formalist discourse). Performed alone in her studio, but photographically documented for posterity, *Escalade* tests the boundaries of the self, making, in Pane's words, a 'critical inscription of the body' on to and within social space. The cuts of her body are the marks of the social upon the body – which, she remarks, 'is never completely "ours"'. The drips of blood are left on the horizontal rungs of the grid, signs of the body's impact on its enfleshed environment.[87]

Pane's enactments of bodily pain – like the culturally and personally specific exorcisms of Athey and Flanagan/Rose – actively produce abjection, thrusting suffering and leakage (blood, piss, mucus) into social visibility. These leaky bodies violently recorporealize the subjects of culture who spew, shit, piss and vomit their woundedness (as female, gay, sick). They politicize the facetious or overtly faked woundedness and grotesqueries of earlier 'abject' works from Marcel Duchamp's semen-stained *Paysage fautif* (1946) to Piero Manzoni's canned artist's shit (*Merda d'artista*, 1961), Andy Warhol's 1978 piss or 'oxidation' paintings and Paul McCarthy's 'bloody', hysterical male body.[88]

Violence and personal pain have been played out differently by other artists who are not aligned with normative (straight, white, masculine) subjectivity; feminists, for example, have reworked images of violence against women (as in the collaborative 1972 *Ablutions* performance mentioned earlier) in order to make the personal political. In fact the phrase 'the personal is political' can be seen as a verbal rendition of the recognition by feminist artists that all bodily experience carries an inescapably social aspect, and that all political engagement has an unavoidably bodily component. In this sense, almost any body artist can be said to enact the personal as political – whether consciously and progressively or not. By definition, the performance of the artist's body as artwork produces this body/self as a means of public communication. Some artists, however, primarily women and artists of colour, have tended to be more 'personal', even more confessional, than others. This is epitomized by Carolee Schneemann's 1975 performance *Interior Scroll*, in which, naked and covered with paint, she pulls a scroll from her vagina in front of a live audience and reads its angry, confessional text aloud. (As Schneemann has so eloquently put it, 'my work has to do with cutting through the idealized [mostly male] mythology of the "abstracted self"'.[89])

Two other projects, one from the 1970s, the other from the 1990s, demonstrate an alternative strand of body-oriented work, which insistently performs particularized bodies. Such bodies are marked, sometimes exaggeratedly, in terms of their ethnic, sexual, gender and other identifications. This work makes public the repressed, 'private' sufferings of racially, ethnically and economically marginalized subjects in US culture. It is epitomized by the flamboyant 1970s masquerades of the Los Angeles-based group ASCO ('nausea' in Spanish); more recently, it is exemplified by the post-colonial performance of artists' bodies as anthropological 'objects' of spectatorial desire in a series of performative tableaux called *Two Undiscovered Amerindians Visit ...* (with the last part of the title to be filled in by the name of the location of each performance), by artists Coco Fusco and Guillermo Gómez-Peña. Both projects negotiate absence by claiming public space for bodies that are now made embarrassingly visible and exaggeratedly particularized.

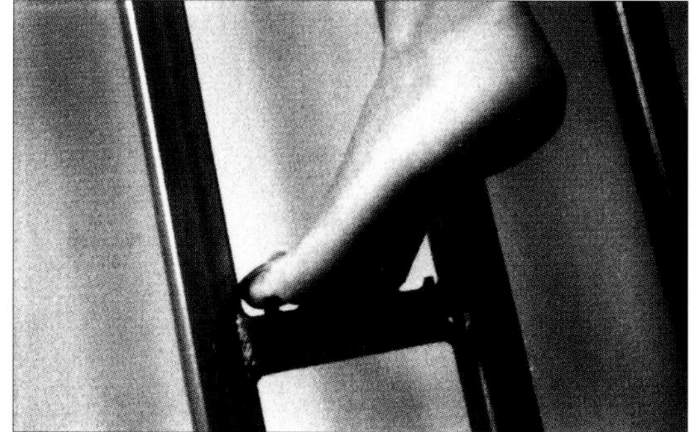

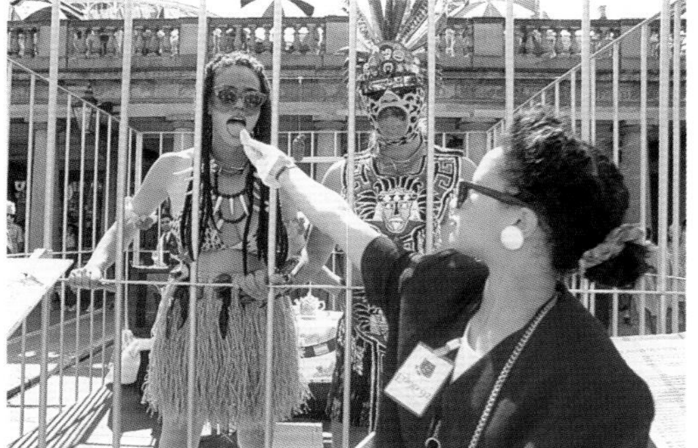

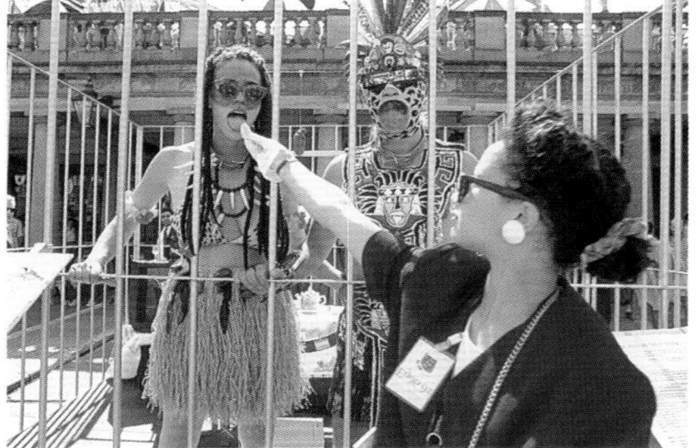

Gina PANE Escalade non-anesthésiée (Non-anaesthetized climb), 1971
Coco FUSCO and Guillermo GÓMEZ-PEÑA Two Undiscovered Amerindians Visit Madrid, 1992
ASCO Walking Mural, 1972

In 1972 ASCO members Patssi Valdez, William F. Herrón III and Gronk seized the public sphere in East Los Angeles, promenading the streets dressed in phantasmagorical costumes as a 'walking mural', with ASCO member Harry Gamboa, Jr. documenting their foray.[90] In flamboyant painted papier mâché, chiffon and make-up, Valdez played the 'Virgin of Guadalupe-in-Black', Herrón a multi-faced mural and Gronk, draped in lime green chiffon and red glass bulbs, a Christmas tree. As art historian Ondine Chavoya has noted, the *Walking Mural* presents the artists as 'both participants and floats' in a public parade. By parodying the static quality of the Chicano/a *Movimiento*'s favoured mode of cultural expression, the public mural, this work acts as a 'counter spectacle intervention' that reclaims social space and configures a new public sphere.[91] (As Gamboa himself has noted, '[s]everal individuals, converted in passing, joined their silent walk through the crowds'.[92]) Through their exaggerated 'rhetoric of walking', ASCO redefines not only the cultural spaces of white LA (including the art world, which has chosen to ignore ASCO in building its identity as cultural centre) but also those of Chicano/a East LA, questioning the idea that Chicano/a art must always appear in the form of heroic murals in the tradition of '*los tres grandes*'.[93]

The LA of ASCO is an LA not only of inclusion (the aim of the 'authentic' activist artist's body) but of discussion, contestation and open-ended self-performance *even in relation to the artist's chosen coalitional identity*. As the shrewd

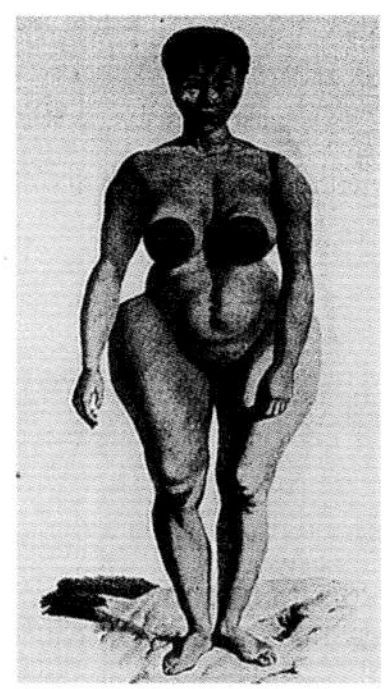
The Hottentot Venus, c. 1815

members of ASCO recognized, it wasn't enough to establish a unified 'Chicano/a' identity to contest white mainstream culture. They had to formulate performative possibilities that could operate effectively 'within a set of social relations largely defined by the mass media and the corporate liberal state'. These possibilities would produce new social spaces of embodiment for young Chicano/a subjects (gay or straight) who were frustrated not only by the disproportionate number of Mexican-American casualties in the Vietnam war but also by the systematic racism perpetrated against them in US culture and the exclusions within the *Movimiento* itself.[94]

Fusco and Gómez-Peña also produce new social spaces, but in this case by turning to the ethnographic paradigm through which the person of colour continues to be given meaning by normative white culture. In their early 1990s performance series *Two Undiscovered Amerindians* ..., Fusco and Gómez-Peña stage a 'reverse ethnography' by mimicking – with their own bodies as agents/objects – the common nineteenth- and early twentieth-century practice of displaying colonialized subjects of Europe and the US as objects of ethnographic desire (as, for example, in the exhibition of the 'Hottentot Venus', a woman from South Africa, in Europe during 1810–15).[95]

In the *Two Undiscovered Amerindians* ... project, the artists planned 'to live in a golden cage for three days, presenting ourselves as undiscovered Amerindians from an island]"Guatinau"] in the Gulf of Mexico that had somehow been overlooked by Europeans for five centuries'. Their daily activities are absurd hybrids of stereotypical 'primitive' behaviours and contemporary mass cultural enthralment: they sew voodoo dolls, lift weights, watch television, work on laptop computers and, for a small fee to be dropped in a donation box, dance to rap music. Gómez-Peña, speaking in gibberish, tells 'authentic' Amerindian tales, while both artists pose for Polaroids with visitors who wish to carry home a souvenir documenting their brush with the primitive.[96]

According to Fusco, the point of the performance is not to interrogate the body/art relation *per se* but to force interactive relationships with audience members – relationships that would expose the nefarious persistence of colonialist belief systems. The original ethnographic exhibits, on the other hand, served to pathologize so-called primitives as bestial, limited in intelligence, overly sexualized and otherwise unformed, so as to raise up Western culture by comparison. Fusco notes as a corollary to this discourse that 'it is the "true" avant-garde artist who becomes a better version of the "primitive", a hybrid or a cultural tranvestite'.[97] *Two Undiscovered Amerindians* ... strategically flips the pathologizing around. Thus, the audience members who – shockingly, to Fusco – believe the piece is a 'real' ethnographic staging of actual primitives are pathologized as dupes as well as bigots via the piece's 'reverse ethnography'.

In *Walking Mural* and *Two Undiscovered Amerindians* ..., specific artistic subjects marked in Western culture as 'other' (marginalized by culture at large, yet marketed by the consumerism of the art world) simultaneously *claim* and *denaturalize* the 'authentic' body of the early, predominantly white 1970s feminists. They enact on a metaphorical scale the pain of discrimination registered in bodies marked culturally other. This work activates the 'personal as political', exposing the private, phantasmagorical side of the self as a way of using cultural 'presence' (in these cases, of embarrassingly overtly self-fetishized bodies) to confront the relationship between the individual and the social in its *specifically ethnic and racial dimensions* (dimensions that are, of course, also always gendered, sexualized, classed, etc.).

Both the ASCO and Fusco/Gómez-Peña projects use humour and humiliation to produce unease in their audiences – in ASCO's case the white masters of high culture in Los Angeles as well as the spectators from their own neighbourhood in East LA; in Fusco/Gómez-Peña's case the unsuspecting street crowds. These projects make use of the power of performativity – its apparent 'realness' and its visceral engagement of the spectator – to produce multiplicitous and excessive variations on both the 'other' to American culture and the norm itself. (Audiences take any number of dislocating positions relative to this work.)

The paradoxical strategy of these body-oriented works is to de-pathologize difference by producing it as excessive and, at the same time, by soliciting the desire *and* identification of their audience. Bodily norms are assumed through a performative, 'reiterative and citational practice' – one that, as Judith Butler claims, 'materialize[s] sexual difference' (as well as, I would insist, racial difference) across the body/self such that otherness is excluded as abject. In this sense ASCO and Fusco/Gómez-Peña exaggeratedly *perform a kind of cultural abjection*. And, while performing abjection, they continue to solicit our identifications and desires. Members of the mainstream art world come to experience the shame of being racist, sexist, classist, heterosexist in such a way that we are abjected in relation to these artists' performative (anti-) normative bodies. Butler's explanation of this dual process of subject/object formation (which must be expanded to encompass racial and ethnic difference) describes the efficacy of the artist's body in such a context: '*As a projected phenomenon, the body is not merely the source from which projection issues, but is also always a phenomenon in the world, an estrangement from the very "I" who claims it. Indeed, the assumption of "sex" [or race], the assumption of a certain contoured materiality, is itself a giving form to that body, a morphogenesis that takes place through a set of identificatory projections. That the body which one "is" is to some degree a body which gains its sexed [and raced] contours in part under specular and exteriorizing conditions suggests that identificatory processes are crucial to the forming of sexed [and raced] materiality.*'[98]

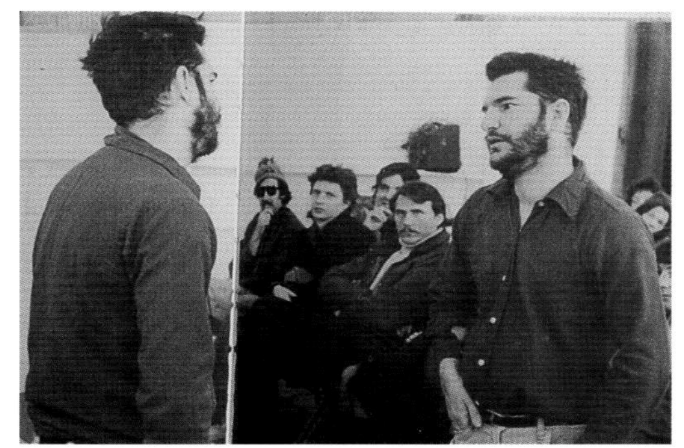

Dan GRAHAM Performance/Audience/Mirror, 1977

Expanding Butler's phenomenological model to encompass the 'raced' or 'ethnic' materiality of the body explains the structures through which *Walking Mural* and *Two Undiscovered Amerindians* ... project abjection on to the viewer, de-pathologizing difference precisely by exaggerating its embodied signifiers to a seemingly untenable degree. In this way, borrowing again from Butler, we could say that ASCO and Fusco/Gómez-Peña claim a kind of racialized 'queerness' as a form of 'citational politics', a 'specific reworking of abjection into political agency' through projection. ASCO and Fusco/Gómez-Peña's body-oriented projects produce the body of the artist – as well as that of the spectator – as both self and other. At the same time these bodies are produced as resolutely social, as bound up in a relationship of complicity such that both become responsible for the production of particular identities as these take shape within the social.[99]

The Simulacral, Self-Reflexive Body

Following from Martin Heidegger's observation regarding the technologization of everyday life in twentieth-century society, wherein the world comes to be 'conceived and grasped as picture', Vivian Sobchack has noted that our bodies 'become increasingly distanced in images, increasingly viewed as "resources", and increasingly lived as "things" to be seen, managed, and mastered'.[100] Many artists have, since the 1960s, deployed imaging technologies to explore this distancing and to return a kind of weighty corporeality to the technologically dematerialized body. Thus, for example, in Dan Graham's *Performance/Audience/Mirror* (1977) the artist stands in front of a wall covered with mirrors and describes in excruciating detail his movements and the audience's behaviour. A video camera tapes this scene of oscillating subject- and objectivity, self-reflexively revealing itself in the mirrors along with the faces of the spectators and Graham's body. The imaging machine becomes itself a kind of 'subject' as it converts Graham and the audience members into framed objects. The audience members perceive themselves in the initial performance as 'pictures', in the mirror, and then are perceived in the resulting video-tape – like Graham himself – as objects of our spectatorial gaze.[101]

From the late 1970s into the 1980s the culture of consumerism reaches new heights in the Euro-American context. The Reagan-Thatcher era in the English-speaking world sees the embrace of untrammelled pancapitalism as federal policy. At the same time the global spread of poverty (facilitated by the corporate downsizing of first-world labour and the exploitation of third-world labour and newly opened third-world markets) and of immune-system diseases such as AIDs goes officially unnoticed. As suggested earlier, this pancapitalist regime consists of a globalized economy (a gargantuan web of commodity exchange of objects and bodies), which forces individuals to submit themselves for remapping, for repositioning within the pancapitalist matrix of commodity exchange, so that they will function more efficiently. Under these imperatives, newly exchangeable bodies – bodies, in Sobchack's terms, that are 'increasingly distanced' and lived as '"things" to be seen, managed and mastered' – are produced.

In this regime body-oriented art practices become a means of either converting the body back into a weighted, cognitively charged self – albeit no longer one of Cartesian certitude – or exaggerating this exchangeability. The sweat, endurance and suffering of the grotesque bodies of artists such as Alastair MacLennan, Ron Athey and the late, cancer-ridden Hannah Wilke, persisting in a somewhat marginalized art world context, have served to thwart the 'efficiency' that pancapitalism demands of the body/self.[102] In contrast, the strategy of exaggerating the simulacral body/self becomes far more common in the 1980s. Such exaggerations by artists such as Cindy Sherman and Jeff Koons characterize a newly reified art world, which itself exploded internationally in the 1980s (from New York to Europe, at least) to encompass a vast celebrity cult of the artist-as-commodity.

On a broader cultural scale the 1980s are marked by the burgeoning of self-conscious discussions about Postmodernism, a term first used in the 1960s but building up to full steam with the publication of theoretical essays by Fredric Jameson and Jean-François Lyotard.[103] Within visual arts discourse Postmodernism is articulated as allegorical, appropriative, deconstructive, as collapsing the boundaries between high and low art. Most importantly for our case, the simulacral artistic bodies of artists such as Sherman and Koons seem to reiterate, if through parodic – and potentially critical – exaggeration, the occlusion of the body as a suffering, pained, smelly, incoherent and chiasmic mode of subjectivication behind the slick, honed bodily surfaces of mass reproduction. Such is also the case with Yasumasa Morimura, a Japanese artist who masquerades in a series of large-scale photographs in the guise of figures ranging from Scarlett O'Hara to those from 'masterpieces' of art history (including Duchamp's own masquerade as a woman in the Rrose Sélavy images [1920–21]). While Sherman, Koons and Morimura still reference the artist's body obsessively, the grotesque, masochistic, suffering artist's body – the body of, say, Paul McCarthy or Gina Pane – goes largely underground again in the 1980s with the demise of the heroic period of body art. As previously noted, performance art proper split off from the visual arts, aligning itself with theatre in the large-scale narrative events orchestrated by artists-turned-celebrities such as Laurie Anderson and Karen Finley.[104]

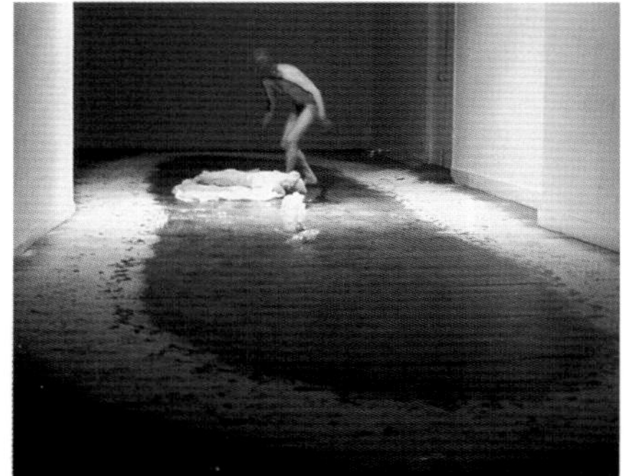

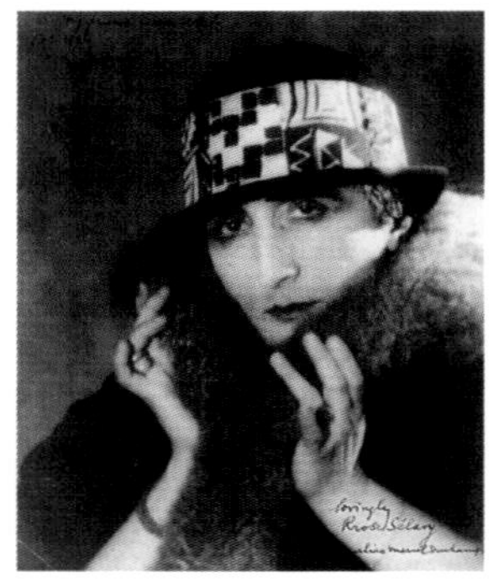

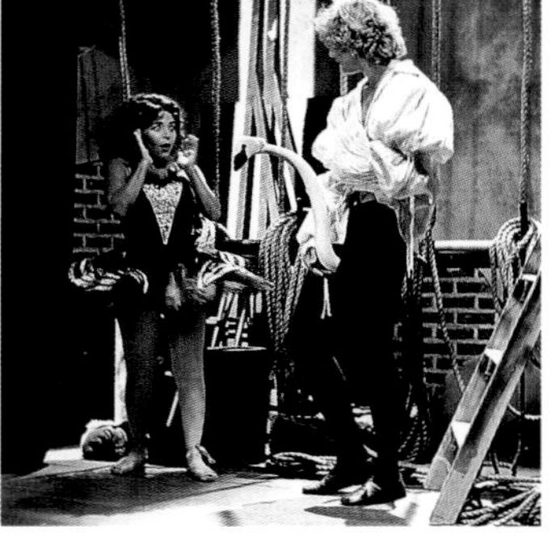

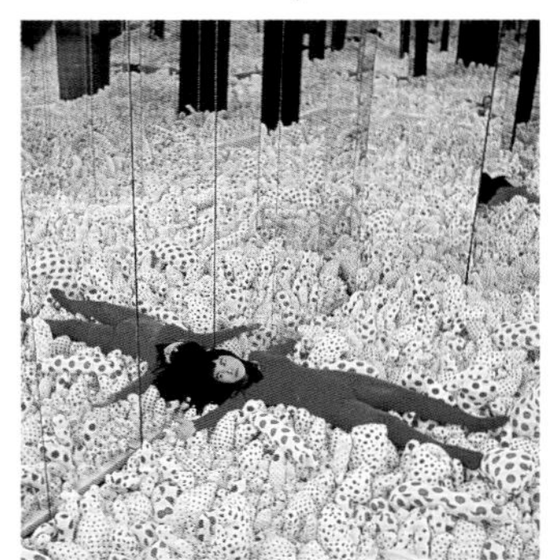

Alastair MACLENNAN Days and Nights, 1981
Marcel DUCHAMP as Rrose Sélavy, photographed by MAN RAY in New York, c. 1920-21
Eleanor ANTIN Swan Lake, 1986
Yayoi KUSAMA Infinity Mirror Room, 1965

What does it mean that the artist's body is oddly 'present' in the 1980s photographic works of highly visible artists such as Sherman, Koons and Morimura but 'present' in a way that merely reinforces its 'absence'? Paralleling the surface emphasis of popular culture's body beautiful cult, when the artist's body did mark its own appearance in the 1980s, it was produced as *simulacral*, as performative, as open to interpretive intervention. In the postmodern regime of what we are calling pancapitalism, as Jean Baudrillard famously pointed out in 1983, 'simulation' ('the generation by models of a real without origin or reality') begins to replace 'representation'.[105]

The self-imaging of Sherman, Koons and Morimura is 'simulacral' rather than 'representational' (the latter implying the existence of a stable or 'real' referent). The 'art history' images of Sherman and Morimura make this point especially clear: by posing themselves in photographic tableaux that mimic 'great works' of the Western art tradition (such as Morimura's doubled mimicry in his posing as Rrose Sélavy, or

Sherman's self-portrait *as* Caravaggio *as* Bacchus in her 1990 *History Painting* series[106]) they mark the absence of an 'original' referent (Rrose Sélavy is no more 'real' than Morimura *as* Rrose Sélavy).[107] This simulacral self-imaging lodges itself as an effect of the 'society of the spectacle'. 'The tangible world' (or at least a world we *believe* is tangible and 'real') is 'replaced by a selection of images which live above it, and which simultaneously impose themselves as the tangible *par excellence*'.[108] The simulacral self in these artists' works marks the effect of the pancapitalist commodification of the body/self, the estrangement of the subject from her or his product – in this case the 'self' itself.

As Duchamp's Rrose Sélavy character or the ambivalently gendered 1920s–30s photographic performances of French artist Claude Cahun make clear, 1980s artists did not invent the idea of photographic self-performance. The earlier performative photographic self-portraits by Eleanor Antin, Yayoi Kusama, Urs Lüthi, Robert Mapplethorpe, Lucas Samaras, Andy Warhol and Hannah Wilke, as well as Duchamp and many others, had begun the process of dislocating the Cartesian notion of the subject transcended in pure thought through a performance, often cross-gendered or otherwise flamboyant, of the self registered photographically.[109] By the 1980s, however, this simulacral concept becomes dominant, positing the body in general – and the artist's body in particular – as always already hypercommodified, *as always already a picture*.

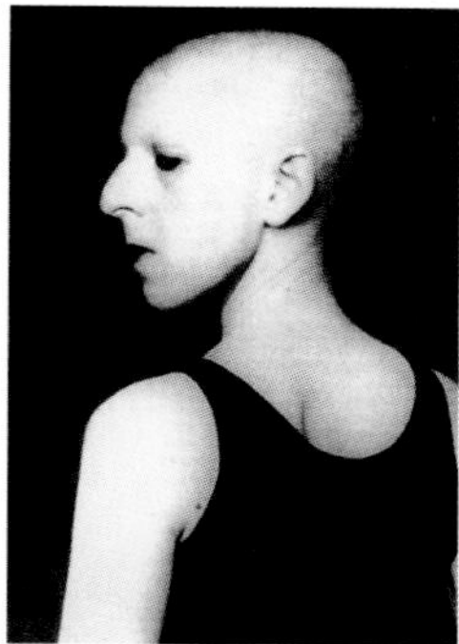

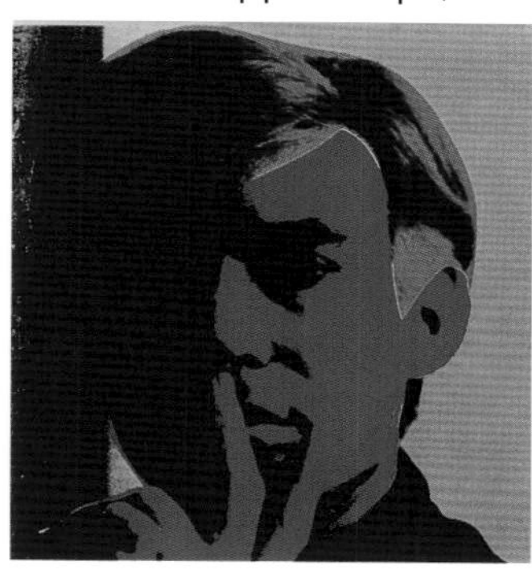

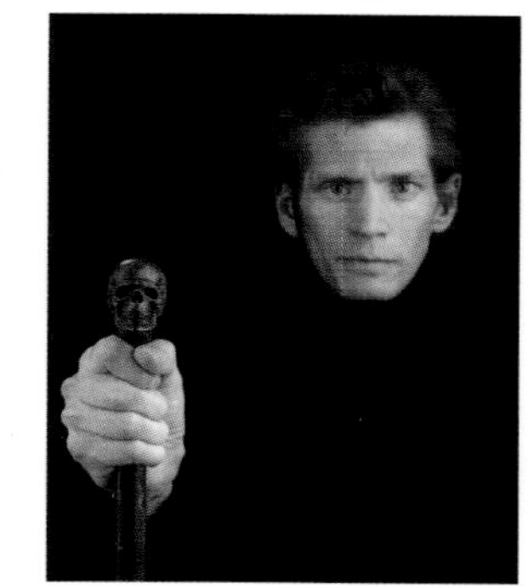

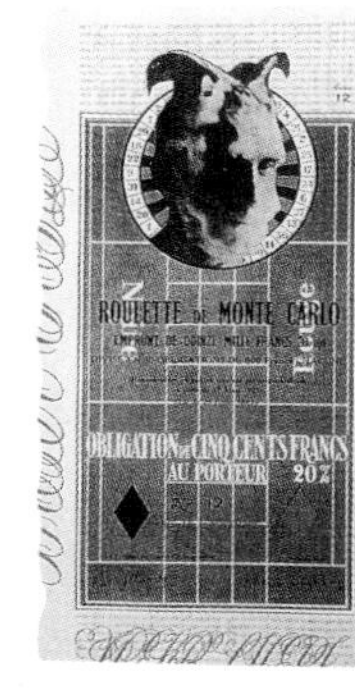

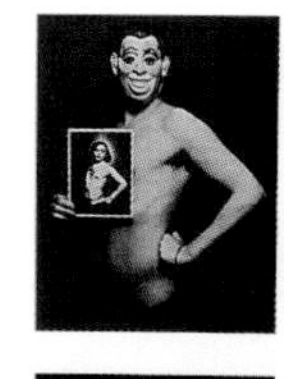

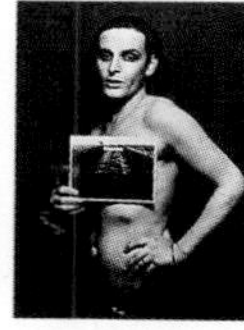

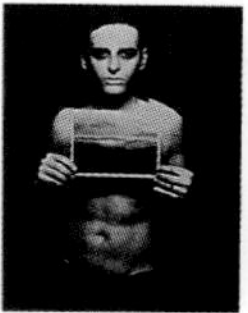

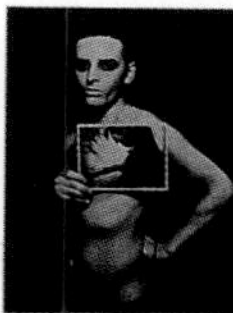

Claude CAHUN Self-portrait, c. 1929
Andy WARHOL Self-portrait, 1967
Robert MAPPLETHORPE Self-portrait, 1988
Marcel DUCHAMP Monte Carlo Bond, 1924
Urs LÜTHI The Numbergirl, 1973

This simulacral self, where ironic disillusionment replaces the self-proclaimed belief in 'authenticity' or cognitive transcendence, perhaps takes its strongest and most estranging form in the visual arts. Rather than projecting the self forwards in socially activist works, implicitly assuming it to be 'self'-evident in its making public of private concerns, artists such as Mapplethorpe articulate the self, as Henry Sayre argues in his 1989 book *The Object of Performance*, as 'a kind of theatre, an ongoing transference of identity, an endless "acting out"'.[110] While the artists' bodies of the 1980s seem to be opposed in every way to the messy, grotesque bodies of earlier body art, in this attachment to 'acting out' there is a strong link between the two. Both are performative; both, whether consciously or not, end up enacting a self that exists only in relation to others – thus opening up meaning and interpretation as an exchange between interrelated, embodied subjects.

Artists from Duchamp and Cahun to Sherman have conveyed and constructed themselves through self-performance as gendered objects of desire in the public realm.[111] By the 1980s it is possible to view Duchamp's 1920–21 masquerade as a woman (Rrose Sélavy) as an early production of the artistic subject *as capital* – as a name and image to be exchanged across cultural boundaries. Perhaps the best example here would be Duchamp's *Monte Carlo Bond* (1924), a scrip on which Duchamp's image and his dually gendered signature (as Marcel and as Rrose) confirm the commodity value of the otherwise worthless 'bond' and, correlatively, of Marcel/Rrose as authenticating 'subject' of the work.

The early 1970s self-performative works of Urs Lüthi and Hannah Wilke inaugurate a newly aggressive exploration of this oscillating, performative, simulacral subject, setting the stage for the obsessive self-posing that reaches its market-friendly apogee in the 1980s. The 'subjects' of Lüthi and Wilke open themselves to the viewer, projecting themselves outward as simulacra. Lüthi's series *The Numbergirl* (1973) and *Un'Isola nell'aria* (*An Island in the Air*, 1975) and Wilke's *S.O.S. – Starification Object Series* (1974) present repetitive series of performative self images. When displayed or reproduced in grids, as both series commonly are, they seem to comment ironically on the evacuated, 'objective' grids of high Modernist painting. They deliberately pollute the purity of these Modernist abstractions with the stench not only of subject matter, but of the most immanent, corporeal kind: the body itself.[112]

By the late 1960s Lüthi, a Swiss artist, was donning various articles of clothing to produce himself in cross-gendered and otherwise travestied ways that set the artistic subject 'Lüthi' in motion, playing him out simulacrally in the guise of multiple 'other' subjects that are none the less still apparently 'him'. 'Everyone', he has noted, 'makes his own little personal spectacle'.[113] In *The Numbergirl* Lüthi poses suggestively, erotically, holding before his emaciated body and sculpted, Garbo-like face earlier photographs from his *oeuvre* – images of himself and of architectural spaces. With each different posture and facial expression – in a repertoire of body language that appears to have originated in an inventory or textbook[114] – Lüthi produces himself as desperate fetish.

With the doubling of his image within the image (the photographed Lüthi holding the photographed Lüthi), he doubles the simulacral effect of the group of pictures, which, in their gridded multiplicity, deny the coherence of Lüthi as 'real' referent, 'real' body or self. This denial is predicated on the simultaneous enticement ('here I am: look and come to know me') and repudiation of desire (there's no 'real' self there). The same denial is emphatically recalled in the oscillatory effects of lack and fullness in *Un'Isola nell'aria*, a series of 'portraits' of what might be Lüthi's own domestic space and its outside environs, but which actually documents the home of a collector, containing many simulacral self-portrait images of Lüthi in drag. In this series architectural space both offers up Lüthi as object of the collector's desire, and refuses his 'actual' presence, for he generally appears within the space only as photographic image on the wall.[115]

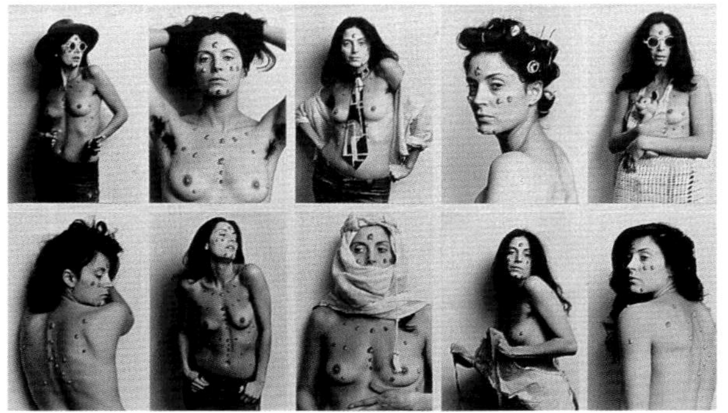

Lüthi is by no means clearly defined as 'artist/origin' in this series: he is offered as object of the collector's and, later, the viewers' fetishizing desires. In these pictures his gender and sexuality are multiplied beyond recognition. As Lea Vergine perceptively remarks, Lüthi 'invert[s] somatic characteristics, thus creat[ing] a crisis in the crystallization of sexual roles'. He 'succeeds in creating a kind of emotional contamination within the spectator who thus becomes either a willing or unwilling partner and collaborator capable of closing the circuit and returning the same interchangeable perception'.[116]

Wilke's repetitious self-imaging in *S.O.S. – Starification Object Series*, part of a career-long project of obsessive posing and self-portraiture, takes a slightly different tack. Like Lüthi, she debunks the individualist belief system of post-Enlightenment Western capitalist (to pancapitalist) patriarchy by insistently performing the self beyond her own singularity. Shown in torso, posing semi- or fully nude, Wilke's flesh is covered with the bubble-gum 'cunts' for which her work during this period became known. These various, highly dramatic, even facetious poses (chest flaunted, head swathed in a veil, body turned away, sunglasses held saucily up to mouth, etc.) partake of the paradox of the mass-marketing of celebrity (usually female) bodies for consumerist desire. The *production* of the celebrity as obtainable object/image is precisely that which flattens and hollows out the celebrity subject, sweeping away the dark, desirable depths of the embodied self in favour of the impenetrable surfaces of the simulacrum.

Wilke's self-reflexive grid – far from delivering her to us through the seemingly inexhaustible range of selves – acts as a kind of fetishistic screen or what Laura Mulvey, film scholar and leading theorist of the objectification of women via the 'male gaze', has called a 'fantasy space' of fetishizing commodity consumption. It is no accident that Mulvey's key example of the intersection of this consumerist regime with the politics of sexuality and of cinematic representation is the degraded grid of identical Marilyn Monroe faces in Andy Warhol's silkscreened, photographically based *Marilyn Diptych* (1962). Another grid, this time its variations exuding only from the vicissitudes of mechanical reproduction, presents the female celebrity self as a 'surface sheen' that 'guards against nameless anxieties associated with the female body outside its glamour mode, which are then repressed, leading to an even more intense reinvestment in the fascination of suface'. The gleam of celebrity subjectivity is marred only by the fragility of the masquerade itself and 'the surface [of the image] starts to crack as the printing process slips and her features distort and decay'.[117]

Wilke's self-scarring with externalized cunts performs the very simulacral production of the self-as-surface that Mulvey identifies in Warhol's *Marilyn Diptych* and which Lüthi has noted he desires to attain with works such as his *Numbergirl*: '[In the self-referential works] I try to explain those things that

Hannah WILKE S.O.S. – Starification Object Series, 1974–82

are on the interior and that I want to transform on the surface.'[118] And yet, the fetishistic dimension of both sets of images testifies to the impossibility of confirming some essential self through the mechanics of simulation. The externalization of the body's interior marks only the fact that the body is 'without organs', installed within a ceaseless flow of desire/commodities.[119] (This is not to say that the body is only object or only fetish; obviously, too, the way in which each body/self negotiates this flow has everything to do with its internally and externally perceived and experienced gender, sexuality and racial, national and class positionalities.)

Extending this interrogation, we might turn to Cindy Sherman's relentless acts of self-production – from the *ingénues* and *femmes fatales* of the 'film stills', which inaugurated 1980s appropriative Postmodernism (or the 'simulacral self' of this period of cultural production), to her more recent performative self-displays as monstrous, abject female body turned inside out – insistently interrogate the process by which the artistic subject takes meaning through her works in the social realm. Sherman's 'women' (not to mention Sherman's 'Sherman') are thus fully embedded in the social relations that give them meaning and economic as well as aesthetic value. For women artists these relations are highly contradictory: the self-portrait images overtly enact the irresolvable conflict between 'woman as object' and 'woman as artist'.

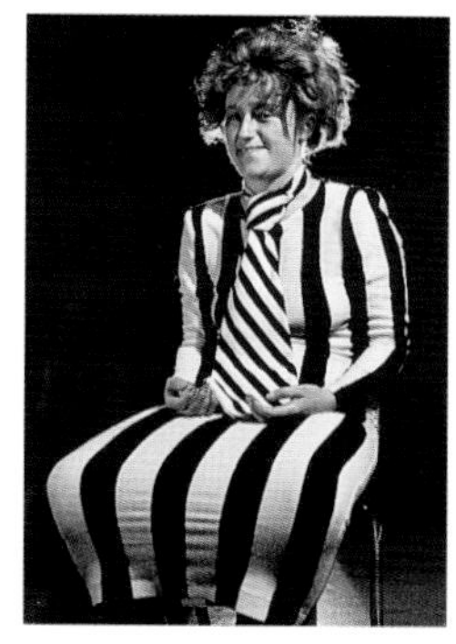

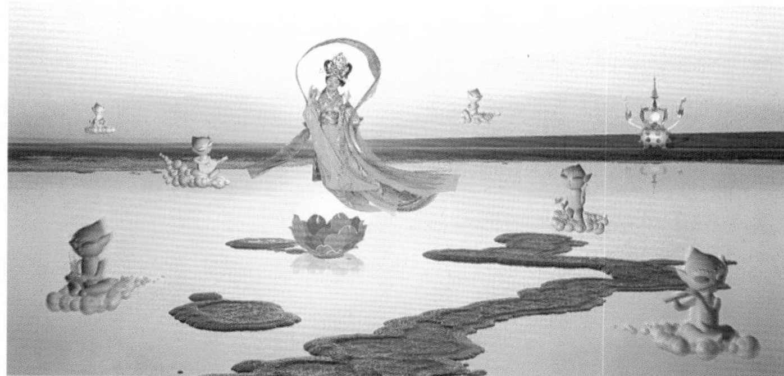

Cindy SHERMAN Untitled No. 138, 1984
Mariko MORI Pure Land, 1997–98

Perhaps especially in her 'fashion' series, commissioned as advertisements and executed in 1983, Sherman opens the gap between these two incompatible selves that any creative woman experiences in patriarchy. Composed through the subverted rhetoric of women's fashion, the images produce Sherman as simulacral 'female model' for bizarre conglomerations of *haute couture*. Her face is marked by the overdrawn makeup or caricatural facial expressions of a lunatic. In *Untitled No.138* (1984), for example, Sherman's 'fashionable' attire – a striped dress and tie – is marred by her leering expression and her hands, which are bloodied by some horrifying homicidal or suicidal act. Through such a violent refusal of passive objectification, Sherman rips the 'feminine' away from its essentialized identification with 'body/object'. Rather than accepting the disempowering potential of the multiplicitous reiteration of the feminine in the society of the spectacle, Sherman wields the spectacle like a sharp knife, simultaneously destroying both the objectified feminine ideal of Western fashion display and the myth of the artist as coherent, masculine, Cartesian subject.

Works by Lüthi, Wilke and Sherman, as noted, mark a mode of production – a mode of negotiating the artist's body – that became dominant in the 1980s: a strategic self-fetishization and obsessive self-imaging that mimics the processes of fetishization (commodity, sexual and photographic) which condition the meaning and experience of the gendered subject in pancapitalism.[120] This strategy takes an exaggerated form in the hyper-artificial photographic tableaux of US artist Jeff Koons, from the 1980s and early 1990s, and the more recent photographic and video tableaux of New York-based Japanese artist Mariko Mori. Mori appropriates ancient to modern Japanese sources from the tea ceremony and Ikebana with their static elegance, to the cyborg culture promoted by the nation's highly advanced technology markets, pressing these symbolic systems through the sieve of Japanese popular culture. In each elaborate morphed landscape, Mori appears, as critic RoseLee Goldberg has noted, 'as a character from a futuristic Japanese cartoon – vinyl-shiny, with pointy hats, plastic tutus, winged anklets and cat's eyes'.[121] Viewed from a Western art world point of view, Mori is the ultimate self-commodifying artist-as-object-of-desire (referring back, whether consciously or not, to the 1960s ebullient self-marketing style of her countrywoman Yayoi Kusama).

In her elaborate, massive (6-m [20-ft] -wide) *Pure Land* of 1997–98 Mori's ceremonial-kimono-clad body hovers, like a divine apparition in plastic, above a glassy seascape peopled by small musician figures that look like a cross between putti, Buddhas and rubber dolls. Mori's 'ethereal, techno/traditional shaman' is both a 'cyborg and a bodhisattva figure from Buddhist Mandala imagery'.[122] The picture is a 1990s version of 1960s psychedelia, merging a hallucinogenic spiritual consciousness with a cyborg mentality. The 'self' Mori produces is resolutely false, if also strongly spiritually symbolic,[123] and occupies a phantasmagorical chemical landscape where the technological *is* the organic.

Mori's self-proclaimed sincerity and utopianism aside, her artifice produces a kind of cybernetic baroque, memorializing a culture of pancapitalist excess where bodies (of artists and others alike) and ideas (spiritual and otherwise) are bought and sold on the art market. Mori's tableaux suggest the impossible instability of the artist's body as anchor of truth or meaning and radically extend the trajectory of simulacral self-representation that I have traced from Duchamp to Sherman. The photographic self-performances of Lüthi, Wilke, Sherman and Mori suggestively expose the way in which our anxiety about the fundamental threat of our emptiness, openness to otherness and existence as 'bodies without organs' motivates the fetishistic reception of works of art.

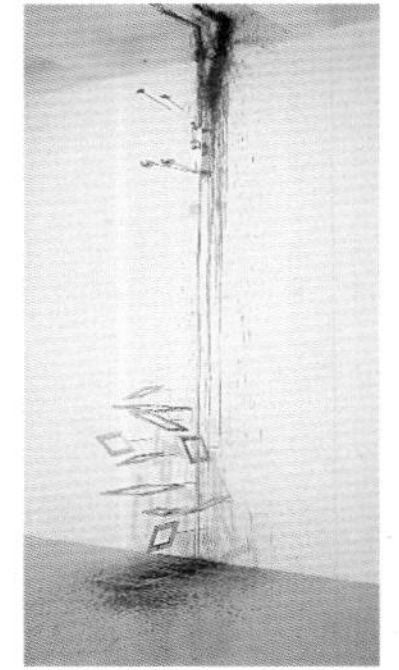

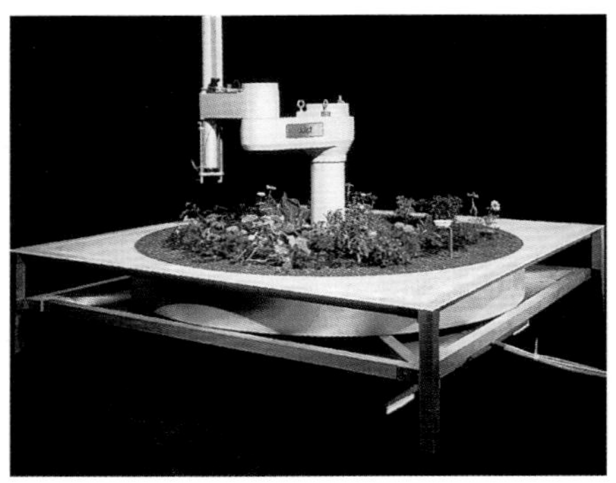

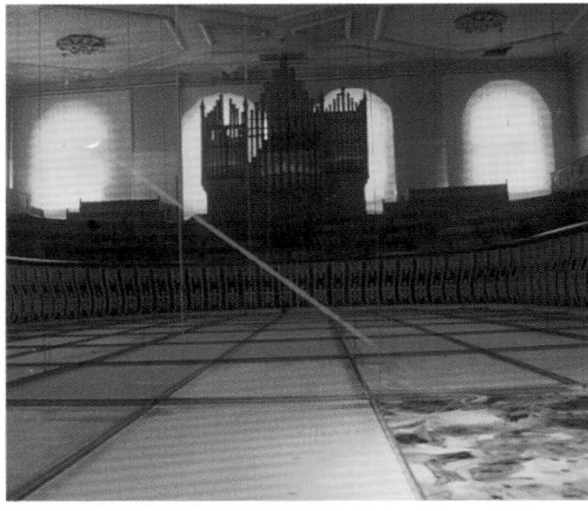

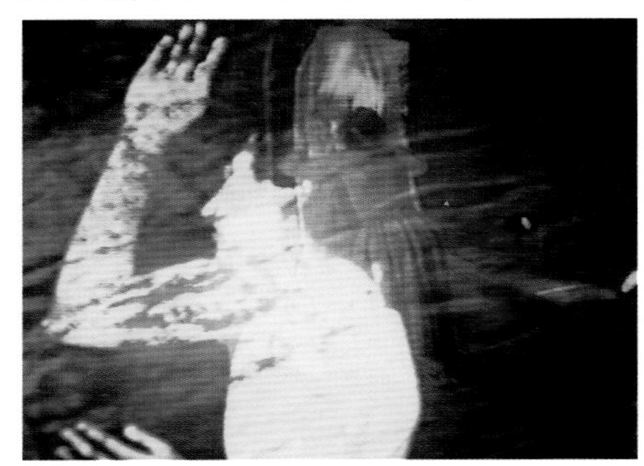

Rebecca HORN Painting Machine, 1988
Joseph SANTARROMANA Telegarden, 1994
Helen CHADWICK Blood Hyphen, 1985
Ulrike ROSENBACH Or-Phelia, 1982

Technologized, Dispersed Artists' Bodies

As these simulacral images suggest, the period since 1960 has been characterized by an increasingly dominant recognition of the conditioning of the contemporary subject through the violent effects of new technologies of representation, communication and medical intervention. From Warhol's deployment of mechanical reproduction, his use of silkscreening techniques, to the mechanized body extensions of Stelarc and the surgically transformed body image of Orlan, artists have exploited and explored the capacity of new technologies to re- and de-form the embodied self. In some cases – such as Rebecca Horn's *Painting Machine* (1988) or Joseph Santarromana's *Telegarden* (1994) – technologized 'bodies' take the place of the artists as makers of the work. In Horn's piece, a machine that paints on command, the body is resolutely mechanical. In Santarromana's, the body is mechanical and cybernetic: web surfers use a computer to activate a robotic arm placed in a garden at the University of Southern California in Los Angeles to plant seeds and tend the seedlings.[124]

The recognition of the conditioning effects of technology took a sophisticated form in the many video and/or installation pieces produced around 1970, especially in the US.[125] These pieces interrogate what we might call the social materiality of the making subject in technologized (videotaped or otherwise mediated) relationship to their audience. This, for instance, is the case in Vito Acconci's video installation piece *Command Performance* (1974), which creates a representational loop between audience, artist and the 'artwork', itself comprised of a situational set-up of monitors showing continually changing representations of artist and audience. The visitor sits on a stool across from a monitor showing an image of Acconci revealing himself to his audience ('I admit it to you ... my work has been too private ...'). Meanwhile, unbeknownst to the visitor, a camera takes footage of her/him watching Acconci on the video and, with instant feedback, plays this on a monitor behind the visitor, who has thus become the subject/object of the work.[126] This piece encapsulates Acconci's brilliance in excavating the chiasmic effects of technologies of representation.

The bodies of 1980s and 1990s artistic production, however, are with increasing frequency performed as technologized, ironicized, fragmented and open to otherness. These bodies must be differentiated from the authentic, activist, 'destroying, mortal, self-reflexive, absent, mechanical and leaking bodies' that this collection of essays in *The Artist's Body* identifies with the 1960s and early 1970s – bodies that rupture in response to the violence of daily life. Thus, while Gina Pane sliced into her own skin in her early 1970s performances, producing her lacerated, bloody body as a metaphor for the violence of contemporary society, by the 1980s body artists Helen Chadwick and Ulrike Rosenbach had begun to produce elaborate video installation works that emphatically registered their bodily fluids as mediated and already symbolic. In Chadwick's *Blood Hyphen* (1985) a red laser beam pierces through the gloomy, mystical ether of a chapel, its annunciatory ray landing on a photograph of cells. In Rosenbach's *Or-Phelia* (1982) corporeal functions are also rendered simulacral: three video monitors, embedded in the floor, show flowing streams of water and bodily fluids.[127] Chadwick's statements regarding her work emphasize the radically technologized nature of her body, which is not simply 'represented' by technologies such as photography but *becomes* them. 'Photography is my skin', she has proclaimed. In photographic imagings of the body, '[p]hysicality is reduced to surface, a mere echo of itself, the corporeal imploded into grains of dust. Dismembered into manifold fragments, the subject shatters, and under the callous intimacy of the reprographic passes into transcience'. At the threshold of representation, '[t]he boundaries have dissolved, between self and other, the living and the corpse'.[128]

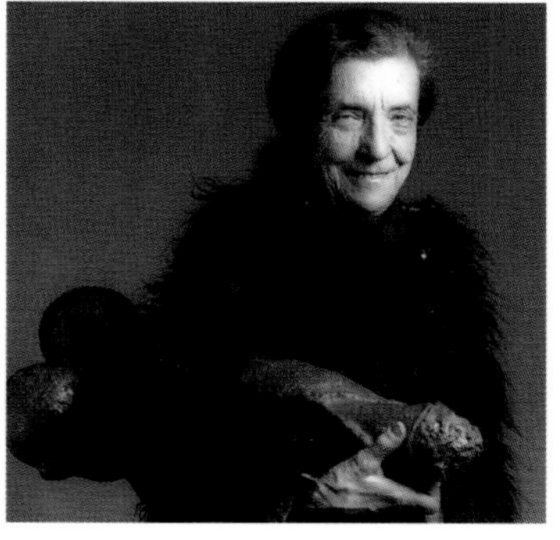

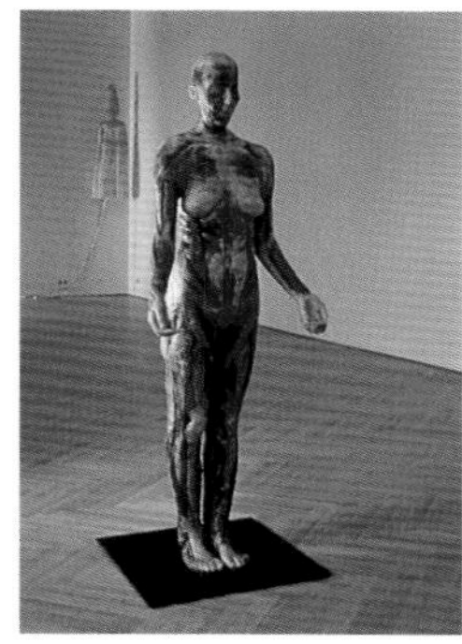

Robert MAPPLETHORPE Portrait of Louise Bourgeois, 1982
Kiki SMITH Virgin Mary, 1992
Lauren LESKO Lips, 1993

This recognition of the 'technologization' of the self in the 1980s and 1990s, linked to the production of simulacral selves in the earlier self-imaging projects, is also connected to a long history of works by artists negotiating the fragmenting effects of industrial and post-industrial age technologies on our experience of our own bodies. While differentiating the varying relationships to technology, we might still trace a trajectory from the creatively revised or industrially produced sexual objects of Surrealist artists Marcel Duchamp, Man Ray and Meret Oppenheim to the fabulous penis/breast forms of Louise Bourgeois' sculptures, to contemporary body-part works by artists (many of whom are explicitly engaged with feminism) such as Senga Nengudi, Kiki Smith, Lauren Lesko, Robert Gober, Louanne Greenwald, Rona Pondick, Byron Kim, Faith Wilding and others.[129]

Such works range from the organic and fleshy (Nengudi's skin/pantyhose pieces and Lauren Lesko's fur 'cunts', for example) to the slick and mechanistic or highly technologized (such as Wilding's technology-invaded wombs).[130] All of these works, deeply informed by feminism, represent a shift away from the celebration of the female body in its fullness common in much US feminist work from the 1970s, and the simulacral multiplication of the self in the 1980s. Instead, they move towards a conception of the gendered body as saturated in and through technology, experienced – in its fragmented, prosthetic forms – through socially inflected technologies of reproduction, communication and medical intervention. These works might be viewed, then, as participating in what British sociologist Celia Lurie calls 'a process of *experimentation* [with technology in] ... a *prosthetic culture*'. Technologies such as photography (which is her focus), enable a 'refiguring of the conventional relations through which the previous [Cartesian] self-understanding of the possessive individual is secured'.[131]

In Marxian terms the merging of the body/self with the social takes a particular alienating form in highly technologized cultures. With the visual arts, reproductive technologies even change the nature of our relationship to the image. As Walter Benjamin, in his signature 1936 essay 'The Work of Art in the Age of Mechanical Reproduction' argues, reproduction evacuates the author's 'presence' and photographic and cinematic technologies reveal 'entirely new structural formations of the subject'. In film in particular the body 'loses its corporeality' and 'evaporates'.[132] Moreover, the more simulacral a culture becomes – the more thoroughly we are technologized (such that we 'become' our mutable, performative image, as in the work of Lüthi and Sherman) – the more we are simultaneously collapsed into the representation and alienated from it. Returning to Heidegger's terms, we begin to experience ourselves, as part of a 'world picture', where all is increasingly unreal or simulacral. As Vivian Sobchack puts it in her extension of Heidegger's formulation:

'*To say we've lost touch with our bodies these days is not to say we've lost sight of them. Indeed, there seems to be an inverse ratio between seeing our bodies and feeling them: the more aware we are of ourselves as the "cultural artifacts", "symbolic fragments" and "made things" that are images, the less we seem to sense the intentional complexity and richness of the corporeal existence that substantiates them.*'[133]

But Benjamin also notes more positively that the 'greatly increased mass of participants has produced a change in the

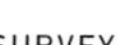

mode of participation'.[134] Thus there is new potential for the production of subjects (bodies/selves) not as only static simulacra but also as in process, open to otherness in a way that promotes rather than suppresses ethical behaviour in relation to others and social spaces.

In this new structure of emphatically embodied selfhood, we would renegotiate our bodies/selves and the social. The social would no longer be conceived as 'out there', as a masculine public sphere that is oppositional to a domestic, feminine, private one – not even in the sense of a pre-existing 'context'.[135] Rather, space is opened up *as itself embodied*. As Chadwick claims, 'the site curves around my presence whilst I in turn mould the geography of space ... The architecture grows corporeal and I am enfleshed.'[136] The body/self is understood as *a kind of social space*. Artists' re-articulations of their bodies as 'in pieces' or networked across cyberspace (no longer 'authentic' or 'mine', or in Lury's terms, no longer self 'possessed' but fully social) produce and relate to new kinds of 'enfleshed' and embodied social space.

It is not a coincidence that these new subjects are never coherent or normative, even if in some cases they may appear at first glance to be economically secure, straight white men. Even the most exaggeratedly normative subjects in this sense are now experienced increasingly as tainted by the very identificatory qualities they attempt to project outward, away from themselves, as abject.[137] As cyber theorist Donna Haraway describes the situation in her important 'Cyborg Manifesto': '*It is no accident that the symbolic system of the family of man – and so the essence of woman – breaks up at the same moment that networks of connection among people on the planet are unprecedentedly multiple, pregnant and complex ... In the "Western" sense, the end of man is at stake. The dichotomies between mind and body, animal and human, organism and machine, public and private, nature and culture, men and women, primitive and civilized are all in question ideologically.*'[138] References to, and performances of, the body in 1990s US and European art increasingly tend to celebrate or explore rather than suppress or render abject the new kind of subjectivity proposed by Haraway's cyborg. This new subject is 'resolutely committed to partiality, irony, intimacy and perversity ... a kind of disassembled and reassembled, postmodern collective and personal self'.[139] Body-oriented practices in the 1990s tend to extend the 'dispersal' of the body/self in pancapitalism, so as to expose, and in some cases momentarily suspend, the flow of capital, whether economic or libidinal.

One overtly technologized artistic project, which references the body, but not as a 'container' of sexual, gender, racial, ethnic and/or class identifications, is Mona Hatoum's *Corps étranger* ('strange' or 'foreign' body, 1994). Here the body (the self) is engaged, projected, even turned inside out. Hatoum, who conceived this project in the 1980s and received support to complete it (from the Centre Georges Pompidou) in the mid 1990s, uses endoscopic and coloscopic cameras to explore the outside and penetrate the inside of her body, adopting an echographic device to capture the sounds of her breathing and her heartbeat.[140] The visitor enters a small cylindrical room, drawn in by an organic, pulsating sound. Projected on to a circular screen extending across the floor of the room are wet, sucking, pulsating tubes and orifices. As she stands and looks down, the visitor realizes she is viewing the internal cavities and exterior contours of a woman's body.

Corps étranger disturbs the equation of 'appearance' and 'identity' that has long supported the mode of exchange characterizing capitalism, pancapitalism and their corollaries (racism, colonialism, imperialism and sexism). In this way the piece also disturbs the antagonists to this mode of exchange, such as 1970s-style coalitional identity politics, which reiterates the appearance/identity equation in order to transform its values. These new artists' bodies are not as codifiable as before, not as 'possessible' or 'exchangeable' within the mechanisms of the art world and cultural scene in general. They are less bounded, catapulting themselves into the blossoming flows of desire/of capital that characterize the technologized realm of the self.

Corps étranger literally turns the normative, objectifying 'male gaze' identified by feminist theory inside out. For a woman, in particular, the sucking vortex of vaginal, throat and other points of bodily entry hits below the belt – we might feel as if *our* insides are being sucked downward into the depthless screen or, in illusion, beneath the floor or the surface of the earth. Our desire to present ourselves (our bodies) as coherent containers of our chosen identity is thwarted through our identification with the mucoid organic tunnels

Mona HATOUM Corps étranger (detail), 1994

beneath us. The sound of sucking and beating plunges us all the more deeply into this chasm of embodiment. For the male viewer the pulsating enfleshing of space might have different, potentially homoerotic or hetero-penetratory, consequences. Debasing the image, literally placing it beneath the feet of the visitor, *Corps étranger* desublimates the human and, in particular, revels in the potentially anarchic, desublimating property of the feminine. Here the naked female body is all *vagina dentata*, all *hole*, with nothing phallic/fetishistic left to palliate the male gaze.

Hatoum highlights the invasive tendencies of medical technologies, graphically displaying their 'ultimate violation of the human body' under our feet, producing an environment that is claustrophobic and sensuous at the same time.[141] The visitor is thus *plunged into* Hatoum's body rather than engaged from the outside. Once the 'gaze' – perhaps against its will – is forced to penetrate the endless entrails that constitute Hatoum's corporeal self, its possessor can no longer

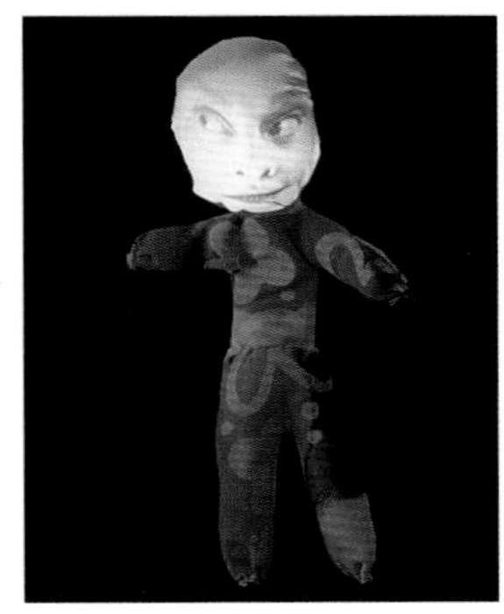

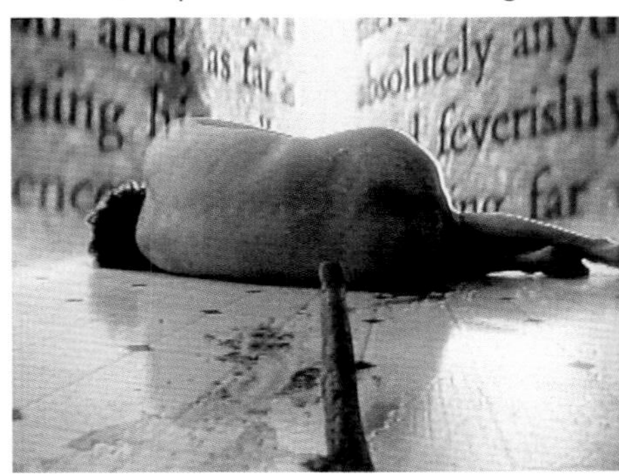

Tony OURSLER Angerotic, 1994
Gary HILL Incidence of Castastrophe, 1987-88

sustain himself in a function of desire.[142] The spectator is himself possessed by the sucking vortex of embodied femininity that is Hatoum's body. Deploying the flat depthlessness of the video screen, *Corps étranger* paradoxically threatens to swallow the (male) viewer into its gooey depths. The apparent 'depth' of Hatoum's body, however, vanishes in the resistant glass surface that delivers up the video image – the body as spectacle.[143]

Like the work of the many other artists – including Gary Hill, Tony Oursler, Joseph Santarromana and Diana Thater – who produce body-video installations that engage the spectator in relationships of desire and, often, repulsion, Hatoum excavates the myth of the subject as Cartesian, centred, full within itself according to specific codes of racial, sexual or gender identity. A Palestinian artist from Lebanon who immigrated to London in the mid 1970s during the Lebanese war, she presses technology through the body and vice versa in order to project new bodies that are not readable as one thing or another. (It is not incidental, in this sense, that there are only a few moments during the *Corps étranger* footage in which we can recognize the body as female.) The subject/object of Hatoum's oeuvre is not easily engaged through pre-existing notions of identity.

At the same time Hatoum insists upon the specificity of the viewer, engaging her or him in her range of identifications. Produced in relation to the video installation works of Hatoum, Thater, et al. are technologized bodies/selves that engage subjects who are as mutable as the technologized imagery (both flat and deep) that video and other technologies of representation make available – but who are never simply 'other'. As French art critic Yves Abrioux has suggested, the most 'foreign' body produced by *Corps étranger* may be the visitor's own: 'As images, allusions and references tumble into consciousness, I come to realize that the foreign body to which the title of the work refers is ultimately my own ... '[144]

Artists working with new technologies engage the network logic of these modes of information exchange (video/TV, the web, CD ROM) to produce themselves (their 'artists' bodies') in ways that make *us* take note of our ever-changing position in the web of intersubjective couplings and disengagements that constitute the social. Thus, artists, through their bodies, have encouraged the rest of us to be more conscious of ours – ours as flesh of the world, as thoroughly part of that social arena we may fantasize as the 'public realm'. In the 1990s, as artists seem to have recognized, the deepest recesses of our bodies/selves are already inhabited by the 'gaze' of technology's new world picture. The 'private' is the 'public' and the artist's body is always and never ours to keep.

1 Carolee Schneemann, in a 1991 performance *Ask the Goddess*, cited by David Levi Strauss, 'Love Rides Aristotle Through the Audience: Body, Image, and Idea in the Work of Carolee Schneemann', *Carolee Schneemann: Up To and Including Her Limits* (New York: New Museum of Contemporary Art, 1996) 33.

2 Marcel Mauss, 'Techniques of the Body' (1934), Jonathan Crary and Sanford Kwinter (eds.) *Incorporations, Zone*, 6 (New York: Zone, 1992) 474; Bryan Turner, *The Body and Society: Explorations in Social Theory* (New York and Oxford: Basil Blackwell, 1984) 7; Jean-Luc Nancy ('We know, we conceive') and Alphonso Lingis paraphrasing Nancy ('The body can') in Lingis' essay 'Bodies that Touch Us', *Thesis Eleven*, 36 (1993) 159, 160.

3 Lea Vergine, *Il corpo come linguaggio* (*La 'Body-art' e storie simili*), trans. Henry Martin (Milan: Giampaolo Prearo Editore, 1974) 3, 9.

4 By 'historic avant-gardes' I am referring to radical politicized movements such as Surrealism and Russian Constructivism and Productivism, as outlined in Peter Bürger's classic model in *Theory of the Avant-Garde*, trans. Michael Shaw (Minneapolis: University of Minnesota Press, 1984). It is primarily in Dada and Surrealism that the unveiling of the artist appears, through performative events such as the nonsense poetry readings at the Cabaret Voltaire in Zurich during the First World War.

5 Henri Lefebvre, *The Production of Space*, trans. Donald Nicholson-Smith (New York and Oxford: Basil Blackwell, 1991).

6 I have previously explored at length the philosophical dimension of this newly invigorated performance of the artist's body in the period after 1960; see Amelia Jones, *Body Art/Performing the Subject* (Minneapolis: University of Minnesota Press, 1998).

7 As Susan Buck-Morss has described the situation, 'Kant's transcendental subject purges himself of the senses which endanger autonomy not only because they unavoidably entangle him in the world, but, specifically, because they make him passive ... instead of active ... susceptible, like "Oriental voluptuaries", to sympathy and tears'. Buck-Morss, 'Aesthetics and Anaesthetics: Walter Benjamin's Artwork Essay Reconsidered', *October*, 62 (Autumn 1992) 9.

8 Rosalind Krauss, a Greenberg follower in the 1960s, recently noted that '[t]he "body" – as it has increasingly surfaced in current theoretical work – is rapidly becoming my phobic object'. Hal Foster, Benjamin Buchloh, Rosalind Krauss, Yve-Alain Bois, Denis Hollier, Helen Molesworth, 'The Politics of the Signifier II: A Conversation on the *Informe* and the Abject', *October*, 67 (Winter 1994) 12.

9 D.N. Rodowick, discussing the work of Raymond Williams, in 'Impure Mimesis, or the Ends of the Aesthetic', in Peter Brunette and David Wills (eds.), *Deconstruction and the Visual Arts: Art, Media, Architecture* (New York: Cambridge University Press, 1994) 96.

10 Simone de Beauvoir's *The Second Sex* (1949) is an analysis of precisely this division of the transcendental, Cartesian (male) subject from the immanent (female) subject in Western thought. Simone de Beauvoir, *The Second Sex*, trans. and ed. H.M. Parshley (New York: Alfred A. Knopf, 1953).

11 As Maurice Merleau-Ponty notes, 'if we rediscover time beneath the subject, and if we relate to the paradox of time those of the body, the world, the thing and others, we shall understand that beyond these there is nothing to understand'; *Phenomenology of Perception* (1962), trans. Colin Smith (New York and London: Routledge, 1995) 362–63, 365.

12 Critical Art Ensemble, *Flesh Machine: Cyborgs, Designer Babies and New Eugenic Consciousness* (Brooklyn: Autonomedia, 1998) 11. I use the term 'pancapitalism' rather than the more common late capitalism because it conveys the enveloping nature of global capitalism; also, for CAE, pancapitalism is defined through its rationalizing relationship to the body or 'flesh machine', while the term 'late capitalism' has tended to entail more abstracted and disembodied formulations.

13 Martin Heidegger, 'The Age of the World Picture' (1938), *The Question Concerning Technology and Other Essays*, trans. William Lovitt (New York: Harper & Row, 1977) 115–54.

14 On the production of the 'high' cultural subject, see Pierre Bourdieu, *Distinction: A Social Critique of the Judgement of Taste* (1979), trans. Richard Nice (Cambridge, Massachusetts: Harvard University Press, 1984).

15 I trace this particular trajectory and artists playing off Pollock's model at length in chapter two, 'The "Pollockian Performative" and the Revision of the Modernist Subject', of *Body Art/Performing the Subject*, *op. cit.*, 53–102.

16 Kathy O'Dell discusses the shift from the 1960s to 1970s work in terms of this mechanics of alienation in her important book *Contract with the Skin: Masochism, Performance Art and the 1970s* (Minneapolis: University of Minnesota Press, 1998) 2, 33.

17 See Judy Chicago, *Through the Flower: My Struggle as a Woman Artist* (Garden City, New York: Doubleday and Co., 1973) 106, 107.

18 This exact wording is from Kathy O'Dell's Ph.D. dissertation, 'Towards a Theory of Performance Art: An Investigation of Its Sites' (City University of New York, 1992) 282. While this material was heavily revised, shortened and published as *Contract with the Skin* (on the Vietnam war and the objecthood of the body in performance, see p. 38), I cite the dissertation directly because it made a crucial impact on my thinking about body art.

19 Vergine, *Il corpo come linguaggio*, *op. cit.*, 1.

20 Michel Feher, 'Of Bodies and Technologies', Hal Foster (ed.), in *Discussions in Contemporary Culture*, 1 (Seattle: Bay Press, 1987) 161. Feher is explicitly drawing on the terms established by Michel Foucault.

21 Kaprow's essay was initially published in *ARTnews* and is reprinted in this volume, along with Harold Rosenberg's 'The American Action Painters' (also originally published in *ARTnews*, 51: 8 [December 1952] 22–23, 48–50), the primary essay responsible for establishing an existentialist reading of an unnamed but clearly Pollockian, performative painting figure [see in this volume pp. 193–94].

22 Rosenberg, 'The American Action Painters', *op. cit.*, 48, 49.

23 Dore Ashton discusses Sartre's importance in relation to Abstract Expressionism in her book *The New York School: A Cultural Reckoning* (London: Penguin, 1972) 181.

24 Thomas McEvilley, 'Art in the Dark', *Artforum*, 12 (Summer 1983) 63–64 [see in this volume pp. 222–27].

25 Thus, the well-known analyses of the marketing of Abstract Expressionism as proof of the freedom of expression within the American democratic system by Serge Guilbaut, Eva Cockroft and others can be viewed via the lens that Pollock – as quintessential 'individual' of action painting's existentialist triumph – provides. See Eva Cockroft's 'Abstract Expressionism: Weapon of the Cold War' (1974) and Serge Guilbaut, 'The New Adventures of the Avant-Garde in America' (1980), both reprinted in Francis Frascina (ed.), *Pollock and After: The Critical Debate* (New York: Harper & Row, 1985) 125–34, 153–66.

26 Mathieu's performances took place in relation to a vertical canvas, unlike Pollock's action painting, always done over a horizontal surface. In this way, while Pollock could be said to be working from a desublimating impulse, returning human creation to a debased, ground-hugging plane, Mathieu remains properly sublimated. Rosalind Krauss has made the desublimating argument in relation to Pollock; see chapter six in *The Optical Unconscious* (Cambridge, Massachusetts and London: MIT Press, 1993) 243–320. Kristine Stiles discusses Mathieu's performances of painting in her wide-ranging essay 'Uncorrupted Joy: International Art Actions', *Out of Actions: Between Performance and the Object, 1949–1979* (Los Angeles: Museum of Contemporary Art; New York: Thames and Hudson, 1998) 287–90. As is characteristic of her work, Stiles backs up her discussion of Mathieu's work with extensive research, noting that he wore dramatic costumes and took on historical personae and that his work was received in the US with a great deal of anxiety.

27 Carolee Schneemann, *More Than Meat Joy: Performance Works and Selected Writings* (New Paltz, New York: Documentext, 1979/1997) 52–53.

28 This paraphrases Helen Molesworth's phrase regarding Robert Rauschenberg's relationship to Pollock – while Pollock is famously 'in the painting', Rauschenberg wants to 'have the painting be on his body and conversely, to have his physicality be on the canvas' – in her essay 'Before *Bed*', *October*, 63 (Winter 1993) 74 [see in this volume pp. 198–200]. Molesworth's description seems to apply more directly to Schneemann than to Rauschenberg.

29 Schneemann, *More Than Meat Joy*, *op. cit.*, 52.

30 Rebecca Schneider, *The Explicit Body in Performance* (New York and London: Routledge, 1997) 35. Schneider also discusses Kubota's *Vagina Painting* in relation to the Schneemann piece; see 38–39.

31 de Beauvoir, *The Second Sex*; see note 10.

32 Schneemann, 'From the Notebooks, 1963–1966', *More than Meat Joy*, *op. cit.*, 55.

33 Ironically, however, because performance takes its place in history through written and photographic documentation, this radicalization is potentially tempered: the photographs that have documented this work art historically press on Schneemann's image, turning it back towards fetish – object of (masculine, heterosexual) spectatorial desire, as per Laura Mulvey's foundational essay 'Visual Pleasure and Narrative Cinema' (1975), *Visual and Other Pleasures* (Bloomington: University of Indiana Press, 1989) 14–26.

34 Lygia Clark from *Book-Oeuvre, 1964–1983*, cited by Paula Terra Cabo, 'Lygia Clark', in Delia Gaze (ed.), *Dictionary of Women Artists*, I (London and Chicago: Fitzroy Dearborn, 1997) 395. See also Guy Brett on Clark and other members of the 'Neo-Concrete' group in Brazil in 'Life Strategies: Overview and Selection, Buenos Aires/London/Rio de Janeiro/Santiago de Chile, 1960–1980', in *Out of Actions*, *op. cit.*, 204–206; Susan Martin and Alma Ruiz (eds.) *The Experimental Exercise of Freedom: Lygia Clark, Gego, Mathias Goeritz, Hélio Oiticica, Mira Schendel* (Los Angeles: Museum of Contemporary Art, 1999) and *Lygia Clark* (Barcelona: Fundació Antoni Tàpies, 1997).

35 Yve-Alain Bois summarizes Clark's beliefs in this way in his introduction to Clark, 'Nostalgia of the Body', *October*, 69 (Summer 1994) 86–88.

36 This is Bois' description in *ibid.*, 87.

37 Lygia Clark, 'About the Act' (1965), trans. Yve-Alain Bois, in 'Nostalgia of the Body', *op. cit.*, 102–104.

38 Clark, as initially quoted in Guy Brett, 'Lygia Clark: The Borderline Between Life and Art', *Third Text*, 1, (Autumn 1987) 87, and cited in Brett's 'Life Strategies: Overview and Selection', in *Out of Actions*, *op. cit.*, 204. Clark describes the 'relational objects' on p. 206.

39 'Jackson Pollock: is he the greatest living painter in the United States?', *Life* magazine (8 April 1949) 42–43, 45.

40 Nelly Richard, 'The Rhetoric of the Body', *Art & Text*, 21 (1986) 65. [see in this volume pp. 244–45].

41 This work is illustrated and discussed in Cabo, 'Lygia Clark', *op. cit.*, 395–96.

42 Maurice Merleau-Ponty, 'The Intertwining – The Chiasm', Claude Lefort (ed.), *The Visible and the Invisible* (1964), trans. Alphonso Lingis (Evanston: Northwestern University Press, 1968) 131.

43 The Living Theater was founded in New York by Judith Malina and Julian Beck in 1947 in order to produce contemporary plays 'performed in such a manner as to move the spectators'; see Pierre Biner, *The Living Theater* (New York: Horizon Press, 1972) 21.

44 Maurice Berger describes these interconnections in *Labyrinths: Robert Morris, Minimalism and the 1960s* (New York: Harper and Row, 1989) 83–84. See also Sally Banes, *Greenwich Village 1963: Avant-Garde Performance and the Effervescent Body* (Durham, North Carolina: Duke University Press, 1993).

45 A closely related body artwork is Robert Morris' 1965 *Site*, in which Morris' heavy manual labour is counterpoised with Schneemann's; Schneemann, who was initially brought on as an equal collaborator, was made to pose nude as a prostitute (specifically Manet's *Olympia*) while Morris struggled across the stage with large pieces of wood. In this way the piece rather problematically divides male (active, physical) from female (passive, sexual) labour. I discuss this piece at greater length in my essay 'Dis/playing the Phallus: Male Artists Perform Their Masculinities', *Art History*, 17: 4 (December 1994) 557, 560 [see in this volume pp. 265–71]. Morris, who worked closely with dancers from the Judson group, provides an obvious link between the use of the everyday in experimental New York

dance from this period, body art and Minimalism.

46 I am indebted to Karen Schaffman, whose two unpublished 1997 papers, 'Contact Improvisation', and 'Fleshing Out: Contact Improvisation and Feminist Phenomenology', from which the quote is taken, have been crucial introductions to Contact Improvisation.

47 Banes, *Greenwich Village 1963*, *op. cit.*, 193.

48 A piece that directly confronts the tragic side of drug culture is Gina Pane's *Hommage à un jeune drogué* (*Hommage to a young drug addict* [1971]), which memorialized the life of a young addict who had overdosed. In the piece Pane empathetically wrung her hands in scalding hot chocolate after describing how the boy's parents calmed their grief by returning to everyday activities. Pane then encouraged a group discussion about drug addiction. See Kathy O'Dell's description of this piece in 'Gina Pane', Delia Gaze (ed.), *Dictionary of Women Artists*, II, (London and Chicago: Fitzroy Dearborn, 1997) 1064.

49 Molesworth situates this impulse to 'register the body' within the Cage and Rauschenberg group at Black Mountain College, one of the key sites for generating the energy for what would become body or performance art around 1960 with the establishment of Happenings and Fluxus. On the interconnections between the Fluxus and Happenings artists (such as George Maciunas and La Monte Young) and Cage as well as the Judson group, see Banes, chapter two, 'The Reinvention of Community', in *Greenwich Village 1963*, *op. cit.*, 33–80.

50 Schneemann, *More Than Meat Joy*, *op. cit.*, 63. This piece was performed three times in 1964 – in Paris, London and at the Judson Church, New York.

51 Herbert Marcuse, *An Essay on Liberation* (Boston: Beacon Press, 1969) vii, 23, 34. Thus, the 'psychedelic search' may hold a 'kernel of truth', potentially bringing release from the rationality of the established system but also presenting the danger of bringing release from 'that other rationality which is to change the established system', p. 37. See also Marcuse's *Eros and Civilization: A Philosophical Inquiry into Freud* (London: Routledge & Kegan Paul, 1956); Gregory Battcock's interesting essay 'Marcuse and Anti-Art', *Arts Magazine*, 43 (Summer 1969) 17–19; and Maurice Berger's chapter two, 'Against Repression: Minimalism and Antiform', in *Labyrinths*, *op. cit.*, 47–75, which discusses Marcuse's impact on the art world.

52 Banes, *Greenwich Village 1963*, *op. cit.*, 194.

53 Michel de Certeau, *The Practice of Everyday Life*, trans. Steven Rendall (Berkeley and Los Angeles: University of California, 1984) 93.

54 Vostell, 'Genesis and Iconography of My Happenings' (1968), cited in Günter Berghaus, 'Happenings in Europe: Trends, Events, and Leading Figures', in Mariellen R. Sandford (ed.), *Happenings and Other Acts* (New York and London: Routledge, 1995) 323.

55 Vostell from 'Neun Nein Decollagen von Wolf Vostell' (1965) and *Happenings und Leben* (1970), both cited in Berghaus, 'Happenings in Europe', *op. cit.*, 323–24; 325.

56 Kaprow, 'Happenings in the New York Scene' (1961), reprinted in Kaprow's *The Blurring of Art and Life*, ed. Jeff Kelley (Berkeley and Los Angeles: University of California, 1993) 20.

57 These incongruous events are then disrupted by the 'eruption' of a 'mountain', with 'tar-paper balls thrown out'. The script is published in Michael Kirby (ed.), *Happenings* (New York: E.P. Dutton, 1966) 105.

58 *Ibid.*, 17.

59 See Kaprow in *Assemblage, Environments, and Happenings* (New York: Harry N. Abrams, 1966) 188–98.

60 In *Ritual Meal*, the meal was presented in a room that was, in Smith's words, 'shattered by films and projections on the walls ... multiple loops of various sounds'; from Smith's description of the work, unpublished text. I am indebted to Smith for sharing this material with me. On Knowles' piece see Kristine Stiles, 'Between Water and Stone/Fluxus Performance: A Metaphysics of Acts', in *In the Spirit of Fluxus* (Minneapolis: Walker Art Museum, 1993) 89. On Fluxus see also George Maciunas, 'Fluxus', in *Happenings and Other Acts*, *op. cit.*, 94–105; and Estera Milman (ed.), 'Fluxus: A Conceptual Country', special issue of *Visible Language*, 26: 1/2 (Winter–Spring 1992–93).

61 Cited by Stiles in 'Between Water and Stone', *op. cit.*, 69. With a far more international cast of characters, Fluxus events tended to be more explicitly political than Happenings – along the lines of the contemporaneous actions of the Situationist International in France, which was explicitly informed by Marxist theories of cultural engagement. The Happenings were typically American in their more oblique relationship to class politics.

62 Antoni's piece is a kind of feminist update of Chris Burden's *White Light/White Heat* (1975), in which Burden installed himself on a high shelf in the gallery, lying there for the duration of the performance out of view from the audience. It is also, as Jennifer Fisher has pointed out, linked to the *Dragon* series by Marina Abramović, where the artist installed herself on a shelf in a gallery with other pedestals and shelves for visitors to pose themselves on as sculpture; Jennifer Fisher, 'Interperformance: The Live Tableaux of Suzanne Lacy, Janine Antoni and Marina Abramović', *Art Journal* special issue on Performance art, 56: 4 (Winter 1997) 31–32. On Burden's *White Light/White Heat* see its documentation in *Chris Burden: A Twenty Year Survey* (Newport Beach Art Museum, 1988) 73. Linda Montano's pieces are documented in *Art in Everyday Life* (Los Angeles: Astro Artz, 1981); this book includes examples of numerous activations and/or denaturalizations of mundane activities – including *Handcuff: Linda Montano and Tom Marioni* (1973), in which she attached herself for extended periods of time to Marioni, with whom she was then destined to perform the minutest actions of everyday life.

63 de Certeau, *The Practice of Everyday Life*, *op. cit.*, 108.

64 Kristine Stiles on Kazuo Shiraga and Saburo Murakami (Gutai artists) and Yves Klein, in 'Uncorrupted Joy: International Art Actions', *op. cit.*, 237. As Catherine Elwes has stated: 'A sense of alienation from oneself and one's environment was seen to be a product of a mechanized, industrialized world. By prompting an audience to take creative responsibility within a work, the artist sought to raise their consciousness and galvanize them into action in the real world of politics.' Elwes, 'Floating Femininity: A Look at Performance Art by Women', in Sarah Kent and Jacqueline Moreau (eds.), *Women's Images of Men* (London: Writers and Readers Publishing, 1985) 169.

65 Smith, unpublished textual description of *Pure Food*, which was performed in response to her better known work *Feed Me* (1973), in which she sat 'naked on a divan surrounded by items of multi-dimensional sensual connection', with a tape loop playing a voice saying 'feed me' over and over. Rumours circulated about this piece that Smith 'intended to make love to every man who entered'; rather, Smith claims, her intention was 'to turn the situation around so the man would have to nurture me' (unpublished textual description of *Feed Me*).

66 Jonathan Benthall, 'The Body as a Medium of Expression: A Manifesto', *Studio International* (July–August 1971) 6–8 [see in this volume, pp. 235–36].

67 Marcuse, *An Essay on Liberation*, *op. cit.*, vii.

68 Martha Rosler in Sayre, *The Object of Performance: The American Avant-Garde Since 1970* (Chicago and London: University of Chicago Press, 1989) 94; Klein in Stiles, 'Uncorrupted Joy: International Art Actions', *op. cit.*, 237.

69 Edelson confirms a certain activist and utopian bent in writing of her attempt to produce ritual images 'connected directly to Goddess as an expanded image of woman as a universal being and not limited to the stereotype of woman as "other" ... Goddess was always a metaphor for me for radical change and change of consciousness and for challenging the daily experience of what is thought of as acceptable social codes while opening other realms of experience.' Edelson, *Shape Shifter: Seven Mediums* (New York: Mary Beth Edelson, 1990) 45. See also illustrations of Edelson's self-construction as goddess in *Mary Beth Edelson: Firsthand/Photographs 1973–1993 and Shooter Series* (New York: Mary Beth Edelson, 1993).

70 On the Art Worker's Coalition as well as the Artists' Protest Committee see Paul Wood, Francis Frascina, Jonathan Harris and Charles Harrison, *Modernism in Dispute: Art since the 1940s* (New Haven and London: Yale University in association with The Open University, 1993) 106–14. The WAR group split off from the AWC due to the latter's lack of concern for gender inequity. A useful source on the women's activist groups is Mary D. Garrard, 'Feminist Politics: Networks and Organizations', in Mary D. Garrard and Norma Broude (eds.), *The Power of Feminist Art* (New York: Harry N. Abrams, 1994) 88–103.

71 See Mary Jane Jacobs, *The 'Silueta' Series 1973–1980* (New York: Galerie Lelong, 1991) 13.

72 See Battcock's discussion in 'Marcuse and Anti-Art', *op. cit.*, 17–18.

73 Suzanne Lacy in an unpublished pamphlet, Linda Macaluso (ed.), 'Three Weeks in May: a Political Performance by Suzanne Lacy, May 7–May 24, 1977, Los Angeles, California', 6; I am indebted to Moira Roth for sharing this and other performance materials from her invaluable archive. In this pamphlet Lacy describes the intersecting discourses of feminism and Kaprow's critique of 'the same closed fraternity of elite art formalism that denied recognition to women artists', *ibid.*, 7.

74 As in all of Lacy's large-scale works, participants in the *Three Weeks of May* events were diverse, coming from a range of economic classes and often not connected to the art world at all. See the description of *Three Weeks of May* in Suzanne Lacy (ed.), *Mapping the Terrain: New Genre Public Art* (Seattle: Bay Press, 1995) 252, and the *In Mourning and Rage* component in Laura Cottingham, 'Eating from the Dinner Party Plates and Other Myths, Metaphors and Moments of Lesbian Enunciation in Feminism and Its Art Movement', in Amelia Jones (ed.), *Sexual Politics: Judy Chicago's* Dinner Party *in Feminist Art History* (Los Angeles and Berkeley: University of California, 1996) 222–23.

75 The classic essay on female imagery is Judy Chicago and Miriam Schapiro's 'Female Imagery', *Womanspace Journal*, 1: 3 (Summer 1973) 11–14. Chicago and Schapiro by no means speak for all California feminists from this period, but their views did become dominant in Southern California in the 1970s due to their pedagogical and institutionally supported positions at California State University, Fresno, California Institute of the Arts and the Women's Building complex.

76 Rosemary Mayer, 'Performance and Experience', *Arts Magazine*, 47: 3 (December 1972–January 1973) 34.

77 See Jean Baudrillard, 'The Precession of Simulacra' (1983), in Brian Wallis (ed.), *Art After Modernism: Rethinking Representation* (New York: New Museum of Contemporary Art; Boston: David R. Godine, 1984) 253–82.

78 From Alphonso Lingis' Marxian phenomenological point of view, in pancapitalism 'bodies are merchandised, transported, positioned, displaced, worn out, replaced. They are known as mechanisms, systems to be geared into other systems, funds of energy, manpower, massed stocks of surplus value, of profit.' Lingis, 'Bodies that Touch Us', *op. cit.*, 164.

79 Catherine Francblin, 'corps-objet, femme-objet', *ARTnews* (1975) 15 (my translation) [see in this volume p. 238].

80 Other absent bodies are found in Howardena Pindell's later *Autobiography* series from 1986 to 1990, wherein she includes a body silhouette (presumably her own given the title of the series) in richly composed, thickly painted and collaged images that recall aspects of Pindell's life as a black woman living in American culture. See *Howardena Pindell: Paintings and Drawings, A Retrospective Exhibition, 1972–1992* (New York: Roland Gibson Gallery at Potsdam College of the State University of New York, 1992) 34, 57 ff.

81 Richard, 'The Rhetoric of the Body', *op. cit.*, 65. On the effects of bodily trauma and war on the subject see also Elaine Scarry, *The Body in Pain* (New York and Oxford: Oxford University Press, 1985).

82 See Blau's lively comments on the state of affairs after Marcuse, in which 'the radical activism of the 1960s [has] abated or [gone] ... underground' only to surface again 'in *theory* as a new erotics of discourse', from '(Re)Sublimating the 1960s', in Sohnya Sayres, Anders Stephanson, Stanley Aronowitz, Fredric Jameson (eds.), *The 1960s Without Apology*

(Minneapolis: University of Minnesota Press, 1988) 318, 319.

83 O'Dell, *Contract with the Skin*, *op. cit.*, 16. In this entire section, I am indebted to Kathy O'Dell's brilliant discussion of masochistic 1970s body art works.

84 On Schwarzkogler's performance see Kristine Stiles' 'Performance and Its Objects', *Arts Magazine*, 65 (November 1990) 35, 37, where she points out that not only is the castration faked, but the body in the photographs is not, as many have assumed, Schwarzkogler's own. On the work of the Actionists see also the exhibition catalogue *Wiener Aktionismus/Viennese Aktionism, Wien/Vienna 1960–1971, Der zertrümmerte Spiegel/The Shattered Mirror* (Klagenfurt: Ritter Verlag, 1989), and Philip Ursprung, '"Catholic Tastes": Hurting and Healing the Body in Viennese Actionism in the 1960s', Amelia Jones and Andrew Stephenson (eds.) *Performing the Body/Performing the Text* (New York and London: Routledge, 1999) 138–152. I discuss Paul McCarthy's work at greater length in my essay 'Paul McCarthy's Inside Out Body and the Desublimation of Masculinity', *Paul McCarthy* (New York: New Museum of Contemporary Art, 2000).

85 Marvin Carlson discusses Athey and Flanagan, both based in Los Angeles, in *Performance: A Critical Introduction* (New York and London: Routledge, 1996) 158–59.

86 I discuss masochism in relation to the ambivalent effects of male castration imagery in body art in my essay 'Dis/playing the Phallus', *op. cit.*, 546–84.

87 Pane's statements are taken from *Gina Pane: Travail d'Action* (Paris: Galerie Isy Brachot, 1980) n.p. Translations from the French are mine. Kathy O'Dell interprets Pane's 'mission' as follows: 'to demonstrate not only the role of the body in social relations but also the ways the body can become more effective as a tool for social change', in *Contract with the Skin*, *op. cit.*, 49. I see Pane's work as having a less instrumental, more phenomenologically charged effect.

88 On Duchamp's *Paysage fautif* see my book *Postmodernism and the En-Gendering of Marcel Duchamp* (New York: Cambridge University Press, 1994) 89–91; Manzoni's cans of *Merda d'artista* are illustrated in *Out of Actions*, *op. cit.*, 48 and in this volume p. 163; Warhol's oxidation paintings are illustrated in Kynaston McShine (ed.), *Andy Warhol: A Retrospective* (New York: The Museum of Modern Art, 1989) 350–51; on Paul McCarthy's works see Carl E. Loeffler and Darlene Tong (eds.), *Performance Anthology: Source Book of California Performance Art* (San Francisco: Last Gasp Press; Contemporary Arts Press, 1989) 320–23; and my essay 'Paul McCarthy's Inside Out Body', *op. cit.* Mike Kelley's shit-smeared, naked adults playing with stuffed animals (*Manipulating Mass-Produced Idealized Objects*, 1990) also relate to this ultimately non-threatening display of abjection; see RoseLee Goldberg, *Performance: Live Art Since 1960* (New York: Harry N. Abrams, 1998) 205. On abjection and the visual arts the obvious source is the catalogue *Abject Art: Repulsion and Desire in American Art* (New York: Whitney Museum of American Art, 1993), which unfortunately oversimplifies the idea of abjection to apply it as a label for virtually any work that investigates 'discursive excess and degraded elements as they relate to the body and society'; Jack Ben-Levi, Craig Houser, Leslie C. Jones and Simon Taylor, 'Introduction', *op. cit.*, 7. Kelley's *Manipulating Mass-Produced Idealized Objects* and John Miller's piles of excremental brown material (such as *Untitled*, 1988) are illustrated in the catalogue as examples of abjection (*op. cit.*, 58; 77); it is interesting to note that the adults in Kelley's piece are Sheree Rose and Bob Flanagan, though they are not identified as such. In my view, this photograph defuses the performative force of Flanagan/Rose's own works: this is reinforced by the fact that this image has become a kind of commodified image of 'abjection' in various exhibitions, including *Abject Art* and *Out of Actions*.

89 From 'Carolee Schneemann', interview with Andrea Juno in *Angry Women* (San Francisco: Re/Search Press, 1991) 69. Schneemann performed *Interior Scroll* several times after its original 1975 performance in Long Island.

90 See Gamboa's illustration of the *Walking Mural* in Chon Noriega (ed.), *Urban Exile: Collected Writings of Harry Gamboa, Jr.* (Minneapolis: University of Minnesota Press, 1998) 73. Ondine Chavoya gives a historical background to the artists, who all came from Garfield High School, in his essay 'Pseudographic Cinema: ASCO's No-Movies', *Performance Research*, 3: 1 (1998) 3.

91 Ondine Chavoya, 'Internal Exiles: The Interventionist Public and Performance Art of Asco', in Erika Suderburg (ed.), *Space, Site and Intervention: Issues in Installation and Site-Specific Art* (Minneapolis: University of Minnesota Press, forthcoming), manuscript, 8.

92 Gamboa in 'Serpents in the City of Angels: After Twenty Years of Political Activism, Has LA Chicano Art Been Defanged?' (1989), *Urban Exile*, *op. cit.*, 79. See also Chon Noriega's description of this event in his 'No Introduction', in *Urban Exile*, *op. cit.*, 10. In 'Serpents in the City of Angels' Gamboa also describes a related performative event, *Stations of the Cross*, produced in East LA in December of the preceding year by Herrón (dressed as Christ/death), Gronk (as Pontius Pilate) and Gamboa (as 'zombie-altar boy'), all in flamboyant costumes, with Herrón carrying a 4.5-m [15-ft] -long crucifix along Whittier Boulevard; see *op. cit.*, 76.

93 The Los Angeles County Museum of Art paid the price of the art world's exclusion in 1972 when the four members of ASCO graffittied their names on the outer wall of the museum; see Chavoya, 'Internal Exiles', manuscript p. 11. Conversely, the difficulty in sustaining the radical empowerment of a resistant, interventionist practice while also fighting marginalization is made clear by the effects of LACMA's incorporation of ex-ASCO member Gronk in a celebratory one-person exhibition in 1994. *Los Tres Grandes* refers to the three great muralists of the modern Mexican tradition, David Alfaro Siqueros, José Clemente Orozco and Diego Rivera. I am indebted in this discussion to Mario Ontiveros' MA thesis, 'Circumscribing Identities: Chicana Muralists and the Representation of Chicana Subjectivity' (University of California, Riverside, 1994).

94 On the 'corporate liberal state' see Chavoya, 'Pseudographic Cinema', *op. cit.*, 3. The *Movimiento* itself refused to acknowledge or negotiate the differences of gender and sexuality within the community. As historian Chon Noriega points out, the *Walking Mural* was threatening to the nationalist discourse in the Chicano/a community in its obvious link to the then burgeoning tradition of gay/lesbian camp, in Noriega, 'No Introduction', *op. cit.*, 10.

95 Fusco on 'reverse ethnography' and the Hottentot Venus in 'The Other History of Intercultural Performance', in her book of collected essays, *English is Broken Here: Notes on Cultural Fusion in the Americas* (New York: The New Press, 1995) 38, 47. Fusco also points out that in the US internally colonized black Americans were sometimes displayed in 'native' dress. I am also indebted in this discussion to Patricia Morton's work on the ethnographic impulse of the 1931 Paris Exposition, *Hybrid Modernities: Architecture and Representation at the 1931 Colonial Exposition, Paris* (Cambridge, Massachusetts and London: MIT Press, 2000).

96 Descriptions of the work are from Fusco's 'The Other History', *op. cit.*, 39. An earlier body art piece by James Luna, a Native-American artist living in Southern California, also brilliantly interrogates the ethnographic impulse. In *The Artifact Piece* (1986) Luna placed his body, naked except for leather breech clout draped over his crotch, in a vitrine in the (unbelievably entitled) 'Museum of Man' in San Diego. Luna included dead-pan labels describing his scars in terms linked to stereotypes about Native Americans (for example, attributing the scars to drunken brawls). Three additional vitrines included his effects – from albums by the Rolling Stones to objects used in tribal rituals on the La Jolla reservation where he lives. See Lucy R. Lippard, *Mixed Blessings: New Art in a Multicultural America* (New York: Pantheon, 1990) 198.

97 Fusco, 'The Other History', *op. cit.* 45.

98 Judith Butler, *Bodies That Matter: On the Discursive Limits of 'Sex'* (New York and London: Routledge, 1993) 17; on the bodily norm and reiterative and citational practice, see *ibid.*, 2; 3.

99 This dynamic highlights the chiasmic intersubjectivity that body art so aggressively surfaces and which makes body art into a collective process of cultural negotiation. As Lea Vergine has noted: 'The public is needed to complete the event; it must be involved in a collective experience that leads it to reconsider its quotidian existence and the rules of its ordinary behaviour ... The relationship between public and artist becomes a relationship of complicity. The artist offers his hand to the spectator and the success of the operation depends upon how and how much the spectator is willing to accept it.' Lea Vergine, 'Bodylanguage', *Art & Artists* (September 1974) 22–27 [see in this volume pp. 236–38].

100 Heidegger, 'The Age of the World Picture', *op.cit.*; Sobchack's statement is from her unpublished 1997 essay '"Is Any Body Home?": Embodied Imagination and Visible Evictions', manuscript, 6; a shorter version of this text appears in Hamid Naficy (ed.), *Home, Exile, Homeland: Film, Media, and the Politics of Place* (New York and London: Routledge, 1998).

101 See Graham's description of the piece in Dan Graham, *Rock My Religion: Writings and Art Projects*, ed. Brian Wallis (Cambridge, Massachusetts and London : MIT Press, 1993) 114–15. Graham points out that the mirror enables the audience to 'perceive itself [instantaneously] as a public mass (as a unity), offsetting its definition by the performer('s discourse)', 115.

102 MacLennan, a Scottish artist living and working in Belfast, is known in Europe for his Beuys-like endurance works in venues from prison cells to office building corridors; his mandate – 'What lies beyond the world of artifice (yet manifests through it)? Communicate from there' – indicates the seriousness of his endeavour, as well as his conviction that a 'real' body/self exists beyond simulation (a conviction specifically denied, I am arguing, by the overtly simulacral self-imaging of an artist such as Cindy Sherman). See Alastair MacLennan, 'Beyond Artifice', *Theatre Ireland*, 23 (1990) 26–29. MacLennan's interest in the everyday is also evident in his statement that his work stems from a belief in 'everyday experience as a key to enlightenment' in the Zen Buddhist sense; see Goldberg, *Performance: Live Art Since 1960*, *op.cit.*, 52. I am indebted to Hilary Robinson and to MacLennan himself for making materials on his work, many of which are difficult to find in the US, available.

103 The best-known texts here are Lyotard's *The Postmodern Condition: A Report on Knowledge*, trans. Geoff Bennington and Brian Massumi (Minneapolis: Minnesota University Press, 1984), and Jameson's 1980s essays, which are collected in *Postmodernism, or The Cultural Logic of Late Capitalism* (Durham, North Carolina: Duke University Press, 1991).

104 Gislind Nabakowski argues provocatively that the concept of 'performance art', which really developed in the late 1970s (the term 'body art' was more common in early 1970s art discourse) was derived 'from the Disco scene in popular music culture' of the 1970s; see Nabakowski, 'The Flirtation with the "It" – On Transgressing the law in the Performance of the 1970s', in A.A. Bronson and Peggy Gale (eds.), *Performance By Artists* (Toronto: Art Metropole, 1979) 250. Important performance venues such as Highways, in Santa Monica (contiguous with Los Angeles), still support smaller-scale performance works, but these are far more narrative and theatrical than the body art works of the 1970s. Artists such as Finley and Anderson do not perform at Highways when they come to LA but, rather, at large capacity venues such as Royce Hall at UCLA.

105 Baudrillard, 'The Precession of Simulacra', *op. cit.*, 253.

106 On Caravaggio's *Bacchus* (also called *Boy with Fruit*; *c.* 1589) as a self-portrait see Walter Friedlander, *Caravaggio Studies* (New York: Schocken Books, 1969) 146. Sherman's picture, *Untitled No. 224*, is reproduced in *Cindy Sherman: A Retrospective* (Los Angeles: The Museum of Contemporary Art; Chicago: Museum of Contemporary Art, 1997) 158.

107 Sherrie Levine's 'After ... ' great photographers' works, in which she rephotographs the works of photographers such as Walker Evans and Edward Weston, perform a similar exercise of excessive simulation on a different register (that of the art

object rather than the more subject-oriented artistic self-portrait). Amy Adler, in her work *After Sherrie Levine* (1994), takes this hollowing out of the signifier one step further by reworking Levine's reworking of Weston in a hand-drawn then rephotographed image of Levine's version of Weston's well-known image of his son's naked torso. Mike Bidlo's 1980s reworkings of Warhol's appropriated images also play out a kind of doubled simulation.

108 Guy Debord, *Society of the Spectacle* (1967) (Detroit: Black and Red, 1983) 38. No translator given. I have added the caveat about the 'belief' in the real as I would not want to imply, as Debord does, that there was a historical moment when we were fully coincident with our actions – versus the alienating situations of capitalism or pancapitalism.

109 On Cahun see François Leperlier, *Claude Cahun* (Paris: Jean-Michel Place, 1992). Warhol and Mapplethorpe, more obsessive about representing the bodies of others in their art works (though they did produce some self-portraits), performed themselves in an overtly public, flamboyant way that makes it appropriate to place them in this category.

110 Sayre, *The Object of Performance*, *op. cit.*, 57.

111 See my extended discussion of the following in *Postmodernism and the En-Gendering of Marcel Duchamp*, *op. cit.*, 146–90; and 'Tracing the Subject with Cindy Sherman', in *Cindy Sherman: A Retrospective*, *op. cit.*, 33–54. See also David Joselit's inspiring discussion of the phenomenon in 'Marcel Duchamp's *Monte Carlo Bond* Machine', *October*, 59 (Winter 1992) 9–26.

112 The Lüthi series is reproduced in a grid of five by four images in *Szene Schweiz: Miriam Cahn, Urs Lüthi, Daniel Spoerri, Aldo Walker* (Cologne: Kunstverein, 1983) 51. I am assuming it was displayed in a similar manner in the exhibition, although a linear installation would give rise to equally interesting interpretations in relation to the negotiation of space and orientation of the human body. The images in Wilke's series have been exhibited and reproduced in a grid; see my *Body Art/Performing the Subject*, *op. cit.*, 183.

113 Lüthi in François Pluchart and Urs Lüthi, 'L'artiste et son double, Entretien avec Urs Lüthi', *Artitudes* 12:14 (1974) 69 (my translation). Appropriately enough a number of these images were included in the important 1973 exhibition 'Transformer: Aspekte der Travestie', which positioned Lüthi's self-images alongside pictures of androgynous pop culture figures such as David Bowie and Lou Reed. See Goldberg, *Performance: Live Art Since 1960*, *op. cit.*, 96.

114 Walter Grasskamp makes this point in the exhibition catalogue *Szene Schweiz*, *op. cit.*, 50.

115 There is only one interior in which 'actual' figures are included but the two seated men are not clearly recognizable. See Rainer Michael Mason, *Urs Lüthi: L'oeuvre multiplié: 1970-1991* (Geneva: Cabinet des Estampes, 1991) 30, 66; the series, 22–25.

116 Vergine, 'Bodylanguage', *op. cit.*, 6. Lüthi's public statements about this type of imagery tend to push in the direction of a yearning for authenticity; per Vergine's suggestion, I am reading against that grain, but with the kind of recognition of intersubjective dynamism Lüthi expresses in an interview with François Pluchart, 'J'ai fait cela pour essayer de voir jusqu-où je pouvais aller dans la relation entre l'homme et la femme ... / Il s'agit de faire sentir au public et d'extérioriser tous mes traits féminins ... / Je me transforme, je change ... / Je n'ai pas l'impression de provoquer ... Il s'agit beaucoup de déclencher quelque chose chez un partenaire éventuel, le spectateur', in Pluchart and Lüthi, 'L'artiste et son double', *op. cit.*, 68. The *Akhnuchik* project by Vulto (1998), in which a man (presumably the artist himself) poses in a series of photographs wearing a false pregnant chest and belly, is an interesting recent counterpart to Lüthi's gender-confusing images. This project is reproduced in the 'Fertility' issue of *New Observations*, 119 (Summer–Autumn 1998) 24–25; the issue is guest edited by Erika Knerr.

117 Laura Mulvey, 'Some Thoughts on Theories of Fetishism in the Context of Contemporary Culture', *October*, 65 (Summer 1993) 14. Mulvey theorizes the 'male gaze' in her well-known article, 'Visual Pleasure and Narrative Cinema' (1975), reprinted in *Visual and Other Pleasures*, *op. cit.*, 14–26. Notably too, in his essay 'The Work of Art in the Age of Mechanical Reproduction', Walter Benjamin writes: 'film responds to the shriveling of the aura with an artificial build-up of the "personality" outside the studio. The cult of the movie star ... preserves not the unique aura of the person but the "spell of the personality", the phony spell of a commodity'; Benjamin, 'The Work of Art in the Age of Mechanical Reproduction' (1936), in Hannah Arendt (ed.), *Illuminations* (New York: Schocken, 1968) 231.

118 Pluchart and Lüthi, 'L'artiste et son double', *op. cit.*, 67 (my translation).

119 The 'body without organs' is Gilles Deleuze and Félix Guattari's term, in *The Anti-Oedipus: Capitalism and Schizophrenia* (Minneapolis: University of Minnesota Press, 1989) 9–15.

120 Both Abigail Solomon-Godeau and Linda Williams have written excellent texts on these intersecting kinds of fetishism. See Solomon-Godeau, 'The Legs of the Countess', *October*, 39 (Winter 1986) 67–68; and Williams, *Hard Core: Power, Pleasure, and the 'Frenzy of the Visible'* (Berkeley and Los Angeles: University of California, 1989) 93–119.

121 Goldberg, *Performance: Live Art Since 1960*, *op. cit.*, 98; and for images, *op. cit.*, 126–27.

122 Dominic Molon, 'Countdown to Ecstasy', *Mariko Mori* (Chicago: Museum of Contemporary Art; London: Serpentine Gallery, 1998) 6.

123 Pure Land is a School of Buddhism prevalent in Japan. On Mori's utopianism and belief in transcendence, see *ibid.*, 15, and Lisa Corrin, 'Mariko Mori's Quantum *Nirvana*', in *Mariko Mori*, *op. cit.*, 19–31.

124 On a related piece by Horn see Caroline Jones, *Painting Machines: Industrial Image and Process in Contemporary Art* (Boston University Art Gallery, 1997) 38–39. *Telegarden*, which Santarromana produced with the technical assistance of Ken Goldberg and a team of assistants, can be accessed at <http://www.usc.edu/dept/garden>

125 A notable exception is the work of Valie Export in Germany; Export produced a number of self-reflexive video and film works in the early to mid 1970s. See chapter 2, 'Performances–Actions–Video–Installations', in Roswitha Müller, *Valie Export: Fragments of the Imagination* (Bloomington: Indiana University Press, 1994) 27–82.

126 For an illustration of Acconci's design of the piece and of the piece installed see Kate Linker's useful monograph *Vito Acconci* (New York: Rizzoli, 1994) 62–63. I write extensively about Acconci's work in my chapter, 'The Body in Action: Vito Acconci and the "Coherent" Male Artistic Subject', in *Body Art/Performing the Subject*, *op. cit.*, 103–50. Bruce Nauman, Robert Morris and Lynda Benglis also made use of instant feedback in video installation works. Rosalind Krauss' 'Video: The Aesthetics of Narcissism' (1978) explores the psychic effects of instant feedback. Reprinted in John Handhardt (ed.,), *Video Culture: A Critical Investigation* (New York: Visual Studies Workshop,1986) 179–91 [see in this volume pp. 277–80].

127 For a description of Chadwick's piece see Oliver Bennet, 'British Performance on the "Edge"', *New Art Examiner* (February 1989) 63; Bennet states that the cells are cancerous cervical cells, which would reinforce the feminist slant of the piece as a comment on the vulnerability of women's bodies to disease. A conflicting description of Chadwick's piece, which states that the laser ends in 'a point marked with Chadwick's own blood', appears in Gray Watson, 'Performance Art's Untapped Potential', *Art International*, 7 (Summer 1989) 41. Either way, Chadwick's piece clearly mobilizes a technologized simulacrum of bodily fluid in a manner that references the annunciation. Maureen Connor's video installation works, like Rosenbach's, press bodily fluids and noises through the sieve of technology; I discuss Connor's works in *Body Art/Performing the Subject*, *op. cit.*, 205–14.

128 'Photography is my skin' is from 'Soliloquy to Flesh', in *Enfleshings* (New York: Aperture, 1989) [see in this volume pp. 280–81]; the remainder of this quotation is from Helen Chadwick, 'Ego Geometria Sum' in *Enfleshings*, *op. cit.*

129 Interestingly, while early 1970s feminist art from the US (especially California) has been characterized as focusing on unified and universalized female bodies to the exclusion of a focus on femininity as fragmented and socially constructed, much of the feminist work from this period engaged body parts in a performative fashion in relation to the full body, which would then be photographed and/or videotaped (such as Lynda Benglis' famous *Artforum* advertisement [November 1974] or the Feminist Art Program's *Cock and Cunt* play [1970], written by Judy Chicago and performed by Faith Wilding and Jan Marie Lester); on the latter, see note 17. The primary exception to this, the infamous vulvar plates from Judy Chicago's *Dinner Party*, are not so much body parts as they are highly symbolic synecdoches of femaleness in general.

130 On Nengudi and Wilding see the 'Fertility' issue of *New Observations*, *op. cit.*, 32–37.

131 Celia Lurie, *Prosthetic Culture: Photography, Memory and Identity* (New York and London: Routledge, 1998) 1. For Lurie the key technology of the prosthetic extension of the self outwards (beyond the self-contained subject of Descartes' 'I think therefore I am') is photography.

132 Benjamin, 'The Work of Art', *op. cit.*, 236, 229. As Don Ihde has pointed out, 'the photograph, more than merely representing, "teaches" a way of seeing', and proffers a kind of 'irrealism' through its immobilizing of the real; Ihde, 'Image Technologies and Traditional Culture', in Andrew Feenberg and Alastair Hannay (eds.), *Technology and the Politics of Knowledge* (Bloomington and Indianapolis: Indiana University Press, 1995) 151.

133 Vivian Sobchack, '"Is Any Body Home?"', *op. cit.*, 1.

134 Benjamin, 'The Work of Art', *op. cit.*, 239.

135 See Mieke Bal and Norman Bryson's critique of the notion of context as a pre-existing 'real' that conditions the cultural product in their essay 'Semiotics and Art History', in Donald Preziosi (ed.), *The Art of Art History: A Critical Anthology* (Oxford and New York: Oxford University Press, 1998) 242–56.

136 Chadwick, 'Soliloquy to Flesh', *op. cit.*, 109.

137 Thus, as I explore in 'The "Pollockian Performative"' (pp. 53–102), in his hyper-masculinity (as a heterosexual, white cowboy and artistic genius rolled into one) Jackson Pollock produces a normative masculinity that is so exaggerated it becomes a parody of itself. Pollock's hyper-masculinity thus slides easily into the performative realm of camp.

138 Donna Haraway, 'A Cyborg Manifesto: Science, Technology, and Socialist-Feminism in the Late Twentieth Century' (1985), *Simians, Cyborgs, and Women: The Reinvention of Nature* (New York and London: Routledge, 1991) 160; 163.

139 *Ibid.*, 151.

140 See Guy Brett, 'Survey', *Mona Hatoum* (London: Phaidon, 1997) 71.

141 These are Mona Hatoum's words in describing the piece; untitled lecture at the J. Paul Getty Museum, 10 September 1996. Orlan's excavation of the invasive, literally body-transforming effects of plastic surgical technologies in her self-mutilation series of public surgeries is closely linked to Hatoum's piece in this regard. See the essays in *Orlan: This is My Body ... This is My Software ...* (London: Black Dog, 1996).

142 These words obviously recall Jacques Lacan's formulation of the intersubjective relation that constitutes the subject in relation to (his desire for) the other; see especially 'The Signification of the Phallus' (1958), in *Écrits: A Selection*, trans. Alan Sheridan (New York: W.W. Norton, 1977) 281–91; and 'Of the Subject Who is Supposed to Know, of the First Dyad, and of the Good' (1964), in *The Four Fundamental Concepts of Psycho-Analysis*, trans. Alan Sheridan (New York: W.W. Norton, 1978) 230–43.

143 See Christine Ross' brilliant discussion of video as a '*mangeuse de profondeur*' in her book *Images de Surface: l'art vidéo reconsidéré* (Montreal: Editions Artextes, 1996). I am indebted to Ross for sharing this work with me and for her excellent thoughts on Hatoum, published as 'To Touch the Other: A Story of Corpo-electronic Surfaces', *Public*, 13 (1996) 55–61. See also Jessica Morgan's interesting discussion of *Corps étranger* in relation to surface and depth in 'The Poetics of Uncovering: Mona Hatoum In and Out of Perspective', *Mona Hatoum* (Chicago: Museum of Contemporary Art, 1977) 2–3.

144 Cited in Guy Brett, 'Survey', *op. cit.*, 71.

WORK-S

MARINA ABRAMOVIC
VITO ACCONCI
BAS JAN ADER
LAURA AGUILAR
ELEANOR ANTIN
JANINE ANTONI
SKIP ARNOLD
RON ATHEY
MIROSŁAW BAŁKA
OLADÉLÉ AJIBOYÉ BAMGBOYÉ
MATTHEW BARNEY
LYNDA BENGLIS
JOSEPH BEUYS
KEITH BOADWEE
LOUISE BOURGEOIS
LEIGH BOWERY
STUART BRISLEY
GÜNTER BRUS
CHRIS BURDEN
JAMES LEE BYARS
CÉSAR
HELEN CHADWICK
JUDY CHICAGO
LYGIA CLARK
JOHN COPLANS
PAUL COTTON
JIM DINE
CHERYL DONEGAN
MARCEL DUCHAMP
JOHN DUNCAN
MARY BETH EDELSON
DIAMELA ELTIT
TRACEY EMIN
PEPE ESPALIÚ
VALIE EXPORT
KAREN FINLEY
BOB FLANAGAN & SHEREE ROSE
SHERMAN FLEMING
TERRY FOX
FRANKO B
HOWARD FRIED
COCO FUSCO & GUILLERMO GÓMEZ-PEÑA
GIDEON GECHTMAN
GILBERT & GEORGE
BRUCE GILCHRIST
ANTONY GORMLEY
LYLE ASHTON HARRIS & RENÉE COX
MONA HATOUM
DICK HIGGINS & ALISON KNOWLES
SUSAN HILLER
HI RED CENTER
REBECCA HORN
JOAN JONAS
MICHEL JOURNIAC
ALLAN KAPROW
MIKE KELLEY
JÜRGEN KLAUKE
YVES KLEIN
MILAN KNÍŽÁK
JEFF KOONS
ELKE KRYSTUFEK
SHIGEKO KUBOTA
TETSUMI KUDO
OLEG KULIK
YAYOI KUSAMA
RACHEL LACHOWICZ
CARLOS LEPPE
BARRY LE VA
RICHARD LONG
JAMES LUNA
URS LÜTHI
PAUL McCARTHY
BRUCE McLEAN
PIERO MANZONI
ROBERT MAPPLETHORPE
GEORGES MATHIEU
ANA MENDIETA
PIERRE MOLINIER
LINDA MONTANO & TEHCHING HSIEH
CHARLOTTE MOORMAN
MARIKO MORI
YASUMASA MORIMURA
ROBERT MORRIS
OTTO MÜHL
TERESA MURAK
SABURO MURAKAMI
BRUCE NAUMAN
SHIRIN NESHAT
HERMANN NITSCH
HÉLIO OITICICA
CLAES OLDENBURG
YOKO ONO
DENNIS OPPENHEIM
ORLAN
LUCY ORTA
RAFAEL MONTAÑEZ ORTIZ
NAM JUNE PAIK
GINA PANE
JAYNE PARKER
MIKE PARR
GIUSEPPE PENONE
ADRIAN PIPER
GIANNI PISANI
JACKSON POLLOCK
MARC QUINN
ARNULF RAINER
EGLĖ RAKAUSKAITĖ
CHARLES RAY
HELI REKULA
KLAUS RINKE
PIPILOTTI RIST
ULRIKE ROSENBACH
NIKI DE SAINT-PHALLE
LUCAS SAMARAS
JENNY SAVILLE
CAROLEE SCHNEEMANN
RUDOLF SCHWARZKOGLER
ANDRES SERRANO
BONNIE SHERK
CINDY SHERMAN
SHOZO SHIMAMOTO
KAZUO SHIRAGA
KATHARINA SIEVERDING
LORNA SIMPSON
BARBARA SMITH
ALAN SONFIST
ANNIE SPRINKLE
STELARC
PETR ŠTEMBERA
STAHL STENSLIE
ATSUKO TANAKA
MIERLE LADERMAN UKELES
ULAY
BEN VAUTIER
BILL VIOLA
WOLF VOSTELL
ANDY WARHOL
ZBIGNIEW WARPECHOWSKI
WILLIAM WEGMAN
PETER WEIBEL
FAITH WILDING
HANNAH WILKE
FRANCESCA WOODMAN
RAÚL ZURITA

PAINTING BODIES

For the Abstract Expressionists working in post-war New York, the canvas was the receptacle for the artist's psychic self-expression. Attention gradually turned away from the painting as an object, and focused on the very act of painting itself; indeed, the movement also became known as 'action painting'. The process of painting was as important as the resulting work, and the artist's chosen method of mark-making on canvas became the subject of the artwork. The artist's presence in the work through the act of painting led to the artist's body becoming a tool for applying paint, akin to the paintbrush, leaving a direct trace of the body in the work. In some works the body itself became the 'canvas' on which to paint. As a reaction to this originally male-dominated art form, epitomized by the 'heroic' status of Jackson Pollock, artists later developed a critique and feminist parody of the macho persona of the paint-flinging male artist.

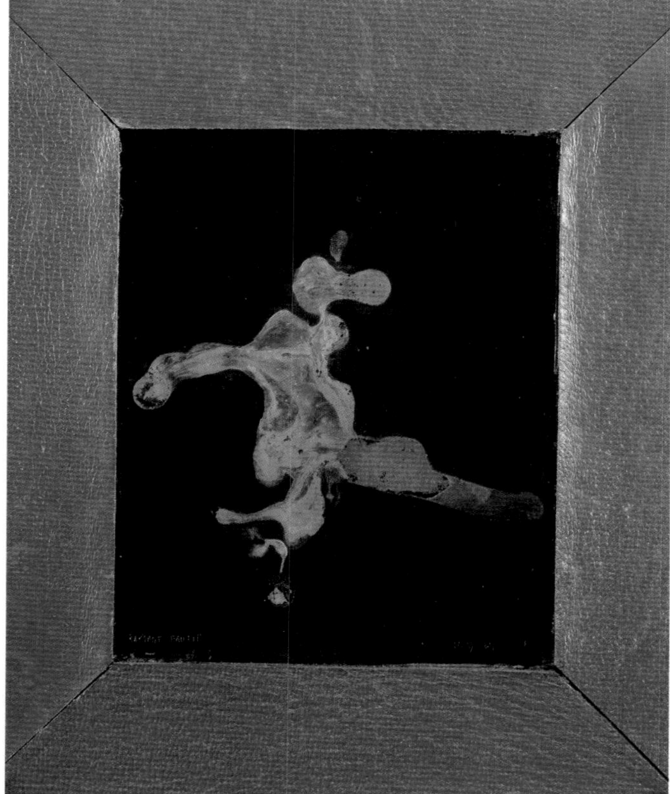

Marcel DUCHAMP
Paysage fautif (Wayward landscape)
1946
Seminal fluid, Astralon, black satin
21 × 17 cm [8 × 7 in]

Between 1941 and 1949, Duchamp made a series of works called *Boîtes-en-valises* (*Boxes-in-valises*), each of which contained sixty-nine miniature reproductions of a selection of his previous works, a handwritten dedication to the recipient and an 'original' artwork. *Paysage fautif* (*Wayward landscape*) was the 'original' included in *Boîte* XII/XX of the de luxe edition. This was dedicated to Maria Martins, the Brazilian artist who was his lover at the time and whose body provided the model for *Etant donnés* (*Given*, 1946–66) and *Prière de toucher* (*Please Touch*, 1947). *Paysage fautif* was a mysterious abstract painting of unknown provenance. In 1989 chemical analysis revealed that it was made with semen, relocating the piece as an ironic addition of a part of the body, both as a medium of direct expression and as a museum-worthy relic.

The only other 'original' from this series to contain material taken directly from the body was *Boîte* XIII/XX, in which clumps of hair (from the head, armpits and pubic region) were taped to a piece of Plexiglas. Duchamp dedicated this *Boîte* to the artist Roberto Matta.

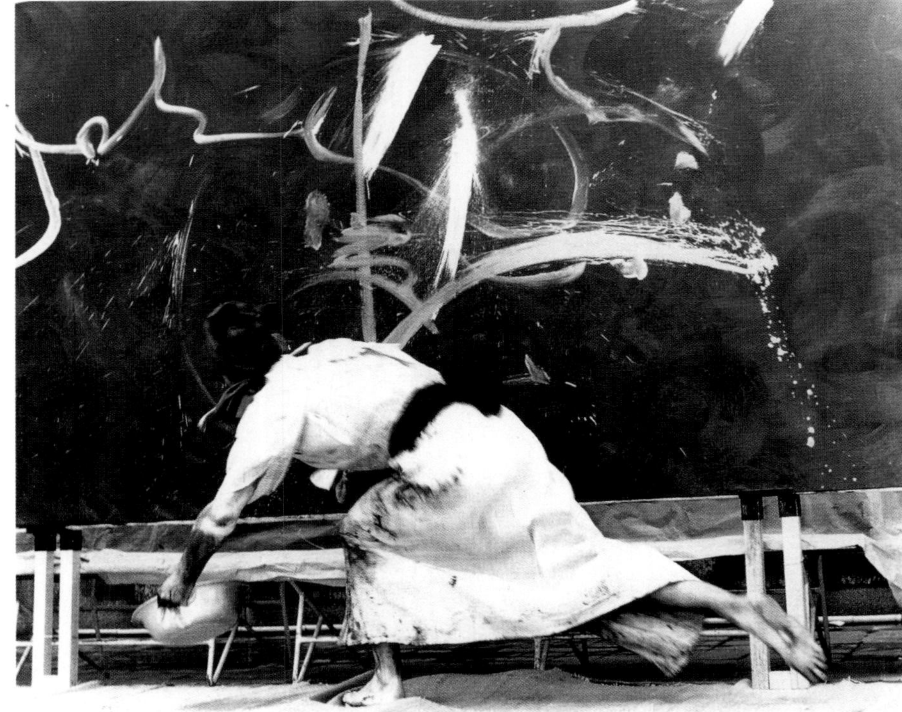

left

Georges MATHIEU

Homage to General Hideyoshi

1957

Osaka, Japan

Mathieu was the first Western artist to stage live action paintings as a performance before a viewing public and as the subject of photography. He executed his monumental paintings in historical costume to reinforce the dramatic effect. Mathieu claimed that the activity of painting needed to be freed-up and transformed through 'speed in execution' to allow it to be spontaneous, direct and uninhibited by the past. His emphasis on improvisation was an attempt to reverse the order in the relationship between sign and meaning: 'The work of art becomes a geometric point of interrogations. Instead of the reduction of the Cosmos to the dimensions of man, the work of art is nothing more nor less than an opening out into the Cosmos.'
– Georges Mathieu, 'Towards a New Convergence in Art, Thought and Science', 1960

opposite

Jackson POLLOCK

Painting in his studio

c. 1950

East Hampton

Photographs of Pollock painting in his studio were published in *Life* magazine and brought Pollock's technique to a wide international audience. A colour film of Pollock's artistic activity, which was shown at The Museum of Modern Art in 1951, presented the artist engaged in a heroic performance, of which the painting became the material embodiment, the product of 'an event'. This placed the emphasis on the activity of painting itself. The canvas, no longer the site of a 'picture' in the traditional sense, began to be experienced as 'an arena in which to act'. As a result of the public presentation of Pollock, the persona of the artist acting in that space began to take on a dimension almost greater than the resultant work.

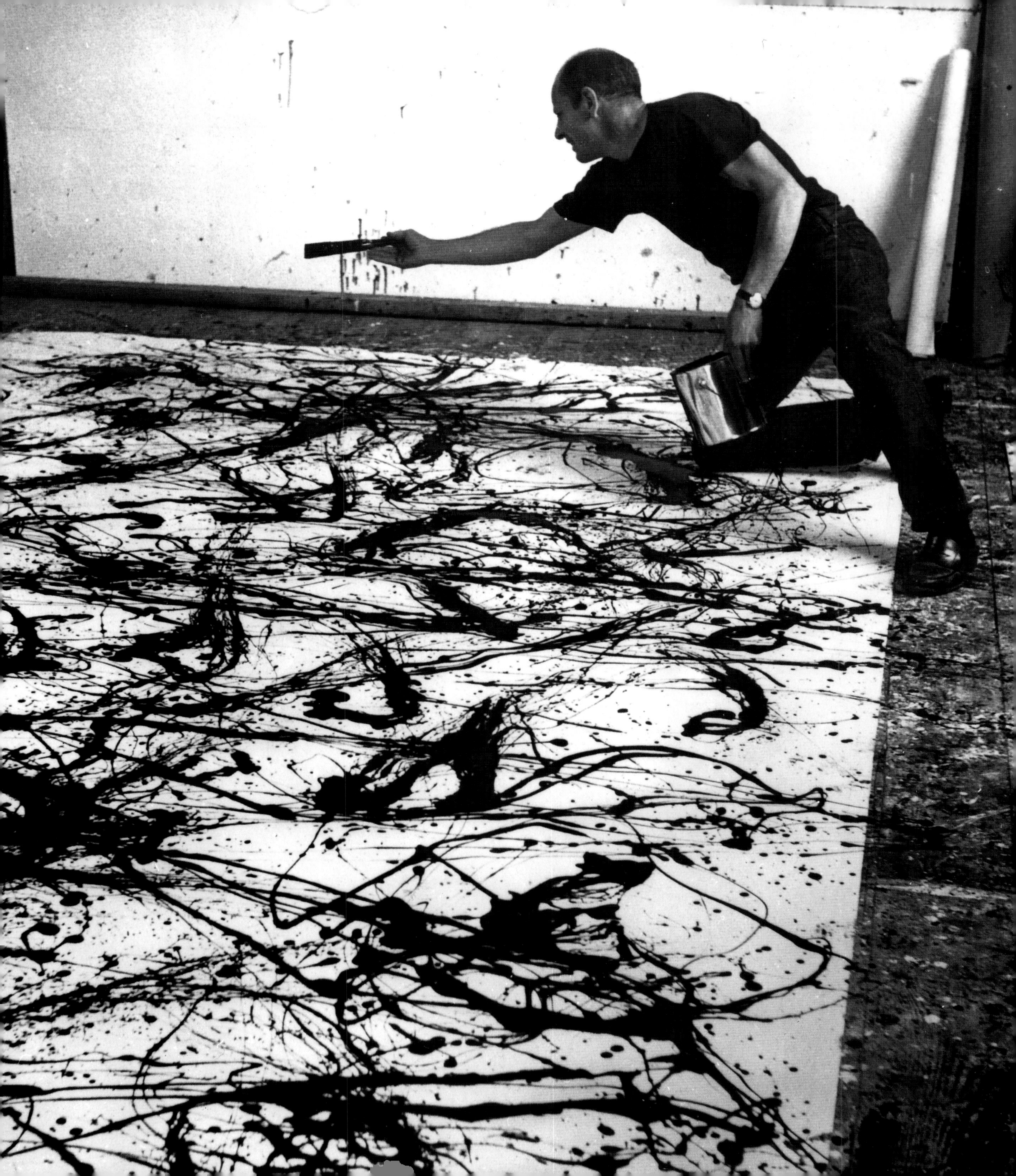

Saburo MURAKAMI

Breaking Through Many Paper Screens

1956

Tokyo

Murakami performed *At One Moment Opening Six Holes* at the First Gutai Art Exhibition at the Ohara Kaikan Hall, Tokyo (1955), and again the following year when it was documented as *Breaking Through Many Paper Screens*. The artist set up a row of paper screens measuring 183 × 366 cm [6 × 12 ft] in wooden frames and then hurled himself through them. His body burst through the traditional flat surface of painted art, dramatically rupturing the picture plane. The work was also a reference to the Japanese martial arts tradition. 'We must not keep on aimlessly adjusting and manipulating the canvas. Instead, our sense must be internally concentrated to a point from which it bursts on to the canvas and assumes a tangible form.'
– Saburo Murakami, *Gutai*, 1955

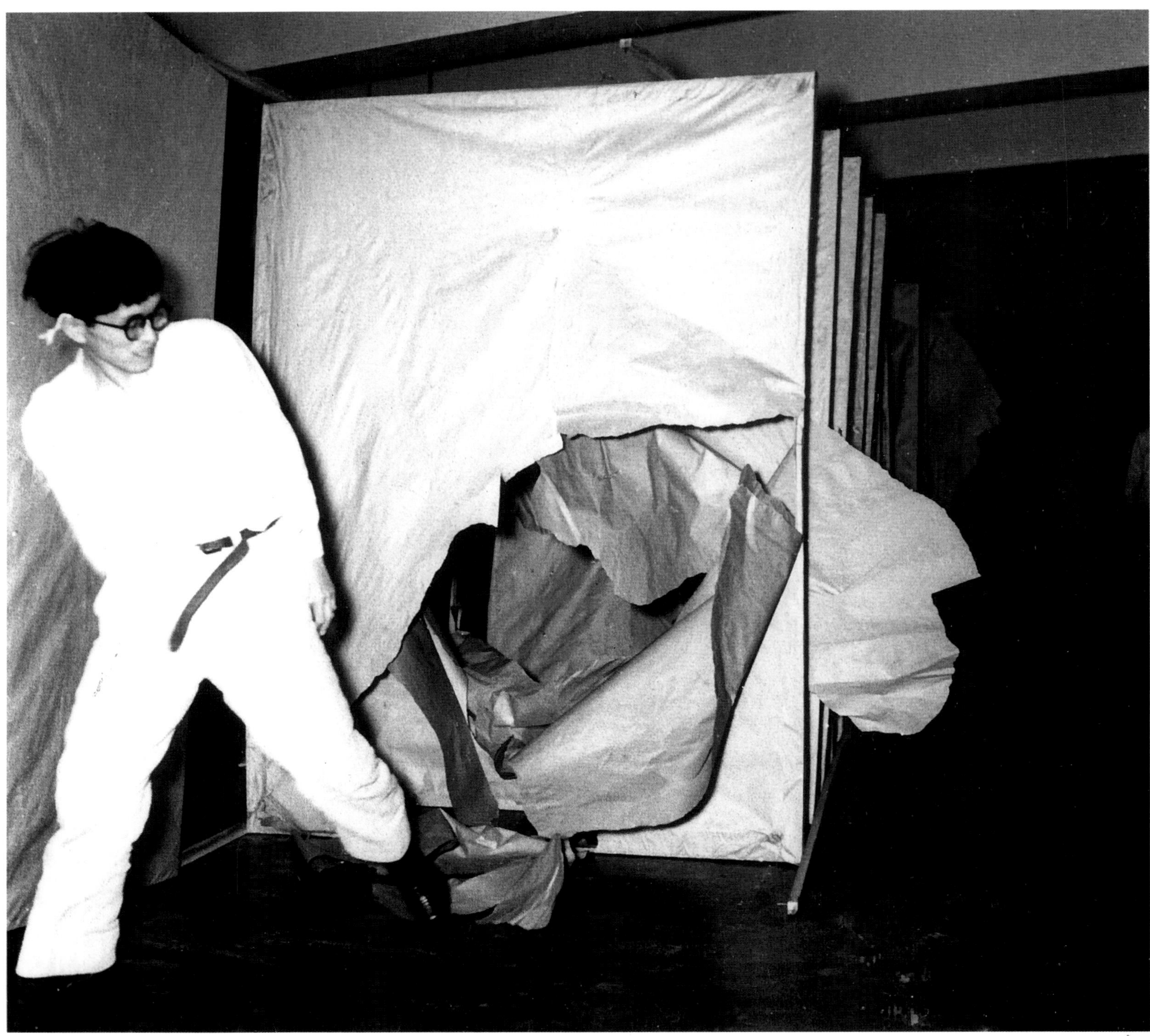

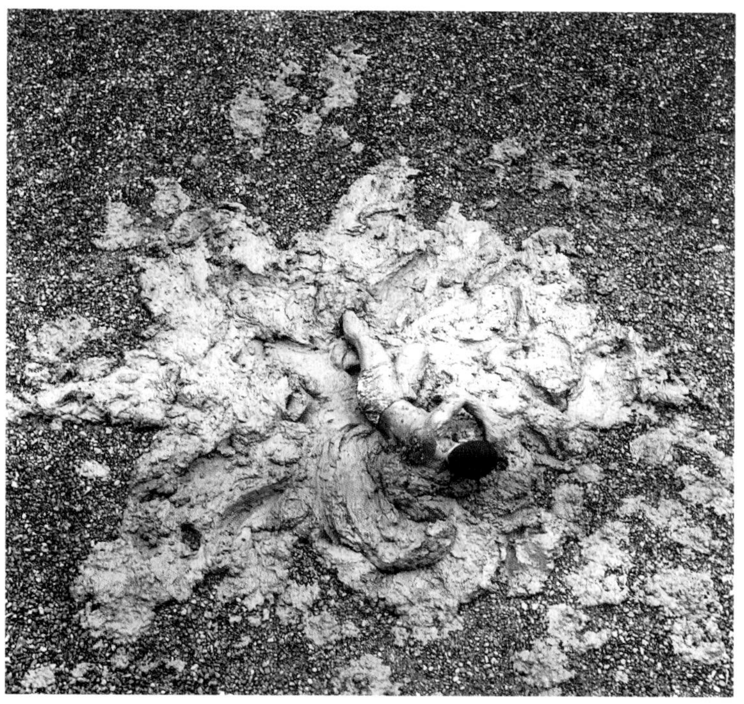

Kazuo SHIRAGA
Challenging Mud
1955
Ohara Kaikan Hall, Tokyo

Shiraga performed *Challenging Mud* by writhing in a pool of thick mud in a primal gestural act, at the First Gutai Art Exhibition at the Ohara Kaikan Hall, Tokyo. Fighting the mud like a wrestler, he produced what was essentially a two-dimensional painting sculpted from mud, which bore the imprint or impression of the artist's physical struggle with matter. Photographic documentation was vital to record the transient activity. Shiraga's transformation of painting into a process-oriented and theatrically inspired medium, 'performed' in temporal space and lived on as photographic documentation, can be seen as a complete and multifaceted embodiment of Gutai, an experimental art group founded in Osaka in 1954 by Jiro Yoshihara. The violent physicality of his painting impulses was expressed through the focus on the movement of his body as both subject and origin of his artistic creativity.

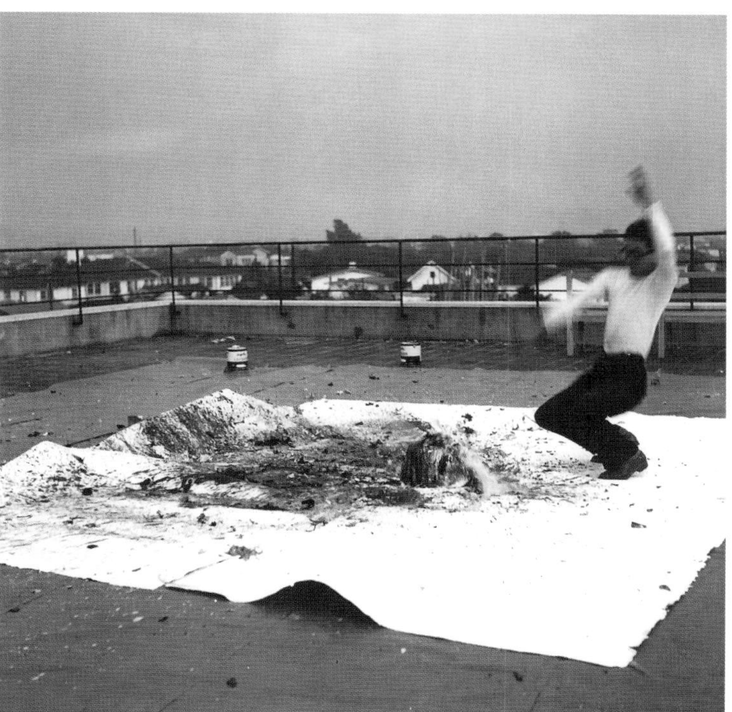

Shozo SHIMAMOTO
Making a Painting by Throwing Bottles of Paint
1956
Ohara Kaikan Hall, Tokyo

This painting was presented at the Second Gutai Art Exhibition at the Ohara Kaikan Hall, Tokyo, in October 1956. Shimamoto hurled jars of paint at unstretched canvases laid on the floor, producing glass-encrusted surfaces in which the reds, oranges and blacks allude to fire and destruction. These projectile paintings provide a direct record of his deliberately violent and theatrical action. Earlier in 1956, in a one-day Gutai exhibition arranged specifically for the photographers of *Life* magazine, Shimamoto had shot paint from a cylinder inside a cannon on to a series of vertical canvases, making paintings through the explosive contact of paint with the pictorial surface. The incorporation of a mechanical process to make marks emphasized the random nature of painting. Very few of these works survived owing to the violence of the process, which literally destroyed them as they were being created. The performative aspect of the process of creation was an essential element of these works.

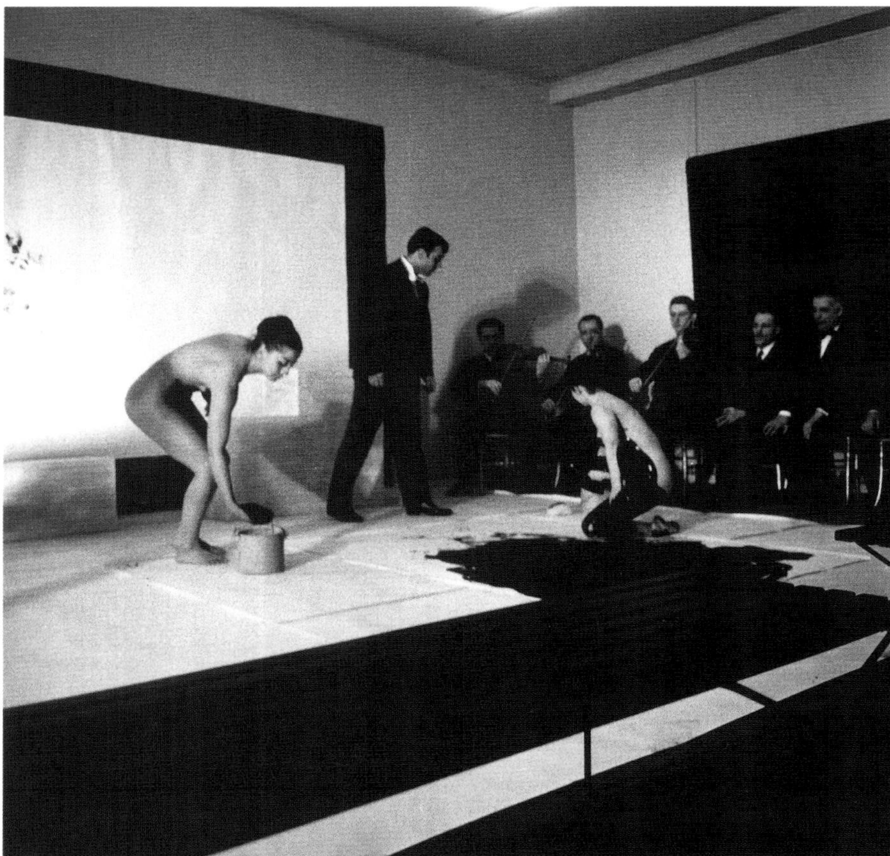

left
Yves KLEIN
Anthropometry of the Blue Epoch
1960
Galerie Internationale d'Art Contemporain, Paris
Klein collaborated with Maurice d'Arquian, the director of the Galerie Internationale d'Art Contemporain, Paris, to produce a spectacle for a hundred members of the art world élite, demonstrating the process of his anthropometry paintings. Dressed in a tuxedo and white tie, Klein directed two nude female models who sponged themselves with his signature blue paint and imprinted markings of their bodies on to large sheets of white paper attached to the wall, climbing on to pedestals of different heights to create a rhythmic composition of silhouettes. A third model was coated with blue paint and dragged across a large sheet of paper on the floor. Throughout the performance, a group of musicians performed Klein's *Monotone Symphony*: twenty minutes of one-note music, followed by twenty minutes of silence. In subsequent performances Klein employed photographers to document his art-making activities, and these documents are an important part of hislegacy.

opposite
Yves KLEIN
Untitled Anthropometry
1960
Dry pigment in synthetic resin on paper on canvas
194 × 127 cm [76 × 50 in]
Collection, Museum Ludwig, Cologne
As a judo expert, Klein believed that the body is the centre of physical, sensorial and spiritual energy. He applied this principle to his work, creating a new painting technique that involved the application of paint directly from the human body, which became a 'living brush'. Klein first publicly used a human body in this way at a dinner party at his friend Robert Godet's apartment in Paris in 1958. A nude female model was covered in Klein's signature ultramarine blue paint (I.K.B., or International Klein Blue). She dragged herself over a gigantic piece of white paper laid on the floor, using her hands and body to spread the paint over the paper and leaving the impression of her body in the texture of the paint. Klein had abandoned the paintbrush in search of complete detachment from, and control over, his paintings: 'I had rejected the brush long before. It was too psychological. I painted with the more anonymous roller, trying to create a "distance" – at the very least an intellectual, unvarying distance – between the canvas and me during the execution. Now, like a miracle, the brush returned, but this time alive. Under my direction the flesh itself applied the colour to the surface and with perfect precision. I was able to remain constantly at the exact distance "X" from my canvas and thus I could dominate my creation continuously throughout the entire execution.'
– Yves Klein, 'Truth Becomes Reality', 1960

The obvious theatrical and sensational aspects of the event shifted the focus from the paintings themselves to the performance of the artist and the bodies he directed. The artist became a conductor whose role was to orchestrate the individuals making his paintings for him in a spectacle of artistic direction.

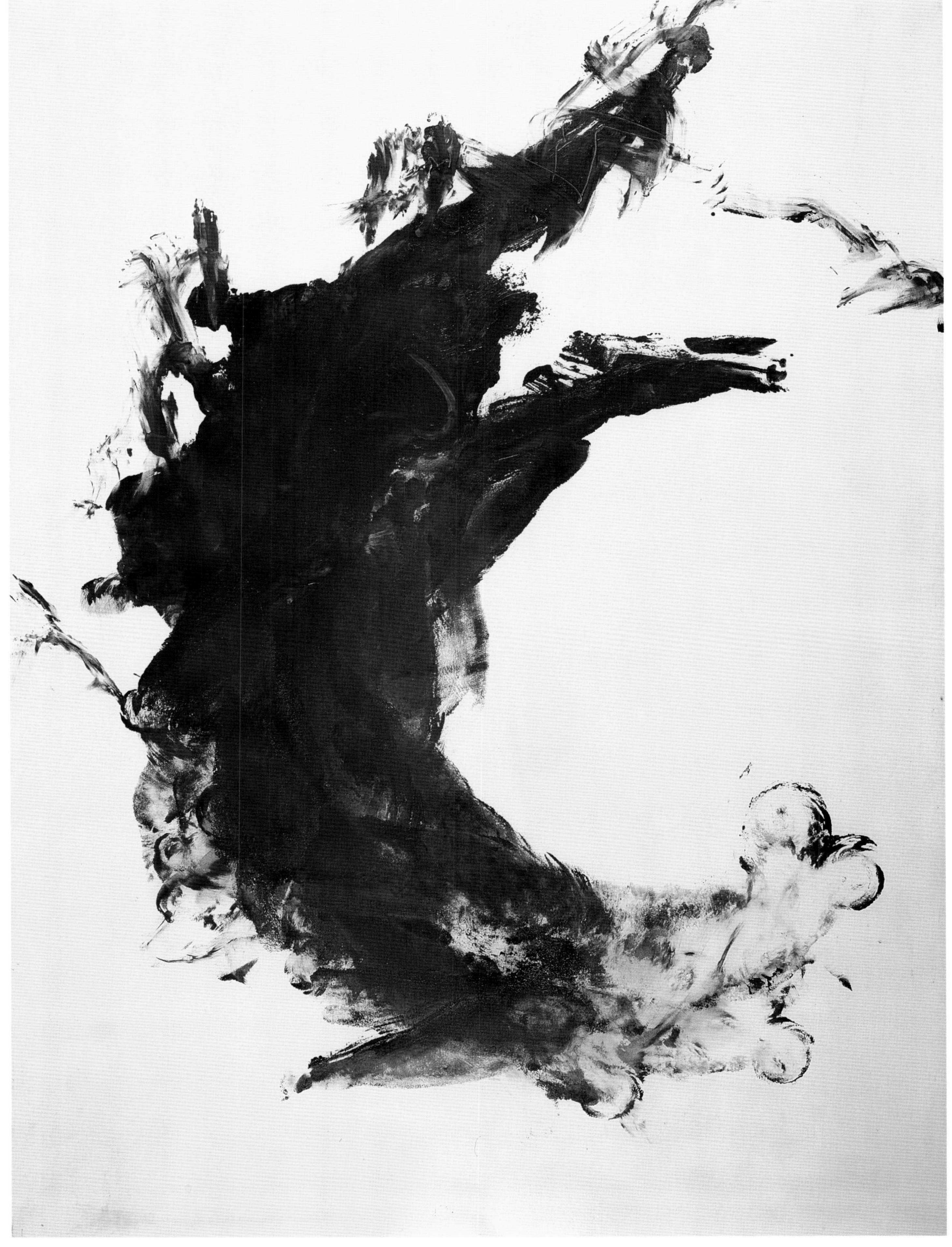

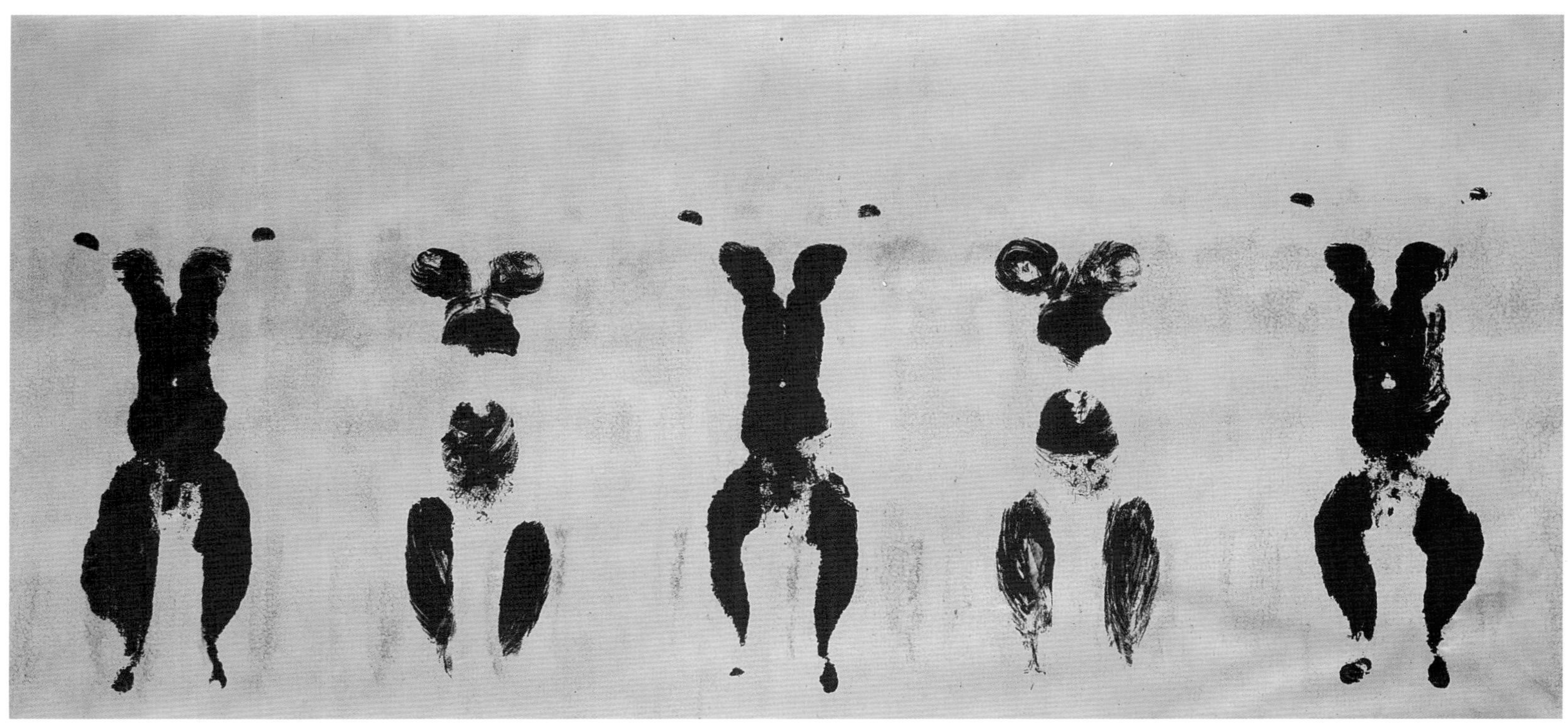

opposite
Yves KLEIN
Untitled Anthropometry with Male and Female Figures
1960
Dry pigment in synthetic resin on paper on canvas
145 × 298 cm [57 × 117 in]

Klein occasionally used his own body to make imprints – as in three of the images in this work. The anthropometries emphasize the artist's interest in using flesh to convey the phenomenological presence of the body, a presence that would reaffirm his belief in the 'resurrection of the body, in the resurrection of the flesh'. Because the body imprints are usually faceless and headless, they do not appear as expressions or even traces of individuality, but instead present the trunk of the body, which for Klein was 'the essential mass', the place where the 'I without the "I" become one with life itself'.
– Yves Klein, 'Truth Becomes Reality', 1960

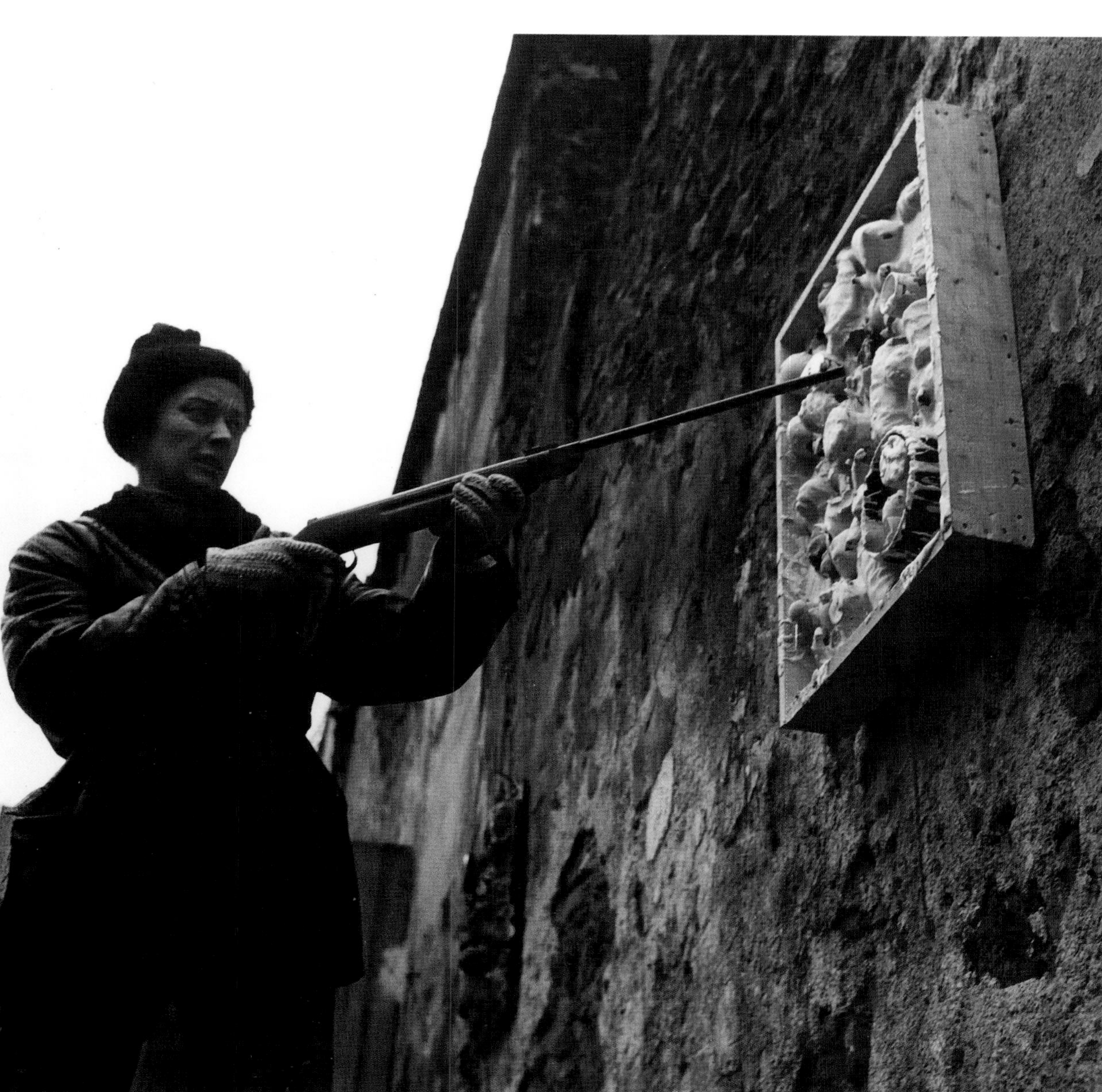

Niki de SAINT-PHALLE
First Shooting Impasse Ronsin
1961
Paris

de Saint-Phalle made a series of these *Tir à Volonté* (*Fire at Will*) paintings. She attached bags of liquid pigment on to their surfaces, which burst when she or others (including artists Robert Rauschenberg and Jasper Johns) fired a .22 calibre rifle at the work. She first presented these 'shoot paintings' publicly at the Galerie J. in Paris in 1961 with the words: 'There are some ideas that cause emotions. My shooting was an emotion that provoked an idea. So my anger became a death ritual without victims.'

Later she wrote: 'I shot because it was fun and made me feel great. I shot because I was fascinated watching the painting bleed and die. I shot for that moment of magic ... Red, yellow, blue – the painting is crying the painting is dead. I have killed the painting. It is reborn.'
– Niki de Saint-Phalle, Artist's statement, 1960

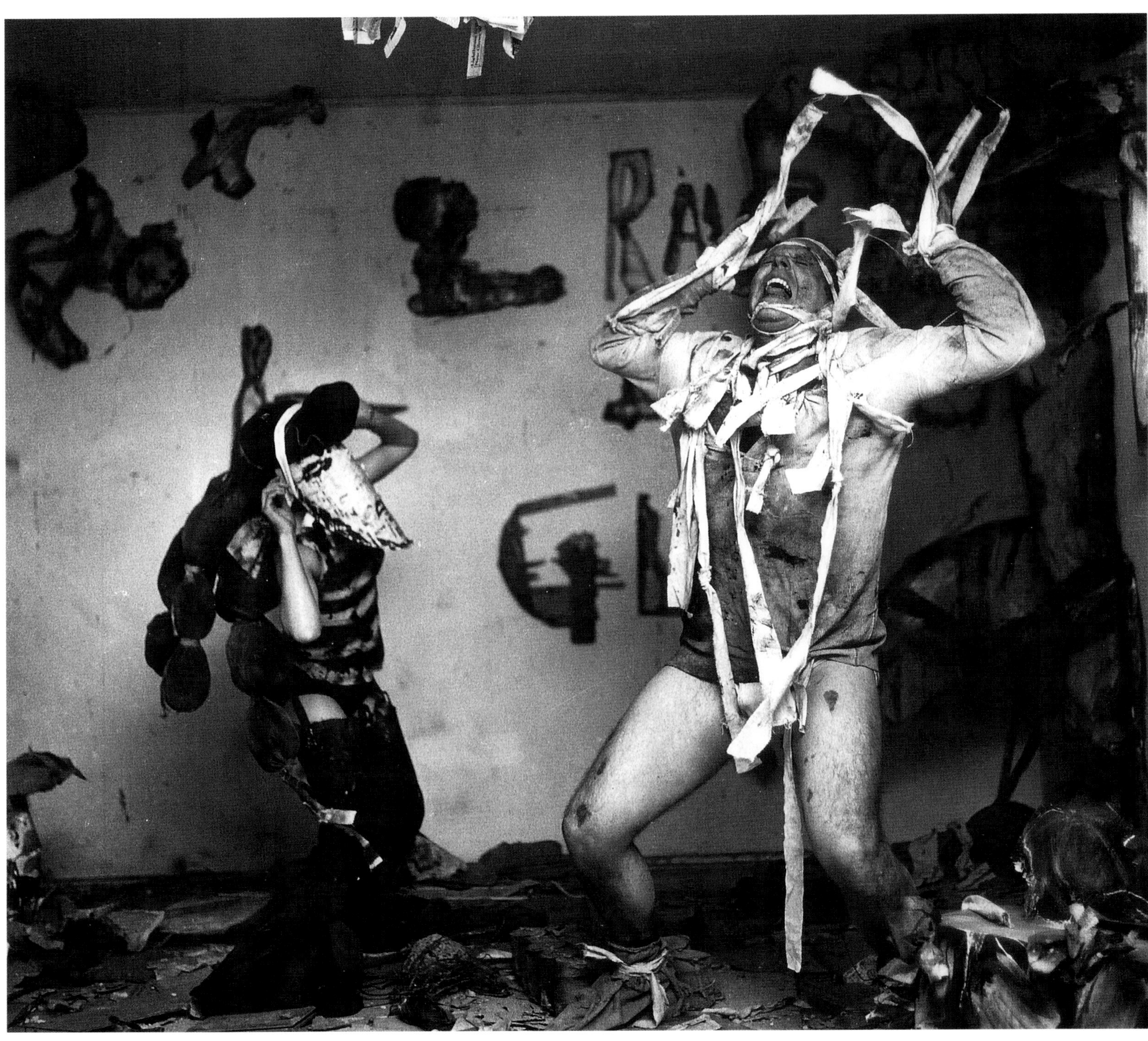

opposite

Claes OLDENBURG

Snapshots from the City

1960

New York

Oldenburg claimed that he became interested in Happenings because he wanted to find new ways to extend traditional painting space, which he had found too limiting. He believed Happenings had the potential to break through in to an exploration of 'total' space. At the Judson Gallery, New York, he installed an environment called *The Street* – a reportage of life in the Lower East Side slums where he performed with Pat Muschinski in a multi-layered confusion of organic matter. Their bodies were presented as human, organic wreckage, wrapped in bandages and covered in dirt, in an environment of cardboard and newspapers and glued and torn paper attached to wire and wooden frames. 'I am for an art that is political-erotical-mystical, that does something other than sit on its ass in a museum ... I am for an art that embroils itself with the everyday crap and still comes out on top. I am for an art that imitates the human, that is comic, if necessary, or violent.'
– Claes Oldenburg, *Store Days*, 1961

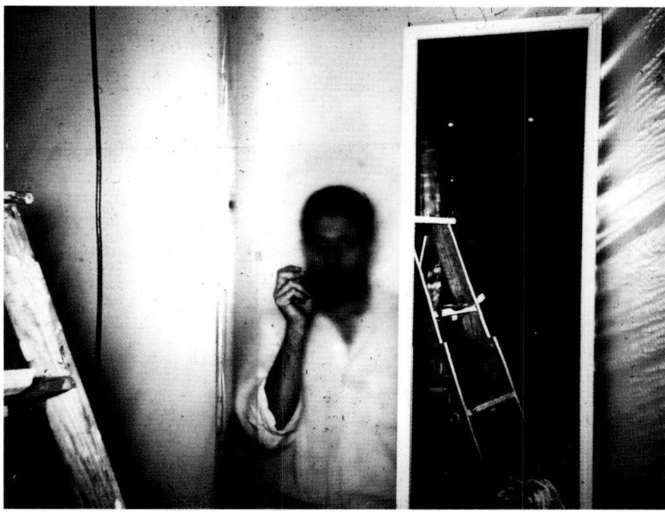

Allan KAPROW

18 Happenings in 6 Parts

1959

Reuben Gallery, New York

In his first groundbreaking 'Happening' presented at the Reuben Gallery in New York, Kaprow created an interactive performance event that synthesized action painting, assemblage and environments. The gallery was divided into three rooms by semi-transparent plastic sheets, which had been painted and collaged, panels on which words were painted, and rows of plastic fruit. Slides and films were projected on to the walls and various musical and non-musical sounds were incorporated into the action, including poetry reading and an orchestra for toy instruments. With no perceptible narrative logic, the 'happening' presented a simultaneous series of activities performed by artists and shared with an audience, which was given instructions on when to applaud, when to change seats and when to move to the next room. In this way viewers were transformed into active participants in the work.

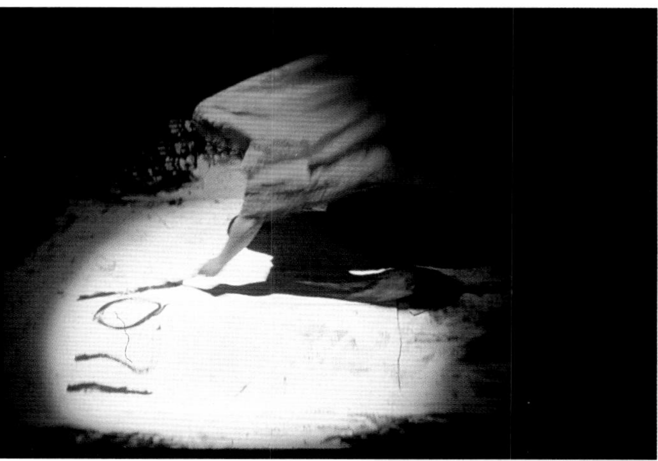

Jim DINE

The Smiling Workman

1960

Judson Memorial Church, New York

The Smiling Workman was presented at Judson Memorial Church as part of a series of Happenings and performances organized by Claes Oldenburg titled the 'Ray Gun Show', which claimed to present 'paintings in the shape of theatre'. Dine performed in a floor-length red smock, his face painted red with a black clown's smile. In front of him was a table with buckets of paint. Behind him was a large sheet of paper stretched like a canvas on which he rapidly scrawled 'I love what I'm doing' in orange and blue. He then drank a bucket of red paint (actually tomato juice), poured more over his head and crashed through the painting. In this work, Dine extended the physical relationship of the artist with his paint and canvas to new levels of bodily connection.

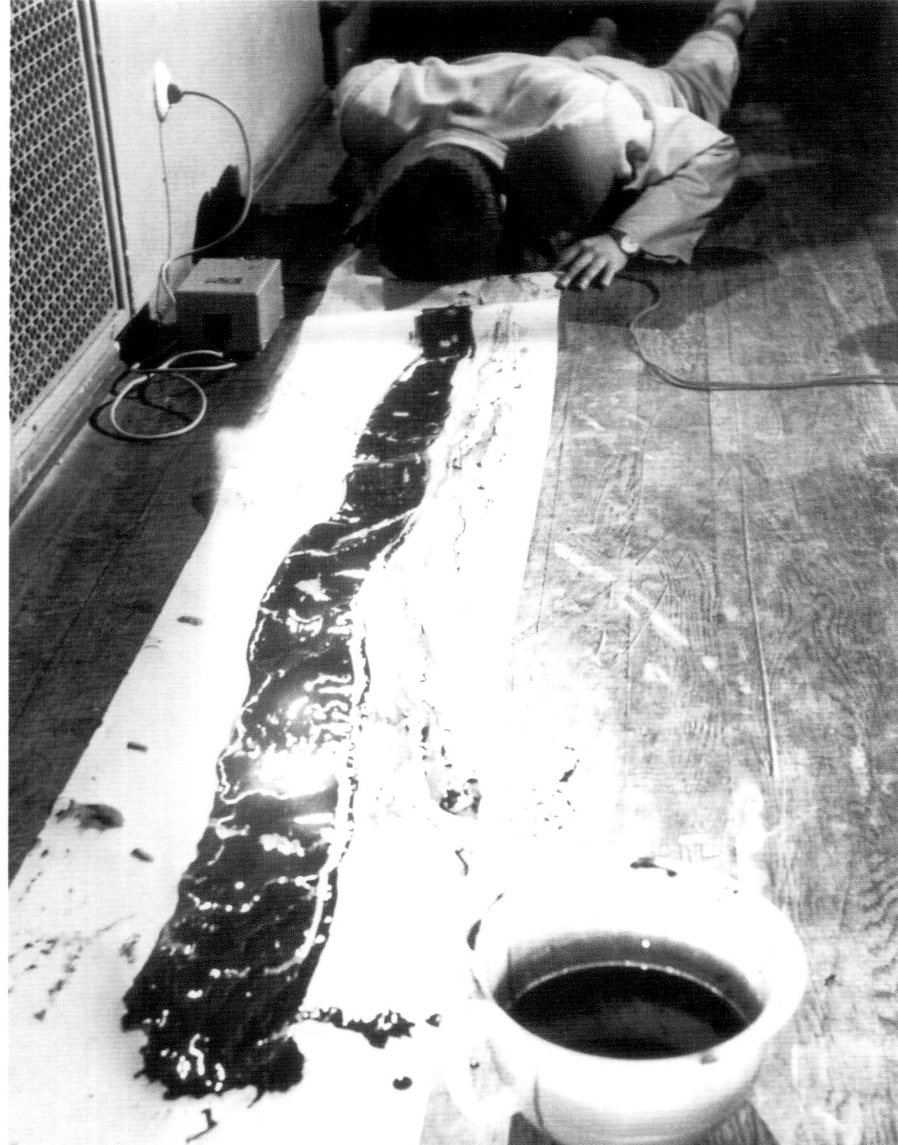

Nam June PAIK

Performing La Monte Young's *Composition 1960 No. 10* to Bob Morris (Zen for Head)

1962

'Fluxus International Festival of New Music', Städtisches Museum, Wiesbaden

Presented at the Städtisches Museum, Wiesbaden, during the 'Fluxus International Festival of New Music' (1962), this performance was Paik's interpretation of La Monte Young's *Composition 1960 No. 10*, dedicated to artist Robert Morris which read 'Draw a straight line and follow it'. Paik dipped his head, hands and tie in a bowl of ink and tomato juice and drew a line by dragging his head along a long narrow piece of paper laid out on the floor. Fluxus was concerned with carrying out deceptively simple actions in order to concentrate on the subtlety of a gesture, bringing about a fusion of art with life. In *Zen for Head*, Paik parodies the notion of meditative art-making by physically enacting a painting gesture using the body as tool rather than the repository of mental and spiritual processes. The head, the source of creative thinking, becomes the mark-maker, actively engaged in the messy processes of material and action.

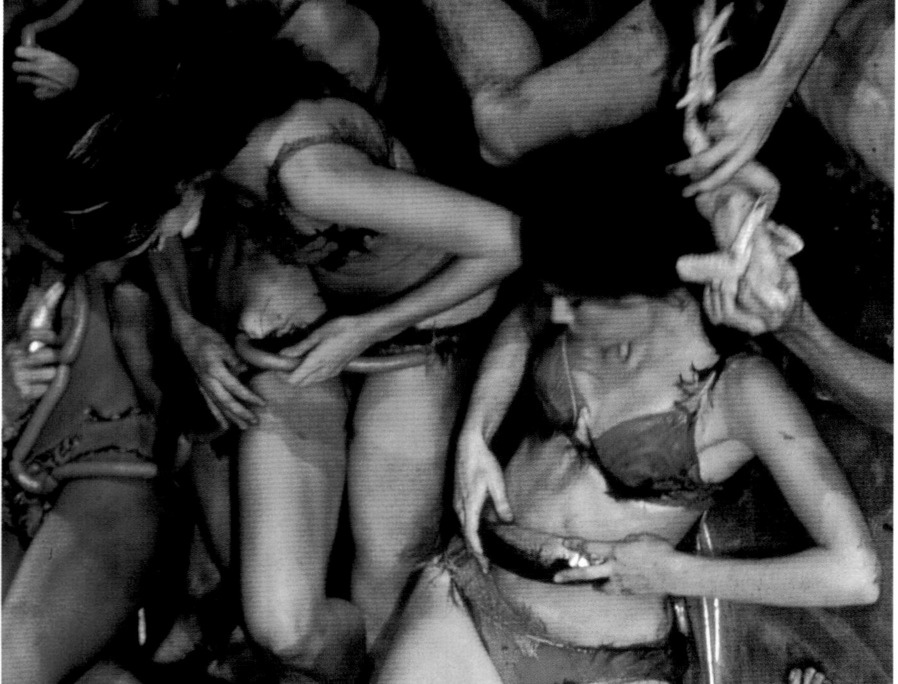

Carolee SCHNEEMANN

Meat Joy

1964

Paris

Meat Joy was an orgiastic happening in which male and female performers grappled with one another and a variety of fleshy, messy materials in close proximity to the audience. It was first performed in Paris in an event called 'Expression' organized by the artist and critic Jean-Jacques Lebel. Subsequently presented in London and New York. *Meat Joy* was made up of gestures and relationships loosely planned by Schneemann during rehearsals; the performers were expected to evolve these instructions in the live situation. Similarly, light and sound technicians were expected to improvise, within certain parameters, following the energy shifts of the performers and the audience. Schneemann had composed a soundtrack of Paris street sounds – traffic noise and the cries of food vendors – superimposed on Motown tunes.

'*Meat Joy* has the character of an erotic rite: excessive, indulgent, a celebration of flesh as material: raw fish, chickens, sausages, wet paint, transparent plastic, rope, brushes, paper scrap. Its propulsion is toward the ecstatic – shifting and turning between tenderness, wildness, precision, abandon: qualities which could at any moment be sensual, comic, joyous, repellent. Physical equivalences are enacted as a psychic and imagistic stream in which the layered elements mesh and gain intensity by the energy complement of the audience.'

– Carolee Schneemann, *More Than Meat Joy*, 1979

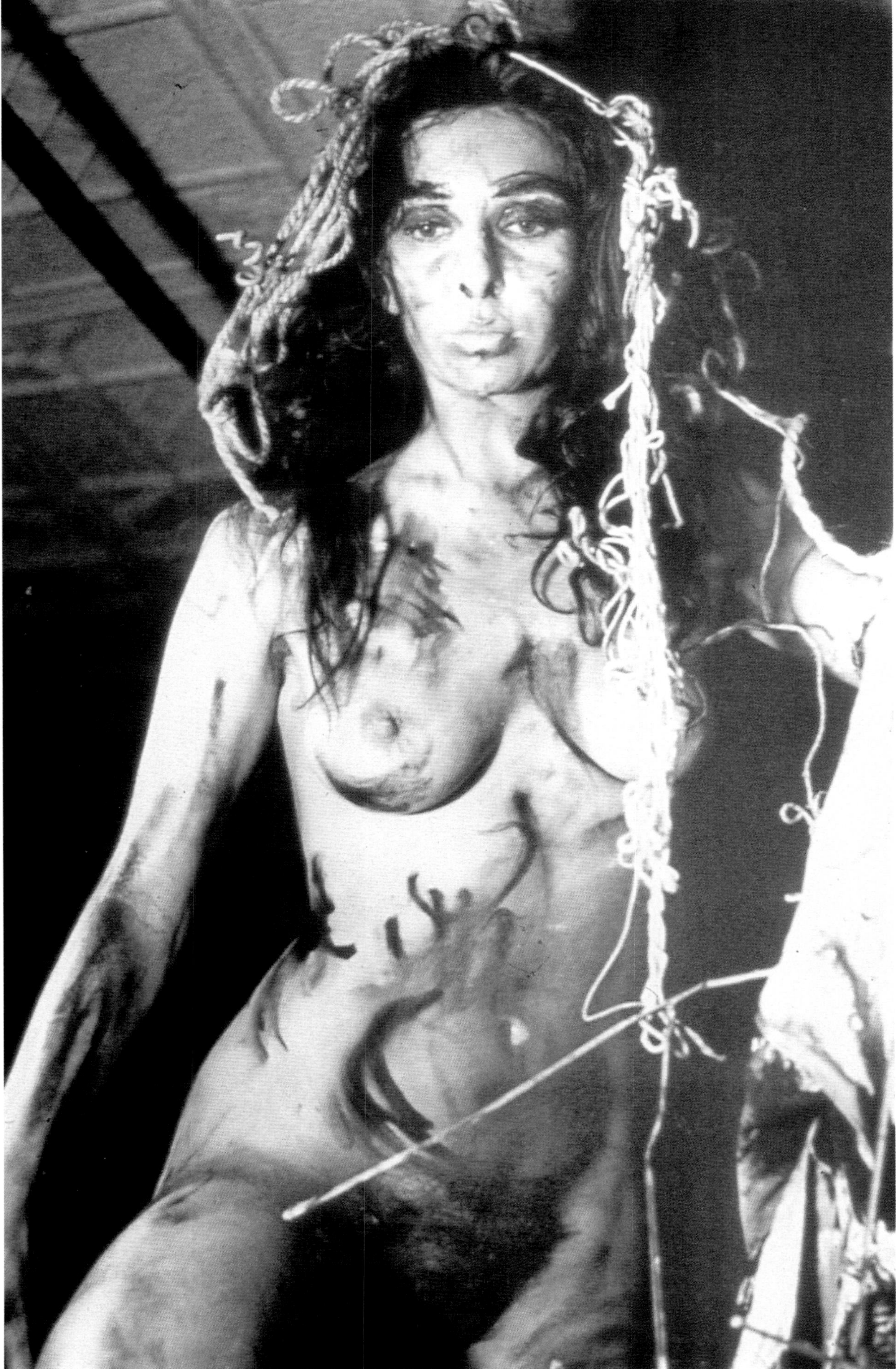

Carolee SCHNEEMANN
Eye Body: 36 Transformative Actions
1963
New York

Schneemann built an environment of large panels, broken mirrors, glass, lights and motorized objects such as umbrellas. This was closely related in scale to her own body. 'I wanted my actual body to be combined with the work as an integral material – a further dimension of the construction ... ' She decided to record a series of physical transformations of her body in her work with the Finnish artist Erró: 'Covered in paint, grease, chalk, ropes, plastic, I establish my body as visual territory. Not only am I an image-maker, but I explore the image values of flesh as material I choose to work with.' For a female artist to use her naked body in her work as an extension of the traditional practices of painting and sculpture/construction was an extremely radical act in 1963, both challenging and threatening to the 'psychic territorial power lines by which women were admitted to the Art Stud Club'.

– all quotes from Carolee Schneemann, *More Than Meat Joy*, 1979

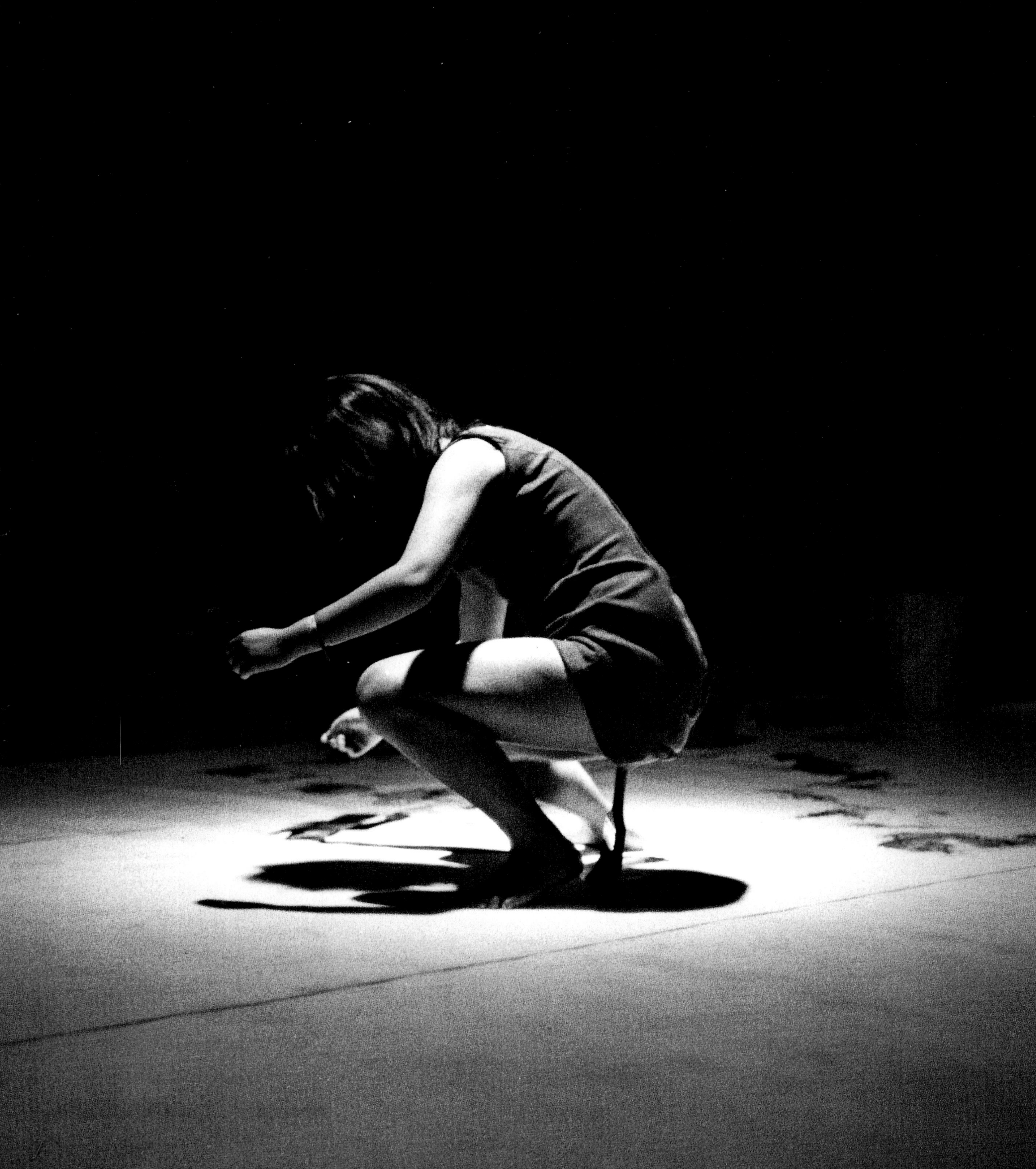

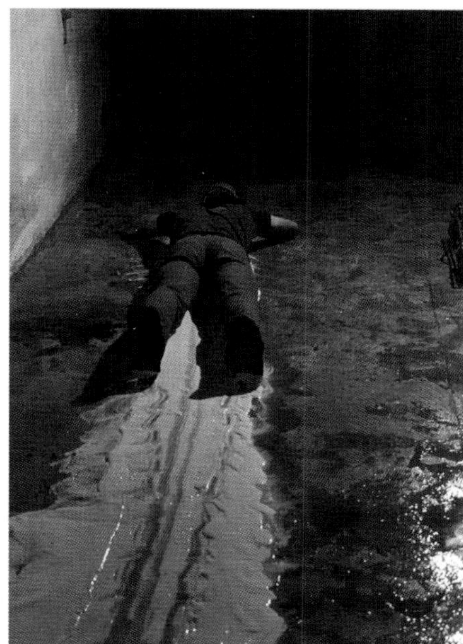

Paul MCCARTHY
Face Painting – Floor, White Line
1972
Los Angeles

In *Face Painting – Floor, White Line*, McCarthy lay on the floor of his studio and pushed a bucket of white paint with his head and torso to make a wide line, which snaked across the room. He had begun 'painting' with substances such as motor oil and ketchup while a student at the University of California in the early 1970s, using different parts of his body in performance-like acts that combined parody with undertones of masochism and self-abasement. Lampooning the macho image of Abstract Expressionists such as Jackson Pollock, McCarthy made private videos and public performances in which he painted using his penis as a brush (for example, *Penis Painting*, 1974). In *Face Painting – Wall, Black Line* he made a black line on the wall using his forehead, pouring paint from a bucket into the place where his face made contact with the wall. In other performances he violently 'whipped' a wall or window with paint, using a large blanket dipped into a mixture of paint and motor oil. These performances involved an element of physical endurance, which showed the artist's body straining to achieve 'heroic status'.

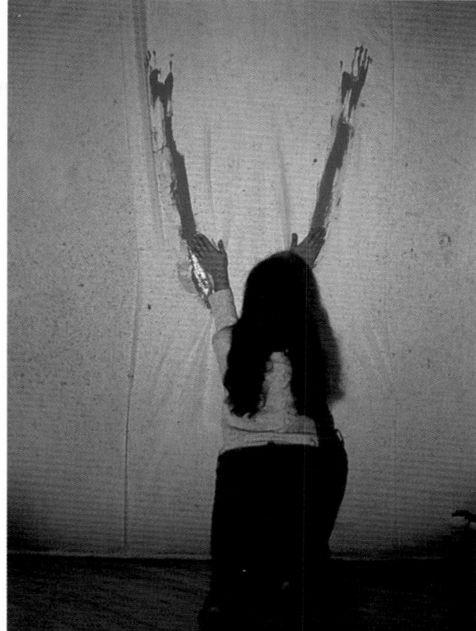

Ana MENDIETA
Body Tracks
1974
University of Iowa, Iowa City

Mendieta covered her hands and arms in blood and then, stretching them out high over her head, pulled down against the wall to a crouching position, leaving smears tracing the body's movement. With prints of her hands at the top, the marks ambiguously suggest both celebratory life and the slipping downwards of a bleeding and tortured body. In a series of 'blood writing' 'action paintings' she painted directly on the wall, pushing her half-clothed, blood-smeared body against it and dragging down to leave the mark of her breasts and a silhouette of her body. The work is reminiscent of Yves Klein's blue *Anthropometries*. In another series made at the same time called *Body Prints* Mendieta covered her naked bloodied body in a black shroud, which was then removed to reveal the red imprints of her body. Some of these performances with blood or red paint were private, filmed events. For Mendieta the use of blood to make body marks was a purifying and empowering affirmation of her status as a female artist: 'I think it's a very powerful magic thing. I don't see it as a negative force.'

– Ana Mendieta, 'Ana Mendieta Plants Her Garden', 1980

opposite
Shigeko KUBOTA
Vagina Painting
1965
'Perpetual Fluxfest', New York

At the 'Perpetual Fluxfest', New York City (1965), Kubota performed another kind of painting that transformed the heroic Pollockian ejaculatory painting into a specifically feminist 'stroke'. Having laid a large sheet of paper on the floor, the artist proceeded to paint red strokes on it with a brush attached to the crotch of her underwear. Subverting action painting in this deliberately 'female' process of gestural, menstrual creativity, Kubota's performance also activated the vagina as a source of inscription and language, inverting the Western cultural designation of female genitalia as a site of 'lack' (lack of the phallus) and the place where language breaks down. By using her own body – specifically her sex – as the tool for artistic production Kubota parodied Yves Klein's use of the female body as a painting tool.

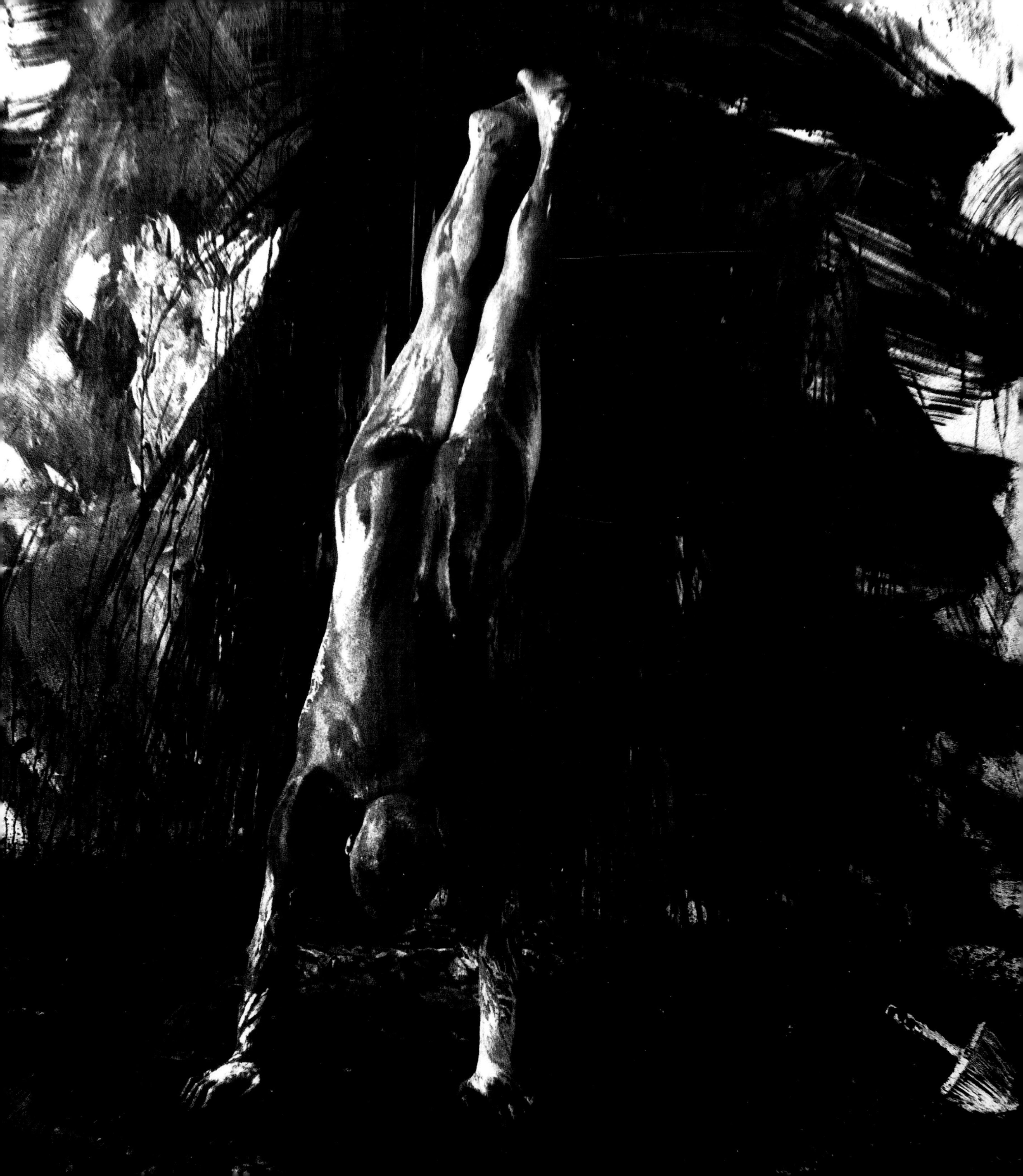

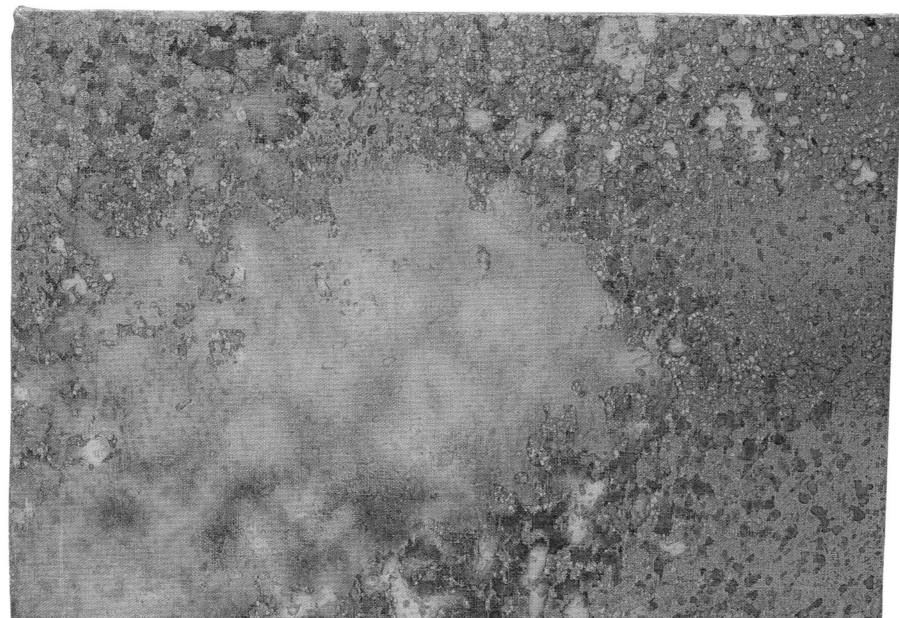

Andy WARHOL
Oxidation Painting
1978
Copper metallic pigment and mixed media on canvas
117 × 203 cm [46 × 80 in]

In the early 1960s Warhol had experimented with his own form of action painting, urinating directly on to a small blank canvas to make *Piss Painting* (destroyed). Nearly twenty years later this process was formalized in a series of monumental paintings in which the chemical processes of urine interacting with copper pigment created a richly coloured and textured surface. As a gesture, making paintings by urinating on canvases laid on the floor was a deeply subversive act which literally pissed on the notion of 'high art', and ridiculed the heroic masculine action painting tradition. In addition, the importance of the artist as personal author of his works was undermined by Warhol's invitation to friends to make their own contributions. The title of this series of works further depersonalizes a gesture which lays primitive claim to the territory of the canvas by focusing attention rather towards a contemplation of the processes and effects taking place on the canvas itself.

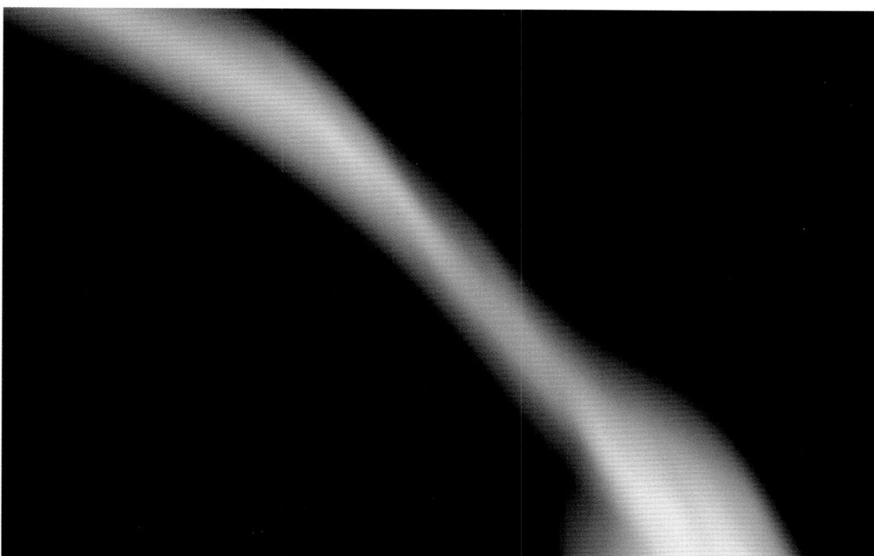

Andres SERRANO
Untitled XIII (Ejaculate in Trajectory)
1989
Cibachrome, silicone, Plexiglas
102 × 152 cm [40 × 60 in]

Serrano photographically captured his ejaculate in motion in order to produce an image of a gesture, the ultimate macho action he could perform. The marks of the artist's body are inscribed on the film in a fragmentary moment, the film becoming the canvas on which he 'paints'. Serrano sees his photographs as 'paintings' in which the sensual surface and materiality of the image challenge the borders between our perceptions of reality and representation. Close-up images of blood, semen and urine emphasize the rich beauty of their substance in order to subvert traditional taboos against these bodily fluids. Their deliberately transgressive titles (*The Unknown Christ* [1984], *Piss Christ* [1987], *Semen and Blood I* [1990]) expose and challenge the distortion of values that has banished the substances of our bodies to the realm of the abject.

opposite
Stuart BRISLEY
Moments of Decision and Indecision
1975
Galeria Teatra Studio, Warsaw

First presented at Galeria Teatra Studio, Warsaw, Brisley's performance took place in one large room and lasted six days. Each day the artist would drench himself in white and black paint to the point at which he could hardly move or see, creating a state of sensory deprivation made more intense by his futile attempts to climb the walls of the room. This generated feelings of frustration and helplessness in the viewers. In the context of its presentation behind the Iron Curtain, *Moments of Decision/Indecision* could be seen as a depiction of the claustrophobia and frustration of a closed political system. It elucidates the individual's need to manoeuvre a position between authority and freedom. The work was performed again at the Tate Gallery in London in 1998.

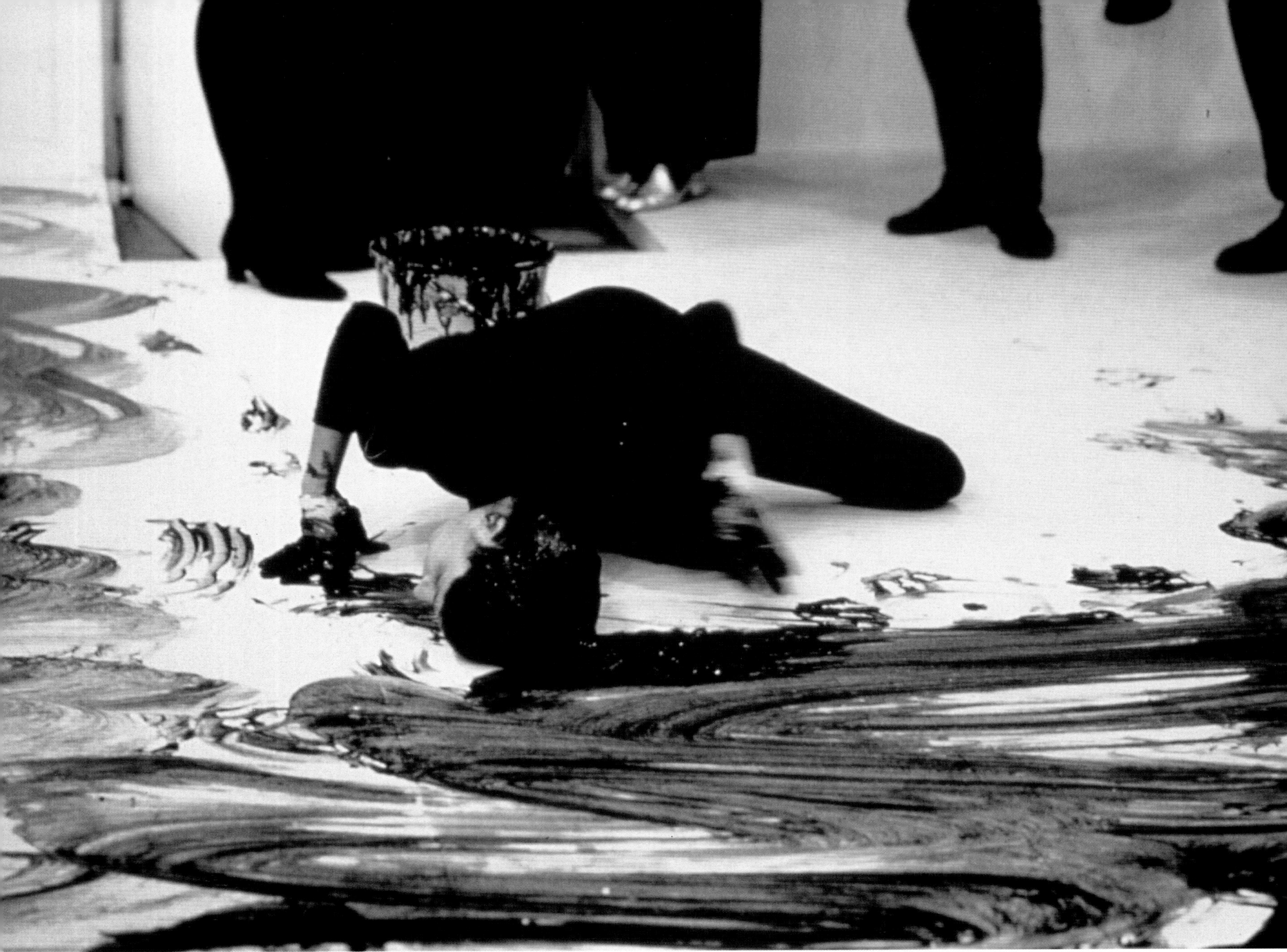

Janine ANTONI
Loving Care
1992
Anthony D'Offay Gallery, London

In this work Antoni dipped her hair into a plastic bucket of 'natural black' hair dye and, using it as a brush, she painted the entire floor of the Anthony d'Offay Gallery, London. The viewers who stood in the square, white-walled room were gradually pushed out of the space by the artist's performance as she simultaneously performed for, and disrupted, the audience's pleasure in looking. As a woman on her hands and knees, sweeping the floor with her hair, she enacted the domestic role of a cleaner. The title, *Loving Care*, which was taken from the commercial brand of hair-dye she used, reinforces the idea of this traditionally female activity of physical labour. As a female artist making marks with her body, Antoni parodies the male-dominated legacy of Abstract Expressionism. 'I feel attached to my artistic heritage and I want to destroy it: it defines me as an artist and it excludes me as woman, all at the same time.'
– Janine Antoni, 'Interview with Laura Cottingham', 1993

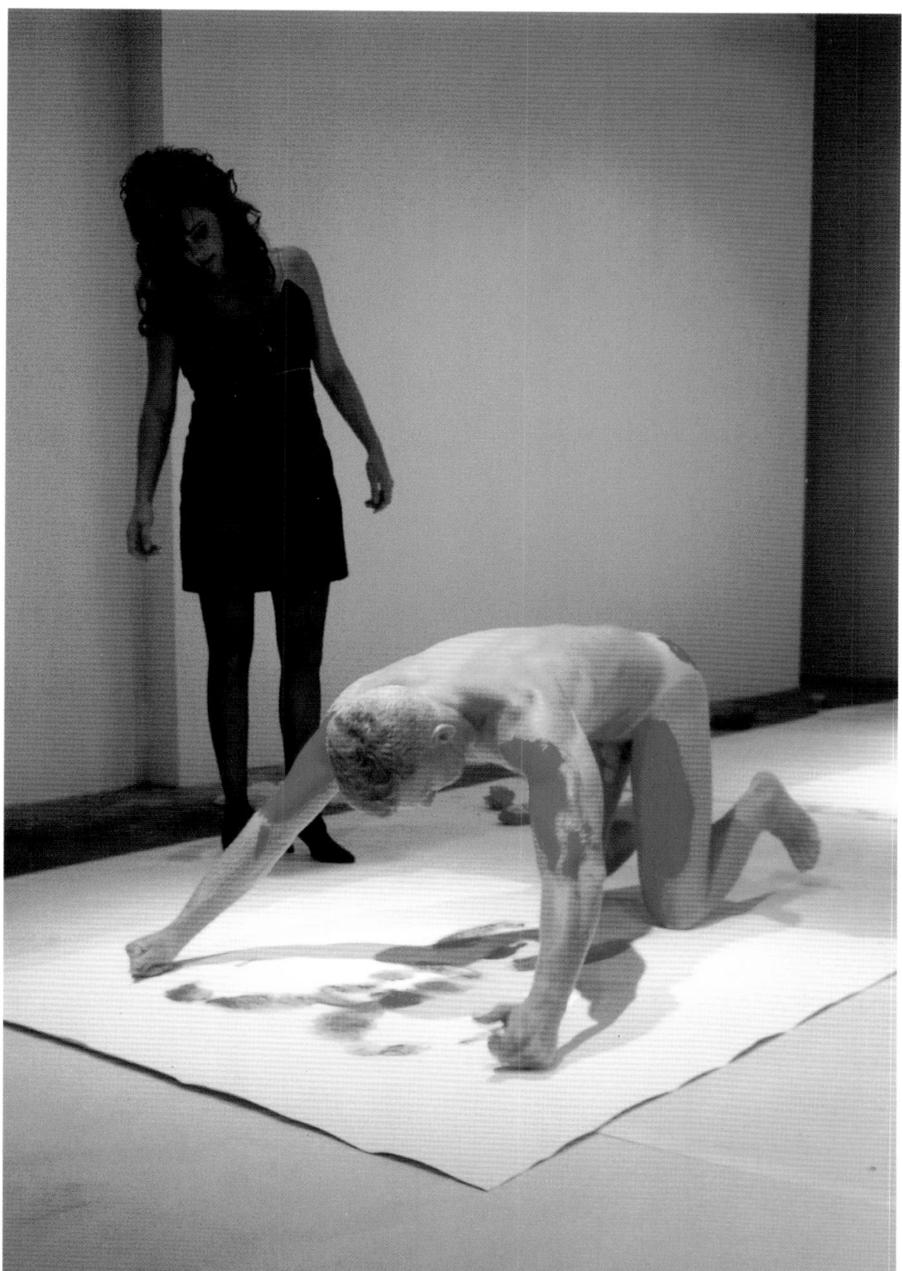

Rachel LACHOWICZ
Red not Blue
1992
Shoshana Wayne Gallery, Santa Monica, California

Lachowicz presented this feminist critique of Yves Klein's *Anthropometries* in a performance at Shoshana Wayne Gallery, Santa Monica. The artist replaced Klein's naked women with muscular men and his signature blue paint with red lipstick. She rubbed this over the models' naked bodies and then dragged them across large sheets of paper placed on the floor. Like Klein, Lachowicz dressed in evening wear and directed the models closely. She also tied a lipstick rod to the penis of one of her models and held it in front of him as they both descended on a scissor lift, making a vertical line down a roll of paper on the wall. The bright red marks resulting from the use of the male body as a tool for painting were both seductively glossy and disturbingly raw, evoking the feminine paradox of beauty aided by art. As curator Bonnie Clearwater has written, 'In many of her recent works, Lachowicz recasts "male" art ... in the gender-specific medium of lipstick. Society conditions women to believe that cosmetics will improve their appearance and make them more desirable. Yet, as Lachowicz has observed, she is taken more seriously when she leaves her face unadorned.'
– Bonnie Clearwater, *The Art of Seduction*, 1994

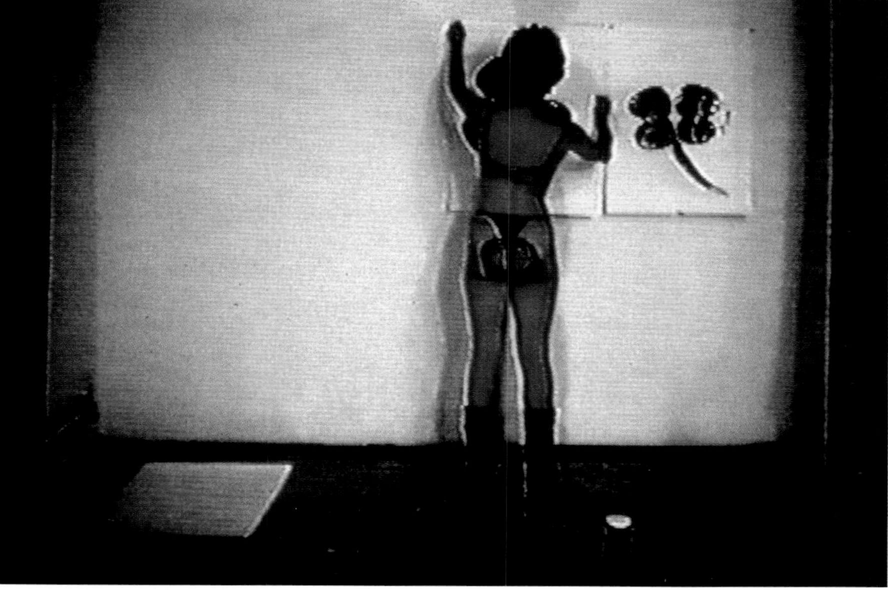

Cheryl DONEGAN
Kiss My Royal Irish Ass (K.M.R.I.A.)
1993
Video still
7 mins., colour, sound

Donegan performed a pastiche of Klein's *Anthropometries* at the Andrea Rosen Gallery, New York. Wearing a green bra and g-string and black engineer boots, she squatted in a puddle of green paint. She then pressed her paint-covered buttocks to sheets of paper on the floor to form shamrock patterns (a four-leaf clover – a lucky charm and the national symbol of Ireland). At the end of the performance she sat on a chair and drank a pint of Guinness – another symbol of Ireland. Masquerading simultaneously as both the macho working man and the erotic feminine woman, Donegan presented her body as both the subject and object of her art-making process in a humorous parody of gender posturing and the 'genderizing' of the creative act. As curator and critic Nancy Spector has said of Donegan's works, '[H]er videotapes, as she has claimed "weave a ... crooked path" through the subjects of sex, gender and creativity; "fanning out, looping back and crossing over" these themes until they coalesce into one or two perfectly absurd moments, when a little bit of truth is revealed, just for an instant.'
– Nancy Spector, 'Rock my Video', 1995

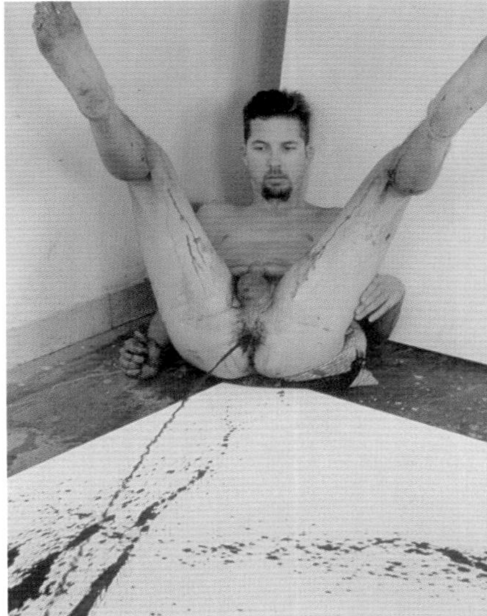

Keith <u>BOADWEE</u>

Untitled (Purple Squirt)

1995

Duraflex print

152 × 122 cm [60 × 48 in]

Boadwee produced two video loops documenting his painting processes in which, either lying on the floor or crouching over the canvas, he ejected streams of paint from his anus to create Pollockian painterly marks. As art historian Amelia Jones has commented, 'Reiterating the Pollockian trope of masculinized action painting, but through a body explicity performed as abject, anal and homosexual, Boadwee exposes the homoerotic as the hidden threat. The anus – *not the penis/phallus* – becomes the site through which male creativity takes place; and yet, far from being phallic and so "transcendent", this site itself is *an orifice* (and one connected in mainstream culture with the most debased aspects of human functioning, as well as with homosexual erotics).'

– Amelia Jones, *Body Art: Performing the Subject*, 1998

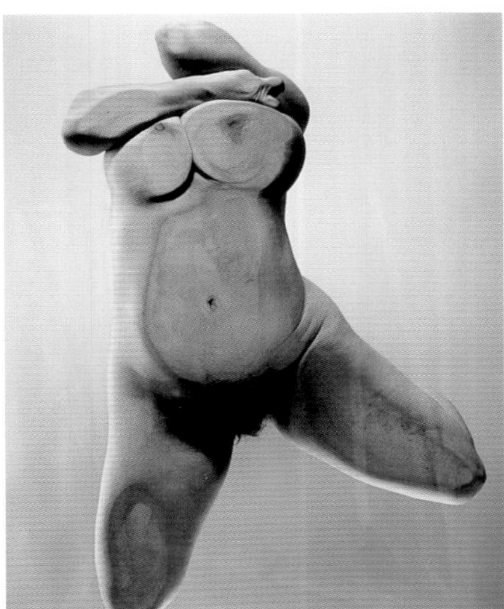

Jenny <u>SAVILLE</u> and Glen <u>LUCHFORD</u>

Closed Contact No. 10

1995-97

C-type print

240 × 180 cm [94.5 × 71 in]

Saville began making her large-scale paintings of female nudes from photographs of parts of her own body as an exploration of what it is to be both model and artist at the same time. In a collaboration that fused the history of the female nude in the tradition of painting with the female body as presented by contemporary fashion media, Saville lay on top of a large sheet of perspex and was photographed from below by fashion photographer Glen Luchford. The resulting images present a female nude distorted by pressing heavily against the perspex but made beautiful through the use of light and the opulent slickness of photography. Seductive and disturbing, Saville's images present the female nude pushing out of the 'canvas' towards the viewer, rather than remaining safely at a distance. The huge scale of the photographs, together with the cropping of her body, which almost completely fills the frame, contribute to the ovewhelming sense of flesh.

Tracey <u>EMIN</u>

Exorcism of the Last Painting I Ever Made

1996

Galleri Andreas Brändström, Stockholm

Emin spent two weeks incarcerated in a room built within the Galleri Andreas Brändström, Stockholm, in an attempt to overcome her six-year block about painting. The audience could watch the naked artist at work through sixteen fish-eye lenses set into the wall. Her first painting, in response to a friend's advice to paint something she would like to own, was a version of Evard Munch's *The Scream*. This was followed by more paintings in homage to other artists, for example a reclining female nude after Egon Schiele, which is also a self-portrait. By presenting herself as both the artist and the model for her paintings Emin confused the role of artist and model, transforming the subjective object – the model – into an active subject – the artist.

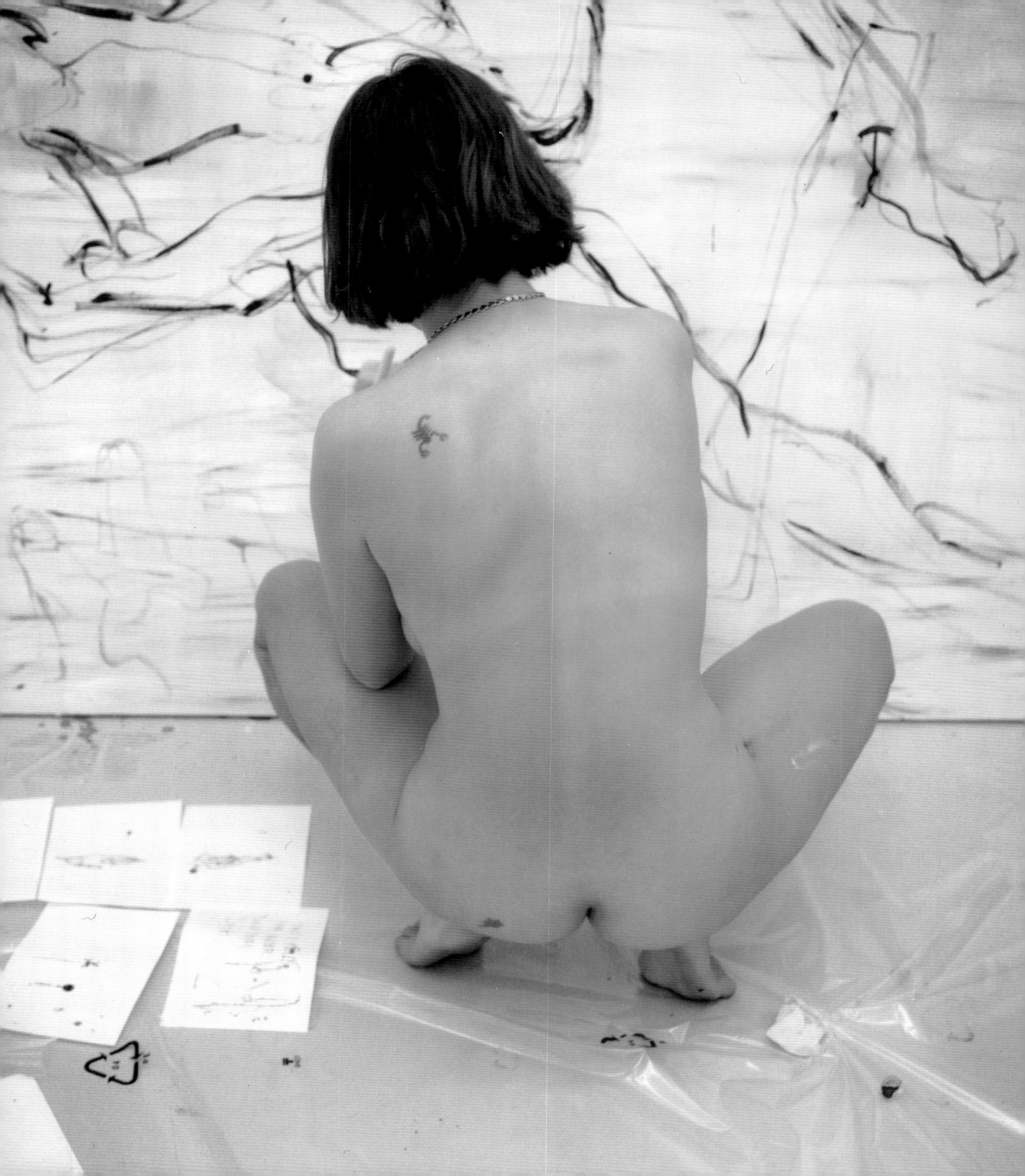

GESTURING BODIES

Painting as action led to an exploration of the artist's gesture as constituting the artwork itself. Artists in the 1960s began to use their bodies as art in performances, events and 'actions'. The ordinary activities of everyday life were also elevated to the status of art. Since the body was presented as the material out of which the artwork was made, the art itself lasted only for the duration of the gesture, and the photograph was used to document this transitory artwork. The artist's dual role as both subject and object developed as a new theme, particularly in Europe and the United States. Through events and Happenings, artists started to bridge the gulf between themselves and the viewer – the creation and reception of art – as the latter became an indispensable participant in the enactment of art. The artists' gestures in public were in the 1960s often transformed into a particular form of activism, which introduced a political dimension to the work.

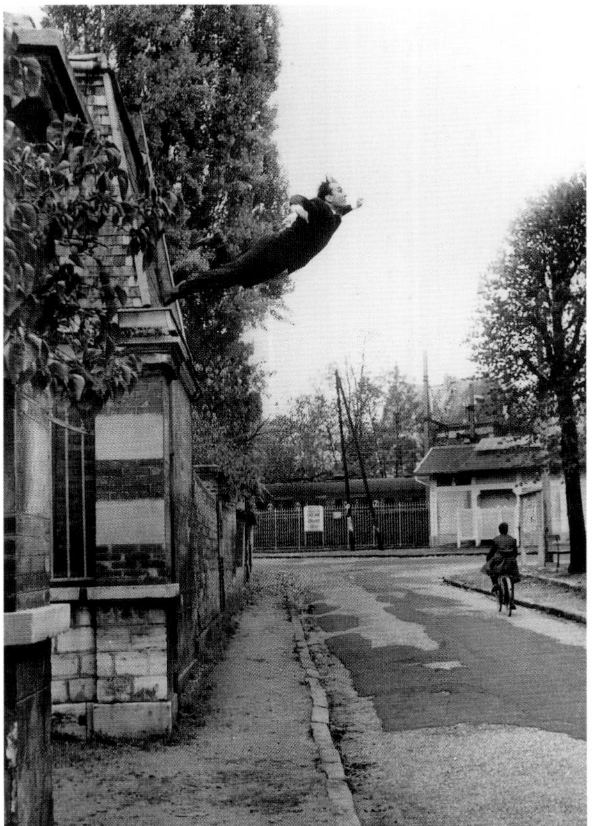

Yves KLEIN
Leap into the Void
1960
Black and white photograph
Dimensions variable

This image appeared in Klein's one-day newspaper *Dimanche* (1960), which he circulated on the day he presented his *Theatre of the Void*. It was captioned with the words, 'A man in space! The painter of space leaps into the void!' Other editions of the photograph were titled with the inscription 'Obsession with levitation'. Klein's preoccupation with levitation at this time coincided with a world-wide interest in space travel as the first satellites completed successful journeys into space. Through his practice of judo, Klein truly believed that levitation was possible but, after injuring himself in a leap from the second storey of a friend's house in January and then again later in the year in a second attempt, he turned his attention away from public performance to the production of a document that would be 'proof' of his ascension into space. This time a tarpaulin was held underneath him to catch him as he fell. Harry Shunk, the photographer responsible for documenting many of Klein's performances, expertly merged separate photographs taken of the jump and of the street into a convincing image. *Leap into the Void* seemingly presents the artist's body poised between life and death.

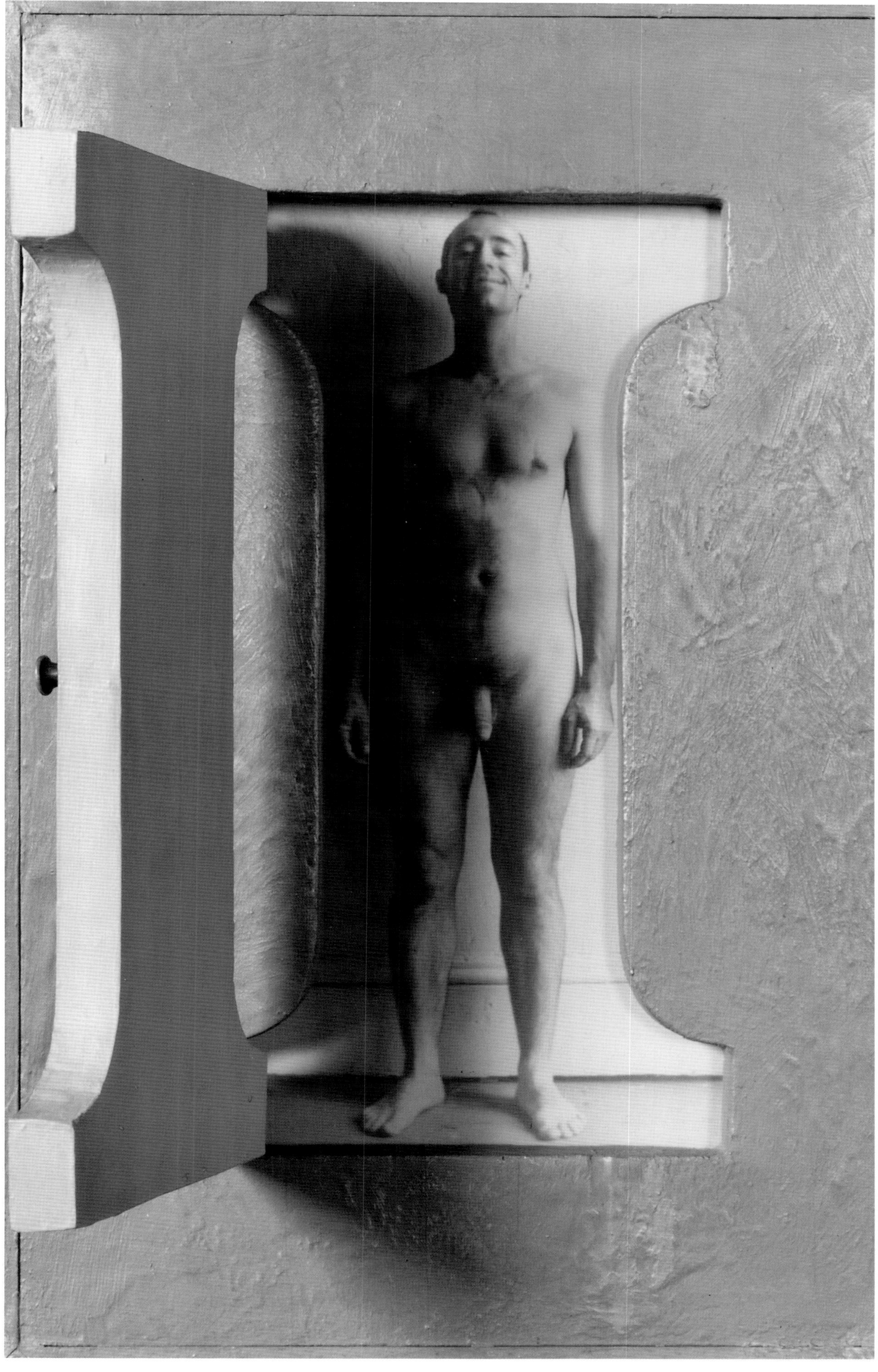

Robert MORRIS
I-Box
1962
Painted plywood cabinet, sculptmetal, photograph
48 × 33 × 4 cm [19 × 13 × 1.5 in]

Morris' work literalized the 'I' of the maker, and also presents the subjective 'I' of art-making as an object-body to be looked at. A photograph of Morris' naked body is discovered behind the I-shaped door of his box. By re-presenting his artistic self through a mechanical process – photography – and disclosing his naked masculine body rather than revealing the products of his creative mind, Morris reverses the tradition of Abstract Expressionist painting in which the canvas is the site of inscription of the artistic 'I' revealed through mark-making. The *I-Box* is also a linguistic play on 'I/eye', which takes the viewer full circle from the subject to the object and back to the subject. Morris smiles back at the viewer, his penis partially erect, implying that at least part of the pleasure in looking is his own. Through this split voyeurism, Morris blurs the discourses of subjectivity and sexual power, suggesting a new position and significance for the artist's masculine body.

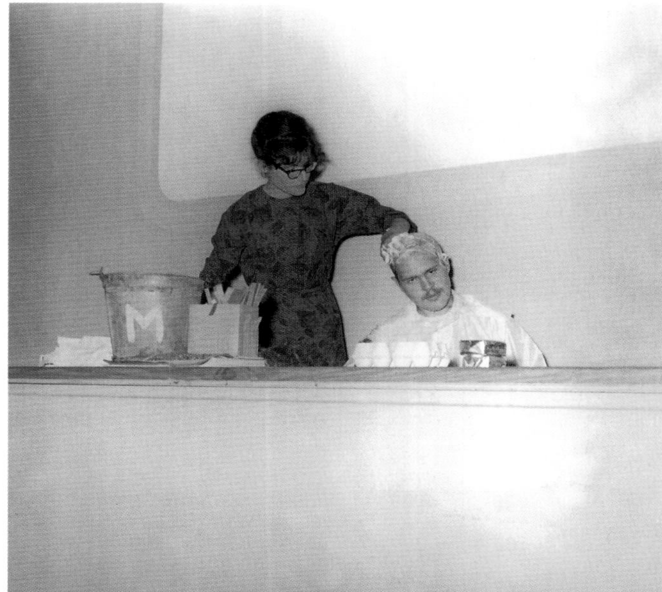

Dick HIGGINS and Alison KNOWLES

Danger Music No. 2

1962

'Fluxus International Festival of New Music', Städisches Museum, Wiesbaden

Danger Music No. 2 was presented at the 'Fluxus International Festival of New Music' (1962). Knowles cut off Higgins' hair in front of an audience. The piece was notated by Higgins as 'Hat. Rags. Paper. Heave. Shave.', emphasizing the idea that the Fluxus artwork never appears as a finished work, but rather as a series of ever-changing ideas. Simple everyday gestures or activities were brought into the environment, where they could be scrutinized in all their simplicity and potential complexity. In the course of this work, Higgins also performed a series of *Danger Music* pieces, actions combined with sound, that brought the audible and the visible together to produce 'action music'.

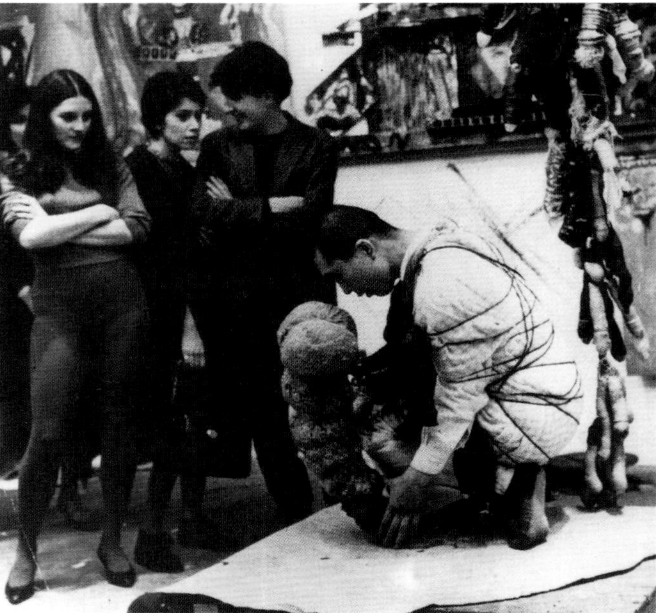

Tetsumi KUDO

Philosophy of Impotence

1962

'To Ward Off the Spirit of Catastrophe', Galerie Raymond Cordier, Paris

For the opening of Jean-Jacques Lebel's event 'To Ward Off the Spirit of Catastrophe' at the Galerie Raymond Cordier, Paris (1962), Kudo recreated an installation entitled *Philosophy of Impotence* , which he had created the year before in Japan. In an environment filled with suspended penis-like rolls, Kudo performed the role of a sex priest, delivering a silent sermon with an immense papier-mâché phallus, then screaming in Japanese, caressing the public with the phallus, and experiencing a 'mystic orgasm' before collapsing. Sculptural representations of fragmented parts of human bodies were combined with plants and insects in an attempt to find a creative solution to humanity's increasing alienation from the natural world through technological advances as epitomized by the destruction of Hiroshima. ' ... the portrait of decomposed man in polluted nature and the flood of technology. The decomposition of man does not mean his death. In fact we are decomposed, metamorphosed and brought to life.'

– Tetsumi Kudo quoted by Keiji Nakamura, *Contestation/Creation*, 1994

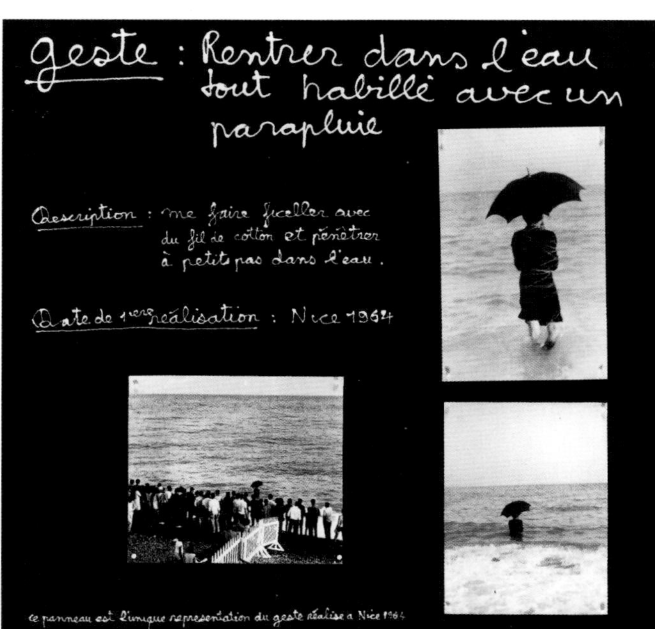

left and opposite

Ben VAUTIER

Geste: Rentrer dans l'eau (Gesture: To enter the water)

1964/72

Nice

Watched by a large crowd of people Vautier walked slowly into the sea, fully clothed and tightly bound with string, carrying an umbrella and an alarm clock. He later mounted the photographic documentation on a board with a hand-written description of the event, including the date, the place and the authentication: 'This board is the unique representation of the gesture carried out in Nice 1964'. In this way he relocated his work of art from the original gesture to its representation. 'The gesture is a work of art which is more limited by time than a natural work of art. The photograph which records it is only its reflection.'

– Ben Vautier, *Ben: The Truth of A to Z*, 1987

Vautier staged his 'Free Expression' gestures in public in order to authenticate as art even the most mundane and mysterious activities – undoing a knot, lifting his hand in the air, picking someone up, lying down in the street – when performed by an artist.

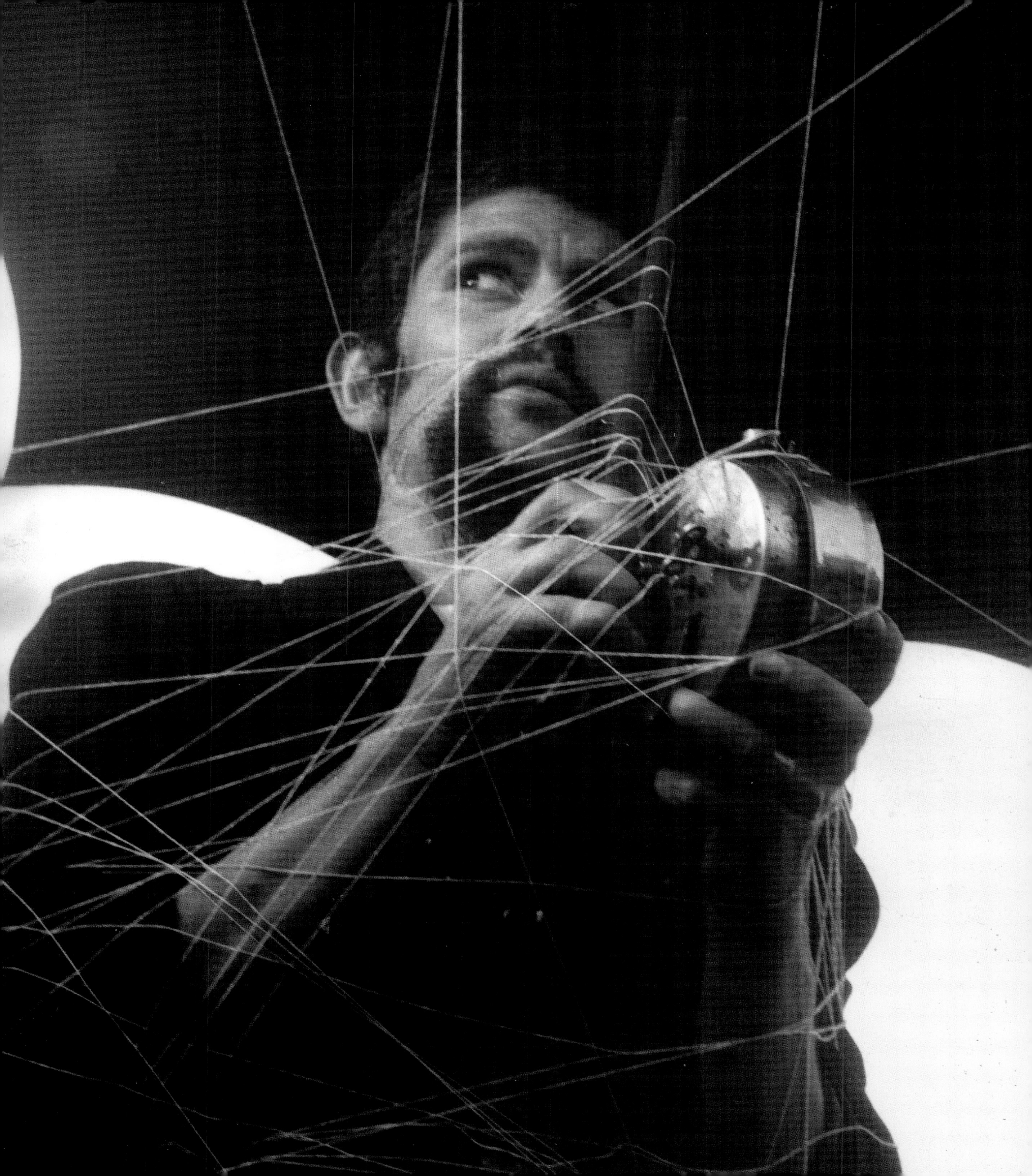

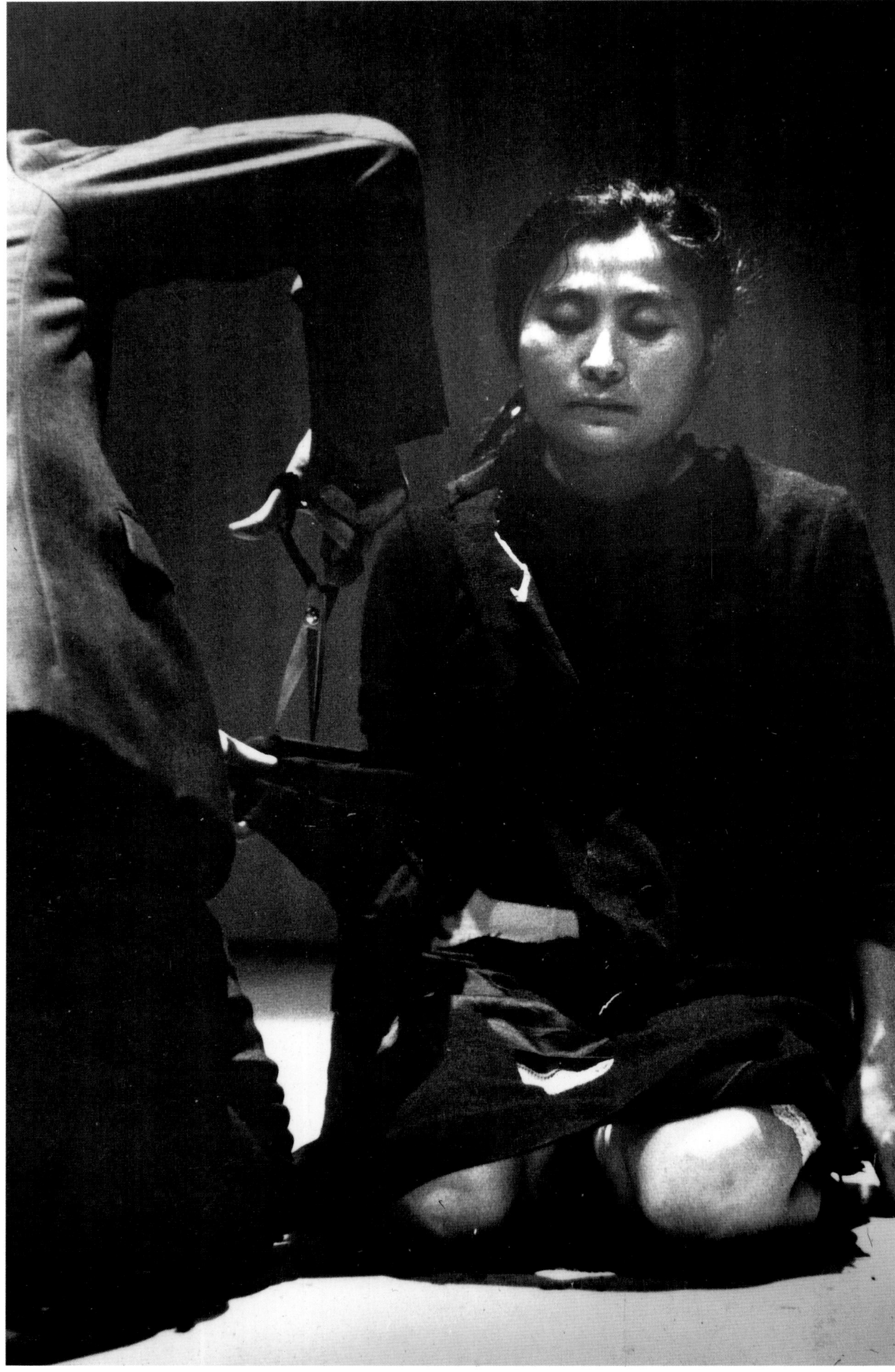

Yoko ONO
Cut Piece
1964
Yamaichi Concert Hall, Kyoto

Ono sat on the stage and invited the audience to come up and cut away her clothing, covering her breasts with her hands as her garments fell away. Deconstructing the supposedly neutral subject/object relationship between the viewer and the art object, Ono presented a situation in which the viewer implicated him/herself in the potentially aggressive act of unveiling the passive body. This was further loaded with gender issues by the fact that that body was female. Emphasizing the reciprocity in the way that viewers and subjects become objects for each other, *Cut Piece* also demonstrates the ways in which viewing without responsibility may cut into and destroy the object of perception. 'People went on cutting the parts they do not like of me. Finally there was only the stone remained of me that was in me but they were still not satisfied and wanted to know what it's like in the stone.'
– Yoko Ono, Artist's statement, 1971

Cut Piece was also performed at the 'Destruction In Art' Symposium in London in 1966.

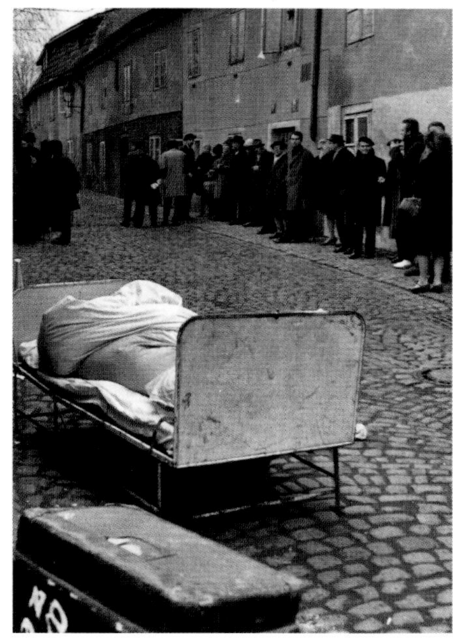

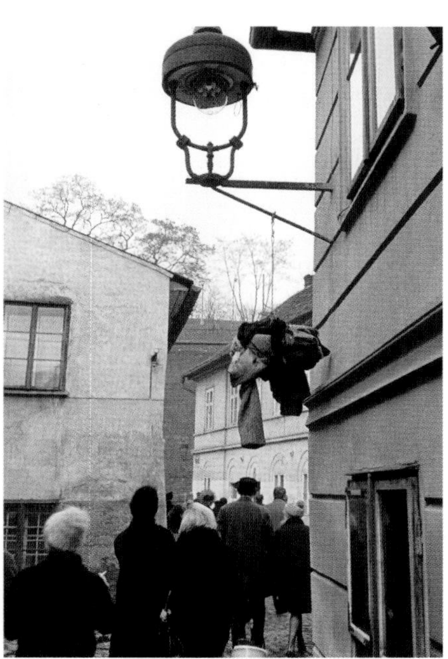

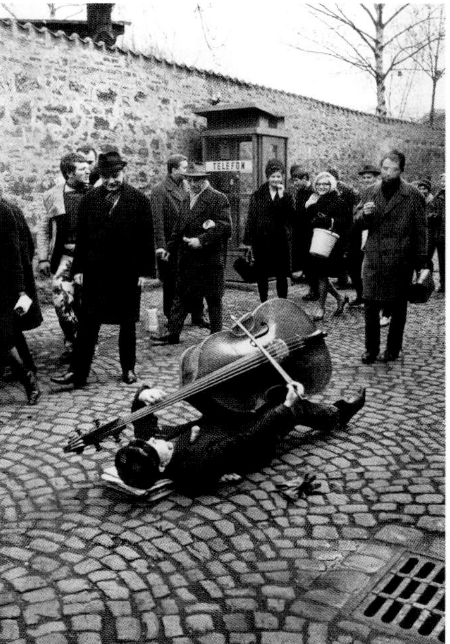

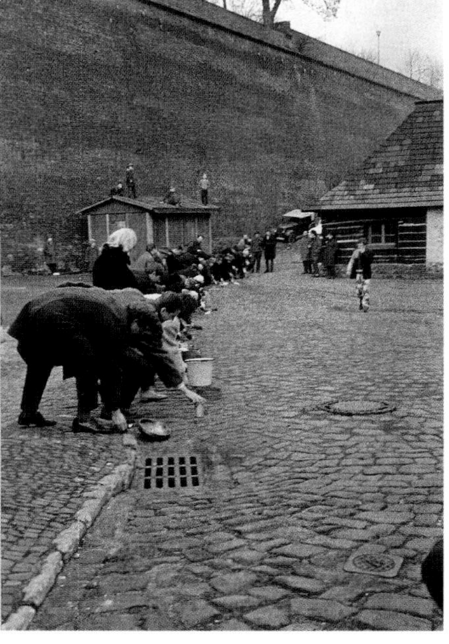

Milan KNÍŽÁK

Demonstration for all the Senses

1964

Prague

Knížák created his 'ceremonies' and 'demonstrations' on the streets of Prague in collaboration with members of the local AKTUAL Community of artists. In this 'demonstration' participants were each given an object (crockery, cutlery, a piece of clothing, etc.) to carry with them as they were taken on a surreal and disorientating walk around the city. 'They ... are led into a small room, where they are locked in and left in inactivity ... A great deal of perfume has been spilled on the floor of the room. They are now let out ... A musician lies on the ground and plays a violin. They reach a small place and are put in the middle of a circle. Around them the organizers of the demonstration run, shouting, roaring, cutting across, driving round on motorcycles and in cars. A chair comes down from above ... A man stands at a wall, glazing a window. As soon as he is finished, he breaks it ... The participants ... are presented with a book, from which each one tears a page. Then they return their objects and leave ... '

– Milan Knížák, Artist's statement, 1978

For Knížák this was only the first part of the 'demonstration' in which he was attempting to fuse art with life. For the following fortnight – the second period of the 'demonstration' – he expected the participants to experience their ordinary lives differently as a result of the disorientation of their senses through the experience of his art.

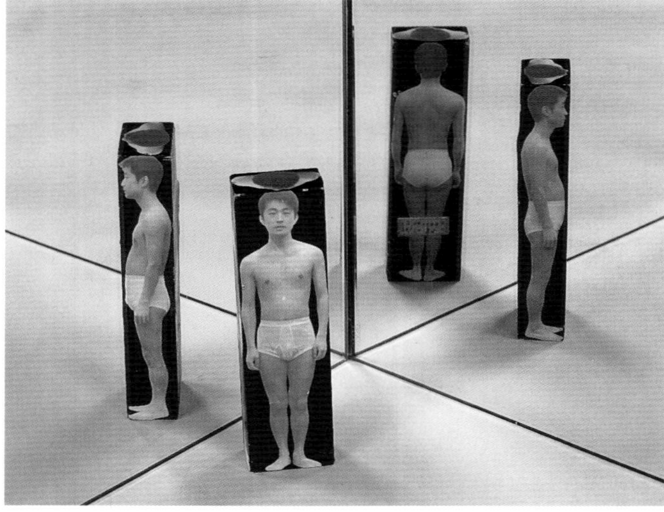

HI RED CENTER
Maquette of the Hi Red Center Shelter (Hotel Event)
1964
Photographs, wood
20.5 × 5.5 × 3.5 cm [8 × 2 × 1.5 in]

In *Hotel Event* Hi Red Center rented a room at the Imperial Hotel in Tokyo where they made life-sized blueprints of visitors, which were used to make custom-built bomb shelters. Visitors were expected to submit to a wide range of inspections in order to obtain the correct measurements including: 'head volume, mouth capacity, difference between shoe and foot length, finger strength, saliva production, length of extended tongue, inflated cheek width, distance from thumb at the end of outstretched arms, length of penis (flaccid), length of penis (erect), depth of vagina, circumference of body at key points (head, neck, shoulders, chest, waist, hips, knees, ankles, elbows, wrists), amount of air filling a balloon as inhaled and expelled in one breath, amount of liquid swallowed in one draught, etc.'
– Hi Red Center, *A Fluxus Performance Workbook*, 1990

Hi Red Center performed a variety of Happenings in the early 1960s that incorporated actions performed in urban areas into everyday life. The idea was to disrupt the boundaries between life and art. Their last activity as a group involved six of them obsessively cleaning a street corner during the Tokyo Summer Olympic Games (1964).

opposite
Joseph BEUYS
How to Explain Pictures to a Dead Hare
1965
Galerie Schmela, Dusseldorf

For his first commercial exhibition, presented at Galerie Schmela, Dusseldorf (1965), Beuys locked himself inside the gallery space. His performance was visible to the public only through the doorway and street window. He covered his head with honey and gold leaf and cradled a dead hare in his arms, silently mouthing words to it. He carried the hare over to the paintings hung on the gallery walls and talked about them, placing the hare's paws on the pictures as he explained their origins and concepts. 'I explained to him because I do not really like explaining them to people ... A hare comprehends more than many human beings with their stubborn rationalism ... I told him that he needed only to scan the picture to understand what is really important about it.'
– Joseph Beuys quoted by Ursula Meyer, 'How to Explain Pictures to a Dead Hare', 1970

Beuys experimented with the artist's role as entertainer/teacher, shaman/professor in many lectures during this period. He heavily influenced artists of the next generation with a sense of responsibility for defining the culture in which they lived.

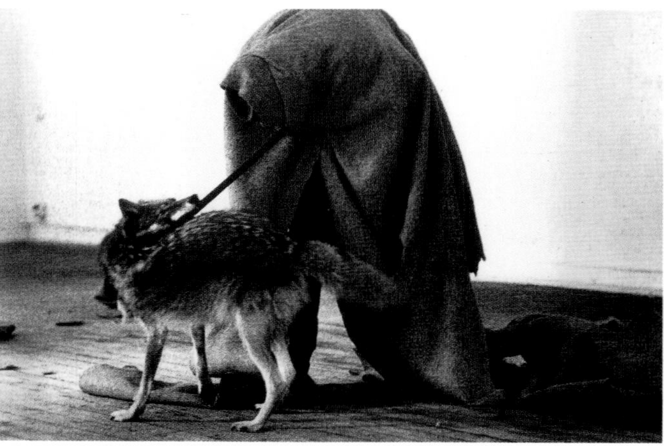

Joseph BEUYS
I Like America and America Likes Me
1974
René Block Gallery, New York

For the opening of the new René Block Gallery, New York (1974), Beuys lived in the space together with a wild coyote named Little Joe for five days. Wrapped in felt on his arrival at JFK Airport and driven to the gallery by ambulance, Beuys entered the hay-strewn space holding a shepherd's staff. Long periods of silence, sleep and mutual watching were occasionally broken when Beuys offered objects to the coyote or executed a sequence of movements and sounds. Beuys played the role of mediator between America's Wild West, as symbolized by the coyote, and its contained and containing capitalism, symbolized by the *Wall Street Journal* and the New York gallery space. At the end of the five-day period he returned to the airport as he had come.

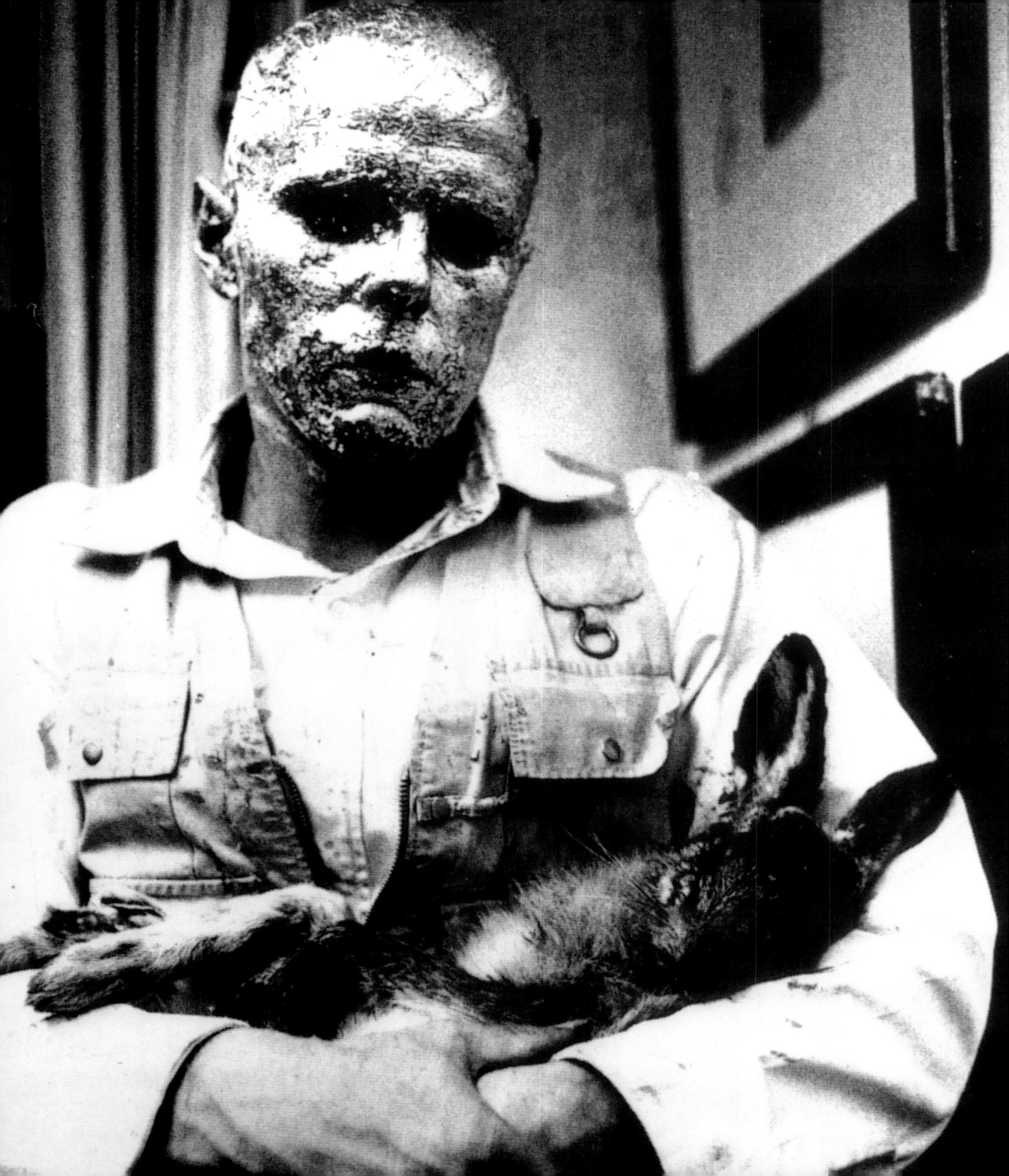

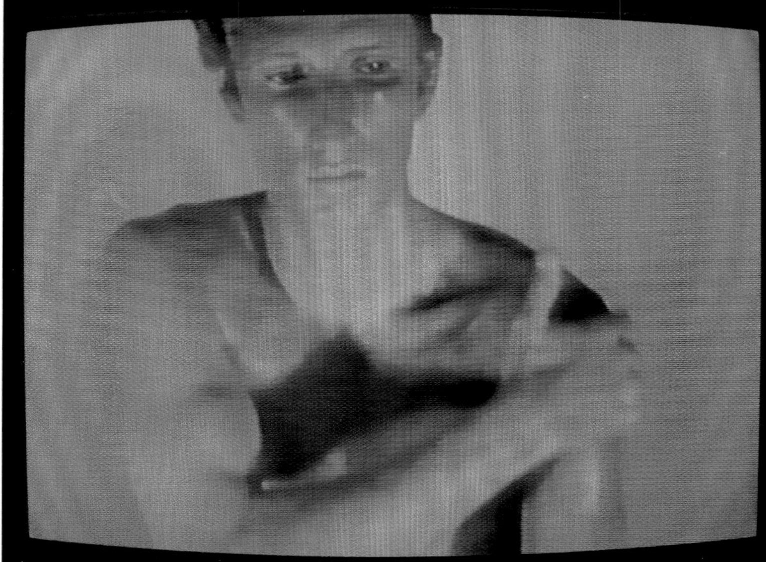

left

Bruce NAUMAN

Art Make-Up Films No. 1; Green

1967-68

Film still

4 parts, 16mm., approx 10 mins. each, colour, silent

Collection, Stedelijk Museum, Amsterdam

In his *Art Make-Up* films Nauman metaphorically effaced himself as part of his investigation of 'withdrawal as an art form'. Applying make-up of different colours to his face and upper body, he self-consciously masked and even erased his identity. He first covered himself with white, then added red, which made pink, before green was layered on to make grey, which was finally covered with black. Bringing a personal tactile activity into the artwork, Nauman used his own body as the surface on which pigment is spread, re-fashioning himself at each mutation into a new character, as if to play another role. Uniting a sense of theatre through the lighting and colours, with a sense of classical sculpture through the simplicity of the image and its focus on the artist's bare torso, Nauman presents himself as an actor who can play several parts. The gleam of the oily make-up on his skin, combined with the rich colour and the intimacy of the cropped frame, enhance the visceral effect of his activity.

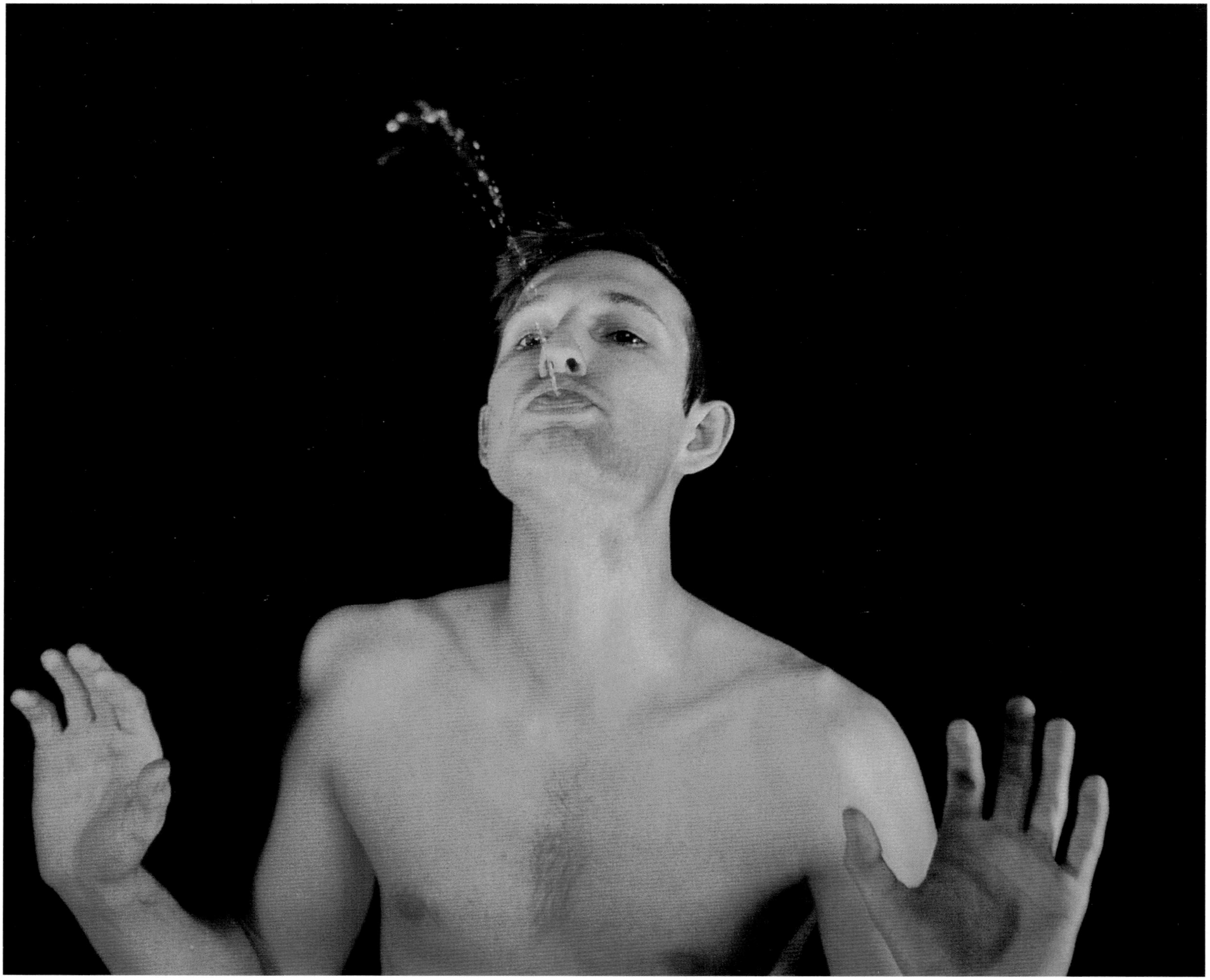

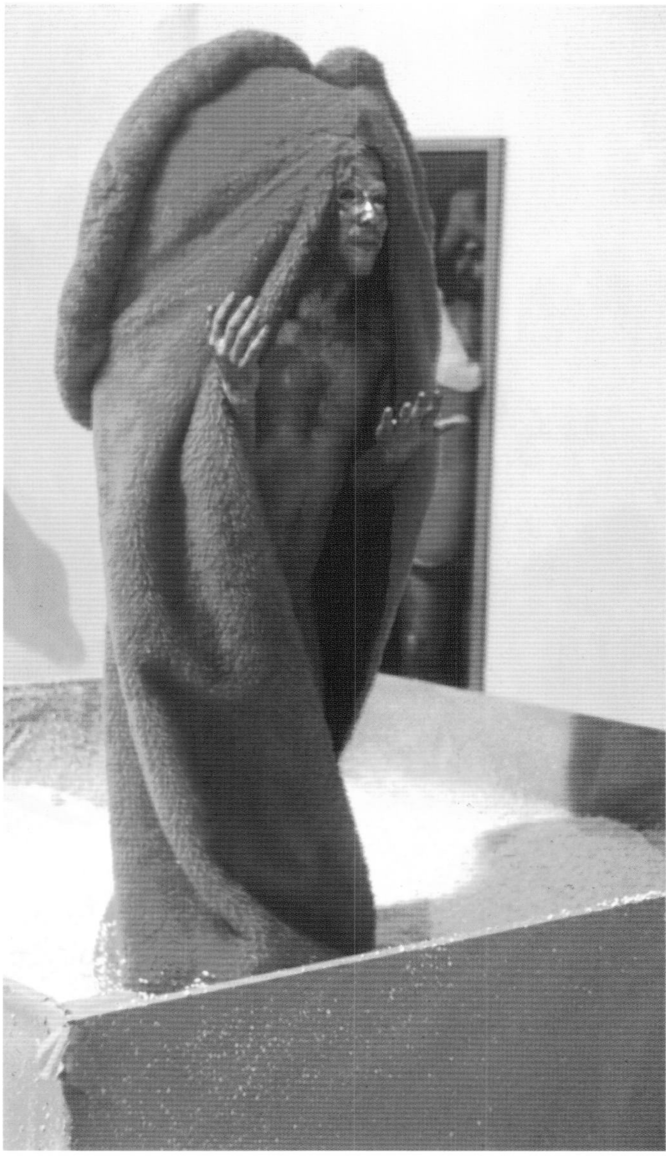

Paul COTTON
The People's Prick
1969
'The Benefit of the Doubt or The Upper Birth of Man Paul Son',
Berkeley, California

'In May 1969 The People's Prick was carried at the head of the People's Park Parade at University, California, Berkeley, as an in-body-meant of the creative vision of the Student Body of the 1960s which had been "cut off" by Governor Ronald Reagan and the National Guard. Two weeks later the People's Prick also "took over the mike in the spirit of revolution" at a poetry reading benefit for the People's Park.'
– Paul Cotton, Artist's statement, 1999

This image shows Paul Cotton in his persona of 'The People's Prick', in a performance called 'The Benefit of the Doubt or The Upper Birth of Man Paul Son'. Cotton's interactive installation and performance pieces challenged the boundaries between individuals, art and life, and humour and high-mindedness.

opposite
Bruce NAUMAN
Self-Portrait as a Fountain
1966-67
Colour photograph
50 × 60 cm [20 × 24 in]

This is one of a series of eleven colour photographs that Nauman made in a period of isolated self-absorption in his studio. During this period he moved from using objects and constructions to the investigation of spatial relationships with a focus on his own body. '[I]f you can manipulate clay and end up with art, you can manipulate yourself in it as well. It has to do with using the body as a tool, an object to manipulate.'
– Bruce Nauman, 'Interview with Willoughby Sharp', 1971

Posing as a self-generating fountain, an art-object ejecting water into the air in a controlled stream from his pursed lips, he parodied the tradition of public sculptors who represent the heroic male nude in poses validating their masculinity. As both the artist and the object, Nauman also presented himself as a metaphorical source of wisdom and fertility. Two text pieces made during the same period read 'The true artist is an amazing luminous fountain' and 'The true artist helps the world by revealing mystic truths.'

Bruce NAUMAN
Walking in an Exaggerated Manner Around the Perimeter of a Square
1967-68
Video still
9 mins., black and white, silent

Nauman made a series of videos in his studio, using his body as both subject and object of the work. He carefully constructed these pieces to create specific physical situations; walking, pacing or dancing is a leitmotif of these early works which focus on the body's encounter with space, and the physiological and emotional effects of time.

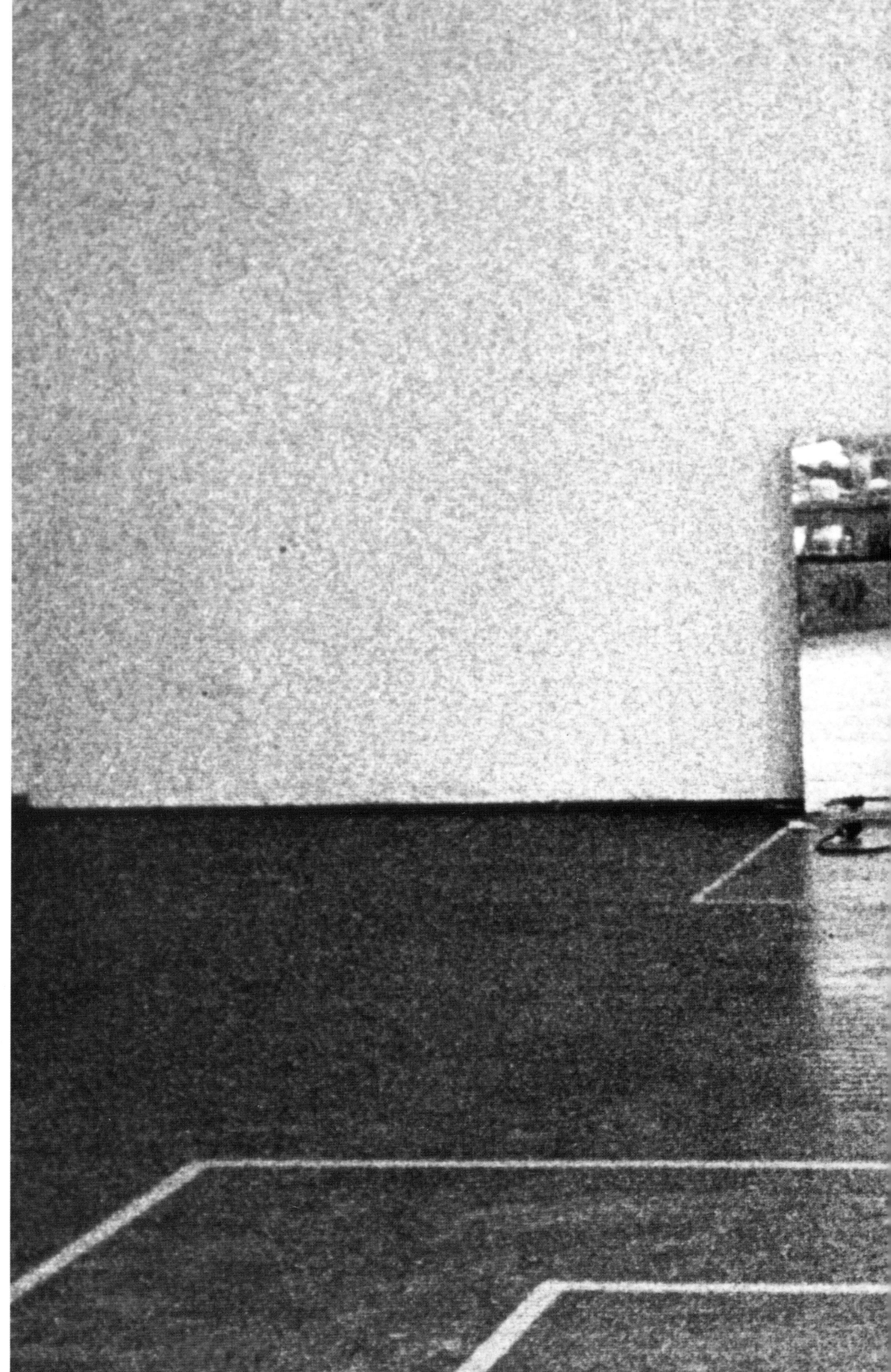

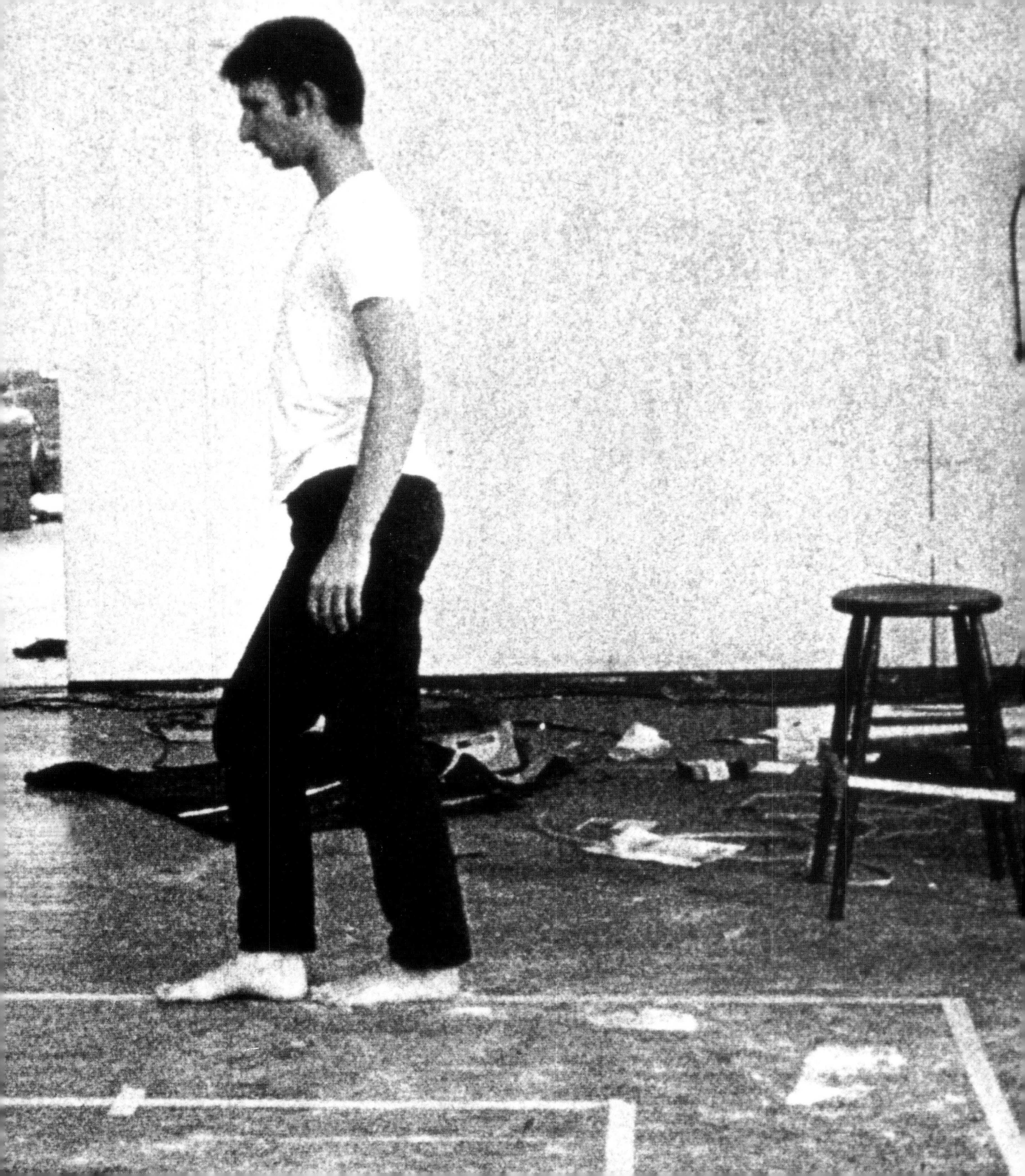

opposite

GILBERT & GEORGE

The Singing Sculpture

1970

Nigel Greenwood Gallery, London

Gilbert & George first performed as human sculptures at several London art schools and two open-air rock concerts in the late 1960s. In buttoned-up suits, with short hair and faces painted metallic silver and gold, they struck robotic poses. Miming the words to a popular Edwardian music-hall song, 'Underneath the Arches', they provided a comic antithesis to the crowds of long-haired hippies. In 1970 Gilbert & George presented 'two sculptors, one stick, one glove and one song' at the Nigel Greenwood Gallery, London. Standing on a small table in their suits and make-up, they posed and sang along to a portable tape-recording, exchanging the walking stick and glove each time the song ended. They performed continually for seven hours a day for five consecutive days, demonstrating the seriousness of their artistic intentions. This performance was revived at the Sonnabend Gallery, New York, in 1991.

'Together with you this sculpture presents as much contact for experiencing as is possible. Human sculpture makes available every feeling you can think of. It is significant that this sculpture is able to sing its message with words and music. The sculptors, in their sculpture, are given over to feeling the life of the world of art.'

– Gilbert & George, 'Six Points Towards a Better Understanding', 1970

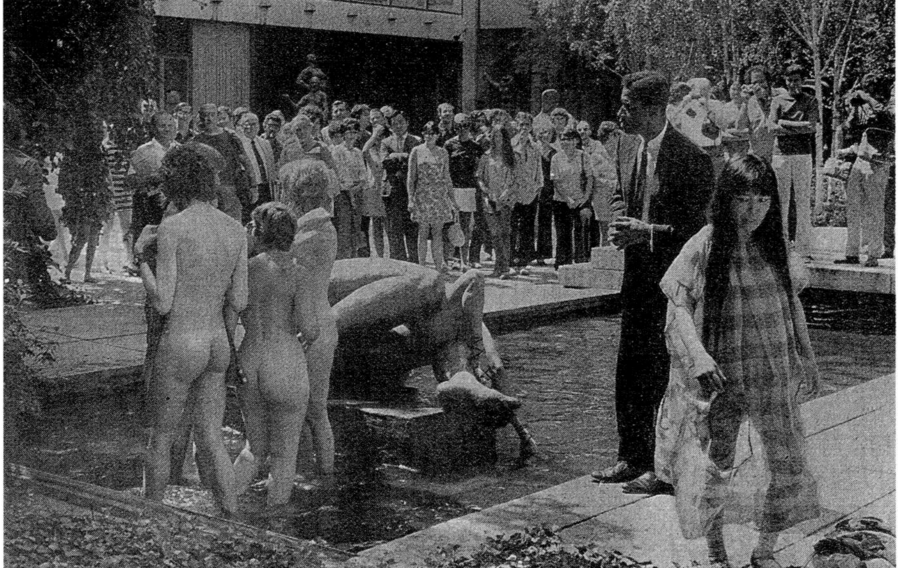

NEWS photo by Mel Finkelstein

But Is It Art? Security officer Roy Williams pleads with nude young men and women to leave Museum of Modern Art fountain, where Maillol's sculpture, Girl Washing Her Hair, reclines. Impromptu nude-in was conception of Japanese artist Yayoi Kusama (right). Crowd takes it in stride. (Some took strides to get closer). *—Story on page 4*

left

Yayoi KUSAMA

Grand Orgy to Awaken the Dead at MoMA (Otherwise Known as The Museum of Modern Art) – Featuring Their Usual Display of Nudes

1969

New York

During the course of 1968 Kusama staged Happenings at locations all over Manhattan, including the New York Stock Exchange, the Statue of Liberty, the United Nations Building, the Board of Elections headquarters, Brooklyn Bridge and the Alice in Wonderland statue in Central Park. Usually these involved a small group of nude men and women covered with Kusama's signature polka-dots, performing a dance on the street until stopped by the police. Kusama presided as dot-painter, choreographer and spokesperson. At The Museum of Modern Art, New York, which Kusama called the 'Mausoleum of Modern Art', eight nude participants struck artistic poses in the fountain of the museum's sculpture garden. Although the art press was by now familiar with Kusama's free-love, anti-war, anti-capitalist, anti-establishment Happenings, the *Daily News* gave her spectacle front-page coverage, reporting that for twenty minutes museum security officers were unable to coax the performers out of the pool. Kusama is quoted as saying, 'What is modern there?... Van Gogh, Cézanne, those other ghosts, all are dead or dying. While the dead show dead artists, living artists die.'

– Yayoi Kusama, 'But Is It Art?', 1969

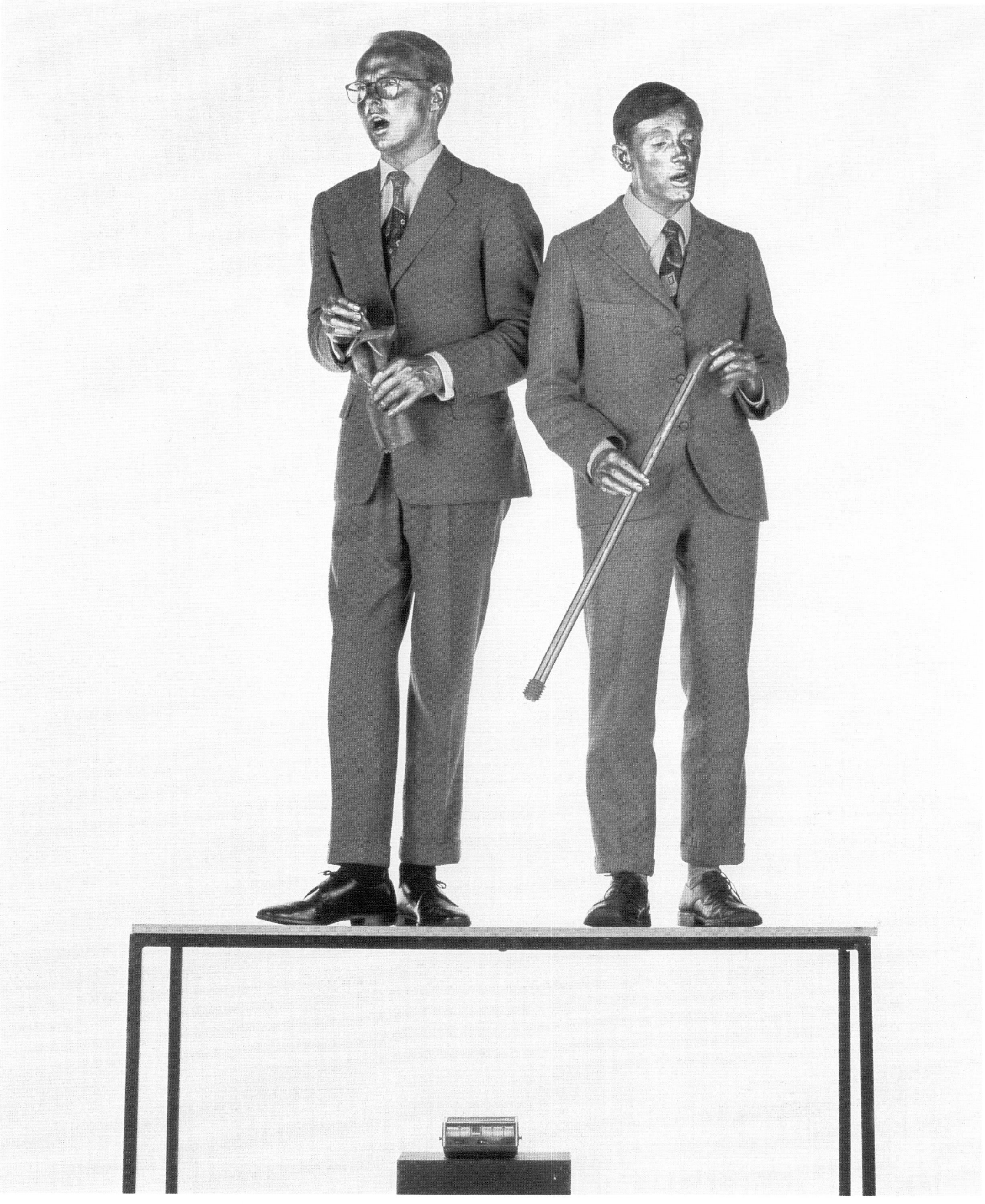

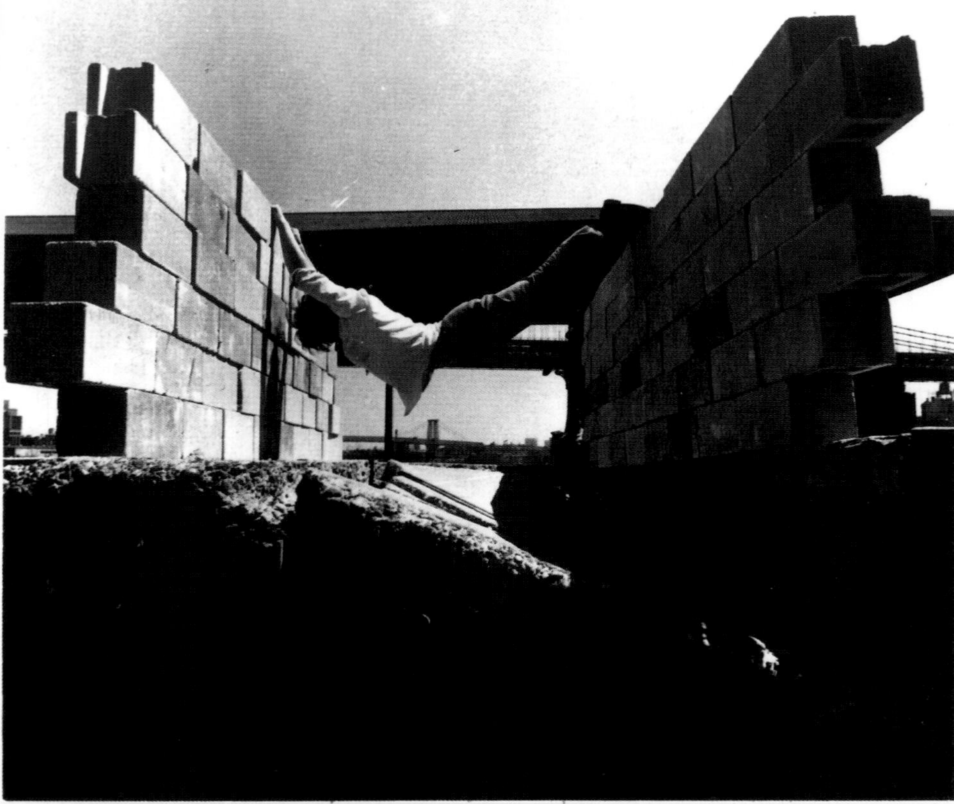

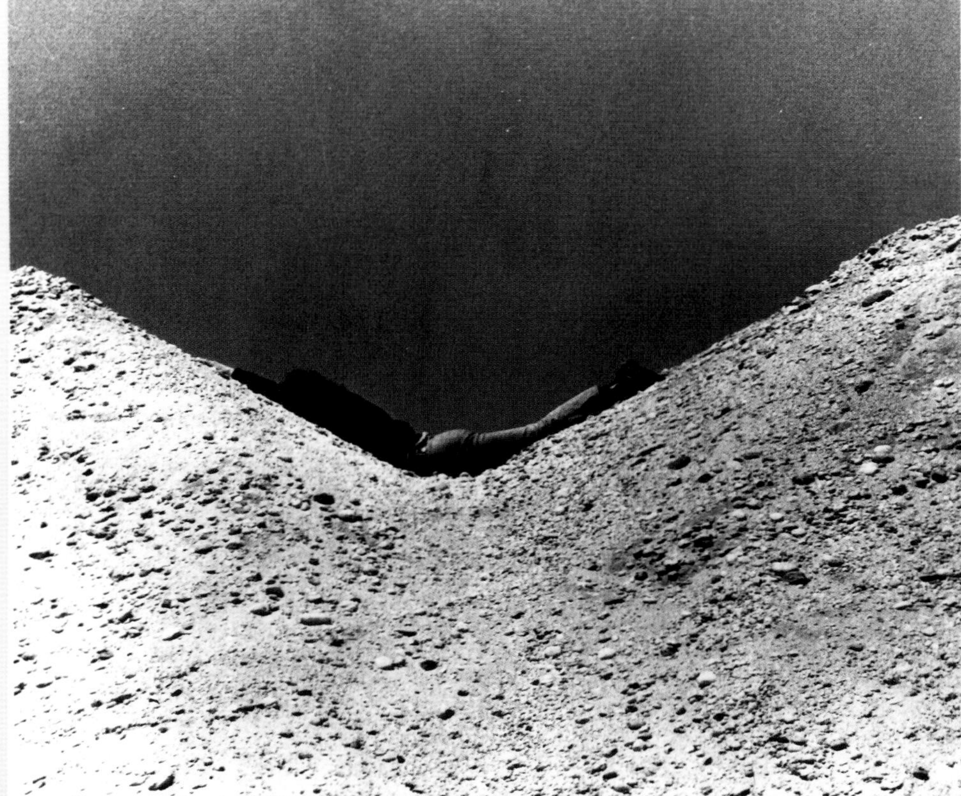

<u>Parallel Stress</u> - A 10 minute performance piece - May 1970
Photo taken at greatest stress position prior to collapse
Location: Masonry-block wall and collapsed concrete pier between Brooklyn and Manhattan bridges
Bottom Photo: Stress position reassumed.
Location: Abandoned sump. Long Island   Photos: Robert K. McElroy

Dennis OPPENHEIM
Parallel Stress
1970
Pier between Brooklyn and Manhattan bridges and an abandoned sump in Long Island, New York

This was a ten-minute performance piece in which Oppenheim suspended his body between a masonry-block wall and a collapsed concrete pier in an industrial space between Brooklyn and Manhattan bridges. He held the position until his body also collapsed. He repeated the position over and over, widening the gap between the walls. The photograph was taken at the point at which his body was in the position of greatest stress. Investigating the human body's relationship to space and the materials of its industrial environment, Oppenheim was using his body to record the stress encountered in bridging two structures, expressed by the position of his body as it arched downwards. In a later work this position was assumed again for one hour in an abandoned sump on Long Island.

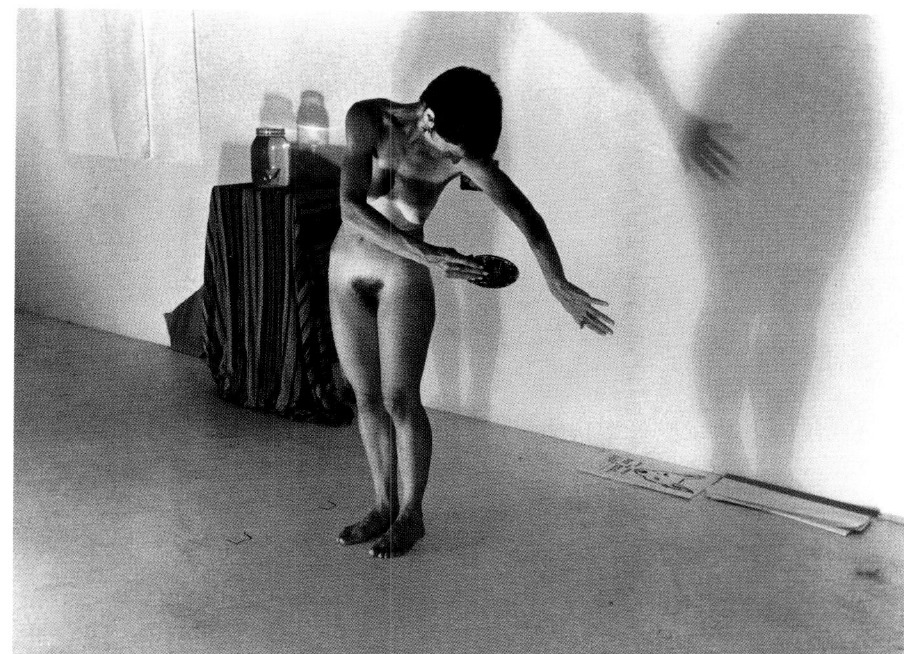

Joan JONAS
Mirror Check
1970
Ace Gallery, Los Angeles

Jonas stood naked in the Ace Gallery, Los Angeles, with a small round hand mirror which she moved around her body, focusing attention on small areas of her body, seen from specific viewpoints, through her own controlling gaze. One of Jonas' earliest investigations into the reflective and reflexive possibilities of the mirror, *Mirror Check* presaged her interest in the search for a visual/metaphorical self through fragmentation, transformation and desynchronization. The mirror is used to present a feminist deconstruction of the relationship between artistic subject and viewer. Only she could see these fragmented views, which she presented verbally to the audience, highlighting the difference in their relative positions of accessibility to the knowledge acquired through looking. The viewer was thus totally dependent on the artist for views of her fragmented self, providing a literal representation of the power of the artist in directing the spectator's eye, here specifically in relation to her female body.

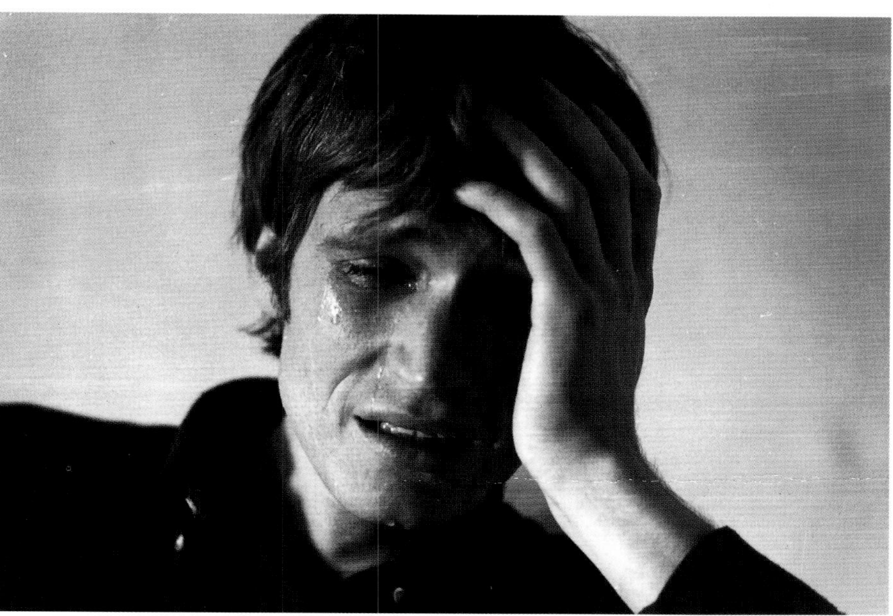

Bas Jan ADER
I'm Too Sad to Tell You
1970
Black and white photograph
9 × 14 cm [3.5 × 5.5 in]

Ader sent this photograph of himself crying in the form of postcards to friends and acquaintances. Only the date and the message, 'I'm too sad to tell you', were written on the reverse. Alternative wording he considered at the time included, 'The space between us fills my heart with intolerable grief' and 'The thoughts of our inevitable and separate deaths fill my heart with intolerable grief.' *I'm Too Sad ...* hinges not on the source of the artist's tears, but on the re-enacting of his private sadness for the camera. The image depends on the artifice and melodrama of the artist's act of placing himself before the camera while crying. As such, it questions our notions of authenticity in expression – how is it that Ader convinces us he is sincere? Through a denial of information – 'I'm too sad to tell you' – Ader creates a sense of limitlessness in the extent and source of grief, an imaginative gap that we are forced to fill for ourselves with our own experience of sadness. As critic James Roberts has written, 'The reason for his (real) crying is "a secret" known only by a few close friends, but it is apparently important that we know there *is* a reason.'
– James Roberts, 'Bas Jan Ader: the artist who fell from grace with the sea', 1994

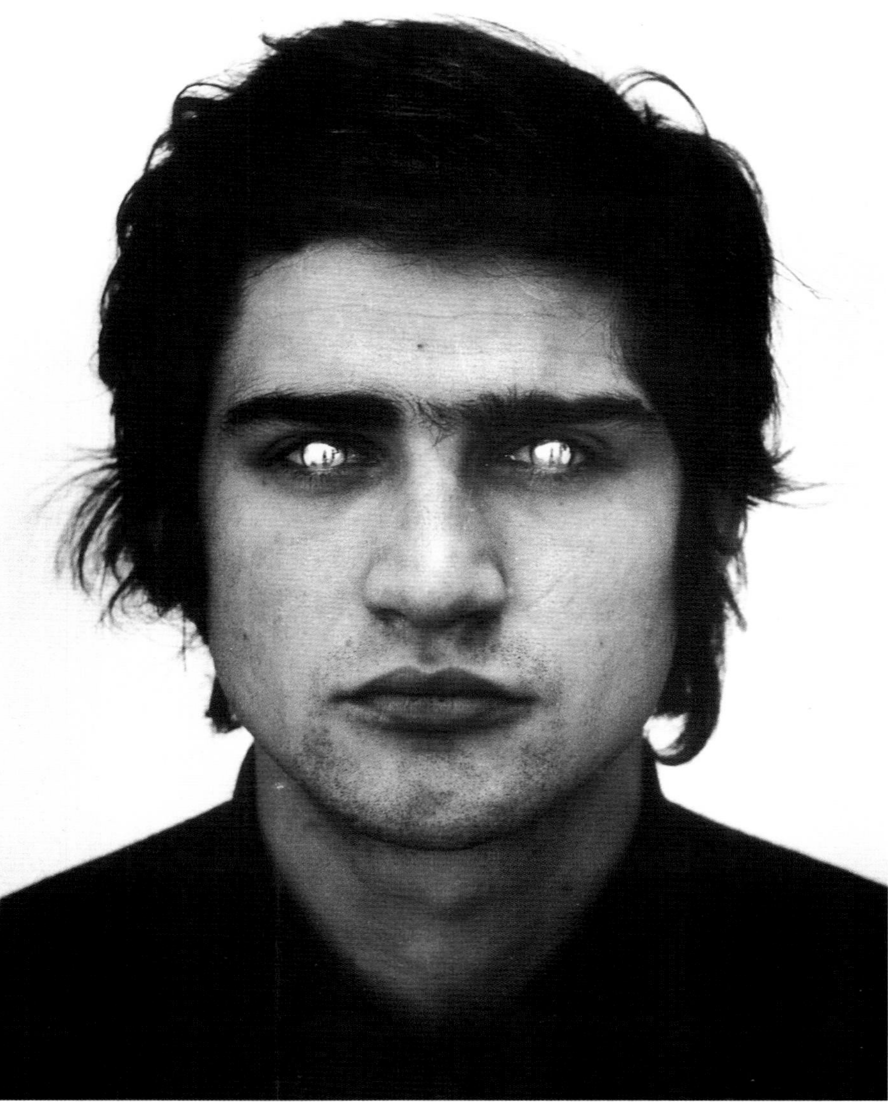

Giuseppe PENONE
Rovesciare i propri occhi (To reverse one's eyes)
1970
Black and white photograph
18 × 13 cm [7 × 5 in]

'Mirrored lenses, when placed over my eyes, indicate the point that separates me from that which surrounds me. They are like a skin, a border element, the interruption of a channel of information ... By blocking my vision I eliminate data necessary for my subsequent behaviour.'
– Giuseppe Penone, Artist's statement, 1977

The mirrored lenses were originally used for an action documented through a series of photographs by Paolo Mussat Sartor. The artist's vision is presented as a literal reflector of his environment. The urban landscape mirrored in the lenses changes as the artist changes his position in relation to it. However, since the lenses effectively blind him, Penone suggests that the artist's relationship with his creativity drives his gaze back into himself.

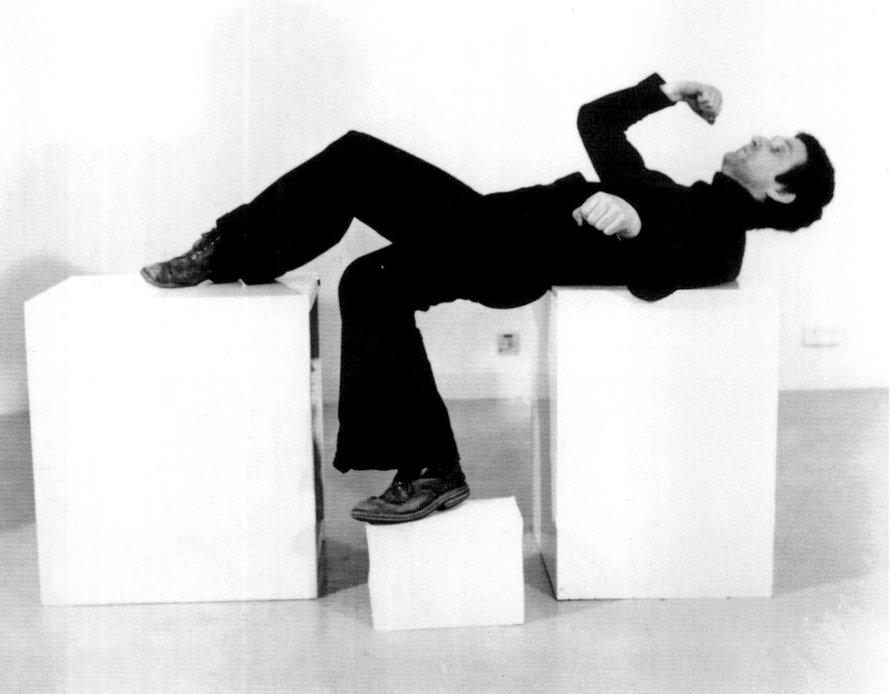

Bruce McLEAN
Pose Work for Plinths
1970
London

Pose Work for Plinths originally occurred in 1970 as a performance staged for 'Situation', a London-based organization devoted to British Conceptual art. McLean posed for the camera in a variety of positions on three white cubes. The resulting prints were then arranged and mounted as a freestanding work, and shown the following year as a 'version' of the original performance. By inserting his living body in place of the art object one would normally see on such plinths, and specifically parodying the dignified reclining maternal figures of Henry Moore, McLean inserted the monumental rhetoric of traditional sculpture. The photographic presentation additionally mocked the self-reflective seriousness of Conceptual-art-as-documentation prevalent at the time, hinting at the possibility of using photography itself as a sculptural medium rather than merely as a means to record and document ephemeral works.

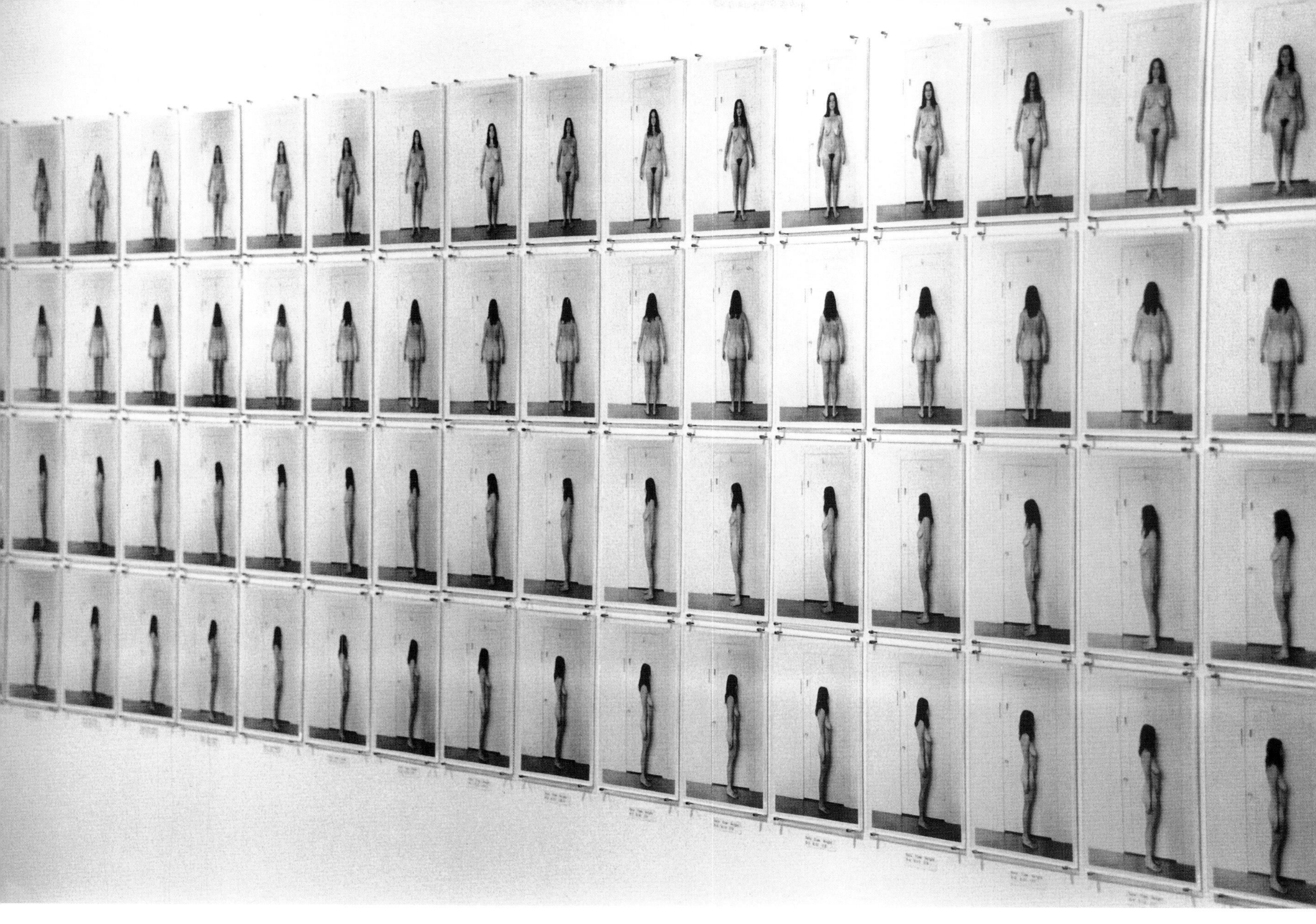

Eleanor ANTIN

Carving: A Traditional Sculpture

1973

Black and white photographs, text

144 photographs, 18 × 12.5 cm [7 × 5 in] each

Collection, Art Institute of Chicago

'This work was carved during the period between 15 July 1972 and 21 August 1972. The material (the artist's body) was photographed every morning in four positions – front, back, right and left profile – to depict the process of "carving" down during a strict dieting regimen.' Parodying the method of traditional Greek scuplture in which the sculptor worked his way round a figure, repeatedly carving a thin layer from all sides in order to 'keep the whole in view', Antin presented her body as the object of her own sculpting activity, through a process that, unlike carving, worked from the inside out. Like the Greek sculptor she could choose when to stop. 'When the image was finally refined to the point of aesthetic satisfaction the work was completed.' There was a proviso that the final result would be determined by '(1) the ideal image towards which the artist aspires, and (2) the limitations of the material'. Antin concludes with a paraphrase of a quote from Michelangelo 'not even the greatest sculptor can make anything that isn't already inside the marble', and ironically points to the primacy of the material internal to her 'sculpted' body, which is precisely what enables her to control that body. – all quotes from Eleanor Antin, Artist's writings, 1973

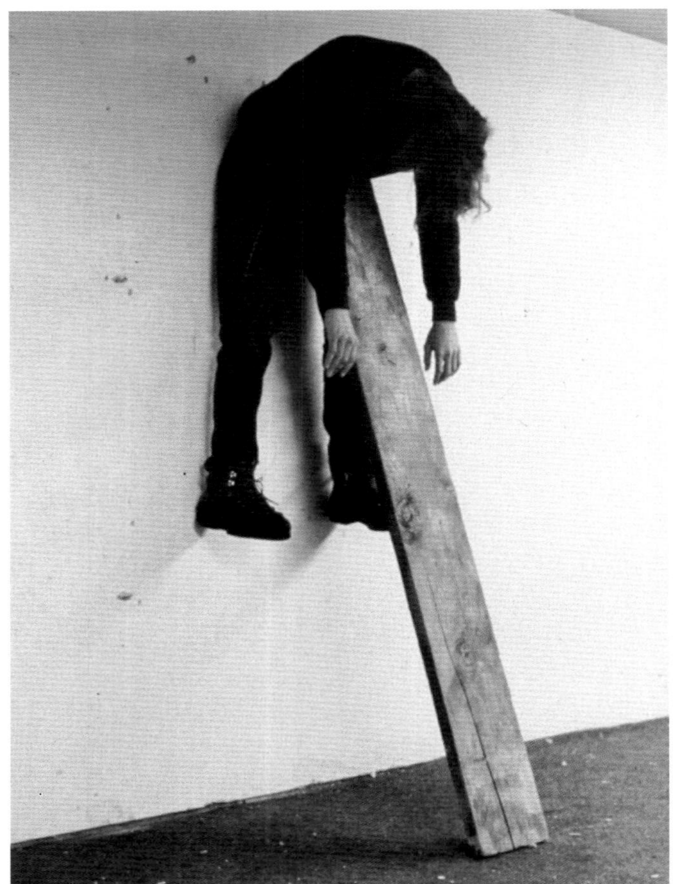

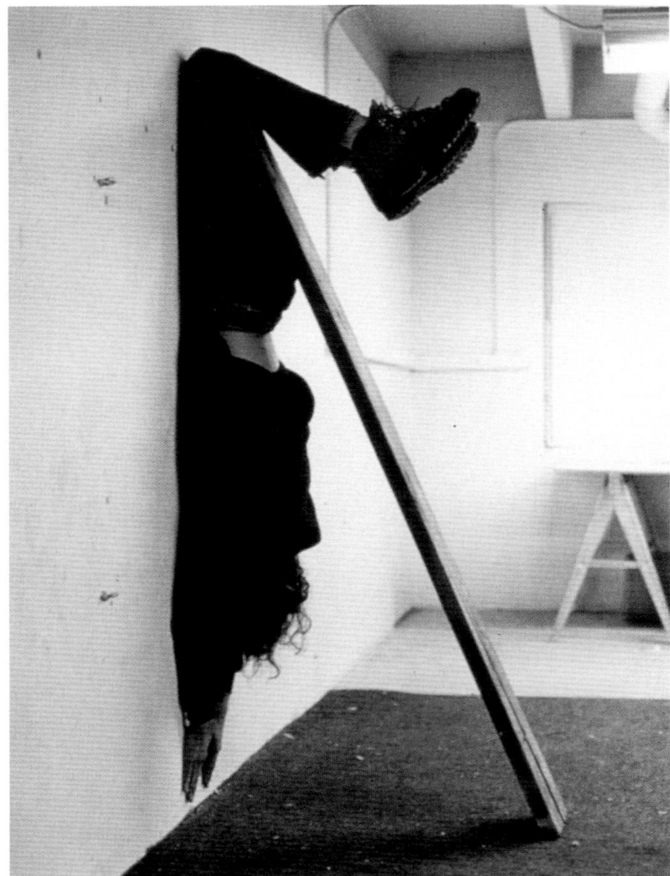

Charles RAY
Plank Piece I & II
1973
Black and white photographs
2 parts, 102 × 76 cm [40 × 30 in] each

This work was an investigation of the plane that simultaneously divides and supports the body. Thinking of sculpture as an activity rather than an object, Ray inserted his body into a simple equation of support, aligning the joints separating his pelvis from his torso, and his calves from his thighs, with the angle of connection between the wall and a plank laid against it.

Mierle Laderman UKELES

Hartford Wash: Washing, Tracks, Maintenance: Outside

1973

Hartford, Connecticut

In a series of thirteen performances between 1973 and 1976 Ukeles carried out 'maintenance' activities in public spaces, cleaning streets and museum floors as well as performing all the duties of the guards in a museum. In her manifesto 'Maintenance Art' (1969), she described the drudgery of maintenance activities while acknowledging their necessity. Her maintenance actions were intended to draw attention to the importance of such activities and to the people who traditionally carry them out, both of which have been ignored in cultural discourse. Having renamed her domestic duties at home 'art' (she had recently become a mother), Ukeles defined women's social role as 'unification ... the perpetuation and maintenance of the species, survival systems, equilibrium', and asked, 'After the revolution, who's going to take out the garbage on Monday morning?'

– Mierle Laderman Ukeles, 'The Garbage Girls', 1991

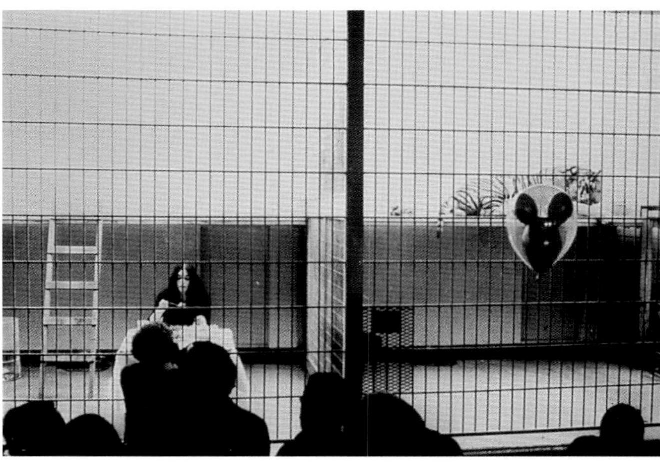

above

Bonnie SHERK

Public Lunch

1971

Lion House, San Francisco Zoo

Sherk sat eating her lunch, prepared by a well-known San Franciscan restaurant, in the feeding cage of the Lion House in San Francisco Zoo. She had previously spent time familiarizing the animals in the next cage with her presence. She claimed that this performance-event came out of a realization of the waste involved in the ceremony of much American public life, which she emphasized through contrasting the staged eating of her expensive restaurant lunch with the dirt and (symbolic) danger of the lion's cage. Sherk later went on to expand her exploration of the relationships between social structures and ecology, humans, plants and animals, setting up a multicultural art and life centre – *The Farm* – in dialogue with governmental systems and city bureaucracy. This was intended to provide a place of unity for all people through a direct and whole experience of nature. It was situated in a large area of land in the middle of a freeway complex, which had been given over to park and garden purposes. Like *Public Lunch*, *The Farm* attempted to integrate the individual more fully both with nature and with city planning.

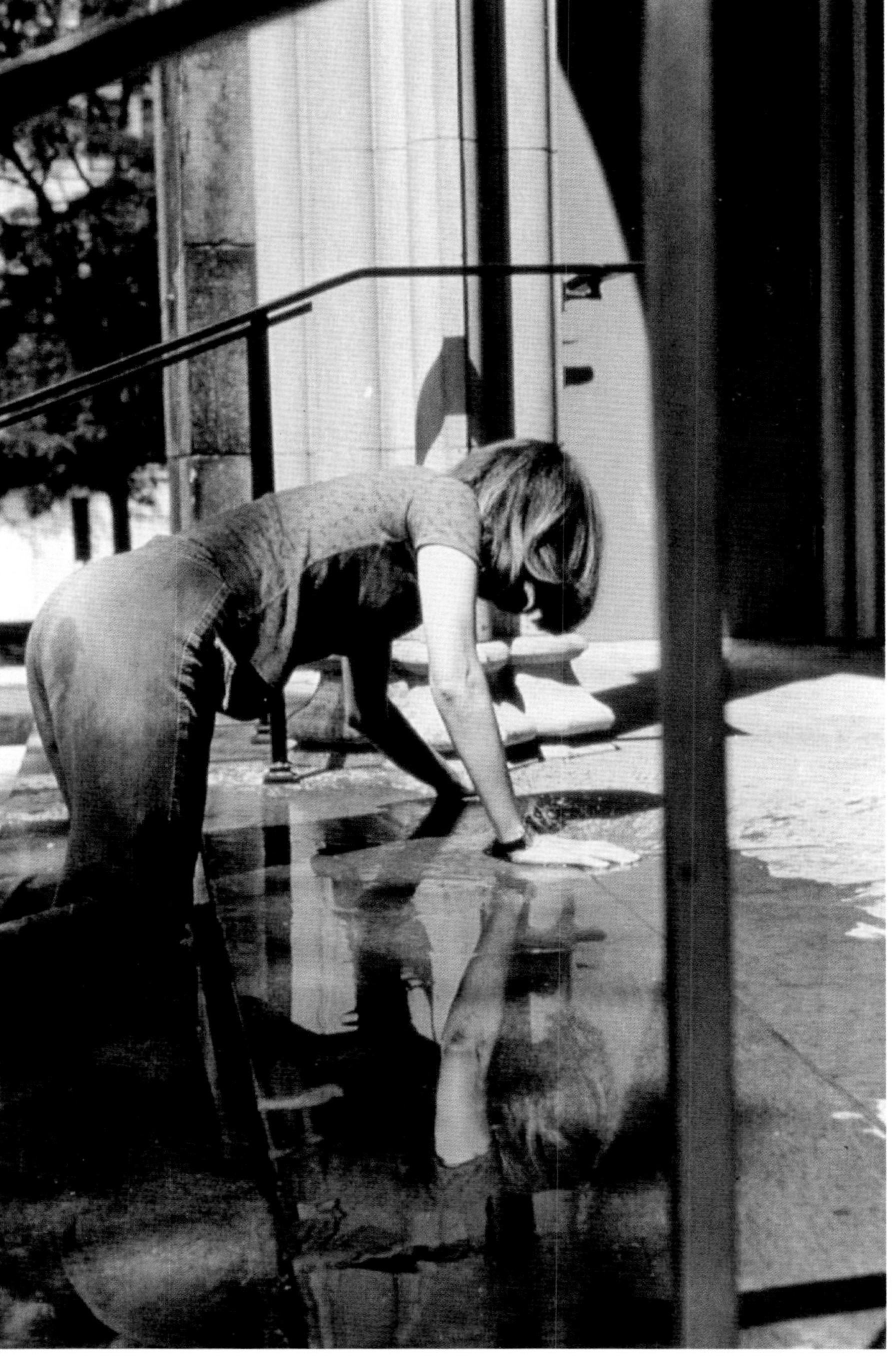

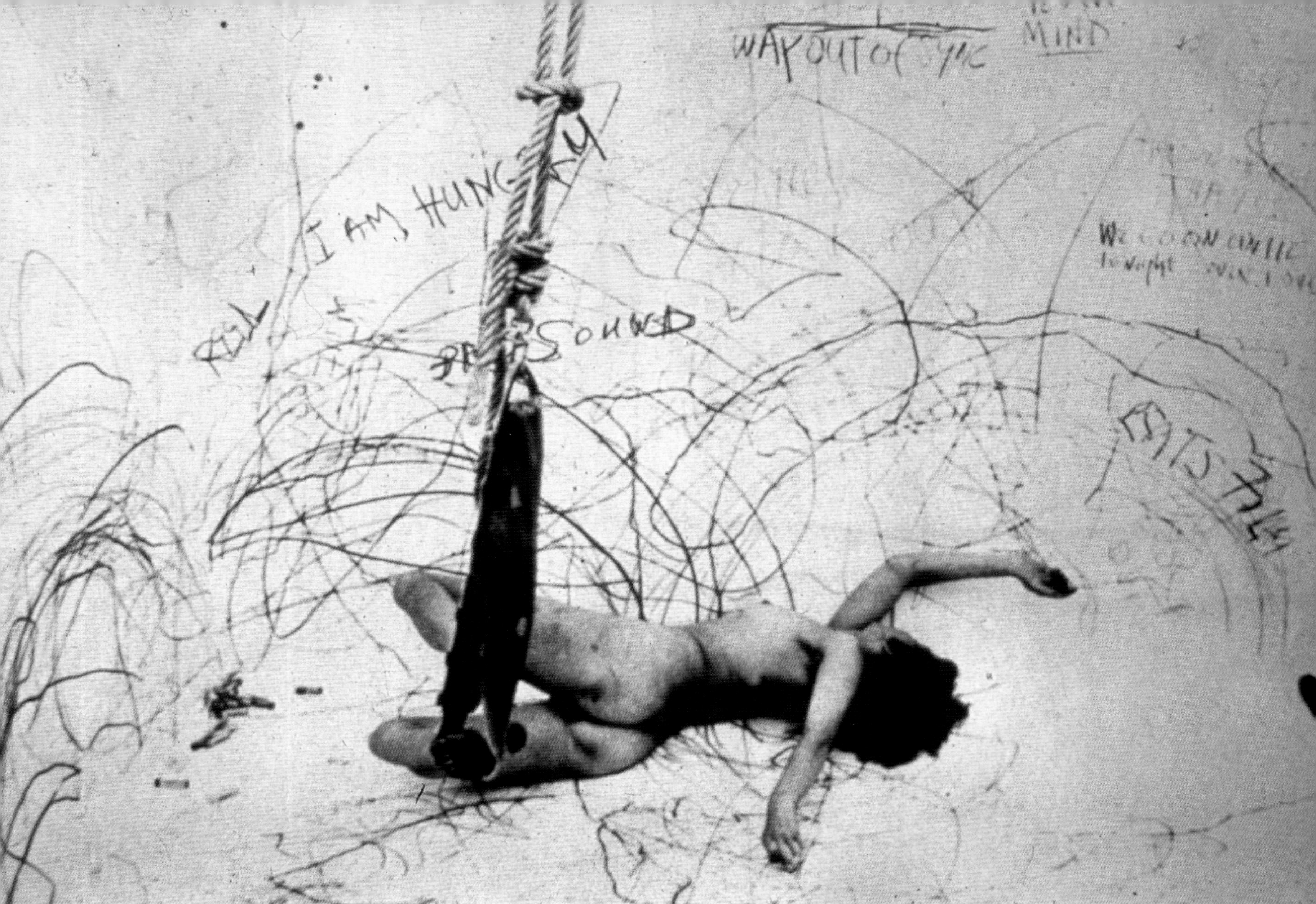

Carolee SCHNEEMANN
Up To And Including Her Limits
1976
Berlin

First performed in an empty boxcar in Grand Central Station, New York, at the Avant-Garde Festival (1973), by 1976 *Up To …* had evolved into a complex installation/performance incorporating projections of super-8 film material previously used by the artist in other works and video compilations of the artist performing the central action of the piece. Swinging naked from a harness, she scrawled on huge sheets of paper attached to the walls, creating drawings from the movement of her body, which could thus 'function as a pencil'. She described the performance as a kind of inwardlooking to reveal her unconscious, 'a private movement meditation, the private life of the artist made public', which required 'concentration, the inward connection to the subtle response and shift of the rope which resulted in the meditation (and a process of what Cage calls "alteration"), in no way performed to an audience, but which they could witness.'
– Carolee Schneemann, *More Than Meat Joy*, 1979

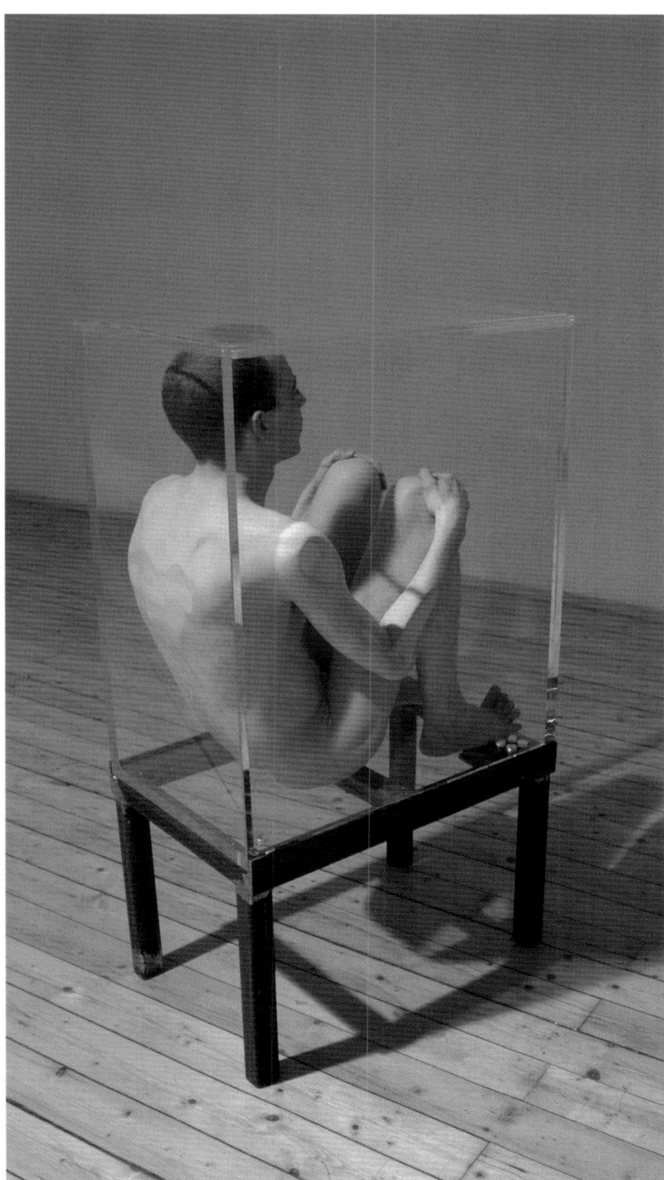

Skip ARNOLD
On Display
1993
Acrylic box, steel stand, the artist
132 × 48 × 72 cm [52 × 19 × 28.5 in]
Installation, 'Performance Relikte & Sedimente', Offens Kulturhaus, Linz, Austia

At 'Performance Relikte & Sedimente', Offens Kulturhaus, Linz, Austia, Arnold sat naked on display in an acrylic box for several hours each day, a living breathing artwork. In another videotaped performance, he perched naked like a gargoyle on the ledge of a building in a parody of architectural sculpture. In a two-day performance art programme in Geneva, Arnold posed nude in a second-storey bay window above the Art and Public Gallery, resulting in the arrest of both the gallery's director and the artist for causing offence to the public. Using his naked body to marry the act of creating art with the literal act of living, Arnold confronts the boundaries between the artist's body as agent and its function as site. Emphasizing meditative endurance in the tradition of 1970s body artists such as Chris Burden and Marian Abramović, Arnold fuses this with conceptual-style documentation, which retains the status of art-relic, ultimately subordinate to the life and body of the artist. In 1996 he used the money he had been awarded for a Guggenheim Fellowship to fund a cruise to the Bermuda Triangle, where he drifted, waiting to vanish. 'My work is not an answer. My only concern is with the impact, the experience, the moment in time. I want people to look beneath the surface of the politics and to go after the image. The viewer should look at the work in its intrinsic integrity. The surface concentration on sexism is an excuse to dismiss the art. It's okay for gays, lesbians and women to display their bodies but not straight men. Straight men are accused of egocentrism, exhibitionism and exploitation. What I am doing is not exposure. I am not showing a spectacle but a body as material.'
– Skip Arnold, 'In Conversation with J.S.M. Willette', 1992

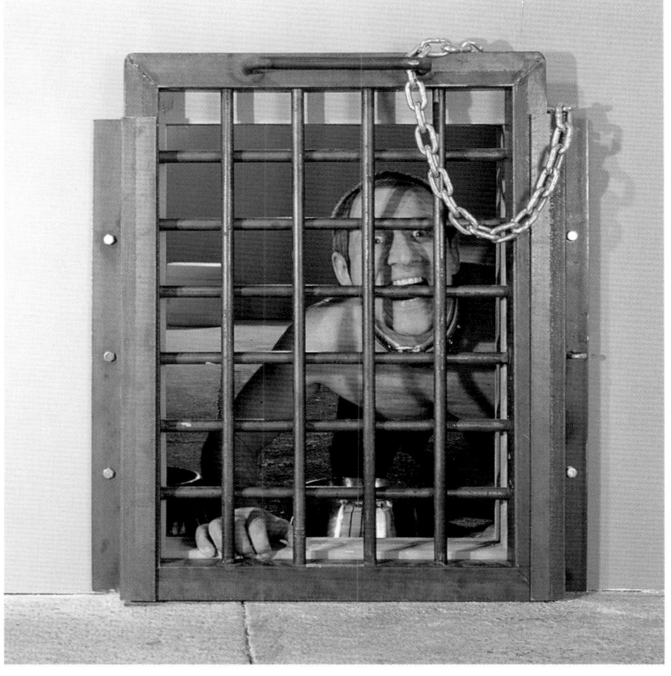

Oleg KULIK
I Bite America and America Bites Me
1997
Deitch Projects, New York

Presented at Deitch Projects, New York, Kulik's performance was staged as a response to Joseph Beuys' work *I Like America and America Likes Me* (1974). On his arrival from Russia at JFK Airport Kulik was escorted to a waiting animal van, where he undressed and assumed his role as 'Dog'. He was then driven to the gallery where his 'keeper' – his wife and collaborator Mila Bredikhina – led him to his pen – a specially constructed cell within the gallery. For two weeks he was on view to the public as a caged animal, crawling around on all fours, eating out of dog dishes, barking, growling and urinating, before being returned to the airport as he had come. As a Russian artist (who apparently cannot speak English) presented as both man and beast, locked up and naked to provide voyeuristic public entertainment, Kulik could be seen to have made an extremely ascerbic comment on American views of Russian culture, more vulnerable to capitalist exploitation since the fall of the Iron Curtain. This transformation of Beuys' mediation between nature and culture into a relationship between America and her old enemies in the East suggests that American cultural imperialism still reduces non-Americans to the status of animals.

RITUALISTIC AND TRANSGRES-SIVE BODIES

During the 1960s, as art began shifting away from the confines of the gallery, it started to be seen as a means of transformation of society at large. Artists such as the Viennese Actionists began to make performances that violated social taboos. The often shocking enactment of these taboos allowed the artist to experience a personal transformation through the event, and the audience was also affected, expected to undergo a mass sense of release. Accepted boundaries regarding sex, food, personal space and bodily fluids were violated in ritualized performances in an effort to bring the artist and the audience to a state of atonement and catharsis. The unhealthy body, particularly since the advent of AIDS, is also a focus of some of the artists in this chapter, for whom art is used as a process of healing and purification. These ritualized actions often mimic traditional religions and cults and can at times present a highly theatrical view of the artist's role as 'shaman', capable of redeeming society.

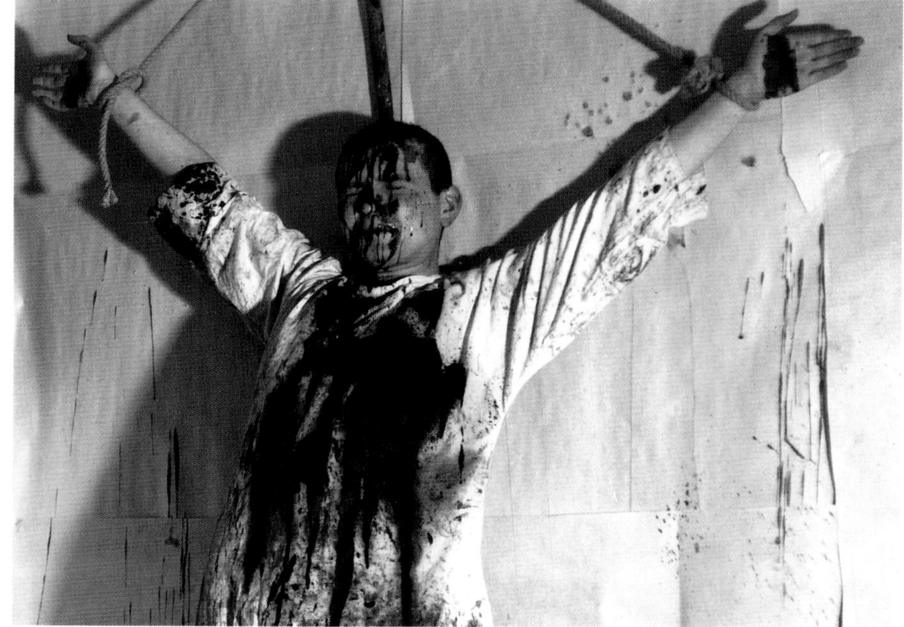

Hermann NITSCH
1st Action
1962
Vienna

Nitsch carried out his first action in Otto Mühl's studio apartment: dressed in a white, alb-like shift, he was tied to rings in the wall as if he were being crucified. Mühl then poured and squirted blood on to his head, letting it run 'in thick rivers down his face and his white alb'. The action was documented by a photographer. Nitsch aimed at an ecstatic redemption through the powerful emotional experience of the physical contact with blood and by assuming the role of Christ. He replaced the canvas with his body and presented the artist as the locus of his work, whose inscription with bloody 'paint' could generate an internal spiritual healing through the enactment of a pagan-Christian rite. In his subsequent actions for a public audience, Nitsch used a slaughtered lamb as a literal replacement for the Christ figure. He would skin and disembowel the carcass, splashing blood and entrails liberally over himself and the surrounding audience in order to provoke a direct visceral sensory experience that would allow emotions to surface and be released.

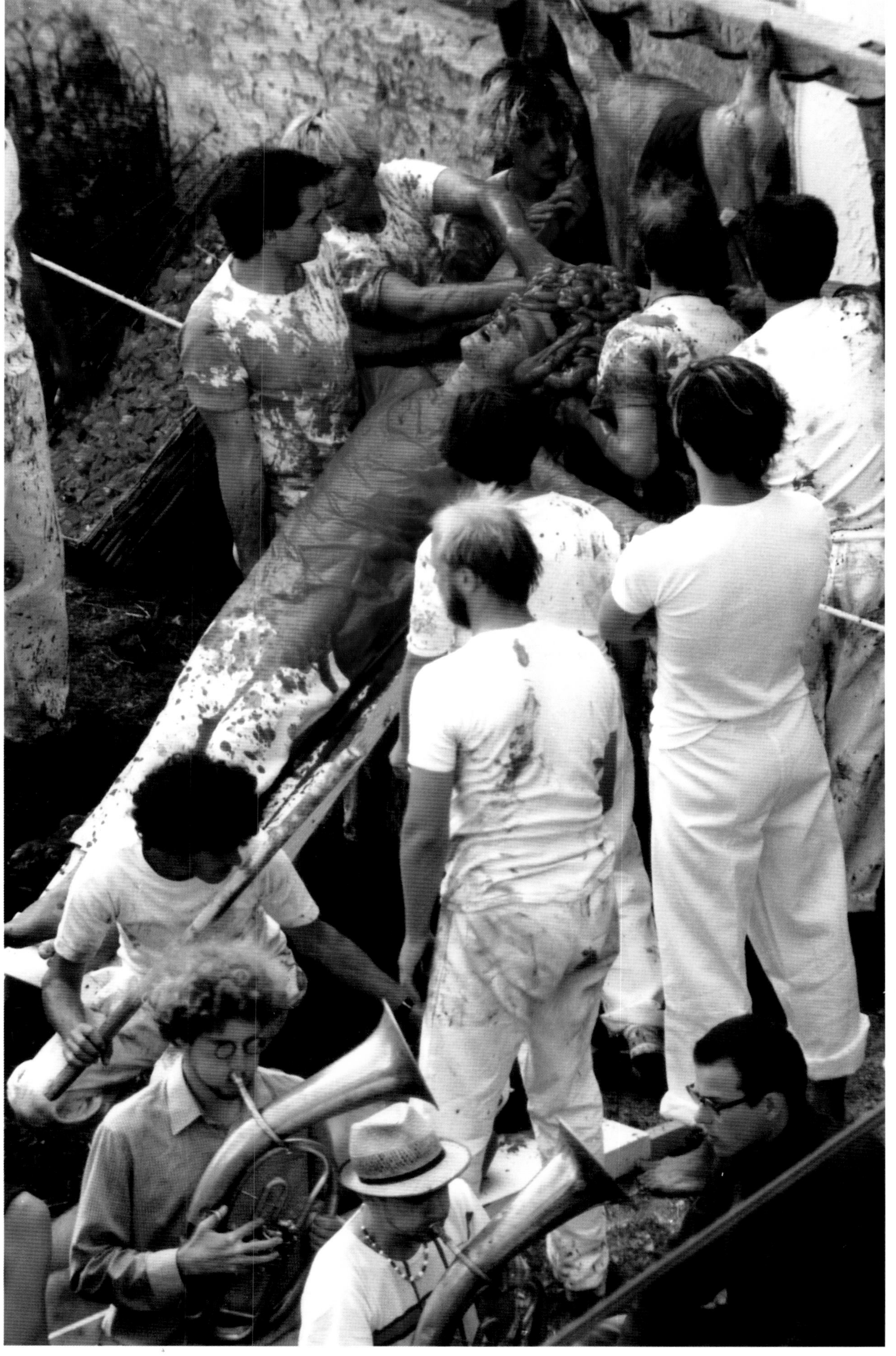

Hermann NITSCH
80th Action: Orgies-Mysteries Theatre
1984
Schloss Prinzendorf, Austria

Nitsch developed his public actions into a series of performative festivals – the *Orgies-Mysteries Theatre* – which incorporated ritual sacrifice and destruction as a vehicle for purging and catharsis. 'Comedy will become a means of finding access to the deepest and holiest symbols through blasphemy and desecration. The blasphemous provocation is devotion ... one must recognize the sacrifice (*Abreaktion*) as a matter of ecstasy, of inspiration for living. The sacrifice is another reversed form of lust, which develops in a changed state out of the unconscious. Forces of the sexual alter and are transposed to the cruelty of the sacrificial process. I accept the absolute jubilation of existence, whose condition is the experience of the cross.'
– Hermann Nitsch, *The Blood Organ*, 1962

Schloss Prinzdorf was acquired by Nitsch as an ideal location for the staging of a huge OMT action. Surrounded by cornfields and vineyards, it accommodated large numbers of performers and spectators for a three-day long Dionysiac orgy of blood and gore. Participants could come and go at will; activities included ritual disembowelments of bulls and sheep, stuffing entrails back into hacked-open carcasses, the treading of huge vats of grapes mixed with entrails, blood and wine, blood-letting on to actors representing Christ and Oedipus, and night-time processions around the castle with pigs, goats, sheep, horses, dogs and cattle and actors bearing flaming torches. Finally, buckets of blood, slime and entrails were dropped from helicopters on to military tanks, which then drove away.

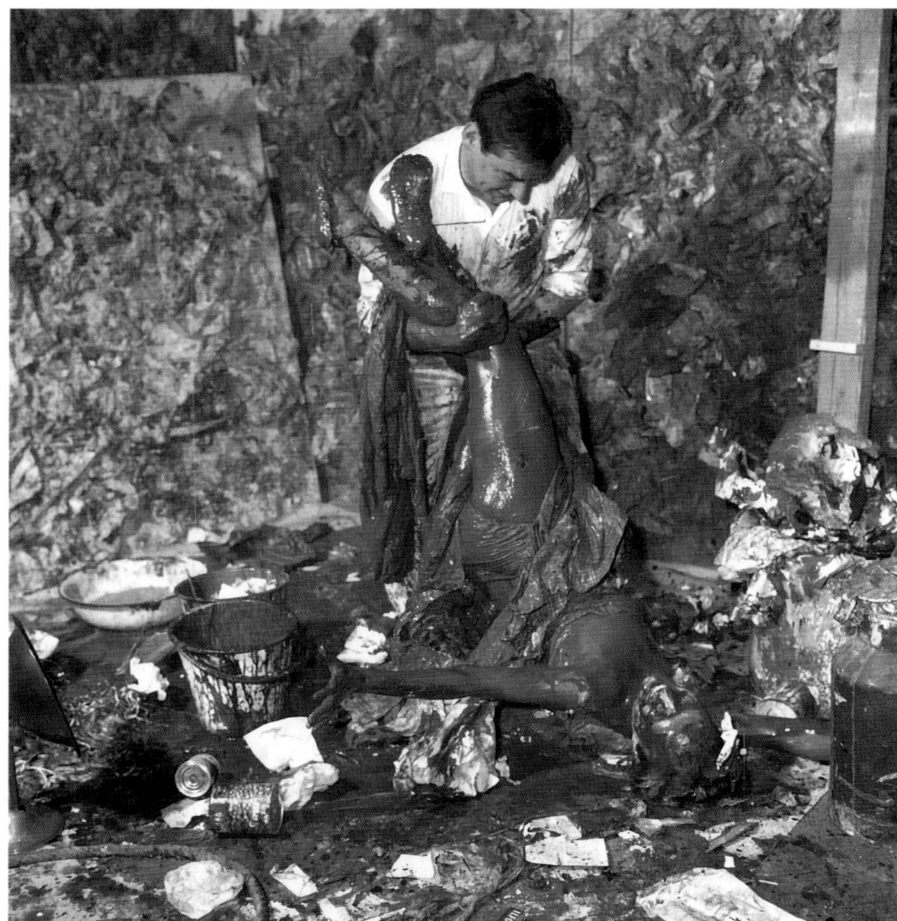

Otto MÜHL

Material Action No.1: Degradation of a Venus

1963

Vienna

'A trough such as bricklayers use to mix mortar (2 × 1.5 m [6.5 × 5 ft]) is already prepared. This trough is everything: bed, grave, pit, picture, sewer, womb. In it the victim is cut up, submerged and buried. I can imagine nothing significant where nothing is sacrificed, destroyed, dismembered, burnt, pierced, tormented, harrassed, tortured, massacred, devoured, torn up, cut up, hanged, stabbed, destroyed or annihilated. We must strive to destroy humanity, to destroy art ... ' Against a background of junk collages and material, Mühl threw paint and rubbish over a woman's body, replacing the act of painting with a psychodramatically constructed performance aimed at lifting the taboo of sexuality and the violent urges it arouses. 'Because I live in a technically civilized world, I sometimes have the need to wallow in mud like a pig. All smooth surfaces incite me to dirty them with intensive life. I crawl on all fours over them and throw the dirt in all directions. I work until the surface is used up ... When I am in heat I hold all valves open and hurl the whole stench of my soul in people's faces. In this way I bring about the redemption of my contemporaries and all future generations.'

– all quotes from Otto Mühl, *Der Psycho-Physische Naturalismus 'Das Intrem'*, 1963

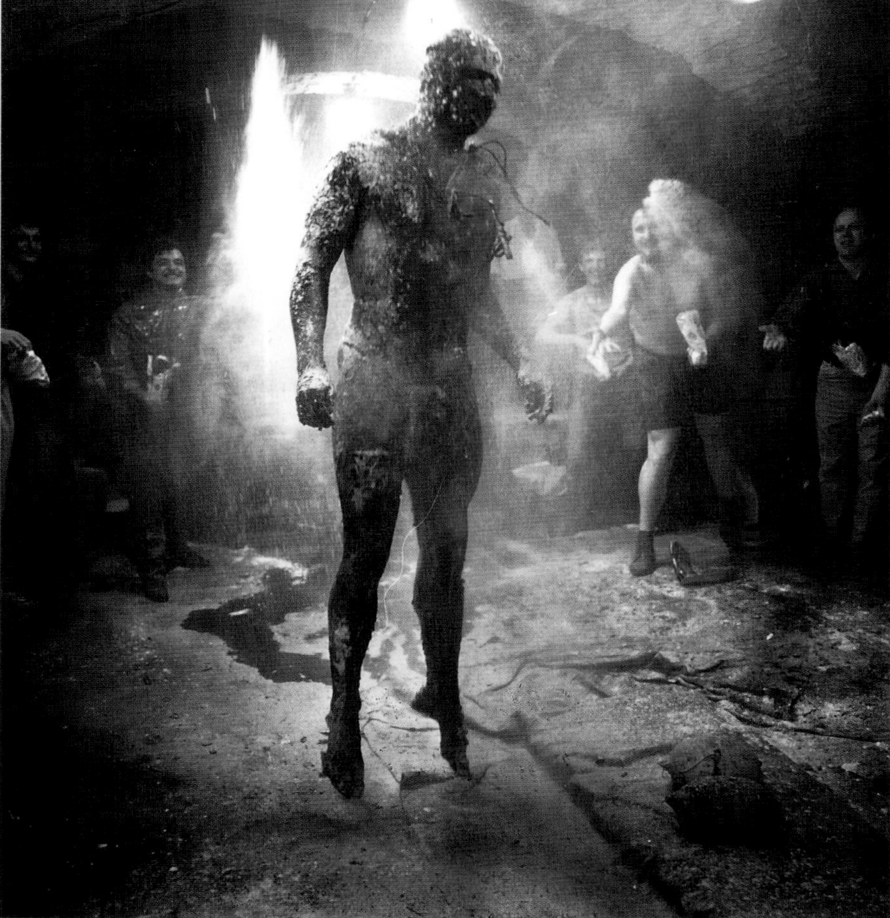

Otto MÜHL

Gymnastics Class in Food

1965

Perinet Cellar, Vienna

This action was performed in the Perinet Cellar to a public audience, alongside films of previous actions. 'It is now a matter of course that in the material action man is not treated as man but as body, even if a body that attracts the most interest to itself ... Man does not appear as man, as person, as sexual being, but as body with certain characteristics. In the material action he is cracked open like an egg and reveals the yoke. The material action is a method to extend reality, to produce reality and to expand the dimension of experience.' Mühl developed his series of chaotic improvised actions as direct and positive experiences of existence that could liberate the artist as much as his audience. A specific material language became successively more concrete in these actions as they became 'Surrealist' dramatic still-lifes, recorded as a series of photographs or as an abstract film. 'By an artist I understand a person who goes down into the earth, tunnels through it and undermines it in all directions, until suddenly somewhere a landslide occurs.'

– all quotes from Otto Mühl, *Otto Mühl: Ausgewählte Arbeiten 1963–1986*, 1986

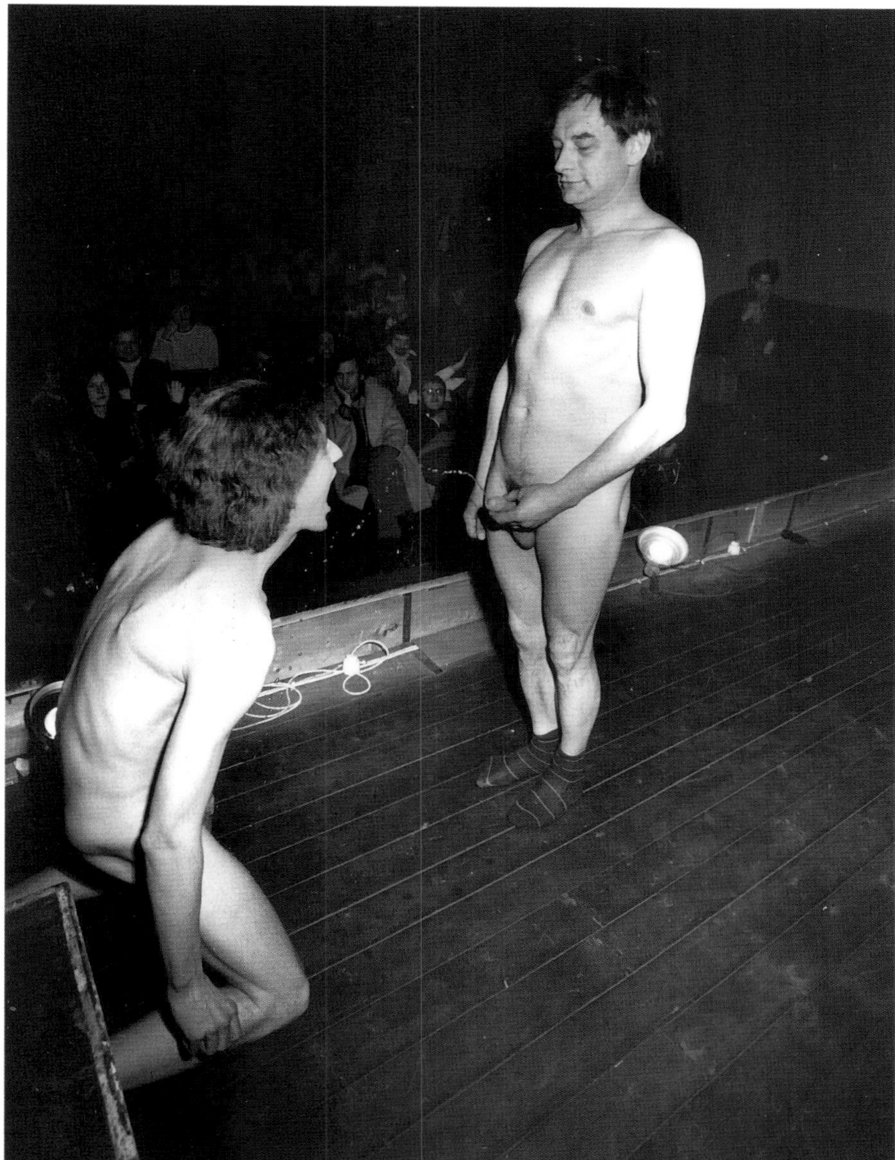

Otto MÜHL
Pissaction
1969
Hamburg Film Festival

Pissaction was first carried out in September 1968 at the public presentation of Mühl's films in Munich. Standing naked on the stage, he urinated into the mouth of his friend and fellow actionist Günter Brus. His particular type of Viennese Actionism embraced 'Direct art', pursuing the chaotic, improvised action of the naked body as positive self-liberation for the individual through the breaking down of taboos. He called for a reduction of man from the personal and the sexual through 'body-awareness' in order to reach the existential more directly, and claimed that 'material action is a method to extend reality, to produce reality and to expand the dimensions of experience'.
– Otto Mühl, *Otto Mühl: Ausgewählte Arbeiten 1963–1986*, 1986

When Mühl carried out a similar action at a student club in Kirchheim-Teck, Germany, he created a scandal, causing the club to be closed by the city administration. At this point, he was already being hunted by the police in Germany. In Austria it was no longer possible for him to perform after he had enraged popular opinion by whipping a masochist who was wrapped in sheets of newspaper.

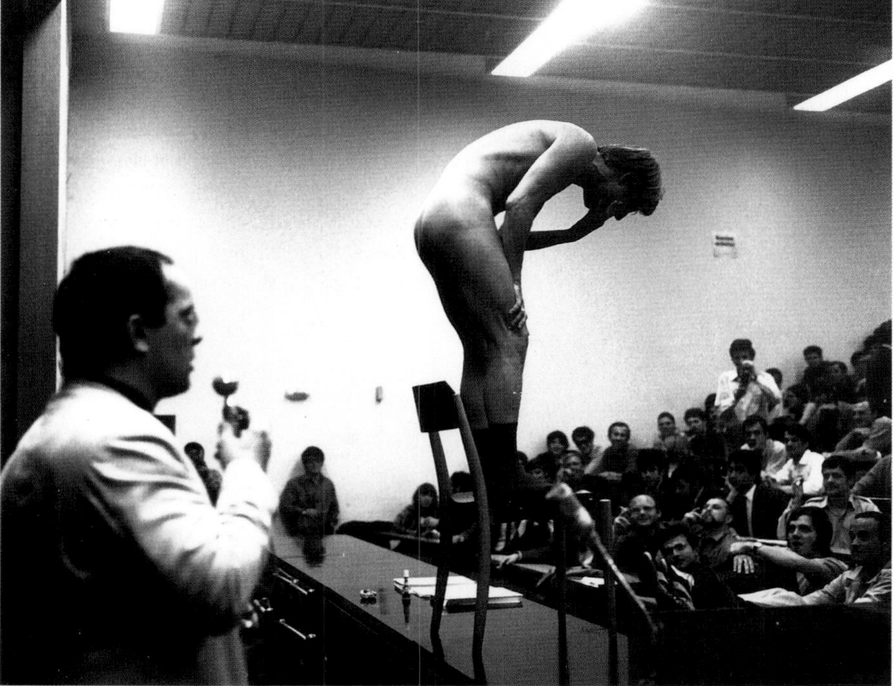

Günter BRUS
Art and Revolution
1968
University of Vienna

Brus and other Actionists had been invited to participate in a political discussion about the position and function of art in late capitalist society by the students' association at the University of Vienna. Brus removed his clothes and stood on a chair in the lecture hall, naked except for his socks. After cutting his chest and thigh with a razor blade, he urinated into a glass and drank from it, defecated and smeared his body with faeces. He then lay on the floor and masturbated while singing the Austrian national anthem. He was arrested for degrading state symbols and had to go into exile in Berlin [on the East German border] in order to escape a six-month prison sentence. Brus claimed that he had planned 'to demonstrate pissing and shitting without excess doings, to record these secretions by photography, as Hitchcock captured the sweat on Cary Grant's brow', but this statement ignored the deeply subversive nature of his actions. In post-Fascist Austria, Brus' activities were seen as highly threatening to the status quo, and he was not pardoned until 1976.
– Günter Brus, *Beiblatt zur Photo Edition*, 1970

Günter BRUS

Self-painting, Self-mutilation

1965

Vienna

'*Self-painting* is a further development of painting. The pictorial surface has lost its function as sole expressive support. It was led back to its origins, the wall, the object, the living being, the human body. By incorporating my body as expressive support, occurrences arise as a result, the course of which the camera records and the viewer can experience ... '

– Günter Brus, quoted in *Le Marais, Sonderheft Günter Brus*, 1965

The collage documenting *Self-painting, Self-mutilation* was presented at the Junge Generation Gallery, Vienna, the day after Brus' first public action. The artist had walked through the centre of Vienna, painted entirely in white, with a black stripe over his face and body. The dark paint was used as a symbol of mutilation. During this action Brus was arrested almost immediately by the police for being potentially disturbing to the public.

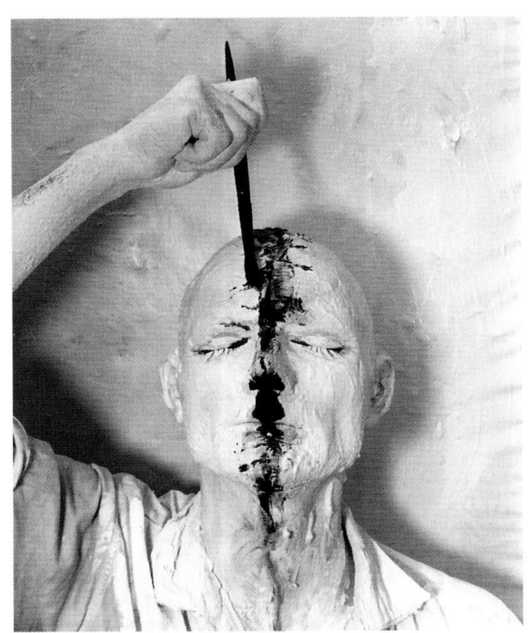

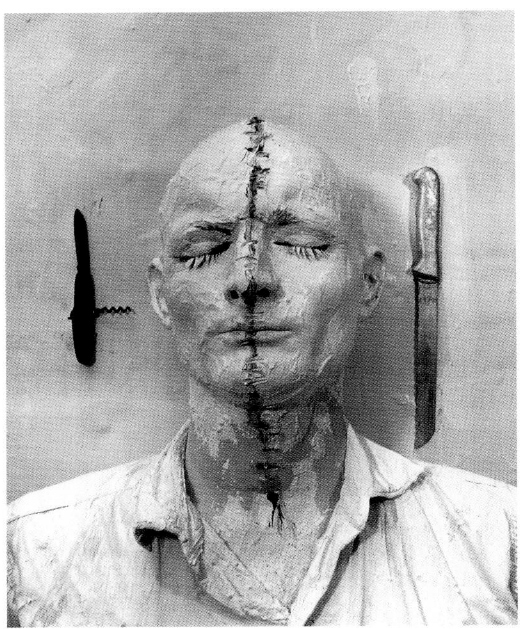

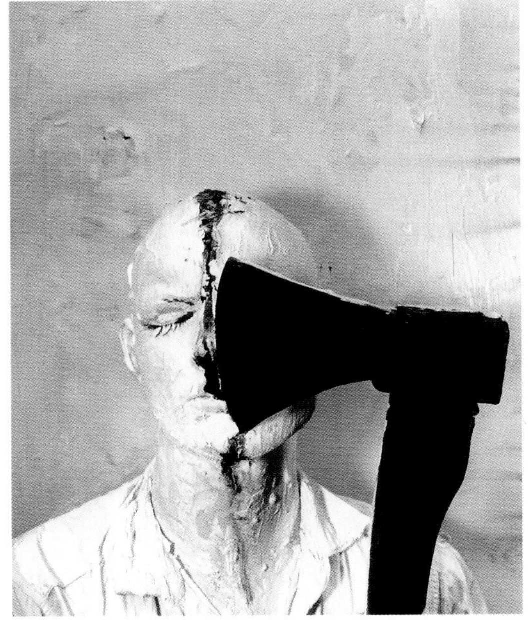

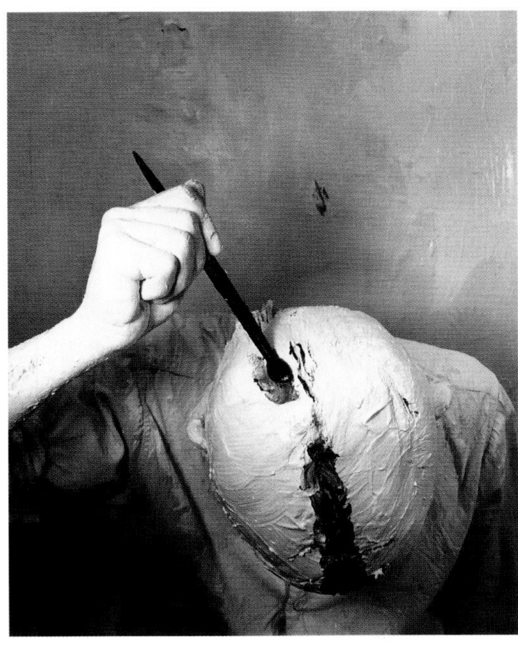

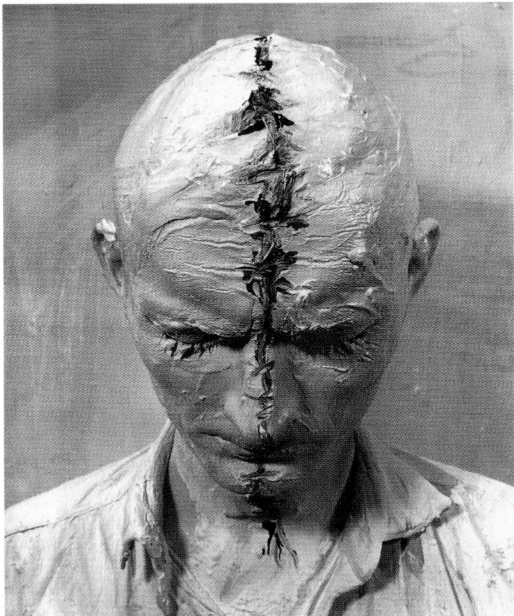

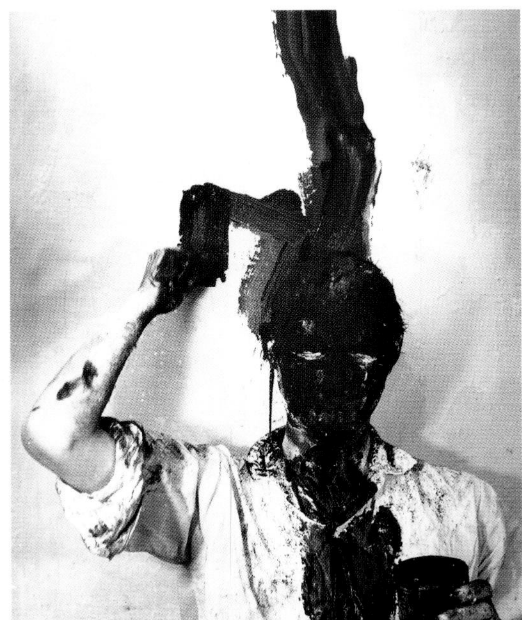

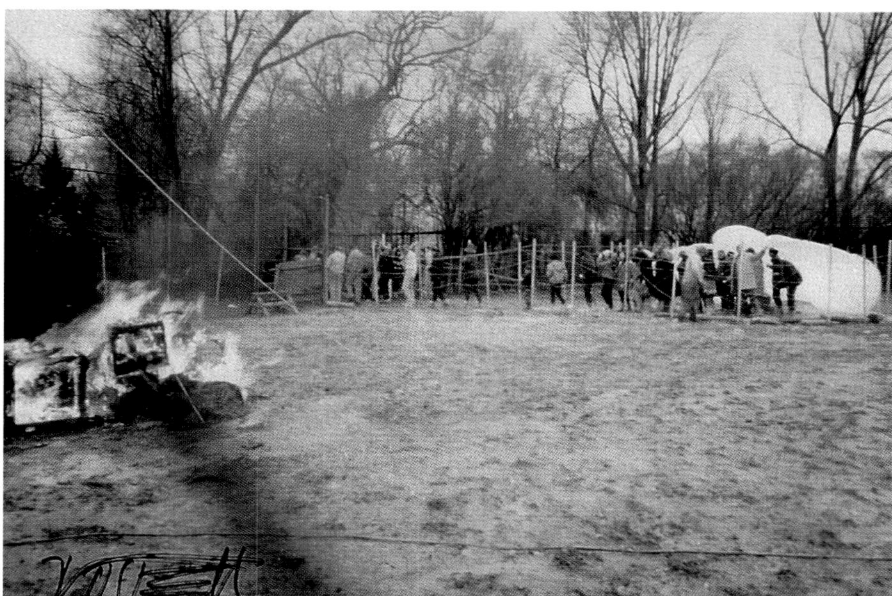

Wolf VOSTELL

You-Happening

1964

King's Point, New York

'The public ... is confronted by the most absurd and repugnant scenes of horror to awaken their consciousness ... Lying on a trampoline, Lette Eisenhauer is enveloped in a transparent, flesh-toned garment upon which are painted the female parts. Two huge beef lungs beside her bounce ... Instructions to the people: please find your way to the swimming pool, either crawling or walking. At the pool, take a pistol filled with colour. Please crawl into the swimming pool. Lie down on the bottom of the pool and build a mass grave. While lying there, decide whether or not you will shoot the other people with the colour ... Put on a gas mask when the TV burns and try to be as friendly as possible to everyone.'

– Wolf Vostell quoted by Allan Kaprow, *Assemblage, Environments and Happenings*, 1966

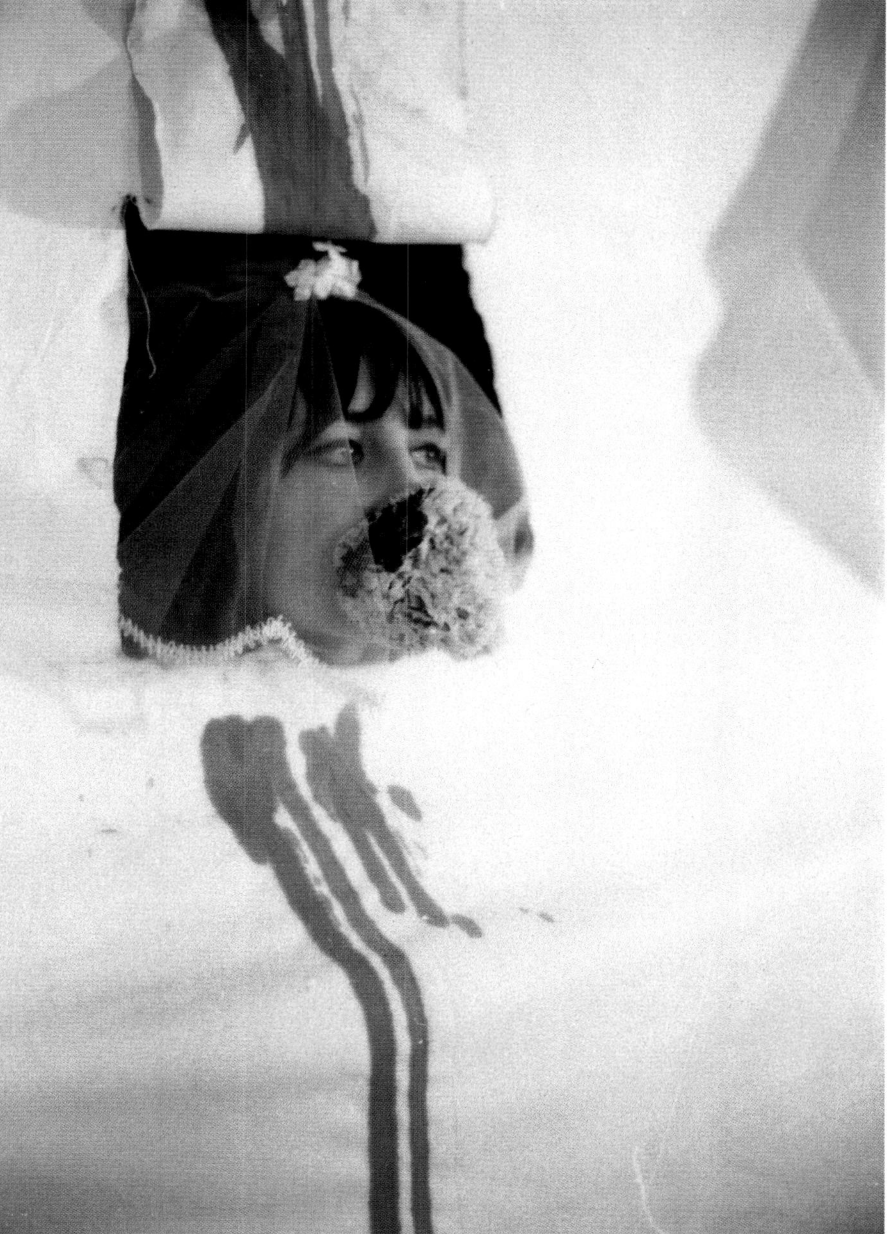

Rudolf SCHWARZKOGLER

Action 1: Wedding

1965

Vienna

Schwarzkogler, Heinz Cibulka and Annie Brus posed for a series of tableaux involving dead fish and chickens, a variety of medical instruments, cosmetic utensils and bright blue paint inspired by Yves Klein's signature ultramarine. Schwarzkogler usually orchestrated his 'actions' specifically for the camera, although *Wedding* took place before invited guests and was conceived of as a 'painting-action'. The resulting photographs record deliberately fictionalized tableaux of enigmatic ritual and symbol along with naturalistic and recognizable gestures. The complex and ambiguous language of objects and actions appearing in the clinical environment of Schwarzkogler's highly aestheticized images communicates an uneasy disjunction of cold formalism with physical and emotional distress. The action was a staging of art-making activity as a means for personal and social redemption, which was expressed through an enigmatic ceremony for cathartic effect.

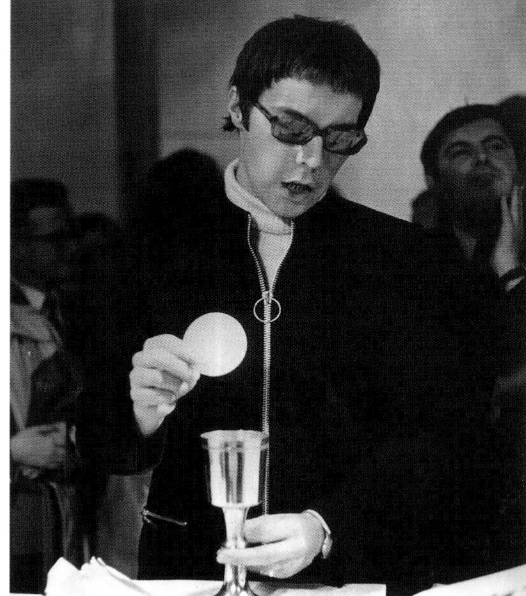

Michel JOURNIAC

Messe pour un corps (Mass for a body)

1969

Paris

During this action, Journiac extracted blood from his own body, which he later used to make *Blood Sausage* (1969). The photographic documentation of this event and the recipe for the sausage were exhibited at the Galerie Stadler, Paris. Journiac explored the possibilities of salvation and liberation from social/sexual restrictions on the body through extreme and often physically painful actions located within the ritualistic traditions of French Catholic society. By presenting himself as both the recipient of the sacrament and the sacrament itself, giving his real blood in place of the metaphoric blood of Christ, Journiac re-presented the artist's body as object of social consumption (particularly by the art world) but also as source of spiritual healing.

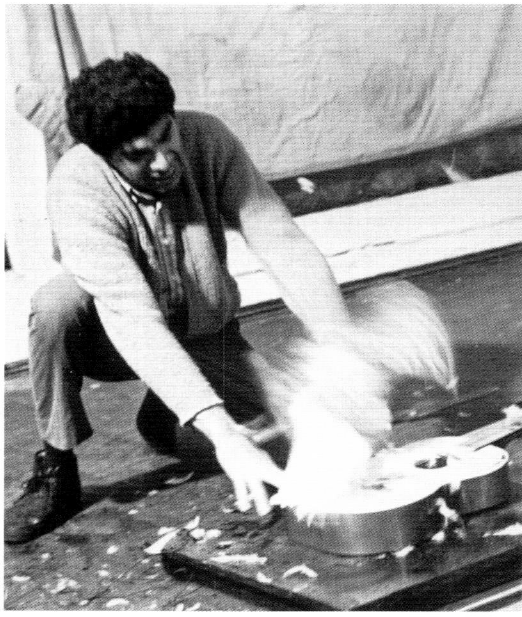

Rafael Montañez ORTIZ

The Birth and Death of White Henny

1967

New York

Ortiz performed a series 'Destruction Ritual Realizations' in which he destroyed objects of furniture such as mattresses, chairs and pianos as part of his theory of destruction as a creative psychological and physical process. He enacted several versions of a birthing and destruction ritual in which he produced a live chicken from the inflated pregnant belly of a female performer. After showing the chicken to the audience, he would tie it by the feet to a rope from the ceiling, and swing it around before snipping off its head with a pair of shears. He would then beat the carcass to shreds on a Flamenco guitar. Finally, the chicken's head was slipped into a plastic bag secreted in the fly of his trousers. Ortiz introduced the ritual destruction of chickens (and later mice) into his performances in a search for a 'more visceral way to relate to art', communicating an intense urgency about the need to unmask and dissolve unconscious repressions – the undercurrent of violence present in family life and social structures. 'Destruction has no place in society – it belongs in our dreams, it belongs to art.'

– Rafael Montañez Ortiz, Artist's statement, 1988

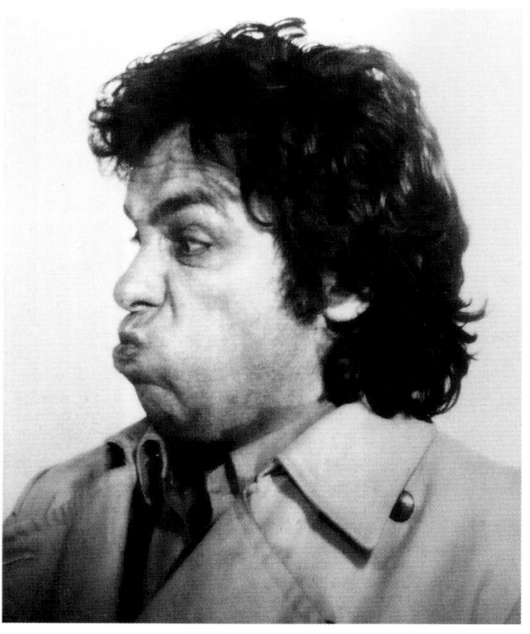

Arnulf RAINER

Face Farces

1969

Black and white photographs

24 × 18 cm [9.5 × 7 in]

During 1968 and 1969 Rainer made regular late-night visits to the photo-booth at his local railway station capturing a series of distorted expressions. 'After a quick glass of wine under the suspicious glances of policemen at the counter, I went to work. A certain feeling of excitement was necessary; an abundance of expression in the facial muscles and nerves. I talked myself into this state all day ...' Rainer explained that he was seeking to locate and express hidden parts of himself.

'Facial tension and physiognomical expressive strain imply not only a formalistic change of character, communication-addiction and nervous exertion, but also a summoning of dormant, or psychopathic, reserves of energy ... These anti-yoga tragi-comic poses, mannered clowneries and tired gestures without grace, chic or charm do not ask for a harmonious physical expression, but for a search for the unlimited possibilities and the unlikely people who are concealed in all of us.'

– Arnulf Rainer, *Face Farces*, 1971

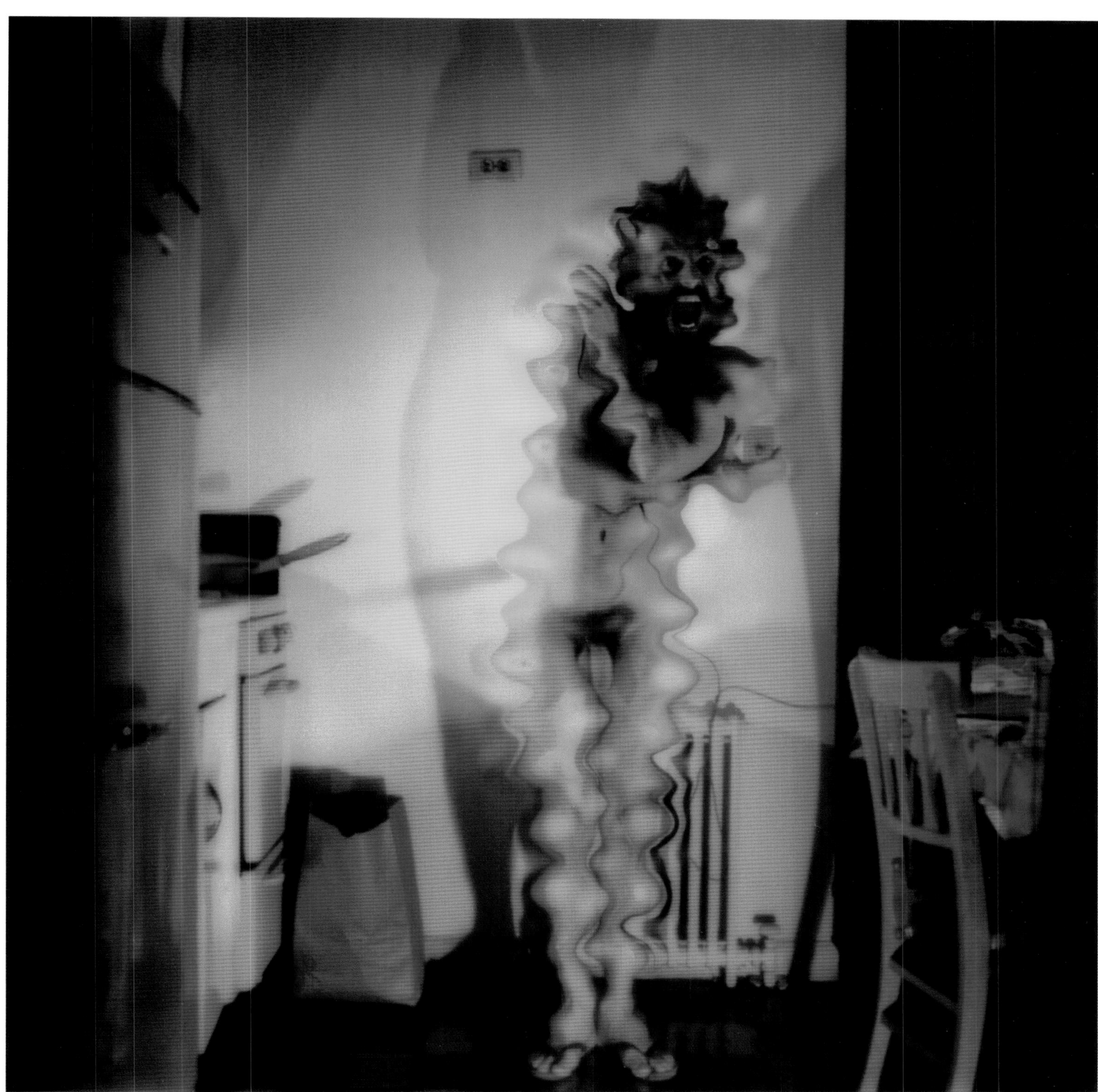

Lucas SAMARAS
Photo-Transformation
1974
SX-70 Polaroid photograph
7.5 × 7.5 cm [3 × 3 in]

Samaras made several series of auto-portraits using a Polaroid camera in which his body appeared distorted or fractured, representing differing states of mind and the effects of his internal forces. Alone in his kitchen with a camera, Samaras was able to break down the barriers of self-censorship. The immediacy of the Polaroid helped him to fuse the immediate surfacing of his subconsious into his conscious and a direct (symbolic) reunification of the mind-body split. In this series of 'photo-transformations' Samaras manipulated the prints by manually blending photo emulsion pigments with a kind of expressionistic finger painting.

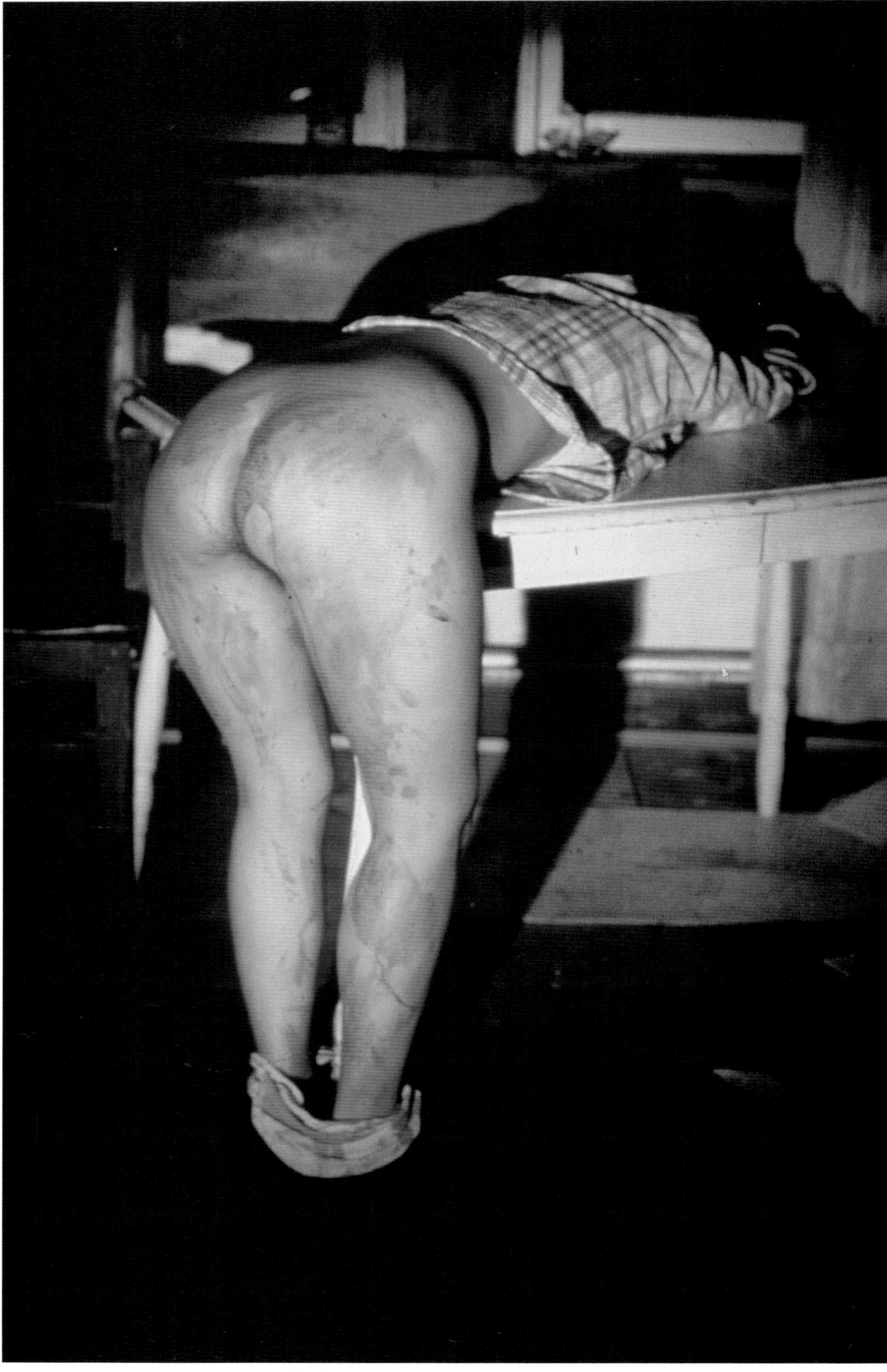

Ana MENDIETA
Rape Scene
1973
Moffit Street, Iowa City, Iowa

Mendieta performed several actions around the subject of rape following an incident on the Iowa University campus where a fellow student had been raped and murdered. She invited friends and fellow students to visit her at her own apartment in Moffit Street, Iowa City. Finding the apartment door slightly open, the visitors entered a darkened room in which a single light illuminated the artist stripped from the waist down, smeared with blood and stretched over and bound to the table. Broken plates and blood lay on the floor beside her. Mendieta later recalled in an interview how the incident had moved and frightened her.

Her direct identification with a specific victim meant that she could not be seen as an anonymous object in a theatrical tableau. Her performance presented the specificity of rape, through which she hoped to break the code of silence that renders it anonymous and general, denying the particular and the personal.

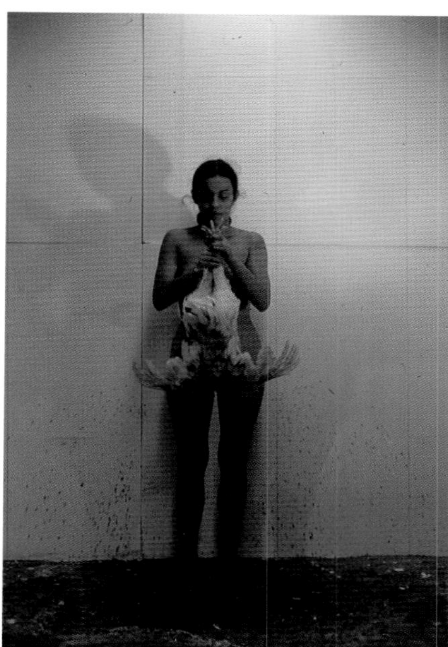

Ana MENDIETA
Death of a Chicken
1972
University of Iowa, Iowa City

Mendieta stood naked, holding a chicken that had just been beheaded. She held the chicken tightly by the legs, away from her body, so that its neck dangled in front of her pubis. Its body jerked about in her hands and, as she closed her eyes, the death throes of the chicken reverberated through her and the blood spurted across her own body. This was one of her earliest performances documented in super-8 film, re-enacting the Cuban Santería ritual of purification through bloodletting, in which a chicken is sacrificed and its blood used to signify initiation into the community. The identification of her female body with that of the sacrificed chicken presents Mendieta as a victim of a social sacrifice, crossing the threshold of social civility with a taboo in which the cultural violence done to her both as a woman and as a Cuban national is symbolized in an overt scene of violation and death.

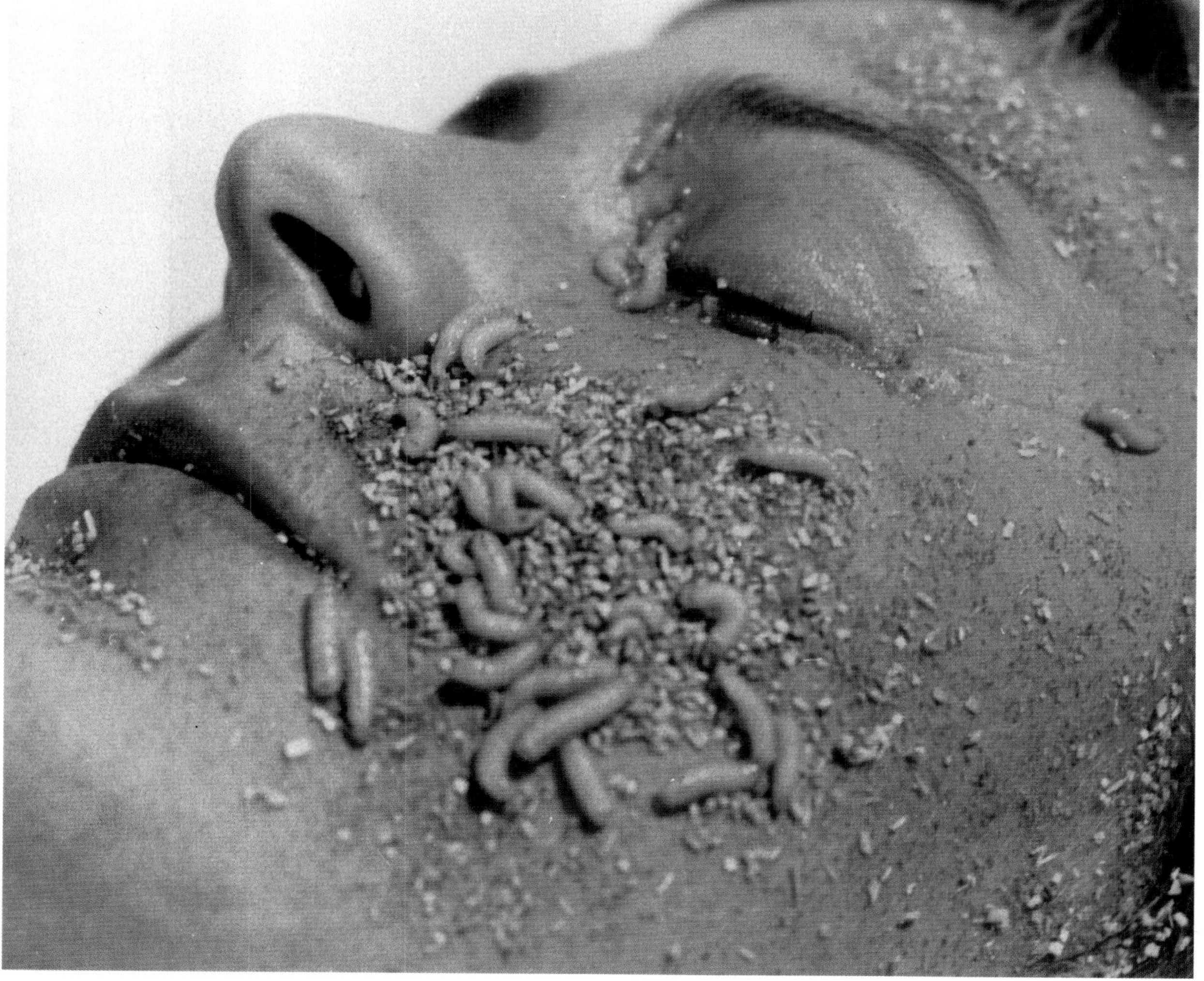

Gina PANE
Death Control
1974
Paris

Two video monitors simultaneously transmitted different images. On the first video tape: 'I was living in posthumous time. Covered with maggots, my flesh detached by maggots: flesh of my flesh, two fleshes living together, one nourishing itself from the other: process of life in a continuum of time. The other video tape showed the event of a birthday experienced by children who were destroying a cake. So it was the juxtaposition of two kinds of time: the time of death and the day we celebrate every year with a party which marks the approach to death ... Death has become a taboo, an intolerable fact, because the dialogue with death begins at birth, so we must meet it with a heightened awareness.'

– Gina Pane, Artist's statement, 1974

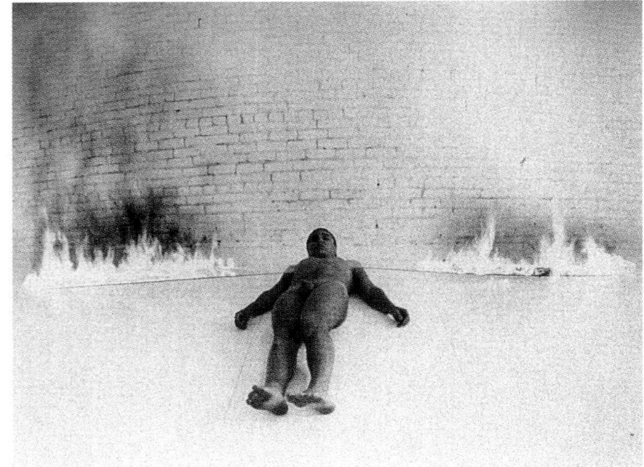

Chris BURDEN
Icarus
1973
Venice, California

Performed for only three spectators in the artist's studio, *Icarus* presented a modern-day inversion of the ancient myth about a failed attempt to fly. Naked, Burden entered the space and stood in the centre while his assistants lifted two 2-m [6-ft] -long sheets of plate glass to his shoulders, propping them at right angles to his body on the floor. They then poured gasoline over the sheets of glass. Stepping back, they lit matches and threw them at the glass 'wings' to ignite the gasoline. 'After a few seconds I jumped up, sending the burning glass crashing to the floor.'
– Chris Burden, *Beyond the Limits*, 1996

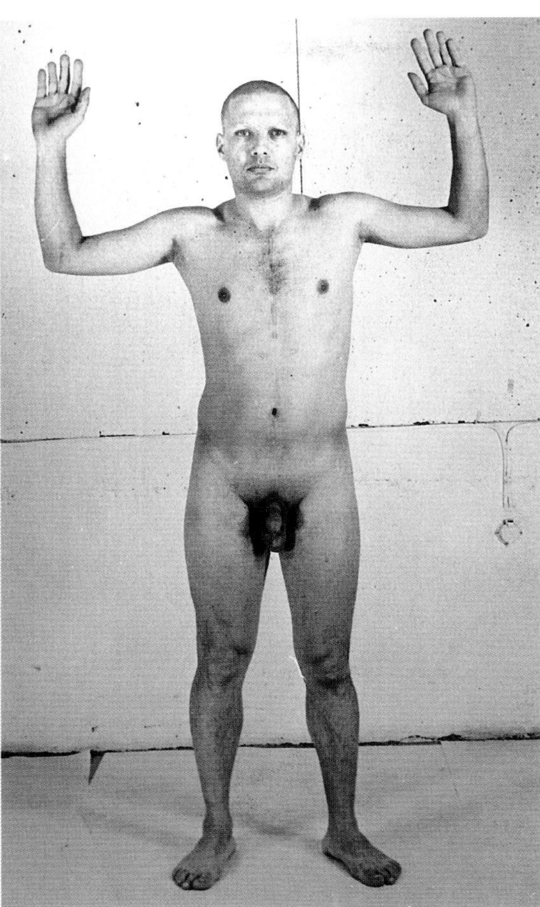

Gideon GECHTMAN
Naked
1974
Black and white photograph, plywood
122 × 103.5 cm [48 × 41 in]

In 'Exposure' at the Yudfath Gallery, Tel Aviv, Gechtman exhibited documentation from an operation he had undergone the previous year to replace a valve in his heart. A kind of personal confession, it violated the unwritten rules of silence surrounding illness. As curator Gideon Ofrat has written: 'Gechtman invites us to peep into a world which unites life and death simultaneously. Death is seen as part of life, disintegration as part of construction. He does not lament, he does not scream in terror. His exhibitions are attempts at reconciliation – because there is no alternative – to this existential condition.'
– Gideon Ofrat, 'The Heart of the Matter', 1986

opposite
Chris BURDEN
Trans-Fixed
1974
Venice, California

Burden stood on the rear bumper of a blue Volkswagen Beetle, laying his body on the car and stretching his arms over the roof. Nails were driven through his palms and the car was pushed from the small garage out on to the street. For two minutes the engine was run at full speed, 'screaming' for the artist, before the car was rolled back into the garage. Burden punned on religious-spiritual experience, countering the intensely emotional resonances of the word 'transfixed' with a live physical enactment of a real transfixion in the form of a crucifixion. Placing himself in a quasi-religious context, Burden presented himself as a modern martyr to contemporary consumerism as represented by the cars in California's burgeoning freeway culture.
'I often think of myself as sort of training for some sort of – you know, outer space programme. I mean, I feel like, in some way, I've done some of the same things.'
– Chris Burden, 'Interview with Robin White', 1978

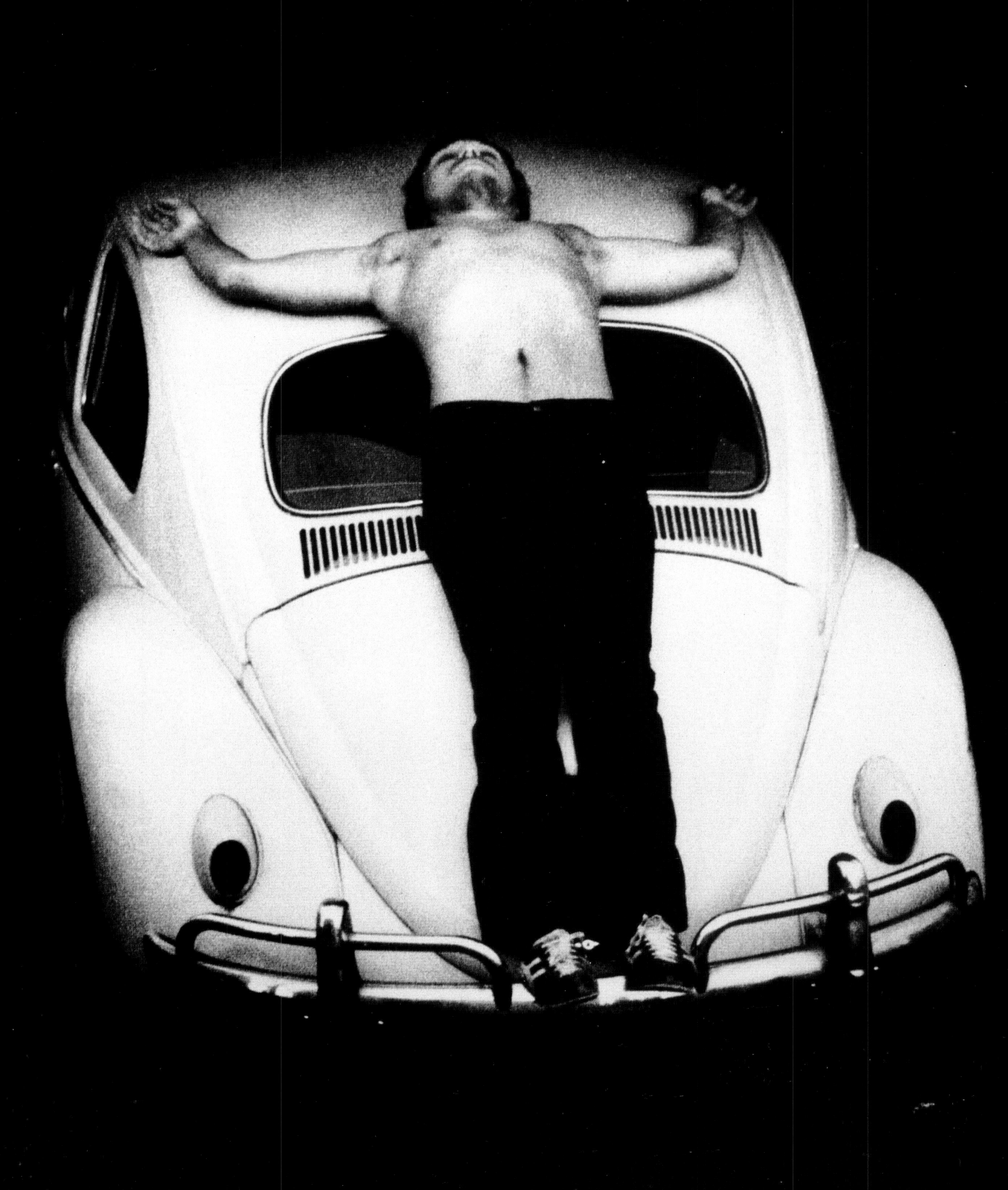

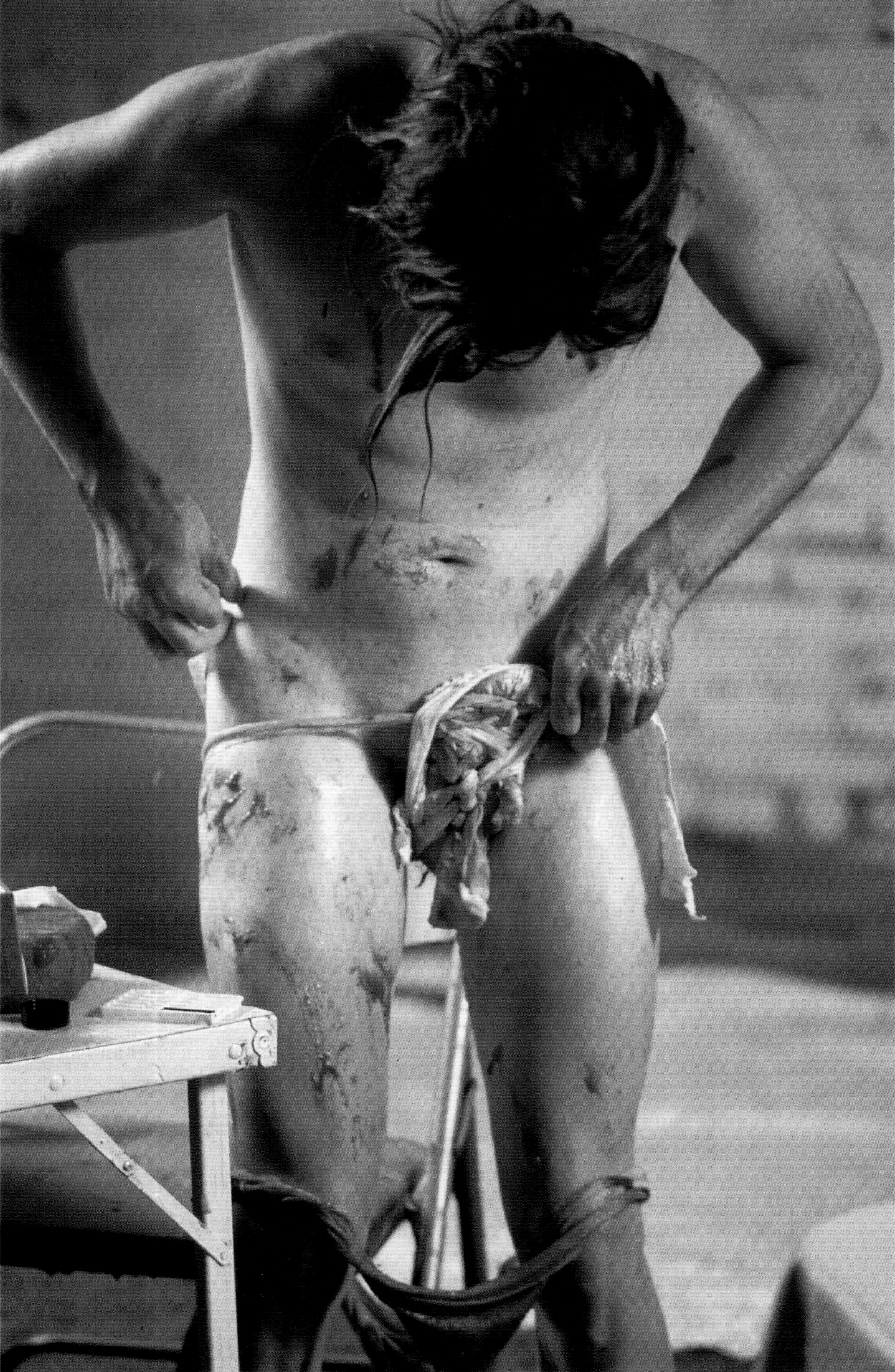

Paul McCARTHY
Hot Dog
1974
Oddfellows Temple, Pasadena, California

Hot Dog was one of McCarthy's earliest performances enacting masochistic culinary rituals. McCarthy stripped and shaved his body in front of a small group of friends in his basement studio. Artist Barbara Smith, present at the event, reported:

'He [then] stuffs his penis into a hotdog bun and tapes it on, then smears his ass with mustard ... He approaches the tables and sits nearby, drinking ketchup and stuffing his mouth with hot dogs ... Binding his head with gauze and adding more hot dogs, he finally tapes his bulging mouth closed so that the protruding mouth looks like a snout ... He stands alone struggling with himself, trying to prevent his own retching. It is apparent that he is about to vomit ... Should he vomit he might choke to death, since the vomit would have no place to go. And should any one of us vomit, we might trigger him to do likewise ... '
– Barbara Smith, 'Paul McCarthy', 1979

McCarthy presented the artist's body constrained and tortured, as an allegory of social conditioning and sexual oppression. Sealing himself off after stuffing himself with food, he can neither digest, nor expel what threatens to suffocate him.

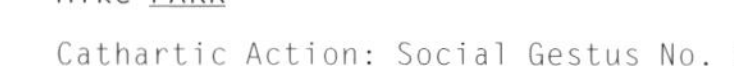

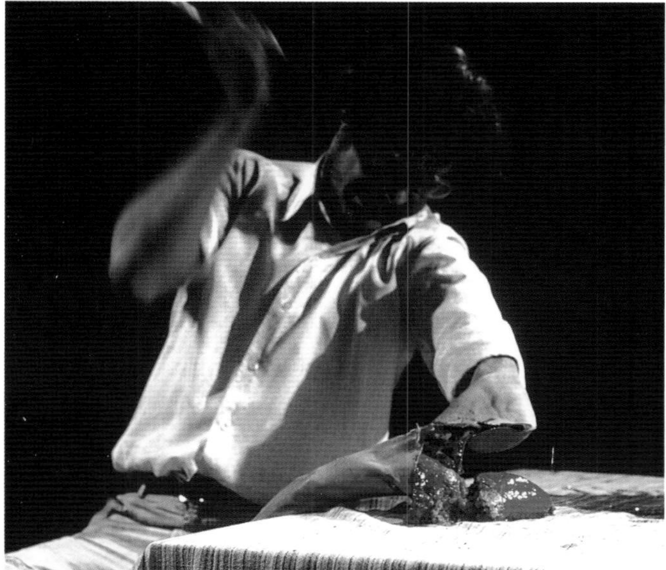

Mike PARR

Cathartic Action: Social Gestus No. 5

1977

10th Paris Biennale

Believing himself to be suffering from a kind of 'social autism' brought about by his relationship with his father and his physical disability (his left arm is amputated below the elbow), Parr made a performance for the 10th Paris Biennale (1977), which 'was about the way in which my disability ... has structured my relationship with my father and how that structure has emerged in my relationship with my wife and daughter. I played again a soundtape that had been fortuitously made as my father and I sat one cold afternoon in the mountains discussing the past and my childhood. The conversation became very intense. Accusations flew back and forth and at the end my father and I were in tears. While I listened to this tape I again cut off my arm (I wore a prosthesis and used a meat cleaver). It was simple, cathartic, but it also dramatized a problem as old as the generations.'
– Mike Parr, Artist's statement, 1977

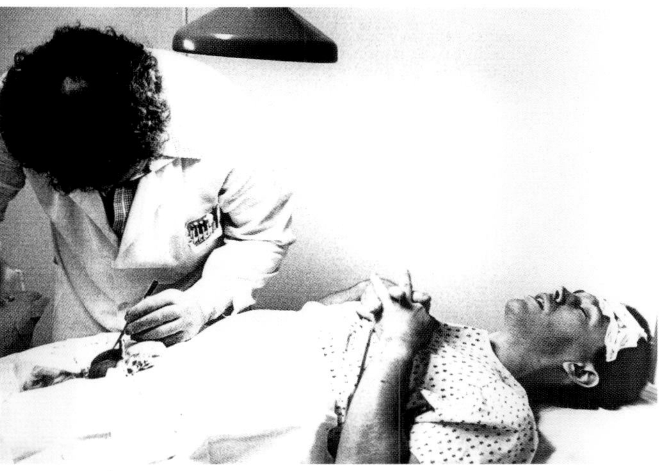

John DUNCAN

Blind Date

1980

California

Duncan bought a female corpse in Mexico and recorded himself performing sexual intercourse with it. Following this experience of 'indescribable intense self-disgust' he returned to California to have a vasectomy in order 'to make sure that the last potent seed I had was spent in a cadaver'. After the operation which he had photographed, he arranged a showing of *Blind Date* in order to explain to the public 'what can happen to men that are trained to ignore their emotions'. A tragic portrayal of masculine impotence, *Blind Date* conflated the traditionally powerful white male as embodied by the artist with his psychological state of disempowerment and death as represented by the lifeless woman he violated. 'I risked the ability to accept myself. I risked the ability to have sex ... and the ability to love.'
– John Duncan, 'Sex with the Dead', 1981

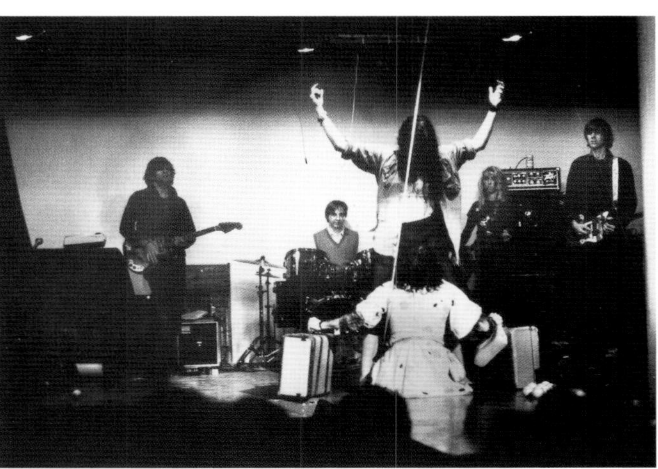

Mike KELLEY

Plato's Cave, Rothko's Chapel, Lincoln's Profile

1986

Artists Space, New York

Kelley's performance at Artists Space, New York, was an attack on the social veneration of history, art and patriotism. The artist adopted the persona of a rock star, haranguing the audience with ranting texts he had written. His tirade, in which he called out the names of states – Arkansas, Florida, Louisiana, etc. – where caves exist, was punctuated by slamming, banging sounds and by a wall of guitar sound produced by the band Sonic Youth, who were concealed behind a curtain on the stage. Kelley also used word association during his rant about sexual liberation which he linked to freedom ('Abraham Lincoln freed the slaves'). He proclaimed he was free, free to be himself, free to take his trousers off, free to play with dolls. The whole action was punctuated by the sound of rock guitars.

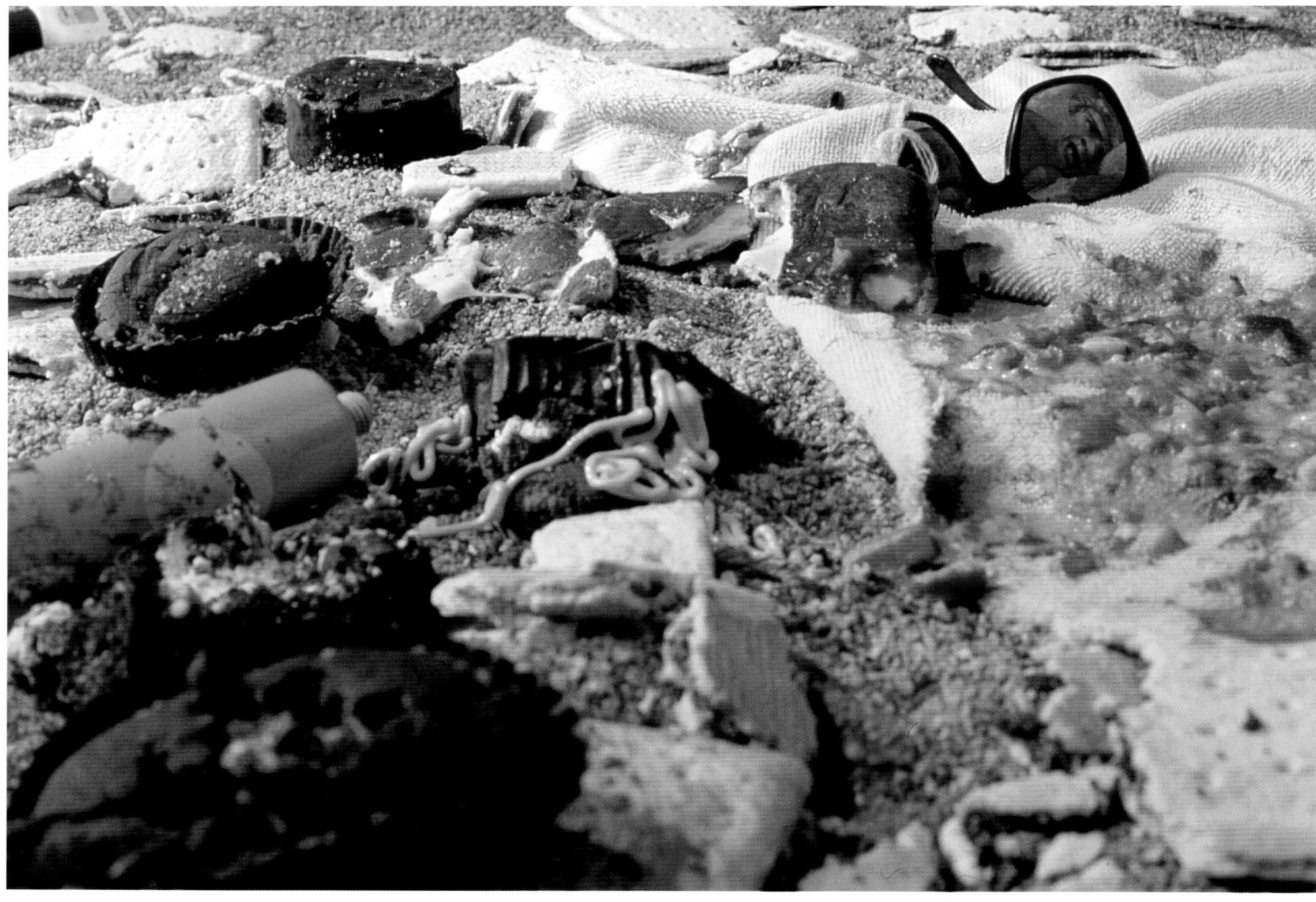

Cindy SHERMAN
Untitled No. 175
1987
Colour photograph
181.5 × 120.5 cm [71.5 × 47.5 in]

Sherman appears as a reflection in a pair of sunglasses, an abused figure, perhaps even a corpse. The pool of vomit issuing from the sunglasses, which are lying in a destroyed landscape, suggests that it is her body that has caused the destruction. Invited by a magazine to make a series of photographs based on fairy tales, Sherman created gruesome images of fantastic hybrid creatures, part doll, part human, grotesquely deformed, fragmented, horrifically grinning, grimacing or with the glazed stare of the dead. Her scenes of excess and abuse critique media images of woman as an object for consumption. All consumption of commodities relating to the body is denied. The food does not look as though it has been consumed, but rather trodden underfoot and crushed, or broken up and thrown about. Similarly, the female body suggested by the face in the lens has already been debased, during a (fictional) narrative that occurred before the moment depicted.

opposite
Andres SERRANO
Piss Christ (detail)
1987
Cibachrome, silicone, Plexiglas
152 × 102 cm [60 × 40 in]

In this photograph a crucifix is immersed in a glass tank filled with Serrano's urine. The title provides a deliberate provocation, linking the sacred with the profane. Serrano uses photography to play with reality and representation: 'The camera lies, it also tells the truth: that's the beautiful contradiction.'
– Andres Serrano, 'In Conversation with Simon Watney', 1993

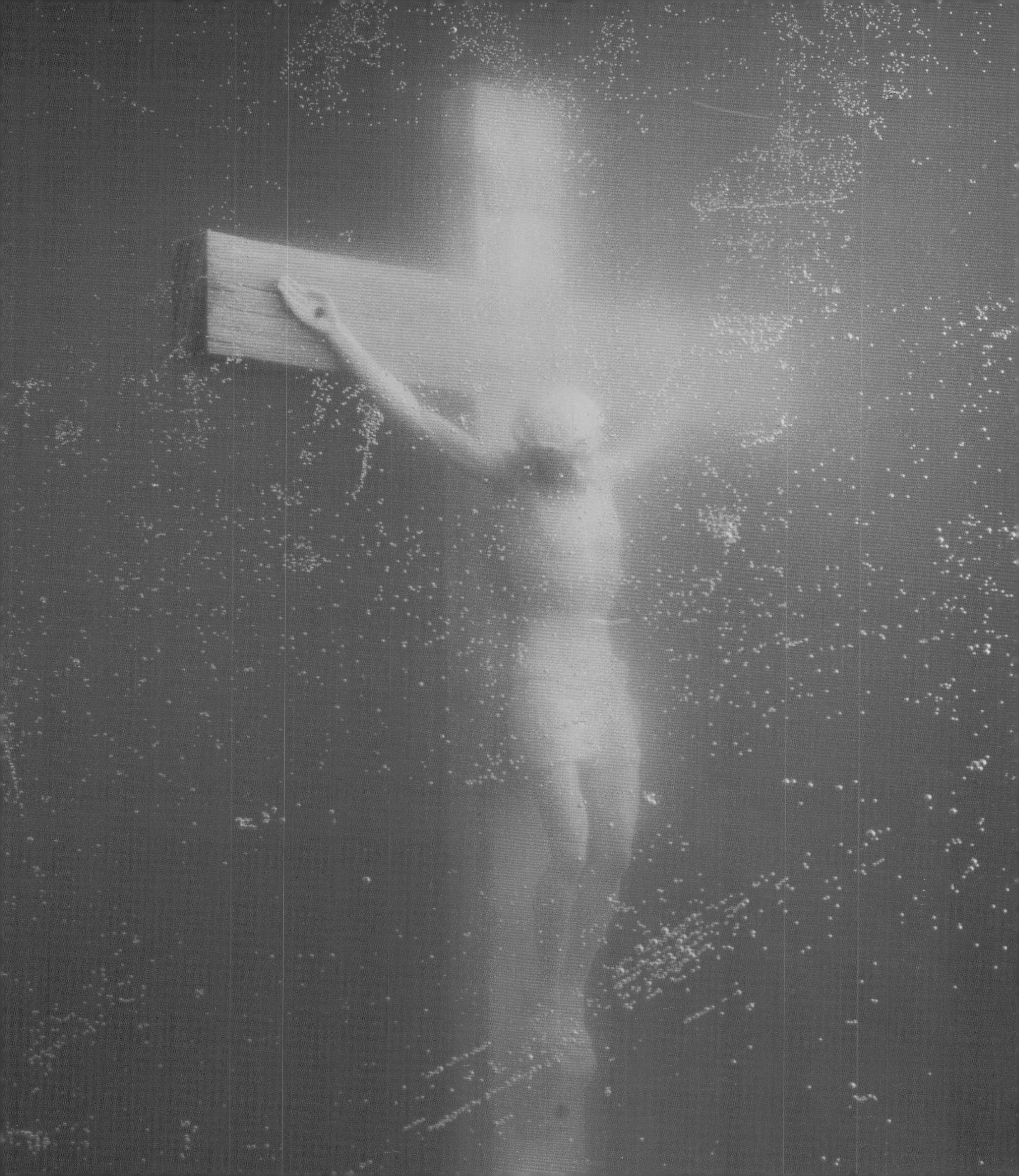

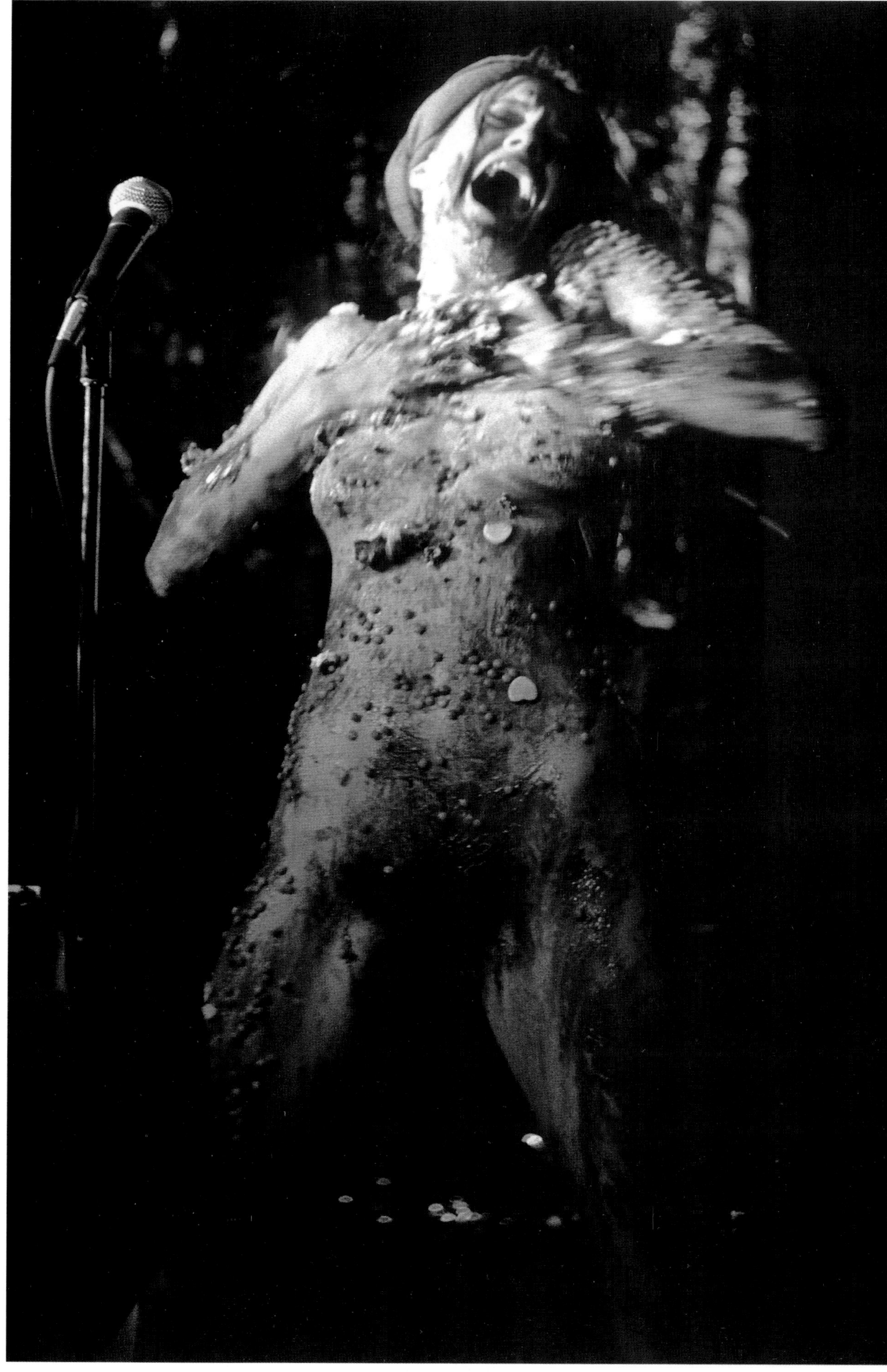

Karen FINLEY

We Keep Our Victims Ready

1989

New York

We Keep Our Victims Ready was partly inspired by the case of a sixteen year-old girl who was found in a trash bag smeared with her own faeces. 'I was so taken by the fact that everyone was blaming [her] and saying that she smeared the faeces on herself. I felt putting chocolate on myself would represent the situation she was in. Then I put on red heart candies to show how, after you're treated like shit, you're loved more. I sprinkle alfalfa sprouts because after you are treated like shit, you're jerked off on. For thousands of years women have been treated like this, but they still know how to dress for dinner.' – Karen Finley, *Uncommon Sense*, 1997

Finley has made performances using her body as a visual field on which fear, desire and violence are projected in order to challenge prevailing attitudes towards women, sex and art. More recently her work has questioned notions of censorship and the rights of artists to speak out about issues such as sexual abuse, incest and the commodification of desire in Western capitalist societies.

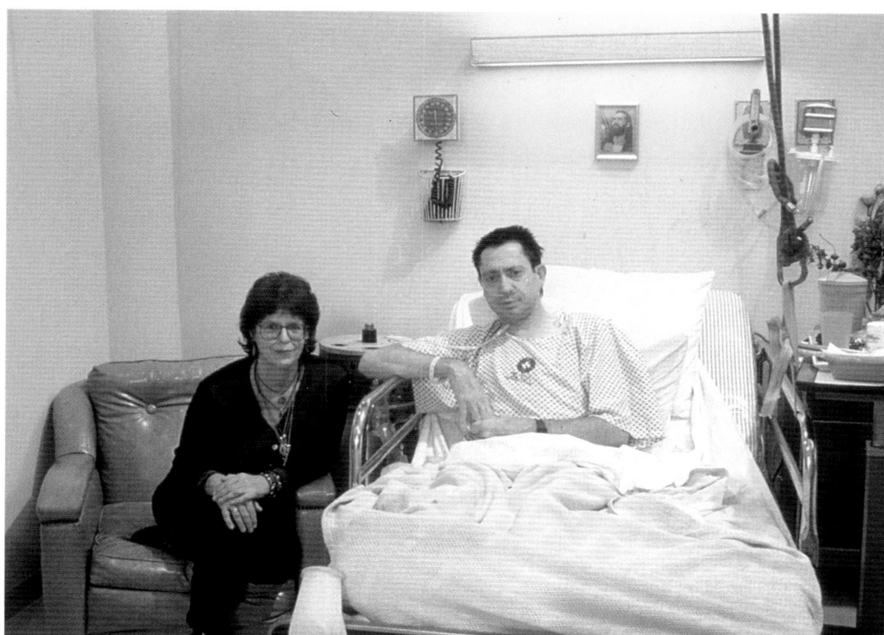

Bob <u>FLANAGAN</u> and Sheree <u>ROSE</u>

Visiting Hours

1992

Santa Monica Museum of Art, California

In *Visiting Hours*, a multimedia presentation of sculpture, video, photography and text set up in the Santa Monica Museum of Art, Flanagan played himself, sitting in a hospital bed and receiving the audience as if they were his visitors in a real hospital.

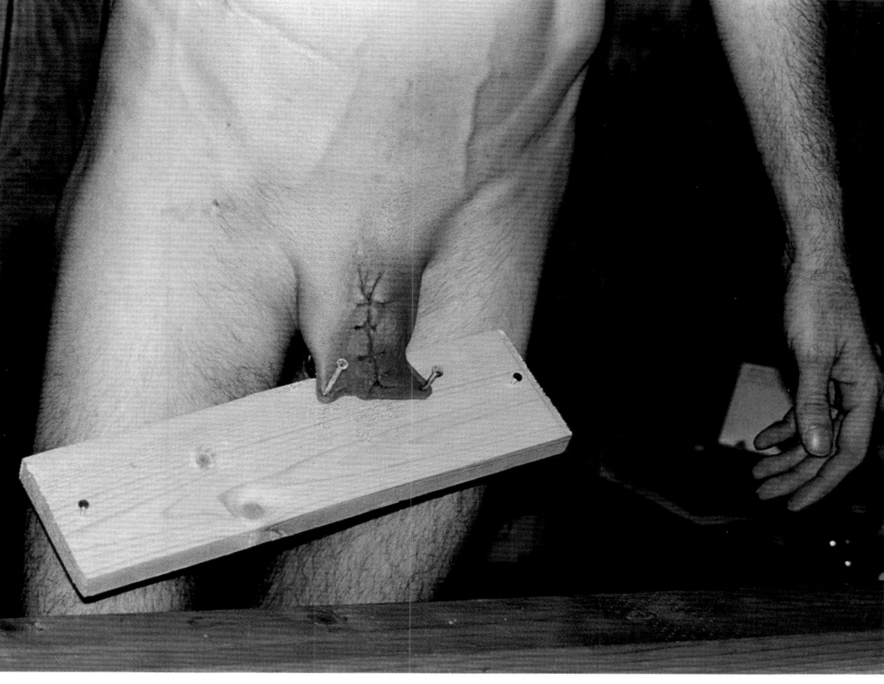

Bob <u>FLANAGAN</u>

Auto-Erotic SM

1989

Los Angeles

A life-long sufferer from cystic fibrosis, Flanagan began to make art in order both to explore and express his masochistic sexual desires, and to combat his physical pain. His ritual performances present his sick and suffering body as both object and subject, revealed objectively through its presentation in medical contexts as distanced and diseased, host to sickness, but also host to Flanagan's subjective self, which treated his situation with candid humour. He openly talked about and enacted the frequently painful S&M practices that provided him with release from his physical pain. With his partner Sheree Rose, Flanagan began to make public their private sexual rituals. The infamous performance *Auto-Erotic SM* began with a series of gory slides of Flanagan's medical condition, followed by the couple enacting various highly stylized S&M acts and concluded with Flanagan nailing his penis to a wooden board.

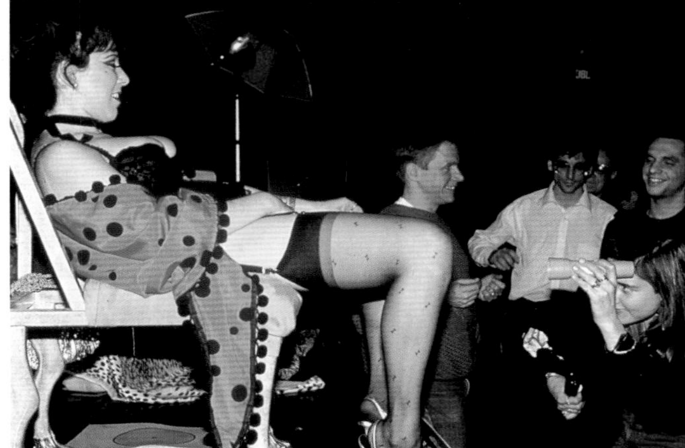

Annie SPRINKLE

Post-Porn Modernist Show

1992

New York

Self-styled 'feminist porn activist'. Sprinkle makes performances informed by her career in the sex industry, in which she worked as prostitute, stripper, porn writer, dominatrix and star of hard-core porn films. In *Post-Porn Modernist*, first performed in a lower-Manhattan burlesque theatre, she presented herself as the complete sex object, empowered by her sexuality. On stage, she talked about her various jobs in the porn industry and evaluated her years of work, illustrating her accomplishments with statistical graphs. The performance also involved Sprinkle masturbating to orgasm with a vibrator. After douching she inserted a speculum and invited the audience to come and look at her cervix, inverting the power relations between subject and object.

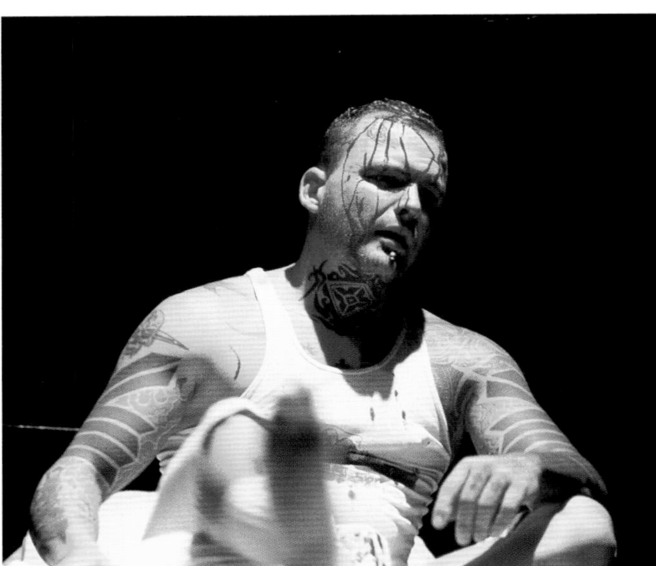

Ron ATHEY

4 Scenes in a Harsh Life

1994

P.S. 122, New York

Raised by Christian fundamentalists and trained to become a pentecostal minister, Athey describes his work as an exploration of fetishism in the service of healing. A series of autobiographical performances staged at P.S. 122, New York, *4 Scenes in a Harsh Life* connects religious fanaticism with pain and suffering, ritualized through body piercing and scarification. In *Suicide/Tattoo Salvation* Athey, who is HIV positive, inserted a series of hyperdermic needles into his arm from wrist to shoulder and then jabbed a 15-cm [6-in] -long needle through his scalp as his history of depression, heroin addiction and suicide attempts was described to the audience. In another part of the performance the artist sliced a design into the back of a collaborator and displayed the resulting blood-prints as art. This was a repeat of a performance of the previous year at the Walker Arts Center, Minneapolis, which caused a scandal over NEA funding, provoked by the public health risk involved in blood-letting and the HIV virus. Athey's exposure of his personal damage through the staging of cathartic rituals raises issues about freedom, pleasure, pain, suffering, disease and survival.

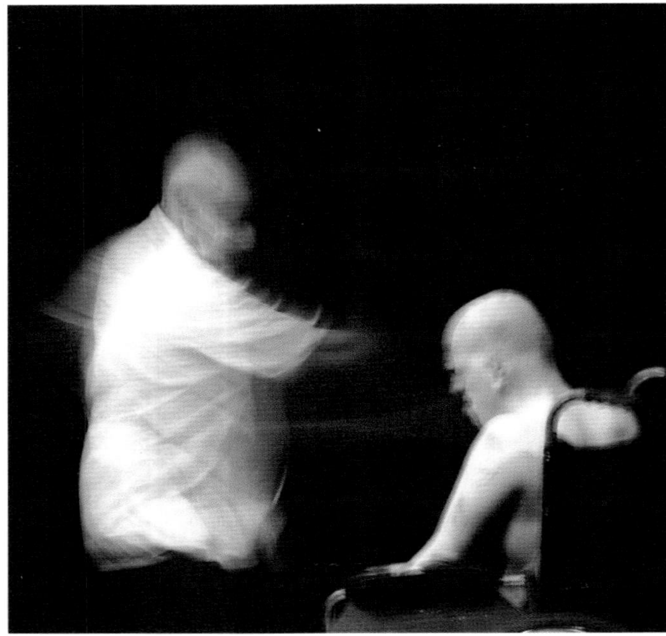

FRANKO B

Mama, I Can't Sing

1996

Institute of Contemporary Arts, London

Franko B started cutting his own skin in protest at a court ruling against the rights of gay adults to make videos of themselves performing sadomasochistic sex. He carved the word DEMOCRACY into his own body and FREEDOM into the skin of his lover. Subsequently, he began using blood in his live performances, which were recorded and shown in video installations and photographs. He reappears in these videos and photographs in different poses, creating dramatic portraits in which he enacts symbols of a degraded life – which the 'Franko B' body claims as his identity – wired to catheter bags, in a wheelchair, in a cage, his body kicked to the ground, repeatedly slapped in the face, on a trolley, covered with his own blood. Abject, naked, abused and smeared with blood and body fluids, the artist presents himself as the physical literalization of the ' ... violence, sadism, perversity, loneliness, desperation, isolation, alienation ... ' of contemporary life.

– Franko B, 'Interview with Dr Rachel Armstrong', 1996

Through the ritual opening-out of his abused and leaking body in degrading, violent activities, there is hope for healing, as the body becomes a metaphor for the violence done by the social body to those who challenge taboos.

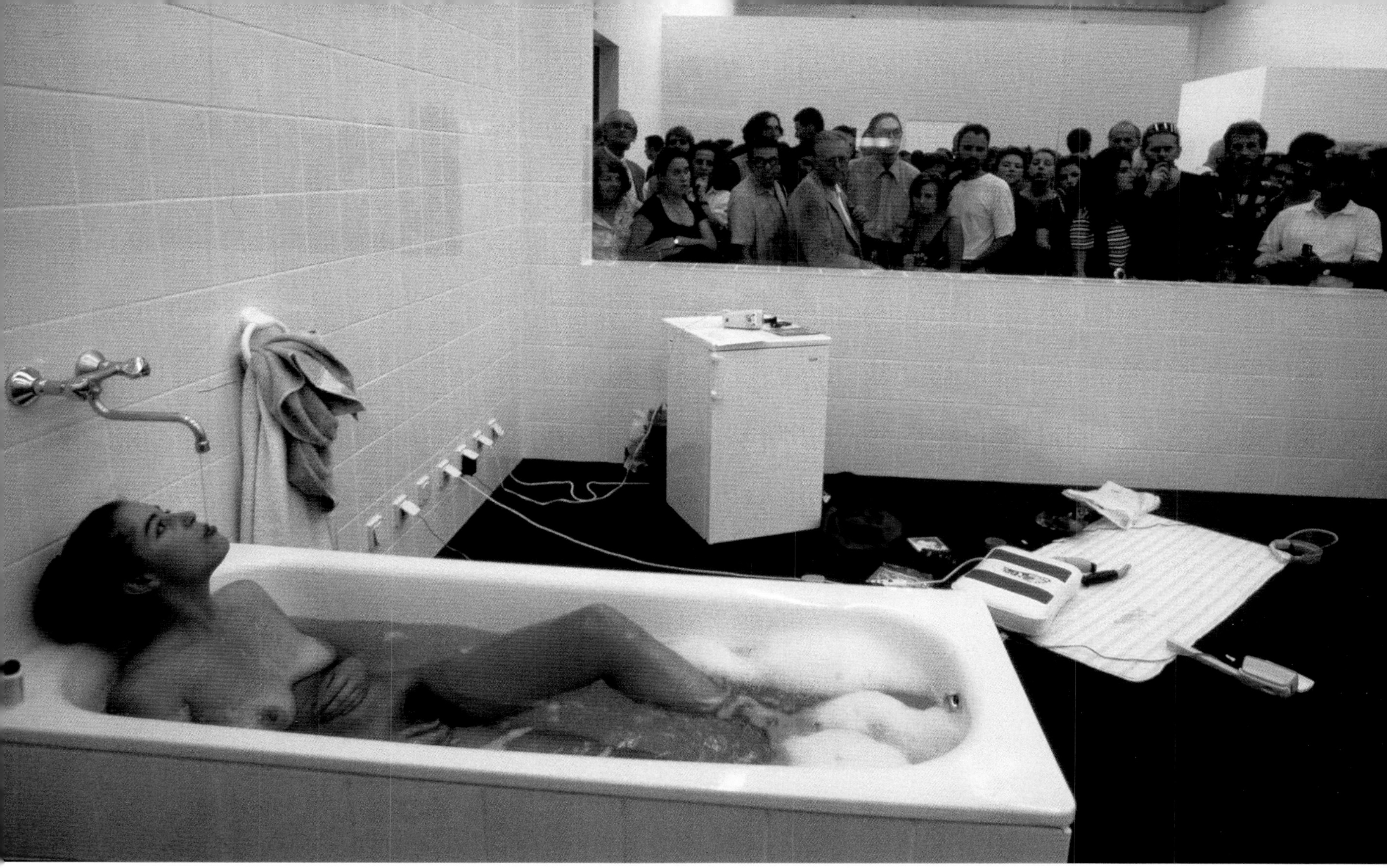

Elke KRYSTUFEK
Satisfaction
1996
Kunsthalle, Vienna

In a group show at the Kunsthalle, Vienna, Krystufek made a performance in which she first bathed and then lay on a mat on the floor and masturbated with a vibrator. By enacting her private rituals in a public space, she opened up issues of intimacy, authenticity and sensationalism, forcing the viewer to confront his/her own position as voyeur. Traditionally the subject matter of the male artist or photographer, the feminine subject glimpsed in her own space has a long history of romantic idealization. Krystufek presented this scenario as a premeditated action in a clinically white and non-erotic space, challenging both what is acceptable in an art venue, as well as who has control over how the intimate female body is observed. Staging self-nurture and pleasure through her own agency, she demonstrated a dynamic of looking that denies rather than creates personal intimacy with the body on display.

Marina ABRAMOVIĆ

Balkan Baroque

1997

XLVI Venice Biennale

Abramović presented this performance at the XLVI Venice Biennale (1997) as a gesture of mourning and healing for the civil wars in the Balkans. Bringing together her personal connection with the history of this community, Abramović enacted a metaphoric rite of passage in order to shed the pain of both her internal conflicts of character (which produce self-destructiveness) and the more generalized (but still intensely personal) tragedy of war. The artist and both her parents appeared on three large video screens in the installation. In a fusion of the theatrical with the real, opposing extremes of scientific rationality and wild emotional dance, masculine aggression and feminine vulnerability were depicted. Three copper bath-like structures filled with water provided a sense of ritual containment and healing. In the centre of the space Abramović sat on a huge pile of 1,500 beef bones, which she cleaned and scrubbed one by one for six hours every day, over five days, continuously singing fragments of folksongs she remembered from her childhood. Abramović described the performance as deeply traumatic.

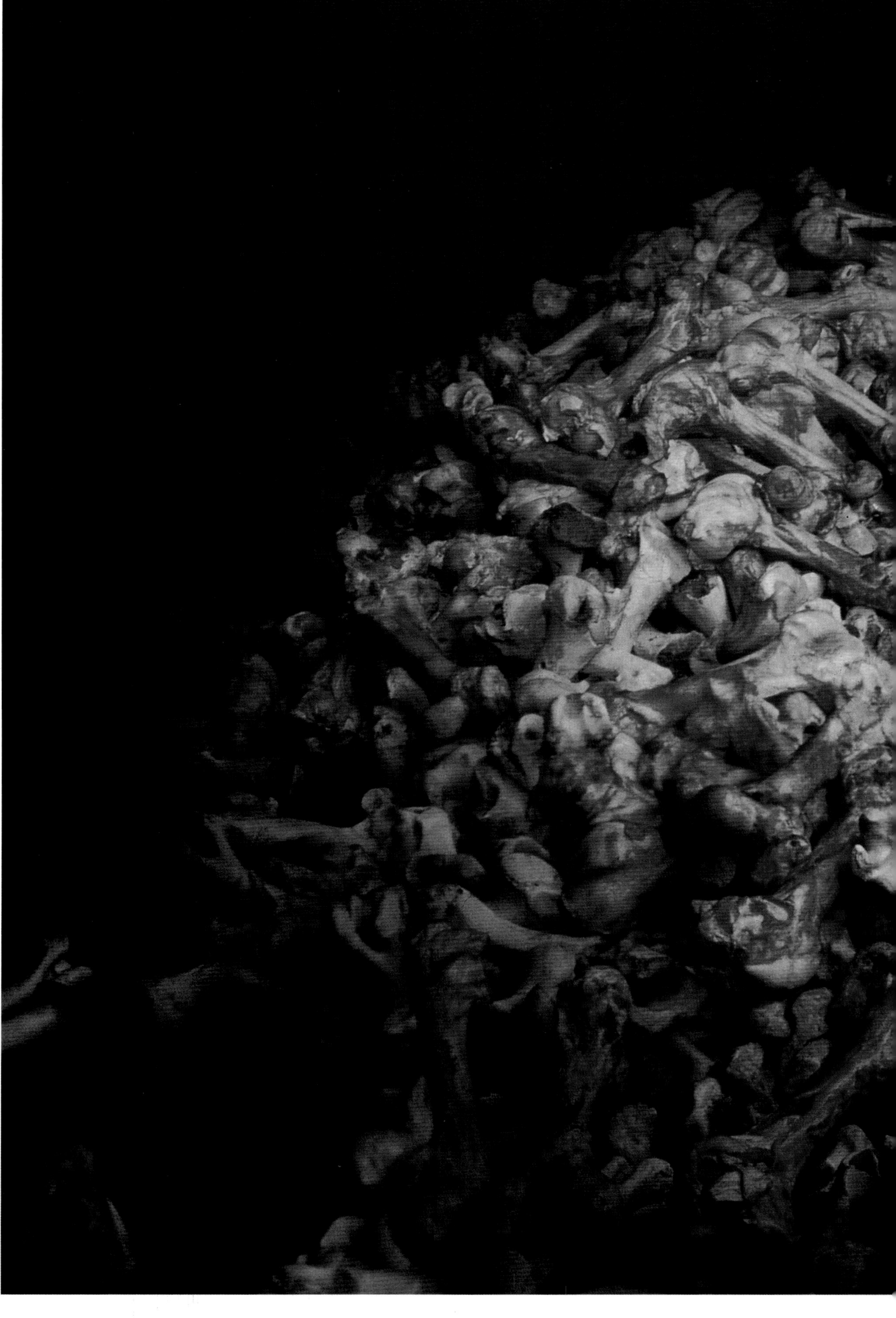

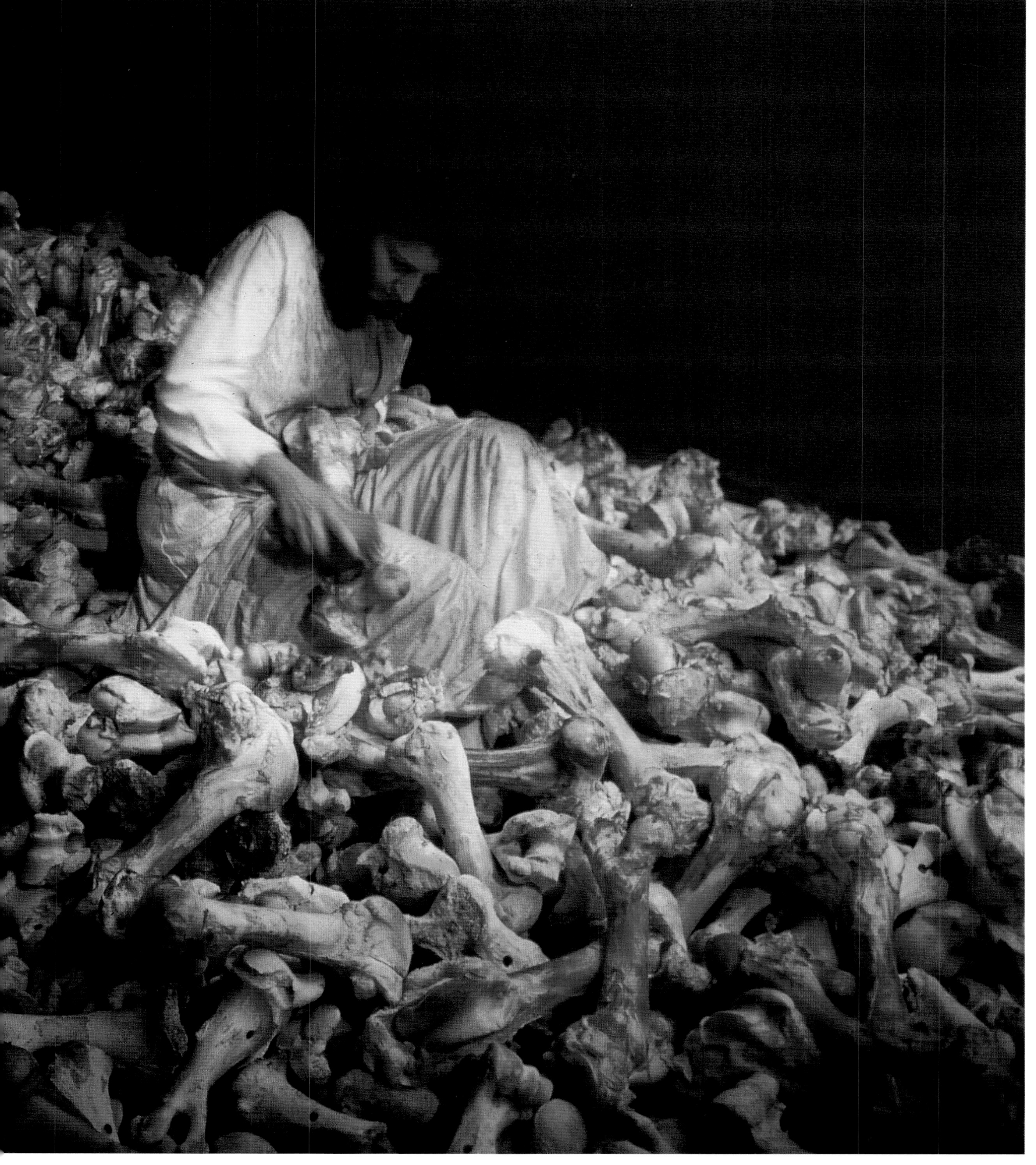

BODY BOUNDARIES

This chapter groups together artists whose work examines the boundaries between the body and its environment: between the individual body and the social or collective body, as well as between the interior and exterior of the body. The body is used as a site that can both be penetrated and that can penetrate – and transform – social spaces. What is considered acceptable on this site is indicative of the physical boundaries placed on the body as well as of the social limitations that constrict the body's behaviour. What is inflicted on the artist's body becomes a metaphor for what is inflicted on the social or collective body: the artist's body becomes a symbol. Frequently the physical (flesh) is a metaphor for the metaphysical (emotion). The work grouped here raises issues of power, control and intimacy regarding the liberties we can and cannot take with our own bodies. It also challenges the moral position of the viewer, who is sometimes given the opportunity to penetrate the boundaries of the artist's own body and explore the limits of his/her own behaviour. Finally, the very boundary between art and its audience – between art and life – is reduced and overtly challenged.

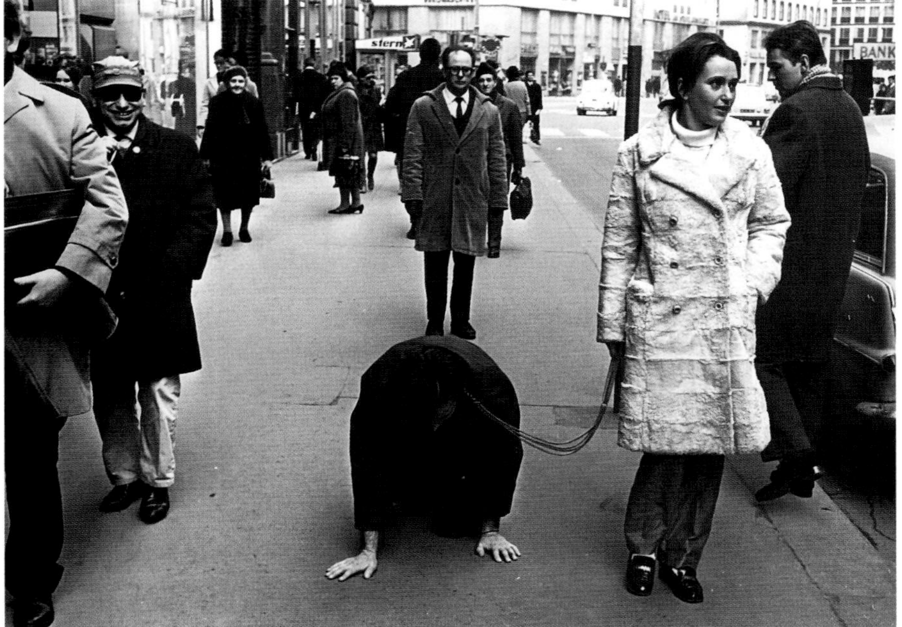

Peter WEIBEL and Valie EXPORT
Aus der Mappe der Hundigkeit (From the Portfolio of Doggishness)
1968
Vienna
In this work Weibel crawled around the city on a lead held by Export. In *Touch and Taste Cinema*, another joint performance in the same year, Export wore a stage-like box over her chest with curtains through which the public were invited to reach in and touch her breasts. Presenting the body as the vehicle of socializing codes, Weibel and Export were pushing the boundaries of such codes through direct action in the public arena. Through its role as a surface on to which our compulsions to communicate are projected and as the place where we enact our objectifying desires, the body in Weibel and Export's collaborations becomes the intermediary space between art and life and is used to question assumptions about social interaction.

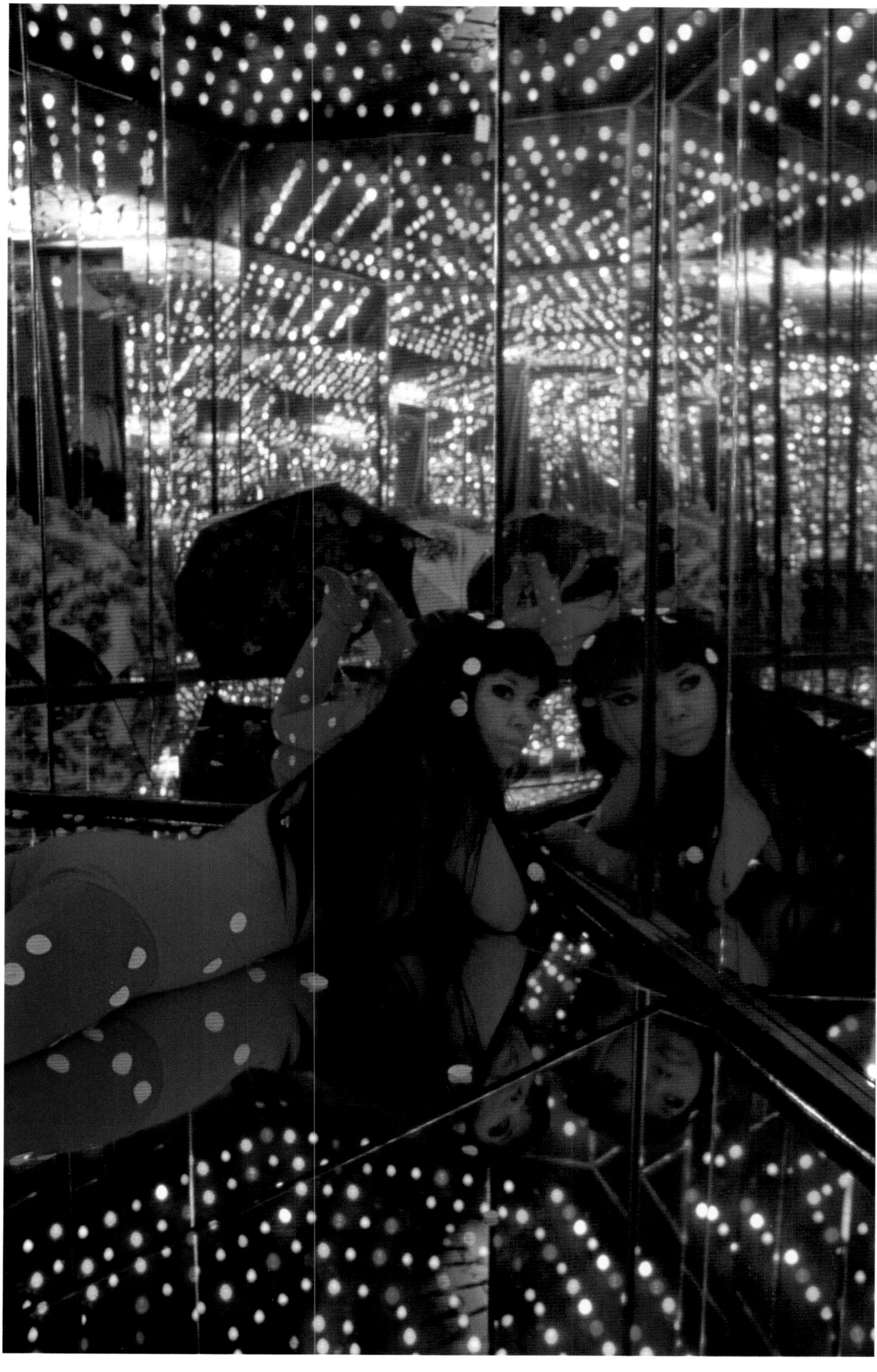

Yayoi KUSAMA
Kusama's Peep Show or Endless Love Show
1966
Mirrors, coloured lights
210 × 240 × 205 cm [83 × 94.5 × 81 in]
Installation, Castellane Gallery, New York

'I feel as if I were driving on the highways or carried on a conveyor belt without ending until my death. This is like continuing to drink thousands of cups of coffee or eating thousands of feet of macaroni ... I feel myself being put into a uniform environment, one which is strangely mechanized and standardized.' *Infinity Mirror Room* used mirrors to replicate endlessly her compulsive obsession with dots and phalluses. 'Infinitely' reflecting an obsessive environment, the work simultaneously replicates the viewer, turning his/her voyeuristic eye back on him/herself and multiplying us into thousands of standardized copies. The physical manifestation of the artist's terrors of 'the obsessions crawling over my body, whether they come from within me or from outside', Kusama's installation re-creates her psychologically split experience for us by placing us in an environment in which we watch ourselves being engulfed.
– all quotes from Yayoi Kusama, 'Interview with Gordon Brown', 1965

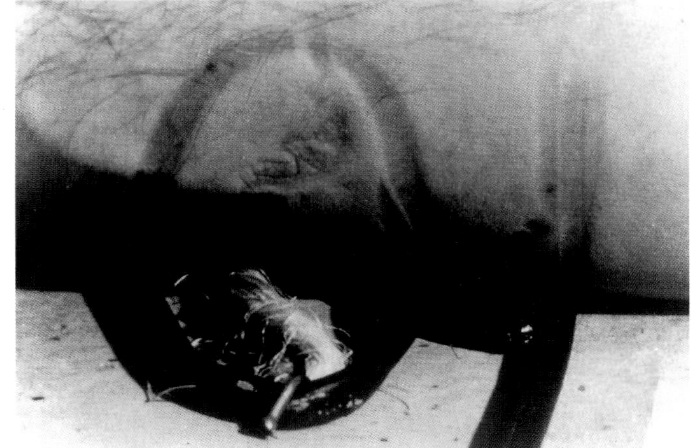

Dennis OPPENHEIM and Bob FIORE
Arm and Wire
1969
Film still
16mm, 8 mins., black and white, silent

In *Arm and Wire* Oppenheim repeatedly rolled the underside of his right arm over several wires, making an impression on his skin. No distinction is made between the material and the tool: his body is both material that is acted upon – receiving an impression from the wire – and the acting material – which rolls back and forth. The close-up shot in which only parts of the arm and the wire are seen emphasizes the lack of distinction between the artist's body and the object that acts on it. The work investigates the relationship between Oppenheim's body and his physical environment and the transactions occurring between them.

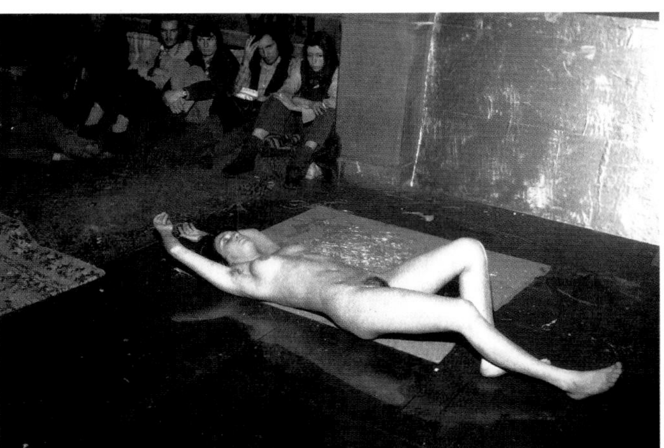

Valie EXPORT
Eros/ion
1971
Vienna

'I first rolled naked on the glass sheet, then in the glass splinters and finally on the paper screen. The cuts in my skin resulting from the slight abrasions caused by the broken glass are openings to the intima, to the inside skin of the veins, the inside of the body ... the body is a projection surface when viewed from outside ... the incisions are openings to the inside, they open up the image, they are the cut on the projection surface of representation, namely the "body", cuts in the image of the "body", surrendering itself to the gaze. The symbolic function of the body is cut open, the signs are expanded, while at the same time they are fragmented to create an expanded chain of signs. In the cut itself the transformation and the difference become visible.'
– Valie Export, *White Cube/Black Box: Video Installation Film*, 1996

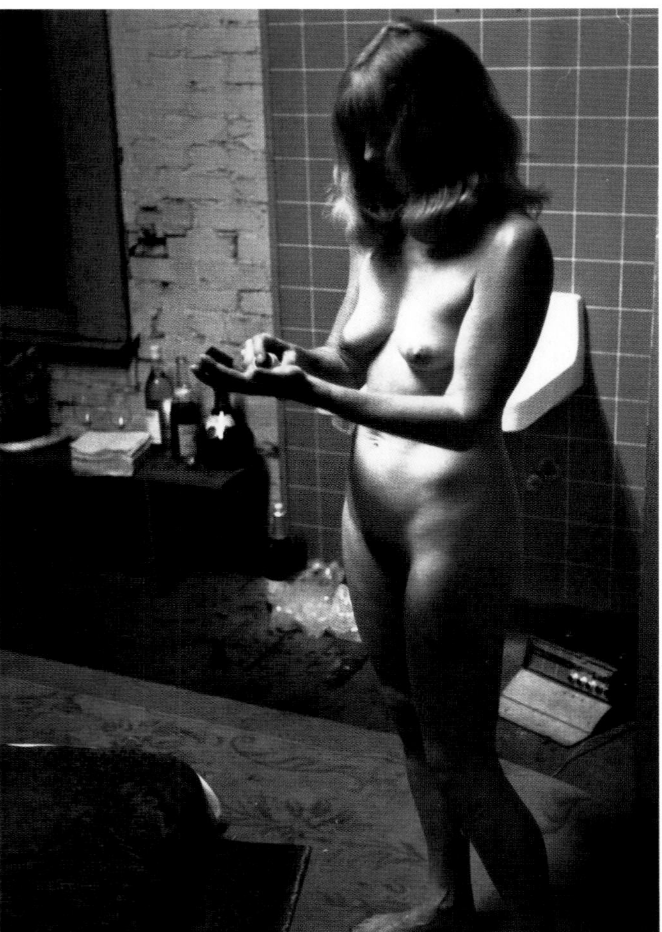

Barbara SMITH
Feed Me
1973
San Francisco Museum of Conceptual Art, San Francisco

Feed Me was staged during an evening event organized at the San Francisco Museum of Conceptual Art in which various male artists enacted noisy projectile activities such as drinking beer and urinating into a metal tub, and firing a rifle at a sawhorse. In contrast, Smith constructed a boudoir-like space, which she inhabited naked, inviting visitor-participants to enter, one at a time, and interact with her. Furnished with a mattress, incense, flowers, body oils, perfume, shawls, wine, tea, marijuana, books, music and a heater to warm the area, the intimate private space created a healing cell in which participants were invited to 'feed' the artist and themselves in an exchange of 'conversation and affection'. Reinforcing gender stereotyping of woman as odalisque, to be accessed in a hot-house environment of nudity and comfort for sympathy, sex and refreshments, Smith explained that such images of women are part of both 'real life' and 'fantasy'. By presenting herself enacting her cultural stereotype in the dual guise of mother and whore, expanded to include the role of the subjective artist, she collapses simple readings of feminine roles, opening a space for multiple co-existing possibilities.

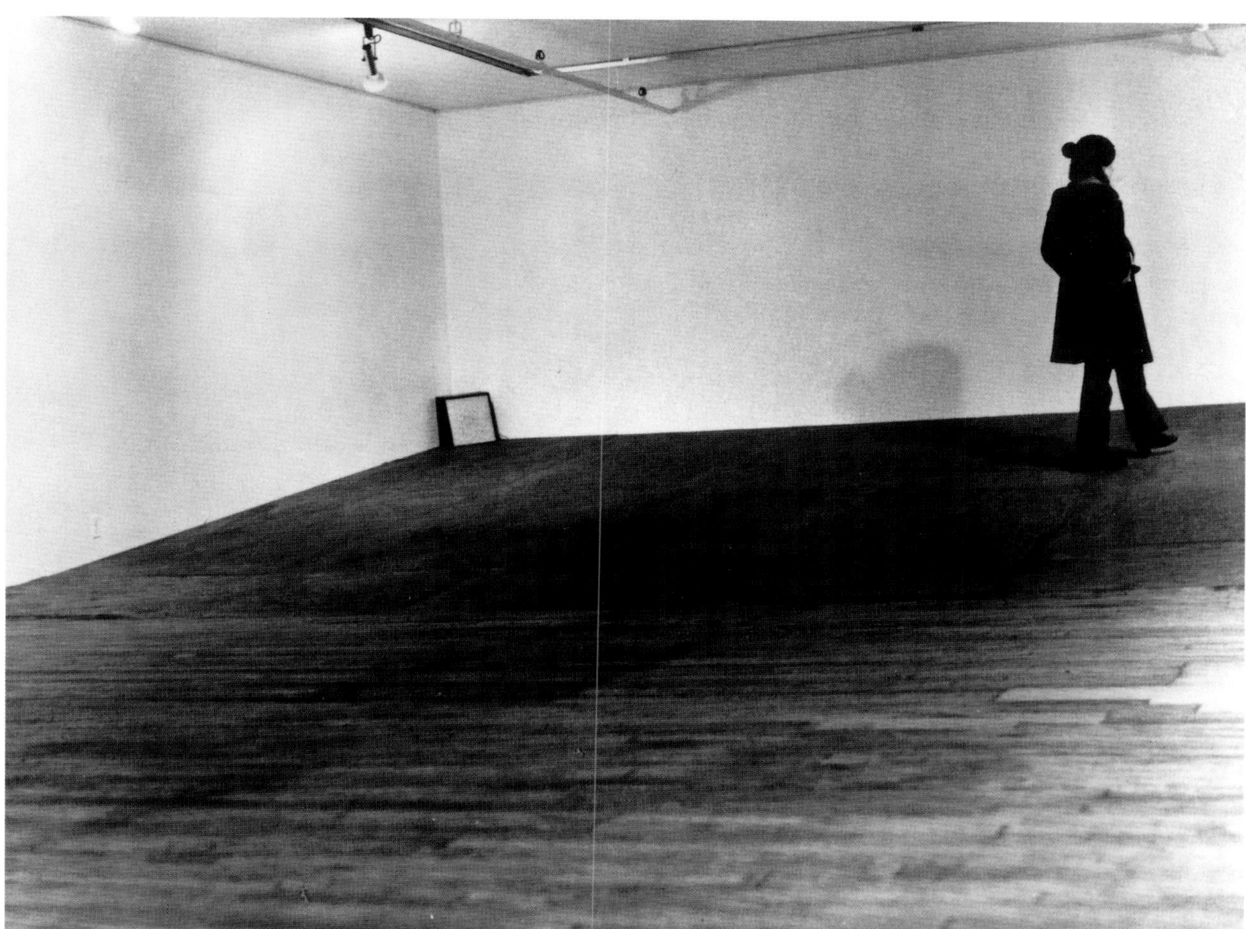

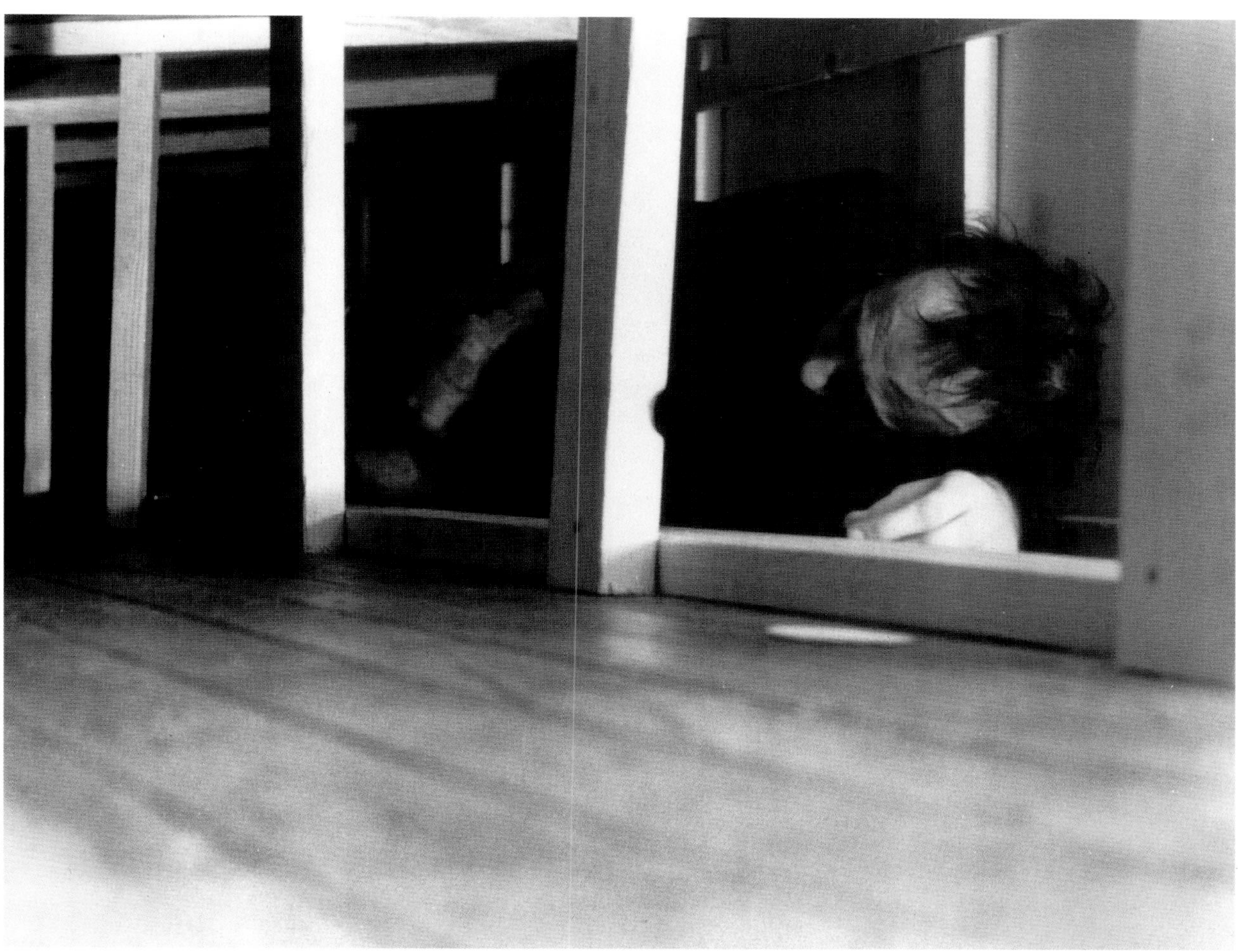

Vito ACCONCI

Seedbed

1972

Sonnabend Gallery, New York

In Sonnabend Gallery, New York, Acconci constructed a low wooden ramp, which merged gently with the floor. Hidden under the ramp for the duration of the exhibition, the artist masturbated in response to the viewers' footsteps above him. He spoke his fantasies about the unknown bodies moving around overhead into a microphone, thereby implicating the viewer as part of the work: ' … You're on my left … you're moving away but I'm pushing my body against you, into the corner … you're bending your head down, over me … I'm pressing my eyes into your hair … I'm doing this with you now … you're in front of me … I'm moving from point to point, covering the floor … I have to continue all day – cover the floor with sperm, seed the floor … You can reinforce my excitement, serve as my medium (the seed planted on the floor is the joint result of my presence and yours).'
– Vito Acconci, 'Power Field – Exchange Points – Transformations', 1972

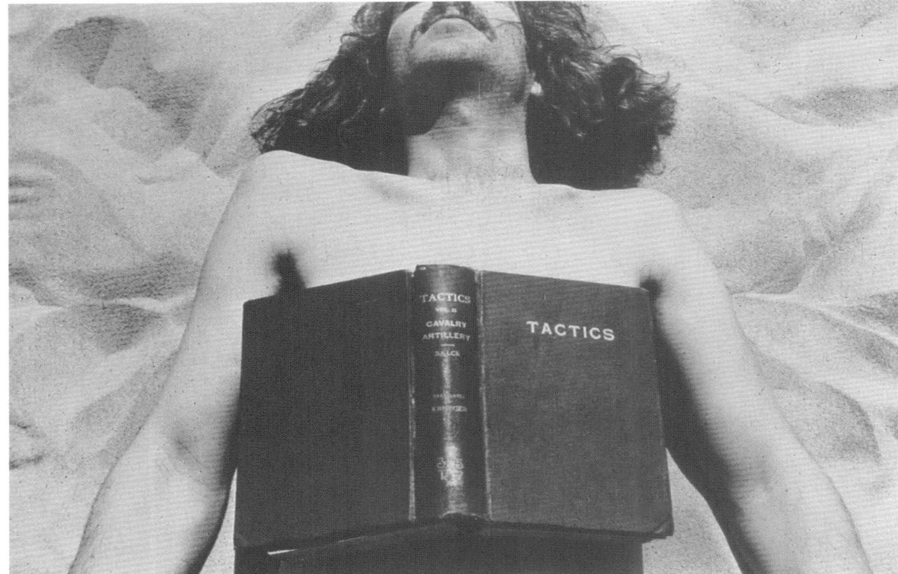

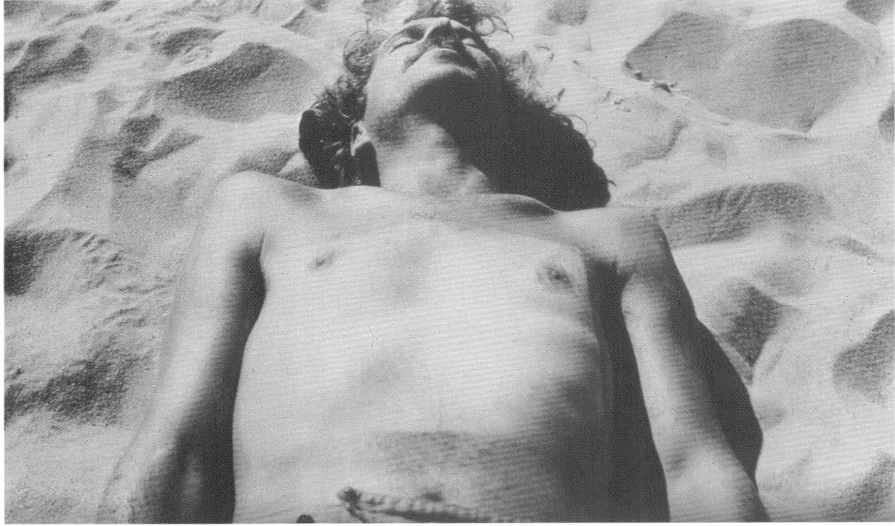

Dennis OPPENHEIM
Reading Position for a Second Degree Burn
1970
Colour and black and white photographs
216 × 152.5 cm [85 × 60 in]

Oppenheim lay on Jones Beach, New York, for five hours, bare-chested, exposing himself to sunburn, with a copy of *Tactics: Cavalry Artillery* open on his chest . 'The piece incorporates an inversion or reversal of energy expenditure. The body is placed in the position of recipient .... an exposed plane, a captive surface. The piece has its roots in a notion of colour change. Painters have always artificially instigated colour activity. I allow myself to be painted – my skin becomes pigment. I can regulate its intensity through control of the exposure time. Not only do the skin tones change, but change registers on a sensory level as well. I feel the act of becoming red.'
– Dennis Oppenheim, 'Another Point of Entry: An Interview with Alanna Heiss', 1990

Presenting his body as a surface for inscription by the sun, Oppenheim reverses the traditional position of artist acting on his environment. The sunburn affects his body both by external marking and by the sensation of pain.

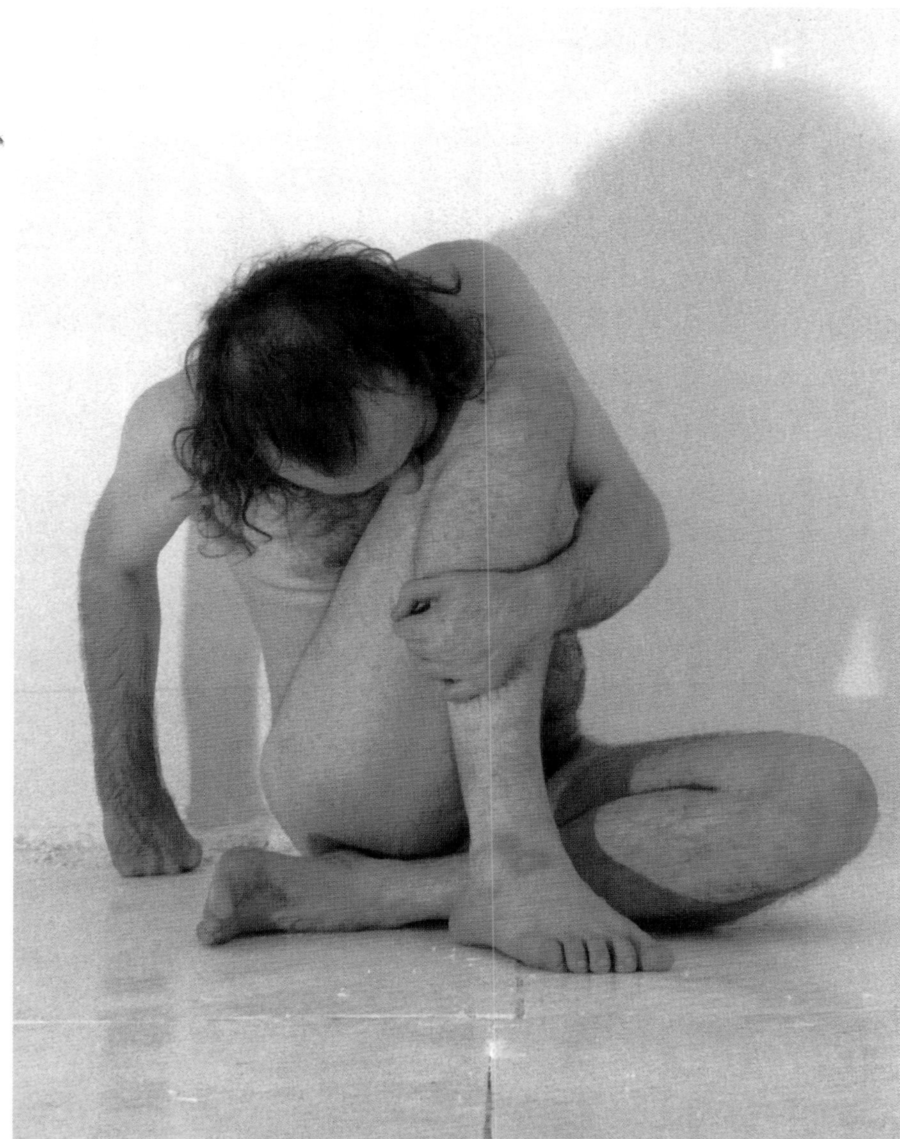

Vito ACCONCI
Trademarks
1970
New York

'Biting myself: biting as much of my body as I can reach. Applying printer's ink to the bites; stamping bite-prints on various surfaces ... Opening a closed region: building up a biography, a public record (bite-print as storage – identity peg – an alibi: I was so involved in myself that I couldn't be somewhere else). Reasons to move – move into myself – move around myself – move in order to close a system. Reasons to move: show myself to myself – show myself through myself – show myself outside. Make my own outside – send my inside outside (I can slip outside, then, because I am still moving inside).'
– Vito Acconci, *Avalanche*, 1972

Acconci described *Trademarks* as an attempt to claim his body as his own. The closed system of self-reflexive gestures presented in this performance conveys a simple and direct message: the artist defines himself by his work, his action on other bodies in the world. Here, the artist's body and his art-making activity are one and the same. Using his teeth to make the identifying marks on his skin, Acconci, a former poet, emphasizes the dual possibilities of the mouth, both as source of spoken language (culture, interaction) and as agent of consumption.

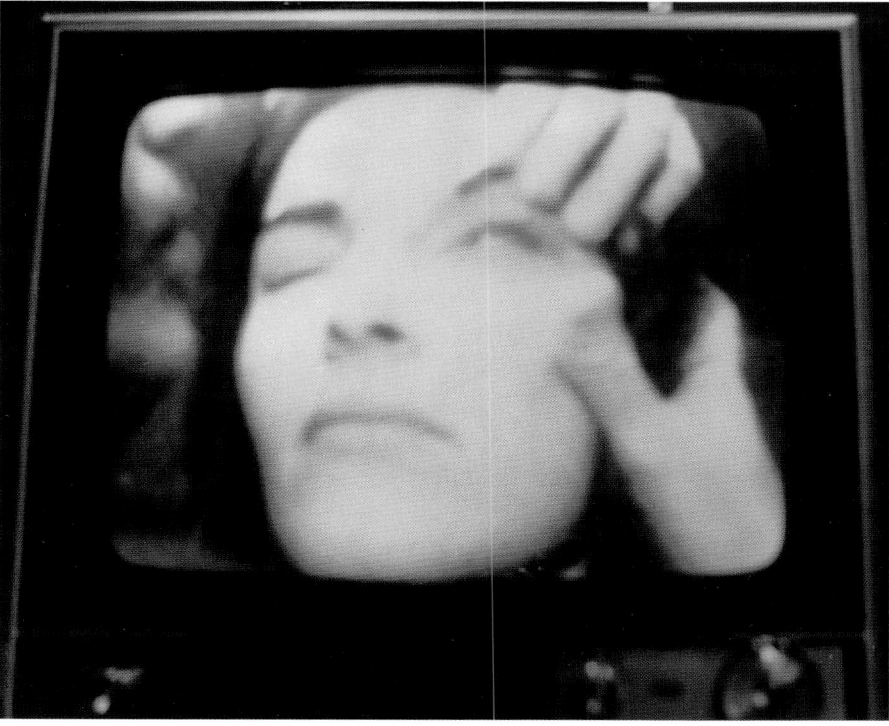

Vito ACCONCI and Kathy DILLON
Pryings
1971
Video still
17 mins., black and white, sound

In *Pryings* Acconci obsessively attempts to prize open Dillon's eyes. She in turn tries to keep her eyes shut. The relentlessness of his attempts to get inside Dillon – her body as metaphor for her mind/soul – and her obstinate refusal to let him in, articulate issues of domination, control, vulnerability and submission.

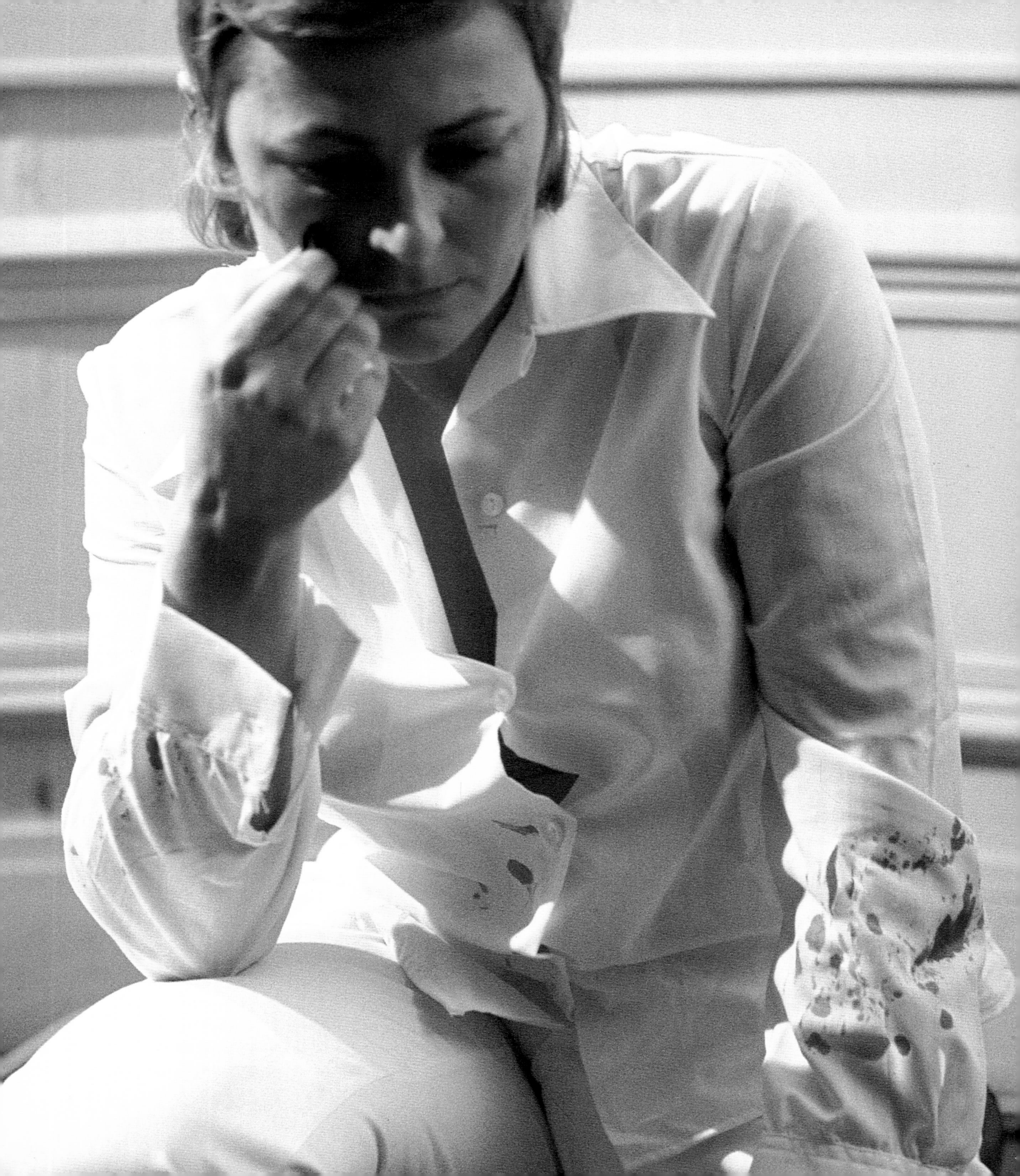

opposite
Gina PANE
Le Lait Chaud (Warm milk)
1972
Paris

In a large Paris apartment, Pane created an installation to the theme 'White Doesn't Exist'. Dressed entirely in white and facing away from the audience, she started to cut her back with a razor blade, allowing the blood to gush on to her shirt. She then interrupted the action by playing with a tennis ball, contrasting the game with the violence of cutting. 'Suddenly I turned to face my public and approached the razor blade to my face. The tension was explosive and broke when I cut my face on either cheek. They yelled "No, no, not the face, no!" So I touched an essential problem – the aestheticism in every person. The face is taboo, it's the core of human aesthetics, the only place which retains a narcissistic power.' After cutting her face, Pane turned the video camera on the audience in order to allow the spectators to witness their own emotional response and 'communicate with themselves'.
– all quotes from Gina Pane, 'Performance of Concern: Gina Pane discusses her work with Effie Stephano', 1973

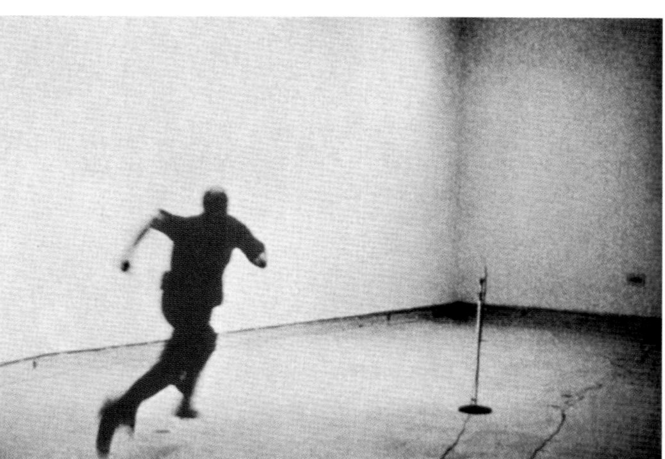

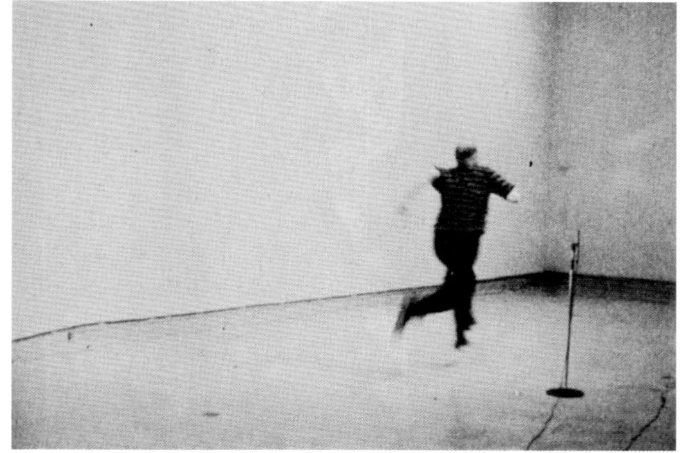

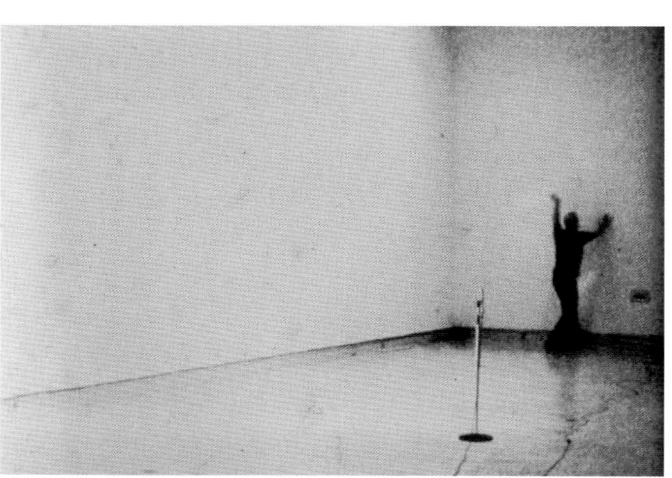

Barry LE VA
Velocity Piece No. 2
1970
La Jolla Museum, Los Angeles

Le Va ran back and forth between two opposite walls 15-m [50-ft] apart, impacting violently against the walls before hurling himself back into space, until he was no longer able to go on. After the performance, evidence of the piece was visible on the blood-spattered walls and in the stereo sound recording. As Le Va explained to curator Liza Bear, 'The energy drain was one of the main purposes of the piece, and that of course increased with time until I was worn out and couldn't move at all ... every part of my body ended up being used.'
– Barry Le Va, '... a continuous flow of fairly aimless movement', 1971

Investigating the relationship between his physical energy and endurance and the external space of an architecturally constructed environment, Le Va used the sound recording to expand the viewer's perceptual awareness of this relationship.

Chris BURDEN
Shoot
1971
Santa Ana, California

In his best-known performance, Burden had a friend shoot him in the arm with a .22 calibre rifle from a distance of 4.5 m [15 ft]. He claimed that all those in the gallery were implicated in this act of self-inflicted violence by their failure to intervene. He later explained that his experiments with extreme and dangerous activities provided a means to gain 'knowledge that other people don't have, some kind of wisdom' through direct experience. 'How do you know what it feels like to be shot if you don't get shot?' he asked in a conversation with curator Paul Schimmel.
– Chris Burden, 'Just the Facts', 1988

Burden's staging of a real shooting in a gallery not far from Hollywood provided a shocking contrast to the artificiality and make-believe of the local film industry, replacing props and acting with real blood and pain.

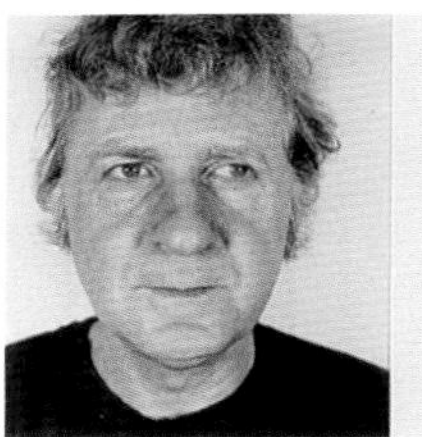
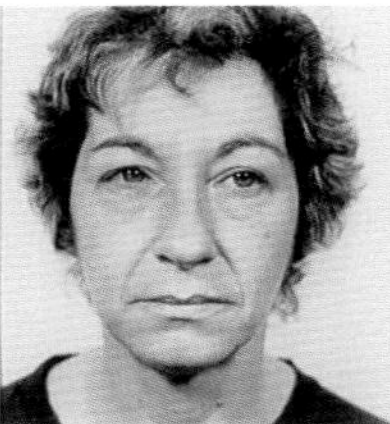
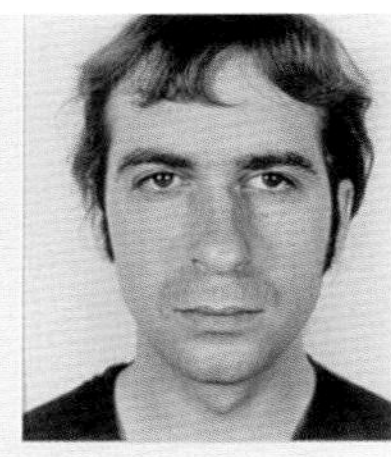
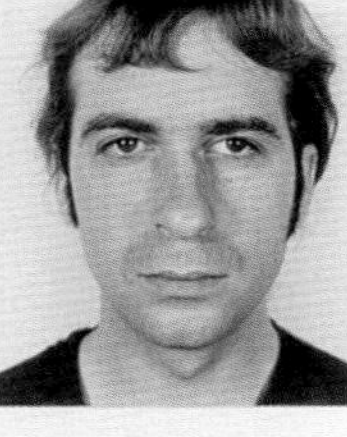
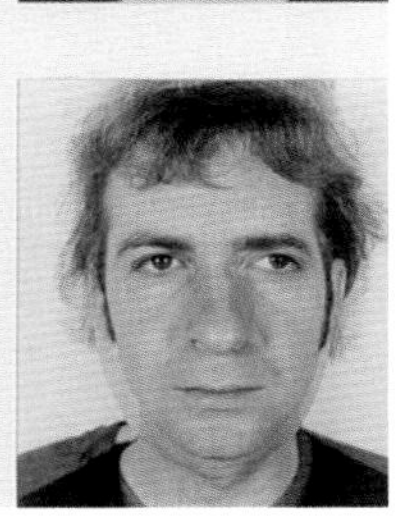

William WEGMAN
Family Combinations
1972
Silver gelatin prints
6 prints, 31 × 26 cm [12 × 10 in] each

Wegman photographed himself and each of his parents, then combined the image of himself first with his father, then with his mother, and finally combined his mother and father alone together. As the difference between the first and sixth image makes clear, the combination of his parents alone does not add up to the artist, even though this is his genetic formation and limitation. While *Family Combinations* demonstrates clear similarities passed on from parent to child, it also points to a subtle but telling difference – the unquantifiable extra elements that cannot be mapped, but whose presence ensure that the individual is always more than the sum of his parts.

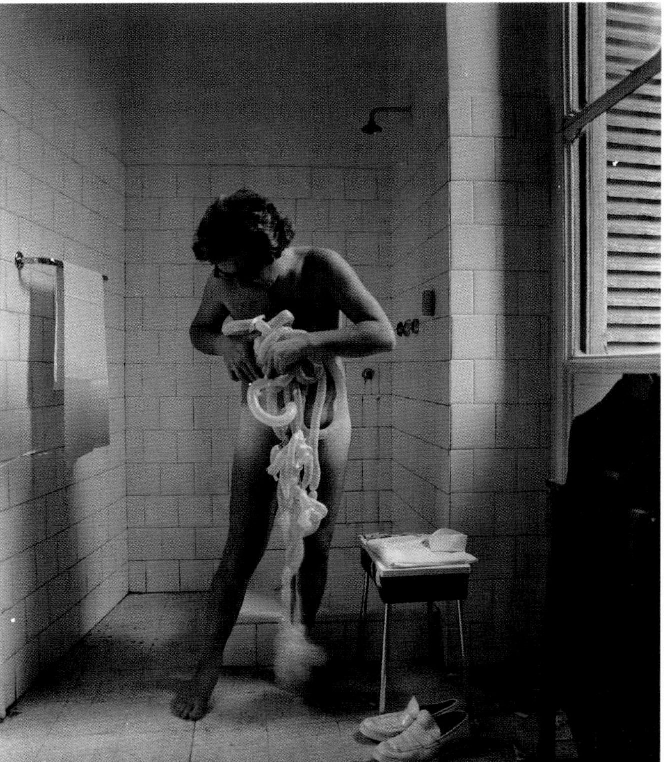

Gianni PISANI
Each Morning Before Going Out
1973
Black and white photographs
10 photographs, 22.5 × 17.5 cm [9 × 7 in] each

'In the morning after a shower, I rewind the umbilical cord on my abdomen (... it is taken from the intestine of a cow, it is that kind of tubular vellum used by butchers to make sausages; I tied it at one end and then I inflated it with a bicycle pump). I arrange this skein under my shirt; as I am buttoning it, I completely conceal the inconvenience which belongs to me. I hide it from the others with my bourgeois clothes which make me no different than the others; I compress it under my daily appearances and go among people.

'The idea of the umbilical cord is tied to my preceding work, from the representation of my suicide to guns, from my old paintings or more recent drawings to the rocking chair or to the destruction of my coffin ... Perhaps the story of the umbilical cord is a return towards life, it is like a need to attach oneself to something, it is the searching for a father-mother-son tie ... the others stay away from it, but these are the fundamental ties ... '
– Gianni Pisani, Artist's statement, 1979

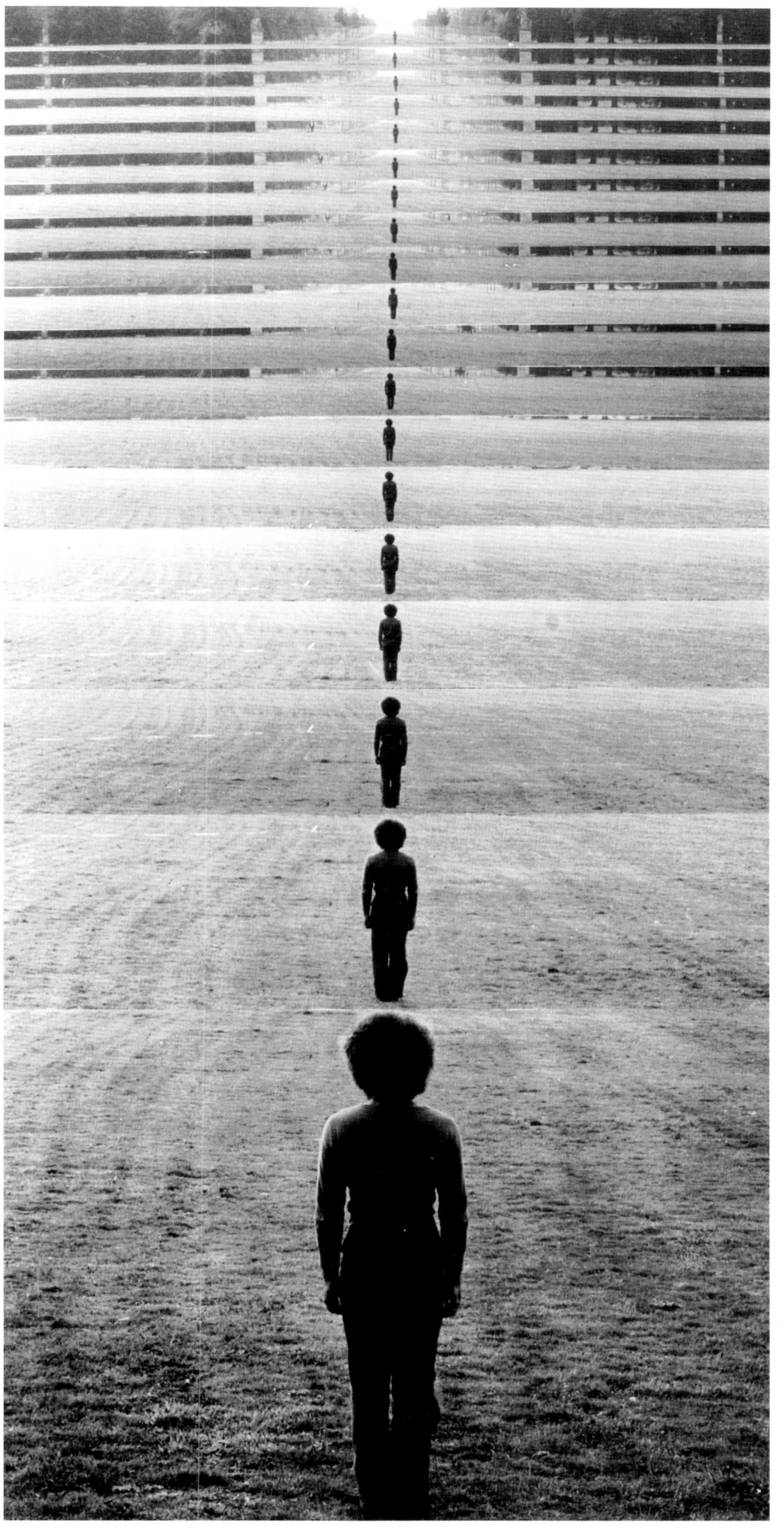

Klaus RINKE

Deplazierung (Changing location according to points in time)

1972

Photo collage on card

c. 180 × 88.5 cm [71 × 35 in]

Deplazierung represents the displacement of a body in space and time through a series of photographs of the artist in a landscape who becomes progressively smaller as the landscape expands. The camera remained in the same position, while the artist advanced 50-m [164-ft] away from it for each photograph taken. Through this device, combining temporal movement with spatial movement, Rinke constructs graph-like axes with his body and the landscape. By collaging the succession of photographs he represents a situation that is impossible to experience in one moment in reality. He saw his work at this time as creating 'a visual mathematics of life, which provokes a regeneration of language as well as an expression of life'. His sculptural actions were intended to invoke existential questions of man's position in the world, a means of coordinating perceptions, and understanding our relationship with time. 'I am presenting a kind of alphabet of looking, of life and of action, thus an alphabet of human existence.'
– all quotes from Klaus Rinke in Evelyn Weiss, *Klaus Rinke: Travaux 1969/1976*, 1976

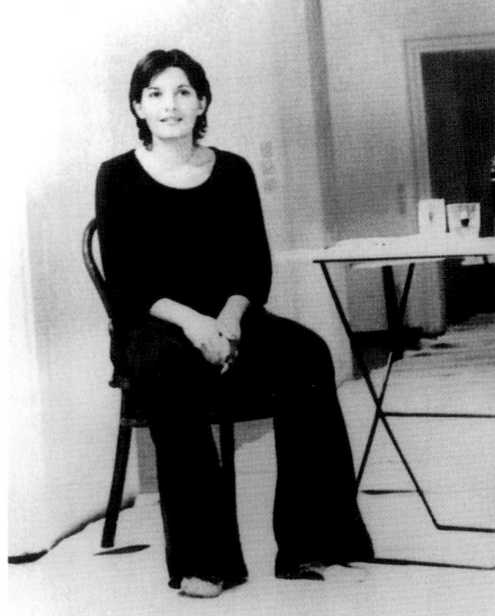

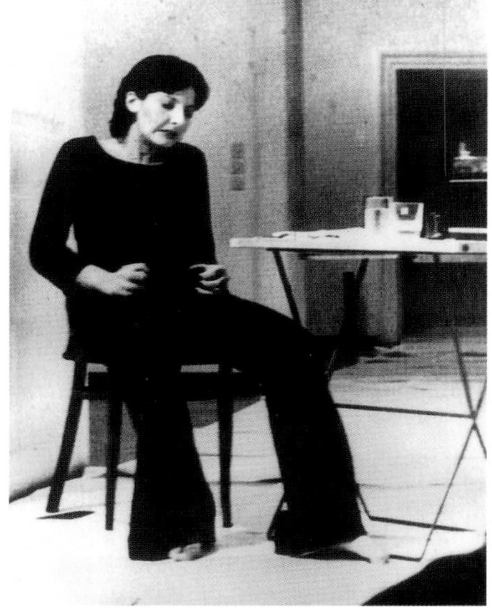

Marina ABRAMOVIĆ

Rhythm 2

1974

Gallery of Contemporary Art, Zagreb

At the Gallery of Contemporary Art in Zagreb, Abramović took psychoactive medications in front of an audience, experiencing and reporting their effects in an open and trusting way. First, she took medication for schizophrenia and experienced the effects for 50 minutes: 'My muscles contract violently and I lose control.' Then she took medication for acute catatonia and sat for six hours: 'I feel cold, then lose consciousness, forgetting who I am and where I am.' By subjecting herself to an experience in which she was passive to the effects of drugs and at the same time watched by the public, Abramović presented herself in a state of extreme vulnerability: with both body and mind distorted by chemical action, she became an object of medical curiosity. This public experience of drugs with powerful physical and psychological effects comprised part of her research into the knowledge gained through loss of control.

– all quotes from Marina Abramović , Artist's statement, 1974

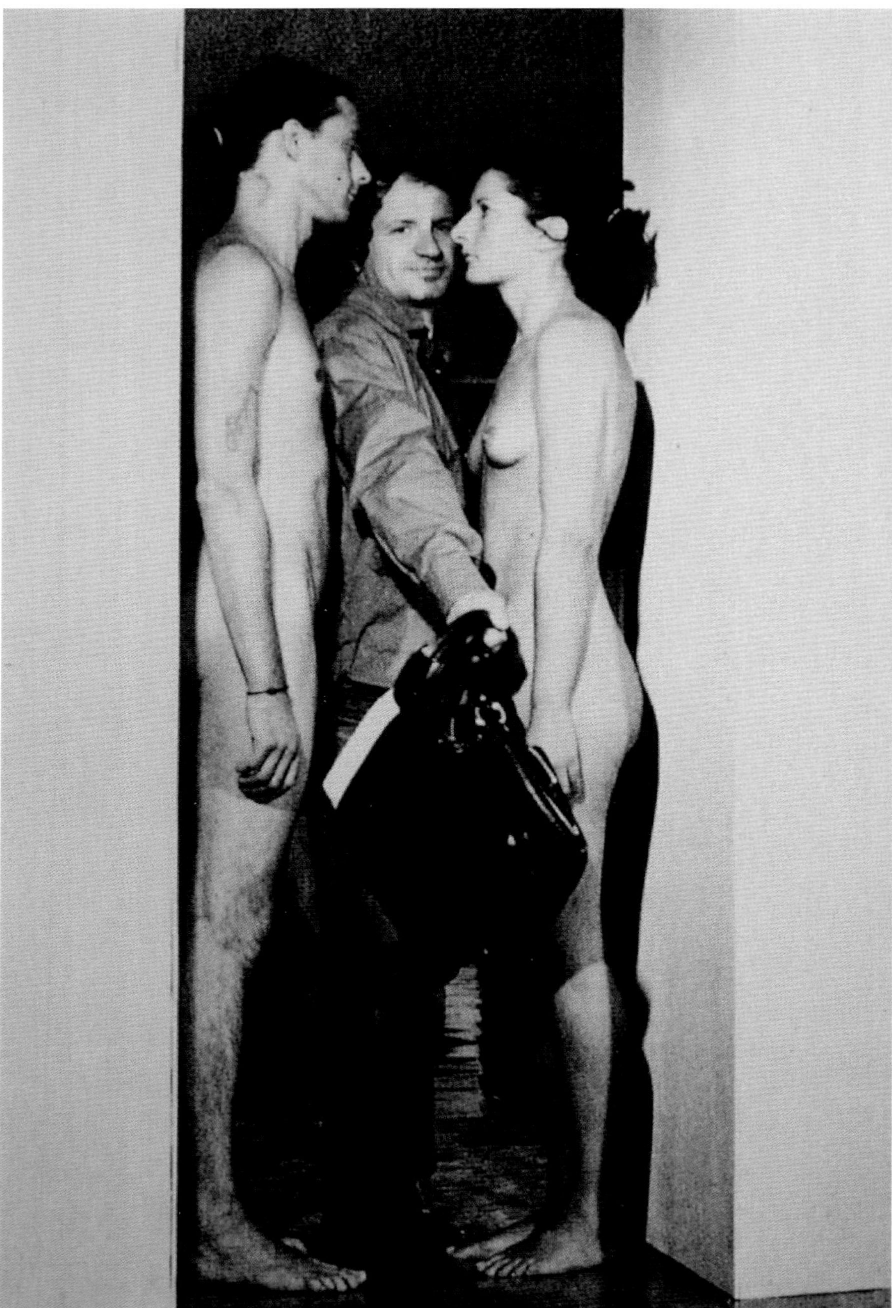

ABRAMOVIĆ /ULAY

Imponderabilia

1977

Galleria Communale d'Arte Moderna, Bologna

Abramović and Ulay collaborated for several years. For an opening at the Galleria Comunale d'Arte Moderna, Bologna, they stood naked, facing each other in the main entrance, forcing the public entering the museum to choose which naked body to face – male or female – as they squeezed through the small space between the two artists. As each member of the public passed awkwardly between the two naked bodies, they were filmed by a hidden camera and saw themselves being projected on monitors placed nearby. Text on the wall by the monitors read:''Imponderable/such imponderable human factors/as one's aesthetic sensitivity/ the overriding importance/of imponderables in determining/human contact.' The piece forced people to confront their attitudes and feelings about gender and sexuality, the body of the 'other', through a direct physical intervention in the architecture of both a building and a social event. They had planned to be the museum's 'living door' for three hours, but after 90 minutes their performance was stopped by the police.

Marina ABRAMOVIĆ

Rhythm 0

1974

Studio Morra, Naples

In an evening performance exploring the dynamics of passive aggression, Abramović stood by a table and offered herself passively to spectators, who could do what they liked with a range of objects and her body. A text on the wall read, 'There are seventy-two objects on the table that can be used on me as desired. I am the object.' The objects included a gun, a bullet, a saw, an axe, a fork, a comb, a whip, lipstick, a bottle of perfume, paint, knives, matches, a feather, a rose, a candle, water, chains, nails, needles, scissors, honey, grapes, plasters, sulphur and olive oil. By the end of the performance all her clothes had been sliced off her body with razor blades, she had been cut, painted, cleaned, decorated, crowned with thorns and had had the loaded gun pressed against her head. After six hours the performance was halted by concerned spectators. Abramović described this piece as the conclusion of her research on the body.

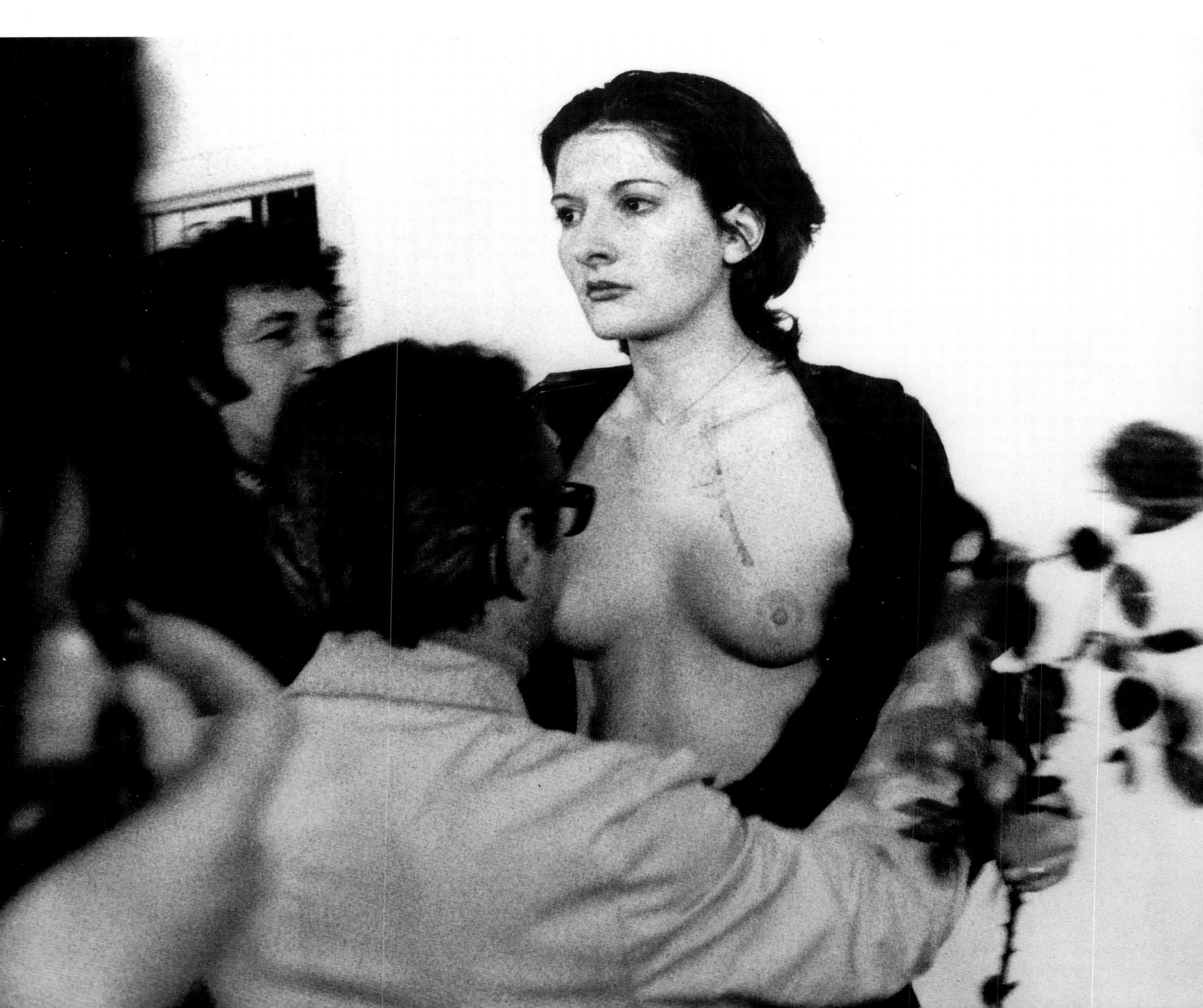

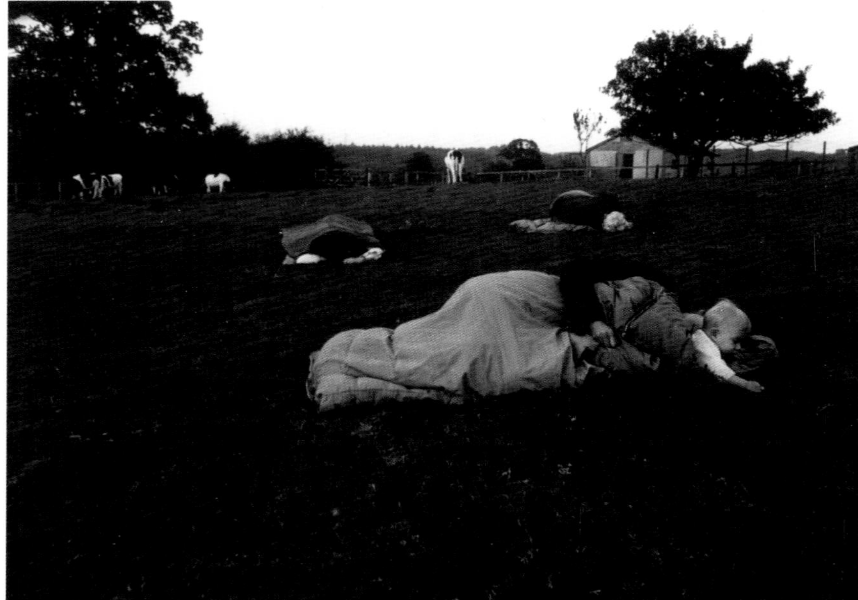

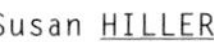

Susan HILLER

Dream Mapping

1974

Hampshire, England

Hiller invited the seven participants in this collective 'live' work to sleep in a Hampshire field for three nights. In the few weeks prior to this they had already learnt to remember and notate their dreams. Each morning they would record and map their dreams; from the individual maps composite ones were created by superimposition. This piece raised questions about the influence of location on the highly specific imagery particular to each dreamer and their personal methods of 'mapping', and about where the individual and the communal intersected. Presenting a parodic application of objective measuring on to insubstantial and subjective dream material, Hiller also stressed the role of the work in sensitizing people to the uncertain nature of the boundary between individual and social, private and public. 'Individual experiences, reactions and expressive acts function as aspects of a structure ... designed to intensify a sense of shared subjectivity.'

– Susan Hiller, 'Dream Mapping', 1981

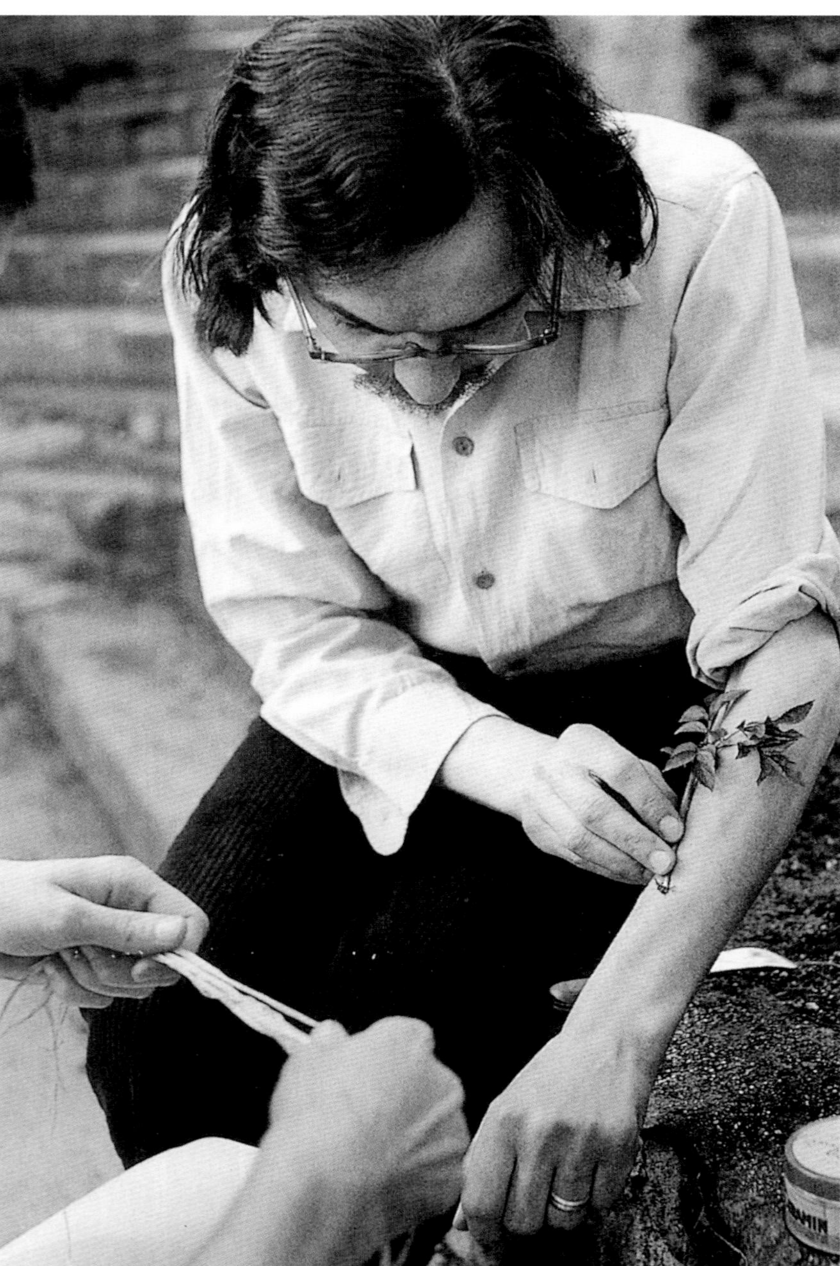

Petr ŠTEMBERA

Grafting

1975

Prague

Štembera attempted to graft a plant to his arm using the normal gardening grafting techniques. This involved cutting his flesh, using poisonous chemicals to encourage the growth of the plant in its new environment and binding its stem to his body. He explained that he wanted 'to make contact with the plant, to put it in my body, to be together with it as long as possible'. His art-making presented increasingly ritualized actions that used his body as a source of energy and power to protect him against 'physical psychological aggression', for which he had prepared himself through the practise of yoga and meditation. Although Štembera claimed that this quest was personal rather than political, the system of repression that arose in his native Czech Republic (former Czechoslovakia) after the Soviet occupation influenced the language he used to express his exploration of physical presence and self-knowledge. His personal acts of communion, joining and self-preservation could be read in this context as metaphors for the need for a wider social healing, the difficulties of assimilating the individual into the collective and of absorbing an alien culture into one's own.

– all quotes from Petr Štembera, Artist's statement, 1975

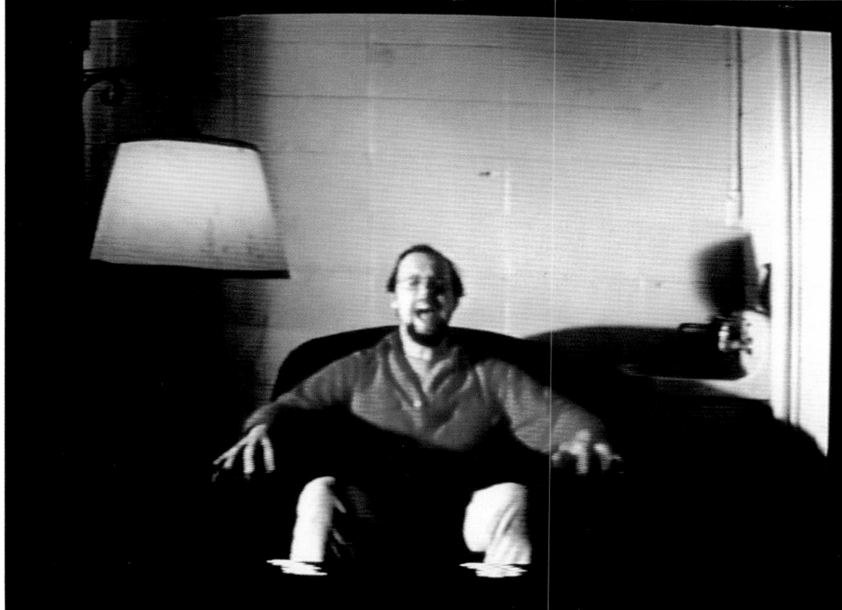

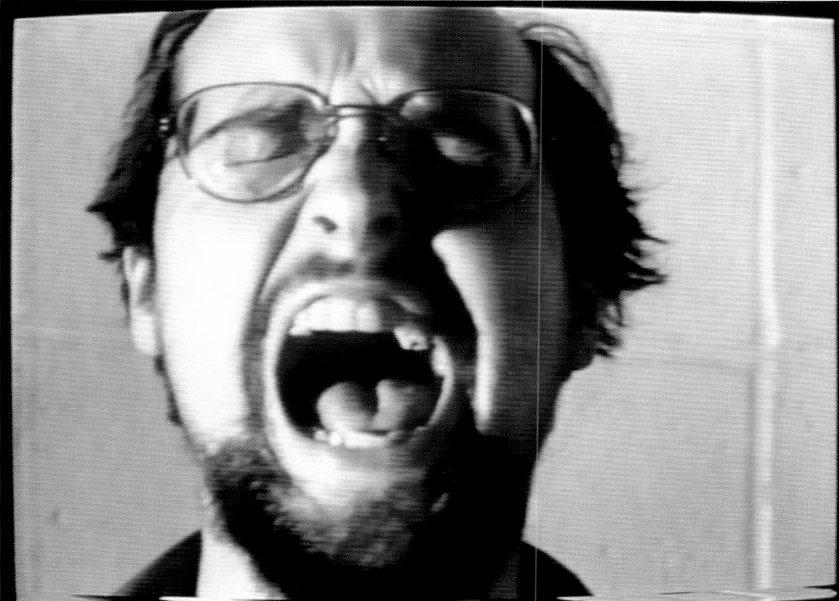

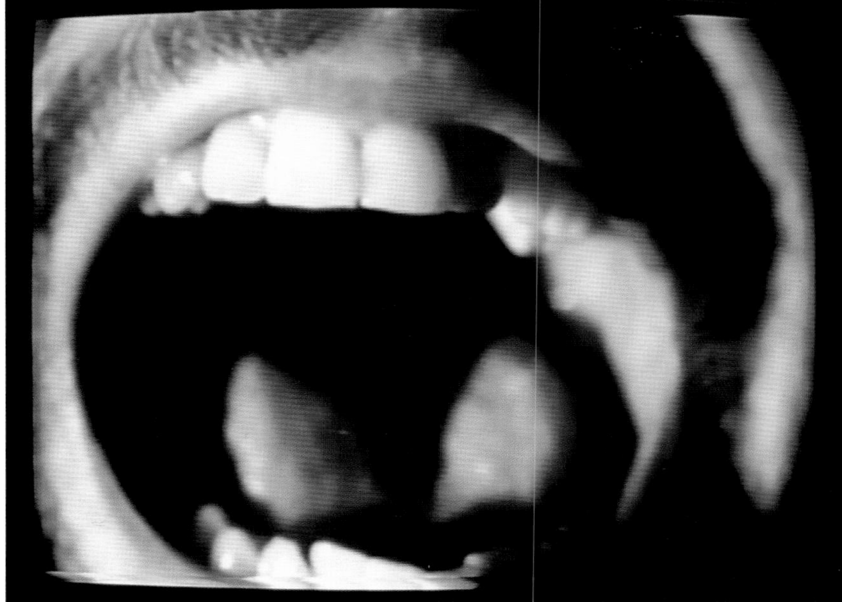

Bill VIOLA

The Space Between the Teeth

1976

Video still

9 mins. 10 secs., colour, mono sound

The camera approaches Viola's screaming face down a long corridor, freezing at the point where it is about to enter his body through the space between his teeth, then falling and emptying the scream into a lake, whose waves wash over it, effectively drowning it. 'The larger struggle we are witnessing today is not between conflicting moral beliefs, between the legal system and individual freedom, between nature and human technology; it is between our inner and our outer lives, and our bodies are the area where this belief is being played out. It is the old philosophical "mind/body" problem coming to a crescendo as an ecological drama where the outcome rests not only upon our realization that the natural physical environment is one and the same as our bodies, but that nature itself is a form of mind.'
– Bill Viola, *Reasons for Knocking at an Empty House*, 1995

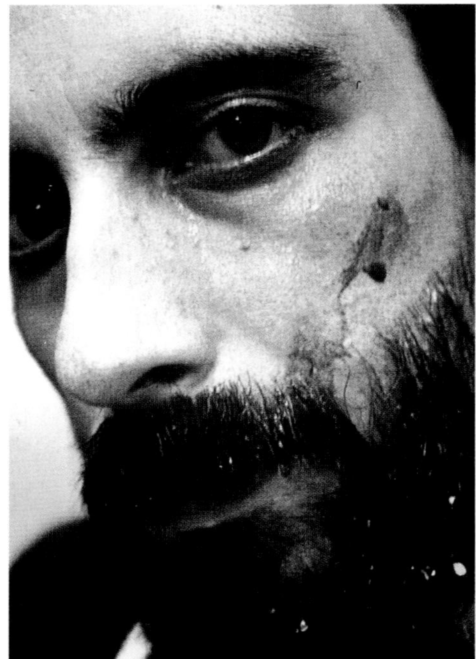

Raúl ZURITA

No, no puedo más (No, I can't stand it any longer)

1979

Galeria Cal, Santiago, Chile

At a forum on the paintings of Juan Davila at the Galeria Cal, Santiago, Zurita responded by ejaculating violently in front of them and then smearing his semen on his cut, bleeding and burnt face. He later claimed that the paintings had appeared subversive to him '... in the fullest sense [...] breaking all the codes. And I thought that any verbal discourse about it would be a type of domestication, and that there were other ways to respond: action instead of words ... ' In order to criticize the function of imposed language and signification, Zurita transcended codes of socially acceptable behaviour – both in regard to his own body, by wounding it, and in respect to the audiences' bodies, by ejaculating publicly – in his art action. Attempting to share an experience that he felt could not be expressed or translated in the terms of existing thought, he used his body as the vehicle for a new series of signs that are pre-verbal and as yet uncodified by any discourse. 'I wished to distinguish between what cannot be written and what has already begun to be written, between what can be talked about and what cannot be talked about. Faced with a personal experience that is extremely violent or painful, the wish to express it, even by going so far as to burn one's face, is already a sign ... '

– all quotes from Raúl Zurita, 'Interview with Samuel Silva', 1982

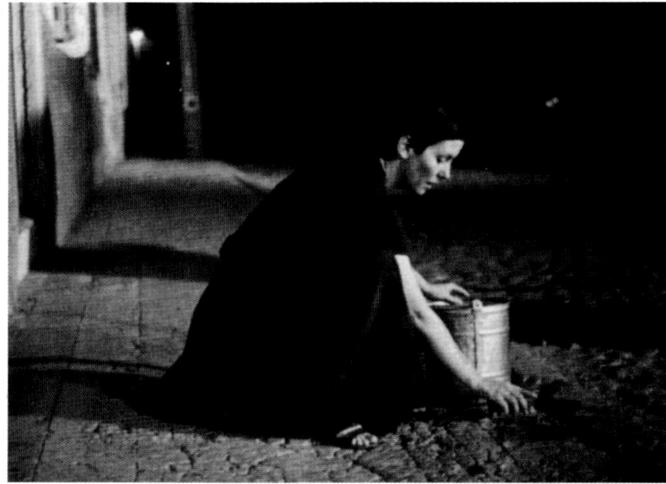

Diamela ELTIT

Maipu

1980

Santiago, Chile

Eltit inflicted cuts and burns on her arms and legs before going to a brothel where she read aloud part of a novel she had written . She then washed the pavement in front of the brothel. Working with what she called 'zones of pain' – marginal areas of social confinement such as brothels, psychiatric hospitals, flophouses and prisons – Eltit used her body to make a connection between individual and collective experience. Her body becomes the physical sign of marginalized people: 'I present my scars as a symptom of exclusion, as a ruptured model [...] superimposing on my wounded body the signs favoured by the system, like clothes, makeup, etc. These signs, by way of contrast, do not resolve but only make manifest the dichotomy that [...] exists between the maltreated body and its submission to the model of appearances.'

– Diamela Eltit, *La Tercera de la Hora* (The third hour), 1982

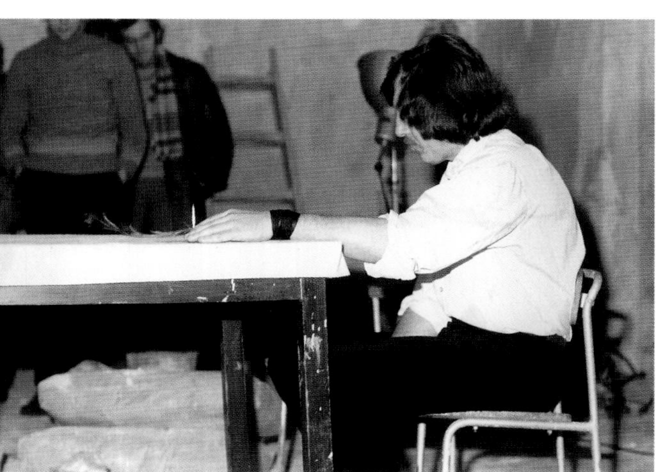

Zbigniew WARPECHOWSKI

Nail Driven Through the Hand

1980

Documenta 8, Kassel, Germany

At Documenta 8 Polish artist Warpechowski undertook a gruelling two-day performance of his work, carrying out ritualized, shamanic actions that both used and rejected Catholic imagery. The final six hours of the performance culminated in the artist hammering a 15-cm [6-in] nail through his own hand, which had a powerful emotive effect on the audience. The artist claims to have performed this same act several times and to be given up to the pain. 'I have done it several times and I am used to it. This hand is like an old potato'.

– Zibigniew Warpechowski quoted by Rob La Frenais, 'The Pit and the Pendulum', 1993

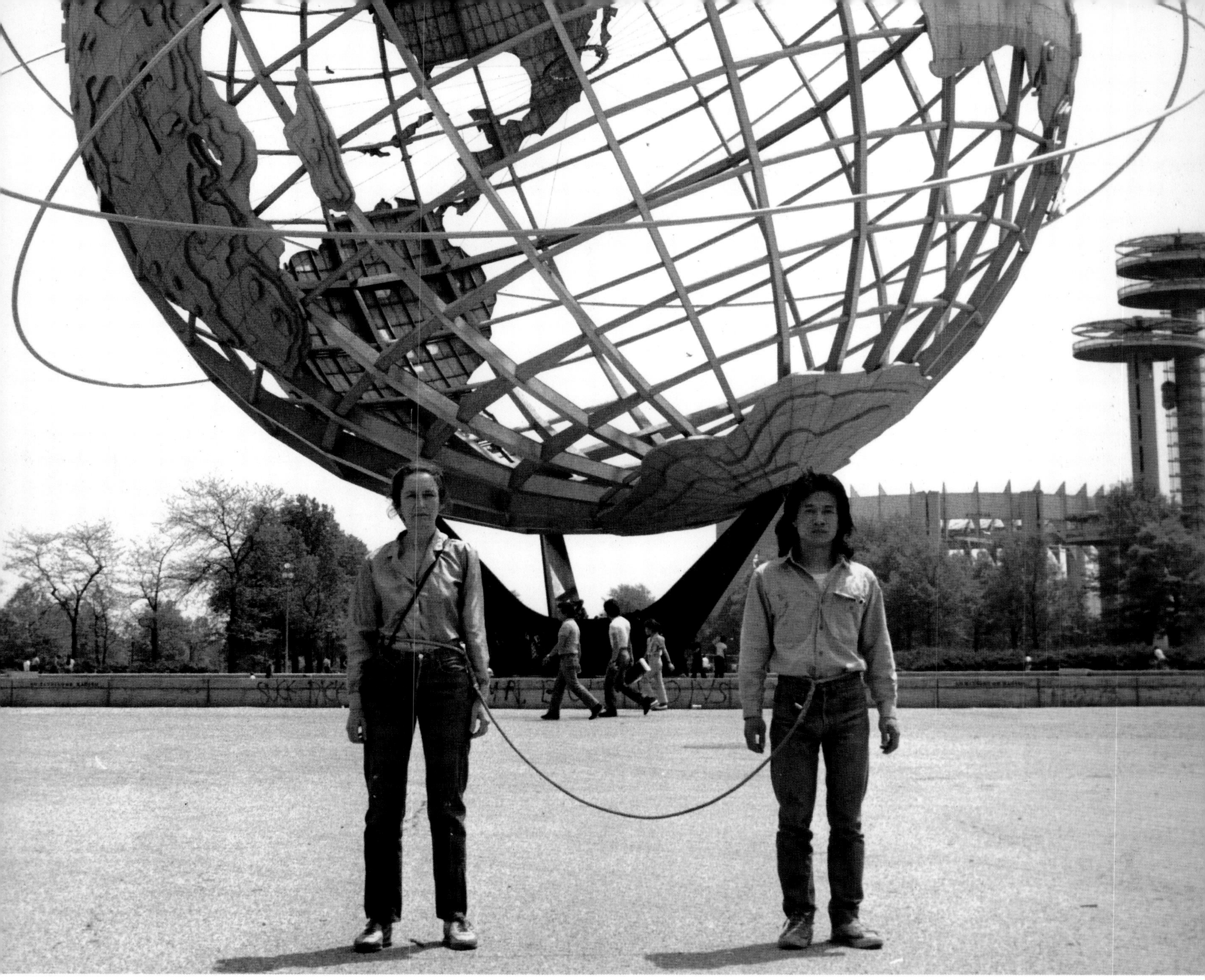

Linda MONTANO and Tehching HSIEH

A Year Spent Tied Together at the Waist

1983-84

New York

In a collaborative one-year performance Montano and Hsieh were tied together at the waist by a 2-m [8-ft] length of rope in order to 'stay together for one year and never be alone'. Ritual performances marked the beginning and end, including the shaving of both artists' heads to eliminate the difference between them and mark time passing through the growth of hair. Daily photographs and the tape recording of every conversation between the two artists provide extensive documentation. Despite their intentions to overcome individual difference, their mutual frustration with conflicting needs and desires made hostility inevitable. Eventually, friends were required to negotiate a mediation between them. For Hsieh, the connection by rope symbolized survival and dependency needs; for Montano the importance lay in what she could learn about herself and her inner life.

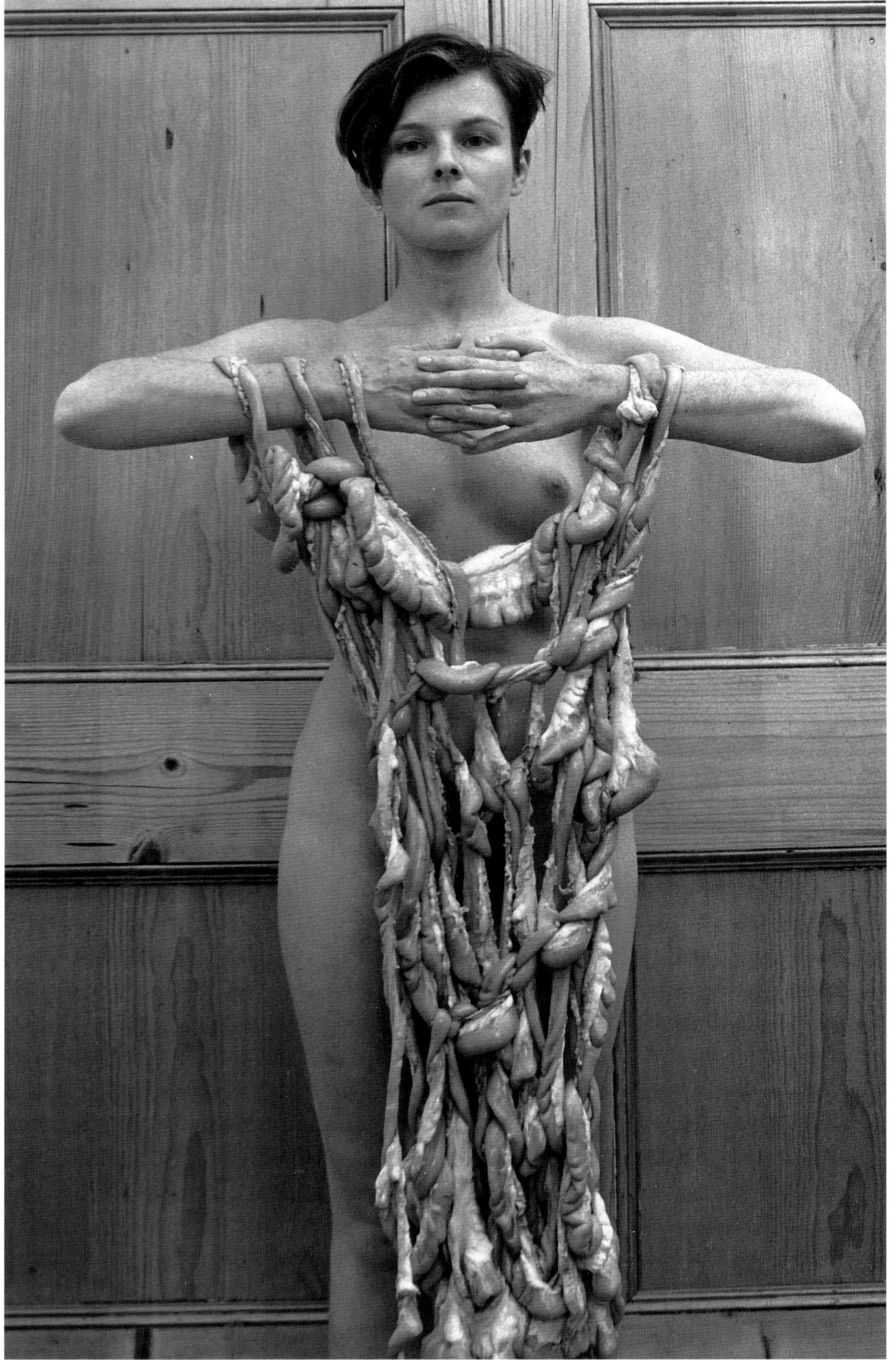

Jayne PARKER
K
1989
Film still
16 mm, 13 mins., black and white, silent

'In *K* I bring my intestine up out of my mouth and let it fall in a pile at my feet. I take the end and proceed to knit, using my arms in the place of knitting needles, until I have knitted the whole length. I hold my knitted intestine in front of my body so that it covers me. I bring out into the open all the things that I have taken in that are not mine, and thereby make room for something new. I make an external order out of an internal tangle.' – Jayne Parker quoted in *Body as Membrane*, 1996

In the second half of the film the artist stands on the edge of a swimming pool and dives in over and over again. She hesitates on the edge, and then the film cuts to her exit from the pool. Finally the last sequence shows a full dive. Parker uses her body to perform gestures that are metaphors for emotional and intellectual experience. *K* presents the embodiment of thought in action, the artist's body bridging the gap between the idea and the (viewer's) emotional experience of it.

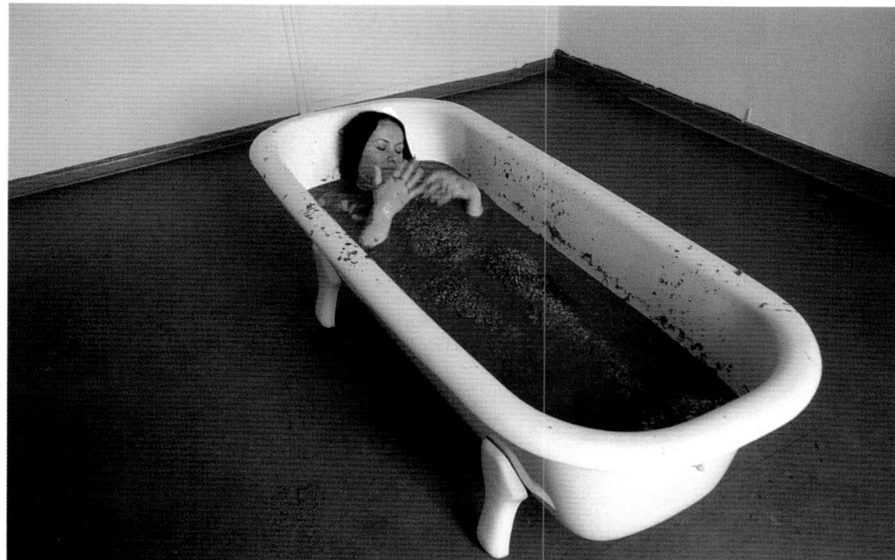
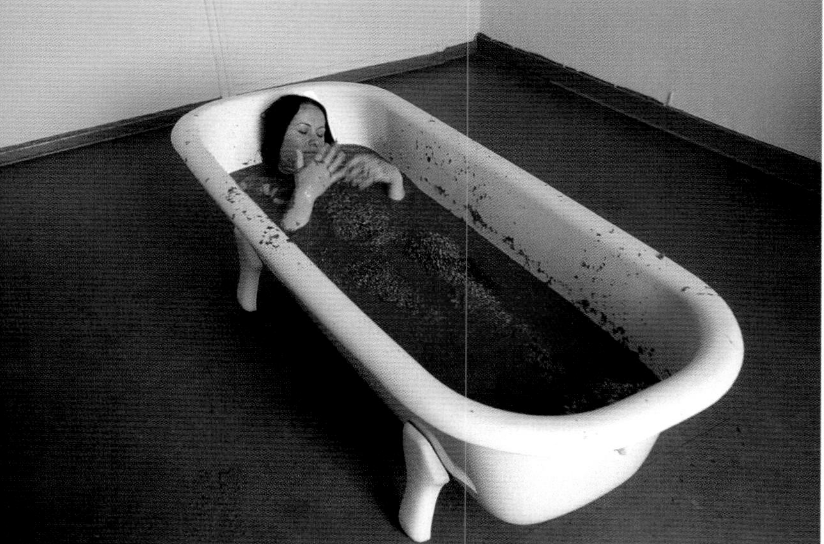

Teresa MURAK
Seed
1989
Künstlerhaus Bethanien, Berlin

In the Künstlerhaus Bethanien, Berlin, Murak lay immersed in a bath of wet seeds for several days, her body's heat stimulating germination. This performance was repeated at P.S. 1, New York, in 1991. Murak grew up in the Polish countryside, moving to Warsaw to go to art school in the early 1970s. She began sewing seeds into garments, which she wore to encourage germination through the warmth of contact with her skin. As an agent for germination and growth, Murak externalizes and expands the internal functions of her body, which through simple ritual become a metaphor for spiritual growth. As critic Andrzej Kostolowski wrote of her work, 'The artist's attitude towards seeds becomes more profound. They were seen as imaginative potential of life's drama; germination was understood as a release of energy; growth itself clearly became in her view a cosmic movement.'
– Andrzej Kostolowski, 'Intimacy Revealed', 1998

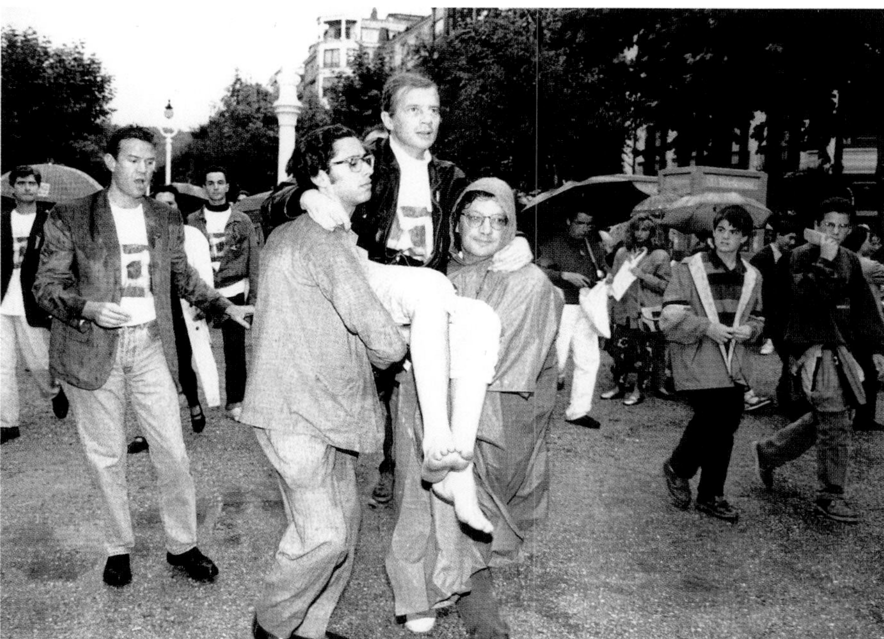

Pepe ESPALIÚ
Carrying
1992
San Sebastián, Spain

Carrying is the title of a series of works made by Espaliú in the last two years of his life when he was dying of AIDS. The title embodies the notion of 'carrying' in the sense of transmission of a virus between bodies as well as in the sense of ideas, of feelings, of care. A line of people split into pairs and then crossed their arms, grasping their partners' wrists to form a kind of seat. Espaliú, barefoot, was held suspended between each couple, his arms round their shoulders, as he was passed along the human chain without ever touching the ground. ' ... Nowadays physicians tell us that the only way is to learn to live with the disease. I think that first and more difficult is to change our attitude towards the social ... [which] aims to transform individuals into islands related to one another by hierarchies interested in competitivity, protagonism, selfishness. Learning to live with AIDS is, however, to reject this atomization, to take over ideas like help, solidarity, love or devotion ... '
– Pepe Espaliú, *Carrying* press release, 1992

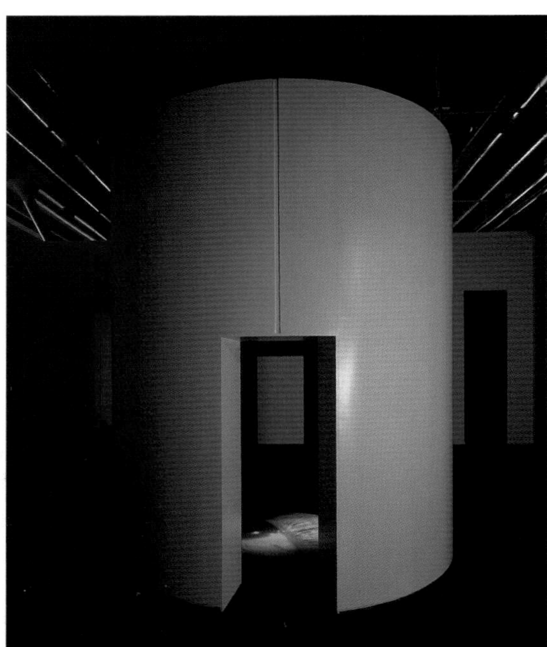

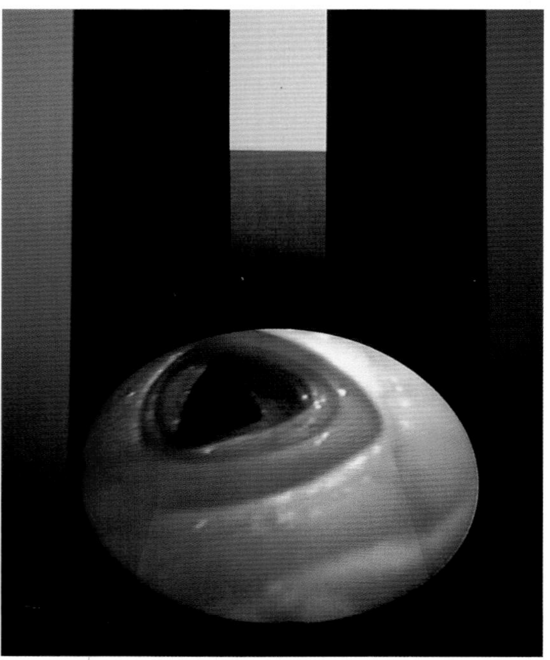

Mona HATOUM
Corps étranger
1994
Video installation
350 × 300 × 300 cm [138 × 118 × 118 in]
Collection, Musée national d'Art Moderne, Centre Georges Pompidou, Paris

Corps étranger consists of a cylindrical white enclosure with two openings through which the viewer may enter to stand over a large circular video projection of a medical scan of the interior of the artist's body. Penetrating into a variety of orifices, the scanner takes the viewer on a dizzying ride along the channels of digestion, reproduction and defecation, through opening and closing valves where liquids gush and swirl, while the body's breathing is manifest through a whistling sound that changes character depending on where the pulse has been taken. At odd moments the camera resurfaces to the outside of the body, where it records giant pores and hairs, only to plunge back inside on its disorienting journey through the internal landscape. Simultaneously penetrating and distancing, the medical gaze of the camera offers an intimate insight into Hatoum's body. At the same time the scale of the projection, enclosed in its womb-like space (the constructed enclosure), threatens to engulf the viewer.

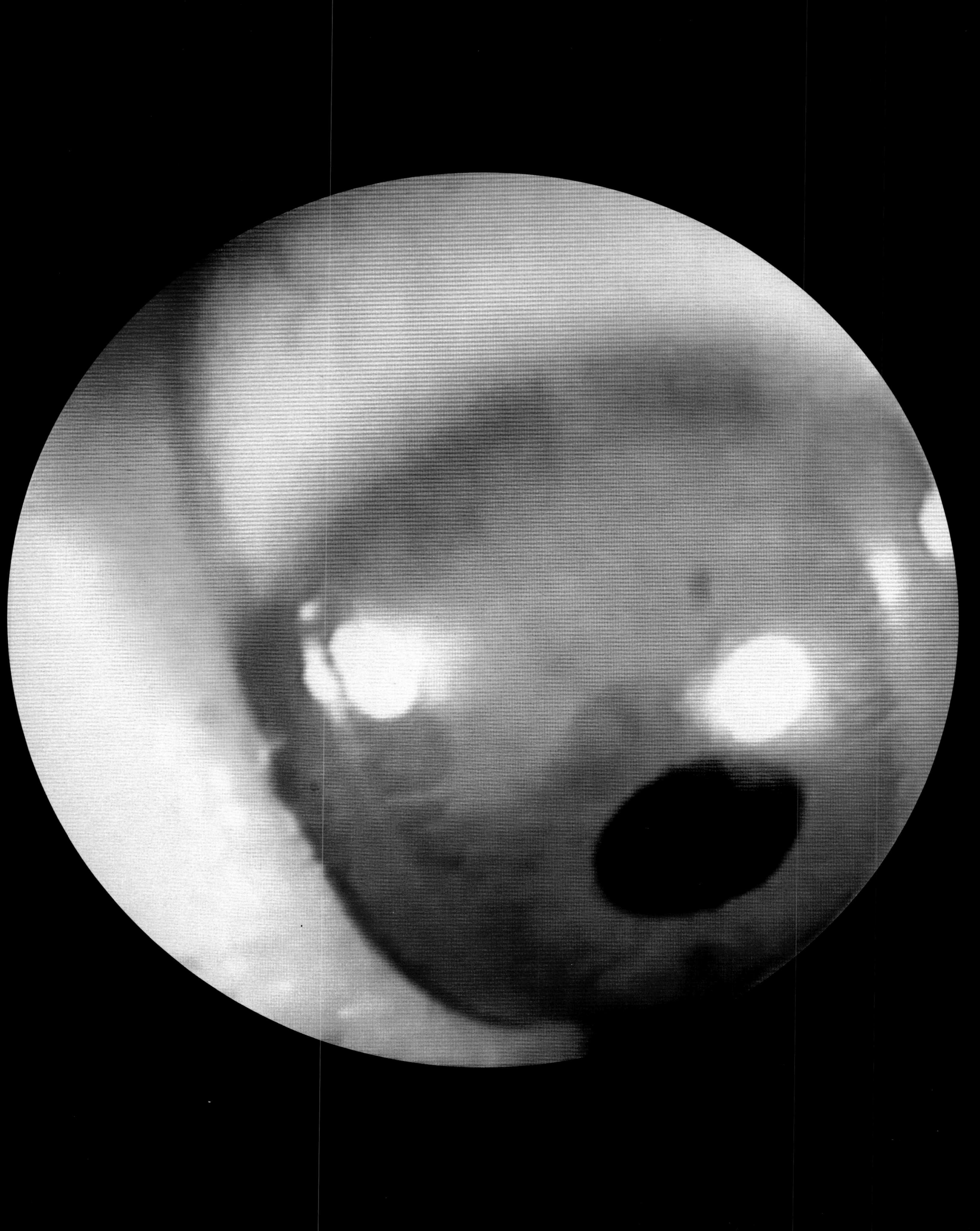

PERFORMING IDENTITY

In this chapter the body is the site where identity as defined by gender, race and sexuality is located, performed and challenged. The artist's body is used as a surface for the inscription of a visual language of identification, both real and projected from stereotypes. Notions of self and identity are acted out in public or brought to light through the artist's use of props, masks, costumes and disguises to become a masquerade of identity, particularly with regard to the crossing of traditional gender roles. By staging and adopting an identity through the use of accepted signs and signifiers, such as clothes, make-up and fake physical attributes, codes of gender and race are investigated.

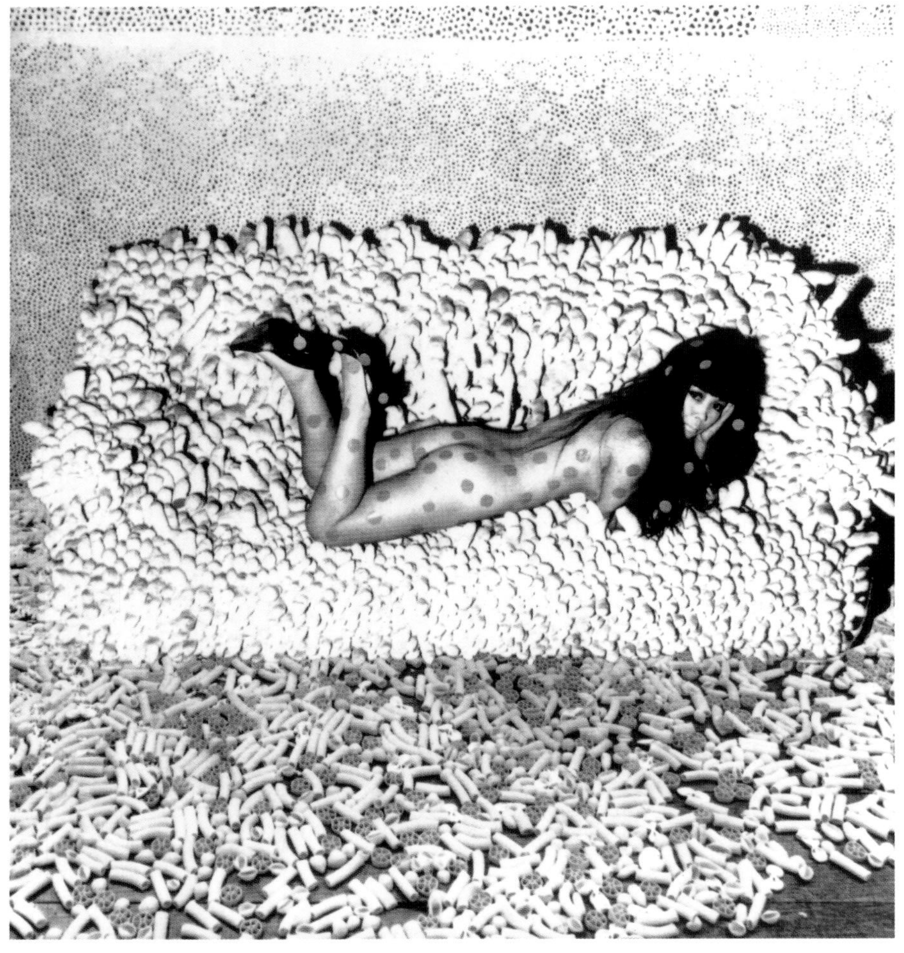

Yayoi KUSAMA
Untitled
c. 1966
Photo collage
Photograph by Hal Reif of the artist reclining on *Accumulation No. 2*, *Infinity Net* background, macaroni carpet
Dimensions unknown

Kusama was photographed reclining on *Accumulation No. 2* in front of one of her *Infinity Net* paintings. She collaged this photograph above a strip of glued-on macaroni which continued the textured, obsessional decorative patterns in the photograph. Presenting herself as both the artist-subject and the explicit body-object of desire, Kusama threatened contemporary attitudes towards her gender. Openly courting publicity, she was criticized for being an exhibitionist by critics, most notably J. F. Rodenbeck who wrote: 'Priestess of Nudity, Psychotic Artist, the Polka-Dot Girl, Obsessional Artist, publicity hound: in the 1960s Yayoi Kusama was the target of a number of epithets, some of them self-inflicted, all of them a part of an exhibitionist's notoriety.'
– J.F. Rodenbeck, 'Yayoi Kusama', 1996

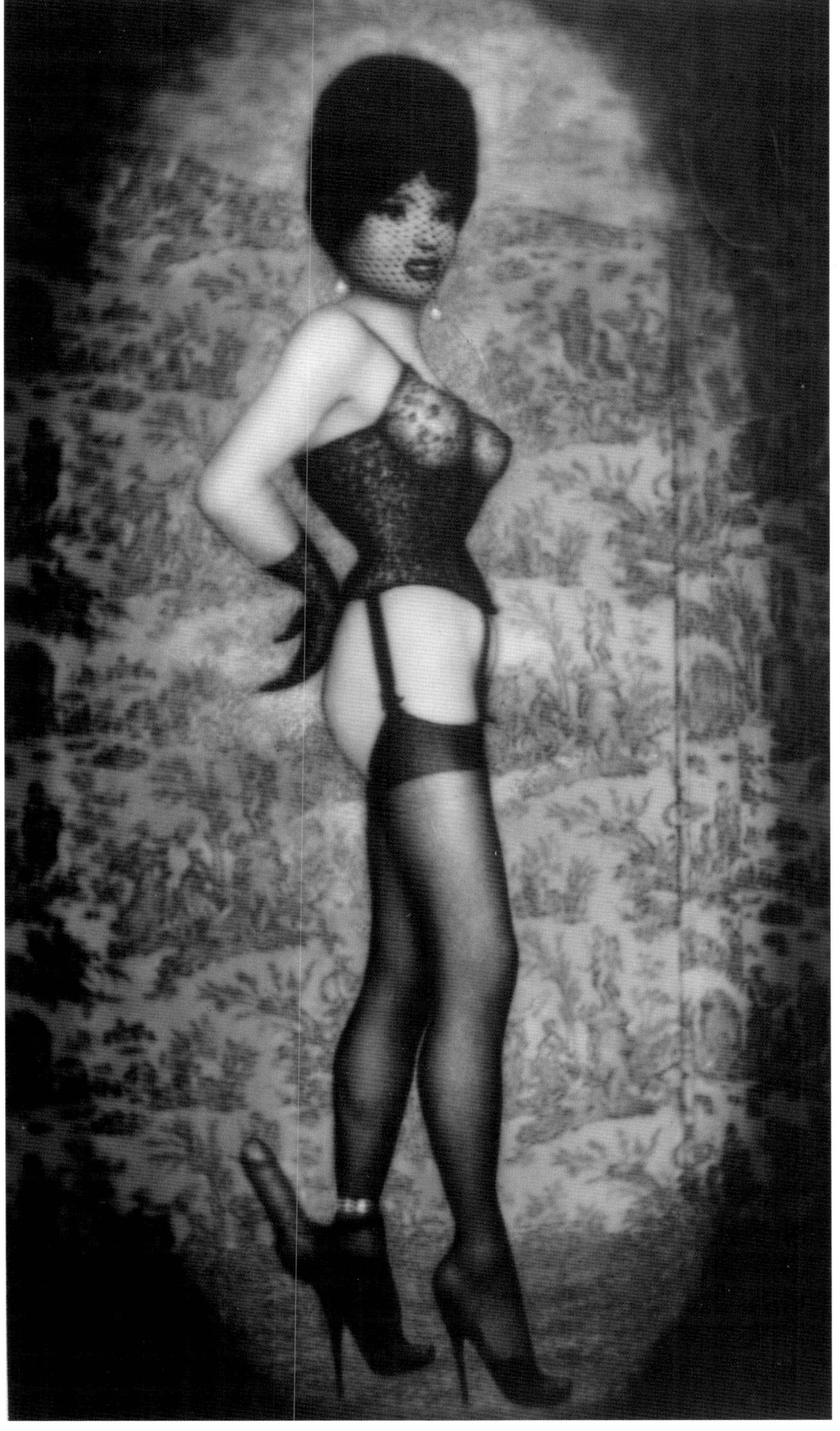

Pierre MOLINIER
The Spur of Love
1966-68
Gelatine-silver print
16 × 9.5 cm [6 × 4 in]

Molinier's photographs depict himself and other models wearing glamorous make-up, female masks, corsets, stockings and stiletto heels, with props such as mannequins or handmade dildos. In *The Spur of Love* he re-creates himself as the image of his own desire. He becomes a hermaphrodite, a state of 'sacred perfection', transfixed for consumption by his own voyeuristic eyes. He transforms his body from male to female through the addition of breasts, by concealing his penis and wearing female underwear. The phallus has been relocated to his heel, where he can use it on himself. By presenting his phallus castrated, reconstructed and attached to a fetishized and 'feminine' garment – his stiletto shoes – he disrupts the system of binary oppositions by which we traditionally understand gender. 'I would prefer to be sodomized by a dildo. And by a woman! Or a beautiful transvestite ... But I believe a woman would be better, because she is what society calls the most *malseine* [dangerous, unwholesome, pernicious].'
– Pierre Molinier quoted by Bernard Marcad, 'Glossaire Orient', 1995

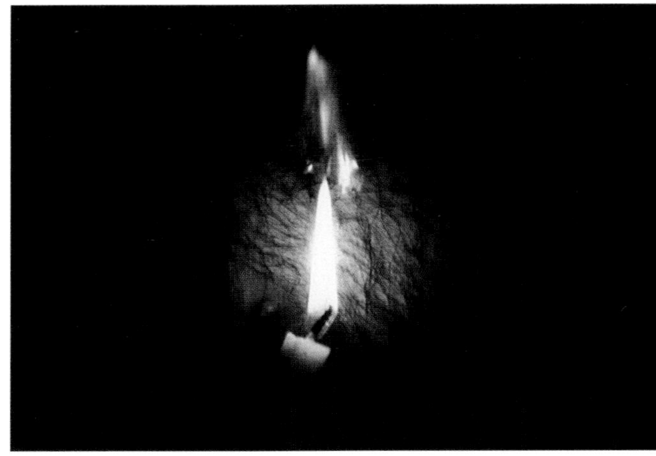

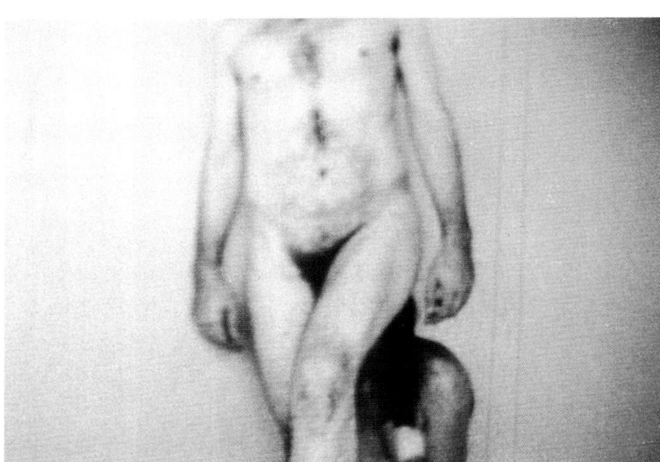

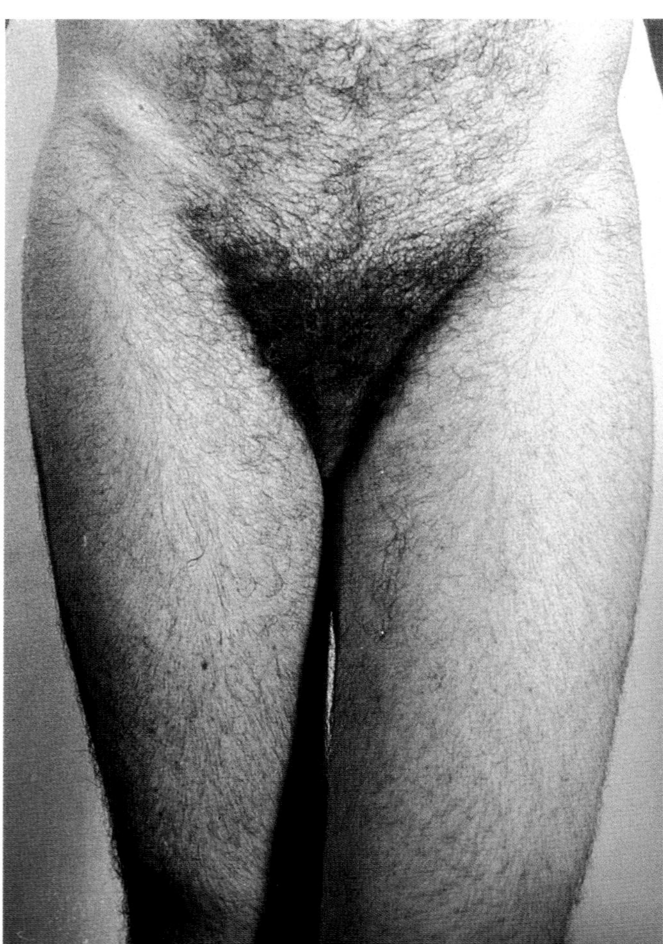

Vito ACCONCI
Conversions
1971
Film still
Super-8 film, 24 mins., black and white, silent

In his series of *Conversions* Acconci attempted a painful alteration of his body, burning the hair off his chest with a candle, pulling at his nipples to form breasts and hiding his penis between his legs in order to assume the sexual identity of a woman. Altering the sexual boundaries of his body in this way, Acconci points to a theme of personal metamorphosis. The elements of comedy and pathos in the artist's conversion of his masculine body into a more feminine one are undercut by the sacreligious violence of burning away body hair (the artist was raised in a strict Catholic-Italian home), as though purging his body for sacrifice. Frequently parodying heroic machismo in his art actions, Acconci here suggests that access to the feminine although desirable, might be both ludicrous and painful.

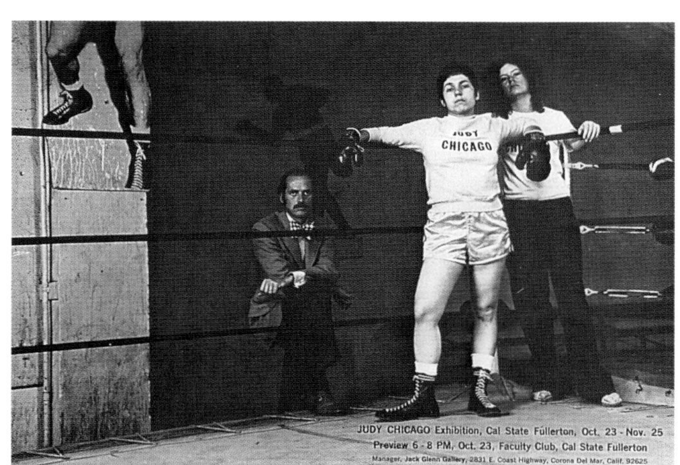

Judy CHICAGO
Boxing Ring
1970
Advertisement
27 × 27 cm [10 × 10 in]

Becoming increasingly frustrated by the difficulties in gaining recognition as a female artist, Chicago decided to change her name publicly from Gerowitz, that of her first husband, to Chicago, as a symbol of her new-found freedom from male dominance. She had a sweatshirt printed with her new name and posed for an advertisement in the boxing ring in which Muhammad Ali had trained. Chicago's parody of the macho announcements and posters used by many male artists at the time heralded an important moment in feminist history: 'the moment when women all over the country came out fighting in an effort to somehow effect a change in the intense discrimination of the art world'.
– Judy Chicago, *Beyond the Flower*, 1996

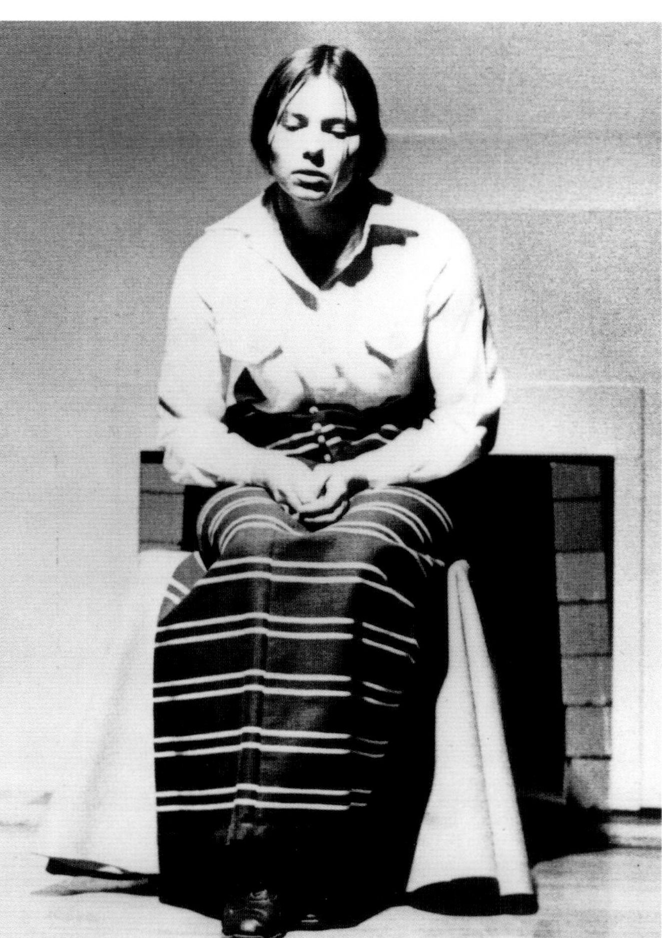

Faith WILDING
Waiting
1971
California Institute of the Arts, Los Angeles

In a performance at Womanhouse, a project of the Feminist Art Program at the California Institute of the Arts, Wilding sat passively with her hands in her lap and rocked back and forth as she listed the endless waiting of a woman's life. 'Waiting ... waiting ... waiting/Waiting for someone to come in/Waiting for someone to pick me up/Waiting for someone to hold me/ Waiting for someone to feed me/Waiting for someone to change my diaper ... Waiting/... Waiting to be a big girl/ ... Waiting to wear a bra/Waiting to menstruate/Waiting to read forbidden books/ ... /Waiting to have a boyfriend/Waiting to go to a party, to be asked to dance, to dance close/Waiting to be beautiful/Waiting for the secret/Waiting for life to begin ... Waiting ...

' ... Waiting to be somebody/ ... Waiting for my pimples to go away/Waiting to wear lipstick, to wear high heels and stockings/Waiting to get dressed up, to shave my legs/Waiting to be pretty ... Waiting .../Waiting for him to notice me, to call me/Waiting for him to ask me out/Waiting for him to pay attention to me/Waiting for him to fall in love with me ...

'Waiting to get married/ ... Waiting for my wedding night/... Waiting for him to come home, to fill my time ... /Waiting for my baby to come/Waiting for my belly to swell/Waiting for my breasts to fill with milk/Waiting to feel my baby move/Waiting for my legs to stop swelling/Waiting for the first contractions/Waiting for the contractions to end/Waiting for the head to emerge/Waiting for the first scream, the afterbirth/ ... Waiting for my baby to suck my milk/Waiting for my baby to stop crying ...

Waiting for him to tell me something interesting, to ask me how I feel/Waiting for him to stop being crabby, to reach for my hand, to kiss me good morning/Waiting for fulfilment ...

'Waiting for my body to break down, to get ugly/Waiting for my flesh to sag/ ... Waiting for a visit from my children, for letters/Waiting for my friends to die .../Waiting for the pain to go away/Waiting for the struggle to end .../Waiting ... '
– Faith Wilding, *Waiting*, 1971

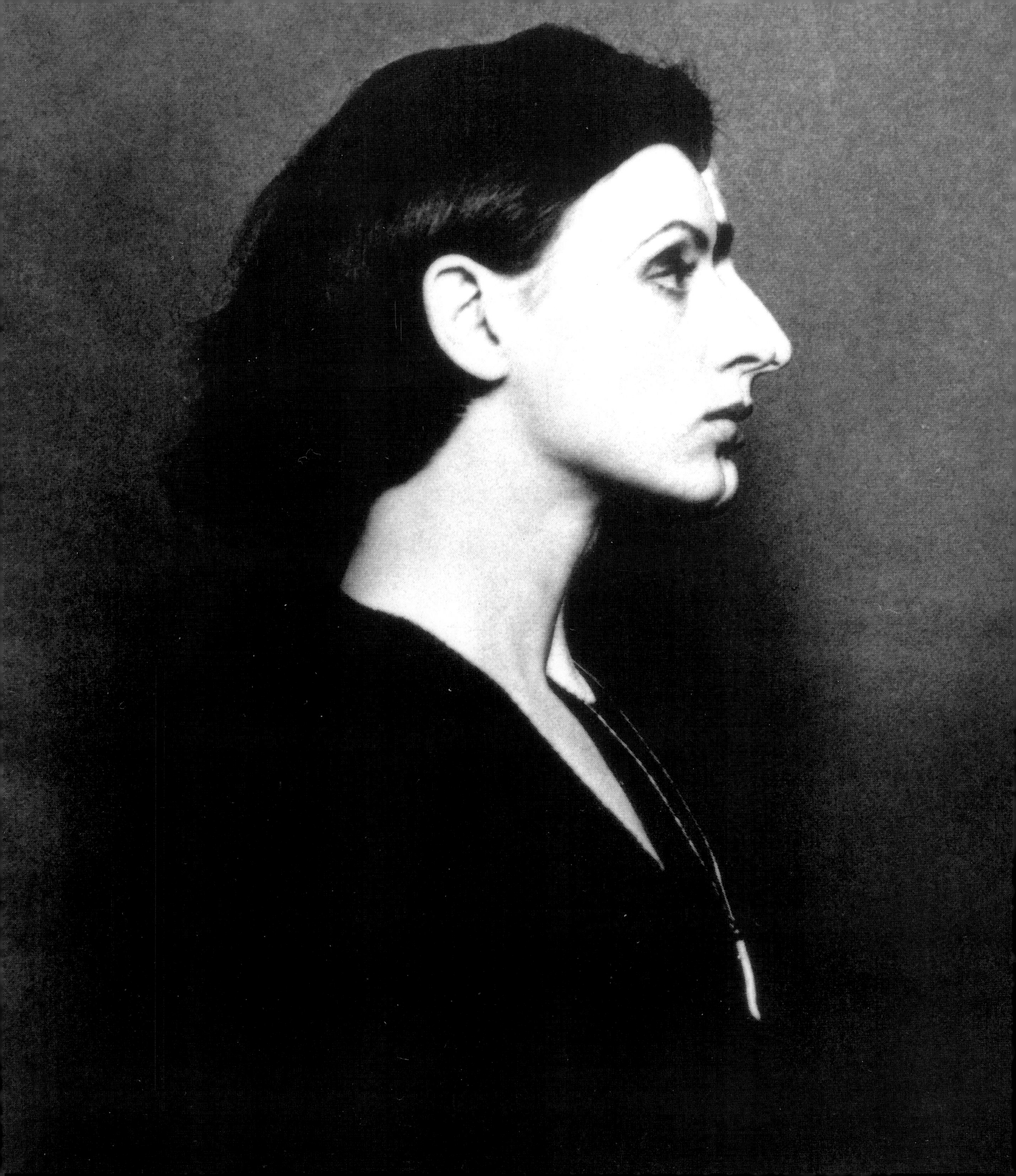

Urs LÜTHI
Self-Portrait with Ecky
1974
Photograph on canvas
90 × 70 cm [35.5 × 27.5 in]

Lüthi photographed himself and his girlfriend standing together, face pressed against face, their identical make-up and clothing making them resemble twins. 'I was trying to identify myself as much as possible with my girlfriend and to slip into her skin in some way.'

Earlier Lüthi had posed as a transvestite for the camera in order to see 'how far I could go in the relationship between a man and a woman'. Motivated by an exploration of his psychological makeup and how it related to his intimate connection with a member of the opposite sex, Lüthi hoped that by communicating 'all that is intimate and personal in me', he would provoke the viewer to reflect upon and question equally personal and contradictory parts of him/herself. The only way he could visually represent his 'feminine features' was by representing himself as a transvestite. Breaking gender stereotyping apart, Lüthi indicates that the connection he feels to the 'feminine' is located somewhere deep inside the psyche, way beyond social appearances and behaviour.

– all quotes from Urs Lüthi, 'The Artist and His Double: Interview with François Pluchart', 1974

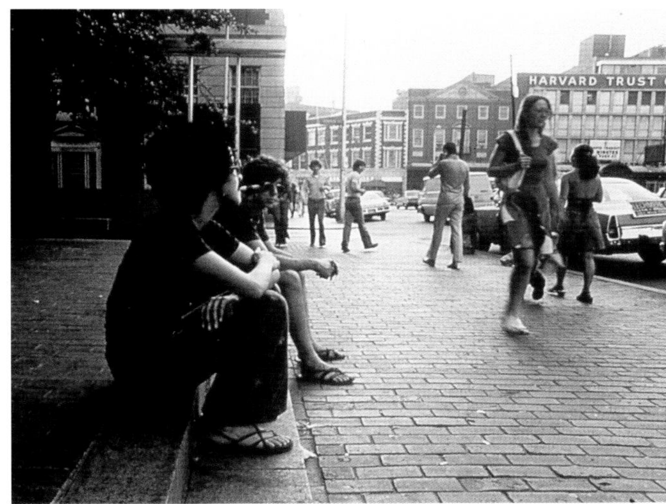

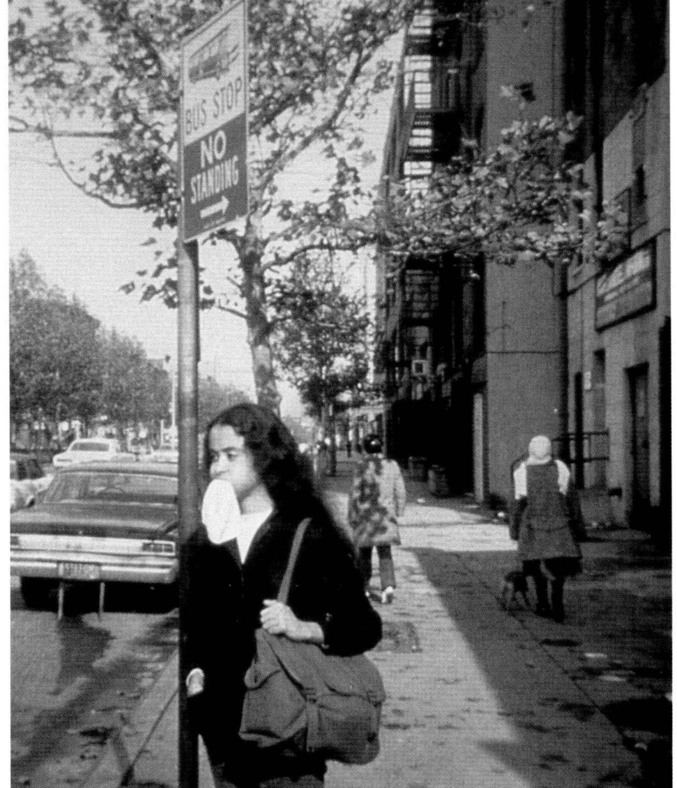

top
Adrian PIPER
The Mythic Being: Cruising White Women
1975
Cambridge, Massachusetts

bottom
Adrian PIPER
Catalysis IV
1970–71
New York

Piper's performances, which took place in the street, on the subway, in museums, bookshops and other public places, demonstrate a desire to question and disrupt general social attitudes towards difference, and how this is read through a person's appearance and gestures. In the *Mythic Being* series Piper disguised herself as an androgynous, racially indeterminate young man, wearing a black t-shirt, flared jeans, big sunglasses, an afro wig and Zapata-style moustache. In her *Catalysis* series her presence, or 'quirky personal activities', were genuinely disruptive. For example, she would appear on the subway in stinking clothes during rush hour or with balloons attached to her ears, nose, hair and teeth. She would go shopping in a smart department store in clothing with sticky white paint letters reading 'WET PAINT' or to a library carrying a concealed tape recording of loud belches. In this way she forced a direct confrontation with the public, which she said caused for her 'some really heavy personality changes'.

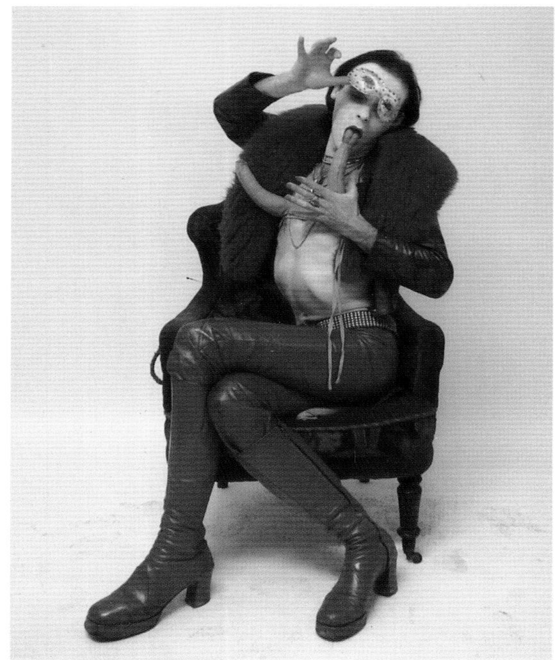

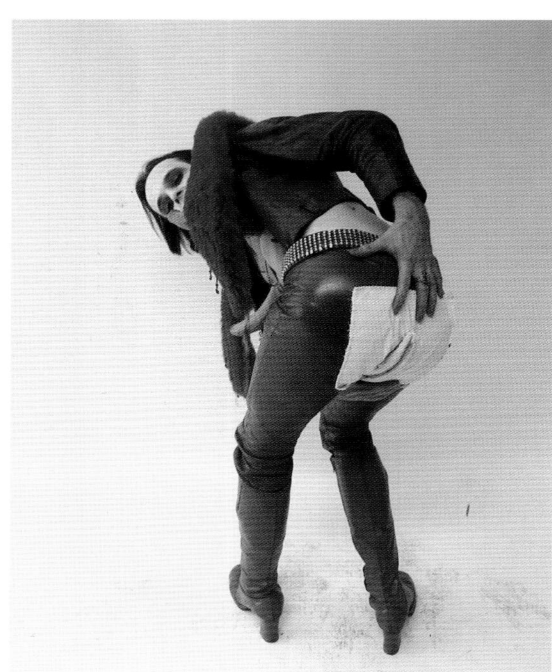

Jürgen KLAUKE

Transformer (detail)

1973

Colour photographs

4 photographs, 120 × 100 cm [47 × 39 in] each

Klauke photographed himself in a variety of poses and costumes signifying a range of cultural labels used to portray an identity in a state of flux. In *Transformer* he enacts 'the passing of one form into the other, in the ever-incompleted character of being', humorously posing as a sexual object in a costume that exaggerates and parodies the hermaphrodite. Klauke portrays himself as a caricature of the visual embodiment of his longing for multiple forms and androgynous gender. He believed that performance of the other's gender enabled a connection with those aspects of the other in himself, and thus an expansion of his internal boundaries and self-knowledge: ' … it's still possible to find your identity through that of others, a raising of consciousness, a reaching out for the limits, and with a little luck perhaps even beyond … I do not assume other roles, I don't want to be a woman or any other person, and I am certainly not striving for unity and divine perfection … if anything, it's a "happy hybrid" … '

– Jürgen Klauke, 'Interview with Peter Weibel', 1994

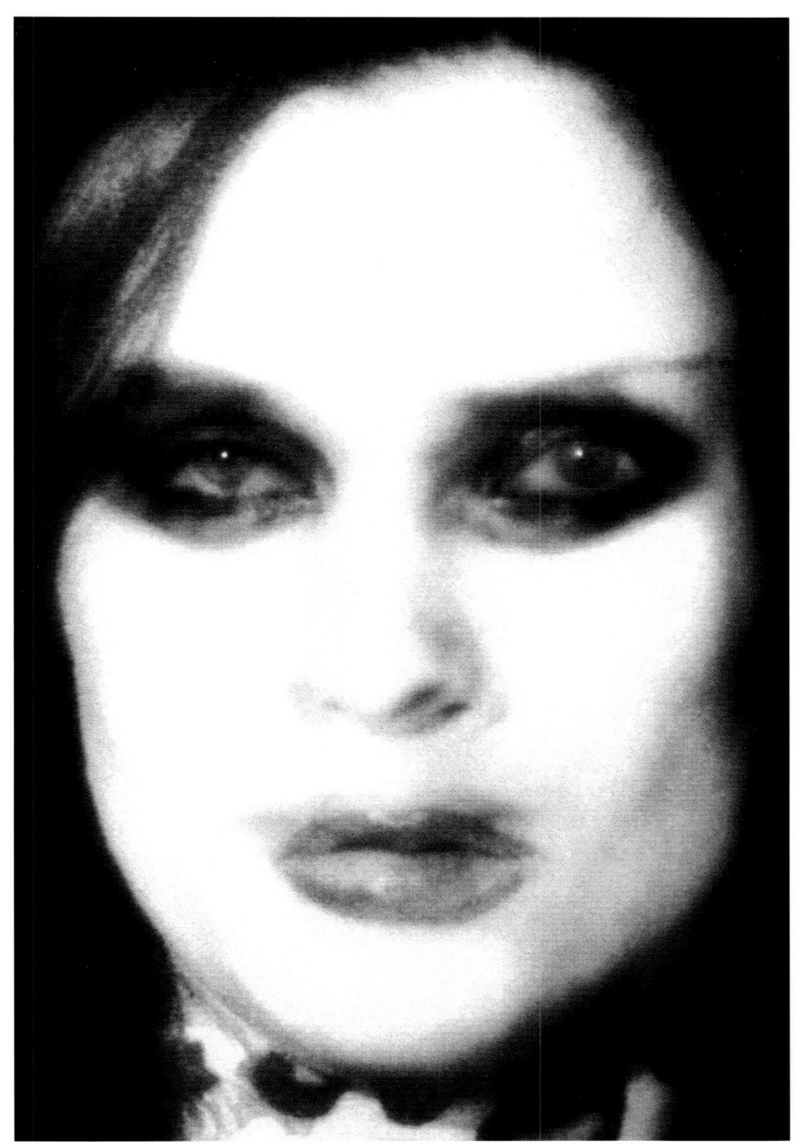

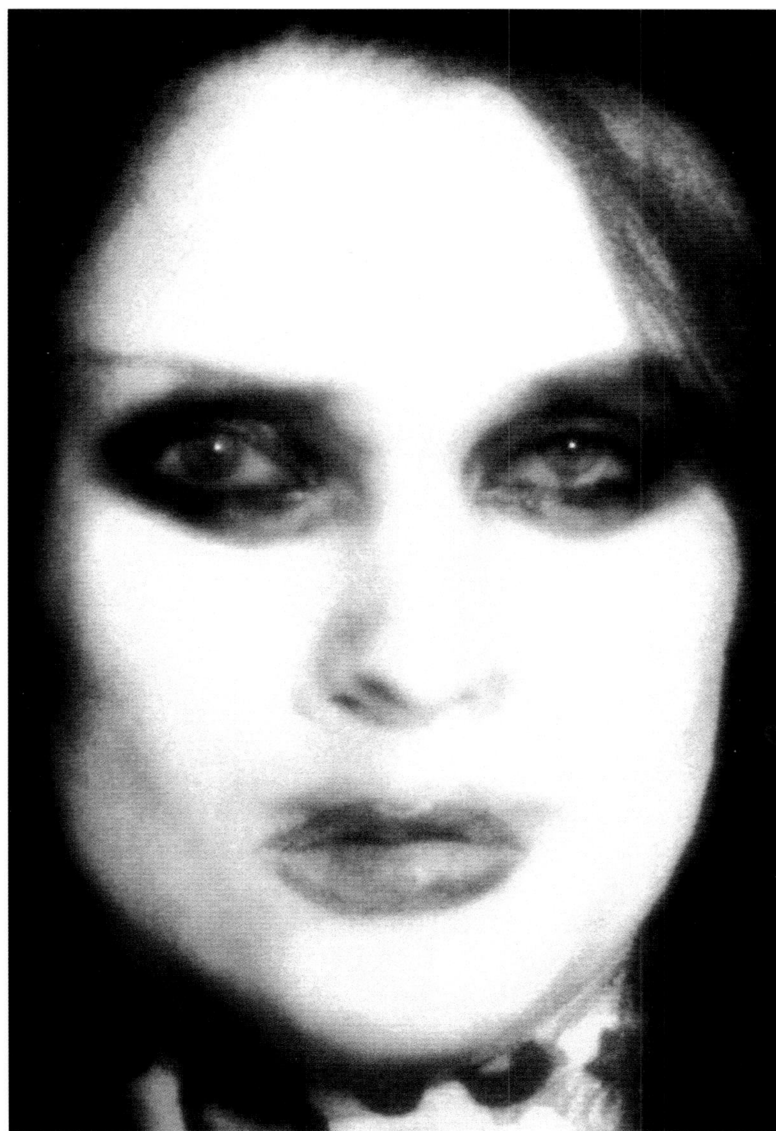

Katharina SIEVERDING
Transformer 1 A/B
1973
Digital analogue, acrylic, Perspex
2 parts, 190 × 125 cm [75 × 49 in] each

In a 1974 exhibition entitled 'Transformer: Aspekte der Travestie' (Transformation: Aspects of the Transvestite), images of Jürgen Klauke, Urs Lüthi and Sieverding were placed alongside those of the similarly androgynous musicians and image-makers David Bowie, Brian Eno and Lou Reed. Sieverding also created photographic montages with her partner Klaus Mettig, in which their male and female faces, similarly made up and coiffed, became almost indistinguishable. In her huge, mask-like, solarized images, the female imitates the male, and the male imitates the female, resulting in 'portraits' whose blurred boundaries and arbitrary distinctions emphasize lack of difference between self and other. Sieverding explained that as a woman she needed to put herself in the masculine position in order to understand the opposite point of view, saying that 'the conquest of another gender takes place in oneself'. While the majority of contemporary female artists working with images of identity were concerned with emphasizing their difference from the masculine, Sieverding, like Lüthi, was concerned with declaring similarity. Transvestism becomes a way to communicate 'roles, repressions ... and self-extension' common to the psychology of both genders.
– all quotes from Lucy R. Lippard, 'The Pains and Pleasures of Rebirth', 1976

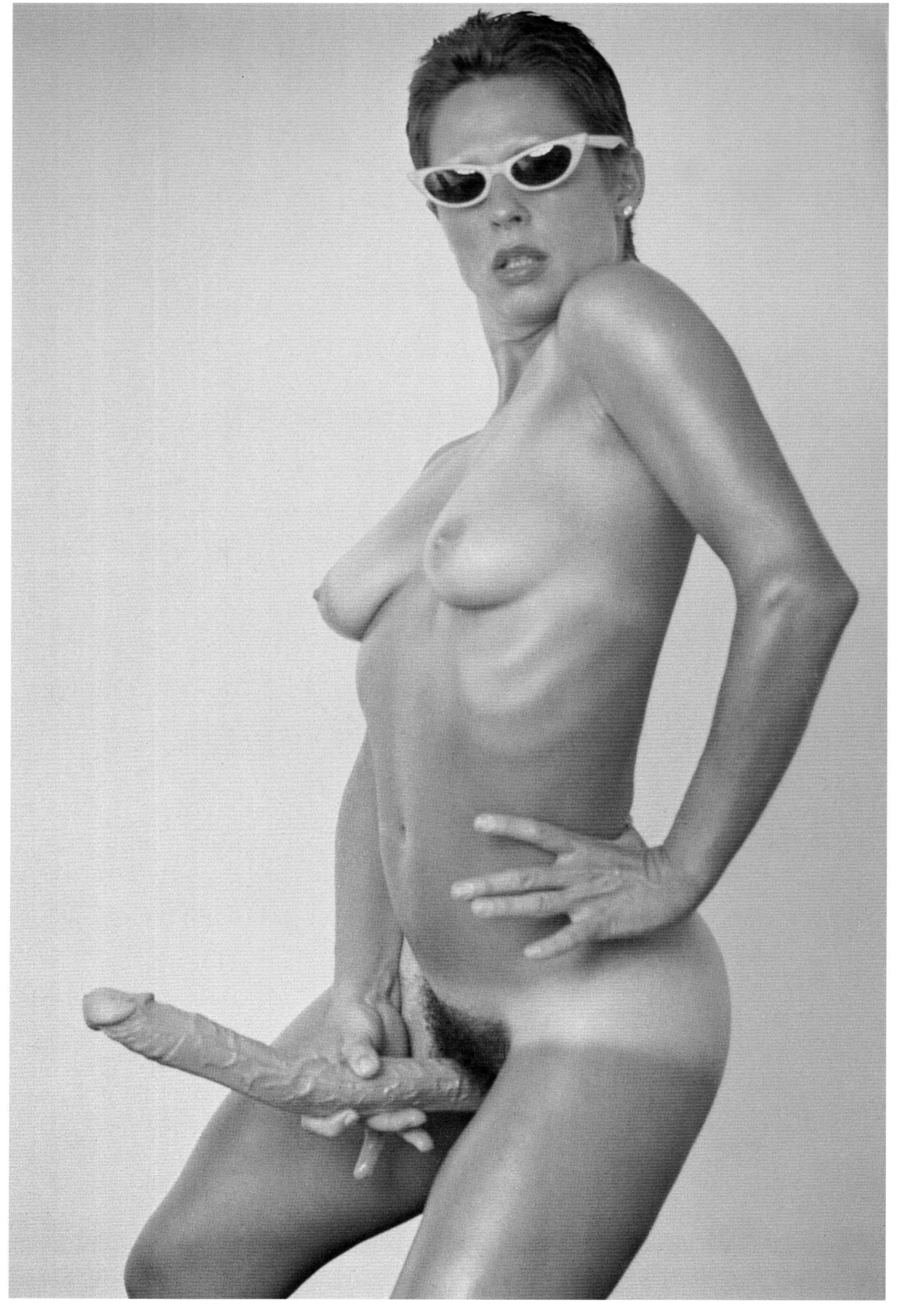

Lynda BENGLIS
Untitled (detail)
1974
Colour photograph
26.5 × 26.5 cm [10.5 × 10.5 in]

For the invitations to her exhibitions Benglis used images of herself in various gender roles: posing like a man with her car, or in a pin-up-style, submissive feminine role, for example. This infamous advertisement placed in *Artforum* was initally intended as a centrefold artist's statement, but it was not permitted by the magazine's editor. She declined the magazine's offer to run her image with an article on her work, instead paying for advertising space under her gallery's name, claiming '... that placing the gallery's name on the work strengthened the statement, thereby mocking the commercial aspect of the ad, the art-star system and the way artists use themselves, their persona, to sell the work. It was mocking sexuality, masochism and feminism. The context of the placement of the ad in an art magazine was important.'
– Lynda Benglis quoted by Susan Keane, 'Dual Natures', 1991

Benglis later explained that her intention had been to mock the idea of having to take sexual sides – of being either a male artist or a female one – and also the hype created by the media.

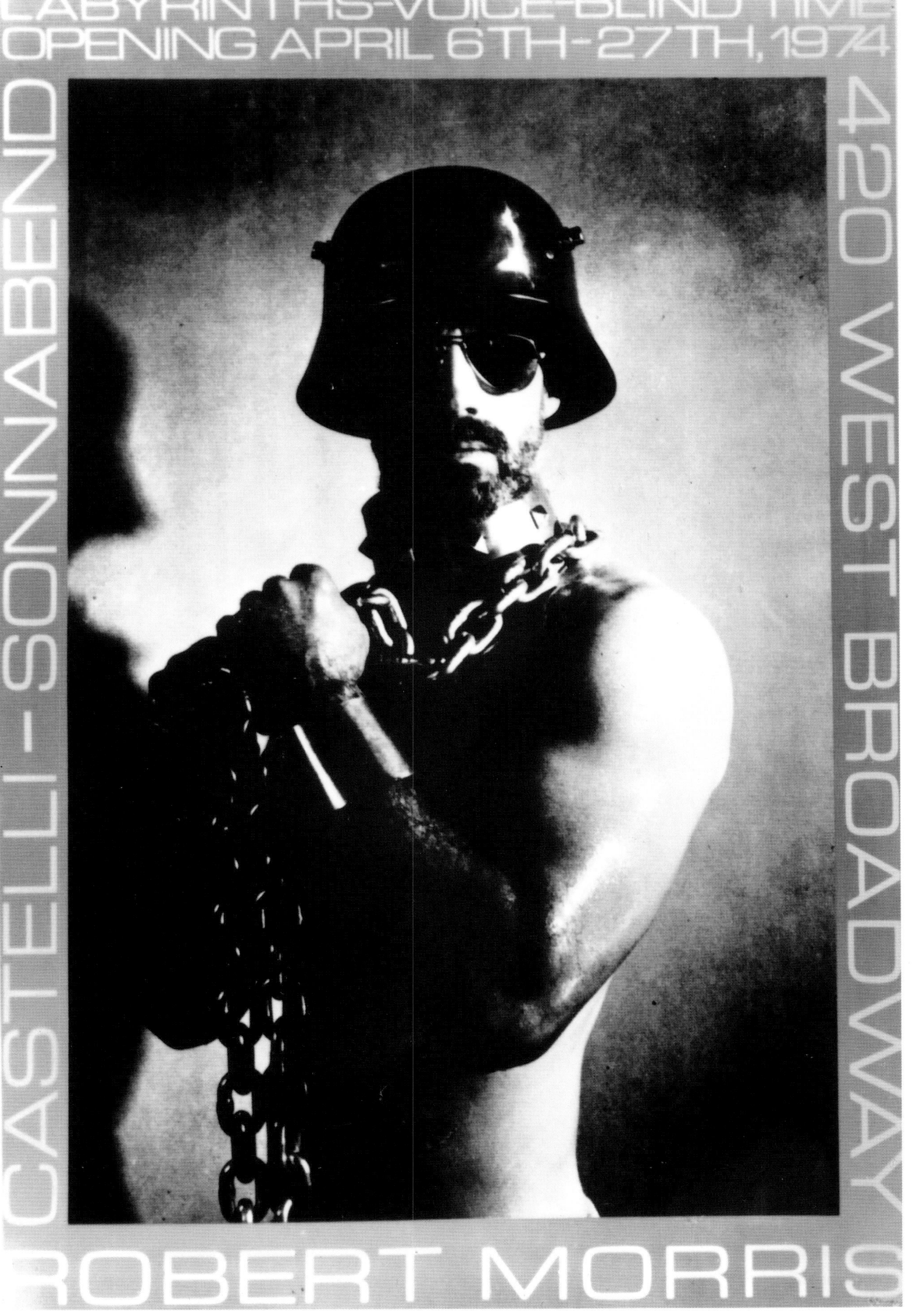

Robert MORRIS
Untitled
1974
Offset lithograph
94 × 61 cm [37 × 24 in]

Morris made this poster-sized self-portrait for his exhibition at Castelli-Sonnabend Gallery, New York. Simultaneously evoking the subjugation of masochism through the heavy chains shackling his neck and wrists and the domination of fascism as signified by the German helmet and dark glasses, Morris' image both parodies and reinforces dominant codes of heterosexual masculinity, while also evoking associations with homosexuality. His powerful muscular build and aggressive stance would seem to confirm a portrayal of 'hyper' masculinity, which the militaristic costume both reinforces and undercuts. At the time he was working in dialogue with Lynda Benglis on themed male and female stereotypical poses and the play between domination and submission. This image presents a masculine 'masquerade' that simultaneously affirms and challenges sexual power.

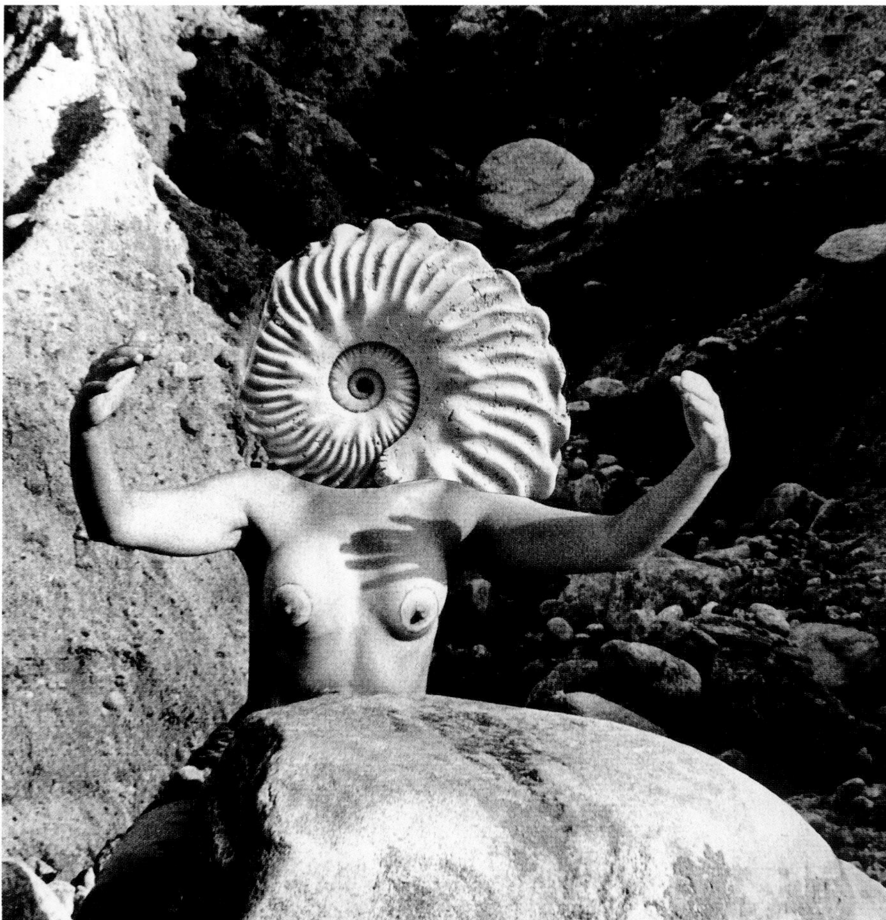

Mary Beth EDELSON
Goddess Head
1975
Photo collage
Approx. 20 × 25 cm [8 × 10 in]

In her collages of the 1970s Edelson looked to the symbols and myths of women's 'lost' history in order to recuperate a sense of female heritage and to bind contemporary woman to a collective feminine community. This essentialist approach attempted to create a new, powerful image of woman based on her primitive alignment with nature and goddess cults. This was a general tendency within the feminist movement of the time, which sought to mend the wrongs of culture with the 'rights of nature'. Referring to the traditional connection of women with the sea (as mother of all creatures), Edelson's human head has been replaced by a shell, which in its fossilized spiral resists penetration and personality and renders the 'goddess' figure as stony and enigmatic as the sphinx. Transforming the female figure from the form of her traditional representation, Edelson presents her body as both receptive and resistant, ancient and modern, monolithic and omnipresent.

opposite
Carolee SCHNEEMANN
Interior Scroll
1975
East Hampton, Long Island

Naked except for a sheet, Schneemann told her audience she would read from her book, *Cézanne, She Was A Great Painter*. She then unwrapped the covering sheet and painted large strokes of mud on the contours of her body and face. She climbed on to a long table and read the text while assuming a series of life-model poses, balancing the book in one hand. Dropping the book, she slowly extracted the scroll from her vagina and read the text inscribed on it, which was taken from feminist texts she had written for a previous work. First performed for an exhibition of paintings and a series of performance works for a largely female audience, called 'Women Here and Now', *Interior Scroll* was a culmination of Schneemann's research into 'vulvic space' and its connection with serpent forms as Goddess attributes in ancient cults. 'I thought of the vagina in many ways – physically, conceptually, as a sculptural form, an architectural referent, the source of sacred knowledge, ecstasy, birth passage, transformation ... a translucent chamber of which the serpent was the outward model: enlivened by its passage from the visible to the invisible, a spiralled coil ringed with the shape of desire and generative mysteries, attributes of both female and male sexual powers. This source of "interior knowledge" would be symbolized as the primary index unifying spirit and flesh in Goddess worship.'
– Carolee Schneemann, *More Than Meat Joy*, 1979

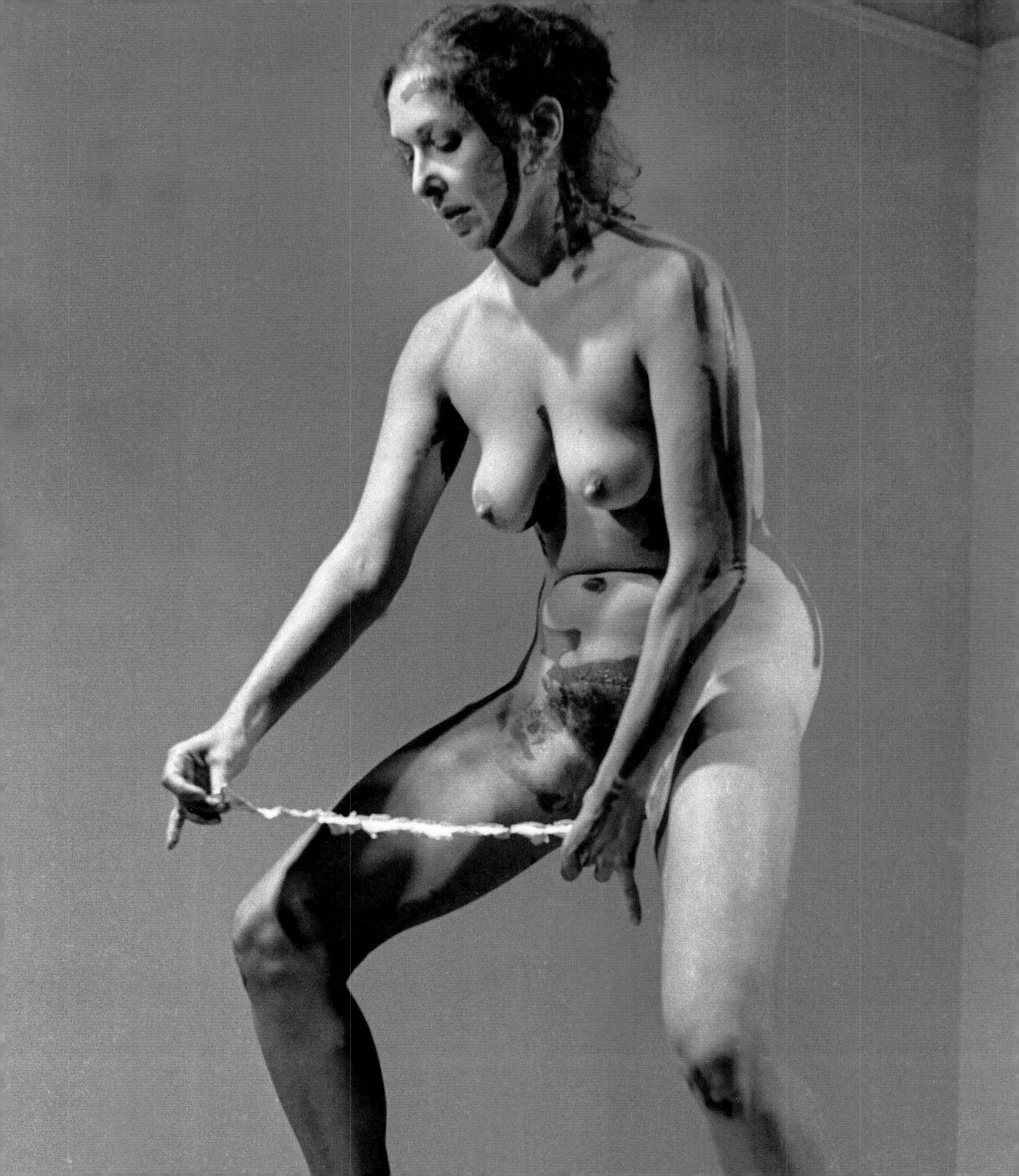

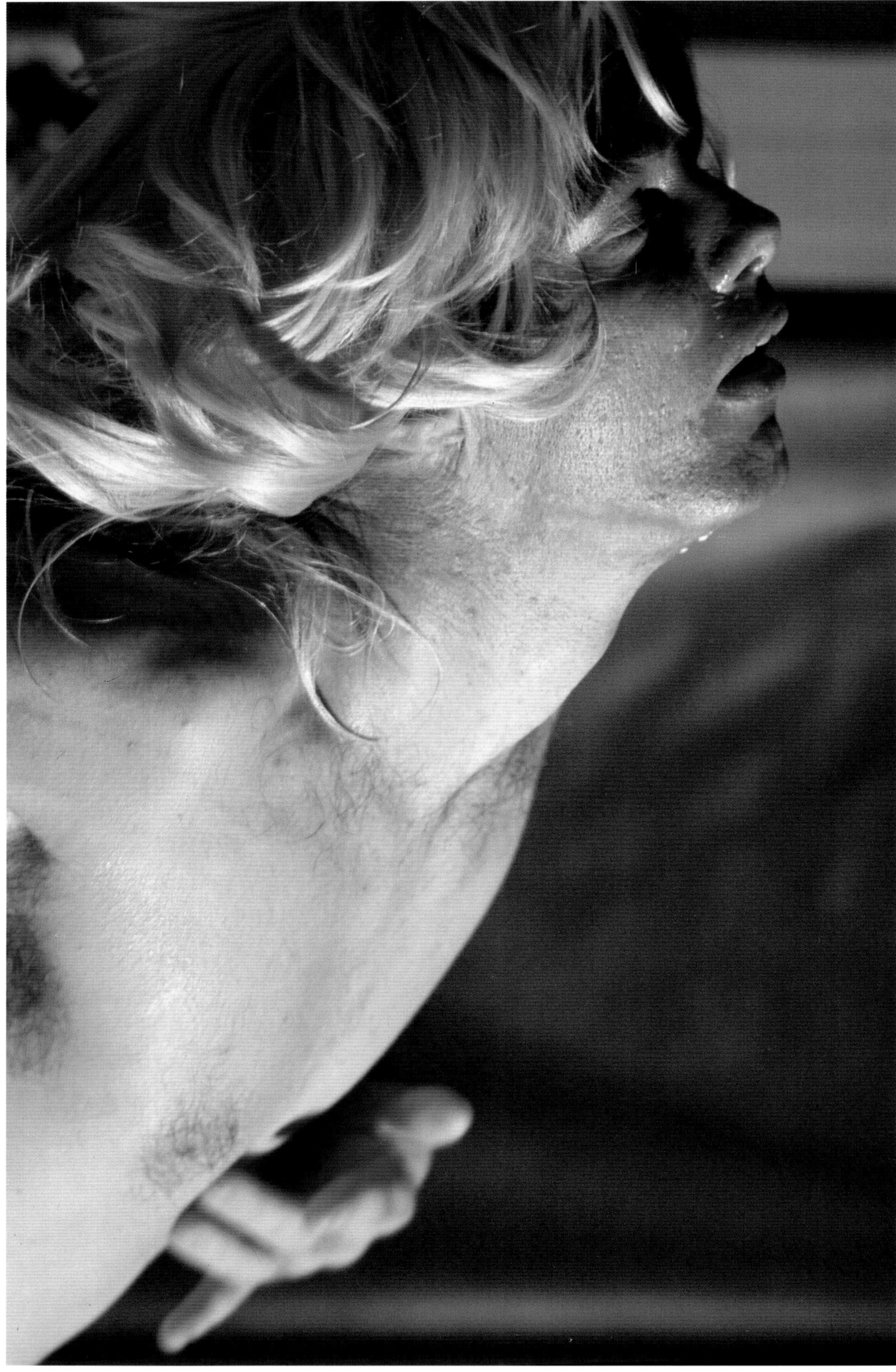

Paul McCARTHY
Sailor's Meat
1975
Los Angeles

McCarthy presents himself both as a female sex object wearing a blond wig, make-up and black bikini panties, and a debased male 'sailor', who copulates with a wad of ground beef and a mayonnaise jar. This is a disruption of the symbolic language of popular culture that references, more particularly, the imagery of soft-core B-movie stills. 'I'm dressed with eye makeup and a wig, but you are very aware that it is a man. It's the image of an androgynous figure. The illusion goes back and forth between watching a male and watching a female, and I think the power of the piece is that you get lost. It's this idea of seducing through an androgynous figure, exploring those sides of myself.'
– Paul McCarthy, 'There's a Big Difference Between Ketchup and Blood', 1993

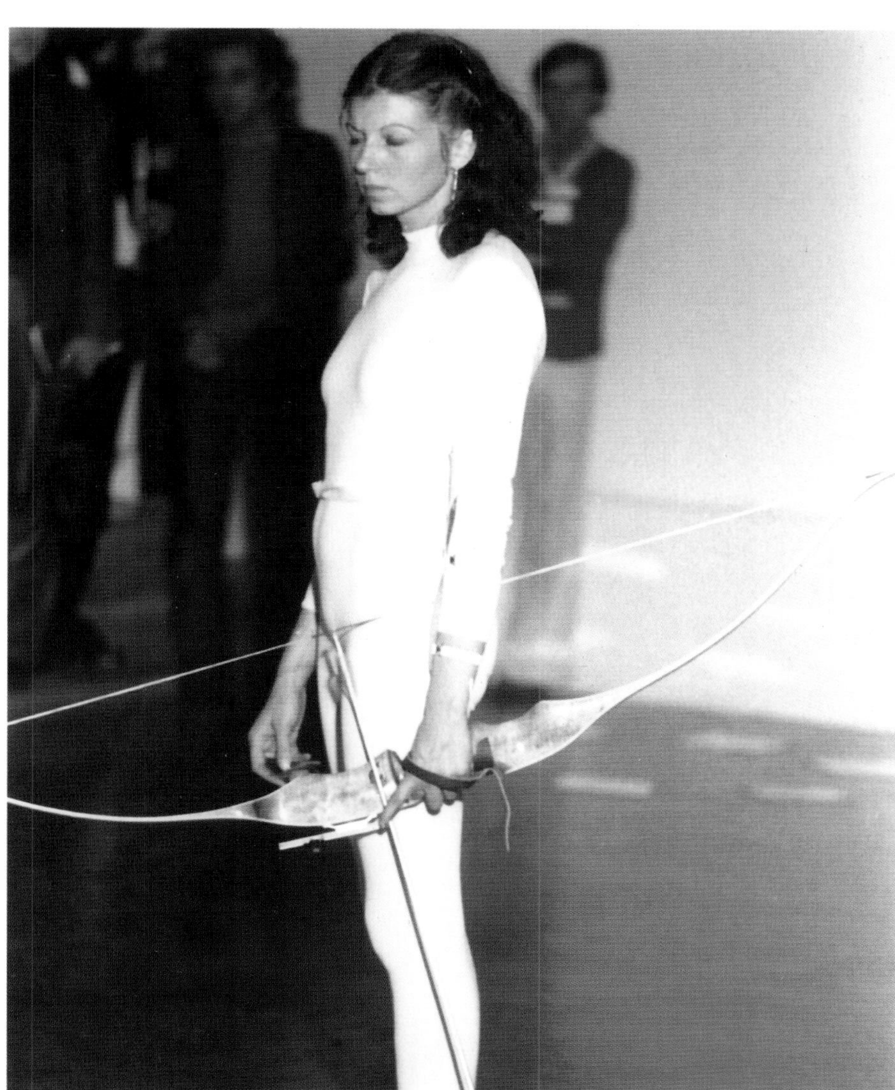

Ulrike ROSENBACH

Don't Believe I Am an Amazon

1975

Kunstmuseum, Dusseldorf

Rosenbach shot fifteen arrows at a target covered with a large black and white reproduction of Shephan Lochner's Renaissance painting *Madonna of the Rose Bower* (*c*. 1435–40). From a square hole cut into the centre of the target, a video camera recorded Rosenbach shooting the arrows. The performance subsequently appeared as a video. The recording made by the camera in the target was superimposed on the image of the Madonna, thus reversing the direction of the shooting arrows so that the artist's own face is superimposed on the Madonna's face as she shoots. The artist thus appears as both victim and torturer, which would seem to point to the multiple nature of feminine roles within society.

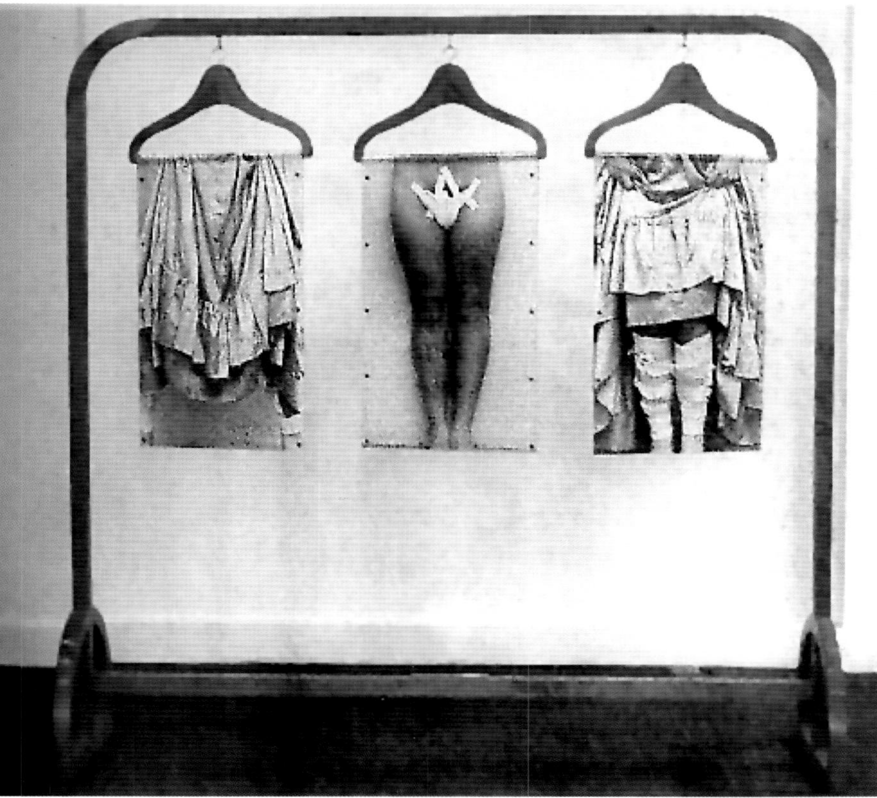

Carlos LEPPE

Perchero (Coat Hanger)

1975

Acrylic, wood, photograph, bronze

180 × 250 cm [71 × 98.5 in]

In a series of performances in the mid to late 1970s (apparently the first live performances in Chile) Leppe challenged the prevailing official order in his country. *Perchero* (*Coat Hanger*), presented at Galería Módulos y Formas, Santiago, was a series of photographs hung on coat hangers on a clothes rack, showing the artist's body being transformed into a woman. In contrast to the heterosexual (macho) norms of the reigning military, Leppe exhibited the transvestite body in terms of vulnerability and struggle. This provided a direct challenge to the highly trained and masculinized body of the status quo.

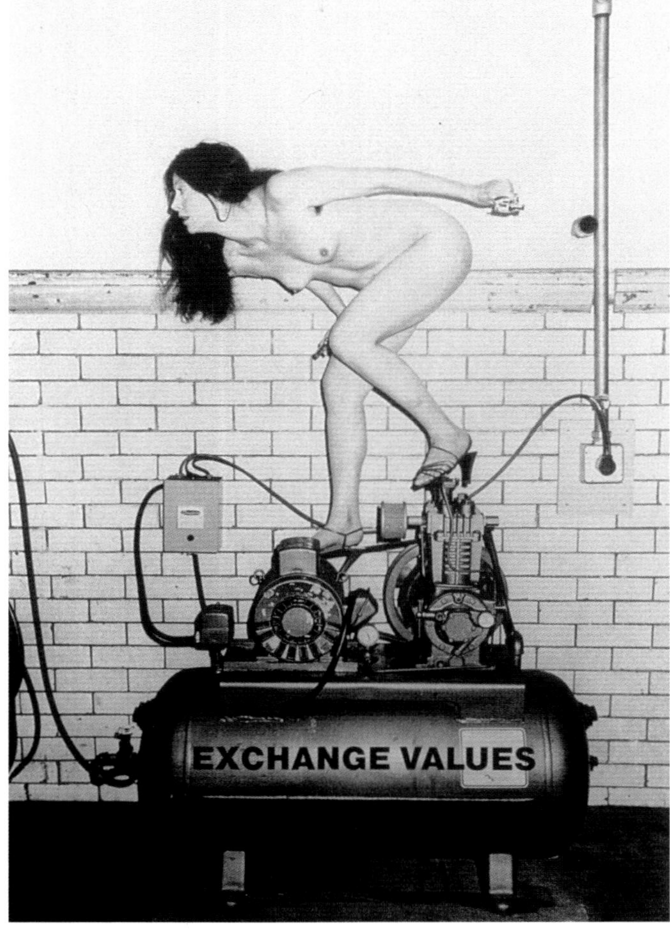

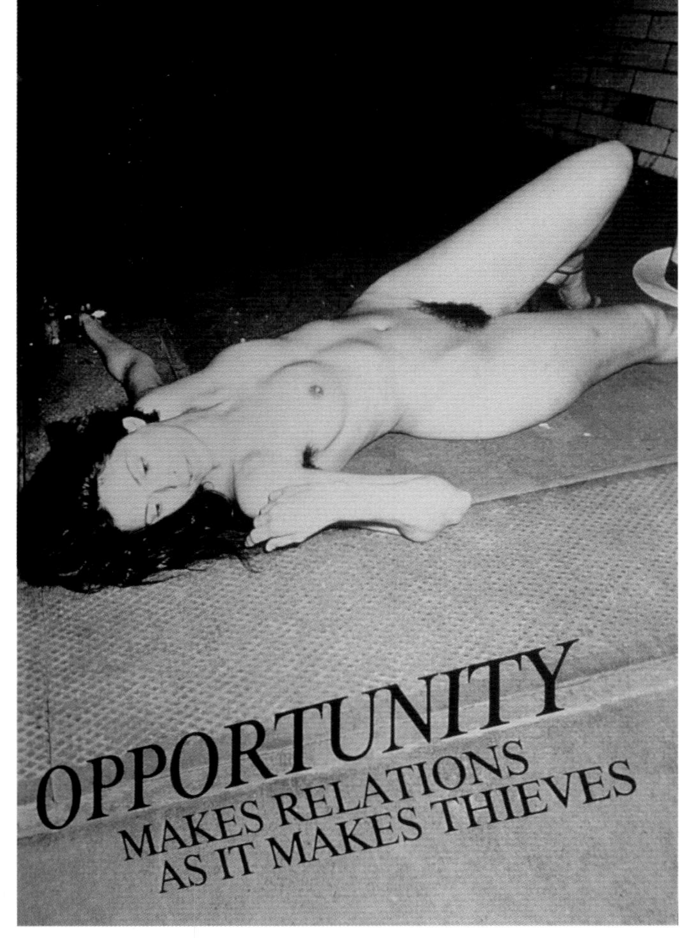

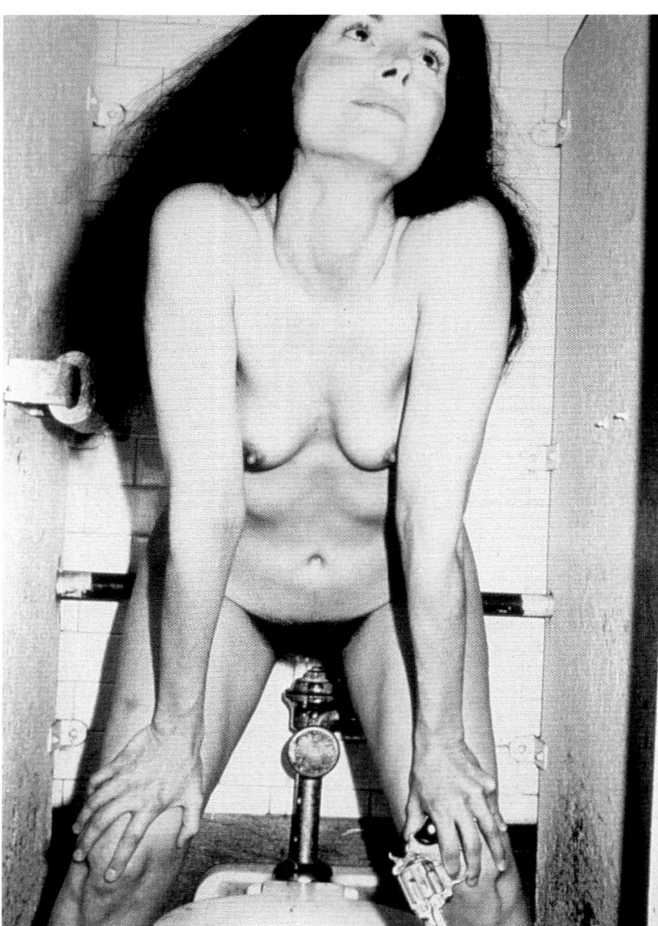

clockwise from top left

Hannah WILKE

Exchange Values (Marx)

1978-84

Black and white photograph

152 × 102 cm [60 × 40 in]

Hannah WILKE

Opportunity Makes Relations as it Makes Thieves (Goethe)

1978-84

Black and white photograph

152 × 102 cm [60 × 40 in]

Hannah WILKE

His Farced Epistol (Joyce)

1978-84

Black and white photograph

152 × 102 cm [60 × 40 in] each

Hannah Wilke made a series of 'performalist self-portrait' photographs at P.S. 1, New York, posing with a gun, naked and in high heels in a variety of run-down spaces. The photographs were overlaid with quotations from texts by male philosophers and artists regarding the relationships among individuals, art and society. The series was called *So Help Me Hannah*. The piece later became a series of videotaped performances in which Wilke moved slowly through the space periodically freezing into poses. This was accompanied by a soundtrack in which she read extensions of the quotations. The work explicitly fuses the female object-body – its objecthood accentuated by the pose, which presents that body as an exposed object – with the mind or 'I' of cultural production, as represented by the texts, and the artist's reappropriation and juxtaposition of them with her image. Wilke's 'feminine' appropriation of the subjective position traditionally held by the male is additionally parodied by the gun she wields, a symbol of masculine potency and destruction that contrasts with the exposure of her vulnerable naked body in order to force the viewer to question assumptions about how we look at the female body.

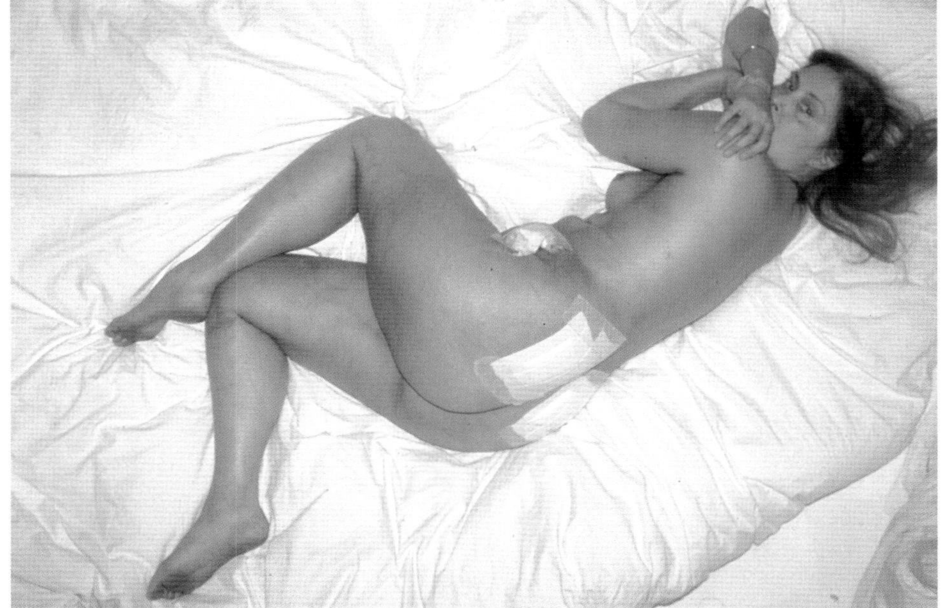

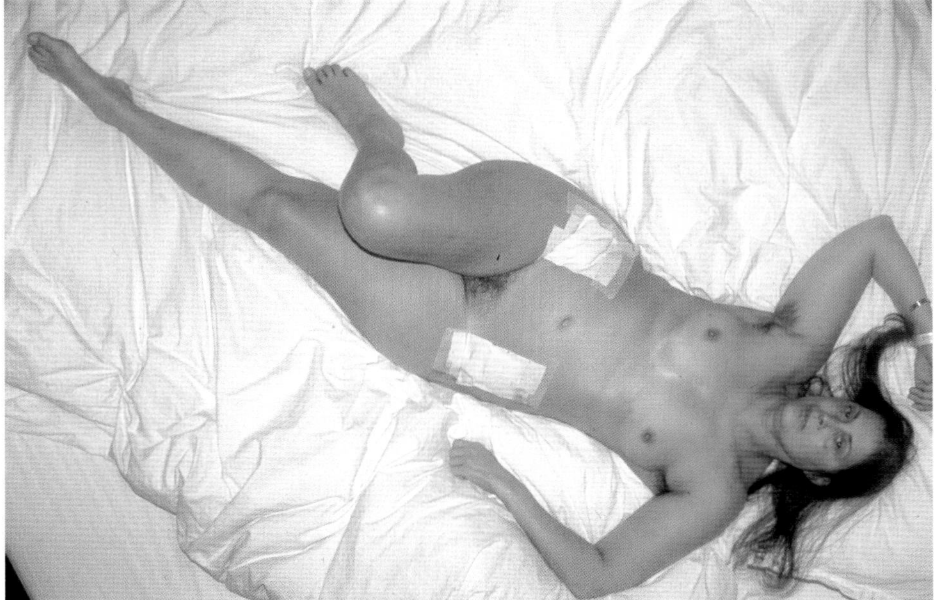

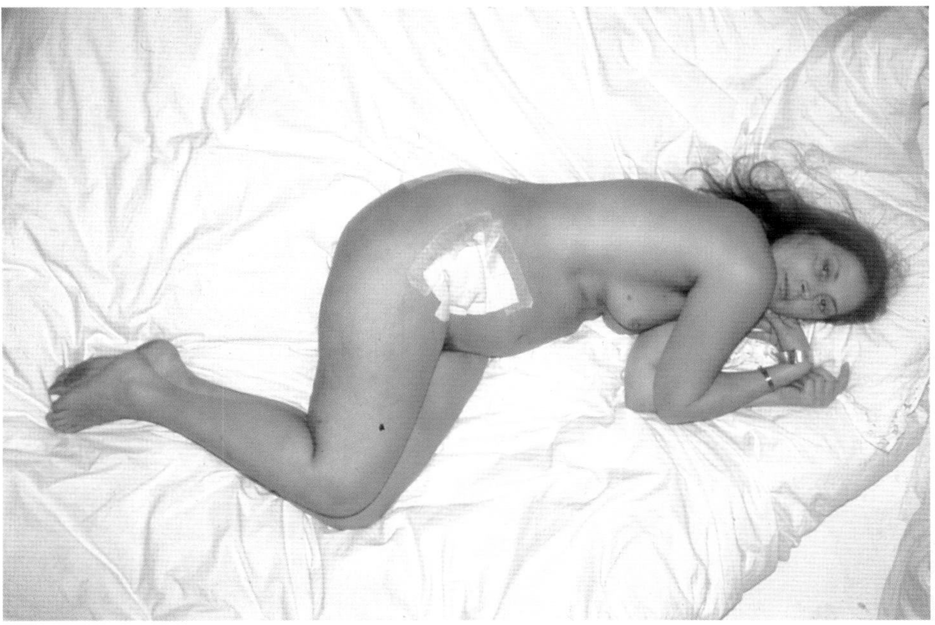

Hannah WILKE (with Donald GODDARD)
Intra-Venus
1993
Chromagenic supergloss photographs
121 × 182 cm [48 × 72 in] each

Intra-Venus was made while Wilke was dying of lymphoma. The work consists of a series of life-sized colour photographs of her swollen and bruised body displaying the deforming effects of cancer treatment, together with self-portrait watercolours, medical object-sculptures and collages made with the hair she lost during chemotherapy. Until _Intra-Venus_ Wilke had been known (and largely discredited) for work using her own face and body. Transformed by her illness, Wilke continued to make work using her body, no longer young and beautiful, no longer conforming to an ideal feminine image. _Intra-Venus_ was exhibited posthumously at the Ronald Feldman Gallery, New York, in 1994.

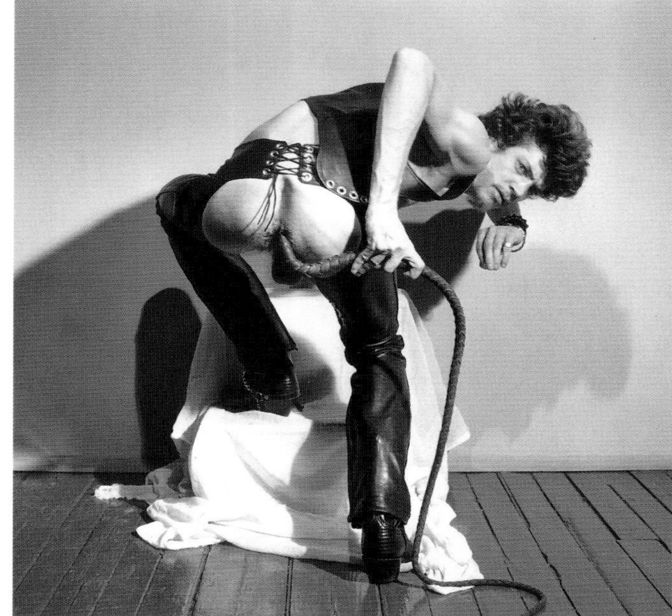

Robert MAPPLETHORPE
Self-Portrait with Bullwhip
1978
Gelatin silver print
41 × 51 cm [16 × 20 in]

Mapplethorpe claimed that his self-portraits expressed that part of himself that was most self-confident, but also which showed him as he really was in everyday life.The formal presentation and classical aesthetic of the photographs contrast powerfully with the subversive content. Mapplethorpe presents his sexual identity graphically and symbolically. The costume he wears, the position he adopts, the bullwhip trailing from an orifice, all provide signs by which to read his social/sexual relations. His pose is at once submissive and defiant. The instrument of cruelty and punishment that penetrates him makes him into an object of masochistic fantasy, while his direct gaze back at the viewer and evident control of the whip demonstrate his full and perhaps ironic control of the situation. Presenting himself as both object and subject of his desire, Mapplethorpe stages a moment of shameless self-revelation, bringing 'deviant' sexual behaviour out of the underworld into the mainstream.

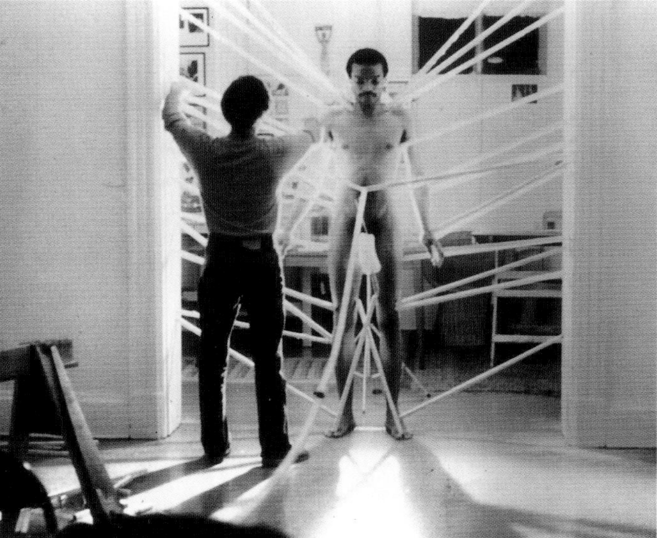

Sherman FLEMING
Something Akin to Living
1979
Washington, DC

Fleming created an ironic alternate persona, RodForce, in which he condensed the representation of black males in popular media into a massive phallic personification of force in order to 'move forward through this morass of power-seeing bodies as the all-powerful Black Male ... unyielding and invulnerable!'
– Sherman Fleming quoted by Kristine Stiles in 'Uncorrupted Joy', 1998

In this performance RodForce, naked except for a large, silver-lamé-covered phallus, positioned himself in a spotlight between a pair of Doric columns in his friend Wayne Higgs' studio gallery. Pieces of wood were measured and cut to fit at various angles between the artist's body and the columns. Standing immobile for the performance duration of 35 minutes, RodForce struggled to support this awkward and imprisoning edifice until he could no longer sustain the strain and simply walked off, leaving the structure to fall to the ground.

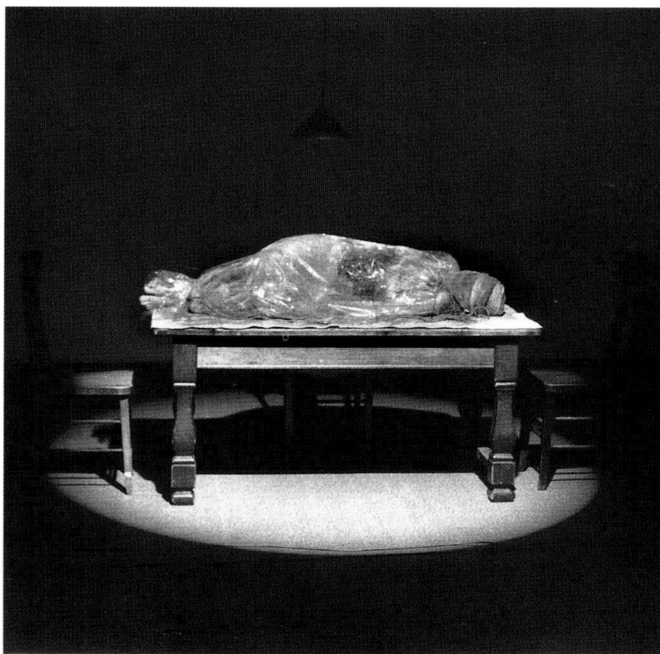

Mona HATOUM
The Negotiating Table
1983
The Western Front, Vancouver

Hatoum lay for three hours on a table under a single light, her body covered with entrails, bandages and blood, and wrapped up in a body bag, representing the victim of the brutal forces of war. A soundtrack of Western political leaders talking about peace filled the empty space around the table and emphasized the pathos of the (symbolically) violated body, and the cold impersonal world it inhabits. The only movement during the performance was the barely perceptible breathing of the artist's body under the plastic wrapper. Spectators standing outside the pool of light were forced to confront their own impotence in the face of destruction, their inaction and passivity contrasting with the rhetorical speeches of the politicians. Hatoum depicted the gulf between the human reality of war and the way in which our culture processes it for consumption by politicians and the media. Lebanese by birth, Hatoum had personal experience of the forces of oppression and resistance that operate between different social groups, both within Lebanon, invaded by Israel in 1982, and within the West, where she found herself identified as an outsider from the Third World.

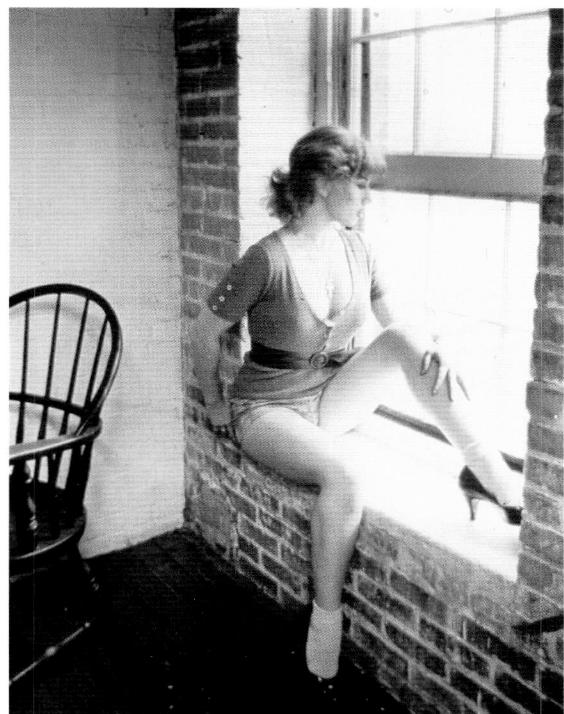

Cindy SHERMAN
Untitled No. 15
1978
Black and white photograph
25 × 20 cm [10 × 8 in]

Sherman began to dress up in different costumes when attending gallery openings and events in her home town of Buffalo, New York State. When she moved to New York City she began a series of photographs documenting her role-playing in the series *Film Stills*, in which she posed as a variety of familiar but unidentifiable film heroines. Characters include a woman in a slip with a Martini glass, a sweet-looking B-movie librarian, a young secretary in the city, a smouldering lower-class woman from an Italian neo-realist film, an innocent runaway, a *film noir* victim, a disturbed woman in a nightdress and several middle-class women in comfortable apartments. In many images Sherman appears as a seductress, caught in a moment of pensive contemplation, looking in the mirror, lying on her bed – traditionally 'feminine' reflective activities. Speaking of these images she said 'to pick a character like that was about my own ambivalence about sexuality – growing up with the women role-models that I had, and a lot of them in films, that were like that character, and yet you were supposed to be a good girl'.
– Cindy Sherman, 'Interview with George Howell', 1995

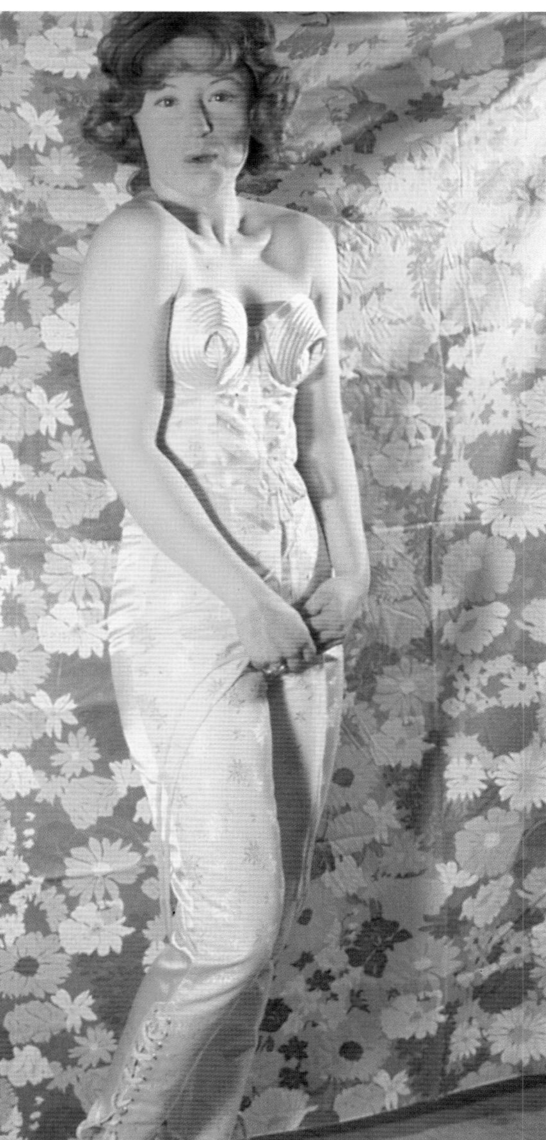

Cindy SHERMAN
Untitled No. 131
1983
Colour photograph
88 × 42 cm [35 × 16.5 in]

Sherman was commissioned by shop owner Diane Benson to make a series of fashion photographs for *Interview* magazine. She was supplied with clothes by designers such as Jean-Paul Gaultier and Comme des Garçons. The resulting images subverted the glamour of high fashion as a masquerade of caricatured 'feminine' stereotypes in exaggerated costumes and highly mannered poses. Other pictures in a second series commissioned by *Vogue* magazine are more sinister: Sherman appears furious, scarred, depressed, possibly abused or assaulted and mad. While these images served to undercut the fantasy identities sold to women by the fashion industry, their theatricality has enabled the fashion industry to appropriate the dark side of feminine identity to advertise their clothes.

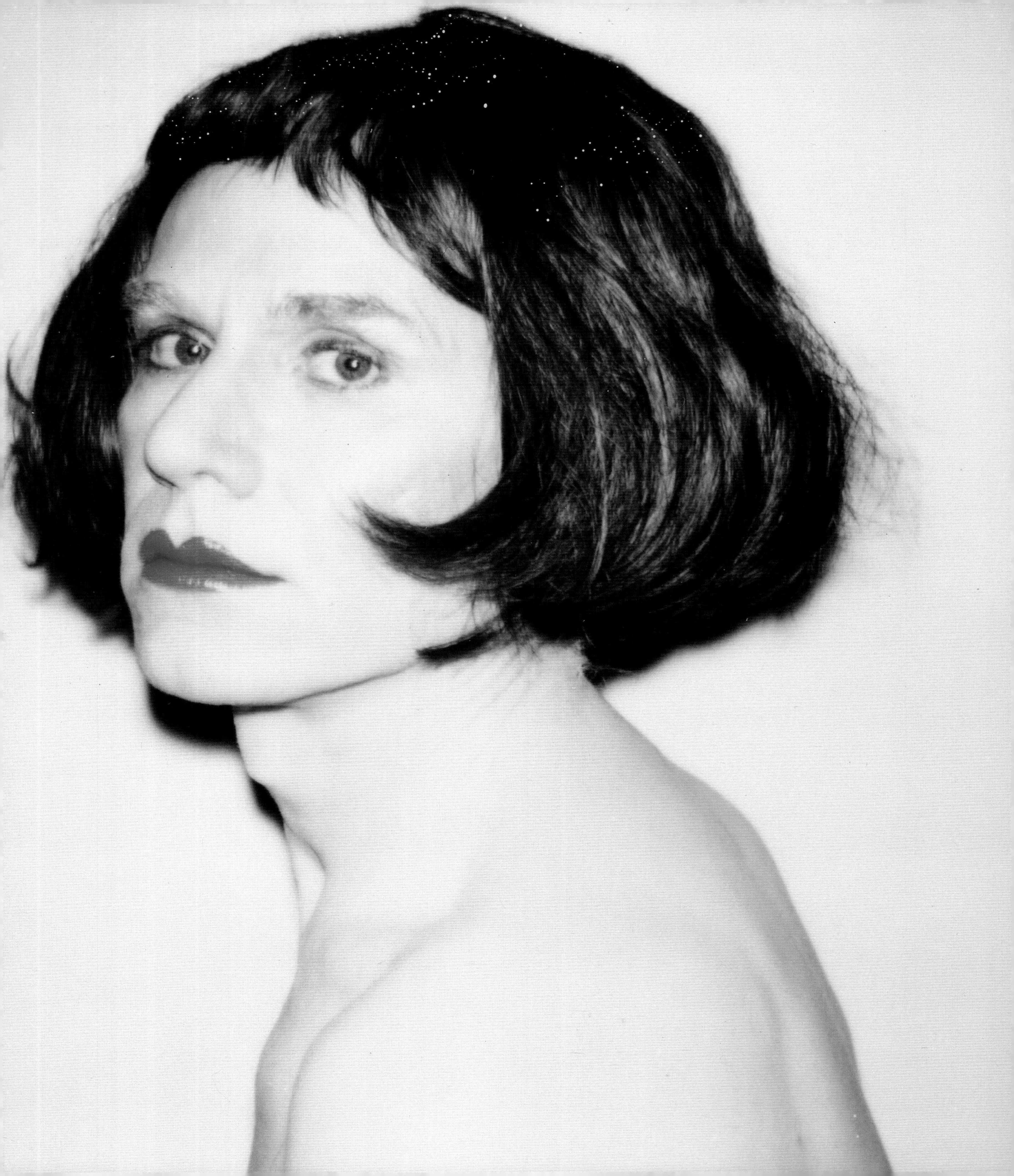

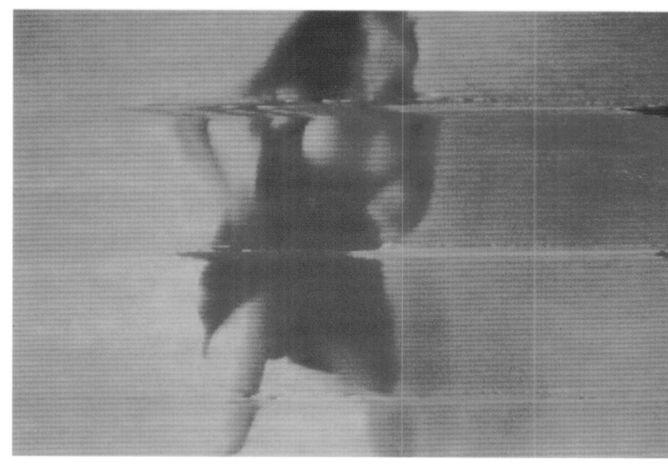

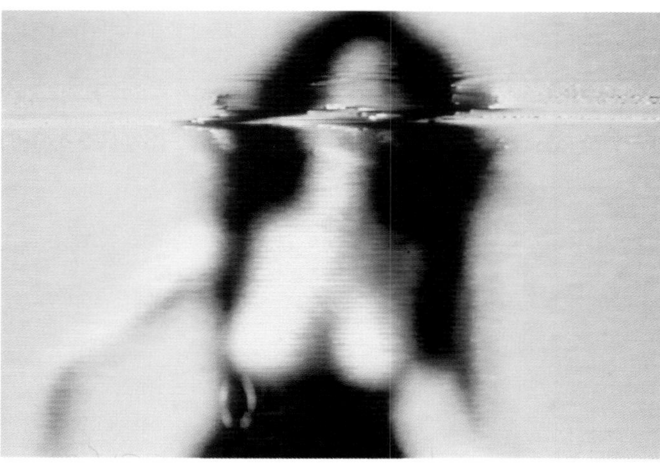

Pipilotti RIST
I'm Not the Girl Who Misses Much
1986
Video stills
5 mins. 2 secs., colour, sound

In her early work Rist appropriated the pop music video format, undercutting it with a feminist agenda. Playing the 'music babe' she moves from objectified love-object – the subject of popular music ballads – to the author of the work itself. This video presents the artist dancing in a dress cut open to reveal her breasts in the style of ancient Cretan goddess figures. The video appears to be on fast-forward: the image is jerky and blurred, while the soundtrack seems to repeat the title again and again very fast and shrill, conveying a sense of desperation. Only at the end of the 5-minute loop is the sample from the Beatles' song 'Happiness is a Warm Gun' revealed as the source. This juxtaposition of the meaning of the words with a feeling of panic undermines the glamour of the standard pop video. Rist re-presents the male musician's muse in terms of insecurity, repetition and hysteria, while reframing his gaze with staccato cutting to render the female body impossible to pin down or hold still.

opposite
Andy WARHOL
Self-Portrait in Drag (detail)
1981
Colour polaroid
11 × 8.5 cm [4 × 3 in]

Warhol played continuously with his own identity, and was heavily influential on the glitter-rock aesthetic in music and culture of the 1960s and early 1970s. Through his films starring flamboyant drag queens and through other artistic activities, he marketed the campy female impersonator as gay or bisexual idol, radically undercutting the rigid patriarchal roles that informed the presentation of public (male) identity. In the early 1980s, in a centrefold project for *Artforum* magazine, Warhol flanked an ambiguous self-portrait in drag with a series of silk-screened dollar signs. The title of the picture, *Forged Image*, indicated that his costumed identity was a counterfeit image. It is impossible to see in this where the 'real' Warhol might be, an uncertainty emphasized by the duality of his sexual identity, which is both dependent on the assumption of camp mannerisms and rendered 'fake' by their performative nature. 'I'm sure I'm going to look in the mirror and see nothing. People are always calling me a mirror and if a mirror looks into a mirror, what is there to see?'
– Andy Warhol, *The Philosophy of Andy Warhol: From A to B and Back Again*, 1975

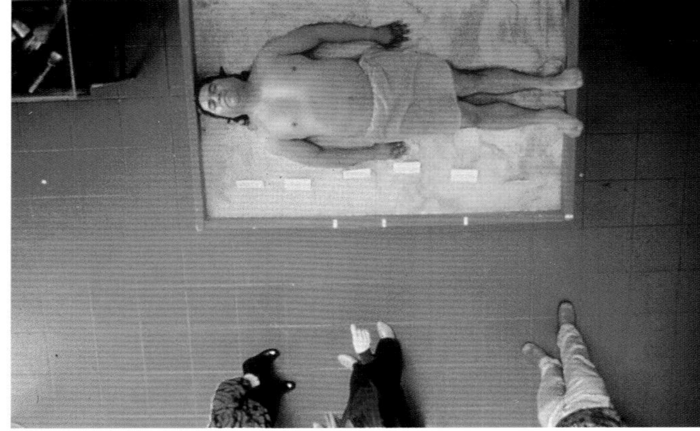

James LUNA

The Artifact Piece

1987

Museum of Man, San Diego

Collection, New Museum of Contemporary Art, New York

At the Museum of Man, San Diego, in the area dedicated to the Kumeyaay tribe, Luna lay on a bed of sand as if he were an ethnographic exhibit. Identified by a name tag, his body was further documented by labels drawing attention to scars on his body – injuries received during a bout of 'excessive drinking'. Two additional cases containing the artist's personal documents and ceremonial items from the Luiseño reservation (his home and place of origin) accompanied his body with legal and cultural 'proof' of his existence. As a Native American, Luna's artistic practice has been informed by the need to find a place for himself within Western discourse where his identity is culturally defined. *The Artifact Piece* parodies the notion of an 'authentic' Native American identity as defined by the objectifying perspective of colonialism, which either romanticizes the Indian as primitive and therefore closer to nature, or condemns him for (Western-determined) social dysfunctionalism – alcoholism, sexuality, unemployment. Luna's literal presence as a museum exhibit disrupts the viewer's ability to observe the ethnic and historical 'other' by the presence of a consciousness and answering gaze. Critic Jean Fisher comments that the artist's body functions as 'less a statement or a representation in the Western sense than a performative act – a "speaking" body continuously retracing the boundaries of self in the world. In such an utterance the art object is not necessarily privileged over the gesture that informs it or the communal space it addresses.'

– Jean Fisher, 'In Search of the "Inauthentic": Disturbing Signs in Contemporary Native American Art', 1992

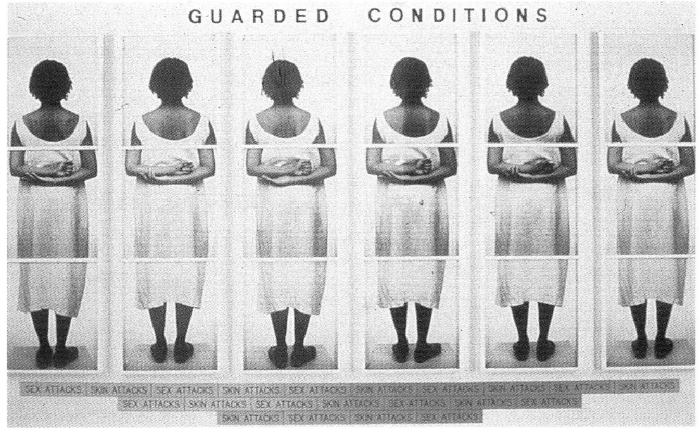

Lorna SIMPSON

Guarded Conditions

1989

Colour Polaroids, plastic plaques

231 × 333 cm [91 × 131 in] overall

Simpson assembled fragmented Polaroid images of her body. With her fist clenched behind her back, face turned away from the viewer, Simpson isolates one gesture to analyse the emotion from which it stems. The repetition of the words 'sex attacks/skin attacks' below the body emphasize the origin of Simpson's pose: her body is in a state of being 'guarded' from the attacks she anticipates as a result of her sexual identity and the colour of her skin. The formal treatment of the image reinforces the sense of attack and protection – the artist's body is severed and serialized, as if ritually segmented, denying the viewer an opportunity to see her whole. Her obdurately turned back and her physical segmentation demonstrate a refusal to be 'framed' within the Western cultural discourses of criminality and pathology associated with her racial and sexual identity. Taking position as subject, the artist forces the viewer to confront the recent history of Western appropriation and consumption of the black female body. Critic Matthew Ritchie has written of her work, ' ...manifesting her singular knack for pushing people's buttons .... Simpson has spent some years successfully operating at the painful interface between identity and politics, using the body and its signs to catalogue the tyrannies of the social gaze.'

– Matthew Ritchie, 'Lorna Simpson', 1996

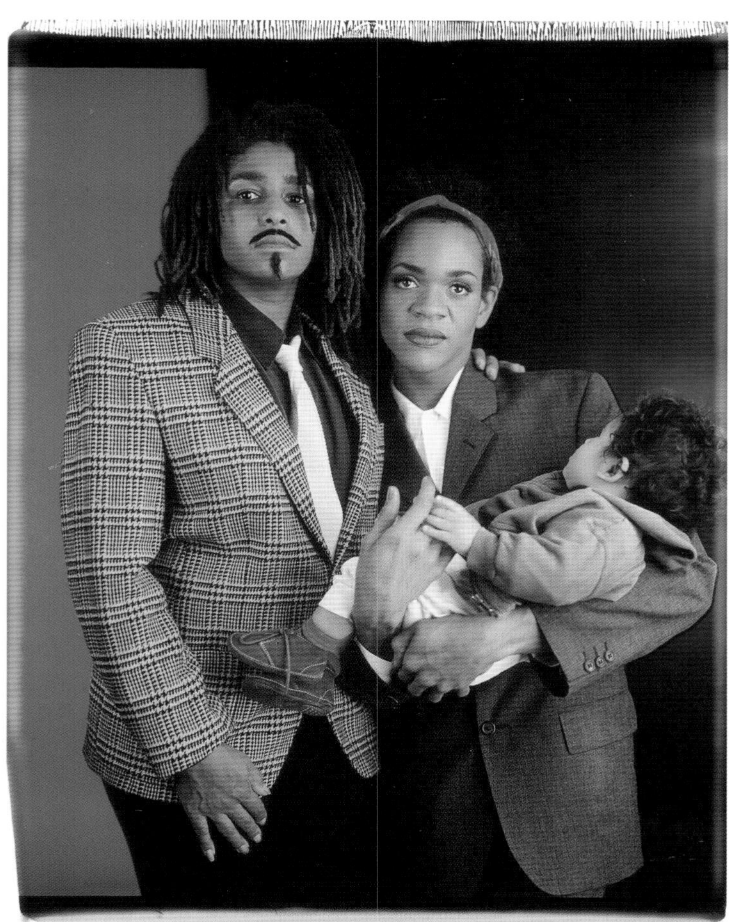

Lyle Ashton HARRIS and Renée COX
Queen, Alias & Id: The Child
1994
Polaroid
61 × 51 cm [24 × 20 in]

In *The Child* artist Renée Cox plays 'father' to Harris' 'mother', while the child, with its non-Afro hair, is presumably adopted. Like the costumes and the roles played by the artists, it suggests that identity and the means of relating are not located in visual signifiers. As Harris explained to critic Michael Cohen, ' ... Using masquerade as our mode of transgression ... we are challenging a construction of African nationalism that positions queers and feminists outside of the black family, the Million Man march and other black institutions.'
– Michael Cohen, 'Lyle Ashton Harris', 1996

Harris made a series of these collaborative works in 1994, contesting the mythology of the European-descended bourgeois nuclear family. Photographed against a tricolour background reminiscent of an African nation's flag, various couples iconically represent possibilities for transformative kinship in which gender roles are swapped or mutated into new structures of relating.

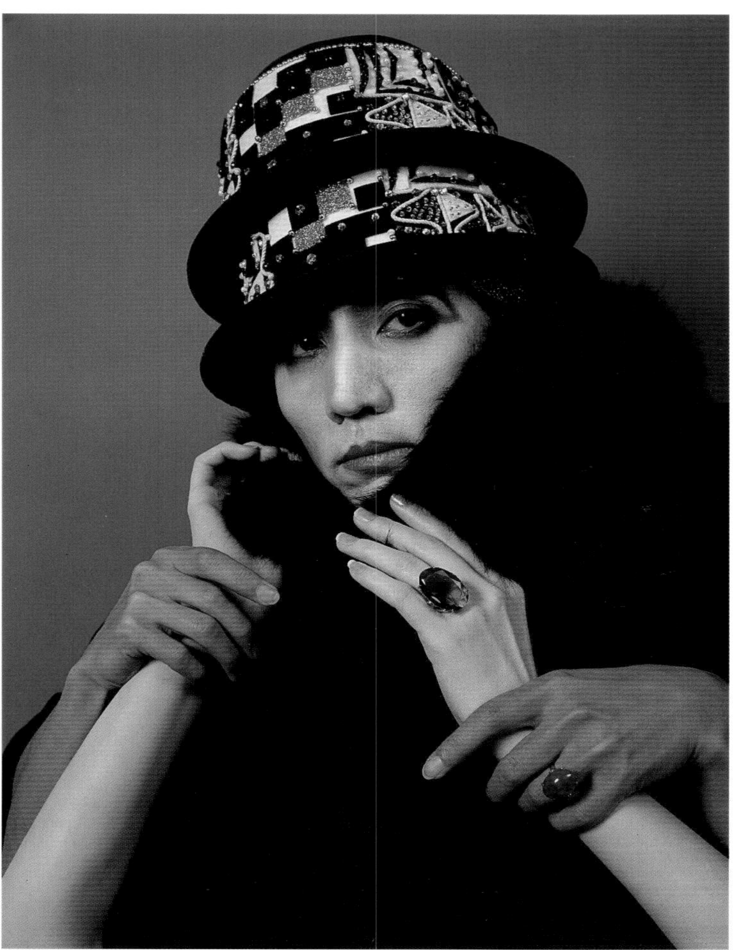

Yasumasa MORIMURA
Doublenage (Marcel)
1988
Colour photograph
152.5 × 122 cm [60 × 48 in]

In the mid 1980s Morimura began making photographs based on masterpieces of art history, such as Manet's *Olympia*. Using himself as the model, he wore costumes that only partially disguised him. *Doublenage* (*Marcel*) refers to Man Ray's famous portrait of Duchamp's female alter-ego Rrose Sélavy. The binary distinctions of the original – male masquerading as female – is expanded into the more contemporary global issues of race and culture, and the manner in which these issues are sexualized. Morimura's male, oriental face at the centre of the image wears a mask of white femininity whose crude artificiality is emphasized by the real white female arms reaching up towards it. These are held – restrained – by hands that could be either feminine or masculine, but certainly aren't white, suggesting that control lies with the non-Western 'other'.

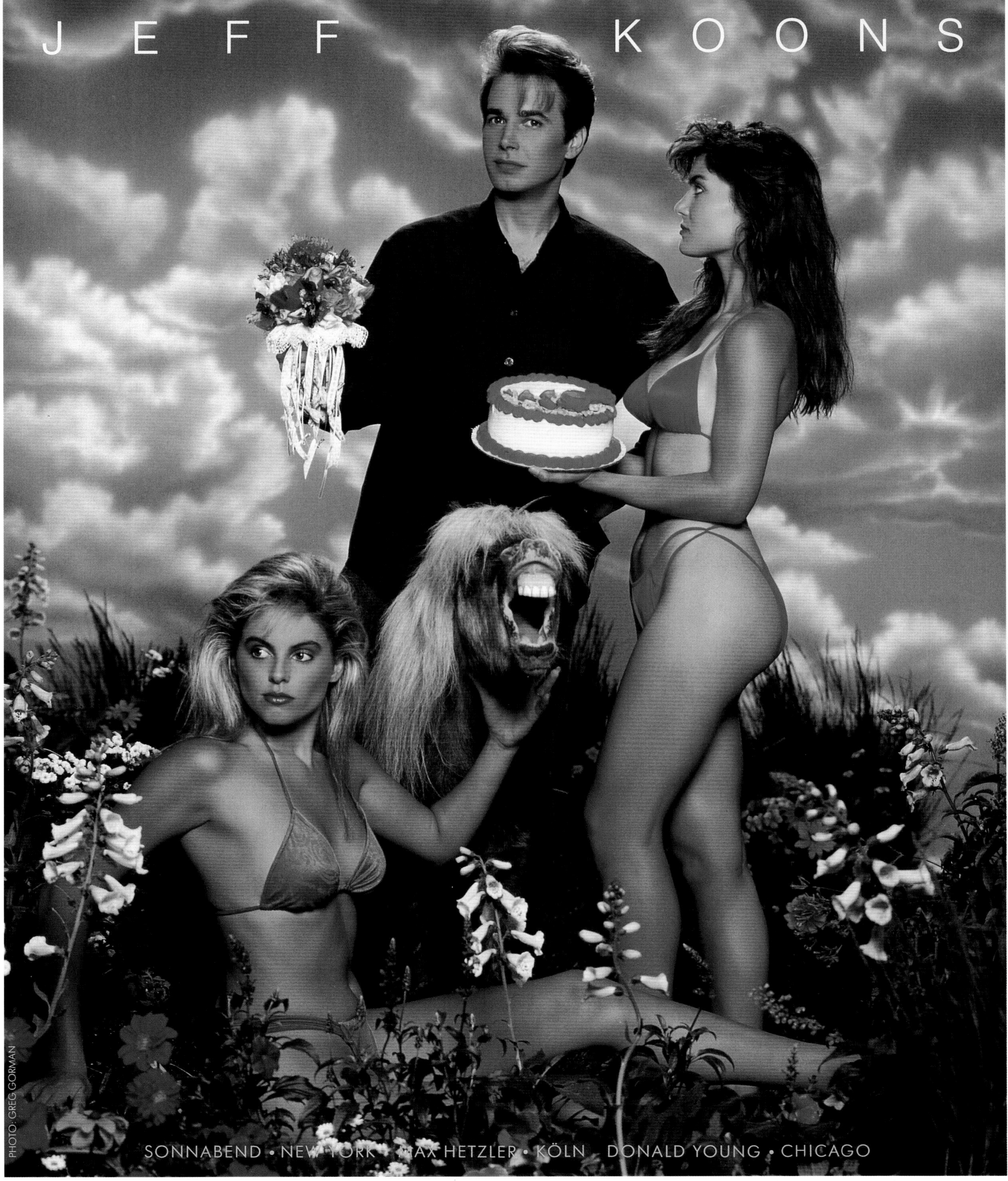
JEFF KOONS
SONNABEND • NEW YORK • MAX HETZLER • KÖLN • DONALD YOUNG • CHICAGO
PHOTO: GREG GORMAN

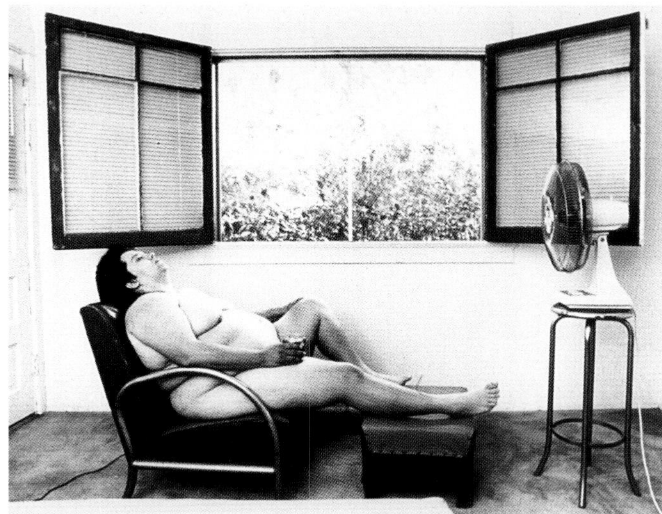

Laura AGUILAR
In Sandy's Room (Self-Portrait)
1991
Black and white photograph
101.5 × 127 cm [40 × 50 in]
Collection, New Museum of Contemporary Art, New York

Aguilar's self-portrait images employ 'documentary' black and white photography to authenticate her body/self identity which, as an overweight 'Latina lesbian', is outside the discourse of desire and acceptability within the dominant American society as well as her own culture. Her work focuses on her psychic pain, her learning disability and the particularities of her organic body – a body that she finds at times a burden, and from which she feels alienated. She presents the body/self as defined and experienced through its relation to others, seeking both to affirm and to transcend it. She explains that, by doing self-portraits 'I've been able to find some comfort and peace through my own body ... I'm a large woman – I'm not supposed to be comfortable with myself. I wonder what people think.'
– Laura Aguilar quoted by Amelia Jones, *Body Art: Performing the Subject*, 1998

opposite
Jeff KOONS
Untitled
1989
Colour advertisement
27.5 × 23 cm [11 × 9 in]

'Perhaps [creating] the most controversial art magazine advertisements since Lynda Benglis ran a photograph of herself with an enormous dildo ... Jeff Koons has personally supervised ads for November issues of four magazines, stirring great debate coinciding with his recent exhibitions ... In keeping with the elaborate preparation and preproduction which Koons orchestrates prior to the fabrication of his sculptural works ... four different full-page ads were created specially by Koons, each targeted at a different magazine – *Arts Magazine*, *Artforum*, *Art in America* and *Flash Art*. Each showed the artist in a different setting contrived for the occasion: a seaside or swimming pool scene with the artist seated betweeen two live seals; the artist in an elementary school classroom, taking questions from eager children, his back to a chalkboard scrawled with inflammatory slogans, "Exploit the Masses"; the artist astride a miniature Shetland pony flanked by two bikini-clad bathing beauties; and beside a fat healthy pig and piglet.

' ... "The highest priority for every artist at this time is to confront the moral crisis that threatens to overwhelm us", said Jeff Koons. "I believe that artists should use all the tools available to them today, all those that the so-called real world – advertising, the record and movie industries – has made available to them. These are our competitors. If the art world doesn't employ all the seductive means at our disposal, it will be devoured by advertising and the entertainment industry."'
– *Flash Art* supplement, 1989

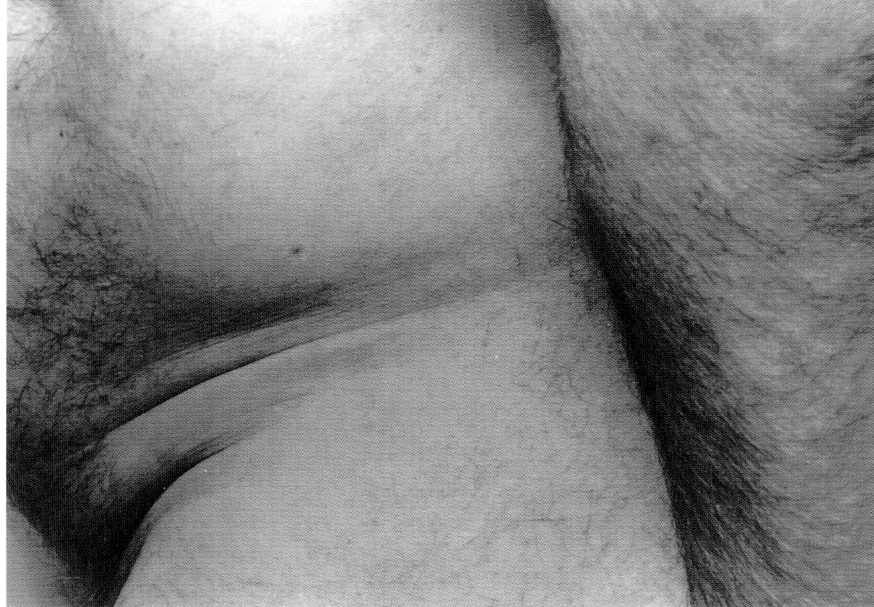

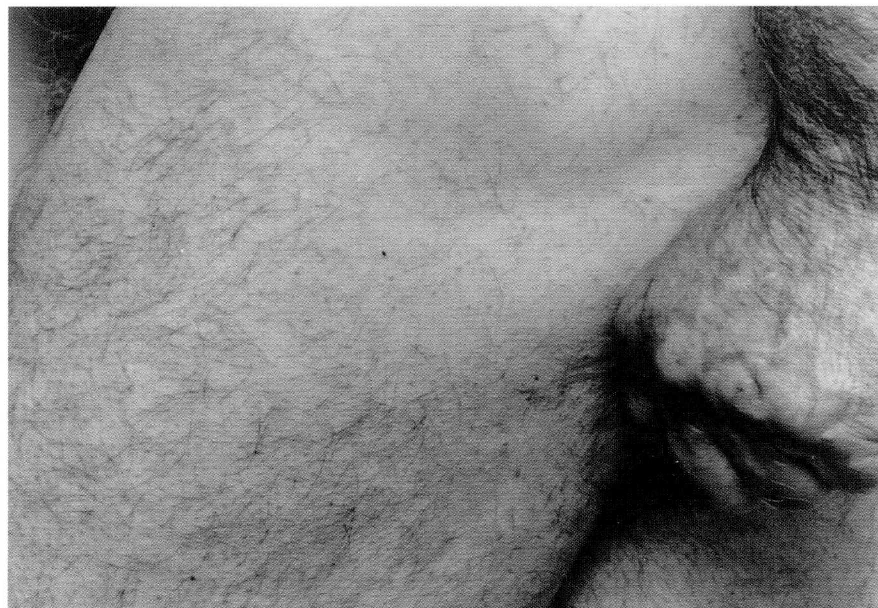

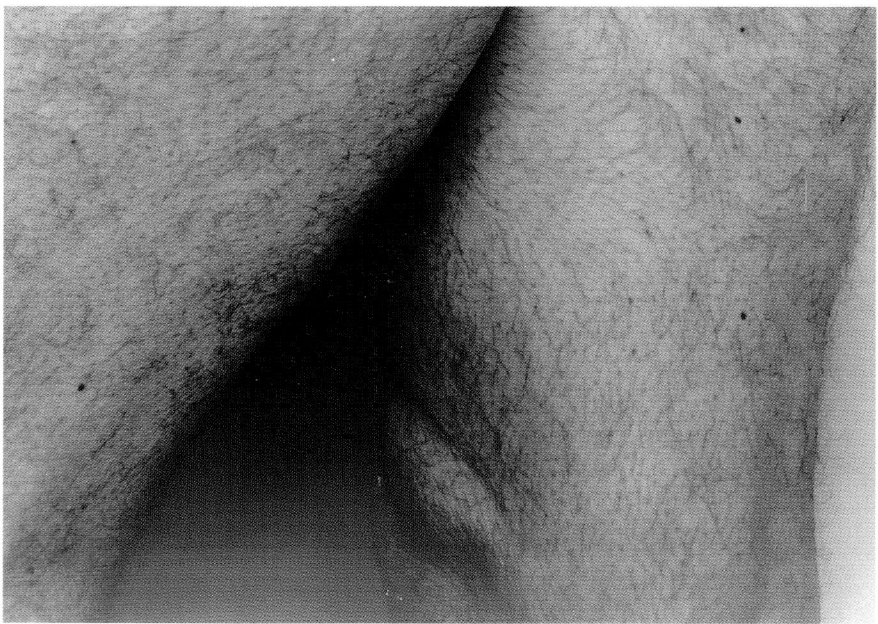

John COPLANS
Self-Portrait (Standing, Side View, Three Panels, No. 5)
1993
Silver print
343 × 145 cm [135 × 57 in]

'... I decided that photography was the medium to try ... It is a medium to build an identity out of a composite personality, to find an artistic identity.' Having been interested in the idea of the primordial and its links to psychoanalysis, Coplans focused his search for identity on the universal – 'being in touch genetically with the inheritance of mankind as an inner thing, something that we all have within'.
– John Coplans, 'Interview with Jean-François Chevrier', 1989

Stripped of face and clothing, Coplans' naked body loses the signifiers of class, culture and era, and turns attention to perception and embodiment. Traditionally taboo within Western culture, his naked, ageing male body is transformed into a landscape of textures and form. Rendering his flesh iconic through the large-scale sumptuousness of his montages, he affirms an identity we have always known but never culturally acknowledged – that of the embodied patriarch.

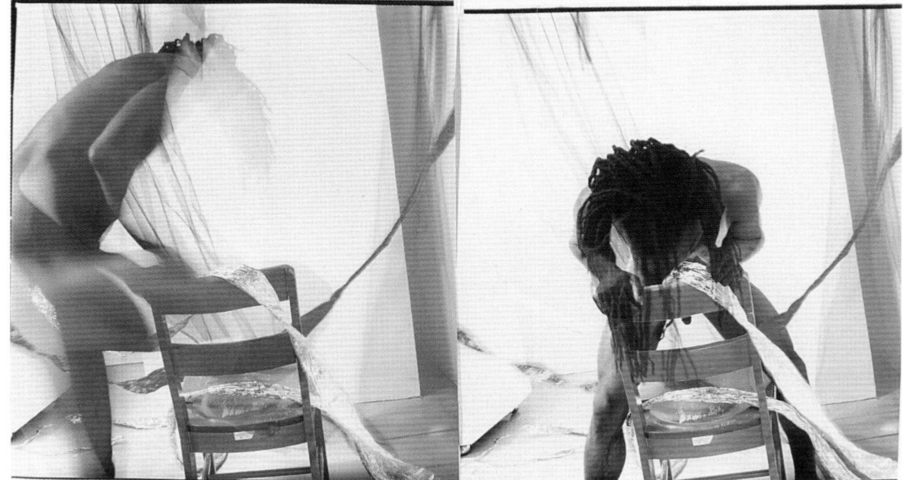

Oladélé Ajiboyé BAMGBOYÉ
1994
Celebrate
C-type print
91 × 110 cm [36 × 43 in] each panel

'I deliberately choose to photograph the male body in the most common, but often under-represented situation: the domestic home. I choose to photograph the nude ... as this is the most natural state of the human body, stripped of all material wealth and status. I concentrate on self-portraiture in order to give me total control over the image-making process and ultimately to be directly responsible for the statements that I make in my work.'
– Oladélé Ajiboyé Bamgboyé, Artist's statement, 1994

For the black artist working within a Western cultural genre, his status as a subject is void. For people of colonial origins representation has limited their status to that of an object, thus defined through their bodies and frequently seen through the prism of an extreme sexuality.

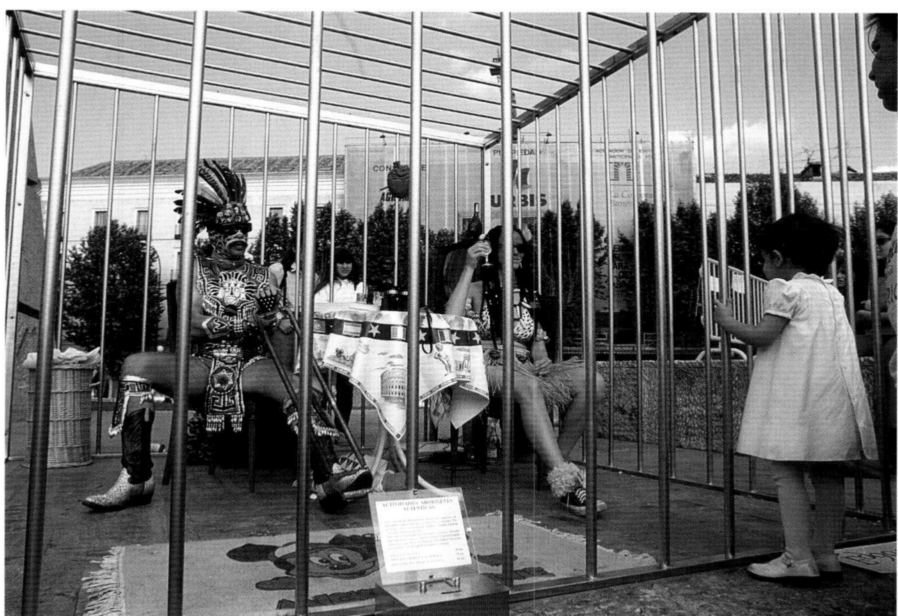

Coco FUSCO and Guillermo GÓMEZ-PEÑA
Two Undiscovered Amerindians Visit Madrid
1992
Plaza de Colón, Madrid

The artists posed as newly discovered 'primitives' on display in a gold cage to crowds at various locations in Spain, here in the Plaza de Colón, Madrid. They spoke a made-up language, had to be taken to the toilet on a leash by an attendant, and if a coin was dropped in a box they would perform a 'native' song and dance. Echoing the historical rape of Latin America by the Spanish and Portuguese conquistadors in the eighteenth century, the gold of the artists' cage underlines the wealth represented by the indigenous peoples of America whose bodies were taken for slavery just as their gold was plundered. Their 'indigenous' identity is a pastiche, a multicultural mix that allies a Western notion of 'primitiveness' – the performing circus animal, or the Victorian curiosity on display – with the ubiquitous signs of Western acculturation (a radio, pictures of Mickey Mouse and so on). The fusion of historical with contemporary elements in this performance underlines a continuation of the cultural objectifying to which indigenous peoples are still subjected by Europe, echoed by the boycotting of the international art world by many indigenous artists in 1992 as a protest against the celebration of Columbus, who had 'discovered' the Americas 500 years earlier.

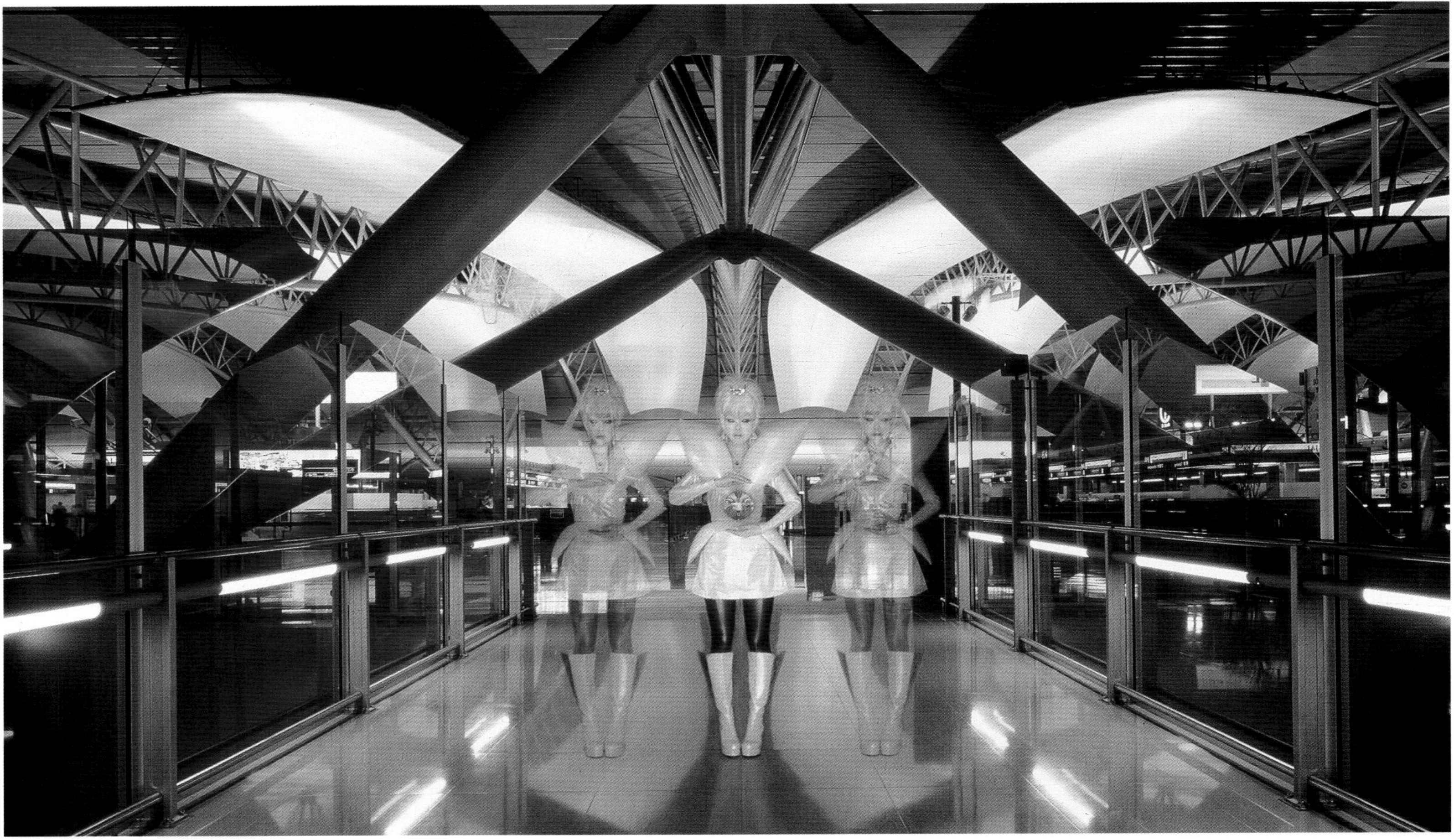

Mariko MORI
1996
Miko no Inori (Last Departure)
Cibachrome print, aluminium, wood, smoked chrome aluminium frame
213 × 366 × 8 cm [84 × 144 × 3 in]

Mori creates and photographs futuristic feminine personas. The photographs are digitally manipulated to present multiple versions of a fantasy identity, which she has referred to as 'someone who needs to be created'. The personas she assumes draw on a fusion of traditional Far Eastern spiritual iconography, Japanese popular culture such as Japanimation, video games and Western cinematic cyborgs in films such as *Bladerunner* (1982) and *Robocop* (1987). Set in Osaka's Kansai International Airport and resonating with ideas of voyage and flight, *Last Departure* shows Mori as a futuristic kaleidoscope-eyed vision holding a crystal ball. Mori the shaman-girl reflects a utopic sense of interconnection through the technology of late twentieth-century global popular culture.

Shirin NESHAT
Faceless (detail)
1994
Black and white photograph, ink
152 × 102 cm [60 × 40 in]

Neshat constructs images of Islamic female identity that bring together and open out the multiplicity of possible meanings embedded in stereotypical representations. Her images challenge the assumptions that the viewer makes about the meaning and status of particular visual symbols, which are heavily loaded with the emotional resonances of power and submission. Neshat juxtaposes images of herself – face peering out of *chador*, her hands, her son's feet – with Arabic text that acts as a second inscription of language over the initial body text. To a Western audience this secondary inscription remains a kind of decoration or ornament, in which an inaccessible meaning is embedded. Its reading is therefore restricted to a purely sensual or visual presence. This double act of inscribing and concealing is echoed by the black *chador*, which for a Western audience is a symbol of suppression and suffering, while in the Islamic world the *chador*, like the gun, makes female entrance into the public sphere possible through erasure of the domestic and the personal as represented by the visible female body.

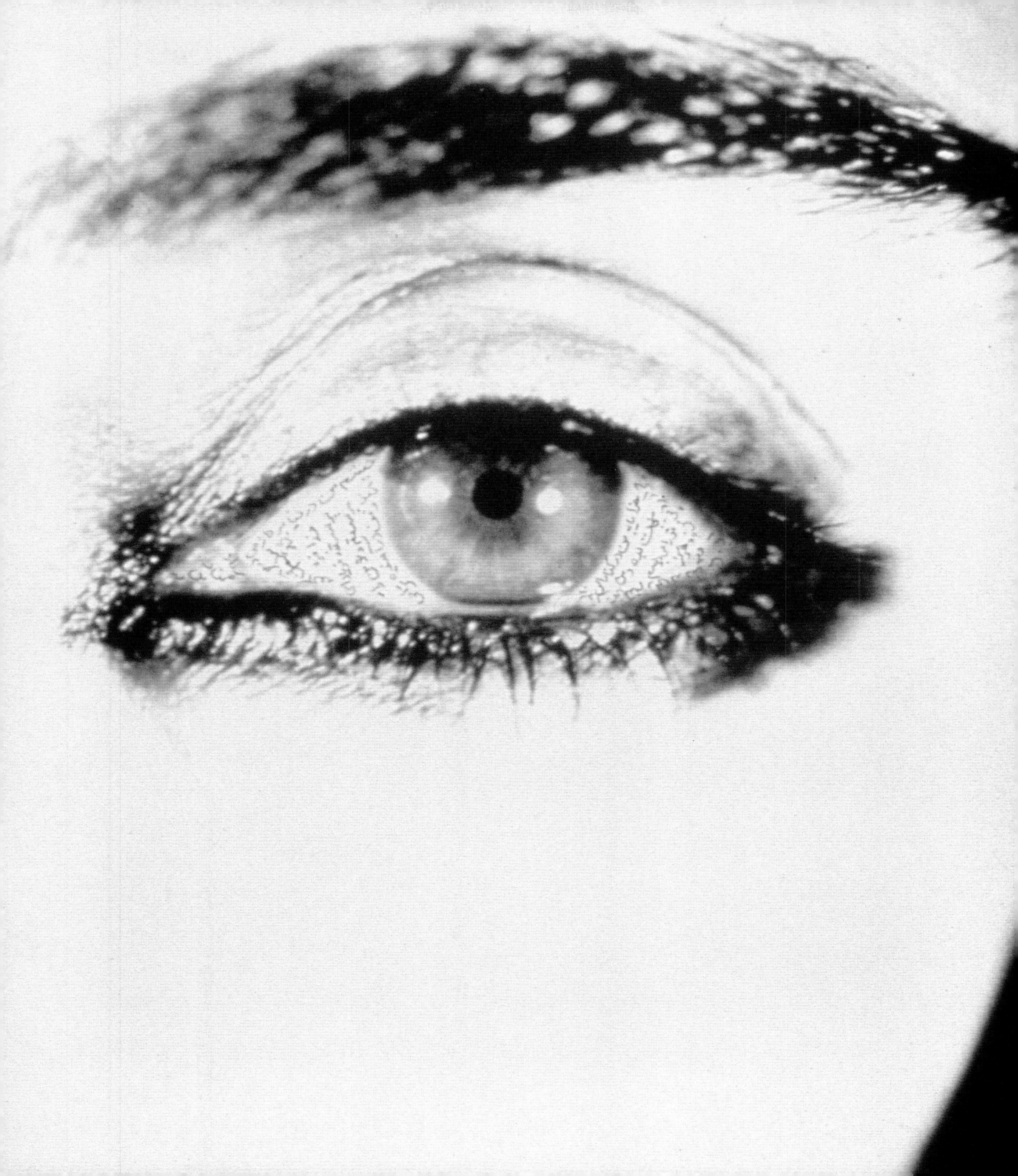

ABSENT BODIES

The artists grouped here use traces of their bodies – casts, imprints, photographs – as stand-ins for their physical presence. The absence of the real body evokes mortality, the transience of the human body in contrast to the more permanent forms of art. The imprint or trace is redolent with memory, absence and the artist's inner life, setting up a contrast between the body's physical manifestation and the spiritual or unconscious.

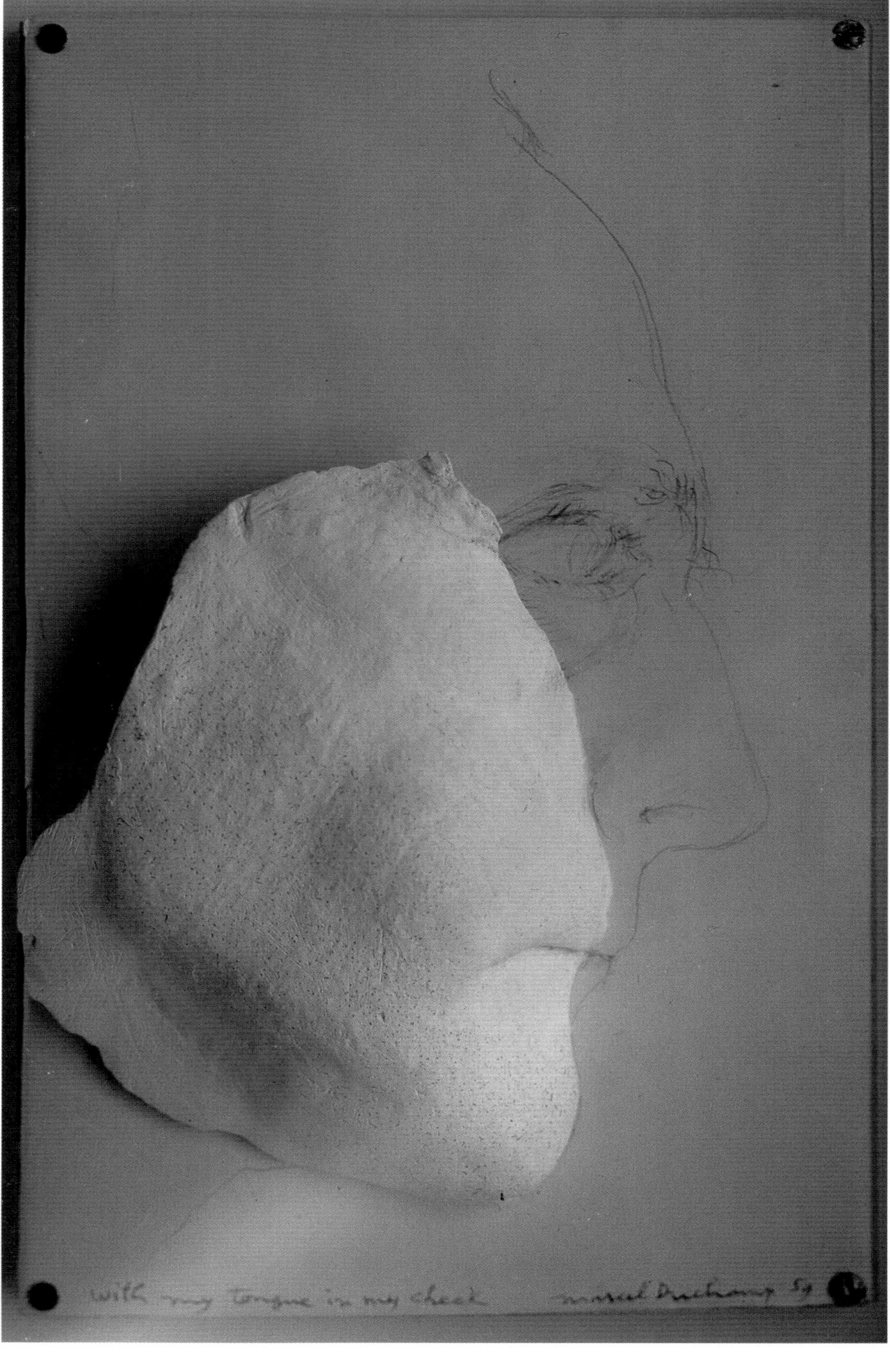

Marcel DUCHAMP
With My Tongue in My Cheek
1959
Collage, plaster, pencil, paper, mounted on wood
25 × 15 × 5 cm [10 × 6 × 2 in]

Duchamp had been commissioned to make illustrations in the spirit of Dada for a magazine article to be written by the critic Robert Lebel. Duchamp's wife, Teeny, made a cast of his cheek, which was puffed out by a walnut in his mouth. Duchamp then glued the cast to a piece of paper on which he had drawn in the rest of his profile, so that he is permanently 'tongue in cheek', perhaps an ironic comment on the role of the artist. He also made a cast of the sole of his foot with several large dead houseflies embedded in it, and called it *Torture-morte* (a play on *nature morte*, meaning still life).

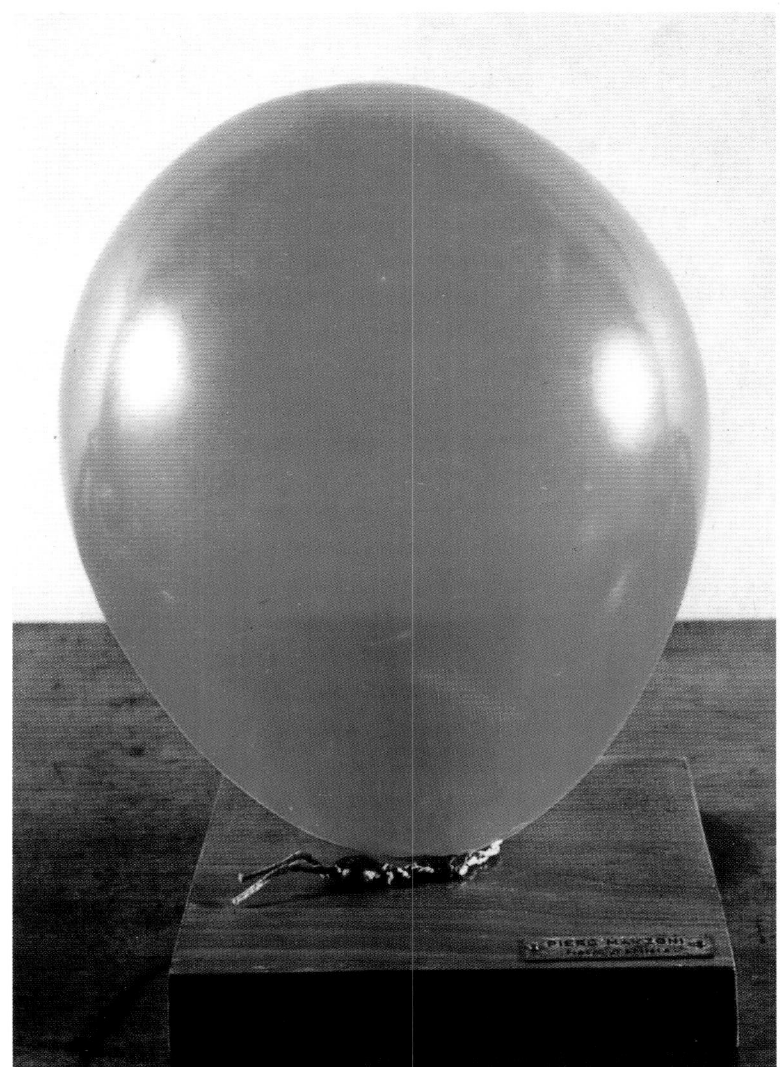

Piero MANZONI
Artist's Breath
1960
Rubber balloon inflated with artist's breath, wood, lead seal
18 × 18 cm [7 × 7 in]

In 1959 Manzoni had presented his 'pneumatic' or 'air sculptures', which consisted of forty-five large white balloons packaged individually in a wooden box with a metal tripod and a mouthpiece so that they could be inflated with breath if no pump was available. Once inflated, the balloons were placed on the tripod to form a sculpture. If the purchaser of one of these *Bodies of Air* wished his sculpture to be inflated by the artist, Manzoni was willing to do this for a small fee. *Artist's Breath* followed directly from these works. A series of small, white, red or blue balloons were inflated by Manzoni and sealed with string and lead seals impressed with his name. These were fixed to wooden bases bearing metal plaques stating: 'Piero Manzoni: Artist's Breath'. Over the years the balloons have gradually deflated, the dry plastic collapsing on to the wooden bases, so providing a relic of the dead artist's body. No longer containing the air he breathed into them, the balloons poignantly illustrate the passing of a life through the decay of the bodily container. Manzoni's tragic death at the age of twenty-nine adds to the pathos of these works.

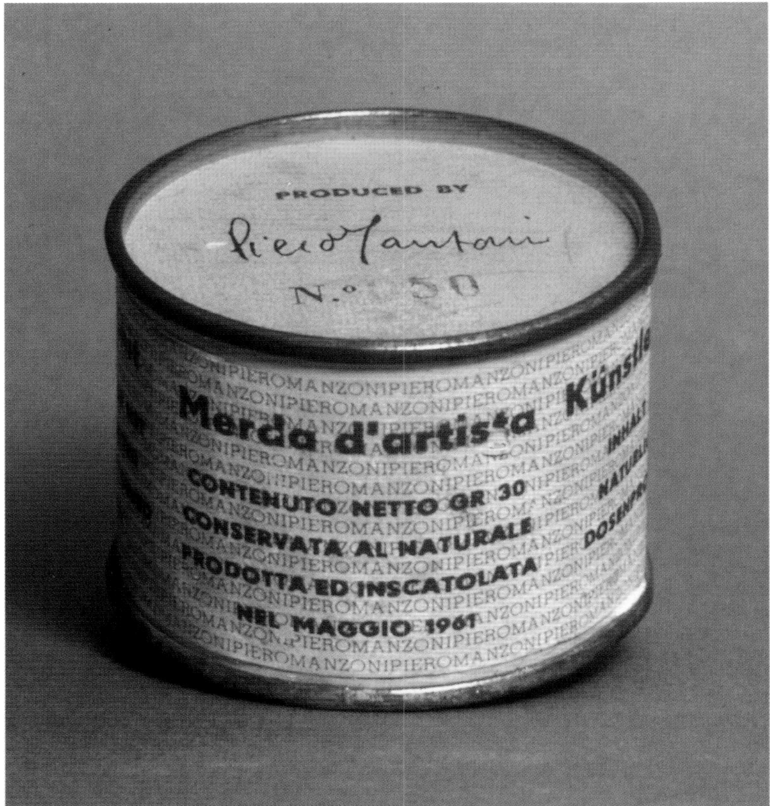

Piero MANZONI
Artist's Shit
1961
Can, paper label, artist's faeces
h. 5 cm [2 in]
ø 6.5 cm [2.5 in]

Manzoni produced ninety tins of his own shit. They were numbered 001 to 090 and labelled '"Artist's Shit", contents 30 gr net freshly preserved, produced and tinned in May 1961' in Italian, French, English and German. Selling them by weight for their equivalent price in gold, Manzoni would issue an authenticating receipt to record the exchange. By bringing the waste products of his body into the realm of factory processing Manzoni enacted a Minimalist reduction of the body's mess into clean containment. Presenting his shit elevated to the status of art object with the literal value of gold, Manzoni was also parodying his own status as an artist, whose creative products were desirable commodities (whatever they were, as long as they were packaged correctly) for which people would pay in gold.

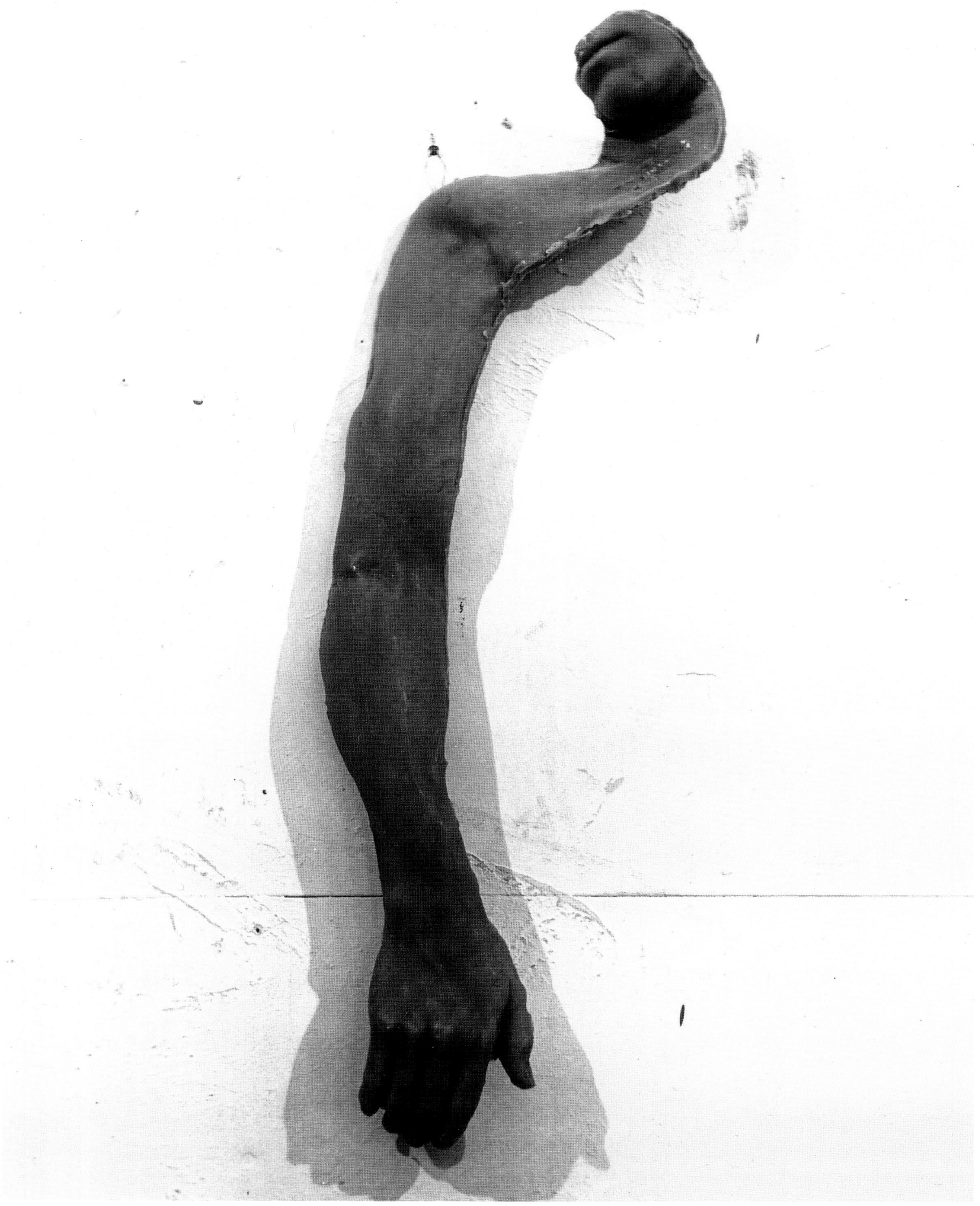

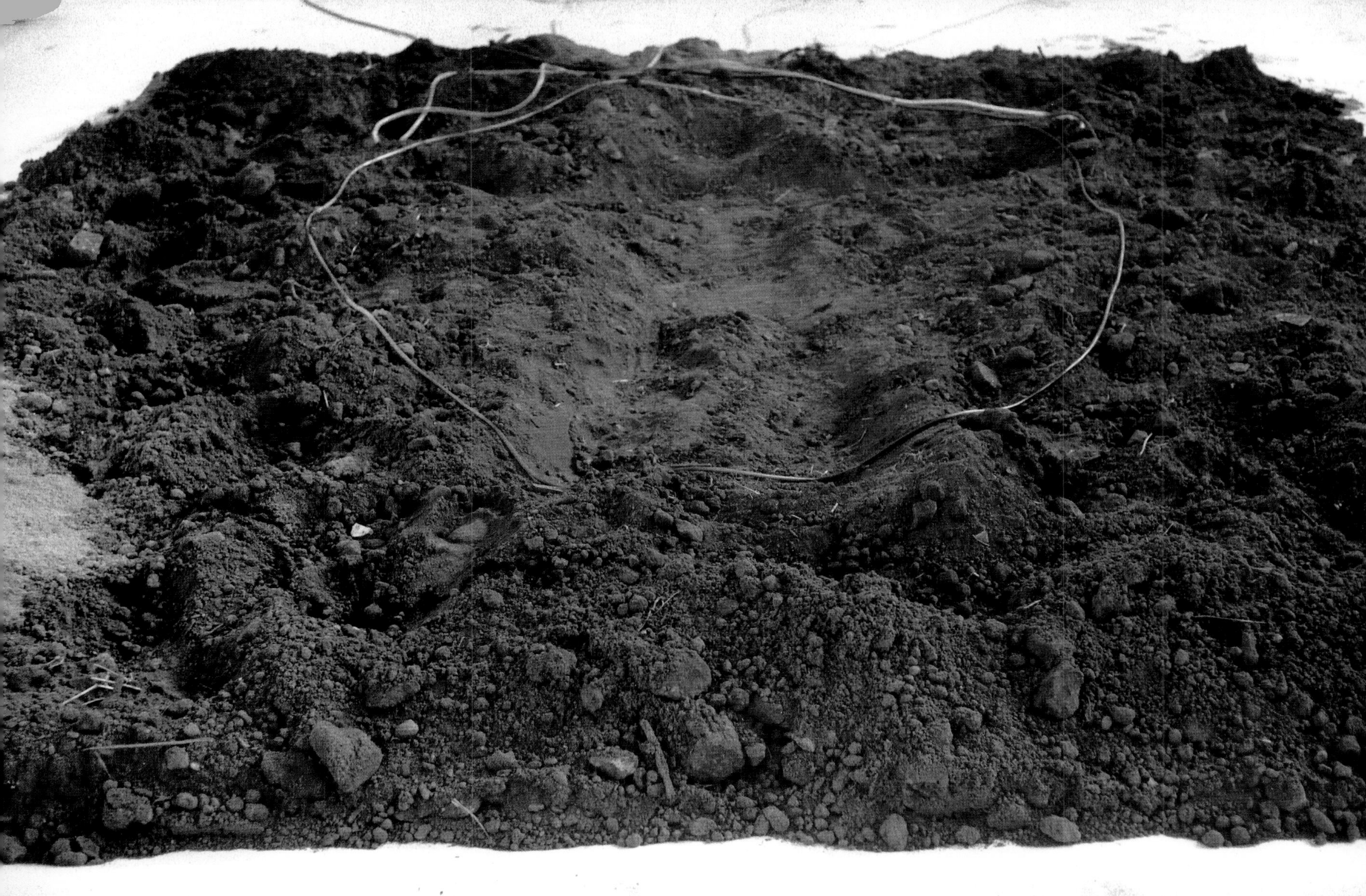

Terry FOX
Levitation
1970
Richmond Art Center, San Francisco

Fox lay on his back in a pile of dirt for six hours at the Richmond Art Center, San Francisco, experiencing a profound sense of being out of his body. 'I drew a circle in the middle of the dirt with my own blood. Its diameter was my height. According to a medieval notion, that creates a magic space. Then I lay on my back in the middle of the circle holding four clear polyethylene tubes filled with blood, urine, milk and water. They represented the elemental fluids that I was expelling from my body. I lay there for six hours with the tubes in my hand trying to levitate. The doors were locked. Nobody saw me. I didn't move a muscle. I didn't close my eyes. I tried not to change my focal point.'
– Terry Fox quoted by Paul Schimmel, 'Leap in the Void: Performance and the Object', 1998

After four hours Fox could no longer feel his body, and concluded that his limbs had gone to sleep. Later visitors were allowed to enter the room and see an imprint of his body in the earth. Fox considered this his most successful sculpture because of its moving quality of absence.

opposite
Bruce NAUMAN
From Hand to Mouth
1967
Cast wax over cloth
71 × 25 × 10 cm [28 × 10 × 4 in]
Collection, Hirshhorn Museum and Sculpture Garden, Washington, DC

From Hand to Mouth was made during a period of intense reflection on how to make art and what it is to be an artist. The sculpture is a literal physical representation of the title. Nauman links utterance to gesture, speech to manual activity. Cutting away the body to isolate a fragment, he has created a form that stands as a sculptural whole in itself, providing a new meaning out of an old cliché. 'The point where language starts to break down as a useful tool for communication is the same edge where poetry or art occurs.'
– Bruce Nauman, 'Interview with Willoughby Sharp', 1970

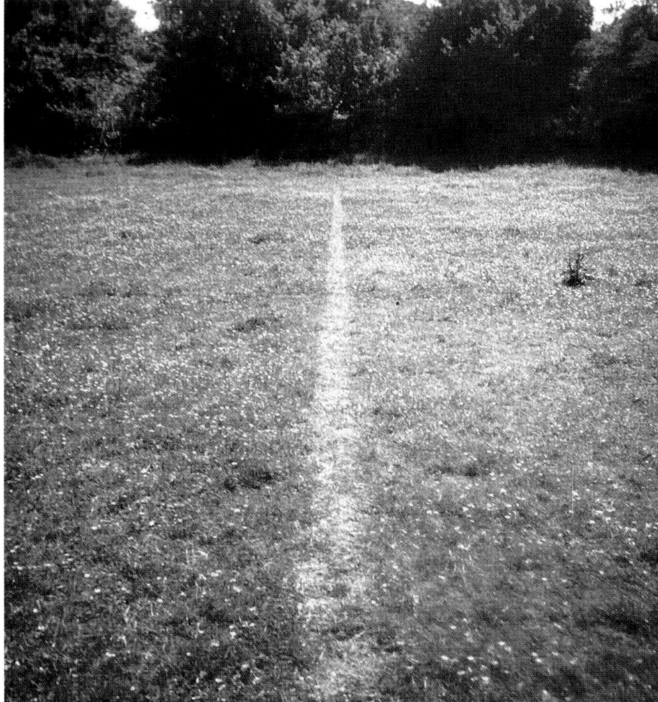

Richard LONG
A Line Made by Walking
1967
Black and white photograph
37.5 × 32 cm [15 × 13 in]
Somerset, England

Long walked repeatedly backwards and forwards along a straight line in a Somerset field, wearing away a path by crushing grass and flowers underfoot. The resulting 'line drawing' bissecting the field would last only as long as it would take for nature to grow back. *A Line Made by Walking* was executed while Long was still a student at London's St Martin's School of Art in the late 1960s and typifies the theme of Long's work over subsequent years: a solitary activity (usually walking) performed in a natural environment coupled with photographic documentation of the artist's ephemeral intervention into the landscape. In other similar actions Long mapped straight lines across the landscape by displacing small stones or twigs along selected stretches of ground. These works require considerable time spent performing repetitive actions. 'My work is real not illusory or conceptual. It is about real stones, real time, real actions.'
– Richard Long, Artist's statement, 1980

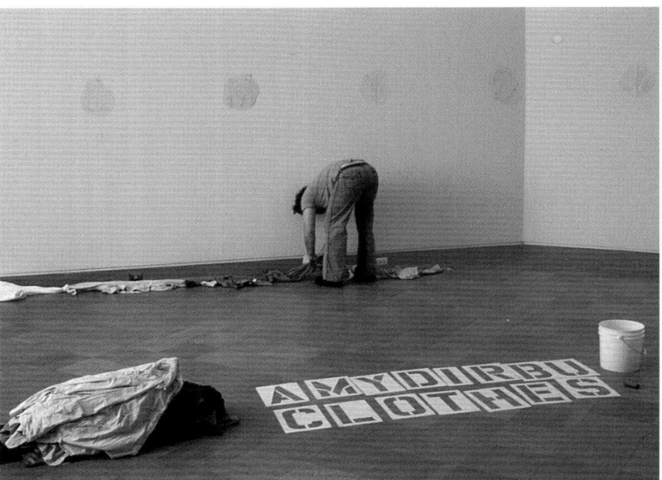

Howard FRIED
All My Dirty Blue Clothes
1970
Oakland Art Museum, San Francisco

Fried tied his dirty blue garments together in a chain along the perimeter of the exhibition space. The installation was divided into three categories relating to the history of the clothes in his life. 'Accumulation' detailed a chronology of acquisition dating from 1957, when he first acquired a long-sleeved polo shirt, to 1969, when he obtained two pairs of trousers. 'Establishment' provided the explanation that he had used clothes as the material in this work because they were the items in closest proximity to his life, and had chosen blue because it was the colour to which he best responded. 'Notification' revealed that he had had to use surrogate garments for all but one of the works. This work revealed Fried's interest in investigating the common details of daily life. He emphasized the significance of personal history and then undermined it by revealing that only one garment had actually been worn by him, parodying the artist as an extraordinary persona and the fetishization of all that touches him or her.

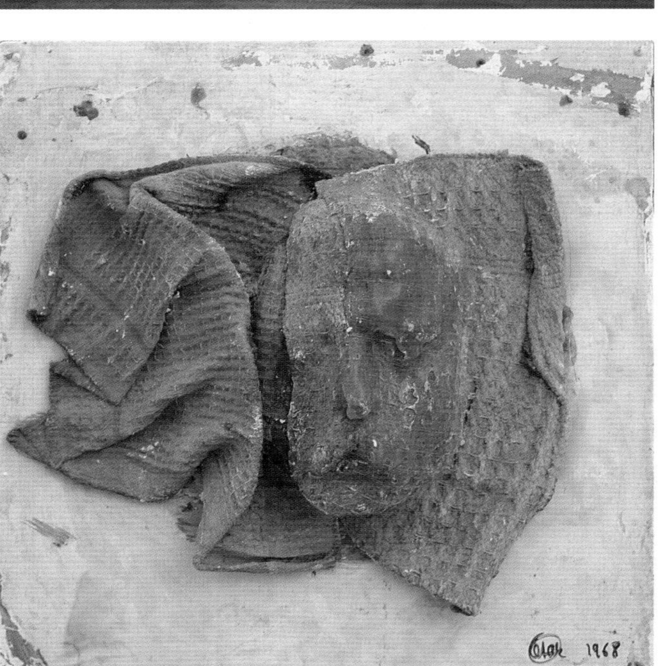

CÉSAR
Masque XXIII (Mask XXIII)
1968
Cloth, polyurethane
45.5 × 45.5 × 10.5 cm [18 × 18 × 4 in]

César had been making 'imprints' of his face, starting with the transfer on to plastic of a photo-portrait of himself by the artist Mimmo Rotella. Reliefs of César's face were moulded in sheets of plastic, then heat-treated to distort and deform the features. Many of the resulting self-portrait masks were cast in bronze and exhibited along with deformed casts in plastic and latex in the show 'Tête-à-têtes' at the Galerie Creuzevault, Paris (1973). At the exhibition's opening, round César-loaves, cast from the original head and made by the specialist bakery Poilâne, were cut up and offered to the guests. Providing a literal connection between bread and the body of the artist, and by analogy the body of Christ, César's humorous presentation of his head as a loaf of bread cleverly anticipated charges of narcissism (the repetitive use of his self-portrait) by pushing that narcissism over the top. The *César-têtes* and masks, stamped with the face of the artist like the head on a coin, provided a very real currency for the consumption of the artist.

Giuseppe PENONE
Piede (Foot)
1972
Plaster cast, hairs, slide projection
20 × 27 × 10cm [8 × 10.5 × 4 in]
Installation, Sperone Gallery, Turin, 1975

In 1971 Penone made a book entitled *Svolgere la propria pelle* (*To unroll one's own skin*) in which he reproduced the surface of six different parts of his body by pressing a glass slide against himself. The following year he made a series of plaster casts of the same parts of his body, on to which he projected slide images of those same parts. During the process of casting his right foot several hairs were torn from his skin, remaining embedded in the plaster replica and therefore absent from the photograph of his foot that was taken shortly after the casting process. The installation bringing slide and cast together restored the hairs missing from the photograph and the natural skin colour absent from the cast, providing a disturbing ambiguity in the viewer's reading of texture and form in two and three dimensions.

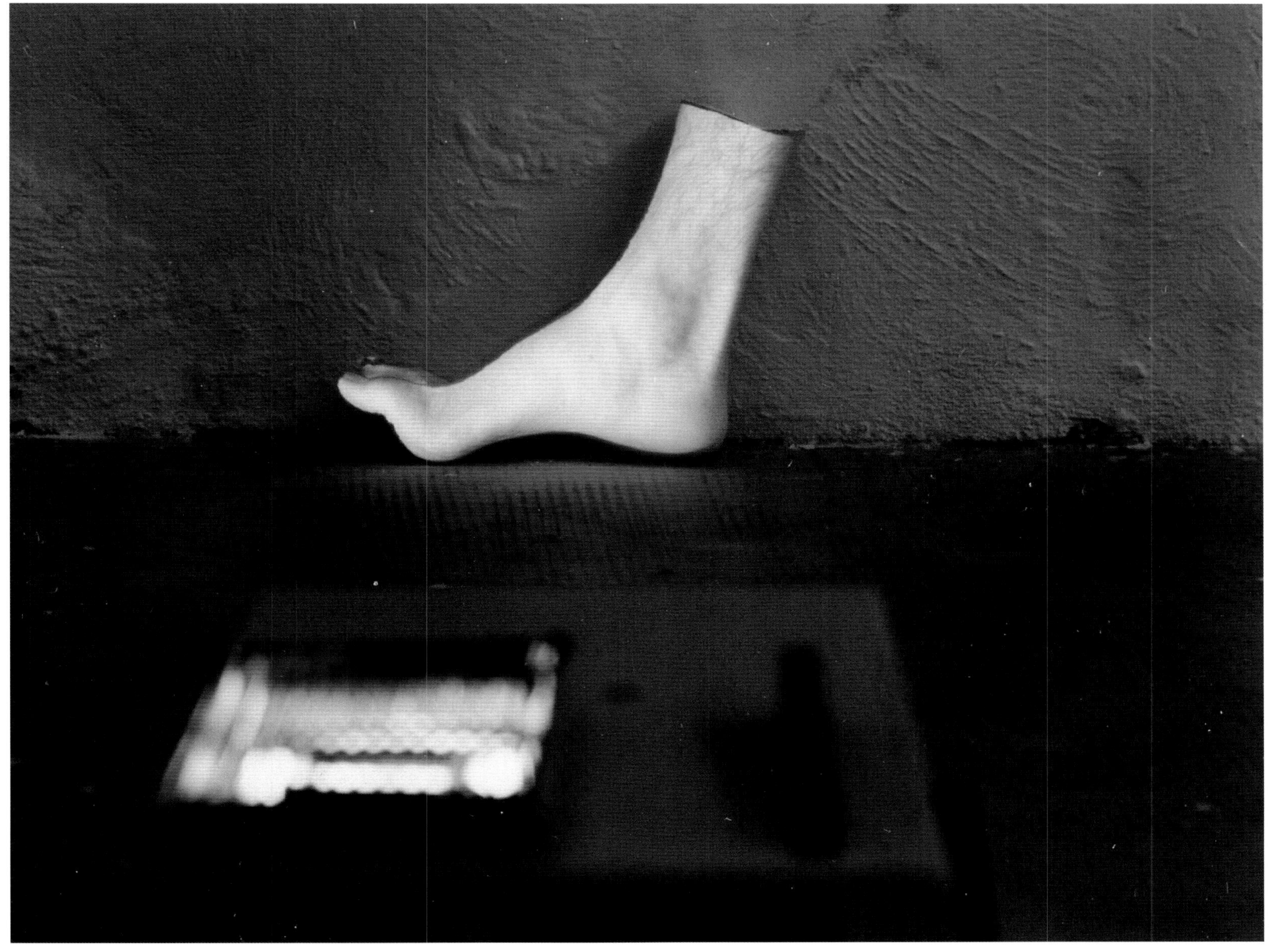

T 182—Will; With Affidavit of Subscribing Witnesses

Julius Blumberg, Inc., Law Blank Publishers
80 Exchange Place at Broadway, New York

I, ALAN SONFIST

being of sound and disposing mind and memory, and considering the uncertainty of this life, do make, publish and declare this to be my last **Will** *and* **Testament** *as follows, hereby revoking all other former Wills by me at any time made.*

First, after my lawful debts are paid, I give my entire estate to my wife except:

Whereas, my body is my museum, it's my history. It collects and absorbs observations - interactions. It is the deciphering of these recordings that I project into the outside world. My boundaries define the world of art. I clarify my own common boundaries in relationship to the outside whether it be the room I exist in, the country I exist in, the universe I exist in. By adding other awarenesses, I am constantly redefining my boundaries and projecting these awarenesses into my art.

My work deals with the idea that the world is always in a state of flux. My art deals with the rhythm of the universe. The pieces are part of that rhythm. A plant grows in cycles- a man moves in cycles - my work tries to bring about awarenesses of these movements. One has to meditate with my work to gain an understanding. It is not the beginning or the end that I am concerned with, but the energy that is given or received through communication with my work.

I therefore provide that a list of proposed works of art from my diary shall be given to the Museum of Modern Art, New York City, upon my death and carried out for them by my agent on a seasonal basis thereafter.

Finally, because the decay and growth of my body will present the continuation of my art work, I bequeath my body in a sealed transparent enclosure to the Museum of Modern Art, New York City to be kept as a work of art accessible to the public.

Alan Sonfist

I hereby appoint Robert Jowanski *to be Executor of this my last Will and Testament.*

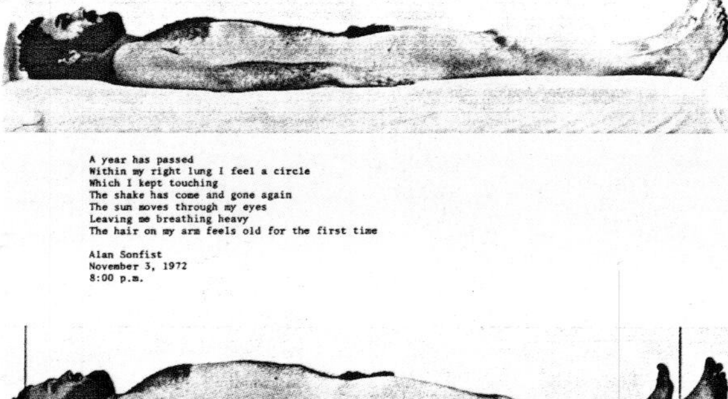

A year has passed
Within my right lung I feel a circle
Which I kept touching
The shake has come and gone again
The sun moves through my eyes
Leaving me breathing heavy
The hair on my arm feels old for the first time

Alan Sonfist
November 3, 1972
8:00 p.m.

A year has passed
My body feels a completeness
Time spent in the openness
Eyes are relaxed
Right side of neck still pain
Lungs opened   soreness gone
Temperature mild
Felt the wind on my skin

Alan Sonfist
October 3, 1973
1:15 p.m.

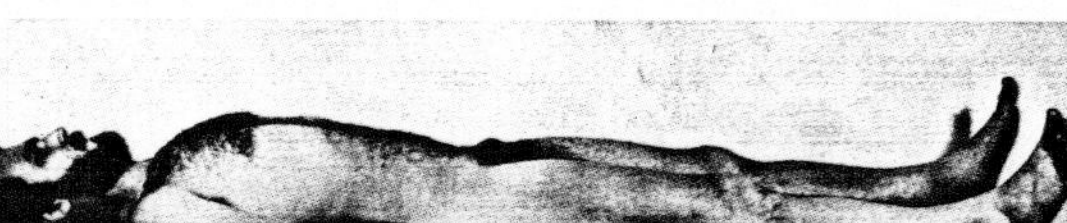

A year has passed
As I breathe my head Fogs
My heart beating my hands
Left side of my body—numbs
From the ridge of my foot to my waist
The intensity has gone
Eyes open and close with equal resistance

Alan Sonfist
November 26, 1974
9:30 a.m.

Alan SONFIST
Last Will and Testament
1973
Black and white photographs, text
2 parts, 28 × 21.5 cm [11 × 8.5 in] each

'I, Alan Sonfist, being of sound and disposing mind and memory, and considering the uncertainty of this life, do make, publish and declare this to be my last Will and Testament as follows, hereby revoking all other former Wills by me at any time made.

'First, after my lawful debts are paid, I give my entire estate to my wife except: whereas, my body is my museum, it's my history. It collects and absorbs observations – interactions. It is the deciphering of these recordings that I project into the outside world. My boundaries define the world of art. I clarify my own common boundaries in relationship to the outside whether it be the room I exist in, the country I exist in, the universe I exist in. By adding other awareness, I am constantly redefining my boundaries and projecting these awarenesses into my art.

'[...] Finally, because the decay and growth of my body will present the continuation of my art work, I bequeath my body in a sealed transparent enclosure to The Museum of Modern Art, New York City, to be kept as a work of art accessible to the public.'

opposite
Ana MENDIETA
Untitled (from the 'Silueta' series)
1976
Red pigment silueta on sand
Life size

Mendieta's earth actions stage a death or a dissolution that implicates a rebirth through reintegration with the maternal body of the earth. 'I have been carrying out a dialogue between the landscape and the female body (based on my own silhouette). I believe this has been a direct result of my having been torn from my homeland (Cuba) during my adolescence. I am overwhelmed by the feeling of having been cast from the womb (nature). My art is the way I re-establish the bonds that unite me to the universe. It is a return to the maternal source. Through my earth/body sculptures I become one with the earth ... I become an extension of nature and nature becomes an extension of my body. This obsessive act of reasserting my ties with the earth is really the reactivation of primeval beliefs ... [in] an omnipresent female force, the after-image of being encompassed within the womb, is a manifestation of my thirst for being.'
– Ana Mendieta quoted in K. Horsfeld, B. Muller and N. García Ferraz, *Ana Mendieta: Fuego de Tierra*, 1988

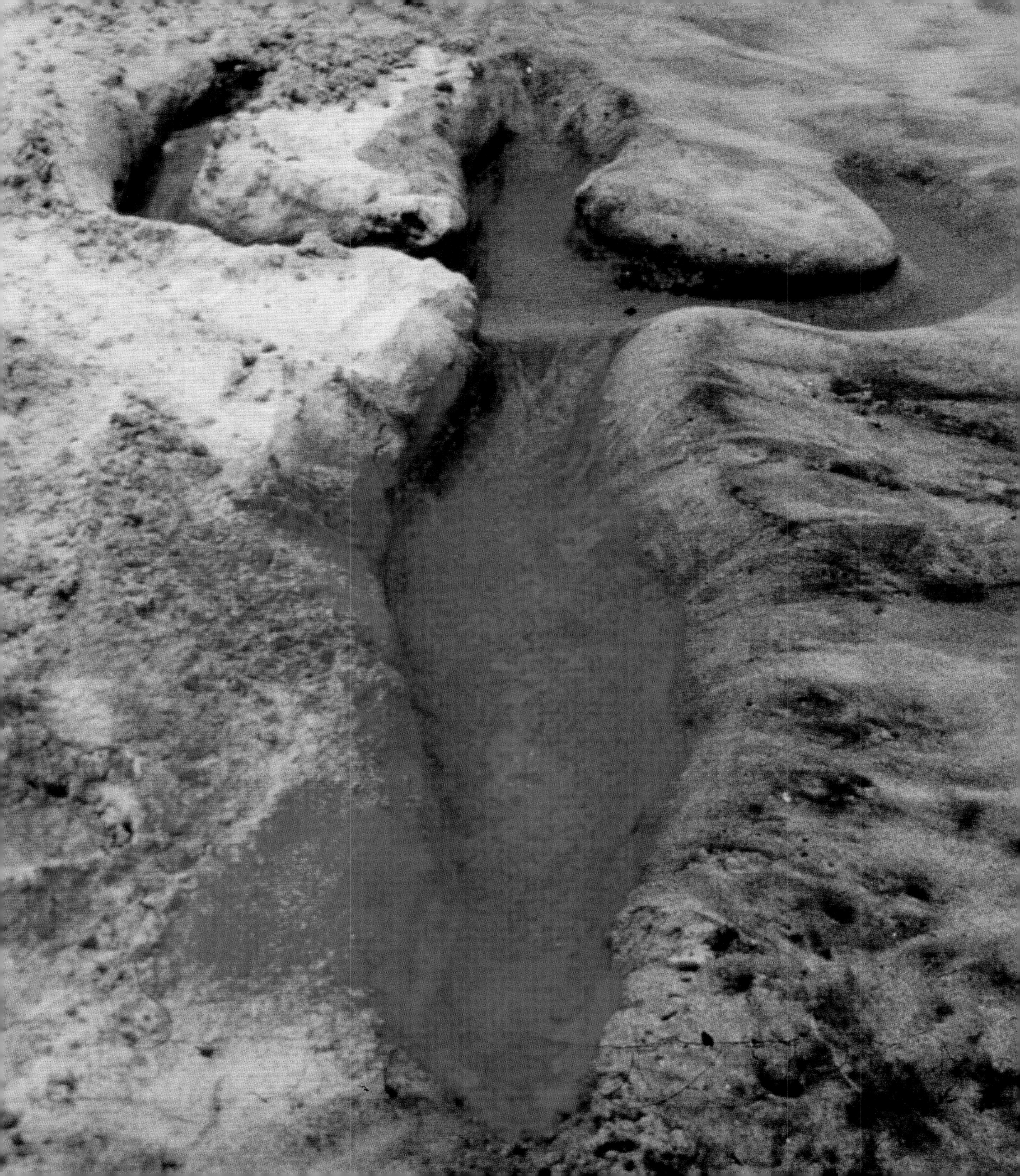

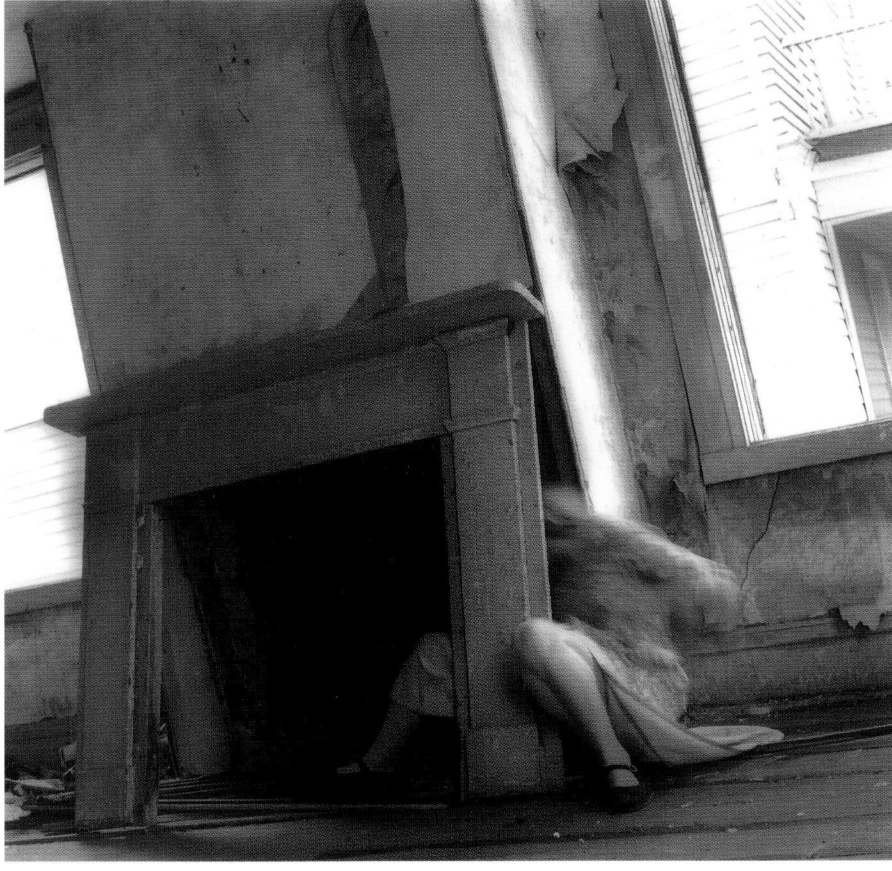

Francesca WOODMAN
House No. 4, Providence, Rhode Island
1975–76
Black and white photograph
20 × 25 cm [8 × 10 in]

While still a student at the Rhode Island School of Design, Woodman made a series of photographs in which her body disappeared into the structure of a dilapidated house, hidden under window frames, behind peeling sheets of wallpaper, or obscured by the dismantled fireplace. Her body is frequently blurred by movement, which conveys a sense of ephemerality and absence. She merges into the building's fragmenting structure, suggesting that she is the spirit of the building her body inhabits. Abandoning overt objecthood to present herself as a non-presence, Woodman removes herself physically from the viewer, discouraging the kind of voyeurism normally invoked by the female body. However, her disappearance into the atmospheric *mises-en-scéne*, which she captures through careful attention to light and space, convey a powerful sense of personal intimacy and a deep self-searching.

opposite
Francesca WOODMAN
Untitled (from the Angel series, Rome)
1977–78
Black and white photograph
20 × 25 cm [8 × 10 in]

Woodman developed the theme of angels while in Rome for a year on a Rhode Island School of Design student-exchange programme. In the 'Angel' series she used her body to create images of a transient, transparent apparition, which seems fragmented and unreal even in its most concrete form. The photographs present a metaphysical presence, a portrait of the invisible, a sense of a life, rather than a record of a person. As such, they disrupt the codes by which we normally read images of the artist, or of a woman, or a woman-artist. Her images present a state of being that is both personal and non-personal, highly particular and utterly general.

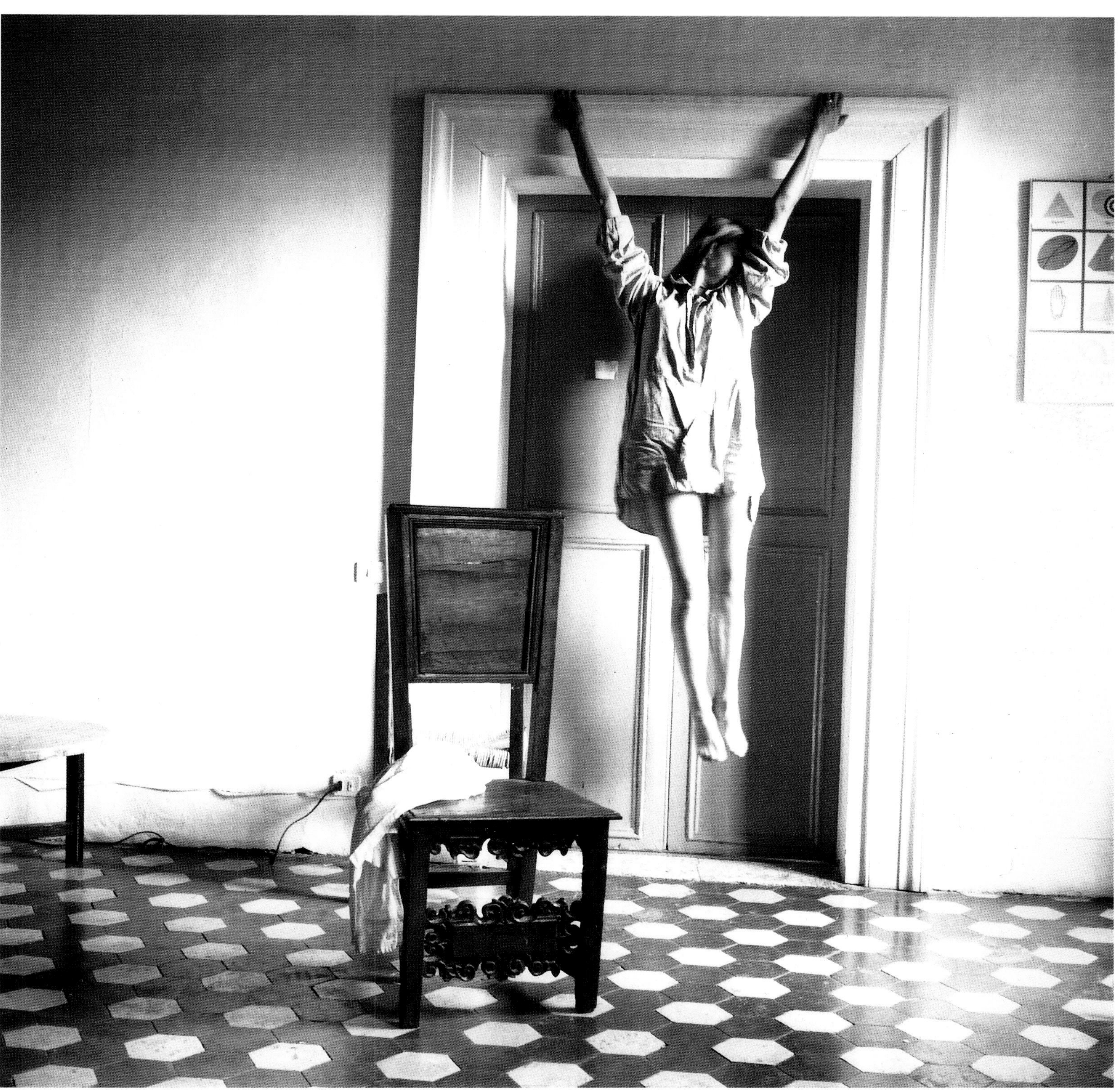

Antony GORMLEY
Bed
1981
Bread, wax
28 × 220 × 168 cm [11 × 87 × 66 in]

In *Bed* the physical body is absent: what is present is a trace of the body configured in layers of sliced bread and wax. Bread is a symbol of both the body and the spirit of Christ, to be eaten in religious ritual. The bread is stacked in the form of a bed, literally containing the invisible body of the artist, whose spirit is present through its absence. For Gormley the body is a force that moves in space; if it is halted hidden elements of the consciousness it contains may be revealed: 'Action can be confused with life. Much of human life is hidden. Sculpture, in stillness, can transmit what may not be seen. My work is to make bodies into vessels that both contain and occupy space.'
– Antony Gormley, Artist's statement, 1985

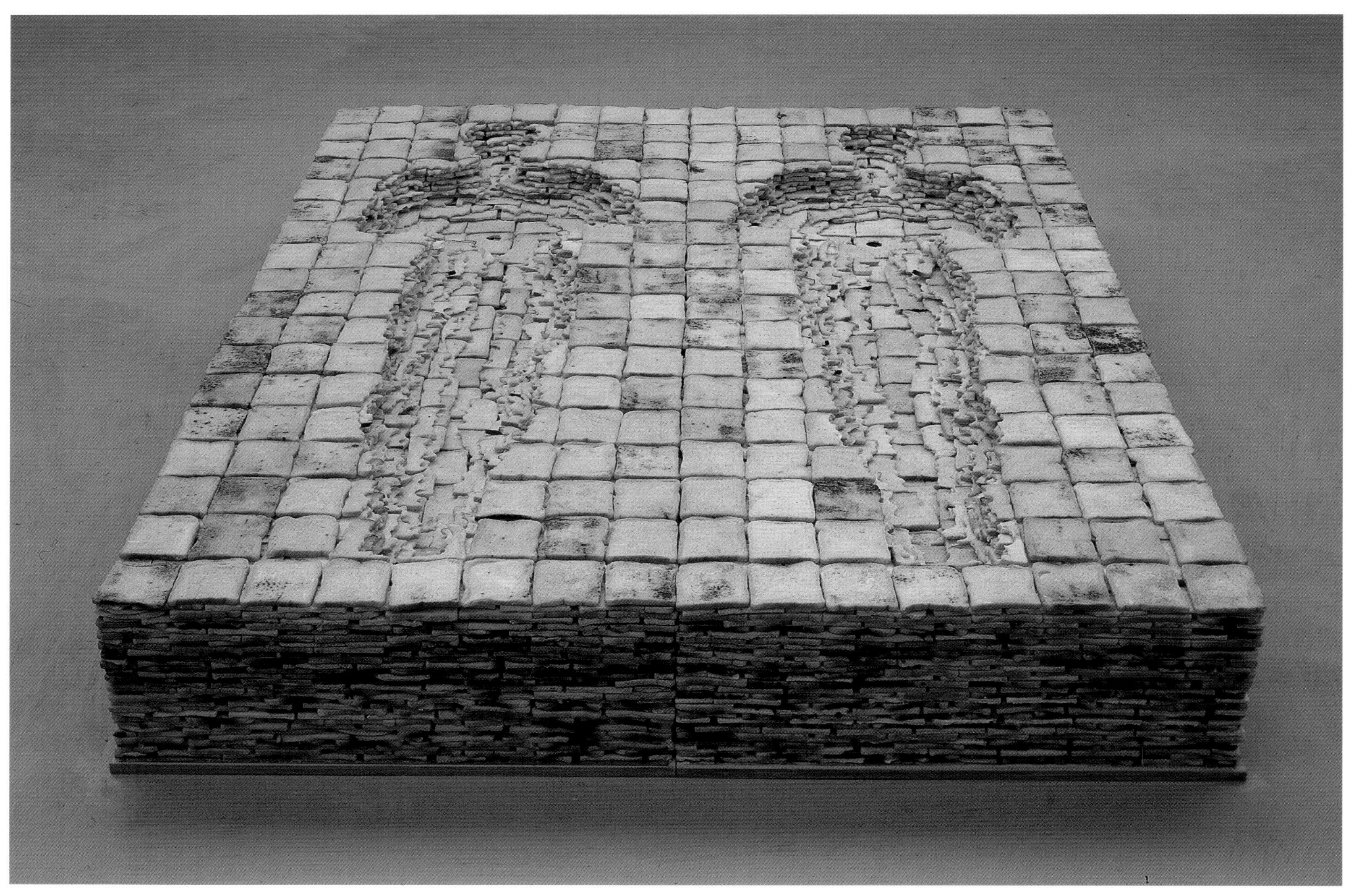

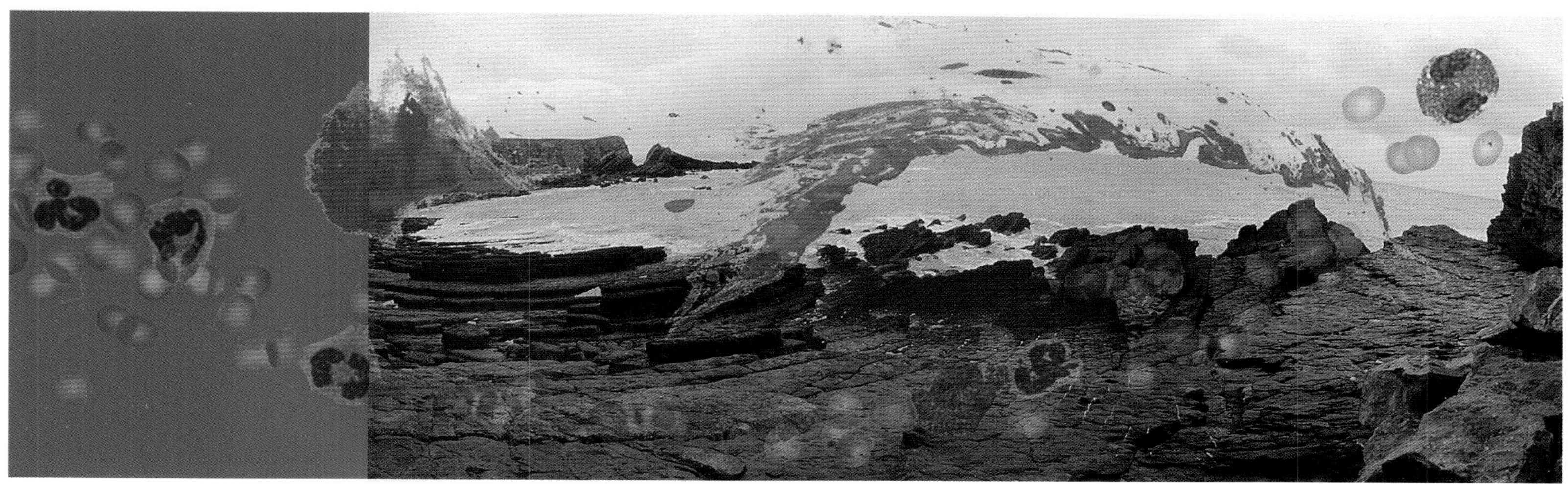

Helen CHADWICK
Viral Landscape No. 3
1988-89
Colour photographic print
120 × 300 cm [47 × 118 in]

Chadwick's *Viral Landscapes* present enlarged images of virus-infected cells from her body printed over photographs of the coastline, the meeting of sea and land symbolizing the coming together of virus and and host cell.

As the cells change with the invasion of the virus the artist's absent body is reconfigured, giving rise to a new body, constantly in flux, which is identifiable only in instants trapped by the camera. 'At its most intimate, the abolition of frontiers renders my body up as cells and tissue, "vulnerable to manifold incursions". Released from the bonds of form and gender, flesh is volatile and free to wander in an aetiology of complete abandon.' Chadwick described the points of contact between a virus and the cells of the body that hosts it as 'territories of a prolific encounter, the exchange of living and informational systems at the shoreline of culture'.
– all quotes from Helen Chadwick, *Enfleshings*, 1989

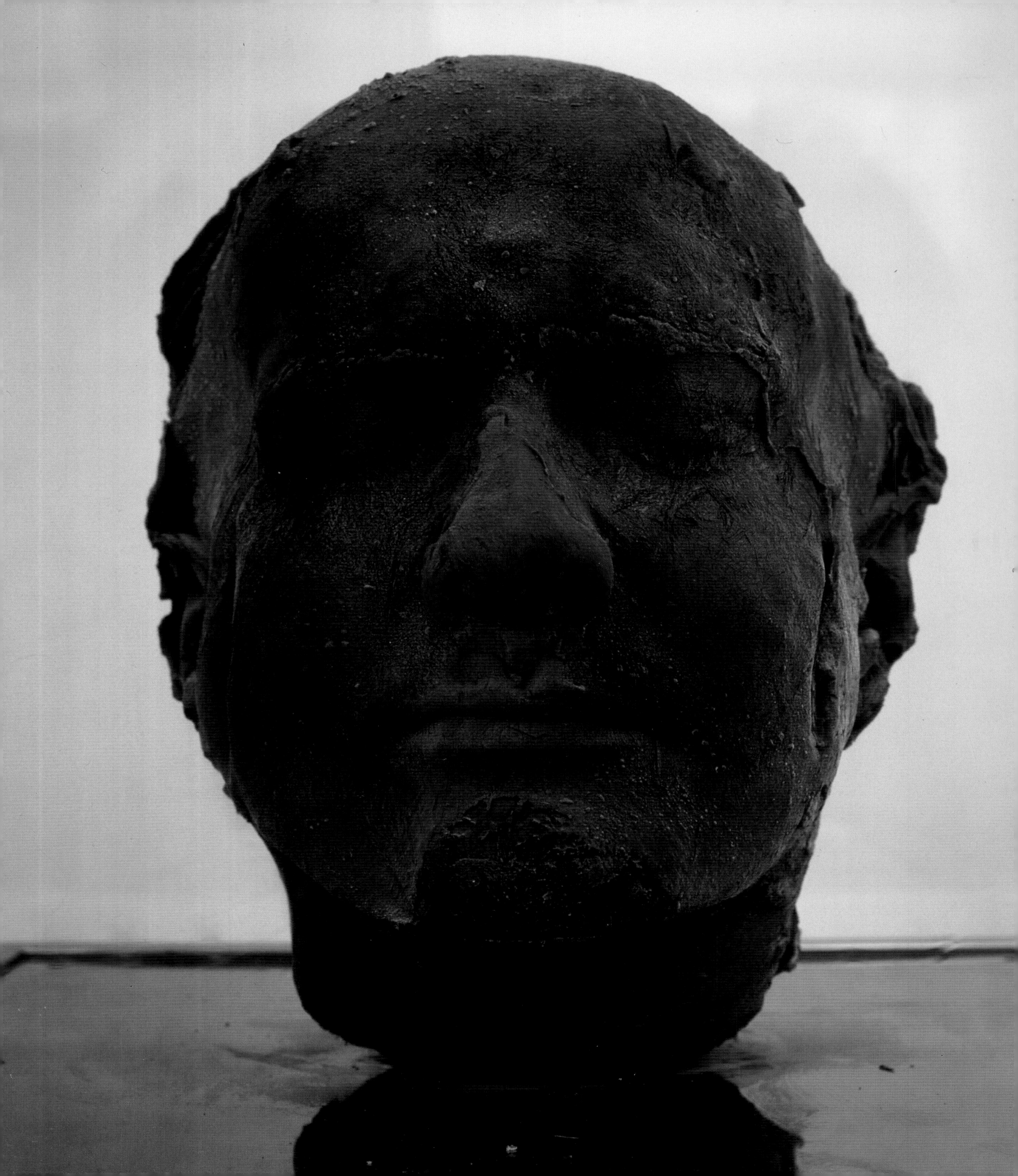

opposite
Marc QUINN
Self
1991
Blood, stainless steel, Perspex, refrigeration equipment
208 × 63 × 63 cm [207 × 25 × 25 in]

Quinn collected 4.5 litres [8 pints] of his own blood – the equivalent of the total blood in the average male body – over a period of five months. He then used it to make a frozen cast of his head, which was installed in a transparent Perspex box connected to refrigeration equipment that keeps it at a constant temperature of -70° C [-94° F]. Producing the ultimate self-portrait, Quinn has made a replica of himself with the substance that constitutes his body. His cast contains the information stored inside the body it mimics – his blood type, genetic identity, the materials for DNA mapping and even cloning. The artist's body is literally present through substance, symbolically through form, but absent in reality. Like the human body from which it comes, *Self* is mortal, stored in suspended refrigeration until someone pulls the plug, when liquefaction and decay set in.

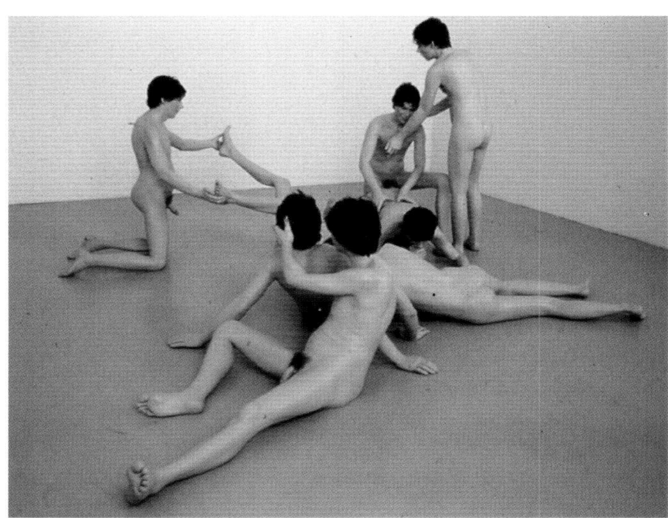

Charles RAY
Oh Charley, Charley, Charley ...
1992
Fibreglass, paint, synthetic hair
68.5 × 457 × 457 cm [72 × 180 × 180 in]

Ray's initial intention was to make his own double, himself as a youth sitting on his own lap. However, the piece developed instead into a complex baroque composition representing an orgy of one in eight parts, as eight stylized, naked representations of the artist seem to engage in non-penetrative sexual play. The cast bodies have been transformed into lifeless facsimiles acting out the most private of activities, masturbation. The static mannequin-bodies are unable to convey a sense of internal life, and so this becomes a desexualized game. Ray explains that part of the tension lies in whether it is 'a flat literary fantasy or a real disturbance in me'.
– Charles Ray quoted by Paul Schimmel, 'Beside One's Self', 1998

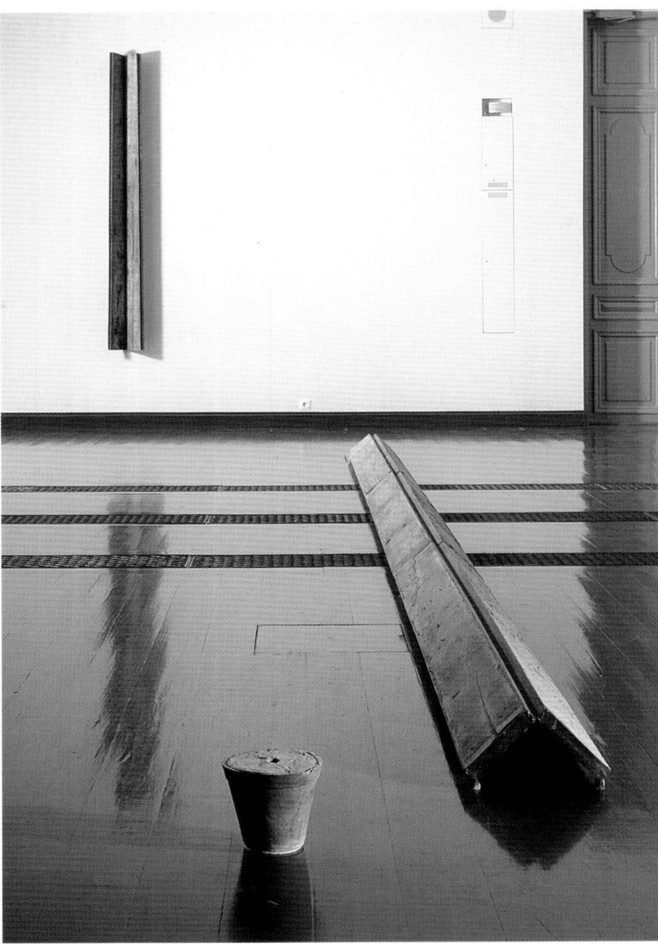

Mirosław BAŁKA
2 × /o2,5 × 167 × 15/
1990
Wood, metal, concrete, flowerpot, pine needle
3 parts, 250 × 30 × 16 cm; 238 × 30 × 15 cm; h. 15 cm, ø 17.5 cm [98.5 × 12 × 6 in; 94 × 12 × 6 in; h. 6 in, ø 7 in]
Installation, Kiasma Museum of Contemporary Art, Helsinki

Bałka has been working with austere geometric forms based on the dimensions of his body since the early 1990s. In his first solo exhibition entitled 'April/My Body Cannot Do Everything I Ask For', at the Foksal Gallery in Warsaw, the viewer entered a space that was empty apart from a few very simple structures. These were fabricated from old wood and metal and erected against the walls or placed in corners to suggest an ordinary table or bed. It is in the dimensions of the individual pieces, quoted as 'titles', that the artist's absent body may be located. Thus *2 × /o2.5 × 167 × 15/* is a pair of metal pipes filled with salty water, positioned at a height and distance from each other to correspond with a pair of human eyes. This structure evokes the presence of the artist's absent, crying body. 'Contemporary time does not exist, we cannot catch the continuous. As we move ever into the future we are always based in the past. This is the state of my sculpture, there is heat from this pillow, and it's impossible to catch this continuous flow. As soon as you touch it it's colder than it was at its source. Everything we touch is coming from the past, it's our access to death. For me the important thing in my art is to try to catch that consciousness of life.'
– Mirosław Bałka, Artist's statement, 1995

opposite top
Janine ANTONI
Eureka
1993
Bathtub, lard, soap
Soap, 56 × 66 × 66 cm [22 × 26 × 26 in]
Bathtub, 76 × 178 × 63.5 cm [30 × 70 × 25 in]

In reference to Archimedes' famous discovery of a method for measuring the volume of an irregular form, Antoni climbed into a bath filled with lard, submerging herself completely in order to displace her body's volume. After removing her body from the bath, Antoni mixed the displaced lard with lye to make a large cube of soap with which she washed herself. *Eureka* comprises the impression of her body in the lard in the bath, and the block of soap, worn away on the upper surface and at the corners by her use. The work cyclically starts with and returns to the artist's absent (female) body simultaneously presenting it as object and agent. Both her objecthood – in the volume of her body – and her gestures – the actions of both making and washing with soap – have contributed to the artwork produced. The absent body is further suggested by the materials used: both lard and soap prompt a tactile and sensory response in the viewer, who can physically empathize with the actions undertaken by the artist.

opposite bottom
Mona HATOUM
Recollection
1995
Hair balls, strands of hair, wooden loom, woven hair, table
Dimensions variable
Installation, Béguinage St. Elizabeth, Kortrijk, Belgium
Collection, De Vleeshal, Middelburg, The Netherlands

First created for the Béguinage Convent of St. Elizabeth in Kortrijk, Belgium, this installation used discarded parts of the artist's body to evoke a nostalgic sense of absence and loss. In a corner of what appeared to be an empty room Hatoum placed a small wooden table, on which was a roughly made miniature loom. As one walked into the large space individual hairs hung from the wooden ceiling beams, in even rows 15 cm [6 in] apart would brush against one's face. The weaving on the loom was also made from hair; hundreds of hair balls floated loose on the floor and window sills. Hatoum, who had collected her own hair from combs and brushes over a long period of time, was using a part of her body – a dead part and in a form that is usually discarded once it has left the body – to reconfigure a physical presence, taking a variety of forms which are both ordered and disordered, from tightly controlled to floating free.

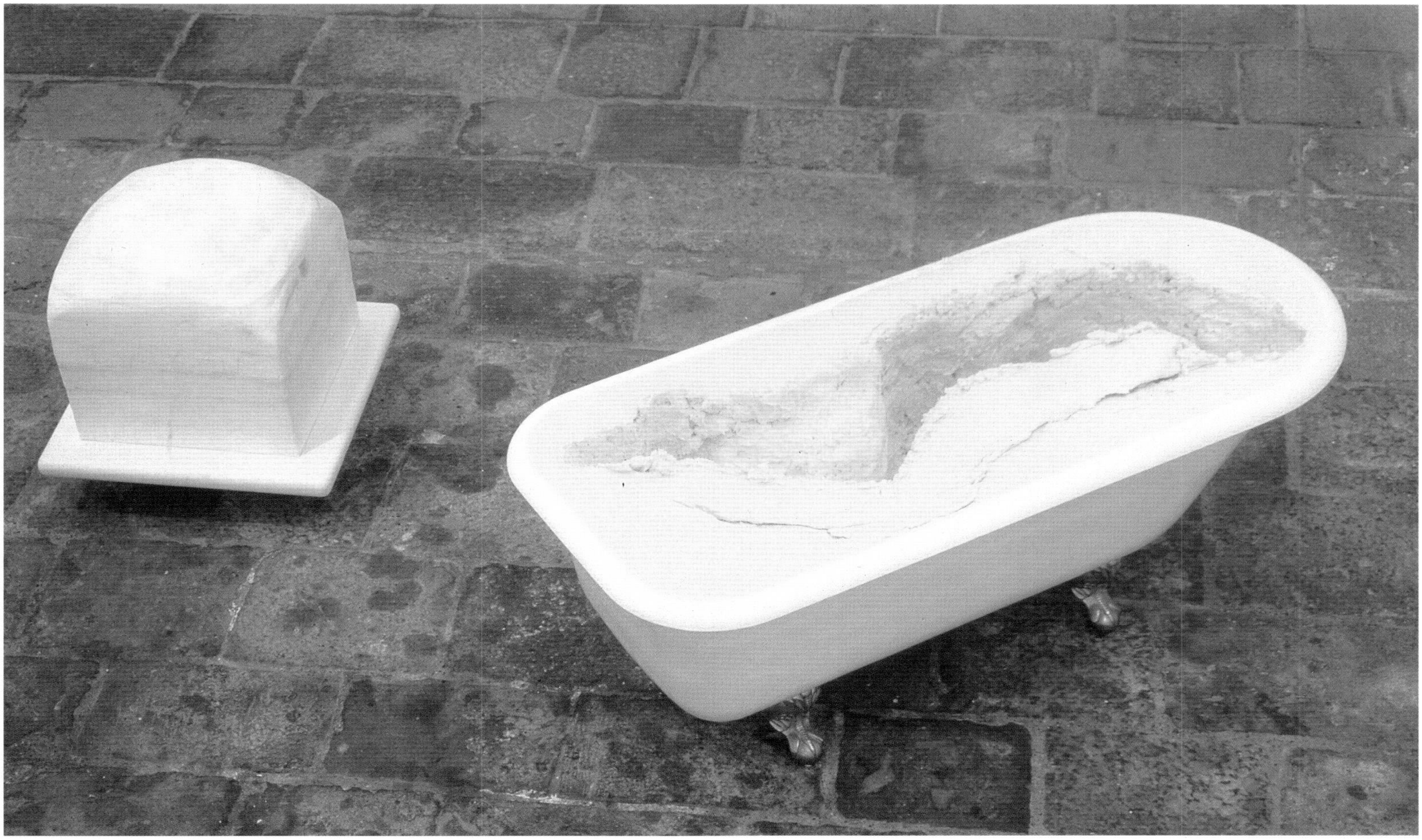

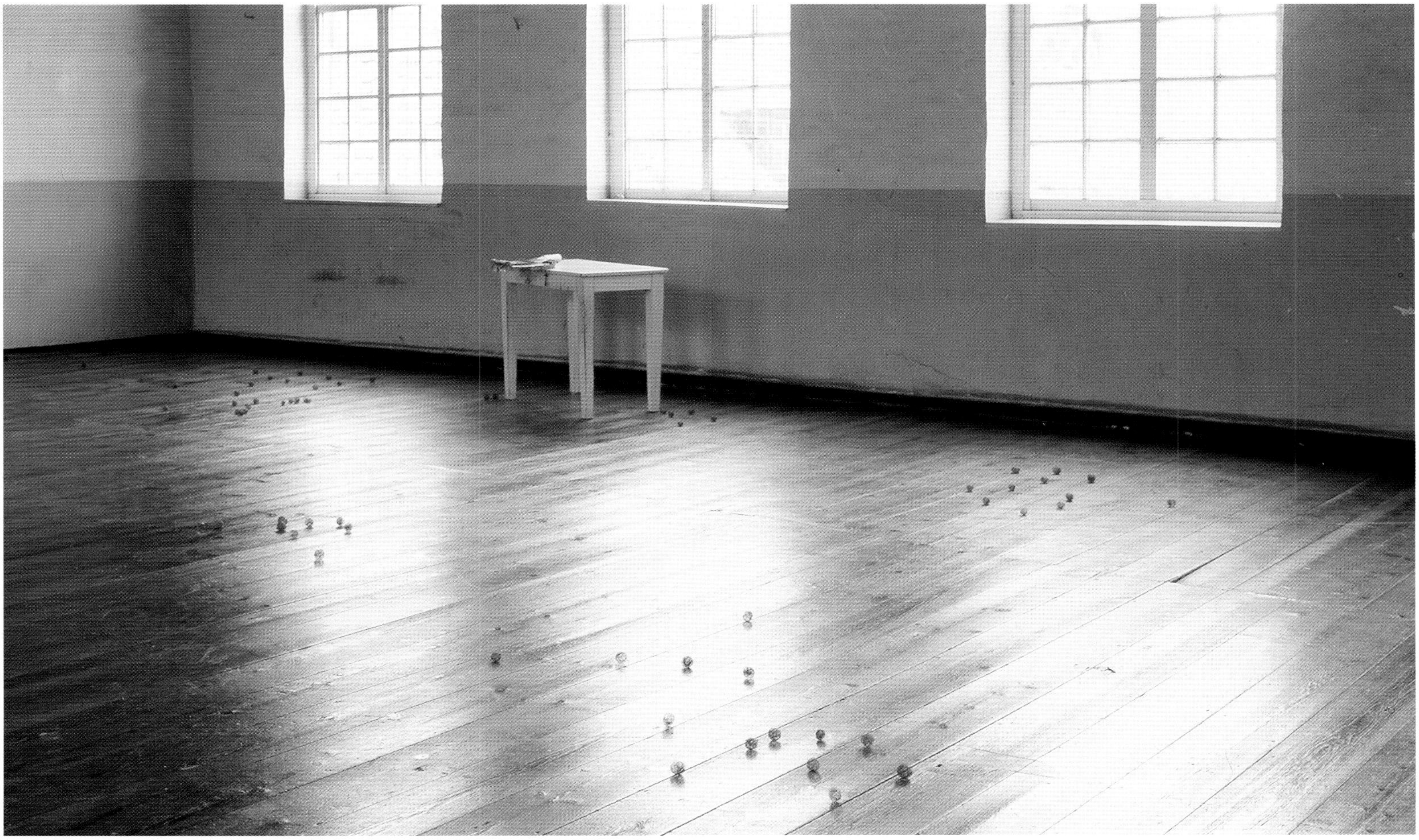

EXTENDED AND PROSTHETIC BODIES

The artists grouped here have extended the body with prosthetics, replacement parts, as it were, for the human. The materials from which these prosthetics are made range from the everyday – such as James Lee Byars' dress – to sophisticated technology – such as Stelarc's mechanized third arm. Some of these prosthetic attachments provide an extension of the body that increases its ability to communicate, thereby creating a new hybrid body beyond the physical limits of the human scale. In other works the body is transformed into a tool or instrument, as can be seen in Nam June Paik's transformation of his body into a cello played by Charlotte Moorman. Artists such as Orlan and Leigh Bowery 'extend' their bodies to create a new identity.

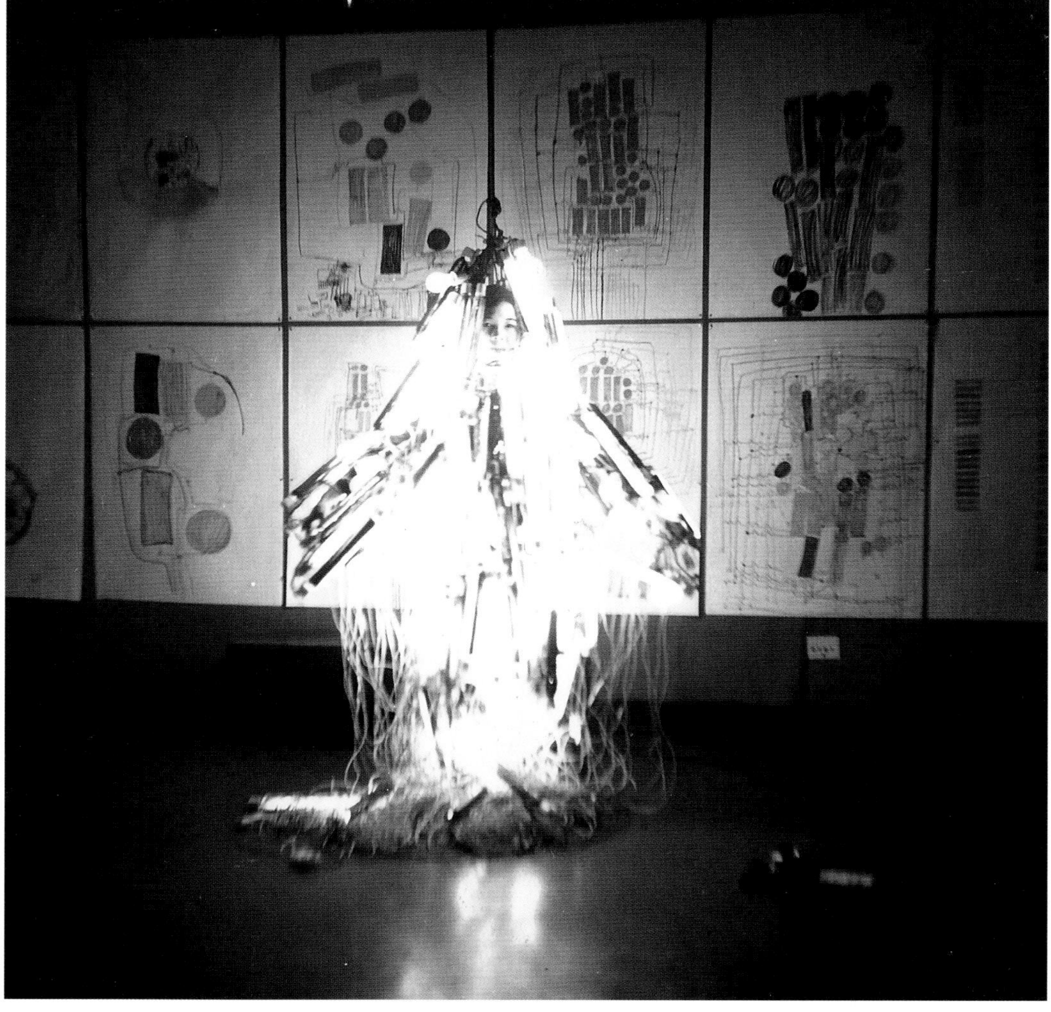

Atsuko TANAKA
Electric Dress
1956
2nd Gutai Exhibition, Ohara Kaikan Hall, Tokyo

Tanaka constructed a garment reflecting the nervous and vascular systems of the human body from an armature of electric wiring to which hundreds of light bulbs painted in primary colours were attached. These lit up along the circulatory and nerve pathways of her body. In 1956, for a performance at the 2nd Gutai Art Exhibition at the Ohara Kaikan Hall, Tokyo, she robed herself with it in the tradition of the Japanese marriage ceremony. As a conflation of the traditional Japanese kimono with modern industrial technology, *Electric Dress* anticipated later investigations into ways of reading and reinterpreting gender, costume and ritual.

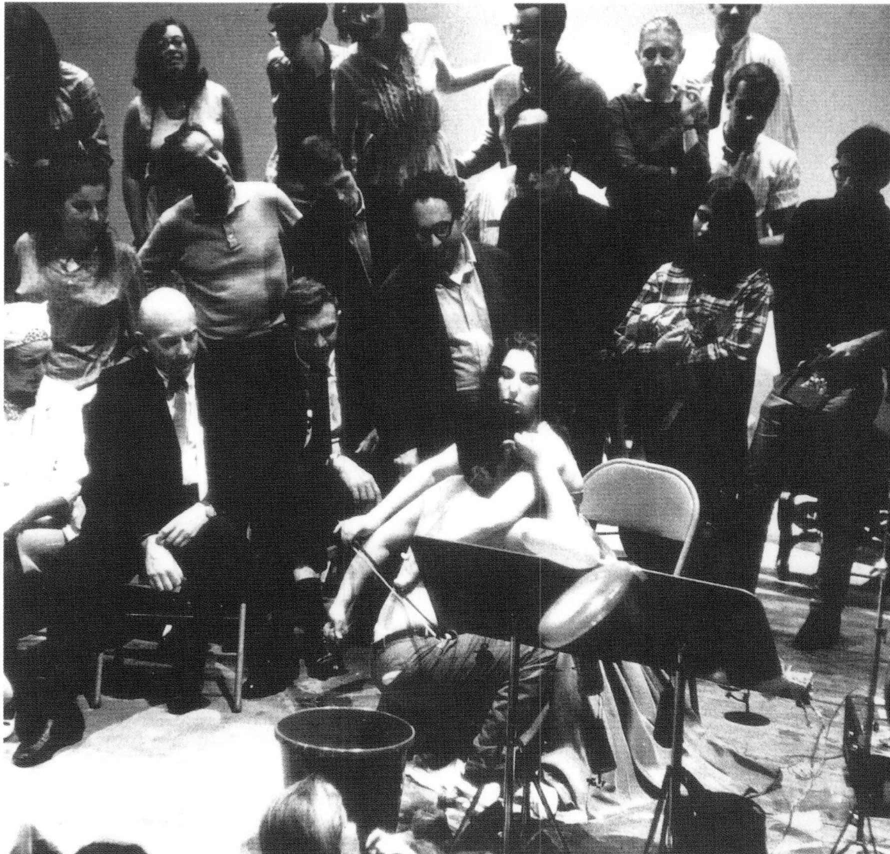

Nam June PAIK and Charlotte MOORMAN
Human Cello
(Interpreting John Cage's '26'1.1499 for a String Player)
1965
New York

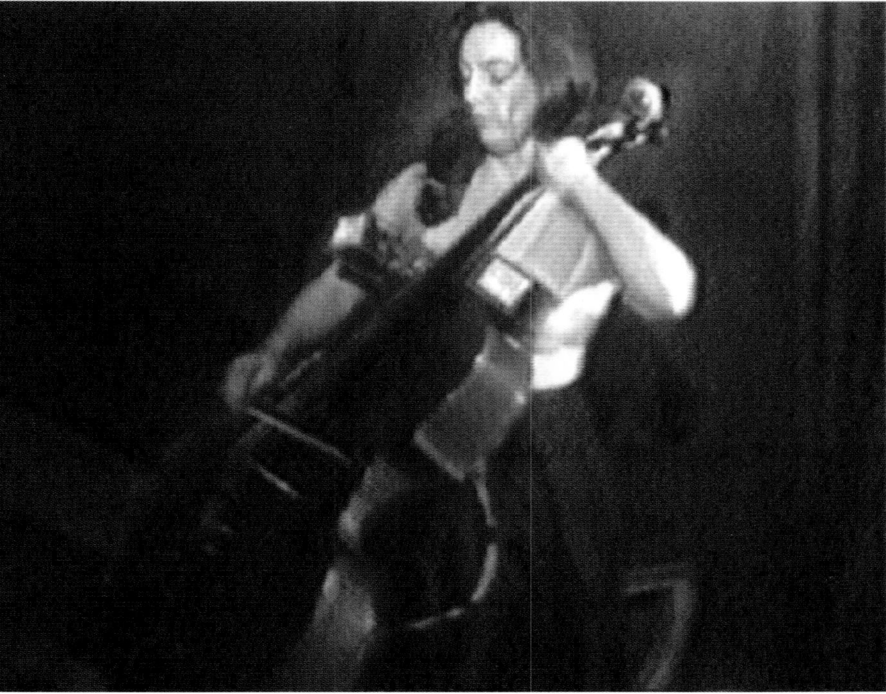

Nam June PAIK and Charlotte MOORMAN
TV Bra for a Living Sculpture
1969
'TV as a Creative Medium', Howard Wise Gallery, New York

Paik's collaborations with Moorman, a professional cellist, fused new music, the body, art and technology. In the performance *Human Cello* the artist's body became an instrument as Moorman held Paik like a cello, playing a string stretched over his bare back. In *TV Bra for a Living Sculpture,* Paik contructed a 'bra' for Moorman consisting of two small television screens covering her breasts, to be worn while she played the cello in a performance for a group show called 'TV as a Creative Medium' at the Howard Wise Gallery, New York. The televisions were occasionally wired up to receive television broadcasts, but more frequently they were connected to a closed-circuit camera within the gallery and to the cello. In this way they reflected the spectators back to themselves, while the notes played on the cello were amplified and transformed into optical signals, which distorted the images on the screens. Moorman almost literally became a television station, receiving and emitting a complex layering of images. Paik stated that his aim was 'to humanize the technology and the electronic medium, which is progressing rapidly, too rapidly', by replacing an intimate part of the female body with a form of technology that was rapidly beloved by American culture.
– Nam June Paik, Artist's statement, 1969

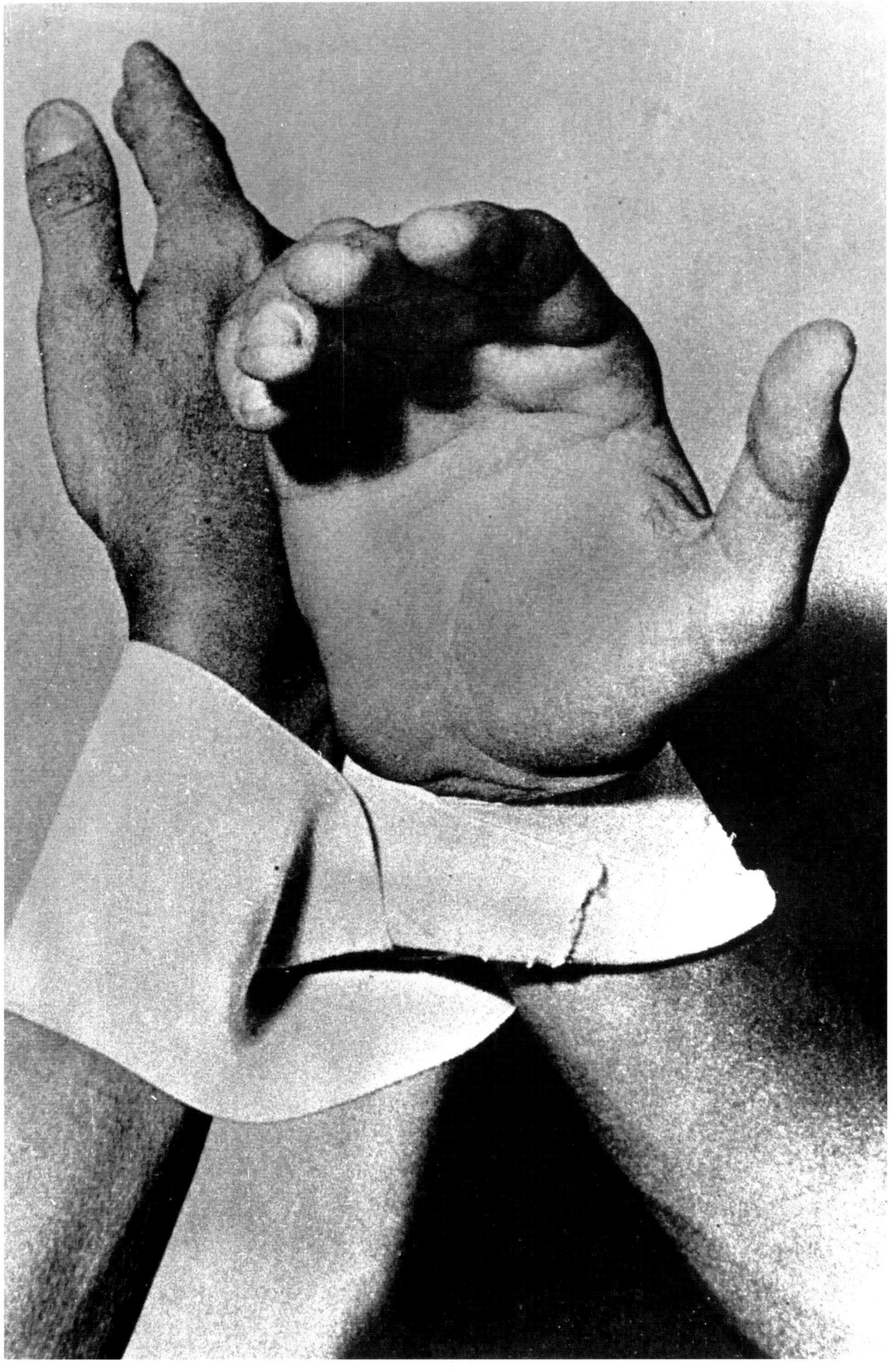

Lygia CLARK
Dialogo de Manos (Dialogue of Hands)
1966
Rio de Janeiro

In *Dialogue of Hands*, two hands are linked by an elastic-band wound around the wrists. Symbolizing the connection of a working relationship in which movement towards, around and away from the other is possible within the limitations of that relationship's elasticity, the Möbius band served to extend the artists' bodies in relation to each other. The idea of endlessness represented by the Möbius strip becomes incorporated into the body, and becomes an embodiment of consciousness and inter-relationality, an extension of body into psyche, rather than out into space.

A member of the Brazilian Neo-Concretist group of the 1960s, Clark made work that was both 'absolutely modern' in its visual language, and absolutely simple in its employment of common and relatively valueless materials culled from her everyday environment in Rio de Janeiro.

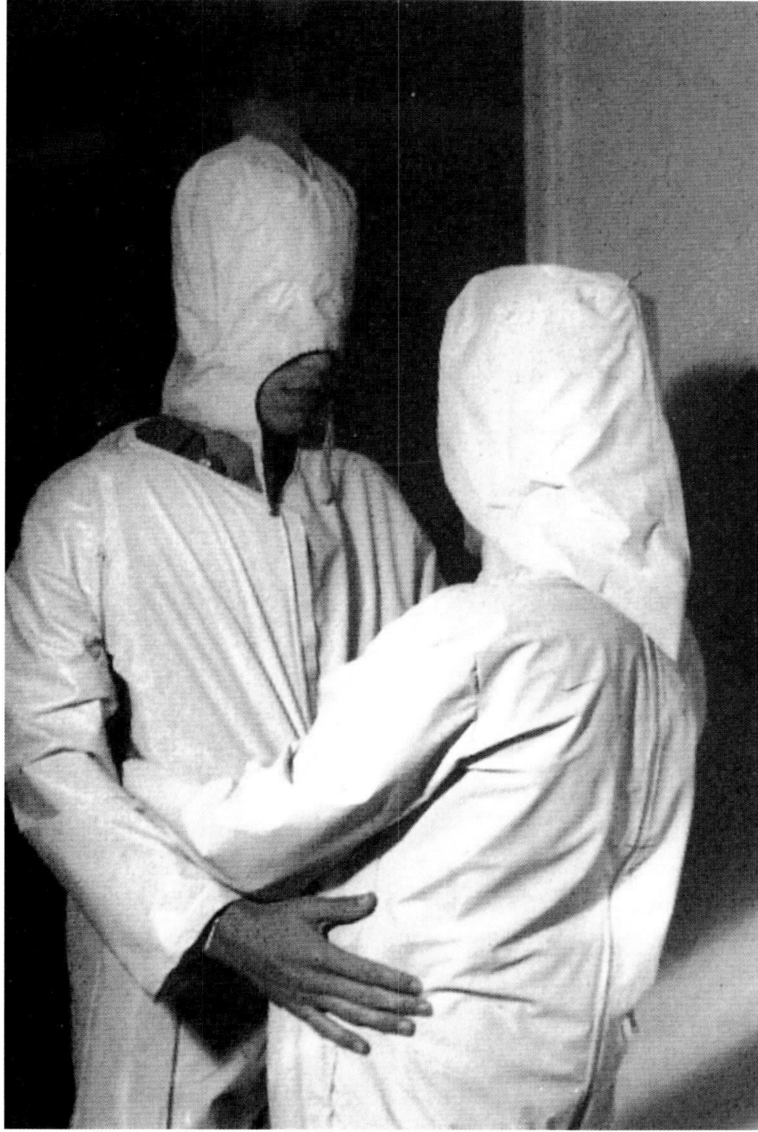

Lygia CLARK

The I and the You: Clothing/Body/Clothing

1967

Rio de Janeiro

'A proposal made for a couple in which both the man and the woman wear a plastic boiler suit. Each boiler suit contains within it a lining made up of different materials (plastic bag with water, vegetable spume, rubber, etc.), which gives the man a feminine sensation and a masculine sensation for the woman. A hood, made of the same plastic, blindfolds the eyes of the participants, and a rubber tube, like an umbilical cord, connects the two boiler suits. When they touch each other, the participants discover small openings in their boiler suits (six zips), which give access to the inner lining, translating them into the sensations felt by their partner. In this manner the man finds himself in the woman and she discovers herself in his body.'
– Lygia Clark, 'The I and the You: Clothing/Body/Clothing', 1967

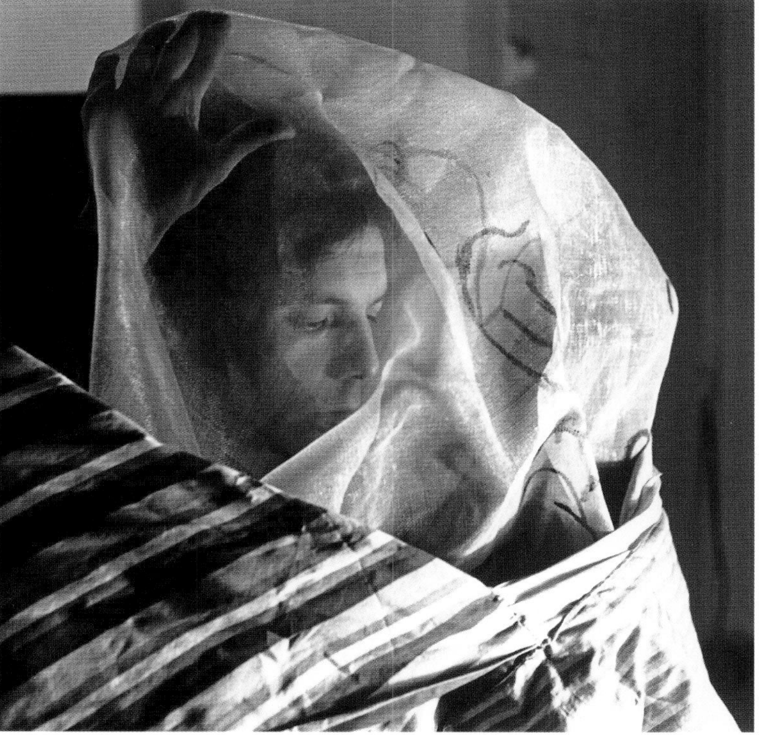

Hélio OITICICA

Wearing Parangolé P19 Capa 15, Gileasa: to Gilberto Gil

1968

London

Oiticica's *Parangole* series involved transformable artworks that were incorporated into the body and personality of the person who interacted with them. Each of the capes he made in this series had a different structure and character, usually inspired by a particular individual, or else were collectively made. Some seemed to evoke pleasure, others provoked more difficult emotions in the wearer. Sometimes inscribed with slogans or images, they were often made for children and friends in the *favelas* or shanty-town wastelands on the margins of the city, where Oiticica drew his inspiration for creative solutions in a 'desperate search for happiness'. 'The cape is not an object but a searching process – it is not a finished object and its spatial sense is not definite. It is more a constructive nucleus, laid open to the spectator's participation, which is the vital thing ... Its structure is unveiled through the direct bodily action of the spectator.'
– Hélio Oiticica, 'Eden', 1969

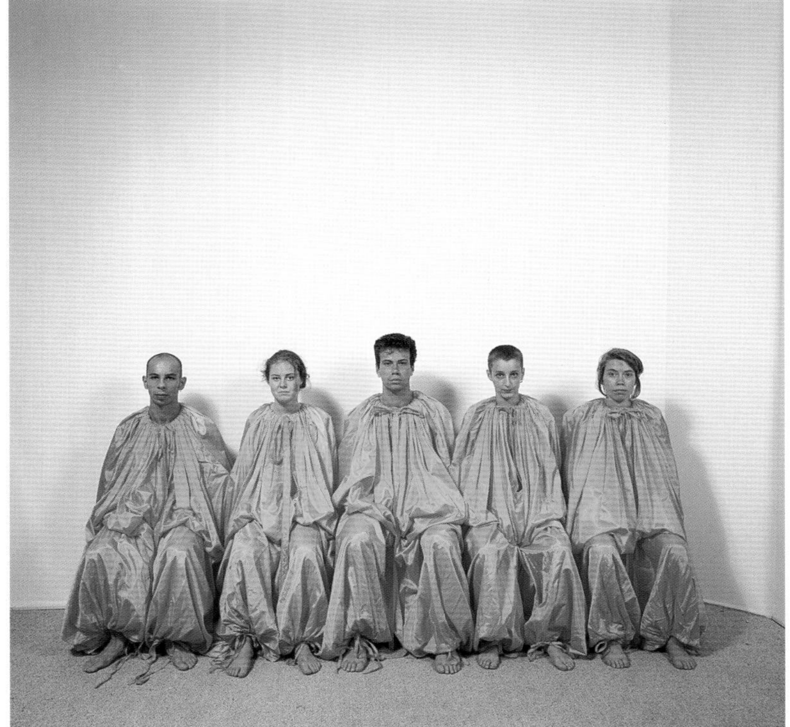

James Lee BYARS

Five in a Dress

1969

Wide White Space Gallery, Antwerp

Five in a Dress records a performative costume consisting of a pink silk circle with holes cut in the material to accommodate five people. A white version was shown and worn in Los Angeles and a black version in New York. Byars' other plural garments included trousers for three, a hat for 100 and a dress for 500, and were intended as a form of 'socializing' that would intensify the symbolic link between people and between the artist and his public. Created for a gathering of participants rather than an audience of spectators, many of the larger garments were later cut up and handed out to those who had 'worn' them, so that they could take home a piece of the experience, a reminder of the socializing connection. Byars described these events as 'thought in performance', bringing the anonymous individual – physically manifest as mere body – literally into the context and content of his sculpture.

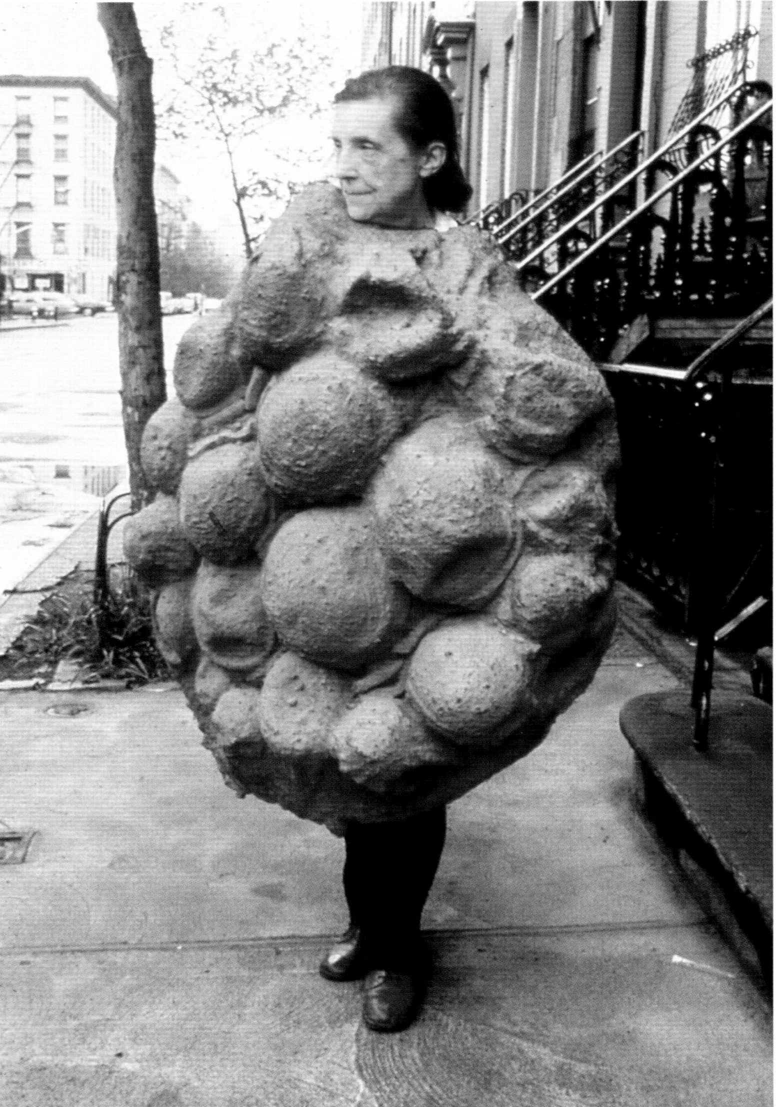

Louise BOURGEOIS

Costume for 'A Banquet'

1978

Latex

Approx. 132 × 96.5 × 12.7 cm [52 × 38 × 5 in]

Referring to her famous sculptural installation *The Destruction of the Father* (1974), Bourgeois recounts the childhood fantasy that generated it: 'at the dinner table my father would go on and on, showing off, aggrandizing himself. And the more he showed off, the smaller we felt. Suddenly there was a terrific tension, and we grabbed him – my brother, my sister, my mother – the three of us grabbed him and pulled him on to the table and pulled his legs and arms apart ... And we were so successful in beating him up that we ate him up.'

– Louise Bourgeois, *Destruction of the Father/ Reconstruction of the Father: Writings and Interviews 1923–1997*, 1998

Like her installation, this costume reflects the artist's desire for powerful maternal femininity to combat and overwhelm patriarchal abuse. Multiple breast-like forms recur throughout her work, sometimes phallic, sometimes like clusters of fingers or eggs. This image of nurturing motherhood that castrates the father recalls statues of the ancient Greek goddess Artemis, whose rituals involved the castration of bulls and the sacrifice of males, and who have clusters of similar rounded forms protruding from their torsos, which could represent castrated testicles as much as breasts. In 1978 she wore her costume in the performance 'The Banquet/ A Fashion Show of Body Parts' in conjunction with her installation *Confrontation*, a later form of the cannibal feast in *Destruction of the Father*.

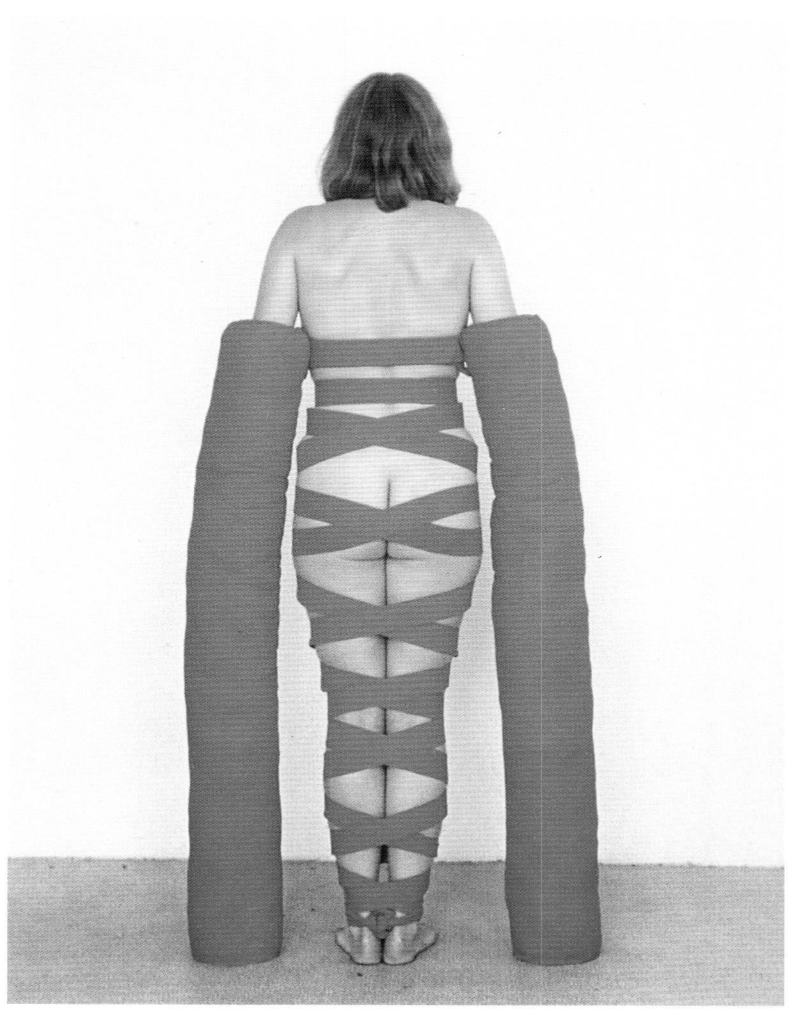

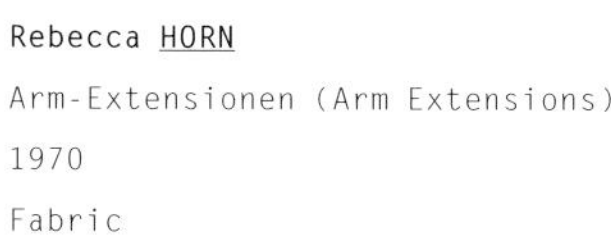

Rebecca HORN
Arm-Extensionen (Arm Extensions)
1970
Fabric
Dimensions variable

Horn started to make fabric body-sculpture pieces when she was forced to spend a year in a sanatorium as a result of lung poisoning from working with polyester and fibreglass at art school. Isolated from the outside world and confined to her bed for long periods, she started to develop ideas for communicating with people through constructions centred on her body. Using cotton, bandages and frequently feathers, she masked, cocooned and extended her body, expressing the paradoxes inherent in the desire for intimacy with another. At times the weight of the garments – as in *Arm Extensions* – renders the wearer clumsy and inert, operating more as a constriction than an expansion. Other garments, like *Finger Gloves*, isolate the wearer from her environment, while allowing her the ability to grasp things from a long way off. The ambiguous nature of these garments, a means of both empowerment and restriction, reveals the dilemma of a fragile embattled self who longs for a comfortable emotional intimacy.

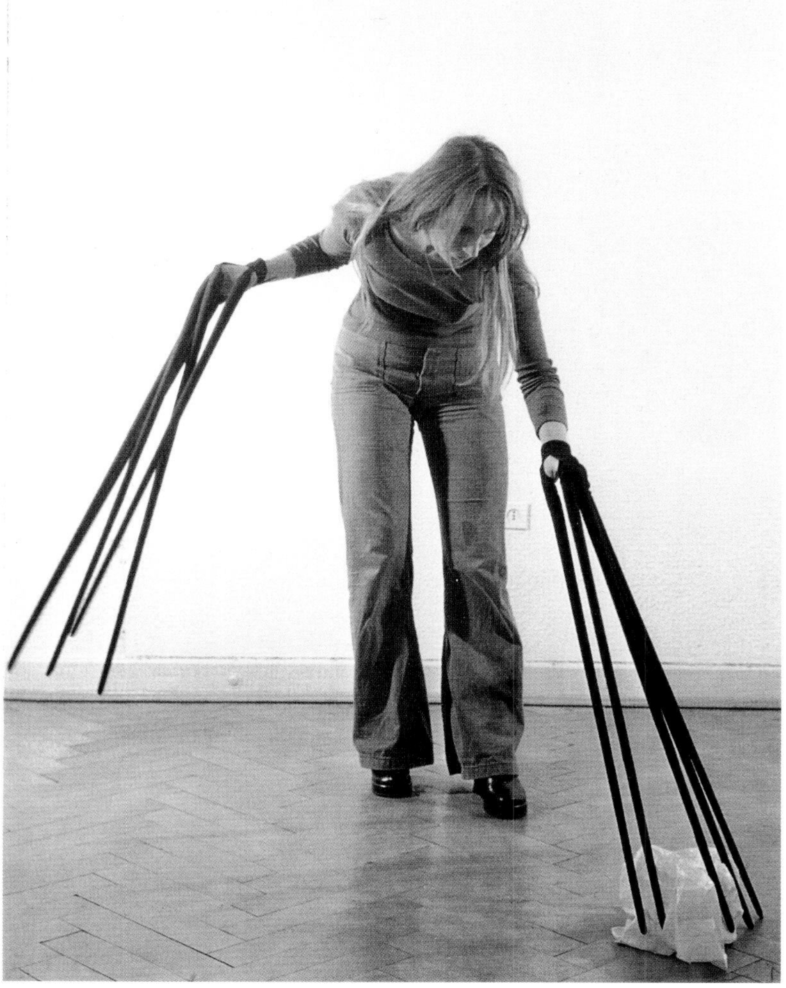

Rebecca HORN
Fingerhandschuhe (Finger Gloves)
1972
Fabric, balsa wood
l. 70 cm [27.5 in]

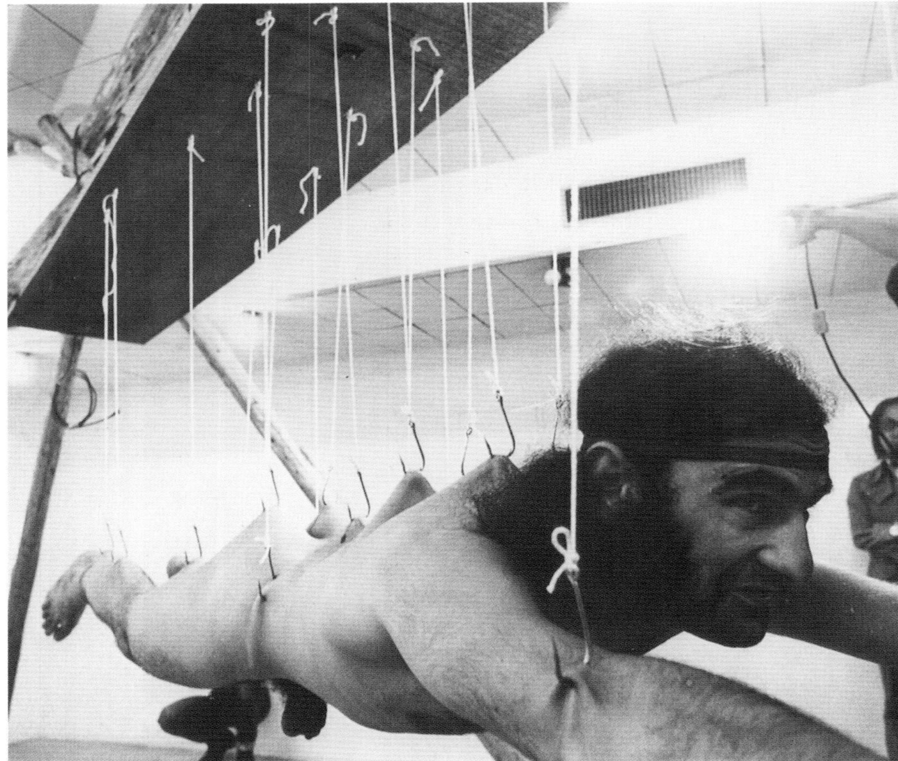

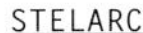

STELARC
Event for Stretched Skin
1976
Maki Gallery, Tokyo

In the early 1970s Australian performance artist Stelarc suspended himself in different spaces with ropes and harnesses. He then discovered that through piercing his skin with hooks, he could reduce the suspension of his body to a minimum of support. He performed twenty-seven suspensions of his body, in which he hung from meat-hooks inserted into the skin on his back. These took place in a variety of different locations, such as over a New York City street during rush-hour and in the Maki Gallery, Tokyo. 'The cables were lines of tension which were part of the visual design of the suspended body, and the stretched skin was a kind of gravitational landscape. This is what it took for a body to be suspended in a 1-G gravitational field. He connects his performances to 'astronauts floating in zero-G' – the twentieth century's expression of a 'primal desire for floating and flying'. For him this becomes a physical reality – a direct bodily experience of a metaphysical idea. 'I think metaphysically, in the past, we've considered the skin as surface, as interface. The skin has been a boundary for the soul, for the self, and simultaneously, a beginning to the world. Once technology stretches and pierces the skin, the skin as a barrier is erased.'

– all quotes from Paolo Atzori and Kirk Wolford, 'Extended-Body: Interview with Stelarc', www.ctheory.com/a29-extended_body.html

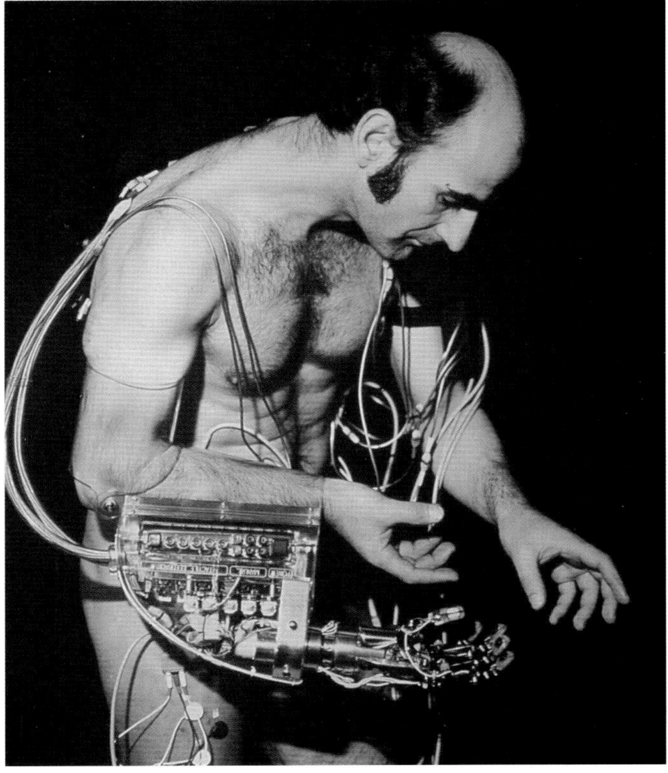

STELARC
The Third Hand
1976–80
Tokyo

Stelarc had a 'third hand' produced for him by Japanese robotic engineers, which matched the size of his own right hand. It was activated directly by the electrical signals of his abdominal and leg muscles, and was able to rotate from the wrist, as well as to grasp and release. It took several months for Stelarc to teach himself the control he needed to be able to write a word using all three hands at once. 'Simply, the body has created an information and technological environment which it can no longer cope with. This ... impulse to continuously accumulate more and more information has created the situation where human cortical capacity just can't absorb and creatively process all this information ... It was necessary to create technology to take over what the body can no longer do. It's created a technology that far surpasses certain capabilities of itself ... The only evolutionary strategy I see is ... to incorporate technology into the body ... technology symbiotically attached and implanted into the body creates a new evolutionary synthesis, creates a new human hybrid – the organic and synthetic coming together to create a new sort of evolutionary energy.'

– Stelarc, 'Obsolete Body/Suspensions/Stelarc', Artist's statement, 1980

ORLAN

Omnipresence

1993

Sandra Gering Gallery, New York

Orlan's seventh 'performance-operation' was broadcast live by satellite from the Sandra Gering Gallery, New York, to fifteen sites worldwide, including the Centre Georges Pompidou, Paris, the McLuhan Center, Toronto, and the Multi-Media Center, Banff. Spectators around the world could ask the artist questions both before and during the operation, to which she responded as the procedure permitted. Elaborately staging the events with colourful drapery, costumes created by famous designers, and extra personnel to translate into English and sign for the deaf, Orlan transformed the operating theatre into her studio, while her operation provided the material for the production of film, video, photographs and objects to be exhibited later. The operation was performed by a feminist plastic surgeon, Dr Marjorie Cramer, who inserted implants above Orlan's eyes and in her cheeks and chin. The artist was conscious but locally anaesthetized, and it is therefore the spectator who suffers as a result of the discomfort produced by images of the operation. The artist retains ultimate (conscious) control of the process of her facial remoulding and thus the representation of her (female) face and body in art. Over the forty-day period directly after the operation, Orlan juxtaposed photographs of her bruised, healing face with computer-morphed images of goddesses from Greek mythology. This emphasized the physical deformity and pain she was undergoing in order to attain a culturally idealized beauty.

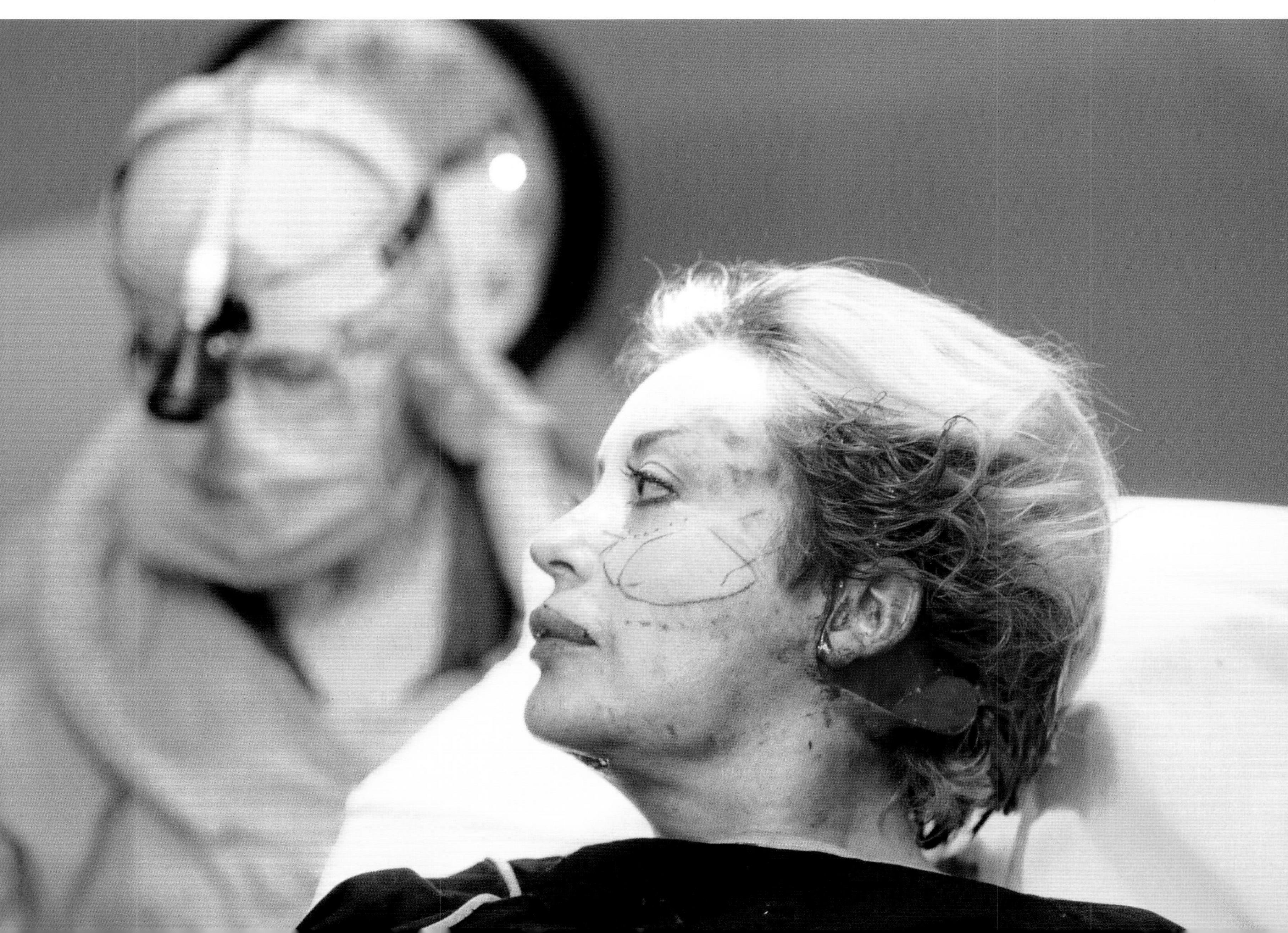

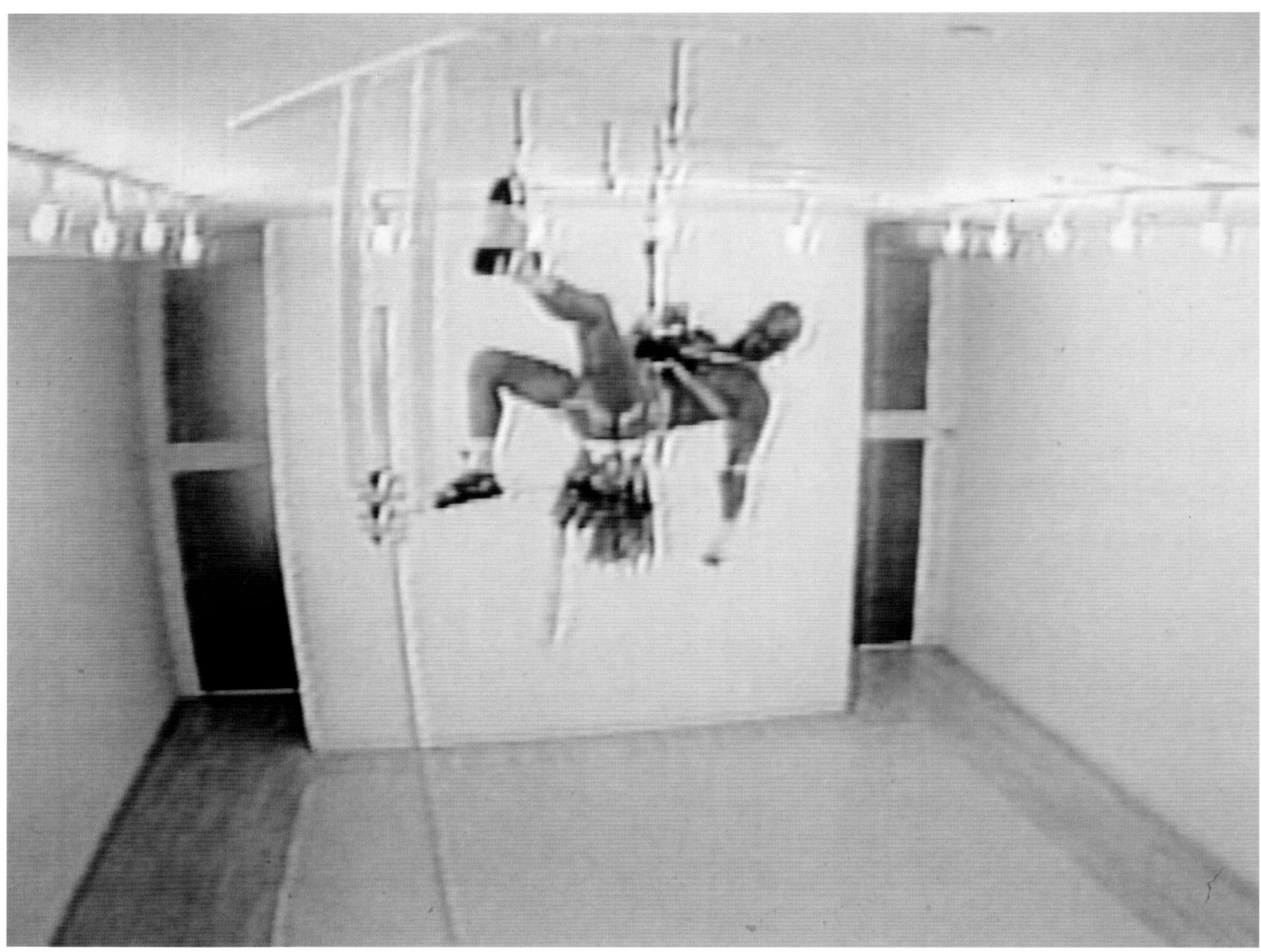

Matthew BARNEY
BLIND PERINEUM
1991
Video still
89 mins. 40 secs., colour, silent

Caught at the threshold between 'hubris and some kind of real but repressed omnipotence, Barney's body appears in his early video actions endlessly scaling the walls and ceiling of an oppressively closed space in a demonstration of physical prowess and endurance'. In BLIND PERINEUM, wearing a full body harness and using the latest technology in climbing gear, Barney presents an athletic male body which, although powerful in itself, is also dependent for its feats on the equipment he uses. Anally penetrated by an ice screw, the artist's body becomes the site of an ambiguous relationship with technology, which both empowers and threatens to dominate him. As Barney explained to critic Thyrza Nichols Goodeve, these actions are 'about an intuitive state with the potential to transcend, and about the kind of intuition that is learned through understanding a physical process'. Locked in an endless repetition without climax, Barney's body appears at once self-punishing and self-pleasuring. Drawing on the tradition of 'heroic' endurance-testing actions by male body artists, Barney presents a new kind of action-hero, whose body is extended outwards but whose focus is entirely internal.
– Thyrza Nichols Goodeve, 'Travels in Hypertropia', 1995

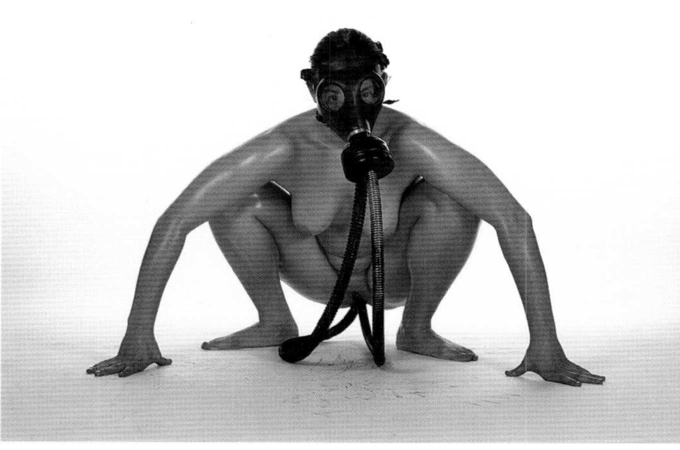

Heli REKULA
Hyperventilation
1993
Cibachrome print
125 × 100 cm [49 × 39.5 in]

Rekula's work deals with the fear of communication and the fear of loss, fears that stem from confusion and anxiety about boundaries, both metaphorical and physical. *Hyperventilation* presents the possible consequence of such fears, sealing her body with a device like an extended gas mask to protect its openings both from penetration and from an emptying out into the external world. Her body becomes a self-contained unit that recycles its own wastes through their reintroduction into the body via the mouth. This self-containment is emphasized by the anonymity offered by masking her face, which renders both communication and loss impossible. But the 'safe' body is sealed and therefore poisons itself by ingesting its own excreta. The title, *Hyperventilation*, which can cause death and is the result of fear, emphasizes the danger of self-containment.

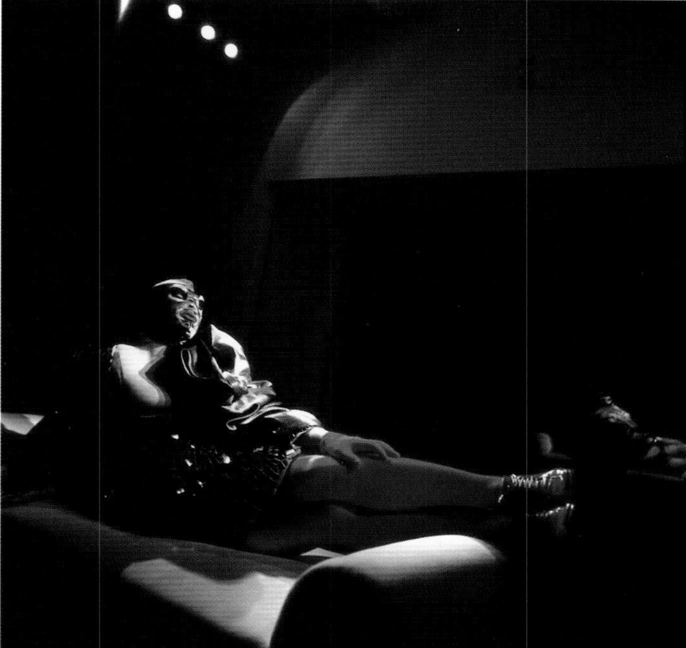

Leigh BOWERY
Leigh Bowery in Performance at the Anthony d'Offay Gallery, 11-15 October 1988
1988
Anthony d'Offay Gallery, London

Bowery designed, made and wore his extraordinary costumes in order to affirm his sense of abnormality (he was a gay man weighing 102 kg [224 lb], and over 2-m [6 -ft] -tall) and to project a confident and powerful persona. Originally involving thick make-up and wigs, as well as platform shoes and huge shoulder-pads, his costumes became increasingly sculptural – with spherical arms, misshapen legs, built-in breasts – while his face disappeared into hoods that entirely covered his head. He manipulated and extended his body, often painfully, in order to create a 'look' that would liberate him from his shyness, and allow him to enact a flamboyant persona on the 'underground' club scene. His commitment to the total theatricalization of the self, using the nightclub as his stage, was in fact an engagement in a form of extreme self-expression, allowing him to explore his fears and desires in outrageous public performances that made him an icon in underground culture. Directly challenging the aesthetics of style and fashion, Bowery's costumes and performances exposed the artist's body as a tool with which to examine prevailing judgements of what is perverse and what is normal.

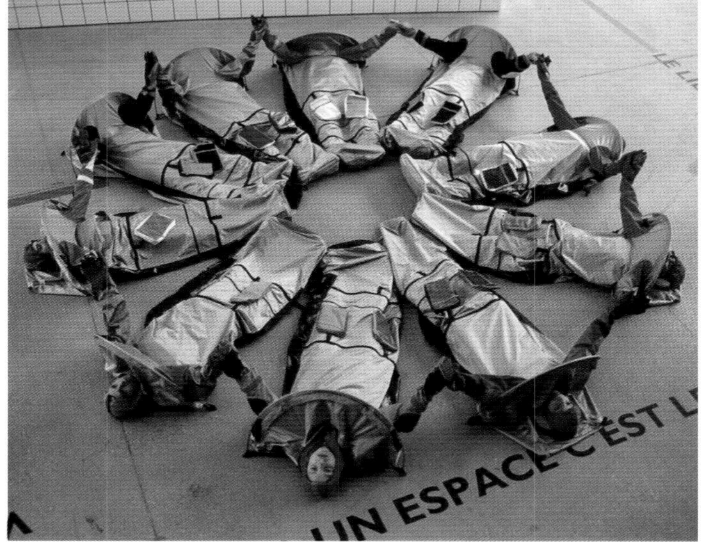

Lucy ORTA
The Unit
1996
Modular Architecture Dance Intervention, Fondation Cartier, Paris

Orta creates 'interventions' in social groups and activities through protective clothing worn and even designed and created by marginalized people on the street. The artist developed her *Refuge Wear* in conjunction with homeless people whom she had followed over a number of years. The multi-functional clothes can be transformed according to an individual's immediate needs: a mobile sleeping sack that turns into an anorak and transport bag, a cocoon that morphs into a tent, for example. Made of the latest materials, experimental fabrics and high-technology prototypes, her *Refuges* are modular architectures, designed to dress, shelter and protect urban nomads confronted with conditions of extreme destitution in a hostile environment. They allow the wearer a small amount of isolated personal space, creating a place of reflection and meditation. Orta has subsequently designed *Survival Kits*, and *Collective Wear* that houses up to sixteen people under one roof.

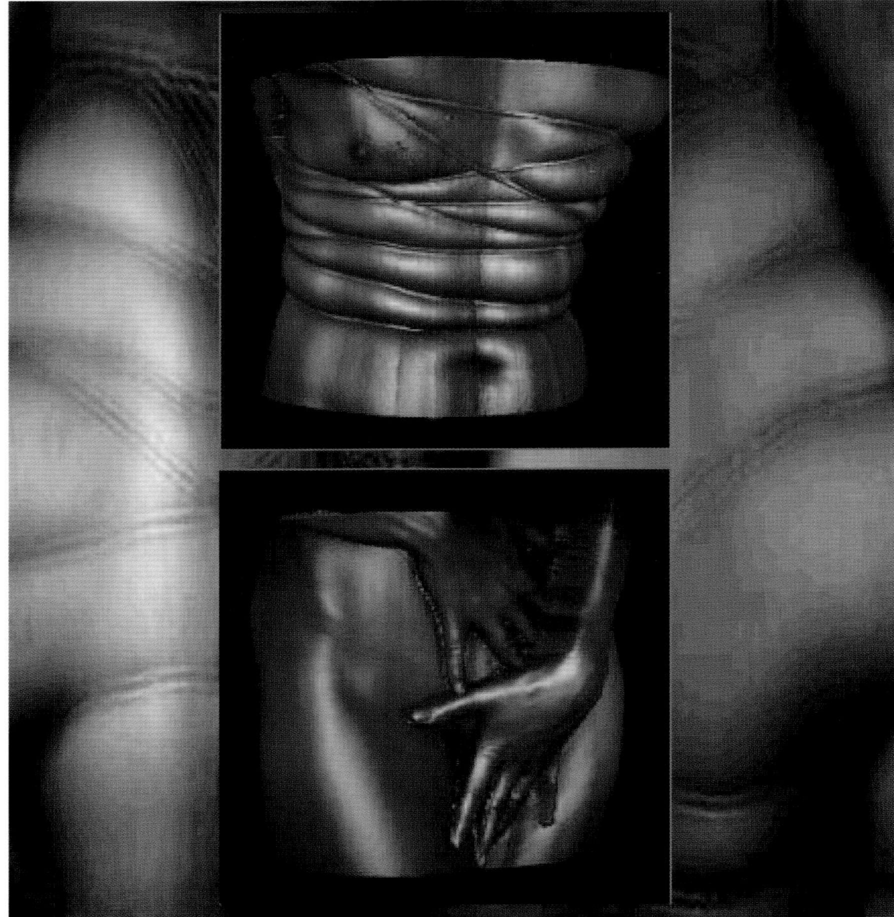

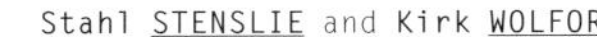

Stahl STENSLIE and Kirk WOLFORD

CyberSM

1994

Cologne

In collaboration with Kirk Wolford, Norwegian artist Stenslie has conducted a number of experiments with Virtual Reality interface design in order to extend the limitations of unitary embodied experience, and to explore ways of using the human body as an interface for a dialogue through touch. The *CyberSM* system functions as a dialogue on the Internet between two participants, in separate locations, wearing specially constructed suits with 'hot zones' that sense the touch of a participant's hand, and generate a variety of physical stimuli. A computer display in front of the participant provides a visual mapping of his/her body as a tactile surface, and translates the varieties of touch stimuli into corresponding sounds. Participants may control the touches they receive by touching their own suits in various ways, or they may speak to the remote participant and ask to be touched in other ways. 'At the end of the millennium, the body has turned into a schizoid corpus. It is on the one hand a single, unitary, physical object with a life span of approximately seventy years, and on the other hand it has done the quantum jump into a transcendental, multiple self of mediated realities. The question is no longer what or who I am, but all that I can be.' – Stahl Stenslie quoted by Joseph Nechvatal, 'Tactiles Technologies: La synesthésie par le cybersexe sur le web de Stahl Stenslie', unpublished article, 1994

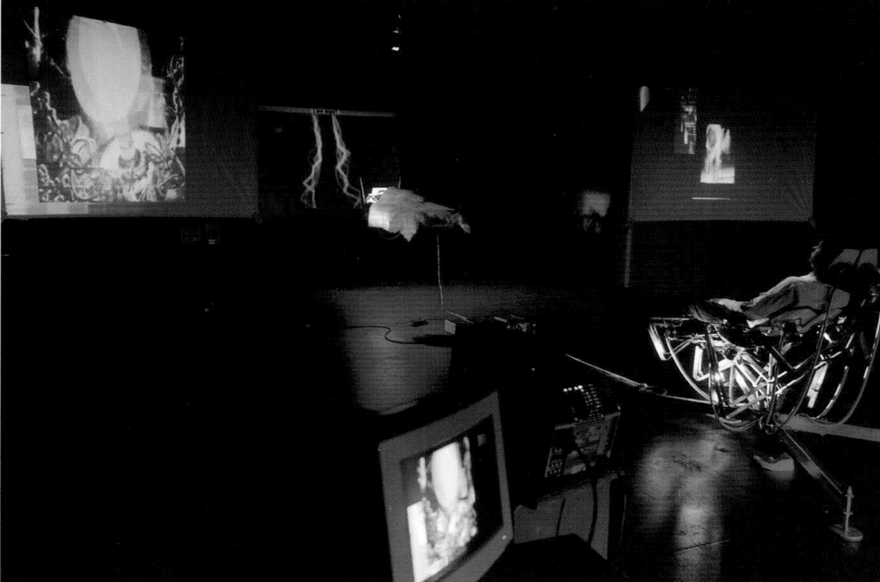

Bruce GILCHRIST (with Jonathan BRADLEY)

Divided by Resistance

1996

Institute of Contemporary Arts, London

In a collaborative performance with software-artist Jonathan Bradley at the Institute of Contemporary Arts, London, Gilchrist slept with his body wired to a unit that scanned his electrical skin resistance. This was then translated into a sound-field. His brain-wave activity was monitored by a digital electroencephalogram and transmitted via fibre-optic cable to a computer, which translated it into imagery displayed on video projectors. Individual members of the public were invited to recline in the 'seat of consciousness', a specially constructed chair that would transmit a codified language in the form of a series of mild electrical currents scanned from the body of the participator back to the sleeping body of the artist. As sound and image changed, the audience were able to feel the palpable effects of the participator's electrical currents on Gilchrist's sleeping body. This work demonstrated the possibility for tangible intervention in the processes of the unconscious mind, using computer software to extend the artist's body/mind out to the literal touch of his/her audience.

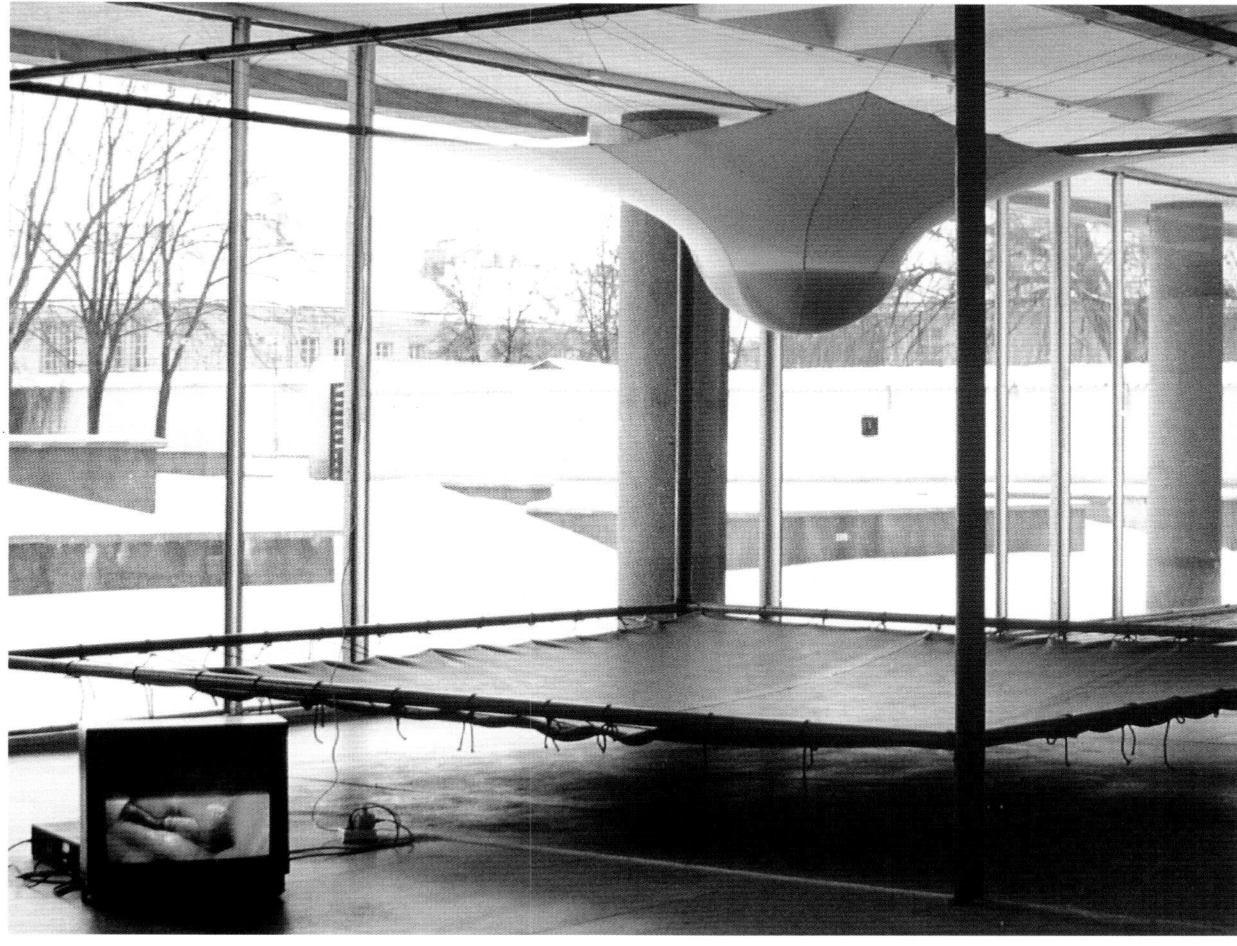

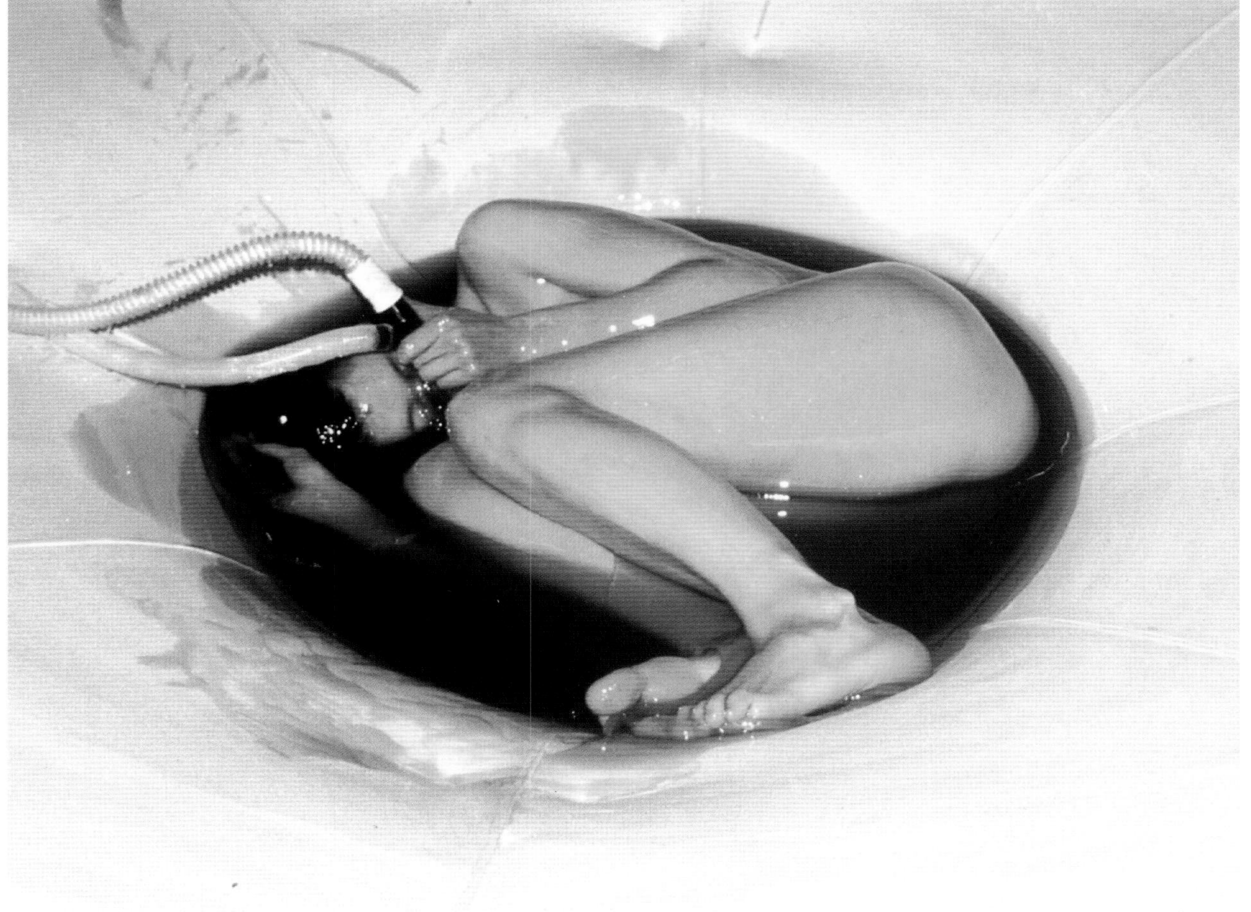

Eglė RAKAUSKAITĖ
In Honey
1996
Performance and video installation
Metal construction, 400 × 400 × 260 cm [157.5 × 157.5 × 102 in]
Cotton construction, 180 × 180 × 95 cm [71 × 71 × 37 in]
Honey, 80 kg [176 lb], rubber cover, 350 × 350 cm [138 × 138 in]
Video, 30 mins., colour, sound
Installation, Municipal Art Museum, Reykjavik, Iceland, 1997

Rakauskaitė focuses on the naked and vulnerable aspects of the body and its means of self-protection. In this performance/installation at the Municipal Art Museum she lay in a foetal position partially submerged in honey, visible to the viewer only on a video monitor. The long tube through which she breathed functioned visually as an umbilical cord, and provided a vital connection to the air she needed. Shiny and yellow like the yolk of an egg, her body was extended through the breathing apparatus to emphasize its connection with, and dependency on, the white space in which she lay. This ultimately transformed the space around her into a giant maternal body upon which she was dependent for life.

DOCU-
MENTS

ART & LANGUAGE
ANTONIN ARTAUD
MIROSŁAW BAŁKA
GEORGES BATAILLE
JONATHAN BENTHALL
JOSEPH BEUYS
FRANCESCO BONAMI
GÜNTER BRUS
JUDITH BUTLER
HELEN CHADWICK
JOHN CHANDLER
MEILING CHENG
LYGIA CLARK
GILLES DELEUZE
CATHERINE FRANCBLIN
SIGMUND FREUD
MICHAEL FRIED
COCO FUSCO
GILBERT & GEORGE
ROSELEE GOLDBERG
DONNA HARAWAY
MONA HATOUM
DICK HIGGINS
AMELIA JONES
LESLIE C. JONES
HOWARD JUNKER
ALLAN KAPROW
MARY KELLY
YVES KLEIN
MILAN KNÍŽÁK
MAX KOZLOFF
ROSALIND KRAUSS
JULIA KRISTEVA
YAYOI KUSAMA
DONALD KUSPIT
MIWON KWON
JACQUES LACAN
ROB LA FRENAIS
JEAN-JACQUES LEBEL
IRA LICHT
LUCY R. LIPPARD
THOMAS McEVILLEY
GEORGE MACIUNAS
PIERO MANZONI
HERBERT MARCUSE
MAURICE MERLEAU-PONTY
HELEN MOLESWORTH
STUART MORGAN
ROBERT MORRIS
OTTO MÜHL
CINDY NEMSER
NEO-CONCRETIST MANIFESTO
HERMANN NITSCH
KATHY O'DELL
GLORIA FEMAN ORENSTEIN
PEGGY PHELAN
ROBERT PINCUS-WITTEN
FRANÇOIS PLUCHART
NELLY RICHARD
HAROLD ROSENBERG
MOIRA ROTH
SEVERO SARDUY
ELAINE SCARRY
CAROLEE SCHNEEMANN
REBECCA SCHNEIDER
RUDOLF SCHWARZKOGLER
EVE KOSOFSKY SEDGWICK
WILLOUGHBY SHARP
SUSAN SONTAG
STELARC
KRISTINE STILES
MARGARET SUNDELL
MARCIA TUCKER
MIERLE LADERMAN UKELES
BEN VAUTIER
LEA VERGINE
PAUL VIRILIO
WOLF VOSTELL
PETER WEIBEL
HANNAH WILKE
JIRO YOSHIHARA

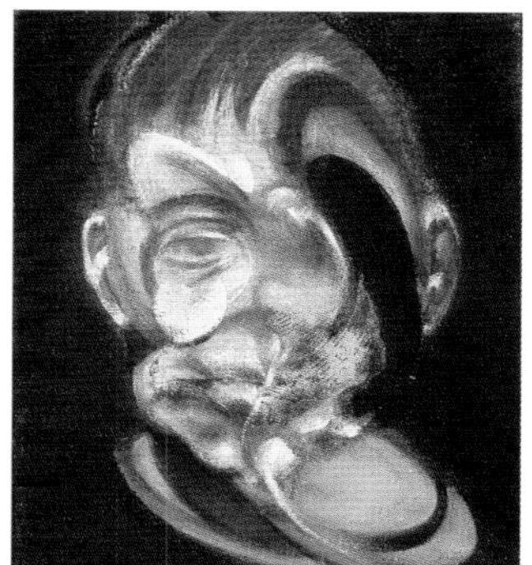

1. [see page 197]
Francis BACON
Self-Portrait
1973
Oil on canvas
34 × 29 cm
[13 × 11 in]

2. [see page 198]
Robert RAUSCHENBERG
Black Painting
1951-52
Oil and newsprint on canvas
183 × 72.5 cm
[72 × 28.5 in]

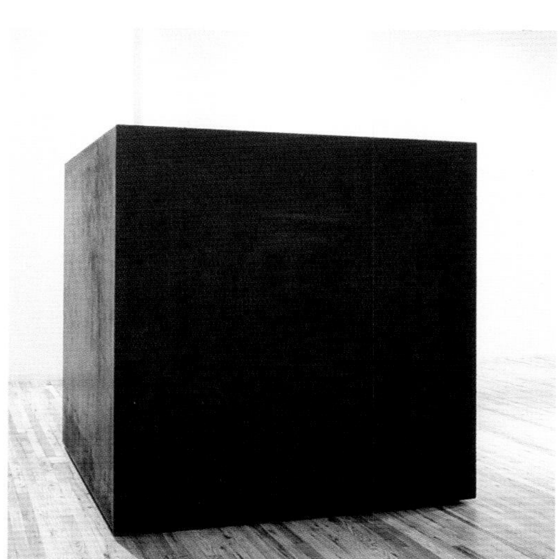

3. [see page 203]
Tony SMITH
Die
1962
Steel
183 × 183 × 183 cm
[72 × 72 × 72 in]

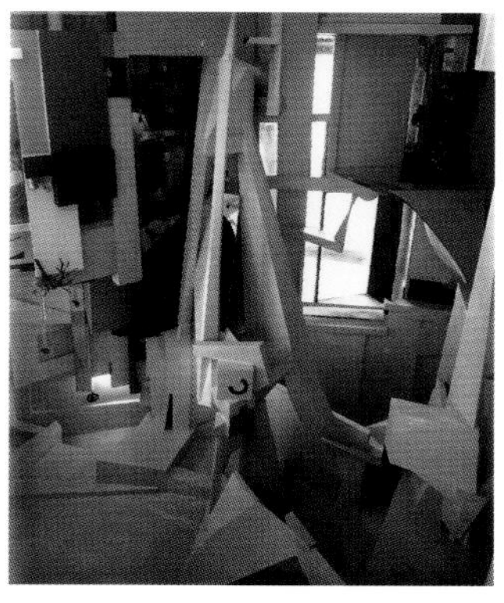

4. [see page 204]
Kurt SCHWITTERS
Merzbau Hanover (Blue Window) (Destroyed)
1923-43
Mixed media

5. [see page 205]
Dan FLAVIN
the nominal three (to William of Ockham)
1963
Flourescent lights
h. 244 cm [96 in]

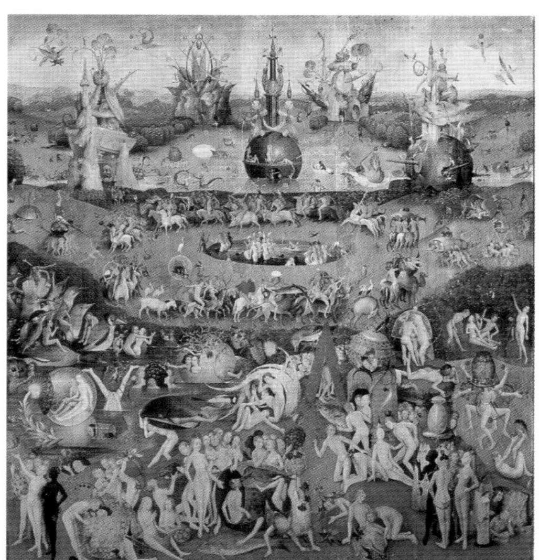

6. [see page 216]
Hieronymus BOSCH
The Garden of Earthly Delights: Allegory of Luxury (detail)
c. 1500
Oil on canvas
220 × 389 cm
[87 × 153 in]

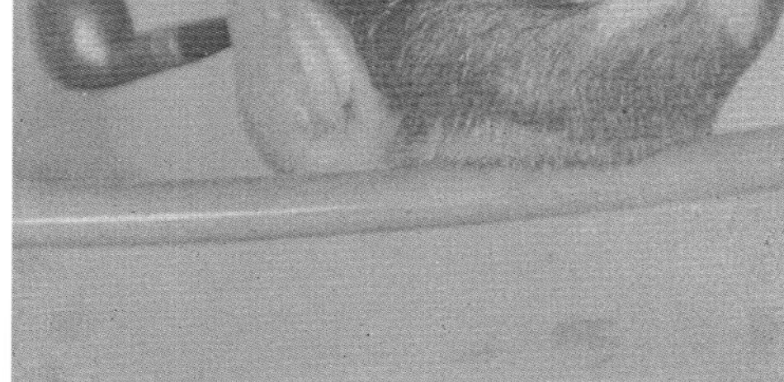

7. [see page 218]
Marcel DUCHAMP
Tonsure
1919
Black and white photograph
9 × 8 cm [3.5 × 3 in]

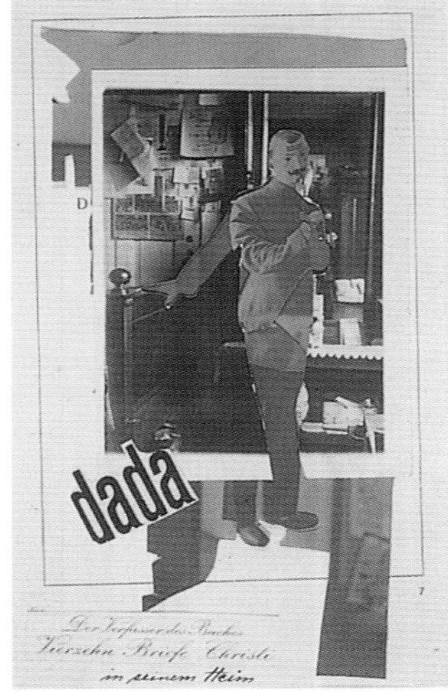

8. [see page 219]
Johannes BAADER
The Author in His Home
c. 1920
Photomontage
22 × 15 cm [8.5 × 6 in]

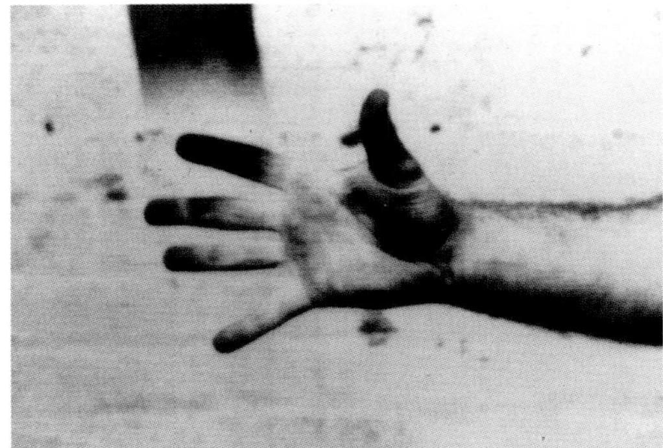

9. [see page 233]
Richard SERRA
Hand Catching Lead
1968
Film still
16 mm, black and white,
3 mins. 30 secs.

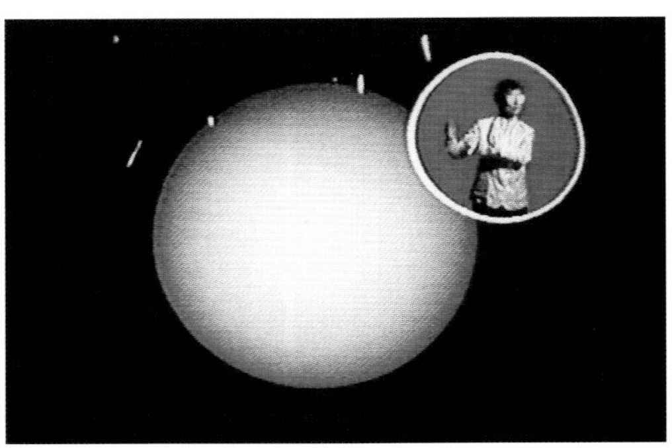

10. [see page 246]
Laurie ANDERSON
O, Superman
1981-83
Video still
8 mins. 40 secs.,
colour, sound

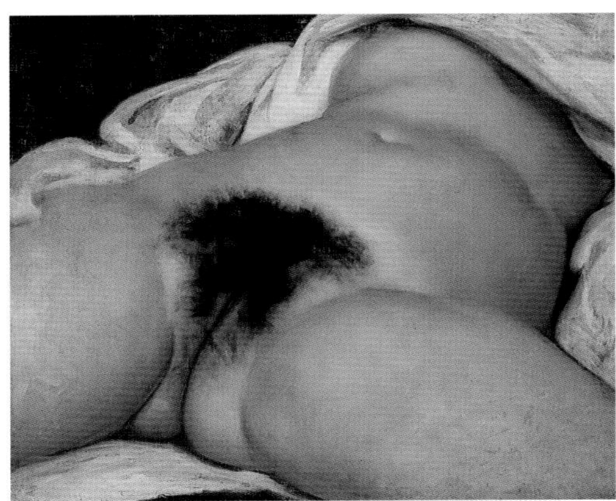

11. [see page 251]
Gustave COURBET
L'Origine du Monde (The origin of the world)
1866
Oil on canvas
46 × 55 cm [18 × 22 in]
Collection, Musée d'Orsay, Paris

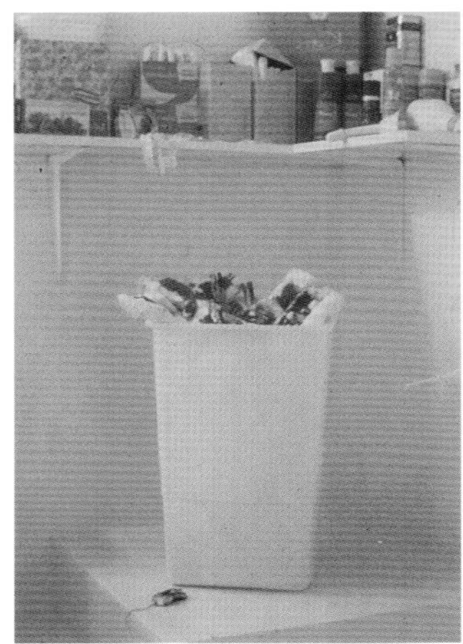

12. [see page 256]
Judy CHICAGO
Menstruation Bathroom
1972
Mixed media
Dimensions variable
Installation,
Womanhouse, Los Angeles

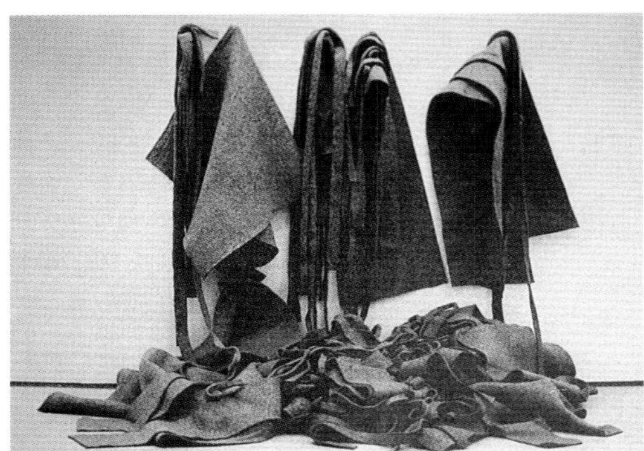

13. [see page 261]
Robert MORRIS
Felt Piece
1967-68
Felt
Dimensions variable

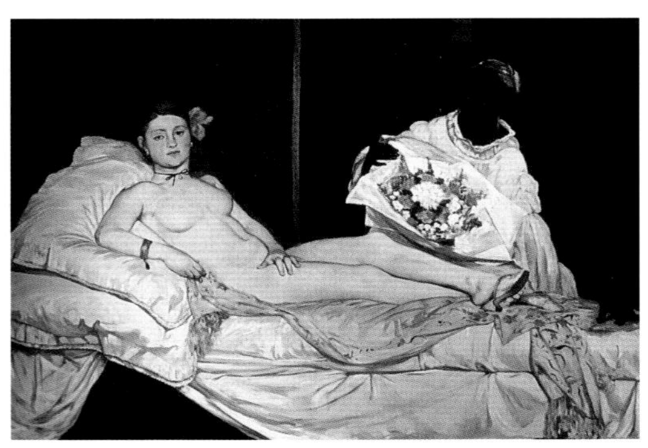

14. [see page 273]
Edouard MANET
Olympia
1863
Oil on canvas
130.5 × 190 cm
[51.5 × 75 in]

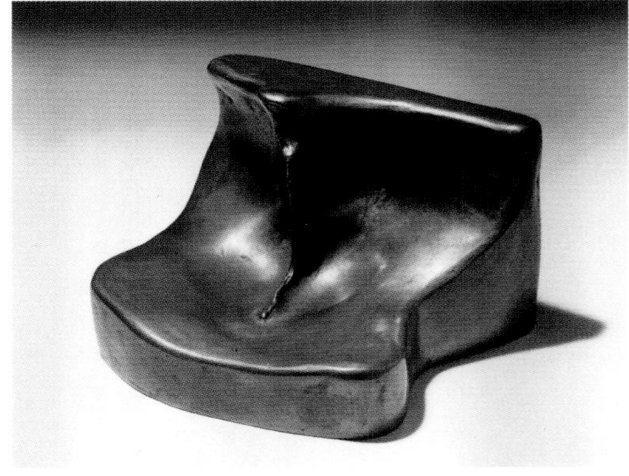

15. [see page 276]
Marcel DUCHAMP
Vigne de femelle (Female Fig Leaf)
1951
Bronze cast plaster
9 × 15 × 13 cm
[3.5 × 6 × 5 in]

PAINTING BODIES

During the 1950s the focus in painting shifted from the formal object to the action or process involved in creating it. Artists developed a more direct contact with the materiality of both the canvas and the paint. As the physical body became increasingly visible in the painting, some artists used the body itself as a brush. The body became increasingly present in the work of artists such as Jim Dine, Claes Oldenburg and Carolee Schneemann, who relocated the 'site' of painting from the surface of the canvas to a three-dimensional environment, in which painting and events 'happened'.

Georges BATAILLE
Primitive Art [1929]

[...] It was from his minute observation of children that Mr Luquet believed he could reconstitute the 'genesis of figurative art' in the far distant period of the Aurignacians. 'Observation of contemporary children', he writes, 'seems to establish ... that heredity, suggestion and example do not exert any appreciable influence and that each of our children begins again for himself the invention of figurative drawing as if he was the first being ever to draw.' The author must recognize however that from the very beginning the child finds himself in the presence of figurative representations to which he generally attributes the same reality as to the objects presented to him. But a factor independent of the desire for figuration may easily be determined: children in particular (but here I suppose that we must also for certain cases bring in the grown-ups) go as far as voluntarily dipping their fingers in colouring materials, for example in pots of paint, in order to leave traces of their passage by walking those fingers over walls, over doors, etc. Such traces do not seem 'to be able to be explained except as unconscious affirmations of the personality of their authors'. And by virtue of this, Mr Luquet compares these marks to one of the rare means which children use to affirm their personality: the destruction of objects, the exploits of 'children who break everything', a comparison which it will be necessary to emphasize further [...]

Georges Bataille, 'L'Art Primitif' (1929), *Documents* (Paris: Éditions Jean-Michel Place, 1991) 389-97. Translated by Elizabeth Manchester.

Harold ROSENBERG
The American Action Painters [1952]

DRAMAS OF AS IF

A painting that is an act is inseparable from the biography of the artist. The painting itself is a 'moment' in the adulterated mixture of his life – whether 'moment' means, in one case, the actual minutes taken up with spotting the canvas or, in another, the entire duration of a lucid drama conducted in sign language. The act-painting is of the same metaphysical substance as the artist's existence. The new painting has broken down every distinction between art and life.

It follows that anything is relevant to it. Anything that has to do with action – psychology, philosophy, history, mythology, hero worship. Anything but art criticism. The painter gets away from Art through his act of painting; the critic can't get away from it. The critic who goes on judging in terms of schools, styles, form, as if the painter were still concerned with producing a certain kind of object (the work of art), instead of living on the canvas, is bound to seem a stranger.

Some painters take advantage of this stranger. Having insisted that their painting is an act, they then claim admiration for the act as art. This turns the act back towards the aesthetic in a petty circle. If the picture is an act, it cannot be justified *as an act of genius* in a field whose whole measuring apparatus has been sent to the devil. Its value must be found apart from art. Otherwise the 'act' gets to be 'making a painting' at sufficient speed to meet an exhibition date [...]

Criticism must begin by recognizing in the painting the assumptions inherent in its mode of creation. Since the painter has become an actor, the spectator has to think in a vocabulary of action: its inception, duration, direction – psychic state, concentration and relaxation of the will, passivity, alert waiting. He must become a connoisseur of the gradations among the automatic, the spontaneous, the evoked.

IT'S NOT THAT, IT'S NOT THAT, IT'S NOT THAT

With a few important exceptions, most of the artists of this vanguard found their way to their present work by being cut in two. Their type is not a young painter but a reborn one. The man may be over forty, the painter around seven. The diagonal of a grand crisis separates him from his personal and artistic past.

Many of the painters were Marxists (W.P.A. unions, artists' congresses) – they had been trying to paint Society. Others had been trying to paint Art (Cubism, post-Impressionism) – it amounts to the same thing.

The big moment came when it was decided to paint ... Just *To Paint*. The gesture on the canvas was a gesture of liberation, from Value – political, aesthetic, moral.

If the war and the decline of radicalism in America had anything to do with this sudden impatience, there is no evidence of it. About the effects of large issues upon their emotions, Americans tend to be either reticent or unconscious. The French artist thinks of himself as a battleground of history; here one hears only of private Dark Nights. Yet it is strange how many segregated individuals came to a dead stop within the past ten years and abandoned, even physically destroyed, the work they had been doing. A far-off watcher, unable to realize that these events were taking place in silence, might have assumed they were being directed by a single voice [...]

Painting could now be reduced to that equipment which the artist needed for an activity that would be an alternative to both utility and idleness. Guided by visual and somatic memories of paintings he had seen or made – memories which he did his best to keep from intruding into his consciousness – he gesticulated upon the canvas and watched for what each novelty would declare him and his art to be.

APOCALYPSE AND WALLPAPER

[...] Once the difficulties that belong to a real act have been evaded by mysticism, the artist's experience of transformation is at an end. In that case what is left? Or to put it differently: What is a painting that is not an object nor the representation of an object nor the analysis or impression of it nor whatever else a painting has ever been – and that has also ceased to be the emblem of a personal struggle? It is the painter himself changed into a ghost inhabiting The Art World. Here the common phrase, 'I have bought an O' (rather than a painting by O) becomes literally true. The man who started to remake himself has made himself into a commodity with a trademark [...]

Harold Rosenberg, 'The American Action Painters', *ARTnews*, 51: 5 (December 1952) 22-23, 48-50; reprinted in Henry Geldzahler, *New York Painting and Sculpture 1940-1970* (London: Pall Mall Press; New York: Metropolitan Museum of Art, 1994) 342-49.

Jiro YOSHIHARA
Gutai Manifesto [1956]

To today's consciousness, the art of the past, which on the whole displays an alluring appearance, seems fraudulent.

Let's bid farewell to the hoaxes piled up on the altars and in the palaces, the drawing rooms and the antique shops.

They are made of the matter called paint, of cloth, metals, earth and marble, which through the casting of the magic spell of 'raw material', through a meaningless act of signification by a human, were made to assume a deceptive appearance. The materials, all slaughtered under the pretence of production of the mind, can now say nothing.

Lock up these corpses in the graveyard.

Gutai art does not alter the material. Gutai art imparts life to the material. Gutai art does not distort the material.

In Gutai art the human spirit and the material shake hands with each other, but keep their distance. The material never compromises itself with the spirit: the spirit never dominates the material. When the material remains intact and exposes its characteristics, it starts telling a story, and even cries out. To make the fullest use of the material is to make use of the spirit. By enhancing the spirit, the material is brought to the height of the spirit.

Art is a place in which creation occurs: however, the spirit has never created the material before. The spirit has only created the spirit. Throughout history, the spirit has given birth to life in art. However, the life thus born always changes and perishes. To us today the great figures of the Renaissance are nothing more than archaeological relics.

Today it is only primitive art and various art movements after Impressionism that manage to convey to us a feeling of life, however inert. Fortunately, these movements could neither successfully distort the material, that is, the paint, nor kill it through using it for the purpose of naturalism as in the case of Pointillism and Fauvism. However, their styles no longer move us at all; they are things of the past.

Now, interestingly, we find a contemporary beauty in art and architecture of the past ravaged by the passage of time or natural disasters. Although their beauty is considered decadent, it may be that the innate beauty of the materials is re-emerging from behind the mask of artificial embellishment. Ruins welcome us unexpectedly with warmth and friendliness; they speak to us through their beautiful cracks and rubble – which might be a revenge of the material that has regained its innate life. In this sense, we highly regard the works of Jackson Pollock and Georges Mathieu. Their work reveals the scream of the material itself, cries of the paint and enamel. These two artists confront us in a way that aptly corresponds to their individual discoveries. Or rather, they even seem to serve the material. Astonishing effects of differentiation and integration take place ...

We have always thought – and still do – that the greatest legacy of abstract art is the opening of an opportunity to create, from naturalistic and illusionistic art, a new autonomous space, a space that truly deserves the name of art.

We have decided to pursue enthusiastically the possibilities of pure abstract art. We believe that by merging human qualities and the material's properties, we can concretely comprehend the abstract space.

When the individual's quality and the selected material melt together in the furnace of automatism, we are surprised to see an emergence of a space unknown, unseen and unexperienced. Automatism inevitably transcends the artist's own image. We endeavour to achieve our own method of creating space rather than relying on our own image ...

Jiro Yoshihara, 'Gutai bijutsu sengen', *Guijutsu Shincho*, 7: 12 (December 1956) 202-204; reprinted in English as 'Gutai Manifesto' in Alexandra Munroe (ed.), *Japanese Art After 1945: Scream Against the Sky*, trans. Reiko Tomii (New York: Solomon R. Guggenheim Museum, 1994) 370.

Allan KAPROW
The Legacy of Jackson Pollock [1958]

[...] Pollock created some magnificent paintings. But he also destroyed painting. If we examine a few of the innovations mentioned above, it may be possible to see why this is so.

For instance, the act of painting. In the last seventy-five years the random play of the hand upon the canvas or paper has become increasingly important. Strokes, smears, lines, dots became less and less attached to represented objects and existed more and more on their own, self-sufficiently. But from Impressionism up to, say, Gorky, the idea of an 'order' to these markings was explicit enough. Even Dada, which purported to be free of such considerations as 'composition', obeyed the Cubist aesthetic. One coloured shape balanced (or modified or stimulated) others, and these in turn were played off against (or with) the whole canvas, taking into account its size and shape – for the most part quite consciously. In short, part-to-whole or part-to-part relationships, no matter how strained, were a good 50 per cent of the making of a picture (most of the time they were a lot more, maybe 90 per cent). With Pollock, however, the so-called dance of dripping, slashing, squeezing, daubing and whatever else went into a work, placed an almost absolute value upon a diaristic gesture. He was encouraged in this by the Surrealist painters and poets, but next to his their work is consistently 'artful', 'arranged' and full of finesse – aspects of outer control and training. With the huge canvas placed upon the floor, thus making it difficult for the artist to see the whole or any extended section of 'parts', Pollock could truthfully say that he was 'in' his work. Here the direct application of an automatic approach to the act makes it clear that not only is this not the old craft of painting, but it is perhaps bordering on ritual itself, which happens to use paint as one of its materials [...]

I am convinced that to grasp Pollock's impact properly, we must be acrobats, constantly shuttling between an identification with the hands and body that flung the paint and stood 'in' the canvas and submission to the objective markings, allowing them to entangle and assault us. This instability is indeed far from the idea of a 'complete' painting. The artist, the spectator and the outer world are much too interchangeably involved here. (And if we object to the difficulty of complete comprehension, we are asking too little of the art.)

Then Form. To follow it, it is necessary to get rid of the usual idea of 'Form', i.e., a beginning, middle and end, or any variant of this principle – such as fragmentation. We do not enter a painting of Pollock's in any one place (or hundred places). Anywhere is everywhere, and we dip in and out when and where we can. This discovery has led to remarks that his art gives the impression of going on forever – a true insight that suggests how Pollock ignored the confines of the rectangular field in favour of a continuum going in all directions simultaneously, *beyond* the literal dimensions of any work. (Though evidence points to a slackening of the attack as Pollock came to the edges of many of his canvases, in the best ones he compensated for this by tacking much of the painted surface around the back of his stretchers.) The four sides of the painting are thus an abrupt leaving-off of the activity, which our imaginations continue outward indefinitely, as though refusing to accept the artificiality of an 'ending'. In an older work, the edge was a far more precise caesura: here ended the world of the artist; beyond began the world of the spectator and 'reality'.

We accept this innovation as valid because the artist understood with perfect naturalness 'how to do it'. Employing an iterative principle of a few highly charged elements constantly undergoing variation (improvizing, as in much Asian music), Pollock gives us an all-over unity and at the same time a means to respond continuously to a freshness of personal choice. But this form allows us equal pleasure in participating in a delirium, a deadening of the reasoning faculties, a loss of 'self' in the Western sense of the term. This strange combination of extreme individuality and selflessness makes the work remarkably potent but also indicates a probably larger frame of psychological reference. And for this reason any allusions to Pollock's being the maker of giant textures are completely incorrect. They miss the point, and misunderstanding is bound to follow.

But given the proper approach, a medium-sized exhibition space with the walls totally covered by Pollocks offers the most complete and meaningful sense of his art possible.

Then Scale. Pollock's choice of enormous canvases served many purposes, chief of which for our discussion is that his mural-scale paintings ceased to become paintings and became environments. Before a painting, our size as spectators, in relation to the size of the picture, profoundly influences how much we are willing to give up consciousness of our temporal existence while experiencing it. Pollock's choice of great sizes resulted in our being confronted, assaulted, sucked in. Yet we must not confuse the effect of these with that of the hundreds of large paintings done in the Renaissance, which glorified an idealized everyday world familiar to the observer, often continuing the actual room into the painting by means of *trompe-l'oeil*. Pollock offers us no such familiarity, and our everyday world of convention and habit is replaced by the one created by the artist. Reversing the above procedure, the painting is continued out into the room. And this leads me to my final point: Space. The space of these creations is not clearly palpable as such. We can become entangled in the web to some extent and by moving in and out of the skein of lines and splashings can experience a kind of spatial extension. But even so, this space is an allusion far more vague than even the few inches of space-reading a Cubist work affords. It may be that our need to identify with the process, the making of the whole affair, prevents a concentration on the specifics of before and behind so important in a more traditional art. But what I believe is clearly discernible is that the entire painting comes out at us (we are participants rather than observers), right into the room. It is possible to see in this connection how Pollock is the terminal result of a gradual trend that moved from the deep space of the fifteenth and sixteenth centuries to the building out from the canvas of the Cubist collages. In the present case the 'picture' has moved so far out that the canvas is no longer a reference point. Hence, although up on the wall, these marks surround us as they did the painter at work, so strict is the correspondence achieved between his impulse and the resultant art.

What we have, then, is art that tends to lose itself out of bounds, tends to fill our world with itself, art that in meaning, looks, impulse seems to break fairly sharply with the traditions of painters back to at least the Greeks. Pollock's near destruction of this tradition may well be a return to the point where art was more actively involved in ritual, magic and life than we have known it in our recent past. If so, it is an exceedingly important step and in its superior way offers a solution to the complaints of those who would have us put a bit of life into art. But what do we do now [...]

Pollock, as I see him, left us at the point where we must become preoccupied with and even dazzled by the space and objects of our everyday life, either our bodies, clothes, rooms, or, if need be, the vastness of 42nd Street. Not satisfied with the suggestion through paint of our other senses, we shall utilize the specific substances of sight, sound, movements, people, odours, touch. Objects of every sort are materials for the new art: paint, chairs, food, electric and neon lights, smoke, water, old socks, a dog, movies, a thousand other things that will be discovered by the present generation of artists. Not only will these bold creators show us, as if for the first time, the world we have always had about us but ignored, but they will disclose entirely unheard-of happenings and events, found in garbage cans, police files, hotel lobbies; seen in store windows and on the streets; and sensed in dreams and horrible accidents. An odour of crushed strawberries, a letter from a friend, or a billboard selling Drano; three taps on the front door, a scratch, a sigh, or a voice lecturing endlessly, a blinding staccato flash, a bowler hat – all will become materials for this new concrete art.

Young artists of today need no longer say, 'I am a painter' or 'a poet' or 'a dancer'. They are simply 'artists'. All of life will be open to them. They will discover out of ordinary things the meaning of ordinariness. They will not try to make them extraordinary but will only state their real meaning. But out of nothing they will devise the extraordinary and then maybe nothingness as well. People will be delighted or horrified, critics will be confused or amused, but these, I am certain, will be the alchemies of the 1960s.

Allan Kaprow, 'The Legacy of Jackson Pollock', *ARTnews*, 57: 6 (1958) 24-26, 55-57; reprinted in Allan Kaprow, *Essays on the Blurring of Life and Art*, ed. Jeff Kelley (Berkeley and London: University of California Press, 1993) 26-47.

Yves KLEIN
Truth Becomes Reality [1960]

... Leave my mark on the world, I have done it! When I was a child ... Hands and feet thick with colour, applied to the surface; suddenly, there I was, face to face with my own psyche. I had the proof of my five senses: I knew I could function. Then I lost my childhood ... just as everyone else (no illusions on that score). And when I tried the same game as an adolescent, I quickly encountered Nothingness.

I did not like Nothingness, and this is how I came to know the void, the deep void, those depths of blue!

As an adolescent I wrote my name on the sky's back in a flight of fantasy – real or imaginary – stretched out one day on a beach at Nice ... I have hated birds ever since that day, I have hated them for trying to pierce great dark holes in my greatest and most beautiful work. Away with all birds!

Having arrived at the monochrome adventure, I no longer needed to force myself to function; I functioned naturally.

I was no longer myself. I, without the 'I', became one with life itself. All my gestures, movements, activities, creations were this life, original or essential in itself. It was at this time that I used to say that 'painting for me is more than a function of the eye'. My works are but the ashes of my art. I monochromed my canvases with devotion. And out of this arose the all-powerful blue, to dominate now and forever. Then I became uneasy. I brought models to the studio, not to work from, but simply to work in their company.

I was spending far too much time in the studio. I did not want to be so alone in the magic blue void that was developing.

Here the reader will smile, no doubt ... but remember, I was still free of the vertigo that all my predecessors had experienced when faced with the absolute void. A void which must be and is the essence of pictorial space ... But how much longer would it last?

In the old days the painter used to go to the subject, work out of doors, in the landscape; he had both feet on the ground. How healthy! Today easel painting, fully academized, imprisons the painter in his own studio, face to face with the terrifying mirror that is his own canvas. In order not to retreat by shutting myself inside the excessively spiritual regions of creative art, with the plain common sense that is so necessary in our bodily condition and that benefits from the presence of flesh in the studio atmosphere, I employed nude models.

The shape of the body, its curves, its colours between life and death, are not of interest to me. The affective atmosphere of the flesh itself is what I value.

The flesh ... !!!

For all that, I took a look at the model now and then ...

... I very quickly perceived that it was the block of the body, that is to say the trunk and part of the thighs, that fascinated me. The hands, the arms, the head, the legs were of no importance to me. Only the body is alive, all-powerful, non-thinking. The head, the arms, the hands are only intellectual articulations around the bulk of flesh that is the body.

The heart beats without thought on our part; the mind cannot stop it. Digestion works without our intervention, be it emotional or intellectual. We breathe without reflection.

True, the whole body is made of flesh, but the essential mass is the trunk and the thighs. It is there that we find the real universe, hidden by the universe of our limited perception.

For a long time, then, the presence of this flesh in the studio steadied me during the enlightenment brought on by the execution of my monochromes. It preserved in me the spirit of health, the health that lets us participate, carefree and yet responsible, in the order of the universe. Strong, tough, powerful and yet fragile, like dreaming animals waking in the perceptual world, like things vegetable and mineral entranced in this world of ephemeral perception ...

... This health that makes us 'exist'. The nature of life itself. All that we are. As I continued to paint in monochrome, I reached the state of disembodiment almost automatically. This made me realize that I really was an Occidental, a proper Christian, believing with reason in the 'resurrection of the body and in the resurrection of the flesh'. An entire phenomenology took shape. But it was a phenomenology without ideas, or rather without any of the recognized conventions.

What appeared was clearly divorced from form. It became immediate experience. The mark of the immediate, that was my need.

... The stages are not hard to understand. At first my models laughed to see themselves transposed in monochrome on my canvas. Then they became accustomed to it and loved the shades, which differed from one painting to another, even during the blue period, when it was always the same hue, the same pigment, the same technique. Then gradually, pursuing the adventure of the immaterial, my work ceased to be tangible. My studio was empty. Even the monochromes were gone. At this moment my models felt they had to help me. They rolled in the pigment and painted my monochromes with their bodies.

They became living brushes.

I had rejected the brush long before. It was too psychological. I painted with the roller, more anonymous, hoping to create a 'distance' between me and my canvases, which should be at least intellectual and unvarying. Now, like a miracle, the brush returned, but this time alive. At my direction, the flesh itself applied the colour to the surface, and with perfect exactness. I could continue to maintain a precise distance from my creation and still dominate its execution. In this way, I stayed clean. I no longer dirtied myself with colour, not even the tips of my fingers. The work finished itself there in front of me with the complete collaboration of the model. And I could salute its birth into the tangible world in a fitting manner, in evening dress. It was at this time that I noticed the 'marks of the body' after each session. They disappeared again at once, since the whole effect had to be monochrome.

These marks, pagans in my religion of the absolute monochrome, hypnotized me at once, and I worked on them secretly, always with the complete collaboration of the models, in order to share the responsibility in the event of spiritual weakness.

My models and I practised a scientifically exact and irreproachable remote control. Thus I was able to present *The Anthropometries of the Blue Period*, first of all privately, at Robert Godet's in Paris in the spring of 1958, and then in a far more perfected form on 9 March 1960, at the Galerie Nationale d'Art Contemporain [...]

Yves Klein, 'Le Vrai devient Réalité' (1960), *Zero*, 3 (July 1961) n.p. (also printed in German, trans. Helmuth de Haas); printed in English as 'Truth Becomes Reality' in Otto Piene and Heinz Mack (eds.), *Zero*, trans. Howard Beckman, (Cambridge, Massachusetts: MIT Press, 1973) 91-94; reprinted in *Yves Klein 1928-1962: A Retrospective* (Houston: Institute of Arts, Rice University; New York: The Arts Publisher, 1982) 229-32.

Maurice MERLEAU-PONTY

Eye and Mind[1] [1961]

[...] The painter 'takes his body with him', says Valéry. Indeed we cannot imagine how a *mind* could paint. It is by lending his body to the world that the artist changes the world into paintings. To understand these transubstantiations we must go back to the working, actual body – not the body as a chunk of space or a bundle of functions but that body which is an intertwining of vision and movement.

I have only to see something to know how to reach it and deal with it, even if I do not know how this happens in the nervous machine. My mobile body makes a difference in the visible world, being a part of it; that is why I can steer it through the visible. Conversely, it is just as true that vision is attached to movement. We see only what we look at. What would vision be without eye movement? And how could the movement of the eyes bring things together if the movement were blind? If it were only a reflex? If it did not have its antennae, its clairvoyance? If vision were not prefigured in it?

In principle all my changes of place figure in a corner of my landscape; they are recorded on the map of the visible. Everything I see is in principle within my reach, at least within reach of my sight, and is marked upon the map of the 'I can'. Each of the two maps is complete. The visible world and the world of my motor projects are each total parts of the same Being [...]

Let us remain within the visible in the narrow and prosaic sense. The painter, whatever he is, *while he is painting* practises a magical theory of vision. He is obliged to admit that objects before him pass into him or else that, according to Malebranche's sarcastic dilemma, the mind goes out through the eyes to wander among objects; for the painter never ceases adjusting his clairvoyance to them. (It makes no difference if he does not paint from 'nature'; he paints, in any case, because he has seen, because the world has at least once emblazoned in him the ciphers of the visible.) He must affirm, as one philosopher has said, that vision is a mirror or concentration of the universe or that, in another's words, the *idios kosmos* opens by virtue of vision upon a *koinos kosmos*; in short, that the same thing is both out there in the world and here in the heart of vision – the same or, if one prefers, a *similar* thing, but according to an efficacious similarity which is the parent, the genesis, the metamorphosis of Being in his vision. It is the mountain itself which from out there makes itself seen by the painter; it is the mountain that he interrogates with his gaze.

What exactly does he ask of it? To unveil the means, visible and not otherwise, by which it makes itself a mountain before our eyes. Light, lighting, shadows, reflections, colour, all the objections of his quest are not altogether real objects; like ghosts, they have only visual existence. In fact they exist only at the threshold of profane vision; they are not seen by everyone. The painter's gaze asks them what they do to suddenly cause something to be and to be *this* thing, what they do to compose this worldly talisman and to make us see the visible [...]

In paintings themselves we could seek a figured philosophy[2] of vision – its iconography, perhaps. It is no accident, for example, that frequently in Dutch paintings (as in many others) an empty interior is 'digested' by the 'round eye of the mirror'.[3] This pre-human way of seeing things is the painter's way. More completely than lights, shadows and reflections, the mirror image anticipates, within things, the labour of vision. Like all other technical objects, such as signs and tools, the mirror arises upon the open circuit [that goes] from seeing body to visible body. Every technique is a 'technique of the body'. A technique outlines and amplifies the metaphysical structure of our flesh. The mirror appears because I am seeing-visible [*voyant-visible*], because there is a reflexivity of the sensible; the mirror translates and reproduces that reflexivity. My outside completes itself in and through the sensible. Everything I have that is most secret goes into this *visage*, this face, this flat and closed entity about which my reflection in the water has already made me puzzle. Schilder[4] observes that, smoking a pipe before a mirror, I feel the sleek, burning surface of the wood not only where my fingers are but also in those ghostlike fingers, those merely visible fingers inside the mirror. The mirror's ghost lies outside my body, and by the same token my own body's 'invisibility' can invest the other bodies I see.[5] Hence my body can assume segments derived from the body of another, just as my substance passes into them; man is mirror for man. The mirror itself is the instrument of a universal magic that changes things into a spectacle, spectacles into things, myself into another and another into myself. Artists have often mused upon mirrors because beneath this 'mechanical trick', they recognized, just as they did in the case of the trick of perspective,[6] the metamorphosis of seeing and seen which defines both our flesh and the painter's vocation. This explains why they have so often liked to draw themselves in the act of painting (they still do – witness Matisse's drawings), adding to what *they* saw then, what *things* saw of them [...]

1 *'L'Oeil et l'esprit'* ('Eye and Mind') was the last work Merleau-Ponty saw published. It appeared in the inaugural issue of *Art de France*, 1: 1 (January 1961). After his death it was reprinted in *Les Temps Modernes*, 184-85, along with seven articles devoted to him. It has now been published, in book form, by Editions Gallimard, Paris (1964). Both the *Art de France* article and the book contain illustrations chosen by Merleau-Ponty. According to Professor Claude Lefort, *'L'Oeil et l'esprit'* is a preliminary statement of ideas that were to be developed in the second part of the book Merleau-Ponty was writing at the time of his death, *Le visible et l'invisible* (part of which was published posthumously by Editions Gallimard in February 1964). The translator wishes to acknowledge his immense debt to George Downing, who spent many long hours working over the final revisions of the translation. Also, thanks are due to Michel Beaujour, Arleen B. Dallery and Robert Reitter for their advice and encouragement.

2 ' ... *une philosophie figurée* ... ', Félix Ravaisson, cited by Henri Bergson, *'La vie et l'oeuvre de Ravaisson'*, in *La pensée et le mouvant* (Paris, 1934) 264-65.

3 Paul Claudel, *Introduction à la peinture hollandaise* (Paris, 1935).

4 Paul Schilder, *The Image and Appearance of the Human Body* (London, 1935; New York, 1950) 223-24. [' ... the body-image is not confined to the borderlines of one's own body. It trangresses them in the mirror. There is a body-image outside ourselves, and it is remarkable that primitive peoples even ascribe a substantial existence to the picture in the mirror' (278). Schilder's earlier, shorter study, *Das Körperschema* (Berlin, 1923), is cited several times in *The Structure of Behaviour* and in *Phenomenology of Perception*. Schilder's later work is of especial interest with regard to Merleau-Ponty's own elaborations of the meaning of the human body; it is worth examining for that reason, as well as for the chance it provides to discern some fundamental coincidences between Merleau-Ponty and certain American pragmatists.]

5 Cf. Schilder, *Image*, *op. cit.*, 281-82.

6 Robert Delaunay, *Du cubisme à l'art abstrait* (Paris:

S.E.V.P.E.N., 1957).

Maurice Merleau-Ponty, 'L'Oeil et l'esprit', *Art de France*, 1: 1 (January 1961); reprinted in English as 'Eye and Mind' in Maurice Merleau-Ponty, *The Primacy of Perception*, trans. Carleton Dallery (Evanston, Illinois: Northwestern University Press, 1964) 159-90.

Susan SONTAG

Happenings: An Art of Radical Juxtaposition [1962]

[...] There has appeared in New York recently a new, and still esoteric, genre of spectacle. At first sight apparently a cross between art exhibit and theatrical performance, these events have been given the modest and somewhat teasing name of 'Happenings'. They have taken place in lofts, small art galleries, backyards and small theatres before audiences averaging between thirty and one hundred persons. To describe a Happening for those who have not seen one means dwelling on what Happenings are not. They don't take place on a stage conventionally understood, but *in* a dense object-clogged setting which may be made, assembled or found, or all three. In this setting a number of participants, not actors, perform movements and handle objects antiphonally and in concert to the accompaniment (sometimes) of words, wordless sounds, music, flashing lights and odours. The Happening has no plot, though it is an action, or rather a series of actions and events. It also shuns continuous rational discourse, though it may contain words like 'Help!', 'Voglio un bichiere di acqua', 'Love me', 'Car', 'One, two, three ...' Speech is purified and condensed by disparateness (there is only the speech of need) and then expanded by ineffectuality, by the lack of relation between the persons enacting the Happening.

Those who do Happenings in New York – but they are not just a New York phenomenon; similar activities have been reported in Osaka, Stockholm, Cologne, Milan and Paris by groups unrelated to each other – are young, in their late twenties or early thirties. They are mostly painters (Allan Kaprow, Jim Dine, Red Grooms, Robert Whitman, Claes Oldenburg, Al Hansen, George Brecht, Yoko Ono, Carolee Schneemann) and a few musicians (Dick Higgins, Philip Corner, La Monte Young). Allan Kaprow, the man who more than anyone else is responsible for stating and working out the genre, is the only academic among them; he formerly taught art and art history at Rutgers and now teaches at the State University of New York on Long Island. For Kaprow, a painter and (for a year) a student of John Cage, doing Happenings since 1957 has replaced painting; Happenings are, as he puts it, what his painting has become. But for most of the others, this is not the case; they have continued to paint or compose music in addition to occasionally producing a Happening or performing in the Happening devised by a friend [...]

Susan Sontag, 'Happenings: An Art of Radical Juxtaposition', *The Second Coming* (1962); reprinted in *Against Interpretation* (New York: Oktagon Books, 1982) 263-74.

Carolee SCHNEEMANN

Eye Body [1963]

In 1962 I began a loft environment built of large panels interlocked by rhythmic colour units, broken mirrors and glass, lights, moving umbrellas and motorized parts. I worked with my whole body – the scale of the panels incorporating my own physical scale. I then decided I wanted my actual body to be combined with the work as an integral material – a further dimension of the construction ...

In December of 1963 I was encouraged by my friend Erró (the Icelandic, Paris-based painter) when I told him I wanted to do a series of physical transformations of my body in my work – the constructions and wall environment. I thought the ritual aspect of the process could put me in a trance-like state.

Covered in paint, grease, chalk, ropes, plastic, I establish my body as visual territory. Not only am I an image maker, but I explore the image values of flesh as material I choose to work with. The body may remain erotic, sexual, desired, desiring but it is as well votive: marked, written over in a text of stroke and gesture discovered by my creative female will.

I write 'my creative female will' because for years my most audacious works were viewed as if someone else inhabiting me had created them – they were considered masculine when seen as aggressive, bold. As if I were inhabited by a stray male principle; which would be an interesting possibility – except in the early 1960s this notion was used to blot out, denigrate, deflect the coherence, necessity and personal integrity of what I made and how it was made.

In 1963 to use my body as an extension of my painting-constructions was to challenge and threaten the psychic territorial power lines by which women were admitted to the Art Stud Club, so long as they behaved enough like the men, did work clearly in the traditions and pathways hacked out by the men. (The only artist I know of making body art before this time was Yoko Ono.)

The nude was being used in early Happenings as an object (often an 'active' object). I was using the nude as myself – the artist – and as a primal, archaic force which could unify energies I discovered as visual information. I felt compelled to conceive of my body in manifold aspects which had eluded the culture around me. Eight years later the implications of the body images I had explored would be clarified when studying sacred Earth Goddess artifacts of 4,000 years ago.

Carolee Schneemann, 'Eye Body' (1963), *More Than Meat Joy: Complete Performance Works and Selected Writings*, ed. Bruce McPherson (New Paltz, New York: Documentext, 1979) 52.

Gilles DELEUZE

The Body, the Meat and the Spirit: Becoming Animal [1981]

The body is the Figure, or rather the material of the Figure. Above all the material of the Figure is not to be confused with the material structure in space which is separate from this. The body is a Figure, not a structure. Conversely, the Figure being a body, is not a face and does not even have a face. It has a head, because the head is an integral part of the body. It can even be reduced to its head. As a portraitist, Francis Bacon is a painter of heads and not of faces. There is a big difference between the two. For the face is a structured spatial organization which covers the head, while the head is an adjunct of the body, even though it is its top. It is not that it lacks a spirit, but it is a spirit which is body, corporeal and vital breath, an animal spirit; it is the animal spirit of man: a pig-spirit, a buffalo-spirit, a dog-spirit, a bat-spirit ... This means that Bacon is pursuing a very special project as a portraitist: unmaking the face, rediscovering or pulling up the head beneath the face.

The deformations which bodies undergo are also *the animal features* of the head. There is in no way a correspondence between animal forms and forms of the face. In fact, the face has lost its form in the process of being subjected to operations of cleaning and brushing which disorganize it and make a head burgeon in its place. And the marks or features of animality are moreover not animal forms, but rather spirits which haunt the cleaned parts, which draw out the head, individualizing and qualifying the head without a face.[1] As procedures used by Bacon, cleaning and features here assume a specific meaning. What happens is that the man's head is replaced by an animal; but this is not the animal as form, it is the animal as *outline*, for example the trembling outline of a bird which spirals over the cleaned area, while the simulacra of face portraits, beside it, serve only as 'witness' (as in the 1976 triptych). What happens is that an animal, a real dog for example, is outlined as the shadow of its master; or conversely the shadow of the man assumes an autonomous and unspecified animal existence. The shadow escapes from the body like an animal to which we give shelter. Instead of formal correspondences, what Bacon's painting constitutes is a *zone of the indiscernible, of the undecidable*, between man and animal. Man becomes animal, but he does not become so without the animal simultaneously becoming spirit, the spirit of man, the physical spirit of man presented in the mirror as Eumenides or Fate. This is never a combination of forms, it is rather a common fact: the common fact of man and animal. To the point that Bacon's most isolated Figure is to begin with a coupled figure, man coupled with his animal in an underlying act of bullfighting.

This objective zone of the indiscernible was to start with the whole body, but the body in terms of flesh or meat.

1. Francis Bacon

Without any doubt the body also has bones, but bones are only spatial structure. Distinctions have often been made between flesh and bones, and even between relationships of flesh and bone. The body only reveals itself when it ceases to be supported by the bones, when the flesh ceases to cover the bones, when they exist in a mutual relation, but each independently, the bones as the material structure of the body, the flesh as the corporeal material of the Figure. Bacon admires Edgar Degas' young woman, *After the Bath* (1885–86), whose broken-up spinal column seems to emerge from the flesh, while the flesh is made the more vulnerable and agile, more acrobatic.[2] In quite a different composition, Bacon painted a similar spinal column for a Figure contorted upside-down. This pictorial tension between flesh and bones is something which has to be achieved. Now to be specific it is meat which brings about this tension in the painting, not least through the splendour of the colours. Meat is that state of the body where the flesh and the bones confront one another locally, instead of entering into composition structurally. Likewise the mouth and the teeth, which are little bones. In meat, it is as if the flesh *drops* from the bones, while the bones rise above the flesh. This is what is specific to Bacon, as opposed to Rembrandt or Soutine. If there is some kind of 'interpretation' of the body in Bacon we find it in his fondness for painting lying figures whose raised arm or thigh stands in for a bone, in such a way that the lulled flesh seems to descend or fall from it. Thus in the central panel of the 1968 triptych, the two sleeping twins flanked by witnesses to the animal spirits; but also the series of the sleeping man with his arms up, of the sleeping woman with the vertical leg, and the sleeping or drugged woman with the raised thighs. Far beyond any apparent sadism, the bones are like gymnastic apparatus (a skeleton-like frame) whose flesh is the acrobat. The athleticism of the body is naturally prolonged in this acrobatics of the flesh. We shall see the importance of falling in Bacon's works. But already in the crucifixions what interests him is the droop, and the sinking head which reveals the flesh. And in those of 1962 and 1965, in the context of an armchair-cross or a trail of bones, we can literally see the flesh dropping from the bones. For Bacon as for Franz Kafka, the spinal column becomes nothing but the sword under the skin which a torturer has slid inside the body of an innocent sleeper.[3] It sometimes even happens that there is a bone just added on in a random spray of paint as an afterthought [...]

But is it possible to say the same thing, exactly the same thing, about meat and the head, namely that it is the objective zone of indecision of men and of animals? Can one say objectively that the head is meat (as much as the meat is spirit)? Of all the parts of the body, is not the head the one closest to the bones? Look at El Greco, and once more at Chaïm Soutine. Now it looks as if Bacon does not experience the head like that. The bone belongs to the face, not to the head. For Bacon there is no death's head. The head is deboned rather than bony. Yet it is not at all soft, but firm. The head is flesh, and the mask itself is not mortuary, it is a firm block of flesh which separates itself from the bones; these are the studies for a portrait of William Blake. Bacon's own head is flesh haunted by a very beautiful gaze without an orbit. And this is how he honours Rembrandt, for having been able to paint a last self-portrait like such a block of flesh without orbits.[4] Throughout Bacon's *oeuvre*, the head-meat relation goes through intensive shifts of scale which make it more and more intimate. At first the meat (flesh on one side, bone on the other) is set on the edge of the track or the balustrade where the Figure-head stands; but it is also the thick, fleshly rain surrounding the head which unmakes its face beneath the umbrella. The scream which issues from the Pope's mouth, the pity which issues from his eyes has meat as its object. Then the meat has a head whereby it flees and descends from the cross, as in the two earlier crucifixions. Later on all of Bacon's series of heads will also declare their identification with meat, and among the finest are those which are painted in the colours of meat, red and blue. Finally, the meat is itself a head, and the head has become the de-localized force of meat, as in the *Fragment of a Crucifixion* of 1950, where all the meat is screaming, with a dog-spirit looking down from the top of the cross. How we know that Bacon does not like this painting is the simplicity of the manifest procedure: all he had to do was dig out a mouth in the middle of the meat. The affinity of the mouth, and of the mouth's interior, with meat still has to be made plain, and it has to reach that point where it has become strictly the section of a cut artery, or even of a jacket sleeve which stands in as an artery, as in the blood-soaked package of the *Sweeney Agonistes* triptych. Then the mouth acquires that power of de-localization which turns all of the meat into a head without a face. It is no longer a specific organ, but the hole through which the entire body escapes, and through which the flesh drops (what is required for this is the procedure of loose involuntary marks). What Bacon calls 'the scream' is the immeasurable pity which extends to the meat.

1 Félix Guattari has analysed these phenomena of facial disorganization: the 'features of faceness' are released and become equally well the features of the head's animality. See Félix Guattari, *L'Inconscient machinique* (Paris: Éditions Recherches, 1979) 75.

2 David Sylvester, *L'art de l'impossible: entretiens avec Francis Bacon*, trans. Michel Leiris and Michaël Pappiatt (Geneva: Editions d'Art Albert Skira, 1976) 92-94.

3 Franz Kafka, 'Das Schwert' (The Sword) in Max Brod (ed.), *The Diaries of Franz Kafka 1914-23*, trans. Martin Greenberg and H. Arendt Schacken (New York: Schoken Books, 1949) 109-10.

4 David Sylvester, *L'Art de l'impossible*, *op.cit.*, 114.

Gilles Deleuze, 'Le corps, la viande et l'espirit, le devenir-animal', *Francis Bacon* (Paris: Éditions de la différence, 1981) 19-22. Translated by Liz Heron.

Helen MOLESWORTH

Before *Bed* [1993]

The *White Paintings*: simple, rectangular canvases, painted a flat, strokeless white and hung side by side, their edges butting tightly up against one another. Robert Rauschenberg made them in 1951 during his second sojourn at Black Mountain College. They were painted after a prolific summer during which he completed the *Night Blooming* series (*c.* 1951): large canvases 2 × 2.5-m [6 × 8-ft] that Rauschenberg took outside, saturated with wet oil paint and pressed into the ground where they picked up the heavy gravel from the road. Night blooming in North Carolina ... jasmine, honeysuckle, sweet gardenia.

John Cage once said, 'The *White Paintings* caught whatever fell on them; why did I not look at them with my magnifying glass?'[1] They hung on the wall ready for viewers to cast their shadows upon them. Cage's question was incomplete, for dust played second fiddle to shadows. The completion of the *White Paintings* demanded the mark of a bodily form – why else would they have needed to be so large? so smooth? so supplicant? so available? Ultimately shadows would not be enough, not because they were too arbitrary but rather because they were too ephemeral. They lacked the full texture and the heady smell of the *Night Blooming*. The first 'Black Painting', made at Black Mountain in 1951, mimicked its white counterparts: black matte paint applied to the canvas with a roller. Rauschenberg knew an uninteresting failure when he saw one. He quickly returned to texture for a sense of touch, an excitation of the senses. The problem emerged: how to create a texture more bodily in nature than gravel, to register the body more concretely than a shadow?

First produced at Black Mountain between 1951 and 1952 and then, after a nine-month hiatus, in 1953, the 'Black Paintings' are patterned canvases with dense, crackling surfaces, laboriously made by tearing sheets of newspaper, dipping them in glue and affixing them to the canvas in a random fashion, where they would be covered by several hues of viscous black paint.[2] In the earliest paintings the newspaper remains hidden under thick paint, resulting in an ambiguous surface texture. *Untitled* ('Black Painting' with *Asheville Citizen*, *c.* 1952) was the first work to expose the newspaper. Rotating the sports and classified pages of the local paper 180 degrees, Rauschenberg spread the full sheets across two joined canvases and painted matte black around their edges. Revealing the newspaper opened a whole new register of meaning for the paintings. For the newspaper is a paradigm of an economy of endless repetition marked by daily consumption and disposability, perhaps best explicated by the popular expression 'same shit, different day'. Its disposability ensures its dailiness, repetition and regularity. In the *Asheville Citizen* painting Rauschenberg exaggerates these aspects of the newspaper by using the sports and classified sections, perhaps the most daily parts of the newspaper (they contain information pertinent only to the immediate present). The 'Black Paintings' became quite repetitious in both appearance and production,[3] mirroring the structure of their ground. Given the number of the paintings, the shadowy newspaper datelines which almost always remain legible, impart a diaristic quality to the works, linking the paintings even more directly to the dailiness and repetition of the newspaper.

Simultaneously, Rauschenberg assiduously photographed the progress of the 'Black Paintings'. The photograph's ability to repeat endlessly and the need to repeat the painting through a photograph of it, as well as

booksandotherprintedma
tterareacurioussymbolo
ffaecespresumablythrou
ghtheassociationwithpa
perandtheideaofpressin
gsmearingimprinting

the indexical capability of the photograph to record the specificity of time and place, has a parallel relation to the newspaper's signification of dailiness. For this purpose, Rauschenberg continually framed the 'Black Paintings' in doorways and doorframes. 'More than simple scaling devices', Walter Hopps has remarked, 'they suggest human presence and establish a literal conjunction of abstract art and the physical factum of everyday life.'[4] Is the 'physical factum of everyday life' merely newspaper and doorways? Or do those traces stand in for dailiness and human presence in another form?

It is hard for me to overlook the way the paintings' textures and colours resonate with faecal matter: the smeared quality of the paint, the varying degrees of viscosity and the colour – shit brown and black. After all, repetition and cycles of consumption and disposal have as much to do with anality as they do with newspapers. And the relation between the two is not so far-fetched. Ernest Jones's landmark essay 'Anal-Erotic Character Traits' discusses the various objects that can signify excrement in unconscious life, with newspapers prominent among them (think of those black smudges left on your hands). 'Books and other printed matter are a curious symbol of faeces', he writes, 'presumably through the association with paper and the idea of pressing smearing, imprinting.'[5] The dirtiness and dailiness, the visual similitude and the compulsive documenting of the paintings against heavily textured brick walls suggest an 'excremental reading' of these works.

In this essay I have given an account of Rauschenberg's early work that engages the uneasiness and disgust that accompany the intense visual pleasure of these paintings. I will also attempt to recapture the profound sense of experimentation with which these works were undertaken. Furthermore I hope to challenge the codification of several standard formalist/biographical/descriptive/ iconographical readings of Rauschenberg.[6] My intention is not to psychoanalyse Rauschenberg or to conflate anality with his sexuality. On the contrary, I feel that 'the body' is presented in Rauschenberg's *oeuvre* as polymorphously perverse. In this regard, my reading engages certain questions concerning the body and the anxieties, fantasies and problems it raises (arouses), especially in the work of artists during the 1950s.[7] Despite the dearth of literature on the topic,[8] Rauschenberg was not alone in this exploration; the problem of registering the body was shared by at least two other key figures at Black Mountain, John Cage and Charles Olson.[9]

'The white paintings came first', Cage once said, 'My silent piece came later.'[10] Yet the exact chronology is not as important as the concern with how to mediate and discuss the body within artistic production. In this regard Cage's recollection of his discovery of silence in a soundproof chamber at Harvard University is striking:

'*I entered one at Harvard University several years ago and heard two sounds, one high and one low. When I described them to the engineer in charge, he informed me that the high one was my nervous system in operation, the low one my blood in circulation. Until I die there will be sounds. And they will continue following my death. One need not fear about the future of music.*'[11]

This revelation locates Cage's most generative musical, artistic and compositional idea within the body itself – more importantly, within the interior of the body, the nervous and circulatory systems, realms of bodily experience of which we are usually not aware. Cage's silence is both located within and driven by the desire to know the body more intimately, to listen to its interior [...]

[T]he 'Black Paintings' were first exhibited at the Stable Gallery in New York in 1953, where Dore Ashton's review saw them as 'black as beasts ... they stir up vaguely primordial sensations, and anxiety. But that is all.'[12] A decade later the Jewish Museum gave Rauschenberg his first retrospective. In the catalogue essay Alan Solomon discussed the paintings' use of colour: 'It supplies an enigmatic field, at once opaque and deep to the furthest reach of space. Shadowed and secretive, it proposes all and discloses nothing, and it became the plasma out of which his present style was formed.'[13] The excremental look of these paintings lay barely beneath the surface of these sensual and tentative descriptions of the 'deep' and the 'primordial' – but the 'anxiety' that it produces is dismissed (Ashton's 'But that is all'; Solomon's it 'discloses nothing').

Rauschenberg's anxiety took a rather different form. Telling an interviewer he went to Black Mountain to be disciplined by Josef Albers, he says:

'*I could have gone on painting with my hands, I think, and making messes forever because I really loved painting. I guess the physicality of my personality was emerging, and so I had to paint with my hands. I couldn't stand a brush coming between me and the canvas. Naturally I cleaned my 'brushes', which were my hands, on my clothes.*'[14]

Rauschenberg does not want to be in the painting – as in Jackson Pollock's famous pronouncement that he could 'literally be *in* the painting'[15] – as much as he wants to have the painting be on his body and, conversely, to have his physicality be on the canvas.

EXCREMENTAL FANTASIES

[...] But if we read the 'Black Paintings' as excremental, as the daily expulsion from the body's interior, can the implications of this instance of *de*sublimation, an instance of a body not successfully overcome, transform the question 'Where do I come from' into 'What is inside of me'? They manifest the desire to explore the interior body through what might be called 'bodily knowledge' – the knowledge, pleasure, curiosity and disgust surrounding that primary bodily product – shit.

Rauschenberg has indeed attempted to turn himself inside out to mark his own body on the canvas.[16] His immersion in an indexical art practice can be well documented by surveying his investment in imprinting the corporeal senses on to the artistic surface. Placing a nude body directly on to light sensitive paper, Rauschenberg and Susan Weil made the *Blueprints* (1950). Taking the wet paintings outside and pressing them in the dirt, he made the *Night Blooming* series. But the questions the 'Black Paintings' ask are: What kind of knowledge do our bodies produce about ourselves? Can knowledge be desublimated and returned to its origin? ... The 'Black Paintings' mark the canvas with the body in the basest of ways. 'The body begins to exist where it *repugnates*, repulses, yet wants to devour what disgusts it and exploits that taste for distaste ... '[17] The paintings enact the body liberated through excretion. They are a narcissistic fantasy of self-birth; they give way to the delirium of the body producing its own knowledge [...]

1 John Cage, *Silence* (Middletown: Wesleyan University Press, 1973) 108.

2 Calvin Tompkins, *Off the Wall: Robert Rauschenberg and the Art World of Our Time* (Garden City, New York: Doubleday and Co., 1980) 71. Tompkins claims that Rauschenberg would randomly drop glue-soaked newspaper on to the canvas, implying that the canvas was horizontal, but no other scholarship makes that assertion.

3 Rauschenberg made at least nine *Black Paintings* during 1952 while at Black Mountain and at least seven at his Fulton Street studio in New York during the spring and summer of 1953.

4 Walter Hopps, *Robert Rauschenberg: The Early 1950s* (Houston: Houston Fine Arts Press, 1991) 62.

5 Ernest Jones, *Papers on Psycho-Analysis* (New York: William Wood and Company, 1918) 676.

6 Two examples are: Roni Feinstein's 'Random Order: The First Fifteen Years of Robert Rauschenberg's Art, 1949-1964', Ph.D. dissertation (New York University, 1990), as primarily descriptive; and Mary Lynn Kotz's monograph *Rauschenberg: Art and Life* (New York: Harry N. Abrams, 1990) as biographical.

7 The importance of the desire to mark bodily form in 1950s art practice is an idea that had its genesis in the context of Rosalind Krauss' seminar 'The Transgressive 1950s' at the CUNY Graduate Center. Krauss' work on Jackson Pollock and Pam Lee's work on Cy Twombly created the space out of which this article grew.

8 The exception is Jonathan Weinberg's 'It's in the Can: Jasper Johns and the Anal Society', *Genders*, 1 (Spring 1988).

9 The relationship between Rauschenberg and Cage has been well documented. See Calvin Tompkins, *The Bride and the Bachelors* (London: Penguin, 1976). The relationship between Rauschenberg and Olson is much less clear. They were both, however, part of *Theater Piece No. 1*, a multimedia event that is often referred to as the first performance-art piece. Among many other activities, Olson read poetry and Rauschenberg's *White Painting* was included.

10 Cage, *Silence*, *op. cit.*, 98.

11 *Ibid.*, 8.

12 Dore Ashton, 'Robert Rauschenberg', *Art Digest* (September 1953) 20, 25.

13 Alan Solomon, *Robert Rauschenberg* (New York: Jewish Museum, 1963) n.p.

14 Barbara Rose, *Robert Rauschenberg* (New York: Vintage Books, 1987) 23.

15 Ellen Johnson (ed.), *American Artists on Art from 1940 to 1980* (New York: Harper and Row, 1982) 4.

16 Roland Barthes, *The Responsibility of Forms*, trans. Richard Howard (Berkeley: University of California Press, 1985) 207. Barthes establishes this idea of turning oneself inside out to discuss the work of the French painter Requichot.

17 *Ibid.*, 210-11.

Helen Molesworth, 'Before *Bed*', *October*, 63 (Winter 1993) 69-82.

GESTURING BODIES

During the 1960s artists increasingly sought to break down the boundaries between art and life and to make a connection between art and society. Art became more and more directly related to the social, economic and historical environment. The artist's body was used as the primary signifying material of the artist's gesture, making the body a site on which ideas could be enacted. Everyday acts and gestures were appropriated as art and the art object began to dematerialize, as the aesthetic object of artistic production became less important. The rethinking of bodily actions through their artistic enactment opened up an alternative reconstruction of thought offering, for example, a commentary on race, class and gender.

Neo-Concretist Manifesto [1959]

[...] *Neo-Concretism*, born from the need to express the complex reality of modern man by means of the structural language of new forms, denies the validity of scientific and positivist attitudes in the arts, and re-convokes the problem of expression in incorporating the new conceptual dimensions created by Constructivist, non-figurative art. *Rationalism strips art of all its autonomy, by substituting notions of scientific objectivity for the irreplaceable qualities of the work of art.* In this way the concepts of form, space, time, structure – which in the language of the arts are tied to an existential, emotional, affective meaning – are confused with the theoretical application science makes of them. In fact, in the name of the prejudices denounced by the philosophy of today (Maurice Merleau-Ponty, Ernst Cassirer, Suzanne Langer), prejudices that are crumbling in all fields – beginning with modern biology's advance over Pavlovian mechanism – *the concrete-rationalists still see man as a machine among other machines, and try to limit art to the expression of this theoretical reality*.

We neither consider the work of art a 'machine' nor an 'object', but rather, an *almost-body*, which is to say, a being whose reality is not exhausted in the external relationships between its elements; a being which, even while not decomposable into parts through analysis, *only delivers itself up wholly through a direct, phenomenological approach*.

For us, the work of art surpasses the materialist mechanics that serve as its support, and this is not at all for metaphysical reasons. If it transcends its mechanical relations (such as Gestalt psychology objectifies them), it's through the creation of an implicit meaning (Merleau-Ponty) which emerged by itself for the first time. *If we must look for an equivalent for the work of art, we will thus find it neither in the machine nor in the object as such, but rather, as Langer and Weidlé did, in living organisms.* However such a comparison would not suffice to express the specific reality of the aesthetic organism. It is because the work of art is not limited to occupying a place in objective space, but transcends it in order to found a new meaning, that the objective notions of time, space, form, structure, colour, etc., are not sufficient to understand the work of art, to account for its reality.

The difficulty of finding a precise terminology to express a world that can't be reduced to formulae has led art criticism to adopt an imprecise vocabulary, the indiscriminate use of which has betrayed the complexity of the work of art. There the influence of technology and of science has again played a role – but in the opposite direction. Certain artists, offended by the critics' imprecise terminology, have tried – in a significant reaction – to make art on the basis of objective notions, trying to apply them as creative methods. This results in a simple illustration of methods given a priori, methods that prescribe the results the work is to realize in advance. Stripping itself of intuitive creation, limiting itself to an objective form in objective space, the painting of the concrete-rationalist evokes nothing but a reaction of stimuli and reflex responses from artist and spectator alike. The concrete work offers itself to the eye in the form of an instrument and *not as a human way of grasping the world and of giving oneself to it*. It addresses itself to the eye-machine and not to the eye-body.

It is because the work of art transcends mechanical space that the notions of cause and effect lose much of their validity in it. The notions of time, space, form, colour, need to be integrated in such a way (in virtue precisely of the fact that as notions they do not pre-exist the work) that it would be impossible to speak of them as isolated terms. Neo-Concrete art, in affirming the absolute integration of its elements, believes that the geometrical vocabulary it uses must take on the expression of complex human reality, in the way that many works by Piet Mondrian, Kasimir Malevich, Nicholas Pevsner, Naum Gabo, Sophie Taeuber-Arp, etc., demonstrate. Even if these artists sometimes confused the concepts of *mechanical form* with those of *expressive form*, it's a matter of clarifying that in the language of art *so-called geometrical forms lose the objective character of geometry in order to become a vehicle for the imagination* [...]

Amilcar de Castro, Lygia Clark, Ferreira Gullar, Reynaldo Jardim, Lygia Pape, Maria Pedrosa, Theon Spanudis and Franz Weissman, 'Manifesto Neoconcreto', *Jornal do Brasil* (March 1959) 4-5; reprinted in English as 'Neo-Concretist Manifesto', trans. Yve-Alain Bois, in *October*, 69 (Summer 1994) 91-95.

George MACIUNAS Fluxus Manifesto [1963]

2. To affect, or bring to a certain state, by subjecting to, or treating with, a flux. '*Fluxed* into another world.' *South*.
3. *Med.* To cause a discharge from, as in purging.
flux (fluks), *n.* [OF., fr. L. *fluxus*, fr. *fluere*, *fluxum*, to flow. See FLUENT; cf. FLUSH, *n.* (of cards).] 1. *Med.* a A flowing or fluid discharge from the bowels or other part: esp., an excessive and morbid discharge: as the bloody *flux* or dysentery. b The matter thus discharged.
Purge the world of bourgeois sickness, 'intellectual', professional and commercialized culture, PURGE the world of dead art, imitation, artificial art, abstract art, illusionistic art, mathematical art –

PURGE THE WORLD OF 'EUROPANISM'!
2. Act of flowing: a continuous moving on or passing by, as of a flowing stream; a continuing succession of changes.
3. A stream; copious flow; flood; outflow.
4. The setting in of the tide towards the shore. Cf. REFLUX.
5. State of being liquid through heat; fusion. *Rare.*
PROMOTE A REVOLUTIONARY FLOOD AND TIDE IN ART.
Promote living art, anti-art, promote NON ART REALITY to be grasped by all peoples, not only critics, dilettantes and professionals.
7. *Chem. & Metal.* a Any substance or mixture used to promote fusion, esp. the fusion of metals or minerals. Common metallurgical fluxes are silica and silicates (acidic), lime and limestone (basic), and fluorite (neutral). b Any substance applied to surfaces to be joined by soldering or welding, just prior to or during the operation, to clean and free them from oxide, thus promoting their union, as rosin.
FUSE the cadres of cultural, social & political revolutionaries into united front & action.

George Maciunas, 'Fluxus Manifesto' (1963), in Jurgen Becker and Wolf Vostell (eds.), *Happenings, Fluxus, Pop Art, Nouveau Réalisme* (Hamburg: Rowohlt, 1965) 203; reprinted in Clive Philpot and John Hendricks (eds.), *Fluxus: Selections from the Gilbert and Lila Silverman Collection* (New York: The Museum of Modern Art, 1988) frontispiece.

Milan KNÍŽÁK

Demonstration for All the Senses [1964]

The organizers of the demonstration wear unusual clothes instead of jewels – articles of daily use or pieces of fancy material sewn on ordinary clothing, parts of clothing painted with some colour, preferably red or white and the like.

Every newcomer is given a thing to carry in his hand at all times, e.g., a piece of cutlery, a plate, glass, vase, teapot, piece of clothing, shoe or the like.

Walking down the street they pass a room with an open window, near which a man sits at a laid table and eats.

They go on, and are led into a small room, where they are locked in and left in inactivity for anything from five minutes up, according to their reaction or indifference. A great deal of perfume has been spilled on the floor of the room.

They are now let out. What has happened to them was only preparation, a disturbance of their normal state of mind.

The walk goes on. They encounter things – parts of furniture, clothes, etc. A musician lies on the ground and plays a violin.

They reach a small place and are put in the middle of a circle. Around them the organizers of the demonstration run, shouting, roaring, cutting across, driving round on motorcycles and in cars.

A chair comes down from above. They look at it and point. Then a man comes and puts the chair on a pedestal.

All fall to the ground. After a minute another man comes, takes the chair down, and sits on it.

All get up.

The participants are appealed to, to arrange a number of objects in a row. Each participant stands behind his own object.

They are then asked to pick up their objects and rebuild the row 20-cm [8-in] farther on. This is repeated as long as desired, according to the reaction of the participants.

Now they walk back. A man stands at a wall, glazing a window. As soon as he is finished, he breaks it. In the middle of the street a woman lies on a mattress, listening to a transistor radio. The participants stop and are presented with a book, from which each one tears a page. Then they return their objects and leave.

The first, active part of the demonstration is now finished. The second ends in a fortnight, and is different for each participant. Everything that happens to him during this period is a second demonstration.

First performed by the Art of the Actual theatrical group in Prague, 1964.

Milan Knížák, 'Demonstrace Pro Všechny Smysly', *AKTUAL ART samizdat* (1964-65) n.p.; published in English as 'Demonstration for All the Senses' (1964), in Allan Kaprow, *Assemblages, Environments and Happenings* (New York: Harry N. Abrams, 1966) 305.

Yayoi KUSAMA

Artist's statement on WABC Radio [1965]

[...] I arrived at my present style after years of experimentation ...

I started when I was a child. I used to tear clothing, papers, even the books I read, into thousands of pieces with scissors and razor blades. I also liked to shatter the windows, mirrors and dishes with stones and hammer ...

Later, I painted intricate pictures of the tiny networks found in leaves, butterfly wings, etc., with Chinese ink. These covered the entire paper and looked like giant webs. Later on, I cut out thousands of little faces from magazines and collected them in a box. Many years afterward, when I was in America, I made collages of these too ...

My *Aggregation Sculpture* is a logical development of everything I have done since I was a child. It arises from a deep, driving compulsion to realize in visible form the repetitive image inside of me. When this image is given freedom, it overflows the limits of time and space. People have said that my *Aggregation Sculpture* presents an irresistible force, a force that goes by its own momentum once it has started. I give to this sculpture the name 'Driving Image'.

I feel as if I were driving on the highways or carried on a conveyor belt without ending until my death.

This is like continuing to drink thousands of cups of coffee or eating thousands of feet of macaroni. This is to continue to desire and to escape all sorts of feelings and visions until the end of my days whether I want to or not. I cannot stop living and yet I cannot escape from death.

This consciousness of living in continuation sometimes drives me crazy. It makes me sick before and after my work. On the other hand, I am deeply terrified by the obsessions crawling over my body, whether they come from within me or from outside. I fluctuate between feelings of reality and unreality. I am neither a Christian nor a Buddhist nor anyone with great control over himself.

I find myself being put into a uniform environment, which is strangely mechanized and standardized. I feel this strongly in highly civilized America and particularly so in New York.

In the gap between people and the strange jungle of civilized society lie many psychosomatic problems. I am deeply interested in the background of problems involved in the relationship of people and society. My artistic expressions always grow from the aggregation of these [...]

Yayoi Kusama, 'Interview with Gordon Brown for WABC Radio', *De niuewe stijl/The New Style*, 1 (1965) 162-64; reprinted in Alexandra Munroe (ed.), *Japanese Art after 1945: Scream Against the Sky* (New York: Solomon R. Guggenheim Museum, 1994) 374-75.

Joseph BEUYS

Statement on How to Explain Pictures to a Dead Hare [1965]

In putting honey on my head I am clearly doing something that has to do with thinking. Human ability is not to produce honey, but to think, to produce ideas. In this way the deathlike character of thinking becomes lifelike again. For honey is undoubtedly a living substance. Human thinking can be lively too. But it can also be intellectualized to a deadly degree, and remain dead, and express its deadliness in, say, the political or pedagogic fields.

Gold and honey indicate a transformation of the head, and therefore, naturally and logically, the brain and our understanding of thought, consciousness and all the other levels necessary to explain pictures to a hare: the warm stool insulated with felt, the 'radio' made of bone and electrical components under the stool and the iron sole with the magnet. I had to walk on this sole when I carried the hare round from picture to picture, so along with a strange limp came the clank of iron on the hard stone floor – that was all that broke the silence, since my explanations were mute, and the radio was on an almost inaudible wavelength.

This seems to have been the action that most captured people's imaginations. On one level this must be because everyone consciously or unconsciously recognizes the problem of explaining things, particularly where art and creative work are concerned, or anything that involves a certain mystery or questioning. The idea of explaining to an animal conveys a sense of the secrecy of the world and of existence that appeals to the imagination. Then, as I said, even a dead animal preserves more powers of intuition than some human beings with their stubborn rationality.

The problem lies in the word 'understanding' and its many levels which cannot be restricted to rational analysis. Imagination, inspiration, intuition and longing all lead people to sense that these other levels also play a part in understanding. This must be the root of reactions to this action, and is why my technique has been to try to seek out the energy points in the human power field, rather than demanding specific knowledge or reactions on the part of the public. I try to bring to light the complexity of creative areas.

This is also a technique to bring about discussion of the human position at a critical time when materialist and rational ideas are still current, coupled with loss of imagination, inspiration and understanding of other things. It's a question again of Which Reality? Is it the limited materialist understanding of *materia*, or is it *substance*? Substance for me is a greater issue and includes evolutionary power which leads ultimately to the real meaning of Materia, with its roots in MATER (mother – as in 'mother earth'), as one pole of spirituality while the other encompasses the whole process of development.

Joseph Beuys, 'Wie man dem toten Hasen die Bilder erkärt' (1965); reprinted in English as 'Statement on How to Explain Pictures to a Dead Hare' in Caroline Tisdall, *Joseph Beuys*, trans. Caroline Tisdall (London: Thames and Hudson, 1979) 105.

Dick HIGGINS

Statement on Intermedia

[1966]

Art is one of the ways that people communicate. It is difficult for me to imagine a serious person attacking any means of communication *per se*. Our real enemies are the ones who send us to die in pointless wars or to live lives which are reduced to drudgery, not the people who use other means of communication from those which we find most appropriate to the present situation. When these are attacked, a diversion has been established which only serves the interests of our real enemies.

However, due to the spread of mass literacy, television and the transistor radio, our sensitivities have changed. The very complexity of this impact gives us a taste for simplicity, for an art which is based on the underlying images that an artist has always used to make his point. As with the Cubists, we are searching for a new way of looking at things, but more totally, since we are more impatient and more anxious to go to the basic images. This explains the impact of Happenings, event pieces, mixed media films. We do not ask any more to speak magnificently of taking arms against a sea of troubles, we want to *see* it done. The art which most directly does this is the one which allows this immediacy, with a minimum of distractions.

Goodness only knows how the spread of psychedelic means, tastes and insights will speed up this process. My own conjecture is that it will not change anything, only intensify a trend which is already there.

For the last ten years or so, artists have changed their media to suit this situation, to the point where the media have broken down in their traditional forms, and have become merely puristic points of reference. The idea has arisen, as if by spontaneous combustion throughout the entire world, that these points are arbitrary and only useful as critical tools, in saying that such-and-such a work is basically musical, but also poetry. This is the intermedial approach, to emphasize the dialectic between the media. A composer is a dead man unless he composes for all the media and for his world.

Does it not stand to reason, therefore, that having discovered the intermedia (which was, perhaps, only possible through approaching them by formal, even abstract means), the central problem is now not only the new formal one of learning to use them, but the new and more social one of what to use them for? Having discovered tools with an immediate impact, for what are we going to use them? If we assume, unlike McLuhan and others who have shed some light on the problem up until now, that there are dangerous forces at work in our world, isn't it appropriate to ally ourselves against these, and to use what we really care about and love or hate as the new subject matter in our work? Could it be that the central problem of the next ten years or so, for all artists in all possible forms, is going to be less the still further discovery of new media and intermedia, but of the new discovery of ways to use what we care about both appropriately and explicitly? The old adage was never so true as now, that saying a thing is so don't make it so. Simply talking about Vietnam or the crisis in our Labour movements is no guarantee against sterility. We must find the ways to say what has to be said in the light of our new means of communicating. For this we will need new rostrums, organizations, criteria, sources of information. There is a great deal for us to do, perhaps more than ever. But we must now take the first steps.

Dick Higgins, 'Statement on Intermedia' (1966), *De-Coll/age* (July 1967); reprinted in *In the Spirit of Fluxus*, ed. Elizabeth Armstrong and Joan Rothfuss (Minneapolis: Walker Art Center, 1993) 172-73.

Michael FRIED

Art and Objecthood [1967]

[...] The presence of literalist art, which Clement Greenberg was the first to analyze, is basically a theatrical effect or quality – a kind of stage presence. It is a function, not just of the obtrusiveness and, often, even aggressiveness of literalist work, but of the special complicity which that work extorts from the beholder [...] The experience of being distanced by the work in question seems crucial: the beholder knows himself to stand in an indeterminate, open-ended – and unexacting – relation as *subject* to the impassive object on the wall or floor. In fact, being distanced by such objects is not, I suggest, entirely unlike being distanced, or crowded, by the silent presence of another *person*; the experience of coming upon literalist objects unexpectedly – for example, in somewhat darkened rooms – can be strongly, if momentarily, disquieting in just this way.

There are three main reasons why this is so. First, the size of much literalist work, as Robert Morris' remarks imply, compares fairly closely with that of the human body. In this context Tony Smith's replies to questions about his 2-m [6-ft] cube, *Die* (1962), are highly suggestive:

3. Tony Smith

Q: Why didn't you make it larger so that it would loom over the observer?

A: I was not making a monument.

Q: Then why didn't you make it smaller so that the observer could see over the top?

A: I was not making an object.[1]

One way of describing what Smith was making might be something like a surrogate person – that is, a kind of *statue* [...] Second, the entities or beings encountered in everyday experience in terms that most closely approach the literalist ideals of the non-relational, the unitary and the holistic are *other persons*. Similarly, the literalist predilection for symmetry, and in general for a kind of order that 'is simply order ... one thing after another', is rooted, not, as Donald Judd seems to believe, in new philosophical and scientific principles, whatever he takes these to be, but in *nature*. And third, the apparent hollowness of most literalist work – the quality of having an *inside* – is almost blatantly anthropomorphic. It is, as numerous commentators have remarked approvingly, as though the work in question has an inner, even secret, life – an effect that is perhaps made most explicit in Morris' *Untitled* (1965–66), a large ring-like form in two halves, with fluorescent light glowing from within at the narrow gap between the two [...]

1 Quoted by Robert Morris as the epigraph to his 'Notes on Sculpture, Part II', *Artforum*, 5: 2 (October 1966).

Michael Fried, 'Art and Objecthood', *Artforum* (June 1967) 12-29.

Lucy R. LIPPARD, John CHANDLER

The Dematerialization of Art

[1968]

During the 1960s the anti-intellectual, emotional/ intuitive processes of art-making characteristic of the last two decades have begun to give way to an ultra-conceptual art that emphasizes the thinking process almost exclusively. As more and more work is designed in the studio but executed elsewhere by professional craftsmen, as the object becomes merely the end product, a number of artists are losing interest in the physical evolution of the work of art. The studio is again becoming a study. Such a trend appears to be provoking a profound dematerialization of art, especially of art as object, and if it continues to prevail, it may result in the object's becoming wholly obsolete.

The visual arts at the moment seem to hover at a crossroad which may well turn out to be two roads to one place, though they appear to have come from two sources:

art as idea and art as action. In the first case, matter is denied, as sensation has been converted into concept; in the second case, matter has been transformed into energy and time-motion. If the completely conceptual work of art in which the object is simply an epilogue to the fully evolved concept seems to exclude the *objet d'art*, so does the primitivizing strain of sensuous identification and envelopment in a work so expanded that it is inseparable from its non-art surroundings. Thus the extremely cool and rejective projects of Donald Judd, Sol LeWitt and others have a good deal in common with the less evolved but perhaps eventually more fertile synesthetic ambitions of Robert Whitman, Robert Rauschenberg and Michael Kirby, or the dance of Yvonne Rainer and Alex Hay, among others. This fact is most clearly illustrated by the work of Robert Morris, who has dealt with idea as idea, idea as object and idea as performance. In fact, the performance media are becoming a no man's or everyman's land in which visual artists whose styles may be completely at variance can meet and even agree.[1] As the time element becomes a focal point for so many experiments in the visual arts, aspects of dance, film and music become likely adjuncts to painting and sculpture, which in turn are likely to be absorbed in unexpected ways by the performing arts [...]

A highly conceptual art, like an extremely rejective art or an apparently random art, upsets detractors because there is 'not enough to look at', or rather not enough of what they are accustomed to looking *for*. Monotonal or extremely simple-looking painting and totally 'dumb' objects exist in time as well as in space because of two aspects of the viewing experience. First, they demand more participation by the viewer, despite their apparent hostility (which is not hostility so much as aloofness and self-containment). More time must be spent in immediate experience of a detail-less work, for the viewer is used to focusing on details and absorbing an impression of the piece with the help of these details. Secondly, the time spent looking at an 'empty' work, or one with a minimum of action, seems infinitely longer than action-and-detail-filled time. This time element is, of course, psychological, but it allows the artist an alternative to or extension of the serial method. Painter-sculptor Michael Snow's film *Wavelength* (1967), for instance, is tortuously extended within its forty-five-minute span. By the time the camera, zeroing in very slowly from the back of a large loft, reaches a series of windows and finally a photograph of water surface, or waves, between two of them, and by the time that photograph gradually fills the screen, the viewer is aware of an almost unbearable anticipation that seems the result of an equally unbearable length of time stretched out at a less than normal rate of looking; the intensity is re-enforced by the sound, which during most of the film is monotonal, moving up in pitch and up in volume until at the end it is a shrill hum, both exciting and painful.

Joseph Schillinger, a minor American Cubist who wrote, over a twenty-five year period, an often extraordinary book called *The Mathematical Basis of the Arts*, divided the historical evolution of art into five 'zones', which replace each other with increasing acceleration: 1) pre-aesthetic, a biological stage of mimicry; 2) traditional-aesthetic, a magic, ritual-religious art; 3) emotional-aesthetic, artistic expression of emotions, self-expression, art for art's sake; 4) rational-aesthetic, characterized by empiricism, experimental art, novel art; 5) scientific, post-aesthetic, which will make possible the manufacture, distribution and consumption of a perfect art product and will be characterized by a fusion of the art forms and materials, and, finally, a 'disintegration of art', the 'abstraction and liberation of the idea'.[2]

Given this framework, we could now be in a transitional period between the last two phases, though one can hardly conceive of them as literally the last phases the visual arts will go through. After the intuitive process of re-creating aesthetic realities through man's own body, the process of reproduction or imitation, mathematical logic enters into art. (The Bauhaus dictum 'Less is More' was anticipated by William of Ockham when he wrote: 'What can be explained by fewer principles is explained needlessly by more'; Nominalism and Minimalism have more in common than alliteration.) From then on, man became increasingly conscious of the course of his evolution, beginning to create directly from principles without the intercession of reproductive reality. This clearly corresponds to the Greenbergian interpretation of Modernism (a word used long before Greenberg, though his disciples insist on attributing it to him). The final 'post-aesthetic' phase supersedes this self-conscious, self-critical art that answers other art according to a determinist schedule. Involved with opening up rather than narrowing down, the newer work offers a curious kind of Utopianism which should not be confused with Nihilism except in that, like all utopias, it indirectly advocates a *tabula rasa*; like most utopias, it has no concrete expression.

Dematerialized art is post-aesthetic only in its increasingly non-visual emphases. The aesthetic of principle is still an aesthetic, as implied by frequent statements by mathematicians and scientists about the *beauty* of an equation, formula or solution: 'Why should an aesthetic criterion be so successful so often? Is it just that it satisfies physicists? I think there is only one answer – nature is inherently beautiful' (physicist Murray Gell-Mann); 'In this case, there was a moment when I knew how nature worked. It had elegance and beauty. The goddam thing was gleaming' (Nobel prizewinner Richard Feynman).[3] The more one reads these statements, the more apparent it becomes that the scientist's attempt to discover, perhaps even to impose order and structure on the universe, rests on assumptions that are essentially aesthetic. Order itself, and its implied simplicity and unity, are aesthetic criteria.

The disintegration Schillinger predicted is obviously implicit in the break-up since 1958 or so of traditional media, and in the introduction of electronics, light, sound and, more important, performance attitudes into painting and sculpture – the so far unrealized intermedia revolution whose prophet is John Cage. It is also implied by the current international obsession with entropy. According to Wylie Sypher, for example: 'The future is that in which time becomes effective, and the mark of time is the increasing disorder towards which our system tends ... During the course of time, entropy increases. Time can be measured by the loss of structure in our system, its tendency to sink back into that original chaos from which it may have emerged ... One meaning of time is a drift towards inertia.'[4]

Today many artists are interested in an order that incorporates implications of disorder and chance, in a negation of actively ordering parts in favour of the presentation of a whole.[5] Earlier in the twentieth century the announcement of an element of indeterminacy and relativity in the scientific system was a factor in the rise of an irrational abstraction. Plato's anti-art statements, his opposition to imitative and representational art, and his contempt for the products of artists, whom he considered insane, are too familiar to review here, but they are interesting to note again in view of the current trend back to 'normalcy', as evidenced by the provocative opening show of the East Village co-operative Lannis Museum of Normal Art, where several of the works discussed here were seen. Actually, the museum would be better called the Museum of Adnormal Art, since it pays unobtrusive homage to the late Ad Reinhardt and to his insistence that only 'art-as-art' is normal for art. (The painter-director, Joseph Kosuth, admits his pedantic tendency, also relatable to Reinhardt's dogmas, in the pun on normal schools.) However, 'no idea' was one of Reinhardt's Rules and his ideal did not include the ultra-conceptual. When works of art, like words, are signs that convey ideas, they are not things in themselves but symbols or representatives of things. Such a work is a medium rather than an end in itself or 'art-as-art'. The medium need not be the message, and some ultra-conceptual art seems to declare that the conventional art media are no longer adequate as media to be messages in themselves [...]

[T]he main twentieth-century sources for a dematerialized art are found in Dada and Surrealism. One can cite the Dada insistence on a *tabula rasa* at the aesthetic as well as the social level, in reaction to the physical emphasis of Cubism which, despite its initial shattering of solid form, aimed at re-creating the object in another, equally physical form. The Dadas adopted the anarchist Bakunin's slogan 'Destruction is Creation'; later even Piet Mondrian declared that the destructive element had been neglected in art. Francis Picabia erased a poem as it was written on a blackboard at a Dada demonstration, and his 1913 Amorphist manifesto was illustrated by blank canvases because total opposition of colour had cancelled out colour and total opposition of form had cancelled out form; in 1920, Max Ernst made an object with a hatchet attached and spectators paid to take whacks at it; Kurt Schwitters hid rather than destroyed the Dada-Expressionist inner core of his first Merzbau by surrounding it with a Stijl-oriented framework. The parallels go on and on. But as is so often the case today, one must return to Marcel Duchamp for the most valid prototype. Younger artists probably do not consider Duchamp a particular influence or force, as Jasper Johns, Jim Dine and others did around 1960; this is due to the almost total absorption and acceptance of Duchamp's aesthetics into the art of the present. He is no longer particular; he is pervasive [...]

4. Kurt Schwitters

The danger, or fallacy, of an *ultra*-conceptual art is that it will be appreciated for the wrong reasons, that it will, like Duchamp's *Bottle Rack* or *Large Glass*, come to be mainly an ingratiating object of aesthetic pleasure instead of the stringently metaphysical vehicle for an idea intended. The idea has to be awfully good to compete with the object, and few of the contemporary ideas (listed above) are finally that good. Nevertheless, the 'thinness', both literal and allusive, of such themes as water, steam, dust, flatness, legibility, temporality, continues the process of ridding art of its object quality. Some of these artists hold that the idea is self-generating and self-conclusive, that building the sculpture or painting the painting is simply the traditional, expected step finally unnecessary to the aesthetic, but very little of their work is really conceptual to the point of excluding the concrete altogether. On the other hand, ideas like Oldenburg's trench or LeWitt's buried cube are both tangible and intangible, simple and complex. They open up art to the intellect without transferring it into any other cultural or trans-cultural area. Visual art is still visual even when it is invisible or visionary. The shift of emphasis from art as product to art as idea has freed the artist from present limitations – both economic and technical. It may be that works of art which cannot be realized now because of lack of means will at some future date be made concrete. The artist as thinker, subjected to none of the limitations of the artist as maker, can project a visionary and utopian art which is no less art than concrete works. Architecture provides many precedents for this kind of unmaterialized art; Wright's mile-high skyscraper is no less art for not having a concrete expression, in fact, had it been made it would have been useful and therefore removed from fine art. Moreover, since dealers cannot sell art-as-idea, economic materialism is denied along with physical materialism.

Non-visual must not be confused with non-visible; the conceptual focus may be entirely hidden or unimportant to the success or failure of the work. The concept can determine the means of production without affecting the product itself; conceptual art need not communicate its concepts. The audience at a Cage concert or a Rainer dance performance will never know what the conceptual framework of the work is. At the other extreme is LeWitt's contention: '*Logic may be used to camouflage the real intent of the artist, to lull the viewer into the belief that he understands the work, or to infer a paradoxical situation (such as logic vs. illogic). The ideas need not be complex. Most ideas that are successful are ludicrously simple. Successful ideas generally have the appearance of simplicity because they seem inevitable.*'[6]

Thus the difficulty of abstract conceptual art lies not in the idea but in finding the means of expressing that idea so that it is immediately apparent to the spectator. In maths or science, the simpler the explanation or formula, the more satisfying it seems to be, and to reduce the great complexity of the universe to a single, simple equation or metaphor is the goal. Even the simple progression of 1, 2, 3, in Dan Flavin's 1963 fluorescent piece *the nominal three (to William of Ockham)*, or the 1, 2, 3, 4, of David Lee's dark hanging Plexiglas panels at Finch Gallery, are enough to satisfy the initial demands of a rational art. Even the most apparently elaborate schemes, such as Larry Poons's multiple inversions, though they require more deliberation to detect, once found are only slightly more complicated than the simple ones. Perhaps this, or the 'camouflage' mentioned by LeWitt, is the reason for the popularity of hermetic motifs today. Hermeticism of one kind or another, manifested as enclosure or monotonality and near invisibility, as an incommunicative blank facade or as excessive duration, helps maintain the desired aloofness in a work confronted by the ordinary or suspiciously avid spectator, while at the same time it satisfies the artist's desire for difficulty and endears itself to the spectator willing to commit himself on a deeper level.

5. Dan Flavin

Much recent conceptual art is illustration in a sense, in the form of drawings or models for nearly impossible projects that will probably never be realized, or in many cases, *need* no further development. According to Joseph Kosuth: 'All I make are models. The actual works of art are ideas. Rather than "ideals", the models are a visual approximation of a particular art object I have in mind'[7] [...]

Idea art has been seen as art about criticism rather than art-as-art or even art about art. On the contrary, the dematerialization of the object might eventually lead to the disintegration of criticism as it is known today. The pedantic or didactic or dogmatic basis insisted on by many of these artists is incorporated in the art. It bypasses criticism as such. Judgement of ideas is less interesting than following the ideas through. In the process, one might discover that something is either a good idea, that is, fertile and open enough to suggest infinite possibilities or a mediocre idea, that is, exhaustible, or a bad idea, that is, already exhausted or with so little substance that it can be taken no further. (The same can be applied to style in the formal sense, and style except as an individual trademark tends to disappear in the path of novelty.) If the object becomes obsolete, objective distance becomes obsolete. Sometime in the near future it may be necessary for the writer to be an artist as well as for the artist to be a writer. There will still be scholars and historians of art, but the contemporary critic may have to choose between a creative originality and explanatory historicism.

Ultra-conceptual art will be thought of by some as formalist because of the spareness and austerity it shares with the best of painting and sculpture at the moment. Actually, it is as anti-formal as the most amorphous or journalistic expressionism. It represents a suspension of realism, even formal realism, colour realism and all the other 'new realisms'. However, the idea that art can be experienced in order to extract an idea or underlying intellectual scheme as well as to perceive its formal essence *continues from* the opposing formalist premise that painting and sculpture should be looked at as objects *per se* rather than as references to other images and representation. As visual art, a highly conceptual work still stands or falls by what it looks like, but the primary, rejective trends in their emphasis on singleness and autonomy have limited the amount of information given, and therefore the amount of formal analysis possible. They have set critic and viewer thinking about what they see rather than simply weighing the formal or emotive impact. Intellectual and aesthetic pleasure can merge in this experience when the work is both visually strong and theoretically complex.

Some thirty years ago, José Ortega wrote about the 'new art': 'The task it sets itself is enormous; it wants to create from nought. Later, I expect, it will be content with less and achieve more.'[8] Fully aware of the difficulty of the new art, he would probably not have been surprised to find that a generation or more later the artist has achieved more with less, has continued to make something of 'nought' fifty years after Malevich's *White on White* seemed to have defined nought for once and for all. We still do not know how much less 'nothing' can be. Has an ultimate zero point been arrived at with black paintings, white paintings, light beams, transparent film, silent concerts, invisible sculpture or any of the other projects mentioned above? It hardly seems likely.

1 See the *Tulane Drama Review* (Winter 1965), which includes articles by John Cage, Claes Oldenburg, Yvonne Rainer, Robert Morris, Allan Kaprow, La Monte Young and a good general essay on 'The New Theatre' by Michael Kirby.

2 Joseph Schillinger, *The Mathematical Basis of the Arts* (New York: Philosophical Library, 1948) 17.

3 Quoted in Lee Edson, 'Two Men in Search of the Quark', *New York Times Magazine* (8 October 1967).

4 Wylie Sypher, *Loss of Self in Modern Literature and Art* (New York: Vintage, 1962) 73-74. The word has also been applied to differing areas of recent art by Robert Smithson and Piero Gilardi; it appears as the title of short stories as well, for instance, by Thomas Pynchon.

5 In the New York art world, the idea seems to have originated with Donald Judd.

6 Sol LeWitt, 'Paragraphs on Conceptual Art', *Artforum* (Summer 1967) 80.

7 *Non-Anthropomorphic Art by Four Young Artists: Four Statements* (New York: Lannis Gallery, 1967).

8 José Ortega y Gasset, *The Dehumanization of Art* (Anchor, New York: Doubleday, 1956) 50.

Lucy R. Lippard and John Chandler, 'The Dematerialization of Art', *Art International*, 12: 2 (February 1968) 31-36.

ART & LANGUAGE

Concerning the Article 'The Dematerialization of Art' [1968]

All the examples of artworks (ideas) you refer to in your article, are, with few exceptions, art-objects. They may not be an art-object as we know it in its traditional matter-state, but they are nevertheless matter in one of its forms ... And it is on this question of matter-state that my caution with regard to the metaphorical usage of dematerialization is centred upon. Whether for example, one calls Carl Andre's 'substance of forms' empty space or not, does not point to any evidence of dematerialization because the term 'empty space' can never, in reference to terrestrial situations, be anything more than a convention describing how space is filled rather than offering a description of a portion of space which is, in physical terms, empty. Andre's empty space is in no sense a void [...]

Matter is a specialized form of energy; radiant energy is

the only form in which energy can exist in the absence of matter. Thus when dematerialization takes place, it means, in terms of physical phenomena, the conversion (I use this word guardedly) of a state of matter into that of radiant energy ... The philosophy of what is called aesthetics relying finally, as it does, on what it has called the content of the artwork is, at the most only fitted with the philosophical tools to deal with problems of an art that absolutely counts upon the production of matter-state entities. The shortcomings of such philosophical tools are plain to see inside this limit of material objects; once this limit is broken these shortcomings hardly seem worth considering as the sophistry of the whole framework is dismissed as being not applicable to an art procedure that records its information in words, and the consequent material qualities of the entity produced ... do not necessarily have anything to do with the idea. That is, the idea 'read about' rather than 'looked at'. That some art should be directly material and that other art should produce a material entity only as a necessary by-product of the need to record the idea is not at all to say that the latter is connected by any process of dematerialization to the former.

Art & Language, 'Concerning the Article "The Dematerialization of Art"' (unpublished letter-essay to Lucy R. Lippard and John Chandler, 1968); printed in Lucy R. Lippard, *Six Years: The Dematerialization of the Art Object* (London: Studio Vista, 1973) 43-44.

Robert MORRIS
Anti-Form [1968]

In recent object-type art the invention of new forms is not an issue. A morphology of geometric, predominantly rectangular forms has been accepted as a given premise. The engagement of the work becomes focused on the particularization of these general forms by means of varying scale, material, proportion, placement. Because of the flexibility as well as the passive, unemphasized nature of the object-type shape it is a useful means. The use of the rectangular has a long history. The right angle has been in use since the first post and lintel construction. Its efficiency is unparalleled in building with rigid materials, stretching a piece of canvas, etc. This generalized usefulness has moved the rectangle through architecture, painting, sculpture, objects. But only in the case of object-type art have the forms of the cubic and the rectangular been brought so far forwards into the final definition of the work. That is, it stands as a self-sufficient whole shape rather than as a relational element. To achieve a cubic or rectangular form is to build in the simplest, most reasonable way, but it is also to build well.

This imperative for the well-built thing solved certain problems. It got rid of asymmetrical placing and composition, for one thing. The solution also threw out all non-rigid materials. This is not the whole story of so-called Minimal or object art. Obviously it does not account for the use of purely decorative schemes of repetitive and progressive-ordering multiple-unit work. But the broad rationality of such schemes is related to the reasonableness of the well-built [...]

The process of 'making itself' has hardly been examined. It has only received attention in terms of some kind of mythical, romanticized polarity: the so-called action of the Abstract Expressionists and the so-called conceptualizations of the Minimalists. This does not locate any differences between the two types of work. The actual work particularizes general assumptions about forms in both cases. There are some exceptions. Both ways of working continue the European tradition of aestheticizing general forms that has gone on for half a century. European art since Cubism has been a history of permuting relationships around the general premise that relationships should remain critical. American art has developed by uncovering successive alternative premises for making itself.

Of the Abstract Expressionists only Jackson Pollock was able to recover process and hold on to it as part of the end form of the work. Pollock's recovery of the process involved a profound rethinking of the role of both material and tools in making. The stick which drips paint is a tool which acknowledges the nature of the fluidity of paint. Like any other tool it is still one that controls and transforms matter. But unlike the brush, it is in far greater sympathy with matter because it acknowledges the inherent tendencies and properties of that matter. In some ways Morris Louis was even closer to matter in his use of the container itself to pour the fluid [...]

In object-type art process is not visible. Materials often are. When they are, their reasonableness is usually apparent. Rigid industrial materials go together at right angles with great ease. But it is the a priori valuation of the well-built that dictates the materials. The well-built form of objects preceded any consideration of means. Materials themselves have been limited to those which efficiently make the general object form.

Recently, materials other than rigid industrial ones have begun to show up. Claes Oldenburg was one of the first to use such materials. A direct investigation of the properties of these materials is in progress. This involves a reconsideration of the use of tools in relation to material. In some cases these investigations move from the making of things to the making of material itself. Sometimes a direct manipulation of a given material without the use of any tool is made. In these cases considerations of gravity become as important as those of space. The focus on matter and gravity as means results in forms which were not projected in advance. Considerations of ordering are not necessarily casual and imprecise and unemphasized. Random piling, loose stacking, hanging, give passing form to material. Chance is accepted and indeterminacy is implied since replacing will result in another configuration. Disengagement with preconceived enduring forms and orders for things is positive assertion. It is part of the work's refusal to continue aestheticizing form by dealing with it as a prescribed end.

Robert Morris, 'Anti-Form', *Artforum* (April 1968) 100-101.

Carolee SCHNEEMANN
Naked Action Lecture [1968]

[In] *Naked Action Lecture* ... I lecture on my visual works and their relations to antecedents in painting while both dressed and undressed, dressing and undressing.

Naked Action Lecture asked the questions: can an artist be an art historian? Can an art historian be a naked woman? Does a woman have intellectual authority? Can she have public authority while naked and speaking? Was the content of the lecture less appreciable when she was naked? What multiple levels of uneasiness, pleasure, curiosity, erotic fascination, acceptance or rejection were activated in an audience?

... In the course of the thirty-minute lecture I undressed and dressed and walked back and forth with a pointer, discussing aspects of perception and spatial organization. I took questions from the audience if they related directly to the content of the lecture.

Naked Action Lecture was performed at the Institute of Contemporary Arts, London, in 1968.

Carolee Schneemann, 'Naked Action Lecture' (1968), *More Than Meat Joy: Complete Performance Works and Selected Writings*, ed. Bruce McPherson (New Paltz, New York: Documentext, 1979) 180.

Mierle Laderman UKELES
Maintenance Art [1969]

[...] A. *The Death Instinct* and *The Life Instinct*.

The Death Instinct: separation, individuality, avant-garde par excellence; to follow one's own part to death – do your own thing, dynamic change.

The Life Instinct: unification, the eternal return, the perpetuation and maintenance of the species, survival systems and operation, equilibrium.

B. Two basic systems: *Development* and *Maintenance*.

The sourball of every revolution: after the revolution who's going to pick up the garbage on Monday morning?

Development: pure individual creation; the new; change; progress; advance; excitement; flight or fleeing.

Maintenance: Keep the dust off the pure individual creation; preserve the new; sustain the change; protect progress; defend and prolong the advance; renew the excitement; repeat the flight [...]

C. *Maintenance is a drag*; it takes all the fucking time, literally; the mind boggles and chafes at the boredom; the culture confers lousy status and minimum wages on maintenance jobs; housewives = no pay.

Clean your desk, wash the dishes, clean the floor, wash your clothes, wash your toes, change the baby's diaper, finish the report, correct the typos, mend the fence, keep the customer happy, throw out the stinking garbage, watch out – don't put things in your nose, what shall I wear, I have no sox, pay your bills, don't litter, save string, wash your hair, change the sheets, go to the store. I'm out of perfume, say it again – he doesn't understand, seal it again – it leaks, go to work, this art is dusty, clear the table, call him again, flush the toilet, stay young.

D. *Art*:
Everything I say is Art is Art. Everything I do is Art is Art. 'We have no Art, we try to do everything well.' (Balinese saying *à la* McLuhan and Fuller.)

Avant-garde art, which claims utter development, is infected by strains of maintenance ideas, maintenance activities and maintenance materials.

Conceptual and Process art especially claim pure development and change, yet employ almost purely maintenance processes.

E. The exhibition of Maintenance Art, 'CARE', would zero in on maintenance, exhibit it, and yield, by utter opposition, a clarity of issues.

'I am an artist ... woman ... wife ... mother (random order). I do a hell of a lot of washing, cleaning, cooking, renewing, supporting, preserving, etc.' Up to now she's also 'done' art, but now Mierle Ukeles is willing to do all that drudgery in a museum on an exhibition basis. 'I will sweep and wax the floors, dust everything, wash the walls (i.e., floor paintings, dust works, soap sculpture, wall paintings, etc.), cook, invite people to eat, clean up, put away, change light bulbs ... My working will be the work.' Second, typed interviews with various people from maintenance professions and museum-goers concerning their views on the piddling but essential tasks of life would be presented. Finally, 'Earth Maintenance', the last part, involves delivering refuse to the museum where it is 'purified, depolluted, rehabilitated, recycled', and conserved by various technical (and/or pseudo-technical) procedures' [...]

Mierle Laderman Ukeles, 'Maintenance Art' (proposal for an exhibition, 1969); printed in Kristine Stiles and Peter Selz (eds.), *Theories and Documents of Contemporary Art: A Sourcebook of Artists' Writings* (Berkeley and London: University of California Press, 1996) 220-21.

Marcia TUCKER
Phenaumanology [1970]

'Experience shows that human beings are not passive components in adaptive systems. Their responses commonly manifest themselves as acts of personal creation.'
– René Dubos, *Man Adapting*

[...] Nauman does not represent or interpret phenomena, such as sound, light, movement or temperature, but uses them as the basic material of his new work. Our responses to the situations he sets up are not purely physical, however. Man alone among animals is able to symbolize, to respond not only to the direct effect of a stimulus on his body, but to a symbolic interpretation of it. This interpretation (and its emotional or psychological corollaries) is conditioned by all other experiences a person has had, and which he involuntarily brings to bear on every new situation. Each person will, therefore, respond to the physical experience of Nauman's work in a different way.

Nauman carefully constructs his pieces to create a specific physical situation. Although he is no longer interested in ways of making art nor the 'interpretation' of a made object, he feels it is still important that a piece be neither over- nor under-refined. In this way focus can be directed to the experience and our response to it, rather than to the object itself.

The structures of sound and movement as a basic function of human behaviour and communication are the phenomena which provide not only the artist, but the linguist, the anthropologist, the philosopher and the social scientist with the sources of our knowledge of man. These are Nauman's concerns, and he sees his art as more closely related to man's nature than to the nature of art. This attitude is evidenced by his evolution from the making of objects and the recording of activities, to his present concern with manipulations of phenomena.

He has utilized progressively intricate 'extensions' of the human body, the same extensions that man has evolved in order to live, to communicate, and to adapt to his environment. They range from writing which extends language and the telephone which extends the voice, to complicated mechanisms like the computer, allowing memory and calculation far beyond the capacity of any human source [...]

Our bodies are necessary to the experience of any phenomenon. It is characteristic of Nauman's work that he has always used his own body and its activities as both the subject and object of his pieces. He has made casts from it (*From Hand to Mouth*, 1967, *Neon Templates of the Left Half of My Body Taken at 10-inch Intervals*, 1966, etc.) and manipulated it (in earlier performances using his body in relation to a T-bar or neon tube, as well as in the holograms). He has made video tapes of his own activities (*Bouncing Balls in the Studio*, 1966–67) and films of parts of his body being acted upon; *Bouncing Balls* (1969) and *Black Balls* (1969) are slow-motion films of Nauman's testicles moving and being painted black. He has questioned, in various pieces, his behaviour as an artist and his attitudes towards himself as such. He has contorted his body and face to the limits of physical action as well as representation. By making audiotapes of himself clapping, breathing, whispering and playing the violin, he has also explored a range of noises made and perceived by his own body.

This concern with physical self is not simple artistic egocentrism, but use of the body to transform intimate subjectivity into objective demonstration. Man is the perceiver and the perceived; he acts and is acted upon; he is the sensor and the sensed. His behaviour constitutes a dialectical interchange with the world he occupies. Maurice Merleau-Ponty, in *The Structure of Behaviour*, stresses that man *is*, in fact, his body, despite the essential ambiguity of its being at once lived from the inside and observed from the outside. Nauman has used himself in this way as a prototypical subject for the pieces. These works are meant, essentially, to be encountered privately by one person at a time. Where earlier the artist was the subject and object of recorded situations, now it is the spectator who becomes both the actor and observer of his own activity [...]

Since the emotional responses to each piece differ according to the receptor, it is almost impossible to name them; loneliness, delight, anxiety, surprise, frustration, serenity and other private feelings provide the sensory poetry of this work.

'Even a long time ago, when I was painting, I could get to a point where everything worked except for one part of the painting which was a mess, and I couldn't figure out what to do with it. One way was to remove that part of the painting. The other way was to make *that* the important part of the painting; that always ended up the most interesting.''

The artist's concern with making the 'difficult' aspect of a work its focus need not be seen as perversity or artistic sadism, but as a viable working method. For example, Nauman has stated that art generally adds information to a situation, and that it seems reasonable to also make art by removing information from a situation. In fact, sensory deprivation experiments have shown that only the essential information needed to identify a thing tends to be picked up from a surrounding group of stimuli [...]

In the audiotapes of breathing, pacing, clapping and playing violin scales, sounds are differentiated from 'noises' by periodicity, which arouses the expectation of pattern in the listener. Intent is thereby revealed through rhythmic structuring. In another tape, he whispers over and over, 'GET OUT OF THE ROOM, GET OUT OF MY MIND'. This highly charged message, delivered regularly and repeatedly, confuses us because we generally associate repetitive messages with a low expressive content.

In a performance at the Whitney Museum of American Art last year, a similar situation was structured by using an abrupt, emotionally charged movement. Nauman, his wife Judy and Meredith Monk each stood about 30.5-cm [1-ft] away from respective corners and bounced the upper part of their bodies into them repeatedly for an hour. In both kinds of work Nauman is also interested in how a movement or sound becomes an exercise, how an exercise becomes a performance and how specific responses to the performance can be controlled.

In some informal and unpublished notes entitled *Withdrawal as an Art Form*, Nauman describes a diverse group of phenomena and possible methods for manipulating them. He is involved with the amplification and deprivation of sensory data; with an examination of physical and psychological responses to simple situations which yield clearly experienceable phenomena; with our responses to extreme or controlled situations, voluntary and involuntary defence mechanisms and biological rhythms.

Among his notes there is a plan for a piece which is, at present, impossible to execute:

'*A person enters and lives in a room for a long time – a period of years or a lifetime.*

'*One wall of the room mirrors the room but from the opposite side; that is, the image room has the same left-right orientation as the real room.*

'*Standing facing the image, one sees oneself from the back in the image room, standing facing a wall.*

'*There should be no progression of images; that can be controlled by adjusting the kind of information the sensor would use and the kind the mirror wall would put out.*

'*After a period of time, the time in the mirror room begins to fall behind the real time – until after a number of*

The structures of sound and movement as a basic function of human behaviour and communication are the phenomena which provide not only the artist, but the linguist, the anthropologist, the philosopher and the social scientist with the sources of our knowledge of man.

Marcia TUCKER Phenaumanology, 1970

years the person would no longer recognize his relationship to his mirrored image. (He would no longer relate to his mirrored image or a delay of his own time.)'

This piece, he says, is related to a dream which he had a long time ago, and could only be done eventually with the aid of a vast computer network.

The experience of such a room, were it possible to build, would slowly alter the way in which we, as human beings, know ourselves in relation to the world we inhabit. If what we know of the world is the sum of our perceptions, and our physical, emotional and intellectual reactions to our environment, then to effectively manipulate these factors is to effect a virtual change in that world.

Nauman's work continues to explore these possibilities. Like the mirror piece, the computer and the dream exemplify the polarities of man's nature, and consequently of his art.

1 All statements by Bruce Nauman are taken from taped interviews with the author, made during August 1970.

Marcia Tucker, 'Phenaumanology', *Artforum*, 9: 4 (December 1970) 38-44.

GILBERT & GEORGE

A Day in the Life of George & Gilbert, the Sculptors [1971]

Being living sculptures is our life blood, our destiny, our romance, our disaster, our light and life. As day breaks over us, we rise into our vacuum and the cold morning light filters dustily through the window. We step into the responsibility-suits of our art. We put on our shoes for the coming walk. Our limbs begin to stir and form actions of looseness, as though without gravity they bounce about for the new day. The head afloat on top levels on the horizon of our thought. Our hearts pound with fresh blood and emotion and again we find ourselves standing there all nerved up in body and mind. Often we will glide across the room, drawn by the window's void. Our eyes are glued to this frame of light. Our mind points ever to our decay. The big happening outside the window floods our vision like a passing film. It leaves us without impressions, giving up only silence and repetitive relaxation. Nothing can touch us or take us out of ourselves. It is a continuous sculpture. Our minds float off into time, visiting fragments of words heard, faces seen, feelings felt, faces loved. We take occasional sips from our water glasses. Consciousness comes along and goes away, slipping from dreaming space into old concrete awareness. The whole room is filled with the mass and the weight of our own history, at times it sees us chained to our chairs and then it will appear like large music, surrounding and intoxicating. We feel briefly but seriously for our fellow artist-men. More than ever complete with our physical, for a time with legs crossed, or arms folded until the elbows ache, a throat is cleared gently but effectively, we then stand for relief pushed up against the wall. Sometimes the room with its size and form and precision of our clarity, its one vase of flowers, its large desk-blackboard of our doing, our two dear faithful green chairs, the black telephone, linked with the world's art-network.

Ring and ring again
Make us happy ever again
Stay as silent as the desk
And be as free and let it be.

The neat ashtray steadily fills with relaxful butts, beside it a fresh yellow packet of cigarettes. Very often the room makes us hurt with real bodily pressure. From time to time we are taken head-first from this room called 'Art for All' out and away, sometimes driven, sometimes drawn to breathe again amongst the people. We stroll with specialized embarrassment and our purpose is only to take the sunshine. The people are all living near to beauty, passing by. Walking is the eternity of our living movement, it can never tell us of an end, it is for nothing but the time passing unnoticed. We give ourselves to this walking and so the houses come towards us and then away behind. We would like to tell of our great pleasure in seeing the early flowers and blossoms, they seem to have a young fresh youth, so fine and coloured. We remark the trees with their tight bursting buds. As our legs take us jauntily along we come to a place where we pause for a cup of poison-nervous tea. We sit over it chatting a little of the normal afternoon when all is usual and well. Nothing breathtaking will occur here, but in the darkness of a picture house, where time is killed, the world explodes realistically into giant action stories, men are killed, women are loved, mountains are blown up, night falls, volcanoes erupt, John Wayne rides again and Caesar speaks anew to the people. All this until the reel is done and viewers drift blinking and reeling out into the bright city. And we happily go back to our art where only tiredness and searching play big roles, where all is thin on the ground, where greatness is made at the stroke of a brush, where something and nothing are both qualities. Art is for the modern world to enjoy the sophistication of decadent living expression. It is our strong belief that in Art there is living, and where there's life there's hope. It is for this reason that we have dedicated our hands, legs, pens, speech and our own dear heads to progress and understanding in art [...]

Gilbert & George, *A Day in the Life of George & Gilbert, the Sculptors Autumn 1971* (London: Gilbert & George, 1971); reprinted in Gilbert & George, *The Words of Gilbert & George With Portraits of the Artists from 1968 to 1997* (London: Thames and Hudson; Violette Editions, 1997) 37-40.

Ben VAUTIER

ART = BEN [1973]

[...] *Ben Vautier* [W]hen I was little, I was already competing, I was an exhibitionist. At school I rolled my 'r's and the other children took the piss out of me. So I decided it was better to be ridiculous than banal. My earliest memory is of walking with a bone attached to my neck. I wanted to be seen.

Then I had a nightclub. I had my band – Ben's band. Then I looked for the new systematically. I was working in a bookshop and I used to go through the pages of the art history books. When I got a shock, it was good. So I developed the theory of shock (I was fifteen or sixteen years old): it had to shock if it was good. The shock was synonymous with personality, with style, synonymous with creation because it signalled an element that wasn't there before. At the point when I shocked someone, I astonished them, I gave them something. You could say it was the basis of my theory of the new. In fact – excepting perhaps a bit in music – I have only ever made art according to this fundamental approach. And in art history I was looking for everything that went with my system. So Duchamp was shocking; he was the man who was the most shocking, so we were friends. Yves Klein made his blue, it was a new absolute, so he was automatically a friend. John Cage said: anything is music; automatically I was for him.

Irmeline Lebeer And your new thing – what is the most original thing that you have contributed to the history of art?

Vautier My new thing has followed several stages. During the first period (from 1960 to 1962) it was appropriation. It was simple: the new thing was to do what had not been done before. So I made lists of things that had been done, and then I took the dictionary and I looked for what hadn't been done. I hit the word 'chicken' – had anybody ever signed a chicken? No? I signed chickens. Kicks. Had anyone done any kicks? No? I gave out kicks signed Ben.

It was a fight, but the rule of the game wasn't mine; since Marcel Duchamp's everything-is-art, you could take anything, so you had to appropriate as many things as you could and it was the game of appropriation, or if you like, super-appropriation – you had to take possession of things before the others got there.

In Nice at the time I knew Klein a little, Arman a little, and since Klein had taken blue, the air, the void, I had to find absolutes more absolute than his. One day I walked up to Yves and I said to him: you have taken the monochrome, you have taken fire, but I have something stronger in my hand. He asked me what and I said: in my hand I have a ping pong ball and in this ping pong ball there is God; you have not signed God. I have just signed God ... I never made a complete systematization like Arman did. A dozen perhaps. Then I signed death, mystery, lack, imbalance, everything, nothing, life, holes [...]

Lebeer You don't think that what has intrigued you most has been things which in reality cannot be appropriated?

Vautier I have always loved absolutes. In other words opposites. Turning situations around. Lack fascinated me, the mystery box fascinated me, in the sense in which they were linked to the notion of absence. I made the absences of artworks: the absence of a work of art = the work of art. How to show the absence of a work of art? By hiding it. And so in order not to make a work of art out of hiding it either, I made a box on which there was an inscription – it's the text that counts – saying: 'In this box there is a work of art, but its value is in its absence. From the moment when you see the work of art, it will lose all aesthetic value.'

Another absolute: the window. I said to myself 'how to beat Klein' again – he was my enemy, I had to fight people, it was simple – Klein had made the monochrome. But stronger than the monochrome is transparency. So I signed windows, at the bottom in the corner. Afterwards I thought about it. Death – very important, death. When you die the whole situation is sorted. It's an absolute work of art – clean, clear. So I signed death.

Lebeer You have also signed other people?

Vautier **Yes, there it was the problem of resemblance which intrigued me. There were artists who made portraits. And I thought that the most resembling portrait that you could do and which was very easy to buy, which we could all have at home, which anybody could put on the wall in a Louis XV or Louis XVI frame, was a mirror. So I made *Your Portrait*: the mirror.**

Then I said to myself: they want sculptures – but what is the most simple sculpture? The clearest? And which moves as well: it's the human being. Instead of spending hours sculpting in marble which will break, there are millions of human beings walking around. I will take one, I will sign it, and this will simplify my life. And so I bought living sculptures. In 1959 someone sold me his head and in 1961 his whole body. This was before Manzoni [...]

Irmeline Lebeer, 'Art = Ben: entretien avec Ben Vautier', *L'Art Vivant*, 42 (August-September 1973) 7-11. Translated by Elizabeth Manchester.

Thomas McEVILLEY Diogenes of Sinope, Selected Performance Pieces [1983]

One day Diogenes was seen sitting in the public square all afternoon gluing shut the pages of a book.

When a play had just ended and the crowds were swarming out, Diogenes made his way into the emptying theatre against the flow. When asked why, he replied, 'This is the kind of thing I practise doing all the time.'

When he was captured by pirates after a shipwreck and put up for sale at a slave auction, the auctioneer asked him what he could do. 'Govern men', he replied and told the crier to call it out in case anyone wanted to buy a master for himself.

One day Diogenes was seen making the rounds of the ornamented porticoes of Athens, begging alms from the public statues.

He would walk backwards through the city streets.

When Plato, investigating species-genera relationships, defined man as a featherless biped, Diogenes walked into the classroom carrying a plucked chicken and said, 'Here is Plato's man.'

Certain ancient Greeks insisted that philosophy should be an activity co-extensive with life – as certain artists in our time have said about art. 'Philosophize more often than you breathe' was the advice of one of the ancient exponents of this view. What he meant is that life lived with a certain focus is philosophy, as in our time it has been claimed that life lived with a certain focus is art.

The process of expanding a limited category into a universal frame involves a willingness to manipulate language directly. The semantic boundaries of the category *word* are broken open and forced, step by step, to the limits of life. Consciousness is violently retextured by the imposition of a new conceptual overlay on its experiences. Some ancient philosophers pursued this goal through enigmatic and challenging public behaviour that was specifically designated as philosophy. 'Performance philosophy' would be an appropriate term for this activity. The classroom philosophers of ancient Greece were no happier to confront this radical expansion of their realm than the established academies in our time were to encounter performance artists who insisted that the artistic frame should not separate one experience from another, but should enclose every moment of life.

The great hero of this tradition, and arguably the great prototype of much performance art, was Diogenes of Sinope, who lived mostly in the fourth century BC.[1] Diogenes designated his entire life as a performance of philosophy. Living in the streets and plazas of Athens and Corinth, he exhibited his every action to public inspection, a lifestyle for which he was called simply 'The Dog'. From that urban stage he devoted himself to the performance of a series of absurdist acts designed to subvert the habitual motivation systems of his viewers.

Diogenes' actions always demonstrated the viability of behavioural options opposite to those of the citizens at large. Thrusting at the cracks of communal psychology, his tiny and quiet gestures laid bare a dimension of hidden possibilities which he thought might constitute personal freedom. His general theme was the complete and immediate reversal of all familiar values, on the ground that they are automatizing forces which cloud more of life than they reveal.

A successor who goes nameless in the literature summed up Diogenes' legacy as he felt it, in a piece repeated always the same. Ascending a platform from which philosophers would customarily address the public, he would simply laugh for the duration of a normal speech, then descend. More than any specific linguistic message, the generalized affirmation of a laugh could point to the unbounded openness that Diogenes had articulated in his gestures.

In our time the category of art has been opened up and deliberately universalized, as the category of philosophy was in Diogenes' day. Artists have performed bizarre and enigmatic public acts and designated them as art. Artists have put themselves on exhibition, and in extreme cases have designated their entire lives as performances. These gestures have dissolved the traditional boundaries of art activity and set new ones at the limits of the life field. In many cases the project has both an artistic goal – the discovery of new art forms beyond the old boundaries – and an ethical one: by refocusing life as art, it is hoped to purge it of conventional motives and restore it to a fresh and disinterested appreciation.

Diogenes redivivus? **'Whoever hears me say that this dog playing here now is the same one that frolicked and romped in this place hundreds of years ago may think of me what he will; but it is a stranger madness yet to imagine that he is fundamentally different.'[2]**

When a rich man took Diogenes into his house and cautioned him not to spit on the rugs and furnishings since they were very expensive, Diogenes spat in the man's face and explained that it was the only thing there cheap enough to spit on.

Diogenes praised people who intended to get married, go on a journey, or enter a profession, and being just about to do so, decided not to.

Alexander the Great, who had heard his notoriety, came and stood beside Diogenes where he was sunning himself in the gutter, and asked if there was anything he could do for him. Diogenes said 'yes; get out of my light'.

One day Diogenes was jerking off in the market place and, when condemned by passers-by, remarked that he wished he could satisfy hunger just by rubbing his stomach.

When a friend dropped a piece of bread in the street and was embarrassed to pick it up, Diogenes tied a rope around the neck of a huge wine jug and spent the afternoon dragging it around the plaza.

One day Diogenes shaved half his head bald, than went to a party where he was accosted and beaten up by young toughs. The next day, bruised and battered, he wrote their names on a slate, hung it around his neck, and spent the day walking around town with it.

Entering a classroom where a professor was lecturing Diogenes stood in plain sight, holding a fish before him. One student after another began to giggle, till the class was in a tumult. 'Look,' said Diogenes, 'this fellow's lectures are less interesting than a twopenny fish.'

When the rats crept up to his table he said, 'See, now even Diogenes keeps pets.'

When he was asked how he wanted to be buried, he said, 'Upside down. For soon down will be up.'

One day he sat down and held his breath until he died.

1 I have retold the Diogenes anecdotes in my own words. For sources and discussions see: Diogenes Laertius, *Lives of Eminent Philosophers*, trans. R.D. Hicks (2 Vols., New York: G.P. Putnam's Sons, 1925) Book VI, Chap. 2; Farrand Sayre, *Diogenes of Sinope: A Study of Greek Cynicism* (Baltimore: J.H. Furst, 1938); Donald Dudley, *A History of Cynicism* (London: Reprografischer Nachdruck der Ausg, 1937); A.J. Malherbe, *The Cynic Epistles: A Study Edition* (Princeton, California: Chico Ca Scholars 1977); Daniel H.H. Ingalis, 'Cynics and Pasupatas the Seeking of Dishonour', *Harvard Theological Review*, 55 (1962); Hermann Diels 'Aus dem Leben des Cynikers Diogenes', *Archiv für Geschichte der Philosophie*, 7 (1894); Kurt von Fritz, 'Quellenuntersuchungen zu Leben

und Philosophie das Diogenes von Sinope', *Philologus*, supplemental 18 (1926); Gunnar Rudberg, 'Zur Diogenes-Tradition', *Symbolae Osloenses*, 14 (1935).

2 Arthur Schopenhauer, *The World As Will and Idea*, ed. David Berman, trans. Jill Berman (London: J.M. Dent, 1995), slightly altered (I have changed Schopenhauer's exemplum from a cat to a dog).

Thomas McEvilley, 'Diogenes of Sinope, Selected Performance Pieces', *Artforum* (March 1983) 58-59.

Kristine STILES

Between Water and Stone – Fluxus Performance: A Metaphysics of Acts [1993]

THE PERFORMATIVE CONDITIONS OF FLUXUS

[...] Fluxus actions may be physical, mental, or linguistic; they may be solitary or collective acts; and they may be single moments or community exchanges. But whether conceptual, corporeal, or verbal, private or public, simple or complex, Fluxus performances often centre around the manipulation and use of objects in the enunciation of auditory and visual experience. The condensation of behavioural signals into simple gestures that are produced in the interchange between action and object enhance the visual character of these performances and, in so doing, engage codes of visual representation that communicate in highly condensed, simultaneous and multiple modes rather than in linear narrative. In this way, the simple, gestural act can serve to communicate complex messages, while collective Fluxus performances and festivals compound the basic unit of expression into complex structures of intersecting events.

Fluxus events constitute 'concerts' of the quotidian, the music of *action* animating *things*. Indeed, objects in Fluxus performances assume a distinctly performative character, and the body, in addition to its role as subject, is itself presented as an object. Together subject and object create a changing and interrelated perceptual field for the investigation of the interchange between actions, language, objects and sounds. Fluxus performances require both performers and viewers to consider the function of thought in the ways in which the body interacts with things: they draw attention to the behavioural processes that relate thinking and doing, and compel both performers and viewers to confront and then, perhaps, revise conditions of being. Such revisions – the results of the reconfiguration of common bodily actions – may give rise to alternative procedures and patterns for the reconstruction of thought. Fluxus events, then, can provide unique models for the rediscovery of the event-value of both actions and objects in the formation of perception and knowledge. For these reasons Fluxus performances must be contemplated within a wider structure of social and collective practices [...]

Fluxus performances situate the body in the centre of knowledge as the principal means by which to interrogate the very conditions in which individuals interact with things and thereby produce social meanings. Each Fluxus action thus contains within itself a 'history' that is both *of* and *for* the body, *of* and *for* society, for as Henri Lefebvre has noted, 'the whole of [social] space proceeds from the body'.[1] I am particularly eager to secure Fluxus performances in this broad context so that the many possible theoretical interpretations they suggest may be grounded in material and historical conditions. For as Lefebvre has also argued, 'The body is establishing itself firmly, as base and foundation, *beyond philosophy*, beyond discourse and beyond the theory of discourse' [in large measure because] 'Western philosophy ... *betrayed* the body; it has actively participated in the great process of metaphorization that has *abandoned* the body; and it has *denied* the body.'[2]

Fluxus performance posits the body, in phenomenological terms, as emergent with the world. In so doing, it suggests a nascent paradigm for social praxis (discussed later in this essay) that both compels a re-evaluation of the human situation and provides revisionist forms for re-evaluating intersubjective connections that enable us to rethink and, thereby, re-enact the social world [...]

RACE, GENDER AND SEX IN FLUXUS EVENTS

Questions of gender and sexuality figure prominently in Fluxus actions, and race – a subject that often had been ignored in the visual arts until recently – is considered. These issues emerged out of the artists' direct personal and social experiences as much as they equally reflected the growing internationality of the period, the nascent feminist movement, the sexual revolution of the 1960s, and most of all the civil rights movement. Strong proto-feminist elements appear particularly frequently in the performances of Japanese women associated with Fluxus and, in the case of Yoko Ono, these feminist aspects are sometimes interlaced with commentary on race and class.[3] Although Fluxus artists did not always fully accept such content in the context of Fluxus performance (Shigeko Kubota remembers that her colleagues hated her performance *Vagina Painting* (1965) and Yoko Ono has explained that she was rejected because her work was 'too animalistic'),[4] it nevertheless was there and was presented often [...]

Ono's performance of *Cut Piece* (*c.* 1964), in which she sat motionless on the stage after inviting the audience to come up and cut away her clothing, brought the theme of physical and emotional pain into the actual interplay of human intersubjectivity. The performance opens itself to a number of interpretations. It may be read as a discourse on passivity and aggression, on the presentation of the self as a victim connected to the reciprocity between abuse and self-denigration, or on the relinquishment of power required in the sadomasochistic exchange. It vividly demonstrates, as well, the potential for objectification of the 'other' in the militarization of feeling that dislocates compassion from acts of brutality. It also comments on the condition of art and becomes that denouement of the relationship between exhibitionism and scopic desires that disrobes the imagined self-referential edifice of art and reveals it to be an interactive exchange between beholder and object. *Cut Piece* visualizes and enacts the responsibility that viewers must take in aesthetic experience [...]

Shigeko Kubota's *Vagina Painting*, however, was the most aggressively proto-feminist performance of Fluxus, although she would not have described it as such at the time. On 4 July 1965, during the Perpetual Fluxfest in New York City, Kubota placed paper on the floor and, squatting over it, began to paint with a brush that she had earlier fastened to her underpants. Moving over the paper, she dipped the brush in red paint to produce an eloquent gestural image that exaggerated female sexual attributes and bodily functions and redefined action painting according to the codes of female anatomy. Kubota performed *Vagina Painting* exactly one year after she arrived in New York. The direct reference to menstrual cycles seems to compare the procreation/creation continuum lodged in the interiority of woman with the temporal cycles of change and growth she experienced in her own art and life after moving from Japan to the United States. Her artistic progeny may be accessed in the action-text of metaphorical blood through which she objectified the immaterial creative biological centre of woman and in the concrete image it manifested of her artistic powers. For, as the literary theorist Elaine Scarry has proposed in *The Body in Pain*, 'To have material form is to have self-substantiating form.'[5]

Kubota's *Vagina Painting* must be understood as an historically daring rejection of the female as muse.[6] In this action, she recovers woman as the source of her own artistic inspiration, as the gender able to produce both actual life and representational form.[7] Kubota's event also posits female bodies as the nexus of art and of life, their material synthesis. Her action gives new and rather poignant, if not psychological, meaning to the desire expressed by so many male artists of her generation 'to act in the gap between' art and life, as Robert Rauschenberg so succinctly imagined it[8] [...]

Despite the very explicit examples that have been discussed here, however, usually when issues of sex, race, class or violence appeared in Fluxus performance they were of a sublimated kind that contrasts starkly with the overtly hedonistic qualities found in other performance practices that coexisted, overlapped and sometimes interlocked with Fluxus in the 1960s. The performances of Al Hansen, Carolee Schneemann, Rafael Montañez Ortiz, Jean-Jacques Lebel, Viennese Actionism, John Latham, Mark Boyle and Gustav Metzger more openly addressed some or all of the issues related to sexuality, destruction, violence and politics. These artists frequently intermingled with Fluxus artists in the early 1960s: Lebel associated with Robert Filiou, Patterson, Nam June Paik, Charlotte Moorman, Williams, and Ben Vautier (who appeared in Lebel's Festivals of Free Expression); Dick Higgins, whose own work often dealt with danger and violence, published Hansen's *A Primer of Happenings & Time/Space Art* in 1965, the same year that Wolf Vostell and Jürgen Becker brought out *Happenings: Fluxus, Pop Art, Nouveau Réalisme: Eine Dokumentation*. Yet despite these associations, and despite the fact that themes of violence and sex were present in Fluxus performances, they were predominantly latent in the realization of most Fluxus practices. By the beginning of the 1970s, the ascetic restraint found in some of the work of George Brecht, La Monte Young, Alison Knowles and George Maciunas had shaped the Fluxus identity to such an extent that a clear separation existed between Fluxus and such artists as Lebel, Schneemann, and Hansen.[9] While Vostell's stridently political, erotic engagement in the creation /destruction dialectic often drew criticism, he maintained a position between the two extremes. None the less, the 'something' that characterizes Fluxus performance must include its concerns, no matter how restrained or sublimated, for gender, sex, race, danger and violence.

FLUXUS PERFORMANCE, A MODEL FOR SOCIAL PRAXIS

[...] In 1954 interpreting and expanding upon the existential aspect of Jackson Pollock's action painting, Georges Mathieu's performances demonstrated how the production of a calligraphic image in action painting provided a concrete, signifying enactment of individual character, emotion and thought.[10] Maciunas recognized how Mathieu's theory and practice connected the body as a producer of signs to the development of human character.[11]

Higgins shifted the location of concrete, 'basic images' from traditional, non-objective and abstract painting and sculpture to a new site 'between' (inter) media, where presentational forms might respond better to historical conditions. He thus seemed to acknowledge that formal shifts carry the primary signifying codes communicating content in art and, operating dialectically between media, intermedia might then synthesize the two concerns central to Modernism – its formal and social projects.[12] His charge that this social dimension of art had been lost in the criticism of 'merely puristic points' appeared just one year before Michael Fried's much debated article 'Art and Objecthood', in which Fried constructed a complex defence of formalism, denouncing 'situational' art as 'theatrical' or 'anti-art'.[13] While the very term *intermedia* is itself formalist, Higgins also pointed out how the cultural impact of mass media and advanced technology rendered formalism alone insufficient to respond to the changed conditions of everyday life. He exhorted artists to seek alternative forms in 'the intermedial approach':

'*Does it not stand to reason, therefore, that having discovered the intermedia (which was, perhaps, only possible through approaching them by formal, even abstract means), the central problem is now not only the new formal one of learning to use them, but the new and more social one of what to use them for?*'

Because of their use of the body as the primary signifying material of performance, artists after 1945 were able to integrate Modernist visual research on the representation of time, the movement of bodies through space, kinetic rhythms, process and change, with the urgent imperative for art to operate in real time and be connected to concrete social and political conditions necessitated by the Holocaust, the atomic bomb and the escalation of the Cold War, with their combined ontological threat of total annihilation.[14] Yves Klein, indebted to his friend Mathieu, realized this trajectory of concrete, non-objective art by collapsing his monochrome painting into the use of the human body as a 'living brush' in 1959 ... For it was not the technological power of 'rockets, Sputniks and missiles' Klein valued, but the 'affective atmosphere of the flesh itself ... [as a] powerful yet pacific force of ... sensitivity.[15]

Earlier, Mondrian had outlined this kind of an extension of art into the environment in his article 'Home-Street-City' (1926), which called for the artist's studio practice to extend out from domestic and work spaces into community practices.[16] Oskar Schlemmer's essay 'Stage' (1927) and his Bauhaus course on 'Man' identified everything in the human organism, from the blood and circulatory system to its position 'between earth and the stars', as proper materials for art: 'We shall observe the appearance of the human figure as an event and recognize that ... each gesture and each movement is drawn into the sphere of significance.'[17] Kaprow summarized the fifty years of modernist research that had anticipated Happenings in this way:

'*The pieces of paper curled up off the canvas, were removed from the surface to exist in their own, became more solid as they grew into other materials and reaching out into the room they filled it entirely. Suddenly, there were jungles, crowded streets, littered alleys, dream spaces ... people moving.*'[18]

Pioneers of performance such as Claes Oldenburg theorized the social import of direct enactment and emphasized the necessity for empathic connection:

'*I am for an art that is political-erotical-mystical, that does something other than sit on its arse in a museum ... for an art that embroils itself with the everyday crap and still comes out on top. I am for an art that imitates the human, that is comic, if necessary, or violent ... I am for the art of conversation between the sidewalk and a blind man's metal stick.*'[19]

Carolee Schneemann, on the other hand, identified the sensate needs of communal exchange:

'*I assume the senses crave sources of maximum information ... If a performance work is an extension of the formal-metaphorical activity possible within a painting or construction, the viewers' sorting of responses and interpretation of the forms of performance will still be equilibrated with all their visual experiences ... The body is in the eye.*'[20]

By introducing presentational means, the artist equally introduced bodily action as a component of aesthetics. But consideration of human action in the context of art also offered a revolutionary means by which artists might directly interact with, intervene in and resist what Higgins described as the 'dangerous forces at work in our world'. Such live art provided an effective means to work constructively for 'what we really care about and love or hate as the new subject matter in our work'. Thus, the aims of 'concrete' art to 'transform the world' as Hans Arp stated it, were empowered in performance by locating art in concrete human imagination, experience and body action in the lived world. In these extraordinary ways, artists' performance collapsed Modernist avant-garde aims into a remarkably unified theory, practice and praxis. But if Fluxus performance contributed to the restoration of a social and political discourse to art, as I believe it has, it was not through conventional activism or partisan rhetoric superficially identified as 'politics'. Fluxus performance – as all performance art – operates by infiltration and by offering alternative perspectives about the nature of identity, use, exchange and what Beuys described as 'ability value'.[21]

As discussed earlier in this essay, a deeply polarized debate formed in Fluxus around the question of whether performative actions should be aimed at direct cultural intervention and aggressive agitprop activities (as Maciunas, Flynt and Schmit argued in 1963) or, as Brecht later articulated in a 1979 interview, in accordance with long-term paradigm shifts.[22] Brecht's kind of view ultimately prevailed[23] and, with it, a notion of change that requires reform in ways of thinking – what Brecht described as the necessity for a new 'history of mind'.[24] Such a history would indicate complex, interrelated and uneven transitions of thought and points of exchange or anomalies where thinking alters ways of being and doing. As Brecht cautioned:

'*It's not always productive to consider things in terms of form. Some things have to be taken as individual members of a galaxy, or as points on a spiral, the form that's important is the form of the whole to which they contribute. This helps to clarify the way different artists work ... What we need today is a new synthesis of all the forces we're in touch with, no matter where they come from, a new synthesis that can be nourishing for all of us.*'[25]

Fluxus performance offers precisely this kind of a synthesis and, as such, might be considered a special kind of social praxis, a mode of action in the world that contributes to radical shifts currently occurring in epistemologies.

The word *praxis* derives from the Greek 'action' or 'doing' and refers to acts, courses of action, interaction or the exercise of practising an art, science or skill. Praxis also implies the therapeutic practice of a specific system or agency. It includes actions in public or political life, and acts aimed at the recovery of something. Nuanced meanings of the word suggest that praxis has the capacity to redress and rehabilitate: praxis is restorative. The distinction between poiesis (the making and production of things) and praxis (affective, rehabilitative action in the public sphere) has been inscribed historically both as language and as institutional practice. This inscription that divides works of art from social action persists in the way creative activity is valued against social doing. What is pertinent here is that Fluxus performances function both as individual works of art *and* as actions of the human body capable of demonstrating the multifarious modes in which consciousness constitutes its objects. Fluxus events collapse poiesis and praxis into a new historical paradigm that the term *intermedia* marks. The principal material of this praxis is the body and its site is the social world [...]

The spirit of Fluxus performance resides in its demonstration of how the body is the meaning-constructing agent of sentience and knowledge. It is the source for the manipulation of objects, social systems and institutions, as well as the invention, reinvention and interrogation of language.[26] Fluxus performances are about the action-structure of things and events as defined both by and through language and the body. Fluxus praxis consists of positing questions in the forum of these performances as they interrogate individual and social meanings and present the body as an object of subjectivity in direct association with other forms of subjectivity. Visual aesthetics traditionally have been restricted to representational codes alone – the conventions of poiesis that perpetuated the aesthetic distance claimed for works of art. Fluxus actions and events extend poiesis into praxis by linking corporeal and ontological significations to actual social and political situations.

When a body of statements, norms and coherent models coalesce in a social practice, Michel Foucault holds, then that body of knowledge functions as a 'threshold' of epistemology, the formation of which is 'neither regular nor homogeneous'.[27] Fluxus artists explored behavioural presentations, objects, enunciations, concepts and sets of choices as alternative means to contribute to knowledge and 'the rebuilding of foundations'. The kinds of actions they proposed, in their consistent challenge of social controls, have unobtrusively contributed to the exposure and dismantling of rigid, arbitrary and relative social formations and univocal morality.

Foucault argued that the ramblings of the 'mad' are paradoxically 'credited with strange powers of ... predicting the future, or revealing ... what the wise were unable to perceive'. Such ramblings are permitted free expression, if 'only in a symbolic sense, in the theatre' where such a figure may step 'forward, unarmed and reconciled, playing his role: that of masked truth'.[28] Fluxus performance, with its codex of meaning-producing enactments, archaeological territories and lessons in perception for the re-evaluation of changing social relations, provided that 'masked truth' that has 'predicted the future' and contributed to the current paradigm shift. Higgins' intermedia, as the space 'between' media, points equally to current researches in genetic engineering, the intersection of nature and machines in the cyborg-body, virtual realities and the endo- and nano-technology of the next century. Fluxus performance, in fact, represents a parallel cultural phenomenon, akin in its unprecedented implications for aesthetic social reform to the development of such new technologies, as well as to the transformations in world politics brought about by the end of the Cold War. Whether cultural, social, scientific or political, each implies radical changes in epistemological paradigms called for in the post-1945 period.

1 Henri Lefebvre, *The Production of Space* , trans. Donald Nicholson-Smith (Oxford and Cambridge, Massachusetts: Blackwell, 1991) 405.

2 *Ibid.*, 407.

3 Yoko Ono and John Lennon were concerned with these issues in their co-authored 'Woman is the Nigger of the World' (1972, recorded on the the albums *Sometimes in New York City* and *Shaved Fish*). Their lyrics acknowledged the repression of women and the psychological and social state of denigration shared by women and blacks.

4 Kubota in a telephone conversation with the author, 12 June 1991; and Yoko Ono, in Melody Summer, Kathleen Burch and Michael Summer (eds.), *The guests go in to supper: John Cage, Robert Ashley, Yoko Ono, Laurie Anderson, Charles Amirkhanain, Michael Pepe, K. Atchley* (Oakland and San Francisco: Burning Books, 1986) 174.

5 Elaine Scarry, *The Body in Pain: The Making and Unmaking of the World* (Oxford and New York: Oxford University Press, 1985) 117.

6 Historically consigned to the passive position of the mythic 'muse', the female in Western culture has served as the creative inspiration for man, stimulating his imagination and redirecting his sexual drive into productive channels that provided his salvation in the creation of music, poetry and visual art. The male Surrealists' obsession with the muse is legendary. Writing about the ways women artists of the Surrealist movement were utilized 'to make the whole psychosexual field of human experience available to the [male] artist', Whitney Chadwick has observed that 'the muse, an externalized source of creative energy and a personification of the female Other, is a particularly male invention'. Whitney Chadwick, *Women Artists and the Surrealist Movement* (New York: A New York Graphic Society Book; Boston: Little, Brown, 1985) 66.

7 In her *Interior Scroll* (1975) Carolee Schneemann made concrete the metaphorical connection between procreation and creation suggested in Kubota's *Vagina Painting*. See Carolee Schneemann, *More Than Meat Joy: Complete Performance Works and Selected Writings*, ed. Bruce McPherson (New Paltz, New York: Documentext, 1979) 234-39 [see in this volume pp. 250-51].

8 Robert Rauschenberg, 'An incentive to paint ... ', *Sixteen Americans* (New York: The Museum of Modern Art, 1959); reprinted in Dore Ashton (ed.), *Twentieth-Century Artists on Art* (New York: Pantheon Books, 1985) 234-39.

9 Schneemann's position *vis à vis* Fluxus, like that of Hansen, Lebel and others, is very complicated. Their exclusion from the context of Fluxus is, on the one hand, arbitrary and distorts the history of the period during which live, performative art developed. Schneemann, in conversation with the author, 9 July 1992, eloquently depicted this context: 'Fluxus is my group: we all came up together and we lived inside each other's pockets for fifteen years. We used to be very precious to each other in the early days.' Certainly such performances as her *Glass Environment for Sound and Motion* (1962) at the Living Theater, in which Dick Higgins, Philip Corner, La Monte Young and others participated, locate her development in the milieu of Fluxus. On the other hand, it is very clear that her work differed dramatically from the direction charted by Maciunas, and her report (in a letter to the author, 11 June 1992) that 'Maciunas sent an excommuncation directive in regard to my work? '65? 66?' is not surprising when one considers the unprecedented direction her art took with *Chromelodeon* (1963) and *Eye Body* (1963). (See Schneemann, *More Than Meat Joy, op. cit.*, 37-46, 52-53). Kubota and Ono were familiar with the radical way in which Schneemann used her body, and these actions, as well as her legendary *Meat Joy* (performed Paris, London and New York in 1964), charted a new direction that anticipated not only the so-called 1960s sexual revolution, but feminism and certainly Kubota and Ono's feminist performance directions.

Neat histories of art and the space limitations of exhibitions and publication often, and must gloss over these kinds of problematic, uneven fits, and this essay is no exception – with a few exceptions! However, it would be historically negligent and art historically false to pretend that while Schneemann, Hansen, Lebel and others may not have been close to the centre of Fluxus, their important incursions into and around its fluctuating core did not contribute greatly to making Fluxus what it is. As Lebel wrote in a letter to the author, 3 August 1991: 'I have heard about a "Spirit of Fluxus" show ... Is it the same old bureaucratic lie pretending that Orthodox Fluxus invented "IT" all (that Gutai or Happenings to Dada never occurred), that it was a purely "Amerika Uber Alles" movement (excluding Asia, Latin America and Europe)?'

10 See Georges Mathieu, 'Toward a New Convergence of Art, Thought and Science', *Art International*, 4: 2 (May 1960) 26-47. See also Georges Mathieu, *Au delà du Tachisme* (Paris: René Julliard, 1963).

11 Maciunas, whose unpublished notes reveal a great interest in Mathieu, was intrigued by the painter's theory that the calligraphic gesture signifies complex emotions and thoughts, and thus is a sign for individual character. See Maciunas' unpublished notes in the Gilbert and Lila Silverman Fluxus Collection.

12 Thomas Crow is particularly instructive on the double articulation of Modernism in his 'Modernism and Mass Culture in the Visual Arts', in ed. Benjamin H.D. Buchloh, Serge Gilbaut and David Solkin, *Modernism and Modernity: The Vancouver Conference Papers* (Halifax: Nova Scotia College of Art and Design, 1983) 257.

13 Michael Fried, 'Art and Objecthood', *Artforum*, 5: 10 (June 1967); reprinted in Gregory Battcock (ed.), *Minimal Art: A Critical Anthology* (New York: E.P. Dutton & Co., 1968) 116-47 [see in this volume p. 203]. Fried attacked any art that 'includes the beholder ... in a situation' and rejected all 'theatricality' as a denigration of art into 'the condition of theatre' (125). A passage paradoxically praising Anthony Caro's sculpture is important not only because it betrays the internal contradiction in Fried's argument, but also because it reveals his deep aversion to the *actual* body and his neo-Platonic insistence upon resemblance: objects must merely re-present the 'innumberable ways and moods [the body] makes meaning' rather than present that body as the concrete self-evidential material in which meaning constantly shifts. During the mid 1960s Donald Judd and Robert Morris' writings and objects clearly moved sculpture in the direction of 'intermedia'. See Judd's influential essay 'Specific Objects', in *Complete Writings 1959-1975* (Halifax: Nova Scotia College of Art and Design, 1975) 181; and Morris' five-part series 'Notes on Sculpture', which appeared in issues of *Artforum* between 1966 and 1968. The debt Morris' work owes to Fluxus has yet to be examined, in part because he suppressed his involvement with Fluxus (see his unpublished letter of 4 April 1964 to Hanns

Sohm, Archiv Sohm, Staatsgalerie, Stuttgart).

14 See Kristine Stiles, 'Survival Ethos and Destruction Art', *Discourse: Journal for Theoretical Studies in Media and Culture*, 14: 2 (Spring 1992) 74-102 [see in this volume pp. 227-29].

15 Yves Klein, 'Truth Becomes Reality', *Yves Klein 1928-1962: A Restrospective* (Houston: Institute for the Arts, Rice University; New York: The Arts Publisher, 1982) 230-31 [see in this volume pp. 195-96].

16 Piet Mondrian, 'Home Sweet City', 1926; reprinted in *Mondrian* (New York: Pace Gallery, 1970) 74-102.

17 Oskar Schlemmer, 'Bühne' [Stage] (originally delivered 16 March 1927 in Dessau, Germany), *Bauhaus Journal*, 3 (1972); excerpts reprinted in Hans M. Wingler, *The Bauhaus: Weimar, Dessau, Berlin, Chicago* (Cambridge, Massachusetts and London: MIT Press, 1984) 473-74.

18 Allan Kaprow, *Assemblage, Environments and Happenings* (New York: Harry N. Abrams, 1966) 165. It is important to note, as Kathy O'Dell reminded me, that Kaprow received his Master's degree in 1952 for a thesis written on Mondrian.

19 Claes Oldenburg, 'I am for an Art ... ' (1960), *Store Days* (New York: Something Else Press, 1967); reprinted in John Russell and Suzi Gablik, *Pop Art Redefined* (New York: Frederick A. Praeger, 1969) 97.

20 Carolee Schneemann, 'Diary Notes from The Notebooks 1958-1963', in Schneemann, *More Than Meat Joy*, *op. cit.*, 9, 13.

21 See a co-authored statement by Beuys and his former student Johannes Stuttgen that discusses 'ability value' in connection to the organization of political alternatives in Beuys' theory of 'Money as the Bloodstream of Society', which was physically demonstrated in his Documenta 6 installation *Honey Pump* (1977). See Caroline Tisdall, *Joseph Beuys* (New York: Solomon R. Guggenheim Museum, 1979) 254, 264.

22 Henry Martin, *Part One: Never change anything. Let changes fall in. Part Two, Never say never. A Conversation with George Brecht* (Milan: Exit Edizioni, 1979) 36-37.

23 A letter from Maciunas to Emmett Williams of 25 June 1963 (The Gilbert and Lila Silverman Fluxus Collection, Detroit), reveals how critical Maciunas felt Brecht's role was to the very identity of Fluxus. 'Bad news!', Maciunas wrote, 'George Brecht wants out of Fluxus, thinks Fluxus is getting too aggressive. So we will have to compromise, find a mid-point between Flynt, Paik and Brecht (if a mid-way can be found!). It would be very bad without Brecht. He is the best man in New York (I think).'

24 Jacques Attali, *Noise: The Political Economy of Music*, trans. Brian Massumi (Minneapolis: University of Minesota Press, 1985) 40.

25 *Ibid.*, 41, 46.

26 See Willougby Sharp, 'Body Works', *Avalanche*, 1 (Autumn 1970) 14-17 [see in this volume pp. 231-33].

27 Michel Foucault, *The Archaeology of Knowledge and The Discourse on Language*, trans. A.M. Sheridan Smith (New York: Harper Colophon, 1972) 186-87. Although Foucault speaks of a 'body of knowledge', it is important to note Lefebvre's critique (*The Production of Space*, *op. cit.*) that this formation identifies an epistemological space that has no reference to actual lived space and the experience of that space, whether in the body itself or its surrounding institutions and activities.

28 *Ibid.*, 217.

Kristine Stiles, 'Between Water and Stone - Fluxus Performance: A Metaphysics of Acts', *In the Spirit of Fluxus* (Minnesota: Walker Art Center, 1993) 64-99.

Jean-Jacques LEBEL Interview by Arnaud Labelle-Rojoux [1994]

Arnaud Labelle-Rojoux As far as your personal route is concerned, it seems to me essential to underline its literal poetic dimension, in the sense that it is about a total return to the dissociation of language by creation itself, since following Rimbaud language is no longer separable from lived experience. To be more precise, you have the expression 'direct poetry' rather than 'happening' to describe the action which you performed at the Paris Biennale ('The arts of language') in 1963, titled *Incidents*. Where does this formulation come from, and why use the word 'poetry'?

Jean-Jacques Lebel **I wanted to make a qualitative leap beyond simple readings of texts in public. I can't stand 'recitation' and literary readings. It was necessary to signal and signify this breaking away from the 'literary soirée' where the text – in some way dramatized – serves as a simple support for actors. Direct poetry, in my sense of it, made reference to Dada, by situating the action in a place which was nomadic, hybrid, undefined, detached from '*Lit et rature*'** [a pun in French, *lit* is both bed and read, *rature* is 'erased'], **which was the title of a Dada magazine.**

To my knowledge no-one had used the expression 'direct poetry' before I coined it after much reflection and deliberation. Naturally, like the word 'happening', like the word 'performance', like the word 'Dada', it can be understood in many different ways. Let us try to tease out a few. For me it was about, on the one hand, in the lineage of the theory and practice of [Antonin] Artaud, a theatre of magical operations, and on the other, in the context of the change introduced by John Cage (the abolition of borders between art and life, listening to the everyday), seizing language from its contexts and conventional supports. You mentioned [Arthur] Rimbaud. In fact it was he who announced the unfurling of the poem into life. The 'derangement of all the senses'. The actual life experience of which the writer 'writes'. All this, it seems to me, is contained in the expression 'direct poetry'. In opposition, quite simply, to 'indirect poetry', in other words poetry which is first written, then printed, then edited, then put in a bookshop. Thus filtered by and through the cultural industry. Direct poetry has a possibility for a 'direct' immediate relating between the reader/speaker or the writer, his or her text, his thought(s), his poetic experience and the hearer/listener/audience or the spectator. The poem is alive equally on the side of the poet and on the side of the audience. This is not all. I was in full visceral libertarian need: I had already made contact, through their texts, with those who were to become the Situationists and, through Benjamin Péret, with the group 'Socialism or Barbarism'. Benjamin had spoken to me with great fervour of what he had experienced at the time of the Durutti column during the Spanish revolution, in other words of the 'revolution from below'. It appeared to me that, in the manner of anarchist 'direct action', the poetic act should 'commit' itself impulsively, without restriction, without asking for permission from any ideological authority, without trying to please or to make propaganda for any cause or party whatsoever, to be outside of the circuits of the dominant culture, so that the poetic experience (I am referring to the Rimbaldian *illuminations*) may be able to generate a work, first it had to exist in a sort of no man's land, beyond the limits of literature and of art.

Labelle-Rojoux 'Direct poetry', out of mistrust for language and for words themselves?

Lebel **In Paris I was mixing with the poets of the Beat Generation – Allen Ginsberg, Gregory Corso, William Burroughs, Brion Gysin (this was in 1958, 1959, 1960). I was already putting together my Anthology of the Poetry of the Beat Generation (of which the postscript was to be titled 'The Mescaline Generation'). Dada and Artaud had exploded 'poetry'. Since that period the poetic state has been, more than anything else, constituted by psychic experiences of volcanic intensity, sometimes sublime, sometimes terrifying, which have blown language to bits [...]**

Acoustic poetry, phonetic poetry, elementary poetry, are, for me, indissociable from the idea of living poetry. This naturally includes Rimbaud as much as the Dadaists, Baudelaire or Henri Michaux. Just as everyday encounters cannot be separated. Encounters with François Dufrêne, or Gherasim Luca or Édouard Glissant – I also saw a lot of these people during the same period. I will not accept restricting myself to exclusive or one-dimensional relationships, to classical confinements, to chapels, to dogmas, in poetry, or in art, or in life. I like forms in poetry, in painting, in music, which are apparently – but only apparently – contradictory. I cannot stand group mentality, nor party patriotism. And even less fundamentalism. The work must remain 'open', and so must the vision or the method of approach. Whence Polyphonix, which – as Deleuze wrote to me – is a 'libertarian souk' [...] Direct poetry, as I understand it, does not operate necessarily on one level – in the framework of a festival – it can equally 'arise' in full reality, in daily life, directly in the social fabric. In the metro, for example (we did it) or in the street (we did that too) [...]

Labelle-Rojoux Why do you think the expression did not take on like the word 'Happening', which you preferred to use more frequently, but which covers, after all, broadly the same thing?

Lebel **Because of the word 'poetry'. Everyone thinks (wrongly) that they know what poetry is. As for the word 'Happening', people did not know, and still do not know what it means. Therefore it works. Because the enigma remains. As with 'Dada'. It is always better to invent or use new words. This is why, later on, I invented the term**

'Polyphonix' to name our nomadic poetry and performance festivals. There is not one meaning, but many meanings. It is not reducible to a single idea. In 1963, at the time of *Incidents* ... even though I was half American in my culture and in my heart, I still hesitated to use the word 'Happening'. Meanwhile, this covered the same kind of activities ... If the word 'Happening' has bloomed, it is because it is used contrary to its true meaning. As soon as there is trouble in the street, an altercation in parliament, a demonstration which is turning into a riot or an active strike which transforms itself into a party, journalists talk about a 'happening'. The government minister Edgar Faure said that May 1968 was a happening. And in fact he wasn't completely wrong. It is a word that is used in everyday language by journalists to signify 'indescribable chaos' or 'uncontrollable situation'. In short, magma in its wild state, or the poetic experience perceived as absurdity, 'madness' and irrationality.

Jean-Jacques Lebel, 'Jean-Jacques Lebel entretien par Arnaud Labelle-Rojoux', *Jean-Jacques Lebel, des happenings à Polyphonix* (Paris: Opus International, 1994); reprinted in *Hors limites: l'art et la vie 1952-1994* (Paris: Centre Georges Pompidou, 1994) 109-15. Translated by Elizabeth Manchester.

Kathy O'DELL

Displacing the Haptic: Performance Art, the Photographic Document, and the 1970s [1997]

[...] Very little photographic documentation of Futurist performances has survived. But cannot the same thing be said of performances produced in today's more highly technologized world? For what do all the photographs taken of any performance really add up to when one considers that each photograph reveals, depending on the camera's f/stop setting, only 1/15th, 1/30th, or even 1/60th of a second of the performed action? This question points to a fascinating, yet complicated problem at the heart of performance art. An epistemological problem, it is what I should like to discuss in this article: How can knowledge of a performed work of art be gained through a document which, due to the technological limitations of the apparatus producing it, so vastly delimits information? Even with the help of supplemental text, which typically accompanies the publication of performance photographs, viewers have to use their imaginations quite vigorously to get at what all might have taken place in and around the split second pictured. It could be said, then, that the history of performance art is one that flickers, one that causes the historian to shuttle back and forth between that which is seen and that which has to be imagined – between the visible and the invisible.[1]

But is this movement back and forth along a trajectory from the visible to the invisible all there is in the experience of performance documents? Or is there more than first meets the eye? To theorize an experience of the *invisible* is tempting, but doesn't adequately resolve the question, I think [...]

What I would like to explore here is an aspect of performance that wreaks a little havoc with the ocularcentrism of the art world, that interrupts the trajectory from the visible to the invisible. My argument is that the reception of performance art – which is to say, the reception of the photographic documents from which performance art is inseparable – is not exclusively dependent on visual experience, but relies heavily on the experience of touch. The proof of my argument lies in the original, material context of these photographic documents. And what I mean here are the actual, tangible publications that brought those performance documents to the attention of viewers who did not have the luxury of attending the live event.

Performance photographs, especially in the decade in which the art form was first named, were primarily circulated in art magazines, journals, or books and catalogues published by the artists themselves.

A few examples would include the photograph documenting Chris Burden's infamous *Shoot* piece, 1971, one of several photographs from the catalogue he published to document his work from 1971 to 1973.

Or a photograph of Carolee Schneemann's 1975 *Interior Scroll*, published in her 1979 book *More Than Meat Joy* – finally published by her, she has reported, because 'nobody else would touch it'.

Or Vito Acconci's 1970 *Trademarks*, published in the Autumn 1972 issue of *Avalanche* magazine.

Or a moment from Gina Pane's 1975 performance *Discours mou et mat*, published in *Studio International*'s special issue on performance, July–August 1976.[2]

Photographs such as these were not, at least initially, fabricated as art objects to be exhibited in galleries or museums where prohibitions on touching apply. Rather, they were meant to be handled as much as they were viewed. It is precisely the question of context, it should be noted, that establishes the difference between these photographs and, say, a modernist photograph framed as an art object. Even a photo-book by a modernist photographer, or by a Postmodernist using photography, comes across more as an art object destined solely for viewing than do the magazines, journals, catalogues, and books in which these photographs appeared. Indeed, these photographs solicited a response both visual *and* haptic.

But the haptic experience has been overlooked in the literature on performance art – displaced, I would argue, on to the visual realm. Later, I shall briefly speculate over reasons for this displacement in relation to the sociopolitical conditions of the 1970s when the art form was given its name. For now, I want to explore haptic experience of photographic documents from a very specific, yet prominent strain of 1970s performance – work that was masochistic in nature. And I want to do so with one more aspect of context in mind.

That the viewing and handling of these photographs would take place primarily in the home – the logical destination of an inexpensive publication that one might purchase – means that the viewer's experience was (and still is) necessarily contextualized as much by the domestic site as the art-world site. The graininess of most of these photographs (taken in dimly lit performance spaces) and the black-and-white film stock (a practical choice in terms of publication) enhance their snapshot quality, which furthers the link to the home by way of their similarity to entries in family photo-albums. Since the domestic site is the context in which the unconscious is originally forged, one's visual and haptic experience of a performance photograph – especially photographs that disturb a normative sense of domestic life or physiognomy, as these do – lends itself to a complicated review of the formation of one's own psychical identity, a review that is actually in progress, I believe, in the performances being documented [...]

1 Of course, my argument here is not unique to performance but applicable to other art forms dependent on photography, such as earth and site works. Thanks to Ann Reynolds for pointing this out to me. See her forthcoming book, *Robert Smithson: Learning from New Jersey and Elsewhere*, for discussion of this topic.

2 The text describing *Shoot*, which Burden printed on the page facing this photograph, reads as follows: '*Shoot*/F Space: November 19, 1971/At 7:45 p.m. I was shot in the left arm by a friend. The bullet was a copper jacket 22 long rifle. My friend was standing about 4.5-m [15-ft] from me.' See Chris Burden, *Chris Burden 71-73* (Los Angeles: Chris Burden, 1974).
The quote from Schneemann is from a conversation with the author, January 1996. *Interior Scroll* was first performed in 1975 at 'Women Here & Now' in East Hampton, Long Island. In the segment pictured, Schneemann extracted from her vaginal 'interior' a long 'scroll' from which she read a text dealing with her experience of being excluded by male structuralist filmmakers of the era who preferred to think of her in the more stereotypically feminine role as a dancer. For a full description of the piece, as well as the text she read from the scroll, see Carolee Schneemann, *More Than Meat Joy: Complete Performance Works and Selected Writings*, ed. Bruce McPherson (New Paltz, New York: Documentext, 1979) 234-39 [see in this volume pp. 250-51]. For more on Schneemann and exclusionary practices, see my article 'Fluxus Feminus', in *TDR (The Drama Review)* 41: 1 (Spring 1997) 43-60.
Trademarks appeared in *Avalanche*, 6 (Autumn 1972), which was a special issue devoted to the work of Vito Acconci.
Pane's *Discours mou et mat* was performed at de Appel, Amsterdam, 1975. See Antje von Graevenitz 'Then and Now: Performance Art in Holland', *Studio International* 192: 52 (July-August 1976)

Kathy O'Dell 'Displacing the Haptic: Performance Art, the Photographic Document and the 1970s', *Performance Research*, 2: 1 (1997) 73-81.

RITUALISTIC AND TRANSGRESSIVE BODIES

Many artists working with the body were aware of rituals and traditions from other cultures brought to attention by anthropological research. American critic Thomas McEvilley writes of the influence the ceremonial and shamanistic practices of other cultures on many artists. Sacrifice, ritual and social and bodily transgression are used as cathartic experiences for both the artist and audience. Viennese Actionist Otto Mühl described his work as 'self therapy made visible'; many artists use their performances as a way to heal social malaise. Violence, suffering and degradation are often employed in their actions. French critic François Pluchart suggests that the risks taken by artists in their performances change established ways of thinking about society, so affecting social norms.

Antonin ARTAUD
Theatre and Cruelty [1933]

[...] In the anguished, catastrophic times we live in, we feel an urgent need for theatre that is not overshadowed by events, but arouses deep echoes within us and predominates over our unsettled period.

Our long-standing habit of seeking diversions has made us forget the slightest idea of serious theatre which upsets all our preconceptions, inspiring us with fiery, magnetic imagery and finally reacting on us after the manner of unforgettable soul therapy.

Everything that acts is cruelty. Theatre must rebuild itself on a concept of this drastic action pushed to the limit.

Infused with the idea that the masses think with their senses first and foremost and that it is ridiculous to appeal primarily to our understanding as we do in everyday psychological theatre, the Theatre of Cruelty proposes to resort to mass theatre, thereby rediscovering a little of the poetry in the ferment of great, agitated crowds hurled against one another, sensations only too rare nowadays, when masses of holiday crowds throng the streets [...]

6. Heironymus Bosch

Practically speaking, we want to bring back the idea of total theatre, where theatre will recapture from cinema, music-hall, the circus and life itself, those things that always belonged to it. This division between analytical theatre and a world of movement seems stupid to us. One cannot separate body and mind, nor the senses from the intellect, particularly in a field where the unendingly repeated jading of our organs calls for sudden shocks to revive our understanding.

Thus on the one hand we have the magnitude and scale of a show aimed at the whole anatomy, and on the other an intensive mustering of objects, gestures and signs used in a new spirit. The reduced role given to understanding leads to drastic curtailment of the script, while the active role given to dark poetic feeling necessitates tangible signs. Words mean little to the mind; expanded areas and objects speak out. New imagery speaks, even if composed in words. But spatial, thundering images replete with sound also speak, if we become versed in arranging a sufficient interjection of spatial areas furnished with silence and stillness.

We expect to stage a show based on these principles, where these direct active means are wholly used. Therefore such a show, unafraid of exploring the limits of our nervous sensibility, uses rhythm, sound, words, resounding with song, whose nature and startling combinations are part of an unrevealed technique.

Moreover, to speak clearly, the imagery in some paintings by Grünewald or Hieronymus Bosch gives us a good enough idea of what a show can be, where things in outside nature appear as temptations just as they would in a saint's mind.

Theatre must rediscover its true meaning in this spectacle of a temptation, where life stands to lose everything and the mind to gain everything.

Besides we have put forward a programme which permits pure production methods discovered on the spot to be organized around historic or cosmic themes familiar to all.

And we insist that the first Theatre of Cruelty show will hinge on these mass concerns, more urgent and disturbing than any personal ones.

We must find out whether sufficient production means, financial or otherwise, can be found in Paris, before the cataclysm occurs, to allow such theatre (which must remain because it is the future) to come to life. Or whether real blood is needed right now to reveal this cruelty.

Antonin Artaud, 'Le théâtre de la cruauté', *14 Rue du Dragon*, 2 (1933); reprinted in English as 'Theatre and Cruelty', trans. Victor Corti, *Collected Works*, 4 (London: Calder & Boyars, 1974) 64-67.

Hermann NITSCH
The Blood Organ [1962]

Through my art production (Form of a live devotion) I take the apparently negative, the unsavoury, the perverse, the obscene, the lust and the victim hysteria resulting from them upon myself to save YOU the polluted, shameless descent into the extreme.

I am expression of the total creation. I have dissolved myself in it and identified myself with it. All agony and lust, mixed to a single state of intoxication, will penetrate me and therefore YOU.

Comedy will become a means of finding access to the deepest and holiest symbols through blasphemy and desecration. The blasphemous provocation is devotion. It is a matter of gaining an anthropologically determined view of existence, through which grail and phallus can be considered two qualified extremes. A philosophy of intoxication, of ecstasies, enchantments shows as result that the innermost of the living and intensely vital is the frenzied excitation, the orgy, which represents a constellation of existence where pleasure, pain, death and procreation are approached and permeated.

As consequence of this way of seeing, one must recognize the sacrifice (Abreaktion) as a matter of ecstasy, of inspiration for living. The sacrifice is another reversed form of lust, which develops in a changed state out of the hectic of the unconscious. Forces of the sexual alter and are transposed to the cruelty of the sacrificial process. I accept the absolute jubilation of existence, whose condition is the experience of the cross. Through completely experiencing and enjoying life to the full can the resurrection festival be obtained.

Hermann Nitsch, *Die Blutorgel*, published for the event of the same name in Perinet Cellar (Vienna: Hermann Nitsch, 1962); reprinted in English as 'The Blood Organ' in Hubert Klocker (ed.), *Viennese Actionism/Wiener Aktionismus 1960-1971*, trans. Keith Hartley, Camilla Neilson, Werner Robitsch (Klagenfurt: Ritter Verlag, 1989) 269.

Otto MÜHL

Materialaktion: Manifesto [1964]

material action is painting represented in action. self therapy made visible. using food stuffs. it works like a psychosis produced by mixing objects, human bodies and material. everything is planned. anything can be used and worked as material.

everything is used as substance.

paint is not a means to colour but is mush, liquid, dust. the egg is not an egg but a gooey substance.

material action exploits the associations which are connected with certain materials, whether deriving from their form, their everyday function or their significance.

actual occurrences are re-created and mixed with material. real events can be jumbled up together or mixed with nonreal, artificial events and then combined with any material. similarly time and place can be changed at will.

a symphony orchestra plays naked in a swimming pool which gradually fills up with jam. an opera performance is sprayed, showered and pelted with foodstuffs and paint. the singers have been instructed to hold out till the end. state visits, parades, marches and other everyday ceremonies can be mixed, transformed, interchanged. real events are re-created. car accidents, floods, conflagrations, scrambled together with other occurrences. combination and transformation follow the method of dreams.

this produces events with deeper meaning. jam, corpses, road-building machines.

events are transformed. material forces its way into reality and loses its everyday connotations, butter turns into pus, jam into blood, they become symbols for other events.

within the predefined possibilities, free association plays a major role. if the audience takes part, it is either accomplice or material.

the material action is structured like a gymnastics lesson in order to prevent instinctual outbursts.

The above text has been reproduced retaining the author's use of capitalization as in the original text.

Otto Mühl, 'Materialaktion: Manifesto' (1964), Peter Weibel and Valie Export (eds.), *wien: bildkempendium wiener aktionismus und film* (Frankfurt: Kohlkunstverlag, 1970) n.p.; reprinted in English in Kristine Stiles and Peter Selz (eds.), *Theories and Documents of Contemporary Art: A Sourcebook of Artists' Writings*, trans. A.C. Brown (Berkeley and London: University of California Press, 1996).

Rudolf SCHWARZKOGLER

Script for a Wedding [1965]

on a table laid in white there are the following objects:

a black mirror with herrings, a knife and scissors

glasses containing red, blue, yellow and white chemical substances

glasses containing blue paint

a yellow bath sponge

eggs

a chicken

a brain

two white-painted potted plants with pink flowers

a pink-painted electric cooking element

muslin bandages

yellow, red and blue films

adhesive tape

A tape-recorder playing Gregorian chants is switched on

S. wraps up a fish in a bandage and places it on to the black mirror

Blue paint is poured out of a glass on to the table

A fish is punctured with the knife and cut open with the scissors. Yellow crystals are poured into it

The chicken, which is covered with a white cloth, has blue paint poured over it.

A pear is cut open and its flesh is pierced by the knife.

An enema is used to bore a hole into a raw egg and to fill it with blue paint.

A flowerpot is broken with a hammer and the earth is knocked off the plant.

Two fish are cut open and filled with pink flowers, wrapped up in blue and red film respectively and nailed on to the wall.

Next to the laid table there is a fairly large wooden board on a footstool. A fish, wrapped up in a bandage and filled with crystals is placed on the board. Blue paint is poured over it from a glass.

A raw brain is placed on the board. Red and blue crystals are poured over it. The whole board is sprayed with blue paint using a paint spray.

White cloth is stretched over a window niche, a tall blue-painted lath is leaning against the wall next to it.

S. cuts into the white, stretched cloth with the scissors, the bride is standing behind it. Using an enema he pours blue paint over the cloth.

The piece of material that has been cut into is held open, the bride looks through the opening. S. puts a party blow-out into the bride's mouth, the bride blows it up.

S. puts a yellow bath sponge into the bride's mouth.

S. pulls the bride's head out and wraps transparent adhesive tape around the head just near the eyes. He tears a bigger opening in the material and pulls and lifts the bride out.

The bride has a bucket of white paint poured over her.

S. tears the top part of the bride's dress down.

A tall blue cylinder with a blue balloon is placed on one side of the bride, on the other side a transparent tube made of soft plastic is leant against the wall.

S. pours a bucket of blue paint over the bride.

S. sprays the chicken blue and hits out at her with it.

S.'s head is swathed in white muslin bandages by C.

S. pours blue paint from a bucket over C.

C. has a cardboard cylinder placed over his head.

The bride is tied up to C. who is standing on a platform playing an accordion. A firework is lit in the cylinder.

The above text has been reproduced retaining the author's use of capitalization as in the original text.

Rudolf Schwarzkogler, 'Script for a Wedding' (1965), transcription by Edith Adam in Hubert Klocker (ed.), *Von der Aktionsmalerei zum Aktionismus: Wien/From Action Painting to Actionism: Vienna 1960-1965*, trans. Keith Hartley, Camilla Neilson, Werner Robitsch (Klagenfurt: Ritter Verlag, 1988)

Günter BRUS

Artist's statement [1965]

I lie white in white in a white bedroom.
I lie white in white in a white toilet.
I sit white in white in a white police office among white policemen.
I make a white speech white in white in the white chamber of parliament among white members.
I preach in a white church white in white.
I dissever my left hand. Somewhere lies a foot. A suture on my wrist-joint bone. I press a drawing-pin into my spinal cord. I nail my large toe to my forefinger. Pubic, underarm and head hairs lie on a white plate. I slit open the aorta with a razor-blade (Smart). I slam a wire-tack into my ear. I split my head lengthwise into two halves. I insert barbed wire into my urethra and by turning it slightly try to cut the nerve (autosystoscopy). I bite open my pimple and suck on it. I have everything photographed and viewed.

Published on the occasion of the action and exhibition at the Junge Generation Gallery, Vienna, 1965

Günter Brus, 'Artist's statement' in *Le Marias, Sonderheft Günter Brus* (Vienna: Junge Generation Gallery, 1965); reprinted in English in Hubert Klocker (ed.), *Viennese Actionism/Wiener Aktionismus 1960-1971*, trans. Keith

Hartley, Camilla Neilson, Werner Robitsch (Klagenfurt: Ritter Verlag, 1989) 118.

Wolf VOSTELL

You: A Decollage Happening For Bob and Rhett Brown

[1964]

THE BASIC IDEA:
The public is brought face to face, in a satire, with the unreasonable demands of life in the form of chaos, and is confronted by the most absurd and repugnant scenes of horror to awaken consciousness. It is not important what I, Vostell, think; what the public itself takes away, as a result of my images and the Happening, is important.

SITUATION AND SITE:
A path, so narrow that only one person can pass at a time, winds towards a swimming pool. The ground underneath is covered with coloured advertisements from *Life* magazine. The path goes through a woods, along a tennis court, through a dark, stinking stable. Here is a hidden loudspeaker that greets each passer-by with 'YOU, YOU, YOU!'

Further on there is a glistening white swimming pool. In the deep end sparkles a pool of water in which stand several typewriters. All around the edge of the pool lie huge, clear plastic sacks filled with brilliant yellow, red, green and blue dye. There is a box of plastic toy water pistols nearby, full of the same bright-coloured dye. Three colour TV sets, each placed upon a white hospital bed, are showing three different baseball games, each with a different distortional pattern. The sound, however, is normal. In a large refrigerator a Beatles record is playing.

Lying on a trampoline, Lette Eisenhauer is enveloped in a transparent, flesh-toned garment upon which are painted the female parts. Two huge beef lungs beside her bounce. On the other side of the pool, a naked girl lies on a table, a vacuum cleaner tank on her body, motor running, embracing and fondling the machine.

Leaving the pool area, the people walk along a blue path at the edge of an orchard, and encounter obstacles of trees, shrubs, vines, etc. You see a large, empty field with bare fruit trees standing in black earth, on which flicker 500 mourning candles. Now you reach the tennis court, painted a bright yellow. At one end of the court stands a bicycle on which there is a playing black-and-white TV set. In the centre of the court is a circular enclosure measuring 21-m (70-ft) in diameter and covered over by a white parachute. Hidden on the yellow court are forty orange-coloured smoke bombs. Lying about on the ground are 181.5 kg [400 lb] of beef bones.

THE UNFOLDING OF THE EVENTS:
All the people crawl or walk along the path. In the swimming pool, a mountain of people is growing and becomes multicoloured from the dye pouring from the burst plastic sacks, human beings, gallons of blue, red and yellow colour, bones, all in a jumble. Some of the people tie bones on their bodies. Lette Eisenhauer bounces on the trampoline beside the beef lungs and becomes blood-smeared.

Down in the dyed water, Tomas Schmidt writes on the typewriter 'YOU, YOU, YOU, YOU ... '

The Beatles record plays in the closed refrigerator. The TV sets are on. Twenty to thirty people snake their way on their stomachs to the tennis court. In the field flicker the white mourning candles.

All the crawling people lie about on the yellow tennis court. All the walking people stand within the circular enclosure and sprinkle yellow paint on the supine bodies. The TV sitting on the bicycle bursts into flame. The people put on gas masks and watch a three-minute programme on the burning set. The TV explodes.

The white parachute floats down upon the people as the whole area fills with orange smoke from the bombs. Everyone within the enclosure receives an envelope. The people are now free to find their way out of the enclosure. They go through the woods back to the buses which will return them to New York City.

INSTRUCTIONS TO THE PEOPLE:
Please find your way to the swimming pool, either crawling or walking.

At the pool, take a pistol filled with colour.

Please crawl into the swimming pool.

Lie down on the bottom of the pool and build a mass grave. While lying there, decide whether or not you will shoot the other people with the colour.

Allow yourself to be tied to the beds where the TVs are playing.

Free yourself.

Crawl or walk down the blue path to the yellow tennis court. Say hello to Bob Brown and ask him for a little bag of yellow colour. Sprinkle the colour on the blue people who are lying on the yellow tennis court.

Open the envelope and read the card inside while the parachute is falling.

Put on a gas mask when the TV burns and try to be as friendly as possible to everyone.

Performed at a swimming pool, orchard and tennis court at King's Point, New York, 19 April 1964.

Wolf Vostell, 'You: A Decollage Happening for Bob and Rhett Brown', in Allan Kaprow, *Assemblages, Environments, Happenings*, trans. Dorothy Schulz (New York: Harry N. Abrams, 1966) 257-58.

François PLUCHART

Body Art [1974]

What it is: the body is the fundamental ground. Pleasure, suffering, illness and death inscribe themselves on it and shape the socialized individual in the course of its biological evolution. In other words, they put it in readiness – hand it formal notice, as we say – to satisfy all the demands and constraints of existing forces. No one can escape this oppression imposed by all on all which decides the morphological course and the formal statement of the condition of the body, which is always ready to be invested with new ideologies, the impregnation of which is so much the deeper the more one wants to escape, resist and control them. On this formal statement of the condition of the individual body, socialized however, depends in return the attitude of the group face to face with all social phenomena, such as strikes, revolutions, wars and the raising of social minority questions, etc.

It is here that painting comes in, or what remains of it since the decisive re-examination by Kasimir Malevich, Marcel Duchamp and most of the Constructivists and Dadaists, and all those who have given up aesthetics as a prerequisite for a work of art. It is here, above the rejects from the prostitutional overvaluing of beauty, that the urgency of body expressiveness appears.

First of all an intellectual provocation but no less an anti-bourgeois contestation, action such as performed by Johannes Baader (preached in November 1918 in the Cathedral of Berlin in order to announce the salvation of the world by Dada) and Marcel Duchamp (*Tonsure in the form of a shooting star*, in 1919) have done more than simply engender what later became the Happening and behavioural art: it opened a breach in the cracked wall of aesthetics and cast away the robes of static beauty. Whatever had been the reactionary will which attempted to refute this finally sociological conception of art, artists such as Piero Manzoni, Kaufner and certain organizers of Happenings have ineluctably removed the former servitude from painting in order to transform it into an instrument of social action and a weapon. From one mistake to another, from one compromise to another, artists have discovered and felt, almost biologically, the impasse of a search which was taking place inside art. Dissidents of Happenings such as Hermann Nitsch and Rudolf Schwarzkogler, and deniers of framework and colour such as Klaus Rinke and Bruce Nauman have assumed the stages which, sometimes violently, sometimes prudently, led to body art such as was able to be foreshadowed and taken up by Michel Journiac and Dennis Oppenheim and in an even more intense manner by Vito Acconci, Gina Pane and Chris Burden, who defined, action by action, the field of an activity where only the power of a speech which disturbs, corrodes and reveals is fundamental.

What it is not: Body Art is not the sewage of the great pictorial abortions of the twentieth century. It is not a new artistic recipe meant to be recorded tranquilly in a history of art which is bankrupt. It is exclusive, arrogant and intransigent. It has no relation whatever with any supposed artistic form unless the latter has first declared itself as sociological and critical. It upsets, rejects and denies the old inherent aesthetic and moral values contained in, or assumed to be belonging to artistic practice, since the power of speech should replace here all other prerequisites of art. Thus for the first time in Western history, an attitude of thought does not want to be an open trend, but on the contrary, to be one which is closed by its own choice, like a community whose only *raison d'être* is to welcome novices who will sing in their turn the coming of a new man building a new society, at last free and harmonious, and rid of false ethics, all dictators of whatever type, repressive ideologies and censors, in other words, cops.

François Pluchart, *L'Art Corporel* (1974) (Paris: Éditions Galerie Stadler, 1975) 4-5.

Peter WEIBEL
Artist's statement [1978]

[...] If an artist beats himself, this does not mean that a sadistic audience is watching a masochistic artist. The problem has to be seen on another level, one on which they are both exposed to the beating. Because the exposed artist can be a substitute for the audience or even for the whole of mankind. The personal exposure to danger in an art context has a semiotic/symbolic quality in the flux of the art process, that goes beyond sadomasochism.

Once you have in mind these two aspects, then you can differentiate other aspects. Is it the crude and unique purpose of an artwork to demonstrate the phenomenon of danger (as in the case of boxing, drinking water to exhaustion, etc.) or is the danger element only part of a greater art context (as in the case of a Günter Brus action)? I prefer to see both in my work and in the work of others the danger element in a larger civilizing context, that is, the artwork embedded in a danger situation which reflects more than the simple demonstration of how to overcome danger or of how long the artist can suffer pain.

Finally, danger in an artist's work can be of a physical, mental/psychic or social nature. The best and most natural way is to combine all three of them. Since the exposure to physical danger alone, without tying it to the cultural context, seems to be pure craftsmanship, not art. Danger is not the purpose in itself. Through the exposure to danger something will be expressed. For example all good art is by its very nature dangerous for society, it is a challenge to conveniences, old *ententes*, old ways of thinking and feeling. To reinforce this aspect of art, danger can be used. The artist exposes himself to danger in order to produce an art work with a danger element, that is, to strengthen the provocation of art, to liberate the consciousness of people.

Danger is also an existential element, and element of life. An artist, who does not want his art to shrink to pure entertainment, an artist who believes in the social function of art in general as well as of single artworks, will use danger sometimes. Danger is not a thrill, but a despair, an energy, a hope, a warning, an insistence – a human quality.

Peter Weibel, 'Artist's statement', *Flash Art* (February-April 1978) 48.

François PLUCHART
Risk as the Practice of Thought [1978]

The staging of risk, of suffering and of death cannot be dissociated from the history of Western art. It even constitutes a sort of archetype, inasmuch as any creation tends to be a metaphysics, or, at least, a transcendence of the hard existential reality. However, beginning with the industrial revolution, in the nineteenth century, let's say since Gustave Courbet, the artist tends to get more and more deeply committed within social struggle and to gamble his safety against his ideas. The movement precipitates during the twentieth century, first with the non-aligned ones from Stalinist orthodoxy, then in relationship to revolutionary or dictatorial situation. This experience of risk, though, is just the most outward aspect – and certainly not the best – of the artist's responsibility, of the danger of being an artist (to play a role in the course of thought). The more or less deeply acquired experience of folly and of disorder of the senses (Arthur Rimbaud, Vincent Van Gogh, Antonin Artaud, etc.), which touches certain mythical temptations, clearly underlines the price an artist must often pay in order to steal an assent and to bend enslaving ideologies.

Generally, risk remains theoretical, a kind of by-product of the masochism inherent in every creative act, and actually one had to wait for the end of the 1960s and the beginning of the 1970s to see the artists endanger their bodies and inflict on themselves a violent physical suffering in order to produce thought.

Except for a few Dadaist provocations, particularly those of Johannes Baader and Arthur Cravan, the first artists who exposed their bodies to public filth and aggressiveness were four Viennese: Hermann Nitsch, Otto Mühl, Günter Brus and Rudolf Schwarzkogler; Mühl with his political actions, Nitsch with ritual ones, Schwarzkogler with sexual disalienation, and, even more so, Brus, with actions which involve defecation and the swallowing of urine. Bodily risk is present as well in some Joseph Beuys actions having a desecrating nature. In all these cases, the aim is to denounce determinisms, taboos, obstacles to freedom and to the individual's expression, whether the latter belongs to social, or family, or other structures.

The artistic use of risk quickly defined itself through the first important statements of Body Art, particularly those by Dennis Oppenheim, Vito Acconci, Michel Journiac, Gina Pane and Chris Burden.

Beginning in 1970, Dennis Oppenheim, in a work called *Parallel Stress*, put his body in danger by hanging in the void from a collapsed concrete casting between the Brooklyn Bridge and Manhattan. And again in 1971, with *Rocked Circle-Fear* and *Reading Position for Second Degree Burn*. In the first of the two, Oppenheim was standing still inside a 152.5-cm (5-ft) diameter circle, a TV camera fastened to his head. A person above him was throwing stones inside the circle while a movie camera was shooting the falling stones. This action had to be interrupted before the artist expected.

In the second, which lasted five hours, Oppenheim in a sense painted his body red by means of sunburn, with the exception of his chest, protected by an open book. Although Oppenheim soon dropped dangerous actions, pain often plays a role in his work: in 1969, in *Arm and Wire*, in which he ran his arm over an electric wire and used a string to mark the trace left on his skin; and in 1970, in *Interchange Material*, in which he ripped off a fingernail and stuck a wood splinter into his finger. The second American artist who used pain as a creative element is Vito Acconci, a poet who, beginning in 1969, progressively abandoned the space of the written page for a place in which the body was assigned the task of going beyond the poetic function. Acconci's body actions at first tried to define the artist's body as a place where he could intervene and create an event by measuring at the same time different types of feelings, such as a pain caused by a burn or a bite, the variations of the biological rhythm during an intellectual or physical effort, his resistance against physical or psychic fatigue, etc. (See *See Through*, 1969; *Rubbing Piece, Trademarks, Hand and Mouth*, 1970). This period was somehow that of his language formation. In a second moment, he started to modify his own body, as in *Conversions*, an action of which he gave two versions with a one-year interval (1970 and 1971) and in which he experienced the possibility to go from the masculine to the feminine, by burning the hair on his chest, by pulling his nipples in the attempt to reach a feminine appearance, by hiding his penis between his thighs and training his body to perform, in this new position, a great number of familiar actions, such as walking, dancing, jumping, sitting down etc., and finally making his penis disappear into the mouth of a young woman kneeling behind him. This work marks an evolution towards the projection of the individual body on another and above all the awareness of the transformation of that individual body through its insertion in society. Starting from this moment and in opposition to what happened in his earlier actions, he tends to elude the spectators' eyes by imposing his presence only through his voice, his body's movements, the inner throb of his biology. As in *Trapping* (1971), where he converses with his penis covered with a white cloth; in *Seedbed*, of the same year, where he masturbates until exhaustion while the audience is walking above him; as in *Anchors* (1972), where he dreams he has a sister.

For Acconci, whose main preoccupation is the body's physical space, the body action tends to modify the individual physically and psychically, as well as to transform it thanks to the practice of a mental tension. The action ends at the ultimate stage of exhaustion, at the approaching of death, which, if it actually came, would be for the artist a kind of setback, a final change which would brutally interrupt a process of potential change, of physical endurance and of self-surmounting. Like many artists of this tendency, Acconci subsequently moved towards more plastic actions, in which he has reintroduced language.

The third American in the most exasperated art trend is Chris Burden. Beyond the violence of their themes, many of his actions constitute a physical provocation as well, in particular *Five Day Locker Piece* (26 to 30 April 1971), a work for which the artist was closed in a locker for five days; *Shoot Piece* of the same year, in which a sharp-shooter at a distance of five steps hit him in the arm with a twenty-two calibre rifle bullet; *Deadman* (1972), in which he placed himself under a tarpaulin at 8 pm, on La Cienega Boulevard in Los Angeles, near a car marked by two danger fire signals of fifteen-minute duration. *Through the Night*

DANGER
IS NOT A THRILL BUT A
DESPAIR
AN ENERGY
A HOPE
A WARNING
AN INSISTENCE – A HUMAN QUALITY

Peter WEIBEL, Artist's statement, 1978

Softly (1973), in which, his hands behind his back, he crawled on broken glass for 14 m [15 yd]. Missed by a sharpshooter, or stopped by the police at the very moment the flares were going out and nothing could have protected him from a real accident, Chris Burden has taken art to the verge of suicide.

In Europe, Michel Journiac has played a determinant role in the definition of a mode of art expression in which thinking, in its most acute sense, takes risks as far as the individual's very existence is concerned. After he defined in a book of poems *le Sang nu* (*Naked blood*, 1968), and an exhibition, the body in its double aspect of flesh and sex, he took to revealing the implications of his political awareness. Many of his events have subsequently aimed at specifying this scandalous definition of the body, an entity despised, derided, disowned by all political or religious forms of government.

Each Journiac certainly, followed or made explicit by an event, is a trap in which he shuts himself up in order to find his own values for liberation. Starting with social travesty and that sexual coadjutant that is attire, he defined at successive times the existence of the body through the faculties of change, offering and desire, its physical and biological components, its being available to mutilations, to being destroyed, to feed a gluttonous society. For Journiac the body can be approached only through rituals. Some of the rituals he created or of which he has diverted the meaning have had a great impact on the evolution of contemporary thinking. It is especially the case of *Messe pour un corps* (*Mass for a body*, 1969), an event in which he stated his solitude by offering a pudding made with his own blood; *Contrat pour une exécution capitale* (*Contract for an execution*, 1971), which is an accusation thrown at the obsolete partisans of capital punishment; and *Piège pour un travesti* (*Trap for a travestite*, 1972), which showed the passing from masculine to feminine mediated by clothing. Whether they are at the deepest level of being, or more immediately physical (for instance: drawing blood in view of making the human blood pudding, from 1969, or cigarette burns in *Rituel pour un mort* [*Ritual for a dead man*] of 1976), pain and risk are present in all Journiac's works, and it is precisely through them that today's art can try to carry out a cathartic action.

After having shown that the body is the most stubborn taboo, that it is manipulated, mutilated by all ideologies, and that body censorship is first of all the denial of the individual, Journiac asserted that the indictment of a castrating and degrading system was of extreme urgency, as well as the only ineluctable duty of the creator, who, at any price, must say no to the restriction of the being. There is no doubt that this attitude permanently puts the artist in a situation of danger: as regards his own balance, but even more so as regards his social insertion. By the doors closing on him, Journiac pays for this provocation day after day.

Deeply present in Journiac's work, risk is inherent in Gina Pane's events, since the very first *Projets de silence* (*Projects of silence*) of 1970, and especially after *Escalade sanglante* (*Bleeding Climb*), a studio work of 1971, for which the artist climbed, with bare feet and hands, a ladder-object with cutting edges. This was followed by actions in which danger played an ever more important role, like: *Sang, lait chaud* (*Blood, hot milk*, 1972), *Transfert* (*Transfer*, 1973), *Psyché* (*Psyche*, 1974) and *Le cas n. 2 sur le ring* (*Case no. 2 in the ring*, 1976).

Every body action by Gina Pane aims at emphasizing, to denounce them and to correct them, certain determinisms according to which each day is identical to the preceding one, and which contribute to throwing man towards a fate of self-mutilation and destruction. In order to restrain this fall, Gina Pane does not take shelter in the abstraction of great philosophical chimeras, but, on the contrary, she takes life in its most daily aspect, that of the banal fact through which great mutations take place, precisely because its anodyne habitual character conceals all the pernicious and determinant sides it carries. To be able to reach a state of discomfort Gina Pane disarranges certain familiar mechanisms, like swallowing half a pound of rotten minced meat while watching TV news in an intentionally uncomfortable position; alternately wounding herself with a razor blade and playing with a tennis ball; gargling endlessly with milk until blood mixes with the spilt liquid; crushing glass with her mouth, or breaking a sheet of glass with her body. The meaning of the body act is channelled by the effects of the perturbing phenomena she creates when doing violence to herself. The wounds, burnings, lacerations of blood vessels and biological disorder the artist inflicts on herself reveal and generate on the rebound in the spectator's mind a state of discomfort that allows him to apprehend a certain behaviour whose cause is at the same time revealed to him. Gina Pane ill-treats herself in order to make one feel that violence is a daily fact, a way of denying both man and life, just as it is proved by torture, war, road accidents or deportation because of one's beliefs, etc. On another level, she swallows rotten meat, laps milk like a dog, licks splinters of glass mixed with mint and milk to show the role played by our nutritional and therefore affective impulsions. During the whole action Gina Pane does not give the spectator a break. By her suffering, her risking, she disrupts his indifference and hostility, she channels his repulsion, making him aware of what they carry. Here, the body is projected as the conscience of the self. It is pure thought, an intellectual and sensitive analysis. Put in the right condition by several months of theoretical preparation (notes, sketches, reading and daily practice of existence), as well as by a physical preparation (swallowing rotten minced meat, prolonged standing over lit candles, physical tension, etc.), the body, having become a thinking and suffering matter, transforms itself in a coadjutant of thought.

Self-imposed pain by artists like Acconci, Burden or Pane has produced a strong echo in several Western artists such as Jan Mlcoch, Petr Stembera and Marina Abramović and Ulay. Petr Stembera, in 1972, started his first actions on physical endurance, like progressively increasing the number of days without eating, drinking or sleeping; studying his muscular resistance by contracting his neck and face muscles; or grafting a rose on his arm, an operation which gave him an infection.

On the other hand, Jan Mlcoch's actions are generally of a symbolic character. However, pain and risk are often present in his work, when, in 1974, he pricked his whole body with a needle so that the sun's rays could penetrate it better; or when, in the same period, he hung from a steel beam, his wrists and ankles tied with a rope.

Marina Abramović and Ulay since 1975 have engaged in a series of actions, in which pain and risk are largely present, as, for example, in a performance presented in Venice in July 1976. In an empty room, two naked bodies clashed frontally full speed and over and over again. In another action, they are back to back attached by their hair.

We could mention many other works, by Barry Le Va, or Mike Parr, by Terry Fox, Ben Vautier or Pinoncelli, which represent danger for the artist, like when Barry Le Va ran over the same straight line for one hour and 43 minutes, in *Velocity Piece* of 1969; when Ben Vautier hit his head against a wall (1970), as well as in several actions where he exposed himself to the audience's aggressiveness and reactions, just as Beuys did many times since 1963; when Pinoncelli, armed with a water pistol, shot red paint at André Malraux during an official party; when he set fire to his own clothes during a street action, or was thrown into the water in the port of Nice, closed in a bag, tied and ballasted (*Hommage à Monte-Cristo* [*Homage to Monte-Cristo*], 1974); or when, shortly afterwards, he attacked a bank, armed with a sawn-off rifle loaded with blanks.

Risk of infection, of poisoning, of a bad wound, of a heart attack, of psychic disorder or of death, but also constant provocation of the social structures which react with rejection, such are some of the main risks run by artists since 1969.

One might question the meaning of such practice and wonder whether the game is worth it. A number of authors, like Georges Bataille in his search for the sacred, and Antonin Artaud in his desperate attempt to give back the theatre its primary cathartic function, show us the way. Depth psychology, psychoanalysis and especially the work by Paul Schilder, give us a better insight. In fact, Paul Schindler, in *The Image of the Body* published in 1935 in London, wrote:

'*Moral laws cannot be applied to human beings but through their bodies. So that moral phenomena are also tightly associated with the images of the body. To say that one never suffers alone is not a simple cliché. The laws of identification and of communication between images of the body make one's suffering and pain everybody's affair.*'

Schindler defines his thought by adding:

'*The fact that the image of the other's body is kept, constructed, elaborated, is the sign, the signal, the symbol of the value of personality. Thus, psychology of the image of the body could lead to an ethical and moral system. Pain, joy, destruction, mutilation, death concern all those who approach them, but there is a magic link which unites the closer to the more distant, and which, therefore extends up to the animal, the plant and inanimate nature.*'

It is at this level of thought that one must find an answer to so much suffering, violence, risk.

François Pluchart, 'Risk as the Practice of Thought', *Flash Art*, 80-81 (February-April 1978) 39-40.

Thomas McEVILLEY

Art in the Dark [1983]

The development of the conceptual and performance genres changed the rules of art till it became virtually unrecognizable to those who had thought that it was theirs. The art activity flowed into the darkness beyond its traditional boundaries and explored areas that were previously as unmapped and mysterious as the other side of the moon. In recent years a tendency has been under way to close the book on those investigations, to contract again around the commodifiable aesthetic object and to forget the sometimes frightening visions of the other side. Yet if one opens the book – and it will not go away – the strange record is still there, like the fragmentary journals of explorers in new lands, filled with apparently unanswerable questions.

When Piero Manzoni, in 1959, canned his shit and put it on sale, in an art gallery, for its weight in gold; when Chris Burden had himself shot in the arm and crucified to the roof of a Volkswagen (in 1971 and 1974, respectively); when two American performance artists, in separate events, fucked human female corpses – how did such activities come to be called art? In fact the case at hand is not unique. Similar movements have occurred occasionally in cultural history when the necessary conditions were in place. Perhaps the most striking parallel is the development, in the Cynic school of Greek philosophy, of a style of 'performance philosophy' that parallels the gestures of performance art in many respects.[1] If this material is approached with sympathy and with a broad enough cultural perspective it will reveal its inner seriousness and meaning.

One of the necessary conditions for activities of this type is the willingness to manipulate linguistic categories at will. This willingness arises from a nominalist view of language which holds that words lack fixed ontological essences that are their meanings; meanings, rather, are seen to be created by convention alone, arbitrary, and hence manipulable. Ferdinand de Saussure pointed towards this with his perception of the arbitrariness of the link between signifier and signified. Even more, Ludwig Wittgenstein, by dissolving fixed meaning into the free-for-all of usage, demonstrated a culture's ability to alter its language games by rotations and reshapings of the semantic field. By manipulating semantic categories, by dissolving their boundaries selectively and allowing the contents of one to flow into another, shifts in cultural focus can be forced through language's control of affection and attitude. In the extreme instance, a certain category can be declared universal, coextensive with experience, its boundaries being utterly dissolved until its content melts into awareness itself. This universalization of a single category has at different times taken place in the areas of religion, philosophy and, in our time, art.

A second necessary condition is a culture that is hurtling through shifts in awareness so rapidly that, like the tragic hero in Sophocles just before the fall, it becomes giddy with prospects of new accomplishments hardly describable in known terms. At such moments the boundaries of things seem outworn; the contents flow into and around one another dizzyingly. In a realm that, like art some twenty-five years ago, feels its inherited boundaries to be antiquated and ineffective, a sudden overflow in all directions can occur.

The tool by which this universalization of the art category was effected is a form of appropriation. In the last few years appropriation has been practised with certain limits; the category as a whole is left intact, though inner divisions such as those between stylistic periods are breached. The model of Francis Picabia is relevant here. But twenty-five years ago appropriation worked on the more universalizing model of Duchamp. In this case, the artist turns an eye upon pre-existing entities with apparent destinies outside the art context, and, by that turning of the eye, appropriates them into the art realm, making them the property of art. This involves a presupposition that art is not a set of objects, but an attitude towards objects, or a cognitive stance (as Oscar Wilde suggested, not a thing, but a way). If one were to adopt such a stance to all of life, foregrounding the value of attention rather than issues of personal gain and loss, one would presumably have rendered life a seamlessly appreciative experience. Art then functions like a kind of universal awareness practice, not unlike the mindfulness of southern Buddhism or the 'Attention!' of Zen. Clearly there is a residue of Romantic pantheistic mysticism here, with a hidden ethical request. But there is also a purely linguistic dimension to the procedure, bound up with the nominalist attitude. If words (such as 'art') lack rigid essences, if they are, rather, empty variables that can be converted to different uses, then usage is the only ground of meaning in language. To be this or that is simply to be called this or that. To be art is to be called art, by the people who supposedly are in charge of the word – artists, critics, curators, art historians and so on. There is no appeal from the foundation of usage, no higher court on the issue. If something (anything) is presented as art by an artist and contextualized as art within the system, then it *is* art, and there is nothing anybody can do about it.[2]

Conversely, the defenders of the traditional boundaries of the realm will be forced to reify language. They will continue to insist that certain things are, by essence, art, and certain other things are, by essence, not art. But in an intellectual milieu dominated by linguistic philosophy and structural linguistics, the procedure of appropriation by designation, based on the authority of usage and the willingness to manipulate it, has for a while been rather widely accepted. During this time the artist has had a new option: to choose to manipulate language and context, which in turn manipulate mental focus by rearrangement of the category network within which our experience is organized.

The process of universalizing the art context goes back at least as far as Marcel Duchamp's showings of Readymades. Dada and Surrealism, of course, had their input. But the tendency came to maturity in the middle to late 1950s, when Alain Robbe-Grillet, for example, insisted that if art is going to be anything it has to be everything.[3] At about the same time Yves Klein, extending the tradition of French dandyism, said, 'Life, Life itself ... is the absolute art.'[4] Similarly, in America, Allan Kaprow suggested that 'the line between art and life should be kept as fluid, and perhaps as indistinct, as possible'.[5] Duchamp had appropriated by signature, as Klein did when, in about 1947, he signed the sky. Later Klein would designate anything as art by painting it with his patented International Klein Blue. Piero Manzoni sometimes designated pre-existing objects as art by signing them, and at other times by placing them on a sculpture base. In 1967 Dennis Oppenheim produced his 'Sitemarkers', ceremonial stakes used to mark off areas of the world as art.

These procedures were sometimes employed in conscious parody of the theological concept of creation by the word. In 1960 Klein, imitating divine fiat, appropriated the entire universe into his Theatre of the Void, as his piece for the Festival d'Art d'Avant-garde in Paris. In the next year he painted a topographical globe International Klein Blue, thereby appropriating the earth into his portfolio; soon Manzoni, responding, placed the earth upon his Sculpture Base (*Socle du Monde*, 1961), wresting it from Klein's portfolio into his own. Any action that takes place in the appropriation zone is necessarily real as itself – yet semantically a kind of shadow-real. In so far as the act's prior category is remembered, it remains what it was, just as a loan-word may retain a trace of its prior meaning – only it is reflected, as it were, into a new semantic category. Thus the process of universal appropriation has certain internal or logical limits; it is based on the assumption that a part can contain the whole, that art, for example, can contain life. But the only way that a part can contain its whole is by reflection, as a mirror may reflect a whole room, or by implication, as a map of a city implies the surrounding nation. The appropriation process, in other words, may rearrange the entire universe at the level of a shadow or reflection, and this is its great power. At the same time, as with the gems strung together in the Net of Indra, only the shadowy life of a reflection is really at issue, and this is its great limit.[6]

The infinite regress implicit in such a procedure was illustrated when, in 1962, Ben Vautier signed Klein's death and, in 1963, Manzoni's, thereby appropriating both those appropriators of the universe. The idea of signing a human being or a human life was in fact the central issue. In 1961 Manzoni exhibited a nude model on his sculpture base and signed her as his work. Later he issued his 'Certificates of Authenticity', which declared that the owner, having been signed by Manzoni, was now permanently an artwork. But it was Klein who most clearly defined the central issue, saying, 'The painter only has to create one masterpiece, himself, constantly.' The idea that the artist *is* the work became a basic theme of the period in question. Ben acted it out, not long after the signing of Klein's death, by exhibiting himself as a living, moving sculpture. Soon Gilbert & George did the same thing. As early as 1959 James Lee Byars had exhibited himself, seated alone in the centre of an otherwise empty room. Such gestures are fraught with strange interplays of artistic and religious forms, as the pedestal has always been a variant of the altar.

It was in part the Abstract Expressionist emphasis on the direct expression of the artist's unique personality that prepared the way for the claim that the artist's person was in fact the art. Through the survival in the art realm of the Romantic idea of the specially inspired individual, it was possible, though in a sort of bracketed parody, to confer on an artist the status of a royal or sacred being who is on exhibit to other humans.

The underlying question (and an insoluble knot in philosophy) is that of the relation between substance and attribute; specifically, how does one tell the agent from the activity? Certain Indian texts, exploring imagistically the relation between god and the world, ask how one can tell the dancer from the dance. In the visual arts the question has always seemed easier, since the painter or sculptor or photographer has traditionally made an object outside him- or herself. But universalizing appropriation has dissolved such a conception, and in performance art, as in the dance, the agent and activity often seem inseparable. In the last twenty years various performance artists (James Lee Byars, Chris Burden, Linda Montano and others) carried this category shift or semantic rotation to its limit by moving into galleries and living there for extended periods as performances. In this situation even the minutest details of everyday life are temporarily distanced and made strange – made art, that is – by the imposition on them of a new category overlay that alters the cognitive focus of both the performer and the beholder. Something parallel, though with fewer possibilities for irony, occurs when novices in ashrams are advised to regard their experiences, at every moment of the day, as sacred and special.

That these creations by designation are linguistic, involving a willed change in the use of the word 'art', does not altogether rob them of mystery and effectiveness. It should be emphasized that category shift by forced designation is the basis of many magical procedures. In the Roman Catholic mass, for example, certain well-known objects – bread and wine – are ritually designated as certain other objects – flesh and blood – which, in the manifest sense of everyday experience, they clearly are not; and the initiate who accepts the semantic rotation shifts his or her affection and sensibility accordingly. Art has often been thought of as exercising a sort of magic; around 1960, some artists adopted an actual magical procedure – basically a linguistic form of what Sir James Frazer called 'sympathetic magic'. At that moment art entered an ambiguous realm from which it has not yet definitively emerged. For the magical rite is already an appropriation of a piece of reality into a sheltered or bracketed zone of contemplation; when it is re-appropriated into the realm of art, a double distancing occurs. Furthermore, the universalization of any category, or the complete submission of its ontology to the process of metaphor, blurs or even erases its individual identity. To be everything is not to be anything in particular. In regard to the universal set, the Law of Identity has no function. The semantical coextensiveness of art and life means either that art has disappeared into life, melting into it everywhere like a new spark of indwelling meaning, or (and this departs at once into theistic metaphor) that life has dissolved into art. In short it means ultimately that the terms have become meaningless in relation to one another, since language operates not by sameness but by difference, and two sets with the same contents are the same set.

The art of appropriation, then, is a kind of shadowy recreation of the universe by drawing it, piece by piece, into the brackets of artistic contemplation. Artists engaged in this pursuit have concentrated on the appropriation of religious forms, of philosophical forms, of political forms, of popular forms, and more recently, of art-historical styles. These enterprises have met different fates. The appropriation of religious contents has been the most unpopular, even taboo, while that based on philosophy, especially linguistic philosophy, for a while acquired a marketable chic. In this discrimination the Apollonian (to use Nietzsche's dichotomy) surfaced over the hidden depth of the Dionysian. Apollo represents the ego and its apparent clarity of identity; Dionysus, the unconscious, in which all things flow into and through one another. In the Apollonian light each thing is seen clear and separate, as itself; in the Dionysian dark all things merge into a flowing and molten invisibility. That our culture, in the age of science, should favour the Apollonian is not surprising. The value of light is beyond question; but where there is no darkness there can be no illumination. Rejection of the Dionysian does not serve the purpose of clear and total seeing.

Universal appropriation has an exacting task if it is to be practised with sufficient range of feeling not to trivialize life. The levity, the sense of the will to entertain, that prevailed when Ben or Gilbert & George displayed themselves as sculptures was balanced by the sometimes horrifying ordeal through which the appropriation of religious forms unfolded. It was necessary to descend from the pedestal, with its Apollonian apotheosis of the ego, into the Dionysian night of the unconscious, and to bring into the light the logic of its darkness.

In Vienna in the early 1960s, Hermann Nitsch began presenting a series of performances that, in 1965, he would consolidate as the OM, or Orgies Mysteries Theatre.[7] His work was a focused exercise to bring the performance genre to its darkest spaces, its most difficult test, at once. In OM presentations the performers tear apart and disembowel a lamb or bull, cover themselves and the environment with the blood and gore, pour the entrails and blood over one another, and so on. These events last up to three hours (though Nitsch is planning one that will last for six days and nights). They have occasionally been shut down by the police. They have occurred in art galleries and have been reported in art magazines and books.

The OM Theatre performances open into dizzyingly distant antiquities of human experience. In form they are essentially revivals of the Dionysian ritual called the *sparagmos*, or dismemberment, in which the initiates, in an altered state produced by alcohol, drugs and wild dancing, tore apart and ate raw a goat that represented the god Dionysus, the god of all thrusting and wet and hot things in nature.[8] It was, in other words, a communion rite in which the partaker abandoned his or her individual identity to enter the ego-darkened paths of the unconscious and emerged, having eaten and incorporated the god, redesignated as divine. In such rites ordinary humanity ritually appropriates the aura of godhood through the ecstatic ability to feel the Law of Identity and its contrary at the same time.

Euripides, an ancient forerunner of the Viennese artists, featured this subject in several works. Like Nitsch, he did so partly because this was the subject matter hardest for his culture, as for ours, to assimilate in the light of day. In the *Bacchae* especially he presents the dismemberment as a terrifying instrument of simultaneous self-abandonment and self-discovery. The Apollonian tragic hero, Pentheus, like our whole rationalist culture, thought his boundaries were secure, his terrain clearly mapped, his identity established. Rejecting the Dionysian rite, which represents the violent tearing apart of all categories, he became its victim. Disguising himself as a Maenad, or female worshipper of Dionysus, he attempted to observe the ritual, but was himself torn apart, and eaten raw. In short, his ego boundaries were violently breached, the sense of his identity exploded into fragments that were then ground down into the primal substrate of Dionysian darkness which both underlies and overrides civilization's attempt to elevate the conscious subject above nature.

Nitsch writes of his work in consciously Dionysian terms as celebrating a 'drunken, all-encompassing rejoicing', a 'drunken ecstasy of life', a 'liberated joy of strong existence without barriers', 'a liturgy of exultation, of ecstatic, orgiastic, boundless joy, of drugged rapture ... '[9] He has created, in fact, a purely classical theory for it, based on Freudian and Jungian reinterpretations of ancient religious forms, on Aristotle's doctrine of catharsis, and on the ritual of the scapegoat as the wellspring of purification for the community.

Another stage of the OM ritual finds a young male standing or lying naked beneath a slain carcass marked with religious symbols and allowing the blood and guts to flow over his naked body. Again an ancient source has been appropriated. In the initiation rite called the *taurobolium*, the aspirant was placed naked in a pit over which, atop a lattice of branches, a bull, representing the god, was slain and disemboweled. When the initiate emerged covered with the bull's blood and entrails, he was hailed as the reborn god emerging from the earth womb.[10]

These works demonstrate the category shift involved in the appropriation process. In part this shift from the zone of religion to that of art represents the residual influence of Romanticism: the artist is seen as a kind of extramural initiation priest, a healer or guide who points the alienated soul back towards the depths of the psyche where it resonates to the rhythms of nature. In addition, it is the neutrality of the unbounded category that allows the transference to occur. Religious structures in our society allow no setting open enough or free enough to equate with that of ancient Greek religion, which was conspicuously nonexclusionary; the art realm in the age of boundary dissolution and the overflow did offer such a free or open zone. Günter Brus, another Viennese performer, has claimed that placing such contents within the art realm allows 'free access to the action'[11] – a free access that the category of religion, with its weight of institutionalized beliefs, does not allow. The assumption, in other words, is that in the age of the overflow the art context is a neutral and open context which has no proper and essential contents of its own. Art, then, is an open variable which, when applied to any culturally bound thing, will liberate it to direct experience. That this was the age of psychedelic drugs, and that psychedelic drugs were widely presumed to do the same thing, is not unimportant. As this tradition advanced along the path to the underworld, it was increasingly influenced by psychopharmacology with its sense of the eternally receding boundaries of experience.

Soon after Nitsch's first performances in Vienna, Carolee Schneemann presented a series of now-classic pieces also based on the appropriation of ritual activities from ancient and primitive sources. The general shape of these works arose, as among ancient shamans and magicians, from a variety of sources, including dream material and experiences with psychedelic drugs. Like Nitsch's works, Schneemann's are based both on depth psychology and on the appropriation of contents from the Neolithic stratum of religious history, especially the religious genre of the fertility rite.

In *Meat Joy* (Paris, 1964) nearly naked men and women interacted, in a rather frenzied, Dionysian way, with one another and with hunks of raw meat and carcasses of fish and chickens. They smeared themselves with blood, imprinted their bodies on paper, tore chickens apart, threw chunks of raw meat and torn fowl about, slapped one another with them, kissed and rolled about 'to exhaustion', and so on.[12] The sparagmatic dismemberment and the suggestion of the suspension of mating taboos both evoke Maenadism and the Dionysian cult. The wild freedom advocated by this ancient cult, as well as its suggestions of rebirth, seemed appropriate expressions of the unchecked newness that faced the art world as its boundaries dissolved and opened on all sides into unexpected vistas, where traditional media, torn apart and digested, were reborn in unaccountable new forms. The Dionysian subversion of ego in the cause of general fertility has become another persistent theme of appropriation performance. Barbara Smith has performed what she calls a Tantric ritual, that included sexual intercourse, in a gallery setting as an artwork.[13]

In general, performance works involving the appropriation of religious forms have fallen into two groups: those that select from the Neolithic sensibility of fertility and blood sacrifice, and those that select from the Palaeolithic sensibility of shamanic magic and ordeal; often the two strains mix. Both may be seen as expressions of the desire, so widespread in the 1960s and early 1970s, to reconstitute within modern civilization something like an ancient or primitive sensibility of oneness with nature.

Though the erotic content of the works based on the theme of fertility has been received with some shock, it is the work based on the shamanic ordeal that the art audience has found most difficult and repellent. Clearly that is part of the intention of the work, and in fact a part of its proper content. But it is important to make clear that these artists have an earnest desire to communicate, rather than simply shock. Seen in an adequate context, their work is not aggression but expression.

In 1965 Nitsch formed the *Wiener Aktionismus* group in conjunction with Otto Mühl, Günter Brus and Rudolf Schwarzkogler. Much of their work focused on the motifs of self-mutilation and self-sacrifice that were implicit, though not foregrounded, both in Klein's career and in the OM Theatre performances. Brus, during his performance period (1964–70), would appear in the performance space dressed in a woman's black stockings, brassiere and garter belt, slash himself with scissors till he ran with blood, and perform various acts ordinarily taboo in public settings, such as shitting, eating his own shit, vomiting and so on. Schwarzkogler's pieces presented young males as mutilated sacrificial victims, often wounded in the genitals, lying foetally contracted and partially mummy-wrapped as if comatose, in the midst of paraphernalia of violent death such as bullet cartridges and electrical wires. Not only the individual elements of these works, but their patterns of combination – specifically the combination of female imitation, self-injury and the seeking of dishonour through the performance of taboo acts – find striking homologies in shamanic activities. The same motifs reappeared, not necessarily with direct influence from the Viennese, in the works of several American performance artists who have stretched audiences' sympathies beyond the breaking point.

Paul McCarthy, a major exponent of the art of the taboo gesture, first heard the calling not from the Viennese but from Klein. As a student at the University of Utah in 1968, he leapt from a second story window in emulation of Klein's *Leap into the Void*.[14] By about 1974 his work had found its own distinctive form, developing into a modernized shamanic style so difficult for audiences to bear that the pieces were usually published only as video tapes. These performances, like Schneemann's, were often developed from dream material, indicating their intimate relation both with shamanic magic and with depth psychology. Like Brus, McCarthy has sometimes appeared dressed as a woman, and has worked, like Rudolf Schwarzkogler, with the themes of self-mutilation and castration; some pieces have acted out the basic female imitation of feigning menstruation and parturition (magical pantomimes that are common in primitive initiation rites). In others McCarthy has cut his hands and mixed the blood with food and water in bowls, clearly echoing various sacramental rites from the Dionysian to the Christian. In still others that, like Nitsch's, have sometimes been shut down by the police, he has acted out the seeking of dishonour as an exploration of the Dionysian-Freudian depths of psycho-biological life. In *Sailor's Meat*, a videotape from 1975, for example, he appeared in a room in a wino hotel wearing black lace panties smeared with blood and a blond female wig and lay on the bed fucking piles of raw meat and ground hamburger with his cock painted red and a hot dog shoved up his ass. As Old Man in *My Doctor* (1978) he slit a rubber mask over his head to form a vagina-shaped opening on it and from the vagina gave birth to a ketchup-covered doll. The piece was a conscious remaking of the myth of the birth of Athena from the cleft brainpan of Zeus, a myth that reverts to the age when male priests and their divinities sought to incorporate the female principle and its powers. In *Baby Boy* (1982) McCarthy gave birth to a doll from between his ketchup-covered male thighs as he lay on his back with his feet in the air like a woman in missionary-style sexual intercourse. In these and other works self-mutilation, female imitation and the performance of taboo acts are combined in a structure roughly parallel to that of Brus' work, though with a greater range of expressiveness.

Similar materials recur in the work of Kim Jones. In a performance in Chicago in 1981, Jones appeared naked except for a mask made of a woman's pantyhose, covered himself with mud (as both African and Australian shamans do when performing) and lay naked on the fire escape in the cold to accumulate energy (a shamanic practice known worldwide but most famous from Tibet). Returning to the performance space, he produced a mayonnaise jar filled with his own shit, smeared himself with it, embraced members of the audience while covered with it and finally burned sticks and green plants till the smoke drove the remaining audience from the gallery. In another piece Jones cut himself with a razor twenty-seven times in a pattern suggesting the body's circulatory system, then pressed himself against the gallery wall for a self-portrait.[15]

Understandably, to audiences habituated to the traditional boundaries of art, to audiences for whom easel painting was still the quintessential art activity, these performances were offensive and even insulting. Of course, the point of such works when they first appeared was in part their seeming to be radically, even horrifyingly, out of context. But for twenty years they have been part of the art scene, if somewhat peripherally, legitimized by art world context and critical designation again and again. In order to understand the wellsprings of such works, in order to approach them with a degree of sympathy and clarity, it is necessary to frame them somewhat in cultural history, where in fact they have a clear context.

Many of the artists discussed here feel that shamanic material and primitive initiation rites are the most relevant cultural parallels to their work. But most of them feel that the tone of their work arose first, often under Freudian or Jungian influence, and was later confirmed and further shaped by some study of shamanic literature.[16] The question of origins, then – whether from shamanic literature, of from the Jungian collective unconscious, or from the Freudian timeless repository of infantile memory, or from all these sources – though it is worthwhile to state, cannot be answered. In any case it is important in terms of any theory of the function of art that these artists have introduced into the art realm materials found elsewhere only in the psychiatric records of disturbed children and in the shamanic thread of the history of religion.[17]

In societies where the shamanic profession is intact, shamans have been perhaps the most fully rounded and powerful cultural figures in history. The poets, mythographers, visual artists, musicians, medical doctors, psychotherapists, scientists, sorcerers, undertakers, psychopomps and priests of their tribal groups, they have been one-person cultural establishments. They have also been independent, uncontrollable and eccentric power figures whose careers have often originated in psychotic episodes – what anthropologists call the 'sickness vocation'.[18] As a result, when societies increase their demands for internal order, the old shamanic role, with its unassimilable combination of power and freedom, is broken up into more manageable specialty professions; in our society, the doctor, the poet, the artist and so on, have each inherited one scrap from the original shaman's robe. Beginning with the Romantic period an attempt was made to reconstitute something like the fullness of the shamanic role within the art realm; poets especially were apt to attribute both healing and transcendentalizing powers to the art experience. This project has been acted out in the last twenty years by those artists whose work appropriates its materials from the early history of religion.

Perhaps the most shocking element in the various performance works mentioned here is the practice of self-injury and self-mutilation. This has, however, been a standard feature of shamanic performances and primitive initiation rites around the world. Siberian shamans cut themselves while in ecstatic states brought on by drugs, alcohol, drumming and dancing.[19] Tibetan shamans are supposedly able to slit their bellies and exhibit their entrails.[20] Related practices are found in the performance art under discussion. Chris Burden crawled through broken glass with his hands behind his back (*Through the Night Softly*, 1973). Dennis Oppenheim did a piece in which for half an hour rocks were thrown at him (*Rocked Circle/Fear*, 1971). Linda Montano inserted acupuncture needles around her eyes (*Mitchell's Death*, 1978). The Australian performance artist Stelarc, reproducing a feat of Ajivika ascetics in India, has had himself suspended in various positions in the air by means of fishhooks embedded in his flesh.[21] The number of instances could easily be multiplied.

The element of female imitation, found in the works of Brus, McCarthy, Burden and others, is also a standard shamanic and initiatory motif, involving sympathetic magic. Male shamans and priests around the world, as well as tribal boys at their puberty initiations, adopt female dress to incorporate the female and her powers.[22] In lineages as far apart as North Asian and Amerindian, shamans have worn women's clothing and ritually married other men.[23] Akkadian priests of Ishtar dressed like their goddess, as did Ramakrishna in nineteenth-century India. A Sanskrit religious text instructs the devotee to 'discard the male (*purusa*) in thee and become a woman (*prakriti*)'.[24] Various tribal rites involve the ritual miming, by men, of female menstruation and parturition, as in the works of McCarthy.[25] Freudian and Jungian theories of the bisexuality of the psyche and the need to realize it are relevant both to archaic and to modern exercises of this sort.[26]

Female imitation and self-mutilation combine in certain practices of ritual surgery found in primitive cultures around the world, though most explicit in Australia. In central Australian initiation rites, for example, a vulva-like opening is cut into the urethral surface of the penis, symbolically incorporating the female principle into the male body.[27] Bruno Bettelheim has observed this motif in the fantasies of disturbed children. Brus, in a performance, once cut a vulva-like slit in his groin, holding it open with hooks fastened to his flesh. Ritual surgery to create an androgynous appearance is common in archaic religious practice generally, as an attempt to combine male and female magical powers into one centre. The emphasis on the mutilation of the male genitals in much of the Viennese work is relevant here. In classical antiquity the priests of Cybele castrated themselves totally (both penis and testicles) in their initiation, to become more like their goddess; thereafter they dressed like women and were called 'females'. In subsequent ecstatic performances they would cut themselves in the midst of frenzied dancing and offer their blood to the goddess.[28]

The public performance of taboo acts is also an ancient religious custom with roots in shamanism and primitive magic. Both art and religion, through the bracketing of their activities in the half-light of ritual appropriationism, provide zones where deliberated inversions of social custom can transpire; acts repressed in the public morality may surface there, simultaneously set loose for their power to balance and complete the sense of life, and held safely in check by the shadow reality of the arena they occur in.

A little-known Sanskrit book called the *Pasupata Sutras* formulates this practice in detail, under the heading of the Seeking of Dishonour.[29] The practitioner is enjoined to court contempt and abuse from his fellow humans by behaviour deliberately contrived as the most inappropriate and offensive for the situation, whatever it may be. In shamanic contexts such practices had demonstrated the shaman's special status beyond convention, his ability to breach at will either metaphysical or ethical boundaries. In yogic terms the goal of the practice was the effacement of ego by the moralization of types of experience usually destructive to the self-image.[30] The shaman, the yogic seeker of dishonour, and the ritual scapegoat figure all offered themselves as targets for calamity, to draw it away from the communities they served. They were the individuals who went out on the razor's edge and, protected in part by the brackets of religious performance, publicly breached the taboos of their times. Today the exhibitionistic breaching of age and gender taboos, as well as other forays into the darkness of the disallowed within the brackets of the art performance, replicates this ancient custom, sometimes with the same cathartic intention. As the shoals of history break and flow and reassemble, to break and flow again, these and other primitive practices have resurfaced, in something like their original combination, in an altogether different context.

The preparation of [the artist's] own body as a magico-sculptural object, for example, is a regular and essential part of the shaman's performance. An Australian shaman may cover his body with mud (symbol of recent arrival from the netherworld) and decorate it with patterns of bird-down fastened on with his own blood; an African shaman may wear human bones, skulls and so forth, and may surgically alter his or her body in various ways; a Central Asian shaman may appear in a skeleton suit with mirrors on it. Frequently the shaman's body is tattooed or scarified or painted with magical symbols. Similarly, Schneemann has presented herself as a 'body collage' decorated with symbols from ancient fertility religions. In a mixture of archaic and Christian materials, Linda Montano in *The Screaming Nun* (1975), 'dressed as a nun, danced, screamed and heard confessions at Embarcadero Plaza [in San Francisco]'.[31] Other pieces by Montano have involved dancing blindfolded in a trance, drumming for six hours a day for six days, shape-changing and identity-changing, self-injury (with acupuncture needles) and astral travel events. Mary Beth Edelson's 'Public Rituals' have involved the marking of her naked body with symbols from ancient goddess cults, the equation of her body with the earth and the declaration of the end of patriarchy (*Your Five Thousand Years Are Up*, 1977).[32] Kim Jones, as Mud Man, or Bill Harding emerging covered with mud from a hole in the ground in the middle of a circle of fire, are reconstituting before our eyes images from the elementary stratum of religious forms.

A motif that is absolutely central to shamanism, and that often also involves body decoration, is the attempt to incorporate the power of an animal species by imitation of it. Shamans in general adopt the identities of their power animals, act out their movements and duplicate their sounds.[33] The claim to understand animal languages and to adopt an animal mind-set is basic to their mediation between culture and nature. Echoes of the practice are, of course, common in the annals of performance art. In Joseph Beuys' conversation with the dead hare the knowledge of an animal language combines with a belief in the shamanic ability to communicate with the dead. In *Chicken Dance* (1972) Montano, attired in a chicken costume, appeared unannounced at various locations in San Francisco and danced wildly through the streets like a shaman possessed by the spirit and moved by the motions of her animal ally. Terry Fox slept on a gallery floor connected with two dead fish by string attached to his hair and teeth, attempting, like a shaman inviting his animal ally to communicate through a dream, to dream himself into the piscine mind in *Pisces* (1971).

In such behaviour a style of decision-making is involved that has much in common with the peculiar arbitrariness and rigour of religious vows in general, and with one called the Beast Vow in particular. Among the Pasupatas of India (the same who formalized the Seeking of Dishonour) the male practitioner commonly took the bull vow. (The bull is the most common shamanic animal by far.) He would spend a good part of each day bellowing like a bull and in general trying to transform his consciousness into that of a bull. Such behaviour was usually vowed for a specific length of time, most frequently either for a year or for the rest of one's life. A person who took the frog vow would move for a year only by squatting and hopping; the snake vower would slither.[34] Such vows are very precise and demanding. The novice, for example, may pick a certain cow and vow to imitate its every action. During the time of the vow the novice follows the cow everywhere: when the cow eats, the novice eats; when the cow sleeps, the novice sleeps; when the cow moos, the novice moos – and so on. (In ancient Mesopotamia cow vowers were known as 'grazers'.) By such actions the Palaeolithic shaman attempts to affect ecology by infiltrating an animal species which can then be manipulated. The yogic practitioner hopes to escape from his or her own intentional horizon by entering into that of another species.

These activities are echoed in performance pieces in various ways. Bill Gordh, as Dead Dog, spent two years learning how to bark with a sense of expressiveness. James Lee Byars wore a pink silk tail everywhere he went for six months. Vito Acconci, in his *Following Piece* (1969), would pick a passerby at random on the street and follow him or her till it was no longer possible to do so.

What I am especially concerned to point out in activities like this is a quality of decision-making that involves apparent aimlessness along with fine focus and rigour of execution. This is a mode of willing which is absolutely creative in the sense that it assumes that it is reasonable to do anything at all with life; all options are open and none is more meaningful or meaningless than any other. A Jain monk in India may vow to sit for a year and then follow that by standing up for a year – a practice attested to in the *Atharva Veda* (about 1000–800 BC)[35] and still done today. In performance art the subgenre known as 'Endurance Art' is similar in style, though the scale is much reduced.

In 1965 Beuys alternately stood and knelt on a small wooden platform for twenty-four hours during which he performed various symbolic gestures in immobile positions. In 1971 Burden, a major explorer of the Ordeal or Endurance genre, spent five days and nights foetally enclosed in a tiny metal locker (61 × 61 × 91-cm [2 × 2 × 3-ft]). In 1974 he combined the immobility vow with the keynote theme of the artist's person by sitting on an upright chair on a sculpture pedestal until, forty-eight hours later, he fell off from exhaustion (*Sculpture in Three Parts*). In *White Light/White Heat* (1975) he spent twenty-two days alone and invisible to the public on a high, shelf-like platform in a gallery, neither eating nor speaking nor seeing, nor seen by, another human being.[36]

The first thing to notice about these artists is that no one is making them do it and usually no one is paying them to do it. The second is the absolute rigour with which, in the classic performance pieces, these very unpragmatic activities are carried out. This peculiar quality of decision-making has become a basic element of performance poetics. To a degree (which I do not wish to exaggerate) it underscores the relationship between this type of activity and the religious vocation. A good deal of performance art, in fact, might be called 'Vow Art', as might a good deal of religious practice. (Kafka's term 'hunger artist' is not unrelated.)

Enthusiasms of this type have passed through cultures before, but usually in the provinces of religion or, more occasionally, philosophy. What is remarkable about our time is that it is happening in the realm of art, and being performed, often, by graduates of art schools rather than seminaries. In our time religion and philosophy have been more successful (or intransigent) than art in defending their traditional boundaries and preventing universal overflow with its harrowing responsibilities and consequences. A classic source on the subject of 'Ordeal Art' is a book called *The Path of Purification* by Buddhaghosa, a fifth-century AD Ceylonese Buddhist.[37] It includes an intricately categorized compendium of behavioural vows designed to undermine the conditioned-response systems that govern ordinary life. Among the most common are the vows of homelessness – the vow, for example to live out of doors for a year. This vow was acted out in New York recently by Tehching Hsieh, who stayed out of doors in Manhattan for a year as a work of art. Hsieh (who also has leapt from the second storey of a building in emulation of Klein's leap) has specialized, in fact, in year-long vows acted out with great rigour. For one year he punched in hourly on a time clock in his studio, a device not unlike some used by forest yogis in India to restrict their physical movements and thus their intentional horizons. The performance piece of this type done on the largest scale was Hsieh's year of isolation in a cell built in his Soho studio, a year in which he neither left the cell nor spoke nor read. Even the scale of this piece, however, does not approach that of similar vows in traditional religious settings. Himalayan yogis as recently as a generation ago were apt to spend seven years in a light-tight cave, while Simeon Stylites, an early Christian ascetic in the Syrian desert, lived for the last thirty-seven years of his life on a small platform on top of a pole.

The reduced scale of such vows in the art context reflects the difference in motivation between the religious ascetic and the performance artist. Religious vows are undertaken for pragmatic purposes. The shaman seeking the ability to fly, the yogi seeking the effacement of ego, the monk seeking salvation and eternal bliss, are all working within intricately formulated belief systems in pursuit of clearly defined and massively significant rewards. Less is at stake for the performance artist than for the pious believer; yet still something is at stake. An act that lacks any intention whatever is probably a contradiction in terms. For some artists (for example, Burden) work of this type has functioned as a personal initiation or catharsis, as well as an investigation of the limits of one's will; others (including Nitsch) are convinced that their performance work is cathartic for the audience as well in that sense serves a social and therapeutic purpose. Rachel Rosenthal describes her performance work as 'sucking diseases from society'.[38]

But in most work of this type attention is directed towards the exercise of will as an object of contemplation in itself. 'Appropriation' art in general (and 'Vow Art' in particular) is based on an aesthetic of choosing and willing rather than conceiving and making. Personal sensibility is active in the selection of the area of the universe to be appropriated, and in the specific, often highly individual character of the vow undertaken; the rigour with which the vow is maintained is, then, like a crafts devotion to perfection of form. Beyond this, the performance is often based on a suspension of judgement about whether or not the act has any value in itself, and a concentration on the purity of the doing. This activity posits as an ideal (though never of course perfectly attaining it) the purity of doing something with no pragmatic motivation. Like the Buddhist paradox of desiring not to desire, it requires a motivation to perform feats of motivelessness. It shares something of Arnold Toynbee's opinion that the highest cultures are the least pragmatic.

In this mode of decision and execution the conspicuously free exercise of will is framed as a kind of absolute. Displays of this type are attempts to break up the standard weave of everyday motivations and create openings in it through which new options may make their way to the light. These options are necessarily undefined, since no surrounding belief system is in place (or acknowledged). The radicality of work in this genre can be appraised precisely by how far it has allowed the boundaries of the art category to dissolve. Many works of the last twenty-five years have reached to the limits of life itself. Such activities have necessarily involved artists in areas where usually the psychoanalyst or anthropologist presides. The early explorations discussed here required the explicit demonstration of several daring strategies that had to be brought clearly into the light. Extreme actions seemed justified or even required by the cultural moment. But the moment changes, and the mind becomes desensitized to such direct demonstrations after their first shock of brilliant simplicity. When an artist in 1983 announces that his or her entire life is designated as performance, the unadorned gesture cannot expect to be met with the enthusiastic interest with which its prototypes were greeted a generation ago.

1 See Thomas McEvilley, 'Diogenes of Sinope (*c.*410-*c.*320 BC): Selected Performance Pieces', *Artforum* (March 1983) [see in this volume, pp. 210-11].

2 For a more detailed discussion of this process see Timothy Binkley, 'Piece: Contra Aesthetics', in Joseph Margolis (ed.), *Philosophy Looks at the Arts* (Philadelphia: Temple University Press, 1978) 25-44.

3 Alain Robbe-Grillet, *For a New Novel* (New York: Grove Press, 1965) 43.

4 For this and other references to Klein the most convenient source is Thomas McEvilley, 'Yves Klein, Conquistador of the Void', in *Yves Klein (1928-1962), A Retrospective* (Houston, Texas: The Institute for the Arts, Rice University; New York: The Arts Press, 1982).

5 Allan Kaprow, *Assemblages, Environments, Happenings* (New York: Harry N. Abrams, 1966) 188.

6 For the image of the Net of Indra see Garma C.C. Chang, *The Buddhist Teaching of Totality* (Philadelphia and London: University Park, 1974) 165-66.

7 In English, see, for example, Hermann Nitsch in *The Spirit of Vienna* (New York: René Block Gallery, 1977) 64.

8 For the *sparagmos* see W.K.C. Guthrie, *The Greeks and Their Gods* (Boston: Beacon Press, 1950) 45, 149, 171-72; and Walter Otto, *Dionysus, Myth and Cult*

(Bloomington: Indiana University Press, 1965) 192ff. For the presence of various drugs in ancient wines, see Carl A.P. Ruck's essay in R. Gordon Wasson, *The Road to Eleusis* (New York: Harcourt Brace Jovanovitch, 1978).

9 *The Spirit of Vienna*, *op. cit.*, 31-32.

10 For the *taurobolium*, see Franz Cumont, *The Oriental Religions in Roman Paganism* (New York: Dover Publications, 1956), 66.

11 Brus in *The Spirit of Vienna*, *op. cit.*, 8.

12 Carolee Schneemann, *More Than Meat Joy: Complete Performance Works and Selected Writings*, ed. Bruce McPherson (New Paltz, New York: Documentext, 1979) 66.

13 'As Above, So Below', *High Performance*, 15: 4: 3 (Autumn 1981) 19-25. Many of the performance works mentioned in this essay were first documented in *High Performance*, a basic source on the subject.

14 I have written about the history of Klein's leaps elsewhere (see note 4 above). The famous photograph is a photomontage of a leap made over a net (tarpaulin, really). But the evidence is indisputable that Klein did, on two occasions before the photographed event, make leaps from comparable heights, sustaining injury both times. It is intriguing to note how resistant people are to accepting this fact; at a panel discussion at the Solomon R. Guggenheim Museum in New York after the opening of the Klein retrospective (21 November 1982), this was the central, and often heated, topic of discussion.

15 The making of blood imprints, which was found also in Schneemann's work and parodied in McCarthy's performances of painting with his penis dipped in ketchup, reverts of course to Yves Klein. In addition to his body prints in ultramarine blue, Klein on two occasions made blood prints of women's naked bodies (once using the model's own menstrual blood), which he subsequently destroyed for fear of their negative magic. The directness of the imprint method influenced neo-primitive performance widely. Recently the Italian performance artist Giuditta Tornetta has made blood imprints of her own pregnant body as performance works.

16 The works most commonly mentioned as influential are Sir James Frazer, *The Golden Bough*, often in the abridgment and revision of Theodore Gaster and Mircea Eliade, *Shamanism* (New York: Bollingen Foundation, Pantheon Books, 1964).

17 The parallels between tribal initiatory customs and the behaviour of disturbed children are brought out by Bruno Bettelheim, *Symbolic Wounds: Puberty Rites and the Envious Male* (New York: Collier Books, 1962).

18 Mircea Eliade, *Shamanism* (New York: Bollingen Foundation, Pantheon Books, 1964) chapters 1 and 2.

19 See, for example, S.M. Shirokogoroff, *Psychomental Complex of the Tungus* (London: K. Paul, Trench, Trubner & Co., 1935) 264; and V.M. Michaelowski, 'Shamanism in Siberia and European Russia, Being the Second Part of Shamanstro', *Journal of the Royal Anthropological Institute of Great Britain and Ireland*, 24 (1894) 66.

20 Fokke Sierksma, 'Tibet's Terrifying Deities', *Art in its Context; Studies in Ethno-Aesthetics, Museum Series*, 1 (1966) 73.

21 For the Ajivika austerity of hanging by hooks inserted in the flesh see Richard Morris, 'Notes and Queries', *Journal of the Pali Text Society* (1884) 95.

22 The classic source for shamanic transvestisism is Robert Briffault, *The Mothers* (London: Allen & Unwin, 1952) 532. For speculations on the female origin of shamanism see Georg Nioradze, *Der Schamanismus bei den sibirischen Völkern* (Stuttgart: Strecker und Schröder, 1925) 51ff.; and Debiprasad Chattopadhyaya, *Lokayatā: A Study in Ancient Indian Materialism* (New Delhi: People's Publishing House, 1959) 285.

23 Waldemar G. Bogoras, *The Chukchee*, *Memoirs of the American Museum of Natural History*, 11: 11 (New York: G.E. Stechert, 1904-1909) 448; and Hans Findeisen, *Schamanentum, dargestellt am beispiel der Bessenheitspriester hordeurasiatischer Völker* (Stuttgart: W. Kohlhammer, 1957) chapter 13.

24 Cited by Chattopadhayaya, *Lokayatā*, *op. cit.*, 284

25 Bettelheim, *Symbolic Wounds*, *op. cit.*, 109-21.

26 See, e.g., Sigmund Freud, 'Some Psychological Consequences of the Anatomical Distinction Between the Sexes', *Three Essays on the Theory of Sexuality and other Essays* (London: Hogarth Press, 1961) 323-44.

27 Subincision is reported by Baldwin Spencer and Francis J. Gillen, *The Native Tribes of Central Australia* (London: Macmillan and Co., 1899) 263, and described in detail by M.F. Ashley-Montagu, *Coming into Being among the Australian Aborigines* (London: G. Routledge and Sons Ltd., 1937) 293; varying psychoanalytical interpretations are given by Géza Róheim, *The Eternal Ones of the Dream* (New York: International Universities Press, 1945); and Bettelheim, *Symbolic Wounds*, *op. cit.*

28 Grant Showerman, *The Great Mother of the Gods* (Chicago, 1969) 16-18. For a psychoanalytic interpretation see E. Weiger-Vowinkel, 'The Cult and Mythology of the Magna Mater from the Standpoint of Pyschoanalysis', *Psychiatry*, 1 (1938) 348-49.

29 The text as a whole is not available in English; for excerpts and summary see Daniel H.H. Ingalls, 'Cynics and pasupatas', *Harvard Theological Review*, 55 (1962).

30 Yoga is primarily a redefining of shamanic practices in terms of later forms of thought. See Thomas McEvilley, 'An Archaeology of Yoga', *Res* (Harvard University: Journal of the Peabody Museum; University of Paris: Laboratoire d'Ethnologie) 1, 44-77.

31 Linda Montano, *Art in Everyday Life* (Los Angeles: Astro Artz Press, 1981).

32 Mary Beth Edelson, *Seven Cycles: Public Rituals* (New York: privately published, 1980). In the feminist branch of performance art this shamanic element has been widely explored. It is well to pause for a moment over the fact of there being a feminist branch at all. There is of course more than a little justification in the history of religion for this development. In fact the prevalence of transvestisism in shamanism has led to an intriguing (but untestable) hypothesis that shamanism was originally a female practice that was adopted by men through the mediation of female dress. Still, the explicitly feminist thrust of some of this work involves it in areas of politics that breach somewhat the neutrality of the appropriation zone.

33 Shirokogoroff, *Psychomental Complex*, *op. cit.*, 309; Wilhelm Radloff, *Aus Sibirien*, 2 (Leipzig: T.P. Weigel, 1884) 20-50; Mary A. Czaplicka, *Aboriginal Siberia: A Study in Social Anthropology* (Oxford: Clarendon Press, 1914) 171ff.; Findeisen, *Schamanentum*, 30ff.; and Adolph Friedrich and Georg Buddruss (eds.), *Schamanengeschichten aus Sibirien* (Munich: O.W. Barth, 1955) 212. Translated by Friedrich and Buddruss.

34 On the Beast Vow see M.G. Bhagat, *Ancient Indian Asceticism* (New Delhi: Munshiram Manoharlal Publishers, 1976) 145; Chattopadhyaha, *Lokayatā*, *op. cit.*, chapter 2; and Ingalls, 'Cynics and Pasupatas', *op. cit.*.

35 *Atharva Veda*, 15: 3; and see Haripada Chakraborti, *Asceticism in Ancient India* (Calcutta: Punthi Pustak, 1973) 368, 371, 437.

36 For the works by Chris Burden cited here see *Chris Burden* (Los Angeles, 1974) 71-73 and *Chris Burden* (Los Angeles, 1978) 74-77.

37 Bhikku Nyanamoli, trans., *The Path of Purification* (*Visuddhimagga*) (Berkeley: Shambhala Publications, 1976). For the parallels drawn here, see, for example, the 'tree-root-dweller's practice' (74), and the 'open-air-dweller's practice' (75).

38 There are countless other examples of artists who might describe their work in such terms; some are omitted due to considerations of space, others because their work seems sensationalist in motivation.

Thomas McEvilley, 'Art in the Dark', *Artforum* (Summer 1983) 62-71.

Kristine STILES

Survival Ethos and Destruction Art [1992]

'The genocidal mentality is neither biologically ordained nor intractable. It is part of a malignant historical direction that extends into general realms of technology, ultimate power and finally illusion. But there are other ways of thinking and feeling, already well under ways which propel us, in fits and starts, towards a change in consciousness, towards a new narrative ... At issue is an expansion of collective awareness, an altered sense of self, that embraces our reality as members of a single species and thereby opens up new psychological, ethical and political terrain.'
– Lifton and Markusen[1]

In their work on the Jewish Holocaust and the psychological effects of 'nuclearism', or the world ethos of nuclear weapons, Robert Jay Lifton and Eric Markusen chart a 'genocidal mentality'. Their findings suggest the emergence of a 'species mentality' that reflects a way of being and knowing in the world which is the result of the vast 'genocidal systems ... of deterrence', the ends of which mean only 'omnicide', or the destruction of all life. 'Genocidal mentality' also manifests itself in massive

'dissociative' behaviour, the psychological term used to suggest 'a broad category of psychological mechanisms, which include psychic numbing, doubling, disavowal and denial'. The various psychological defence mechanisms belonging to dissociation also serve, Lifton and Markusen observe, 'as psychological facilitator(s) for deterrence, helping to reduce the kind of psychic stress that would be morally useful and appropriate' to combat the pervasive threat to survival. Such dissociative behaviour also has been proven clinically to be a marked symptom of those who have been raised in an environment of alcoholism, or suffered physical and sexual abuse, and dissociative behaviour is, as well, a characteristic response to racism. Given the staggering numbers of individuals worldwise who experience some or all of these dissociative-provoking experiences, 'genocidal mentality' appears nearly ubiquitous and the conditions of survival ever more precarious.

Certain kinds of presentational art forms have demonstrated a predisposition for and an ability to convey the ontological effects of the technology, phenomenology and epistemology of destruction and the ways in which individuals and the collective negotiate the resulting crisis of survival. These performances and/or public events often feature advanced technology and/or use the body or body surrogates. Robots and other mechanized body-substitutes sometimes serve as the aesthetic site for the representation of the conjunction of social and political practices and interrelationships that collude in destruction. The tacit agreement among certain artists to situate the body at the centre of the discourse of destruction and survival cannot properly be called a 'tendency' and it is certainly *not* an 'art' movement, or 'ism', or aesthetic. Rather it is a response to the 'genocidal mentality', an answer or countercharge that is cross-cultural, postindustrial, interdisciplinary and multinational, and which shares no unified aesthetic, method or technique. Examples of this work are found in disparate performative practices throughout the twentieth century, but the subject of destruction and its relation to survival has been explored increasingly and systematically since the Second World War in Europe, the United States, Japan and the industrialized countries of South America.

Destruction art is the term I have adapted to identify the presentational works that situate the body in the centre of the question of destruction and survival. Indeed, such art might just as appropriately be called 'survival art' if it did not originate in the terminology, aesthetic and theoretical practices of Gustav Metzger and Rafael Montañez Ortiz ... The term 'destruction art', then, is merely an identificatory device, a concise index of a wide anthropological field. Destruction art, like such broad tendencies as Arte Povera, is inclusive rather than exclusive, defies narrow definitions and is found at moments in the practices of diverse artists [...]

Because destruction art is not a 'movement', it has never been systematically organized or methodically publicized and thus resists categorization for the lack of a manageable identity. The result is that, in many ways, it is culturally invisible. On the one hand, obscurity permits these artists' actions and survivalist messages to infiltrate social and political spheres without being co-opted into the market system. On the other hand, concealment within culture makes it vulnerable to mystification, neglect and disappearance. Often those who do work on questions of survival do not know of the intent of these artists. Thus, even Lifton, who has made unique contributions to these concerns, can state: 'In my work I take three dimensions that you can roughly connect with ... our contemporary situation. The first is the breakdown of traditional symbols and of modern parallels or developments of those symbols; the second is the mass media revolution; and the third is imagery of extinction or threat of extinction. *This last is the most difficult for art to confront, and I don't know if it's really been represented yet.*'[2]

In destruction art artists present the 'imagery of extinction' localized in the body, the object which is offered both as a destructible material and/or an agent of that destruction. In this sense, the performative practices which I associate with destruction art recapitulate the technological conditions, effects, processes and epistemologies of terminal culture. But destruction art is not only about the presentation of the conditions of destruction. It is also one of the means by which a world consciousness is being formed that may contribute to the construction of an 'altered sense of self' which is necessary to insure human survival.

[...] Western society and its most compelling aesthetic productions continue to perpetuate the epistemological ethos of destruction. But art that once reflected, mirrored and passively *represented* the abstract conventions and patterns of knowledge now actively *presents* the literal embodiment of psychic wounds, urban bedlam and militarized consciousness at the crisis core of terminal culture. But this epistemology also has healing roots, traditions, that are intertwined in the very technology, languages and practices of destruction.

Foucault recovered the Greek term *epimeleia heautou* which stood for the psychological and intellectual condition of being interested in taking care of one's self, of work on the self. The term equally described the responsibilities of power. *Epimeleia heautou* implied attention, knowledge, technique, a work of meditation that required understanding the necessities of the world, not imposed upon the individual by civil law or religious obligation, but rather as a choice about existence made by the individual who decided whether or not to care for the self, and thereby, to care for the world. Foucault pointed out that *epimeleia heautou* described a condition in which individuals 'acted so as to give to their lives certain values [for] it was a question of making one's life into an object for a sort of knowledge, for a *techné* – for an art'.

Destruction art communicates the visual knowledge that may recuperate the materiality of life from the violent, discontinuous destructions that imperil survival. The body may be a tool in the *techné* of survival and may function as a transit between agency and process, language, experience and their objects to close the lesion between *techné* and *logia* (word, speech or knowledge) that has inhered in the modern concept of technology.

I have proposed often that the primary communicating codes of the visual arts were transformed in the presentation of the body. The unprecedented achievement of the body as an active agent in art has been to visualize the perpetually shifting but mutually identifiable relations of power and need within the exchange of subject/object relations. When the body becomes the material support, subject and content of art, it holds the possibility of shifting the determined and fixed relations demanded by the prior objective status of art into an interplay of subjectivities established and transmitted in body gestures, systems and relations. The private body is utilized as formal material, subject matter and content into which the experiences and institutions of the body politic are collapsed. I want to suggest that in these terms, *the body holds the possibility for becoming both an aesthetic and social sign that also commutes political power.* Lifton believes that the task of the artist is 'to reveal the exquisite details of the experience of desymbolization' and 'the breakdown of viable relationships with symbols and symbolic forms [that] is an impairment in the "psychic action" of the "formative process" ... associated with severe manifestations of psychic numbing'. In destruction art, the body conveys the interdependent, interconnected and contingent state of the individual and the collective in survival. That embodiment holds the potential to reconnect experience to the objects of that experience and thereby to intervene in the destructive practices, institutions and technologies threatening extinction.

When faced with extinction, the artist must, if s/he takes responsibility for his/her trust, put art in the service of survival. This does not imply that all art must assume the task of destruction art, but it does mean that art has a particular social function which requires an ethical position on the question of survival, no matter what formal resolution that work finally assumes. In this sense I believe destruction art recovers the social force of art from instrumental reason and the economies of late capitalism. For destruction art constantly re-inscribes the profound significance of the survival of the body in the oppositions it deconstructs. In this sense, destruction art is a warning system, an aesthetic response to human emergency that occurs in the lapse between theory and practice in terminal culture; it presents the pain of bodies, the anxiety of minds, the epistemology of technology, the specious claims of ideology, the absence of ecological responsibility, the loss of human integrity and compassion, and the violence that structures both gender and sexual relations. Just as destruction art is the image of resistance in the form of an event, it is also an important means to survival that must be continuously explored.

1 I am grateful to Susan Roth, professor of psychology specializing in trauma and stress disorders at Duke University, for introducing me to Robert Jay Lifton's work. See Robert Jay Lifton, *Boundaries: Psychological Man in Revolution* (New York: Vintage, 1969); *The Future of Immortality and Other Essays for a Nuclear Age* (New York: Basic, 1987); and Robert Jay Lifton and Eric Markusen, *The Genocidal Mentality: Nazi Holocaust and Nuclear Threat* (New York: Basic, 1990). See also, Kristine Stiles, 'Shaved Heads and Marked Bodies:

Representations from Cultures of Trauma', *Strategie II: Peuples Mediterranéens*, 64-65 (July-December 1993) 95-117; reprinted with a new 'Afterword' in *Talking Gender: Public Images, Personal Journeys, and Political Critiques*, ed. Jean O'Barr, Nancy Hewitt, Nancy Rosebaugh (Chapel Hill: University of North Carolina Press, 1996) 36-64.

2 Lifton, *The Future of Immortality*, *op. cit.*, 238, my emphasis.

Kristine Stiles, 'Survival Ethos and Destruction Art', *Discourse: Journal for Theoretical Studies in Media and Culture*, 14: 2 (Spring 1992) 74-102. Parts of this essay first appeared in *Out of Control* (Linz: Ars Electronica, 1991).

Meiling CHENG

Bob Flanagan's Body Double

[1998]

'In a bizarro, alternative universe kind of way', muses the Los Angeles body artist Bob Flanagan. 'I sort of resemble Superman. Look, up in the sky, suspended by his wrists and sporting a huge erection – it's me. Yes, it's me ... And despite my skinny physique and frail sensitivities, I possess certain powers and abilities far beyond those of so-called normal human beings.'[1] The citation serves as the caption for a wall-size installation for *Visiting Hours*, a 1992 retrospective exhibition of Flanagan's artworks in the Santa Monica Museum of Art. Against the background of a blue sky with wholesome, white clouds, a full-size portrait entitled 'Bob Flanagan: Super-Masochist' floats in the centre. Sporting a flipped hospital gown as a cape, Flanagan stands in a frontal view with his arms akimbo and legs apart, his body adorned by a collage of accessories including both medical equipment and the paraphernalia from S&M sex games [...]

Dark humour: the self-parodic apotheosis of Bob Flanagan as a Terrestrial Superman comments on the extremity of his life condition, one that registers the habitual pressures of dealing with a therapeutic institution that attempts at cure by enforcing discipline. He manages to transmute the overwhelming presence of ailment and the corollary brutality of its medical treatments into live performances that feature the eroticism of mutilated body. His existential and aesthetic tasks are intertwined to such an extent that there is barely any distinction between the struggles for expression and those for survival. The art practised by Flanagan is then simultaneously an engagement with life traumas and a search for body healing. In this context, the manifest masochism in his performances of sensual violence is a self-prescribed homeopathic medicine that confronts the pain caused by the invading foreign bodies – be they organic, chemical or mechanical – by producing self-willed pain. Such a strategy does not so much reflect a sensorial substitution of pain with pleasure than to suggest an instant translation of self-determination, however painful, into pleasure.[2] As the arbitrary autonomy of his disease prevents him from owning a large portion of his body, he turns to his most prodigious body part, the penis, and renders it into *a surrogate self*, a cooperative *body double* solely under his control.[3] His torso in bondage and his tortured penis then project two types of pain: the first type is mimetic, imitating the effects caused by the medical machine's aggressive architectonics; the second type is volitional, appropriating his most frequent sensation to be a demonstrative, ecstatic release. The aetiology of Flanagan's masochism can be boiled down to one self-avowing sentence: 'I've learned to fight sickness with sickness'[4] [...]

1 The entire caption is published in *Bob Flanagan: Supermasochist*, ed. M. Andrea Juno and V. Vale (San Francisco: Re/Search, 1993) 3.

2 My observation is inspired by Gilles Deleuze's questioning of the conflation between pain and pleasure assumed by general studies on masochism. According to Deleuze, pleasure is a result from the painful exertion of the masochistic will. See 'Coldness and Cruelty' in *Masochism* (New York: Zone Books, 1991) 9-138.

3 For my concept of Flanagan's penis as a surrogate self, I am indebted to Joseph Roach's theory of performance as surrogation, effigy and fetish in *Cities of the Dead: Circum-Atlantic Performance* (New York: Columbia University Press, 1996).

4 In *Bob Flanagan: Supermasochist*, *op. cit.*, 3.

Meiling Cheng, 'Bob Flanagan's Body Double' (1998) in *Body Acts: Writing Extreme Performances* (Middletown: Wesleyan University Press, 2001).

BODY BOUNDARIES

The body is perhaps the primary metaphor for a society's perception of itself. The individual and spoken language are what make up the social body; the physical body is a kind of boundary between biology and society, between drives and discourse. Man can only know himself through his environment. Our awareness of self heightens our awareness of the world around us. Through a deeper understanding of what it means to live within one's own body, we understand better that we are all connected and related to one another. For critic Nelly Richards the body is the 'site par excellence for transgressing the constraints of meaning or what social discursivity prescribes as normality', and the site where questions of sexuality and its categorization in terms of power, biography and history, are played out.

Herbert MARCUSE An Essay on Liberation: Introduction [1969]

Up to now, it has been one of the principal tenets of the critical theory of society (and particularly Marxian theory) to refrain from what might be reasonably called utopian speculation. Social theory is supposed to analyze existing societies in the light of their own functions and capabilities and to identify demonstrable tendencies (if any) which might lead beyond the existing state of affairs. By logical inference from the prevailing conditions and institutions, critical theory may also be able to determine the basic institutional changes which are the prerequisites for the transition to a higher stage of development: 'higher' in the sense of a more rational and equitable use of resources, minimization of destructive conflict and enlargement of the realm of freedom. But beyond these limits, critical theory did not venture for fear of losing its scientific character.

I believe that this restrictive conception must be revised, and that the revision is suggested, and even necessitated, by the actual evolution of contemporary societies. The dynamic of their productivity deprives 'utopia' of its traditional unreal content: what is denounced as 'utopian' is no longer that which has 'no place' and cannot have any place in the historical universe, but rather that which is blocked from coming about by the power of the established societies.

Utopian possibilities are inherent in the technical and technological forces of advanced capitalism and socialism: the rational utilization of these forces on a global scale would terminate poverty and scarcity within a very foreseeable future. But we know now that neither their rational use nor – and this is decisive – their collective control by the 'immediate producers' (the workers) would by itself eliminate domination and exploitation: a bureaucratic welfare state would still be a state of repression which would continue even into the 'second phase of socialism', when each is to receive 'according to his needs' [...]

Freedom would become the environment of an organism which is no longer capable of adapting to the competitive performances required for well-being under domination, no longer capable of tolerating the aggressiveness, brutality and ugliness of the established way of life. The rebellion would then have taken root in the very nature, the 'biology' of the individual; and on these new grounds, the rebels would redefine the objectives and the strategy of the political struggle, in which alone the concrete goals of liberation can be determined.

Is such a change in the 'nature' of man conceivable? I believe so, because technical progress has reached a stage in which reality no longer need be defined by the debilitating competition for social survival and advancement. The more these technical capacities outgrow the framework of exploitation within which they continue to be confined and abused, the more they propel the drives and aspirations of men to a point at which the necessities of life cease to demand the aggressive performances of 'earning a living', and the 'non-necessary' becomes a vital need. This proposition, which is central in Marxian theory, is familiar enough, and the managers and publicists of corporate capitalism are well aware of its meaning; they are prepared to 'contain' its dangerous consequences [...]

For the world of human freedom cannot be built by the established societies, no matter how much they may streamline and rationalize their dominion. Their class structure, and the perfected controls required to sustain it, generate needs, satisfactions, and values which reproduce the servitude of the human existence. This 'voluntary' servitude (voluntary inasmuch as it is introjected into the individuals), which justifies the benevolent masters, can be broken only through a political practice which reaches the roots of containment and contentment in the infrastructure of man, a political practice of methodical disengagement from and refusal of the Establishment, aiming at a radical transvaluation of values. Such a practice involves a break with the familiar, the routine ways of seeing, hearing, feeling, understanding things so that the organism may become receptive to the potential forms of a nonaggressive, nonexploitative world.

No matter how remote from these notions the rebellion may be, no matter how destructive and self-destructive it may appear, no matter how great the distance between the middle-class revolt in the metropoles and the life-and-death struggle of the wretched of the earth – common to them is the depth of the Refusal. It makes them reject the rules of the game that is rigged against them, the ancient strategy of patience and persuasion, the reliance on the Good Will in the Establishment, its false and immoral comforts, its cruel affluence.

Herbert Marcuse, 'Introduction', *An Essay on Liberation* (Boston: Beacon Press, 1969) 3-6.

Willoughby SHARP

Body Works: A Pre-critical, Non-definitive Survey of Very Recent Works Using the Human Body or Parts Thereof [1970]

On Saturday 20 September 1969 at 4:20 PM on Barnes High Street outside London, Bruce McLean smiled. Shortly after that at the nearby Bull's Head Tavern he executed *Three Part Installation for the Body*.

The previous year Bruce Nauman made a series of 20 × 25-cm [8 × 10-in] holograms, *Making Faces*. On the afternoon of Tuesday 12 May 1970 he went into a vacant Pasadena lot and clapped his hands.

On Sunday 10 January 1970 William Wegman sat in his Madison, Wisconsin, studio and stuck toothpicks into his gums. Eleven photographs, each with a typewritten inscription, became *Eleven Toothpick Expressions*.

Dennis Oppenheim selected several of his sculptural works for cinematographic reproduction. In *Arm and Wire*, a six-minute 16mm black and white film shot by Bob Fiore, Oppenheim repeatedly rolled the underside of his right forearm over some wire.

During the morning of Monday 18 May, just prior to the opening of his one-man show at the Reese Palley Gallery, San Francisco, Terry Fox executed a three part-piece *Asbestos Tracking*. In one part, *Skipping*, he laid down a broken line of black footmarks on the grey concrete floor.

Early this year Larry Smith cut a 15-cm [6-in]-long *Line* into his left arm.

On at least three separate occasions this spring Vito Acconci repeatedly put his right hand as far down his throat as it would go until he gagged: *Hand and Mouth Piece*.

The videotape *Hand* was a part of Keith Sonnier's exhibition last March at the Castelli warehouse.

For *Beyond the Vanishing Point* (1969) Dan Graham, with his legs outspread, walked a V on a Nova Scotia beach, photographing every step. Sixteen photos, four to a row, taken from above, behind and either side comprise the photo-documentation of the piece.

These nine works share a common characteristic – the use of the artist's own body as sculptural material. Variously called actions, events, performances, pieces, things, the works present physical activities, ordinary bodily functions and other usual and unusual manifestations of physicality. The artist's body becomes both the subject and the object of the work. The artist is the subject and the object of the action. Generally the performance is executed in the privacy of the studio. Individual works are mostly communicated to the public through the strong visual language of photographs, films, videotapes and other media, all with strong immediacy of impact.

Aesthetic considerations aside, it is not surprising that under the present repressive socio-economic situation young artists have turned to their most readily available source, themselves, for sculptural material with almost unlimited potential, capable of doing exactly what the artist wants, without the obduracy of inanimate matter. In this respect it is significant that many of the artists under discussion have made earthworks, a fact which may partially explain the emphasis on the physical manipulation of pre-existing materials. Some of these artists have turned from cutting into the land to cutting into their own bodies.

In focusing on the creative act itself, body works are yet another move away from object sculpture. If objects are used, they only serve to reinforce aspects of the body. But body works do not represent a return to figuration. At most their relation to figurative art is ironic. Assumptions about our modes of being are questioned and explored, often with a wry sense of humour. Picking one's nose is presented as an artistic statement.

On another level, the new work can be seen as a reaction to Conceptual art which tries to remove experience from sculpture. This does not mean that body works are a return to some kind of expressionism. This is definitely not the case. The artists feel no need to vent their personal emotions in their work. The artist's own body is not as important as the body in general. The work is not a solitary celebration of self. As someone said, 'It's more about using a body than autobiographical.' The personality of the artist refines itself out of the work, impersonalizes itself. The artist, James Joyce observed, 'remains within or behind or beyond or above his handiwork, invisible, refined out of existence, indifferent, paring his fingernails'.

The Body as Tool. Hands have traditionally been used to make sculpture. Recently feet have come into their own. In 1967 Richard Long began a series of works by pacing up and down a straight line in an English meadow. In later walking works, like the recent one in Wiltshire, Long walked four increasingly large concentric squares, noting the time taken to complete each. In the first piece photographs documented the line on the ground. In the second a map was used to indicate the content of the work. For *Place and Process* Long contributed a photograph of footprints in the dusty Kenya ground. In the same show Dennis Oppenheim also used his feet for a work. *220 Yard Dash – Condensed* consisted of the artist running in a muddy lot and then making plaster casts of his footprints. Oppenheim has done at least a dozen works of this order. Some of these include *Condensed Hop Step and Jump* (1969) in which a 8-m [28-ft] leap was cast in plaster; *Two Jumps for Dead Dog Creek* executed in silt last April for his show at John Gibson's; and *Ground Level* (1970), push-ups on mud to indicate 'energy in the form of ground pressure'. Since last Autumn, Oppenheim has been wearing specially incised rubber soles which leave lines on the ground. A selection of 300 photos of these imprints was gathered together in *Ground Manoeuvers* (1969). An extension of this principle is a work in which Oppenheim wants 'to catch the patterns made by thousands of marchers in the landscape by photographing them from above, in a plane'. This work and a film *Backtrack* (1969), in which the artist's body was dragged along the sand to make marks, might be called an assisted body work since others are needed for its execution. In some ways it is reminiscent of Yves Klein's imprints (1961) using bodies of nude models to apply paint to canvas, but Klein was more interested in the theatrics of the works which were generally done as performances. He also kept the physical contact with his materials down to a minimum and wore white gloves so as not to get paint on his hands.

Another use of whole body as a marking instrument was seen at 'Projections: Anti-Materialism' at the La Jolla Museum in May. Barry Le Va did a piece which consisted of running full speed into one of the museum's walls as often as he could. John Van Saun extended this idea in *Breakthrough*, recently executed in MOMA's garden. He ran through an especially built, wall-like, wood partition. The penetrated structure and two photographs showing him falling through were exhibited in 'Information'. Terry Fox has done both indoor and outdoor works with his feet. In *Skipping* he dipped his shoes in black tar and skipped over a concrete floor leaving a 9-m [30-ft] trail of black residue. Two other parallel lines were made, one dragging one foot and the second shuffling.

The Body as Place is a common condition of body works. Oppenheim's 1969 earthworks extended Andre's conception of 'sculpture as place' to the point where, as he said, 'a work is not put in a place, it is that place'. This sentiment applies equally to Oppenheim's body works. In several works his body is treated as a place. Generally the body as place acts as a ground which is marked in ways quite similar to those employed in earthworks. In *Wound 1* (1970) he transferred the configuration of his healing skin on to a small piece of land. In *Arm and Asphalt*, a film of 1969, he rolled his underarm over sharp bits of asphalt. Intercuts of land mass related the action back to the original site of the earth material. It is not surprising then to find that Oppenheim's 'concern for the body came from constant physical contact with large bodies of land'. He also feels that working with land 'demands an echo from the artist's body'. This echo can literally be perceived in his *Reading Position for Second Degree Burn* (1970). Oppenheim went to a Long Island beach and exposed his body to the sun. He placed a large, leather-bound book entitled *Tactics* over his chest. In this work represented by two photos, one colour shot shows the artist lying on the beach before the burn and the other after, without the book. An unburned rectangle occupies the place where the book was. A related work is *Hair Piece* (1970), in which Oppenheim exposed parts of his scalp to a video camera. In *Material Interchange* (1970), Oppenheim is concerned with intimate transactions between his body and the environment. The work consists of four photographs, two of which show the artist wedging a fingernail between floorboards, and the others the same finger into which a long splinter from the same floorboard has been introduced.

Vito Acconci, who has executed several outdoor land pieces, has also treated his body as a place. In May he carried out *Rubbing Piece*. Sitting at a table in a restaurant, he rubbed his left inside forearm with the fingers of his right hand for one hour. Every five minutes a colour photograph was taken 'recording the development and progress of the resultant sore'. When the body is used as a place it is marked. Sometimes these marks are temporary, sometimes permanent. If they are permanent, this is an unavoidable consequence of the work rather than a desirable effect. The result of Larry Smith's *Line* was that it left a 15-cm [6-in] scar on his arm but the purpose of the piece was to explore a part of the body as potential sculptural material. This work seems to have antecedents in the tattoo and other body decorations which were thought to indicate a person's value in primitive cultures – a practice, incidentally, that seems to be coming back into favour now. (Janis Joplin recently had herself tattooed, and Charles Manson carved a cross into his forehead with his fingernails to signify that he had X-ed himself out of society.)

But body works executed directly on the body are never intended to either beautify or disfigure the artist. These are not sculptural concerns.

When the body is used as a backdrop, it is set off by an object or a number of objects which serve to articulate it. These objects are either placed in front of or in the body. In normal circumstances the body is always in a specific spatial-temporal framework surrounded by objects which define its relationship to the macrocosm and with which it interacts. But in some body works the outside parameters are unknown. No clues to site or situation are given in photographs like Bruce Nauman's *Portrait of the Artist as a Fountain* (1967) or William Wegman's *Eleven Toothpick Expressions* (1970). Another work by Wegman, *Wound*, shows five close-up photos of his face each with a letter, W.O.U.N.D. spelled out over his eyes and nose in bandaids. In these works only engaged parts of the body are visible. This tends to isolate the works further from their broadest context leaving the whole piece somewhat enigmatic, to the point that the interesting aspect of these works is the questions they provoke. This could also be said of Bruce McLean's *Three Part Installation for the Body* (1969).

The body as prop is related to the use of the body as a backdrop in that the body is presented in relation to other physical objects. But here the body exists in an identifiable field, as one particular among other particulars. Consequently, the works are slightly more theatrical. In Keith Sonnier's *Hand*, a part of a long videotape in which the body is seen with a variety of foam rubber shapes, the extension of the hand into the body, while not seen, can always be clearly inferred. A conditioning factor here is the fact that this videotape is immediately followed by a section with feet, and others where the whole body is evident. But even if this were not the case, the body would be inferred because the medium makes it difficult to see things as isolated. Another element of this medium is that it stimulates greater empathy than still photography or films. In Joseph Beuys' *How to Explain a Painting to a Dead Hare* (1965), in which the artist painted his face gold and sat immobile on a stool cradling a dead rabbit in his left arm, his body acts as a prop. The whole took on the character of a living tableau with Beuys as a frozen statue. This is an example of work that in a sense exists outside time, although it was visible throughout the opening of the artist's 1969 exhibition at the Schmela Gallery in Dusseldorf. While the work has the superficial appearance of a theatrical event, Beuys considers it one of his 'actions' or sculptural works similar to *Fettecke*.

The artist generally presents his body in certain circumstances and certain costumes in order to indicate how the work should be understood. Beuys has been able to make his work seem somewhat neutral because for more than a decade he has always worn the same clothes. This reinforces the impression that the artist is just another inanimate object. Steve Laub's *Smile Support* (1970) carries similar overtones. The artist stands with his hands stiffly at his sides and his back against a wall. His mouth is stretched open into a forced smile by two hooks attached to plastic bags filled with meat bones. The work has a coldly detached quality which makes a bleak comment on the plasticity of the human body. Nauman has used his body to similar effect. In the super slow-motion film *Making a Face* (1970) a long roll of gauze is slowly unrolled from Nauman's mouth. In real life we experience the world through our bodies and other people's bodies are viewed among material objects. In some of these works which use the body as a prop the artist has almost succeeded in transforming his own body into an object, albeit a human object, even for himself.

Strictly speaking it is impossible to use the body as an object. The only case in which a body approaches the status of an object is when it becomes a corpse. Nevertheless, several artists have proposed works which utilize cadavers while others have presented their own bodies as if they were dead. Shortly before he died Yves Klein did several works in which he lay outstretched either under a monogold covered with flowers or in a blue box pretending to be dead. Keith Arnatt, influenced by Oldenburg's Central Park grave, did a *Self-Burial* (1969) which was filmed for German television last October. He stood on a patch of ground and slowly sank into the earth. John Baldessari recently proposed a piece in which a corpse was to be exhibited in a refrigerated glass container in the Museum of Modern Art. Fox, who has been pushing parts of his body into walls and corners of rooms, is trying to procure a corpse for his next show at the Richmond Art Center in the Autumn. Much of this work, especially Fox's, reveals a sober acceptance of physical facts of death and a willingness to exploit their artistic potential.

One extension of Duchamp's found object is the found body or the body in normal circumstances. While Duchamp recognized the integrity and power of ordinary ready-made objects and their aesthetic relevance, a number of artists have presented simple physical functions like breathing and sneezing as works of art. Bruce McLean has done more than thirty works of this nature: walking, running, jumping and smiling. The last subject is a favourite: *Smile Piece* (1969), is a vertical sequence of three photographs of the artist in different stages of smiling. Most body works presented through still photos show various views of an ongoing process and approach the effect of films. But even if a single photo is offered as the work, one is still very conscious of a continuous process.

Nauman's first body work was done at the University of California at Davis in 1965 while he was still a graduate student there. He gave a performance resembling calisthenics. For thirty minutes he put himself through a series of bodily exercises like standing, leaning, bending, squatting, sitting and lying down. It was easier to continue this work alone in his Pasadena studio, so he did these performances in front of a 16mm camera that he generally operated by himself. A number of shorts of straight-forward, simple activities like *Bouncing a Ball*, *Playing a Violin*, *Pacing in the Studio* and *Pacing* followed. These films are extraordinary in that while Nauman goes through these regular procedures in a hyperconscious manner, he doesn't appear in the least bit self-conscious. Even the more artificially structured events, like dancing on a taped square on his studio floor, Nauman executes in the most natural way, giving an appearance of studied relaxation. Vito Acconci engaged in a similar activity each morning for a month. He used a small stool as a step and stepped up and down it at the rate of thirty steps a minute as long as he could without stopping. Although the piece was performed at his home, the public was invited to visit him any morning at 8:00 am during the time it was being executed. If he wasn't home, he performed the activity wherever he happened to be.

There is a 1924 photograph of Marcel Duchamp with his face covered in shaving lather and his hair drawn out into two horns. In spirit it resembles Nauman's series of holograms *Making Faces* (1968) in which the artist distorts his face by pulling and pushing it with his fingers as if he were testing the limits of its flexibility. Another hologram shows him falling through air while each hand holds on to one toe. In both the facial expressions and the falling piece, the tone is cool and unemotional. More recent works of the body in unusual situations are the slow motion films *Bouncing Balls* and *Black Balls*. In the former, a continual displacement of the artist's gonads is effected with his fingers. In the latter they are covered with black cream. These two films also show the body used to find out something about itself, exploratory since it is undergoing an experience yielding information about its performance levels and how it functions. This is also true about Acconci's *Steps* (1970) and a number of the other works. Acconci is very concerned with this improvement aspect of body works which seems to parallel the learning of language by training, a Wittgensteinian notion. In *Breathing In* (1969) which consisted of taking deep breaths, holding them for as long as possible and exhaling, Acconci's performance improved in time. As opposed to McLean's breathing piece which concentrates on this as a unique bodily function, Acconci is concerned with both raising his level of awareness of breathing and his control over this function. Discipline was not the concern of Richard Serra's short film of his hand grasping and catching flat pieces of lead which he then squeezes and drops. Serra did not try to control the strain on his hand muscles or regulate his performance as this operation progressed. He was interested in finding out what was happening to a part of his body. Fox's *Push Wall Piece* (1970) was similar in that he wanted to experience a special bodily sensation. He wanted to test the wall's massiveness in relation to his own body.

In body works the body *per se* is not as important as what is done with the body. An erased videotape of late last year by William Wegman shows an almost unidentifiable image of the artist's body with head and feet cut off at the top of the screen. He stands with his arms pressed close to his sides and flashes finger signs, first two, then four, which seem to be trying to communicate some strange pre-linguistic (body) sign language. In another work Wegman photographed himself with his head stuck in the ground like an ostrich. The work is a literalist enactment of a verbal metaphor, similar to Nauman's *Feet of Clay* (1967–70), and again shows the influence of Wittgensteinian language games.

As a body of work body works are still very much in the process of defining themselves. One indication of the increasing subtlety and complexity of the works being produced is to be found in Vito Acconci's *Room Situation (Proximity)* (1970), his proposal for the *Software* show at the Jewish Museum this Autumn. Acconci's proposal states: '*Every day, during the exhibition, I will be present at the exhibition area, from opening time to closing time, going randomly from room to room. Subjects will be chosen who are standing in relative privacy at one of the exhibits; I will stand beside the person, or behind him, so that he might shift his posture, attempt to move away, etc. (I will stand beside him until he moves away.)*'

Willoughby Sharp, 'Body Works: A Pre-critical, Non-definitive Survey of Very Recent Works Using the Human Body or Parts Thereof', *Avalanche* (Autumn 1970) 14–17.

Cindy NEMSER
Subject – Object: Body Art
[1971]

'Our body is not in space like things; it inhabits or haunts space. It applies itself to space like a hand to an instrument, and when we wish to move about we do not move the body as we move an object. We transport it without instruments as if by magic, since it is ours and because through it we have direct access to space. For us the body is much more than an instrument or a means; it is our expression in the world, the visible form of our intentions. Even our most secret affective movements, those most deeply tied to the humeral infrastructure, help to shape our perception of things.'
– Maurice Merleau-Ponty[1]

Since the beginning of recorded history, artists, men endowed with exceptionally sensitive perceptual apparatus, have continued to make visual images of both man's physical and psychological states. In the *Hidden Dimension* Edward Hall views these visual recreations of man as a recapitulation of his growing awareness 'first of himself, second of his environment, then of himself scaled to his environment, and finally of the transaction between himself and his environment'.[2]

Indeed, it is this last mentioned phase of historical awareness that is engaging most advanced thinkers today. Scientists, philosophers and psychologists, as well as artists, have come to realize that man is no passive receiver of environmental signs and signals: on the contrary, he is an active agent involved in a never-ending dialogue between himself and the world around him. The problem now is how to record and express these active environmental transactions as part of man's simultaneously subjective-objective existence. For artists such as Bruce Nauman, Dennis Oppenheim and Vito Acconci, among others, the immediate solution is to go back and explore the primary source material, their own bodies. These artists would concur with psychologist James J. Gibson's basic thesis that man can only know his environment through the perceptual systems of his own body.

They would also accept Gibson's contention that 'words and pictures are at best man-made substitutions for direct stimuli language'[3] ... Knowledge *about* the world rests on *acquaintance* with the world.

If we look into the history of twentieth-century art, we will see that the decision to work directly on the body is the logical outgrowth of a series of ongoing developments. In 1921 Marcel Duchamp lathered his scalp and shaved off his hair in the form of a star. With his gesture the masterful Marcel revealed his knowledge that the artist and his object are in reality one and the same. Then Duchamp went a step further and by dressing up as a woman, Rrose Sélavy, attempted, within a limited range, to experience the opposite sex role.

Thirty years later Jackson Pollock, coming out of Surrealism and psychoanalysis, followed through on Duchamp's idea of making the artist's entire being part of his work by literally putting himself into his paintings as he created them. However, after the action was over Pollock withdrew physically from his work, leaving behind only the residue of his activities. Other artists after him strove to create a closer union between the objectified remains of their bodily acts and their subjective physical and psychological states. Members of the Japanese Gutai group, in the 1950s, and various creators of Happenings, in the 1960s, used their entire bodies, often in theatre presentations, to make their artworks. Allan Kaprow, in events like *An Individual Demonstration,* performed in Prague, and *Tree Man Topples Pole,* both in 1964, not only focused on himself as simultaneously acting and being acted upon, but also brought his body out into the everyday world of the street and the countryside. Yet Kaprow, along with the other creators of Happenings, still viewed the body primarily as a prop to be moved about into various spatial positions along with other inanimate objects.

At the same time as the Happenings were occurring, Jasper Johns was trying to create a subjective-objective record of himself and his activities and still continue to make paintings and sculptures. He began to leave physical traces of his own body in his work. A little later on Donald Judd and Robert Morris worked out a particularly extreme solution to the problem Johns was investigating. Minimal art was an attempt to force the artist and viewer to deal with his subjective being by disengaging him from the materials and craftsmanship that came between him and his awareness. According to Morris in his 'Notes on Sculpture'[4] his specific objects did away with 'intimacy producing relationships' and 'traces of the artist's hand'. As a result of these eliminations, the object, writes Morris, is 'more reflexive because one's awareness of oneself existing in the same space is stronger than in previous work'.

Yet, since this perceptual interaction took place after the fact of execution, the artist as prime mover was still left out of his own work. This artificial dichotomy did not last long. By 1966 Bruce Nauman, realizing the full implications of Duchamp's star image, began to incorporate his body, both as phenomenon and as activator into the total conception of his artwork. He had himself photographed with water squirting out of his mouth in the *Portrait of the artist as a Fountain*. Then in 1968 Richard Serra went a step further and made a film entitled *Hand Catching Lead*, in which the body in the act of creating the artwork, simultaneously became the artwork. Finally the actor and the acted upon came together, the processor became the processed, the verb and the subject were one. Both Nauman and Serra had grasped the implications of James Gibson's assertion that 'the equipment for *feeling* is automatically the same equipment as for doing'.[5]

This premise is the essential element that unites all the body works that have been executed in the past three years. Body artists also have several other features in common. First of all, they work within real time and space and with themselves in terms of their own identities. Secondly, whether their works use the media of live performance, film, photographic documentation, tape recording, videotapes or written information, these pieces are not considered to be actualized unless carried out by the body itself. They are not conceptual in the recent art sense of the word.

Although body artists operate within this common framework, their pieces seem to divide into two major categories. Sometimes the artist's body is viewed as a closed system acting and being acted on by itself alone. At other times, the artist gives primary attention to having his body interact with the various elements and aspects of his environment.

In approaching the body as a closed system Bruce Nauman has explored the different attitudes the body can assume. According to Dan Graham, in such works as *Body as a Cylinder* or *Body as a Sphere* (1970), Nauman is 'engaged in studying the rules by which the body is expressive'. In *Pulling Mouth* (1969), he continues his research in this direction by using a slow-motion film (2,000 frames per second) in order to concentrate on the process of face-making as well as the phenomenological aspect of it. Nauman's art has definite affinities with the sound compositions of Steve Reich, who writes in the 1969 *Anti-Illusions: Procedures/Materials* catalogue, that 'to facilitate really close perception a process should happen very gradually ... so slowly and gradually that listening to it resembles watching a minute hand on a watch. You can perceive it moving after you stay with it a little while'.

The desire to effect physical and psychological change is often implicit in the works of artists who use their bodies as a closed system. In a piece called *Deformity*, Dennis Oppenheim attempts to restructure the deformed keratin tissue of an injured toe by scraping away at it with a rock. He views this re-formation process as a circular in-put out-put energy system since 'the residue is recorded in body change and is therefore feed back to the source'.

Vito Acconci, in a piece entitled *Openings* (1970), concerns himself more with a psychic transformation rather than a physical restructuring. In this work the artist weeds out an area around his navel by plucking out one hair at a time. The strain of his pulling action produces an accumulation of perspiration in and around the navel which causes this 'opening' to resemble a vagina. Therefore, by effecting a physical change the artist feels he has, to some degree, undergone a sexual identity transformation similar to the one experienced by Duchamp when he masqueraded as Rrose Sélavy. A variation on this re-formation theme is a piece by Tom Moroni called *Focus Pocus*, performed at the Berkeley Museum in 1971. After playing out a recording of a heartbeat brought to a dead stop, Moroni took off his clothes and became Allan Fish, thus effecting a total identity change.

While there are many other body works developed out of this closed system approach, more often body artists utilize other environmental elements to explore various aspects of their subject-object relationships. Chris Burden uses gym equipment, tailor-made to interact with his own body, in order to investigate his specific sensual experiences. Mowry Baden, with his long belts bolted to the ground, is involved in similar kinds of research. Sometimes a body artist will use a particularly forceful prop to insure empathy on the part of the viewer. When Bruce Nauman, in a slow-motion film, extracts a long roll of gauze from his mouth, or when William Wegman jams toothpicks into his gums or ties up his tongue, the viewer cannot help but feel the vibrations of these actions in his own body.

As the body, used simultaneously as raw material and tool, interacts with a deliberately selected environment, real time and specific place are more thoroughly incorporated into the work. In his *Velocity Piece*, first performed at the University Museum at Columbus, Ohio, in 1969, and then at La Jolla, in 1970, Barry Le Va ran back and forth crashing into two opposite walls 15-m [50-ft] apart for as long as he was able to go on. With the help of stereo equipment his movements in that particular space were precisely recorded while visual recordings of his activity were left on the blood-spattered walls. After the event had taken place those viewers who were invited to hear the results of his ordeal were able to follow the sound of his progress step by step as evidenced by the ping pong movements of their heads. Le Va had truly become a ghostly presence, a body haunting space.

Terry Fox's use of his own body is even more complex as it deals with a specific space spiritually as well as physically. In a work called *Pisces* (1971) the artist perpetrated a 'murder' and experienced the victim's death throes by reclining on the floor while his prey, two sea bass, one tied to his tongue and the other to his penis, were allowed to expire. Then Fox drove to his 'opening' at the Santa Clara museum where he lay down, shrouded in white canvas sheets, with the decaying fish fastened to his teeth and hair, surrounded by dimming flashlights, and slept for three hours. Visitors were able to view this tableau from another room, but were not permitted to intrude upon the death sequence. Fox, whose work has many affinities with that of Joseph Beuys, states that his intention is to 'charge a space with feeling so powerful that after the performance the space remains "charged" enough to have some effect on future visitors'.

Some of the most complex and provocative bodyworks occur when the artist uses his body to interact with other human beings on both a physical and psychological level. Dan Graham, in a piece called *Correlated Rotations* (1969), has himself and another participant walk about in a circle as they film each other simultaneously. Then the films, which are of necessity slightly out of synchronization, are shown on opposite walls and the audience's eyes must constantly gravitate from one screen to the other in response to the visual re-creation of the feedback interaction process being played out before them. The artist sees each *I* as extended through the *eye* of the person who holds the camera.

Dennis Oppenheim has also explored the subjective-objective states of fear, aggression and trust through interpersonal transactions. In a piece called *Rocked Circle* (1971), he planted himself in the centre of a 1.5-m [4.5-ft] circle while his wife Phyllis, located above him, attempted to fill this circumscribed area with ice-encapsulated rocks. In the midst of this dangerous downfall Oppenheim made a video tape of his changing facial expressions. His aim was to record the physical result of an ambivalent psychological state generated out of a precariously balanced combination of fear, anger and trust.

Physical movement is often linked to experiments in psychological control in the recent works by Vito Acconci. In a piece called *Pull*, performed at the Loeb Center in 1971, the artist placed Kathy Dillon in the centre of a circle while he located himself on its circumference. The goal of each participant was to hold the other's eye while each decided whether or not either to initiate a movement or to follow one. As opposed to earlier Happenings and later minimal dance performances, the people involved were not props going through the motions of making formal patterns in space. Their movements were determined by both their subjective and objective knowledge of what the other person might do or was doing. In this simple, almost ritualistic battle of wills, we see the essence of the entire perceptual process in which the subject is continuously transformed into the object and then back into the subject through his ongoing physical interaction with the environment.

Now, while the desire to know oneself as both subject and object in relation to one's surroundings is certainly a positive goal, we cannot help but notice the strain of bizarre, sado-masochistic exhibitionism that runs through this account of body art. Yet when interviewed, none of these artists admitted to any personal sense of pleasure or pain while acting out their works. They all regarded their bodies simply as materials or instruments with which to discover real physical or psychological processes. Vito Acconci, who is interested in vulnerability, states that 'shock tactics are convenient means of showing how the body can be intruded on'. Oppenheim and Le Va view their bodies as tools and materials for the exploration of energy drain. The latter declared that upon hearing the playback recording of his bruised, bloody body ploughing into the wall he could not believe it was he who was actually suffering.

This clinical attitude towards pain seems quite rational if one looks upon these artists as researchers working under laboratory conditions. For, according to Gibson, painful touch is 'a kind of obtainable stimulus information about the environment'.[6] Yet despite the benefits gained from such research, one cannot help but recoil from some of these acts of physical and psychological torture. After all, these are not laboratory animals, but human beings who have somehow come to look upon themselves as guinea pigs upon whom they are entitled to inflict these terrible torments. Indeed, the detached manner in which they view their bodily discomforts seems to be at odds with the primary goal of body art, the desire to bring the subjective and objective self together as a totally integrated entity.

Now, why should there be such a disparity between these artists' intentions and their actions? Well, artists are both reflectors and reflections of the culture in which they operate. If our culture is as alienated and schizoid as R.D. Laing and Rollo May, among many others, maintain, then it is hardly surprising that artists, particularly those working with their own bodies, exploring both their inner and outer selves, are simultaneously acting out as well as reflecting that condition.

Edward Hall suggests that artists can help us to know ourselves in relation to our environment because 'they can abstract those parts which, if properly organized, can stand for the whole and constitute a more forceful, uncluttered statement than the layman might make for himself'.[7] If this is true, then today's body artists are functioning at a higher level of rationality than the rest of us since they make coherently structured images out of our fragmented, alienated society. Indeed, the logical validation of their body activities is that they reflect the most basic of human impulses. For as Claude Lévi-Strauss tells us in his *Structural Anthropology*, among primitive tribes face and body decorations are not only ornaments. '... They are messages fraught with spiritual and moral significance ... to stamp on the mind all the traditions and philosophy of the group.'[8]

Right now, the body artists, openly alternating between states of intense body sensation and extreme cerebral detachment, are attempting to give us a message about the frightening and dangerous aspects of our own society. As a simultaneous re-creation and mirror of the chaotic structure of contemporary Western culture this disturbing art form faces two major obstacles. On one hand, due to the unpleasant nature of the content of body art, the public may refuse to read it intelligently. On the other hand, these bodyworkers, with their self-destructive impulses, may not survive long enough as artists to get their message through. The question is, if they don't make it, will we?

1 Maurice Merleau-Ponty, 'An Unpublished Text: Prospectus of his Work', *The Primacy of Perception*, ed. James Edie, trans. Arleen B. Dallery (Urbana: Northwestern

University Press, 1964) 5.

2 Edward Hall, *The Hidden Dimension* (New York: Doubleday & Co., 1966) 90.

3 James J. Gibson, *The Senses Considered as Perceptual Systems* (Boston: Houghton Mifflin Co., 1966) 28.

4 Robert Morris, 'Notes on Sculpture', *Artforum* (October 1966).

5 Gibson, *The Senses Considered*, *op. cit.*, 99.

6 *Ibid.*, 132.

7 Hall, *Hidden Dimension*, *op. cit.*, 81.

8 Claude Levi-Strauss, *Structural Anthropology*, trans. Claire Jacobson and Brooke Gundfest Choepf (New York: Doubleday & Co., 1963) 251-52.

Cindy Nemser, 'Subject-Object: Body Art', *Arts Magazine* (September 1971) 14-17.

Jonathan BENTHALL

The Body as a Medium of Expression: A Manifesto [1972]

'The body is the first and the most natural instrument of man.'
– Marcel Mauss

'The body ... the great central ground underlying all symbolic reference.'
– A.N. Whitehead

'It is not to the physical object that the body may be compared, but rather to the work of art.'
– Maurice Merleau-Ponty

[...] The ICA programme will explore the body's role in interactional contexts as a mechanical, topographic and symbolic complex. A variety of specialists will cover the following aspects of the body:
(a) gesture, posture and the study of movement (kinesics)
(b) face-to-face behaviour and the means whereby everyone manages his 'personal front' (a field pioneered by Erving Goffman)
(c) proximity studies (proxemics)
(d) deaf-sign languages
(e) paralinguistics – the 'greasy' parts of speech such as hesitation, vocalization, etc.
(f) animal signal systems (mainly primates but also dolphins and whales as representing another branch on the evolutionary tree)

But this is just the start. The lecture series will attempt to subject some of this specialist research to a sociological and anthropological critique.

Recent American sociological trends will be touched on,[1] but we have been more guided by European social anthropology: the *Année sociologique* school (Émile Durkheim, Mauss, Gustave Hertz), Claude Lévi-Strauss and particularly Mary Douglas.[2] These and other theorists have tackled the vast question of the possibility of consonance between all layerings of experience – the physical, the psychological, the social and the cosmic. Douglas has suggested that 'the achievement of consonance between different realms of experience is a source of profound satisfaction'. The body is perhaps the foremost of all metaphors for a society's perception of itself, recurring constantly in myths and cosmogonies, art and literature. One lecture in the series will be given by Philip Rawson on the Indian cult of Tantra, where the body becomes a metaphor perhaps more explicitly all-embracing than in any other social situation. The ambiguous attitude of Christianity to the body – oscillating between glorification and mortification – is particularly close to home and should not be forgotten.

Body behaviour and body imagery differ so widely from culture to culture that it is impossible to unscramble those biological or genetic constituents of any given behaviour which might fairly be called 'culture-independent' or 'specific to the human species'. It is doubtful whether any formal attempt to unscramble the biological/genetic dimension from the social and psychological dimensions would be a profitable exercise (since the notion of an asocial human nature is an abstraction); but such ethnographic field-data as exists – about such cultures as Bali, Navaho, Southern Italy – is useful for testing all theories about the body.

We shall also investigate various 'aids' to the body-medium such as clothing, adornment, body mutilation, hair-styling, bathing and care of the body; and the use of the dead body as an art-form. These 'aids' need to be studied in relationship to images and ideas of the body.

But the most urgent and radical aspect of the subject is what John O'Neill, author of *Sociology as a Skin-Trade*, calls 'body politics'. O'Neill refers to Marx and Freud, but also to the activists – such as Norman Brown, Jerry Rubin, Cassius Clay, Eldridge Cleaver and Fritz Fanon – who have between them 'taught us to understand the deep political structures of sex, language and the body'. According to Rubin, 'Nobody really communicates with words any more.' Demonstrations, street art and sit-ins are literally and palpably *embodying* arguments to challenge verbal mystification and lies. (Polhemus will speculate that it is the 'arbitrariness'[3] of verbal language which makes it the most 'alienating' form of communication.)

O'Neill writes of the 'non-verbal rhetoric' of political dissidents. Developing his case, we are working on the hypothesis that, since our society uses words as its primary means of social control, all repressed groups will tend to find their most effective and confident expression through the body's wider resources rather than within the enclosure of verbal language, in so far as they opt for self-assertion rather than for integrating with the norms of the majority. There are three clear test-cases: blacks, male homosexuals and the deaf. (Other test-cases – such as women, female homosexuals, artists, lunatics, children – are not so clear but could be brought into the argument at a later stage.)

***Blacks* Any student of the history of white attitudes to the negro will be aware of the intense interest in the negro's body and his place in the Great Chain of Being.[4] Racial theory attempted to define scientifically how exactly the black body was set off from the white body. In reaction to stereotyping by the whites as a mindless brute, or a phallic symbol, the black has recently asserted his relationship with his body as different from that of the white. This is articulated in the ideologies of *négritude* and of Black Power.**

***Male Homosexuals* Epithets implying unnaturalness or animality have been used in our culture to crush sexual deviance, as 'nigger' has been used to repress the blacks. Even in more sophisticated discourse, the homosexual is taught to regard himself as doomed to *miss* essential human experiences such as the procreation of children. The ethos of the Western homosexual sub-culture is celebrated today in the world of dance and ballet.**

***The Deaf* Lacking a sense – claimed by the dominant speaking-hearing majority as essential to full human communication – the deaf often communicate by manual signing which to the speaker-hearers is a crude – almost animal – version of verbal language. Aaron Victor Cicourel has brilliantly criticized this logocentric view, reminding us that all the notations used to describe deaf-sign languages are invented by speaker-hearers. He imagines an anthropologist from another planet who can only make a field-study of the earth people by using the deaf people as his informants. The anthropologist ends up feeling sympathy with the deaf for having to live with such a barbaric community as the speaker-hearers [...]**

This article was written with the help of some colleagues at the Institute of Contemporary Arts, London, in particular Ted Polhemus.

1 Aaron V. Cicourel, 'Ethnomethodology', *Current Trends in Linguistics*, 12.

2 Cicourel belongs to a new school of sociologists called 'ethnomethodologists' who study the rational properties of everyday mundane experience and 'indexical' practice. Such research necessarily returns frequently to the body as the source of such experience and practice. Harold Garfinkel's paper 'Passing and the managed achievement of sex status in an "intersexed" person' - the case-history of "Agnes", a psychiatric patient of ambiguous sexual status - is a classic of sociological reportage, complete with a narrative twist at the end that makes most contemporary fiction seem pale. Garfinkel's experiments - which he prefers to call 'demonstrations' or 'aids to a sluggish imagination' - recall the practices of certain avant-garde artists today; for instance, 'Students were instructed to select someone other than a family member and in the course of an ordinary conversation, and without indicating that anything unusual was happening, to bring their faces up to the subject's until their noses were almost touching ... ' (H. Garfinkel, *Studies in Ethnomethodology* [New Jersey: Prentice-Hall, 1967]).

3 Especially Lévi-Strauss's *La Pensée Sauvage* (*The Savage Mind*, 1962); and Mary Douglas' *Natural Symbols* (Barrie and Rockcliffe, 1970); and 'The Social Control of Cognition: Some Factors in Joke Perception' (*Man*, 3: 3 [September 1968]).

4 See Winthrop Jordon, *White Over Black: American Attitudes Toward the Negro, 1550-1812* (Baltimore: Penguin, 1971).

Jonathan Benthall, 'The Body as a Medium of Expression: A Manifesto', *Studio International* (July-August 1972) 6-8; reprinted in Jonathan Benthall and Ted Polhemus (eds.), *The Body as a Medium of Expression* (London: Allen Lane, 1975).

Lea VERGINE

Bodylanguage [1974]

The body is being used as an art language by an ever-greater number of contemporary painters and sculptors, and even though the phenomenon touches upon artists who represent different currents and tendencies, who used widely differing art techniques and who come from a variety of cultural and intellectual backgrounds, certain characteristics of this way of making art are none the less to be found in all of its manifestations. It always involves, for example, a loss of personal identity, a refusal to allow the sense of reality to invade and control the sphere of the emotions and a romantic rebellion against dependence upon either people or things.

Tenderness is always the goal aimed for and missed and therefore surrounded by frustration. And all of this is always accompanied by the anguish that derives from the absence of an 'adult' and altruistic form of love.

At the basis of 'body art' one can discover the unsatisfied need for a love that extends itself without limit in time – the need to be loved for what one is and for what one wants to be – the need for a kind of love that confers unlimited rights – the need for what is called *primary love*. This is what gives this art its dimension of inevitable delusion and failure. This unobtained love is what transforms itself into the aggressivity that is typical of all of these actions, events, photo sequences and performances. It is also redirected to other versions of the self, and the self is doubled, camouflaged and idealized. It is turned into the love of the romance of the self. This avid need for love becomes narcissism in the foetus that we continue to be, but to be loved in this way is the only power that might once again give sense to the lives of so many of us.

Narcissus protests (and thus finds gratification) through the agency of himself. The feeling of the 'diary' becomes (once again?) fundamental: the souvenir, the search for the impression lost and protected in memory, the reconstruction of the span of time in which certain events to be re-evoked actually took place, the association between image as stimulus and image as reaction. Tape recorders, movie cameras, photos, measurements and graphs drawn on maps are the means that are used in order to *freeze* any number of tiny private episodes. And thus the artist becomes his object. Or better, the artist is the thesis with respect both to himself and his subject, this is to say that he *posits* himself as object since he is conscious of the process in which he is involved.

What emerges is an appeal to asceticism, a form of worldly mysticism, and a kind of negative theology. The attitude of ritualism gives further strength to a search for relationship between aesthetic activity and *regressive pleasure*. The discomfort of unrequited desire, the hazard implicit in our precarious existence, and the continuous tension that is experienced when faced with the prospects of hypotheses that may never become realizable are all understood to be *quotidian* situations that lead inevitably to a state of anguish for the *being-in-the-world* and likewise to the pain that results from the impossibility of finding a real relationship with the world. This, then, is what gives rise to the *catastrophe reaction* and the *protection delirium*.

'*With respect to the bodies of others as well as with respect to my own, I have no way of knowing the human body other than by living it – which means to assume responsibility for the drama that flows through me and to merge my identity into it.*'
– Maurice Merleau-Ponty

Thus, the significant terms of this art are the things that are outside of us, our bodies, what happens inside of us and what happens *to* us.

Objects have the task of being the proof that others are either *together* with us or not, and the nature of the situation in which we find ourselves is communicated to us by the physiognomy of objects. The relationship between the artist and the other is a question of being close to or distant from objects. And this leads to the self-satisfied cohabitation of a certain group with itself as well as to a situation of affectionate self-observation for the spectator.

We observe the recuperation of the love object (which is always, finally, an elaboration of the original maternal image that we have lost) and we also observe the refurbishment of this image in the external world as a kind of compensation for the charges of affective energy that have remained deluded within us.

One's own life, the proofs of one's own existence and the entire sphere of everything 'private' are used as repertory material. Anything and everything can be pressed into service – any action from any moment of any day – photographs of oneself, or X-rays, or medical test graphs – one's own voice – all of the possible relationships one can have with one's excrement or one's genitals – reconstructions of one's past or the theatrical presentation of one's dreams – the inventory of the events of family history – gymnastics, mime and acrobacy – blows and wounds.

'*The body is a part of every perception. It is the immediate past in so far as it still remains present in the present that flees away from it. This means that it is at one and the same time a point of view and a point of departure – a point of view and a point of departure that I am and that I also go beyond as I move off towards what I must become.*'
– Jean-Paul Sartre

Some of the artists activate a displacement, an inversion or a censure through anthropological citations or inventions; others bring forth paradoxical and terrifying fabulations; still others give themselves over to the elaboration of their personal myths and turn their attention to infantile shocks and adolescent transfers. We end up with the individual who is nothing more than an individual. *Homo* is neither *faber*, nor *ludens*, nor *sapiens*. He is simply man without the myth, without morality, apology or allegory; he is only a man full of the fear of uninterrupted banality, full of damning affections and disaffections. He lives with his acts of piety and obscenity, with his red and impure intestines, with his taste for decadence and expiration.

In the same way that many small children use their excrement as a tool for affirming themselves in the eyes of the adults around them, many of the artists involved in body art and performances also exalt the excretory functions and the uses and abuses of all of the body's orifices. Obsessive neuroses are no longer renounced nor is coprophilia censured; everything that derives from anal eroticism is accepted and put to use. And this is not as if to say '*homo sum, humani nihil a me alienum puto*'; it is rather an alarming documentation of a pernicious autism and of a frenzied and sadistic self-satisfaction not only with respect to the artist in performance but also with respect to the spectator – true and proper neoplasms of sado-masochistic perversion.

These artists do not 'take a long look at life' and their forms of expression are not genteel. They make no a priori exclusion and in most of them suffering is not transformed into mysticism. This is particularly true when they are involved in the investigation of our infirmities and the monstrous organization of the real, and this is their way of avoiding the cunningly flaccid co-existence of the Pharisees and the hypocrisy of Tartuffe. It's a question of facing up to death through life, rummaging around in the under and seamy sides of life, bringing to light the *secret* and the hidden. Only by experimenting a little at a time with death does one come to understand a little bit more about life – only by showing the precariousness of everything that we are accustomed to call normal (Michael Fried, Trotta, Allen Ruppersberg, etc.). Instead of giving us a story and a character, these artists become both story and character. They are looking for the human being who isn't castrated by the functionalism of society – the man who lives outside of the laws of profit. What's important is not to know, but to know that one knows. This is a state in which culture is no longer of any conceivable use. Once the productive forces of the unconscious have been liberated, what follows is a continuous and hysterical dramatization of the conflicts between desire and defence, licence and prohibition, latent content and manifest content, memory and resistance, castration and self-conservation, life impulses and death impulses, voyeurism and exhibition, impulses towards sadism and masochistic pleasure, destructive fantasy and cathartic fantasy. If we were interested in looking for analogies in psychopathology, we could find them in the intemperances of neurolability, in hysterical crises (emotional reactions that lack proportion to their external causes), in abandonment neuroses, in inhibitions with respect to adult development, in autoeroticism, in obsessive mania, in aspirations to omnipotence, in oral avidity, in sadistic allusivity. If we were interested in relations to perversion, we could talk about fetishism, transvestism, voyeurism, kleptomania, paedophilia, necrophilia, sado-masochism, rupophobia [*sic*], scatophagia. A search for psychotic symptoms would lead our attention to the aspects of the work connected to dissociation, melancholy, delirium, depression and persecution manias. But this procedure would lack commitment. The use of a terminology borrowed from psychopathology is incapable of leading to an understanding of the appeal of this *reductio ad absurdum* that many of the artists now considered avant-garde are intent upon practising and practising at their own risk.

The representation of the theme of bisexuality and thus the simultaneous presence of tendencies, attitudes, affective goals and contrasting impulses is likewise frequently an attempt to keep a distance from repressed traumatic experiences that continue to make their presence felt in our lives. One holds them at bay or even exorcizes them thanks to the pleasure of reproducing the variants of the experiences of conquering them. All of this becomes a narration that is directed to us and that concerns both us and the others who must participate in the same experience in order to enter into contact with us. As we know, there is a certain level of anatomic hermaphroditism to be found in all of us, but for most of us the dominant sex has repressed the psychic representation of the vanquished sex. But this is not so for everyone.

'*The transvestite is the man or the woman who utilizes the* toilettes *that are not traditionally allowed to their sex. It is not so much the questioning of the masking or concealment of a man or a woman as rather a question of a human being who transcends the limits of his own body and who becomes what he desires to be and not what his society would force him to be.*'
(One might remember De Sade's Juliet, who wants to be married twice in one day, first dressed as a woman and then dressed as a man.) Transvestism is not 'misunderstood' – in the society we live in it is *forbidden* and the destruction of this barrier is important. Having broken the wall of silence and circumspection (that always renders it difficult to see who to be or not to be) and having individuated a tenuous convention that separates the confines of the roles, several of the artists (Urs Lüthi, Leo Castelli, Katharina Sieverding, Annette Messager, etc.) place the accent upon the comparison and the confusion of man and woman, masculine and feminine, and thus invert the somatic characteristics, grotesquely accentuating appearances of bisexuality, inventing fictitious personalities for themselves, and thus create a crisis in the crystallization of sexual roles. In any case, however, there remains the difficulty of accepting the combinations that simulate or that *are identity*. (Here the individual searches only for himself but in a guise that permits the lie.)

As was said shortly above, the desire is to create a crisis in roles. Lüthi, for example, is truly extraordinary in bringing to the surface the most hidden of the vibrations of the unconscious of others. He gives himself to our gaze with extreme seductivity of dress and attitude and, thanks as well to a subtle telepathic current, he succeeds in creating a kind of emotional contamination within the spectator who thus becomes either a willing or unwilling partner and collaborator capable of closing the circuit and returning the same interchangeable perception. No one is better than Lüthi in the use of the spell of the androgyne; he sexualizes and desexualizes both himself and the others in precisely the same way and always through the means of an intent attention that strikes out directly towards the doubts and the desires that have been hidden out of consciousness.

The artist's attempt to function in a *different* or *alternative* manner is an expression of the desire to eliminate the habitual position of prestige that his role comports. It is also an attempt to clear the field of interpersonal relations from the forms of alienation that art and culture continually produce and that help to render relations frustrating and non-emancipatory. The objective is to eliminate aesthetic specificity and cultural deprivation. Competitivity, destructivity and the guilt feelings that accompany them are exasperated by the civilization of automation. Thus the enjoyment of something tragically total or absolute, along with what might be called the nostalgia for a prenatal situation (to be found transferred into the relationship between artist and public), eliminates or distances the suspicion that the goals of the communication are obscured or secretive. The public is needed to complete the event; it must be involved in a collective experience that leads it to reconsider its quotidian existence and the rules of its ordinary behaviour. This is seen as the end of the norms of passive contemplation and now the public is to serve as a sounding box. The relationship between public and artist becomes a relationship of complicity. The artist offers his hand to the spectator and the success of the operation depends upon how and how much the spectator is willing to accept it. The gesture of the artist who makes the proposition acquires significance only if his actions are met by an act of *recognition* on the part of the spectator. The artist needs to feel that the others are receptive to him, that they are willing to play the game of accepting his provocations and that they will give him back his 'projections'. It is indispensable that the public cooperate with the artist since what he needs is to be confirmed in his identity. The behaviour of the spectator is a gratification for the artist just as the behaviour of the artist is a gratification for the spectator. When the public allows itself to be *used*, the artist has found an 'other' who is willing to give him reassurance in the fantasy or utopianizing world that he is attempting to make visible and the experiment works the other way round as well. But sometimes the situation becomes a question of 'anything goes' and we end up with reciprocal deception. This is due to the fact that the spectator is a masochist desirous of being punished. (The function of the punishment would be to eliminate feelings of guilt and the possibility for a successive moment of pleasure.) And thus we approach a kind of aesthetic terrorism that considers itself based upon a vigorous opposition to the phenomena of elitist and consumer art. But it is legitimate to ask a question. One wonders if these new ceremonials haven't continued to be rechannelled, commercialized and instrumentalized in ways that are as new as the art itself.

And there is yet another question. This manner of populating the real world with the spectres that haunt us, this conversion of neurotic and psychotic formations into surrogate cultural activities, these representations that aim less at the need of awareness than at the awareness of need ... to what extent can all this create a *space* in which men will be able to meet with each other for the formulation of a comprehensive and all-inclusive form of communication? To what extent is this anti-art capable of transforming itself into a real possibility of the transformation of the very language of art?

The uninhibited exhibition of their physical psychic weaknesses is the only road that can permit many of the artists to make some sort of intervention upon their lives. Gina Pane, for example, always presents situations that are connected to antecedents or memories that are symbolically re-evoked in each of her pieces. Thus she manages to liberate herself from charges of blocked-up affect in a manner so clamorous as to come close to the edges of the pathological. The degree of excitation achieved finally reaches trauma. She presents situations of such great emotional discharge that one asks oneself if she is liberating herself from the weight of the traumatic event or trying to bring it back to life so as better to be able to hold on to it. Frequently, her themes have to do with filling up some unsupportable emptiness – an emptiness that is also a kind of mourning for a lost love object. For Gina Pane it's a question of love that is no longer understood as a solution that compensates existence, but rather as a kind of collision, a laceration and a transcendence – it is love as an interpersonal and intersexual relationship, both selective and elective, love as the desire to vanquish death, love as union and reconjunction of the *self* and the *other*. Love, as Sartre wrote is:
'*the desire to place oneself outside of the entire system of values that has been created by others, and this is understood to be the necessary condition for any and all new valorizations ... I am no longer to be permeated with finitude, nor is my being any longer immobilized in simply* what I am ... *The possession of the transcendence of the other, and in any case as a body.*'
The body – and especially so in Gina Pane's representations – is the cause of sensation. It is more than an instrument of action and it contributes to the life of consciousness and memory in a psychophysical parallelism of processes that assume meaning and relief only when they are connected.

At this point what is required of the spectator is an act of *intelligence*. If we find the work resistant or repulsive, there is obviously still some diaphragm to be broken before being able to come to complete understanding. The public is asked for an act of the will that comports an interest that is not simply an aesthetic interest. If we so desire, we stand within the magic circle. In accordance with the ability of the artist, we can enter into the game, give ourselves without reserve and penetrate together into a different dimension where the *I* of the artist becomes another, turns itself into phenomenon and spectacle, gives itself entirely to its interlocutor and thus realizes its objective in precisely this manner of *being for the others*.

In what way does it establish a true climate of *empathy* that allows the transmission of apperceptions so as in turn to prevent emotional participation from becoming an end in itself, thus permitting it to become an instrument for political struggle? In *The Obscene Dimension*, Peter Gorsen analyses the ideological content of amoral rebellion and the revolutionary or pseudo-revolutionary meaning of attacks upon constituted morality and he asks himself: '*if this aggressive subculture can be considered a form of alternative culture or if it doesn't in fact remain a prisoner of repressive society and if it isn't thus more of a contradiction on the inside of a repressive tolerance that renders us all equal in a neurotic un-freedom*'.

Two poles remain. On the one hand there is opposition (even if lived dramatically) and transgression (the totality of one's being, which is the being of a *divided* subject, is placed into question) that do not go past the state of paranoia, that do not connect the past to the future and that thus move away from authentic possibilities of communitarian significance. On the other hand there is the possibility that the flow of revolutionary schizoid impulses could cause a great deal more than a simple confusion of superficial structures.

Lea Vergine, 'Bodylanguage', *Art & Artists* (September 1974) 22-27.

Catherine FRANCBLIN Body–Object, Woman–Object [1975]

The refusal expressed by Western women at encountering an economic-ideological structure which reduced them to a position in which they had no other libidinal stature than that declared woman-object – this refusal and its development, although still in their initial stages, seem to have been marked by one of those figures of speech privileged in the discourse of the forbidden – in other words irony. Afterwards, and to keep to the work on the body which characterizes the [artistic] activity of most of the women invited this year to the [Paris] Bienniale, their rejection of this function of woman-object – now both named and repeated – appears to me to have perfectly expressed what has been repressed, without doubt, not only in the whole social body, but also perhaps more particularly – and as a result of the complexified relationship between a woman and her mother – in a specifically feminine field. So much so that the present declaration of protest could now be reheard as an increase in censorship of a whole zone of memory in women: I mean the moment of separation from being with the mother or the object of desire – the first substitute, the first object; this the [female] subject must now find in her own body. If it is true that our society works in such a way that what is expressly forbidden by the community as a whole comes to a head in the institution of art in a kind of return to that which has been repressed, then we will be able to measure the weight of feminine guilt aroused by all reactivation of primitive autoerotic pleasure. Because in the field of art – here within the framework of this Bienniale – what women, for the most part, are showing, is the complete opposite of a denial of the woman-object, because the object of desire (to portray) is precisely the woman's body itself.

'A PITY THAT I CANNOT GIVE MYSELF A KISS'[1]

The photographic images exhibited by Natalia LL are centred on the oral area: lips, tongue, palate, teeth. Here the artist shows the movement back and forth of an object of pleasure, one which is either originally separate from her body (food which is tenderly chewed, swallowed, dribbled), or an object external but not separate (tongue licking the lips and teeth, finger coaxing the mouth, being sucked, teased, kissed). It is clear in these images that the oral pleasure and privation of early infancy is being staged. It is the passage from one to other – in other words, the traumatic moment of separation from the maternal body (breast, mouth), to be succeeded by the sucking of a substitute object – which these images are reactivating. The game of Natalia LL recalls the playful activity of 'fort-da' in which the infant, instead of submitting to the departure and return of its mother, gradually makes itself agent of the process, by assuming itself the role of the mother in relation to the object lost to the infant. Still to take pleasure from ingestion, not to renounce the eroticized absorbed material [...]

THE GREAT RESERVOIR

If it is indeed as I suggest, that the female repression originating in the oral stage is making a return here, it is inevitable that in the same movement sadistic impulses will reappear. Because the fear of separation from the mother attaches itself no less to what she represents in terms of desire than it does to the destructive aggression of which she is the object. This is evident in the voracity of Natalia LL, but also in Nancy Kitchell's patient labour of identification – in so far as an incorporation of the whole object, as a symbolic equivalent to cannibalism, could be considered identification. The transferences of identity which the artist attempts to accomplish by imitating other women (a grandmother, a friend who had taken her boyfriend, the woman who was her lover's first lover), which she recounts in an exercise book appropriately titled *Exorcism*, graphically demonstrate the ambivalent nature of these introjective processes. That these are experienced through mime is no doubt because it offers only a weak resistance to the liberation of aggressive fantasies.[2] Nancy Kitchell's fantastical acts of devouring aim as much at preserving the link of love (for example with the grandmother) as destroying it, and it is not so much in order to take the place of these women near to the Father, but more exactly in order somehow to take up position in the place where pleasure springs: in this great libidinal reservoir from which the mother appears to draw only to squander.[3] Keeping the great reservoir full means being economical with what desire expends in its infinite quest – this seems to me to be the demand repeated by these artists. Quite clearly it is about a demand touching the return to a potential for narcissism or autoeroticism. But beyond that, if we respect what it represents in terms of preservation from loss of identity, what it means in terms of withdrawal, in the face of an explosion and dispersal of the subject coming to grips with the object world, I would be tempted to think of this great narcissistic reservoir as pleasure passed on from a maternity which has become divine – or, to put it another way, utopic. Perhaps a winged femininity would have the appearance of the body-fan exhibited by Rebecca Horn. Body from nowhere, always balanced, always impelled by a rhythm which would have, as Jacques Lacan wrote of impulse, neither day or night, spring nor summer.

SOMEWHERE ELSE TO CUT?

On their faces and on their bare bodies the women of the Caduveo tribe in Brazil trace blue-tinted arabesques. This pictorial surgery which 'grafts art on the human body'[4] is the operation which re-speaks access to the symbolic, the passage to sociality. Body writing. In another sort of heat, in 1974 in the United States Judith Stein attached herself to a crazy machine whose only function was to measure, because 'menstration is the act of art'. A text results from this 'parade of conscience', it is a page which could have been extracted from a medical dictionary and which describes menstruation quantitatively, without the least emotional charge (ages of starting and ending, periodicity, length of duration of flow, volume, etc.). Here the analytical voice, parodying femininity, ironizes corporeal disinvestment, the loss of feeling (for the sensitive) which scientific sociality brings about. Here disaffection with the body-life is parodied; the compulsive affectation of the feminine body which motivates the research of Nancy Kitchell or Marina Abramović – both artists who revive actions similar to ritual magic and initiations – contests the same thing in different ways: the disappropriation of the sexual object. Or again: entry into the written. This refusal speaks the pain of separation from that very object, and an accompanying resistance to processes of substitution, deplacement and sublimation, which that separation demands.

Desire for something beyond the substitution from which the symbolic is created? Desire for something beyond the differentiation object/subject, for some place other than separation? Ethnologists used to dream of it. They returned from their voyages sad.

1 This is what Freud said to the child constrained to give up continued maternal kisses. Sigmund Freud, 'Three Essays on the Theory of Sexuality' (1905), see *On Sexuality: Three Essays on the Theory of Sexuality and Other Works* (London and New York: Penguin Books, 1977).

2 Melanie Klein, *Essais*.

3 On the big reservoir which constitues the libido of self, cf. Freud, *op. cit.*

4 Claude Lévi-Strauss, *Tristes tropiques*.

Catherine Francblin, 'corps-object, femme-object', *Art Press*, 20 (September-October 1975) 14-15. Translated by Elizabeth Manchester.

Moira ROTH Towards a History of California Performance: Part One [1978]

[...] In the later 1960s performance appeared simultaneously in different parts of the Bay Area [of California]. Least known, then or now, were the performances in the Berkeley sector. Why so little known? Were they so integral to the life of the artist that the 'art frame' was less perceptible? Or did artists deliberately prefer unpublicized and undocumented events for a closed circle of friends? Certainly, at that time, if the artists had ambitions towards fame in the art world, these ambitions were latent or ambivalent. In any event, the early pieces in Berkeley were some of the most inventive in all the Bay Area [...]

Michael Haimovitz, Paul Cotton and Stephen Laub were prominent within the group of these early Berkeley artists. They were all loosely connected with the University of California Berkeley graduate Art Department – a dissatisfying experience for most except for their relationship with Jim Melchert, an artist and teacher whose intelligence and kindness were highly supportive. Basically these artists operated outside graduate school, working within a larger group of imaginative friends who frequently served as participants in their performances. Among this larger circle were the musician-composer Charles McDermed[1] and the poet Daniel Moore, who ran the Floating Lotus Magic Opera Company, a ritual theatre group. Mysticism, mystery and mockery formed communal bonds among these artists, composers and poets. They were not overtly political in their art; rather, there was a social Utopian vision implicit in their work, and surely Utopian visions inspired much of the political activity of the decade [...]

Paul Cotton, part of the same circle, was equally inventive but, unlike Haimovitz, has caught more public attention from time to time including an invitation of Documenta in 1972. Cotton was and is obsessed with breaking boundaries: between people, between art and life and between humour and high-mindedness – and two central means for conveying these ideas are 'framing' and 'nudity' [...] Miming and play often took place, and anyone who stepped through the frame was invited to ... this event: *One Reel Altar-Native*. Three days after the astronauts had returned to Earth, Cotton, in a self-designed costume (the People's Prick),[2] placed a flag on the Earth proclaiming it the domain of Eye-Magi-Nation. Part of the event was a broadcast telephone conversation between the artist and his parents (who lived on the East Coast), a family reference to which Cotton returned in another event that Christmas Eve. The Dilexi Foundation flew Cotton's mother out to Oakland so that she might participate in this second event at Cotton's studio, located in an old nursery. Some hundred people watched a series of spectacles, ranging from wild comedy to haunting imagery that focused around a ritualistic scene.

Cotton is often provoked into action by what he considers discrepancies between theory and practice, most typified for him by the difference between the writings and lifestyle of Norman O. Brown. With Norman O. Brown as an unwilling participant, Cotton has engaged in an extended encounter with the author of *Love's Body* through such performances as *The Battle of the Books* (1969) and *The 'Second' Norman Invasion* (1976). As another didactic act, Cotton once marched down the corridors of the Los Angeles County Museum of Art, nude, totally shaven and painted white, and presented himself to the startled curator Maurice Tuchman as a 'Living Sculpture'. Cotton gave a statement to Tuchman and both signed it, the artist as 'Witness to the Free Act' and the curator as 'Figure-Head'. The text acknowledged that all human life, including 'this being at play', was more important than any man-made object in the museum. Cotton still lives in Oakland and continues to make performances and punning texts [...]

In San Francisco in the late 1960s, independent of school affiliations, other performance artists were converging. Terry Fox had just returned from Europe where he had been living for several years. Tom Marioni had been in the city since 1959 'doing sculpture for ten years and it was getting nowhere'.[3] Marioni and Fox, Paul Kos, Mel Henderson and other artists began to present Conceptual and performance art in public places and in certain permissive and supportive gallery spaces, notably the Reese Palley Gallery (run by Carol Lindsley),[4] the Richmond Art Center (under the curatorship of Marioni 1968–71),[5] and the Museum of Conceptual Art, commonly known as MOCA, set up in 1970 by Marioni [...]

In 1967 a young American artist in Paris heard that Bill Wiley was interested in a dust exchange. In this *Dust Exchange* Terry Fox sent dust collected from a sarcophagus in the Louvre and received in return dust from Wiley's piano top in San Francisco. For years Fox oscillated between gentle and blunt imagery, including material that often referred to his long, painful encounter with illness. Returning to San Francisco in 1968, Fox did a series of Public Theatre Events which included asking a blind singer, whom he admired, to sing at a certain street corner at an appointed time and for whose 'concert' he sent out announcements. In *Cellar* (1970) the rubbish-covered, dusty basement of New York's elegant Reese Palley Gallery was occupied during the performance by a Bowery bum who drank and slept there briefly while Fox himself performed a ritualistic encounter with the physical and psychological aspects of the space. In that same year he did his *Levitation* piece in Richmond. For six hours Fox lay on his back in a pile of dirt, surrounded by a circle drawn with his own blood, holding four clear polyurethane tubes filled with blood, urine, milk and water. As the time went on, Fox reports experiencing a prolonged sense of being out of his body.

Ritual and sound have always drawn Fox, and both were present in the labyrinth-maze design on the floor of Chartres Cathedral, an image and idea central to Fox's studies and art for the last five years. In 1977 he did an installation and tape called *The Labyrinth Scored for the Purrs of 11 Different Cats*. In the tape single cats purr, conjuring up scenes of comfortable domesticity. The sound gradually changes until their purring merges to create the sound, indeed the image, of a jungle cat; and it is this sound which, according to Fox, is to be heard at the centre of the labyrinth. From tapes of purring cats, from the sounds of voices and environment noises in a river tunnel, and from his 'found' and handmade musical instruments (which he often plays with a violin bow), Fox produces music as if from a new and different world. Using unorthodox means and in secular settings, he works like a great mediaeval master of sacred sound.

Howard Fried, who came out of Davis and was also quickly acclaimed, began his performance work with *All My Dirty Blue Clothes* (1969), in which he placed all the dirty blue clothes he possessed around a room until he ran out of material. The piece had been commissioned but then got turned down by the organizers of the 1970 'Pollution' show at the Oakland Museum. Fried, who shows an ironic and often pleasingly malicious sense of wit in his art, printed a huge poster with all the facts about the piece, including the letter of rejection.

Basic to Fried's work are his intellect, wit and brilliance as a master of metaphor. Perpetually ambivalent, intellectually taut and inventive, his intelligence ranges widely, sometimes entangling itself in its own complexities and expresses itself in everything Fried takes on, including object-making, live performances, video and film. A famous example of his psychological and visual metaphor is *Synchromatic Baseball* (1971). Framed in a lively vaudeville atmosphere, this piece took place on the roof of Fried's studio. The two teams were chosen by Fried according to what he sensed about their psychological character, and he anticipated correctly which team would win.

Fried himself often makes reference to the 'Approach-Avoidance' syndrome in his art. This mixture of enticement and rejection is clear in such works as *40 Winks* (1971) in which Fried performed before an audience in a gallery space – much of the material of the piece had to do with riddles and questions – and then encouraged them to follow him out of the gallery and on to an extended 'journey' through the city streets. With a single exception, the audience one by one slowly fell away exhausted from their Pied Piper [...]

The works of Tom Marioni have, over the years, moved from humour to psychic and mystical concerns. His early performances were loose, casual and often flaunted conventional definitions and expectations, as in *The Act of Drinking Beer with Friends is the Highest Form of Art* (done by the artist and a group of friends for the Oakland Museum in 1970) and in *Pissing*, part of a 1970 MOCA group show 'Sculpture Sound As'. The success of MOCA hinged not only on Marioni's obvious organizational abilities but also on his imaginative and creative choice of topics, such as the sound sculpture one, for the MOCA group shows. The redefining of art itself as well as challenging its conventions underlay much of his activities, and he periodically sought a fine distinction between sculpture-as-action and performance pieces. For example, in *Lecture*, an engaging event staged at the University Art Museum in Berkeley, he had a janitor, a dancer, an actor and himself, in sequence, sweep the floor of the Museum. Marioni remembers: 'We all did the same activity using the same broom, but we saw the world differently and it was a totally different action. It was sweeping the floor for the janitor, it was a dance for the dancer, it was a performance for the actor and it was a sculpture piece for me.'[6]

Since 1973 Marioni has directed himself increasingly towards sound as a medium for telepathic communication. Drumming for extended periods of time, Marioni slowly puts himself into a meditative trance. A frequent by-product is his drum brush drawings made with gold and silver-plated snare drum brushes being 'played' upon a piece of paper [...]

Two other artists who moved into public spaces were Bonnie Sherk and Linda Montano, both artists admired and accepted by MOCA. A student of Henderson's at San Francisco State, Bonnie Sherk graduated in 1970 and immediately began highly independent and offbeat work. Her *Portable Parks* series of 1970 introduced artificial palm trees and live animals into public places. In the same year in another series, *Sitting Still* (which has been well recorded in photographs), we see her sitting, beautiful and alone in choicely selected sites of the city. In one photograph in the series she appears formally dressed and seated in an armchair that has been plunked down in the middle of a flooded city dump. For me the most moving of all the images is the bizarre *Public Lunch* (1971). By some bureaucratic miracle Sherk gained access to an empty cage in the lion and tiger section of the San Francisco Zoo. Precisely at feeding time when the largest number of spectators would naturally be present, she sat alone at a formal dinner table with elegant silver and tablecloth and, with deliberate grace and ceremony, ate lunch. Other of her early pieces placed less stress on isolation and rather involved Sherk's relationship with animals and with life cycles in nature.

The early work of Linda Montano, like Sherk's, often conveys a sense of isolation. In Rochester, where she had worked in sculpture, Montano had already begun to use gauze material, whiteness, stillness and public settings – and chickens – in a 1971 series in which she lay in state, a Sleeping Beauty wearing tap shoes. Dancing was the theme of her 1972 *Chicken Dance* series in which she strutted about energetically on the streets of San Francisco, dressed in a self-designed chicken costume and accompanied by the sound of Vivaldi's *Four Seasons*. Whitened face and large gauze wings were part of the *Chicken Dance* costume, as was a blue prom dress. In contrast to such lively pieces, but still using costumes, Montano did many performances in a state of trance or meditation. She like others has done 'Living Art' pieces in which time is set aside and everything that happens within that time is framed as art; in some of these she is alone, in others she lives briefly with a friend. The most dramatic of these pieces was with Marioni during which they were handcuffed together for three days in 1973 [...]

Lynn Hershman's interests are wide-ranging, [but] much of her work revolves around the concept of portraiture – whether of a person, a site, a city or, recently, a continent. Because sculpture was her initial field, she began her events with wax figures set among objects and sounds. In her 1973 *Dante Hotel* installation two figures lay in bed surrounded by references to their life in that room. To reach the exhibition one had to enter a randy North Beach Motel in San Francisco, obtain a key from the desk clerk, and open the room oneself. The desolate psychological state conjured up by that hotel room became a base for a *persona*, Roberta, played by Hershman herself. As Roberta, the artist interacts with the real world – Roberta keeps a diary, has her own bank account, advertises for room-mates and meets people. Roberta began in 1975, the same year as the Floating Museum was founded, and in the following year Hershman did a brilliant installation for the Bonwit Teller Store in New York. In the twenty-six Bonwit Teller windows she created an entire world of people and events and of times, past, present and future. During the week the show was mounted huge crowds thronged around looking at the multi-media environments occupied by real people and mannequins. In one window mannequins re-enacted a recent New York city crime, the killing of a balloon-peddler; in another a panel of experts discussed prognoses for the future. A mannequin had thrust her hand through a window, and Plexiglas chips lay on the sidewalk; she was next seen travelling on the subway and sitting on a park bench [...]

1 Haimovitz has acknowledged a debt to McDermed for introducing him to the creative possiblities inherent in large-scale events arranged through collective action and designed for a particular person. In the mid 1960s McDermed adbucted Haimovitz, blindfolded him and stuffed him into a crowded car. He was driven to various sites and unblindfolded to find presents waiting for him in a cave or on the slope of a steep street. While travelling, McDermed played with the rhythm of the car, 'making it musical, playing the horn, changing speed, etc.' (From taped interview between Haimovitz and myself, 29 October 1977)

2 Cotton had reinvented the costume, the 'People's Prick', in order to take part in a parade for the People's Park in 1969 and has worn this costume since then on numerous occasions. He has also made miniature stuffed penises from various fabrics as presents for friends and as props for performances.

3 Quoted from taped interview between Tom Marioni and myself (28 October 1977).

4 During this time (1968-72) Carol Lindsley was in charge of the Reese Palley Gallery (San Francisco branch). She presented performances and exhibitions by Bruce Nauman, Steve Kaltenbach, Dennis Oppenheim, Howard Fried, Paul Kos, Terry Fox and Jim Melchert, among others. In 1972, Reese Palley closed the San Francisco branch.

5 In 1969 at the Richmond Art Center Marioni did *Invisible Painting and Sculpture* and *Return of Abstract Expressionism*, both Conceptual art shows; Marioni presented the first one-person show of Paul Kos (1969), and finally, under his curatorship, Fox's *Levitation* was done at Richmond in 1970. Incidentally, in order to make clear the distinction between himself as an artist and as a curator, Marioni invented an alter ego, Allan Fish, who signed his works until 1971, when *A Collaboration between Tom Marioni and Allan Fish* exposed the persona.

6 From a taped interview between Marioni and myself (7 September 1977).

Moira Roth, 'Towards a History of California Performance: Part One', *Arts Magazine* (February 1978) 94-103.

Moira ROTH
Towards a History of California Performance: Part Two [1978]

[...] Cal Arts, an ambitious and experimental art school with a strong East Coast bias, brought out several artists whose bent was towards event-making (Alison Knowles, Dick Higgins, Nam June Paik, Simone Forti and others), and their teachings and performances, together with Kaprow's career and performances by Cal Arts students, made the campus a major centre for Southern California performance art in the early 1970s.

Other East Coast visitors were Steve Paxton, Alex Hay and Yvonne Rainer, all connected with the Judson Memorial Church dance/theatre experiments. They organized performances and workshops in the late 1960s which acted as catalytic situations for early Los Angeles performance artists, notably Barbara Smith and John White [...]

Smith began a steady production of performances. In 1969 she staged *Ritual Meal*, a major work, at the home of the art collectors Elyse and Stanley Grinstein. Sixteen elegantly dressed guests were led into the dining room while the sound of an amplified heartbeat throbbed throughout the house. They were given elaborate makeup supplies and dressed in surgical gowns and caps. Silent costumed figures served them a six-course dinner lasting some four hours. No conventional utensils were provided; instead, the table was set with an assortment of surgical implements (forceps, scalpels, plasma bottles, beakers, Bunsen burners, etc.). Wine was served in a test tube held by clamps. Food was eaten either with bare hands – washed ritualistically by the waiters after each course – or by the guests donning rubber gloves and using the various operating-room tools. In this piece Smith intended to suggest sacrament and ritualistic dismemberment. Characteristically for her, it was a blend of Christian, pagan, mythological and psychological references. Armed with such symbol and rituals, Smith moved away from Los Angeles in 1969 to attend the University of California at Irvine, some 112 km [70 miles] south of Los Angeles [...]

Lacy has sustained the most consistent, prolonged and acclaimed career in feminist performance on the West Coast. Her work has been shaped by several factors, including her training in biology, her graduate studies in psychology, the liberating experiences of the Fresno Feminist group and, above all, her own reflections on what it means to live within one's own body and how, through our physical possession of our own bodies, we are all connected and related to each other.

This goes far to explain two recurring themes in her work, namely the incorporation into her ritualistic performances of animal organs and bodies – which for her function as 'metaphors for physicality, universally recognized and used in primitive ritual forms' – and, second, the theme of tying together or binding figures through netlike entrapments. For her these entrapments conjure up associations with 'fibrous connective tissue, veins, spider webs, and the like'. From her earliest work in performance art up until her recent pieces, in which she transforms herself into an old woman, a fundamental concern has been 'the exploration of what it means to be a consciousness trapped inside a physical, decaying, often unpredictable body. In this my real predecessors are the medical anatomists and illustrators of the Middle Ages, and people like Bruce Conner, Ed Kienholz, Lucas Samaras and Stan Brakhage, all of whom I recognize as having similar pain and comprehension of the irony of being conscious inside a time bomb.'

This is one side of Lacy – her concern with universal and timeless attempts to connect people, things and history and to express ephemeral states of being – but another equally strong aspect of her work is a hard-hitting set of feminist goals evident in both her teaching and her performance. As part of Lacy's continuous attempt to overcome 'otherness', as well as, to my way of reading the piece, an attempt to widen her feminist context, Lacy tried in 1977 to make a liaison with the women's community in San Francisco's Chinatown and finally collaborated with a Chinese actress Kathleen Chang in a costumed event on San Francisco's Angel Island. In *The Life and Times of Donaldina Cameron*, Lacy as Cameron, a well-known nineteenth-century white missionary in Chinatown, tried to rescue and convert a Chinese prostitute (Chang), who sneered at her efforts and motives. The piece ended with the two performers turning to the audience and conversing on problems in the collaboration caused by conflicting goals between Chinese and white women and between art and politics.

Political action, media coverage and collaboration increasingly characterize Lacy's current performances. In 1977 she organized *Three Weeks in May*, a tough, dramatic and moving piece as protest – both personal and general, on behalf of all women – against the high incidence of rape in Los Angeles. She placed a 15-m [50-ft] map in City Hall recording, with a red stamp, each day's rapes and their location. City officials, feminist groups and artists participated in this three-week series of public meetings demanding better protection for women. The events included self-defence classes and performances protesting about rape. Lacy herself designed a cathartic three-part event for women who had experienced various forms of sexual violence [...]

Rachel Rosenthal is an amazing woman who has been involved in myriad lives and arts. Born in Russia and brought up in Paris, she arrived in New York to dance with Merce Cunningham. Like Byrd, Rosenthal brought news of New York when she came West in 1955 to escape from 'the vortex of supercharged energy' of the Cage, Johns, Rauschenberg, Cunningham circle. Settled in Los Angeles, she co-founded the improvisatory Instant Theater group in 1956. In 1975 she reminisced about these early days: 'At first, for instance, the lights were hand-held and part of the action. Visually we achieved a Neo-Dada collision of gas masks, Japanese umbrellas, chains, tutus, periscopes, army boots and strings of fake salami. We made masks, and we and the stage were giant, living assemblages.'[1] The art community, to a greater extent than regular theatregoers, was fascinated by Instant Theater, which ran from 1956 to 1966, and reappeared briefly in 1976–77.

Rosenthal has also begun to make excursions into autobiographical performances, mining her own life for bizarre and haunting episodes. First came *Charm* (1976), where she and members of the Instant Theater used the improvisatory techniques of their group to act out Rosenthal's 'charmed' childhood. *Charm* referred to the literal and symbolic aspects of her three-storeyed house in Paris. The ground floor was the setting for the elegant and charming public life of her parents; the middle for the less charming, private encounters of the family; on the third floor the child, Rachel, lived terror with the servants and a sadistic governess. Below, Rosenthal lived as a little princess; above, servants dismissed her as stupid and an idiot. Throughout the piece Rosenthal told of her 'charming' childhood, while the bizarre figures appeared and disappeared, 'enacting all the things I'm not talking about, all the underneath stuff, the nightmare. They're being sadistic and sadomasochistic.'[2] She accompanied her story by eating throughout the duration of the performance. At the beginning she daintily ate little French pastries served in porcelain and silver containers, but towards the end her eating was 'more and more gluttonous and animal-like, finally totally like a pig'. She performed this piece only once. Rosenthal continued her autobiographical tale with *The Story of O*, and she would like to do more with the play of truth and imagination upon her autobiography [...]

For Smith the ritual meal is both a literal means and a symbol of psychic/social communion and sensuality, two major concerns in her art and life. In 1973 Smith confronted an audience with one of her most demanding events, *Feed Me*, in the group show 'All Night Sculptures' at the Museum of Conceptual Art in San Francisco. Smith created a comfortable room with incense, oils, pillows, rugs, flowers, music, food and books. She sat in it nude. Participants entered one at a time. Each was confronted with the conflict of rumoured sexual expectations and the reality of entering a room to find a real person on her own terms. Smith had set up the context to require acknowledgement and involvement of *all* the senses. Complex and subtle interactions occurred. Smith's next performance, *Pure Food*, was in total contrast to *Feed Me*. As its setting, Smith found a small clearing in a large field in Orange Country. In this eight-hour piece, Smith meditated for a long time and 'from then on it was a matter of passing the time and noticing the directions my attention would take'.[3] *Pure Food* drew upon Smith's longstanding and serious immersion in Eastern mysticism, often of a sparse and solitary nature. These meditative interests are sometimes at variance with her needs for communion and sensuality. Another aspect of Smith's mind and personality is a wild humour which she enjoys for itself as well as for its function as a lens through which she and the audience can explore complex, often painful subject matter.

In 1977, after years of intense and psychically draining performance, Smith created *Ordinary Life, Part I* and *Part II*. This two-part piece, performed in Los Angeles and San Francisco, was the outcome of Smith's examining the effects of her performance on her personal life. *Ordinary Life* combines ritual, theatre and plain talk. In it Smith told her audience of her erstwhile hopes that art would 'repair my life, find me a lover, a home and give me personally what I need'. She ended her long monologue with the speculation: 'What if I said I was no longer afraid?'

Paul McCarthy was brought up as a Mormon on the outskirts of Salt Lake City. He took up painting at the University of Utah and speedily transformed it into a process akin to performance. With only a reading knowledge of what was happening elsewhere – and a particular admiration for Yves Klein – McCarthy subjected his paintings to destruction – burning or cutting the canvases. Since then McCarthy has existed artistically on a consistent diet of bizarre violence which, as he moved into both live and video performance, has been directed against himself and his audience.

McCarthy began performance work in Utah in the late 1960s. In one, he crammed masses of furniture on to a stage and placed mannequins in the set. The University of Utah audience watched in disbelief as he attacked this scene with chain saw and hatchet. Shortly afterwards he left for Utah for San Francisco and, in 1970, moved to Los Angeles where he now lives. While in San Francisco he experimented with film-making and jazz and created a theatre set using little dolls (carved from soap) and real animals. For several years he has worked with his self-image, scrutinizing it physically and psychologically. He transforms himself in his performances through primeval behaviour, masks and smearing himself with gobs of ketchup, soap and the like. Often his little soap dolls act as props and actors in his world. He intimidates, disgusts and occasionally arouses the audience as he runs them and himself through a gauntlet of primitive states of being. He appears nude, often masked, spitting, vomiting, gyrating, clambering, crawling and grovelling on the floor [...]

Eleanor Antin's artistic presence in the area was apparent long before she joined the UCSD faculty full-time in 1975. Since the late 1960s she had lived in Solana Beach and had used that locale as backdrop for many of her *100 Boots* images – a series of postcards of episodes in the lives of her hundred boots who lived, worked and loved in the area. In 1973 the King of Solana Beach began to appear: Eleanor Antin, dressed in medieval king's garb, bearded and beguiling, sauntering around and chatting with his subjects.

The King, the Black Movie Star, the Ballerina and the various guises of the Nurse are Antin's personae. She has built them up through their 'own' writings and art-making and through their appearance in still photographs, narrative video tapes and live performances. They relate to her idea of the world as theatre and are allegorical as well: in Antin's eyes the King stands for power, the Nurse for romance and service and the Ballerina for the professional artist. Theatrical exposures of these personae to a live audience are frequently integral to their essence. The King's character, glimpsed in interaction with his Solana Beach subjects and pinned down by photographs, video and the *King's Meditations*, was crucially fleshed out when he appeared before live audiences in *The Battle of the Bluffs*, strutting and vigorously defending his territory against his enemies.

In 1974 Antin created an autobiographical piece called *Eleanor 1954* to 'confront my four selves, trying to reach a real self'.[4] Presented to a supportive audience at the Los Angeles Woman's Building – 'a perfect audience. They just spurred me on to one of the greatest improvisations I've ever made' – it used videotape to show stills of her personae as well as glamorous cheesecake poses of herself as an aspiring young actress (authentic photographs of Antin in 1954), while in the narration Antin shifted back and forth between her past and present selves, her attitude moving from mockery to analysis to compassion towards her younger self.

Over the past few years Antin has shifted from an improvisational and loosely structured style of performance to more rehearsed events with texts. In her words, 'I am now into theatre' – a return to her stage aspirations of 1954. Additional characters appear increasingly to accompany her through her world, as in, most recently, *The Angel of Mercy* (1977). In this event she appeared on stage dressed as Eleanor Nightingale, together with forty-two other members of the cast, life-size – or almost so – cut-out painted figures mounted on rollers for rapid rearrangement, representing the characters in her saga of Victorian England and the Crimean War. Antin's movements and her 'dialogue', talking both as herself (a nurse) and, in altered voice, on behalf of her masonite companions, constitute an amazingly elegant and polished presentation. The theatrical aspects of Antin's art indeed fit into the recurring Southern California theatrical impulse in , but hers has an exceptional professionalism to it [...]

1 Quoted from an essay by Rachel Rosenthal in *Journal*, 4 (February 1975) Los Angeles Institute of Contemporary Art. This issue, edited by Eleanor Antin, is devoted to a fascinating collection of essays by 'immigrant-artists' in Los Angeles.

2 Quoted from a taped interview between Rachel Rosenthal and myself (23 November 1977). In it she describes the early audience of Instant Theater frequently including Walter Hopps, Wallace Berman, George Herms and Edward Kienholz.

3 Quoted from an edited interview between Barbara Smith and myself, printed in the catalogue *Barbara Smith* (San Diego: Mandeville Art Gallery, University of California, 1974).

4 This and other Eleanor Antin quotes are drawn from a taped interview between Antin and myself (4 November 1977).

Moira Roth, 'Towards a History of California Performance: Part Two', *Arts Magazine* (June 1978) 10-23.

Julia KRISTEVA
Approaching Abjection [1980]

'No Beast is there without glimmer of infinity,
No eye so vile nor abject that brushes not
Against lighting from on high, now tender, now fierce.'
– Victor Hugo, *La Légende des siècles*

NEITHER SUBJECT NOR OBJECT

There looms, within abjection, one of those violent, dark revolts of being, directed against a threat that seems to emanate from an exorbitant outside or inside, ejected beyond the scope of the possible, the tolerable, the thinkable. It lies there, quite close, but it cannot be assimilated. It beseeches, worries and fascinates desire, which, nevertheless, does not let itself be seduced. Apprehensive, desire turns aside; sickened, it rejects. A certainty protects it from the shameful – a certainty of which it is proud holds on to it. But simultaneously, just the same, that impetus, that spasm, that leap is drawn towards an elsewhere as tempting as it is condemned. Unflaggingly, like an inescapable boomerang, a vortex of summons and repulsion places the one haunted by it literally beside himself.

When I am beset by abjection, the twisted braid of affects and thoughts I call by such a name does not have, properly speaking, a definable *object*. The abject is not an ob-ject facing me, which I name or imagine. Nor is it an ob-jest, an otherness ceaselessly fleeing in a systematic quest of desire. What is abject is not my correlative, which, providing me with someone or something else as support, would allow me to be more or less detached and autonomous. The abject has only one quality of the object – that of being opposed to *I*. If the object, however, through its opposition, settles me within the fragile texture of a desire for meaning which, as a matter of fact, makes me ceaselessly and infinitely homologous to it, what is *abject*, on the contrary, the jettisoned object, is radically excluded and draws me towards the place where meaning collapses. A certain 'ego' that merged with its master, a superego, has flatly driven it away. It lies outside, beyond the set, and does not seem to agree to the latter's rules of the game. And yet, from its place of banishment, the abject does not cease challenging its master. Without a sign (for him), it beseeches a discharge, a convulsion, a crying out. To each ego its object, to each superego its abject. It is not the white expanse or slack boredom of repression, not the translations and transformations of desire that wrench bodies, nights and discourse; rather it is a brutish suffering that 'I' puts up with, sublime and devastated, for 'I' deposits it to the father's account [*verse au père – père-version*]: I endure it, for I imagine that such is the desire of the other. A massive and sudden emergence of uncanniness, which, familiar as it might have been in an opaque and forgotten life, now harries me as radically separate, loathsome. Not me. Not that. But not nothing, either. A 'something' that I do not recognize as a thing. A weight of meaninglessness, about which there is nothing insignificant, and which crushes me. On the edge of non-existence and hallucination, of a reality that, if I acknowledge it, annihilates me. There, abject and abjection are my safeguards. The primers of my culture [...]

THE ABJECTION OF SELF

If it be true that the abject simultaneously beseeches and pulverizes the subject, one can understand that it is experienced at the peak of its strength when that subject, weary of fruitless attempts to identify with something on the outside, finds the impossible within; when it finds that the impossible constitutes its very *being*, that it *is* none other than abject. The abjection of self would be the culminating form of that experience of the subject to which it is revealed that all its objects are based merely on the inaugural *loss* that laid the foundations of its own being. There is nothing like the abjection of self to show that all abjection is in fact recognition of the *want* on which any being, meaning, language or desire is founded. One always passes too quickly over this word, 'want', and today psychoanalysts are finally taking into account only its more or less fetishized product, the 'object of want'. But if one imagines (and imagine one must, for it is the working of imagination whose foundations are being laid here) the experience of *want* itself as logically preliminary to being and object – to the being of the object – then one understands that abjection, and even more so abjection of self, is its only signified. Its signifier, then, is none but literature. Mystical Christendom turned this abjection of self into the ultimate proof of humility before God, witness Elizabeth of Hungary who 'though a great princess, delighted in nothing so much as in abasing herself'.'

The question remains as to the ordeal, a secular one this time, that abjection can constitute for someone who, in what is termed knowledge of castration, turning away from perverse dodges, presents himself with his own body and ego as the most precious non-objects; they are no longer seen in their own right but forfeited, abject. The termination of analysis can lead us there, as we shall see. Such are the pangs and delights of masochism.

Essentially different from 'uncanniness', more violent, too, abjection is elaborated through a failure to recognize its kin; nothing is familiar, not even the shadow of a memory. I imagine a child who has swallowed up his parents too soon, who frightens himself on that account, 'all by himself', and, to save himself, rejects and throws up everything that is given to him – all gifts, all objects. He has, he could have, a sense of the abject. Even before things for him *are* – hence before they are signifiable – he drives them out, dominated by drive as he is, and constitutes his own territory, edged by the abject. A sacred configuration. Fear cements his compound, conjoined to another world, thrown up, driven out, forfeited. What he has swallowed up instead of maternal love is an emptiness, or rather a maternal hatred without a word for the words of the father; that is what he tries to cleanse himself of, tirelessly. What solace does he come upon within such loathing? Perhaps a father, existing but unsettled, loving but unsteady, merely an apparition but an apparition that remains. Without him the holy brat would probably have no sense of the sacred; a blank subject, he would remain, discomfited, at the dump for non-objects that are always forfeited, from which, on the contrary, fortified by abjection, he tries to extricate himself. For he is not mad, he through whom the abject exists. Out of the daze that has petrified him before the untouchable, impossible, absent body of the mother, a daze that has cut off his impulses from their objects, that is, from their representations, out of such daze he causes, along with loathing, one word to crop up – fear. The phobic has no other object than the abject. But that word, 'fear' – a fluid haze, an elusive clamminess – no sooner has it cropped up than it shades off like a mirage and permeates all words of the language with nonexistence, with a hallucinatory, ghostly glimmer. Thus, fear having been bracketed, discourse will seem tenable only if it ceaselessly confronts that otherness, a burden both repellent and repelled, a deep well of memory that is unapproachable and intimate: the abject.

BEYOND THE UNCONSCIOUS

Put another way, it means that there are lives not sustained by *desire*, as desire is always for objects. Such lives are based on *exclusion*. They are clearly distinguishable from those understood as neurotic or psychotic, articulated by *negation* and its modalities, *transgression, denial* and *repudiation*. Their dynamics challenge the theory of the unconscious, seeing that the latter is dependent upon a dialectic of negativity.

The theory of the unconscious, as is well known, presupposes a repression of contents (affects and presentations) that, thereby, do not have access to consciousness but effect within the subject modifications, either of speech (parapraxes, etc.), or of the body (symptoms), or both (hallucinations, etc.). As correlative to the notion of *repression*, Freud put forward that of *denial* as a means of figuring out neurosis, that of *rejection* (*repudiation*) as a means of situating psychosis. The asymmetry of the two repressions becomes more marked owing to denial's bearing on the object whereas repudiation affects desire itself (Lacan, in perfect keeping with Freud's thought, interprets that as 'repudiation of the Name of the Father').

Yet, facing the ab-ject and more specifically phobia and the splitting of the ego ... one might ask if those articulations of negativity germane to the unconscious (inherited by Freud from philosophy and psychology) have not become inoperative. The 'unconscious' contents remain here *excluded* but in strange fashion: not radically enough to allow for a secure differentiation between subject and object, and yet clearly enough for a defensive *position* to be established – one that implies a refusal but also a sublimating elaboration. As if the fundamental opposition were between I and Other or, in more archaic fashion, between Inside and Outside. As if such an opposition subsumed the one between Conscious and Unconscious, elaborated on the basis of neuroses.

Owing to the ambiguous opposition I/Other, Inside/Outside – an opposition that is vigorous but pervious, violent but uncertain – there are contents, 'normally' unconscious in neurotics, that become explicit if not conscious in 'borderline' patients' speeches and behaviour. Such contents are often openly manifested through symbolic practices, without by the same token being integrated into the judging consciousness of those particular subjects. Since they make the conscious/unconscious distinction irrelevant, borderline subjects and their speech constitute propitious ground for a sublimating discourse ('aesthetic' or 'mystical', etc.), rather than a scientific or rationalist one.

AN EXILE WHO ASKS, 'WHERE?'

The one by whom the abject exists is thus a *deject* who places (himself), *separates* (himself), situates (himself), and therefore *strays* instead of getting his bearings, desiring, belonging, or refusing. Situationist in a sense, and not without laughter – since laughing is a way of placing or displacing abjection. Necessarily dichotomous, somewhat Manichaean, he divides, excludes and without, properly speaking, wishing to know his abjections is not at all unaware of them. Often, moreover, he includes himself among them, thus casting within himself the scalpel that carries out his separations.

Instead of sounding himself as to his 'being', he does so concerning his place: '*Where* am I?' instead of '*Who* am I?' For the space that engrosses the deject, the excluded, is never *one*, nor *homogeneous*, nor *totalizable*, but essentially divisible, foldable and catastrophic. A deviser of territories, languages, works, the *deject* never stops demarcating his universe whose fluid confines – for they are constituted of a non-object, the abject – constantly question his solidity and impel him to start afresh. A tireless builder, the deject is in short a *stray*. He is on a journey, during the night, the end of which keeps receding. He has a sense of the danger, of the loss that the pseudo-object attracting him represents for him, but he cannot help taking the risk at the very moment he sets himself apart. And the more he strays, the more he is saved [...]

1 Francis de Sales, *Introduction to a Devout Life*, trans. Thomas C. Kepler (New York: World, 1952) 125. [Modified to conform to the French text which reads, 'l'abjection de soy-mesme'.]

Julia Kristeva, 'Approches de l'abjection', *Pouvoirs de l'horreur: Essai sur l'abjection* (Paris: Éditions du Seuil, 1980); reprinted in English as 'Approaching Abjection' in *Powers of Horror: An Essay on Abjection*, trans. Leon S. Roudiez (New York and Oxford: Columbia University Press, 1982) 1-31.

Elaine SCARRY The Structure of Belief and Its Modulation into Material Making [1985]

[...] If one compares the living human body with the altered surrogate of the body residing in the material artifact, one can say that the second almost always has this advantage over the first: human beings can direct the changes the second undergoes much more easily than they can the first. Two versions of the body stand side by side and the one is in its susceptibility to control an improved version of the other. The chair (which assists the work of the skeleton and compensates for its inadequacies) can over centuries be continually reconceived, redesigned, improved and repaired (in both its form and its materials) much more easily than the skeleton itself can be internally reconceived, despite the fact that the continual modifications of the chair ultimately climax in, and thus may be seen as rehearsals for, civilization's direct intervention into and modification of the skeleton itself. Even before the climactic moment of medical miracle, the redesigning of the chair allows the benefits of 'repairing the live body' to accrue to the body without jeopardizing the body by making it subject to the not yet perfected powers of invention. So, too, to return to the body location of greatest interest to Marx and Engels,[1] the hand may itself be altered, redesigned, repaired through, for example, an asbestos glove (allowing the hand to act on materials as though it were indifferent to temperatures of 500°), a baseball mitt (allowing the hand to receive continual concussion as though immune to concussion), a scythe (magnifying the scale and cutting action of the cupped hand many times over), a pencil (endowing the hand with a voice that has more permanence than the speaking voice, and relieving communication of the requirement that speaker and listener be physically present in the same space) and so on, through hundreds of other objects. The natural hand (burnable, breakable, small and silent) now becomes the artifact-hand (unburnable, unbreakable, large and endlessly vocal) [...]

What differentiates men and women from other creatures is neither the natural acuity of our sentience nor the natural frailty of the organic tissue in which it resides but instead the fact that ours is, to a vastly greater degree than that of any other animal, objectified in language and material objects and is thus fundamentally transformed to be communicable and endlessly sharable.[2] The socialization of sentience – which is itself as profound a change as if one were to open the body physically and redirect the path of neuronal flow, rearrange the small bones into a new pattern, remodel the ear drum – is one of Marx's major emphases. Sense organs, skin and body tissue have themselves been re-created to experience themselves in terms of their own objectification. It is this now essentially altered biological being that, in going on to remake himself or herself in other ways, enters into that act of remaking as one whose sentience is socialized, fundamentally restructured to be relieved of its privacy: '[The objects of civilization and culture] are thereby posited as property, as the organic social body within which the individuals reproduce themselves as individuals, but as social individuals. The conditions which allow them to exist in this way in the reproduction of their life, in their productive life's process, have been posited only by the historic economic process itself.'[3]

To say that this subsequent process of self-artifice entails the continual re-creation not just of the body but of the spirit and mind is tautological; for the very notion of spirit and mind – the very fact that a person looking straight forward at her physical image in the mirror or looking down at her own embodied circumference 'sees' that she is 'not just' and 'much more than' a body – is itself at its origins a profound registration of the fact that physical sentience has, after first projecting itself outward, then absorbed back into its own interior content the externalized objectifications of itself. That is, human beings project their bodily powers and frailties into external objects such as telephones, chairs, gods, poems, medicine, institutions and political forms, and then those objects in turn become the object of perceptions that are taken back into the interior of human consciousness where they now reside as part of the mind or soul, and this revised conception of oneself – as a creature relatively untroubled by the problem of weight (chair), as one able to hear voices coming from the other side of a continent (telephone), as one who has direct access to an unlimited principle of creating (prayer) – is now actually 'felt' to be located inside the boundaries of one's own skin where one is in immediate contact with an elaborate constellation of interior cultural fragments that seem to have displaced the dense molecules of physical matter. Behind the surface of the face in the mirror is blood and bone and tissue but also friends, cities, grandmothers, novels, gods, numbers and jokes; and it is likely to be the second group (the socialization of sentience) rather than the first (the privacy of sentience) that she at that moment 'senses' as the washcloth in the mirror moves back and forth over the illuminated surface of the skin.

The notion that everyone is alike by having a body and that what differentiates one person from another is the soul or intellect or personality can mislead one into thinking that the body is 'shared' and the other part is 'private' when exactly the opposite is the case. The mute facts of sentience (deprived of cultural externalization) are wholly self-isolating. Only in the culture of language, ideas and objects does sharing originate. For Marx, the more extended and sublimated sites of making should extend this attribute of sharebility: the interaction made possible by a freestanding object is amplified as that object now becomes a 'commodity' interacting with other objects and so increasing the number of persons who are in contact with one another; the socialization of sentience should continue to be amplified as one moves to more extended economic (money, capital) and political artifacts. Marx's whole work is devoted to his belief that this does not happen. If extended economic sites continued this work of amplification, they would collectively constitute a 'socialist economy', one compatible with and magnifying the 'socialization of sentience' occurring at the earlier sites. Instead, the 'capitalist economy' reverts to an emphasis on 'privacy', contracting rather than extending the number of human makers who will be disembodied by their own acts of making, and thereby subverting the essential impulse and intention of what imagining was at its origins [...]

1 The hand has this same kind of primacy in the scriptures as well, for it is referred to many hundreds of times, far more than any other bodily part, such as face, head, or heart.

2 The stipulation that this is a difference in degree is important, for animals have not only *verbal* or vocalized forms of communication but also the rudimentary equivalents of *materialized* objectification, artifacts or tools. Engels, for example, mentions in his essay the spider's weaving of a web, as does Marx as well (*Capital 1*, 284). The web is a tool that not only assists the catching of prey but does so by extending the range of the creature's sentience: that is, just as a person may literally feel different surfaces at the end of a walking stick or scissors, so it is today recognized that some spiders, by poising their legs on the threads of the weave, feel in the vibrations of the threads the approach of another creature; thus the threads act as literal extension of their nervous systems. Frequently cited instances of *instinctual* animal construction include the arch of the termite, the habit of some birds to use their own feathers to fish with, and the fact that some fish have a growth on their bodies that acts as a 'fishing lure' to attract other fish, either for food or reproductive processes. As an example of the last, see Stephen Jay Gould's discussion of the *Lampsilis ventricosa* ('The Problem of Perfection, or How Can a Clam Mount a Fish on Its Rear End?' in *Ever Since Darwin: Reflections in Natural History* (New York: Norton, 1979) 103f. After saying that human beings are, in their capacity for objectification, differentiated from other animals by a difference in degree, one must then go on to acknowledge that the degree is itself so vast a one that the difference comes to seem almost as qualitatively great as if there has been no point of identification.

3 Karl Marx, *Gundrisse: Foundations of the Critique of Political Economy*, trans. and introd. Martin Nicolaus (New York: Random Vintage, 1973) 832.

Elaine Scarry, 'The Structure of Belief and Its Modulation into Material Making' in *The Body in Pain: The Making and Unmaking of the World* (Oxford and New York: Oxford University Press, 1985) 181-277.

Nelly RICHARD
The Rhetoric of the Body
[1986]

It is at the level of what we understand as everyday life, namely the intersubjective microcircuits existing within the couple or the family, work, domestic organization, urban movements, etc., that the division between *the public* (the sphere of social productivity) and *the private* (everything outside that sphere) can be traced. This division is necessarily strategic in countries like Chile: here authoritarianism penetrates the everyday (for example, through the familial myths surrounding the woman)[1] because it abolishes the distinction between the political and the apolitical, and disguises the fact that this distinction is itself inherently political.

The body is the stage on which this division primarily leaves its mark. It is the meeting-place of *the individual* (or one's biography and unconscious) and *the collective* (or the programming of the roles of identity according to the norms of social discipline). That is why its utilization as a support for art practice entails the dismantling of the ideological use of the body as a vehicle for images or representations of the rituals of day-to-day living, as a material bearer of the means of social reproduction and the models of sexual domination.

The body is the physical agent of the structures of everyday experience. It is the producer of dreams, the transmitter and receiver of cultural messages, a creature of habits, a desiring machine, a repository of memories, an actor in the theatre of power, a tissue of affects and feelings. Because the body is at the *boundary* between biology and society, between drives and discourse, between the sexual and its categorization in terms of power, biography and history, it is the site *par excellence* for transgressing the constraints of meaning or what social discursivity prescribes as normality.

Contrary to what happened in the case of urban interventions, there is no significant record of any use of the body in Chilean art prior to 1973. Then in 1975 two major works appeared, triggering the whole discussion of the body which took place after that time within the *avanzada* scene. One was Carlos Leppe's *Perchero* (*Coat Hanger*), performed at the gallery Modulos y Formas in 1975, which marked the first photographic treatment of the male nude disguised as a woman in Chilean art. The other was Raúl Zurita's act of self-atonement in burning part of his face, thus initiating the form of poetry which he later on came to develop in his first book *Purgatorio* (1979), which showed his mutilated face on the cover. These two events anticipate and encapsulate the double reference to the body that remained active (if only for a few, like Adasme and Andres Serrano) during this whole period: the body as a place of sacrifice or painful acts (Zurita and Diamela Eltit), and the body as a place of mimesis or the use of simulacra (Leppe), one bordering on literature while the other on theatricality.

After his first live body performance, *Happening de las gallinas* (*Happening of the Chickens*), in 1973 at the gallery Carmen Waugh, Carlos Leppe continues to stage photographic self-portraits. The pose in his 1975 *Retrato con hilos* (*Portrait With Strings Attached*), which frustrates any indulgence in narcissism, shows his identity somewhat constrained in a social web of resignations and compromises, as a metaphor of the blackmailing of self suffered by the Chilean subject. The same severe presentation occurs in his 1977 performance at Cromo, *Reconstitución de escena* (*Scene of the Crime*), where the photographic document, again a self-portrait, is reflected in a whole arrangement of objects emphasizing the repressive social landscape of a body traversed by zones of incarceration (prisons or psychiatric hospitals), or by places of sexual exploitation (brothels).

This first series of photographic references to the socially violated body was followed by a long period of video performances. Different techniques appear for disguising identity (the pose, makeup, theatrical costumes and impersonations) as a response to the tyranny of social roles. This fantasy of touching up one's image defies that form of identity which remains identical to itself in the imitation of a model, which remains unique and definitive through unalterable marks of itself.[2]

Leppe's performances present a self which is always self-parodying: this disguising of identity or role changing is a strategy of appearances, of altering or metamorphosing the substance of the body. Here the face is an expressive ruse of a merely rhetorical self, playfully falsifying that rogue's gallery or demand for identity expressed by society in its photographic inventories. Leppe's 'mountain of lies' is a response to the pressure to remain faithful to the roles which society deems fixed or inexchangeable.

From his first quotation of the male nude in *Perchero* to his use of feminine rhetoric or artifice of signs Leppe postulates the body as a *tissue of quotations*, interweaving photographic, theatrical and cosmetic references to different models of the body, and constructing identity in a game of otherness. His body quotations refer to a fragmented self that is never psychological or interiorized, but one which defies all depth and challenges the hermeneutic interpretations of the essentialist notion of the self. His use of the body defines the subject as a combinatory of signs of collective identity within the discontinuous perimeter of the individual.

Whereas Leppe postulates the body as a game of appearances and reinvents its image by manoeuvring its external signifiers, Zurita and Eltit promote the body's 'concrete substance of pain' in acts of resignation and self-denial. Their various mortifications of the body signal a type of subjectivity that is modelled on *sacrifice* or martyrdom: Raúl Zurita burns his face (1975) or attempts to blind himself (1980), Diamela Eltit cuts and burns herself and then turns up at a brothel where she reads part of her novel (1980). By inflicting upon themselves these emblems of the wounded body Zurita and Eltit appeal to pain as a way of approaching that borderline between individual and collective experience: *their self-punishment merges with an 'us' that is both redeemer and redeemed*. The threshold of pain enables the mutilated subject to enter areas of collective identification, sharing in one's own flesh the same signs of social disadvantage as the other unfortunates. Voluntary pain simply legitimates one's incorporation into the community of those who have been harmed in some way[3] – as if the self-inflicted marks of chastisement in the artist's body and the marks of suffering in the national body, as if pain and its subject could unite in the same scar.

The acts of mortification used by Zurita and Eltit belong to that primitive tradition of communal sacrifice, or the *ritual exorcism of violence*. Even though not every manifestation of marginality need pass through a process of self-torture, it still enables one to purge oneself through the mystical experience of going beyond the self. The register of the sacred in Zurita and Eltit, to which most of their rhetorical figures of the body refer, undoubtedly explains the fascination with their work in Chile. At a time when the real is forbidden, there is a demand for the symbolic, a demand which their Christian message is able to satisfy [...]

1 'The Chilean military regime extends its definition of "being a woman" to the specific sense of "being a patriot". Thus any questioning of the patriarchal order is neutralized by the very discourse that treats politics as chaotic. The masculine is reinstated as an (apparently) apolitical sphere dominated by the figure of the Fatherland. Politics is conceived in similar hierarchical terms to those of the domestic sphere: the referent is no longer the *polis* of Greek democracy, but the paterfamilias of the Roman Empire ... If the patriarchal order was previously based on the exclusion of woman from the political and public world, it now relies on the restriction of woman to the private or apolitical (familial-patriotic) sphere as the only legitimate one.' Norbert Lechner-Susana Levy, *El disciplinamiento de la mujer* (*Disciplining the Woman*) (Santiago: Flacso, 1984).

2 'Carlos Leppe's *Sala de espera* shows his body transformed through the medium of television and imprisoned in a plaster cast, with his face made up as the opera singer heard in the video. This particular kind of transvestism, already a transgressive act, presents an imaginary woman in a body which is also trapped in plaster. Thus it is not an act of exhibitionism or of personal liberation (which is proven by the plaster cast), but a statement on the fragmentation of identity. Its staging problematizes sexual identity in general, despite its performance by an individual. Its aim extends beyond the no less pertinent analogy between masculinity/authority and femininity/affectivity ... Perhaps we can add that a programme of personal transformation is necessary to begin any attempt at social transformation. The work of Leppe points to the establishment of a creative subject capable of recognizing in his own body the social conflicts which traverse him and which make him conform to society.' Fernando Balcells, *Análisis* (December 1980).

3 'Diamela Eltit herself works with what she calls "zones of pain", or marginal areas of social confinement: brothels, psychiatric hospitals, flophouses, jails, etc. "My concern is to expose these places, to become one with them by my physical presence. My wish is not to morally change them, but only to show that they actually exist ... It is a form of individual pain confronting the collective pain. Then you can grow and fuse with it."' CADA, 'Como matar el arte y, de paso, cambiar el mundo' ('How to kill art and, by the way, change the world'), *La Tercera de la Hora* (November 1982).

Nelly Richard, 'The Rhetoric of the Body', *Art & Text*, 21 (May-July 1986) 65-73.

Rob LA FRENAIS
The Pit and the Pendulum: An Anatomy of Real Performance [1993]

[...] There have been many attempts to approximate a form that can be defined as 'real' performance. I have in my personal memory a small number of performances I have attended where a 'moment' has occurred where I am conscious of a mixture of fear, pleasure, excitement, questioning, displacement which appears to have no causal basis, but is instead the effect of the artists acting as a kind of 'transmitter' of energy, the human acting as material for elemental forces. This may explain why performance has occupied in recent times an end point, one of the final nodes of Modernism, where the tricks of arranging paint and material are replaced by pure meat. But why do performances happen as they do? Why are some 'actions' mere rituals, relying on art history, techniques of theatre, or simply a desire for a celebration, but others strike through to the essence, requiring an emotional and spiritual safety net?

I'd like first to look more closely at the linked questions of myth and personal experience. There is a turning point at which private performance becomes public performance and that is powered by myth, which has many facets. The principal observation to be made from the era of happenings, Fluxus, 'queer theatre', merry pranks, acid awakenings, sex, blood and flesh rituals, formation of early cults, pre-celebrity pop-bonding escapades, poetry reading, encounter groups and orgies (to cast a deliberately wide net around the worldwide formation of art-based mythological culture during 1960–75) is that only the survivors exist to tell the tale, which soon becomes the basis for a vast academic, commercial and journalistic industry [...]

The question of myth leads to an unstable definition of the nature of a 'real' performance moment. The apparent relationship to the spirit of the age can be heightened by the presence of celebrities, critics or TV crews. Perceptions can be altered by the artists themselves, by introducing the format of a journey, a kidnap, the possibility of danger, heat, light and overcrowding. What is most reliable is the quality of the recollection of the 'witness' and that is a role I have often played. The only way to effectively 'witness' a performance is to somehow move in a direction to meet the subjectivity of the unstable forces which are being witnessed. This is a dilemma which has been thoroughly exhausted by contemporary anthropologists. However, I suppose that my view is no better or worse than the average art-accustomed person and it will have to suffice.

To look at the mechanics of myth and personal experience ... I'd like to take as a particular example the work of Zbigniew Warpechowski ... is a performance artist whose work developed from the early 1960s poetry movement in Poland and continued throughout the years of the Cold War and martial law, physically in isolation, yet umbilically connected to performance movements in the West. Shamanistic and animistic in form, it both uses and rejects Catholic imagery ... [In] Warpechowski's performance, a 15-cm (6-in) nail is hammered by the artist through his own hand ... To put a sharp object through the hand in itself, while shocking to the squeamish and sensitive, is in effect no more than a stunt. As Warpechowski himself put it to me once, 'I have done it several times and I am used to it. This hand is like an old potato.' What was to later puzzle me was the explosive effect this could have on the psyche of certain of the audience – as if there had been some kind of shamanistic energy release. Would a religious background affect the perceptor of the piece, with its clear simulacrum of crucifixion [...]

Let us look at the theatre for a moment and go briefly over that well-trodden distance between performance art and theatre. Many of the effects sought after in a work of performance art – or indeed a work of static art – can be replicated or codified in the theatre. Much of what passed for performance art, particularly in New York in the 1980s, was simply theatre adapting to the economies of scale or the particular environment – the club scene, for example. That does not mean to say that theatre and performance art do not in some way share some of the strategies – surprise, alienation, distortion of time and space, visual aesthetics. The only tangible way to compare the two is via repeatability and formula. This does not just mean scripting – it is just simply that in the theatre the team providing the performance sets out with a given formula which is more or less designed to achieve certain effects at the end of the day, that this can be done again and again (with varying success, admittedly) and that generally the distance from point A to B is covered [...]

I think it is important to state that while I believe it is possible to isolate moments of 'real' performance, the conditions are never truly stable or formulaic ... I've tried to point out that there are numerous rogue inputs, connected with myth, expectancy, state of mind of the audience, reminiscent of the popular perception of the results of the 'cold fusion' breakthrough in physics that was apparently discredited a few years back. However ,it could be said that the drawbacks of these rogue inputs are by definition more active and influential when 'real' performance is taking place. In a sense this kind of work allows a clear zone for entropy to seep in and thrive. Theatre, however, while recognizing entropy (as for example in the Wooster Group's use of LSD during rehearsal), tends by nature to need to crystallize, formalize it, to turn it into a sub-routine that can be reliably called upon [...]

Until now, I have spoken from the point of view of witness, in that I have spoken of performances which I have seen. As I have stated, the role of witness in performance is a peculiar one, and should perhaps be separated from the role of critic. In order to play this role a certain amount of distance must be removed between subject and object, just as a work of art can be only usually appreciated when the viewer puts in a certain amount of spadework. Also, by nature, this form is not practically available to large numbers of people. Artists may, as Laurie Anderson or Jan Fabre did, experiment with works for large crowds, but the forms of entropy to be admitted are of a different nature. Otherwise the riot would be the formal structure [...]

10. Laurie Anderson

Mapping out an anatomy of a 'real' performance, then – avoiding surrounding imposters – leaves us with a web of myth, surrounding a calculated unreliability of witnesses, with a central point – a moment of shamanic release – highlighting at the same time the precise nature of the performative action. The unparalleled technician of all of these was, of course, Joseph Beuys, although whether the forces of entropy could break through his iconic status alive or dead is now a matter for history.

What I do believe the thirty years of 'real' performance practice could have achieved is the ability to conduct 'thought experiments' with the nature of life itself, as I think Warpechowski, for example, has achieved. The recent acceleration of contact between artists, scientists and technologists has led to the exposure of an enormous thirst on behalf of artists for the techniques and discoveries of science. In particular, the question of the simulation of forms of life on an algorithmic basis has been a debate to which artists have been recently admitted. However, I'm not convinced that artists have given back to science anything more than a taste for the exotic, a notion that science has something to do with aesthetics, or at best the sense of a target audience, a mirror from which to reflect science's internecine theoretical disputes. By looking at the gap between life-actions and the imitation of life, by taking a non-mystical angle on the workings of magic, by wrestling with forces of life and death before witnesses, 'real' performance artists are laying down the groundwork using only the technology they find between the soles of their feet and the tops of their heads. They are starting the journey before the body has died.

Rob La Frenais, 'The Pit and the Pendulum: An Anatomy of Real Performance' (1993), published in German as 'Die Grube und Das Pendel in *Relikte & Sedimente*, ed. and trans. Gottfried Hattinger (Linz: Offenes Kulturhaus, 1993) 11-15.

RoseLee GOLDBERG
Here and Now [1995]

[Marina Abramović's] performances in 1974 and 1975, many titled simply *Rhythm* and numbered, were exercises in passive aggression. At *Rhythm 0* (1975, in Naples), an evening performance at a well-known gallery, the audience's responses developed into an ugly surge of cruelty; however, a small group banded around the artist to protect her from the impending violence, and finally put a stop to the event. Abramović had been inviting trouble when she set out a table with various instruments of provocation. 'There are seventy-two objects on the table that can be used on me as desired. I am the object', she later wrote. As she stood passively alongside the table, viewers turned her around, moved her limbs, stuck a thorny rose stem in her hand. By the third hour they had cut all her clothes from her body with razor blades and nicked bits of flesh from her neck. Later, someone put a loaded gun in her hand and pushed its nozzle against her head.

'Real experience' in the gallery was in keeping with Conceptual art's aesthetic experiments. The *experience of space and of time* (concepts in constant circulation and part of the critical vocabulary of the time) reflected the motivation behind many paradoxical pieces of the period: to engage both viewer and artist directly in the work itself. The most aesthetic examples of this included works such as Bruce Nauman's *Corridor* (1972), through which the visitor had to squeeze in order to undergo a changed physiological perception of the colour of light when exiting from the other end. Chris Burden's *Shoot* (1974), which entailed Burden being shot in the arm with a bullet by a marksman 6-m [20-ft] away, like Abramović's work, confronted the audience with undiluted violence that provoked ethical questions and fierce criticism. For artists such as Abramović and Burden the point was to push the physical limits of the body, in order to reach a different mental state.

Abramović's solo performances – wild, sometimes desperate, always frightening to the audience (and sometimes also perhaps for the artist) – irritated scars from a period that was peculiarly her own: a politically-aware adolescence in post-war Yugoslavia, the extremes of her parents' secular partisanship on the one hand and the Serbian Orthodox rituals of her grandmother (with whom she lived during her early years) on the other, and the intensity of a complicated home life where she continued to live until she was twenty-eight years old. Bojana Pejić described the effects of growing up in Yugoslavia, with its annual socialist rituals such as the May Day Parade or the May 25th celebration of President Tito's birthday, and its image of society as a 'collective body' under the banner of the Red Star, as 'living between Marx and God'.[1] Family disputes and a restrictive political dogma provided a hazardous environment for the young artist, and she channelled the adrenaline resulting from their combustion into creating scandalous public ceremonies of her own [...]

By the time she visited Amsterdam in 1975 to attend an international gathering of conceptual artists and performers, where she met Uwe Laysiepen (known as Ulay), she had begun research into a range of Eastern philosophies and how their rituals and ceremonies could raise the participant into heightened states of self-awareness. These rituals seemed to correspond to unconscious desires which lay behind many of her instinctually executed performances. Ulay was equally absorbed in Tibetan Buddhism, Tantric, Sufi and Indian philosophies, and both artists created performances that aimed to move both artist and viewer along a pathway of enlightenment. Shocking an audience was less of an issue than was the creation of situations, the dramatic architectural settings of which combined to provide a sense of ceremony of sufficient duration for the nervous energy of the artists to be transferred to the audience. 'In extreme situations you can make a kind of mental jump, to another state of mind', Abramović has said of her and Ulay's early performances [...]

A work such as *Imponderabilia* (1977), was a canny illustration of the tension between the two: standing naked in the doorway of a museum, facing one another, the artists created a narrow passageway through which viewers would be forced to pass sideways in order to enter the museum and they would have to make a split-second decision as to which naked body, male or female, they would brush up against frontally as they passed [...]

From her birth in Belgrade in 1946, Abramović's life has been the subject of her work. The relationship between the two has always been inseparable, and for the viewer, information about her life provides many helpful insights. For Abramović's performances are propelled as much by her desire to transform her own fears and emotions into startling images, distended in time, as they are by her wish to unravel the perceptions and fears of viewers. Catharsis is the outcome of such highly charged events, and it carries with it the notion that staged pain or crisis is a learning tool for the examined life [...]

1 Bojana Pejć, Being-in-the-body: On the Spiritual in Marina Abramović's Art', *Marina Abramović* (Berlin: Edition Cantz, 1993).

RoseLee Goldberg, 'Here and Now', *Marina Abramović: Objects, Performance, Video, Sound*, ed. Chrissie Iles (Oxford: Museum of Modern Art, 1995) 11-18.

PERFORMING IDENTITY

During the 1970s there was an increasing awareness of identity which continues today. The body is a primary communicator of gender, race and class, and body art reflects the 'role crisis' within contemporary society. Artists use their bodies to blur and cross boundaries of identity and to explore the implications of identity. Critic Lucy R. Lippard explores the different ways in which men and women use their bodies and how this work is received by both audience and critics. Women are often labelled narcissistic while men are not. Donald Kuspit examines Cindy Sherman's depiction of many socially accepted and familiar female roles, which she presents as redundant. The notion of ethnic identity and its place in the cultural mainstream are examined through, for example, the work of Coco Fusco and Yasumasa Morimura.

Sigmund FREUD
Parapraxes: Introduction
[1916]

[...] Two of the hypotheses of psychoanalysis are an insult to the entire world and have earned its dislike. One of them offends against an intellectual prejudice, the other against an aesthetic and moral one. We must not be too contemptuous of these prejudices; they are powerful things, precipitates of human developments that were useful and indeed essential. They are kept in existence by emotional forces and the struggle against them is hard.

The first of these unpopular assertions made by psychoanalysis declares that mental processes are in themselves unconscious and that of all mental life it is only certain individual acts and portions that are conscious.[1] You know that on the contrary we are in the habit of identifying what is psychical with what is conscious. We look upon consciousness as nothing more nor less than the *defining* characteristic of the physical, and psychology as the study of the contents of consciousness. Indeed it seems to us so much a matter of course to equate them in this way that any contradiction of the idea strikes us as obvious nonsense. Yet psychoanalysis cannot avoid raising this contradiction; it cannot accept the identity of the conscious and the mental.[2] It defines what is mental as processes such as feeling, thinking and willing, and it is obliged to maintain that there is unconscious thinking and unapprehended willing. In saying this it has from the start frivolously forfeited the sympathy of every friend of sober thought, and laid itself open to the suspicion of being a fantastic esoteric doctrine eager to make mysteries and fish in troubled waters [...] The question whether we are to make the psychical coincide with the conscious or make it extend further sounds like an empty dispute about words; yet I can assure you that the hypothesis of there being unconscious mental processes paves the way to a decisive new orientation in the world and in science.

You cannot have any notion ... of what an intimate connection there is between this first piece of audacity on the part of psychoanalysis and the second one, which I must now tell you of. This second thesis, which psychoanalysis puts forward as one of its findings, is an assertion that instinctual impulses which can only be described as sexual, both in the narrower and wider sense of the word, play an extremely large and never hitherto appreciated part in the causation of nervous and mental diseases. It asserts further that these same sexual impulses also make contributions that must not be underestimated to the highest cultural, artistic and social creations of the human spirit.[3]

In my experience antipathy to this outcome of psychoanalytic research is the most important source of resistance which it has met with. Would you like to hear how we explain that fact? We believe that civilization has been created under the pressure of the exigencies of life at the cost of satisfaction of the instincts; and we believe that civilization is to a large extent being constantly created anew, since each individual who makes a fresh entry into human society repeats this sacrifice of instinctual satisfaction for the benefit of the whole community. Among the instinctual forces which are put to this use the sexual impulses play an important part; in this process they are sublimated – that is to say, they are diverted from their sexual aims and directed to others that are socially higher and no longer sexual. But this arrangement is unstable; the sexual instincts are imperfectly tamed, and, in the case of every individual who is supposed to join in the work of civilization, there is a risk that his sexual instincts may refuse to be put to that use. Society believes that no greater threat to its civilization could arise than if the sexual instincts were to be liberated and returned to their original aims.[4] For this reason society does not wish to be reminded of this precarious portion of its foundations. It has no interest in the recognition of the strength of the sexual instincts or in the demonstration of the importance of sexual life to the individual ... That is why it will not tolerate this outcome of psychoanalytic research and far prefers to stamp it as something aesthetically repulsive and morally reprehensible, or as something dangerous [...]

1 *Unbewusst* and *bewusst*. It should be realized from the first that in German these words have a passive grammatical form and, generally speaking, a passive sense. In English 'conscious' and 'unconscious' *may* be used passively but as often as not are used *actively*: 'I am conscious of a pain in my toe' or 'he was unconscious of his hatred'. The German usage would rather speak of the *pain* as conscious and the *hatred* unconscious, and this is the usage adopted regularly by Freud.

2 The first section of Freud's paper on 'The Unconscious' (1915*a*) discusses this question at great length.

3 The sexual instincts form the topic of Lecture 20.

4 The antagonism between civilization and the instinctual forces received its fullest treatment by Freud in *Civilization and its Discontents* (1930*a*).

From a lecture series delivered at the University of Vienna, 1915-17.

Sigmund Freud, *Vorlessungen zur einführung in die psychoanalyse* (Leipzig and Vienna, 1916-17); reprinted in English as 'Parapraxes: Introduction' in *Introductory Lectures on Psychoanalysis*, trans. James Strachey (London: Penguin, 1991) 39-49.

Jacques LACAN
The Mirror Stage as Formative of the Function of the I as Revealed in Psychoanalytic Experience [1949]

The conception of the mirror stage that I introduced at our last congress, thirteen years ago, has since become more or less established in the practice of the French group. However, I think it worthwhile to bring it again to your attention, especially today, for the light it sheds on the formation of the *I* as we experience it in psychoanalysis. It is an experience that leads us to oppose any philosophy directly issuing from the *Cogito*.

Some of you may recall that this conception originated in a feature of human behaviour illuminated by a fact of comparative psychology. The child, at an age when he is for a time, however short, outdone by the chimpanzee in instrumental intelligence, can nevertheless already recognize as such his own image in a mirror. This recognition is indicated in the illuminative mimicry of the *Aha-Erlebnis*, which Köhler sees as the expression of situational apperception, an essential stage of the act of intelligence.

This act, far from exhausting itself, as in the case of the monkey, once the image has been mastered and found empty, immediately rebounds in the case of the child in a series of gestures in which he experiences in play the relation between the movements assumed in the image and the reflected environment, and between this virtual complex and the reality it reduplicates – the child's own body, and the person and things, around him.

This event can take place, as we have known since Baldwin, from the age of six months, and its repetition has often made me reflect upon the startling spectacle of the infant in front of the mirror. Unable as yet to walk, or even to stand up, and held tightly as he is by some support, human or artificial (what, in France, we call a *trotte-bébé*), he nevertheless overcomes, in a flutter of jubilant activity, the obstructions of his support and, fixing his attitude in a slightly leaning-forward position, in order to hold it in his gaze, brings back an instantaneous aspect of the image [...]

We have only to understand the mirror stage *as an identification*, in the full sense that analysis gives to the term: namely, the transformation that takes place in the subject when he assumes an image – whose predestination to this phase-effect is sufficiently indicated by the use, in analytic theory, of the ancient term *imago*.

This jubilant assumption of his spectacular image by the child at the *infans* stage, still sunk in his motor incapacity and nursling dependence, would seem to exhibit in an exemplary situation the symbolic matrix in which the *I* is precipitated in a primordial form, before it is objectified in the dialectic of identification with the other and before language restores to it, in the universal, its function as subject.

This form would have to be called the Ideal-I,[1] if we wished to incorporate it into our usual register, in the sense that it will also be the source of secondary identifications, under which term I would place the functions of libidinal normalization. But the important point is that this form situates the agency of the ego, before its social determination, in a fictional direction, which will always remain irreducible for the individual alone, or rather, which will only rejoin the coming-into-being (*le devenir*) of the subject asymptotically, whatever the success of the dialectical syntheses by which he must resolve as *I* his discordance with his own reality [...]

I am led, therefore, to regard the function of the mirror-stage as a particular case of the function of the *imago*, which is to establish a relation between the organism and its reality – or, as they say, between the *Innenwelt* and the *Umwelt*.

In man, however, this relation to nature is altered by a certain dehiscence at the heart of the organism, a primordial Discord betrayed by the signs of uneasiness and motor uncoordination of the neonatal months. The objective notion of of the anatomical incompleteness of the pyramidal system and likewise the presence of certain humoral residues of the maternal organism confirm the view I have formulated as the fact of a real *specific prematurity of birth* in man.

Lecture delivered at the 16th International Congress of Psychoanalysis, Zurich, 17 July 1949.

1 Throughout this article I leave in its peculiarity the translation I have adopted for Freud's *Ideal-Ich* [i.e. 'je-idéal'], without further comment, other than to say that I have not maintained it since.

Jacques Lacan, 'Le stade du miroir comme formateur de la fonction de Je' (1949), *Écrits* (Paris: Éditions du seuil, 1966); reprinted in English as 'The Mirror Stage as Formative of the Function of the I as Revealed in Psychoanalytic Experience' in *Écrits: A Selection*, trans. Alan Sheridan (New York and London: Routledge, 1977) 1-7.

Max KOZLOFF
Pygmalion Revisited [1975]

'To know oneself is to foresee oneself; to foresee oneself amounts to playing a part.'
– Paul Valéry

Question: can a work of art ever be in pain? Answer: yes, if it is *incarnated* in a body; if, somehow, the body acts as the ground upon which an art meaning may be inscribed. Naturally, theatre and dance employ human bodies, in the sense of being staffed by them. But we would not say a play is *composed* of people, as for example, a painting is composed of paint. The script or notation, whatever plan has been decided on or improvised, directs bodies on a stage. It is usually that direction we call the work, interpreted by performers. Actors, of course, may well experience wear and tear, but covertly, in the illusive enactment of behaviour represented as other than that of their own lives. A complex alliance exists, however, between some variants of these performance media and a form that has been influenced by dramatic values, but whose premises should be judged radically different, in that the body is placed in overt jeopardy. I refer to a phenomenon called Body art, or bodyworks, whose origins are obscured in recent Process and Conceptual art, the Minimal sculpture of ten, the Happenings of fifteen and the Dada and Futurism of sixty years ago.

Fashioned out of these sources, some very contemporary work has emerged. It may be distinguished, for the moment, by what I imagine to be a peculiar-sounding hypothesis. Generally speaking, a visual work of art has been bodily executed by its maker. What we see is an artifact that has been put together by certain muscular activities – not the literal sum of these activities, certainly, but a thing effectuated through them. Let it now be supposed that an array of artists construes the 'thing' materialized as endowed with consciousness – specifically, that of their own persons. What had earlier been the hidden instrumentality of the work becomes, not so much its visible motif, but the receptacle of the art action, the corporeal base that has been acted upon by the artists' process.

Their bodies and ours: they're conscious, animate, sensitive and mortal organisms. The artist's flesh often gives the impression of having been exposed to damaging conditions, or of having taken into itself something of the work, and possibly the force necessary to have made an object presentable as art. Empathy has been defined as the identification of the self with the other. But we never had to empathize, as we do now, with the physical violence that materializes art because it has become dramatized by the artist who plays the role of its victim. In an environment that puts a higher premium on 'activity' than on objects, this mirror-of-process theory is the short route to explaining why one of the prevalent themes – or outright conditions – of such work is self-inflicted pain.

An extended literature has grown in support of efforts that include bodyworks. But we only tentatively understand such art, even at this mature stage in its development, because the criteria for separating it from other forms are not clear. An artist may do an ephemeral 'piece' for a necessarily small audience, an event often completely dependent on media transmission for broadcast to the art world. Or the artist may conceive a media-form – photos, optionally accompanied by words – as the prime stimulus for the viewer. In the one instance, the evidence is fragmentary and, in the other, exclusive

and sufficient. This reliance on graphics cum literature permits the enlargement of extremely small-scale incidents, such as Dennis Oppenheim running a sliver through his thumb. Photos sometimes become records of occurrences the artist felt no need to have presented to an initially present audience. And they may even be of situations that never existed, such as Willliam Wegman's and Vicenzo Agnetti's face mutations. So the literature, heavily contributed to by the artists themselves, invariably reverts to a reportorial discourse. Most typically it carries bibliographical entries, compiled data, scenario descriptions; and it comes in the form of interview, catalogues and informative materials published by galleries and museums. To leaf through these documents is simultaneously to be impressed by the richness of their ideas and frustrated by their lack of any felt need to evaluate the convergences of such art. Neutral in the extreme, the tone of this literature would appear detached from its object, until we recognize its characteristic cool as a publicity function. Just as the body is artistically dissociated from the person, so critical regard is isolated from warmth, in a reading too close to serve as cultural perspective.

Bodyworks are international. Aside from a sprinkling of essays in the art press, the American magazine that has most consistently attended to them is *Avalanche*. A small, hesitant survey exhibition, 'Bodyworks', took place last spring at the Museum of Contemporary Art, Chicago. Though a first of its kind in the US, it skimped on its offerings. In contrast, Europe has developed an enormous and well-organized institutional support of body-art activities. A roster of periodicals has featured the mode: *Interfunktionen, Flash Art, Data* and *Magazin Kunst*. Two large compendia, *Kunst als Lebens*, edited by Gerhard Horst Haberl, have appeared from Graz, Austria. And serious viewers will know of the quite mammoth 'Documenta '72' and *Kunst bleibt Kunst*, the catalogue of the 'projekt '74' show in Cologne. A recent notable entry into the field is *Il corpo come linguaggio (La Body-art e storie simili)*, a bilingual Italian-English book by Lea Vergine.[1]

This paperback has collected work and statements, accompanied by biographical records and a critical preface. An augmented brochure, it does not pretend to give an historical account of evolving forces, nor does it situate them within the cerebral and technical context of avant-garde theory. It is a product of an almost maniacally radicalized European artistic and intellectual milieu; it shares some of the jargon of this ambience, but finally not all the remoteness, the concern with the generalities of political right thinking over the health of people. If, for Lea Vergine, a socio-cultural unity depends on the stable psychology of individuals, body art is seen as an inevitably divisive, but compelling index of breakdown. Except for some Austrian work of 1965, the period covered dates from 1968 to 1974. This moment opens in France with a revolt of Parisian students exasperated with Pompidolian oppression, and 'concludes' when plans for the Centre Beaubourg, a highly ambitious and state-financed museum of experimental arts, staffed in part by quasi-Maoists, is shortly to open. In 1972 artists made the old official nationalisms and corrupt marketeering of the prize system at the Venice Biennale so uncomfortable as to finish them off, but they also staged, in 1974, a gigantic, populist and polysyllabic Biennale of their own, while tolerating the Basel art fairs.

Il corpo ... does not knowingly detect the ironies of this background, a serious flaw, but it is sensitive to the alarms that a reactive art expresses. 'At the basis of body art', writes Lea Vergine, '... one can discover the unsatisfied need for a love that extends itself without limit in time ... for a kind of love that confers unlimited rights.' This need sounds disturbing, and the text, as it proceeds, wrestles less and less successfully with what it perceives to be the emotional twistedness of its subject. For its attack against deceitful, bourgeois culture, its accent on self-knowledge and the liberating exposure of personal shame, the author gives credit to Body art, or rather, thinks it credible. She goes further, too, in praising its aim to 'communicate something that has been previously felt but that is lived in the very moment of communication'. She makes a case for this standard ethic, but at the same time leans uneasily towards the idea that, in practice, it represents a vivid symptomatology of the damned. Familiar with the work, she is impelled to list the illnesses with which much of it is absorbed: hysteria, autism, paranoia, fetishism, sado-masochism, delirium, schizophrenia – an endless, sad list of mental disorders, inadequately described by labels. Just the same, one must honour those artists who resist being alienated from what they produce in the capitalist scene by making the integrity of their own bodies, which no one else may possess, an artistic barrier against the social disease of the economy. On the other hand, the body seems 'liberated' only to be coiled by a raving consciousness. Presumably on the far side of that malaise viewers are brought into complicity with it, and do not know whether the aesthetic context secures them against its lumpen terrorism. We engage in a war of nerves, and wander in the realm of berserk caperings where accidents are encouraged and someone could get hurt. Yet, as if this fear weren't enough, Vergine strongly suspects that the attraction of exhibiting the self has overmastered any political animus and thrives well as a commercial instrument. Bad faith is one sickness, then, that would weaken the authenticity of the others, though whether that is a relief or not is hard to tell. 'And so it goes', as Kurt Vonnegut says in *Slaughterhouse 5* [...]

Dominating a contained environment, the body, with maximized attention given its features, gestures, potentials and roles, has been the main subject in homocentric Western art. But the values of that tradition are usurped, since bodily events, though now self-enacted, are deprived of the confidence and integral sufficiency associated with them. The body, a spotlit organism in an alien world, is so thoroughly impinged upon by a merciless voyeurism which it assents to (or rather, sets up), that it becomes an object even to the consciousness of the one who possesses the body. The artistic search for indecency has often been justified by the need to lacerate the repressions that numb genteel order. But I believe that the urge to dissociate and depersonalize the body, to split it from awareness, flirts with a more profound indecency – since it leads to considering others as less than human. Crimes that violate bodies depend, in one degree or another, on our propensity to turn people into things. It is by no means certain that some bodyworks even pretend to such derangement because they are directed inward. But at times the aura of it seems incipiently there, in reserve.

Still, this is to confuse a possible effect with artistic rationale. A photographer needs to be unfeeling of others when 'shooting' them at close range; a surgeon requires a certain desensitized bearing when cutting with the scalpel. Their skills, and those of countless others, could never be activated without the distancing mechanism peculiar to their aims. Art in the twentieth century deals with psychic transmissions and occlusions, in covert, internalized forms, constructed for their own sake. Bodyworks show great impatience with the elliptical canons of those forms, but are still aligned with their basic self-reflexiveness. Compared with the earlier Happenings, they are far more ascetic and essentializing fruits of the Minimalist experience that had intervened between them.

One should say of a number of them that they are interested in exposing the root conditions of self-regard, and of providing contemporary metaphors of that classic modern theme: consciousness rounding upon itself [...]

It is a pity that in its more extreme reaches Body art seeks to invert a humane enlightenment into moral cretinism. But that potential always exists in modern 'with-it' aesthetic attitudes. As a matter of course, such attitudes install such elastic boundaries of permissibility that they offer too much slack to test anything very conclusive. The Western art ritual simply does not convey so much honour on its actors and its viewers that they should consider themselves exempt from the excesses to which it alludes. It may be in covert recognition of this that our artists have often reverted to religious poses in which fantasies of death and regeneration are pseudosanctified by assumptions of omniscience, the Adamic demi-urge.

In that art area where sexual and political neuroses masquerade, the most revealing images or presences are of males transposing themselves into females.

'*Many of my theatre actions are like births. And a birth is like a crucifixion and resurrection together. There is blood and meat and pain, and then comes the newly born child, and he cries and begins to live ... I want to celebrate existence.*' (Hermann Nitsch)

This 'birth envy' (of the female) was recorded long after the Surrealists pondered it in their art ... The myths of Narcissus and the androgyne, once made to intersect forty years ago, ride again, from Duchamp to Acconci, in more atomized form, among artists who do not have altogether the same historical experience. The chief difference comes out of what happens to Pygmalion. Instead of the fable of the stone statue that changed into a living body, we now have the story of the animate body that doubles back into inanimate art. The religion of quiet has supplanted the religion of movement. An artist (Alan Sonfist) shows a photograph of himself as a naked corpse lying on a mortician's couch, and titles it *Last Piece* (1973). He thereby appropriates Minimalism, if you will, to a continuous chain of thought whose hopefulness – the immortality of art – frankly foresees the denial of life.

1 Lea Vergine (Milan: Giampaolo Prearo, 1974)

Max Kozloff, 'Pygmalion Revisited', *Artforum* (November 1975) 29-37.

Severo SARDUY
The Transvestites. Kallima on a Body: Painting, Idol [1975]

KALLIMA

The Indonesian butterfly: as soon as it is placed on a bush – each variety has its 'own' – it begins its conversion: appendages, which a genetic knowledge 'destines' for the mirage, immobilize themselves into leaf stalks; the upper wings, already lanceolate, turn into leaves: a median vein traverses them; patches which are dark or transparent, matt or glistening, smooth or granulous and rough, organize themselves on both sides of the axis. Fixity. Or, a light swaying, oscillation, movement back and forth which is almost imperceptible: the wind.

The simulation, at this point, has been carried out, the change given. This disguise would suffice: no bird, however perspicacious, would be able to see through it, nor any snake; placed on the stalk, symmetrical with the real leaf – the temptation, already, to write this last 'real' in inverted commas – the theatre of dissimulation has been accomplished: the representation of invisibility.

But they – the theatre, the insect – go further. The leaf, as it is, is not enough: the wings will emanate, exude – image in accelerated motion, mockery for the 'patience' of a wall – minuscule spots, greyish, like those which a lichen's leprosy draws on the leaves. Miming until the price is death: leaves which are sick, anaemic, indented, mouldy, barred with these transparent scars which predatory insects leave, and which are stitched in by a meticulous work of mother of pearl.

And more: black spots, imitating caterpillar droppings; or white: excrement from a bird half effaced by the rain. A useless addition: holes or 'windows' with elytron leaves, only visible in the course of flight, just when it is superfluous to resemble a leaf. A deployment of excess in the mechanics of simulation which is sometimes fatal: 'the Surveyor caterpillars simulate the growing shoots of a shrub so well that the gardeners prune them with their secateurs; the situation of the Phyllies is even more miserable: they graze amongst themselves, taking each other for real leaves'.

A movement, therefore, of excess, of ostentation, in vain: even on the non-edible wings appear concentric motifs, peacocks' eyes, terrifying pupils or frightening veins: a whole register of venomous or lethal threats. Baroque or mannered drawings, of a compulsive or hypnotic density. Layout with an ephemeral script/design. The law of wastefulness.

And thus the transvestite: it would be too convenient, or ingenuous, to reduce their performance to simple simulation, to a fetishism of inversion: not to be perceived as man, to become the appearance of woman. Their quest, their compulsion to ornament, their luxurious existence, go further. Woman, in fact, is not the limit point where their simulation ends. Hyper-telos: they go beyond their end: towards the absolute of an abstract image – an image which is religious, iconic, mortal/lethal. To the point where – go and see the Carrousel – women imitate them.

Hyper-woman, said Gallia, a transvestite; 'Fantasy', Lacan would answer: it is about being (all) the woman, when woman is in fact not to be all.

To reconnect the body work of the transvestite to a simple cosmetic obsession, to effeminacy or to homosexuality would be equally naive: these are only the apparent boundaries between a metamorphosis without limits and its 'natural' screen.

A subsidiary detail: the Javanese butterfly mentioned above which is officially identified according to its varieties – Inachis or Parallecta – is known, more popularly, by a beautiful name for a transvestite: Kallima.

ON A BODY

[...] Mimesis effaces the borders, dissolves the body into the space which surrounds it, assimilates it and renders it transparent over its prop; body writing remarks it, signals it, detaches it like an encoded object belonging to language, the pose separate from all that which surrounds it – men and things. Mimesis, fixing the animal, identifying it with the vegetal, takes it down a notch; body writing, drawing a dead letter on mobile skin, situates man at the pinnacle of his attributes, in the place where the symbol reigns.

A 'cosmetic' passion ... but on the condition of returning to this word its original meaning in the Greek: it is derived from 'cosmos'.

PAINTING

Like the painter of the hyperreal, the transvestite and the author with connotations which are manifestly, insolently, narcissistic – such as the photos of Urs Lüthi, for example, of which the only object is Urs Lüthi himself, or rather the programmed oscillation between his him and his her – obey the compulsion to represent a fantasy. Simply, for the painter, the support of this representation is external to his body, foreign to his nature; for the transvestite, it is tauto-topical [*tauto-topique*]. There is another relationship which is historical: cross-dressing is a continuation, and better still, the radicalization of the Happening; it recovers the accent placed, since action painting, on gesture and the body.

It has never been a better time to show a fantasy, and even to impose it on reality: today, the Polaroid and the time-delay shutter release make it possible to make accessible to representation one of the paradoxical features of fantasy (and one which was hardly imaginable): the presence – as in a dream – of the subject inside the image which he has there, before him. The transvestite, or more generally the one who works on his body and exhibits it, both invests and constrains the reality of his make-believe, by means of arrangement, reorganization, mixing up or make-up, so that it passes – albeit by mimetic and ephemeral means – as part of his game. In the territory of the transvestite, in the field magnetized by his metamorphosis, in the gallery where he makes his 'painting', everything is phallus. It is a game of the denial of castration: everything is [has] a hard-on, even in the softness of boas and mousselines. Or rather, throughout this cosmetic simulation, the phallus will be attributed, like a sumptuous and unexceptionable gift, to everything. The ceremony of cross-dressing – public or private, but always photographed, as if to affirm over and above every suspicion, that this has been – does not fête, nor ritualize, nor dress up anything but the chronicle of an instant: that in which, through the efficacy of the make-up, the intolerable absence of the phallus has failed.

The *mise-en-scène* of the transvestite has its reverse and its contrary – another triumph of the deception – in what, apparently, most resembles it: the passion – in so far as the Christian sense of the word: 'correction' and sacrifice of the body – of the transsexual, who, in remodelling himself, produces the imaginary.

For the transvestite the dichotomy of the sexes is abolished, returned to untimely or archaeological criteria; for the transsexual, it is maintained, the opposition underlined, accepted: simply, he himself has jumped, taking the cut according to the letter, on the other side of the barrier.

The transvestite returns to archaeology, to another complementary and comforting myth, that of the androgyne, which situates itself in a time 'of Adam', a time before time – before the anatomical separation of the sexes, time of their sleeping undifferentiation; while the transvestite places himself at the end of the race between the sexes: in their vacillation, at the point where their contradiction is both maintained, accentuated and erased.

I took the characteristics of Kallima from Roger Caillois, *The Myth and Man*, *Legendary Mimesis and Psychastenia* (Paris: Idées/Gallimard); the analytical difference between transvestite and transsexual from M. Safouan, *Studies of Oedipus* (Paris: Éditions Seuil); Gallia's Hyper-woman, from a broadcast by the Atelier de Création Radiophonique, 'To be male, without knowing what to do with it'.

Severo Sarduy, 'Les travestis. Kallima sur un corps: toile, idole', *Art Press*, 20 (September-October 1975) 12-13. Translated by Elizabeth Manchester.

Carolee SCHNEEMANN
Interior Scroll [1975]

I first wrote about 'vulvic space' in 1960 as a result of an art history assignment on symbolism. I chose to do research on the 'Transmigration of the Serpent', never suspecting that the transmutation of serpent symbolism in the wall paintings, carvings, inscriptions of ancient cultures – this traditionally 'phallic' symbolism would lead me to a concept of vulvic space and this in turn to the disappearance and mis-attribution of Goddess artifacts and imagery, to a total inversion and reinterpretation of myth and symbol. Once begun, my studies continued as a 'secret project', for nothing at that time confirmed the inter-relations I saw and the fury and anguish they inspired (the relief of substantiation by Gould Davis, Gertrude Levy, H.R. Hays, Helen Diner, etc. ten or twelve years later was indescribable). Nevertheless it was usually the works of male scholars who first intensified my study – both by keys, links they established and by denials and obfuscations. In MacKenzie I read that: Cro-Magnon people believed in a Mother Earth Goddess; their cave paintings exaggerate the female sexual characteristics. Water and wind were of fundamental importance and were symbolized by natural spirals. The snake symbolized whirlpool, whirlwind, cosmic energy. Snakes originally symbolized the cosmic energy of the female womb which protected and nourished the embryo as they believed the ocean originally did the earth ... (school notes from MacKenzie's *The Migration of Symbols*, 1926).

From my identification with the symbology of the female body I made the further assumption that carvings and sculptures of the serpent form were attributes of the Goddess and would have been made by women worshippers (artists) as analogous to their own physical, sexual knowledge. I thought of the vagina in many ways – physically, conceptually: as a sculptural form, an architectural referent, the source of sacred knowledge, ecstasy, birth passage, transformation. I saw the vagina as a translucent chamber of which the serpent was an outward model: enlivened by its passage from the visible to the invisible, a spiralled coil ringed with the shape of desire and generative mysteries, attributes of both female and male sexual powers. This source of 'interior knowledge' would be symbolized as the primary index unifying spirit and flesh in Goddess worship. I related womb and vagina to 'primary knowledge'; with strokes and cuts on bone and rock by which I believed my ancestor measured her menstrual cycles, pregnancies, lunar observations, agricultural notations – the origins of time factoring, of mathematical equivalences, of abstract relations. I assumed the carved figurines and incised female shapes of Palaeolithic, Mesolithic artifacts were carved by women – the visual-mythic transmutation of self-knowledge to its integral connection with a cosmic Mother – that the experience and complexity of her personal body was the source of conceptualizing, of inter-acting with materials, of imagining the world and composing its images.

The message I read for *Interior Scroll* is from the feminist texts in *Kitsch's Last Meal*.[1] The image occurred as a drawing; this image seemed to have to do with the power and possession of naming – the movement from interior thought to external signification, and the reference to an uncoiling serpent, to actual information (like a ticker tape, rainbow, torah in the ark, chalice, choir loft, plumbline, bell tower, the umbilicus and tongue).

I think the action was also influenced by two films seen at the 'Women In Film and Video' conference.[2] First, Sharon Hennessey's *What I Want*, in which she appears in a fixed frame shot for the duration it takes her to read from a paper endlessly unfolding like a scroll: the text is one simple statement after another of what a woman wants in her life – direct and full of rich contradiction. The other film was Anne Severson's *Near The Big Chakra*, in which a continual relay of thirty or more different vaginas are filmed in close focus. Like *Fuses* it becomes a film about nature and confronts, dismantles the convention of the genital being 'obscene', that is, forbidden to be seen. Our three films presented an ethic about knowledge itself – received from and in the body.

Interior Scroll was performed twice. Each 'reading' required a ritual preparation for the action, a gradual inhabitation of the space, increasing concentration. For 'Women Here and Now' I placed a long table under two dimmed spotlights, in a corner of the exhibition/performance hall of the old town meeting house. The audience was largely composed of other women artists who work during summers in East Hampton, and they assembled during the exhibit of paintings for a series of performance works. I approached the table dressed and carrying two sheets. I undressed, wrapped myself in one sheet, spread the other over the table and told the audience I would read from *Cézanne, She Was a Great Painter*.[3] I dropped the covering sheet and, standing there, painted large strokes defining the contours of my body and face. The reading was done on top of the table, taking a series of life model 'action poses', the book balanced in one hand. At the conclusion I dropped the book and stood upright on the table. The scroll was slowly extracted as I read from it, inch by inch.

1 *Kitsch's Last Meal*, super 8mm diary film, double projection, colour, sound, 5 × 25 min. units, 1973-76.

2 Center for Media Study, Buffalo University, February 1974.

3 Carolee Schneemann, *Cézanne - She Was a Great Painter - Unbroken Words to Women* (New Paltz, New York: Trespass Press, 1975).

Carolee Schneemann, 'Interior Scroll' (1975), *More than Meat Joy: Complete Performance Works and Selected Writings*, ed. Bruce McPherson (New Paltz, New York: Documentext, 1979) 234-35.

Ira LICHT
Bodyworks [1975]

Artists using their own bodies as their primary medium of expression is the most significant artistic development of the 1970s. The importance of 'Bodyworks' lies as much in the ways it revises the relationship among artist, subject and public as it does in the particular qualities intrinsic to this new activity, which has already produced an estimable corpus of work and suggests a reconsideration of the definitions of visual art.

Distinct from the theatricality of Happenings and the formality of contemporary dance, by both of which it has been influenced, and unlike performance art, with which it has certain similarities, 'Bodyworks' is primarily personal and private. Its content is autobiographical and the body is used as the very body of a particular person rather than as an abstract entity or in a role. Action oriented artists such as Vito Acconci, Joseph Beuys, Chris Burden and Rudolf Schwarzkogler, whose attitudes are extrapolations from the physical activity of art-making into performance situations, may admit audiences; nevertheless the content of the performance is intimately involved with the artist's psychological condition and personal concerns. Those artists – Urs Lüthi, Bruce Nauman and Lucas Samaras, for example – who are in the tradition of the cult of the self, pose privately just for the photographic record. In either case it is the artist's physical being which bears the content and is both subject and means of aesthetic expression.

One must consider the artists themselves as art objects. While these artists' attitudes towardsvisual records differ, for the most part what is seen in galleries can be considered documentation. Even in those works expressly created to exist only in photographic or videotape form, the power of the physicality and the psychological directness of the gesture transcend its pictorial representation, which we are habituated to interpret more as facsimile than as object. So there is a minimum of physical intervention in the communication between the artist and his audience.

Eliminating the traditional art object – the painting or sculpture presented to the public independent of the circumstances of its creation – the 'Bodyworks' artist offers in its stead his corporeal reality, activities and psyche. Rather than an intermediary object informed by the artist's personality and left to the interpretation of an audience ignorant of the psychology of its creator, 'Bodyworks' delivers information directly through confrontation and is able to effect and control emotional response while retaining in the person of the performer much of the mystery and metaphor of the object. The autobiographical content which has become characteristic of much of Modernism may have found its most appropriate form.

Since the middle of the nineteenth century when church and state could no longer provide either ideals or patronage sufficient to support progressive artists, they turned increasingly to painting for themselves and the general public and subject matter shifted from classical myths, kings and cardinals to the individual and especially to the artist himself. An important result of this was that the artist became a hero and moral exemplar. The cult of self in art may be said to have begun with Gustave Courbet's egocentric paintings, his radical political activities and his public posturing which included the cultivation of a singular Assyrian-style beard. Certainly, the Romantic idea of the artist as an extraordinary being – genius, rebel and prophet – has descended through Charles Baudelaire, Frederich Nietzsche, Paul Gauguin and Vincent Van Gogh to Jackson Pollock and Joseph Beuys. We believe that the artist has something to tell us, something that we do not know or cannot express, and that we can learn also from his anguish and alienation, from that deeper self with which only the creative are in touch. Society accepts the psychological idiosyncrasies of the artist and appreciates his ability to express fully, or even create, his self. And his self can be a guide to ourselves.

11. Gustave Courbet

These beliefs underlie 'Bodyworks'. It is implicit that the ideas and feelings of the artist as a specific personality are of at least equal value to his achieved artistic products and that if we knew the man as well as the art we would be richer. For the contemporary manifestations of the merging of art and life, art and artist, Marcel Duchamp's influence is seminal. It is his career that certified the possibility that the artist himself has an aesthetic reality. In his *Readymades*, in which he designated with a signature certain commercial products (a urinal, a snow shovel and a coat rack among others) as art, and *The Green Box*, wherein he presented as a finished work random notes of his ideational processes for one, Duchamp renounced the physical creation of art, finally 'retiring' from art in a gesture that became legendary. Thus, in denying the work of art, Duchamp substituted a life of art. Of special pertinence to the brief history of body art are his celebrated impersonations of Rrose Sélavy, his female alter ego, in several photographs by Man Ray (1921) which presage much of Vito Acconci's, Lüthi's and Samaras' transvestite and androgynous investigations. And with his head shaved in the form of a star, Duchamp, like Hugo Ball in Dada costume, and the Russian Futurist David Burliuk, with painted face and a wooden spoon in his lapel, himself became the art object.

The context of 'Bodyworks' was further established in the 1960s by artists influenced by Duchamp, among them Andy Warhol, Robert Morris and the Europeans Yves Klein, Piero Manzoni and Ben Vautier. Warhol rivalled Duchamp's celebrity as a public figure and his work demonstrated that when art objects become nearly indistinguishable from commercial products the artist's attitude can stand for the object's intrinsic interest. Klein and Manzoni matched Warhol in the cult of personality, the latter proving his point by selling a limited edition of his canned excrement and signing nudes as works of art (1961). Klein used nudes as 'living paintbrushes' applied to canvas (1960) and hurled his body from a building to express the void. Ben Vautier went on sale as 'a living, moving sculpture' in 1962. Morris' two-fold contribution was almost certainly of greater impact on American artists, however. The important early *I-Box* (1962) dealt in a Duchampian way with the ambiguity of verbal and visual references by placing a frontal nude photograph of himself behind an I-shaped door; his dance activities were a vital conjunction between the visual and performance arts. Of the major body artists Acconci, Nauman and William Wegman developed Duchampian ideas, though Acconci's activities evolved more from his poetic investigations. But to isolate these few names would be to distort the development of 'Bodyworks' and deny the richness of its sources.

'Bodyworks' was also partially grounded on the heroic myth of Jackson Pollock and on Allan Kaprow's interpretation of his painting technique (swirling paint over a large canvas on the floor, and occasionally stepping into the picture) as 'a quasi-environment', which interpretation led to Happenings and environments in which ambulatory movement was imperative. Lucas Samaras, Joseph Beuys and Arnulf Rainer have all had important experience in Happenings, while the work of Rudolf Schwarzkogler and Günter Brus is related to the ritual theatre of their compatriot Hermann Nitsch.

More recently, 'Anti-Form' or 'Process art' has been another formative factor in the evolution of Body art. Its emphasis was on the physical activities of creation in real time and space, and on the artist's operations and behaviour rather than on what he made. Both Process art and 'Bodyworks' share a sensibility in opposition to the hermetic and depersonalized Minimal art object which preceded them and to the invisibility and rarefaction of purely Conceptual art. Each of these recent approaches to art is part of the modern attack on the object which dates back at least to Wagner's theory of a total synthetic art form which would merge art, music and drama, for it is only through the destruction of the physical limits of the art object that restrictive definitions of art forms can subsequently be challenged. Parenthetically, one might note that Wagner claimed 'the gestures of the mime will amply compensate us for the cessation of sculpture', thus nicely predicting the present situation.

But 'Bodyworks' is significantly a product of a larger intellectual and social context as well. It is a result of the same sensibilities and attitudes that account for the acceptance of public relations-packaged demagogues and the popularity of grotesque and sexually ambiguous performers such as Alice Cooper. We require superstars, gurus and personalities. We join groups in order to encounter each other and find ourselves; our trust in astrologers and cults demonstrates a lack of faith in our own individuality. Dehumanized, we seek out and celebrate assertive personalities interestingly presented. Body artists confront us with our neurotic needs and pathologic behaviour in an artistically controlled and ritualized manner. It may be occasionally repellent but the need for it exists, and it is aesthetically stimulating, vigorous and magnetic.

Psychological content is certainly not new to art. Anguished introspection, sexual fantasies and fetishes already appeared at the turn of the century in Edvard Munch, Max Klinger and others. The Surrealists based their aesthetic on Freudian principles, and his thought has long been absorbed into the mainstream of modern art. 'Bodyworks' already reflects the thinking and strategies of Norman O. Brown, R.D. Laing and Erving Goffman.

The major themes of body artists: rituals of self-transformation, social interaction and the inter-relationship of creativity, sexuality and dying, all find reflection, if not their sources, in these men. Brown recognizes madness, hostility and alienation as the general condition of mankind, and Laing advises that madness 'may also be breakthrough'. Goffman in two celebrated sociological studies, *The Presentation of Self in Everyday Life* and *Interaction Ritual*, the titles of which well represent the concerns of Body art, establishes a performance model for social situations in which the self is a dramatic character created to suit each particular situation.

The strengths of 'Bodyworks' lie just in how much it draws from the dramatic contexts of everyone's customary social role playing as well as the way it touches one's innermost fantasy life. That it does not observe traditional artistic forms and conventions may disturb some, as might the intimacy of its themes and frankness of treatment. Nevertheless, in its return to the expression of very basic human concerns, emotional experiences, psychological phenomena and personal communication, 'Bodyworks' is essentially humanitarian; its values are not vested in things but in society.

Ira Licht, *Bodyworks* (Chicago: Museum of Contemporary Art, 1975).

Lucy R. LIPPARD

The Pains and Pleasures of Rebirth: Women's Body Art [1976]

The 1970s have seen the proliferation of a new type of art in which the primary image and/or medium is the artist's own body [...]

When women began to use their own faces and bodies in photo-works, performance, film and video, rather than appearing as props in pieces by men, it was inevitable that body art would acquire a different tone. Since 1970, when the women's movement hit the art world, it has; and the questions it raises concern not only form and content, but context and political climate. Although the Western world is habitually considered a cultural whole, varying points of view on women's body art have emerged on both sides of the Atlantic, on the two American coasts, and particularly from the two sexes.

I have no strict definition of body art to offer, since I am less interested in categorizing it than in the issues it raises and in its relationship to feminism. Early on, the term 'body art' was used too loosely, like all art labels, and it has since been applied to all performance art and much autobiographical art rather than just to that art which focuses on the body or body parts. Usually the artist's own body is the medium, but at times, especially in men's work, other bodies are used, envisioned as extensions of the artist him/herself. The differences between men's and women's body art are differences of attitude, which will probably be neither seen nor sensed by those who resist or are simply unaware of the possibility (and ramifications) of such an approach. I am not setting out to draw any conclusions, but to provoke thought and discussion about sexual and gender-oriented uses of the body in Conceptual art by women.

As Lea Vergine has pointed out in her book *Il Corpo come Linguaggio*,[1] body art originated in Europe, though not with the expressionist Happenings of the sado-masochistic Viennese school in 1962, as she states, but with Yves Klein's use of nude women as 'living brushes'.[2] In the US, something like body art was an aspect of many Happenings from the late 1950s on, but Body works as entities in themselves only emerged in the late 1960s as an offshoot of Minimalism, Conceptualism, film, video and performance art. Virtually no women made Body art in New York during the late 1960s, although it had been an important element in the *oeuvres* of Carolee Schneemann, Yayoi Kusama, Charlotte Moorman, Yvonne Rainer, Joan Jonas and others. In the early days of the new feminism, the first art by women to be taken seriously and accepted into the gallery and museum structure rarely differed from the prevailing, primarily abstract styles initiated by men. If it did reflect a different sensibility beneath an acceptable facade, this was hardly noticed by either men or women.

Body works by women, and art dealing with specifically female or feminist issues, materials, images and experience, whatever style they were couched in, became publicly visible with more difficulty than mainstream art and have therefore acquired a 'radical' image in some circles. Although such 'women's work' eventually suffered a brief vogue, it was initially considered clever or pretty, but not important, and was often relegated to the category of naive art or craft. This despite the fact that the autobiographical and narrative modes now fashionable were in part inspired by women's activities, especially consciousness-raising. Indeed, since much women's work came out of isolation or feminist enclaves rather than from the general 'scene', and since it attempted to establish a new iconography, it was justifiably perceived as coming from an 'other' point of view, and it was frequently labelled retrograde for its lack of compliance with the 'evolutionary' mainstream.

In a parallel development, the concept of 'female imagery' arose on the West Coast through the ideas and programmes of Judy Chicago and Miriam Schapiro. The initial notion (central-focus abstraction, boxes, spheres, ovals) emphasized body identification and biologically derived forms, primarily in painting and sculpture. This idea met strong resistance when it reached the East Coast and in New York – the Minimal/Conceptual stronghold – it was diffused into more deadpan styles and 'avant-garde' media. Nevertheless, all kinds of possibilities were opened up to women artists here who had recently espoused feminism, wanted change in their art as well as in their lives, and were mustering the courage to deal publicly with intimate and specifically female experience. If the results on the East and West Coasts were somewhat different, the motivations were the same. Now, six years later, body art with a feminist consciousness is still considered to be more subversive than neutral art by women that ignores the sexual identity of its maker and/or its audience.

In Europe, on the other hand, an opposite situation seems to have developed. 'Neutral' art made by women still has little chance of making it into the market mainstream, while the male establishment, unsympathetic to women's participation in the art world as equal competitors, has approved (if rather patronizingly and perhaps lasciviously) of women working with their own, preferably attractive, bodies and faces. Of the handful of women artists who currently appear at all in vanguard European magazines and exhibitions, the large majority deal with their own faces and figures. This was borne out by last Autumn's 'Biennale des Jeunes' in Paris. I have been told that both the male editor of an Italian art tabloid and a male French neo-Duchampian artist have discouraged women from working in other ways by publicly and powerfully applauding women's art which limits itself to these areas. Perhaps as a result, female critics like Catherine Francblin have had negative reactions to women's body art. In an interesting article in *Art Press*,[3] she sees it as a return to infantilism and an inability to separate one's own identity from that of the mother, or subject from object. She blames these artists for: '*reactivation of primitive autoerotic pleasures. For what most women expose in the field of art ... is just the opposite of a denial of the woman as object insamuch as the object of desire is precisely the woman's own body*' [...]

It is no wonder that women artists deal so often with sexual imagery, consciously or unconsciously, in abstract, representational and Conceptual styles. Even now, if less so than before, women are raised to be aware that our faces and figures will affect our fortunes and to mould these parts of ourselves, however insecure we may feel about them, into forms that will please the (male) audience. When women use their own bodies in their art work, they are using their *selves*: a significant psychological factor converts these bodies or faces from object to subject. However, there are ways and ways of using one's own body, and women have not always avoided self-exploitation. A woman artist's approach to herself is necessarily complicated by social stereotypes. I must admit to a personal lack of sympathy with women who have themselves photographed in black stockings, garter belts and boots, with bare breasts, bananas and coy, come-hither glances. Parody it may be (as in Dutch artist Marja Samsom's 'humorous glamour pictures' featuring her alter ego 'Miss Kerr', or in Polish artist Natalia LL's red-lipped, tongue-and-sucking 'Consumption art'), but the artist rarely seems to get the last laugh. A woman using her own face and body has a right to do what she will with them, but it is a subtle abyss that separates men's use of women for sexual titillation from women's use of women to expose that insult.

It was not just shyness, I suspect, that kept many women from making their own Body art in 1967 to 1971 when Bruce Nauman was 'Thighing', Vito Acconci was masturbating, Dennis Oppenheim was sunbathing and burning himself and Barry Le Va was slamming into walls. It seemed like another very male pursuit, a manipulation of the audience's voyeurist impulses, not likely to appeal to vulnerable women artists just emerging from isolation. Articles and books on Body art include frequent pictures of nude females, but few women artists.[4] Men can use beautiful, sexy women as neutral objects or surfaces,[5] but when women use their own faces and bodies they are immediately accused of narcissism. There is an element of exhibitionism in all body art, perhaps a legitimate result of the choice between exploiting oneself or someone else. Yet the degree to which narcissism informs and affects the work varies immensely. Because women are considered sex objects, it is taken for granted that any woman who presents her nude body in public is doing so because she thinks she is beautiful. She is a narcissist, and Acconci, with his less romantic image and pimply back, is an artist.

Yet Vergine has noted that 'generally speaking, it is the women, like Joan Jonas, who are the least afraid to know their own body, who don't censor it. They make attempts at discovery beyond acculturation'.[6] I must say I admire the courage of the women with less than beautiful bodies who defy convention and become particularly vulnerable to cruel criticism, although those women who *do* happen to be physically well endowed probably come in for more punishment in the long run. Hans Peter Feldmann can use a series of ridiculous porno-pinups as his art,[7] but Hannah Wilke, a glamour girl in her own right who sees her art as 'seduction', is considered a little too good to be true when she flaunts her body in parody of the role she actually plays in real life. She has been making erotic art with vaginal imagery for over a decade, and since the women's movement, has begun to do performances in conjunction with her sculpture, but her own confusion of her roles as beautiful woman and artist, as flirt and feminist, has resulted at times in politically ambiguous manifestations which have exposed her to criticism on a personal as well as on an artistic level.

Another case in point is Carolee Schneemann, known in the early 1960s as a 'body beautiful' because she appeared nude in Happenings – her own as well as those of Claes Oldenburg and others, though for years she was labelled more comfortably 'dancer' than 'artist' – 'an image, but not an Image-Maker, creating my own self-image' (1968). Schneemann's work has always been concerned with sexual (and personal) freedom, a theme still often considered unacceptable from a woman: she intends to prove that 'the life of the body is more *variously* expressive than a sex-negative society can admit. I didn't stand naked in front of 300 people because I wanted to be fucked, but because my sex and work were harmoniously experienced. I could have the audacity or courage to show the body as a source of varying emotive power' (1968). 'I use my nude body in *Up To and Including Her Limits* as the stripped-down, undecorated human object' (1975). 'In some sense I made a gift of my body to other women: giving our bodies back to ourselves. The haunting images of the Cretan bull dancer – joyful, free, bare-breasted, skilled women leaping precisely from danger to ascendancy, guided my imagination' (1968).[8]

A similarly defiant narcissism or 'vulgarity' resulted when Lynda Benglis confronted the double standard head-on in some advertisements for herself, which provided the liveliest controversy the art world has had for years. A respected sculptor (whose imagery is, incidentally, as abstract as it is sexual[9]) and video artist (here the imagery is autobiographical and autoerotic), Benglis has published a series of photographic ads for her exhibitions that included: herself in a Greek boy's skirt; herself leaning butchly on a car; herself as a pin-up in a famous Betty Grable pose, but with her jeans dropped around her ankles; and finally – the *coup de grâce* – herself as a greased nude in sunglasses, belligerently sporting a gigantic dildo. The uproar that this last image created proved conclusively that there are still things women may not do. The notion of sexual transformation has, after all, been around for some time. No such clamour arose in 1970 when Vito Acconci burned hair from his chest, 'pulling at it, making it supple, flexible – an attempt to develop a female breast', then tucked his penis between his legs to 'extend the sex change' and 'acquired a female form' by having a woman kneel behind him with his penis 'disappearing' in her mouth.[10] Nor was there any hullabaloo when Scott Burton promenaded Fourteenth Street in drag for a 1969 Street Work, or when he flaunted a giant black phallus in a static performance in 1973, when William Wegman made his amusing *trompe-l'oeil* 'breast' piece (on video, with his elbows) or when Lucas Samaras played with himself in front of his Polaroid camera.

It has often been remarked that body art reflects the 'role crisis' in contemporary life. The urge to androgyny, in fact, has been frequently expressed by artists of both

I must say
I admire the
courage of the
women with
less than
beautiful
bodies
who defy
convention
and become
particularly
vulnerable to cruel
criticism, although
those women
who do
happen
to be
physically
well
endowed
probably
come in for more
punishment in
the long run.

Lucy R. **LIPPARD** The Pains and Pleasures of Rebirth: Women's Body Art, 1976 sexes, though more often by men than by women (oddly, given the advantage of being male in this society). Urs Lüthi, the Swiss artist who makes campy transvestite photodramas starring himself, says that ambivalence is the most significant aspect of his work, and that he sees himself as a stranger. Katharina Sieverding, in Dusseldorf, has made photoworks on 'Aspects of Transvestism' which she sees not as a pathological phenomenon but as 'communications material', exposing roles, repression, ambiguity, possibility and self-extension: 'The conquest of another gender takes place in oneself.'[11] Such a positive approach has more in common with the traditional (Platonic, Gnostic, etc.) myth of the androgyne as two in one, 'the outside as the inside and the male with the female neither male nor female'[12] than with contemporary art's emphasis on separation instead of union of the two sexes. A woman working with androgyny these days would not be 'accused' of being a lesbian, because gay women no longer want to be men, but see themselves as the last word in woman-identified women.

In 1972,in Halifax, Martha Wilson made a 'drag' piece in which she transformed herself first into a man and then into a man dressed as a woman. Suzy Lake, in Montreal, transforms herself into her friends, both male and female, in two ways – with cosmetics and through photo-retouching. In *Suzy Lake as Gary Smith* the documentation is organized 'with reference to a binary logic: the first row = female, augmentation, transformation done on the actual subject; the second row = male, diminution, transformation done at a distance on the photo image.'[13] In Annette Messager's albums of found photographic images of women's lives, she has created *femmes-hommes* and *hommes-femmes* whose disguises are lightly laid over their dominant characteristics; men are still men (although with long lashes and red lips), and women are still women (although with beards and moustaches). Jacki Apple's *Identity Exchanges*, *Transfers* and *Redefinitions* also involve impersonation of both sexes and 'the relationship between the many views of a single person and the varying positions of the viewers to the object'.[14] Eleanor Antin's several art personae include one man – a seventeenth-century king in whose beard, boots, cape and sword she visits her subjects on the streets of Solana Beach, California. Adrian Piper too has a male ego – the 'Mythic Being' with Afro, shades and moustache, who also walks the streets in a continuation of Piper's several years of exploration of the boundaries of her personality. 'The fact that I'm a woman I'm sure has a great deal to do with it ... at times I was "violating my body"; I was making it public. I was exposing it; I was turning me into an object ... '[15] Dressed as the Mythic Being, she re-enacts events from her own life but re-experiences them as a man. One of the many things the Mythic Being is to his creator is 'a therapeutic device for freeing me of the burden of my past, which haunts me, determines all my actions ... '[16]

For the most part, however, women are more concerned with female than with male roles and role models.[17] Ulrike Rosenbach, in Germany, has made a series of videotapes of herself dressed in the high hat, or *Haube,* worn in the fourteenth century by married women and made a symbol of self-confidence and equality in the Renaissance; she uses it 'to transcend the conventional erotic context of contemporary women'. In a 1974 performance called *Isolation is Transparent*, dressed in a black net leotard, she combined erotic 'coquetry with the female body' and 'man's work with hammer and nails', weaving a rope skirt around herself from the corners of the space until she became 'the centre of the earth'.[18] Also in performance, Yugoslavian artist Marina Abramović recorded her reactions after swallowing pills intended to cure schizophrenia. Two cameras, one pointed at the artist and the other at the audience, emphasized the subject/object relationship and the perfectly natural desire to see yourself as others see you. Camera and video monitor have multiplied the mirrors into which for centuries women have peered anxiously before going out to confront the world [...]

Men, however, when not using themselves, are using women. Vergine has written about the 'acute gynaephobia' demonstrated in much male body art, and sees many of its manifestations as an 'envy of the uterus as capacity for creation'. Hermann Nitsch, in a destructive male imitation of the constructive female ability to give birth, smears blood and animal guts on himself and other men, calling this a 'birth ... like a crucifixion and resurrection together'.[19] Stanislao Pacus seems to speak for many of his colleagues when he declares that, 'Woman annuls creativeness. She is the dualistic model of love-hate in which the artist loses himself and from which, with intellectual effort, he escapes. To reconquer his professional conscience the artist derides the loved-hated woman's nakedness'.[20] Vettor Pisani chains women in his performances and archaically equates the female with 'darkness'. Such statements are parried by Tania Mouraud, who has written that,

'*Women, who create, know what creation is. I started to paint after bringing my daughter into the world; the male argument which sees the maternal sensibility as an obstacle to creation seems inverse. On the contrary, the male's fixation on his sex, the fundamental which animates him of one day finding himself impotent, has completely falsified the very notion of art. Women do not act out of fear, but out of love and knowledge.*'[21]

European men, less conscious of feminism than Americans and less intimidated by women's consciousness of themselves, are particularly guilty of exploitation of women's bodies in their art, but the US is not far behind. Acconci has tied up and otherwise manipulated women psychologically and physically; James Collins, as his own voyeur hero, 'watches' women as erotic objects on film; Roger Cutworth makes pallid films which use naked women as though we still lived in the Renaissance; Chris Burden has thrown burning matches on his wife's nude body in performance. In fact, it is difficult to find any positive image whatsoever of women in male body art.

Much of the work discussed above clearly rises from a neurotic dissatisfaction with the self. There are exceptions on both sides, but, whereas female unease is usually dealt with hopefully, in terms of gentle self-exploration, self-criticism or transformation, anxiety about the masculine role tends to take a violent, even self-destructive form. Acconci and Oppenheim burned, scarred, irritated their own bodies around 1970; Burden has taken the lead since then by having himself shot in the arm, locking himself in a baggage locker for five days, nearly electrocuting himself, nearly immolating himself, nearly being run over, and so forth. Though lacking the horror-show theatricality of the Viennese S&M school, the deadpan masochism of American male body artists has a decidedly chilling effect.

Almost the only woman who engages in such practices is Gina Pane, in Paris, who has cut herself with razor blades, eaten until she got sick and subjected herself to other tortures. Her self-mutilation is no less repellent than the men's, but it does exist within a framework which is curiously feminine. Take, for instance, her *Sentimental Action 1973*, a performance she describes as the 'projection of an "intra" space' activated by the sentiments of 'the magic mother/child relationship, symbolized by death ... a symbiotic relationship by which one discovers different emotional solutions'. Using her body as a 'conductor', she takes apart 'the prime image – the red rose, mystic flower, erotic flower, transformed into a vagina by reconstitution into its most present state: the painful one'.[22] Photodocumentation shows the artist dressed in white with her face hidden in a bunch of roses and her bleeding arm, pierced by a line of tacks, stretched out before her.

If few women artist inflict pain on their own bodies, the fear of pain, cruelty and violence surfaces frequently in their work. Hannah Wilke's *S.O.S* (*Starification Object Series*) 1974 includes a performance in which, shirtless, she flirts with the audience while they chew bubblegum, which she then forms into tiny loops resembling vaginas and sticks in patterns on her nude torso. She calls these 'stars', in a play on the celebrity game, but they are also scars, relating on the positive side to African rituals through which women gain beauty and status, and on the negative side to the anguish of the artist's real 'internal scarification'. In German artist Rebecca Horn's strange, mechanically erotic films, her body is always protected by bizarre contraptions resembling medieval torture apparatuses; she makes contact with objects or people but only at a remove; in her elongated, stiff-fingered gloves, tickling feathered headdresses, cages and harnesses, she achieves a curiously moving combination of potential sadism and tenderness [...]

In Iowa City, Ana Mendieta has made brutal rape pieces where the unwarned audience enters her room (or a wooded area) to discover her bloody, half-naked body. She has also used herself as a symbol of regeneration in a series of slide pieces. In one she is nude in an ancient stone grave in Mexico, covered by tiny white flowers which seem to be growing from her body; in another she lies nude over a real skeleton to 'give it life'; and in another she makes herself into the 'white cock', a Cuban voodoo fetish, covered with blood and feathers. She has traced her skeleton on her nude body to become 'Visible Woman' and ritually outlined her silhouette in flowers, flames, earth and candles.

A good deal of this current work by women, from the psychological makeup pieces to the more violent images, is not so much masochistic as it is concerned with exorcism, with dispelling taboos, with exposing and thereby defusing the painful aspects of woman's history. The prototypes may have been several works by Judy Chicago – her *Menstruation Bathroom* at Womanhouse (1972),[23] her notorious photo-lithograph *Red Flag* (1971), a self-portrait from the waist down showing the removal of a bloody Tampax (often read by male viewers as a damaged penis) and her 'rejection drawings' which demand: 'How Does it Feel to be Rejected? It's Like Having Your Flower Split Open.' In a recent two-woman exhibition at the College of St. Catherine in Saint Paul, Betsy Damon and Carole Fisher showed, respectively, drawings, collages and reliefs titled *Mutilation Images: A Garden* and *Self Images: Terrible Mother of the Blood River*. Many of these took, however, the hopeful shape of the butterfly – female transformation *par excellence* – also introduced into feminist iconography by Judy Chicago. The visual resemblance of a butterfly to the Great Goddess' double-edged axe is not coincidental, for Chicago has made a series of painted-china plaques which deal with the 'butterfly vagina' and its history as passage, portal, Venus of Willendorf and so forth. Edelson, in photographs of herself as a symbol of 'Woman Rising' from the earth, from the sea, her body painted with ancient ritual signs, adopts these images to a new feminist mythology. She also incorporates into her work stories written by the audience of her shows; mother stories, heroine stories, menstruation and birth stories, all of them part of her search for ancient woman's natural, shameless relationship to her body.

12. Judy Chicago

One curious aspect of all of this woman's work, pointed out by Joan Simon, is the fact that no women dealing with their own bodies or biographies have introduced pregnancy or childbirth as a major image. Sex itself is a focal point; Edelson has done ritual pieces with her son and daughter (as has Dennis Oppenheim); a Womanhouse performance included a splendidly choreographed group birth scene and a number of women photographers have dealt fairly often with pregnant nudes, but for individual Conceptual artists, this mental and physical condition unique to women exists in a curious void. Is it because many of these artists are young and have yet to have children? Or because women artists have traditionally either refused to have children or have hidden them away in order to be taken seriously in a world that accuses wives and mothers of being part-time artists? Or because the biological aspect of female creation is an anathema to women who want to be recognized for their art? Or is it related to narcissism and the fact that the swollen belly is considered unattractive in the male world? But if this were so, why wouldn't the more adamant feminists have taken up the theme of pregnancy and birth along with monthly cycles and ageing? None of these explanations seems valid. The destruction of derogatory myths surrounding female experience and physiology appears to be one of the major motives for the recent surge in body art by feminist artists. Perhaps procreativity is the next taboo to be tackled, one that might make clearer the elusive factors that divide body art by women from that by men.

1 Lea Vergine, *Il Corpo come Linguaggio* (Milan: Giampaolo Prearo, 1974).

2 The Gutai group in Japan also made similar events in the late 1950s, and Carolee Schneemann's *Eye Body* (*Nude in Environment*) dates from 1963.

3 Catherine Francblin, 'Corps-objet, femme-objet', *Art Press*, 20 (September-October 1975) [see in this volume p. 238].

4 This continues. Max Kozloff's 'Pygmalion Revisited' in *Artforum* (November 1975) is the latest example. A few women body artists are mentioned and no women are reproduced in twelve illustrations. He also seems unaware of the existence of a large selection of such art by women and complains that there are 'very few artists … to exploit dress, ornament or headgear … ' [see in this volume pp. 248-49].

5 In the course of my research in European art magazines I found: a woman with her blouse open, a woman's body signed as art, a woman with a gallery announcement written on her two large bare breasts, a provocative 1940s pin-up captioned 'Subscribe to me - I'm Extra' to advertise an 'artists' magazine of that name.

6 Lea Vergine, *Data* (Summer 1974).

7 Hans Peter Feldmann, *Extra*.

8 The 1968 quotations are taken from Schneemann's book *Cézanne She Was a Great Painter* (1975); the 1975 quotation was from another self-published book, *Up To and Including Her Limits* (1975).

9 Benglis' wax totems are acknowledged labial imagery; her sparkle-covered knot pieces are named after strippers and all the knot pieces have sexual connotations.

10 *Avalanche* special edition (Autumn 1972). Susan Mogul, in Los Angeles, has made a delightful feminist parody of Acconci's masturbatory activities in her vibrator video piece.

11 Katharina Sieverding, *Heute Kunst* (April-May 1974).

12 This is a quotation from Gnostic mysticism in 'The Myth of the Androgyne' by Robert Knott, *Artforum* (November 1975). The subject is also treated in the same issue by Whitney Chadwick, who notes that throughout the nineteenth century 'the myth of "the man/woman" … emblemized the perfect *man* of the future' (my italics), thus absorbing the female altogether, which seems to be the point of most male androgynous art.

13 Paul Heyer in *Camerart* (Montreal: Galerie Optica, 1974).

14 Jacki Apple, unpublished artist's statement (1973).

15 Adrian Piper, *The Drama Review* (March 1972).

16 Adrian Piper,'Notes on the Mythic Being, I' (March 1974).

17 I have written on costume, autobiographical and role-playing art by women in 'Transformation Art' (unpublished manusript, October 1975).

18 Ulrike Rosenbach in *Avalanche* (May 1974).

19 Nitsch, quoted in Kozloff, *op. cit.*, The Knott article, *op. cit.*, relates the relationship of androgyny and 'countless fertility myths' which employ violent dismemberment. Chadwick, *op. cit.*, sees debasement of women and androgyny as ways male artists have used to 'desexualize the female's natural procreative functions' - from sadism to the making of art as competition with the mother and her ability to create the artist himself.

20 See Vergine, *Il Corpo*, *op.cit.*

21 Tania Mouraud, *Actuel*, 3 (1974).

22 Pane quoted in Vergine, *Il Corpo*, *op.cit.*

23 Leslie Labowitz and Friederike Pezold in Germany have also made menstruation pieces, as have Judith Stein, Jacki Apple in a terrifying autobiographical text, and Carolee Schneemann in her important orgiastic happening, *Meat Joy* (1964).

Lucy R. Lippard, 'The Pains and Pleasures of Rebirth: Women's Body Art', *Art in America*, 69: 3 (May-June 1976) 73-81.

Hannah WILKE
Intercourse With … [1976]

Since 1960 I have been concerned with the creation of a formal imagery that is specifically female, a new language that fuses mind and body into erotic objects that are nameable and at the same time quite abstract. Its content has always related to my own body and feelings, reflecting pleasure as well as pain, the ambiguity and complexity of emotions. Human gestures, multi-layered metaphysical symbols below the gut level translated into an art close to laughter, making love, shaking hands … Eating fortune cookies instead of signing them, chewing gum into androgynous objects … Delicate definitions … Rearranging the touch of sensuality with a residual magic made from laundry lint, or latex loosely laid out like love vulnerably exposed … continually exposing myself to whatever situation occurs … Gambling as well as gambolling.

My interest in developing a specifically female iconography for both sexes in the early 1960s was in direct conflict with a society that prohibited its citizens from and sometimes arrested them for using the words *fuck*, *cock* and *prick*. In the United States the state of nudity is still a problem. My concern is with the word translated into form, with creating a positive image to wipe out the prejudices, aggression and fear associated with the negative connotations of pussy, cunt, box.

As an American girl born with the name Butter in 1940, I was often confused when I heard what it was like to be used, to be spread, to feel soft, to melt in your mouth. To also remember that as a Jew, during the war, I would have been branded and buried had I not been born in America. Starification-scarification/Jew, Black, Christian, Moslem … Claes, Richard, Donald … Labelling people instead of listening to them … Judging according to primitive prejudices. 'Marks-ism' and art. Fascistic feelings, internal wounds, made from external situations. Sticks and stones break our bones, but names more often hurt us … Yet to name a thing wherein I caught the conscience of the king, as well as the queen … to keep on naming a thing … to wear my hat, the memory of all that, until that thing is really something. To exist instead of being an existentialist, to make objects instead of being one. The way my smile just gleams, the way I sip my tea. To be a sugar giver instead of a salt cellar, to not sell out … The memory of all that, now that's really something … Oh, no they can't take that away from me … no, they can't take that away from me.

Text used in a videotape performance and lecture at the

London Art Gallery, Ontario, 17 February 1977; originally written for the Guggenheim Memorial Foundation Grant, 1976. Hannah Wilke, 'Intercourse With ... ', *Hannah Wilke: A Retrospective*, ed. Thomas H. Kochheiser (Columbia: University of Missouri Press, 1989) 139.

Gloria Feman ORENSTEIN

The Re-emergence of the Archetype of the Great Goddess in Art by Contemporary Women [1978]

[...] Mary Beth Edelson's work has long been intimately involved in the explorations of the Goddess. In 1961 her painting of Madonna and Child entitled *Godhead* introduced concentric circles as sources of energy from the Madonna's head. In these early paintings' her women were frequently depicted with their arms uplifted, reminiscent of the posture of many early Goddess figures. The primal image of the outstretched arms of the ancient Goddess, whose power must be reclaimed by women for themselves today, is seen by Edelson not only as a spiritual signifier, but as a contemporary symbol of our political activism.

In 1969 she began to evolve a more defined and specific area of archetypal imagery, out of which emerged the exhibition *Woman Rising*, revolutionary in the way it brought to consciousness psychic material about the Great Goddess. Her most innovative images for today have been the body images she has created through performing private body rituals where the body itself is the house of wisdom. In these the artist calls upon Goddess energy, using her own body as a stand-in for the Goddess and as a symbol for Everywoman, whose expanded states of body-consciousness and multiple transformations are evoked through contact with powerful natural energies.

On 1 March 1977 Edelson performed a mourning ritual ceremony for her exhibition, *Your 5000 Years Are Up*, entitled *Mourning Our Lost Herstory*, at the Mandeville Gallery, University of California at La Jolla. Ten women sat in a circle in the centre of a fire ring, the only source of light, chanting and wailing while seven silent 20-m [8-ft] high black-draped figures, which had previously seemed to be an uninhabited formal sculptural installation on the back wall, came alive and began to move around the cavernous gallery. More recently she performed a mourning-reclamation ritual at A.I.R. Gallery, New York City, entitled *Proposals For: Memorials to the 9,000,000 Women Burned as Witches in the Christian Era*. This ritual, based on research about witch burning in relation to women who were Goddess worshippers, evoked the spirits of individual women who were tortured during the Inquisition. Edelson is not content, however, to exorcize the past; her art is about mythic recreation of holy spaces for women's culture today [...]

1 'Mary Beth Edelson's Great Goddess', *Arts Magazine* (November 1975)

Gloria Feman Orenstein, 'The Re-emergence of the Archetype of the Great Goddess in Art by Contemporary Women', *Heresies*, 5 (Spring 1978) 74-84.

Mary KELLY

Woman – Desire – Image [1984]

Pre-panel anxiety seems to encapsulate the Lacanian notion of desire as desire of the other since it consists of repeatedly posing the question: what does she want of me? – the organizer, the panel moderator, the woman in the audience. Lacking the reassuring presence of the imaginary mother 'who would tell me what to do' I grasped my transitional object – the seminar flyer.

Here I noted that 'in consumer advertising as well as in high art, the female body has traditionally been the site of desire'. But I thought to myself, discourses of the body and of sexuality do not necessarily intersect. In recent high art, for example, it is the phenomenological body that takes precedence; what belongs to me, my body, the body of the self-possessing artistic subject whose guarantee of aesthetic truth is grounded in actual experience, often in the painful state. Considering this, it then becomes significant to point out that, alternatively, the contribution of feminists, mainly in the field of performance, has been to pose the question of sexuality across that discourse of the body in a way which focuses on the construction of the sexual subject. So the body is not perceived as the repository of an artistic essence; it is seen as a kind of hermeneutic image: the enigma of femininity – formulated as the problem of images of women, how to change them and resolved by the discovery of a true identity behind the patriarchal facade – 'the essence in woman'.

But here again the predominant forms of feminist art continue to counterpose a visible form and a hidden content; excavating a different, yet similarly fundamental order of truth – the truth of the woman, her original feminine identity.

What persistently emerges as a result of foregrounding the question of sexuality and representation as images of women – particularly the notion of positive images, is more in the order of an underlying contradiction than an essential content. The woman artist 'sees' her experience as a woman particularly in terms of the 'feminine position' – what some writers have referred to as her narcissistic over-identification with the object of the look – but she must also account for the 'feeling' she experiences as the artist, occupying the so-called 'masculine position' as subject of the look. The former she defines as the socially prescribed position of the woman, one to be questioned, exercised or overthrown, while the implications of the latter – (that there can be only one position with regard to active looking and that is masculine) – cannot be acknowledged and is construed instead as a kind of psychic truth; a natural, instinctual, pre-existent and possibly unrepresentable femininity.

I think these remarks help to put the flyer's next statement in perspective. 'Feminine artists have refused the image of the maternal body, creating significance out of its absence.' I look at this not as a tendency, not yet, anyway, but specifically as a reference to my own work. So, I would like to say that it seemed crucial, not in the sense of a moral imperative, but as a *historical strategy*, to avoid the literal figuration of mother and child, that is, to avoid any means of representation which risked recuperation as 'a slice of life'. Using the body of the woman, her image or person, is not impossible but problematic for feminism. In my work I have tried to cut across the predominant representation of woman as the object of the look in order to question the notion of femininity as a pre-given entity, and foreground instead its social construction as a representation of sexual difference within specific discourses. Above all I am trying to picture the woman as subject of her own desire. This is not a new form of iconoclasm but an aspiration I share not only with feminists, but with certain Postmodernists who are making a critique of the kind of creative essentialism that predominates in much current art and criticism.

Barbara Kruger's strategy of appropriating images, for instance, contests notions of originality, genius, artistic authorship, but at the same time subverts the division of the visual field into sexually fixed positions: women 'seen', man subject of the appropriating gaze. In *We won't Play Nature to Your Culture* she refuses to return the look; she speaks instead of turning a familiar mode of advertising address against itself – an aggressive assertion of self-possession. But what about the flyer's assertion that Robert Mapplethorpe's work is an aggressive assertion of male virility? Perhaps some general remarks on fetishism should precede my comments on this case.

Sexual identity is said to be the outcome of a precarious passage called the Oedipus complex; a passage which is in a certain sense completed by the acceptance of symbolic castration. But castration is also inscribed at the level of the imagery, that is in fantasy, and this is where the fetishistic scenario originates and is continually replayed. The child's recognition of difference between the mother and the father is above all an admission that the mother does not have the phallus. In this case seeing is not necessarily believing, since what is at stake for the child is really the question of his or her own relation to having or being. Hence the fetishist, conventionally assumed to be male, postpones that moment of recognition, although certainly he has made the passage – he knows the difference, but denies it. In terms of representation, this denial is associated with a definite iconography of pornographic images where the man is reassured by the woman's possession of some form of phallic substitute or alternatively by the shape, the complete arrangement of her body.

Mapplethorpe's fashionable muscular 'lady' does not subvert the genre. The heightened ambivalence of an eccentrically framed crotch is not distanciation, nor is it particularly progressive to objectify black men. All of these devices explore the genre in a way which effects an aesthetized closure, rather than questioning how sexual identity is produced. An alternative exploration of 'male' voyeurism is found for instance in Victor Burgin's *Zoo* series. But since he is here on this panel, I will not elaborate on his views.

The question of masculine perversions is an important one. But it would be a mistake to confine women to the realm of repression, excluding the possibility, for example, of female fetishism. The woman, in so far as the outcome of the Oedipal moment has involved at some point a heterosexual object choice (that is, she has identified with her mother and has taken her father as a love object) will also postpone the recognition of lack in view of the promise of having the child. In having the child, in a sense she has the phallus. So the loss of the child is the loss of that symbolic plenitude – more exactly the ability to represent lack.

When Freud describes castration fears for the woman, this imaginary scenario takes the form of losing her loved objects, especially her children; the child is going to grow up, leave her, reject her, perhaps die. In order to delay, disavow, that separation she has already in a way acknowledged, the woman tends to fetishize the child: by dressing him up, by continuing to feed him no matter how old he gets, or simply by having another 'little one'. So perhaps in place of the more familiar notion of pornography, it is possible to talk about the mother's memorabilia – the way she saves things – first shoes, photographs, locks of hair or school reports. My work starts from this site; instead of first shoes, first words set out in type, stained liners, hand imprints, comforter fragments, drawings, writings or even the plants and insects that were his gifts; all these are intended to be seen as transitional objects; not in Derek Winnicott's sense of surrogates but rather in Lacan's terms as emblems of desire. That is, I think that Lacan's insistence on the fact that desire is caused, not by objects, but in the unconscious according to the peculiar structure of fantasy, is crucial to this discussion because it emphasizes that the question of desire is not simply synonymous with images of desirable women.

Desire is repetitious, it resists normalization, ignores biology, disperses the body. So when the flyer asks 'How are we to understand the seductiveness of the image?', perhaps it is precisely the replay, the repetition, the representation of moments of separation and loss which captivate us more than the promise of plenitude. As to what is involved in 'the deconstruction of desire' (flyer again) I am completely baffled, but this leads me to pose a different set of questions in place of concluding remarks.

What does it mean to say we have refused the image of the woman? Can the notion of the image be reduced to the representational image or iconic sign? What about the possibility of the indexical or symbolic sign to invoke the non-specular within the visual field. Invoke precisely the configuration of desire associated with the invocatory drives; create waves against the current of a culturally overdetermined scopophilia. Would this release the so-called 'female spectator' from her hysterical identification with the male voyeur? What is implied by suggesting that women have a privileged relation to narcissism or that fetishism is an exclusively male perversion? Surely, the link between narcissism and fetishism is castration. For both the man and the woman this is the condition for access to the symbolic, to language, to culture; there can be no privileged relation to madness. But still there is difference. There is still that irritating asymmetry of the Oedipal passage. This must be negotiated in reading visual representations. Is it possible to produce pleasure differently for women? Perhaps, by representing a very specific loss – the loss of her imagined closeness to the mother's body (that archaic, anal, oral or concentric organization of the drives which Michele Montrelay has called 'her precocious femininity') – pleasure, then, would be produced in the representation of exactly that which was assumed to be outside of language, unspeakable, invisible, unrepresentable. Recalling the first session in this series I asked myself again what did Dora enjoy in the image of the Sistine Madonna if not the possibility of imagining the woman as subject of desire without transgressing the socially acceptable representation of the woman as mother? To have the child as phallus, to be the phallic mother, or perhaps to have the mother in being once again the child. Is there in that image a duplication of identification and desire that only the body of another woman can sustain?

Finally, another type of question altogether keeps imposing itself as I look at that image. What does it mean to acknowledge that the Madonna was the most popular picture of its type in the early sixteenth century, occupying a place not dissimilar to the stars of narrative cinema in more recent times? Clearly there is a dimension to desire which is not reducible to questions of sexuality, the body or the image, but to what is ambiguously referred to as *power*; that is, the institutional context that determines the distribution, definitions and conditions of existence for artistic texts. Can art forms, especially critical art forms, ever be considered outside of those constraints? At this point, however, I think I may be in danger of deconstructing your desire to consider my previous questions, so I will pause here and let the discussion continue.

Mary Kelly, 'Woman – Desire – Image', *ICA Documents: Desire*, ed. Lisa Appignanesi (London: Institute of Contemporary Arts, 1984) 30-31.

Donald KUSPIT
The New Subjectivism: Inside Cindy Sherman [1987]

[...] Cindy Sherman creates a scatter effect of objects, almost to the point of chaos. One can perversely say she is 'deconstructing' the world of the (female) subject, but the effect of the deconstruction is a sense of total abandonment. Her pictures are scenes of primitive abandonment, all the more terrifying because of the promise of happiness latent in the scenes – the glamour of happiness, promised by the glamour of the colour. She shows us not fear of abandonment but its actuality – its fundamentality, whether in a generalized sense of vulnerability or in the broken promise of happiness that life made. Sometimes it is the abandonment implicit in the forced intimacy of rape, which speaks for the sense of the nothingness of oneself all human relationships sooner or later give, especially love relationships. The scenes often show a promise of pleasure become painful. The blood-red in many of the pictures suggests the generally destructive character of intimacy, whose debris is pictured. Sexuality is clearly the implied theme of a number of these works, as the picture of the destroyed bed with the figure watching the creatures on it suggests. (The bed suggests the lost paradise of love, from which the figure is exiled, a paradise whose lostness is confirmed by the fact that the creatures have turned to stone – become garden statuary.) In general, these works convey the sense of coming upon the dregs of some decadent, violent Bacchanalia. The pictures are more or less conspicuously scenes of a crime, as in the image where a woman's hand, bloody underwear and fallen head, seen from the back, are visible on a forest floor.

The pictures are stills from Hollywood horror film scenes, their constructed look and mechanisms of representation are self-evident – in the picture just mentioned what is seen from the back is a woman's wig, and the leaves and pine cones look glossily fake – but they are none the less, as mentioned, emotionally effective. In fact, their very artificiality serves their emotional effectiveness, because it becomes a safe area from which we can explore its horror and the emotions aroused by it with a certain contemplative aloofness. And, as with the colour, the general artificiality – the readability of the picture as artificial, a construction, with the attendant Eureka sense of 'I get it (intellectually, aesthetically)!' – lures us into the destructive fantasy, and stimulates our own unconscious fantasy. By attending to the pictures intellectually and aesthetically, which they blatantly invite us to do, we anchor ourselves more firmly in their fantasy. It is the trick of the major artist: we are given the sense of being wide awake in the nightmare, carefully noticing the stuff out of which it is constructed, which makes it all the more convincingly an emotionally gripping nightmare. In a sense, our very alertness to the way the picture is made is a sign of our possession by its horror.

Sherman's pictures are an astonishing mix of paranoid and depressive fantasies. That is, they reveal the anxiety aroused by fear of destruction of the self by the other, and the anxiety aroused by the self's desire to destroy the other. Her pictures are an unholy mix of cruelties, in which there is no reparation for the self that feels vulnerable, or for the other broken on the rack of the self's fantasies of destruction. Sherman's work has been interpreted as a feminist demonstration of the variety of female roles – the lack of fixity of female, or for that matter any, identity, although instability seems to have been forced more on women than men. Sherman in a sense is destroying an already destroyed – bankrupt – social identity. Behind the masquerade of identities, none of them binding, and none of them invented by and belonging to woman, but forced upon her by man, there is supposedly a void, a faceless cipher – a nonentity and nonidentity. But this interpretation is a very partial truth. Sherman shows the disintegrative condition of the self as such, the self before it is firmly identified as male or female. This is suggested by the indeterminate gender of many of the faces and figures that appear in these pictures, and the presence of male or would-be male figures in some of them. Female attributes – for example, the woman's clothes in one untitled work (all are of 1987) – are just that, dispensable attributes, clothes that can be worn by anyone. The question is what the condition of the self is that will put them on – reach into the mess of the room and decide that they're for it because they'll reflect, even substantialize, it. These clothes exist within a repudiated world. Sherman is in fact thrusting the repudiated and abhorrent in our faces – especially in one startling picture of bulging flesh as full of sores as the flesh of the dead Christ in Grünewald's Isenheim Altarpiece.

It is not just the repudiated as such that Sherman represents – whether the repudiated as symbol of the victimized, annihilated female (repudiated and abhorrent because her very presence is a glorified nothingness) – but inwardly repudiated death, the abhorrent death she manifests in her pictures, the outlawed death lurking in herself. The sense of violent decay – of the inherent violence of decay – that permeates these pictures suggests Sherman's destructive aggression: that is the repressed repudiated and abhorrent that returns with a vengeance in these works. There is a certain violence in Sherman's constant shifting of roles, endless playing of endless roles – an aggression which mocks and finally destroys each role in the act of filling it, discards it in the very act of demonstrating it. Nobody else can play it after Sherman has, which means there is nothing left to play – only the play of the colour, the play of the artistic construction.

Sherman is an ultra-elegant nihilist. One can understand her nihilism through Heinz Kohut's conception of aggression as the product of the self's fragmentation and disintegration: Sherman is in effect announcing her own lack of integral selfhood through her nihilistic, aggressive playing and transformation of roles, each the fragment of a self that does not add up to a whole, that is less than the sum of its parts. Or it can be understood in Melanie Klein's terms as a manifestation of primal destructiveness, where the impulse to play a new role implies a desire to appropriate its power (every act of appropriation being an act of destruction and over-powering). In either case, there is no denying the underlying sense of destructive rage in Sherman's works.

This disintegrative rage is in no way denied by the theatrical, 'egoistic' manner in which it is made manifest. What the theatrical 'egoism' – the strong aesthetic flair – of the execution suggests is a certain ego strength; it is a survivor's strategy in the midst of the maelstrom of destructive rage. Sherman makes us not only complicitous detectives at the scene of a crime – the crime of the aggression a woman is not supposed to have, yet is regularly the victim of – but asks us to believe that we can be strengthened by the charnel house experience. We sift the ruins of Sherman's pictures in search of her identity, and we find it in the tension between the erotic, glamorized pleasure of the colour that is part of the ingeniousness of the artistic construction, and the thanatopsistic scene. The split personality of these pictures, which so readily and fully reveal the elegance of their methods yet harbour a mysterious, blank-faced violence – which with extraordinary power bring repulsive, ugly scenes under aesthetic control, make them aesthetically appetizing – surely signals Sherman's profound ambivalence about her experience of her womanhood, something she abhors yet enjoys, and brings under control by putting it to artistic use. It is this artistic use – her wish to excel with a certain aesthetic purity as well as to represent inventively – that reveals her wish to heal a more fundamental wound of selfhood than that which is inflicted on her by being a woman.

Donald Kuspit, 'The New Subjectivism: Inside Cindy Sherman', *Artscribe* (September-October 1987) 41-43; reprinted in Donald Kuspit, *The New Subjectivism: Art in the 1980s* (Ann Arbor: UMI Research Press, 1988) 381-96.

Francesco BONAMI
Yasumasa Morimura [1992]

[...] To consider Yasumasa Morimura's work as an indignant accusation towards Japan's abandoning its own roots would be a hasty simplification and trivialization of an *oeuvre* which has developed through the Eurocentric filter with which Asian contemporary art is systematically perceived. Paradoxically, the influence that Europe wields over Japanese art has always been subject to, rather than imposed, a hybrid metamorphosis. Tsuguharu Foujita's 1950s canvases were an emblematic representation of the anguish of a transition whereby the origins painfully survived the desire to forget. Born in an era when Japanese memory was being revived, Osaka-born Morimura is well aware that enemies lurk not only in the tradition that exists all around him but also far outside his homeland. The use of photography and the computer express this awareness and a certain willingness to accede to a privileged vantage point from which to witness this collision of cultures.

Armed with a neutral medium, Morimura takes up his course from within Japanese tradition. By imposing his face on to Diego Velázquez's *Infant Margaret, (Daughter of Art History, Princess B*, 1990), the artist injects a spirit of *onnagata* – the traditional wearing of women's clothes in Kabuki theatre – into a Western icon. The allusion to a history which could be overturned is extremely subtle, offering his own traits to Vincent Van Gogh's self-portrait, suggesting the influence that Japanese *ukiyo-e* prints had on Impressionism and balancing an otherwise overly descriptive critique of the excesses of Japanese collector culture. By subjecting European masterpieces to such a disconcerting metamorphosis, Morimura gradually eradicates the spectator's belief that the artist's critical eye is set exclusively on the cultural establishment of his own country. In the multiplication of his own face within the image (*Portrait, Nine Faces*, 1990), his procedure becomes increasingly disquieting and the visual hierarchy to which we were mentally accustomed, by means of an unchallenged cognitive process, is wiped out. Moreover, through the extension of his own physiognomy, a symbolic equality is established with the roles that the postwar Japanese population adopted: Corpse, Student and later, Master [...]

Morimura understands how the perception of images around us is formed by our guilty conscience. By assuming responsibility for every role, the artist explores the potential for both civilizations to beat a parallel path towards a common point.

Francesco Bonami, 'Yasumasa Morimura', trans. Christopher Martin, *Flash Art*, 25: 163 (March-April 1992) 82-83.

Peggy PHELAN
Developing the Negative [1993]

[...] Robert Mapplethorpe often declared his antipathy towards photography. Trained as a sculptor, much of Mapplethorpe's work aspires towards three-dimensionality. Borrowing the canvas of painting and printing his photographs on linen soaked in platinum, he created a geometrical alphabet of shapes draped in silk and velvet which he hung above or behind the 'printed' canvas. Lush, large and lyrical, Mapplethorpe's photographs are images angling to be objects.[1] In a 1987 interview Mapplethorpe remarked: 'I never liked photography ... I like the object. I like photographs when you hold them in your hand.' Like the desire to transform the phallus into the penis, changing the image into an object seems to hold a promising payoff – 'you [can then] hold them in your hand'.

Much of Mapplethorpe's photography depicts the male nude, and a significant part of that *oeuvre* is devoted to black men. His photography is shot through with a heady classicism, a reverential attitude towardsthe statuesque pose of the Greeks and a rigorous formalism. What distinguishes his work from painting is the way in which photography's mechanical ontology transforms the attitude of his compositions. Like other artists working in the epoch presaged by Walter Benjamin's 'art in the age of mechanical reproduction', Mapplethorpe's work uses the camera eye to investigate subjectivity, that in fact, the two are synonymous. For him, men's – and especially gay men's – most dramatic confrontations involve the battle between the mechanical 'objective' and the sexual-subjective. The gaze ravages the print, the eye accosts the model: the lure for the looker is to touch him – to hold him in your hand. Mapplethorpe's cool camera serves the model up untouched; the image's impression on the paper invites the spectator to fantasize the pressure of that touch. Erotic photography solicits the touch and defers it; instead of skin, paper. Instead of sex, the devouring gaze[2] [...]

1 For a fine analysis of Mapplethorpe's long interest in the photograph as object see Richard Marshall, *Robert Mapplethorpe* (New York: Whitney Museum of American Art in Association with New York Graphic Society Books, 1989).

2 This is the connection between Mapplethorpe's 'art' photography and fashion photography. Unable to touch the model's skin, the looker settles for the touch of the fabric that the model wears – and so the spectator buys the clothes the fashion model wears.

Peggy Phelan, 'Developing the Negative', *Unmarked: The Politics of Performance* (New York and London: Routledge, 1993) 34–70.

Leslie C. JONES
Transgressive Femininity: Art and Gender in the 1960s and 1970s [1993]

'When the age-long slavery of woman shall have ended, when she will be able to live by and for herself; then man – hitherto abominable – having given her her freedom, she will be a poet too. Woman will discover things that will be strange and unfathomable; repulsive and delicate. We shall take them from her and we shall understand them.'
– Arthur Rimbaud[1]

[...] It was not until the 1960s and 1970s, exactly that period when 'the age-long slavery of woman' was being challenged, that women artists began to openly proclaim their difference from their male counterparts. The explicit gendering of the artist was a consequence of the demand of the women's movement for equal rights and for the endorsement of a distinct female voice. The movement's motto, 'The personal is political', urged women to publicly assert their difference as a means to greater understanding and, ultimately, to unbiased recognition. In line with this feminist discourse, many women artists chose to engage in a strictly feminist art practice aimed at expressing their difference from men through visual imagery. When Judy Chicago proposed that 'maybe the existing forms of art for the ideas men have had are inadequate for the ideas women have', she was promoting an art of difference.[2] The initial source for 'the ideas women have' were those practices that had made women different in the past, as well as what made them different physically – their bodies. For this reason, many women chose to valorize previously marginalized female art practices such as weaving, quilting, embroidery and ceramics, as well as daily female activities – ironing, cooking and cleaning. Many also adopted vaginal iconography as a means to uncover and celebrate the biological source of woman's difference.

Womanhouse, for example, a multimedia environment created in 1971 by the Feminist Art Program at the California Institute of the Arts, Valencia, exposed the regular, but otherwise invisible, sites and activities of a woman's daily life. The programme was headed by Miriam Shapiro and Judy Chicago, and participating artists included Faith Wilding, Mira Schor, Sandra Orgel, Nancy Youdelman, Karen LeCoque and Chris Rush. The environment comprised rooms and performances created by the individual artists. In *Menstruation Bathroom*, Judy Chicago installed a trash can overflowing with bloodied tampons and pads under a counter displaying a selection of all the 'liberating' and 'refreshing' accoutrements marketed for female consumption at 'that time of the month'. Chicago exposed the bloody reality of menstruation underneath the adman's pretty pastel packaging. But more important than her critique of the advertising industry and ultimate subversion of the patriarchal notion (or non-notion) of menstruation, was her use of the abject. The exhibition of menstrual blood threatens the patriarchy with its fear of the maternal body. In discussing the work of Kristeva, Elizabeth Gross explains: 'Horror of menstrual blood is a refusal to acknowledge the subject's corporeal link to the mother ... It marks the site of an unspeakable and unpayable debt of life, of existence, that the subject (and culture) owes to the maternal body.'[3] In Kristeva's terms, Chicago uses 'nature' to confront 'culture' and thus disturbs identity, system, order [...]

Although bold and explicit in its subversive imagery, *Womanhouse* has remained marginal in the pages of art history. While women were free to proclaim their sexuality and difference through their art practice, they were not free from the practice of critical legitimation, which demanded an interpretation based on the patriarchal concepts of woman as nature, woman as amorphous, woman as passive, etc. The interpretation of the work of women artists during this period suffered tremendously because critics and art historians chose either, as in the case of *Womanhouse*, to completely isolate the artists as feminists, thus disregarding their contributions, or, as we shall see, to interpret their works solely in the terms of the concepts of femininity described above, so that all individuality was repressed.

This period of transgression and gendering in the arts corresponds to the emergence of Eccentric Abstraction and Anti-Form, concepts that privileged the amorphous and the visceral, and of Happenings, body and performance art, which privileged the use of the artists, own body. What these diverse practices had in common was a capacity to disturb viewers, to draw them 'towards the place where meaning collapses'[4] through the incorporation of untraditional substances, amorphous forms and the artist's body itself. In the case of most artists the intent was to shock, to repulse in order to blur the boundaries of propriety and social strictures imposed on art, on women and on society as a whole. It is my intention to re-examine the artistic practice of women who, during this period, incorporated abject materials or imagery; and, more important, to examine how this art was received relative to that of men also employing the abject.

By the early 1960s certain artists were already engaged in an art practice that privileged 'feminine' forms and imagery. The works of Lee Bontecou, Yayoi Kusama and Claes Oldenburg represent highly influential precedents for the development of Eccentric Abstraction and Anti-Form [...]

[The] trace of a sewn stitch in the work of a male artist, namely Claes Oldenburg, became the focus of critical attention and proceeded to revolutionize art practice. (Although it was, in fact, Pat Oldenburg, the artist's wife, who did the actual sewing of his soft sculptures.) Whether in terms of sewing, softening or sensualizing, Oldenburg was clearly concerned with feminizing his forms as a transgressive practice in his art. 'It is important', he stated, 'to operate out of the forces in us, forces and counterforces and not to be afraid to use them. Just now I am indulging in my femininity.'[5] Because vision has often been privileged as the superior sense in Modernism and therefore constitutive of the male subject, the experience of the other senses of the body has been denigrated and relegated to the realm of the feminine. Oldenburg adopts the language of the body 'to offset the tendency to vagueness and abstraction. To remind people of practical activity, to suggest the senses and not escape from the senses, to substitute flesh and blood for paint.'[6] Oldenburg's soft sculptures, such as *Soft Toilet* (1966), testify to his 'desire for every kind of contact sensation for his sculpture (eating, touching, sitting on, caressing) ... visceratonic impulses'.[7] Oldenburg's success in the manipulation of amorphous forms needs no testimony. As we shall see, however, the exploration of 'feminine' spaces in the art practice of men was received quite differently from that in the work of women.

Yayoi Kusama, like Bontecou and unlike Oldenburg, was rarely acknowledged for the sewing of her soft sculptures. For Kusama, who claims to have been the first to make sewing-machine sculpture, this was a grave oversight.[8] The act of sewing, stitching or knitting in Kusama's work signified the repetitive or monotonous tasks performed by women on a daily basis, and has been a figural reference in her work since her *Infinity Paintings* of the late 1950s. Kusama's sewing machine 'protuberances' – pieces of material sewn into narrow pouches and stuffed into phallic shapes – have often been likened to the soft sculptures of Oldenburg. But even though both artists soften quotidian objects, the majority of Kusama's objects are more specifically concerned with the everyday life of women. Moreover, the furniture, mixing bowls, high-heeled shoes and frying pans that she softens and envelopes with protuberances appear less affable than Oldenburg's sculptures and more as if diseased by phallic fungi. The tumorous sculptures infect and spread over the object, rendering it useless for sitting, eating, walking, whatever.

Critics have attempted to 'disinfect' the malignant nature of Kusama's work by interpreting it as evocative of 'elemental feelings'[9] and the 'eternal processes of growth and generation in nature'.[10] Such interpretations clearly deny the threat of disease and reveal the nature of society's fear of contamination and, more broadly, of the unclean and the improper. Kusama's use of wild, spreading protuberances could be associated with her later use of polka dots: 'red polka dots ... suggest spots like the spots of disease. This disease is the attitude of the human race towardssex, which is sick. I used mirrors to show that the problem goes on and on without stopping.'[11] The problem that goes 'on and on without stopping' is, fundamentally, the abject. Like the threat of disease, it is ever-present. 'A certain "ego" that merged with its master, a superego, has flatly driven it away. It lies outside, beyond the set, and does not seem to agree to the latter's rules of the game. And yet, from its place of banishment, the abject does not cease challenging its master.'[12]

The 1966 'Eccentric Abstraction' exhibition, curated by Lucy R. Lippard for the Fischbach Gallery, New York, brought together artists 'allied to the non-formal tradition devoted to opening up new areas of materials, shape, colour and sensuous experience'.[13] Lippard referred to the Freudian concept of 'body ego' in describing the viewer's response to the work:

'*Body ego can be experienced two ways: first through appeal, the desire to caress, to be caught up in the feel and rhythms of a work; second, through repulsion, the immediate reaction against certain forms and surfaces which take longer to comprehend.*'[14]

The opposing reactions of repulsion and desire are also indicative of the state of abjection, the state of the ambiguous where all 'meaning collapses'. According to Lippard, the experience provoked 'giggles of uneasiness and perhaps even awe, like the giggles provoked by aspects of death, love, sex, excretion, any natural function too naturally exposed'.[15] In the work of Kristeva these 'aspects' are theorized as 'dark revolts of being', the abject.[16]

In 1968, two years after the 'Eccentric Abstraction' exhibition, Robert Morris published 'Anti-Form', an influential essay that defined the radical practice of process-oriented art in opposition to the idealizing notions of art based on form, or art for art's sake.[17] He was responding to Herbert Marcuse's proposition that 'art remains alien to the revolutionary praxis by virtue of the artist's commitment to Form: Form as art's own reality, as *die Sache selbst*'.[18]

Morris rallied for a revolutionary art practice based on Anti-Form through a 'disengagement with preconceived enduring forms and orders'.[19] Such a disengagement would dictate the exclusion of the durable materials and geometric morphology that had dominated Western art practice. Morris, like Lippard, cites Oldenburg as a precursor in the use of alternative materials and forms. Oldenburg's soft materials make process visible. 'The focus on matter and gravity as means results in forms which were not projected in advance.'[20]

13. Robert Morris

In *Felt* (1967–68), Morris attaches strips of thick felt to a single point on the wall so that they limply cascade into a random pool on the gallery floor. Removing the material and structural support, he allows gravity to determine the form of the object. In the words of one critic, 'they are not "upright", "straight", "firm" or "strong" ... [but] they could be called "sociable", suggesting, as they do, comfort and invitation. They are extremely tactile. They *want* to be touched.'[21] Other critics found Morris' works to have 'gone soft';[22] and later they were described as 'unmistakably vaginal'.[23] Anti-Form, with its emphasis on process and the natural and unpredictable orientation of the actual materials, confronted the senses. 'Under the predominance of rationalism', Marcuse wrote, 'the cognitive function of sensuousness has been constantly minimized ... Sensuousness, as the "lower" and even "lowest" faculty', was thus an ideal means of representation to challenge the Modernist art practice based on vision.[24] Morris, like Oldenburg, chose to explore 'feminine' spaces, to 'indulge his femininity' as a transgressive means to counter Modernism.

The work of Eva Hesse, Lynda Benglis and Louise Bourgeois also explored 'feminine' spaces. For these women, unlike their male counterparts, however, the process was regarded as stereotypically feminine. Critics received it as a natural phenomenon rather than as a willed intellectual strategy [...]

Lynda Benglis' art has often been exclusively discussed in terms of patriarchal notions of femininity. Benglis' brown polyurethane foam sculptures ooze out of the gallery walls and freeze suspended just inches above the gallery floor, simultaneously evoking sensations of awe and disgust. While reminiscent of lava and the mysterious generative powers of nature, these sculptures are clearly scatological. Thomas B. Hess equated Benglis with a different force of nature: 'Nature can change states – freeze water, melt rocks; Benglis, too, can congeal or liquefy matter ... '[25] And Klaus Kertess described her as '*intensely concerned with process and with images. Excessive images. Images concerned with organic, liquid phenomena (the ocean, body fluids and flow). Images involved with flesh and physicality ... Images that openly declare a very strong female sensuality.*'[26]

As with the work of Kusama, critics have attempted to confine the threatening readings of Benglis' work to the safe realms of nature and feminine excess. They ignore its obvious scatology, which in fact is confrontational, challenging us with the fear of excrement, with 'the danger to identity that comes from without: the ego threatened by the non-ego, society threatened by its outside, life by death'.[27]

As excrement threatens all social beings from without, the fluids issuing from the vagina threaten sexual identity from within. In *Travel Agent* (1966/1977–78) the viewer is confronted with a distinctly vaginal icon that valorizes as well as threatens. Benglis' icon is threatening not only because it uncovers patriarchy's historical concealment and thus domination of female sexuality, but because it is aroused. The tender surface of dripping wax clearly eroticizes the icon. In fact, Benglis has discussed the creation of the wax paintings, the steady stroking of wax over masonite, as 'masturbating in [her] studio',[28] a clear reclamation of a woman's right to her own sexual pleasure.

As early as the 1940s Louise Bourgeois was working with amorphous and biomorphic forms that often suggested female and/or male genitalia. But it was not until the 1960s, when amorphousness and the visceral had been legitimated by male art practice, that she began to receive critical recognition. That recognition, however, was concentrated on references to nature and fertility. One critic described Bourgeois' work as 'evocative of a world of forests, of hills, of oceans, caves, hollow echoes of the sound of waves ... created by a strikingly fertile imagination'.[29] William Rubin called *Molotov Cocktail* (1968) 'a pregnancy' and noted that when surrounded by Bourgeois' work 'we are in the world of germination and eclosion – the robust sexuality of things under and upon the earth'.[30] Clearly, the 'robust sexuality' is often human sexuality, and Rubin comes to fear that 'when themes of sexuality are pressed too literally, a set of emotions interposes itself between the viewer and the work in a manner unconducive to aesthetic contemplation'.[31] Rubin represents patriarchal society and its institutions' fear of contamination; Bourgeois' bold imagery threatens because it is not 'savoured and absorbed, like the sexuality of Brancusi and Arp'.[32] The voice of patriarchy could not be clearer; human sexuality must be bordered up and sublimated. The work of Bourgeois 'talks about things we don't want talked about, acknowledges forces we don't want broadcast loudly and certainly not let loose'.[33] It talks about the abject.

Bourgeois' forms are suggestive of the body, both male and female, and its interior spaces. The symbolic merging of the male and female in the fusing of breast and/or vagina and penis is a theme that began in Bourgeois' totemic wood figures of the 1940s and has continued in more recent work, such as *Nature Study* (1984), where the squatting dog/demon betrays both swelling breasts and a penis. Bourgeois' latex pieces of the 1960s evoke associations with living flesh, more precisely with the interior side of flesh, as within a mouth or vagina. The viewer is threatened by these mutations and interior spaces because they are at once recognizable and foreign, attractive and repulsive. The art of Louise Bourgeois, perhaps like that of no other artist working in the 1960s and 1970s, continues to transgress by its insistence on representing visceral and sexual body in the face of patriarchal demands for sublimation. In response to *Nature Study*, for example, one critic noted how it 'makes you avert your gaze; you turn away with a sickened feeling ... to meet another pair of staring eyes, emblematic of Bourgeois' unflinchingness'.[34]

The transgression of order through the use of the abject was also demonstrated in the 1960s Happenings and Body art and in performance art of the next decade. All three practices used the human body as the medium in choreographed or semi-choreographed events. Happenings and Body art were dominated by men, but during this same period the innovational dance of Yvonne Rainer and Simone Forti, the Fluxus activities of Yoko Ono and Alison Knowles, and the music of Charlotte Moorman were preparing the way for the great surge of women performance artists in the 1970s.

Carolee Schneemann was one of the few women to actively engage in the conception of Happenings (or Kinetic Theatre, as she called it) and was most likely the first to incorporate her own nude body in her work. In discussing the development of *Eye Body* (1963), Schneemann emphasized how the decision to use her own body represented empowerment:

'*I wanted my actual body to be combined with the work as an integral material ... Covered in paint, grease, chalk, ropes, plastic, I establish my body as visual territory. Not only am I an image maker, but I explore the image values of flesh as material I choose to work with.*'[35]

Schneemann was well aware of the taboos associated with the nude female body and chose to expose them as a means of transgressing gender-specific norms:

'In 1963 to use my body as an extension of my painting-construction was to challenge and threaten the psychic territorial power lines by which women were admitted to the Art Stud Club, so long as they behaved enough *like the men, did work clearly in the traditions and pathways hacked out by men.'*[36]

Schneemann offered her self-stripped, self-emblazoned body as a banner for other women in their struggle to reclaim their bodies and their identities.

In the following year, Schneemann turned to the taboo subject of human sensuality. She described her most famous (or infamous) theatre piece, *Meat Joy* (1964), as 'an exuberant sensory celebration of the flesh'.[37] To arrive at such a state of abandon, she introduced abject materials into the choreography. Nude participants frolicked, rolled around and danced in piles of paper scrap; gradually other substances such as wet paint, raw fish, chickens and sausages were added to the writhing mass of bodies, resulting in an erotic ritual, both sensual and repellent. It was an experiment in pushing the limits of sensuality – pushing them to the frontier of the disgusting in the hope of making the disgusting pleasurable. The goal was to 'dislocate, compound and engage our senses, expanding them into unknown and unpredictable relationships'.[38] Schneemann wanted these new relationships to question and ultimately destroy social taboos.

By the early 1970s, at the height of the women's movement, many more women artists found Body and performance art – the literal use of one's own body – to be an ideal means of self-exploration and self-expression. A woman artist's use of her own nude body, however, ignited controversy by emphasizing the social taboos that continued to surround representation of the female sex. In the same period, 'Bruce Nauman was "Thighing", Vito Acconci was masturbating, Dennis Oppenheim was sunbathing and burning and Barry Le Va was slamming into walls'.[39] Men were free to manipulate their bodies as they pleased, women were not; the great irony being that certain male artists, among them Vito Acconci, had attempted to become women by altering their bodies in their art practice. In *Conversions* (1971), for example, Acconci burned the hair off his chest, tried to develop female breasts by pulling on his own and finally hid his penis between his legs.[40] Although his engagement in transgressive femininity and his attempt to 'become' a woman were perceived as a valid art practice, body manipulations by Hannah Wilke and Lynda Benglis were deemed narcissistic or pornographic.

Wilke offered the viewer only blemished or demeaning images of herself. The constant accusations of narcissism and pornography were unjustified: from a more objective vantage, Wilke's work presented an extremely critical picture of the status and representation of women. In *S.O.S. (Starification Object Series)* (1974) Wilke 'scarred' her nude body with vaginally shaped sculptures made from chewed gum, and then photographed herself in poses that mock those of magazine models. The effect of these scars on the viewer is not unlike that of Cindy Sherman's dismembered mannequins, as in *Untitled* (1992):

'Automatic scopophilic consumption, whether narcissistic or voyeuristic, is interrupted. By rendering the body problematic, and exposing what is conventionally hidden, Sherman infuses the desirous look with a sense of dread and disease.'[41]

Two decades earlier, Wilke, too, had exposed what was conventionally hidden – the vagina – and she did it with a non-art medium – chewing gum. The proliferation of vagina gums was Wilke's attempt to make visible the 'invisible' sex, reinstating visually the presence of woman so long repressed within patriarchal society. As Debra Wacks observes, Wilke 'embraces and builds upon the connotations that are associated with chewing gum ... For gum is sticky and messy, and chewing gum is often considered a disgusting, even obsessive habit.'[42] The incorporation of such an abject substance as chewed gum not only subverts the notion of high art materials, but also sensualizes the experience: the chewing gum is in fact worked into its malleable state by the spectators, who thus partake in the taste, smell and sound of the creative process [...]

Lynda Benglis' gallery advertisement for *Artforum* in November 1974 was a bold attempt to confront the issue of gender bias in the art world. In the self-conceived photograph, Benglis slicks up her nude body, places a larger-than-life dildo at her groin and with one hand on her hip turns belligerently to confront the viewer. According to Benglis, her 'intention was to mock the idea of having to take sexual sides – to be either a male artist or a female'.[43] In the controversy that ensued Benglis was accused of narcissism, pornography and penis envy. Her critique of gender bias in the art world was lost on critics who failed to see past a nude female body. According to one, 'Benglis' sexual photographs are not to be confused with Vito Acconci's performances on erotic themes ... Superficially, Benglis' work reveals the tasteful, the glossy and the narcissistic, while Acconci's secret sexual systems are more populist, and tend towardsthe squalid, the exorcistic and the puritanical.'[44] This bias becomes even clearer when compared to the perhaps less aggressive yet equally threatening photo of Robert Morris in S&M gear, used as a poster for his April 1974 exhibition at Castelli/Sonnabend Galleries. Jeremy Gilbert-Rolfe observed that the poster was an 'ironic encapsulation of [Morris'] own position in contemporary art'.[45] And what about the position of the artist if she is a woman? Is not Benglis' image of an 'ironic encapsulation' of the state of woman as an artist in a male-dominated art world?

Clearly this world, by accusing women artists like Schneemann, Wilke and Benglis of narcissism and pornography, has pre-empted a more legitimate association of their work with the abject. Similarly, Kusama, Hesse, Bourgeois and Benglis again, working in abject materials and imagery that have a bold transgressive force, were often subjected to one-dimensional interpretations that referred to nature and emotional excess. For male artists like Oldenburg, Morris and Acconci, on the other hand, the incorporation of abject material or imagery – what I have termed the practice of transgressive femininity – earned them the accolade of rebel-innovator.

Transgressive femininity is not an option for the woman artist. As I said earlier, the privileging of the feminine in a transgressive discourse by no means guarantees liberation. Rather, as in the art practice of the 1960s and 1970s, women are presumptuously categorized and thereby rendered mute and invisible as individuals. In 'Femininity and Mas(s)querade', Tania Modleski concludes:

'Not the least of the problems involved in equating the masses and mass culture [or in our case, nature and the body] with the feminine is that it becomes much more difficult for women to interrogate their role within that culture.'[46]

Nor is transgressive masculinity an option for the woman artist. Such a concept was boldly parodied by Benglis. By appropriating an obviously *faux* phallus, Benglis likened the notion of a woman obtaining power or legitimacy to that of a man having a 60-cm [24-in] penis.

In the 1970s a feminist art practice emerged that attempted to deconstruct the patriarchal notions of femininity through the use of theory. Of distinct note in this practice is the absence of a direct representation of the female body. In *Post-Partum Document* (1974–79), for example, Mary Kelly uses Lacanian analysis to deconstruct patriarchal concepts of motherhood. In *Documentation I*, she deconstructs the notion of woman as nurturer. Rather than depict a mother feeding a child, Kelly juxtaposes feeding charts and Lacanian diagrams with stained diaper liners as a record of the nurturing procedure, the non-verbal mother/child means of communication. The stain marks a successful response to the child's request for nourishment.

The work of artists like Mary Kelly set a precedent for another generation to pursue theoretically based art practices critical of the representation of women and notions of femininity. As recently as 1991, however, in her essay discussing the critical reception of the work of Cindy Sherman, Abigail Solomon-Godeau asks how 'the work of a woman artist, whose work has long been preoccupied with constructions of femininity, is ... textually dispatched with an exclamatory invocation to the masculine'.[47] Solomon-Godeau is responding to the interpretation of Sherman's work as 'humanistic' and concludes that:

'in ascending to that pantheon where, as we all know, genius has no gender, what gets deflected in the criticism, if not relegated to critical oblivion altogether, are all those elements in the work that constitute its difference.'[48]

Arthur Rimbaud's prophecy concerning women's contributions to poetry (and, in our case, art) still rings uncannily true: 'We shall take them from her and we shall understand them.' The adoption and consequent erasure of meaning in women's art continues to persist even today.

I would like to thank Linda Nochlin and Mira Schor for sharing their thoughts on and enthusiasm for women's art practice of the 1960s and 1970s. Richard Meyer, Mignon Nixon and Debra Wacks generously made their unpublished works available to me.

1 Arthur Rimbaud, letter to Paul Demeny, 15 May 1871, in Enid Starkie, *Arthur Rimbaud* (New York: New Directions Books, 1961) 124-24. The last clause reads in French 'nous les prendrons, nous les comprendrons'; *comprendre* here seems better translated as 'to incorporate' or 'encompass'.

2 Quoted in Lucy R. Lippard, *From the Centre: Feminist Essays on Women's Art* (New York: E.P. Dutton & Co., 1976) 6.

3 Elizabeth Gross, 'The Body of Signification', in John Fletcher and Andrew Benjamin (eds.), *Abjection, Melancholia and Love: The Work of Julia Kristeva* (New York and London: Routledge, 1990) 92.

4 Kristeva, *Powers of Horror: An Essay in Abjection*, trans. Leon S. Roudiez (New York and Oxford: Columbia University Press, 1984) 2.

5 Claes Oldenburg and Emmett Williams, ed., *Store Days: Documents from the Store (1961) and Ray Gun Theatre (1962)* (New York: Something Else Press, 1967) 65.

6 *Ibid.*, 141.

7 Harris Rosenstein, 'Climbing Mt. Oldenburg', *ARTnews*, 64 (February 1966) 57.

8 Kusama's remark is cited in Alfred Carl, 'Call Her Dotty', *New York Sunday News* (13 August 1967) 36.

9 Anita Feldman, 'Somthing Rich and Strange', unidentified clipping, Yayoi Kusama artist's file, Whitney Museum of American Art, New York.

10 'Kusama: The First Obsessional Artist', unidentified typescript, Yayoi Kusama artist's file (New York: Whitney Museum of American Art).

11 Quoted in 'Kusama's Show', *New York Post* (14 November 1965).

12 Julia Kristeva, *Powers of Horror*, *op. cit.*, 2 [see in this volume pp. 242-43].

13 Lucy R. Lippard, 'Eccentric Abstraction', *Art International* (November 1996); reprinted in Richard Armstrong and Richard Marshall (eds.), *The New Sculpture 1967-75: Between Geometry and Gesture* (New York: Whitney Museum of American Art, 1990) 54.

14 *Ibid.*, 55.

15 *Ibid.*, 58.

16 Kristeva, *Powers of Horror*, *op. cit.*, 1.

17 Robert Morris, 'Anti-Form', *Artforum*, 6 (April 1968) 33-35 [see in this volume p. 206].

18 Herbert Marcuse, *An Essay on Liberation*, quoted in Maurice Berger, *Labyrinths: Robert Morris, Minimalism and the 1960s* (New York: Harper & Row, 1989) 47.

19 Morris, 'Anti-Form', *op. cit.*, 35.

20 *Ibid.*

21 Ralph Pomeroy, 'Soft Objects', *Arts Magazine*, 43 (March 1969) 28.

22 Grace Glueck, 'A Feeling for Felt', *New York Times* (28 April 1968) 28.

23 Pepe Karmel, 'The Evolution of the Felt Works' in *Robert Morris: The Felt Works* (New York: Grey Art Gallery and Study Center, New York University, 1989) 57.

24 Herbert Marcuse, *Eros and Civilization*, quoted in Berger, *Labyrinths*, *op. cit.*, 67.

25 Thomas B. Hess, 'Abstract Acrylicism', *New York Magazine* (8 December 1975) 114.

26 Klaus Kertess, 'Foam Structures', *Artforum*, 10 (May 1972); reprinted in Armstrong and Marshall, *The New Sculpture*, *op. cit.*, 283.

27 Kristeva, *Powers of Horror*, *op. cit.*, 71.

28 Quoted in Robert Pincus-Witten, 'Lynda Benglis: The Frozen Gesture', *Artforum*, 13 (November 1974); reprinted in Armstrong and Marshall, *The New Sculpture*, *op. cit.*, 310. Benjamin Buchloh has suggested that Benglis' comment may also refer to Bruce Nauman's films of the late 1960s, which recorded activities in his studio such as breathing, tossing a ball, clapping or painting his testicles black.

29 Daniel Robbins, 'Sculpture by Louise Bourgeois', *Art International*, 8 (October 1964) 30, 31.

30 William S. Rubin, 'Some Reflections Prompted by the Recent Work of Louise Bourgeois', *Art International*, 13 (April 1969) 17.

31 *Ibid.*, 19-20.

32 *Ibid.*, 20.

33 Donald Kuspit, 'Louise Bourgeois: Where Angels Fear to Tread', *Artforum*, 25 (March 1987) 115.

34 Jeanne Silverthorn, 'Louise Bourgeois', *Artforum*, 22 (December 1984) 81.

35 Carolee Schneemann, 'Eye Body', *More Than Meat Joy: Complete Performance Works and Selected Writings*, ed. Bruce McPherson (New Paltz, New York: Documentext, 1979) 52 [see in this volume p. 196].

36 *Ibid.*

37 Quoted in 'Carolee Schneemann: Image as Process', *Creative Camera*, 76 (October 1970) 304.

38 *Ibid.*

39 Lippard, *From the Center*, *op. cit.*, 125.

40 Vito Acconci, 'Drifts and Conversions', *Avalanche*, 2 (Winter 1971) 82-95.

41 Jan Avgikos, 'Cindy Sherman: Burning Down the House', *Artforum*, 38 (January 1993) 78.

42 Deborah Wacks, 'Feminism/Humanism in Hannah Wilke's *S.O.S. - Starification Object Series*' (unpublished paper, Institute of Fine Arts, New York University, 1992) 7.

43 Quoted in Susan Krane, *Lynda Benglis: Dual Natures* (Atlanta: High Museum of Art, 1990) 42.

44 Pincus-Witten, 'Lynda Benglis', in Armstrong and Marshall, *The New Sculpture*, *op. cit.*, 312.

45 Jeremy Gilbert Rolfe, 'Robert Morris: The Complication of Exhaustion', *Artforum*, 13 (September 1974) 44.

46 Tania Modleski, 'Femininity as Mas(s)querade' in *Feminism Without Women: Culture and Criticism in a 'Postfeminist' Age* (New York and London: Routledge, 1991) 34.

47 Abigail Solomon-Godeau, 'Suitable for Framing: The Critical Recasting of Cindy Sherman', *Parkett*, 29 (1991) 112.

48 *Ibid.*, 115.

Leslie C. Jones, 'Transgressive Femininity: Art and Gender in the 1960s and 1970s', *Abject Art: Repulsion and Desire in American Art*, ed. Jane Philbrick (New York: Whitney Museum of American Art, 1993) 33-57.

Judith BUTLER
Bodies That Matter [1993]

INTRODUCTION

'Why should our bodies end at the skin, or include at best other beings encapsulated by skin?'
– Donna Haraway, 'A Cyborg Manifesto', 1985

'If one really thinks about the body as such, there is no possible outline of the body as such. There are thinkings of the systematicity of the body, there are value codings of the body. The body, as such, cannot be thought, and I certainly cannot approach it.'
– Gayatri Chakravorty Spivak, 'In a Word', interview with Ellen Rooney

'There is no nature, only the effects of nature; denaturalization or naturalization.'
– Jacques Derrida, *Donner le Temps*

Is there a way to link the question of the materiality of the body to the performativity of gender? And how does the category of 'sex' figure within such a relationship? Consider first that sexual difference is often invoked as an issue of material differences. Sexual difference, however, is never simply a function of material differences which are not in some way both marked and formed by discursive practices. Further, to claim that sexual differences are indissociable from discursive demarcations is not the same as claiming that discourse causes sexual difference. The category of 'sex' is, from the start, normative; it is what Foucault has called a 'regulatory ideal'. In this sense, then, 'sex' not only functions as a norm, but is part of a regulatory practice that produces the bodies it governs, that is, whose regulatory force is made clear as a kind of productive power, the power to produce – demarcate, circulate, differentiate – the bodies it controls. Thus, 'sex' is a regulatory ideal whose materialism is compelled, and this materialization takes place (or fails to take place) through certain highly regulated practices. In other words, 'sex' is an ideal construct which is forcibly materialized through time. It is not a simple fact or static condition of a body, but a process whereby regulatory norms materialize 'sex' and achieve this materialization through a forcible reiteration of those norms. That this reiteration is necessary is a sign that materialization is never quite complete, that bodies never quite comply with the norms by which their materialization is impelled. Indeed, it is the instabilities, the possible for materialization, opened up by this process that mark one domain in which the force of the regulatory law can be turned against itself to spawn rearticulations that call into question the hegemonic force of that very regulatory law [...]

PERFORMATIVITY AS CITATIONALITY

When, in Lacanian parlance, one is said to assume a 'sex', the grammar of the phrase creates the expectation that there is a 'one' who, upon waking, looks up and deliberates on which 'sex' it will assume today, a grammar in which 'assumption' is quickly assimilated to the notion of a highly reflective choice. But if this 'assumption' is *compelled* by a regulatory apparatus of heterosexuality, one which reiterates itself through the forcible production of 'sex', then the assumption of sex is constrained from the start. And if there is *agency*, it is to be found, paradoxically, in the possibilities opened up in and by that constrained appropriation of the regulatory law, by the materialization of that law, the compulsory appropriation and identification with those normative demands. The

forming, crafting, bearing, circulation, signification of that sexed body will not be a set of actions performed in compliance with the law; on the contrary, they will be a set of actions mobilized by the law, the citational accumulation and dissimulation of the law that produces material effects, the lived necessity of those effects as well as the lived contestation of that necessity.

Performativity is thus not a singular 'act', for it is always a reiteration of a norm, or set of norms, and to the extent that it requires an act-like status in the present, it conceals or dissimulates the conventions of which it is a repetition. Moreover, this act is not primarily theatrical; indeed, its apparent theatricality is produced to the extent that its historicity remains dissimulated (and, conversely, its theatricality gains a certain inevitability given the impossibility of a full disclosure of its historicity). Within speech act theory, a performative is that discursive practice that enacts or produces that which it names.[1] According to the biblical rendition of the performative, i.e., 'Let there be light!', it appears that it is by virtue of *the power of the subject or its will* that a phenomenon is named into being. In a critical reformulation of the performative, Derrida makes clear that this power is not the function of an originating will, but is always derivative: '*Could a performative utterance succeed if its formulation did not repeat a "coded" or iterable utterance, or in other words, if the formula I pronounce in order to open a meeting, launch a ship or a marriage were not identifiable as conforming with an iterable model, if it were not then identifiable in some way as a "citation"? ... in such a typology, the category of intention will not disappear; it will have its place, but from that place it will no longer be able to govern the entire scene and system of utterance* [*l'énonciation*].'[2]

[...] If the formulation of a bodily ego, a sense of stable contour and the fixing of spatial boundary is achieved through identificatory practices, and if psychoanalysis documents the hegemonic workings of those identifications, can we then read psychoanalysis for the inculcation of the heterosexual matrix at the level of bodily morphogenesis? What Lacan calls the 'assumption' or 'accession' to the symbolic law can be read as a kind of *citing* of the law, and so offers an opportunity to link question of the materialization of 'sex' with the reworking of performativity as citationality. Although Lacan claims that the symbolic law has a semi-autonomous status prior to the assumption of sexed positions by a subject, these normative positions, i.e., the 'sexes', are only known through the approximations that they occasion. The force and necessity of these norms ('sex' as a symbolic function is to be understood as a kind of commandment or injunction) is thus functionally *dependent on* the approximation and citation of the law; the law without its approximation is no law or, rather, it remains a governing law only for those who would affirm it on the basis of religious faith. If 'sex' is assumed in the same way that a law is cited – an analogy which will be supported later in this text – then 'the law of sex' is repeatedly fortified and idealized as the law only to the extent that it is reiterated as the law, produced as the law, the anterior and inapproximable ideal, by the very citations it is said to command. Reading the meaning of 'assumption' in Lacan as citation, the law is no longer given in a fixed form *prior* to its citation, but is produced through citation as that which precedes and exceeds the mortal approximations enacted by the subject.

In this way, the symbolic law in Lacan can be subject to the same kind of critique that Nietzsche formulated of the notion of God: the power attributed to this prior and ideal power is derived and deflected from the attribution itself.[3] It is this insight into the illegitimacy of the symbolic law of sex that is dramatized to a certain degree in the contemporary film *Paris Is Burning*: the ideal that is mirrored depends on that very mirroring to be sustained as an ideal. And though the symbolic appears to be a force that cannot be contravened without psychosis, the symbolic ought to be rethought as a series of normativizing injunctions that secure the borders of sex through the threat of psychosis, abjection, psychic unlivability. And further, that this 'law' can only remain a law to the extent that it compels the differentiated citations and approximations called 'feminine' and 'masculine'. The presumption that the symbolic law of sex enjoys a separable ontology prior and autonomous to its assumption is contravened by the notion that the citation of the law is the very mechanism of its production and articulation. What is 'forced' by the symbolic, then, is a citation of its law that reiterates and consolidates the ruse of its own force. What would it mean to 'cite' the law to produce it differently, to 'cite' the law in order to reiterate and co-opt its power, to expose the heterosexual matrix and to displace the effect of its necessity?

The process of that sedimentation or what we might call *materialization* will be a kind of citationality, the acquisition of being through the citing of power, a citing that establishes an originary complicity with power in the formation of the 'I'.

In this sense, the agency denoted by the performativity of 'sex' will be directly counter to any notion of a voluntarist subject who exists quite apart from the regulatory norms which she/he opposes. The paradox of subjectification (*assujetissement*) is precisely that the subject who would resist such norms is itself enabled, if not produced, by such norms. Although this constitutive constraint does not foreclose the possibility of agency, it does locate agency as a reiterative or rearticulatory practice, immanent to power, and not a relation of external opposition to power.

As a result of this reformulation of performativity (a) gender performativity cannot be theorized apart from the forcible and reiterative practice of regulatory sexual regimes; (b) the account of agency conditioned by those very regimes of discourse/power cannot be conflated with voluntarism or individualism, much less consumerism, and in no way presupposes a choosing subject; (c) the regime of heterosexuality operates to circumscribe and contour the 'materiality' of sex, and that 'materiality' is formed and sustained through and as a materialization of regulatory norms that are in part those of heterosexual hegemony; (d) the materialization of norms requires those identificatory processes by which norms are assumed or appropriated, and these identifications precede and enable the formation of a subject, but are not, strictly speaking, performed by a subject; and (e) the limits of constructivism are exposed at those boundaries of bodily life where abjected or delegitimated bodies fail to count as 'bodies'. If the materiality of sex is demarcated in discourse, then this demarcation will produce a domain of excluded and delegitimated 'sex'. Hence, it will be as important to think about how and to what end bodies are constructed as it will be to think about how and to what end bodies are *not* constructed and, further, to ask after how bodies which fail to materialize provide the necessary 'outside', if not the necessary support, for the bodies which, in materializing the norm, qualify as bodies that matter.

How, then, can one think through the matter of bodies as a kind of materialization governed by regulatory norms in order to ascertain the workings of heterosexual hegemony in the formation of what qualifies as a viable body? How does that materialization of the norm in bodily formation produce a domain of abjected bodies, a field of deformation, which, in failing to qualify as the fully human, fortifies those regulatory norms? What challenge does that excluded and abjected realm produce to a symbolic hegemony that might force a radical rearticulation of what qualifies as bodies that matter, ways of living that count as 'life', lives worth protecting, lives worth saving, lives worth grieving?

1 See J.L. Austin, *How to Do Things With Words*, ed. ed. J. O. Urmson and Marina Sbisà (Cambridge, Massachusetts: Harvard University Press, 1955), and *Philosophical Papers* (Oxford: Oxford University Press, 1961), especially pp. 233-52; Shoshana Felman, *The Literary Speech-Act: Don Juan with J.L. Austin, or Seduction in Two Languages*, trans. Catherine Porter (Ithaca, New York: Cornell University Press, 1983); Barbara Johnson, 'Poetry and Performative Language: Mallarmé and Austin', in *The Critical Difference: Essays in the Contemporary Rhetoric of Reading* (Baltimore: Johns Hopkins University Press, 1980) 52-66; Mary Louise Pratt, *A Speech Act Theory of Literary Discourse* (Bloomington: Indiana University Press, 1977); and Ludwig Wittgenstein, *Philosophical Investigations*, trans. G.E.M. Anscombe (New York: Macmillan, 1958) part 1.

2 Jacques Derrida, 'Signature, Event, Context', *Limited, Inc.*, ed. Gerald Graff, trans. Samuel Webster and Jeffrey Mehlman (Evanston, Illinois: Northwestern University Press, 1988) 18.

3 Nietzsche argues that the ideal of God was produced '[i]n the same measure' as a human sense of failure and wretchedness, and that the production of God was, indeed, the idealization which instituted and reinforced that wretchedness; see Friedrich Nietzsche, *On the Genealogy of Morals*, trans. Walter Kauffman (New York: Vintage, 1969), section 20. That the symbolic law in Lacan produces 'failure' to approximate the sexed ideals embodied and enforced by the law, is usually understood as a promising sign that the law is not fully efficacious, that it does not exhaustively constitute the psyche of any given subject. And yet, to what extent does this conception of the law produce the

very failure that it seeks to order, and maintain an ontological distance between the laws and its failed approximations such that the deviant approximations have no power to alter the workings of the law itself?

Judith Butler, 'Introduction', *Bodies That Matter: On the Discursive Limits of 'Sex'* (New York and London: Routledge, 1993) 1-23.

Coco FUSCO

The Other History of Intercultural Performance [1994]

In the early 1900s Franz Kafka wrote a story that began, 'Honoured members of the Academy! You have done me the honour of inviting me to give your Academy an account of the life I formerly led as an ape.'[1] Entitled 'A Report to an Academy', it was presented as the testimony of a man from the Gold Coast of Africa who had lived for several years on display in Germany as a primate. That account was fictitious and created by a European writer who stressed the irony of having to demonstrate one's humanity; yet it is one of many literary allusions to the real history of ethnographic exhibition of human beings that has taken place in the West over the past five centuries. While the experiences of many of those who were exhibited is the stuff of legend, it is the accounts by observers and impresarios that constitute the historical and literary record of this practice in the West. My collaborator, Guillermo Gómez-Peña, and I were intrigued by this legacy of performing the identity of an Other for a white audience, sensing its implications for us performance artists dealing with cultural identity in the present. Had things changed, we wondered? How would we know, if not by unleashing those ghosts from a history that could be said to be ours? Imagine that I stand before you then, as did Kafka's character, to speak about an experience that falls somewhere between truth and fiction [...]

Our original intent was to create a satirical commentary on Western concept of the exotic, primitive Other; yet, we had to confront two unexpected realities in the course of developing this piece: 1) a substantial portion of the public believed that our fictional identities were real ones; and 2) a substantial number of intellectuals, artists and cultural bureaucrats sought to deflect attention from the substance of our experiment to the 'moral implications' of our dissimulation, or in their words, our 'misinforming the public' about who we were. The literalism implicit in the interpretation of our work by individuals representing the 'public interest' bespoke their investment in positivist notions of 'truth' and depoliticized, ahistorical notions of 'civilization' [...]

Our plan was to live in a golden cage for three days, presenting ourselves as undiscovered Amerindians from an island in the Gulf of Mexico that had somehow been overlooked by Europeans for five centuries. We called our homeland Guatinau, and ourselves Guatinauis. We performed our 'traditional tasks', which ranged from sewing voodoo dolls and lifting weights to watching television and working on a laptop computer. A donation box in front of the cage indicated that, for a small fee, I would dance (to rap music), Guillermo would tell authentic Amerindian stories (in a nonsensical language) and we would pose for Polaroids with visitors. Two 'zoo guards' would be on hand to speak to visitors (since we could not understand them), take us to the bathroom on leashes and feed us sandwiches and fruit. At the Whitney Museum in New York we added sex to our spectacle, offering a peek at authentic Guatinaui male genitals for $5. A chronology with highlights from the history of exhibiting non-Western peoples was on one didactic panel and a simulated Encyclopaedia Britannica entry with a fake map of the Gulf of Mexico showing our island was on another. After our three days in May 1992 we took our performance to Covent Garden in London. In September, we presented it in Minneapolis and in October at the Smithsonian's National Museum of Natural History. In December we were on display in the Australian Museum of Natural History in Sydney, and in January 1993 at the Field Museum of Chicago. In early March we were at the Whitney for the opening of the biennial, the only site where we were recognizably contextualized as artwork. Prior to our trip to Madrid, we did a test run under relatively controlled conditions in the Art Gallery of the University of California, Irvine [...]

1 Franz Kafka, *The Basic Kafka* (New York: Washington Square Press, 1979) 245.

Coco Fusco, 'The Other History of Intercultural Performance', *The Drama Review*, 38: 1 (Spring 1994); reprinted in Coco Fusco, *English is Broken Here: Notes on Cultural Fusion in the Americas* (New York: New Press, 1995) 37-64.

Amelia JONES

Dis/playing the Phallus: Male Artists Perform Their Masculinities[1] [1994]

The phallus, according to the new Random House Dictionary, is '1: an image of the male reproductive organ, esp. that carried in procession in ancient festivals of Dionysus, or Bacchus, symbolizing the generative power in nature; 2: *Anat.*, the penis, the clitoris, or the *sexually undifferentiated* embryonic organ out of which either of these develops.' The principal function of the phallus, then, is to celebrate the primacy of the male subject by symbolizing his genital prowess in public rituals. Its secondary meaning, and I have to say I was shocked to find such egalitarianism accorded to this usually unilaterally biased term, implies a collapse of sexual difference into a nebulous, 'undifferentiated' pre-genital state.

This anatomically based yet radically amorphous phallus contrasts dramatically with that famous concept-cum-organ defined in coyly ambiguous terms by Jacques Lacan:

'The phallus is not a fantasy ... nor is it such an object (part, internal, good, bad, etc. ...) in so far as this term tends to accentuate the reality involved in a relationship. It is even less the organ, penis or clitoris, which it symbolizes.'

As many feminists have pointed out, while Lacan thus imputes a radical unfixability to the phallus, he also continues to characterize it as the means of accessing the symbolic – the order of the law and the father. The relations between the sexes, he claims, 'will revolve around a being and a having which ... refer to a signifier, the phallus ...'[2] Although we all know who 'has' and who 'is' in patriarchal culture, Lacan's system arguably allows for the ambiguities and complexities of subjectivity and sexual identity and, potentially, for an understanding of the culturally specific nature of the penis/phallus conflation. The phallus is not (or not *simply*) the penis, though, as Jane Gallop has noted:

'the masculinity of the phallic signifier [phallus being masculine in gender in the French language] serves well as an emblem of the confusion between phallus and male which inheres in language, in our symbolic order.'

Lacan's phallus implies that while '[m]an is threatened with loss, woman is deprived'; it is a sign of the fact that the 'subject that knows cannot be separated from the subject that can mistake the phallus for a penis'.[3]

This paper addresses masculinity as a negotiated system of identities that are accomplished through the ritual display of phallic attributes, specifically in relation to the masculinized function of the artist – a function that could be said to exaggerate the attributes of masculinity affording power to the male subject in patriarchal culture. As many feminist art historians have pointed out, the artist in modern western culture is a quintessentially phallic figure, one who exaggerates the characteristics of the fictional unified subject of modernism[4] (that subject Michel Foucault has theorized as 'modern man'[5]). The male artist is paradigmatic of the ideologically centred subject of modernism, acting as a paternal origin for subsequent lineages of artistic production, a genius whose fully intentional creative acts are invested with transcendental value by art history – a discipline that, not incidentally, developed within the period designated by Foucault as the modern episteme (beginning roughly in 1800 and extending towards the present). Within this period the artist has come to epitomize the centring of the modern subject upon himself – the construction of the masculine self as a coherent individual at the expense of female subjectivity, which is thus rendered impossible to conceive.[6] The artist has become a guarantor of Kantian transcendentality through what Jacques Derrida has called the 'divine teleology' of Western aesthetics – a teleology founded in the figure of the artistic genius, who is given 'surplus value' by God, his inspiration.[7] The artist might be said to replace God in the modern episteme, the period of God's demise, if Nietzsche is to be believed.

In this essay I explore the intersection of the masculine and authorial fields of subjectivity by examining the work of male artists who, in the 1960s and early 1970s, used their own bodies in or as their art: Yves Klein, Robert

Morris, Vito Acconci and Chris Burden. I argued that, by displaying and performing their own bodies, these 'body artists' shift to varying degrees away from the transcendental and singularly masculine conception of artistic authority put into place within Modernism – a conception that relies on the veiling of the actual body of the artist such that his divinity (his phallic prowess) can be ensured. As Lacan writes: '... the phallus can only play its role as veiled ';[8] the artist's authority is most effectively confirmed when the function of the phallus is masked, hidden under art-historically sanctioned symbols of artistic genius. Art history provides this veiling function both by celebrating genius as if it is divinely endowed and inherent rather than a system of attributes displaced by the artist and given value through the interpretive act, and by occluding its own investments behind a facade of objectivity. Through this veiling of the authorial and interpretive phallus, art history pretends that artistic and interpretive authority are gender neutral.

Whether consciously or not, these male body artists exaggerate the phallic properties of masculinity and authorial subjectivity to various effects. They 'play' the phallus, exploiting its conventional alignment with the male body to reinforce their own artistic authority and/or they 'display' its anatomical corollary, the penis, to potentially deconstructive ends. At the very least, through this exaggerated dis/play, they could be said to complicate the Modernist strategy of disguising or occluding the link between the symbolic function of the phallus and the penis: that link that simultaneously obscures and guarantees the privileging of the anatomically male subject within Western culture. It is through *performing* the normative attributes of masculinity that these attributes are played out as contingent rather than inherent.

It may seem problematic that I continue to focus here on the blatantly heterosexist and binary terms of the phallic division. I hope that the reasons for this focus will become clear as I re-create in my own terms various projects of male artists, all of whom performed themselves as heterosexual in their lives and work. While interrogating this work in terms of conventional masculinity, then, I do not mean to imply that masculinity is a fixed term, much less that the phallus is an anatomical thing that can be visually determined as its attribute. Rather, I hope to suggest that, while this work still operates within 1960s and 1970s assumptions about gender difference, it can also be interpreted as in some ways rupturing the very binary model of gender that it engages with – opening provocative cracks in the fabric (or flesh?) of masculinity.

Subtending this analysis will be an interest in historical concerns. I examine this work as instantiating what I see to be a shift towards a more critical approach among male artists to the phallus (to modernism's heroic artist genius figure), an approach marked by a transformation of the firmly heterosexual, masculine conception of artistic authority into a *performative* relationship with subjectivity and identity in general. Certainly not coincidentally, this shift coincides with the rise of the second wave of feminism and of the civil rights and gay rights movements, all of which attacked the politics of normative subjectivity in white, male-dominated Euro-American culture, as well as with the development of poststructuralist critiques of modernist conceptions of subjectivity and meaning.[9] It also, as Kathy O'Dell has argued in her extensive examination of masochistic performance art, parallels an increasing scepticism towards the state – a transformation in individuals' relationships with the social contract resulting from the Vietnam war.[10]

I am placing these artists, then, within a particular social and theoretical context – one in which subjectivity begins to be articulated not in terms of a Cartesian centring, but rather as a continually negotiated exchange among individuals. I am reading body art as constitutive and exemplary of a profound shift in conceptions of the self in Western culture – a shift that we might characterize as Postmodern. In the visual arts, where Postmodernism is generally discussed only in relation to the productive strategies employed in contemporary art practices – such as the dematerialization of the object, fragmentation and allegory, appropriation and the merging of high and low culture – Postmodernism has not been examined in relation to questions of subjectivity in any sense.[11] This essay – and the book project on body art and artistic performativity to which it relates, aim to begin to fill this lacuna by exploring the vicissitudes of artistic subjectivity and interpretation within Postmodernism.[12] Because body artworks actively perform the embodied and sexualized object of the artist in relation to a viewing audience, they provide a paradigmatic locus for an inquiry into shifts in authorial and interpretive subjectivity and conceptions of the body/self in the last thirty years [...]

[W]hile it would be easier simply to condemn this work as unequivocally masculinist, I take it as a challenge to offer desiring and performative feminist readings that acknowledge both its seductiveness (in its sexualization of the male body and potential dislocation of phallic mastery) and my own participation as an Anglo heterosexual feminist in determining particular values for it.[13] What I hope to add to an understanding of the meanings of body art and Postmodernism here is an acknowledgement of the *performative aspect of interpretation itself* and thus of the implication of interpretive desire in the production of meaning for this work. I view this production as differing from that involved in paintings or other static objects to the extent that, when the interpreter actually experiences the body in performance rather than its representations, she/he faces a different type of identificatory bond with the performer: not a more 'essential' or more 'radical' one necessarily, but one whose effects may well be more difficult to reorder or repress due to the temporal aspects of performance (particularly its unpredictability as an open-ended narrative form) and to the immediate proximity of artist and interpreter – such that the two can potentially interact and respond to one another's reactions. My interpretive framework, then, is posed as a feminist alternative to conventional and eminently phallocentric models of interpretation that require a repression of the question of the engaged body; by addressing practices of body art and the interpretive pleasures it evokes, I am stressing the need to open out this repression. My point is that body art is neither inherently anti-feminist nor immediately phallocentric but rather – *as I exchange with it here* – can be read as raising important questions about the intimate relationship between masculinity and artistic and interpretive authority.

The shift towardsa performative conception of artistic subjectivity has been marked broadly in art discourse and practice since 1960 or so.[14] Strikingly, for example, in paging through issues of art magazines from the late 1960s and early 1970s, one finds a proliferation of self-performative advertisements on the part of both male and female artists. It is important to note that the productive and receptive contexts of these images are decidedly different from those of photographs stemming from public performances – they lack the 'spontaneity' common to the photograph of a performance (the spontaneity that, even when staged, seems to act as 'proof' of the duration, immediacy and proximity that presumably existed at the time the photographs were taken). These advertisements are, rather, the result of privately enacted poses presented within commercial venues. While we thus encounter these photographs on different grounds, they still offer us the opportunity to engage and negotiate with a playfully performative artistic figure who complicates the gender and class-coded terms of artistic subjectivity.

This self-consciously ironic subject-in-representation contrasts dramatically with the Modernist artist, who is generally constructed – and constructs himself – as a fixed, masculine subject. For example, in the infamous 1949 presentation of Jackson Pollock as 'the greatest living painter in *Life* magazine, he is aligned with a blatantly romanticized and masculine artistic authority.[15] Pollock's representation dramatically contrasts with the majority of images of post-Abstract Expressionist artists, who often parody or otherwise undermine this histrionic notion of artistic genius as divinely endowed (and inevitably masculine) through photographic posing. Thus, in an advertisement dating from September 1970 in *Artforum* Robert Rauschenberg perches casually on a ladder in front of a large-scale lithograph in a bourgeois plaid suit, subverting the alignment of artistic authority with a transcendentialized phallic power by refusing the macho poses and self-consciously anti-bourgeois clothing of Pollock (but also, arguably, maintaining the prerogative of masculine authority by projecting an image of himself as imbricated within his heroically monumental artwork).

Notably, this performativity is not gender neutral; the strategic self-fashioning of male artists contrasts sharply with that of women artists, as we can see by comparing Judy Chicago's advertisement for an exhibition at California State University, Fullerton, to Ed Ruscha's coy promotional picture (both published in *Artforum*, December 1970 and January 1967 respectively). While Chicago fashions herself as a butch pugilist, wearing boxing gloves, satin shorts and leaning back against the ropes of a boxing ring, humorously and aggressively transforming the image of a woman artist as retiring and passive, Ed Ruscha constructs himself as a bad boy art stud, lying in bed between two seemingly naked women. In case the reader misses the point, Ruscha's picture is captioned 'Ed Ruscha says goodbye to college joys'.

Both ads ironicize artistic subjectivity; Chicago and Ruscha adopt the attributes of a phallic masculinity, enacting sexual difference as an element of artistic subjectivity. But they produce this masculinity – and we read it today – from radically different perspectives. Chicago, as a woman artist in the early 1970s, had a large stake in undermining the conflation of the artist with masculinity and authority (the penis with the phallus); knowing she is a woman, we read her image as a critique of this conflation. Because he is a man, we can assume that Ruscha had an even larger stake in nurturing it; certainly the effects of his parodic gesture are to empower him as both phallic (heterosexually virile) and ironically anti-Modernist. Even under the regime of Postmodernism, which is ostensibly critical of the masculocentrism, such male self-display is rewarded (the relative economic value of Ruscha's and Chicago's paintings, and their contrasting levels of acceptance by art-historical institutions will confirm which artist is viewed more favourably by the market). What I am defining as the Postmodern performativity of the artist subject, then, still often maintains relatively conventional gender codes.

Similarly, Klein, Morris, Acconci and Burden have also performed themselves in relation to the phallic attributes of masculinity. Again, it must be stressed that the dynamics of self-display I examine here generally took place initially within a theatrical context (Acconci alone of the four often performed for film or video cameras in private). While I was not present for the live performances, I read the still photographs and textual descriptions documenting these events as moments taken from the extended narrative. Most of the still images I discuss here, like the advertisements I introduced above, are the result of carefully choreographed actions that were monitored, staged and distributed by the artist in question; key to this discussion, then, will be the issue of *self-construction*.

As is evident in the still photographs taken of his public performances and in the portraits he posed for throughout his career, Yves Klein, for example, could be described as a master of performativity, a brilliant fashioner of the artistic self.[16] Early on in his life, Klein was a self-trained Rosicrucian, living a life of self-discipline to attain the transfiguration of the body promised by the esoteric theories of Max Heindel. In Klein's words, he wanted to create 'in the ego the power to purify the physical body and the astral body and the body of desire'.[17] When he decided he was an artist, somewhat late in his brief life of thirty-four years, Klein transferred his Rosicrucian training into Romantic models of artistic genius, with figures such as Delacroix and Van Gogh functioning as levers to shift the orgasmic spiritualism of his religious training into modernism's more practical spiritualism of artistic genius. Thus, in his writings Klein makes inflated, romantic claims of artistic production – such as, the artist '*puts a soul in his creation*'[18] [...]

It is perhaps in his performative actions that we can most directly examine the ways in which Klein made masculinity function for himself – both ironically and deadly seriously at the same time. Klein's most notorious self-promotional art is perhaps his photographic *Leap into the Void* from 1960. Publicly claiming these pictures as documents of a single, high-risk, metaphysical leap into space, Klein none the less published two different versions, exposing his own charade by allowing the viewer to see that darkroom manipulations were required to attain such a mysterious scene. Subsequent research has shown that, indeed, Klein invited only close friends and photographers to the event, then made several leaps into a tarpaulin held by judo colleagues, attempting to get the desired transcendent expression on his face. Klein reproduced the first photograph (including a man riding by on a bicycle) on the front page of his egocentric version of the Parisian paper *Dimanche*, and the second version (*sans* bicyclist) in the catalogue accompanying a retrospective of his work.[19]

While Klein's contemporaneous statements suggest that this piece was initially conceived as an extension of the Rosicrucian ideal of bodily and mental transcendence, the history of the photographs suggests that he was savvy enough by 1960 to recognize that the Parisian art world would not buy such mysticism. Translating such metaphysical fantasies into phenomenological ideas, particularly those of Gaston Bachelard, Klein counted on ambiguity to veil the direction of his efforts. The resulting images of his leap could be viewed by a spiritualist or advocate of artistic romanticism as sincere attempts to encounter the void of infinity, or, by the presumably more sophisticated Parisian art world, as ironic comments on artistic genius. Needless to say, subsequent interpreters, imbued with the values of Postmodernism, have tended to celebrate the irony, legitimizing Klein as a 'master' of the critique of modernism. Through this ambiguity, Klein manages both to *critique* the phallus and to *possess* it, with this photographically rendered act paradoxically celebrated as exemplary of the Postmodern critique of Modernism's emphasis on existential risk [...]

There are easier ways for the male artist to ensure his authorial prowess than to die, however. While other European artists such as Joseph Beuys and Hermann Nitsch seem to have abandoned irony completely in their appeals to Christian ritual and the militaristic attributes of masculinity, male artists from the United States during the 1960s and 1970s tended to work, like Klein, in ironic and overtly sexualized ways, both against and with the grain of phallic authority. The US artist Robert Morris, for example, also contrived performative images of himself that play with conventional masculine artistic subjectivity. As with Klein, Morris' ironic self-constructions allowed him to empower himself through ambivalence, his smug parading of the attributes of masculinity placing him in the paradoxical position of anti-Modernist mastery.

In 1962, for example, Morris executed his *I-Box*.[20] Here, Morris flaunts his disrobed body, blatantly contextualizing its alignment, as anatomically male, with the authoritative 'I' of artistic production. Smirking, as if enjoying his defiance of the conventional system of veiling by which the body of the male artist is covered up and/or hidden away to further its claims to phallic mastery, Morris stands unabashed behind the wooden 'I'. In fact, the very structure of the piece, with its hinged door that the viewer must open to gain access to the photograph of the fully exposed figure of the artist, intensifies (yet reverses) the voyeuristic relation implicated in the ascription of phallic power to the male subject: it is the artist, normatively the possessor of the so-called 'male gaze' (and the authorial 'I'), whose body is given to the scopophilic and fetishizing look of the viewer.

In his infamous self-constructed image on a Castelli/Sonnabend Gallery poster from 1974 Morris appears overtly to enact the alignment of the male body *as* penis with the empowering phallus. In this image, as Mira Schor has written in her essay 'Representations of the Penis', Morris 'turns himself into a penis, a GI helmet forming the head, and his bare, oiled pecs and biceps the shaft. But, decorously, he is shot from the waist up and for good measure you can spot his BVDs waistband at the bottom edge of the photograph.'[21] Schor stresses that Morris' body operates a phallus only through the occlusion of his anatomical penis. Furthermore, because of his access to authorial power as a male subject in patriarchy, Morris' self-phallicization has radically different effects from that more common fetishization of the female body in western art as substitute for her ostensibly lacking phallic organ – as a comparison with Lynda Benglis' *Artforum* advertisement from 1974, which quickly became the more infamous of the two, was made in dialogue with Morris' poster and the two were lovers at the time.[22] Hoisting a huge plastic dildo (a 'phallus' that could hardly be more artificial) against her taut, greased and clearly female body, Benglis explicitly illustrates the culturally determined disjunction between being a woman and wielding the phallus.

Morris, conversely, adopts the excessive attributes of a specific type of masculinity (working-class tough guy, his S&M garb also signalling the dangerous marginality of gay male subjectivity). By doing do, one could argue that he dislocates the signifiers of masculinity, exposing it as a construction. One could just as easily make the point, however, that he shows as constructed a *particular type* of masculinity – one that is distant from his actual experience, and so does not threaten his artistic subjectivity as a middle-class, straight, white male artist.[23] Either way, Morris also affords himself a knowledge of masculine authority that Benglis can only mimic. It must be strongly stressed again that because of our identification of Morris as a male artist, we read his adoption of phallic attributes differently. As a male artist, Morris, while certainly projecting an ironic awareness of the constructedness of masculinity, also has an entirely different relationship to the masculine than do feminist body artists such as Benglis – artists who, perhaps particularly in the 1970s, had far more of a stake in thoroughly dismantling the tropes of masculine genius. Feminists under patriarchy have often been forced to access knowledge at least in part through the aggressive appropriation of phallic attributes that are not seen as properly theirs; for Morris the phallus is ostensibly always already 'his'. While the women enact themselves in self-exploratory scenarios, Morris – *as* male artist – takes on the role of master, of teacher, of the subject who supposedly knows.[24]

Morris' power comes from his carefully measured

parody of masculine authority. Benglis' power, if momentary and ambiguous, stems from her exposure of the deep prohibitions surrounding artistic objectivity (the prohibition against women playing the role of the artist, and that against unveiling the artificiality of the phallus of artistic authority). The effects of this asymmetry are reflected in contemporaneous and subsequent interpretations of the two artists and their performative actions. While Morris' poster is generally discussed as an amusing and intelligent critique of masculinity, Benglis' has engendered hostile if not hysterical responses. Thus, in a letter published in the subsequent issue of the magazine by a group of *Artforum* editors, the ad is condemned as an 'object of extreme vulgarity'.[25] Benglis' 'extreme vulgarity' is precisely that which exposes the masculinism of artistic and critical authority, prompting the frantic attempts to devalue the piece on the part of the editors, who have a stake in keeping this masculinism (the phallus of critical authority) veiled. While Benglis and other feminist body artists (such as Carolee Schneemann and Hannah Wilke) have been marginalized from histories of contemporary art, Morris, conversely, is incorporated within mainstream art history as a critic of the mastery of the male artist subject and as a Minimalism genius – perhaps because he still remains familiarly (rather than threateningly) phallic in doing so.

The performative pieces I have discussed so far display the male artist's body to the exclusion of others – building up a narcissistic relationship to conventional artistic masculinity that is simultaneously critical and exploitative of the phallic attributes of male authorial prowess. Both Morris and Klein, however, also performed their relationship to the female body directly in several pieces from the 1960s. The productive as well as receptive aspects of these pieces tell us more about how masculinity operates ambivalently, if still empoweringly, in relation to male body art [...]

I would like to turn now to a number of performative works that more directly and violently enact the alignment between phallic attributes, including the male artist's penis, and the power assigned to the male creative subject. The other male body artists I am addressing here – Vito Acconci and Chris Burden – exposed their bodies in masochistic rituals, raising the question of how violence operates in relation to masculinity: do violent acts perpetrated on the male body build up its image as an inviolable vessel of unified subjectivity, or dislocate the strategic coherence of masculinity through the desecration of its physical repository? Extending my earlier points, I insist that potentially they do both – the particular effects of each performative act are contingent on its productive and receptive contexts – particularly, here, on my own interpretive exchanges with the photographic, textual and filmed traces that remain to document these male bodies in performance.

In Vito Acconci's best-known performance piece, the infamous *Seedbed* of 1972, he lay under a ramp in the Sonnabend Gallery three days a week and masturbated when visitors entered the gallery, magnifying his moans and whispers over a loudspeaker.[26] Mira Schor's essay 'Representations of the Penis' discusses Acconci's piece as exemplary of the way in which male artists explored masculinity in the early 1970s only to reaffirm its privileges. She argues that in determining his goal as 'the production of seed', Acconci makes the gallery the site for the production and display (although unseen) of male sexuality ... There is reference and allusion to the penis, but the artist and his penis ... remain hidden in a mantle of art.'[27] And yet, one could also argue that Acconci is surfacing the erotics of the marketing of art: the commodification of male procreative prowess via a hidden mechanics of transference, whereby masculinity is most valuable when it is carefully hidden behind (and conflated with) the objects of art. Either way, one must agree with Schor that in the performance itself Acconci hid his penis from view (although one can strain to view it in one of the photographs used to document the event).[28]

Acconci published a statement about *Seedbed*, part of which reads as follows: 'Whenever I reach a climax, the viewer might want to pick himself or herself out of the crowd; the viewer might want to think: he's done this for me, he's done this with me, he's done this because of me.'[29] On the one hand, in specifying the interpolated visitor as female *or* male, it would seem that Acconci further opens the subject/object exchange of artistic production to a radicalizing, polymorphous erotics of viewing and hearing. On the other hand, Acconci's statement makes clear the narcissism his interest in intersubjective exchange involves: 'he's done this for me', etc. While enthralled by the observer's response to him, Acconci's fascination returns to himself – and particularly the power of seduction he can wield, as an artist, over a gallery audience. This performance, then, can be interpreted as being both masculinizing – in its narcissistic empowerment of the performing male subject, and feminizing – in that his performative, masturbatory act positions him as object of (and desiring of) the viewer's desire, exposing a 'desire to desire' on his part that aligns him with the 'problematic relation to language and [its] ... signifier *par excellence* (the phallus)', that defines and circumscribes the female subject in patriarchy.[30] As object of the viewer's desires (themselves anticipated and projected by Acconci), Acconci feminizes himself, staging an oscillatory circuit of bisexualized desires between himself and his audience.

In *Conversions I–III*, his performative films from 1970–71, Acconci brutalizes his hairy, clearly masculine body directly, ostensibly in an attempt to transform it into a feminine one. First he takes a candle and burns off his chest hair, in his published statement explaining that 'once my chest is hairless ... I pull each breast in a futile attempt to develop a woman's breast'. The second part of *Conversions* consists of Acconci 'walking, running, jumping, bending over, ... all the while', he explains, 'attempting to keep my penis "removed", held between my legs'. Finally, in *Conversions III*, in an apotheosis of his feminization, a woman kneels behind him and he pushes his penis back into her mouth. Acconci describes this act as follows: 'when I'm seen from the front, the woman disappears behind me and I have no penis, I become the woman I've cancelled out'.[31] Schor interprets this act as simply misogynist, writing, 'the phallus reinscribes itself over the erased/lacking woman, even as the penis is hidden, as usual'.[32] And yet, in its effacement of both masculinity (the hiding of his penis) and femininity (the 'cancelling out' of the woman) could this ritual not be said to enact the reciprocity of gender identity and the fundamental lack installed at the core of all subjectivity? Again, I would argue that both dynamics are at play in Acconci's works, which I read here as attempts to take apart systems of gender difference through performative displays of his sexual body and thus as far more sceptical of conventional masculinity than the body artworks of Klein, Morris or Burden. Acconci projects himself as ejaculating yet victimized, the directing subject of the action *and* the receptive object of spectatorial desire – marking the ultimate exchangeability and interdependence of each element in the supposedly oppositional categories of viewer/viewed, male/female, subject/object.

In discussing the work of Acconci, and comparing it to that of an artist such as Chris Burden, the role of masochism in the dis/play of male artistic subjectivity needs to be addressed. It must be stressed, however, that these artists' masochistic acts are carefully staged for viewing audiences; masochism in their case, then, is to be understood in a metaphoric rather than a clinical sense.[33] According to Freud, masochism is a perversion experienced by the male subject, one characterized by a passive attitude towardsthe sexual life, or a narcissistic and feminized relation towardssexual pleasure (a dynamic that would, of course, correspond to Acconci's feminization as described above).[34] The masochistic subject fantasizes about being beaten or tortured, the object of another, usually female, subject of violence. For Freud, male masochists 'invariably transfer themselves into the part of a woman; that is to say, their masochistic attitude corresponds with a *feminine* one'.[35] And yet, as other theorists of masochism have argued, this perversion can also function as a means of ensuring the coherence and power of the masochistic subject. Theodor Reik, for example, writes, 'The masochist ... cannot be broken from the outside. He has an inexhaustible capacity for taking a beating and yet knows unconsciously he is not licked.'[36] Hence, the masochist's self-mutilations serve to reinforce the impenetrability of the heroic male body, its survivability under any violent circumstance [...]

In *Movie on the Way Down* of 1973, Burden's exhibitionism is at its most direct and revealing; to my knowledge, this is the only piece among his works in which Burden actually exposed his penis. As the audience members entered a gymnasium at Oberlin College in Ohio to the accompaniment of light piano music, they were confronted by the body of Burden, completely naked, suspended by his feet from the ceiling and holding a camera pointed at the floor. As soon as the music stopped, in Burden's words, 'an assistant in the rafters severed the rope with an axe blow. I crashed to the floor, got up, dressed and left.'[37] Apparently, nothing but the macho drama of an axe blow could symbolize the risks of the artistic process for Burden. While constructing a situation of extreme vulnerability, exposing his flesh to the desiring and surely horrified gazes of his audience, Burden still maintained an explicitly masculine relationship to pleasure, pain and creative risk.[38]

And yet, this exhibitionism of the unclothed male artist's body, in explicitly *displaying* the flaccid penis, makes its alignment with the phallus of artistic authority potentially difficult, to say the least. In addition, as Kaja Silverman has argued, 'Christian masochism has radically emasculating implications, and is in its purest forms intrinsically incompatible with the pretensions of masculinity' because of its reliance on the spectatorial gaze.[39] I would argue as well, however, that the exhibitionism of Christian masochism, as epitomized in the case of Jesus Christ, assigns the sufferer an incomparable role of centrality and power in relation to those who view him. Furthermore, while Christ can hardly be said to have controlled his torturers, Burden certainly does; like Yves Klein – and like Deleuze's masochist – he rigorously directs situations of putative danger in order to construct himself as both heroically martyred and bravely surviving [...]

In closing I would like to reiterate my argument that one can approach and interpret each of these practices in a number of ways. Far from being simply radical and subversive, or simply regressive and phallocentric, each of these pieces both strategically unhinges the phallus/penis/artist equation and, in some ways, reinforces it. The moments that are the most eroticizing and disruptive of the penis/phallus conflation for me are those in which a charged relationship with the interpreter is allowed to surface – in which, in Paul Smith's terms, the male body returns to exceed the narrative processes of interpretation such that, for example, my investments and desires are exposed as I re-create these moments for the reader of my text.

One could argue provisionally along the lines of a model of masochism offered by Kaja Silverman that these moments mark instances of 'heteropathic identification', a situation in which a radical transference of subjectivity is encouraged, such that the self is located in the site of the other[40] [...]

Finally, it is *my* relationship with these works, and the reader's with my text, that determines their meanings here and now. Returning to my own subjective responses, I can only continue to stress the ambivalence and undecidability of any male subject's relationship to masculinity. For masculinity, like any other subject position, is a condition whose significances and radical or regressive effects are contingent on the contexts in which it is produced and in which it is read. And my relationship to masculinity, as a feminist but also as a heterosexual, is one of ambivalence itself: I have a critical disdain for certain of its aspects, but a flagrant and irrepressible desire for others.

1 I initially presented a version of this paper in London at the 1993 Association of Art Historians meeting as part of the 'Visualizing Masculinities' session organized by Andrew Stephenson. I am grateful to Andrew Stephenson for inviting me to present this material, and to Nancy Ring, Marcia Pointon and Paul Binski for their excellent suggestions towards revising the essay. I would also like to express my gratitude to the University of California, Riverside, for providing me with an Affirmative Action Career Development Award, which enabled my completion of this essay.

2 Jacques Lacan, 'The Meaning of the Phallus' (1958), *Feminine Sexuality: Jacques Lacan and the école freudienne*, ed. Juliet Mitchell and Jacqueline Rose, trans. Jacqueline Rose (New York and London: W.W. Norton, 1982) 79, 83-84.

3 Jane Gallop, *Reading Lacan* (Ithaca, New York and London: Cornell University Press, 1985) 140, 146, 156. Kaja Silverman has also examined this mutually sustaining relationship between the penis and phallus, this 'dominant fiction' of masculine subjectivity, which 'urges both the male and the female subject ... to deny all knowledge of male castration by believing in the commensurability of penis and phallus, actual and symbolic father'. Kaja Silverman, 'The Dominant Fiction', *Male Subjectivity at the Margins* (New York and London: Routledge, 1992) 42. Furthermore, as Judith Butler has argued, Lacan inadvertently deconstructs his own phallocentric formulation by positing the phallus as both originating significations, as the origin of the symbolic order (he theorizes it thus in his 'The Meaning of the Phallus'), but also as initially determined in relation to the male genitals (through the susceptibility initiated, according to Lacan's essay 'The Mirror Stage', within the mirror stage of the subject's development). Butler reads these two essays against one another in order to exacerbate this deconstruction (the phallus cannot be both the originary fiction of the symbolic, presumably a 'neutral', pre-social function, and the always ready masculine [socialized, penile] organizing force of the body's coherence as initially perceived in the mirror stage). She uses this contradiction to expose the phallus as a *symptom*, arguing that its conflation with the penis is a 'transvaluative denial of [the penis'] ... substitutability, dependency, diminutive size, limited control, partiality', rather than its symbolic guarantor. Judith Butler, 'The Lesbian Phallus and the Morphological Imaginary', *Differences: A Journal of Feminist Cultural Studies*, 'The Phallus Issue', 4: 1 (Spring 1992) 153, 155.

4 See, for example, Jo-Anna Isaak, 'Seduction without Desire', *Vanguard*, 16: 3 (Summer 1987) 11-14.

5 In *The Order of Things*, Foucault defines modern man as a figure developing in the late eighteenth century and characterized his own desire to centre himself upon his own origin (the male gender pronoun is particularly fitting in this case, given Foucault's blindness to sexual difference). Needless to say, then, modern man is a masculine subject – a figure endowed symbolically and provisionally (though, as Lacan would insist, never in any actual sense) with the phallus. Lacan places the development of the mythical unified 'I' in the early seventeenth century, with the development of Cartesianism. See 'The Subject and the Other: Aphanisis' (1964), *The Four Fundamental Concepts of Psycho-Analysis*, ed. Jacques-Alain Miller, trans. Alan Sheridan (New York and London: W.W. Norton, 1981) 216-29. In Silverman's terms, this coherent, Cartesian 'I' instantiates the 'dominant fiction' of masculine subjectivity, wherein the male subject (who, I would add, is implicitly straight, white and upper-middle class), 'refuses to recognize an unwanted feature of the *self* by projecting it on to the other, i.e. by relocating' – a process exemplified by the male artist's conventional objectification of the female body as fetish to palliate his anxious fear of lack. Silverman, 'The Dominant Fiction', *op. cit.*, 45.

6 This is meant as a deliberate reference to Luce Irigaray's critique of phallocentrism in 'How to Conceive (of) a girl', in *Speculum of the Other Woman* (1974), trans. Gillian C. Gill (Ithaca, New York: Cornell University, 1985) 160-67.

7 Jacques Derrida, 'Economimesis', trans. R. Klein, *Diacritics*,11: 2 (Summer 1975) 3-25, especially p. 9. See also Roland Barthes on the 'Author-God', in 'The Death of the Author' (1968), *Image-Music-Text*, trans. Stephen Heath (New York: Hill & Wang, 1977) 146, 147.

8 Lacan, 'The Meaning of the Phallus', *op. cit.*, 82.

9 Of course other social, political and economic shifts have been noted as characteristic of the Postmodern by theorists such as Jean Baudrillard, Andreas Huyssen and Frederic Jameson – including the radicalization of new technologies of representation and the culture of the simulacrum fostered by late capitalist economic relations.

10 In her sophisticated study, O'Dell unfortunately reduces the historical picture to this one event, which she treats rather simplistically as *the* motivating factor for performance art – particularly masochistic performance – in the early 1970s. Kathy O'Dell, 'Toward a Theory of Performance Art: An Investigation of Its Sites' (Ph.D. dissertation, The City University of New York, 1992).

11 'Dematerialization' is Lucy R. Lippard's term; see her book *Six Years: The Dematerialization of the Art Object* (New York: Praeger, 1973). On allegory and appropriation as Postmodern strategies, see Craig Owens, 'The Allegorical Impulse: Towards a Theory of Postmodernism', *October*, 12 (Spring 1980) 67-86; *October*, 13 (Summer 1980) 59-80; and Benjamin Buchloh, 'Allegorical Procedures: Appropriation and Montage in Contemporary Art', *Artforum*, 21 (September 1982) 43-56. A notable exception to this avoidance of the question of subjectivity in discussions of Postmodernism in the visual arts is the work of Thierry De Duve, who has theorized Postmodernism, with all of its contradictions, as a 'paradoxical performative' in his book *Au nom de l'art* (Paris: Les Éditions de Minuit, 1989) see especially pp. 68-89. In De Duve's terms, Postmodernism is that which is spoken as beyond the Modern (entailing the embodied act of speaking). And yet, this act of speaking exposes the investment of the speaker in the drive to periodization and interpretive mastery that characterizes Modernism. This very speaking, then, defines the speaker as *both* modern and Postmodern. See also my more detailed discussion of the performativity of Postmodernism in 'Concluding Remarks', chapter 6 of my book *Postmodernism and the En-Gendering of Marcel Duchamp* (New York and Cambridge: Cambridge University Press,

1994) 205-13.

12 My book will be a feminist history and theory of body art and the performativity of the artistic subject from the 1960s to the present. I employ the term 'body art' rather than 'performance art' throughout this project because the former is a broader term and I wish to encompass in the larger study not only performance art pieces *per se* but also images and other artistic projects that perform the artist in various ways (such as the advertising portraits I discuss below).

13 On performative feminist readings see Tania Modleski, 'Some Functions of Feminist Criticism, or the Scandal of the Mute Body', *October*, 49 (Summer 1989) 15.

14 The shift from an investment in the modernist artist/genius to what we might call a *post*modern culture with a 'distinct performative and theatrical mode [in contemporary art ... such that] the objects of such a performative or theatrical production are not immanent. They are, rather, contingent, fragmentary, even disembodied. As such, they evoke, rather than an aura of full presence ... their own *absence*.' For Sayre, it is the performative act in contemporary art that most dramatically challenges the phallocentrism of modernism by exposing the contingency of artistic meaning on its conditions of interpretation. Henry Sayre, *The Object of Performance: The American Avant-Garde Since 1970* (Chicago and London: University of Chicago Press, 1989) 9. For an interesting discussion of how performativity is enacted in relations of artistic production, particularly those centred in the site of the studio, see also Caroline Jones, 'The Romance of the Studio and the Abstract Expressionist Sublime', chapter 1 of 'Machine in the Studio: Changing Constructions of the American Artist, 1945-1968' (Ph.D. dissertation, Stanford University, 1992) 1-71; see too Robert Weimann's rather abstruse discussion of performativity, Postmodernism and questions of authority, '(Post)Modernity and Representation: Issues of Authority, Power, Performativity', *New Literary History*, 23 (1992) 955-81.

15 Pollock is represented in worker's denims, arms and legs crossed, leaning defiantly against a drip painting, on the opening spread of 'Jackson Pollock: Is he the greatest living painter in the United States?', *Life*, 27: 6 (8 August 1949) 42. I examine in greater detail Pollock's conventional masculine performativity in my unpublished essay, '"The Clothes Make the Man": The Male Artist as a Performative Function'.

16 For reproduction of the images of Klein I discuss here, see *Yves Klein 1928-1962: A Retrospective* (Houston: Institute for the Arts; New York: The Arts Publisher, 1982). Klein is one of the few male artists whose performances are discussed within the broader context of his work. More often, art histories suppress this aspect of male artists' work – certainly because of its intransigence *vis-à-vis* historical documentation, but also, I would argue, because of the difficulties it opens up for the interpretive model.

17 Yves Klein, 'Transfiguration' (1954), cited by Thomas McEvilley, 'Yves Klein: Conquistador of the Void', in *ibid.*, 33-34.

18 Cited by McEvilley, 'Yves Klein: Conquistador of the Void', *ibid.*, 46. McEvilley points out that Klein 'read Delacroix's [notion of] "indefinable" as equivalent to Heindel's [Rosicrucian notion of] "Spirit". The indefinable, said Delacroix, is "what the soul [of the artist] has added to the lines and colours to reach out to the soul [of the viewer]".' Similarly, McEvilley continues, 'Van Gogh (whom Yves also enlisted on his side in the Battle, because he "foresaw the monochrome") wrote to his brother Theo that "paintings have their own life which comes entirely from the soul of the painter ... The artist, then, is truly godlike".'

19 The retrospective, in Krefeld, was entitled *Yves Klein: Monochrome und Feuer*. The switch was deliberate: Klein wrote twice to the museum director to specify that the second version be used, arguing that it was '*plus nette*'; see Nan Rosenthal, 'Assisted Levitation: The Art of Yves Klein', in *Yves Klein 1928-1962, op. cit.*, 128; both pictures are reproduced in *ibid.*, 204.

20 All Morris' pieces discussed here are reproduced in Maurice Berger, *Labyrinths: Robert Morris, Minimalism, and the 1960s* (New York: Harper & Row, 1989).

21 Mira Schor, 'Representations of the Penis', *M/E/A/N/I/N/G*, 4 (November 1988) 9.

22 For reproductions of both images see Susan Krane, *Lynda Benglis: Dual Natures* (Atlanta: High Museum, 1991) 40, 41. According to Krane, Morris accompanied Benglis to buy the dildo she used in the piece and the two artists posed with it in a group of staged Polaroids (42). See my extended discussion of this image and other feminist body art projects in 'Feminist Pleasures and Embodied Theories of Art', *New Feminist Criticism: Art/Identity/Action*, ed. Cassandra Langer, Joanna Freuh and Arlene Raven (New York: Harper Collins, 1994).

23 Of course, built into the masculinity of the artist function is an implicit heterosexuality; this is the case even for homosexual artists such as Rauschenberg and Jasper Johns, whose 'deviant' sexual orientation is suppressed in art-historical constructions of them in relation to their work. Their authority is purely (i.e. heterosexually) masculine if their actual sexuality is not.

24 As Lucy R. Lippard has pointed out, 'when women use their own faces and bodies, they are immediately accused of narcissism' due to the assumption that 'any woman who presents her nude body in public is doing so because she thinks she is beautiful', but the male artists who are doing so are considered pioneering and bravely exhibitionistic. Lucy R. Lippard, 'European and American Women's Body Art', *From the Center: Feminist Essays on Women's Art* (New York: E.P. Dutton & Co., 1976) 125.

25 Rosalind Krauss, Annette Michelson, Lawrence Alloway, Max Kozloff and Joseph Mascheck, 'Letter to the Editor', *Artforum*, 13: 4 (December 1994) 9.

26 The works of Acconci discussed here are reproduced in Mario Diacono, *Vito Acconci: Dal testo-azione al corpo come testo* (New York: Out of London Press, 1975).

27 Schor, 'Representations of the Penis', *op. cit.*, 7.

28 See the photograph reproduced within Robert Pincus-Witten's article, 'Vito Acconci and the Conceptual Performance,' *Artforum*, 10: 8 (April 1972) 47. This is an interesting case *vis-à-vis* the issue of photographic documentation versus the 'actual' experience of the event itself, as the photograph gives information (the unveiled body of the artist) that was specifically withheld in the performance.

29 In Judith Russi Kirshner, *Vito Acconci A Retrospective: 1969 to 1980* (Chicago: Museum of Contemporary Art, 1980) 17.

30 These terms are Mary Ann Doane's, in *The Desire to Desire: The Woman's Film of the 1940s* (Bloomington and Indianapolis: Indiana University Press, 1987) 13.

31 Acconci in 'Body and Soul', special issue of *Avalanche* on Acconci, 6 (Autumn 1972) 28; and in Krishner, *Vito Acconci A Retrospective, op. cit.*, 15.

32 Mira Schor, 'Representations of the Penis', *M/E/A/N/I/N/G*, 4 (November 1988) 8. Contrary to Schor, I read Acconci's exaggerated performances of his relationship to his penis as dislocating, rather than confirming, the veiled penis/phallus conflation that conventionally empowers the male artist. In another piece, *Reception Room* (1973), in which he lay naked on a table rolling back and forth underneath a white sheet exposing himself periodically, Acconci literalized and ironicized this desire to hide his penis, intoning in an audiotape played simultaneously, 'What I am really ashamed of is the size of my prick, but I won't show them', 205-11.

33 O'Dell discusses the use of metaphor within masochistic performance at great length in 'Towards a Theory of Performance Art'. Here she theorizes masochism in performance as deconstructive of the social order because of its metaphoric representation of Oedipal and pre-Oedipal moments from the modern subject's developmental past – moments that, because they take place in the domestic site, where the law of the father takes hold, necessarily link up to the social contract. By confronting the traumas of individual development, O'Dell argues, the masochistic performer inevitably critiques the failure of the social contract. While her insights are suggestive, O'Dell tends to assume an *inherent* meaning for performance art, arguing, for example, that masochistic performances by Gina Pane and others are necessarily radical – that, 'motivated by the structural breakdown in contractual agreements between state and citizens' in the early 1970s, they necessarily 'deconstruct' the social contract (279), that masochistic acts are 'inherently alienating' and that they necessarily force the viewers to become 'automatic participants' in the work, and thus to acknowledge their complicity in the psychological states performed (349). My reservations *vis-à-vis* this kind of interpretive authoritarianism lead me to insert myself into my interpretations so as to make clear my investment in reading body artworks in relation to masculine subjectivity. Thus, as a feminist, I obviously have an interest in artworks that I see as critiquing masculinity; others – fans of pro-male media misogynists Rush Limbaugh or Howard Stern, for example – might see as negative this capacity to critique masculinity, and still others might doubt my readings of them as critical

in the first place. My point here is that, particularly in practising a feminist art history, since feminism had worked to question the notion of cultural value, and/or in attempting to situate performance as critical of modernist value systems and notions of historical or aesthetic truth, it behoves me to complicate my own processes of determining value for this work. O'Dell, who claims an anti-Modernist value for masochistic performance, would be more convincing in this argument if she were to question her interpretive system, which still – as it claims anti-Modernism for the works – maintains a thoroughly Modernist investment in inherency and artistic intentionality.

O'Dell also makes recourse to the notion that the performance work (particularly the masochistic performance piece) is necessarily more radical than non-performative work because it 'literalizes and metaphorizes the figurative split' in the subject experienced during the Lacanian mirror stage, 'profoundly accelerat[ing] … the questioning process' (243-44). This tendency to claim priority for performance work because of the artist's body within it is questionable in that it reinforces the very Modernist metaphysics of presence – and particularly the notion of the coherent individual – that performance art is supposed to critique. It is, however, almost impossible to resist making recourse to some notion of ontological priority when discussing the effects of performance art. I have attempted to negotiate and theorize this aspect of performance (its seductive promise of presence) without succumbing to its wiles, but there are certainly moments here when I, too, am guilty of drawing on its appeal to substantiate my arguments.

34 See Freud's first examination of masochism, 'Sadism and Masochism' (1905), *Three Essays on the Theory of Sexuality*, trans. James Strachey (New York: Basic Books, 1962).

35 Sigmund Freud, 'A Child is Being Beaten' (1919), in *Sexuality and the Psychology of Love*, trans. Alix and James Strachey (New York: Macmillan, 1963) 126. See also Jean-Paul Sartre's discussion of the inevitable failure of the masochist's desire to exist as pure object (as, in Freud's terms, purely feminine), in *Being and Nothingness* (1943), trans. Hazel Barnes (New York: Washington Square Press, 1956) where he describes the masochist's dilemma as follows: 'I attempt … to engage myself wholly in my being-as-object. I refuse to be anything more than an object. I rest upon the Other … As the Other apprehends me as an object by means of *actual desire*, I wish to be desired, I make myself in shame an object of desire'; but, through this apprehension, the Other 'has referred me to my own unjustifiable subjectivity' (491, 492). This is the failure that I interpreted Acconci as enacting in this performative references to the penis and spectatorial desire.

36 Theodor Reik, *Masochism in Modern Man*, trans. Margaret H. Beigel and Gertrud M. Kurth (New York: Farrar, Strauss and Co., 1941) 163.

37 Burden, in *Chris Burden: a Twenty-Year Survey* (Newport Harbour Museum of Art, 1988) 61.

38 O'Dell argues that Burden's work – in particular his performances involving bed-like structures – 'fall[s] short' of playing the 'deconstructive role' she attributes to masochistic performance in general (see note 33, above, for my critique of the essentialism I feel this analysis implies). For O'Dell, Burden's performances work only to unrepress the formerly repressed aspects of the social contract, rather than setting up a more productive negotiatory relationship with the audience.

39 Silverman, 'Masochism and Male Subjectivity', *op. cit.*, 198. Paul Smith argues that 'in much occidental cultural production the Christ figure could be said to have operated chronically as a privileged figure of the pleasurable tension between the objectification and what I will call the masochizing of the male body … ' in 'Action Movie Hysteria, or Eastwood Bound', *Differences*, 1: 3 (1989) 98-99.

40 Kaja Silverman, 'Masochistic Ecstasy and the Ruination of Masculinity in Fassbinder's Cinema', *Male Subjectivity at the Margins*, *op. cit.*, 264-65.

Amelia Jones, 'Dis/playing the Phallus: Male Artists Perform Their Masculinities', *Art History*, 17: 4 (December 1994) 546-84.

Eve Kosofsky SEDGWICK
Queer Performativity: Warhol's Whiteness/ Warhol's Shyness [1996]

The jokes that mean the most to you are the ones you don't quite get; that's one true fact I've figured out over the years. Another is, the people with the most powerful presences are the ones who aren't all there. Like going to hear Odetta at the Cookery some years ago and having her – I don't know what was going on with her – in the middle of one song, still *singing*, wander off for a brief tour of the restaurant kitchen, her machinelike, perseverating voice winding from its distance outward towardsthe excruciated and rapt audience: now *that* was *presence*: presence like the withdrawal of a god.

Andy Warhol had presence of that revelatory kind – revelatory not in the sense that it revealed 'him' but rather that he could wield it as a sharp, insinuating heuristic chisel to pry at the faultlines and lay bare the sedimented faces of his surround. As with Odetta at the Cookery, excruciation – the poetics, politics, semiotics and somatics of shame – provided the medium for this denuding sculpture at once so intimate, so public. Shame, in Warhol's case, as crystallized in a bodily discipline of florid shyness:

'There are different ways for individual people to take over space – to command space. Very shy people don't even want to take up the space that their body actually takes up, whereas very outgoing people want to take up as much space as they can …

'I've always had a conflict because I'm shy and yet I like to take up a lot of personal space. Mom always said, "Don't be pushy, but let everybody know you're around". I wanted to command more space than I was commanding, but then I knew I was too shy to know what to do with the attention if I did manage to get it. That's why I feel that television is the media I'd most like to shine in.'[1]

From shame to shyness to shining – and, inevitably, back and back again: the candour and cultural incisiveness of this itinerary seem to make Warhol an exemplary figure for a new project, an urgent one I think, of understanding how the dysphoric affect shame functions as a nexus of production: production, that is, of meaning, of personal presence, of politics, of performative and critical efficacy. What it may mean to be a (white) queer in a queer-hating world, what it may mean to be a white (queer) in a white-supremacist one, are two of the explorations that, for Warhol, this shyness embodied.

Both *POPism* and *The Philosophy of Andy Warhol* include extended arias specifically on the shy and, *not* incidentally, on the queer and on the white, in which the illusion of Warhol's presence gets evoked in shimmeringly ambiguous, shame-charged linguistic space of utterance and address. In *POPism*, in a scene from the Factory in 1966, Warhol describes Silver George impersonating Andy Warhol over the phone:

'"You want me to describe myself?" Silver George was saying. He looked at me as if to say, "You don't care if I do this, right?" I asked who it was and when he said it was a high school paper I motioned for him to go ahead.

'"Well, I wear what everybody else around the Factory wears", he said, looking over at me as a reference. "A striped T-shirt – a little too short – over another T-shirt, that's how we like them … and Levi's … " He listened for a few moments. "Well, I would call myself – youthful-looking. I have slightly faggy air and I do little artistic movements … " I looked up from painting. I'd thought all they wanted was a fashion description, but it didn't matter …

'"Well, I have very nice hands", he said, "very expressive … I keep them in repose or touching each other, or sometimes I wrap my arms around myself. I'm always very conscious of where my hands are … But the first thing you notice about me is my skin. It's translucent – you can really see my veins – and it's grey, but it's pink, too … My build? Well, it's very flat, and if I gain any weight, it's usually all in my hips and stomach. And I'm small-shouldered and I'm probably the same dimension at my waist as I am at my chest … " Silver George really had momentum now … "And my legs are very narrow and I have tiny little ankles – and I'm a little birdlike from my hips down – I sort of narrow in and taper down towards my feet … 'Birdlike', right … and I carry myself very square, like a unit. And I'm rigid – very conservative about my movements; I have a little bit of an old-lady thing there … And my new boots have sort of high heels, so I walk like a woman, on the balls of my feet – but actually, I'm very … hardy … Okay?"

' … "No, it was no trouble … "

"When Silver George hung up, he said they were really thrilled because they'd heard I never talked and here I'd just said more to them than anybody they'd ever interviewed. They'd also said how surprised they were that I could be so objective about myself."[2]

Day after day I look in the mirror and I still see something – a new pimple. If the pimple on my upper right cheek is gone, a new one turns up on my lower left cheek, on my jawline, near my ear, in the middle of my nose, under the hair on my eyebrows, right between my eyes. I think it's the same pimple, moving from place to place. If someone asked me, 'What's your problem?', I'd have to say, 'Skin'.

Andy WARHOL in Eve Kosofsky SEDGWICK Queer Performativity: Warhol's Whiteness/Warhol's Shyness, 1996

What Warhol does in publishing this account in 1980 under his own name – his own and Pat Hackett's, not to let things get too oversimplified! – is a bit like what he's done in *Philosophy* in 1975, retelling a phone conversation between himself, as 'A', and one of the several interlocutors he brings together under the designation 'B': '*"Day after day I look in the mirror and I still see something – a new pimple. If the pimple on my upper right cheek is gone, a new one turns up on my lower left cheek, on my jawline, near my ear, in the middle of my nose, under the hair on my eyebrows, right between my eyes. I think it's the same pimple, moving from place to place." I was telling the truth. If someone asked me, "What's your problem?", I'd have to say, "Skin".*

'*"I dunk a Johnson and Johnson cotton ball into Johnson and Johnson rubbing alcohol and rub the cotton ball against the pimple ..."*

'*"When the alcohol is dry", I said, "I'm ready to apply the flesh-coloured acne-pimple medication that doesn't resemble any human flesh I've every seen, though it does come pretty close to mine ... So now the pimple's covered. But am I covered? I have to look into the mirror for some more clues. Nothing is missing. It's all there. The affectless gaze. The diffracted grace ..."* [...]'[3]

I can't do justice to the comic sublimity of these passages, in which an uncanny and unmistakable presence wills itself into existence in the flickering, holographic space of Warhol's hunger to own the rage of other people to describe him – to describe him as if impersonally, not to say sadistically. The effect of this shy exhibitionism is, among other things, deeply queer. ('Remember the 1950s?' Lilly Tomlin used to ask in a comedy routine. 'Nobody was gay in the 1950s; they were just shy.') Some of the infants, children and adults in whom shame remains the most available mediator of identity are the ones called shy. And *queer*, as I've suggested elsewhere, might usefully be thought of as referring in the first place to this group or an overlapping group of infants and children, those whose sense of identity is for some reason tuned most to the note of shame [...]

Thanks to Hall Sedgwick for the Odetta story.

This essay is part of a larger project on shame, performance and performativity. Some of its language overlaps with another, related essay of mine that emerges from the same project, 'Queer Performativity: Henry James's *Art of the Novel*', *GL9*, 1: 1 (Summer 1993) 1-16.

1 Andy Warhol, *The Philosophy of Andy Warhol* (New York: Harcourt Brace Jovanovich, 1975) 246-47.

2 Andy Warhol and Pat Hackett, *POPism: The Warhol Sixties* (New York: Harcourt Brace Jovanovich, 1980) 199-200.

3 Andy Warhol, *The Philosophy*, *op. cit.*, 7-10.

Eve Kosofsky Sedgwick, 'Queer Performativity: Warhol's Whiteness/Warhol's Shyness', *Pop Out, Queer Warhol*, ed. Jennifer Doyle, Jonathan Flately and José Esteban Muñoz (Durham, North Carolina: Duke University Press, 1996).

Rebecca SCHNEIDER

Gender in Perspective: Have We Really Gone Beyond?

[1997]

In league with the humanist ideals of the Renaissance, perspective secularized the godhead into the eye of the beholder, and gendered that beholder after the gender of God. As John Berger remarks of this transformation, 'The visible world is [in perspectivalism] arranged for the spectator as the universe was once thought to be arranged for God.'[1] Like God, the viewer is unseen. Conventions of perspective instituted and humanized the distantiation of omniscience, veiling and dislocating the viewer from the viewed by the secular science of mathematical proportion. As Martin Jay has noted, 'The painter's own body ... was effectively banished',[2] even as the painter (and by extension the viewer) was presumed to be gendered, like God, male. The marker of the viewer/artist's godly gender was veiled, displaced on to his prerogatives of vision. In contrast, the given to be seen was rendered embodied object, reproducible by mathematical proportion and calculable distance: located, fixed and blinded. The scopic field was feminized as passive – as accessible as it was, by virtue of the vanishing point, inaccessible. Men and women who appeared in the scopic field were fixed – sometimes in poses of pride and arrogance, as their portraits rooted their propriety into recessive eternity, beckoning an envy on the part of the viewer. Women were often undressed and spread across the terrain as emblems of the scopic field itself, beckoning the viewer to sense both the power of his gaze and the insatiability of his desire. She stretched across the field as an emblem of his desire to acquire that which, again by logic of the vanishing point, could never be fully acquired.

Classic perspective orients the field of vision to the viewer's veiled or vanished body, as if the scene itself emanates from the viewer's own gaze. The scene is subservient to that eye, at the same time that that eye is erased from implication in the visual field. Within the terms of perspective, there is no reciprocity – the seen does not see back. Classically, even if the seen is presented so as to be looking at the viewer (as in Titian's *The Venus of Urbino* or Edouard Manet's *Olympia*), what is acknowledged by the direction of her gaze (whether defiant or compliant) is the viewer's sight marking her as seen. She can only acknowledge that she is seen, but she cannot author vision, cannot see back. She does not render the viewer visible. Rather, she renders him sighted. Emblematic of the scopic field itself, she *is* the vision and he *has* the vision – she is the vision he has – just as Lacan would engender the logic of the fetish at the base of the Symbolic Order: she is the (fetishized) phallus, he has the phallus, she is the phallus he has.

Interestingly, the institution of perspective actually theatricalized the field of vision, creating 'scenographic space' in which all that is given to be seen is, in a sense, staged for the viewer – laid out before him like his own future. In this sense, importantly, the seen became spectacle, an always already theatrical masquerade, a parade of desire, a dreamscape of wishes spread for potential consumption. This scenographic orientation in perspectivalism is, as Jay notes, 'a notion of space congenial not only to modern science, but also, it has been widely argued, to the emerging economic system we call capitalism'.[3] The given to be seen grants an access to an 'actual' marked by distance from the viewer. That distance beckons and simultaneously denies, invoking possession at the same time that it expands into an infinite, inaccessible dreamscape of masquerade hinged on the vanishing point. It is an inscription of distance and penetrability – a distance across which desire can be constructed as insatiable, and so constructed, can work its magic as the unending drive to accumulate, appropriate, possess and acquire.

Despite any number of attempts to find ourselves beyond the grip of perspectivalism or to locate nonperspectival roots in Western concepts of representation – such as Martin Jay's (1993) thesis that the denigration of vision in the twentieth century has led to the end of ocularcentrism, or Svetlana Alpers's attention to generally ignored nonperspectival traditions in painting – the historical primacy of perspectivalism, at the very least in our historicizing of art, is indisputable. Works which wrestle with the legacies of perspective reckon with the ghosts of those habituations. Sitting, watching, we conjure these ghosts, whenever we look for narrative line.[4] 'Woman', whenever we recognize her signs, rebounds with the cultural construction of desire as insatiable, a narrative linked to the feminization of the scopic field as open for possession – a narrative replete with the heterosexual imperative[5] which renders the 'phallic ghost' as modus operandi of seeing[6] [...]

In late capitalist renditions of perspective, then, insatiability still reigns: the image/commodity does not 'give' what it promises, the viewer does not 'get' what he desires – he is destined to spend himself unseen, un(re)marked by the blinded object of his gaze, to try and try again, ritually stabbing at his own eyes like Oedipus. Ultimately he imagines he can give up on vision altogether in orgasmic thrall with his narrative of loss. The image, the object, is what must be 'gotten' or abandoned. The given to be seen, like the commodity itself, is never considered to 'get', but only to 'give' or to deny.

To return to the roots of perspective, it is not inconsequential that the institution of the vanishing point and its logic of insatiability marked the institution, the 'discovery', of a previously inconceivable notion of infinity.[7] As Erwin Panovsky has explained, the vanishing point in perspective is relative to a shift in worldview from the concept of a closed universe to an infinite expanse, a never-ending recession and expansion of space, endlessly purveyable by an enterprising, colonizing and capitalizing subject/gaze.[8] The vanishing point, as mirror site of the viewer's dislocation, services enterprise and is elusively contained within the terrain of the envisioned, the commodified, as thus the feminine. The feminine, as emblematic of the given to be seen, became terrain, virgin territory made passive before a veiled masculine gaze. 'She' is thus figured both as that which is traversable, the object possessable, and the inaccessible, the vanishing point of present knowledge – that which infinitely recesses, endlessly escaping the boundaries of phallocratic ordering. As that which is rendered visible as well as that which slips beyond vision, woman became emblematic of the modernist paradox of a possessable infinite – she is given to be origin as well as death in a universe which, paradoxically, contains no beginning and admits no end. Thus in the broad symbolic picture woman became, as Freud would acknowledge, a riddle – a riddle marked, above all, by sexuality.

As woman, like the horizon, contains the vanishing point of her difference – her sex marked as lack – then the aim to possess her could never be fully satiated, propelling infinite exchange, and the consumer's quest for the feminized object of masculinized desire became, as Luce Irigaray put it, a 'game of Chinese boxes. Infinitely receding'.[9] We read the female body as sex, but dominant tropes of heterosexuality play on both the overly visible terrain of bodily matter and on the slippery slope of language, 'engenderment', the arena of language and its limits. Lacan placed language in symbolic league with the scopic field, catching language and vision in a thoroughly tangled embrace. To quote Jacqueline Rose, explicating Lacan, sexuality is conceived as 'the vanishing point on meaning'.[10] And thus, as feminist criticism has so often pointed out, 'woman' – the traversable field, the site of sex – is constantly caught as that which cannot be caught, known as that which cannot know or be known, meant as that which cannot mean. Emblem of consumptive desire and designated capitalist consumer, she sets out to consume *herself* in an anotectic frenzy of the logic of the vanishing point – attempting to consume her own inaccessible image, chasing after disappearance infinitely.

1 John Berger, *Ways of Seeing* (New York: Penguin Books, 1972) 16.

2 Martin Jay, *Downcast Eyes: The Denigration of Vision in Twentieth-Century Thought* (Berkeley: University of California Press, 1993) 56.

3 *Ibid.*, 57.

4 On the deeply ingrained link between habits of vision and habits of verbalization see Michael Argyle and Mark Cooke, *Gaze and Mutual Gaze* (Cambridge University Press, 1976) 88-89. See Teresa de Lauretis on the gendering of narrative structure, 'Desire in Narrative', in *Alice Doesn't* (Bloomington: Indiana University Press, 1985).

5 The heterosexual imperative is actually, in Luce Irigaray's terms, a ruse of the more 'hom(m)osexual' imperative of the market by which women are insignia of desire exchanged fundamentally between men. See *This Sex Which Is Not One* (Ithaca, New York: Cornell University Press, 1985) 170-97.

6 Jacques Lacan, *Four Fundamental Concepts of Psychoanalysis*, trans. Alan Sheridan (New York: W.W. Norton and Co., 1981) 88.

7 Alexandre Koyre, *From the Closed World to the Infinite Universe* (Baltimore: Johns Hopkins University Press, 1957).

8 Erwin Panovsky, *Perspective as Symbolic Form* (New York: Zone Books, 1991) 57. Though point of view was stable in early modern perspectivalism as opposed to its dislocation in later capitalism, a dislocation linked interestingly to the poststructural dislocation of subjectivity itself, there is nevertheless a lineage of perspectival detachment and, perhaps less reconfigured, a lineage of the crucial notion of infinite. In the later modern model of dislocation, the infinite is no longer strictly relative to the vanishing point within the scopic field but becomes, as well, a property of the viewing subject in his infinite deferral. Implicit in this analysis, articulated in Crary's work, is the suggestion that this infinity is enhanced by the submission of both subject and object to the increasingly dislocating terms of the phantasmic commodity and its relentlessly desire-deferring opticality.

9 '[T]he "object" is not as massive, as resistant, as one might wish to believe. And her possession by a "subject", a subject's desire to appropriate her, is yet another of his vertiginous failures. For where he projects a something to absorb, to take, to see, to possess … as well as a patch of ground to stand upon, a mirror to catch his reflection, he is already faced by another specularization, whose twisted character is her inability to say what she represents. The quest for the object becomes a game of Chinese boxes. Infinitely receding.'

10 For Lacan, men and women exist always already in language, and that language institutes women as the negative term (man is not woman, woman, therefore, is 'not'). Relative to Lacan's larger critique of the 'subject-presumed-to-know' as situated already in language, woman, as the negative term of language, in part escapes the Symbolic Order. Her *jouissance* exceeds the phallus, and exceeds language. But because knowledge, or the presumption of knowledge, is situated in language, woman cannot know that very negativity she is presumed to possess. Thus, she can have her jouissance, figured as excess or 'something more' than phallic, but cannot know her own *jouissance*. See 'God and the *Jouissance* of the Woman' in Lacan's *Feminine Sexuality* (New York: W.W. Norton and Co., 1982). This, however, continues the mystification of woman that Lacan simultaneously attempts to expose.

Rebecca Schneider, 'Permission to See – Gender in Perspective: Have We Really Gone Beyond?', *The Explicit Body in Performance* (New York and London: Routledge, 1997) 67-71.

ABSENT BODIES

The absence of the body is a poignant reminder of the transience of life. Artists have registered the body's absence in different ways – as casts, imprints, photographs or traces – and for different reasons. The absent body can be used to explore what it is like to be, to sense, to act. Critic Robert Pincus-Witten discusses the use of the body, and its trace, as a readymade. Art-historian Rosalind Krauss talks of loss of self in self through the reflection of self, and the drama of this self-reflexiveness. Looking at the trace of the body can also be said to point to an obsession with the past and where we came from. Artist Mirosław Bałka describes an attempt to define human existence through the body's dimensions. For critic Margaret Sundell Francesca Woodman's often fleeting images of the body point to its transient nature and instability.

Piero MANZONI Some Realizations, Some Experiments, Some Projects [1962]

My first *Achromes* date from 1957, and are of canvas impregnated with kaolin and glue. In 1959 the seams of the *Achromes* consisted of machine stitching. In 1960 I made some in cotton wool and expanded polystyrene. I experimented with phosphorescent pigment and with other surfaces soaked in cobalt chloride that would change colour with the passage of time. In 1961 I carried on with still more surfaces in straw and plastic and with a series of paintings, also white, made of balls of cotton wool, and then some that were furry like clouds, made of natural or artificial fibre. I also made a rabbit-skin sculpture. In 1959 I prepared a series of 45 *Bodies of Air* (pneumatic sculptures) of maximum diameter 80-cm [31-in] (height including base 120-cm [47-in]): if the purchaser wished, he could, in addition to the membrane and the base (closed in the small pencil box provided), buy my breath too, in order to conserve it in the membrane.

At the same period I planned a group of spherical bodies of air of approximate diameter 2.5-m [8-ft] to go in a park. By means of an air compressor these were to pulsate with a slow unsynchronized rhythm of breathing (experimental example with a membrane of small dimensions, 1959). On the same principle I made an architectural proposal of a pneumatically pulsating ceiling and wall. As another scheme for a park I had thought of a cluster of pneumatic cylinders, elongated in shape, like stele, which would vibrate in the blowing of the wind. (As part of the same project there would have been other very high steel stele which would have produced sounds in the wind.)

In 1959–60 I studied the idea of a moving, autonomous sculpture for outdoors. This mechanical animal would be independent because it would draw its nourishment from nature (solar energy). At night it would shut down and close in on itself. In the day it would move and emit sounds, rays and antennae in order to seek energy and avoid obstacles. It would also have the ability to reproduce itself.

In 1960 I realized an old project: the first sculpture in space. A sphere held suspended by a jet of air. On the same principle I worked on a number of 'bodies of absolute light': spheroids held up by suitably directed jets of air that turned giddily on their own axes to create a virtual volume.

At the beginning of 1959 I carried out my first lines, at first short, then longer and longer (19.11-m, 33-m, 63-m, 1,000-m, etc. ... [67-ft, 108-ft, 207-ft, 3,280-ft, etc. ...]): the longest one I have done to date is 7,200-m [23,622-ft] (Herning, Denmark, 1960). All these lines are placed in sealed containers.

I would also like to draw a white line around the entire Greenwich Meridian!

In 1960 in the course of two manifestations (in Copenhagen and Milan) I consecrated a number of hard-boiled eggs to art by placing my thumb print on them: the public was able to make contact with these works by swallowing the entire exhibition in seventy minutes.

From 1960 onwards I have been selling prints of my right and left thumbs. In 1959 I thought of exhibiting a number of living people (I wanted to enclose and conserve other, dead, bodies in blocks of transparent plastic). In 1961 I began to sign people for exhibition. I give a certificate of authenticity to accompany these works. In January 1961 I also constructed the first 'magic base', as long as any person or any object stayed on this base he, or it, was a work of art. I realized a second 'magic base' in Copenhagen. The earth is held up by the third one which is of large scale and made of iron standing in the park at Herning (Denmark, 1962): this is the 'base of the world'.

In the month of May 1961 I produced and tinned ninety tins of artist's shit (30 grams [1 oz] each) naturally preserved (made in Italy). A previous project had been to produce phials of artist's blood.

Between 1958 and 1960 I prepared a series of *tables of assessment* of which eight have been published as lithographs presented in a folder (maps, alphabets, finger prints ...).

In the field of music I composed, in 1961, two *Alphonie* the *aphonia Herning* (for orchestra and public), and the *aphonia Milan* (heart and breath). At the present moment (1962) I am studying an electronically controlled labyrinth which will be of use for psychological tests and brainwashing.

Piero Manzoni, 'Alcune realizzazioni, Alcuni esperimenti, Alcuni progetti' (Milan: Piero Manzoni, 1962), n.p.; reprinted in English as 'Some Realizations, Some Experiments, Some Projects', *Manzoni: Paintings, Reliefs and Objects*, ed. Germano Celant, trans. Caroline Tisdall and Angela Bozzola (London: Tate Gallery, 1974) 84-85.

Robert PINCUS-WITTEN

Theatre of the Conceptual: Autobiography and Myth

[1973]

The posthumous revelation of the diorama *Etant Donnés* gave lie to the canard that Marcel Duchamp abandoned art for chess in 1923, when he left the *Large Glass* unfinished. For twenty years at least (*c.* 1946–66) Duchamp had been intensely engaged by the continued elaboration of the mythology that had occupied him between 1912 and 1923 – the arcana of the *Large Glass*. Duchamp scholars now realize that the imagery of *Etant Donnés* represents a working towards nature from the mechanomorphic elements of the *Large Glass* – empirical representationalism deduced from diagrammatic terms instead of the reverse.

15. Marcel Duchamp

The title *Etant Donnés* as an expression indicates those syllogistic premises that are 'given' or 'granted' in a logical argument. When we say so and so is 'granted', in French we say '*étant donné*'. In *Etant Donnés*, the granted elements are identical to those of the *Large Glass* – the waterfall and the illuminating gas – physical and metaphorical sources of energy.

Significant to the development of *Etant Donnés* are three small erotic objects of 1951, the *Objet-Dard*, the *Female Fig Leaf* and the *Wedge of Chastity*. All the titles of these familiar and curiously ambiguous talismans play with literary conceits and/or outright puns. The pun is the touchstone of Duchamp's thought – a circular process of reasoning that thriftily returns to the same place while releasing fresh insights.

These three sexual objects account for certain inferences that clarify the mode of Conceptual art that deals with autobiography and/or myth [...]

We witnessed, for example, as part of conceptual theatre, work by the so-called body artist, Vito Acconci. He extrapolated the mythical type perfected by Duchamp – the androgyne – on to a behaviourist examination of his own psychology, seen in *Seedbed*, a work developed during the period of 1970–72.

Despite scandalized outcries, *Seedbed* presents a bare *mise-en-scène*. Its setting is a ramp or wedge sloping up the corner of a gallery floor.[1] Certainly it was not the external aspect of the work that proved provocative, but that the artist, fed by airholes drilled into the ramp's surface, isolated himself below the slanted floor and engaged in masturbation. The fantasy accompanying this act was faintly audible in the larger gallery space as it was transmitted through a loudspeaker in the corner of the chamber.

Seedbed takes as its metaphor one that Duchamp earlier had attributed to the *Large Glass*. *Seedbed*, like Duchamp's subtitle for the *Large Glass*, is 'an agricultural machine' – Acconci's seed, so to speak, now being cast upon the floor.

The *Large Glass* – the work must here be referred to by its proper name *The Bride Stripped Bare by her Bachelors, Even* – records an ongoing series of physical changes, effected through the actions of complex mechanomorphic machinery. Owing to the functions of the mechanomorphs depicted on the glass, physical states are at one point seen as gaseous – the cloud or liquid – the 'love juice' dripped from the 'Bride' in the upper portion of the glass into the realm of the 'Bachelors' below. At length, the love juice falls into the 'Nine Malic Moulds' and therein presumably solidifies. Among still other possibilities, this altered physical matter may be pulverized by the 'Chocolate Grinder', as it once again may be turned into light energy while passing through the lenses of the 'Optical Witnesses'.

In arcane lore, the person capable of enforcing the change of physical matter from one state to another is the alchemist or the androgyne – the latter being a fusion of male and female. He-She corresponds to a notion of God, that is, a coincidence of opposites. Throughout highly disparate cultures such a person is often assigned the role of shaman or seer, the see-er of the future, like Tiresias of Greek tragedy, or the Seller or Salt, the Salt Merchant of *kabbalism* and alchemy.

By an exiguous and circumstantial argument the salt merchant appears to correspond to the medieval alchemist, i.e., the person capable of effecting the change of matter from one physical state to another. The 'salt' of the salt merchant may well be symbolized by the philosopher's stone of the alchemist – the esoteric catalyst without which such changes in matter cannot be made. The arcane knowledge, the gnosis needed to effect this change – say, for example, the secret name of God – and the actual enactment of these changes constituted for the alchemist, the cabbalist or the magus, *la grande œuvre*, the great work of magic. Duchamp's *The Large Glass* as completed by the *Etant Donnés* is his great work of magic and his life work as well.

In French the Salt Merchant is called '*Le Marchand du Sel*', a transpositional pun on the four syllables of the name of Marcel Duchamp. Duchamp knew the name of the androgyne – Rrose Sélavy (the secret name of God?) as well as the androgyne's appearance – the artist himself in transvestiture. Man Ray photographed Marcel Duchamp in such cross-garb in 1920, when preparing the punning label for the perfume bottle *La Belle Haleine* – beautiful breath, beautiful Helen. The label displays a photograph of Rrose Sélavy, a punning name meaning 'life is okay'. She is the female side of Duchamp's nature.

All of this background is essential to an understanding of *Seedbed*. Acconci's earlier attempts to deal with the projection of an androgynous personality were realized through performances of such actions as the burning away of the artist's body hair, the tugging at his breasts, and the hiding of his penis between his legs. These performances indicate publicly that Acconci projected a notion of the androgyne that had earlier been set by Duchamp within his conception of his mythical alter ego, Rrose Sélavy.

It is important to note the difference between the conceptual theatre of Acconci's *Seedbed* and Dennis Oppenheim's *Adrenochrome* of 1973. *Adrenochrome*, like *Seedbed*, deals with the emission of chemicals – in Oppenheim's case, the chemical necessary to reconstitute the normal blood-cell structure of a schizophrenic – in Acconci's work, human sperm. *Adrenochrome* illuminates a particle of the chemical at the apex of a pyramid, while at the same time, a slide of the microscopic structure of the chemical is projected against a gallery wall. Both *mises-en-scène* are lent credibility owing to a parallel support system for abstract forms, the ramp and the pyramid.

While both the above works were generated by personal crises, *Adrenochrome* remains a *pro forma* work that insists on a one-to-one relationship to the artist's biography. *Seedbed*, by contrast, is a highly non-formal and secretive work whereby the autobiographical element is transposed to the plane of myth on the basis of Duchamp's lore.

The ontological artist, therefore, as Duchamp had anticipated and indicated, is the one whose work is completed in the public psyche. It must be noted that the psyche is primed by a literature of myth. In the absence of this acculturation nothing appears to happen except the work itself and the viewer's subjective experience of it.[2]

The mythical personage of the androgyne, it seems to me, is the exteriorization of Duchamp himself, expressed through the surrogate adventure that began when the Nude Descended the Staircase, became the Bride, was Stripped Bare by her Bachelors – female and male personae who ultimately united in the androgyne as impersonated by Duchamp in transvestiture.

An important 'proof' for this, apart from the visual evidence, derives from the French name of *The Large Glass: La Mariée mise à nu par ses célibataires, même*. La MARiée mise à nu par ses CELibataires – MAR-CEL, the first three letters of the French word for bride and the first three letters of the French word for bachelors comprise the letters of Duchamp's first name.

The by now obvious fact that Marcel Duchamp is both Bride and Bachelor at the same instant allows one to recognize something of a mythical core in, say, Vito Acconci's work, as well as to understand why Bruce Nauman may have used his name as a Readymade – *My Name As If It Were Bounced Off The Surface Of The Moon* or *My Name Enlarged Vertically 14 Times*.

Similarly, as Duchamp had regarded the three sexual objects in terms of morphological transfer – most particularly the *Female Fig Leaf* – so too Nauman casts against his body in unanticipated ways. It was this aspect of Duchamp's work that licenses for us Nauman's move into behaviouristic performance, video work, laser stereoptics and architectural situations. At first, Nauman's attention focused on the external effect made by his body upon some malleable substance, as in the *Template of the Left Hand of My Body at Ten Inch Intervals*. From this Nauman was able to project an art in which no external object was actually formed but which internalized the process back into his body – intangible substances such as space, light, warmth, acting in time – were now re-forming his body.

This shift between the mould and that which is moulded has influenced much of the open and often seemingly unpurposeful aspects of the conceptual performance [...]

In the absence of myth and autobiography the conceptual performance becomes purely behavioural. This appears to be another reason why, in Conceptual art, the behavioural appears to bridge the ontological and epistemological branches of the movement. Contrary to what I have previously thought, behaviourism is abstract conceptual theatre.

When Nauman investigated the artistic possibilities of his body or his name as a readymade, he drew away from an art based on the pun and simple language towards what has been loosely called 'phenomenology' – perhaps an abuse of the term, but one that none the less has entered art talk.

'Phenomenology', used this way, indicates a kind of physiological behaviourist activity and self-examination. What is it like to be? To do? To sense? To enact certain kinds of experiences and activities? Many of the experiences thus examined tend to be those attributed to inanimate things – residual Minimalism again – an underpinning derived from abstraction. What is it like to be immobile for long durations? To mechanically repeat physical activities? In such ways, artists as disparate as Nauman, Gilbert & George, recent Keith Sonnier, Robert Morris and Lynda Benglis can be bracketed, if only momentarily.

Moreover, Nauman regarded his body as a medium – trying to find in his body the very vehicle of his art – in the way that earlier artists had discovered the media of their art in watercolour, gouache, oil paint, etc. This may relate to Johns' connection between seeing and orality in many forms – speaking, masticating, ingesting [...]

Certainly, the *sine qua non* – traces of sensitively stroked surface executed with paint-loaded brush – has been fundamentally undermined, perhaps irrevocably. While such activity is, can and does remain art for many, other artists feel impelled to investigate looser modes and media, such as laser beam photography, video and film, behavioural phenomenology, dance, storywriting and telling. The latter are all being explored as viable in their own right as alternatives to sensibility drawing and sensibility painting, and as an alternative to the structures of thought of the pure Conceptualists.

In part this is why there has been such a resurgence of dance. Not necessarily dance practised as a classically defined discipline, but rather as an art of rudimentary movement: walking as dance, amateur as dancer, another way of painting and sculpting – an alternative. Painting without painting, sculpture without sculpture.

This may be a polemical generalization. That today we happen to see many dancers performing in ways suggestive of modes of painting and sculpture does not necessarily mean that the dancer is a painter or sculptor. When dance – and music too, for that matter – engages a wide reach in relation to painting and sculpture, it is tacitly assumed that this kind of dance or music is in some sense an expression *formative* of painting and sculpture. This is by no means a clear question today [...]

1 See my 'Vito Acconci and the Conceptual Performance', *Artforum* (April 1972).

2 The recognition, therefore, of 'public psyche' does not take place as a mystical necessity – the overtones of Jungian archetypes – but as a conclusion drawn from a liberal education. Were this not so when I would be sponsoring an art of mysticism and intuition qualities, if they exist, that are the paths of madness.

Robert Pincus-Witten, 'Theatre of the Conceptual: Autobiography and Myth', *Artforum* (October 1973) 40-46.

Rosalind KRAUSS
Video: The Aesthetics of Narcissism [1976]

It was a commonplace criticism in the 1960s that a strict application of symmetry allowed a painter 'to point to the centre of the canvas' and, in so doing, to invoke the internal structure of the picture-object. Thus 'pointing to the centre' was made to serve as one of the many blocks in that intricately constructed arch by which the criticism of the last decade sought to connect art to ethics through the 'aesthetics of acknowledgement'. But what does it mean to point to the centre of a TV screen?

In a way that is surely conditioned by the attitudes of Pop art, artists' video is largely involved in parodying the critical terms of abstraction. Thus when Vito Acconci makes a video tape called *Centers* (1971), what he does is literalize the critical notion of 'pointing' by filming himself pointing to the centre of a television monitor, a gesture he sustains for the 20-minute running time of the work. The parodistic quality of Acconci's gesture, with its obvious debt to Duchampian irony, is clearly intended to disrupt and dispense with an entire critical tradition. It is meant to render nonsensical a critical engagement with the formal properties of a work, or indeed, a genre of works – such as 'video'. The kind of criticism *Centers* attacks is obviously one that takes seriously the formal qualities of a work, or tries to assay the particular logic of a given medium. And yet, by its very *mise-en-scène*, *Centers* typifies the structural characteristics of the video medium. For *Centers* was made by Acconci's using the video monitor as a mirror. As we look at the artist sighting along his outstretched arm and forefinger towards the centre of the screen we are watching, what we see is a sustained tautology: a line of sight that begins at Acconci's plane of vision and ends at the eyes of his projected double. In that image of self-regard is configured a narcissism so endemic to works of video that I find myself wanting to generalize it as *the* condition of the entire genre. Yet, what would it mean to say, 'The medium of video is narcissism?'

For one thing, that remark tends to open up a rift between the nature of video and that of the other visual arts. Because that statement describes a psychological rather than a physical condition: and while we are accustomed to thinking of psychological states as the possible subject of works of art, we do not think of psychology as constituting their medium. Rather, the medium of painting, sculpture or film has much more to do with the objective, material factors specific to a particular form: pigment-bearing surfaces; matter extended through space; light projected through a moving strip of celluloid. That is, the notion of a medium contains the concept of an object-state, separate from the artist's own being, through which his intentions must pass.

Video depends – in order for anything to be experienced at all – on a set of physical mechanisms. So perhaps it would be easiest to say that this apparatus – both at its present and future levels of technology – comprises the television medium, and leave it at that. Yet with the subject of video, the ease of defining it in terms of its machinery does not seem to coincide with accuracy; and my own experience of video keeps urging me towards the psychological model.

Everyday speech contains an example of the word 'medium' used in a psychological sense; the uncommon terrain for that common-enough usage is the world of parapsychology: telepathy, extrasensory perception and communication with an afterlife, for which people with certain kinds of psychic powers are understood to be mediums. Whether or not we give credence to the fact of mediumistic experience, we understand the referents for the language that describes it. We know, for instance, that configured within the parapsychological sense of the word 'medium' is the image of a human receiver (and sender) of communications arising from an invisible source. Further, this term contains the notion that the human conduit exists in a particular relation to the message, which is one of temporal concurrence. Thus, when Freud lectures on the phenomenon of telepathic dreams, he tells his audience that the fact insisted upon by reports of such matters is that the dreams occur at the *same time* as the actual (but invariably distant) event.

Now these are the two features of the everyday use of 'medium' that are suggestive for a discussion of video: the simultaneous reception and projection of an image; and the human psyche used as a conduit. Because most of the work produced over the very short span of video art's existence has used the human body as its central instrument. In the case of work on tape this has most often been the body of the artist-practitioner. In the case of video installations it has usually been the body of the responding viewer. And no matter whose body has been selected for the occasion, there is a further condition which is always present. Unlike the other visual arts, video is capable of recording and transmitting at the same time – producing instant feedback. The body is therefore as it were centred between two machines that are the opening and closing of a parenthesis. The first of these is the camera; the second is the monitor, which re-projects the performer's image with the immediacy of a mirror.

The effects of this centring are multiple. And nowhere are they more clearly named than in a tape made by Richard Serra, with the help of Nancy Holt, who made herself its willing and eloquent subject. The tape is called *Boomerang* (1974), and its situation is a recording studio in which Holt sits in a tightly framed close-up wearing a technician's headset. As Holt begins to talk her words are fed back to her through the earphones she wears. Because the apparatus is attached to a recording instrument, there is a slight delay (of less than a second) between her actual locution and the audio-feedback to which she is forced to listen. For the ten minutes of the tape Holt describes her situation. She speaks of the way the feedback interferes with her normal thought process and of the confusion caused by the lack of synchronism between her speech and what she hears of it. 'Sometimes', she says, 'I find I can't quite say a word because I hear a first part come back and I forget the second part, or my head is stimulated in a new direction by the first half of the word.'

As we hear Holt speak and listen to that delayed voice echoing in her ears, we are witness to an extraordinary image of distraction. Because the audio delay keeps hypostatizing her words, she has great difficulty coinciding with herself as a subject. It is a situation, she says, that 'puts a distance between the words and their apprehension – their comprehension', a situation that is 'like a mirror-reflection ... so that I am surrounded by me and my mind surrounds me ... there is no escape'.

The prison Holt both describes and enacts, from which there is no escape, could be called the prison of a collapsed present, that is, a present time which is completely severed from a sense of its own past. We get some feeling for what it is like to be stuck in that present when Holt at one point says, 'I'm throwing things out in the world and they are boomeranging back ... boomeranging ... eranginging ... anginging'. Through that distracted reverberation of a single word – and even word-fragment – there forms an image of what it is like to be totally cut off from history, even, in this case, the immediate history of the sentence one has just spoken. Another word for that history from which Holt feels herself to be disconnected is 'text'.

Most conventional performers are of course enacting or interpreting a text, whether that is a fixed choreography, a written script, a musical score or a sketchy set of notes around which to improvise. By the very fact of that relationship, the performance ties itself to the fact of something that existed before the given moment. Most immediately, this sense of something having come before refers to the specific text for the performance at hand. But in a larger way it evokes the more general historical relationship between a specific text and the history constructed by all the texts of a given genre. Independent of the gesture made within the present, this larger history is the source of meaning for that gesture. What Holt is describing in *Boomerang* is a situation in which the action of the mirror-reflection (which is auditory in this case) severs her from a sense of text: from the prior words she has spoken: from the way language connects her both to her own past and to a world of objects. What she comes to is a space where, as she says, 'I am surrounded by me'.

Self-encapsulation – the body or psyche as its own surround – is everywhere to be found in the corpus of video art. Acconci's *Centers* is one instance, another is his *Air Time* of 1973. In *Air Time* Acconci sits between the video camera and a large mirror which he faces. For thirty-five minutes he addresses his own reflection with a monologue in which the terms 'I' and 'you' – although they are presumed to be referring to himself and an absent lover – are markers of the autonomous intercourse between Acconci and his own image. Both *Centers* and *Air Time* construct a situation of spatial closure, promoting a condition of self-reflection. The response of the performer is to a continually renewed image of himself. This image, supplanting the consciousness of anything prior to it, becomes the unchanging text of the performer. Skewered on his own reflection, he is committed to the text of perpetuating that image. So the temporal concommitant of this situation is, like the echo-effect of *Boomerang*, the sense of a collapsed present.

Bruce Nauman's tapes are another example of the double effect of the performance-for-the monitor. In *Revolving Upside Down* (1968) Nauman films himself through a camera that has been rotated so that the floor on which he stands is at the top of the screen. For sixty very long minutes Nauman slowly moves, turning on one foot, from the depths of his studio forwards towards the monitor and then back again, repeating this activity until the tape runs out.

In Lynda Benglis' *Now* there is a similar levelling out of the effects of temporality. The tape is of Benglis' head in profile, performing against the backdrop of a large monitor on which an earlier tape of herself doing the same actions, but reversed left and right, is being replayed. The two profiles, one 'live' the other taped, move in mirrored synchrony with one another. As they do, Benglis' two profiles perform an autoerotic coupling, which, because it is being recorded, becomes the background for another generation of the same activity. Through this spiral of infinite regress, as the face merges with the double and triple re-projections of itself merging with itself, Benglis' voice is heard either issuing the command 'Now!' or asking 'Is it now?' Clearly, Benglis is using the word 'now' to underline the ambiguity of temporal reference: we realize that we do not know whether the sound of the voice is coming from the live or the taped source, and if from the latter, which level of taping. Just as we also realize that because of the activity of replaying the past generations, all layers of the 'now' are equally present.

But what is far more arresting in *Now* than the technological banality of the question 'which "now" is intended?' is the way the tape enacts a collapsed present time. In that insistence it connects itself to the tapes by Nauman and Acconci already described, and ultimately to *Boomerang*. In all these examples the nature of video performance is specified as an activity of bracketing out the text and substituting for it the mirror-reflection. The result of this substitution is the presentation of a self understood to have no past, and as well, no connection with any objects that are external to it. For the double that appears on the monitor cannot be called a true external object. Rather it is a displacement of the self which has the effect – as Holt's voice has in *Boomerang* – of transforming the performer's subjectivity into another, mirror, object.

It is at this point that one might want to go back to the proposition with which this argument began, and raise a particular objection. Even if it is agreed, one might ask, that the medium of video art is the psychological condition of the self split and doubled by the mirror-reflection of synchronous feedback, how does that entail a 'rift' between video and the other arts? Isn't it rather a case of video's using a new technique to achieve continuity with the modernist intentions of the rest of the visual media? Specifically, isn't the mirror-reflection a variant on the reflexive mode in which contemporary painting, sculpture and film have successively entrenched themselves? Implicit in this question is the idea that auto-reflection and reflexiveness refer to the same thing – that both are cases of consciousness doubling back upon itself in order to perform and portray a separation between forms of art and their contents, between the procedures of thought and their objects.' In its simplest form this question would be the following: Aside from their divergent technologies, what is the difference, *really*, between Vito Acconci's *Centers* and Jasper John's *American Flag*?

Answer: The difference is total. Reflection, when it is a case of mirroring, is a move towardsan external symmetry; while reflexiveness is a strategy to achieve a radical *a*symmetry, from within. In his *American Flag* Johns uses the synonymy between an image (the flag) and its ground (the limits of the picture surface) to unbalance the relationship between the terms 'picture' and 'painting'. By forcing us to see the actual wall on which the canvas hangs as the background for the pictorial object as-a-whole, Johns drives a wedge between two types of figure/ground relationships: the one that is internal to the image; and the one that works from without to define this object as Painting. The figure ground of a flat, bounded surface hung against a wall is isolated as a primary, categorical condition, within which the terms of the process of painting are given. The category 'Painting' is established as an object (or a text) whose subject becomes this particular painting – *American Flag*. The flag is thus both the object of the picture *and* the subject of a more general object (Painting) to which *American Flag* can reflexively point. Reflexiveness is precisely this fracture into two categorically different entities which can elucidate one another in so far as their separateness is maintained.

Mirror-reflection, on the other hand, implies the vanquishing of separateness. Its inherent movement is towardsfusion. The self and its reflected image are of course literally separate. But the agency of reflection is a mode of appropriation, of illusionistically erasing the difference between subject and object. Facing mirrors on opposite walls squeeze out the real space between them. When we look at *Centers* we see Acconci sighting along his arm to the centre of the screen we are watching. But latent in this set-up is the monitor that he is, himself, looking at. There is no way for us to see *Centers* without reading that sustained connection between the artist and his double. So for us as for Acconci video is a process which allows these two terms to fuse.

One could say that if the reflexiveness of modernist art is a *dédoublement* or doubling back in order to locate the object (and thus the objective conditions of one's experience), the mirror-reflection of absolute feedback is a process of bracketing out the object. This is why it seems inappropriate to speak of a physical medium in relation to video. For the object (the electronic equipment and its capabilities) has become merely an appurtenance. And instead, video's real medium is a psychological situation, the very terms of which are to withdraw attention from an external object – an Other – and invest it in the Self. Therefore, it is not just any psychological condition one is speaking of. Rather it is the condition of someone who has, in Freud's words, 'abandoned the investment of objects with libido and transformed object-libido into ego-libido'. And that is the specific condition of narcissism.

By making this connection, then, one can recast the opposition between the reflective and reflexive into the terms of the psychoanalytic project. Because it is there, too, in the drama of the couched subject, that the narcissistic re-projection of a frozen self is pitted against the analytic (or reflexive) mode.[2] One finds a particularly useful description of that struggle in the writing of Jacques Lacan.

In *The Language of the Self* Lacan begins by characterizing the space of the therapeutic transaction as an extraordinary void created by the silence of the analyst. Into this void the patient projects the monologue of his own recitation, which Lacan calls 'the monumental construct of his narcissism'. Using this monologue to explain himself and his situation to his silent listener, the patient begins to experience a very deep frustration. And this frustration, Lacan charges, although it is initially thought to be provoked by the maddening silence of the analyst, is eventually discovered to have another source: '*Is it not rather a matter of a frustration inherent in the very discourse of the subject? Does the subject not become engaged in an ever-growing dispossession of that being of his, concerning which – by dint of sincere portraits which leave its idea no less incoherent, of rectifications which do not succeed in freeing its essence, of stays and defences which do not prevent his statue from tottering, of narcissistic embraces which become like a puff of air in animating it – he ends up by recognizing that this being has never been anything more than his construct in the Imaginary and that this construct disappoints all his certitudes? For in this labour which he undertakes to reconstruct this construct* for another, *he finds again the fundamental alienation which made him construct it* like another one, *and which has always destined it to be stripped from him* by another.'[3]
What the patient comes to see is that this 'self' of his is a projected object, and that his frustration is due to his own capture by this object with which he can never really coincide. Further, this 'statue' which he has made and in which he believes is the basis for his 'static state', for the constantly 'renewed status of his alienation'. Narcissism is characterized, then, as the unchanging condition of a perpetual frustration.[4]

The process of analysis is one of breaking the hold of this fascination with the mirror; and in order to do so the patient comes to see the distinction between his lived subjectivity and the fantasy projections of himself as object. 'In order for us to come back to a more dialectical view of the analytic experience,' Lacan writes, 'I would say that the analysis consists precisely in distinguishing the person lying on the analyst's couch from the person who is speaking. With the person listening [the analyst], that makes three persons present in the analytical situation, among whom it is the rule that the question ... be put: Where is the *moi* of the subject?'[5] The analytic project is then one in which the patient disengages from the 'statue' of his reflected self, and through a method of reflexiveness, rediscovers the real time of his own history. He exchanges the atemporality of repetition for the temporality of change.

If psychoanalysis understands that the patient is engaged in a recovery of his being in terms of its real history, modernism has understood that the artist locates his own expressiveness through a discovery of the objective conditions of his medium and their history. That is, the very possibilities of finding his subjectivity necessitate that the artist recognize the material and historical independence of an external object (or medium).

In distinction to this, the feedback coil of video seems to be the instrument of a double repression: for through it consciousness of temporality and of separation between subject and object are simultaneously submerged. The result of this submergence is, for the maker and the viewer of most video-art, a kind of weightless fall through the suspended space of narcissism.

There are, of course, a complex set of answers to the question of why video has attracted a growing set of practitioners and collectors. These answers would involve an analysis of everything from the problem of narcissism within the wider context of our culture, to the specific inner workings of the present art market. Although I would like to postpone that analysis for a future essay, I do wish to make one connection here. And that is between the institution of a self formed by video feedback and the real situation that exists in the artworld from which the makers of video come. In the last fifteen years that world has been deeply and disastrously affected by its relation to mass-media. That an artist's work be published, reproduced and disseminated through the media has become, for the generation that has matured in the course of the last decade, virtually the *only* means of verifying its existence as art. The demand for instant replay in the media – in fact the creation of work that literally does not exist outside of that replay, as is true of conceptual art and its nether side, body art – finds its obvious correlative in an aesthetic mode by which the self is created through the electronic device of feedback.

There exist, however, three phenomena within the corpus of video art which run counter to what I have been saying so far. Or at least are somewhat tangential to it. They are: 1) tapes that exploit the medium in order to criticize it from within; 2) tapes that represent a physical assault on the video mechanism in order to break out of its psychological hold; and 3) installation forms of video which use the medium as a sub-species of painting or sculpture. The first is represented by Richard Serra's *Boomerang*. The second can be exemplified by Joan Jonas' *Vertical Roll*. And the third is limited to certain of the installation works of Bruce Nauman and Peter Campus, particularly Campus' two companion pieces *mem* and *dor*.

I have already described how narcissism is enacted in *Boomerang*. But what separates it from, say, Benglis' *Now*, is the critical distance it maintains on its own subject. This is primarily due to the fact that Serra employs audio rather than visual feedback. Because of this the angle of vision we take on the subject does not coincide with the closed circuit of Holt's situation, but looks on to it from outside. Further, the narcissistic condition is given through the cerebrated form of language, which opens simultaneously on to the plane of expression and the plane of critical reflexiveness.

Significantly, Serra's separation from the subject of *Boomerang*, his position outside it, promotes an attitude towards time that is different from many other works of video. The tape's brevity – it is ten minutes long – is itself related to discourse: to how long it takes to shape and develop an argument; and how long it takes for its receiver to get the 'point'. Latent within the opening situation of *Boomerang* is its own conclusion; when that is reached, it stops.

Vertical Roll is another case where time has been forced to enter the video situation, and where that time is understood as a propulsion towards an end. In this work access to a sense of time has come from fouling the stability of the projected image by desynchronizing the frequencies of the signals on camera and monitor. The rhythmic roll of the image, as the bottom of its frame scans upward to hit the top of the screen, causes a sense of decomposition that seems to work against the grain of those 525 lines of which the video picture is made. Because one recognizes it as intended, the vertical roll appears as the agency of a will that runs counter to an electronically stabilized condition. Through the effect of its constant wiping away of the image, one has a sense of a reflexive relation to the video grid and the ground or support for what happens to the image.

Out of this is born the subject of *Vertical Roll*, which visualizes time as the course of a continuous dissolve through space. In it a sequence of images and actions are seen from different positions – both in terms of the camera's distance and its orientation to a horizontal ground. With the ordinary grammar of both film and video these shifts would have to be registered either by camera movement (in which the zoom is included as one possibility) or by cutting. And while it is true that Jonas has had to use these techniques in making *Vertical Roll*, the constant sweep of the image renders these movements invisible. That is, the grammar of the camera is eroded by the dislocating grip of the roll. As I have said, the illusion this creates is one of a continuous dissolve through time and space. The monitor, as an instrument, seems to be winding into itself a ribbon of experience, like a fishing line being taken up upon a reel, or like magnetic tape being wound upon a spool. The motion of continuous dissolve becomes, then, a metaphor for the physical reality not only of the scan-lines of the video raster, but of the physical reality of the tape deck, whose reels objectify a finite amount of time.

Earlier, I described the paradigm situation of video as a body centred between the parenthesis of camera and monitor. Due to *Vertical Roll*'s visual reference through the monitor's action to the physical reality of the tape, one side of this parenthesis is made more active than the other. The monitor side of the double bracket becomes a reel through which one feels prefigured the imminence of a goal or terminus for the motion. That end is reached when Jonas, who has been performing the actions recorded on the tape, from within the coils of the camera monitor circuit, breaks through the parenthetical closure of the feedback situation to face the camera directly – without the agency of the monitor's rolling image.

If it is the paired movement of the video scan and the tape-reel that is isolated as a physical object in *Vertical Roll*, it is the stasis of the wall-plane that is objectified in Campus' *mem* and *dor*. In both of the Campus works there is a triangular relationship created between: 1) a video camera, 2) an instrument that will project the live camera image on to the surface of a wall (at life- and over-life-size), and 3) the wall itself. The viewer's experience of the works is the sum of the cumulative positions his body assumes within the vectors formed by these three elements. When he stands outside the triangular field of the works, the viewer sees nothing but the large, luminous plane of one of the walls in a darkened room. Only when he moves into the range of the camera is he able to realize an image (his own) projected on to the wall's pictorial field. However, the conditions of seeing that image are rather special in both *mem* and *dor*.

In the latter the camera is placed in the hallway leading to the room that contains the projector. Inside the room the viewer is out of the range of the camera and therefore nothing appears on the wall-surface. It is only as he leaves the room, or rather is poised at the threshold of the doorway, that he is both illumined enough and far enough into the focal range of the camera to register as an image. Since that image projects on to the very wall through which the doorway leads, the viewer's relation to his own image must be totally peripheral; he is himself in a plane that is not only parallel to the plane of the illusion, but continuous with it. His body is therefore both the substance of the image and, as well, the slightly displaced substance of the plane on to which the image is projected.

In *mem* both camera and projector are to one side of the wall-plane, stationed in such a way that the range of the camera encompasses a very thin corridor-like slice of space that is parallel to, and almost fused with, the illumined wall. Due to this, the viewer must be practically up against the wall in order to register. As he moves far enough away from the wall in order to be able to see himself, the image blurs and distorts, but if he moves near enough to place himself in focus, he has formed such closure with the support for the image that he cannot really see it. Therefore in *mem*, as in *dor*, the body of the viewer becomes physically identified with the wall-plane as the 'place' of the image.

There is a sense in which we could say that these two works by Campus simply take the live feedback of camera and monitor, which existed for the video artist while taping in his studio, and re-create it for the ordinary visitor to a gallery. However, *mem* and *dor* are not that simple. Because built into their situation are two kinds of invisibility: the viewer's presence to the wall in which he is himself an absence; and his relative absence from a view of the wall which becomes the condition for his projected presence upon its surface.

Campus' pieces acknowledge the very powerful narcissism that propels the viewer of these works forwards and backwards in front of the muralized field. And, through the movement of his own body, his neck craning and head turning, the viewer is forced to recognize this motive as well. But the condition of these works is to acknowledge as separate the two surfaces on which the image is held – the one the viewer's body, the other the wall – and to make them register as absolutely distinct. It is in this distinction that the wall-surface – the pictorial surface – is understood as an absolute Other, as part of the world of objects external to the self. Further, it is to specify that the mode of projecting oneself on to that surface entails recognizing all the ways that one does not coincide with it.

There is, of course, a history of the art of the last fifteen years into which works like *mem* and *dor* insert themselves, although it is one about which little has been written. That history involves the activities of certain artists who have made work which conflates psychologistic and formal means to achieve very particular ends. The art of Robert Rauschenberg is a case in point. His work, in bringing together groupings of real objects and found images and suspending them within the static matrix of a pictorial field, attempts to convert that field into something we could call the plane of memory. In so doing, the static pictorial field is both psychologized and temporally distended. I have argued elsewhere[6] that the impulse behind this move arose from questions that have to do with commodity-fetishism. Rauschenberg, among many other artists, has been working against a situation in which painting and sculpture have been absorbed within a luxury market – absorbed so totally that their content has been deeply conditioned by their status as fetish-prizes to be collected, and thereby consumed. In response, Rauschenberg's art asserts another, alternative, relationship between the work of art and its viewer. And to do this Rauschenberg has had recourse to the value of time: to the time it takes to read a text, or a painting, to rehearse the activity of cognitive differentiation that that entails, to get its point. That is, he wishes to pit the temporal values of consciousness against the stasis of the commodity-fetish.

Although responsive to the same considerations, the temporal values that were built into the Minimalist sculpture of the 1960s were primarily engaged with questions of perception. The viewer was therefore involved in a temporal decoding of issues of scale, placement or shape – issues that are inherently more abstract than, say, the contents of memory. Pure, as opposed to applied psychology we might say. But in the work of certain younger sculptors, Joel Shapiro for example, the issues of Minimalism are being inserted into a space which, like Rauschenberg's pictorial field, defines itself as mnemonic. So that physical distance from a sculptural object is understood as being indistinguishable from temporal remove.

It is to this body of work that I would want to add Campus' art. The narcissistic enclosure inherent in the video-medium becomes for him part of a psychologistic strategy by which he is able to examine the general conditions of pictorialism in relation to its viewers. It can, that is, critically account for narcissism as a form of bracketing-out the world and its conditions, at the same time as it can reassert the facticity of the object against the grain of the narcissistic drive towards projection.

1 For example, this completely erroneous equation allows Max Kozloff to write that narcissism is 'the emotional correlate of the intellectual basis behind self-reflexive modern art'. See 'Pygmalion Revisited', *Artforum*, 14 (November 1975) 37 [see in this volume pp. 248-49].

2 Freud's pessimism about the prospects of treating the narcissistic character is based on his experience of the narcissist's inherent inability to enter into the analytic situation: 'Experience shows that persons suffering from the narcissistic neuroses have no capacity for transference, or only insufficient remnants of it. They turn from the physician, not in hostility, but in indifference. Therefore they are not to be influenced by him; what he says leaves them cold, makes no impression on them, and therefore the process of cure which can be carried through with others, the revivification of the pathogenic conflict and the overcoming of the resistance due to the repressions, cannot be effected with them. They remain as they are.' Sigmund Freud, *A General Introduction to Psychoanalysis*, trans. Joan Rivere (New York: Permabooks, 1953) 455.

3 Jacques Lacan, *The Language of the Self*, trans. Anthony Wilden (New York: Delta, 1968) 11.

4 Explaining this frustration, Lacan points to the fact that even when 'the subject makes himself an object by striking a pose before the mirror, he could not possibly be satisfied with it, since even if he achieved his most perfect likeness in that image, it would still be the pleasure of the other that he would cause to be recognized in it', *ibid.*, 12.

5 *Ibid.*, 100. Although *moi* translates as 'ego', Wilden has presumably retained the French here in order to suggest the relationship between the different orders of the self by the implicit contrast between *moi* and *je*.

6 See my 'Rauschenberg and the Materialized Image', *Artforum*, 13 (December 1974).

Rosalind Krauss, 'Video: The Aesthetics of Narcissism', *October*, 1 (Spring 1976) 57-64.

Helen CHADWICK
Soliloquy to Flesh [1989]

My apparatus is a body × sensory systems with which to correlate experience. Not exactly solid and real, I am none the less conscious, via physicality, of duration, of passing through. The sense of motion is emphatic, positing flesh-hood not as matter or image, but as process, a sequence of

quantities of action. Like a bout of the hiccups, interactions keep making me happen, piecemeal. As links in a chain of reflex, I cannot be fixed in absolute terms, I can only present myself as variable, as event within the dynamic of place. What-is is what happens, made intelligible by charting the relations of perception to the physical.

On impulse, I plan an incidence of self, in other words, a building site to develop in. As I proceed, things appear to change. The site curves around my presence while I in turn mould the geography of space. In mutual circumnavigation, the terrain waxes open and, following the path of least resistance, performs new convolutions. I mirror these curvatures. The architecture grows corporeal and I am enfleshed. In stories of origin and memory, cycles of transformation and decay, I narrate myself as envelopes of feeling quantized into flesh. There at the heart of these inscapes are enucleate abstracts eluding definition, stubbornly refusing to cohere.

Photography is my skin. As membrane separating this from that, it fixes the point between, establishing my limit, the envelope in which I am. My skin is image, surface, medium of recognition. Existing out there, the photograph appears to duplicate the world, disclosing me within its virtual space. But its range is elsewhere. Beyond the likeness I perceive another in-between, dilating in waves of harmony and dissonance, the tension of me for other. In parabolas, complementary functions of inside-outside, I plot the amplitude of difference, criss-crossing through this permeable screen. Pulled back and forth as message, the semblances are sinusoidal writing. Inside is outside is inside.

The eye reads these signals in the cool far retinal distance. Yet they occurred and are still in the knowing realm of touch. Intimate events of the moment of contact, happening once, are continually secured in place. This is not just light falling on to film, but tactile photography, the very sensitizing of surface itself. The vital interface is here, where substance quickens to sensation in the eros of the moment. I graze the emulsion and by a process of interpenetration am dynamically returned: echoes of my falling on to picture are irradiated back as me again.

All these are propositions for being in the world, like physics. It seems I cannot distinguish anything as separate from myself so perhaps after all, I am the anything I observe. I use this eye/I reluctantly. Consciousness itself implicates me, moving out from what feels central to form relations with place, time, image, others, everything. There is nothing to explain, I have just to form the interruptions, this sequence of partial and approximate episodes which are self-consistent with my co-incidence. If I exist, it is a discontinuity, a transient state of interrelations, pulse-like jumps in the illusion of things unfolding into fabricated space ... pages turning in associated time.

Helen Chadwick, 'Soliloquy to Flesh', *Enfleshings* (1982-84) (London: Martin Secker & Warburg Ltd., 1989) 109.

Mirosław BAŁKA

Conversation with Jaromir Jedliński [1991]

Jaromir Jedliński I'd like to begin our conversation by asking you a question [about] your attitude towards the place, space and human body, and about the way you approach those issues in your sculpture as well as in your installations.

Mirosław Bałka **My attitude towardsthe space, place and human body in my art is defined by the relationship between myself and the place where I work. It's not an indifferent interior. I work in a deserted room where once somebody lived and died.[1] This room has its own atmosphere and its own definite dimensions. My body has definite dimensions, there are relationships between my body and the room, between myself and the corners in this particular interior.**

Jedliński Could you develop this theme of the human body and comment on this element of your earlier work when you employed the projection of the human figure, and upon the moment when the breakthrough in your work took place? This change concerned the language of sculpture relating to a human body. The figure disappeared from your works and the presence of the human body manifested itself in a different way.

Bałka **In my earlier works I employed the body in the very literal way. Very sensual [...] I think that it resulted from hunger or rather primeval hunger for a body. After some time I satisfied my hunger for the form of the human body. I took an interest in the forms that accompany the body and in the traces the body leaves: a bed, a coffin, a funeral urn.**

Those earlier figures, in a sense, died. There appeared the problem of dimensions which begin to be really important at the moment of death when the coffin has to be built or the urn has to be of a certain capacity to contain the ashes. Departure from the figure occurred in a narrative way in the case of the sculpture *River*. The work [...] was in the form of a coffin whose shape resembled this swimming figure with its hand extended over its head. The dimensions of the coffin were smaller than the ones of the body so that the coffin could not play a utilitarian role. I mainly intended it as a metaphor. Then my works began to relate to dimensions in a more disciplined way. Since the beginning of 1990 I have been using dimensions as the titles of my works. Since I am 190-cm [6-ft] tall, this dimension appeared in my works.[2] An attempt to define human existence by dimensions became important to me. Traces of a man can be measured somehow. These works were not 'untitled'. Concrete dimensions served as a title. I have introduced through it a certain degree of register and at the same time these works have a certain anonymity. On one hand, they were difficult to recognize through the number, on the other hand, they were very clearly defined, and related, due to the same number. A measurement from both the outside and the inside.

Jedliński The presence of the human body in a whole series of works which you entitle, or rather – subtitle – using the dimensions of its individual elements, are submitted to one general English motto: *My Body Cannot Do Everything I Ask For*, a title under which you have already exhibited them several times. And earlier when you had shown the works from your artistic quest, you used the title *Good God* which is I assume, a play on words. I would like you to say something more about your way of perceiving the body in your works, not only with relation to dimension, but also to the materials and substances you use, which also relate to the human body – the use of salt, salty water, a board, a sponge, a pillow, etc.

Bałka **I want to emphasize that this refers to definite titles. The cycle *My Body Cannot Do Everything I Ask For* got its title by coincidence. It is a sentence I noticed on a scrap of English newspaper. I was struck by the content and conciseness of this information. All my individual exhibitions in 1991 have as their main title *My Body Cannot Do Everything I Ask For*, and the months of subsequent shows constitute the subtitles of this cycle. It's an attempt to define a state, a condition, understood very broadly. I don't intend to represent my mood according to the seasons of the year.[3]**

The works presented in the Foksal Gallery relate directly to the body and to the traces it leaves. Salt appears in it in a non-metaphysical but concrete way, as dried sweat. By filling a steel pipe of my height with salt, I undertook an attempt to preserve a trace (sweat) that a particular man can leave.

By filling two steel pipes that are at my eye level with salty water I tried to measure and preserve tears. I begin with a certain anecdote and create an abstract object. This object, through the information it carries, is not indifferent to reality. In my earlier works I was interested in the problem of the history of objects; in information that an old floorboard may contain. It is internal information never revealed to us until the last moment but appearing along with the floorboard itself. Cutting this plank to a specific length, my own dimension, I involve it in my own matters. Two histories begin to overlap: the plank's and my own [...]

1 The artist worked there from 1985 until 1992. Next he began to work in the house where he grew up and spent his childhood. Now this house is his studio.

2 Part of a conversation between Maria Morzuch and Mirosław Bałka published in *Muzeum Sztuki w Lódzi 1931-1992. Collection-Documentation-Actualité* (Lyons: Musée d'Art Contemporain and ELAC, 1992) 262.

3 His first exhibition in 1992 was entitled *No body* (Vienna: Galerie Peter Pakesch).

Mirosław Bałka, 'Conversation between Jaromir Jedliński' (1991), *Die Rampe* (Eindhoven: Stedelijk Van Abbemuseum; Lódź: Muzeum Sztuki, 1994) 64-70; revised 1998.

Francesco BONAMI

Charles Ray: A Telephone Conversation [1992]

In *Vox*, Nicholson Baker's most recent book, the author suggests that the telephone creates a certain distance, it is

not simply a means. Two people living 13,000 km [8,000 miles] apart who speak to one another over the phone without ever seeing each other create a particular kind of intimacy; another kind of dialogue takes place when these same people share a common space. Perhaps, in the end, a more sincere intimacy arises over the phone, one which is not mitigated by the inherent, mutual judging which occurs when speaking face to face. In an interview, for example, you write your questions in advance but then can sense that the voice on the phone is too close for the questions you've prepared. You can't interview somebody by whispering things into his or her ear. What results is simply an informal conversation, no matter who is on the other end of the line. Conversations in a single physical space tend to narrow; on the phone they tend to expand and make themselves understood. Whether you're wearing a three-piece suit or lying around in your underwear changes nothing in your relationship with the speaker; all awkwardness is overcome.

I know Charles Ray only through his work – through the bodycasts he has produced – and so enjoy as intimate a relationship with him as I might with, say, a wax dummy of Margaret Thatcher. The words alone, spoken over the phone, tell me more about him than if I were to stare into his eyes or shake his hand. The table in some New York bar which would have come between us had we met in person seems, after our phone call, an unsurmountable distance.

'What I'm doing now is a figurative sculpture called *Oh! Charley, Charley, Charley* ... : eight figures, all bodycasts of myself. It's a sex orgy and I'm the only participant. They are cast from plaster and then made in fibreglass. They don't have anywhere near the resolution of a Duane Hanson, but they have much more resolution than a mannequin. They have painted flesh, wigs and some pubic hair. When I first began the project a year ago the notion of different sex positions was really in the forefront of my mind. Each figure touches another someplace, but it's not a daisy chain *per se*. In a way this work isn't about sex; I made some abstract pieces that I think are much more about sex ... I was getting divorced from my wife, I was involved with different girlfriends and partners, you know. You realize at a certain point that you just ... you just like sleeping with yourself [...]

'I, like many people in the 1970s, experimented with drugs; they did something for me in this relation with the world but I wouldn't recommend them, I don't think they are necessary. What I do now, you know, is sailing, or I go shopping. When you go to the fucking mall, talk about taking a lot of speed. Just go in a department store; it's a very similar experience really, you know, the fishing poles, the leather belts, women's underwear, tennis shoes ... In a way, a lot of work from the 1980s got this thing wrong, quite wrong. What that first mannequin, my self-portrait, was trying to do in this weird way was reclaim consumer space on an erotic level. I don't mean erotic by taking my dick out, I mean by being a physical being. I see the revolution that happened in the East, and in a weird way it wasn't political, was it? It was a consumer revolution; people want to *buy* fucking *things*. The critique of the 1980s is right on, it's true; the continuous, rapid growth of the economy is a bunch of bullshit. But at the same time there's another world to look at it. I think that somehow it's attached to sex, desire and eroticism. So maybe it is with us and the answer is, somehow, reclaiming it in some other way, reclaiming that space. I'm not talking about being a yuppie. With that mannequin I wasn't doing a critique but creating moral territory, putting myself in the department store. I can't really put it into that type of intellectual discourse; my intellect is whatever comes out of the work.'

And then we hung up.

Francesco Bonami, 'Charles Ray: A Telephone Conversation', *Flash Art*, 25: 165 (Summer 1992) 98-100.

Miwon KWON
Bloody Valentines: Afterimages by Ana Mendieta [1996]

'There is no original past to redeem: there is the void, the orphanhood, the unbaptized earth of the beginning, the time that from within the earth looks upon us. There is above all the search for origin.'
– Ana Mendieta[1]

[...] Of the *Silueta* series, perhaps the most reproduced if not the most powerful set of Mendieta's works, the artist wrote in 1981, 'My art ... is a return to the maternal source. Through my earth/body sculptures I become one with the earth ... I become an extension of nature and nature becomes an extension of my body. This obsessive act of reasserting my ties with the earth is really the reactivation of primeval beliefs ... [in] an omnipresent female force, the after-image of being encompassed within the womb, in a manifestation of my thirst for being.'[2] Both male and female critics, perhaps taking their cues from the artist, continue to view the strength of Mendieta's work as essentially female – as artistic imagery and power exclusive to women. William Zimmer commented rather crudely in 1979, 'Mendieta offers photographs of alterations she has made on landscape sites. These marks are dubbed 'silhouettes' but are really vaginas on the hillside or on the grass. The Abstract Expressionists wished to identify their bodies with the earth but, as men, couldn't come this close.'[3] A more recent reviewer stridently asserted: 'Mendieta hails women as omnipotent creators, not slavish biological reproducers ... Female body one with the earthen core, the feminine creative spirit reasserts her fertile sovereignty. The female force becomes primary mover.'[4] Fellow artist Nancy Spero in a tribute to Ana Mendieta noted the timeless quality of this feminine creative force: 'If one of her sculptures were sent to a distant planet, or were kept sealed for thousands of years on earth, it would still convey the imagery, strength, mystery and sexuality of the female human form – woman's body and spirit inscribed.'[5]

Countless others have interpreted Mendieta's schematic and iconographic use of the female body in her earth/body works of the 1970s as an 'affirmation of female power, the female body, the female will, and women's bonds and heritage'.[6] But often projected as a kind of (feminist) primitivist fantasy, this female power has been configured as a primordial natural force, exceeding historical and cultural specificities. In characterizations like 'Ana Mendieta's Primal Scream: With Fire, Water, Blood, and Earth as Her Medium, This Cuban-Born Artist was the High Priestess of Performance Work',[7] and 'Ana *became* the earth and the earth goddess became Ana. By 1980, when the [*Silueta*] series ended, Ana and the goddess were one',[8] the wilful identification of the artist with some elemental, (super)natural feminine power was emphatic. Recruiting the imagery, ritual and symbolism of various goddess-worshipping religions and traditions, Mendieta, like many other women artists of the period, claimed power through a process of self-othering – a self-primitivizing that located the 'feminine' and 'woman' anterior to historical time (moving to *pre*history) and outside 'civilized' cultural spaces (siting the work in the 'other' space of nature or treating the body as a natural site).[9] Mendieta, of course, did both. And the allure of her identity as a Third World woman artist surely added to the exoticism of her works in light of the entrenched primitivist tendencies of 1970s feminist discourse and in the general discourse on Western modernism.

Yet something enigmatic remains, especially concerning the configuration of the *Silueta* series, a peculiarity that spills over and exceeds this feminist framing. Mendieta's use of her/the body almost always approached erasure or negation: her 'body' consistently disappeared. This is striking given that most feminist artists during the 1970s vied for visibility and self-affirming expression through figurative, literal, sometimes 'in-your-face' presence. It is curious that Mendieta traced her absence instead. Even when considered within a broader context of other contemporary experiments in earth/body works, such as Dennis Oppenheim's *Rocked Hand* (1970) or Charles Simonds' *Landscape–Body–Dwelling* (1970), Mendieta's substitution of negative imprints for positive figures seems anomalous. Her sensibility as expressed in exemplary works like the *Silueta* series, in other words, cannot be attributed simply to her sex [...]

1 Undated note by Ana Mendieta, as cited by Robert Katz in 'Naked by the Window: The Fatal Marriage of Carl Andre and Ana Mendieta', *Atlantic Monthly Press* (1990) 123.

2 Ana Mendieta, as quoted by John Perreault in 'Earth and Fire, Mendieta's Body of Work', *Ana Mendieta: A Retrospective* (New York: New Museum of Contemporary Art, 1987) 10.

3 William Zimmer, 'Artists Only', *SoHo Weekly News* (1979), as quoted by Petra Berraras del Rio in 'Ana Mendieta: A Historical Overview', *Ana Mendieta: A Retrospective*, *op. cit.*, 33.

4 Nancy Shalala, 'Artist Gets Physical for Feminism', *Japan Times* (27 September 1992) 11.

5 Nancy Spero, 'Tracing Ana Mendieta', *Artforum* (April 1992) 77.

6 Whitney Chadwick, *Women, Art and Society* (London: Thames and Hudson, 1990) 324. See also Lucy R. Lippard, *Overlay: Contemporary Art and the Art of Prehistory* (New

York: Pantheon, 1983), for a similar characterization.

7 Title of an article by Heidi Rauch and Federico Suro in *Américas*, 44: 5 (1992) 45-48.

8 Rachel Mendieta, 'Ana Mendieta: Self-Portrait of a Goddess', *Review: Latin American Literature and Arts* (January-June 1988) 39.

9 Of course, many male artists of the period invoked and searched for 'other' sites, too, often in nature – Charles Simonds, Dennis Oppenheim, Robert Morris, Robert Smithson, Richard Long and Michael Heizer, among others. But as many feminist art historians have noted, their works tended to be gestures of control and domination of nature rather than respectful homages to it. Such a critique, however, is based on a problematic identification of the female body with the earth, which puts into equivalence women's itinerant vulnerability, in sociopolitical terms, with the earth's physical vulnerability. In contradistinction to the male artists' ventures into nature, Nancy Spero wrote of Mendieta's work: 'Ana did not rampage the earth to control or dominate or create grandiose monuments of power and authority. She sought intimate, recessed spaces, protective habitats signalling a temporary respite of comfort and meditation.' *op. cit.*, 77.

Miwon Kwon, 'Bloody Valentines: Afterimages by Ana Mendieta', *Inside the Visible: An Elliptical Traverse of Twentieth-Century Art*, ed. M. Catherine de Zegher (Cambridge, Massachusetts and London: MIT Press, 1996) 165-71.

Margaret SUNDELL Vanishing Points: The Photography of Francesca Woodman [1996]

I was shown a small book with pictures. Francesca Woodman: born 1958. First photograph 1970. Suicide 1981. The points of life like a chart, graphed on a line from A to B to C. But the pictures inscribed a geometry that was far more complex. Like tangents, they shot off, sometimes dipping back to meet the line but, in the end, always slipping beyond its strictures.

Helen Wilson, a painter and close friend of Francesca Woodman, calls her photographs 'diary pictures'. The term refers to their intimate scale (with the exception of a series of monumental blueprints, none exceed 20 × 25-cm [8 × 10-in] and many are smaller still), but even more to their exceedingly personal sensibility. There are few close-ups; views of Woodman's face are rare, and she often used friends as models. Yet it is hard not to read these works, produced during Woodman's late teens and early twenties, as an ongoing series of self-portraits, a map of the artist's own evolution – both as a potential object of others' desire and as a creator of images.

Behind the search for self in Woodman's photographs, however, lies the insistent cultivation of a liminal space. Woodman's frequent use of serial images pushes the limits of the photographic frame, as does the voyeuristic complicity that many of her works establish with the viewer. In content, Woodman's photographs seek out and surpass the borders between subject and object, self and environment, and in sensibility they reveal a moment hovering precariously between adolescence and adulthood. The *House* series (1975–76) exemplifies this play of physical and psychic limits. Crouching beneath a fireplace, or blurring her body into a ghostly spectre through overly long exposures, Woodman stages an elaborate game of hide-and-seek with the peeling walls and chipped floors of an abandoned dwelling. Like Charlotte Perkins' *The Yellow Wallpaper*, this series can be seen as a nightmare of femininity, the literal engulfing of a woman by her domestic role. But Woodman's childish attire – her flowered dress, white stockings and black Mary Janes – recall a second work of fiction, *Alice in Wonderland*. In addition to the potentially feminist message, the series conveys a sense of 'playing house', of the way a child feels at once overwhelmed and omnipotently invisible when infiltrating a place that adults once owned.

If Woodman's preoccupation is limits, the examination of them is consistently grounded in the body or, more precisely, in the act of bringing the body into relation with an outside element that destabilizes it and renders it liminal. Rosalind Krauss has defined Woodman's aesthetic strategy as 'the subjectification of the objective language, the immediate instinct to register the formal within the "support" of the body'.[1] Ann Gabhart's statement that 'fascinated by the sensuous and tactile qualities of objects, she always saw them in relation to the soft aloofness of flesh'[2] stands as a corollary to Krauss' emphasis on the objective language of visual form. In her photographs Woodman sets the body first against the material surfaces of the world that surrounds it and then against the geometry that contains it. In *Space Squared* (1975–76), for example, space becomes both metaphor and fact of the body at its limits, as Woodman pushes herself against the confines of the glass case that encloses her. The material and the formal come together to comprise the external reality either inscribed on to Woodman's body or animated through association with her presence [...]

Describing Woodman's work, curator Matthew Teitelbaum states that, 'It is as if, by making herself a subject to be looked at, she makes herself disappear. Indeed, many of her photographs convey a tension between bodily presence and bodily absence. In works from the *Angel* series (1977) for example, or from the *Self-Deceit* series (1978), she often reaches out of the picture frame, spins out of focus, hides behind an object, or twists her body away from the viewer.'[3] The fragility of self-recognition necessitates an endless restaging of the subject's autonomy. The tension and strength of Woodman's work lies in her ability to return again and again to this precise point of instability, to simultaneously create and explode the fragile membrane that protects one's identity from being absorbed by its surroundings [...]

For all the penetration of limits, Woodman's photographs ultimately lead the viewer to a perimeter that cannot be traversed. As a genre, the self-portrait seems to promise self-knowledge and mastery of one's image in the world. But if Woodman's photographs initially aim at knowing the self, they attest finally to the limits of such knowledge – or rather, to the knowledge that the self, no matter how often approached, is never fully captured by its representations. A picture from the series *I Stopped Playing the Piano* (1977), entitled *I Could No Longer Play I Could Not Play by Instinct*, makes this revelation startlingly clear. Woodman, chest bared and face cropped from the frame, wields a knife while a string of photo-booth self-portraits drips from her breast like blood. Echoing the self-consciousness of its title, the photograph presents the quest for self-knowledge as an act of mutilation that results not in the capturing of a 'true' self but in the production of a never-ending chain of images.

I would like to thank Betty and George Woodman for supporting my interest in their daughter's work. I am also grateful to Rosalind Krauss and Mary Kelly for their comments on an earlier version of this essay, which appeared under the same title in *Documents*, 3 (Summer 1993).

1 Rosalind Krauss, 'Problem Sets', in *Francesca Woodman: Photographic Work*, ed. Ann Gabhart (Massachusetts: Wellesley College Museum, 1986) 47.

2 Ann Gabhart, 'Francesca Woodman 1958-1981', in *Francesca Woodman: Photographic Work*, *op. cit.*, 54.

3 Matthew Teitelbaum, 'Absent Bodies' (Boston: Institute of Contemporary Art, 1992) n.p.

Margaret Sundell, 'Vanishing Points: The Photography of Francesca Woodman', *Inside the Visible: An Elliptical Traverse of Twentieth-Century Art*, ed. M. Catherine de Zegher (Cambridge, Massachusetts and London: MIT Press, 1996) 435-49.

EXTENDED AND PROSTHETIC BODIES

Due to late twentieth-century technological advances, the body can be extended in extraordinary ways. Artists have used these advances to extend their bodies. In some cases, for example Lygia Clark and James Lee Byars, this extension is used as a new means to communicate, opening different channels. Lygia Clark also extends the body through her concentration on states of consciousness and dreams. Lucy Orta extends the body for protection, creating clothes which act to shelter and protect. Scientist and theorist Donna Haraway explores our physical relationship with technology. She believes that man has become a hybrid between a machine and an organism, and that we have all become cyborgs in a post-gendered world, a 'condensed image of imagination and material reality'. Cyborgs and technology herald a new age, in which there is a new logic behind our being, no longer based solely on our idea of ourselves as an organism.

Lygia CLARK

About the Act [1965]

For the first time I have discovered a new reality not in myself but *in the world*. I encountered a *Trailing*, an internal journey *outside myself*. Before, the *Beast* emerged from me, bursting out in an obsessional explosion, in all directions. Now, for the first time, with the *Trailing*, it's just the opposite. I perceive the whole of the world as a single, global rhythm that stretches from Mozart to the footwork of a soccer game on the beach.

Architectural space overwhelms me. To paint a picture on a surface or to make a sculpture is so different from living in architectural terms! Now, I am no longer alone. I am pumped up by others. Perception so powerful that I feel myself torn up from my roots. Unstable in space. I feel as though I were in the process of disintegrating. To live perception, *to be* perception ...

These days I am almost continually ill. I can swallow nothing and my body deserts me. Who is the *Beast* – myself? I become an abstract existence. I sink in real depths, without connections to my work – which looks at me from a distance and from outside myself. 'Is it I who did that?' Upheavals. A hysterical sense of leaking. Only a thread holds me fast. My body has left me – *trailing*. Dead? Living? I am extinguished by odours, sensations of touch, the heat of the sun, dreams.

A monster surges up from the sea, surrounded by living fish. The sun shines intensely when suddenly it begins to go out. The fish: dead, their white bellies upward. Then the sun shines again, and the fish are alive. The monster has disappeared into the depths, the fish along with him. I am saved.

Another dream: in the inside which is the outside, a window and myself. Through this window I want to pass to the *outside* which is the *inside* for me. When I wake up, the window of my room is the one from my dream; the *inside* I was looking for is the space outside. The *Beast* which I called 'inside and outside' was born from this dream. It's a stainless-steel structure, supple and deformable. There's a void at the centre of the structure. When you manipulate it, this inner void gives the structure completely new aspects. I consider 'inside and outside' as the completion of my experiments with the *Beasts* (just before 'inside and outside', I worked out another *Beast* without hinges which I called 'before and after').

Often I awaken before the window of my room – looking for the exterior space as though it were 'inside'. I am afraid of space – but I reconstruct myself by means of it. During crises, it escapes me. It's as though we played – myself and it – at cat and mouse, at winner loses.

I am before and after, I am the future now.

I am inside and outside, front and back.

What strikes me in the 'inside and outside' sculpture is that it transforms my perception of myself, of my body. It changes me. I am elastic, formless, without definite physiognomy. Its lungs are mine. It's the introjection of the cosmos. And at the same time it's my own ego crystallized as an object in space. 'Inside and outside': a living being open to all possible transformations. Its internal space is an affective space.

In a dialogue with my 'inside and outside' work, an active subject encounters his or her own precariousness. No more than does the *Beast*, the subject no longer has a static physiognomy that is self-defining. The subject discovers the ephemeral in opposition to all types of crystallization. Space is now a kind of *time ceaselessly metamorphosed through action*. Subject and object become essentially identified within the act.

Fullness. I am overflowing with meaning. Each time I breathe, the rhythm is natural, fluid. It adheres to action. I have become aware of my 'cosmic lungs'. I penetrate the world's total rhythm. The world is my lung. Is this fusion death? Why does this fullness have the taste of death? I am so incredibly alive ... How to connect these two poles always? Often in my life I have discovered the identity of life and death. A discovery which none the less has a new flavour each time. One night, I had the perception that the absolute was this 'full-void', this totality of the interior with the exterior I've spoken of so often. The 'full-void' contains all potentialities. It's the *act* which gives it meaning.

The act in the process of happening is time. I wonder if

the absolute is not the sum of all acts? Would this be space -time – where time, trailing along, continually makes and remakes itself? This absolute time would be born of itself.

We are a spatio-temporal totality. In the immanent act we see no temporal limit. Past, present, future, mix together. We exist before the afterward – but the afterward anticipates the act. The afterward is implied in the act in the process of happening. If time lives in the instant of the act, what comes out of the act is incorporated into the perception of absolute time. There is no distance between the past and the present. When one looks backward, the distant past and the recent past fuse.

Perhaps none of this is clear. But the proof of the perception I had is the only thing I cling to.

Lygia Clark, 'De l'act', *Robho*, 4 (1965) 17; reprinted in English as 'About the Act', trans. Yve-Alain Bois, *October*, 69 (Summer 1994) 102-104.

Rebecca HORN

Arm Extensions [1968]

From her chest to her feet she is wrapped in criss-crossing bandages like a mummy. All movement becomes impossible. Both arms are imbedded in thickly wadded stumps, which serve as balancing props for her body. After being tied up for a while, the subject gains the impression that, in spite of her erect posture, her arms are gradually touching the ground, as if they were actually growing into the floor and turning into 'isolating columns' fixed to her own body.

Rebecca Horn, 'Arm-Extensionen' (1968), in *Zeichnungen, Objekte, Video, Filme* (Cologne: Kunstverein, 1977) 24; reprinted as 'Arm Extensions' in *Rebecca Horn* (New York: Solomon R. Guggenheim Foundation, 1993) 69.

STELARC

Artist's statement [1977]

THIS PLANET IS CRUSHING MY CORTEX
I'm tired of my 64-kg [141-lb] weight, I'm tired of this gravitational conspiracy, I want to unplug my body from this planet.
My hemispheres want to hover, but this gravity is containing me.
This paranoid planet is crushing my vortex.
VICARIOUS VICIOUSNESS ASSAULTS THE ENICSTASY
We inhabit a planet of data and documentation. Data has become destructive, content has been consumed by complexity.
The role of information has changed – information now is so fragmentary, so conflicting and so overwhelming that it tends to confuse rather than clarify. External excessive information mystifies; danger – this documentation is deceptive.
FREEDOM OF FORM
In this age of information overload, only physical commitment is meaningful. In this age of information overload, what is significant is not freedom of ideas, but rather freedom of form.
Will society allow you freedom of form, freedom to tamper with your body? [...]
PHYSICAL COMMITMENT FRIGHTENS
In this age of global communications the tyranny of brainwashing becomes obsolete.
The tyranny of the future will not be changing your mind, but rather preventing you from changing your body, keeping you confined within your limited genetic parameters.
SUBSTANCE SUPERSEDES SYMBOL
In this age of vicarious viciousness symbols are no longer adequate. Modification of the body is the ritual for its ultimate mutation. Conscious modification and mutation compresses evolution in time. Conscious evolution will not be evolution of the mass by chance, but rather evolution of the individual by choice.
Evolution by the individual, for the individual.
TECHNOLOGY IMPLANTED – EVOLUTION EXTERNALIZED
NASA's act is not the accumulation of extra-terrestrial data. When NASA thought it was blasting off probes to explore the solar system, it was, in fact, imploding miniaturized technology back to the body. Technology is hurtling back towards our bodies with increasing speed and inevitable accuracy, focusing physical change on each individual body and its micro-structure, modifying our DNA destiny. NASA is an evolutionary planetary surgeon imploding, implanting. Technology, emanating from the human body, now returns, physically modifying it, creating a creature to supersede the human species.
We are obsolete, and we know it.
The body as an organization is obsolete.
THIS PLANET IS CRUSHING MY CORTEX
I'm tired of this gravitational conspiracy. I want to unplug my body from this planet. I want to by-pass this planet. I want to bypass this body [...]
My hemispheres want to hover in Zero G.

Stelarc, 'Artist's statement' (1977), *Flash Art*, 80-81 (February-April, 1978) 54.

Howard JUNKER

James Lee Byars: Performance as Protective Colouration [1978]

[...] For Byars art is the way, perhaps the only way, of being in and of this world. He is thus the archetypical artist-in-resident ... wherever he is. In 1969 he commandeered Eugenia Butler's gallery in Los Angeles, had its door sealed, its skylight covered and one wall painted red. He solicited statements about himself from friends and acquaintances, and the piece, according to Thomas H. Garver, became a celebration of 'the cult of James Byars': viewers crawled through a small round hole into darkness to listen to Byars reading quotes by and about Byars.

All this may seem terribly self-indulgent – for Garver, the 'idea ... of an epicentre of the thought by and about James Lee Byars is more interesting than the actuality'. And during the 1970s, self art/body art became quite trivial. But Byars was not using himself as material the way Acconci did, burning the hair off his chest, or as Burden did, having his arm shot with a 22-calibre gun. Byars was making a gesture towards talking about himself, about sharing himself with friends. He called the piece, *The Ghost of James Lee Byars Speaking*. And it was the gesture of an extremely withdrawn man, a man who could produce signals only at great cost, at great danger to himself.

These signals, therefore, had to be disguised, had to be presented where they would probably escape unnoticed or, if noticed, would easily be waved off. Above all, their desperate urgency could not be admitted.

In *The Perfect Kiss* Byars presents himself with the absolute certainty that no one will kiss him back and with near certainty that most people will miss the alleged act, the kiss, completely, because it goes by so fast, Byars will be noticed – he insists on it – but only as long as he is simultaneously not noticed. He is not an autobiographical artist; he is profoundly anti-confessional.

The Perfect Kiss was accompanied at Berkeley by a performance-sculpture Byars had had made in Japan in 1963, but had never been asked to perform ... The piece is 1,000 squares of 'perfect' white rice paper, folded into a 46-cm [1.5-ft] cube. Unfolded on the main floor of the museum into a giant comb-shape, this dazzling piece, extraordinarily delicate, like an Ad Reinhardt black painting, the antipodes of a Carl Andre, became – somewhat to Byars' dismay, since he much prefers perfection – a series of ridges and valleys, a rectilinear Mercator projection of a snowy world, the perfect paper equivalent of a Japanese sand garden.

One day, after the piece had been deployed, statements were read by four men in tuxedos standing at the corners. (One reader was the curator of the exhibit, another the director of the museum – it is difficult not to become implicated in Byars' 'fat projects'.) The key statement was from Kafka's story, 'The Great Wall of China', the parable of the messenger sent 'to give you a message' from the Emperor who may or may not have been executed. The messenger is defeated by the distance to be travelled, by the labyrinth of the city. In short, 'nobody could fight his way through here even with a message from a dead man. But you sit at your window when evening falls and dream it to yourself.'

So it is with Byars: the message (from the dead man?) is impossible to deliver, but it can be apprehended in reverie. Others – The Other – can only be approached with caution, if at all; probably it is best to remain at a great distance or, at least, to begin any encounter with pre-emptive violence.

Beuys, for example, once invited Byars to his show at the ICA in London. Byars went with his friend, a 41-kg [90-lb] German woman whom Byars had trained in the martial art of throwing people to the ground. As Beuys approached them, she threw him to the ground, pinned his arms and whispered in his ear.

According to Jacqueline Barnitz, in *Can't*, a play Byars

proposed in 1969, 'a man and a woman unknown to each other' stand at either end of a mile-long strip of red acetate. They keep the fabric taut: 'If either participant moves, the other will know it by the change in the fabric's tension. At the end of the play, its two participants leave without ever meeting' [...]

Howard Junker, 'James Lee Byars: Performance as Protective Colouration', *Art in America* (November-December 1978) 109-13.

Donna HARAWAY

A Cyborg Manifesto: Science, Technology and Socialist-Feminism in the Late Twentieth Century [1985]

AN IRONIC DREAM OF A COMMON LANGUAGE FOR WOMEN IN THE INTEGRATED CIRCUIT

[...] By the late twentieth century, our time, a mythic time, we are all chimeras, theorized and fabricated hybrids of machine and organism; in short, we are cyborgs. The cyborg is our ontology; it gives us our politics. The cyborg is a condensed image of both imagination and material reality, the two joined centres structuring any possibility of historical transformation. In the traditions of 'Western' science and politics – the tradition of racist, male-dominant capitalism; the tradition of progress; the tradition of the appropriation of nature as resource for the productions of culture; the tradition of reproduction of self from the reflections of the other – the relation between organism and machine has been a border war. The stakes in the border war have been the territories of production, reproduction and imagination. This is an argument for *pleasure* in the confusion of boundaries and for *responsibility* in their construction. It is also an effort to contribute to socialist-feminist culture and theory in a Postmodernist, non-naturalist mode and in the utopian tradition of imagining a world without gender, which is perhaps a world without genesis, but maybe also a world without end. The cyborg incarnation is outside salvation history. Nor does it mark time on an oedipal calendar, attempting to heal the terrible cleavages of gender in an oral symbiotic utopia or post-oedipal apocalypse. As Zoe Sofoulis argues in her unpublished manuscript on Jacques Lacan, Melanie Klein and nuclear culture, *Lacklein*, the most terrible and perhaps the most promising monsters in cyborg worlds are embodied in non-oedipal narratives with a different logic of repression, which we need to understand for our survival.

The cyborg is a creature in a post-gender world; it has no truck with bisexuality, pre-oedipal symbiosis, unalienated labour, or other seductions to organic wholeness through a final appropriation of all the powers of the parts into a higher unity. In a sense, the cyborg has no origin story in the Western sense – a 'final' irony since the cyborg is also the awful apocalyptic *telos* of the 'West's' escalating dominations of abstract individuation, an ultimate self untied at last from all dependency, a man in space. An origin story in the 'Western', humanist sense depends on the myth of original unity, fullness, bliss and terror, represented by the phallic mother from whom all humans must separate, the task of individual development and of history, the twin potent myths inscribed most powerfully for us in psychoanalysis and Marxism. Hilary Klein has argued that both Marxism and psychoanalysis, in their concepts of labour and of individuation and gender formation, depend on the plot of original unity out of which difference must be produced and enlisted in a drama of escalating domination of woman/nature. The cyborg is resolutely committed to partiality, irony, intimacy and perversity. It is oppositional, utopian and completely without innocence. No longer structured by the polarity of public and private, the cyborg defines a technological *polis* based partly on a revolution of social relations in the *oikos*, the household. Nature and culture are reworked; the one can no longer be the resource for appropriation or incorporation by the other. The relationships for forming wholes from parts, including those of polarity and hierarchical domination, are at issue in the cyborg world. Unlike the hopes of Frankenstein's monster, the cyborg does not expect its father to save it through a restoration of the garden; that is, through the fabrication of a heterosexual mate, through its completion in a finished whole, a city and a cosmos. The cyborg does not dream of community on the model of the organic family, this time without the oedipal project. The cyborg would not recognize the Garden of Eden; it is not made of mud and cannot dream of returning to dust. Perhaps that is why I want to see if cyborgs can subvert the apocalypse of returning to nuclear dust in the manic compulsion to name the enemy. Cyborgs are not reverent; they do not re-member the cosmos. They are wary of holism, but needy for connection – they seem to have a natural feel for united front politics, but without the vanguard party. The main trouble with cyborgs, of course, is that they are the illegitimate offspring of militarism and patriarchal capitalism, not to mention state socialism. But illegitimate offspring are often exceedingly unfaithful to their origins. Their fathers, after all, are inessential.

I will return to the science fiction of cyborgs at the end of this chapter, but now I want to signal three crucial boundary breakdowns that make the following political-fictional (political-scientific) analysis possible. By the late twentieth century in United States scientific culture, the boundary between human and animal is thoroughly breached. The last beachheads of unique-use, social behaviour, mental events, nothing really convincingly settles the separation of human and animal. And many people no longer feel the need for such a separation; indeed, many branches of feminist culture affirm the pleasure of connection of human and other living creatures. Movements for animal rights are not irrational denials of human uniqueness; they are a clear-sighted recognition of connection across the discredited breach of nature and culture. Biology and evolutionary theory over the last two centuries have simultaneously produced modern organisms as objects of knowledge and reduced the line between humans and animals to a faint trace re-etched in ideological struggle or professional disputes between life and social science. Within this framework, teaching modern Christian creationism should be fought as a form of child abuse.

[...] The second leaky distinction is between animal-human (organism) and machine. Pre-cybernetic machines could be haunted; there was always the spectre of the ghost in the machine. This dualism structured the dialogue between materialism and idealism that was settled by a dialectical progeny, called spirit or history, according to taste. But basically machines were not self-moving, self-designing, autonomous. They could not achieve man's dream, only mock it. They were not man, an author to himself, but only a caricature of that masculinist reproductive dream. To think they were otherwise was paranoid. Now we are not so sure. Late twentieth-century machines have made thoroughly ambiguous the difference between natural and artificial, mind and body, self-developing and externally designed, and many other distinctions that used to apply to organisms and machines. Our machines are disturbingly lively, and we ourselves frighteningly inert.

[...] The third distinction is a subset of the second: the boundary between physical and non-physical is very imprecise for us. Pop physics books on the consequences of quantum theory and the indeterminacy principle are a kind of popular scientific equivalent to Harlequin romances (the US equivalent of Mills & Boon) as a marker of radical change in American white heterosexuality: they get it wrong, but they are on the right subject. Modern machines are quintessentially microelectronic devices: they are everywhere and they are invisible. Modern machinery is an irreverent upstart god, mocking the Father's ubiquity and spirituality. The silicon chip is a surface for writing; it is etched in molecular scales disturbed only by atomic noise, the ultimate interference for nuclear scores. Writing, power and technology are old partners in Western stories of the origin of civilization, but miniaturization has turned out to be about power; small is not so much beautiful as pre-eminently dangerous, as in cruise missiles. Contrast the TV sets of the 1950s or the news cameras of the 1970s with the TV wrist bands or hand-sized video cameras now advertised. Our best machines are made of sunshine; they are all light and clean because they are nothing but signals, electromagnetic waves, a section of a spectrum, and these machines are eminently portable, mobile – a matter of immense human pain in Detroit and Singapore. People are nowhere near so fluid, being both material and opaque. Cyborgs are ether, quintessence.

Donna Haraway, 'A Cyborg Manifesto: Science, Technology and Socialist-Feminism in the Late Twentieth Century' (1985), *Simians, Cyborgs and Women: The Reinvention of Nature* (New York and London: Routledge, 1991) 149-81.

Stuart MORGAN

Matthew Barney: Of Goats and Men [1995]

[...] By 1991, when Barney's 'New Work' exhibition was presented at the San Francisco Museum of Modern Art, titles were turgid and drawings were obscure, but the sense of an evolving private language was unmistakable. Titling had become poetry, cross-referencing had lurched out of control until every work seemed part of every other, the tone was humorous, and the joke was a smutty one. Penetration, masturbation, constipation and lubrication featured in the terminology, as well as obscure puns ... And if the regalia of the male figure in Barney's performances was sportsmanlike and heroic, with swimming, baseball, rock-climbing and gymnastics merging into one activity, his female counterpart, played by Barney posing in a white robe, toque and 1950s swimsuit, seemed the epitome of nimbleness and grace. Not even her white gloves and dark glasses could prevent her bouncing a pearl into an elaborately stretched hole designed to receive it by cutting through a skin-like fabric and holding the incision open with a clamp. Shifts between conventional sexual roles, between states and conditions (hard and soft, frozen and liquid, captivity and freedom); the references to protection by coated surfaces (Pyrex, Teflon, Silicon): above all the use of materials such as 'human chorionic gonadotropin', relate to the sex act. But *which* sex act, exactly? As in Duchamp's work – if the works in drag and the halving of *The Large Glass* are taken into account – the theme was gender itself, the test of gender being desire. For perhaps only desire can resolve the whole idea of sexing and of what 'masculine' or 'feminine' could mean [...]

A drum roll introduces a view of an impossibly long, Victorian pier jutting from a rocky, green landscape. To the drone of a bagpipe, the familiar CREMASTER logo is seen at speed, before Barney himself appears in a white performance space, his face more animal than human, the bright red hair offsetting the whiteness of the room, his suit and the white mistletoe in his buttonhole. As he combs his hair over them, we cannot help but notice the two strange holes in his head where his horns once were. The room is a pavilion at the very end of a mile-long pier, leading to a beach and a road. For the setting is the Isle of Man, a place where it comes as no surprise to encounter mutations. For man, on Man, may have become as much of a hybrid as the elaborately horned goats to be seen there or the rambling route of the Tourist Trophy motorcycle races. In this white room in the white pavilion, near the end of the long pier, three naked, muscled, red-haired, epicene figures pander to their master's every need [...]

The Isle of Man is an obvious place to make a film about masculinity. Or is it? Inbreeding produces freakish anomalies. Where did the idea of that three-legged man come from? Could it be a sign of rampant masculinity? (Do Manxmen have members the same length as their legs?) Or its opposite? (Three legs leave no room for genitalia.) Or some third alternative? In *Drawing Restraint 7*, flirtation or sport leads to the removal of the satyr's horns, which must be restored, for what would a satyr be without horns? That the creature Barney plays is not a goat is crucial, since the sign that he has successfully achieved his aim in his confrontation with a real regimental goat in tartan, the first thing to be seen as he emerges from his undersea journey. Perhaps a goat is to a satyr what a woman is to a drag queen: an object of envy and pity in equal quantities. For sexually, it is a primitive version of Barney's satyr: suave, fashionable, but lacking animal attraction. You are not born a woman; you become one, Simone de Beauvoir argued. That also applies to heroes. The undersea journey is paralleled in every mythology in the world. And, like this particular baptism, it takes place in tight spots. Crawling with difficulty up a symbolic sphincter is the last stage of the rebirthing process. Or is it a ritual of definition? ... As the action draws to a close, two separate objects, both elliptical like the two zeroes of the Jim Otto motif, appear and reappear: on the strange, symbolic tyre; on the ramps built to display the motorcycles after the race; above all, in the disturbing, mobile objects placed in the drivers' pockets, organs which take on a life of their own and crawl up the bodies of the duelling drivers [...]

Stuart Morgan, 'Matthew Barney: Of Goats and Men', *frieze*, 20 (January-February 1995) 35-38.

Paul VIRILIO

Urban Armour [1996]

I was first attracted to the work of Lucy Orta because of its situational nature. The problem of art today is one of delocalization. Art is no longer found in galleries and museums; it is found where ever-changing social situations condense. Art is one of the elements of a world vision and this relationship with the world is a constantly changing one. I first came across Lucy Orta's work where this relationship changes the most – in the street [...]

Lucy's work is an appeal to take on board a new relationship with the body. I recall that art has its origins in the body: dance and theatre, war paint and tattoos. Lucy Orta's work struck me as a style of rock painting inscribed on the body. Enveloped in Lucy's overalls, the being bears witness to the threat towards the body. This threat is linked not only to problems of unemployment and precariousness, factors which, as an architect, interest me a lot, but also to the drowning of the body in virtuality, to the creation of clones and to a remote intimacy. Lucy's collective wear reminds me of collective body practices which exist in the world of survival. The survival of most animals depends on running with the pack. The concept of the pack is linked to animality [...]

Each individual keeps an eye on, and protects, the other. One individual's life depends on the life of the other. In Lucy's work the warmth of one gives warmth to the other. The physical link weaves a social link. Revealed here are signs; symptoms which contradict the myth of comfort and also the desire to preserve the body, to save it from solitude and from death in solitude. I believe that Lucy's work can never be separated from the threat of regression that it invokes. Behind the innovation of this collective wear, overalls designed to protect from a real social threat, there is, at the same time, a sense of novelty and a fear of regression; a tragedy and a dramatic art form [...]

Paul Virilio, 'Urban Armour', *Lucy Orta: Refuge Wear* (Paris: Éditions Jean-Michel Place, 1996) n.p.

ARTISTS' BIOGRAPHIES

Marina ABRAMOVIC [b. 1946, Belgrade] lives in Paris and Amsterdam. She began using her body in performance in 1972, exploring themes of pain and physical resistance. From 1976-1988 she collaborated with East German artist Uwe Laysiepen (known as Ulay) making works which tested relationships between bodies. More recent work includes sculpture, video, installation and performances. She was included in Documenta 6, Kassel [1977] and the 47th Venice Biennale [1997]. Solo exhibitions include 'Freeing the Voice', De Appel Gallery, Amsterdam [1975], and 'Spirit House', Sean Kelly Gallery, New York [1998].

Vito ACCONCI [b. 1940, New York] lives in New York. Shifting from 'the page' of poetry to 'the body as the page' he began to make performance pieces in the 1960s in which he explored voyeurism and fantasy, and deconstructed the persona of the heroic male artist. He occasionally collaborated with artist Cathy Dillon. In the late 1970s-90s he moved on to create environments and architecture. Group exhibitions include 'Video Art', University of Pennsyvannia, Philadelphia [1975], and Documenta X, Kassel [1997]. Solo exhibitions include 'Headlines and Images', Stedelijk Museum, Amsterdam [1978], and Barbara Gladstone Gallery, New York [1998].

Bas Jan ADER [b. 1942, Winschoten, Holland; d. 1976] lived in Amsterdam and California. A Conceptual artist making photographs of himself as documents of staged events, he frequently presented sadness, failure and nostalgia. In a performance at Art & Project, Amsterdam [1972], he read aloud from the *Reader's Digest*. While undertaking the second part of a proposed three-part work in a solo voyage across the Atlantic Ocean [1976], he disappeared at sea. A retrospective of his work was shown at Openbaar Kunstbezit, Amsterdam [1988].

Laura AGUILAR [b. 1959, San Gabriel, California] makes work about her identity and status as a lesbian Hispanic-American, using black and white photographs and video. Her work was included in 'Shifting Terrains', Zone Gallery, Newcastle, England [1997], and 'Sexual Politics: Judy Chicago's *Dinner Party* in Feminist Art History', UCLA/Armand Hammer Museum of Art, Los Angeles [1996].

Eleanor ANTIN [b. 1935, New York] lives in California. She is best known for performances and photographic work in which she presents herself as historical archetypes, as allegories for explorations of the self and essentialist notions of female power. She was included in 'Video Art USA', São Paolo Biennale [1975], and 'Myths', The Museum of Modern Art, New York [1990]. A major retrospective was held at the Los Angeles County Museum of Art [1999].

Janine ANTONI [b. 1964, Freeport, Bahamas] lives in New York. She uses her body in relation to sculptural installations as a feminist intervention in art discourse, enacting daily rituals such as eating, cleaning and bathing on objects and materials with a specific art historical reference. Her work was shown at the 45th Venice Biennale [1993]. Solo exhibitions include 'Swoon', Whitney Museum of American Art, New York [1998].

Skip ARNOLD [b. 1957, Binghampton, New York] lives in California. He presents his life and his body as unmediated art, posing naked as sculpture in public spaces. His work was featured in the Osnabruck Medai Festival, Ontario [1991], and he held a solo show at Spencer Brownstone Gallery, New York [1997].

Ron ATHEY [b. 1961, Groton, Connecticut] lives in California. His work is informed by his fundamentalist upbringing in the Pentecostal church and subsequent depression and drug-abuse. His performances involve S&M practices, piercing and bloodletting and take place in nightclubs and venues such as LACE, Los Angeles, and P.S. 122, New York, where he performed *Four Scenes in a Harsh Life* [1994].

Mirosław BAŁKA [b. 1958, Warsaw, Poland] lives in Poland. His early works were figurative sculptures. Later work based on his body dimensions became more austere, using metal rods and wooden planks to suggest rather than delineate his presence. He participated in the 1998 São Paulo Biennale. Solo exhibitions include De Appel, Amsterdam [1991], and 'Revision', IVAM Centre del Carma, Valencia, Spain [1997].

Oladélé Ajiboyé BAMGBOYÉ [b. 1963, Nigeria] lives in London. He makes photographs, videos and films informed by the experience of growing up as a Nigerian immigrant in Scotland. He presents identity as multiple and ultimately subjective. He was included in documenta X, Kassel [1997]. Solo exhibitions include the Künstlerhaus Bethanien, Berlin [1998].

Matthew BARNEY [b. 1967, San Francisco] lives in New York. He presents sculptural installations made with props from his videos and films. His *Cremaster* film series allegorizes the stages in the sexual differentiation of an embryo through elaborate use of costume, prosthetics and role-play. His work was exhibited in 'Viral Infection: The Body and its Discontents', Hallwalls Contemporary Art Center, Buffalo [1990], and the 46th Venice Biennale [1995]. Solo shows include Boymans-van Beuningen Museum, Rotterdam [1996].

Lynda BENGLIS [b. 1941, Lake Charles, Louisiana] lives in New York. Her early work examined the relation between painting and sculpture. Work in the 1970s explored power relations between the sexes, both alone and in collaboration with Robert Morris. In the 1980s she began making organic sculptures. Her work was included in 'Contemporary Women: Consciousness and Content', Brooklyn Museum, New York [1977]. Solo shows include Paula Cooper Gallery, New York [1970], and Cheim & Read Gallery, New York [1998].

Joseph BEUYS [1921-86, Germany] became one of the most influential figures in Germany's post-war artistic revival. His actions, sculptural installations (using fat and felt) and political activities, combined the metaphors of his personal symbolism with a quest for spiritual healing. He represented Germany in the Venice Biennale [1976] and participated in Documenta 7, Kassel [1982]. Major retrospectives of his work were held at the Solomon R. Guggenheim Museum, New York [1979], and the Musée national d'Art Moderne, Centre Georges Pompidou, Paris [1994].

Keith BOADWEE [b. 1961, Mississippi] lives in California. His work deconstructs the traditional macho identity of the action painter through videos and photographs of his painting practice. He was included in 'Bad Girls', New Museum of Contemporary Art, New York [1994]. His solo exhibitions include Gallery 207, Los Angeles [1999].

Louise BOURGEOIS [b. 1911, Paris] lives in New York. Much of her work features the organic body and embattled feminine identity. Her work was included in many group exhibitions at The Museum of Modern Art, New York [from 1943 to present]. She represented the US at the 45th Venice Biennale [1993]. Solo shows include an exhibition of paintings at Bertha Schaefer Gallery, New York [1945], and the Tate Gallery of Modern Art, London [2000].

Leigh BOWERY [b.1961, Melbourne, Australia; d. 1994, London] came to London in 1980. He appeared in extraordinary costumes and makeup in the London fashion and underground clubbing scenes. In 1993 he formed the rock band Minty, and performed his notorious 'birth' piece at numerous venues and events including the 'Fête Worse Than Death', Hoxton Square, London [1994]. A posthumous exhibition was held at Tanya Bonakdar Gallery, New York [1995].

Stuart BRISLEY [b. 1933, Surrey, England] lives in London. His performances address issues of socio-political power through deprivation, physical endurance and repetition. His work was included in the São Paolo Biennale [1985]. Solo shows include a retrospective at the Institute of Contemporary Arts, London [1981], and the Serpentine Gallery, London [1987].

Günter BRUS [b. 1938, Ardning, Austria] lives in Berlin. In the early 1960s he joined the Viennese Actionists and began to perform 'actions' using his body as the site for increasingly violent processes, which he named 'Body Analysis'. Since his last action *Zereissprobe* [1970] he has made drawings and literary works. He was included in 'Limite du visible', Musée nationale d'Art Moderne, Centre Georges

Pompidou, Paris [1993]. An exhibition of his drawings was shown at the Whitechapel Art Gallery, London [1980].

Chris BURDEN [b. 1946, Boston] lives in California. His early performances using his own body as material were shocking for their realism and danger. Since the 1980s his work has evolved into monumental sculptures and installations. He was included in 'l'art corporel', Galerie Stadler, Paris [1975], and in Whitney Biennales, New York [1977; 1989; 1993]. Solo exhibitions include 'B-Car', Ronald Feldman Fine Arts, New York [1977], and 'Beyond the Limits: Machines and Models. Power, Time and Distance', Museum of Applied Arts, Vienna [1996].

James Lee BYARS [b. 1932, Detroit; d. 1997, Cairo] lived and worked in the US and Japan. Informed by Western philosophy and Eastern spiritualism, Byars' art-making investigated perfection and ephemerality through performance, photography, books, objects and installations. His later works used precious materials such as gold and marble. His work was shown at Documentas 5, 6, 7 and 8, Kassel [1977; 1982; 1987; 1992]. Solo shows include 'The Perfect Love Letter', Palais des Beaux-Arts, Brussels [1974], and 'JLB - The Epitaph of Conceptual Art is Which Questions Have Disappeared?', Kestner Gesellschaft, Hannover [1999].

CÉSAR [b. César Baldaccini, 1921, Marseille] lives in Paris. He is a sculptor who works principally with scrap metal and plastics. In the 1960s he created a new sculptural concept by presenting compressed car bodies as art. He represented France at the 46th Venice Biennale [1995]. Solo shows include retrospectives at the Stedelijk Museum, Amsterdam [1966], and the Galerie nationale du Jeu de Paume, Paris [1997].

Helen CHADWICK [b. 1953, Croydon; d. 1996, London] made sculpture, installations and photographic works investigating feminine identity in art history and contemporary culture. She was included in 'ARS '95', Museum of Contemporary Art, Helsinki [1995]. Solo shows include 'Growing Up', National Portrait Gallery, London [1983], and the Museum of Modern Art, Tel Aviv [1997].

Judy CHICAGO [b. 1939, Chicago] lives in New Mexico. She was a vital figure in the feminist art movement in California in the 1970s, and was a founding member of Womanhouse [1972]. Her work encompasses painting, sculpture and needlepoint and focuses on images of female sexuality. She has published autobiographical books including *Through the Flower: My Struggle as a Woman Artist* [1973]. She was included in 'Sexual Politics: Judy Chicago's *Dinner Party* in Feminist Art History', UCLA/Armand Hammer Museum of Art, Los Angeles [1996]. Solo exhibitions include 'Trials and Tributes', Florida State University Museum of Fine Arts, Tallahassee, Florida [1999].

Lygia CLARK [b. 1920, Belo Horizonte, Brazil; d. 1988, Rio de Janeiro] studied and worked in Paris and Rio de Janeiro. She co-founded the Neo-Concrete movement [1959]. Her later work was informed by her practice as a psychologist. Retrospectives of her work were shown at the Venice Biennale [1968], the São Paulo Biennale [1994] and Fundació Antoni Tàpies, Barcelona [1997].

John COPLANS [b. 1920, London] lives in New York. He gave up painting to work as a critic and curator, founding *Artforum* and contributing to *ARTnews*, *Art in America* and *Art International*. In 1984 he began making black and white photographs of his own naked body. His work has been shown at the Art Institute of Chicago [1981] and at P.S. 1/Andrea Rosen Gallery, New York [1997].

Paul COTTON [b. 1939, Fitchburg, Massachusetts] lives in Oakland, California. He uses his body as a 'living sculpture'. Among his group exhibitions are 'Live in Your Head: When Attitudes Become Form', Kunsthalle, Bern [1969], and 'Out of Actions: Between Performance and the Object', Museum of Contemporary Art, Los Angeles [1999], and touring. One-person actions include 'The World Made Flesh', Los Angeles County Museum of Art [1969], and Berkeley Zen Center [1998].

Renée COX [b. 1958, New York] lives in New York. Her photographic work subverts her identity as a female African-American. She has been included in 'Body as Membrane', Kunsthallen Brandts Klaedefabrik, Odense, Denmark [1996], and in 'Sexual Politics: Judy Chicago's *Dinner Party* in Feminist Art History', UCLA/Armand Hammer Museum of Art, Los Angeles [1996].

Jim DINE [b. 1935, Cincinnati, Ohio] lives in New York. Originally a painter, he produced several Happenings [1959-60], before returning to painting, sculpture, collage and assemblages. He was included in Documenta 4, Kassel [1968] and in a travelling exhibition 'Made in the USA: Between Art and Life, 1940-1970', Fundaciao 'La Caixa', Barcelona [1999]. Retrospectives include the Whitney Museum of American Art, New York [1970], and 'Walking Memory, 1959-68', Solomon R. Guggenheim Museum, New York [1999].

Cheryl DONEGAN [b. 1962, New York] lives in New York and makes videos subverting gender stereotypes and art-making processes. She was included in the 45th Venice Biennale [1993]. Her first solo show was at Elizabeth Koury Gallery, New York [1993].

Marcel DUCHAMP [b. 1887, Blainville-Crevon, France; d. 1968, Neuilly] lived in Neuilly, Paris, New York and Argentina. He abandoned painting to make sculptural and conceptual works, and invented the notion of the 'readymade' in which the ordinary objects of everyday life became invested with a new and often incongruous significance. He pioneered gender subversion with his alter-ego Rrose Sélavy and introduced word-play as a means of influencing and altering the reading of artworks. He was included in 'Fantastic Art, Dada, Surrealism', The Museum of Modern Art, New York [1936]. A major retrospective of his work 'The Almost Complete Works of Marcel Duchamp' was held at the Tate Gallery, London [1966]. Later retrospectives include the Philadelphia Museum of Modern Art and The Museum of Modern Art, New York [1973].

John DUNCAN [b. 1953, Wichita, Kansas] lives in San Leonardo, Italy. He makes work encompassing performance, music and installations. Group shows include Yokohama City Art Museum, Japan [1983] and 'Out of Actions: Between Performance and the Object', Museum of Contemporary Art, Los Angeles [1999], and touring. Among his solo shows are 'John Duncan: Drawings', Daily Planet Gallery, Tokyo [1982], and 'John Duncan: Events', Contained, Vöest Alpina Steel Works, Linz [1995].

Mary Beth EDELSON [b. 1933] lives in Chicago. In her early performances and photographs she enacted ancient goddess mythology to subvert patriarchy. More recent work uses symbols of contemporary aggression. She was included in 'International Feministische Kunst', Stichting de Appel, Amsterdam, and touring [1979]. Solo shows include 'The Nature of Balancing', A.I.R. Gallery, New York [1979], and 'A Non-Survey in Two Parts', Nicole Klagsbrun Gallery and A/C Project Room, New York [1993].

Diamela ELTIT lives in Santiago. She is primarily a poet, but collaborated with Raúl Zurita during the Chilean dictatorship in a group called Colectivo de Acciones de Arte, making actions of political protest. Since the early 1980s she has been making actions involving people on the margins of society. Wounds she inflicts on herself symbolize the communal body of suffering, and connect her female body with the socially outcast.

Tracey EMIN [b. 1963, London] lives in London. Her artmaking centres entirely around her traumatic life experiences, expressed in live and video performances, through text and installation, often with a sensationalist slant. She was included in 'Life's a Bitch', De Appel Gallery, Amsterdam [1998]. Solo exhibitions include 'My Major Retrospective', White Cube, London [1993].

Pepe ESPALIÚ [b. 1956, Cordoba, Spain; d. 1993] lived in Madrid and Cordoba. He was first known for his paintings and for his poetry and writings for the Seville-based art magazine *Figura*. His later work in performance and sculpture was informed by his experience of AIDS, questioning identity and mortality. He was included in 'Rites of Passage', Tate Gallery, London [1995]. Solo exhibitions include Brooke Alexander, New York [1989].

Valie EXPORT [b. 1940, Linz] lives in Vienna and makes work investigating the body as a bearer of meaning and communication. Many of her early performances involved direct interaction with people on the street. In the 1970s she began making video-performances, videotapes and 16mm film, sometimes collaborating with Peter Weibel. She was included in Documenta 6, Kassel [1977]. Solo shows include 'Psycho-Prognose', Neuer Aachener Kunstverein, Aachen, Germany [1998].

Karen FINLEY [b. 1956, Chicago] lives in New York. Her performances address social taboos such as domestic abuse, rape, suicide, homophobia, racial intolerance and AIDS. They operate through impersonation bordering on possession in which she enacts both aggressor and victim. She was included in 'Uncommon Sense', Los Angeles Museum of Contemporary Art [1997]. She performed *The Constant State of Desire*, The Kitchen, New York [1986], and *Strangling Baby Birds*, P.S. 122, New York [1987].

Bob FLANAGAN [b. 1952; d. 1996] and Sheree Rose [b. 1952] worked in collaboration. Flanagan's work was informed by his life-long suffering from cystic fibrosis which he combatted through extreme S&M practices in collaboration with his dominatrix partner and documentor, Rose. His performance-installation *Visiting Hours*, originally shown at the Santa Monica Museum of Art [1992], featured the artist suspended by his feet surrounded by video monitors showing various parts of his sick body. *Sick: The Life and Death of Bob Flanagan, Supermasochist* [1996], a film directed by Kirby Dick, was a commemoration of the couple's sixteen-year partnership.

Sherman FLEMING [b. 1953, Richhmond, Virginia] lives in Washington, DC, and makes performances using childhood games and ritual dance actions informed by African and Afro-Carribean cultures. His body-actions focus on balance and strength to investigate black male identity in American society. He performed REDBEDGREATCAVE in collaboration with Kristine Stiles at Franklin Furnace, New York [1989], and 'Pretending to be Rock' at S.U.N.Y., New Paltz, New York [1997].

Terry FOX [b. 1943, Washington] lives in Liège, Belgium. He uses his body in performances which explore the role and nature of consciousness. He was included in the Sydney Biennale [1990]. Solo shows include De Appel, Amsterdam [1977], and Otis College of Art and Design, Los Angeles [1994].

FRANKO B [b. 1960, Milan] lives in London. His S&M performances use the body metaphorically to provoke a visceral, emotional response from his audience. He participated in 'Rosso Vivo', Padiglione d'arte contemporanea, Milan [1999]. Solo performances include *Mamma I can't sing*, Institute of Contemporary Arts, London [1995], and *Aktion 398*, South London Gallery [1999].

Howard FRIED [b. 1946, Cleveland, Ohio] lives in San Francisco. His performance, video and film works operate through metaphor to test and illustrate the psychology of social interaction. His work was shown in Documenta 5, Kassel [1972], and in 'In Site: Five Conceptual Artists from the Bay Area', Amherst University Gallery, University of Massachusetts [1990].

Coco FUSCO [b. 1960, New York] lives in Los Angeles. She is an artist and cultural critic and curator. Her book *English is Broken Here: Notes on Cultural Fusion in the Americas* [1994] includes essays, scripts and poems about cultural relations between North and South America. Her installation 'Better Yet When Dead' was shown at YYZ Artists Outlet, Toronto [1997].

Gideon GECHTMAN [b. 1942, Alexandria, Egypt] lives in Israel. His work is concerned with his body's illness and advance towards death. He was included in 'Makom: Zeitgenossische Kunst aus Israel', Museum moderner Kunst Stiftung Ludwig, Vienna [1993]. Solo exhibitions include 'Yotam', Herzliya Art Museum, Israel [1999].

GILBERT & GEORGE [Gilbert Proesch, b. 1943, the Dolomites, Italy; George Passmore, b. 1942, Devon, England] live in London. They began their joint career as 'living sculptures' in 1968, making their life together their art. They were included in Documentas 5, 6 and 7, Kassel [1972; 1977; 1982]. Solo exhibitions include Baltimore Museum of Art [1980], and touring, and Musée d'art Moderne de la Ville de Paris [1997-98].

Bruce GILCHRIST [b. 1959, Glasgow, Scotland] lives in London. His performative work explores the dichotomy of experience between artist and audience, consciousness and unconsciousness, using cutting-edge technologies. He has collaborated with computer software artist Jonathan Bradley. His work has been shown in 'Twilight', Contemporary Art Centre, Vilnius [1998], and 'Totally Wired', Institute of Contemporary Arts, London [1996].

Guillermo GÓMEZ-PEÑA [b. 1955 in Mexico City] lives in New York and San Diego/Tijuana. He makes hybrid performance installations which parody colonial practices of representation and take place in public spaces. He performed *BORDERscape 2000* at the New World Theater, University of Massachusetts, Amherst [1998].

Antony GORMLEY [b. 1950, London] lives in London. Since the early 1980s he has been making human and large-scale sculptures in metal cast from, or based on, his own body. He was included in 'Aperto', Venice Biennale [1982], and Documenta 8, Kassel [1987]. Solo shows include Serpentine Gallery, London [1981], and 'Koji Ogura', Nagoya, Japan [1995].

Lyle Ashton HARRIS [b. 1965, New York] lives in Los Angeles. His photographs question fictions of race, gender and sexuality. He was included in 'Black Male: Representations of Masculinity in Contemporary Art', Whitney Museum of American Art, New York [1994]. Solo shows include Jack Tilton Gallery, New York [1994].

Mona HATOUM [b. 1952, Beirut, Lebanon] lives in London. Her work in performance, video, installation and sculpture deals with issues of culture and identity. She was included in 'Foreign Body', Museum für Gegenwartskunst, Basel [1996]. Solo exhibitions include Musée national d'Art Moderne, Centre Georges Pompidou, Paris [1994], and the New Museum of Contemporary Art, New York [1998].

Dick HIGGINS [b. 1938, Cambridge, England; d. 1998, Quebec City] lived in New York. A founder member of the Fluxus group, his work is a synthesis of literary, visual and musical genres. His imprint, Something Else Press, published artists' books; he established the Something Else Gallery with Alison Knowles in 1966. He was included in 'Ubi Fluxus, Ibi Motus', 44th Venice Biennale [1990]. Solo shows include Galerie René Block, Berlin [1973], and a retrospective at the Donja Henie-Niels Onstad Museum, Oslo [1995].

Susan HILLER [b. 1940, Tallahassee, Florida] lives in London. Her art is informed by a training in anthropology and encompasses painting, sculpture, video, photography, installation and artist's books. Her work was included in 'The Hayward Annual', Hayward Gallery, London [1978]. Solo shows include the Serpentine Gallery, London [1976], and 'Wild Talents', Institute of Contemporary Art, University of Pennsylvania, Philadelphia [1998].

HI RED CENTER was an artist's group, active in Tokyo [1962-64]. The three founding members were Genpei Akasegawa, Jiro Takamatsu and Natsuyuki Nakanishi. They staged Happenings, which they called 'agitations', throughout Tokyo. In *Miniature Restaurant* [1963] they served food on toy plates to visitors at the Yomiuri Indépendent, and in their last action, *Movement to Promote the Cleanup of the Metropolitan Area (Be Clean!)* [1964] they cleaned a street corner in Tokyo.

Rebecca HORN [b. 1944, Michelstadt, Germany] has lived in Berlin, Hamburg and New York. Her early works used the body as a vehicle for sculptural extensions presented in ritualized performances documented on film. Later she developed mechanically-supported installation-type works. In 1974 she began working in 16mm film. Her first solo show was at the René Block Gallery, Berlin [1973]. She had a major retrospective at the Solomon R. Guggenheim Museum, New York [1993].

Tehching HSIEH [b. 1950, Taiwan] lives in New York. He is a conceptual performance artist specializing in ritualized actions which take place over a long time span and result in detailed documentation. In *Punching the Time Clock on the Hour, One Year Performance* [1980-81] he punched a time clock in his studio every hour (day and night) for a year.

Joan JONAS [b. 1936, New York] lives in New York. She is a performance artist who uses video in combination with live action to enable the audience to view different aspects of the work simultaneously. She frequently used the camera lens as a mirror, or as a device to interrupt as well as convey vision. She was included in Documenta 5, Kassel [1972]. Solo shows include the Walker Arts Center, Minneapolis [1974], and the Stedelijk Museum, Amsterdam [1994].

Michel JOURNIAC [b. 1943, Paris] lives in Paris. Since the 1960s he has explored the body, performing rituals informed by Catholicism and exhibiting photographic and sculptural work which challenge gender stereotypes. His work was included in 'l'art corporel', Galerie Stadler, Paris

[1975], and 'Hors Limites', Musée national d'Art Moderne, Centre Georges Pompidou, Paris [1994]. A retrospective exhibition was held at the Museo de Bellas Artes, Bilbao [1995].

Allan KAPROW [b. 1927, Atlantic City] lived in New York and California. He invented the term 'Happening' for his actions involving painted and collaged environments, lights, sound and audience participation, which aimed to break down the traditional distinctions between life and art. In 1952 he co-founded the Hansa Gallery, New York. Publications include *Assemblage, Environments and Happenings* [1966] and *Essays on the Blurring of Art and Life* [1993].

Mike KELLEY [b. 1954, Detroit] lives and works in Los Angeles. He is a sculptor, performance and installation artist who combines the aesthetics of handicraft, illustration and psychedelia with modern sculpture, painting and architecture. Group exhibitions include 'Sound', Los Angeles Institute of Contemporary Art, and P.S. 1, New York [1979], and 'On the Sublime', Rooseum, Centre for Contemporary Art, Malmo [1999]. Among his solo shows are 'The Poltergeist, A Work between David Askevold and Mike Kelley', Foundation for Art Resources, Los Angeles [1979], and Metro Pictures, New York [1999].

Jürgen KLAUKE [b. 1943, Kliding, Germany] lives in Cologne. His early photographic and performance works explored unconventional representations of gender, sexuality and role-play. He was included in 'Transformer: Aspekete der Travestie', Kunstmuseum, Lucerne [1973]. Solo exhibitions include Galerie d'Appels, Amsterdam [1975], and Kunstmuseum, Dusseldorf [1992].

Yves KLEIN [b. 1928, Nice; d. 1962] lived in Paris. A seminal figure in the development of non-art genres, he chose the sky for its dimension of infinity as his theme, and created his signature 'International Klein Blue'. He studied judo in Japan and believed he could perform the impossible. He was a co-founder of the Nouveau Réalistes. He showed with Jean Tinguely in 'Vitesse pure et stabilité monochrome', Galerie Iris Clert, Paris [1959], and a solo show was held at the Stedelijk Museum, Amsterdam [1965]. A major touring retrospective of his work was organized by the Hayward Gallery, London, and the Museum Ludwig, Cologne [1995].

Milan KNÍŽÁK [b. 1940, Pilsen, Czech Republic] lives in Prague. A performance and conceptual artist, he has a long involvement in dissident politics. He co-founded the art-action group Aktual in Prague [1964] and participated in 'Happenings and Fluxus' at the Kunstverein, Cologne [1970]. He was included in 'After the Spring: Contemporary Czech and Slovak Art', Sydney Museum of Contemporary Art [1994], and touring. His work has been shown at the Kunsthalle, Hamburg [1986], and Mudima, Milan [1990].

Alison KNOWLES [b. 1933, New York] lives in New York. A visual artist, composer and poet, she began her involvement in Fluxus activities in 1962. She co-founded the Something Else Gallery with Dick Higgins in 1966. 'Twenty Years of Performance Art: Dick Higgins and Alison Knowles' was shown at the University of Massachussetts Gallery, Amherst [1980]. Solo exhibitions include the Galerie René Block, Berlin [1974], and 'Indigo Island', State Gallery, Sarbrüken [1997], and touring.

Jeff KOONS [b. 1955, York, Pennsylvania] lives in New York. His practice is founded on the commingling of high and low art expressed in sculptural installations and photographic images. Group exhibitions include the Whitney Biennial [1989] and the 47th Venice Bienniale [1997]. A travelling retrospective was organized by the San Fransisco Museum of Modern Art [1992-93].

Elke KRYSTUFEK [b. 1970, Vienna] lives in Vienna. Her work explores multiplicitous self-portraiture through photography, performance, video, drawing, painting and collage. Her work was included in 'feminin/masculin', Musée national d'Art Moderne, Centre Georges Pompidou, Paris [1995]. Solo shows include 303 Gallery, New York [1998].

Shigeko KUBOTA [b. 1937, Niigata, Japan] lives in New York. First known for her involvement in Fluxus, she specializes in innovative video installations combining sculptural forms with video technology. *Duchamp's Grave* was shown at The Kitchen, New York [1975]. She was included in Documenta 7, Kassel [1977]. Solo exhibitions include the National Museum of Art, Osaka [1992].

Tetsumi KUDO [b. 1935, Aomori, Japan; d. 1990, Tokyo] lived in Paris. He made sculptures and installations invoking the natural world as a source of healing after industrial desolation. His work was included in 'Happenings and Fluxus', Kunstverein, Cologne [1970], and 'Reconstruction: Avant Garde Art in Japan 1945-65', The Museum of Modern Art, New York [1985]. A major retrospective, 'Contestation/Création', was held at the National Museum of Art, Osaka [1994].

Oleg KULIK [b. 1961, Kiev, Ukraine] lives in Moscow. A performance artist, his recent work has investigated man's animal nature. In *Fourth Dimension* performed at the Wiener Seccession, Vienna [1997], he adopted his alter-ego as a dog to interact with visitors to his space. The encounters were simultaneously broadcast on a monitor in the centre of the room. He was arrested for his performance as a dog at the opening night of 'Interpol – a global network from Stockholm and Moscow', Centre for Contemporary Art, Stockholm [1996], after causing a scandal by viciously attacking members of the audience.

Yayoi KUSAMA [b. 1929, Matsumoto, Japan] moved to New York in 1957, returning to Tokyo in 1973. Her life's work has been the expression of an obsessional fear of being engulfed by her environment, expressed through paintings, sculptures and installations. In the 1960s and 1970s she organized naked Happenings, opened clothing boutiques and made films. She has also published poetry and novels. Exhibitions include 'International Watercolour Exhibition', Brooklyn Museum, New York [1955], and 'Out of Actions: Between Performance and the Object', Museum of Contemporary Art, Los Angeles [1999], and touring. Among her solo shows are Takemiya Gallery, Tokyo [1955], and Serpentine Gallery, London [2000].

Rachel LACHOWICZ [b, 1964, San Francisco] lives in Los Angeles. She makes sculptural installations in which she recasts the works of male Minimalist sculptors such as Richard Serra and Carl Andre in feminine materials such as lipstick. She was included in 'The Art of Seduction', Dade Community College, Miami [1994]. Solo exhibitions include Shoshana Wayne Gallery, Santa Monica [1992], and Fawbush Gallery, New York [1995].

Carlos LEPPE [b. 1952, Chile] lives in Santiago, Chile. In the 1970s he made performances, photographs and videos referencing the socially violated body through the adoption of multiple identities. His first performance *Happening of the Chickens* took place at Galeria Carmen Waugh, Santiago [1973]. Other shows include Galeria Sur, Santiago [1980 and 1981].

Barry LE VA [b. 1941, Long Beach, California] lives in New York. A conceptual performance artist working with installation and sound, he presents ambiguous structures expressive of thinking processes which challenge the viewer's ability to piece disparate elements together. He was included in Documenta 7, Kassel [1982]. Solo exhibitions include the New Museum of Contemporary Art, New York [1979], and Danese, New York [1997].

Richard LONG [b. 1942, Bristol, England] lives in Bristol. He has based most of his work on the activity of walking, documented through photographs, maps and lists. He also makes large sculptural installations and mud-paintings. His first exhibition experience was in '19:56-21:55', Dorothy Loehr, Frankfurt [1967]. Solo exhibitions include the Museum of Modern Art, Oxford [1971], and the National Museum of Modern Art, Kyoto [1996].

James LUNA [b. 1950, Orange, California] lives in La Jolla Indian Reservation, North County, San Diego, California. His work is concerned with his identity as a Native American Indian. Group exhibitions include 'Native American Art', Office of the Governor of California, Sacramento, California [1975], and UCLA/Armand Hammer Museum of Art, Los Angeles [1998]. Solo exhibitions include Tozzer Library, Peabody Museum, Harvard University, Cambridge, Massachusetts [1999].

Urs LÜTHI [b. 1947, Lucerne, Switzerland] lives in Zurich and Munich. He makes photographs of himself and his friends which depict ambivalent gender roles and relations. His work was shown in 'l'art corporel', Galerie Stadler, Paris [1975], and in 'Hors Limites', Musée national d'Art Moderne, Centre Georges

Pompidou, Paris [1994]. Solo shows include Galerie nächt St Stephan, Vienna [1973], and the Kunstverein, Bonn [1993].

Paul McCARTHY [b. 1945, Salt Lake City] lives in Los Angeles. His performance, video and installation works confront the viewer with violence and perversion as a critique of American culture and its TV and media obsession. *Penis Painting* was performed at the San Fransisco Art Institute [1980]. A number of his recent works have been made in collaboration with Mike Kelley. Exhibitions include 'California Performance Now and Then', Museum of Contemporary Art, Chicago [1981], and 'Painter', Projects Room, The Museum of Modern Art, New York [1995].

Bruce McLEAN [b. 1944, Glasgow] lives in London. His work in performance and painting has focused on witty deconstructions of the heroic pose. In 1971 he co-founded Nice Style, the World's First Pose Band and performed *Deep Freeze: The Pose that took us to the Top at the Hannover Grand Hotel, London* [1973]. His work was included in the 39th Venice Biennale [1980]. Solo exhibitions include Galerie Fortlaan, Ghent, Belgium [1994].

Piero MANZONI [b. 1933, Soncino, Italy; d. 1963, Milan] lived in Milan. A leading avant-garde artist of the 1950s and early 1960s, his sculptures and performances brought unconventional objects into the realm of art. He was a founder member of Galerie Azimuth, Milan [1959]. His work was shown in 'Zero', Fine Art Museum of Philadelphia [1964]. Major retrospectives include the Stedelijk Museum, Amsterdam [1970] and the Serpentine Gallery, London [1998].

Robert MAPPLETHORPE [1946-1989, New York] lived in New York. He challenged the norms of permissible portraiture through his depiction of sadomasochistic activities and homoerotic acts. His photographs were exhibited in Documenta 6, Kassel [1977], and 'Mirrors and Windows: American Photography Since 1960', The Museum of Modern Art, New York [1978], and touring. Solo exhibitions include Light Gallery, New York [1973, 1976], and the Hayward Gallery, London [1996].

Georges MATHIEU [b. 1921, Boulogne-sur-Mer] lives in Paris. A pioneer of lyrical abstraction, in 1948 he developed his own form of action painting – spontaneous calligraphic large-scale paintings executed at high speed in public. Solo exhibitions include the Institute of Contemporary Arts, London [1956], and Galerie Semiha Huber, Zurich [1990].

Ana MENDIETA [b. 1948, Havana, Cuba; d. 1986, New York] lived in Iowa and New York. Her work was informed by her youthful exile from her home and culture. She recorded private rituals of reconnection with the earth by carving, sculpting, immersing and burning her silhouette into natural settings in Iowa and Mexico. She was included in 'Inside the Visible', Whitechapel Gallery, London [1998]. Her work was exhibited at 112 Greene Street Gallery, New York [1976], and at the New Museum of Contemporary Art, New York [1987].

Pierre MOLINIER [b. 1900, Agen, France; d. 1976, Bordeaux] lived in Bordeaux. His photographic work depicts an autoerotic relationship with his own body, costumed and made up as a woman. He was included in 'Transformer: Aspekete der Travestie', Kunstmuseum, Lucerne [1973]. Solo exhibitions include l'Etoile Scellée, at André Breton's Surrealist gallery, Paris [1956], and a retrospective at the Musée national d'Art Moderne, Centre Georges Pompidou, Paris [1979].

Linda MONTANO [b. 1942, Kingston, New York] lives in Austin, Texas. Her early performances, such as *Dead Chicken, Live Angel* [1971] involved the transformation of her persona through endurance, meditation and ritual. She began 'art-life counselling' in 1980. In 1984 she undertook a project called *14 Years of Living Art* [1984-98]. Her recent work is an evolution from her study of Zen buddism and Indian philosophy. She was included in 'The Incident', Institute of Contemporary Arts, London [1997].

Charlotte MOORMAN [b. 1933, Arkansas; d. 1991] was a cellist. She lived in New York and co-founded the New York Avant-Garde Festival at Carnegie Music Hall with John Cage in 1963. She and Nam June Paik worked in a long-term creative partnership, 'humanizing' and 'sexualizing' technology. After a 1967 performance of *Opéra Sextronique* at the Filmmakers' Cinémathique, Paris, they were arrested and charged with obscenity.

Mariko MORI [b. 1967, Tokyo] lives in Tokyo. She presents herself in large colour photographs and video installations costumed as a futuristic deity figure, usually in Japanese urban environments. Her work was shown at the 47th Venice Biennale [1997]. Solo exhibitions include 'Made in Japan', Shiseido Gallery, Tokyo, and Deitch Projects, New York [1995], and the Serpentine Gallery, London [1998].

Yasumasa MORIMURA [b. 1951, Osaka] lives in Osaka. Using photography, overpainting and computer imaging he makes self-portraits in which he deconstructs categories of race, gender, age and culture. His work was included in 'Rrose is a Rrose is a Rrose', Solomon R. Guggenheim Museum, New York [1998]. Solo exhibitions include the Fondation Cartier pour l'Art Contemporain, Paris [1993].

Robert MORRIS [b. 1931, Kansas City, Missouri] lives in New York. He made conceptually inspired sculpture and later earthworks which investigated the physical and psychological conditions of viewing. This extended to works in experimental theatre and performance which deconstructed heroic masculinity. His work was included in 'American Sculpture of the 1960s', Los Angeles County Museum of Art [1967], and the 39th Venice Biennale [1980]. Solo exhibitions include Corcoran Gallery of Art, Washington, DC [1967], and 'Robert Morris: The Mind/Body Problem', Solomon R. Guggenheim and SoHo Guggenheim Museum, New York [1994].

Otto MÜHL [b. 1925, Grodnau] lived in Austria until his imprisonment in 1991 (with a seven year sentence) for sexual offences against minors. He now lives in Portugal. One of the Viennese Actionists, he initially made collages and junk sculptures but shifted to making performative actions in which he and collaborators wallowed in foodstuffs and dirt. He participated in the 'Destruction in Art Symposium', London [1966]. In 1972 he set up a commune in Friedrichshof which developed into an experimental society practising free sexuality, collective ownership and child-rearing and encouraging creative self-expression. It closed in 1990.

Teresa MURAK [b. 1949, Kielczewicze, Poland] lives in Warsaw. She has been making performances and sculptural installations since the early 1970s, in which she germinated the seed of the lady smock plant on garments or directly on her body. More recent performances involve leaven (bread dough), river mud and the construction of earthworks. Exhibitions include 'Lady's Smock', Galeria Sztuki MDK Labirynt, Lublin, Poland [1975], and 'Body and the East', Museum of Modern Art, Ljubljana, Slovenia [1998].

Saburo MURAKAMI [b. 1925, Kobe, Japan] lives in Nishinomiya. One of the central members of the Gutai group of artists, he made gestural performances which intervened on a variety of surfaces to produce traces of the gestures. At the 'Second Gutai Art Exhibition', Ohara Kaikan Hall, Tokyo [1956], he presented conceptual objects which demanded audience interaction. He was included in 'Out of Actions: Between Performance and the Object 1949-79', Museum of Contemporary Art, Los Angeles [1998], and touring.

Bruce NAUMAN [b. 1941, Fort Wayne, Indiana] lives in New Mexico. Originally a sculptor, he began applying his conceptual theories to film and performance pieces in the mid 1960s. Group exhibitions include 'American Sculpture of the 1960s', Los Angeles County Museum of Art [1967] and touring, and 'American Art in the Twentieth Century', Martin-Gropius-Bau, Berlin [1993], and touring. His first solo show was at Leo Castelli, New York [1968]. Major retrospectives include the Musée national d'Art Moderne, Centre Georges Pompidou, Paris [1998], and touring.

Shirin NESHAT [b. 1957, Qazvin, Iran] lives in New York. Her signature black and white photographs inscribed with arabic text explore the contradictory roles of women in Muslim society. She also works in video. She was included in 'Beyond the Borders: Art by Recent Immigrants', Bronx Museum of Arts, New York [1994]. Solo exhibitions of her work include the Maison Européene de la Photographie, Paris [1998].

Hermann NITSCH [b. 1938, Vienna] lived in Vienna, then Prinzendorf. A principal member of the Viennese Actionists, his goal has been to invent participatory modern rituals to put men and women in touch with their emotional and sexual sensibilities, based on Dionysian mythology, Catholic liturgy and psychoanalytic theory. He created his *Orgies Mysteries Theatre* in 1957. He first performed in London at the 'Destruction in

Art Symposium', Institute of Contemporary Arts [1966]. Recent actions were performed at his castle in Prinzendorf, Austria, such as *Six-Day-Play* [1998], which can be viewed on the internet.

Hélio OITICIA [1937-1980 Rio de Janeiro] lived in Rio de Janeiro and New York. Associated with Lygia Clark and the Neo-Concrete artists from 1954, he first presented his *Parangoles (Capes)* at the Museum of Modern Art, Rio de Janeiro, in 1965. His exhibition 'Eden', Whitechapel Gallery, London [1969], was an environment of tactile materials. A travelling retrospective of his work was organized by the Walker Art Center, Minneapolis, and the Witte de With Centre for Contemporary Art, Rotterdam [1992-94]. A centre for contemporary art bearing his name has been established in Rio de Janeiro.

Claes OLDENBURG [b. 1929, Stockholm] lives in New York. In the early 1960s he was involved with the group of New York artists making Happenings. In 1961 he opened *The Store* on the Lower East Side to sell plaster replicas of food and other commodities. He is best known for his giant soft sculptures of everyday objects. Recent works include giant monuments at urban sites. He was included in 'The Museum as Muse', The Museum of Modern Art, New York [1998]. A retrospective of his work was organized by the Solomon R. Guggenheim Museum, New York and the Hayward Gallery, London [1996-97].

Yoko ONO [b. 1933, Tokyo] lives in New York. She is a Conceptual artist making installations, performances, films and poetry, and was associated with the Fluxus artists, contributing to the 'Alchemical Wedding' event, Royal Albert Hall, London [1967]. Her book of 'mind poems' and other writings, *Grapefruit*, was published in 1964 and reprinted in 1971. Her work was included in 'Crossings', Kunsthalle Wien, Vienna [1998]. Solo shows include Everson Museum, Syracuse, New York [1971], and a retrospective at the Museum of Modern Art, Oxford [1998], and touring.

Dennis OPPENHEIM [b. 1938, Electric City, Washington] lives in New York. In the 1960s and 1970s he created conceptual installations, Land art, videos and performances investigating the relationship of his body to the environment and their effects upon each other. In 1979 he began making machine constructions. He exhibited in 'Body Art', Museum of Contemporary Art, Chicago [1975], and at the 39th Venice Biennale [1980]. Solo shows include the Pennsylvania Art Museum, Philadelphia [1970], and the Fundaciao de Serralves, Porto, Portugal [1996].

ORLAN [b. 1947, Saint-Etienne, France] lives in Paris. A multi-media performance artist, she has been working on the relationship between her image as a contemporary woman and that of women in art history. Performances include *The Reincarnation of Saint Orlan*, 'Edge 90', Newcastle [1990], in which she re-enacted earlier poses as a saint. In her touring exhibition 'This is my body … this is my software' [1996], she presented video and cd-ROM documentation of her latest plastic surgery operation.

Lucy ORTA [b. 1966, Birmingham, England] lives in Paris. Her performances and clothing are collaborative works which critique the inadequacies of social policies and urban life. Her work was shown at the 46th Venice Biennale [1995] and at the Hayward Gallery, London [1999]. 'Identity and Refuge Project: Shopping' was created at The Salvation Army, SoHo, and Deitch Projects, New York [1996].

Rafael Montañez ORTIZ [b. 1934, Brooklyn] lives in Brooklyn. Ortiz' performances are based on rituals of ancient cultures often combined with electronic media. Among his group exhibitions are 'Five from New York', Boston Museum of Fine Arts School [1962], and El Museo del Barrio, New York [1982]. Solo exhibitions include a performance of *Henny Penny Daddy*, Ecco Homo Gallery, New York [1967], and 'Physio-Psshycho-Alchemy', Völkerunde Museum, Gallery of the Artists, Munich [1987].

Nam June PAIK [b. 1932, Seoul, Korea] has lived in Hong Kong, Tokyo, New York and Germany. A central member of Fluxus, he inaugurated video art in 1963 with his exhibition of altered TVs in 'Participation TV', Galerie Bruce Kurz, Wuppertal. Major exhibitions of his work include a retrospective at the Whitney Museum of American Art, New York [1982], and 'The Electronic Super Highway: Travels with Nam June Paik', Columbus Museum of Art, Ohio [1995], and touring.

Gina PANE [b. 1936, Biarritz; d. 1990, Paris] lived in Paris. Working with her body, she began making actions in nature before shifting her focus more exclusively to actions on her body. She presented a number of performances at the Galerie Stadler, Paris, in the 1970s. She was included in Documenta 6, Kassel [1977], and 'Hors Limites', Musée national d'Art Moderne, Centre Georges Pompidou, Paris [1994]. Solo shows include 'La Pêche Endeuillée', Galleria Diagramma, Milan [1975], and 'Partitions: Opera Multimedia 1984-85', Padiglione d'Arte Contemporanea, Milan [1986].

Jayne PARKER [b. 1957, Nottingham, England] lives in London. Her film and video works are enactments of disturbing rituals as metaphors of internal processes. Her work was included in the 'Biennial of Independent Film and Video', Institute of Contemporary Arts, London [1990], and touring, and in 'I-Dish', Musée national d'Art Moderne, Centre Georges Pompidou, Paris [1987].

Mike PARR [b. 1945, Sydney] lives in Alexandria, Australia. In 1970 he set up Inhibodress, an artists' cooperative and prototype space for Conceptual art, performance work, sound and video. Having focused on written conceptual works, sculpture and performances, from 1979 he shifted to environmental installations involving large drawings. He was included in 'An Australian Accent', P.S. 1, New York [1984], and in 'No Exit: The Guinness Contemporary Art Project', Art Gallery of New South Wales, Sydney [1996].

Giuseppe PENONE [b. 1947, Garessio, Italy] lives in Turin. An Arte Povera artist, his work explores notions of empirical knowledge and experience. Gestures such as touching, shaping and moulding give rise to imprints and sculptural reliefs bearing witness to the body's interaction with the environment. His work was included in the Venice Biennale [1978]. Major solo shows include the Kunstmuseum, Lucerne [1977], and the Municipal Museum of Art, Toyota [1997].

Adrian PIPER [b. 1948, New York] lives in New York and Wellesley, Massachusetts. She works in numerous media, including performance, drawing, text, video and installation. Her early interventionist performance and photographic works explored issues of racism, gender and class exploitation. Among her group exhibitions is 'Contested Histories', Carpenter Center, Harvard University [1998]. Solo shows include the Whitney Museum of American Art, New York [1990], and John Weber Gallery, New York [1997].

Gianni PISANI [b. 1935, Naples] has been Director of the Fine Arts Academy of Naples since 1984. Initially a painter, he began making performances in the early 1970s. Exhibitions include 'Irritationart', Galleria Milano, Milan [1972], and 'Terrae Morus', Lucio Amelia Foundation, Royal Palace, Caseria, Italy [1994]. Among his solo shows are Galleria Galatea, Turin [1958], and Studio Morra, Naples [1990].

Jackson POLLOCK [b. 1912, Wyoming; d. 1956, Easthampton] lived in California, New York and Easthampton. One of the most influential American artists of his generation, he pioneered action and gesture in painting. His famous 'drip' painting technique, began in 1947, was enacted for photographs and films by Hans Namuth and brought him world-wide fame. Major retrospectives of his work were held at The Museum of Modern Art, New York [1956; 1967], and at The Museum of Modern Art, New York, and Tate Gallery, London [1998].

Marc QUINN [b. 1964, London] lives in London. He uses a variety of casting and moulding techniques and materials on his own body to depict embodied metaphyical concepts. His work was shown at the Sydney Biennale [1992]. He had a solo exhibition 'Marc Quinn Incarnate', Gagosian Gallery, New York [1998].

Arnulf RAINER [b. 1929, Baden, Austria] lives in Vienna. After making abstract paintings he began body-painting in a performance at the opening of the 'Pinotarium' exhibition in Munich [1967]. His work was included in 'Photography and Performance', Photographic Resource Centre, Boston [1989]. He had a solo show at the Galerie Michael Haas, Berlin [1997].

Eglė RAKAUSKAITĖ [b. 1967, Vilnius, Lithuania] lives in Vilnius and works in performance, video and installation. Group shows including her work are 'Footnotes', Reykjavik Municipal Art Museum, Iceland [1997], and 'Recent Documents', Balzekas Museum, Chicago [1995]. A solo exhibition of her work was held at the Contemporary

Art Centre, Vilnius [1998].

Charles RAY [b. 1953, Chicago] lives in Los Angeles. In early work he introduced his body into sculptural installations, forcing the monumentalism of the Minimalist tradition back down to human size. He made a series of mannequins in which the figure is enlarged, reduced or replicated. He also works with photographs. His work was included at the Whitney Biennale, New York [1993]. Major solo shows include the Newport Harbor Art Museum [1990], and the Rooseum Center for Contemporary Art, Malmo [1990] and touring.

Heli REKULA [b. 1963, Helsinki, Finland] lives in Helsinki. She makes photographic work which investigates the boundaries of identity and the dark side of social order. Group shows include 'Body as Membrane', Kunsthallen Brandts Klaedefabrik, Odense, Denmark [1996]. Solo exhibitions include Fotogalleriet, Oslo, Norway [2000].

Klaus RINKE [b. 1939, Wattenscheid, Germany] lives in Dusseldorf. In 1966 he gave up painting and started to make installations, performances and photographic work. He was included in 'l'art corporel', Galerie Stadler, Paris [1975], and in 'The Promise of Photography', Kestner-Gesellschaft, Hannover [1998], and touring. A retrospective, 'Klaus Rinke 1954-1991', was held at the Kunsthalle, Dusseldorf [1992].

Pipilotti RIST [b. 1962, Schweizer Rheintal, Switzerland] lives in Zurich. She works with video, film and video installation, using her own body as a model for a more generalized image of contemporary woman. Her work was included in the 47th Venice Biennale [1997]. Solo exhibitions include 'Himalaya Pipilotti Rist, 50kg', Kunsthalle, Zurich, and Musée d'Art Moderne de la Ville de Paris [1999].

Ulrike ROSENBACH [b. 1943, Bad Saizdetfurth, Germany] lives in Cologne. She began making video and live performances dealing mainly with feminist subjects in the early 1970s. She was included in Documentas 6 and 8 [1975 and 1987]. Solo shows include 'Last Call for Engel', Kunstmuseum, Heidenheim [1996], and touring.

Niki de SAINT-PHALLE [b. 1930, Neuilly-sur-Seine] has lived in New York and Paris. In the early 1960s she showed 'target' pieces: sculptures and assemblages incorporating small bags of paint which she shot at, splattering the paint beneath the plaster. She was invited to join the Nouveau Réalistes in 1961. Her later work is sculptural. Her work was shown in 'Zero et Paris 1960, et aujourd'hui', Musée d'Art Moderne et d'Art Contemporain de la Ville de Nice [1998]. Solo exhibitions include Musée national d'Arte Moderne, Centre Georges Pompidou, Paris [1980], and 'Un Univers à Découvrir', displayed throughout the city of Luxembourg [1995].

Lucas SAMARAS [b. 1936, Kastoria, Greece] lives in New York. He has made work in painting, sculpture, assemblage, film, photography and performance informed by his interest in psychology. His work was included in 'Worlds in a Box', City Art Centre, Edinburgh [1994], and touring. Solo exhibitions of his work have been shown at the Whitney Museum of American Art, New York [1973], and The Museum of Modern Art, New York [1992].

Jenny SAVILLE [b. 1970, Cambridge] lives in London. Her paintings depict the female body in monumental scale as a feminist response to the objectification of female flesh in art history. More recently she has started to make photographs in collaboration with Glen Luchford. Her work appeared in 'Contemporary '90', Royal College of Art, London [1990]. Solo exhibitions include 'Territories', Gagosian Gallery, New York [1999].

Carolee SCHNEEMANN [b. 1939, Fox Chase, Pennsylvania] lives in New Paltz, New York. A seminal figure in 1960s performance and Body art, her works centred around her own body and her position as (female) subject and object of her art making. She published a catalogue of her work, *More than Meat Joy*, in 1979. Her work appeared in 'Body as Membrane', Kunsthallen Brandts Klaedefabrik, Odense, Denmark [1996]. Retrospectives include 'Carolee Schneemann: Early Work 1960-1970', Max Hutchinson Gallery, New York [1982], and 'Carolee Schneemann: Up To and Including Her Limits', New Museum of Contemporary Art, New York [1998].She has published *The Body Politics of Carolee Schneemann* [MIT Press: 2000].

Rudolf SCHWARZKOGLER [b. 1940, Vienna; d. 1969] lived in Vienna. Associated with the Viennese Actionists, his most of his *oeuvre* consists of staged photographs, the documentation of his 'actions'. Most of these were made using his friend Heinz Cibulka as his model, and recorded private rituals of redemption and healing. He was included in 'The Shattered Mirror', Museum Ludwig, Cologne [1989]. Solo shows include the Museum moderner Kunst Stiftung Ludwig, Vienna [1992], and touring, and the Hirshhorn Museum, Washington, DC [1996].

Andres SERRANO [b. 1950, New York] lives in New York. He makes colour photographs exploring body-related taboos. Group exhibitions include '(Not So) Simple Pleasures', List Visual Arts Center, Cambridge, Massachusetts [1990-91], and ARS 95, Helsinki [1995]. He has held individual exhibitions at the Institute of Contemporary Art, Philadelphia [1994], and the New Museum of Contemporary Art, New York [1994].

Bonnie SHERK [b. 1945, New Bedford, Massachusetts] lives in New York. She is an environmental designer, educator and artist who was a pioneer in bringing the experience of nature to an urban population. She founded *Crossroads Community* (*The Farm*), an urban farm and community environmental education and arts centre in San Francisco in 1974. Group exhibitions include 'The Four', De Saisset Museum, Santa Clara, California [1973], and 'Out of Actions: Between Performance and the Object', Museum of Contemporary Art, Los Angeles [1998]. A solo exhibition of her work was held at the Civic Center, San Francisco [1996].

Cindy SHERMAN [b. 1954, New Jersey] lives in New York. Her early *Untitled Film Stills* [1977-80] were exhibited at The Kitchen [1978] and Metro Pictures [1979], both in New York. With them she established the basis of an *oeuvre* built on photographing herself in particular guises and settings to portray diverse aspects of the image of woman in contemporary culture. She was included in 'Four Artists', Artists' Space, New York [1978], and 'A/drift', Center for Curatorial Studies, Bard College, New York [1996]. Solo shows include Hallwalls Contemporary Arts Center, Buffalo [1979] and the Whitney Museum of American Art, New York [1998], and touring.

Shozo SHIMAMOTO [b. 1928, Osaka] lives in Nishinomiya, Japan. A member of the Gutai group, his experimental painting techniques included bursting through the canvas surface, shooting paint at vertical canvases from a cannon, and then throwing jars of paint against unstretched canvases laid on the floor. At 'The First Gutai On-Stage Art Show' [1957], he smashed a huge white cylinder with a stick causing an explosion of falling balls. Solo exhibitions have been held at Nishinomiya Art Space [1977], and The Mainichi Shimbun, Tokyo [1994].

Kazuo SHIRAGA [b. 1924, Amagasaki City, Japan] lives in Amagasaki. A member of the Gutai group, he experimented with many forms of action painting using diverse implements. From the mid 1950s he established his signature technique of painting with his feet. His work was shown at the 'Exhibition of International Contemporary Art', Bridgestone Museum, Tokyo [1957], and in 'Gutai Group', Gallery of Modern Art, Rome [1990]. He had a solo exhibition at Galerie Nothelfer, Berlin [1992].

Katharina SIEVERDING [b. 1944, Prague] has lived in Dusseldorf, Hamburg and Berlin. Her early photographic work features large-scale, close-up self-portraits with endless subtle variations. In the mid 1970s she began making monumental photographic tableaux which combine image and text and refer to political events. She was included in 'Transformer: Aspekte der Travestie', Kunsthalle, Lucerne [1973], and she represented Germany at the 47th Venice Biennale [1997]. Solo exhibitions include the Stedelijk Van Abbemuseum, Eindhoven [1979].

Lorna SIMPSON [b. 1960] lives in New York. She was included in 'Mistaken Identities', University Art Museum, Santa Barbara [1992], and 'Other Narratives', Contemporary Arts Museum, Houston [1999]. She had a solo show 'Interior/Exterior, Full/Empty', Wexner Center for the Arts, Ohio State University, Columbus [1997].

Barbara SMITH [b. 1931, Pasadena] lives in California. She has been making performances since the late 1960s, mainly exploring an image of woman which negotiates between patriarchal and feminist discourses, and often involving ritual meals. She presented the inaugural exhibit at Womanspace, Los Angeles, with her performance *The Bird Flies* [1973]. Her work was included in '1960-80', Stedelijk Museum, Amsterdam [1982]. Solo exhibitions include San Diego Art Gallery [1974] and Tortue Gallery, Los Angeles [1981].

Alan SONFIST [b. 1946, New York] lives in New York. His work is concerned with man's interaction with and preservation of the environment. From the early 1960s he has developed the idea of Time Landscape™ which reintroduces indigenous flora and fauna into a reclaimed urban site. He participated in Documenta 6, Kassel [1977]. Solo exhibitions include Institute of Contemporary Arts, London [1972] and Diane Brown Gallery, New York [1986].

Annie SPRINKLE [b. 1955, New York] lives in New York. After working in the porn industry for sixteen years, she was 'discovered' and moved into performance as a cast member of Deep Inside Porn Stars at Franklin Furnace, New York [1985]. She now writes and makes film and video performances. She was included in 'Body as Membrane', Kunsthallen Brandts Klaedefabrik, Odense, Denmark [1996]. Her extensive web-site may be accessed at www.heck.com/annie.

STELARC [b. 1946, Limassol, Cyprus] lived in Japan and now Melbourne. He has used medical, robotic and virtual reality systems to explore, extend and enhance the body's performance parameters. Group exhibitions include 'Edge 92', London [1992], and ISEA 94, Helsinki [1994]. He performed at The Kitchen, New York in 1993.

Petr ŠTEMBERA [b. 1945, Pilsen, Czech Republic] lives in Prague. He began to make body actions in the early 1970s, recalling shamanistic and voodoo practices, using ritual as a means of self-protection. He was included in 'Polar Crossings: 3 Europeans', Los Angeles Institute of Contemporary Art [1978], and in 'Body and the East', Museum of Modern Art, Ljubljana [1998].

Stahl STENSLIE [b. 1965, Norway] lives in Oslo and Cologne. He is a media artist working on cognition-and perception-manipulative projects within the fields of art, media and network-research. In collaboration with specialists in hard and software construction, including Kirk Wolford, Knut Mork and Marius Watz, he has created on-line, real time, virtual tele-experiments which use the body as interface and data source. His work was exhibited at ISEA 94, Helsinki [1994].

Atsuko TANAKA [b. 1932, Osaka] lives in Asuka-mura, Nara, Japan. One of the Gutai group of artists, her work in the 1950s focused on garments and light, anticipating feminist art. In addition to the group Gutai shows, her solo exhibitions include Gutai Pinachotheca, Osaka [1963], and Gallery Kuranuki, Osaka [1991].

ULAY [b. Uwe Laysiepen, 1943, Solingen, Germany] has lived in Germany and Amsterdam. He collaborated on a book of photographs with Jürgen Klauke, *Ich & Ich* [1971], exploring androgyny. He collaborated for twelve years with Marina Abramović [1976-88]. Performances include 'Relation in Space', Venice Biennale [1976] and 'The Lovers – The Great Wall Walk', Great Wall of China [1988].

Ben VAUTIER [b. 1935, Naples] lives in Nice. He was a founder of Total Art and was active with the *Nouveau Réalistes* and the Fluxus group of artists. He declared that 'everything is art' and centred his actions and performances on daily routines. He was included in 'Hors Limites', Musée national d'Art Moderne, Centre Georges Pompidou, Paris [1994]. His work has been shown at René Block, Berlin [1971], and a retrospective, 'Ben "pour ou contre"', was held at MAC - galeries contemporaines des musées de Marseille [1995].

Bill VIOLA [b. 1951, New York] lives in California. He makes video and sound which explore themes of mortality, mysticism and spiritual transformation. He represented the US at the 46th Venice Biennale [1995]. He had his first solo show at The Kitchen, New York [1974]. A major retrospective of his work was shown at the Whitney Museum of American Art, New York [1998].

Wolf VOSTELL [b. 1932, Leverkusen, Germany; d. 1998] lived in Germany and Spain. A co-founder of Fluxus, he created some of the earliest Happenings in Europe. He published the magazine *De-coll/age* from 1962. In 1976 he built his Museum for the Conception of Art in the Second Half of the Twentieth Century in Malpartida, Spain. His work was shown at the Museum of Contemporary Art, Chicago [1975], and the Institute of Contemporary Art, Los Angeles [1980]. A major retrospective of his work toured Germany in 1992.

Andy WARHOL [b. 1928, Pittsburgh; d. 1987, New York] lived in New York. In the early 1960s he was the leading exponent of Pop art, becoming a cult figure. He established the Factory in 1963, a large studio frequented by young cultural activators, where his films such as *Empire* [1964] were made. An exhibition of his work was shown at the Tate Gallery, London [1971], and The Museum of Modern Art, New York, held a retrospective of his work in 1989. The Andy Warhol Museum was established in Pittsburgh in 1994.

Zbigniew WARPECHOWSKI [b. 1938, Ploski, Poland] lives in Lodz and Sandomierz, Poland. He makes poetry, paintings and performances informed by shamanistic ritual and animistic primitivism. He has presented work in 'Edge 88', London [1988], and 'Empedokles', Kassel [1992]. He was included in 'Transgressions II', Muzeum Narodowe, Wroclaw, Poland [1993].

William WEGMAN [b. 1943, Holyoke, Massachusetts] lives in New York. His early work comprised witty black/white photographs and videos focusing on simple poses and actions which undercut the heroic status of the artist. Since the 1970s he has been making humourous photographic and film work in colour using his dog, Man Ray, and others, as his models. Group exhibitions include 'Altered Egos', Phoenix Art Museum [1986], and 'Reel Work: Artists' film and video of the 1970s', Miami Museum of Contemporary Art [1996]. He had solo shows at the Rooseum, Malmö [1998], and at the Massachusetts College of Art, Boston [1999].

Peter WEIBEL [b. 1945] lives in Karlsruhe, Germany. His early work was influenced by the Wiener Gruppe and Parisian Structuralism, and was a conceptual analysis of the communicative potential of texts and technical media. He collaborated with Valie Export and others. He participated in 'Ars Electronica', Linz [1984], and held an exhibition 'From Globe to Glove', Contemporary Art Museum, University of South Florida, Tampa [1994], in which he presented interactive installation together with sculptures and sketches.

Faith WILDING [b. 1943, Primavera, Paraguay] lives in Pittsburg, Pensylvannia. She was an important member of the Californian women's movement in art in the 1970s, making performances and installations, teaching and writing critical texts. She made *Crocheted Environment or Womb Room* [1972] for the feminist art space Womanhouse, Los Angeles. She was included in 'Sexual Politics: Judy Chicago's *Dinner Party* in Feminist Art History', UCLA/Armand Hammer Museum of Art, Los Angeles [1996]. Solo shows include 'Embryoworlds', State University of New York, Old Westbury [1999].

Hannah WILKE [1940-93] lived in New York. Originally a sculptor, she invented her own iconography based on vaginal imagery, using clay, latex and then chewing-gum. Her own body became increasingly the focus of her work, and featured in 'performalist portraits'. Her posthumous exhibition 'Intra-Venus' was shown at Ronald Feldman Gallery, New York [1994], and the Santa Monica Museum of Art, California [1996]. A retrospective of her work was held at the Copenhagen Contemporary Art Centre and Helsinki City Art Museum [1999].

Francesca WOODMAN [b. 1958, Denver, Colorado; d. 1981, New York] lived in New York and Italy. Most of her work was produced while a student at the Rhode Island School of Design, Providence, and while working in Rome, Italy, and features her own body in decaying interiors. Her book, *Some Disordered Interior Geometries*, was published in 1981. Retrospectives include Wellesley & Hunter College Art Gallery [1986], and the Fondation Cartier pour l'art contemporain, Paris [1998], and touring.

Raúl ZURITA [b. 1950, Santiago] lives in Santiago. He is primarily a poet whose early work, reacting to the repressive dictatorship in Chile, consisted of transgressive acts of self-atonement through disfigurement and pain, such as burning his face and attempting to blind himself. He collaborated with Diamela Eltit in a group called Colectivo de Acciones de Arte, which made actions protesting against the political regime. His book *Purgatorio* [1979] reproduced a psychiatric report on his 'psychosis' and three encephalographs, together with his poetry.

AUTHORS' BIOGRAPHIES

ART & LANGUAGE [Michael Baldwin, b. 1945, Chipping Norton, Oxfordshire; Mel Ramsden, b. 1944, Ikestone, Derbyshire] was the name given in 1968 to the collaborative practices developed by Baldwin and Ramsden. It was subsequently used to reflect the conversational basis of their activity. They were included in 'Language II', Dwan Gallery, New York [1968], and held a solo show at the Lisson Gallery, London [1994].

Antonin ARTAUD [1896-1948] lived in Paris. A dramatist, artist, poet and theorist, his book *The Theatre and its Double* [1938] was highly influential to artists and critics of the 1950s and 1960s.

Georges BATAILLE [1897-1962] lived in Paris. A novelist, philosopher and theorist, he was influenced by the Surrealist movement. Publications include *The Story of the Eye* [1928] and *Visions of Excess: Selected Writings 1927-1939*, which was published posthumously in 1985.

Jonathan BENTHALL [b. 1941, Calcutta] lives in London. He has been Director of the Royal Anthropological Institute, London, since 1974. His books include *Science and Technology in Art Today* [1972] and *Disasters, Relief and the Media* [1993].

Francesco BONAMI [b. 1955, Florence] is a critic and curator based in New York. Curatorial projects include Site, Santa Fe, New Mexico [1995], and 'Unfinished History', Walker Art Center, Minneapolis [1998].

Judith BUTLER [b. 1956] is Professor of Comparative Literature and Rhetoric at the University of California, Berkeley, specializing in theories of gender difference and sexuality. Books include *Gender Trouble* [1990] and *Bodies that Matter* [1993].

Meiling CHENG [b. 1960, Taipei, Taiwan] teaches at the School of Theater, University of Southern California, Los Angeles. She writes poetry, short stories and art criticism specializing in performance art. Her essay 'Renaming Untitled Flesh/Marking the Politics of Marginality' was published in *Performing the Body/Performing the Text*, edited by Amelia Jones and Andrew Stephenson [1999].

Gilles DELEUZE [1925-95] lived in Paris. A philosopher and writer on art and film studies, he collaborated with French psychoanalyst Felix Guttari [1936-92]. Their book *Anti-Oedipus: Capitalism and Schizophrenia* [1972] brought international acclaim. They published *What is Philosophy?* in 1991.

Catherine FRANCBLIN [b. 1945] is a French critic. Publications include *Les Nouveaux Réalistes* [1998], and monographs on Daniel Buren [1987] and Bertrand Lavier [1999].

Michael FRIED [b. 1939] was associated with Clement Greenberg and was profoundly influenced by his theories of Modernism. Fried claimed that the techniques of Minimalism led to a focus on process which neglected the finished product. His books include *Courbet's Realism* [1990] and *Manet's Modernism* [1996].

Sigmund FREUD [b. 1856, Freiburg, Moravia; d. 1939, London] lived in Vienna and London. The father of psychoanalysis, he revolutionized medical treatment of the emotionally disturbed by his attention to the patient's spoken word. *The Standard Edition of the Complete Psychological Works of Sigmund Freud* were first published in English in 1963.

RoseLee GOLDBERG is a critic and curator living in New York. She pioneered the study of performance art with her book *Performance Art from Futurism to the Present* [1979]. *Performance: Live Art since the 60s* was published in 1998.

Donna HARAWAY [b. 1944, Denver, Colorado] lives in Santa Cruz. A professor in the History of Consciousness Department at the University of California, she teaches feminist theory, cultural studies and the history of science. Her books include *Primate Visions: Gender, Race and Nature in the World of Modern Science* [1989] and *Simians, Cyborgs and Women: The Reinvention of Nature* [1991].

Leslie C. JONES [b. 1966, California] is an art historian and independent curator based in New York. She co-curated 'Abject Art', Whitney Museum of American Art, New York [1993]. Jones lectures at The Museum of Modern Art, New York. Her dissertation is on the paintings of Henri Michaux for the Institute of Fine Arts, New York University.

Howard JUNKER [b. 1940, Port Washington, New York] lives in San Francisco where he is editor of *ZYZZYVA*, a journal of West Coast writers and artists. He has edited anthologies taken from the journal, including *Lucky Break: How I Became A Writer* [1999]. He contributes to *Artforum*, *Art in America*, *Arts Magazine* as well as *Harper's Bazaar*, *Esquire*, *The Nation* and *Newsweek*.

Mary KELLY [b. 1942, Fort Dodge, Iowa] lives and works in Los Angeles. Kelly's work was pivotal to the development of both Conceptual art and feminism. She is best known for her work *Post Partum Document* [1976], which examined her relationship with her infant. Exhibitions include 'Sexual Politics: Judy Chicago's *Dinner Party* in Feminist Art History', UCLA/Armand Hammer Museum of Art, Los Angeles [1997]. Publications include *Imaging Desire* [1996].

Rosalind KRAUSS [b. 1940] is Meyer Schapiro Professor of Art and Theory at Columbia University, New York. A founding editor of *October* magazine, she is also an independent curator. Publications include *The Originality of the Avant-Garde and other Modernist Myths* [1985] and *The Optical Unconscious* [1993].

Julia KRISTEVA [b. 1941, Bulgaria] is a literary theorist, linguist, writer and teacher at the University of Paris-VII. She has been a practising psychoanalyst since 1979, and is an editor of the structuralist journal *Tel Quel*. Important publications include *Semiotic* [1969] and *Powers of Horror* [1982].

Max KOZLOFF [b. 1933, Chicago] lives in New York. In the 1960s he was the art critic at *The Nation*. He was executive editor of *Artforum* [1974-76], and still contributes regularly. Publications include *Photography and Fascination* [1979] and *The Privileged Eye* [1987].

Donald KUSPIT lives in New York and is Professor of Art History and Philosophy at the State University of New York, Stony Brook, and Andrew Dixon White Professor at Large at Cornell University. He is editor of *Art Criticism*, *Artforum* and *Centennial Review*. Books include *The Cult of the Avant-Garde Artist* [1993] and *Idiosyncratic Identities* [1996].

Miwon KWON [b. 1961, Seoul, Korea] is a writer living in New York. She is a co-founder and editor of *Documents* and Assistant Professor in the Department of Art History at UCLA, Los Angeles. She is also a faculty member in the Museum of Fine Arts Program in Visual Art at Vermont College.

Jacques LACAN [b. 1901; d. 1981] was a psychoanalyst whose influence has extended into all areas of the humanities and social sciences. He theorized language as a structure which provides a model for reading the human psyche. In 1964 he founded *l'Ecole Freudienne de Paris*. Publications include *Écrits - A Selection* [1966].

Rob LA FRENAIS [b. 1951, Rickmansworth, England] lives in London. A founding editor of *Performance Magazine* [1979-87] he works as a curator and critic. He co-curated the 'Edge Biennales' [1988-92], and is curator at Arts Catalyst. La Frenais is writing a doctorate on performance art and consciousness.

Jean-Jacques LEBEL [b. 1936, Paris] lives in Paris. An artist and political activist, he organized festivals of Free Expression in cities throughout Europe, including *Dechirex at the Festival of Free Expression*, Paris [1965], and *Fluxus: une conférence-demonstration*, Nanterre [1967].

Ira LICHT was an American art historian, critic and curator. He worked at the Museum of Contemporary Art, Chicago, and at the Lowe Art Museum, Miami. Publications include *Robert Irwin* [1975].

Lucy R. LIPPARD [b. 1937, New York] is a freelance writer, curator and activist based in New York. She has written extensively for many art magazines. Publications include *Six Years: The Dematerialization of the Art Object from 1966-72* [1973] and *The Pink Glass Swan: Selected essays on feminist art* [1995]. She collaborated with John Chandler to write their famous article, 'The Dematerialization of Art'.

George MACIUNAS [b. 1931, Kaunas, Lithuania; d. 1978, New York] lived in New York. He was the chief co-ordinator and promoter of the activities and philosophy of Fluxus, having invented the term in 1961 to describe a growing body of collaborative work by artists involved in performance, Conceptual art and new music. He founded the AG Gallery, New York, in 1960.

Herbert MARCUSE [1898-1979], a student of Martin Heidegger, was a German philosopher and sociologist. He emigrated to the US in 1936 where he taught at Columbia University, New York. Among his most important books are *Soviet Marxism: A Critical Analysis* [1958], *Eros and Civilization* [1955] and *Culture and Society* [1965].

Thomas McEVILLEY [b. 1939, Cincinnati] lives in New York and is Professor of Art History at Rice University, Houston. He is a contributing editor of *Artforum* and has published articles, catalogue essays and reviews of contemporary art. Publications include *Art and Discontent: Theory at the Millennium* [1991] and *Art and Otherness: Crisis and Cultural Identity* [1992].

Maurice MERLEAU-PONTY [1908-61] lived in Paris. A philosopher, he taught at the Sorbonne and other French colleges. He co-edited the journal *Les Temps Modernes* with Jean-Paul Sartre and Simone de Beauvoir. Publications include *The Phenomenology of Perception* [1942] and *In Praise of Philosophy* [1963].

Helen MOLESWORTH [b. 1966, New York] is Curator of Contemporary Art at the Baltimore Museum of Art. Her publications include catalogue essays on artists such as Mark Dion and Wolfgang Tilmans. She is a founding editor of *Documents*, and contributes frequently to *October*, *Artjournal* and *frieze*.

Stuart MORGAN lives in London. A curator and critic, he has been editor of *Artscribe* and consulting editor of *Contemporanea* (New York). He contributes regularly to magazines such as *Artforum* and *frieze*. *What the Butler Saw: Selected Writings 1977-1995* was published in 1996.

Cindy NEMSER [b. 1937, New York] lives in New York. A critic and writer, she has contributed to *Artforum*, *Arts Magazine* and *Changes*. She was editor of *The Feminist Art Journal* [1972-77]. She started making taped interviews with artists in the late 1960s, and this material appeared in *The Feminist Art Journal*, and later in her publication *Art Talk: Conversations with 15 Women Artists* [1975].

Kathy O'DELL is Associate Professor of Art History and Theory at the University of Maryland, Baltimore. She is one of the founding editors of *Link: A Critical Journal on the Arts in Baltimore and the World*, and contributes to *Artforum*, *Art in America*, *Arts Magazine*, *Art Text*, *Performance Research Journal* and *The Drama Review*. Her book *Contract with the Skin: Masochism, Performance Art and the 1970s*, was published in 1998.

Gloria Feman ORENSTEIN is a Professor of Gender Studies and Comparative Literature in the College of Letters, Arts, and Sciences, University of Southern California, Los Angeles. Her research and teaching cover ecofeminism and art history. Books include *The Theater of the Marvelous: Surrealism and the Contemporary Stage* [1975] and *Multi-Cultural Celebrations: The Paintings of Betty LaDuke* [1994].

Peggy PHELAN is Assistant Professor and Associate Chair of Performance Studies at Tisch School of the Arts, New York University. She specializes in critical theory with a feminist slant, and co-edited *Acting Out: Feminist Performances* [1993]. Published books include *Unmarked: The Politics of Performance* [1993] and *Mourning Sex: Performing Public Memories* [1997].

Robert PINCUS-WITTEN [b. 1935, New York] is an educator and writer. He was associate editor of *Arts Magazine* [1963-90] and editor of *Artforum* [1966-76]. He is director of the Gagosian Gallery, New York. His books include *Post-Minimalism: Art of the Decade* [1977] and *Eye Contact: Twenty Years of Art Criticism* [1984].

François PLUCHART lived in Paris. A cultural theorist specializing in Body art in the 1970s, he curated and promoted artists such as Gina Pane and Michel Journiac. He was editor of and contributor to *ArTitudes*. Publications include *Gina Pane: Partitions et dessins* [1983] and *Pop Art et Cie* [1971].

Nelly RICHARD [b. 1948, France] has lived in Chile since 1970. A critic, editor and curator, she specializes in marginal cultures, particularly that of Latin America. Publications include *Un Margen de Escritura Critica* [1981].

Harold ROSENBERG [1906-78] lived in New York and was an art and literary critic. His focus on action painting as an event which transcended the need for an aesthetic provided an important opposition to Clement Greenberg. He was art critic for the *New Yorker* magazine, and edited *Locations* during the 1960s and 1970s. Publications include *The Anxious Object* [1966] and *Art on the Edge: Creators and Situations* [1976].

Moira ROTH [b. 1933, London] lives in Berkeley, California. She is a feminist art historian, critic, curator and educator, and is Trefethen Professor of Art History at Mills College, Oakland, California. Books include *The Amazing Decade* [1983] and *Travelling Companions/Fractured Worlds* [2000].

Severo SARDUY [1937-93] a writer of Afro-Cuban and Chinese heritage, he left Cuba for Paris in 1960, never to return. He was the author of novels, poetry, essays and plays, as well as co-editor of the French *Editions du Seuil*, in which he introduced contemporary Latin American fiction to European readers. Publications include *Big Bang* [1974] and *Daquiri* [1980].

Eve Kosofsky SEDGWICK [b. 1950 Dayton, Ohio] is Newman Ivey White Professor of English at Duke University, North Carolina and one of the founders of gay and lesbian studies in America. Publications include *Between Men: English Literature and Male Homosocial Desire* [1985] and a volume of poetry, *Fat Art, Thin Art* [1994].

Elaine SCARRY lives in Massachusetts. A philosopher and literary critic, she is the Cabot Professor of Aesthetics at Harvard University, New York. Her books include *The Body in Pain: the Making and Unmaking of the World* [1985] and *Resisting Representation* [1994].

Rebecca SCHNEIDER [b. 1959, San Francisco] teaches Performance Studies in the Theater, Film and Dance Department, Cornell University. She is the author of *The Explicit Body in Performance* [1997], and has published numerous essays in anthologies and journals. She is a contributing editor to *The Drama Review* and Vice President of the Women and Theater Program in the American Theater in Higher Education Association.

Willoughby SHARP [b. 1938, New York] teaches at the School of Visual Arts, New York. He is a founding editor of *Avalanche*, and curated the influential survey show 'Information' at The Museum of Modern Art [1970].

Susan SONTAG [b. 1933, New York] lives in New York. She has written novels, stories and innovative essays covering a wide range of aesthetic, cultural and political issues. Her books include *The Style of Radical Will* [1969], *On Photography* [1976], and *AIDs and Its Metaphors* [1989].

Kristine STILES [b. 1956, Denver, Colorado] lives in North Carolina. A critic, curator and artist, she is Associate Professor of Art History at Duke University, North Carolina. She has published essays on, among others, Fluxus, Actionists and Paul McCarthy. She co-edited *Theories and Documents of Contemporary Art* [1996] with Peter Selz.

Margaret SUNDELL [b. 1965, New York] is a New York-based writer completing a Doctorate at Columbia University on the work of Man Ray. She is a founding editor of *Documents*.

Marcia TUCKER [b. 1940, New York] lives in New York. She was a founding director and curator of the New Museum of Contemporary Art, New York [1977-91]. Publications include *Robert Morris* [1970] and *Bad Girls* [1994].

Lea VERGINE [b. 1938, Naples] is a critic and curator who lives in Milan. She contributes to *Corriere della Sera and Il Manifesto*, *Modo*, *Domus* and *Art and Artists*. Her publications include *Body Art and Similia* [1974] and *L'altra metà dell'avanguardia 1910-1940* [1980-82].

Paul VIRILIO [b. 1932, Paris] lives in Paris. As an educator he is involved with the Ecole Speciale d'Architecture, Paris, and the College International de Philosophie, Paris. Publications include *Bunker archéologie* [1975] and *War and Cinema: the Logistics of Perception* [1984].

Jiro YOSHIHARA [b. 1905, Osaka City, Japan; d. 1972] was a founding member of the Gutai Art Association in Japan. Among his exhibitions are the first and second Gutai exhibitions, Tokyo [1954], and 'International Contemporary Art', National Museum of Modern Art, Tokyo [1969].

BIBLIOGRAPHY

Abramović, Velimir, *Marina Abramović: Artist Body – Performances 1969–98* (Milan: Charta, 1998)

Ades, Dawn, *Art in Latin America: The Modern Era 1820–1980* (New Haven, Connecticut and London: Yale University Press, 1989)

Allsop, Ric; deLahunta, Scott, *The Connected Body: An Interdisciplinary Approach to the Body and Performance* (Amsterdam School of Arts, 1996)

Ammann, Jean-Christophe, *Transformer* (Lucerne: Kunstmuseum, 1974)

______, *Giuseppe Penone* (Lucerne: Kunstmuseum, 1977)

Antin, Eleanor, *The Angel of Mercy* (California: La Jolla Museum of Contemporary Art, 1977)

______, *Ghosts* (Winston-Salem, North Carolina: Southeastern Center for Contemporary Art, 1996)

Armstrong, Elizabeth; Rothfuss, Joan (eds.), *In the Spirit of Fluxus* (Minneapolis: Walker Art Center, 1993)

Armstrong, Rachel, 'Franko B', *Totally Wired: Science, Technology and the Human Form* (London: Institute of Contemporary Arts, 1996)

Arnold, Skip, 'A Conversation with J.M.S. Willette', *Artweek* (19 November 1992)

Badura-Triska, Eva; Klocker, Hubert, *Dal Profundo: Brus, Nitsch, Rainer* (Milan: Mazotta, 1986)

Baerwaldt, Wayne; Gorsen, Peter; Watson, Scott, *Pierre Molinier* (Winnipeg: Plug In Editions, 1993)

Balsamo, Anne Marie, *Technologies of the Gendered Body: Reading Cyborg Women* (Durham, North Carolina: Duke University Press, 1996)

Barney, Matthew, *Matthew Barney: New Work* (San Francisco Museum of Modern Art, 1991)

Bataille, Georges, *Visions of Exc[illegible] Selected Writings 1927–1939*, ed. Allan Stoekl, trans. Allan Stoekl, Carl R. Lovitt and Donald M. Leslie, Jr. (Minneapolis: University of Minnesota Press, 1985)

Bear, Liza; Sharp, Willoughby, 'Chris Burden: The Church of Human Energy', *Avalanche*, 8 (Summer–Autumn 1973)

Becker, Jurgen; Vostell, Wolf (eds.), *Happenings, Fluxus, Pop Art, Nouveau Réalisme* (Hamburg: Rowohlt, 1965)

Benjamin, Andrew (ed.), *The Body* (London: Academy Editions/Ernst & Sohn, 1993)

Bersani, Leo, *The Freudian Body: Psychoanalysis and Art* (New York: Columbia University Press, 1986)

Blessing, Jennifer (ed.), *Rrose is a Rrose is a Rrose: Gender Performance in Photography* (New York: Solomon R. Guggenheim Museum, 1997)

Bois, Yve-Alain, 'Lygia Clark: Nostalgia of the Body', *October*, 69 (Summer 1994)

______; **Krauss, Rosalind**, *Formless: A User's Guide* (New York: Zone Books, 1997)

Bonami, Francesco, 'Elke Krystufek', *Flash Art* (November–December 1992)

Brecht, George, *Chance-Imagery* (New York: Something Else Press, 1966)

Breidenbach, Tom, 'Renée Cox', *Artforum*, 36: 10 (Summer 1998)

Brett, Guy, *Susan Hiller* (London: Institute of Contemporary Arts, 1986)

______, 'Lygia Clark: The Borderline Between Art and Life', *Third Text*, 1 (Autumn 1987)

______, 'Lygia Clark: In Search of the Body', *Art in America*, 82: 7 (July 1994)

______; **Klocker, Hubert; Schimmel, Paul; Osaki, Shinichiro; Stiles, Kristine**, *Out of Actions: Between Performance and the Object 1949–1979* (California: Museum of Contemporary Art; London: Thames & Hudson, 1998)

Brett, Philip; Case, Sue-Ellen; Leigh Foster, Susan, *Cruising the Performative Interventions into the Representations of Ethnicity, Nationality and Sexuality* (Bloomington: Indiana University Press, 1995)

Brisley, Stuart; Overy, Paul; Roberts, John, *Stuart Brisley* (London: Institute of Contemporary Arts, 1981)

Brittain, David, 'Jenny Saville Interviewed by David Brittain', *Creative Camera* (June–July 1995)

Bromfield, David, *Identities: A Critical Study of the Work of Mike Parr 1970–1990* (Nedlands, Alexandria, New South Wales: Western Australian University Press, 1991)

Bronson, A.A.; Gale, Peggy (eds.), *Performance by Artists* (Toronto: Art Metropole, 1979)

Brus, Günter, *Beiblatt zur Photo Edition (Korperanalyse)* (Berlin: Armin Hundertmark, 1970)

Butler, Judith, *Gender Trouble, Feminism and the Subversion of Identity* (New York and London: Routledge, 1990)

Byars, James Lee; Fuchs, Rudi, *The Palace of Good Luck* (Turin: Castello di Rivoli, 1989)

______, *James Lee Byars* (Bern: Kunsthalle, 1978)

Cage, John, *Silence: Lectures and Writings* (Middletown, Connecticut: Wesleyan University Press, 1961)

Cameron, Dan, *Carolee Schneemann: Up to and Including her Limits* (New York: New Museum, 1996)

Camnitzer, Luis, 'Ana Mendieta', *Third Text*, 7 (Summer 1979)

Carlson, Marvin, *Performance: A Critical Introduction* (New York and London: Routledge, 1996)

Carr, C., *On Edge: Performance at the End of the Twentieth Century* (Hanover, New Hampshire: University Press of New England, 1993)

Case, Sue-Ellen, see **Brett, Philip**

Caumont, Jacques; Gough-Cooper, Jennifer (eds.), *Yves Klein: Selected Writings*, trans. Barbara Wright (London: Tate Gallery, 1974)

Celant, Germano (ed.), *Giuseppe Penone* (Amsterdam: Stedelijk Museum, 1980)

______; **Spector, Nancy**, *Rebecca Horn* (New York: Solomon R. Guggenheim Foundation, 1993)

______, *Robert Mapplethorpe* (London: Hayward Gallery; Milan: Electa, 1996)

______ (ed.), *Piero Manzoni* (London: Serpentine Gallery; Milan: Charta, 1998)

Chandès, Hervé, *Francesca Woodman* (Paris: Fondation Cartier pour l'art contemporain; Actes Sud, 1998)

Charles, David, *For the Birds: John Cage in Conversation* (Boston and London: Marion Boyars, 1981)

Chevrier, Jean-François, *Another Objectivity* (Paris: Centre National des Arts Plastiques, 1989)

Chicago, Judy, *Beyond the Flower: My Struggle as a Woman Artist* (Garden City, New York: Doubleday, 1975)

Childs, Nicky; Walwin, Jeni (eds.), *A Split Second of Paradise: Live Art, Installation and Performance* (London: Rivers Oram, 1998)

Chipp, Herschel B. (ed.), *Theories of Modern Art: A Sourcebook by Artists and Critics* (Berkeley, California and London: University of California Press, 1968)

Cohen, Michael, 'Lyle Ashton Harris', *Flash Art*, 29: 188 (May–June 1996)

Cottingham, Laura, 'Janine Antoni: Biting Sums Up My Relationship to Art History', *Flash Art*, 26: 171 (Summer 1993)

Crow, Thomas E., *The Rise of the 1960s: American and European Art in the Era of Dissent* (London: Weidenfeld and Nicolson, 1996)

Curtis, Penelope (ed.), *Helen Chadwick: Elective Affinities* (Liverpool: Tate Gallery, 1993)

deLahunta, Scott see **Allsop, Ric**

Derrida, Jacques, *Of Grammatology* (1967), trans. Gayatri Chakravorty Spivak (Baltimore and London: Johns Hopkins University Press, 1976)

de Saint-Phalle, Niki, *Niki de Saint-Phalle: Exposition Rétrospective* (Paris: Éditions du Centre Pompidou, 1980)

de Zegher, Catherine M. (ed.), *Inside the Visible: An Elliptical Traverse of Twentieth-Century Art in, of, and from the Feminine* (Cambridge, Massachusetts and London: MIT Press, 1996)

d'Harnoncourt, Anne; McShine, Kynaston (eds.), *Marcel Duchamp* (Philadelphia Museum of Art; New York: The Museum of Modern Art, 1973)

Diamond, Elin (ed.), *Performance and Cult Politics* (New York and London: Routledge, 1996)

Donegan, Cheryl, 'Artist's statement', *Audience 001. International Video* (Milan: Giancarlo Politi Editore, 1994)

Durant, Mark Alice, 'Lost (and Found) in a Masquerade: The Photographs of Pierre Molinier', *Exposure*, 29: 2–3 (1994) 27–35

Elliott, David (ed.), *The Perfect Thought: Works by James Lee Byars* (Houston: Contemporary Arts Museum; Berkeley: University Art Museum, University of California, 1990)

Export, Valie; Justessen, Kirsten, 'Jayne Parker', *Body as Membrane* (Odense: Kunsthallen Brandts Klaedefabrik, 1996)

Feher, Michel; Naddaff, Ramona; Tazi, Nadia (eds.), *Fragments of a History of the Human Body, Parts 1–3* (New York: Zone Books, 1989)

Ferguson, Bruce W., *Charles Ray* (Malmo: Rooseum Center for Contemporary Art; London: Institute of Contemporary Arts, 1994)

Finley, Karen, *Uncommon Sense* (Los Angeles Museum of Contemporary Art, 1997)

Foster, Stephen C. (ed.), *Event Arts and Art Events* (Ann Arbor and London: UMI Research Press, 1988)

Fox, Terry, *Metaphorical Instruments* (Essen: Museum Folkwang; Berlin: Berliner Künstlerprogramm des Deutschen Akademischen Austauschdienstes, 1982)

Freud, Sigmund, *The Standard Edition of the Complete Psychological Works of Sigmund Freud*, 24 Vols., ed. James Strachey, et al. (London: The Hogarth Press and the Institute of Psycho-Analysis, 1974)

Freuh, Joanna, *Erotic Faculties* (Berkeley and London: University of California Press, 1996)

Friedman, Ken (ed.), *Fluxus Performance Workbook* (Trondheim: El Djarida, 1990)

Fuchs, Rudi see **Byars, James Lee**

Fusco, Coco, 'The Border Art Workshop, Interview with Guillermo Gómez-Peña and Emily Hicks', *Third Text*, 7 (Summer 1979)

_____, 'Uncanny Dissonance: The Work of Lorna Simpson', *Third Text*, 22 (Spring 1993)

_____, *English is Broken Here: Notes on Cultural Fusion in the Americas* (New York: New Press, 1995)

Goldberg, RoseLee, *Performance Art: From Futurism to the Present* (London: Thames & Hudson, 1988)

_____, *Performance: Live Art Since 1960* (London: Thames & Hudson, 1998)

Goodeve, Thyrza Nichols, 'Travels in Hypertrophia: Interview with Matthew Barney', *Artforum*, 33: 9 (May 1995)

Gorsen, Peter see **Baerwaldt, Wayne**

Gough-Cooper, Jennifer see **Caumont, Jacques**

Gray, John (ed.), *Action Art: A Bibliography of Artists' Performance from Futurism to Fluxus and Beyond* (Westport, Connecticut and London: Greenwood Press, 1993)

Grenier, Catherine, *Günter Brus: Limite du Visible* (Paris: Éditions du Centre Pompidou, 1993)

Grosz, Elizabeth, *Volatile Bodies: Toward a Corporeal Feminism* (Bloomington: Indiana University Press, 1994)

Guldemond, Jaap, *Ulay/Abramović Performances 1976-88* (Eindhoven: Stedelijk Van Abbemuseum, 1997)

Gumpert, Lynn, 'Glamour Girls', *Art in America*, 84: 7 (July 1996)

Halberstame, Judith; Livingston, Ira, *Posthuman Bodies* (Bloomington: Indiana University Press, 1995)

Hamilton, Ann, *The Body and the Object: Ann Hamilton 1984-1996* (Columbus, Ohio: Wexner Center for the Arts, 1996)

Hanhardt, John G. (ed.), *Nam June Paik* (New York: Whitney Museum of American Art; W.W. Norton, 1982)

Hansen, Al, *A Primer of Happenings and Time Space Art* (New York: Something Else Press, 1965)

Harrison, Charles; Wood, Paul (eds.), *Art in Theory 1900-1990* (Oxford: Blackwell, 1992)

Hart, Lynda; Phelan, Peggy, *Acting Out: Feminist Performances* (Ann Arbor: University of Michigan Press, 1993)

Hatoum, Mona, 'Body and Text', *Third Text*, 1 (Autumn 1987)

Heathfield, Adrian; Templeton, Fiona; Quick, Andrew, *Shattered Anatomies: Traces of the Body in Performance* (Bristol: Arnolfini, 1997)

Heiss, Alanna (ed.), *Dennis Oppenheim, Selected Works, 1967-90* (New York: P.S. 1 Museum, 1990)

Hendricks, Jon; Phillpott, Clive (eds.), *Fluxus: Selections from the Gilbert and Lila Silverman Collection* (New York: The Museum of Modern Art, 1988)

Henri, Adrian, *Environments and Happenings* (London: Thames & Hudson, 1974)

Hiller, Susan (ed.), *The Myth of Primitivism* (New York and London: Routledge, 1991)

Hollier, Dennis (ed.), *Against Architecture: The Writings of Georges Bataille*, trans. Betsy Wing (Cambridge, Massachusetts and London: MIT Press, 1989)

Hutchinson, John, et al., *Antony Gormley* (London: Phaidon Press, 1995)

Jahn, Wolf, *The Art of Gilbert & George, or An Aesthetic of Existence*, trans. David Britt (New York: Thames & Hudson, 1989)

Janus, Elizabeth, 'Private Functions', *frieze* (December 1994)

Johns, Jasper, 'Sketchbook Notes', *Art and Literature* (Spring 1965)

Johnston, Jill, 'Hardship Art', *Art in America* (September 1984)

Jones, Amelia, *Postmodernism and the En-gendering of Marcel Duchamp* (Cambridge University Press, 1994)

_____, *Body Art: Performing the Subject* (Minneapolis and London: University of Minnesota Press, 1998)

_____, 'Tracing the Subject with Cindy Sherman', *Cindy Sherman Retrospective* (New York and London: Thames & Hudson; Chicago: Museum of Contemporary Art; Los Angeles: Museum of Contemporary Art, 1997)

_____; **McKaskell, Robert**, *Hannah Wilke: Intra-Venus* (New York: Ronald Feldman Fine Arts, 1995)

Junker, Howard, 'James Lee Byars: Performance as Protective Coloration', *Art in America*, 66: 6 (November 1978)

Juno, Andrea; Vale, V. (eds.), *Bob Flanagan: Supermasochist* (San Francisco: Re/Search Publications, 1993)

Justessen, Kirsten see **Export, Valie**

Kaprow, Allan, *Assemblage, Environments and Happenings* (New York: Harry N. Abrams, 1966)

_____, *Essays on the Blurring of Art and Life*, ed. Jeff Kelley (California & London: University of California Press, Berkeley, 1993)

Kardon, Janet, *Laurie Anderson: Works from 1969 to 1983* (Philadelphia: Institute of Contemporary Arts, University of Pennsylvania, 1983)

_____, *Robert Mapplethorpe: A Perfect Moment* (Philadelphia: Institute of Contemporary Art, University of Pennsylvania, 1988)

Keane, Susan, *Lynda Benglis: Dual Natures* (Atlanta: High Museum of Art, 1991)

Kirby, Michael (ed.), *Happenings: An Illustrated Anthology* (London: Sidgwick and Jackson, 1965)

Klauke, Jürgen, 'Interview with Peter Weibel', *Jürgen Klauke, Cindy Sherman* (Munich: Sammlung Goetz; Ostfildern: Canz, 1994)

Klocker, Hubert (ed.), *Otto Mühl: Ausgewählte Arbeiten 1963-86* (Vienna: Hubert Klocker-Kunsthandel, 1986)

_____ (ed.), *Viennese Actionism/Wiener Aktionismus 1960-1971* (Klagenfurt: Ritter Verlag, 1989)

_____ see **Brett, Guy**

Koch, Stephen, *Andy Warhol Photographs* (New York: Robert Miller Gallery, 1986)

Kochheiser, Thomas H. (ed.), *Hannah Wilke: A Retrospective* (Columbia and London: University of Missouri Press, 1989)

Kontova, Helena, 'The Wound as a Sign: An Encounter with Gina Pane', *Flash Art* (August 1979)

Koons, Jeff, *Flash Art*, 144 (January-February 1989) supplement

Kostelanetz, Richard, *Dictionary of the Avant-Gardes* (Pennington, New Jersey: Capella, 1993)

Kostolowski, Andrzej, 'Intimacy Revealed', *Teresa Murak* (Warsaw: Galeria Bielska BWA, 1998)

Krauss, Rosalind, *The Originality of the Avant-Garde and Other Modernist Myths* (Cambridge, Massachusetts and London: MIT Press) 1985

_____, *The Optical Unconscious* (Cambridge, Massachusetts and London: MIT Press) 1993

_____ see **Bois, Yve-Alain**

Kroker, Arthur; Marilouise, Kroker (eds.), *Body Invaders: Sexuality and the Postmodern Condition* (Basingstoke: Macmillan, 1988)

Kulturmann, Udo, *Art-Events and Happenings*, trans. John William Gabriel (London: Mathews Miller Dunbar, 1971)

Kuspit, Donald, *Chris Burden: A Twenty-Year Survey* (Newport Harbor Art Museum, 1988)

_____, *The New Subjectivism: Art in the 1980s* (Ann Arbor, Michigan and London: UMIST Research Press, 1988)

_____, 'Joseph Beuys', *Artforum*, 27: 6 (1989)

_____; **McEvilley, Thomas; Smith, Roberta**, *Lucas Samaras: Objects and Subjects 1969-1986* (New York: Abbeville Press, 1988)

_____; **Mendieta, Ana**; et al., *Ana Mendieta* (Barcelona: Fundació Antoni Tàpies, 1997)

Lacan, Jacques, *Ecrits: A Selection*, trans. Alan Sheridan (London and New York: Routledge, 1977)

Leigh Foster, Susan see **Brett, Philip**

Lifson, Ben, *Lucas Samaras: Photographs 1969-1986* (New York: Aperture, 1988)

Linker, Kate, *Vito Acconci* (New York: Rizzoli, 1994)

Lippard, Lucy R., *From the Center: Feminist Essays on Women's Art* (New York: E.P. Dutton & Co., 1976)

_____, *Overlay: Contemporary Art and the Art of Prehistory* (New York: Pantheon, 1983)

Livingston, Ira see **Halberstame, Judith**

Loeffler, Carl E.; Tong, Darlene (eds.), *Performance Anthology: Source Book of Californian Performance Art* (San Francisco: Last Gasp Press; Contemporary Arts Press, 1989)

Loers, Viet; Schwarz, Dieter (eds.), *Vienna 1960-1965: From Action Painting to Actionism* (Klagenfurt: Ritter Verlag, 1988)

Loisy, Jean de (ed.), *Hors Limites: l'art et la vie 1952-1994* (Paris: Centre Georges Pompidou, 1994)

Lyotard, Jean-François, *Les TRANSformateurs Duchamp* (Paris: Galilée, 1977)

McEvilley, Thomas see **Kuspit, Donald**

McKaskell, Robert see **Jones, Amelia**

Marcad, Bernard, 'Glossaire Orient', *Femininmasculin: Le sexe de l'art* (Paris: Éditions du Centre Pompidou; Gallimard/Electa, 1995)

Marshall, Richard, *Robert Mapplethorpe* (New York: Whitney Museum of American Art; New York Graphic Society Books, 1988)

McShine, Kynaston see **d'Harnoncourt, Anne**

Melzer, Annabelle, *Dada and Surrealist Performance* (Baltimore and London: Johns Hopkins University Press, 1994)

Mendieta, Ana see **Kuspit, Donald**

Mercer, Kobena (ed.), 'Dark and Lovely: Black Gay Image Making', *Welcome to the Jungle: New Positions in Black Cultural Studies* (New York and London: Routledge, 1994)

_____, 'Home from Home: Portraits from Places in Between', *Self-Evident* (Birmingham: Ikon Gallery, 1995)

Meschede, Friedrich; Pejič, Bojana; von Drathen, Doris, *Abramovič* (Stuttgart: Edition Cantz, 1993)

Metzger, Gustav, *Damaged Nature: Auto-destructive Art* (London: Coracle, 1996)

Meyer, Ursula, 'Joseph Beuys: How To Explain Pictures to a Dead Hare', *ARTnews*, 68: 9 (January 1970)

Morgan, Stuart, *Susan Hiller* (London: Institute of Contemporary Arts, 1986)

Morris, Frances, *Miroslaw Balka* (London: Tate Gallery, 1995)

Munroe, Alexandra (ed.), *Japanese Art After 1945: Scream Against the Sky* (New York: Harry N. Abrams, 1994)

Naddaff, Ramona see **Feher, Michel**

Nakamura, Keiji, *Contestation/Creation* (Osaka: National Museum of Art, 1994) 117

Ninio, Moshe (ed.), *Gideon Gechtman: Works*

1971-1986, trans. Richard Flantz (Tel Aviv: Stavit Editions, 1986)

Noever, Peter (ed.), *Chris Burden: Beyond the Limits* (Vienna: Oesterreichishes Museum für angewandte Kunst, 1996)

Nyman, Michael, 'George Brecht: Interview', *Studio International*, 192: 984 (November-December 1976)

Obrist, Hans Ulrich (ed.), *Louise Bourgeois: Destruction of the Father/Reconstruction of the Father: Writings and Interviews 1923-1997* (London: Violette Editions, 1998)

Oldenberg, Claes, *Store Days: Documents from The Store, 1961, and Ray Gun Theater, 1962* (New York: Something Else Press, 1967)

______, et al., 'Claes Oldenberg, Roy Lichtenstein, Andy Warhol: A Discussion (Moderated by Bruce Glaser)', *Artforum*, 4: 6 (February 1966)

Ono, Yoko, *Grapefruit* (London: Sphere, 1971)

Orlan, *This is my Body - This is my Software* (London: Black Dog, 1996)

Osaki, Shinichiro see **Brett, Guy**

O'Dell, Kathy, *Contract with the Skin: Masochism, Performance Art and the 1970s* (Minneapolis: University of Minnesota Press, 1998)

Paffrath, James D.; Stelarc (eds.), *Obsolete Body/Suspensions/Stelarc* (Davis, California: J.P. Publications, 1983)

Paik, Nam June, 'To Catch Up or Not to Catch Up with the West: Hijikata and Hi Red Center', in Alexandra Munroe (ed.), *Japanese Art After 1945: Scream Against the Sky* (New York: Harry N. Abrams, 1994)

Parr, Mike, 'Artist's statement', *Flash Art* (February-April 1978)

Pazzini, Karl-Josef, *Elke Krystufek* (Vienna: Wiener Secession, 1997)

Phelan, Peggy, *Unmarked: The Politics of Performance* (London and New York: Routledge, 1993)

______, *Ends of Performance* (New York University Press, 1998)

______ see **Hart, Lynda**

Phillpott, Clive see **Hendricks, Jon**

Piper, Adrian, 'Catalysis: An Interview with Lucy Lippard', *The Drama Review* (March 1972)

______, *Out of Order, Out of Sight* (Cambridge, Massachusetts and London: MIT Press, 1996)

Pluchart, François, 'l'Artist et son double: Entretien avec Urs Luthi', *Artitudes*, 12-14 (July-September 1974)

Poetter, Jochen (ed.), *Jürgen Klauke: Sonntagneurosen* (Ostfildern: Cantz; Baden-Baden: Staatliche Kunsthalle, 1992)

Pollock, Griselda (ed.), *Generations and Geographies in the Visual Arts: Feminist Readings* (London and New York: Routledge, 1996)

Quick, Andrew see **Heathfield, Adrian**

Rainer, Arnulf, *Arnulf Rainer* (Cologne: Galerie Ariadne, 1971)

Ratcliff, Carter, *Gilbert & George: The Complete Pictures 1971-1985* (New York: Rizzoli, 1986)

Ricard, René, 'No Dice', *Artforum* (October 1997)

Richard, Nelly, 'Art in Chile Since 1973', *Third Text*, 2 (Winter 1987-88)

Richardson, Brenda, 'Howard Fried: The Paradox of Approach-Avoidance', *Arts Magazine* (Summer 1971)

______ (ed.), *Gilbert and George* (Baltimore Museum of Art, 1984)

Ritchie, Matthew, 'Lorna Simpson', *Flash Art*, 187 (March-April 1996)

Roberts, James, 'Bas Jan Ader: The Artist Who Fell from Grace with the Sea', *frieze*, 17 (1994)

Rodenbeck, J.F., 'Yayoi Kusama: Surface, Stitch, Skin', in Catherine de Zegher (ed.), *Inside the visible: An Elliptical Traverse of Twentieth-century Art; in, of and from the Feminine* (Cambridge, Massachusetts and London: MIT Press, 1996) 149-56

Rosenbach, Ulrike, *Körpersprache* (Berlin: Haus am Waldsee, 1975)

Roth, Moira (ed.), *The Amazing Decade: Women and Performance Art in America 1970-80* (Los Angeles: Astro Artz, 1983)

Rubin, William, 'Jackson Pollock and the Modern Tradition', *Artforum*, 5 (February-May 1967)

Rugoff, Ralph, et al., *Paul McCarthy* (London: Phaidon Press, 1996)

Ruhe, Harry, *Fluxus: The Most Radical and Experimental Art Movement of the 1960s* (Amsterdam: 'A', 1979)

Saltz, Jerry, 'The Next Sex', *Art in America*, 84: 10 (October 1996)

Sandford, Mariellen R. (ed.), *Happenings and Other Acts* (London and New York: Routledge, 1995)

Sartre, Jean-Paul, *Being and Nothingness: An Essay on Phenomenological Ontology* (London: Methuen, 1969)

Sayre, Henry M., *The Object of Performance: The American Avant-Garde since 1970* (University of Chicago Press, 1989)

Schimmel, Paul, 'Just the Facts', *Chris Burden: A Twenty-Year Survey* (Newport Harbor Art Museum, 1988)

______, 'Beside One's Self', *Charles Ray*, (Los Angeles: Museum of Contemporary Art, 1998)

______ see **Brett, Guy**

Schlemmer, Oskar, *Man: Teaching Notes from the Bauhaus*, trans. Krishna Wintson (London: Lund Humphries, 1971)

Schneede, Uwe M., *Joseph Beuys die Aktionen* (Stuttgart: Ostfidern-Ruit, 1994)

Schneemann, Carolee, *More than Meat Joy: Performance Works and Selected Writings*, ed. Bruce R. McPherson (Kingston, New York: McPherson & Co., 1997)

Schwabsky, Barry, 'Shirin Neshat', *Artforum* (December 1995)

Schwartz, Arturo, *The Complete Marcel Duchamp* (London: Thames & Hudson; New York: Harry N. Abrams, 1969)

Schwarz, Dieter see **Loers, Viet**

Schwarzkogler, Rudolf, *Photographies d'actions, Vienna 1965-66* (Paris: Éditions du Centre Pompidou, 1993)

Selwyn, Marc, 'There's a Big Difference between Ketchup and Blood', *Flash Art*, 170 (May-June 1993)

Selz, Peter; Stiles, Kristine (eds.), *Theories and Documents of Contemporary Art: A Sourcebook of Artists' Writings* (Berkeley, California and London: University of California Press, 1996)

Sharp, Willoughby, 'Interview with Bruce Nauman', *Arts Magazine*, 44: 5 (March 1970)

______ see **Bear, Liza**

Shiraga, Kazuo, 'Only Action', *Gutai*, 20 (October 1955)

Simon, Joan (ed.), *Bruce Nauman* (Minneapolis: Walker Arts Center, 1994)

Smith, Barbara, 'Paul McCarthy', *Journal*, 21 (January-February 1979)

Smith, Roberta see **Kuspit, Donald**

Sohm, H. (ed.), *Happenings and Fluxus: Materialen* (Cologne: Kunstverein, 1970)

Spector, Nancy, 'Rock my Video', *frieze* (January-February 1995)

______ see **Celant, Germano**

Stachelhaus, Heiner, *Joseph Beuys*, trans. David Britt (New York: Abbeville Press, 1987)

Stembera, Petr, 'Artist's statement', *Flash Art* (February-April 1978) 49

Stephano, Effie, 'Gina Pane: Performance of Concern', *Art and Artists* (April 1973)

Stich, Sidra (ed.), *Yves Klein* (Ostfildern: Cantz, 1994)

Stiles, Kristine, 'Raphael Montañez Ortiz', *Years of the Warrior, Years on the Psyche 1960-1988* (New York: El Museuo Del Barrio, 1988)

______ see **Brett, Guy; Selz, Peter**

Stone, Rosanne Allucquere, *The War of Desire and Technology at the Close of the Mechanical Age* (Cambridge, Massachusetts and London: MIT Press, 1995)

Sussman, Elizabeth, *Mike Kelley: Catholic Tastes* (New York: Whitney Museum of American Art, 1993)

Schwabsky, Barry, 'Shirin Neshat', *Artforum* (December 1995)

Tannenbaum, Judith, *PerForms: Janine Antoni, Charles Ray, Jana Sterbak* (Philadelphia: Institute of Contemporary Art, University of Pennsylvania, 1995)

Tarkka, Minna (ed.), *ISEA '94: The Fifth International Symposium on Electronic Art* (Helsinki: University of Art and Design, 1994)

Tazi, Nadia see **Feher, Michel**

Templeton, Fiona see **Heathfield, Adrian**

Tisdall, Caroline, *Joseph Beuys* (London: Thames & Hudson, 1988)

Tong, Darlene see **Loeffler, Carl E.**

Townsend, Chris, *Vile Bodies: Photography and the Crisis of Looking* (Munich: Prestel, 1998)

Triscott, Nicola (ed.), *Body Visual* (London: Arts Catalyst, 1996)

Vale, V. see **Juno, Andrea**

Vergine, Lea, *Gianni Pisani* (Naples: Museo Diego Aragona Pignatelli Cortes, 1979)

Violette, Robert (ed.), *Reasons for Knocking at an Empty House* (London: Thames & Hudson; Anthony d'Offay Gallery, 1995)

Vito, Acconci, 'Vito Acconci', *Avalanche*, 6 (Autumn 1972)

Volkart, Yvonne, 'Medusa and Co', *Flash Art* (May-June 1994)

von Drathen, Doris see **Meschede, Friedrich**

Vostell, Wolf, *Aktionen: Happenings und Demonstrationen seit 1965* (Reinbek bei Hamburg: Rowohlt, 1970)

______ see **Becker, Jurgen**

Vowinckel, Andreas; Weiss, Evelyn (eds.), *Jurgen Klauke: An Eternal Smile: Drawings, Photographical Works, Performances 1970-86* (Cologne: DuMont Buchverlag, 1986)

Walwin, Jeni see **Childs, Nicky**

Watson, Scott see **Baerwaldt, Wayne**

Weibel, Peter see **Klauke, Jürgen**

Weiss, Evelyn, *Klaus Rinke Travaux, 1969/76* (Cologne: Museum Ludwig; Paris: Musée d'Art Moderne de la Ville de Paris, 1976)

Weiss, Evelyn see **Vowinckel, Andreas**

Welton, Donn (ed.), *Body and Flesh: A Philosophical Reader* (Oxford: Blackwell, 1997)

Wilding, Faith, 'Waiting', *Ms.* (December 1973); reprinted in Judy Chicago, *Through the Flower* (Garden City, New York: Doubleday & Co, 1975)

______, Faith Wilding, *Art Journal* (Spring 1995)

Wood, Paul see **Harrison, Charles**

Wright, Beryl J., *Options 44: Yasumasa Morimura* (Chicago: Museum of Contemporary Art, 1992)

Yasumasa, Morimura, *Morimura Yasumasa: The Sickness unto Beauty - Self-Portrait as Actress* (Yokohama Museum of Art, 1996)

Zaya, Octavio, 'Women of Allah', *Creative Camera* (October-November 1996)

INDEX

Abramović, Marina 91, 221, 238, 255; *Balkan Baroque* [1997] 112, *112*; *Rhythm 0* [1974] 125, 246, *125*; *Rhythm 2* [1974] 124, *124*
Abstract Expressionism 23-24, 28, 49, 63, 65-66, 71, 193, 206, 212, 222, 266, 282
Abrioux, Yves 43
Acconci, Vito 21, 32, 218, 221, 226, 231, 232-234, 249, 251-253, 255, 266-267, 277-78, 285; *Conversions* [1970-71] 136, 219, 262, 268, *136*; *Pryings* (with Kathy Dillon) [1971] 119, *119*; *Seedbed* [1972] 117, 219, 268, 276, *117*; *Trademarks* [1970] 119, 215, 219, *119*
Ader, Bas Jan, *I'm Too Sad to Tell You* [1970] 85, *85*
Aguilar, Laura, *In Sandy's Room (Self-Portrait)* [1991] 157, *157*
Albers, Josef 200
Anderson, Laurie 22, 32, 36, 246; *O, Superman* [1981-83] *192*
Andre, Carl 205, 231, 285
Anti-form 252, 260, 261
Antin, Eleanor 22, 37, 241-42, 255; *Carving: A Traditional Sculpture* [1973] 87, *87*; *Swan Lake* [1986] *36*
Antoni, Janine *Eureka* [1993] 176, *176*; 'Interview with Laura Cottingham' 66; *Loving Care* [1992] 66, *66*; *Slumber* [1994] 29, *29*
Arman (Armand Fernandez) 209
Arnatt, Keith, *Self-Burial* [1969] 232
Arnold, Skip 'In Conversation with J.S.M. Willette' [1992] 91; *On Display* [1993] 91, *91*
Arp, Jean 261
Art & Language, 'Concerning the Article "The Dematerialization of Art"' [1968] 205-206
Artaud, Antonin 214, 219, 221, 'Theatre and Cruelty' [1933] 216
Arte Povera 228
ASCO *Walking Mural* [1972] 33-35, *33*
Ashton, Dore 200
Athey, Ron 14, 32-33, 36; *4 Scenes in a Harsh Life* [1994] 110, *110*
Atzori, Paul, 'Extended-Body: Interview with Stelarc' (with Kirk Wolford) 184

Baader, Johannes 218, 219; *The Author in His Home* [c. 1920] *192*
Bachelard, Gaston 267
Bacon, Francis 197-98; *Self-Portrait* [1973] *191*
Bakhtin, Michel 27
Bakunin, Mikhail 204
Baldessari, John 232
Bałka, Mirosław 275; *2 x /o2.5 x 167 x 15/* [1990] 176, *176*; 'Interview with Jaromir Jedliński' 281
Ball, Hugo 252
Bamgboyé, Oladélé Ajiboyé, *Celebrate* [1994] 159, *159*
Banes, Sally 26-27
Barney, Matthew 287; BLIND PERINEUM [1991] 186, *186*
Barthes, Roland 12
Bataille, Georges 221; 'L'Art Primitif' [1929-30] 193
Baudelaire, Charles 214, 251
Baudrillard, Jean 36
Bear, Liza 121
Beauvoir, Simone de 24
Benglis, Lynda 21, 143, 157, 253, 261-62, 267-268, 277-279; *Untitled* [1974] 142, *142*
Benjamin, Walter 259; 'The Work of Art in the Age of Mechanical Reproduction' [1936] 41-42
Benthall, Jonathan, 'The Body as a Medium of Expression: A Manifesto' [1972] 29, 235-36
Berger, John 273
Beuys, Joseph 219, 221, 225-26, 234, 246, 251-52, 267, 285; *I Like America and America Likes Me* [1974] 76, 91, *76*; 'Statement on How to Explain Pictures to a Dead Hare' [1965] 76, 202-203, 232, *76*
Blake, William 198
Blau, Herb 31
Boadwee, Keith, *Untitled (Purple Squirt)* [1995] 68, *68*
Bonami, Francesco 'Charles Ray: A Telephone Conversation' [1992] 281-82; 'Yasumasa Morimura' [1992] 259
Bontecou, Lee 260
Bosch, Hieronymus 216; *The Garden of Earthly Delights: Allegory of Luxury* [c. 1500] *191*
Bourgeois, Louise 41, 261; Costume for 'A Banquet' [1978] 182, *182*; *Destruction of the Father/Reconstruction of the Father: Writings and Interviews 1923-1997* [1998] 182
Bowery, Leigh 178; *Leigh Bowery in Performance at the Anthony d'Offay Gallery, 11-15 October 1988* [1988] 187, *187*
Brancusi, Constantine 261
Brecht, Bertolt 28
Brecht, George 196, 212
Brisley, Stuart, *Moments of Decision and Indecision* [1975] 65, *65*
Brown, Norman O. 235, 239, 252
Brus, Günter 12, 219, 223-25, 252; *Art and Revolution* [1968] 95, *95*; *Beiblatt zur Photo Edition* [1970] 95, *95*; *Self-painting, Self-mutilation* [1965] 96, *96*; *Vienna Walk* [1965] *32*
Burden, Chris 13, 21, 91, 218, 221, 223, 225-26, 234, 251, 255, 266-69; *Icarus* [1973] 102, *102*; 'Interview with Robin White' [1978] 102; 'Just the Facts' [1988] 122; *Shoot* [1971] 32, 122, 215, 219, 246, 285, *122*; *Trans-Fixed* [1974] 102, 222, *102*
Burgin, Victor, *Zoo* series 258
Burroughs, William 214
Butler, Judith 14, 35; 'Bodies That Matter' [1993] 263-65
Byars, James Lee 178, 222-23, 226, 284, 285-86; *Five in a Dress* [1969] 182, *182*

Cage, John 12, 26, 90, 196, 198, 200, 204-205, 209, 214, 241
Cahun, Claude 37; *Self-portrait* [c. 1929] *37*
Campus, Peter 279-80
Caravaggio, Michelangelo da 37
Cassirer, Ernst 201
Castelli, Leo 237
Certeau, Michel de 28, 29
César, *Masque XXIII (Mask XXIII)* [1968] 166, *166*
Cézanne, Paul 82
Chadwick, Helen 42; *Blood Hyphen* [1985] 41, *40*; *Enfleshings* [1989] 173; 'Soliloquy to Flesh' [1989] 280-81; *Viral Landscape No. 3* [1988-89] 173, *173*
Chandler, John see **Lippard, Lucy R.**
Cheng, Meiling, 'Bob Flanagan's Body Double' [1998] 229
Chevrier, Jean-François see **Coplans, John**
Chicago, Judy 253, 266-67; *Ablutions* [1972] 22, 33, *21*; *Beyond the Flower* [1996] 137; *Boxing Ring* [1970] 137, *137*; *Cock and Cunt Play* [1970] 22, *22*
Menstruation Bathroom [1972] 256, 260, *192*
Clark, Lygia 13; 'About the Act' [1965] 284-85; *Ar e Pedra (Air and Stone)* [1966] 25, *25*; *Dialogo de Manos (Dialogue of Hands)* [1966] 180, *180*; *Relational Objects: Dialogue* [1968] 24, *24*; 'The I and the You: Clothing/Body/Clothing' [1967] 26, 181, *181*
Clearwater, Bonnie, *The Art of Seduction* [1994] 67
Cohen, Michael, 'Lyle Ashton Harris' 155
Conceptual art 86, 239, 246, 248, 252-53, 277
Conner, Bruce 241
Constructivism 201, 218
Contact Improvisation 26-28
Cooper, Alice 252
Coplans, John 'Interview with Jean-François Chevrier' [1989] 158; *Self-Portrait (Standing, Side View, Three Panels, No. 5)* [1993] 158, *158*
Cottingham, Laura see **Antoni, Janine**
Cotton, Paul *The Battle of the Books* [1969] 239; *The People's Prick* [1969] 79, 239, *79*
Courbet, Gustave 219, 251; *L'Origine du Monde (The origin of the world)* [1866] *192*
Cox, Renée, *Queen, Alias & Id: The Child* (with Lyle Ashton Harris) [1994] 155, *155*
Cravan, Arthur 219
Cubism 193-95, 204, 206
Cunningham, Merce 241; *Rain Forest* (with Andy Warhol) [1968] 26

Dada 11, 13, 20, 26, 28, 162, 194, 204, 214, 218-19, 222, 248, 252
Degas, Edgar, *After the Bath* [1885-86] 198
Delacroix, Eugène 267
Deleuze, Gilles 214, 269, 'The Body, the Meat and the Spirit: Becoming Animal' [1981] 197-98
Derrida, Jacques 264-65
Descartes, René 19-20
Destruction art 228
Dillon, Kathy 234
Dine, Jim 12, 193, 196, 204; *The Smiling Workman* [1960] 59, *59*
Donegan, Cheryl, *Kiss My Royal Irish Ass [K.M.R.I.A.]* [1993] 67, *67*
Douglas, Mary 235
Duchamp, Marcel 12-13, 40-41, 204, 209, 222, 232, 249, 251-52, 277, 287; *Etant donnés (Given)* [1946-66] 49, 276; *Vigne de femelle (Female Fig Leaf)* [1951] 276, *192*; *Monte Carlo Bond* [1924] 37, *37*; *Paysage fautif (Wayward landscape)* [1946] 33, 49, *49*; as Rrose Sélavy [c. 1920-21] 36, 155, 23-34, 252, 276, *36*; *Tonsure in the form of a shooting star* [1919] 218, 233, *191*; *With My Tongue in My Cheek* [1959] 162, *162*
Duchamp, Teeny 162
Duncan, John; *Blind Date* [1980] 105, *105*; 'Sex with the Dead' [1981] 105
Durkheim, Émile *235*

Edelson, Mary Beth 30, 32, 225, 256, 257; *Goddess Head* [1975] 144, *144*
Eisenhauer, Lette 97, 218
El Greco 198
Eltit, Diamela 244, 245; *Maipu* [1980] 128, *128*
Emin, Tracey, *Exorcism of the Last Painting I Ever Made* [1996] 68, *68*
Engels, Friedrich 243
Ernst, Max 11, 204
Erró 61, 196
Espaliú, Pepe, *Carrying* [1992] 131, *131*
Export, Valie *Eros/ion* [1971] 116, *116*; *Genital Panic* [1969] *21*
Expressionism 204, 252

Fabre, Jan 246
Fanon, Fritz 235
Fauvism 194
Feher, Michel 14, 22-23
Feminist Art Program, California Institute of the Arts 30, 137, 260; Womanhouse 256
Filiou, Robert 211
Finley, Karen 36; *We Keep Our Victims Ready* [1989] 108, *108*
Fiore, Bob see **Oppenheim, Dennis**
Fisher, Jean, 'In Search of the "Inauthentic": Disturbing Signs in Contemporary Native American Art' [1992] 154
Flanagan, Bob 32-33; *Auto-Erotic SM* [1989] 109, *109*; *Visiting Hours* (with Sheree Rose) [1992] 109, 229, *109*
Flavin, Dan, the nominal three (to William of Ockham) [1963] 205, *191*
Fleming, Sherman, *Something Akin to Living* [1979] 150, *150*
Fluxus 13, 21-22, 24, 26-29, 72, 211-14, 245, 261
Flynt, Henry 212
Forti, Simone 240, 261
Foucault, Michel 213, 228, 263, 265
Fox, Terry 221, 225, 231-34; *Levitation* [1970] 165, 239, *165*
Francblin, Catherine 13, 31, 253; 'Body-Object, Woman-Object' [1975] 238
Franko B 'Interview with Dr Rachel Armstrong' [1996] 110; *Mama, I Can't Sing* [1996] 110, *110*
Freud, Sigmund 11, 223-25, 235, 243, 261, 268, 274, 277, 279; 'Parapraxes: Introduction' [1916] 247-48
Fried, Howard *All My Dirty Blue Clothes* [1970] 166, 239, *166*
Fried, Michael 236; 'Art and Objecthood' [1967] 203, 212
Fusco, Coco 247; 'The Other History of Intercultural Performance' [1994] 265; *Two Undiscovered Amerindians Visit Madrid* (with Guillermo Gómez-Peña) [1992] 33, 34-35, 159, *33*, *159*
Futurism 215, 248, 252

Gabo, Naum 201
Gallop, Jane 265
Gauguin, Paul 251
Gechtman, Gideon, *Naked* [1974] 102, *102*
Gilbert & George (Gilbert Proesch and George Passmore) 222-23, 277; 'A Day in the Life of George & Gilbert, the Sculptors' [1971] 209; 'Six Points Towards a Better Understanding' [1970] 82; *The Singing Sculpture* [1970] 82, *82*
Gilchrist, Bruce 14; *Divided by Resistance* (with Jonathan Bradley) [1996] 188, *188*
Ginsberg, Allen 214
Godet, Robert 54, 196
Goffman, Erving 235; *Interaction Ritual* 252; *The Presentation of Self in Everyday Life* 252
Goldberg, RoseLee 39; 'Here and Now' [1995] 246
Gómez-Peña, Guillermo 265; *Two Undiscovered Amerindians Visit Madrid* (with Coco Fusco) [1992] 33, 34-35, 159, *33*, *159*
Goodeve, Thyrza Nichols, 'Travels in Hypertropia' [1995] 186
Gorky, Arshile 194
Gormley, Antony, *Bed* [1981] 172, *172*
Gorsen, Peter 237-38
Graham, Dan 231, 234; *Performance/Audience/Mirror* [1977] 35, *35*
Greenberg, Clement 12, 23-24, 203-204
Grooms, Red 196
Gross, Elizabeth 260
Grünewald, Matthias 216
Guerrilla Art Action Group 22
Guerrilla Girls, Poster [1989] *22*
Gutai group 12, 23, 53, 194, 233
Gysin, Brion 214

Haimovitz, Michael 239
Hall, Edward 233-34
Hansen, Al 196, 211-12
Hanson, Duane 282
Happenings 13, 21, 26-29, 59, 70, 76, 82, 196, 212, 214-15, 218, 233-34, 245, 248, 250-53, 260, 261
Haraway, Donna 14, 284; *A Cyborg Manifesto: Science, Technology and Socialist-Feminism in the Late Twentieth Century* [1985] 42, 263, 286
Harris, Lyle Ashton 22; *Construct No. 10* [1989] *23*; *Queen, Alias & Id: The Child* (with Renée Cox) [1994] 155, *155*
Hatoum, Mona, *Corps étranger* [1994] 42-43, 132, *42*, *132*; *Recollection* [1995] 176, *176*; *he Negotiating Table* [1983] 150, *150*

Hay, Alex 204, 240
Heidegger, Martin 21, 35, 41
Heiss, Alanna see **Oppenheim, Dennis**
Henderson, Mel 239
Hennessey, Sharon 251
Hershman, Lynn 240
Hess, Thomas B. 261
Hesse, Eva 261
Hi Red Center 13, 22; *A Fluxus Performance Workbook* [1990] 76; *Maquette of the Hi Red Center Shelter (Hotel Event)* [1964] 43, 76, *76*
Higgins, Dick 196, 211-13, 240; *Danger Music No. 2* (with Alison Knowles) 72, *72*; 'Statement on Intermedia' [1966] 203
Hill, Gary 43
Hiller, Susan *Dream Mapping* [1974] 126, *126*; 'Dream Mapping' [1981] 126
Holt, Nancy, *Boomerang* (with Richard Serra) [1974] 277-79
Hopps, Walter 200
Horn, Rebecca 238, 255; 'Arm Extensions' [1968] 285; *Arm-Extensionen (Arm Extensions)* [1970] 183, *183*; *Fingerhandschuhe (Finger Gloves)* [1972] 183, *183*; *Painting Machine* [1988] 40, *40*
Hsieh, Tehching 226

Impressionism 194
Irigaray, Luce 274

Jameson, Fredric 36
Jay, Martin 273
Jedliński, Jaromir see **Bałka, Mirosław**
Johns, Jasper 57, 204, 233, 278
Jonas, Joan 252-53, 279-80; *Mirror Check* [1970] 85, *85*
Jones, Amelia 14; *Body Art: Performing the Subject* [1998] 68, 157; 'Dis/playing the Phallus: Male Artists Perform Their Masculinities' [1994] 265-71; 'Tracing the Subject with Cindy Sherman' [1997] 106
Jones, Ernest 200
Jones, Kim 224-25
Jones, Leslie C., 'Transgressive Femininity: Art and Gender in the 1960s and 1970s' [1993] 260-63
Journiac, Michel 218, 219; *Messe pour un corps (Mass for a body)* [1969] 98, 221, *98*
Joyce, James 231
Judd, Donald 203-204, 233
Judson Dance Group 26
Jung, Carl Gustav 223, 225
Junker, Howard, 'James Lee Byars: Performance as Protective Coloration' [1978] 285-86

Kafka, Franz 226, 265, 285
Kant, Immanuel 20, 265
Kaprow, Allan 12, 196, 222, 233, 252; *18 Happenings in 6 Parts* [1959] 59, *59* *Assemblage, Environments and Happenings* [1966] 97; *The Courtyard* [1962] 28, *28* 'The Legacy of Jackson Pollock' [1958] 23, 194-95
Keane, Susan, 'Dual Natures' [1991] 142
Kelley, Mike, *Plato's Cave, Rothko's Chapel, Lincoln's Profile* [1986] 105, *105*
Kelly, Mary 13, 262; 'Woman - Desire - Image' [1984] 257-58
Kienholz, Edward 241
Kim, Byron 41
Kinetic Theatre 261
Kitchell, Nancy, 238
Klauke, Jürgen 13, 141; 'Interview with Peter Weibel' [1994] 140; *Transformer* [1973] 140, *140*
Klein, Melanie 259, 286
Klein, Yves 12-13, 21, 23-24, 30, 63, 67, 97, 209, 212, 222, 231, 241, 252, 260, 266, 269; *Anthropometry of the Blue Epoch* [1960] 54, *54*; *Leap into the Void* [1960] 70, 224, 226-67, *70*; 'Truth Becomes Reality' [1960] 54, 57, 195-96; *Untitled Anthropometry* [1960] 54, *54*; *Untitled Anthropometry with Male and Female Figures* [1960] 57, *56*
Knížák, Milan, 'Demonstration for all the Senses' [1964] 75, 202, *75*
Knowles, Alison 29, 212, 240, 261 *75*; *Identical Lunch* [1973] 28, *28*
Kooning, Willem de, *Woman IV* [1952-53] 25, *25*
Koons, Jeff 22, 36, 39; *Untitled* [1989] 157, *157*
Kostolowski, Andrzej, 'Intimacy Revealed' [1998] 131
Kosuth, Joseph 204-205
Kozloff, Max, 'Pygmalion Revisited' [1975] 248-49
Krauss, Rosalind 275, 283; 'Video: The Aesthetics of Narcissism' [1976] 277-80
Kristeva, Julia 260-61; 'Approaching Abjection' [1980] 242-43
Kruger, Barbara 257
Krystufek, Elke, *Satisfaction* [1996] 111, *111*
Kubota, Shigeko 21; *Vagina Painting* [1965] 24, 63, 211, *63*
Kudo, Tetsumi, *Philosophy of Impotence* [1962] 72, *72*
Kulik, Oleg, *I Bite America and America Bites Me* [1997] 91, *91*
Kusama, Yayoi 22, 37, 39, 252, 260-61; *Accumulation No. 2*, *134*; 'But Is It Art?' [1969] 82; *Grand Orgy to Awaken the Dead at MoMA* [1969] 82, *82*; *Infinity Mirror Room* [1965] 115, *36*; 'Interview with Gordon Brown for WABC Radio' [1965] 115, 202; *Kusama's Peep Show or Endless Love Show* [1966] 115, *115*; *Untitled* [c. 1966] 134, *134*
Kuspit, Donald 247; 'The New Subjectivism: Inside Cindy Sherman' [1987] 258-59
Kwon, Miwon, 'Bloody Valentines: Afterimages by Ana Mendieta' [1996] 282-83

La Frenais, Rob 14; 'The Pit and the Pendulum' [1993] 128, 245-46
Labelle-Rojoux, Arnaud see **Lebel, Jean-Jacques**
Labowitz, Leslie see **Lacy, Suzanne**
Lacan, Jacques 243, 250, 258, 262-66, 273-74, 279, 286; 'The Mirror Stage as Formative of the Function of the I as Revealed in Psychoanalytic Experience' [1949] 248
Lachowicz, Rachel, *Red not Blue* [1992] 67, *67*
Lacy, Suzanne 22, 31, 240; *In Mourning and in Rage* (with Leslie Labowitz) [1977] 30, *30*; *Three Weeks in May* [1977] 30, 241
Laing, R.D. 234, 252
Lake, Suzy 255
Latham, John 211
Laub, Stephen 232, 239
Le Va, Barry 221, 231, 234, 253, 262; *Velocity Piece No. 2* [1970] 121, *121*
Lebeer, Irmeline see **Vautier, Ben**
Lebel, Jean-Jacques 60, 211-12; 'Interview by Arnaud Labelle-Rojoux' [1994] 214-15
Lebel, Robert 162
LeCoque, Karen 260
Lee, David 205
Lefebvre, Henri 19, 211
Leppe, Carlos 13, 245, *Perchero (Coat Hanger)* [1975] 147, 244, *147*
Lesko, Lauren *Lips* (1993) 41, *41*
Lester, Jan 22, *22*
Lévi-Strauss, Claude 235
LeWitt, Sol 204-205
Licht, Ira, 'Bodyworks' [1975] 251-52
Lifton, Robert Jay 227-28
Lippard, Lucy R. 247; 'The Dematerialization of Art' (with John Chandler) [1968] 203-205; 'The Pains and Pleasures of Rebirth: Women's Body Art' [1976] 141, 252-56
LL, Natalia 238, 253
Long, Richard, *A Line Made by Walking* [1967] 166, *166*
Louis, Morris 206
Luchford, Glen see **Saville, Jenny**
Luna, James, *The Artifact Piece* [1987] 154, *154*
Lüthi, Urs 13, 41, 141, 237, 250-52, 255; *Self-Portrait with Ecky* [1974] 139, *139*; *Tell Me Who Stole Your Smile* [1974] *22*; 'The Artist and His Double: Interview with François Pluchart' [1974] 139; *The Numbergirl* [1973] 37-38, *37*
Lyotard, Jean-François 36

McCarthy, Paul 12-13, 32-33, 36, 225, 241; *Face Painting - Floor, White Line* [1972] 63, *63*; *Hot Dog* [1974] 104, *104*; *Sailor's Meat* [1975] 146, 224, *146*; 'There's a Big Difference Between Ketchup and Blood' [1993] 146; *Whipping a Wall and a Window with Paint* [1974] *21*
McEvilley, Thomas 23, 216; 'Art in the Dark' [1983] 221-27; 'Diogenes of Sinope. Selected Performance Pieces' [1983] 210-11
Maciunas, George 13, 29, 212; 'Fluxus Manifesto' [1963] 201-202
McLean, Bruce, 232, *Pose Work for Plinths* [1970] 86, *86*
MacLennan, Alastair 36; *Days and Nights* [1981] *36*
McLuhan, Marshall 203, 207
Malevich, Kasimir 201, 205, 218
Malraux, André 221
Manet, Édouard, *Olympia* [1863] 155, 273, *192*
Man Ray 41, *Marcel Duchamp as Rrose Sélavy* [c. 1920-21] 155, 252, 276, *36*
Manzoni, Piero 13, 21, 24, 210, 218, 252; *Artist's Breath* [1960] 163, *163*; *Merda d'artista* [1961] 33, 163, 222, 275, *163*; 'Some Realizations, Some Experiments, Some Projects' [1962] 275; *To Devour Art* [1960] *4*
Mapplethorpe, Robert 22, 257, 259; *Portrait of Louise Bourgeois* [1982] *41*; *Self-portrait* [1988] *37*; *Self-Portrait with Bullwhip* [1978] 150, *150*
Marcad, Bernard, 'Glossaire Orient' [1995] 135
Marcuse, Herbert 29, 31, 261; *An Essay on Liberation* [1969] 27, 30, 230
Marioni, Tom 29, 239; *Free Beer on Friday* [1979] *29*
Markusen, Eric 227-28
Marx, Karl 235, 243-44, 246
Mathieu, Georges 23-24, 194, 212; *Homage to General Hideyoshi* [1957] 50, *50*; 'Towards a New Convergence in Art, Thought and Science' [1960] 50
Matisse, Henri 197
Matta, Roberto 49
Mauss, Marcel 18, 235
Mendieta, Ana 21, 30, 32, 255; 'Ana Mendieta Plants Her Garden' [1980] 63; *Body Tracks* [1974] 63, *63*; *Death of a Chicken* [1972] 101, *101*; *Rape Scene* [1973] 100, *100*; *Silueta de Cenizas (Silhouette of Ashes)* [1975] 31, *31*; *Untitled* (from the Silueta series) [1976] 168, *168*
Merleau-Ponty, Maurice 21, 26, 201, 207, 233, 235-236; 'Eye and Mind' [1961] 196-97
Messager, Annette 237, 255
Metzger, Gustav 211, 228
Meyer, Ursula see **Beuys, Joseph**
Michaux, Henri 214
Michelangelo *87*
Minimalism 63, 204, 206, 233, 248-49, 252-53, 268, 280
Mitchell, Joan 24, *Chez ma Soeur* [1981-82] *24*
Mlcoch, Jan 221
Modernism 19, 20, 23-25, 33, 37, 204, 212, 245, 251, 260-61, 266-67, 278
Modleski, Tania, 'Femininity and Mas[s]querade' 262
Molesworth, Helen 27; 'Before Bed' [1993] 198-200
Molinier, Pierre, *The Spur of Love* [1966-68] 135, *135*
Mondrian, Piet 201, 204, 212
Monet, Claude 24
Monk, Meredith 207
Monroe, Marilyn *38*
Montano, Linda 29, 223, 225, 240; *A Year Spent Tied Together at the Waist* (with Tehching Hsieh) [1983-84] 129, *129*
Moore, Henry 86
Moorman, Charlotte 178, 211, 252, 261
Morgan, Stuart, 'Matthew Barney: of Goats and Men' [1995] 287
Mori, Mariko *Miko no Inori (Last Departure)* [1996] 160, *160*; *Pure Land* [1997-98] 39-40, *39*
Morimura, Yasumasa 36-37, 247, 259; *Doublenage (Marcel)* [1988] 155, *155*; *Portrait (Futago)* [1988] *2-3*
Morris, Robert 60, 203-204, 262, 267-68, 277; 'Antiform' [1968] 206, 261; *Felt Piece* [1967-68] 261, *192*; *I-Box* [1962] 71, 252, 267, *71*; 'Notes on Sculpture' [1966] 233; *Untitled* [1974] 143, *143*
Mouraud, Tania 255
Mühl, Otto 12, 92, 216, 219, 224; *Ausgewählte Arbeiten 1963-1986* [1986] 94-95; *Der Psycho-Physische Naturalismus 'Das Intrem'* [1963] 94; *Gymnastics Class in Food* [1965] 94, *94*; *Material Action No.1: Degradation of a Venus* [1963] 94, *94*; *Materialaktion: Manifesto* [1964] 217; *Pissaction* [1969] 95, *95*
Mulvey, Laura 38
Munch, Edvard 68, 252
Murak, Tersa, *Seed* [1989] 131, *131*
Murakami, Saburo, *Breaking Through Many Paper Screens (At One Moment Opening Six Holes)* [1956] 52, *52*

Namuth, Hans 23
Nancy, Jean-Luc 18
Nauman, Bruce 21, 209, 218, 231-33, 234, 246, 251-53, 262, 276-79; *Art Make-Up Films No. 1; Green* [1967-68] 78, *78*; *From Hand to Mouth* [1967] 165, 207, *165*; 'Interview with Willoughby Sharp' [1971] 79, 165; *Self-Portrait as a Fountain* [1966-67] 79, 232, 233, *79*; *Walking in an Exaggerated Manner Around the Perimeter of a Square* [1967-68] 80, *80*
Nechvatel, Joseph, 'Tactiles Technologies: La synesthésie par le cybersexe sur le web de Stahl Stenslie' [unpublished] [1994] 184
Nemser, Cindy, 'Subject - Object: Body Art' [1971] 233-35
Nengudi, Senga 41; *Studio Performance with R.S.V.P.* [1976] 26, *26*
Neo-Concretist Manifesto 201
Neshat, Shirin, *Faceless* [1994] 160, *160*
Nietzsche, Friedrich Wilhelm 223, 251, 264-65
Nitsch, Hermann 12, 216-19, 223-24, 226, 249, 252, 255, 267; *80th Action: Orgies-Mysteries Theatre* [1984] 93, *93*; *1st Action* [1962] 92, *92*

O'Dell, Kathy 22, 32, 266; 'Displacing the Haptic: Performance Art, the Photographic Document, and the 1970s' [1997] 215
Ofrat, Gideon, *The Heart of the Matter* [1986] 102, *102*
Oiticica, Hélio *Wearing Parangolé P19 Capa 15, Gileasa: to Gilberto Gil* [1968] 181, *181*
Oldenburg, Claes 13, 193, 196, 205-206, 212, 232, 253, 260-62; *Snapshots from the City* [1960] 59, *59*
O'Neill, John 235
Ono, Yoko 13, 21, 196, 261; *Cut Piece* [1964] 74, 211, *74*
Oppenheim, Dennis 218, 222, 225, 232-34, 249, 253, 255-56, 262, 276, 282; 'Another Point of Entry: An Interview with Alanna Heiss' [1990] 118; *Arm and Wire* (with Bob Fiore) [1969] 116, 219, 231, *116*; *Parallel Stress* [1970] 84, 219, *84*; *Reading Position for a Second Degree Burn* [1970] 118, 219, 231, *118*
Oppenheim, Meret 41
Orenstein, Gloria Feman, 'The Re-emergence of the Archetype of the Great Goddess in Art by Contemporary Women' [1978] 257
Orgel, Sandra 260
Orlan 13-14, 40, 178, *Omnipresence* [1993] 185, 32, *185*
Orta, Lucy 284, 287, *The Unit* [1996] 187, *187*
Ortiz, Rafael Montañez 211, 228; *The Birth and*

Death of White Henny [1967] 98, *98*
Oursler, Tony, *Angerotic* [1994], *43*

Paik, Nam June 12, 211, 240; *Human Cello (Interpreting John Cage's 26'1.1499 for a String Player)* (with Charlotte Moorman) [1965] 179, *179*; *Performing La Monte Young's Composition 1960 No. 10 to Bob Morris (Zen for Head)* [1962] 60, *60*; *TV Bra for a Living Sculpture* (with Charlotte Moorman) [1969] 179, *179*
Pane, Gina 13, 36, 40, 215, 218-19, 221, 237, 255; *Death Control* [1974] 101, *101*; *Escalade non-anesthésiée (Non-anesthesized climb)* [1971] 32-33, *33*; *Le Lait Chaud (Warm milk)* [1972] 121, *121*; 'Performance of Concern: Gina Pane discusses her work with Effie Stephano' [1973] 121
Panovsky, Erwin 273
Parker, Jayne, *K* [1989] 130, *130*
Parr, Mike 221; *Cathartic Action: Social Gestus No. 5* [1977] 105, *105*
Pejić, Bojana 246
Penone, Giuseppe *Piede (Foot)* [1972] 167, *167*; *Rovesciare i propri occhi (To reverse one's eyes)* [1970] 86, *86*
Pevsner, Nicholas 201
Phelan, Peggy 14; 'Developing the Negative' [1993] 259-60
Picabia, Francis 204, 222
Picasso, Pablo, *Les Demoiselles d'Avignon* [1907] 11
Pincus-Witten, Robert 275; 'Theatre of the Conceptual: Autobiography and Myth' [1973] 276-77
Piper, Adrian 255; *Catalysis IV* [1970-71] 139, *139*; *The Mythic Being: Cruising White Women* [1975] 139, *139*
Pisani, Gianni, *Each Morning Before Going Out* [1973] 122, *122*
Pluchart, François 216; 'Body Art' [1974] 218-19; 'Risk as the Practice of Thought' [1978] 219, 221
Pollock, Jackson 12, 21, 24-25, 49, 63, 68, 193-95, 200, 212, 233, 251-52, 266; photographed by Hans Namuth [1960] *23*; Painting in his studio [*c.* 1950] 50, *50*
Poons, Larry 205
Pop art 277
post-Impressionism 193
Postmodernism 31, 36, 39, 266-67
Process art 248, 252

Quinn, Marc, *Self* [1991] 175, *175*

Rainer, Arnulf 252; *Face Farces* [1969] 98, *98*; 'Face Farces' [1971] 98
Rainer, Yvonne 204-205, 240, 252, 261
Rakauskaitė, Eglė, *In Honey* [1996] 189, *189*
Rauschenberg, Robert 57, 204, 211, 241, 266, 280; *Black Paintings* [1951-52] 198, 200, *191*; *Reservoir* [1961] *26*
Ray, Charles 282; *Oh Charley, Charley, Charley ...* [1992] 175, 282, *175*; *Plank Piece I & II* [1973] 88, *88*
Reagan, Ronald 22, 31, 35, 79
Reich, Steve 233
Reinhardt, Ad 204, 285
Rekula, Heli, *Hyperventilation* [1993] 187, *187*
Rembrandt van Rijn 24, 198
Richard, Nelly 25, 230; 'The Rhetoric of the Body' [1986] 244-45
Rimbaud, Arthur 214, 219, 260, 262
Rinke, Klaus 218; *Deplazierung (Changing location according to points in time)* [1972] 123, *123*
Rist, Pipilotti, *I'm Not the Girl Who Misses Much* [1986] 153, *153*
Ritchie, Matthew, 'Lorna Simpson' [1996] 154
Roberts, James, 'Bas Jan Ader: the artist who fell from grace with the sea' [1994] 85
Rodenback, J.F., 'Yayoi Kusama' [1996] 134
Romanticism 23, 222-23, 225, 251, 267
Rose, Jacqueline 274
Rose, Sheree 32, 33; *Visiting Hours* (with Bob Flanagan) [1992] 109, *109*
Rosenbach, Ulrike 40, 255; *Don't Believe I Am an Amazon* [1975] 147, *147*; *Or-Phelia* [1982] 41, *40*
Rosenberg, Harold 23, 24; 'The American Action Painters' [1952] 193-94
Rosenthal, Rachel 226, 241
Rosler, Martha 21, 30; *Semiotics of the Kitchen* [1975] *29*
Roth, Moira; 'Towards a History of California Performance: Part One' [1978] 238-40; 'Part Two' [1978] 240-42
Ruppersberg, Allen 236
Ruscha, Ed 266-67

Sade, Marquis De 237
Saint-Phalle, Niki de, *First Shooting Impasse Ronsin* [1961] 57, *57*
Samaras, Lucas 37, 241, 251-53; *Photo-Transformation* [1974] 99, *99*
Santarromana, Joseph, *Telegarden* [1994] 40, *40*
Sarduy, Severo, 'The Transvestites. Kallima on a Body: Painting, Idol' [1975] 250
Sartre, Jean-Paul 21, 23, 236
Saussure, Ferdinand de 222
Saville, Jenny, *Closed Contact No. 10* (with Glen Luchford) 68, *68*
Sayre, Henry, *The Object of Performance* [1989] 37
Scarry, Elaine 211; 'The Structure of Belief and Its Modulation into Material Making' [1985] 243-44
Schapiro, Miriam 253
Schiele, Egon 68
Schilder, Paul 197
Schillinger, Joseph 204
Schimmel, Paul 122; 'Beside One's Self' [1998] 175; 'Leap in the Void: Performance and the Object' [1998] 165
Schindler, Paul, *The Image of the Body* [1935] 221
Schlemmer, Oskar 12; 'Stage' [1927] 212
Schneemann, Carolee 12-13, 17, 193, 211-12, 225, 252, 260; *Eye Body: 36 Transformative Actions* [1963] 24-25, 61, 196, 261, *24*, *61*; *Interior Scroll* [1975] 33, 144, 215, *144*; 'Interior Scroll' [1975] 250-51; *Meat Joy* [1964] 21, 27, 60, 224, 262, *27*, *60*; *More Than Meat Joy* [1979] 24, 60-61, 90, 144, 215; 'Naked Action Lecture' [1968] 206; *Up To And Including Her Limits* [1976] 90, 253, *90*
Schneider, Rebecca, 'Gender in Perspective: Have We Really Gone Beyond?' [1997] 273-74
Schor, Mira 260; 'Representations of the Penis' 267, 268
Schwarzkogler, Rudolf 218-19, 224, 251-52; *Action 1: Wedding* [1965] 97, *97*; *Aktion 3* [1965] *32*; 'Script for a Wedding' [1965] 217
Schwitters, Kurt 11, 204, *Merzbau Hanover [Blue Window]* [1923-43] *191*
Sedgwick, Eve Kosofsky, 'Queer Performativity: Warhol's Whiteness/Warhol's Shyness' [1996] 271-73
Serra, Richard 232; *Boomerang* (with Nancy Holt) [1974] 277-79; *Hand Catching Lead* [1968] 233, *192*
Serrano, Andres 244; 'In Conversation with Simon Watney' [1993] 106; *Piss Christ* [1987] 65, 106, *106*; *Untitled XIII (Ejaculate in Trajectory)* [1989] 65, *65*
Shapiro, Joel 280
Shapiro, Miriam 260
Sharp, Willoughby, 'Body Works' [1970] 231-33
Sherk, Bonnie *Public Lunch* [1971] 89, 240, *89*
Sherman, Cindy 13, 22, 36, 37, 40-41, 247; 'Interview with George Howell' [1995] 151; *Untitled No. 15* [1978] 151, *151*; *Untitled No. 131* [1983] 151, *151*; *Untitled No. 138* [1984] 39, *39*; *Untitled No. 175* [1987] 106, *106*
Shimamoto, Shozo, *Making a Painting by Throwing Bottles of Paint* [1956] 53, *53*
Shiraga, Kazuo 12; *Challenging Mud* [1955] 53, *53*; *Painting with his Feet* [1956] *23*
Sieverding, Katharina 237, 255; *Transformer 1 A/B* [1973] 141, *141*
Silva, Samuel see **Zurita, Raúl**
Simon, Joan 256
Simonds, Charles, *Landscape-Body-Dwelling* [1970] 282
Simpson, Lorna, *Guarded Conditions* [1989] 154, *154*
Smith, Barbara 29, 224; *Feed Me* [1973] 116, 241, *116*; 'Paul McCarthy' [1979] 104; *Ritual Meal* [1968] 28, 240, *28*
Smith, Kiki, *Virgin Mary* [1992] 41, *41*
Smith, Larry, *Line* [1970] 231-32
Smith, Tony, *Die* [1962] 203, *191*
Sobchack, Vivian 35, 36, 41
Solomon-Godeau, Abigail 262
Sonfist, Alan 249; *Last Will and Testament* [1973] 168, *168*
Sonnier, Keith 231-32, 277
Sontag, Susan 12; 'Happenings: An Art of Radical Juxtaposition' [1962] 196
Spector, Nancy, 'Rock my Video' [1995] 67
Spero, Nancy 282
Spivak, Gayatri Chakravorty 263
Sprinkle, Annie, *Post-Porn Modernist Show* [1992] 110, *110*
Stelarc 14, 40, 178, 225; *Event for Stretched Skin* [1976] 184, *184*; 'Obsolete Body/ Suspensions/Stelarc' [1980] 184; *The Third Hand* [1976-80] 184, *184*
Štembera, Petr 221; *Grafting* [1975] 126, *126*
Stenslie, Stahl 14; *CyberSM* (with Kirk Wolford) [1994] 188, *188*
Stiles, Kristine 30; 'Between Water and Stone – Fluxus Performance: A Metaphysics of Acts' [1993] 211-14; 'Survival Ethos and Destruction Art' [1992] 227-29; 'Uncorrupted Joy' [1998] 150
Sundell, Margaret 275; 'Vanishing Points: Photography of Francesca Woodman' [1996] 283
Surrealism 11, 41, 194, 204, 222, 233, 252

Taeuber-Arp, Sophie 201
Tanaka, Atsuko, *Electric Dress* [1956] 178, *178*
Teitelbaum, Matthew 283
Thater, Diana 43
The Hottentot Venus [*c.* 1815] 34, *34*
Tomlin, Lilly 273
Tucker, Marcia, 'Phenaumanology' [1970] 207-209
Tzara, Tristian 11

Ukeles, Mierle Laderman 21, 22; *Hartford Wash: Washing, Tracks, Maintenance: Outside* [1973] 89, *89*; 'The Garbage Girls' [1991] 89; 'Maintenance Art' [1969] 89, 206-207
Ulay (Uwe Laysiepen) 221, 246
Ulay/Abramović; *Imponderabilia* [1977] 124, 246, *124*; *Interruption in Space* [1977] *32*

Valéry, Paul 248
Van Gogh, Vincent 82, 219, 251, 259, 267
Van Saun, John 231
Vautier, Ben 211, 221-23, 252; 'Art = Ben' (interview with Irmeline Lebeer) [1973] 209-10; 'Ben: The Truth of A to Z' [1987] 72; *Geste: Rentrer dans l'eau (Gesture: To enter the water)* [1964/72] 72, *72*
Velázquez, Diego de Silva y 259
Vergine, Lea 18-19, 21-22, 38, 253, 255; 'Bodylanguage' [1974] 236-38; 'Il corpo come linguaggio' (La Body-art e storie simili) [1974] 249, 252
Viennese Actionism 12, 32, 72, 92, 95, 211, 216
Viola, Bill *Reasons for Knocking at an Empty House* [1995] 127; *The Space Between the Teeth* [1976] 127, *127*
Virilio, Paul, 'Urban Armour' [1996] 287
Vonnegut, Kurt 249
Vostell, Wolf 28, 29, 212; *Happenings: Fluxus, Pop Art, Nouveau Réalisme; Eine Dokumentation* (with Jürgen Becker) [1965] 211; 'You: A Decollage Happening For Bob and Rhett Brown' [1964] 218; *You-Happening* [1964] 97, *97*

Wacks, Debra 262
Warhol, Andy 33, 37-38, 40, 153, 252; *Oxidation Painting* [1978] 65, *65*; *Self-Portrait* [1967] *37*; *Self-Portrait in Drag* [1981] 153, *153*; *The Philosophy of Andy Warhol: From A to B and Back Again* [1975] 153, 271-73
Warpechowski, Zbigniew 246; *Nail Driven Through the Hand* [1980] 128, 245, *128*
Wegman, William 231-34, 249, 252-53; *Family Combinations* [1972] 122, *122*
Weibel, Peter 114, 219; *Aus der Mappe der Hundigkeit (From the Portfolio of Doggishness)* (with Valie Export) [1968] 114, *114*
Weiss, Evelyn, *Klaus Rinke: Travaux 1969/1976* [1976] 123
White, John 240
Whitehead, A.N. 235
Whitman, Robert 196, 204
Wilde, Oscar 222
Wilding, Faith 22, 41, 260; *Waiting* [1971] 137, *137*
Wiley, Bill 239
Wilke, Hannah 13, 21-22, 31-32, 36, 39-40, 253, 268; *Exchange Values (Marx)* [1978-84] 148, *148*; *His Farced Epistol (Joyce)* [1978-84] 148, *148*; 'Intercourse With...' [1976] 256-57; *Intra-Venus* (with Donald Goddard) [1993] 149, *149*; *Opportunity Makes Relations as it Makes Thieves* (Goethe) [1978-84] 148, *148*; *S.O.S. – Starification Object Series* [1974-82] 37, 38, 255, 262, *38*
Willette, J.S.M. see **Arnold, Skip**
Wilson, Martha 255
Winnicott, Derek 258
Wittgenstein, Ludwig 222, 232-33
Woodman, Francesca 275, 283; *House No. 4, Providence, Rhode Island* [1975-76] 170, *170*; *Untitled* (from the 'Angel' series, Rome) [1977-78] 170, *170*
Wooster Group 246
Wright, Frank Lloyd 205

Yoshihara, Jiro 53; 'Gutai Manifesto' [1956] 194
Youdelman, Nancy 260
Young, La Monte 196, 212

Zimmer, William 282
Zurita, Raúl 244-45; 'Interview with Samuel Silva' [1982] 128; *No, no puedo más (No, I can't stand it any longer)* [1979] 128, *128*

PUBLISHER'S ACKNOWLEDGEMENTS

We would like to thank all those who gave their kind permission to reproduce the listed material. Every effort has been made to secure all reprint permissions prior to publication. However, in a small number of instances this has not been possible. The editors and publisher apologize for any inadvertent errors or omissions. If notified, the publisher will endeavour to correct these at the earliest opportunity.

We would like to thank the following for their kind assistance:

AKG, London; Rasheed Araeen, London; Skip Arnold, Los Angeles; Arteleku, Donostia-San Sebastián, Spain; Arts Catalyst, London; Franko B, London; Keith Boadwee, Emeryville, California; Bridgeman Art Library, London; Gunter Brus, Graz, Austria; Chris Burden, Topanga, California; Stuart Brisley, London; Matthew Barney/ Barbara Gladstone Gallery, New York; Basilico Fine Arts, New York; Galleria Blu, Milan; Rudolph Burckhardt, New York; Leo Castelli Gallery, New York; Helen Chadwick Estate, London; Cheim & Read, New York; Judy Chicago/ Through the Flower Archives, Belen, New Mexico; Sadie Coles, London; Giorgio Colombo, Milan; Conexion, Santiago; Bill Cook, Atlanta; Paula Cooper Gallery, New York; Corbis, London; Paula Court, New York; Paul Cotton, Oakland, California; Cristinerose Gallery, New York; Deitch Projects, New York; DPA/ Photoreporters, Frankfurt/London; Anthony d'Offay Gallery, London; John Duncan, Udine, Italy; Mary Beth Edelson, New York; Thomas Erben Gallery, New York; Valie Export, Cologne; Feature, Inc. New York; Ronald Feldman Fine Arts, New York; Karen Finley, Nyack, New Jersey; Rose Finn-Kelcey, London; Sherman Fleming, Washington; Howard Fried, Vallejo, California; Collection Friedrichshof, Vienna; Fuji Television Gallery, Tokyo; Coco Fusco, New York; Gagosian Gallery, New York; Harry Gamboa Jr., Los Angeles; Gideon Gechtman, Rishon-le-Zion, Israel; The Getty Research Institute, Los Angeles; Gilbert & George, London; Barbara Gladstone Gallery, New York; Antony Gormley, London; Dan Graham, New York; Mona Hatoum, London; Susan Hiller, London; Tehching Hsieh, New York; Israel Museum, Jerusalem; Joan Jonas, New York; Jay Jopling/ White Cube, London; Georg Kargl Gallery, Vienna; Mike Kelley, Los Angeles; Sean Kelly Gallery, New York; Yves Klein Archives, Paris; Milan Knížák, Prague; Alison Knowles, New York; Robert Koch Gallery, San Francisco; Jeff Koons, New York; Yayoi Kusama, Tokyo; Suzanne Lacy, Oakland, California; Jean-Jacques Lebel, Paris; Lenono Photo Archive, New York; Lauren Lesko, New York; London Projects, London; Richard Long, Bristol; Luhring Augustine Gallery, New York; Urs Lüthi, Münich; Alastair MacLennan, Belfast; Archivio Opera Piero Manzoni, Milan; The Estate of Robert Mapplethorpe, New York; Anne Marchand, Paris; Tom Marioni/ The Museum of Conceptual Art, San Francisco; Georges Mathieu, Paris; Paul McCarthy, Altadena, California; The Estate of Ana Mendieta and Galerie Lelong, New York; Metro Pictures, New York; Victoria Miro Gallery, London; The Estate of Joan Mitchell, City Island, New York; Teresa Murak, Warsaw; Museu de Arte Moderna/ Estate of Lygia Clark, Rio de Janeiro; The Museum of Contemporary Art, San Diego, California; Museum Moderner Kunst Stiftung Ludwig, Vienna; Nagoya City Art Museum, Nagoya, Japan; The Estate of Hans Namuth/ Pollock-Krasner House and Study Center, East Hampton, New York; Nelson-Atkins Museum of Art, Kansas City, Missouri; Shirin Neshat, New York; Archiv Nitsch, Prinzendorf, Austria; Projeto Hélio Oiticica, Rio de Janeiro; Claes Oldenburg, New York; Dennis Oppenheim, New York; Orlan, Paris; Lucy Orta, Paris; Osaka Contemporary Art Center, Ashiya City Museum of Art and History and the former members of Gutai Art Association, Ashiya, Japan; PaceWildenstein Gallery, NewYork; Patrick Painter Inc./ Estate of Bas Jan Ader, Vancouver; Jayne Parker, London; Giuseppe Penone, Turin; Philadelphia Museum of Art; Gianni Pisani, Naples; Robert del Principe, New York; Eglė Rakauskaitė, Vilnius, Lithuania; Ulrike Rosenbach, Bornheim-Rosberg, Germany; Martha Rosler, New York; Klaus Rinke, Haan, Germany; The Saatchi Gallery, London; Joseph Santarromana, Los Angeles; Jenny Saville, London; SCAC, Paris; Scharlatt Family, Los Angeles; Carolee Schneemann, New Paltz, New York; Anna Schwartz Gallery, Melbourne; Richard Serra, New York; Bonnie Sherk, New York; Robert J. Shiffler Foundation Collection and Archive, Greenville, Ohio; Harry Shunk, New York; Katharina Sieverding, Dusseldorf; The Gilbert and Lila Silverman Fluxus Collection, New York; Barbara Smith, Venice, California; Archiv Sohm, Staatsgalerie, Stuttgart; Holly Solomon Gallery, New York; Solomon R. Guggenheim Museum, New York; Alan Sonfist, New York; Sprengel Museum, Hanover; Galerie Stadler, Paris; Stedelijk Museum, Amsterdam; Stelarc, Victoria, Australia; Galerie Tokoro, Tokyo; Torch Gallery, Amsterdam; Ubu Gallery, New York; Galerie Ulysses, Vienna; Ben Vautier, Nice; Bill Viola, Long Beach, California; Rafael Vostell, Berlin; The Andy Warhol Foundation Inc./ Art Resource, New York; Betty and George Woodman, New York; Zbigniew Warpechowski, Sandomierz, Poland; Shoshana Wayne Gallery, Santa Monica, California; William Wegman, New York; Donald Young Gallery, Seattle, Washington

PHOTOGRAPHERS

J. Akehurst and M.H. LeNy p. 187 (bottom); Art Centrum p. 77; BACCI p. 163 (top, bottom); Leslie Barany p. 110; Peter Barker pp. 33 (middle), 159 (bottom); Bonieventure p. 188; Ed Bowes p. 119 (bottom); Dirk Buwalda p. 86; Javier Campano p. 29 (middle); Central Art Archives, Helsinki p. 176; Helen Chadwick and Edward Woodman p. 173; Bill Cook p. 135; Prudence Cuming Ass. Ltd. p. 86 (bottom); Anthony Cunha p. 174; Anny de Decker p. 182; D. James Dee p. 38; John Delacour p. 105 (top); DPA/ Photoreporters p. 62; Augustin Dumage p. 98 (top); Erro p. 24 (second from left); Fotostudio Eshof p. 177; Henrik Gaard p. 90; Al Geise p. 62 (bottom); Donald Goddard p.149; John Goldblatt p. 181 (bottom); Lloyd Hamrol p. 137; David Harris p. 191; Leslie Haslam p. 66; J. Wayne Higgs p. 150; Ludwig Hoffenreich p. 32 (second from left); Ludwig Hoffenreich/ Walter Kindler p. 97 (bottom); Martha Holmes p. 60; Ricardo Iriarte p. 131 (bottom); Elizabeth Jappe p. 131 (top); Mimmo Jodice p. 122 (bottom); Marin Karras p. 30 (right); Richard Kilgroe p. 116 (bottom); James Klosty p. 26 (middle); Erich Lessing p. 192; George Macunius p. 64; Attilo Maranzano p. 111; Francoise Masson pp. 33 (left), 101; Dona Ann McAdams p. 108; Anthony McCall p. 145; Robert R. McElroy pp. 61 (bottom), 84; Vincente de Mello p. 25; Eric Metcalfe p. 150 (bottom); Klaus Mettig p. 141; Philippe Migeat pp. 132, 133; Peter Muscato p. 88; Roberta Neiman p. 85 (top); Niederbacher p. 92; Otis Niles p. 79; Ellen Page Wilson p. 99; Kevin Parker p. 29 (left); Kira Perov p. 127; William Ransom p. 28 (middle); Hartmut Rekort p. 74 (top); Sheree Rose p. 109 (top); Paolo Mussat Sartor p. 86 (top); Harry Shunk pp. 23 (right), 59, 72; Lawrence Shustak p. 31 (right); Sichov SIPA Press p. 185; P. Stietmann p. 186; Alain Tarica p. 37 (second from right); Caroline Tisdall p. 78 (bottom); Aufnahme von W. Vogel p. 79; Charles Wilp p. 58 (bottom); Dorothy Zeidman pp. 80-81, 164; Zeitpunktueller Standortwechsel p. 123

AUTHOR'S ACKNOWLEDGEMENTS

I would like to thank those friends, colleagues and institutions whose guidance and assistance helped make this project possible, and particularly Iwona Blazwick, who initiated this project with me.

Thanks to the many artists, galleries and museums who co-operated with picture research requests, as well as those which allowed me personal access to their archives.

The editorial team at Phaidon led by Gilda Williams, who guided me through the initial stages of this book and oversaw its completion; Clare Manchester and Audrey Walen, who held the project together against the odds and pulled the book together for publication; Elizabeth Manchester, who researched and wrote the extended captions and biographies; the superb team of editors and researchers, Clair Joy, John Stack and Zöe Stollery, without whose expertise and equanimity this book would not exist; designer Stuart Smith; and production controller Veronica Price.

Other individuals also made contributions both large and small to the process, whose assistance is gratefully acknowledged. I would especially like to mention Stelarc, Marina Abramović, Kathleen Rogers, Bruce Gilchrist, Georges Mathieu, the Hélio Oiticica Foundation, Rudolf Stadler Gallery, Rob La Frenais, Hubert Klocker, Gail Elson, Sara Perry, Bob Simillie, Tine Bech and my family, Lola Warr, Maureen Warr, Eddie Warr, Sylvia Neale, Julie Turley and Lee Warr. I am grateful to The Surrey Institute of Art & Design and Oxford Brookes University where research posts enabled me to complete work on the book.

THEMES AND MOVEMENTS The development of modern and contemporary art has been dominated by fundamental, revolutionary movements and recurring themes. The Themes and Movements series is the first fully to examine post-war art by combining expert narrative, key works and original documents. Each book is introduced by a comprehensive Survey by a distinguished scholar who provides a thorough analysis of the theme or movement. The second section is dedicated to numerous images of the Works themselves. A selection of key artworks is illustrated and accompanied by an extended caption describing the principal ideas and the process behind it, as well as exhibition history. Finally, with the Documents section, the series also offers direct access to the voice of the artist and to primary texts by critics, historians, curators, philosophers and theorists. A unique archive of the innovations, discourses and controversies that have shaped art today, these books are as exhaustive as a full-scale museum overview, presenting many of the most significant works of art associated with a particular tendency.